UNDERSTANDING CONTRACTS

UNDERSTANDING CONTRACTS

Third Edition

Jeff Ferriell
Professor of Law
Capital University Law School

print ISBN: 978-0-7698-9808-7
eBook ISBN: 978-0-7698-9809-4

Library of Congress Cataloging-in-Publication Data

Ferriell, Jeffrey Thomas, 1953-
   Understanding contracts / Jeffrey T. Ferriell, Professor of Law, Capital University Law School. -- Third Edition.
    p. cm.
  Includes index.
    ISBN 978-0-7698-9808-7
  1. Contracts--United States. I. Title.
  KF801.Z9F46 2014
  346.7302'2--dc22

                           2014015445

NOTE TO USERS
To ensure that you are using the latest materials available in this area, please be sure to periodically check the LexisNexis Law School web site for downloadable updates and supplements at www.lexisnexis.com/lawschool.

Editorial Offices
121 Chanlon Rd., New Providence, NJ 07974 (908) 464-6800
201 Mission St., San Francisco, CA 94105-1831 (415) 908-3200
www.lexisnexis.com

MATTHEW◆BENDER

Preface

This book is about the law of broken promises. It is designed primarily for use by law students enrolled in the traditional first-year law school course in contract law. I also hope that practitioners, judges, and scholars who need an overview of the doctrine and theory of contract law will also find it useful.

The text relies on established common law principles as reflected primarily by case law and the Restatement (Second) of Contracts, as well as on relevant provisions of Article 2 of the Uniform Commercial Code (U.C.C.), governing domestic sales of goods, which is covered extensively. The second edition also covers the United Nations Convention on the International Sale of Goods (CISG), UNIDROIT Principles on International Commercial Contracts (PICC), and Principals of European Contract Law (PECL), at a level appropriate to a basic course in the law of contracts, and modern statutes regarding methods of electronic contracting.

The text is limited to the range of material I might discuss with one of my more ambitious students who is seeking help in understanding contract law during a detailed conversation in my office or online. To that end I have used several recurring fact patterns involving common situations that arise in the basic contracts course. Readers will quickly become familiar with the cast of characters and their deals: Sam's contract to sell his car to Barb; Industrial Supply's agreement to sell a quantity of new frimulators to Franklin Manufacturing; Julie's various agreements with Rhonda's Roofing and Winkler Builders to repair or renovate her home; and Karen's contract to sell her house to Phil, to mention a few. In addition, the book frequently refers to cases that are included in many of the most popular Contracts casebooks. They are the best examples of the core principles of the law of contracts, and nothing I could do here would serve as a substitute for reading these cases carefully.

Modern contract law practice includes a much wider variety of situations than those represented by these basic transactions. However, most of the development of contract law has involved one variation or another on three basic themes: contracts for the sale of land, contracts for the sale of goods, and contracts for construction or employment services. Where appropriate, I have added more elaborate details to these and other recurring situations to enable students to understand the wide variety of circumstances in which issues in contract law may arise.

In addition, I have tried to carefully explain concepts that students frequently struggle with. Thirty years of classroom teaching have left me with clear impressions of the topics that students have the most difficulty with. I have attempted to describe these subjects with clear explanations and pointed examples, reflecting the type of fact patterns students are likely to encounter both in the classroom and on final exams. These explanations frequently use the leading cases that are included in many Contracts casebooks.

The book includes a detailed table of contents that is intended to serve as a basic outline of the course. I hope that students will find it useful in organizing their own comprehensive outlines. However, it is no substitute for the hard and useful work of organizing the material on your own. Included as well is an extensive set of internal cross-references in the hope that students will find them useful in drawing connections between the various strands of the course. Finally, the book includes an extensive set of

Preface

footnotes with citations that provide readers not only with support for the statements made in the text, but also refers them to supplemental resources that can be consulted for further study or for a more elaborate explanation of the topics covered by the text.

I enjoyed the assistance of many individuals in the production of this book. First and foremost were the efforts of my friend and co-author of the first edition, the late Penn State, Dickinson School of Law Professor Michael Navin. My sadness, as well as that of everyone who knew him, at his untimely passing, just weeks before the manuscript for the first edition was submitted to the publisher, is profound. I know that he would have liked to have participated in the corrections and improvements made in this edition and that he is frustrated over his inability to draw my attention to further improvements that could still be made. Not just the second edition of this book, but every other aspect of the lives of those who knew him, suffer from his conspicuous absence from our midst.

I received valuable assistance in preparing the third edition from Capital University Law School students Erin Porta and Eric Cass. I received similar help with the second edition from Capital University Law School student research assistants Bryn Beers, Kristin Chek, David Lynch, Deborah Auten Schrader, and Andrew Zamensky. Dickinson Law School student Matthew Stone and Capital University Law School students Katherine Johnson, Britton Atchley, Matthew Barkhurst, Damien M. Clifford, and Christina Lyons provided assistance with the first edition. Financial and other support from Capital University Law School and from both Capital University Law School Dean Jack Guttenberg and Associate Dean Shirley Mays was also key.

I owe a particular debt of gratitude to Professors Alan Sheflin and Gary Neustadter at Santa Clara University Law School, and to Professor Emeritus David R. Warner III at Ohio Northern University College of Law, who provided instruction and guidance when I was first a law student and later a neophyte Contracts instructor. I am also grateful for the capable editorial assistance of Ellen Boyne and Cristina Gegenschatz of LexisNexis, who pored over the manuscript and discovered and corrected many embarrassing mistakes.

Thanks is also owed to all of my contracts students over the past 30 years, primarily at Capital, Ohio State, Seattle University, and Ohio Northern, whose efforts to learn the law of contracts inspired this work. Their many questions have made it necessary for me to refine my understanding of the law of contracts and have prompted me to always seek to provide clearer explanations and useful examples of how the law applies.

Finally, work on this project could not have been maintained without the steady support and constant patience of my wife, Shawnee State University General Counsel, Cheryl Hacker. She suffered through many early mornings, late evenings, and grouchy moods, both at our home in Columbus and at our cottage on Martha's Vineyard, Massachusetts, while both editions of this book were being prepared.

The inevitable mistakes, of course, are entirely my own.

Jeff Ferriell
Columbus, Ohio & Oak Bluffs, Massachusetts
February 2014

Table of Contents

Table of Contents

Table of Contents

Table of Contents

Table of Contents

Table of Contents

Table of Contents

Table of Contents

Table of Contents

Table of Contents

Table of Contents

Table of Contents

Table of Contents

Table of Contents

Table of Contents

Table of Contents

Table of Contents

Table of Contents

Table of Contents

Table of Contents

Chapter 1

INTRODUCTION

§ 1.01 THE MEANING OF CONTRACT

A contract is a promise that the law will enforce.[1] More precisely, and to paraphrase the Restatement (Second) of Contracts, a contract is a promise for the breach of which the law either provides a remedy or recognizes as a duty.[2] Thus, a promise that is enforceable is a contract; a promise — and there are many of them — that is not enforceable, is not a contract.

Defining a contract in this simple fashion, as a promise that the law will enforce, is far more complex than it appears. The variety of situations in our society in which promises are made and broken, combined with the complexity of the public policies that might affect the enforceability of a particular promise, makes the question of whether the law will enforce a promise challenging. As will be seen, a great deal of contract law deals with the distinctions between agreements or promises that the law will enforce and those which, for various reasons, the law will not enforce.

The law of contracts involves several key features. As Sir Henry Maine famously noted in 1861: "the movement of the progressive societies has hitherto been a movement from Status to Contract."[3] Our freedom of contract, both the freedom to enter into legally binding agreements that advance our own purposes, and the freedom to avoid obligations unless we express our consent, is a key organizing principle of our free society.[4] Not only is freedom of contract a key aspect of a free society, it has also been the great engine of commerce in the world. One of the principal topics in the law of contracts is the extent of this freedom and the

---

[1] RESTATEMENT (SECOND) OF CONTRACTS § 1 (1981) ("contract is a promise . . . for the breach of which the law gives a remedy.").

[2] *Id.*

[3] HENRY MAINE, ANCIENT LAW 182 (Sir Frederick Pollock ed. 1930). *See also* Friedrich Kessler, *Contracts of Adhesion — Some Thoughts About Freedom of Contract*, 43 COLUM. L. REV. 629, 641 (1943) (on the return to the significance of status).

[4] P.S. ATIYAH, THE RISE AND FALL OF FREEDOM OF CONTRACT (1979); MICHAEL J. TREBILCOCK, THE LIMITS OF FREEDOM OF CONTRACT (1993); Neil B. Cohen & William H. Henning, *Freedom of Contract vs. Free Alienability: An Old Struggle Emerges in a New Context*, 46 GONZ. L. REV. 353 (2010); Harold C. Havighurst, *Limitations upon Freedom of Contract*, 1979 ARIZ. ST. L.J. 167; Friedrich Kessler & Edith Fine, *Culpa in Contrahendo, Bargaining in Good Faith, and Freedom of Contract: A Comparative Study*, 77 HARV. L. REV. 401, 407–09 (1964); Friedrich Kessler, *Contracts of Adhesion — Some Thoughts About Freedom of Contract*, 43 COLUM. L. REV. 629, 641 (1943). *See* Mark Pettit Jr., *Freedom, Freedom of Contract, and the "Rise and Fall,"* 79 B.U.L. REV. 263, 265 (1999); Samuel Williston, *Freedom of Contract*, 6 CORNELL L.Q. 365, 379 (1921).

restraints that are imposed on it. Nearly every major aspect of contract law involves some balancing of the principle supporting freedom of contract and societal restraints on that same freedom.[5]

A second key feature of contract law is the manner in which it enforces contracts — the remedies it deploys to give teeth to the notion of a contract as a promise that the law will enforce.[6] The nature and extent of the legal and equitable remedies available to enforce promises are not just an important part of contract law, they are in many ways the central part. As Justice Oliver Wendell Holmes once famously declared: "The duty to keep a contract at common law means a prediction that you must pay damages if you do not keep it, — and nothing else."[7] Accordingly, an understanding of the law of contract remedies is crucial to obtain a complete understanding of contract law generally. Without an understanding of the consequences of a breach of contract it is impossible to understand the meaning of a contract in the first place.[8]

Another central feature of the law of contracts is the manner in which it determines which promises are enforceable, and those that are not.[9] As will be seen, our free market economy depends on the predictable enforceability of promises that are part of an agreed exchange. Thus, ordinary exchange transactions of the type that occur millions of times each day in the marketplace for property and services are usually enforceable. These exchanges must be predictably enforceable in order for our market economy to function efficiently.[10] Promises to make gifts, on the other hand, while of great concern to the one who will receive the gift, are of lesser importance to the functioning of a vital economy. For this and other reasons, contract law draws a sharp dividing line between promises made as part of an exchange and promises made as an intended gift.[11]

The distinction between promises that are part of an exchange, and those that involve a mere promise to make a gift, raises another key feature of the law of contracts: the significance of reliance. People tend to rely on promises that others make. They change their plans, take action, and refrain from taking action, because they count on promises being kept. In the view of many, promises are enforceable primarily because they are relied upon — or at least because of the foreseeable likelihood that they may be relied upon. As will be seen, reliance on a promise provides both an alternative basis for enforcing the promise as well as a mechanism for calculating the amount of damages available for breach of the promise.

---

[5] Anthony T. Kronman, *Paternalism and the Law of Contracts*, 92 YALE L.J. 763 (1983).

[6] Oliver Wendell Holmes, *The Path of the Law*, 10 HARV. L. REV. 457, 462 (1897) ("The duty to keep a contract at common law means a prediction that you must pay damages if you do not keep it — and nothing else.") (*reprinted in* OLIVER WENDELL HOLMES, COLLECTED LEGAL PAPERS 174 (1920)). Later, however, he seemed to recant: "Breaching of a legal contract without excuse is wrong . . . and if a State adds to civil liability a criminal liability to fine, it simply intensifies the legal motive for doing right." Bailey v. Alabama, 219 U.S. 219, 246 (1911) (dissent).

[7] Oliver Wendell Holmes, *The Path of the Law*, 10 HARV. L. REV. 457, 462 (1897).

[8] *See infra* Chs. 12–15.

[9] *See infra* Chs. 2 and 3.

[10] *See infra* § 2.03 Consideration — A Bargained-For Exchange.

[11] *See infra* § 2.04 Promises to Make a Gift.

Another critical feature of the law of contracts is that liability is based on the parties' voluntary assumption of a legal duty. Promises are, by their very nature, voluntarily made. Contractual obligations, therefore, are voluntarily assumed. In this respect, contract law makes it possible for us to transform our intentions into legally binding obligations as an extension of the voluntary expression of our free will.[12] In this key respect, contract law is fundamentally different from the law of torts, which deals with obligations that are imposed on us externally by the society in which we live.

Promises are not only voluntary, they are also outwardly manifested through words and actions; they are not based on secret subjective intent.[13] The parties' words (whether spoken, written, or both) and actions often must be interpreted to determine whether they involve a promise, and if so, the meaning of the promise. Consequently, another important feature of the law of contracts is its principles for determining the meaning and legal effect of people's words and actions.

These key features of the law of contracts will be encountered throughout your course in the law of contracts, and throughout this book. As you study the law of contracts, you are likely to find it useful to consider how these features are reflected in the details of the rules you study, as well as in how they apply to specific fact patterns.

§ 1.02 TYPES OF CONTRACTS

Contracts can be classified in many different and sometimes overlapping ways. Contracts are sometimes characterized as express or implied, as bilateral or unilateral, as void or voidable, or as executory. These characterizations are frequently helpful in resolving issues related to the characterizations.

[A]   Express and Implied Contracts[14]

Courts sometimes characterize contracts as "express" or "implied." Implied contracts are sometimes further characterized as implied "in fact" or implied "in law." The distinction is sometimes important, as it may affect the remedy available to the injured party.

If a contract is made in express oral or written terms it is sometimes said to be an "express contract." Express contracts take many forms, ranging from a detailed multi-page contract negotiated over many months for the sale of a large business[15] to a simple agreement for the sale of a used car concluded with a handshake. On the other hand, contracts "implied in fact" are created far more informally,

---

[12] *See generally* J. WILLARD HURST, LAW AND THE CONDITIONS OF FREEDOM IN THE NINETEENTH CENTURY UNITED STATES (1968); JAMES GORDLEY, CONTRACT PROPERTY, AND THE WILL — THE CIVIL LAW AND COMMON LAW TRADITIONS, IN THE STATE AND FREEDOM OF CONTRACT 66, 79–83 (H. Scheiber ed. 1998).

[13] *See infra* § 4.02 Objective Theory of Contract Formation.

[14] Willard L. Boyd III & Robert K. Huffman, *The Treatment of Implied-in-Law and Implied-in-Fact Contracts and Promissory Estoppel in the United States Claims Court*, 40 CATH. U.L. REV. 605, 629 (1991).

[15] *E.g.*, Empro Mfg. Co. v. Ball-Co Mfg., Inc., 870 F.2d 423 (7th Cir. 1989).

perhaps through nothing more than a nod of the head or a wave of the hand. The traditional elements of contract implied in fact are: (1) the defendant requested the plaintiff to perform work, (2) the plaintiff expected the defendant to compensate him or her for those services, and (3) the defendant knew or should have known that the plaintiff expected compensation.[16] For example, a patron in a bar might hold up two fingers, indicating to the bartender that he wants to purchase another round of drinks for him and his companion, thus implying his agreement to pay the standard price for the drinks. Or, more commonly (litigation over payment for a round of drinks being rare), an owner of a building might ask his builder to make a change to an ongoing construction project, and the builder completes the requested work. As one court explained:

> A contract implied in fact is not created or evidenced by explicit agreement of the parties, but is inferred as a matter of reason or justice from the acts or conduct of the parties. However, all of the elements of an express contract must be shown by the facts or circumstances surrounding the transaction — mutuality of intent, offer and acceptance, authority to contract — so that it is reasonable, or even necessary, for the court to assume that the parties intended to be bound.[17]

There is no legal difference between an express contract and a contract implied in fact. Both are true contracts, based upon the expressed intentions of the parties to enter into a voluntary obligation. The only distinction between the two is the manner in which the parties' intent is expressed.

A contract "implied in law" on the other hand, is not really a contract at all.[18] A contract implied in law, or a "quasi-contract" as it is sometimes called, is based on the law of restitution.[19] The law of restitution seeks to prevent "unjust enrichment" and thus does not depend on the voluntary consent of the parties.

A clear example of this is found in *Cotnam v. Wisdom*.[20] The plaintiffs were

---

[16] Ramsey v. Ellis, 484 N.W.2d 331 (Wis. 1992). *See* Comment, *Implied in Fact Contracts and Mutual Assent*, 33 Harv. L. Rev. 376, 389–90 (1926).

[17] Prudential Ins. Co. v. United States, 801 F.2d 1295, 1297 (Fed. Cir. 1986), *cert. denied*, 479 U.S. 1086 (1987). *See also* B. & O. Ry. Co. v. United States, 261 U.S. 592, 597 (1923) where the United States Supreme Court said:

> The "implied[-in-fact] agreement" . . . is not an agreement "implied in law," more aptly termed a constructive or quasi contract, where, by fiction of law, a promise is imputed to perform a legal duty, as to repay money obtained by fraud or duress, but an agreement "implied in fact," founded upon a meeting of minds, which, although not embodied in an express contract, is inferred, as a fact, from conduct of the parties showing, in the light of the surrounding circumstances, their tacit understanding.

[18] *See* Martin v. Little, Brown and Co., 450 A.2d 984, 988 (Pa. Super. Ct. 1981); Cont'l Forest Prods. v. Chandler Supply Co., 518 P.2d 1201, 1205 (Idaho 1974).

[19] *See* Ramsey v. Ellis, 484 N.W.2d 331 (Wis. 1992); Paffhausen v. Balano, 708 A.2d 269 (Me. 1998); Callano v. Oakwood Park Homes Corp., 219 A.2d 332 (N.J. Super. Ct. 1966).

[20] 104 S.W. 164 (Ark. 1907). Students may wonder why so many older cases are used as illustrations of modern contract doctrine. One reason is to illustrate the heritage of the rules that continue to govern us today. But, most of the time, these cases involve simple facts, which provide clear examples of the underlying doctrine, uncluttered by complexities that might bring other rules and policies into play. These cases continue to be studied, not so much because of their clear articulation of the rules that they

physicians who performed emergency surgery on Mr. A.M. Harrison, who hit his head when he was thrown from a street car. Mr. Harrison never became conscious and was never able to express his willingness to pay for the emergency medical services he received in the effort to save his life. Mr. Harrison's estate was nevertheless liable, on a theory of quasi-contract, for the value of the benefit he received as a result of the doctors' efforts, even though there was no agreement between the parties and thus no real contract.

When the parties are both conscious and capable of expressing their consent, the distinction between a contract implied in law and a contract implied in fact is more difficult to draw. When the owner of a house undergoing renovation asks the contractor to make a change or makes a request for additional work, it might be unclear whether the contractor's claim for payment for the extra work is based on the unjust enrichment to the owner that would otherwise occur or on the owner's implied consent to pay for the additional work.[21] Not only may the remedy be slightly different, but the existence of an express contract dealing with the project might impose a barrier to recovery based on a contract implied in law.[22]

Other cases are more clearly based on unjust enrichment and not on the parties' informal expressions of assent. In *Schott v. Westinghouse Electric Corp.*,[23] an employee submitted a suggestion to his employer pursuant to a company program that encouraged employees to make suggestions by holding out the possibility of a cash award. The suggestion form signed by the employee contained an express disclaimer of contractual liability, making it clear that there was no agreement by the employer to pay for the suggestion. Thus, the only possible basis for the employee's recovery was on a theory of quasi-contract based on any unjust enrichment of the employer who used the suggestion to its benefit.

Another important distinction between express contracts and contracts implied in fact on the one hand, and contracts implied in law on the other, is the remedy provided. In a true contract, based on the voluntary assent of the parties, remedies are based on the injured party's expectations.[24] When the court finds a quasi-contract, the remedy is based on the value of the benefit conferred on the party who was enriched, in an effort to prevent any enrichment that otherwise would be unjust.[25]

A further, sometimes confusing distinction is also made between quasi-contract and "quantum meruit." Quantum meruit literally means "as much as he deserved." It is used to obtain compensation for work or labor performed. Although courts sometimes mistakenly use the term to refer to an action to recover the value of goods delivered, "quantum valebant" was the term that was traditionally used to refer to such an action. Quantum meruit is sometimes used to refer to a contract

---

propound, but rather because of the simplicity of the facts, which makes the rules easier to understand.

[21] *See* Assoc'd Builders, Inc. v. Oczkowski, 801 A.2d 1008 (Me. 2002).

[22] Hall Contracting Corp. v. Entergy Serv., Inc., 309 F.3d 468 (8th Cir. 2002).

[23] 259 A.2d 443 (Pa. 1969).

[24] *See infra* § 12.02 Damages Based on the Injured Party's Expectations.

[25] *See infra* § 12.01[B] Expectation, Reliance, and Restitution Interests.

implied in fact, and at other times used to refer to a contract implied in law.[26] The distinction is important. As one court explained: "[D]amages in an unjust enrichment claim are measured by the benefit conferred upon the defendant, while damages in a quantum meruit claim are measured by the reasonable value of the plaintiff's services."[27] Despite this, courts frequently use the terms "quasi-contract," "unjust enrichment," "restitution," and "quantum meruit" interchangeably. Because of this, and because of the confusion between "contracts implied in fact" and "contracts implied in law," some scholars have suggested elimination of both terms.[28]

[B] Formal and Informal Contracts

The distinction between "formal" and "informal" contracts has two meanings. The traditional distinction was based on whether the formation of the contract adhered to certain ritualistic formalities,[29] such as the impression of melted wax on a written contract with an impression known as a "seal."[30] In this sense, the term "formal contract" was used to refer to the form of the agreement and played a critical element in its enforceability.[31] Modern examples are negotiable instruments, negotiable documents, and letters of credit, all of which are governed by special provisions of the Uniform Commercial Code.[32] In this context, "informal contract" referred to all other contracts, regardless of whether they were written or oral, or whether they were simple or complex.[33]

Today, a formal contract is one that is carefully negotiated and expressed (or "memorialized") in a formal final written document.[34] An informal contract is one formed more casually, possibly not bothering with any kind of a writing.[35] Thus, when your author hired a local home renovation construction firm to build an addition to his house he signed an elaborate printed contract covering a wide variety of possible contingencies and allocating responsibilities between the parties

---

[26] RESTATEMENT (THIRD) OF RESTITUTION AND UNJUST ENRICHMENT § 49 cmt. f (Tentative Draft No. 5, 2007). *See* Candace SaariKovacic-Fleischer, *Quantum Meruit and the Restatement (Third) of Restitution and Unjust Enrichment*, 27 REV. LITIG. 127, 129 (2007).

[27] Ramsey v. Ellis, 484 N.W.2d 331, 333–34 (Wis. 1992). *See also* Maglica v. Maglica, 66 Cal. App. 4th 442 (1998) (reversing trial court's award of damages measured by the amount of the benefit received by the defendant, in favor of the reasonable value of the plaintiff's services).

[28] Doug Rendleman, *Quantum Meruit for the Subcontractor: Has Restitution Jumped off Dawson's Dock?*, 79 TEX. L. REV. 2055, 2060 (2001).

[29] *See, e.g.*, Harold D. Hazeltine, *The Formal Contract of Early English Law*, 10 COLUM. L. REV. 806 (1910).

[30] *See* RESTATEMENT (SECOND) OF CONTRACTS § 6(a) (1981); *infra* § 2.02[B] The Seal.

[31] *See* ARTHUR LINTON CORBIN, 1 CORBIN ON CONTRACTS § 1.5 (1993); Peter Linzer, *Rough Justice: A Theory of Restitution and Reliance, Contracts and Torts*, 2001 WIS. L. REV. 695, 696 n.5.

[32] *See* RESTATEMENT (SECOND) OF CONTRACTS § 6 (1981).

[33] Peter Linzer, *Rough Justice: A Theory of Restitution and Reliance, Contracts and Torts*, 2001 WIS. L. REV. 695.

[34] *See* William C. Whitford, *The Role of the Jury (and the Fact/Law Distinction) in the Interpretation of Written Contracts*, 2001 WIS. L. REV. 931, 938.

[35] *See* Robert Childres & Stephen J. Spitz, *Status in the Law of Contracts*, 47 N.Y.U. L. REV. 1, 4 (1972); Wendell H. Holmes, *The Freedom Not to Contract*, 60 TUL. L. REV. 751, 790 (1986).

with respect to many details associated with the project. On the other hand, the agreement he made with his landscaper to install an array of perennial flowers, shrubs, and trees consisted of little more than a drawing with a price scribbled in the corner. Moreover, his wife's agreement (she is also an attorney) to pay a caterer for a small private party was even more informal: they discussed and settled on a date, a time, a place, a menu, the number of people who would be attending, and a price. The differences in the degrees of formality do not affect the enforceability of the agreement, though, as will be seen, they may have a bearing on the admissibility of evidence of promises that were never incorporated into any final written version of the parties' agreement.[36]

[C]   Bilateral and Unilateral Contracts

Contract law sometimes distinguishes between "bilateral" and "unilateral" contracts.[37] A bilateral contract involves two promises; a unilateral contract involves only one. Although the distinction was abandoned by the Restatement (Second) of Contracts,[38] and was never found in the Uniform Commercial Code, courts still commonly refer to it.[39]

Its most common use is in connection with the manner in which a contract is created. In a bilateral contract, a contract is formed through an exchange of promises. Thus, when Rhonda's Roofing promises to install a new roof on Julie's house, in exchange for Julie's promise to pay for the work, a bilateral contract is formed. The contract exists as soon as the parties' promises are exchanged for one another. Both parties have made an enforceable promise: Rhonda's Roofing will be liable to Julie if Rhonda fails to perform the promised work and Julie will owe a debt to Rhonda's Roofing if she fails to make timely payment for the work.

In a unilateral contract, only one of the parties makes an offer that can only be accepted by performance: "If you find my lost cat, and return him to me safely, I'll pay you $100." The owner of the cat has made a promise, but has not sought a return promise in exchange. The contract is not concluded by an exchange of promises. Instead, it is concluded when the requested performance is complete — when the cat is found and safely returned. Until the cat is found, there is no binding contract.[40] Thus, the offeree is free to abandon his search for the missing cat at any time, without liability for breach.

Modern decisions treat the distinction primarily as a question of the manner in which acceptance is made. If the offer does not invite acceptance in the form of a return promise, but instead insists on performance as the exclusive manner of acceptance, the contract is not generally regarded as formed until completion of

---

[36] *See* Robert Childres & Stephen J. Spitz, *Status in the Law of Contracts*, 47 N.Y.U. L. REV. 1 (1972).

[37] RESTATEMENT OF CONTRACTS § 12 (1932).

[38] *See* RESTATEMENT (SECOND) OF CONTRACTS § 1 (1981).

[39] Brannan & Guy, P.C. v. City of Montgomery, 828 So.2d 914, 921 (Ala. 2002); Conference Am., Inc. v. Conexant Sys., Inc., 508 F. Supp. 2d 1005, 1013–14 (M.D. Ala. 2007); Garcia v. Sonoma Ranch East II, LLC, 298 P.3d 510, 517 (N.M. Ct. App. 2013).

[40] *See, e.g.*, Dahl v. HEM Pharm. Corp., 7 F.3d 1399 (9th Cir. 1993); Hamer v. Sidway, 27 N.E. 256 (N.Y. 1891).

the requested performance.[41] Still, as will be seen, where a promisee begins performance in reliance on an offer, the promisor may be prevented from attempting to revoke the promise until a reasonable time for completion has passed.[42]

[D]   Executory Contracts

In the law of contracts, an "executory contract" is one that has not yet been substantially performed.[43] An "executed contract" on the other hand, is one in which the obligations have been at least substantially, if not fully, performed.[44] If Karen and Phil enter into an agreement that Phil will purchase Karen's home for $225,000, the contract is still fully "executory" during the time between the creation of the contract and the "closing," when Karen delivers a deed to the house to Phil and Phil pays Karen the $225,000.

A contract may be fully executory, with both parties having substantial duties remaining to be performed, or it might be performed by one party with the other having material duties remaining to be performed. Thus, if Sam promises to sell his auto to Barb for a price of $20,000, Sam may have delivered the car on Monday and waited for Barb to pay him for the car on Tuesday.[45] Likewise, a construction company may have completed work on the owner's house but not yet received payment for its work.

Whether a contract remains fully or partially executory is relevant to several issues, including the enforceability of a modification made without consideration,[46] the avoidance of a contract entered into by a party who is intoxicated[47] or affected by a mental disability,[48] and whether the contract can be rescinded[49] or modified after it has been assigned.[50] Whether the contract remains fully executory also affects the doctrine of anticipatory repudiation.[51]

Courts sometimes also refer to the "execution" of a written contract to refer to whether the contract has been signed, using "executed" as synonymous with "signed" or "authenticated."[52]

---

[41] *See* RESTATEMENT (SECOND) OF CONTRACTS § 32 cmt. b (1981).

[42] *See* RESTATEMENT (SECOND) OF CONTRACTS § 45(1) (1981). *See generally infra* § 4.05[B][3] Acceptance by Performance Alone: Unilateral Contracts.

[43] *E.g.*, Gaugert v. Duve, 579 N.W.2d 746 (Wis. Ct. App. 1998).

[44] Smith v. Allen, 436 P.2d 65 (Cal. 1968).

[45] As Wimpy from the cartoon "Popeye" frequently said: "I will gladly pay you Tuesday, for a hamburger today."

[46] *See* RESTATEMENT (SECOND) OF CONTRACTS § 89 (1981).

[47] *See* RESTATEMENT (SECOND) OF CONTRACTS § 16 cmt. b (1981).

[48] *See* RESTATEMENT (SECOND) OF CONTRACTS § 15(2) (1981).

[49] *See* RESTATEMENT (SECOND) OF CONTRACTS § 148 (1981).

[50] *See* RESTATEMENT (SECOND) OF CONTRACTS § 338 cmt. f (1981).

[51] *See* RESTATEMENT (SECOND) OF CONTRACTS § 253 cmt. c (1981). *See also infra* § 9.05 Anticipatory Repudiation.

[52] *See also* U.C.C. § 9-102(a)(7) (2012).

[E]   Adhesion Contracts

Adhesion contracts are those in which one of parties has little or no opportunity to bargain over the specific terms of the agreement.[53] Instead, the party who has drafted the contract presents it on a "take-it-or-leave-it" basis, leaving the other party with the choice of entering into the contract as written, or walking away from the transaction completely. Such contracts are usually in a "standardized form" with the same terms offered to every customer.

Insurance policies are good examples of adhesion contracts. The insured has a choice of whether to agree to the terms of the policy or to shop around for a better deal from some other insurance company. Apart from the availability of a limited number of standardized additional protections, or "riders," the purchaser is not usually able to negotiate over the specific terms of the protection offered by the policy. Likewise, many employment contracts are contracts of adhesion, with the employee bound by the terms supplied by the employer to all of its employees, and not usually susceptible to negotiation by the employee.[54]

When the terms of a contract of adhesion are oppressive or overly one-sided, they are sometimes unenforceable under the doctrine of "unconscionability." The contract in *Henningsen v. Bloomfield Motors, Inc.*[55] contained terms purporting to limit the liability of the seller of a defective automobile. Even though the provision was standard, throughout the automobile industry, it was held unenforceable, partially due to the oppressive nature of the provision and the gross inequality in bargaining power between the parties.[56]

Despite decisions like *Henningsen*, life would be both difficult and expensive if contracts of adhesion were unenforceable.[57] Imagine, for a moment, if it were necessary to separately negotiate all of the terms of a life insurance contract for its terms to be binding — the insured might die before the contract was concluded. The use of standardized forms simplifies the contracting process by reducing the transaction costs associated with creating many contracts. Likewise, their use permits institutional parties who enter into many similar transactions, with a wide variety of customers, to plan the delivery of the goods and services they provide. Tailoring the terms of each individual transaction to the particular and sometimes idiosyncratic desires of every customer would make the process of entering into contracts time-consuming and the process of fulfilling the terms of those contracts cumbersome. Standardized contracts avoid these problems. This is particularly

---

[53] *See generally* Robert A. Hillman & Jeffrey J. Rachlinski, *Standard-Form Contracting in the Electronic Age*, 77 N.Y.U. L. Rev. 429 (2002); Edwin Patterson, *The Delivery of a Life Insurance Policy*, 33 Harv. L. Rev. 198, 222 (1919); Todd D. Rakoff, *Contracts of Adhesion: An Essay in Reconstruction*, 96 Harv. L. Rev. 1173 (1983).

[54] *E.g.*, Fittante v. Palm Springs Motors, Inc., 105 Cal. App. 4th 708 (2003). Your own agreement with your law school is just such a contract. You are not able to negotiate over which courses you will take, at least during your first year; nor are you likely to find the school's tuition structure subject to negotiation — apart, at least, from whatever financial aid award you have received.

[55]   161 A.2d 69 (N.J. 1960).

[56]   *Id.* at 75. *See generally infra* § 10.05 Unconscionability.

[57]   Michael I. Meyerson, *The Reunification of Contract Law: The Objective Theory of Consumer Form Contracts*, 47 U. Miami L. Rev. 1263, 1269–70, 1275 (1993).

true when most customers desire essentially the same terms. The costs savings experienced as a result of the advantages of employing standardized terms will be passed on, at least in a competitive market, to customers in the form of lower prices.[58] The law recognizes these advantages and, accordingly, most contracts of adhesion are fully enforceable.

Although most adhesive contracts are enforceable, they are nevertheless subject to closer scrutiny than contracts in which all or most of the terms have been separately negotiated by the parties. For example, ambiguities in contracts of adhesion are usually construed against the party who drafted the unclear language.[59] Likewise, courts might insist that adequate notice be provided with respect to particularly one-sided or otherwise onerous terms, such as a forum selection clause that would force the party lacking any bargaining power to pursue any litigation in a distant and inconvenient forum.[60] However, despite these occasional limitations, adhesive contracts are generally fully enforceable according to their terms.

[F] Void, Voidable, and Unenforceable Contracts

Some contracts are illegal.[61] Some otherwise legal contracts might be tainted by the lack of capacity of the parties, due either to their age or mental condition,[62] or because of the use of improper means of obtaining consent, including fraud, duress, undue influence, or unconscionability.[63] On other occasions performance is excused due to mistake, impossibility, or frustration of purpose.[64] These circumstances may either make the contract "void ab initio" (void from the outset) and thus completely invalid, or, on the other hand, merely "voidable" at the election of one of the parties.[65] When a contract is said to be "unenforceable" it means that there is no remedy for breach, but that the existence of the contract may be recognized in some other way,[66] such as the basis for an action in tort for interference with a contractual relationship.[67] When the agreement between the parties is completely illegal, such as an agreement to commit a crime or a tort, the agreement is "void."[68]

---

[58] *See* Carnival Cruise Lines v. Shute, 499 U.S. 585, 594 (1991) (enforceability of forum selection clause in vacation cruise contract).

[59] *E.g.*, Grinnell Mut. Reinsurance Co. v. Jungling, 654 N.W.2d 530, 536 (Iowa 2002); Howard v. Fed.Crop Ins. Corp., 540 F.2d 695 (4th Cir. 1976).

[60] *See, e.g.*, Hunt v. Sup. Ct., 81 Cal. App. 4th 901 (2000). *See also* Carnival Cruise Lines, Inc. v. Shute, 499 U.S. 585 (1991).

[61] *See infra* § 10.02 Contracts Contrary to Public Policy; Illegal Contracts.

[62] *See infra* § 10.03 Incapacity.

[63] *See infra* § 10.04 Obtaining Assent Improperly: Fraud, Duress, and Undue Influence.

[64] RESTATEMENT (SECOND) OF CONTRACTS § 7 cmt. b (1981). *See infra* Ch. 11 Excuse: Mistake and Change of Circumstances.

[65] *See* RESTATEMENT (SECOND) OF CONTRACTS § 7 (1981).

[66] *See* RESTATEMENT (SECOND) OF CONTRACTS § 8 (1981).

[67] *See* Daugherty v. Kessler, 286 A.2d 95, 97 (Md. 1972); ARTHUR LINTON CORBIN, 1 CORBIN ON CONTRACTS §§ 1.6, 1.7 & 1.8 (Interim ed. 1993); Abraham M. Levin, *The Varying Meaning and Legal Effect of the Word "Void,"* 32 MICH. L. REV. 1088 (1933).

[68] *See infra* § 10.02 Contracts Contrary to Public Policy; Illegal Contracts.

There might have been an agreement, but there was never a "contract." Neither party can enforce the agreement, and there is nothing the parties can do to make the agreement valid. Such agreements are sometimes referred to as "void contracts" even though this term is a bit of a misnomer.

When there is some other problem with the agreement, but it is still enforceable by one of the parties, the contract is said to be "voidable." However, until the party with the right to disaffirm the contract acts to exercise its right, the contract remains valid. And, the party with the right to disaffirm the contract, seeing advantages in the deal, might decide to ratify the contract and go ahead with its performance.

A good example of a contract that is voidable at the election of one of the parties is an agreement with someone who, like a child or a person suffering from a mental disability, lacked the legal capacity to enter into the contract.[69] For example, the court-appointed guardian of an Alzheimer's patient may seek to disaffirm a contract the patient previously entered into with a nursing home, on the grounds that the patient was not capable of understanding the nature of the agreement she made. Or the victim of a brain injury may, after his full recovery, seek to disaffirm a contract made while he was suffering from his injuries.

On the other hand, there may be no reason to disaffirm the contract. If the nursing home is providing the patient with good care at a reasonable price, it may make more sense to leave the contract in place. Likewise, a 17-year-old, who is satisfied with the car he agreed to buy, may want to keep it despite his legal power to disaffirm the deal and give the car back to the seller. In these situations, where the contract is merely voidable, not void, the party suffering from the lack of contractual capacity will have the option of disaffirming the contract or enforcing it. If the party lacking capacity wants to enforce the contract, the other party remains bound.

[G]   Contracts Involving "Merchants" or "Consumers"

The law of contracts does not apply uniformly to everyone. Article 2 of the Uniform Commercial Code in particular, frequently draws distinctions between contracts involving one or more business professionals, or "merchants," and those lacking any particular business expertise. In addition, special statutory provisions or common law rules are frequently applicable to transactions involving consumers.

[1]   Rules Governing Merchants[70]

Special rules apply to merchants because of their expertise in connection with either the subject matter of the transaction or with the practices involved in the transaction. U.C.C. § 2-104 defines a merchant as

---

[69] *See infra* § 10.03[B] Mental Incapacity.

[70] Zipporah Batshaw Wiseman, *The Limits of Vision: Karl Llewellyn and the Merchant Rules*, 100 Harv. L. Rev. 465 (1987); John F. Dolan, *The Merchant Class of Article 2: Farmers, Doctors, and Others*,

a person who deals in goods of the kind or otherwise by his occupation holds himself out as having knowledge or skill peculiar to the practices or goods involved in the transaction or to whom such knowledge or skill may be attributed by his employment of an agent or broker or other intermediary who by his occupation holds himself out as having such knowledge or skill.[71]

Thus, a person may acquire the status of a merchant due to knowledge or skill he or she has that is particular to the goods involved in the transaction. Likewise, depending on the context, a person may be a merchant because of his expertise in connection with the business practices involved in the transaction, even though these are general business practices that would be familiar to anyone in business.[72] Moreover, an unsophisticated person, without expertise, may be saddled with the responsibilities of a merchant by representing himself as a person with special knowledge or skill. One's occupation alone may be sufficient for this purpose. Finally, a person may be treated as a merchant if he engages an employee or other agent who represents himself as having specialized knowledge or skill relevant to the transaction.

Where applicable, these specialized rules rest on the premise that greater reliance is usually placed on a person who either has expertise or who represents himself or herself as having expertise related to the transaction.

Whether someone is a merchant sometimes depends on the context in which the issue arises. The Official Comments to U.C.C. § 2-104 point out three separate contexts in which designating someone as a merchant may be important.[73] The definition of a merchant applies somewhat differently in each setting.

Although Article 2 of the U.C.C. generally governs all contracts for the sale of goods, several provisions of Article 2 of the U.C.C. impose special rules governing the contract formation process when one or both of the parties qualifies as a merchant. These rules include the statute of frauds,[74] rules relating to firm or irrevocable offers,[75] the "battle of the forms,"[76] and modifications of contracts.[77] All of these rules require little expertise beyond that which would normally be expected of anyone who is in business, such as the usual business practice of responding to mail.[78] A second context in which a person's status as a merchant is important is in connection to the implied warranty that goods will be of merchantable quality.[79]

1977 WASH. U.L.Q. 1; Larry T. Garvin, *Small Business and the False Dichotomies of Contract Law*, 40 WAKE FOREST L. REV. 295 (2005).

[71] U.C.C. § 2-104(1) (2012).

[72] U.C.C. § 2-104 cmt. 2 (2012).

[73] *Id.*

[74] U.C.C. § 2-201 (2012). *See infra* § 5.06[C] Confirmatory Memorandum in Transactions Between Merchants.

[75] U.C.C. § 2-205 (2012). *See infra* § 4.09[D] Firm Offers Under U.C.C. § 2-205.

[76] U.C.C. § 2-207 (2012). *See infra* § 4.10 Mirror-Image Rule and the Battle of the Forms Under U.C.C. § 2-207.

[77] U.C.C. § 2-209(2) (2012). *See infra* § 5.09[B] Agreements Requiring Modifications in Writing.

[78] U.C.C. § 2-104 cmt. 2 (2012).

[79] U.C.C. § 2-314 (2012). *See infra* § 7.03 Implied Warranty of Merchantability.

The warranty applies only if the seller is not only a merchant but is a "merchant with respect to goods of [the] kind" involved in the transaction.[80] A third set of rules impose slightly elevated responsibilities on merchants in a variety of general and specialized settings, ranging from the overall duty of good faith[81] to the specific duties imposed on a merchant to follow the seller's instructions with respect to defective goods in the merchant buyer's possession.[82] When used in these and other contexts, the more general or specific sense of the definition of merchant can apply.[83]

[2]   Rules Governing Transactions with Consumers

[a]   Consumer Protection Legislation

Special rules sometimes also apply to transactions with consumers. Most of these rules are not part of the general law of contracts. Instead, they are found in a myriad of state and federal legislative and regulatory provisions that afford greater protections to consumers than are available under the common law of contracts. Foremost among these rules are those found in federal Consumer Credit Protection Act, which includes provisions related to consumer loan transactions,[84] credit reporting,[85] debt collection practices,[86] and electronic funds transfers.[87] The federal Magnuson-Moss Warranty Act is responsible for the form in which many consumer product warranties appear.[88] Many of these statutes are accompanied by complex administrative regulations.[89]

Likewise, the Federal Trade Commission (FTC) has adopted trade regulation rules pursuant to its authority under the Federal Trade Commission Act.[90] The FTC's Regulations for Sales Made at Homes[91] are particularly important. They give consumers the right to rescind a sale made at the consumer's home if the consumer cancels the transaction within three business days after the contract is made.[92] This three-day right of rescission, applicable only to sales concluded in the consumer's home, is the source of the common misconception that any consumer transaction can be rescinded within a three-day period.[93] A similar three-day

---

[80] U.C.C. § 2-314 (2012). *See infra* § 7.03[A] Seller a Merchant with Respect to Goods of the Kind.

[81] U.C.C. § 1-304 (2012).

[82] U.C.C. § 2-104 cmt. 2 (2012).

[83] *Id.*

[84] The Truth in Lending Act, 15 U.S.C. §§ 1601–1667f (2006).

[85] The Fair Credit Reporting Act, 15 U.S.C. §§ 1681–1681u (2006).

[86] The Fair Debt Collection Practices Act, 15 U.S.C. §§ 1692–1692o (2006).

[87] Electronic Funds Transfer Act, 15 U.S.C. §§ 1693–1693r (2006).

[88] 15 U.S.C. §§ 2301–2312 (2006).

[89] *See generally* HOWARD J. ALPERIN & ROLAND F. CHASE, CONSUMER LAW (1986).

[90] 15 U.S.C. § 45 (2006).

[91] 16 C.F.R. §§ 429.0–429.3 (2008).

[92] 16 C.F.R. § 429.1 (2008).

[93] Nearly every year a Contracts student approaches your author seeking information "for a friend" about the friend's ability to rescind a contract for the purchase of an automobile.

cooling-off period is available for certain home equity mortgage loan transactions.[94]

In addition, there are many special state consumer protection statutes covering a wide variety of topics, such as home renovation contracts,[95] automobile repairs,[96] and various types of consumer loans,[97] to name a few. These statutes vary considerably from state to state. The most important of these statutes are the Uniform Consumer Credit Code,[98] adopted in seven states,[99] and the Uniform Consumer Sales Practices Act,[100] adopted in only three states.[101]

With minor variations, the scopes of these various statutes are quite similar. They apply to agreements intended for personal, family, or household purposes.[102] Thus, it is not the inherent nature of the goods that controls whether consumer protection law applies to the transaction. Instead, it is the purpose of the agreement. For example, the purchase of a computer at an electronics store for installation in the buyer's home to be used to play games, keep track of the family checking account, and to surf the Internet for fun and amusement is intended for personal, family, or household purposes and would be subject to most consumer protection laws. The purchase of an identical computer for use in a home office for exclusively business purposes would not be covered by these statutes.

An important exception is the Magnuson-Moss Consumer Warranty Act.[103] It is the source of the language found in most consumer product warranties conspicuously indicating that the warranty is either a "FULL" or "LIMITED" warranty and disclosing the duration of the warranty's protection. Most of its provisions apply to transactions involving products *normally used* for personal, family, or household purposes."[104] Thus, because personal computers are "normally used" for personal, family, or household purposes, the sale of a computer for use in either a home office, or a conventional office located at a business, would be governed by the Act.

---

[94] Truth in Lending Act § 125, 15 U.S.C. § 1635 (2006).

[95] *E.g.*, Ohio Rev. Code Ann. § 1345.21–1345.28 (Anderson 2002); FTC Door-to-Door Sales Regulations 16 C.F.R. §§ 429.0–429.3 (2008).

[96] *E.g.*, 107 Ohio Admin. Code § 109:4-3-13 (2001).

[97] *See* Elizabeth R. Schiltz, *The Amazing, Elastic, Ever-Expanding Exportation Doctrine and Its Effect on Predatory Lending Regulation*, 88 MINN. L. REV. 518 (2004).

[98] *See, e.g.*, Colo. Rev. Stat. Ann. §§ 5-1-101 to 5-9-103 (LexisNexis 2003).

[99] Colorado, Idaho, Indiana, Iowa, Kansas, Maine, Oklahoma, South Carolina, Utah, Wisconsin, and Wyoming. It has also been enacted in Guam.

[100] *See, e.g.*, Ohio Rev. Code §§ 1345.01–1345.51 (Anderson 2002).

[101] Ohio, Kansas, and Utah.

[102] *E.g.*, Truth in Lending Act § 103(h), 15 U.S.C. § 1602 (2006).

[103] 15 U.S.C. §§ 2301–2312 (2006).

[104] 15 U.S.C. § 2301(1) (2006) (emphasis added).

[b]   Unconscionability

Apart from these types of statutory and regulatory provisions, contract law usually applies uniformly to consumers and non-consumers. A possible important exception is the law of "unconscionability."[105] A contract or one of its terms may be unenforceable due to unconscionability if the terms of the agreement unreasonably favor one party and if, due to an inequality in bargaining power or other flaws in the bargaining process, the other party was unable to make a reasonable choice about entering into the transaction.[106]

Although this doctrine is not strictly limited to contracts with consumers,[107] it is most frequently applied to transactions made for personal, family, or household purposes.[108] Many courts have been unwilling to apply the unconscionability doctrine to contracts between businesses.[109]

[H]   Contracts for the Sale of Goods

Domestic contracts for the sale of goods are governed by Article 2 of the Uniform Commercial Code. If the parties are located in different countries, and neither is a consumer, the transaction is probably governed by the United Nations Convention on the International Sale of Goods (CISG).

[1]   Domestic Sales Under U.C.C. Article 2

Most first-year Contracts courses include coverage of significant portions of U.C.C. Article 2, which governs contracts for the sale of goods entered into between residents of the United States. As explained in more detail elsewhere, the Uniform Commercial Code is state law, adopted on a largely uniform basis in all 50 states, the District of Columbia, the U.S. Virgin Islands, Puerto Rico, and Guam.

It applies to *all* domestic contracts for the sale of goods, regardless of whether the parties are merchants or consumers.[110] The plain language of U.C.C. § 2-102 specifies that Article 2 "applies to transactions in goods."[111] Although some of the Code's provisions contain special rules that apply to merchants, most of its rules apply with equal force to transactions between one consumer and another, between a consumer and a merchant, and between two merchants.

---

[105] *See infra* § 10.05 Unconscionability.

[106] *See* Williams v. Walker-Thomas Furniture Co., 350 F.2d 445 (D.C. Cir. 1965).

[107] *See* Campbell Soup Co. v. Wentz, 172 F.2d 80 (3d Cir. 1948).

[108] *See generally* Jane P. Mallor, *Unconscionability in Contracts Between Merchants*, 50 Sw. L.J. 1065 (1986).

[109] *E.g.*, Zapatha v. Dairy Mart, Inc., 408 N.E.2d 1370 (Mass. 1980). *But see* A & M Produce Co. v. FMC Corp., 135 Cal. App. 3d 473 (1982).

[110] Scott J. Burnham, *Why Do Law Students Insist That Article 2 of the Uniform Commercial Code Applies Only to Merchants and What Can We Do About It?*, 63 Brook. L. Rev. 1271 (1997).

[111] U.C.C. § 2-102 (2012).

[a]　　　Defining Goods

Article 2 goes further and defines goods as "all things (including specially manufactured goods) which are movable at the time of identification to the contract for sale other than the money in which the price is to be paid, investment securities . . . and things in action."[112] It goes on to specify that goods includes "the unborn young of animals and growing crops."[113] Section 2-107 further explains that it applies to a sale of minerals, oil, gas, and structures to be removed from real estate "if they are to be severed by the seller."[114] Thus, a contract for the sale of coal, in a mine, is governed by Article 2 if the coal is to be removed by the seller. If the buyer will extract it from the ground, it is governed by other law. On the other hand, a contract for the sale of growing crops, or of timber to be cut, is within Article 2, regardless of whether the crops will be harvested or the timber will be cut by either the buyer or the seller.[115] The same is true of any other thing that will be removed from real estate without "material harm" to the realty.[116] Thus, a contract to sell old blackboards hanging on a school wall is governed by Article 2, because the blackboards can be removed from the building without substantial harm to the structure.

Article 2 applies to contracts for the sale of goods even when the goods are to be "specially manufactured" by the seller.[117] For example, in *Propulsion Technologies, Inc. v. Attwood Corp.*,[118] the buyer agreed to purchase certain propeller castings from Attwood, which Attwood was to fabricate and manufacture for delivery to the buyer. The seller resisted enforcement of the contract under Article 2's statute of frauds provision, which requires contracts for the sale of goods to be in writing.[119] The trial court rejected this effort, holding that, because Attwood was to manufacture the items, the contract was for services, and neither Article 2 nor its statute of frauds rule applied. On appeal, the court reversed, noting that U.C.C. § 2-105 expressly includes "specially manufactured goods" within Article 2's scope.[120] Thus, Article 2 applies regardless of whether the seller will deliver goods it has purchased from others, or manufactures the goods itself. If the rule were otherwise, a purchase of a loaf of bread from the bakery would be governed by the common law, but a purchase of the same loaf of bread from the grocery store would be governed by Article 2 — this would be an absurd result.

---

[112] U.C.C. § 2-205(1) (2012).

[113] *Id.*

[114] U.C.C. § 2-107(1) (2012).

[115] U.C.C. § 2-107(2) (2012).

[116] *Id.*

[117] U.C.C. § 2-105(1) (2012).

[118] 369 F.3d 896 (5th Cir. 2004).

[119] *See* U.C.C. § 2-201 (2012).

[120] Oddly, however, the court failed to notice the "specially manufactured goods" exception to the statute of frauds, in U.C.C. § 2-201(3). *See infra* § 5.06[D] Specially Manufactured Goods.

[b]   Hybrid Transactions

The more difficult issue in connection with the scope of Article 2 is the extent to which it applies to hybrid transactions, involving a mixture of goods and something else — usually services. For example, if Connie purchases a new large-screen television from Big Box Electronics, and arranges to have Big Box deliver it, there are some services associated with the deal — delivery. But, this is primarily a contract for the sale of goods, and most courts would have no trouble concluding that the "predominant purpose" of the transaction was to transfer ownership of the TV from Big Box to Connie, and that the services were purely incidental to the sales transaction.[121] For example, *Bonebrake v. Cox* involved the sale and installation of bowling equipment to a bowling alley.[122] Even though there were substantial services involved in the transaction, its predominant purpose was for the transfer of the bowling equipment to the buyer.

On the other hand, if Julie hires Winkler Construction Co. to build an addition to her home, the court is likely to conclude that the contract is primarily one for services, and therefore governed by the common law, even though Winkler Construction Co. will use a large quantity of ordinary building materials — goods — to complete the addition. For example, *DiIorio v. Structural Stone & Brick Co., Inc.*[123] concerned a construction contract that included the delivery and installation of stone on both the interior and exterior of a house that was being built for the plaintiff; it was a contract for services and thus governed by the common law, not a contract for the sale of the stone governed by Article 2.

Most hybrid transactions involve a mixture of goods and services. But, other hybrids might also exist. One example is a contract for the sale of a business. Although it does not involve a mixture of goods and services, it is still a hybrid transaction, because something besides goods is involved: the transaction might include a sale of inventory and equipment (goods), real estate, the name (or "trademark") of the business, and other intellectual property such as customer lists, and possibly accounts receivable owed to the business. Because the contract involves a mixtures of goods and other rights, the predominant purpose test applies. In some cases, the transaction is predominantly a sale of the tangible assets of the business, such as the equipment and inventory. In these cases, Article 2 controls. However, if other assets, such as real estate, receivables, trademarks, and goodwill predominate, the transaction is governed by the common law of contracts.[124]

Despite this, Article 2 has regularly been applied to franchise or distributorship agreements. While long-term distributorship contracts are nothing more than long-term contracts for the sale of goods,[125] others, particularly those where trademarks, advertising, and other features of the franchisor's product line

---

[121] *See* Worrell v. Barnes, 484 P.2d 573 (Nev. 1971) (purchase and installation of hot water tank).

[122] Bonebrake v. Cox, 499 F.2d 951 (8th Cir. 1974).

[123] 845 A.2d 658 (N.J. Super. Ct. App. Div. 2004).

[124] Monarch Photo, Inc. v. Qualex, Inc., 935 F. Supp. 1028 (D.N.D. 1996) (film processing business).

[125] *E.g.*, Custom Commc'n Eng'g, Inc. v. E.F. Johnson Co., 636 A.2d 80 (N.J. Super. Ct. App. Div. 1993).

predominate, are less clearly defined as such. Thus, in *Alesayi Beverage Corp. v. Canada Dry Corp.*, the court held that a soft-drink bottling franchise agreement was not governed by Article 2, even though the transaction involved the sale of some soft-drink syrup and other goods, where the predominant purpose of the transaction was "the establishment of a bottling business."[126]

Courts sometimes take a different approach and, instead of applying the predominant purpose test, apply Article 2 or the common law based on whether the dispute between the parties arises from the goods component of the transaction or some other aspect of the deal. This happened in *J.O. Hooker & Sons v. Roberts Cabinet Co.*,[127] in a contract to sell and install kitchen cabinets in numerous units of a public housing project. The court said that "whether or not the contract should be interpreted under the U.C.C. or our general contract law should depend upon the nature of the contract and also upon whether the dispute in question primarily concerns the goods furnished or the services rendered under the contract." Because the particular dispute dealt with which party was responsible for disposing of the old kitchen cabinets, which the plaintiff had removed, the court applied the common law, not Article 2.[128]

Although this approach seems tempting, and might work in circumstances, like those in *J.O. Hooker & Sons*, involving defective performance, it presents serious difficulties in cases where the issue is whether a contract has been formed at all. If, for example, the question is whether the statute of frauds has been satisfied, the court may need to determine whether Article 2 or the common law applies, as part of its initial inquiry over whether a writing is required at all. Under Article 2, contracts for the sale of goods, with a price of $500 or more, must be evidenced by a writing.[129] Construction contracts, on the other hand, do not usually need to be in writing at all.[130] In this kind of dispute, as well as in those involving the offer and acceptance process, among other issues, the predominant purpose test makes more sense.

Goods that are specially manufactured for a buyer have proven particularly difficult, both for students and courts. For example, in *Propulsion Technologies, Inc. v. Attwood Corp.*,[131] the outcome of the dispute depended on whether Article 2's statute of frauds provision applied.[132] The trial court concluded that Article 2 did not govern, and that therefore no writing was required, because the transaction

---

[126] 947 F. Supp. 658 (S.D.N.Y. 1996).

[127] 683 So. 2d 396 (Miss. 1996).

[128] *See also* Foster v. Colorado Radio Corp., 381 F.2d 222 (10th Cir. 1967); H. Hirschfield Sons Co. v. Colt Indus. Operating Corp. v. Machala, 309 N.W.2d 714 (Mich. Ct. App. 1981).

[129] U.C.C. § 2-201(1) (2012).

[130] The statute of frauds would apply to a services contract only if performance were contractually required to take longer than a year — such as an 18-month employment contract. Even if a construction contract has a deadline of a more than a year from the time the contract is made, the contract usually does not *require* performance to continue until the deadline, and thus the branch of the statute of frauds that requires a writing for contracts that cannot be performed within a year of the time they are made, would not apply. *See infra* § 5.03[B] Contracts That Cannot Be Performed Within a Year.

[131] 369 F.3d 896 (5th Cir. 2004).

[132] *See* U.C.C. § 2-201 (2012); *infra* § 5.06 Sale of Goods.

involved manufacturing services rather than goods. The court of appeals reversed, and reached the right conclusion, explaining that U.C.C. § 2-105[133] expressly places contracts for "specially manufactured goods" within the scope of Article 2. Any other outcome would lead to chaos, with contracts for the same items being governed by different laws, depending on whether the goods were purchased from a wholesaler or retailer, or from the manufacturer.

Another issue that has proven difficult is whether to apply Article 2 to computer software. The problem is exacerbated by the fact that software is usually not sold, but licensed. Courts have drawn differing conclusions, with some courts applying Article 2 directly to the transactions, other courts applying it by analogy, and still other courts applying common law principles. Recently there has been a trend toward treating contracts for prepackaged software as contracts for goods, but contracts for custom software as involving services.[134]

[2]   International Sales

The United Nations Convention on the International Sale of Goods (CISG) applies to sale-of-goods transactions between parties located in countries that have adopted the treaty. Article 1(1) specifies that the CISG "applies to contracts of sale of goods between parties whose places of business are in different States (a) when the States are Contracting States; or (b) when the rules of private international law lead to the application of the law of a Contracting State."[135] In this context, "state" means country. Thus, CISG never applies to transactions between businesses that are both located in the United States, even if performance of the transaction will occur in another country.

Article 1(1)(a) is predicated on the parties' businesses being located in countries that are "Contracting States" — countries that have adopted the CISG. As of March 2013, 79 countries have adopted the CISG, including the United States and most of its principal trading partners, such as Canada, Mexico, Germany, France, Italy, China, South Korea, and Japan.[136] Thus, if a buyer in California and a seller in South Korea enter into a contract for the purchase of commercial manufacturing equipment, the CISG applies. Moreover, if a New York firm and a Belgian firm enter into a contract for the sale of goods, and agree that the Belgian seller will deliver goods from its warehouse in Frankfurt to one of the buyer's stores in Munich, the CISG applies even though performance of the contract will occur entirely in Germany. The parties are located in Belgium and the United States, both of which are "Contracting States." The fact that the transaction will occur entirely in one country does not matter.

If one of the parties is not located in a contracting state, the CISG may still apply under Article 1(1)(b). Its language makes the CISG applicable if "the rules of private international law lead to the application of the law of a Contracting

---

[133] U.C.C. § 2-105 (2012).

[134] *See* Robyn L. Meadows, Carolyn L. Dessin & Larry T. Garvin, *Uniform Commercial Code Survey: Sales*, 59 Bus. Law. 1557, 1558 (2004).

[135] CISG Art. 1(1) (1980).

[136] *See* http://www.cisg.law.pace.edu/cisg/countries/cntries.html (last viewed September 6, 2013).

State."[137] Oddly, the United Kingdom has not ratified the CISG.[138] Thus, if a Canadian business enters into a contract with a British enterprise, calling for the British company to ship goods to Quebec, the CISG may apply even though both parties are not located in contracting states. Because negotiation and performance of the contract occurred in Canada, general principles of private international law are likely to lead to the application of Canadian law. Because Canada is a contracting state, Article 1(1)(b) could dictate that the Canadian court would apply the CISG.

Matters are somewhat complicated by CISG Article 95. It specifies that a Contracting State may create a "reservation" that it will "not be bound by subparagraph (1)(b) of article 1."[139] When the United States adopted the CISG, it declared such a reservation.[140] Thus, if the transaction were between a Detroit buyer and a British seller, a Michigan court would not apply the CISG but would instead apply either the law of the United Kingdom or the state law of Michigan, presumably U.C.C. Article 2.

The CISG does not apply to transactions with consumers. There are several other transactions it does not govern. CISG Article 2 provides, in this regard:

This Convention does not apply to sales:

(a) of goods bought for personal, family, or household use, unless the seller, at the time before or at the conclusion of the contract, neither knew nor ought to have known that the goods were bought for any such use;

(b) by auction;

(c) on execution or otherwise by authority of law;

(d) of stocks, shares, investment securities, negotiable instruments, or money;

(e) of ships, vessels, hovercraft or aircraft; or

(f) of electricity.[141]

With respect to the substantive scope of the CISG, Article 1(1) indicates that it applies to "contracts for the sale of goods."[142] However, unlike the U.C.C., it contains no further definition of what constitutes "goods." In the absence of any further definition of goods, CISG Article 7 provides guidance about how a court should proceed. First, it indicates that in interpreting the Convention "regard is to

---

[137] CISG Art. 1(1)(b) (1980).

[138] Sally Moss, *Why the United Kingdom Has Not Ratified the CISG*, 25 J.L. & Com. 483, 483–85 (2005).

[139] CISG Art. 95 (1980).

[140] *See* Message from the President Containing a Legal Analysis of the UN Convention on Contracts for the International Sale of Goods. S. Treaty Doc. No. 98–9, Sept. 21, 1983, pp. 21–22, *reprinted in* 22 Int'l Legal Mat'l 1368, 1380 (1984).

[141] CISG Art. 2 (1980).

[142] CISG Art. 1(1) (1980).

be had to its international character and to the need to promote uniformity in its application and the observance of good faith in international trade."[143] Thus, interpretive decisions from courts in other countries are to be given considerable regard, in an effort to maintain the uniformity of the treaty's scope. However, this should not lead later courts to give weight to poorly reasoned earlier decisions with results that do not further the other goals of the Convention of advancing the development of international trade.[144]

Article 7 further directs that "matters governed by this Convention which are not expressly settled in it are to be settled in conformity with the general principles on which it is based, or in the absence of such principles, in conformity with the law applicable by virtue of the rules of private international law."[145] This leaves room for countries, consistent with the principle of uniformity, to use their own domestic law to resolve issues such as how to handle hybrid transactions involving a mixture of goods and services, and whether to apply the convention to leases of goods.

With respect to hybrid transactions in particular, Article 3 makes it clear that contracts for specially manufactured goods are covered. It provides: "Contracts for the supply of goods to be manufactured or produced are to be considered sales unless the party who orders the goods undertakes to supply a substantial part of the materials necessary for such manufacture or production."[146] Thus, the Convention does not apply if the buyer is supplying the components and relying on the seller to fabricate them into a completed product. This makes some sense — if the buyer is providing the materials for someone else to assemble, the seller is providing little more than manufacturing services.

Article 3(2) also specifies that the Convention does not apply to contracts where "the preponderant part of the obligation of the party who furnishes the goods consists in the supply of labor or other services."[147] This should resolve many questions about hybrid transactions, such as construction contracts, where services predominate, but it does not speak clearly to other hybrid agreements, such as those for the sale of a business where a sale of goods is not combined with services, but with other types of real and intangible property.

A further complication is derived from the freedom provided by the CISG for the parties to elect not to apply its provisions to their contract. Article 6 of the CISG provides: "[t]he parties may exclude the application of this Convention, or . . . vary the effect of any of its provisions."[148] However, parties who have attempted to avoid application of the CISG have sometimes been surprised by the effect of their language, particularly if they have not been sufficiently specific. For example, in *BP Oil International Ltd. v. Empresa Estatal Petroleos de Ecuador*,[149] the contract indicated that the law of Ecuador would apply to their contract. In interpreting this

---

[143] CISG Art. 7(1) (1980).

[144] *See* CLAYTON P. GILLETTE & STEVEN D. WALT, SALES LAW: DOMESTIC AND INTERNATIONAL 35–36 (1999).

[145] CISG Art. 7(2) (1980).

[146] CISG Art. 3(1) (1980).

[147] CISG Art. 3(2) (1980).

[148] CISG Art. 6 (1980).

[149] 332 F.3d 333, 337 (5th Cir. 2003).

provision, the court determined that because Ecuador had adopted the CISG for international sale-of-goods contracts, the effect of the parties' contract was to make the CISG applicable to their deal.[150] However, in *American Biophysics Corp v. Dubois Marine Specialities*,[151] the court concluded that a contractual term providing for application of Rhode Island law was sufficient to prevent the CISG from governing the contract. Given these disparate rulings, parties who wish to invoke CISG Article 6 and avoid the application of its other provisions should specify that they wish to apply the substantive domestic law of a particular jurisdiction and not the CISG. They should leave no room for ambiguity about their intent.

§ 1.03 HISTORY OF CONTRACT LAW[152]

An entire history of the law of contracts is far too detailed and complex to be covered in more than a cursory fashion here. However, a basic understanding of the origins and development of contract law in England and the United States will be of help to those attempting to learn its intricacies today.

[A] Roman Law of Contracts[153]

The Roman law of contracts, like all contract law, distinguished between promises that were legally enforceable and those that were not. However, Rome never developed a comprehensive set of rules governing contracts.[154] Instead, Rome had a wide variety of doctrines that made promises of various types enforceable.

One of the most important was "stipulatio," or in modern parlance, "stipulation." Stipulatio was a type of unilateral contract. It imposed an obligation on one party and created a corresponding right in favor of the other party. It was created by exchanging a precise series of formal questions and answers,[155] similar in fashion to the manner in which very traditional Christian baptismal ceremonies are still performed.[156] What we would recognize today as a bilateral contract could be accomplished only through an exchange of two separate sets of questions and

---

[150] *See* Keith A. Rowley, *The U.N. Convention on Contracts for the International Sale of Goods*, in Howard O. Hunter, Modern Law of Contracts §§ 23:01–23:07 (rev. ed. 2007).

[151] 411 F. Supp. 2d 61 (D.R.I. 2006).

[152] P. Atiyah, The Rise and Fall of Freedom of Contract (1979); E. Allan Farnsworth, *The Past of Promise: An Historical Introduction to Contract*, 69 Colum. L. Rev. 576 (1969); Grant Gilmore, The Death of Contract (1974); W.S. Holdsworth, *Debt, Assumpsit, and Consideration*, 11 Mich. L. Rev. 347 (1913); Morton Horwitz, *The Historical Foundations of Modern Contract Law*, 87 Harv. L. Rev. 917 (1974); A.W.B. Simpson, *The Horowitz Thesis and the History of Contracts*, 46 U. Chi. L. Rev. 533 (1979); A.W.B. Simpson, A History of the Common Law of Contract (1987); Tony Weir, *Contracts in Rome and England*, 66 Tul. L. Rev. 1615, 1620 (1992).

[153] Malcolm P. Sharp, *"Pacta Sunt Servanda,"* 41 Colum. L. Rev. 783 (1941).

[154] Russ Versteeg, Law in the Ancient World 349 (2002).

[155] W.W. Buckland & Arnold D. McNair, Roman Law and Common Law 194–95 (2d ed. 1965). *See also* Robert W. Lee, The Elements of Roman Law 345–46 (1956).

[156] Tony Weir, *Contracts in Rome and England*, 66 Tul. L. Rev. 1615, 1620 (1992).

answers, with each party taking his turn in making a reciprocal "stipulationes."[157]

Roman law also provided for a number of so-called "real" contracts: mutuum, commodatum, depositum, and pignus.[158] They are referred to as "real" because they were based on the delivery of a thing or a "res" and thus the obligation to return the thing or its value.[159] *Mutuum* involved the delivery of money or goods and the corresponding obligation to deliver an equivalent quantity (but not necessarily the same items) of money, or goods of the same kind, at a later date. *Commodatum* was akin to a bailment or lease of goods, with the bailee required to return the specific goods that had been delivered.[160] *Depositum*, on the other hand, was more akin to a modern bailment, or even, as the name suggests, a deposit in a bank account, where the res was delivered for safekeeping.[161] Finally, *pignus* was similar to the modern possessory security interest or "pledge," with the creditor's obligation to return the goods dependent on the debtor's payment or performance of an obligation.[162]

The Romans also recognized a variety of more informal consensual contracts that resembled many modern transactions, including contracts for the sale of goods (emptio venditio), agreements for the lease of land or goods (locatio conductiorei), contracts for the completion of a specific task, such as construction of a building (locatio operus faciendi), or for more unskilled tasks (locatio conductio operarum).[163] This category included partnership agreements or joint ventures (societas).[164]

There were, as well, a variety of unnamed or "innominate" contracts, which were enforceable so long as one of the parties had already performed its side of the bargain.[165] However, these more informal obligations never expanded to make a simple exchange of executory promises legally enforceable.[166]

---

[157] W.W. Buckland & Arnold D. McNair, Roman Law and Common Law 195 (2d ed. 1965); Parviz Owisa, *The Notion and Function of Offer and Acceptance Under French and English Law*, 66 Tul. L. Rev. 871, 874 n.3 (1992).

[158] Russ Versteeg, Law in the Ancient World 351 (2002); Alan Watson, The Law of Obligations in the Later Roman Republic 157, 167, 179 (1984).

[159] E. Allan Farnsworth, *The Past of Promise: An Historical Introduction to Contract*, 69 Colum. L. Rev. 576, 589 (1969).

[160] Russ Versteeg, Law in the Ancient World 352 (2002).

[161] Russ Versteeg, Law in the Ancient World 352 (2002); W.W. Buckland & Arnold D. McNair, Roman Law and Common Law 277 (2d ed. 1965).

[162] W.W. Buckland & Arnold D. McNair, Roman Law and Common Law 314 (2d ed. 1965).

[163] Russ Versteeg, Law in the Ancient World 352 (2002).

[164] *Id.* at 353.

[165] W.W. Buckland & Arnold D. McNair, Roman Law and Common Law 310 (2d ed. 1965).

[166] E. Allan Farnsworth, *The Past of Promise: An Historical Introduction to Contract*, 69 Colum. L. Rev. 576, 590 (1969).

[B]   Early English Writs

One might have thought that English law would have picked up where Roman law left off. However, this did not occur.[167] Instead, the English system, which we inherited, developed along a different track.

The early English common law writ system was not particularly hospitable to the enforcement of promises. To obtain relief, a plaintiff had no alternative but to frame his complaint within the scope of one of the available forms of action. If the wrong the plaintiff had suffered did not fit within one of the available writs, there was no relief for his complaint. Accordingly, much of the history of the development of the our modern law of contracts is the history of the stretching and manipulation of the forms of action that existed in England in the fifteenth and sixteenth centuries to accommodate the needs of society for a general theoretical foundation for enforcing promises.

The principal difficulty encountered by the forms of action was that none of the existing writs fit the common modern circumstances of breach of an unperformed executory exchange of promises. An owner of goods who had promised to sell them to a buyer simply had no recourse if the buyer reneged on his promise to pay for them when the time for delivery arrived.[168]

The common law writ of "covenant" made the parties' promises enforceable, but only if they were made in a writing to which the promisor had affixed his wax "seal."[169] Physical production of the sealed document eventually became a necessity, thus limiting the general utility of the writ of covenant for more informal promises.[170] Furthermore, like the Roman sitpulatio, the form of the promise completely governed its substance.[171]

The writ of "debt" was also available to enforce a promise to repay a loan of a specific sum of money. However, it was not available if the sum of money owed was uncertain. Moreover, liability was based more on the injustice that would result if the debtor were permitted to retain the value of the money loaned than on the debtor's liability for breach of his promise to pay. While it was useful for creditors attempting to collect loans they had made, or for sellers attempting to collect the price of goods that had been sold and already delivered,[172] "debt" was simply unavailable to enforce an executory exchange of promises where neither party had yet performed.[173]

The writ of "detinue" was available in even more limited circumstances, to

---

[167] *Id.* at 591.

[168] *See, e.g.*, Neri v. Retail Marine Corp., 285 N.E.2d 311 (N.Y. 1972).

[169] E. Allan Farnsworth, *The Past of Promise: An Historical Introduction to Contract*, 69 Colum. L. Rev. 576, 593 (1969).

[170] *See* John H. Langbein, *Historical Foundations of the Law of Evidence: A View from the Ryder Sources*, 96 Colum. L. Rev. 1168, 1183 (1986).

[171] *See* Lon Fuller, *Consideration and Form*, 41 Colum. L. Rev. 799 (1941).

[172] F.B. Ames, *Parol Contract Prior to Assumpsit*, 8 Harv. L. Rev. 252, 260–61 (1894).

[173] W.S. Holdsworth, *Debt, Assumpsit, and Consideration*, 11 Mich. L. Rev. 347, 348 (1913).

recover goods that had been delivered to a bailee and then wrongfully withheld.[174] A buyer who had paid the price of goods, but had not yet received them from the seller, had an action in "debt," not "detinue." The rigidity of the common law writ system would not permit even this degree of flexibility.

The ultimate problem with all of these forms of action was that none of them provided relief for breach of an informal bilateral contract involving purely executory promises. Covenant was available only if the contract was in the form of a sealed writing. Detinue permitted recovery only to recover chattels previously delivered to a bailee. Moreover, debt was available only to recover a fixed sum owed to a plaintiff who had already fully performed. If neither party had yet performed, the law provided no relief.

Apart from these structural limits, the writ system suffered from a more serious failing. The defendant could successfully avoid liability, regardless of the weight of the evidence, by utilizing the procedure of "wager of law."[175] If the defendant could find 12 individuals to swear (truthfully or not) that they believed the defendant's version of the facts, the defendant would prevail.[176]

These limitations were ultimately surmounted largely as a result of the success of the common law courts in their competition with the ecclesiastical[177] and chancery courts[178] for the lion's share of jurisdiction.[179]

[C]   The Writ of Assumpsit[180]

The first word of the first case in Professor Lon Fuller's original Contracts casebook,[181] at the beginning of *Hawkins v. McGee*,[182] foretells for first-year law students the entire history of the modern law of contracts: "Assumpsit." Assumpsit developed not from the early law of contracts, but instead from the law of torts.

The early common law of torts distinguished between "trespass," which was available for wrongs involving some actual or implied physical force, such as assault, battery, false imprisonment, abduction, or physical injury to land or goods;[183] and "trespass on the case," which was available for injuries not involving any kind of force,[184] including defamation or breach of warranty.[185]

---

[174] B. SHIPMAN, HANDBOOK OF COMMON LAW PLEADING 114–17 (3d ed. 1923).

[175] JOHN H. BAKER, AN INTRODUCTION TO ENGLISH LEGAL HISTORY 64–65, 265, 268 (2d ed. 1979).

[176] *See* F. MAITLAND, THE FORMS OF ACTION AT COMMON LAW 34 (1909).

[177] E. Allan Farnsworth, *Parables About Promises: Religious Ethics and Contract Enforceability*, 71 FORDHAM L. REV. 695, 702 (2002).

[178] *See generally* Timothy S. Haskett, *The Medieval English Court of Chancery*, 14 LAW & HIST. REV. 245 (1996).

[179] W.S. Holdsworth, *Debt, Assumpsit, and Consideration*, 11 MICH. L. REV. 347, 349 (1913).

[180] ROY KREITNER, CALCULATING PROMISES: THE EMERGENCE OF MODERN AMERICAN CONTRACT DOCTRINE 15–42 (2007).

[181] LON L. FULLER, BASIC CONTRACT LAW 1 (1947).

[182] 146 A. 641 (N.H. 1929).

[183] *See* BENJAMIN J. SHIPMAN, HANDBOOK OF COMMON-LAW PLEADING 68 (3d ed. 1923).

[184] *Id.* at 83. *See* James B. Ames, *The History of Assumpsit*, 2 HARV. L. REV. 1, 8 (1888).

An action for trespass on the case could be brought against someone who undertook to render a performance and then performed it badly. The classic example, drawn from an early case, involved a carpenter's promise to build a house "good and strong and of a certain form, and yet [who made] a house which is weak and bad and of another form."[186] The analogy to the modern construction contract, involving defective work, is readily apparent.[187] Thus, a subcategory of trespass on the case, known as "special assumpsit," became available for breach of a promise by poor performance or "misfeasance."[188]

In cases involving nonperformance (nonfeasance), rather than poor performance (misfeasance), an action for special assumpsit was not at first available, or in the language of the day, "would not lie,"[189] unless one of the parties had already performed.[190] The earlier misfeasance cases were based on the premise that the promisee had suffered a detriment in reliance on the promise.[191] This made it easy to draw an analogy, in cases where no performance had been rendered, permitting enforcement of the promise where the promisee had changed his or her position in reliance on the promise.[192] By the end of the sixteenth century the necessity of detrimental reliance had disappeared, and an action in assumpsit was available merely as a result of an exchange of promises, on the theory that the promise made by the plaintiff was a sufficient detriment to make the promisor's promise enforceable.[193]

By the outset of the seventeenth century — when Elizabeth I was Queen — an action could be brought to recover damages for breach of a simple contract even though neither party had yet performed.[194] Thus, the owner of a house could sue a contractor for the contractor's failure to commence the promised work even though no payment had been made by the homeowner and was not yet due.

The final ascent of the writ of assumpsit occurred in *Slade's Case* in 1602.[195] *Slade's Case* established that an action could be brought in assumpsit, with its attendant right to a jury trial, to recover an obligation to pay a previously

---

[185] BENJAMIN J. SHIPMAN, HANDBOOK OF COMMON-LAW PLEADING 95 (3d ed. 1923).

[186] Y.B. 14 Hy 6 [1679 ed.], at 18 (1436), 3 HOLDSWORTH, HISTORY OF ENGLISH LAW 430 (4th ed. 1935). *See* E. Allan Farnsworth, *The Past of Promise: An Historical Introduction to Contract*, 69 COLUM. L. REV. 576, 594 (1969).

[187] *See, e.g.*, K & G Constr. Co. v. Harris, 164 A.2d 451 (Md. 1960).

[188] James B. Ames, *The History of Assumpsit*, 2 HARV. L. REV. 1, 5 (1888).

[189] E. Allan Farnsworth, *The Past of Promise: An Historical Introduction to Contract*, 69 COLUM. L. REV. 576, 595 (1969).

[190] James B. Ames, *The History of Assumpsit*, 2 HARV. L. REV. 1, 13 (1888).

[191] *Id.*

[192] *Id.*

[193] *Id.* at 596.

[194] *E.g.*, Strangeborough v. Waener, 74 Eng. Rep. 686 (Q.B. 1588).

[195] Slade's Case, 76 Eng. Rep. 1074 (1602). *See* 3 WILLIAM HOLDSWORTH, A HISTORY OF ENGLISH LAW 451 (7th ed. 1965).

liquidated sum.[196] Such an action could previously only have been brought as an action under the writ of "debt," in which the defendant could avoid liability through "wager of law" with its accompanying risk of perjury.[197] Thus, the writ of "indebitatus assumpsit," or "general assumpsit," was available for the recovery of debts in an action in which a jury would serve as the finder of fact.[198] The right to a jury trial resulted in shifting away from the merchants courts and to the common law courts any jurisdiction over disputes in cases involving what we would today recognize as a commercial contract.[199]

Between *Slade's Case* and the first decade of the twenty-first century, the law of the contracts grew and prospered with the market economy that developed during the last 400 years. The nineteenth century's industrial revolution necessitated its further development and expansion.[200] A clear set of rules helps facilitate economic development through private exchanges.[201] Accordingly, the law must change when business and society changes. Thus, although it sometimes may seem as if contract law is difficult to adjust, the Internet and the information revolution of today spurs its continued adaptation to a constantly changing world.

§ 1.04 SOURCES OF CONTRACT LAW

There are many sources of contract law. When it first emerged from the primal swamp of the law of torts,[202] contract law was common law, made by judges. Today, although much of contract law remains dominated by judges' common law decisions, statutory and regulatory rules now play a prominent role both in the general law of contracts and in the law regarding specific types of transactions. In particular, Article 2 of the Uniform Commercial Code, which governs contracts for the sale of goods in all 50 states, has had a profound effect on contract law in general. More recently, the United Nations Convention on the International Sale of Goods has begun to have a similar effect on transactions in international commerce.

Another important source of contract law is the Restatement of Contracts. There are two versions of it: the original Restatement of Contracts, promulgated in 1932,[203] and the Restatement (Second) of Contracts, completed in 1981[204] by the

---

[196] A.W.B. Simpson, *The Place of* Slade's Case *in the History of Contracts*, 74 Law. Q. Rev. 381 (1958).

[197] Andrew N. Adler, *Can Formalism Convey Justice? — Oaths, "Deeds," & Other Legal Speech Acts in Four English Renaissance Plays*, 72 St. John's L. Rev. 237, 238–39 (1998).

[198] *See* Val D. Ricks, *The Sophisticated Doctrine of Consideration*, 9 Geo. Mason L. Rev. 99, 101 n.11 (2000).

[199] Michael E. Tigar, *Address, Litigators' Ethics*, 67 Tenn. L. Rev. 409, 410 (2000).

[200] Mark L. Movsesian, *Formalism in American Contract Law: Classical and Contemporary*, 12 Ius Gentium 115, 116 (2006) (describing American formalism in contract law from 1870–1930).

[201] James Gordley, *The Common Law in the Twentieth Century: Some Unfinished Business*, 88 Calif. L. Rev. 1815, 1847–50 (2000).

[202] *See supra* § 1.03 History of Contract Law.

[203] Restatement of Contracts (1932).

[204] Restatement (Second) of Contracts (1981).

American Law Institute.[205] As the work of a private group of lawyers, judges, and scholars, the Restatements are not controlling authority.[206] Nevertheless, they have had a powerful influence on courts and are sometimes expressly adopted as definitive statement of the common law of their state. The Restatement (Second) is sufficiently important that you may be assigned to obtain a supplement containing its text. In other Contracts courses you may refer to Principles of International Commercial Contracts (PICC), promulgated by the International Institute for the Unification of Private Law (UNIDROIT), or Principles of European Contract Law (PECL), promulgated by the Commission on European Contract Law, both of which provide resources similar to the Restatements, but for international transactions.

Finally, contract law has been greatly influenced by the work of contracts scholars. Their work includes the great contracts treatises of the twentieth century, by Samuel Williston and Arthur Linton Corbin, as well as more recent and shorter works by Chancellor John E. Murray Jr., the late Professor E. Alan Farnsworth, and Professors John D. Calamari and Joseph M. Perillo. These basic resources are supplemented by a wealth of other books and law review articles by scholars representing a wide range of theoretical perspectives.

[A]   Common Law

The most important source of contract law is the common law, developed by judges as necessary to resolve disputes before them. The most important basic principles of contract law are found in the last 600 years of English and American judicial decisions, in cases seeking to enforce one sort of promise or another. Much of your first-year course in contracts law will consist of reading, briefing, and discussing these decisions.

[1]   Stare Decisis[207]

Our common law system is based on the rule of established precedent or "stare decisis."[208] This doctrine, which takes its name from the Latin maxim, "stare decisis et non quietamovere" or "stand by the thing decided and do not disturb the

---

[205] John P. Frank, *The American Law Institute, 1923–1998*, 26 Hofstra L. Rev. 615 (1998).

[206] Michael Greenwald, *American Law Institute*, 79 Law Lib. J. 297 (1987). *See also* Natalie E. H. Hull, *Restatement and Reform: A New Perspective on the Origins of the American Law Institute*, 8 Law & Hist. Rev. 55 (1990).

[207] William O. Douglas, *Stare Decisis*, 49 Colum. L. Rev. 735 (1949); Oona A. Hathaway, *Path Dependence in the Law: The Course and Pattern of Legal Change in a Common Law System*, 86 Iowa L. Rev. 601 (2001); Lewis A. Kornhauser, *An Economic Perspective on Stare Decisis*, 65 Chi.-Kent L. Rev. 63 (1989); Jody S. Kraus, Essay, *From Langdell to Law and Economics: Two Conceptions of Stare Decisis in Contract Law and Theory*, 94 Va. L. Rev. 157 (2008); James C. Rehnquist, *The Power That Shall Be Vested in a Precedent: Stare Decisis, the Constitution, and the Supreme Court*, 66 B.U.L. Rev. 345, 347 (1986).

[208] *See, e.g.*, Richard H. Fallon Jr., *Stare Decisis and the Constitution: An Essay on Constitutional Methodology*, 76 N.Y.U. L. Rev. 570 (2001); Caleb Nelson, *Stare Decisis and Demonstrably Erroneous Precedents*, 87 Va. L. Rev. 1 (2001).

calm,"[209] means that judges are expected to follow the rulings of judges who have resolved similar disputes in the past. The rule of stare decisis supports several important values associated with the rule of law, including fairness, stability, predictability and efficiency.[210] Applying the law consistently ensures equal justice.[211] Likewise, it prevents the law from changing unexpectedly, thus ensuring stability in the law and fostering public confidence in its administration.[212] It also serves as a limit on the discretion of judges who might otherwise administer the law in a manner consistent with their own values, beliefs, or interests.[213] Of particular importance in contract law is the effect that the adherence to precedent has on the economy, by permitting parties to successfully predict how the law will be applied to transactions they might enter into in the future. Thus, the rule of stare decisis reduces risk for people engaged in business transactions.[214] Finally, adherence to precedent makes the administration of justice more efficient. Judges do not need to fully consider rules governing problems that have already been resolved. Instead, they may simply apply established rules to recurring situations without the necessity of reinventing the wheel on every occasion.[215]

At the same time, as Justice Benjamin Cardozo, a famous scholar of contract law, once remarked: "Law, like the traveler, must be ready for the morrow."[216] Contract law, like all law, must be prepared to adapt to social change. Accordingly, the rule of stare decisis and the policies it fosters are constantly at odds with the value of adaptability.

The development of the common law of contracts provides an excellent example of the relationship and tension between these two values. Any course in contract law inevitably follows the development of the law in response to the industrial revolution of the nineteenth century, the mass marketing of goods and services that developed in its wake, the availability of consumer credit, the development of modern financial markets, instantaneous means of communication, and other technological change, such as the Internet.

[2]   Common Law Decision-Making

Confronted with the need for change or adaptation, judges might take one of several approaches. They might, of course, simply overrule a past decision.[217] Although examples of this strategy are found, they are rare, particularly in the

---

[209] John Paul Stevens, *The Life Span of a Judge-Made Rule*, 58 N.Y.U. L. Rev. 1, 1 n.2 (1983).

[210] *See* Michael Stokes Paulsen, *Abrogating Stare Decisis by Statute: May Congress Remove the Precedential Effect of Roe and Casey?*, 109 Yale L.J. 1535 (2000); Bradley Scott Shannon, *May Stare Decisis Be Abrogated by Rule?*, 67 Ohio St. L.J. 645 (2006).

[211] William O. Douglas, *Stare Decisis*, 49 Colum. L. Rev. 735, 736 (1949).

[212] James C. Rehnquist, *The Power That Shall Be Vested in a Precedent: Stare Decisis, the Constitution and the Supreme Court*, 66 B.U.L. Rev. 345, 347 (1986).

[213] *Id.* at 348.

[214] William O. Douglas, *Stare Decisis*, 49 Colum. L. Rev. 735 (1949).

[215] Benjamin N. Cardozo, The Nature of the Judicial Process 149 (1928).

[216] Benjamin N. Cardozo, The Growth of the Law 19–20 (1924).

[217] *See* E. Allan Farnsworth, Changing Your Mind: The Law of Regretted Decisions (2000).

context of the common law of contracts, where other alternatives exist. Overruling a past decision, even though it was wrong, disrupts most of the values associated with the doctrine of stare decisis. Furthermore, most decision makers are reluctant to admit that a past decision was wrong and thus admit to the possibility of error (readers with children, or those who have observed their parents or teachers, will understand).

However, not all precedent is binding on everyone. The courts of one state are not usually bound by the decisions of the courts of another state. Likewise, and somewhat surprising to those not versed in the federalist nature of our constitution, state courts are not bound by the decisions of federal courts regarding matters of state law. Nor are higher courts bound by the decisions of lower courts. In similar fashion, lower courts may not be bound by the decisions of their peers in different parts of the same state. Thus, a court might ignore the previous decision of another court if the decisions of that other court are merely "persuasive" (or unpersuasive), but not "binding." At an earlier stage of our common law history, courts sometimes "doubted" a precedent, indicating that it was not required to be followed, possibly because the unofficial report of the decision did not accurately reflect the court's decision, or simply that the decision was not a true reflection of the "brooding omnipresence" of the common law.[218]

An obvious and frequently encountered alternative to overruling a decision is to distinguish its facts from those of the case currently before the court. Distinguishing earlier decisions can be a complex task. It is usually important not just to distinguish the facts of the earlier case from the one before the court, but to do so in a way that is consistent with the reasons given for the earlier decision. It would be completely unacceptable, for example, for a judge to rule differently in an otherwise similar fact pattern, simply because the plaintiff's eyes (or skin) were a different color than those of the plaintiff in the decision establishing the earlier precedent.

To the contrary, distinguishing cases usually requires a careful examination of the rationale of the past court's decision to determine whether the facts presented in the new case fit within the rationale of the established precedent, or whether they fall outside the reasons for the earlier decision.[219] This effort is sometimes complicated by the presence of either an incomplete or an exaggerated rationale in the earlier decision. Judges are sometimes unaware of all of the reasons for their conclusions and thus fail to articulate a complete rationale for their conclusion. In other cases, much like parents, they supply makeweight justifications, based on facts present in a case, which might seem compelling, but which are not really the basis for their decision. In still other cases, judges are disingenuous about the reasons for their decision, making the principled resolution of subsequent disputes even more complicated.

---

[218] In *Southern Pacific Co. v. Jensen*, 244 U.S. 205, 222 (1917), Justice Oliver Wendell Holmes remarked that "(t)he common law is not a brooding omnipresence in the sky, but the articulate voice of some sovereign."

[219] *E.g.*, Magallanes Inv., Inc. v. Circuit Sys., Inc., 994 F.2d 1214, 1218 (7th Cir. 1993) (distinguishing Empro Mfg. Co. v. Ball-Co Mfg., Inc., 870 F.2d 423 (7th Cir. 1989)); McCarthy Well Co. v. St. Peter Creamery, Inc., 410 N.W.2d 312, 314–15 (Minn. 1987).

In deciding cases of "first impression," or in attempting to distinguish earlier decisions, courts sometimes refer to "public policies." These public policies are sometimes broad and sweeping, such as "promoting justice," which is not much more precise than "doing good and avoiding evil."[220] On other occasions the court will refer to a somewhat more concrete public policy such as "encouraging efficient breach" or "preventing unjust enrichment." These "policies" sometimes disguise deeper and sometimes more controversial political, social, or moral values that provide the real rationale for the court's decision.

Moreover, judges, who are supposed to "decide cases," but who are not usually entitled to "make law," are more reluctant than other governmental decision makers to reveal the policies on which their decisions are based, lest their decisions appear to inappropriately reflect partisan political concerns, or, worse yet, concerns about the outcome of the next judicial election. Still, on rare occasions, judges will wear their policies on their sleeves, and base their decisions on clearly articulated values about the proper organization of society.[221]

[3]   The Law Merchant[222]

During the eleventh and twelfth centuries, medieval merchants developed a modern and practical set of rules, based on customary practice, for resolving disputes between members of the mercantile class.[223] The lex mercatoria or "law merchant," used by private tribunals of the mercantile class, was gradually incorporated into the common law of contracts in the mid-eighteenth century, largely through the efforts of Lord Mansfield, who became Chief Justice of the King's Bench in England in 1756.[224] The law merchant survives and has had a significant impact on modern commercial law. The Uniform Commercial Code explicitly incorporates the law merchant into the Code, and thus permits resort to it where necessary to resolve an issue not governed by the express language of the Code.[225]

[B]   Uniform Law

Complex economic systems function more efficiently under a uniform system of standardized rules. A nation with 50 separate states, each with its own legislature and court system, can easily create inefficiencies by imposing different and

---

[220] 1 Thessolosians 5: 21–22 (King James); THOMAS AQUINAS, AN AQUINAS READER: SELECTIONS FROM THE WRITINGS OF THOMAS AQUINAS 241 (ed. Mary T. Clark 2000). *In re* George Cindrich General Contracting, Inc., 130 B.R. 20, 22 (Bankr. W.D. Pa. 1991) (recognizing that courts are not "granted 'carte blanche' to do good and avoid evil").

[221] *See, e.g.*, Williams v. Walker-Thomas Furniture Co., 350 F.2d 445 (D.C. Cir. 1965).

[222] J.H. Baker, *The Law Merchant and the Common Law Before 1700*, 38 CAMBRIDGE L.J. 295 (1979); L. TRAKMAN, THE LAW MERCHANT: THE EVOLUTION OF COMMERCIAL LAW (1983); I. Trotter Hardy, *The Proper Legal Regime for "Cyberspace"*, 55 U. PITT. L. REV. 993, 1019–21 (1994).

[223] BRUCE L. BENSON, THE ENTERPRISE OF LAW: JUSTICE WITHOUT THE STATE 60–62 (1990).

[224] J.H. Baker, *The Law Merchant and the Common Law Before 1700*, 38 CAMBRIDGE L.J. 295 (1979); Paul R. Milgrom, Douglass C. North & Barry R. Weingast, *The Role of Institutions in the Revival of Trade: The Law Merchant, Private Judges, and the Champagne Fairs*, 2 ECON. & POL. 1 (1990).

[225] U.C.C. § 1-103(b) (2012).

sometimes unclear rules on parties to transactions that cross state boundaries. The same kinds of inefficiencies can easily occur in international trade due to the conflicting laws of different countries.

Despite the overall inefficiencies of varying and uncertain law, states and nations have incentives to develop their own legal rules, irrespective of the laws of their trading partners. Local laws are sometimes better suited to local conditions. They also leave lawmakers more directly accountable to their citizens.[226] Among their disadvantages, however, include the risk that factions may capture the local law-making process and oppress a minority,[227] or that local governments might adopt local laws that operate to the advantage of local businesses at the expenses of trading partners in other jurisdictions.[228]

The development of cooperatively created uniform laws, such as the Uniform Commercial Code and the United Nations Convention on the International Sale of Goods, can avoid these problems, at least where consensus can be achieved.[229] The development of uniform laws has the further advantage of bringing together individuals with expertise,[230] and diminishes the influence of local factions who otherwise might capture the law-making process.[231] It has the potential for the development of standardized rules that operate in an efficient manner for all of the interested parties.[232]

It was in this spirit that the uniform law movement first developed in the United States in the late nineteenth century. It has resulted in a wide variety of uniform state laws and international treaties, many of which govern various aspects of contract law.[233]

[1]   Uniform Commercial Code[234]

The Uniform Commercial Code (U.C.C.) is the singularly most successful example of uniform law in the United States, and perhaps in the world. A joint product of the American Law Institute (ALI)[235] and the National Conference of

---

[226] Ted Janger, *The Public Choice of Choice of Law in Software Transactions: Jurisdictional Competition and the Dim Prospects for Uniformity*, 26 Brooklyn J. Int'l L. 187, 190 (2000).

[227] *Id.* at 190. *See* The Federalist No. 10 (James Madison).

[228] Edward J. Janger, *Predicting When the Uniform Law Process Will Fail: Article 9, Capture, and the Race to the Bottom*, 83 Iowa L. Rev. 569 (1998).

[229] *Id.* at 580, 583 (1998).

[230] James J. White, *Ex ProprioVigore*, 89 Mich. L. Rev. 2096, 2096 (1991).

[231] Edward J. Janger, *Predicting When the Uniform Law Process Will Fail: Article 9, Capture, and the Race to the Bottom*, 83 Iowa L. Rev. 569, 579–80 (1998).

[232] *Id.*

[233] *See* www.uniformlaws.org (last viewed June 13, 2013).

[234] Peter A. Alces & David Frisch, *On the UCC Revision Process: A Reply to Dean Scott*, 37 Wm. & Mary L. Rev. 1217 (1996); Robert Braucher, *The Legislative History of the Uniform Commercial Code*, 2 Am. Bus. L.J. 137 (1964); Allison Dunham, *A History of the National Conference of Commissioners of Uniform State Laws*, 30 Law & Contemp. Probs. 233 (1965); Eugene F. Mooney, *Old Kontract Principles and Karl's New Kode: An Essay on the Jurisprudence of our New Commercial Law*, 11 Vill. L. Rev. 213 (1966); John E. Murray Jr., *The Emerging Article 2: The Latest Iteration*, 35 Duq. L. Rev. 533 (1997);

Commissioners on Uniform State Law (NCCUSL),[236] it has been adopted in all 50 states and in the District of Columbia.[237]

The U.C.C. started out in 1938 as an effort to revise the Uniform Sales Act, which had been promulgated by NCCUSL in 1906 and was eventually adopted in 37 states. It was transformed into an effort to develop not just a revision of the law relating to the sale of goods, but to promulgate a comprehensive statute governing a wide variety of commercial transactions, including negotiable instruments, bank deposits, letters of credit, bulk sales, documents of title, securities transfers, and security interests in personal property.

A draft of the Code was first submitted to the states for enactment in 1952, but was subsequently revised, in large part as a result of amendments promulgated by the New York Law Revision Commission.[238] The 1962 version that emerged from this process was ultimately adopted throughout the nation. It has since been expanded and revised numerous times, and now covers an expanded range of topics.

The Uniform Commercial Code is comprised of 11 separate Articles covering a variety of consumer and commercial transactions. Although these articles are distinct, many complex consumer and business transactions will implicate rules derived from several articles. A sale of goods on credit to a consumer might easily involve issues arising under Article 2 (with respect to the sale), Article 3 (with respect to any promissory note the consumer signs), and Article 9 (with respect to the creditor's right to repossess the item sold if the buyer fails to make a payment). Likewise, a business deal involving a documentary sale of goods, in which goods are shipped from the seller to the buyer via an independent trucking company, and in which the purchase is financed by the buyer's bank, might easily be governed by

---

D. Murray, *Under the Spreading Analogy of Article 2 of the Uniform Commercial Code*, 39 FORDHAM L. REV. 447 (1971); Linda J. Rusch, *A History and Perspective of Revised Article 2: The Never Ending Saga of a Search for Balance*, 52 SMU L. REV. 1683 (1999); William A. Schnader, *A Short History of the Preparation and Enactment of the Uniform Commercial Code*, 22 U. MIAMI L. REV. 1 (1967); Symposium, *Is the UCC Dead, or Alive and Well?*, 26 LOY. L.A. L. REV. 535 (1993); Symposium, *Is the UCC Dead, or Alive and Well? An Introduction to the Practitioners' Perspectives*, 28 LOY. L.A. L. REV. 89 (1994).

[235] The American Law Institute was formed in 1923 for the purpose of preparing the Restatements, and joined NCCUSL in the U.C.C. project in 1945. William A. Schnader, *A Short History of the Preparation and Enactment of the Uniform Commercial Code*, 22 U. MIAMI L. REV. 1 (1967).

[236] The National Conference of Commissioners on Uniform State Laws is a quasi-governmental body, organized in 1892 to promote the development of uniform laws. Commissioners are appointed by each state and vote, as a state unit, on proposals submitted to them. Ted Janger, *The Public Choice of Choice of Law in Software Transactions: Jurisdictional Competition and the Dim Prospects for Uniformity*, 26 BROOKLYN J. INT'L L. 187, 188 n.4 (2000). *See also* Allison Dunham, *A History of the National Conference of Commissioners on Uniform State Laws*, 30 LAW & CONTEMP. PROBS. 233 (1965). Your author serves as a member of the National Conference, representing Ohio.

[237] Louisiana, with its civil law tradition based on the Napoleonic Code, was the last holdout. However, by 1988 it had adopted all of the Code's Articles apart from Article 2. William D. Hawkland, *The Uniform Commercial Code and the Civil Codes*, 56 LA. L. REV. 231, 242–43 (1995).

[238] Allen R. Kamp, *Downtown Code: A History of the Uniform Commercial Code 1949–1954*, 49 BUFF. L. REV. 359 (2001). *See also* Allen R. Kamp, *Uptown Act: A History of the Uniform Commercial Code: 1940–1949*, 51 SMU L. REV. 275 (1998).

provisions contained in Article 1 (General Provisions), Article 2 (Sales), Article 3 (Negotiable Instruments), Article 4 (Bank Deposits & Collections), Article 5 (Letters of Credit), Article 7 (Documents of Title), and Article 9 (Secured Transactions). Thus, in practice, it is often necessary to consult provisions in several articles to resolve all of the issues involved in a single deal. Fortunately, at least for the time being, law students (and particularly first-year law students) are not usually confronted with the intricacies of these more complicated commercial transactions.

Article 1, "General Provisions," includes numerous definitions applicable throughout the Code[239] and supplies a set of guiding principles to be used in interpreting the remaining 10 substantive Articles of the Code.[240] Of particular importance is section 1-103, which, unless displaced by the particular provisions of the Code, incorporates "the principles of law and equity, including the law merchant and the law relative to capacity to contract, principal and agent, estoppel, fraud, misrepresentation, duress, coercion, mistake, bankruptcy, or other validating or invalidating cause."[241] Thus, when the Code does not speak to an issue, or is not exhaustive in its treatment of a problem, other sources of law may be consulted to resolve the issue at hand.[242]

In 2001, NCCUSL and the ALI approved a comprehensive set of revisions to Article 1. Although some of its more controversial provisions have been rejected by the states, and subsequently eliminated from its provisions, these revisions are effective in 45 states and seem likely to be adopted nearly everywhere soon.[243]

Article 2, "Sale of Goods," governs all domestic contracts for the sale of goods.[244] Even though law students sometimes develop the mistaken belief that it applies only to sales of goods involving merchants, it applies to all sales of goods in the United States, including those between merchants, those between a merchant and a consumer, and those between one consumer and another.[245]

Most first-year law school courses in contract law include some coverage of many of Article 2's most important provisions, though law schools sometimes also offer an advanced course in the law of sales. This advanced course might also cover international sales transactions under the United Nations Convention on the International Sale of Goods and perhaps Article 2A on leases of goods, or other uniform laws. A substantial revision of Article 2 began in 1996 and in 2003 resulted in approval of a new version of Article 2. It is now clear that opposition to several key provisions of the new version makes it unlikely that it will be adopted anywhere.[246] Accordingly, this book refers almost exclusively to the unrevised

---

[239] U.C.C. § 1-201 (2012).

[240] U.C.C. §§ 1-101 to 1-310 (2012).

[241] U.C.C. § 1-103(b) (2012).

[242] *Cf. infra* § 6.05 The Parol Evidence Rule.

[243] *See* www.uniformlaws.org (last viewed, June 13, 2013).

[244] U.C.C. § 2-102 (2012).

[245] Scott J. Burnham, *Why Do Law Students Insist That Article 2 of the Uniform Commercial Code Applies Only to Merchants and What Can We Do About It?*, 63 BROOK. L. REV. 1271, 1271 (1997).

[246] Amelia H. Boss, *The Future of the Uniform Commercial Code Process in an Increasingly*

original version of Article 2.

Article 2A deals with leases of goods. Like Article 2, it was amended in 2003, but the revisions have not been adopted. Your first-year Contracts course may occasionally refer to Article 2A, but you are unlikely to study it in detail.

Articles 3, 4, and 4A deal respectively with "Negotiable Instruments,"[247] "Bank Deposits and Collections,"[248] and "Funds Transfers."[249] Together, these articles deal with various ways in which payment obligations are created and satisfied. Their provisions are considered in law school courses in Commercial Law, Commercial Paper, or more recently Payment Systems. Revisions to Articles 3 and 4 were approved by NCCUSL and the ALI in 2002, but thus far have been adopted in only 10 states.[250] You may study Article 3's provision on the use of a check to accomplish an "accord and satisfaction"; otherwise you are unlikely to delve into Articles 3, 4, or 4A until after your first year.

Article 5, "Letters of Credit," governs promises by a bank or another "issuer" to make payment to a "beneficiary" of the letter of credit when the detailed conditions contained in the letter are satisfied.[251] Article 5 was substantially revised in 1995. It is sometimes covered in a variety of law school courses in Commercial Law, Secured Transactions, or Payment Systems (sometimes still referred to as Commercial Paper).

Letters of credit were traditionally used to facilitate contracts for the sale of goods. A bank would issue a "commercial letter of credit" promising to pay the seller for goods shipped to the buyer, but only on the condition that the seller presented the bank with certain specified documents showing that the goods purchased by the buyer had been shipped for delivery to the buyer. Sellers were more willing to ship goods to geographically distant buyers if assured of eventual payment by a bank rather than taking the risk that a geographically distant buyer with an unknown and unknowable credit history would eventually pay for them.

More recently, banks have issued "standby letters of credit" to guarantee payment of a wide variety of obligations, such as the obligation to complete a construction project[252] or repair farmland damaged by a strip-mining operation. In a standby-letter-of-credit transaction, unlike that with a traditional commercial letter of credit, the issuer of the letter of credit does not usually anticipate being asked to honor its commitment to pay. Instead, the beneficiary of the letter of credit will only demand payment or "draw on the letter of credit" if there is some

---

International World, 68 OHIO ST. L.J. 349 (2007) (regarding the breakdown of the uniform law process and the failure of Article 2 revisions); Linda Rusch, *A History and Perspective on Revised Article 2: The Never Ending Saga of a Search for Balance*, 52 SMU L. REV. 1683 (1999); Alan Schwartz & Robert E. Scott, *The Political Economy of Private Legislatures*, 143 U. PA. L. REV. 595, 651 (1995) (discussing "capture" of the uniform laws process by "powerful interests").

[247] U.C.C. § 3-101 (2001).

[248] U.C.C. § 4-101 (2012).

[249] U.C.C. § 4A-101 (2012).

[250] *See* www.uniformlaws.org.

[251] U.C.C. § 5-101(a)(10) (2012).

[252] *E.g.*, W. Sur. Co. v. Bank of S. Or., 257 F.3d 933 (9th Cir. 2001).

problem in the underlying construction or other transaction that necessitates payment. In this respect, a standby letter of credit operates much like a payment or performance bond of the type that might be issued by an insurance company or a commercial surety firm.

However, a letter of credit is different from a guarantee. The obligation of a guarantor to pay a debt owed by another is usually dependent on the nature and extent of the obligation of the principal debtor.[253] The obligation of the issuer of a letter of credit is independent of any underlying obligation that may have inspired the creation of the letter of credit.[254]

Significantly, Article 5 is expressly subject to the agreement between the parties to the letter of credit. Many letters of credit provide that they are governed by the "Uniform Customs and Practices for Documentary Credits" (or UCP),[255] promulgated by the International Chamber of Commerce, or, in the case of standby letters of credit, by the Convention on Independent Guarantees and Standby Letters of Credit, promulgated by UNCITRAL.[256] Another source of law dealing with standby letters of credit is "ISP98," the International Standby Practices published by the Institute for International Banking Law and Practice.[257] Thus, Article 5 should be considered as a set of default rules available to fill the gaps left by the UCP or to apply to letters of credit that are not made subject to these documents by the parties.[258]

Article 6, "Bulk Sales," was designed to ensure that unsecured creditors received advance notice of the sale of a substantial part of a debtor's inventory. Subject to wide criticism, upon NCCUSL's recommendation, it has been repealed nearly everywhere, except California and Virginia, where watered-down versions of it persist.[259]

Article 7, "Documents of Title," covers bills of lading,[260] warehouse receipts,[261] and other similar documents issued in connection with goods in the possession of a bailee, such as a public warehouse or a common carrier. These documents of title are frequently used in connection with contracts for the sale of goods to facilitate

---

[253] *See* Mary Pappas, *Reconciling Standby Letters of Credit and the Principles of Subrogation in Section 509*, 7 BANK. DEV. J. 227, 238 (1990).

[254] U.C.C. § 5-103 cmt. 1 (2012). *See generally* Philadelphia Gear Corp. v. FDIC, 751 F.2d 1131 (10th Cir. 1984).

[255] Uniform Customs and Practice for Documentary Credits of the International Chamber of Commerce, Pub. No. 600 (2007).

[256] United Nations Convention on Independent Guarantees and Standby Letters of Credit (United Nations 1995).

[257] Janet Koven Levit, *Bottom-Up Lawmaking Through a Pluralist Lens: The ICC Banking Commission and the Transnational Regulation of Letters of Credit*, 57 EMORY L.J. 1147 (2008).

[258] Scott E. Nutter and Bryan T. Pratt, *A Practitioner's Guide to Revised Articles 5 and 8 of the Uniform Commercial Code*, 63 MO. L. REV. 325, 362–69 (1998); Janet K. Levit, *A Bottom-Up Approach to International Lawmaking: The Tale of Three Trade Finance Instruments*, 30 YALE J. INT'L L. 125 (2005).

[259] *See* www.uniformlaws.org (last viewed Sept. 12, 2013).

[260] U.C.C. § 1-201(b)(6) (2012).

[261] U.C.C. § 1-201(b)(42) (2012) (formerly § 1-201(45)).

delivery of the goods to the buyer. Article 7 is sometimes covered in advanced law school courses in sales or in other courses in commercial law. Revisions to Article 7 were promulgated in 2003 and have been adopted nearly everywhere in the country.[262]

Article 8, on "Investment Securities," governs the mechanisms for transferring investment property, such as stocks and bonds, whether held in the form of a "security certificate," an "uncertificated security" or a "security entitlement." Because of the rapid changes in the manner in which investment property is held, Article 8 has twice been amended, once in 1978, and again in 1994. Some aspects of Article 8 are sometimes covered in law school courses in secured transactions.

Article 9, "Secured Transactions," governs the law of security interests in personal property.[263] Security interests are interests in personal property that are given, like real estate mortgages, to secure payment of an obligation.[264] Article 9 also covers the outright sale of certain types of rights to receive payment.[265] Thus, it governs certain aspects of contract law dealing with "assignments" of these rights to receive payment. Likewise, it governs certain consignments and statutory agricultural liens, and liens arising under U.C.C. Article 2.[266] Most Contracts casebooks contain materials dealing with several aspects of such assignments, but not every course manages to cover these materials. The vast majority of Article 9 is typically covered in law school courses in secured transactions or commercial law.

[2]   UN Convention on International Sales of Goods[267]

The United Nations Convention on Contracts for the International Sale of Goods, or CISG,[268] applies to contracts for the sale of goods between parties located in different countries. It governs only if either both countries have adopted the treaty,[269] or, even if only one of the countries has adopted the treaty, if the general rules of private international law would result in the application of the law

---

[262] *See* www.uniformlaws.org (last viewed June 13, 2013).

[263] U.C.C. § 9-109(a)(1) (2012).

[264] U.C.C. § 1-201(b)(35) (2012) (formerly § 1-201(37)).

[265] U.C.C. § 9-109(a)(3) (2012).

[266] U.C.C. § 9-109(a) (2012).

[267] Michael Joachim Bonel, *The CISG, European Contract Law and the Development of a World Contract Law*, 56 Am. J. Comp. L. 1 (2008); Filip De Ly, *Sources of International Sales Law: An Eclectic Model*, 25 J.L. & Com. 1 (2005); Elizabeth D. Lauzon, Annotation, *Construction and Application of United Nations Convention on Contracts for the International Sale of Goods (CISG)*, 200 A.L.R. Fed. 541 (2005); Roland Loewe, *The Sphere of Application of the United Nations Sales Convention*, 10 Pace Int'l L. Rev. 79 (1998); Marlyse McQuillen, Note, *The Development of a Federal CISG Common Law in U.S. Courts: Patterns of Interpretation and Citation*, 61 U. Miami L. Rev. 509, 520–23 (2007); Richard E. Speidel, *The Revision of UCC Article 2, Sales in Light of the United Nations Convention on Contracts for the International Sale of Goods*, 16 Nw. J. Int'l L. & Bus. 165, 166 (1995); Symposium, *Ten Years of the United Nations Sales Convention*, 17 J.L. & Com. 181 (1998).

[268] Apr. 11, 1980, S. Treaty Doc. No. 98-9 (1983), 19 I.L.M. 668 (1980) [hereinafter CISG] (entered into force on Jan. 1, 1988), available in 15 U.S.C.A. app. at 49 (West Supp. 1996), 52 Fed. Reg. 6262–80, 7737 (1987), U.N. Doc. A./Conf. 97/18 (1980).

[269] CISG Art. 1(1)(a) (1980).

of the nation that has adopted the treaty.[270] It was promulgated in 1980 under the auspices of the United Nations Commission on International Trade Law (UNCITRAL).[271] Also referred to as the "Vienna Convention," the CISG was ratified by the United States in 1986 and as of September, 2013, had been adopted by 79 nations.[272]

Unlike Article 2 of the U.C.C., the CISG does not apply to every contract for the sale of goods.[273] Significantly, it does not apply to transactions involving consumer goods unless the seller had no reason to know that they were bought for personal, family, or household purposes.[274] Nor does it apply to the sales of ships, vessels, hovercrafts, or airplanes.[275]

Moreover, the CISG does not contain rules governing every aspect of an international contract for the sale of goods. Although it provides rules governing formation[276] and performance of such agreements, it is silent with respect to rules governing a wide variety of defenses to the enforceability of a contract such as fraud, undue influence, mistake, or unconscionability.[277]

In addition, the CISG provides contracting states with an important escape hatch for parties who, consistent with the principle of freedom of contract, may agree that the convention will not apply at all to their transaction or may vary the application of any of its provisions.[278]

Because of its significance in a growing variety of sales transactions, some Contracts courses include coverage of the CISG. Several popular contracts casebooks include references to its provisions, and it is included in many statutory supplements assigned for use in first-year Contracts courses.

---

[270] CISG Art. 1(1)(b) (1980).

[271] UNCITRAL was established in 1966 by the United Nations General Assembly to promote harmonization in the area of international trade law. *See* G.A. Res. 2205, U.N. GAOR, 21st Sess., Supp. No. 16, at 99, U.N. Doc. A/6316 (1967). The Commission is composed of 60 Member States, representing the world's various geographical regions, elected by the General Assembly for six-year terms. *See* United National Commission on International Trade Law. http://www.uncitral.org/uncitral/en/about_us.html (last viewed Sept. 6, 2013).

[272] *See* http://cisgw3.law.pace.edu/cisg/countries/cntries.html (last viewed Sept. 6, 2013).

[273] JOHN O. HONNOLD, UNIFORM LAW FOR INTERNATIONAL SALES UNDER THE 1980 UNITED NATIONS CONVENTION § 56 (1999).

[274] CISG Art. 2(a) (1980).

[275] CISG Art. 2(e) (1980).

[276] John E. Murray Jr., *An Essay on the Formation of Contracts and Related Matters Under the United Nations Convention on Contracts for the International Sale of Goods*, 8 J.L. & COM. 11 (1988).

[277] *See generally* Peter Winship, *The Scope of the Vienna Convention on International Sales Contracts, in International Sales: The United Nations Convention on Contracts for the International Sale of Goods*, ch. 1 (1984).

[278] CISG Art. 6 (1980). *See generally* JOHN O. HONNOLD, UNIFORM LAW FOR INTERNATIONAL SALES UNDER THE 1980 UNITED NATIONS CONVENTION § 74 (1999).

[3] UNIDROIT Principles of International Commercial Contracts[279]

A further source of rules for contracts in international trade is found in the UNIDROIT Principles of International Commercial Contracts,[280] originally promulgated in 1994 by the International Institute for the Unification of Private Law, or "UNIDROIT," and subsequently revised in 2004.[281] Unlike the CISG, the UNIDROIT Principles are not a treaty, but instead are designed to be followed in much the same manner as the American Restatement (Second) of Contracts.[282] The parties to a contract in international trade are permitted to enter into an agreement that the Principles will govern their transaction.

[4] Principles of European Contract Law[283]

The Principles of European Contract Law (PECL) were developed between 1990 and 2003 by the Commission on European Contract Law.[284] They are similar to UNIDROIT'S Principles of International Commercial Contracts. Their purpose was to articulate a set of comprehensive rules of contract law that applied throughout the European Union.[285] Rather than serving as a comprehensive civil code governing contract law, PECL is more of a Restatement that legislators, judges, and scholars can draw on to discern the underlying principles upon which

---

[279] MICHAEL JOACHIM BONELL, AN INTERNATIONAL RESTATEMENT OF CONTRACT LAW: THE UNIDROIT PRINCIPLES OF INTERNATIONAL COMMERCIAL CONTRACTS (3d ed. 2005); Michael Joachim Bonell, *The CISG, European Contract Law and the Development of a World Contract Law*, 56 AM. J. COMP. L. 1 (2008); Herbert Kronke, *The U.N. Sales Convention, the UNIDROIT Contract Principles and the Way Beyond*, 25 J.L. & COM. 451, 458 (2005); Joseph M. Perillo, *UNIDROIT Principles of International Commercial Contracts: The Black Letter Text and a Review*, 63 FORDHAM L. REV. 281 (1994).

[280] http://www.unidroit.org/english/principles/contracts/main.htm (last viewed May 27, 2009).

[281] UNIDROIT was first established in 1926 as an arm of the League of Nations. It was subsequently re-established in 1940 as an independent intergovernmental organization. Ted Janger, *The Public Choice of Choice of Law in Software Transactions: Jurisdictional Competition and the Dim Prospects for Uniformity*, 26 BROOKLYN J. INT'L L. 187, 189 n.5 (2000).

[282] *See generally* Louis F. Del Duca, Albert H. Kritzer & Daniel Nagel, *Achieving Optimal Use of Harmonization Techniques in an Increasingly Interrelated 21st Century World — Consumer Sales: Moving the EU Harmonization Process to a Global Plane*, 41 UCC L.J. 1 (2008); Joseph M. Perillo, *UNIDROIT Principles of International Commercial Contracts: The Black Letter Text and a Review*, 63 FORDHAM L. REV. 281 (1994).

[283] *See, e.g.,* Principles of European Contract Law (PECL), prepared by the Commission on European Contract Law (Lando Commission), http://www.jus.uio.no/lm/ eu.contract.principles.parts.1.to.3.2002/ (last viewed Sept. 12, 2013). *See* Michael Joachim Bonell, *The CISG, European Contract Law and the Development of a World Contract Law*, 56 AM. J. COMP. L. 1 (2008); Larry A. DiMatteo, *Contract Talk: Reviewing the Historical and Practical Significance of the Principles of European Contract Law*, 43 HARV. INT'L L.J. 569, 570 (2002); Henry D. Gabriel, *Introduction to the Special Issue on the Comparison of the Principles of European Contract Law with the Uniform Commercial Code*, 13 PACE INT'L L. REV. 257 (2001); Ole Lando, *Salient Features of the Principles of European Contract Law*, 13 PACE INT'L L. REV. 339 (2001).

[284] PRINCIPLES OF EUROPEAN CONTRACT LAW, PARTS I AND II (Ole Lando & Hugh Beale eds. 2000); Part III (Ole Lando, et al. eds., 2003).

[285] Michael Joachim Bonell, *The CISG, European Contract Law and the Development of a World Contract Law*, 56 AM. J. COMP. L. 1 (2008).

the law is based.[286] Its provisions are similar, in many respects, to those of the UNIDROIT Principles, though they sometimes provide greater detail about specific situations.[287]

[5]   Electronic Contracting: UETA and E-Sign[288]

Electronic commerce has expanded dramatically in the past 15 years. Until recently there were few rules specifically addressing the formation of agreements across the Internet. Worse yet, existing statutes required many types of contracts to be "in writing,"[289] making these electronic agreements of questionable enforceability.

In response to the need for a set of rules to facilitate electronic means of entering into contracts, the National Conference of Commissioners on Uniform State Laws (NCCUSL) promulgated the Uniform Electronic Transactions Act[290] (UETA), which, by 2013, has been adopted in nearly every state. In 2000, recognizing the need for a uniform standard, and before quite so many states had adopted UETA, Congress stepped into what at the time was a relative void by adopting the Electronic Signatures in Global and National Commerce Act popularly known as "E-Sign."[291]

Both E-Sign and UETA assist the development of electronic commerce by eliminating some of the uncertainty over the enforceability of contracts created over the Internet. Both statutes permit the use of an electronic record and signature in place of a signed writing.[292] Likewise, both statutes make the use of

---

[286] Christian von Bar, *A Common Frame of Reference for European Private Law — Academic Efforts and Political Realities*, 23 Tul. Eur. & Civ. L.F. 37, 41 (2008).

[287] Lars Meyer, *Soft Law for Solid Contracts? A Comparative Analysis of the Value of the UNIDROIT Principles of International Commercial Contracts and the Principles of European Contract Law to the Process of Contract Law Harmonization*, 34 Denv.J. Int'l L. & Pol'y 119 (2006).

[288] Stephen E. Blythe, *Digital Signature Law of the United Nations, European Union, United Kingdom and United States: Promotion of Growth in E-Commerce with Enhanced Security*, 11 Rich. J. L. & Tech. 6 (2005); Jean Braucher, *Rent-Seeking and Risk-Fixing in the New Statutory Law of Electronic Commerce: Difficulties in Moving Consumer Protection Online*, 2001 Wis. L. Rev. 527; Jean Braucher, *Under the Surrounding Circumstances: Amended Article 2's Redundant (or Worse) Electronic Commerce Provisions*, 68 Ohio St. L.J. 115 (2007); Ronald J. Mann, Essay, *Just One Click: The Reality of Internet Retail Contracting*, 108 Colum. L. Rev. 984 (2008); Wolfgang Hahnkamper, *Acceptance of an Offer in Light of Electronic Communications*, 25 J.L. & Com. 147 (2005); Michael J. Hays, *The E-Sign Act of 2000: The Triumph of Function over Form in American Contract Law*, 76 Notre Dame L. Rev. 1183 (2001); John M. Norwood, *A Summary of Statutory and Case Law Associated with Contracting in the Electronic Universe*, 4 DePaul Bus. & Com. L.J. 415 (2006); Minyan Wang, *The Impact of Information Technology Development on the Legal Concept — A Particular Examination on the Legal Concept of 'Signatures,'* 15 Int'l J.L. & Info. Tech. 253 (2007); Jay M. Zitter, Annotation, *Construction and Application of Electronic Signatures in Global and National Commerce Act (E-Sign Act), 15 U.S.C.A. §§ 7001 to 7006*, 2006 A.L.R. Fed. 2d 13.

[289] *See, e.g.*, U.C.C. § 2-201 (2012).

[290] Uniform Electronic Transactions Act (1999); 7A U.L.A. 21 (Supp. 2001); http://www.uniformlaws.org/shared/docs/electronic%20transactions/ueta_final_99.pdf (last viewed June 13, 2013).

[291] 15 U.S.C. §§ 7001–7031 (2006).

[292] Robert A. Wittie & Jane K. Winn, *Electronic Records and Signatures Under the Federal E-SIGN*

electronic signatures and documents voluntary between the parties.[293]

E-sign requires express consent from a consumer before electronic records can be used to comply with statutes or regulations requiring information to be provided to the consumer in writing.[294] UETA, on the other hand, specifies that a legal requirement to provide information to another person in writing is satisfied if the information is sent in an electronic form capable of being retained by the recipient of the information.[295]

To the extent that the statutes conflict, E-Sign prevails, except to the extent that E-Sign has deferred to state statutes, such as UETA.[296] Significantly in this regard, E-Sign contains a variety of consumer protection provisions missing from UETA.[297] In other respects, however, UETA is more comprehensive than E-Sign, covering a range of issues not addressed by the federal statute.[298]

[C]   The Restatement (Second) of Contracts[299]

The American Law Institute (ALI), one of the co-sponsors of the Uniform Commercial Code, was originally formed in 1923 to develop a set of comprehensive summaries of the common law. The ALI is comprised of a select group of lawyers, judges, and scholars. The Restatement of Contracts, adopted in 1932, was the first project the ALI completed.[300] It was subsequently replaced, in 1981, by the Restatement (Second) of Contracts.

Cast almost in the form of a statute, the Restatement provides a comprehensive set of more or less definitive statements of contract law, which purport to summarize the relevant case law on the law of contracts. These rules are supplemented by both commentary and examples, most of which are drawn from actual decisions.

Legislation and the UETA, 56 Bus. Law. 293, 298 (2000).

[293] *Id.* at 299.

[294] E-Sign, 15 U.S.C. § 101(c)(1) (2006).

[295] UETA § 8(a) (1999).

[296] Robert A. Wittie & Jane K. Winn, *Electronic Records and Signatures Under the Federal E-SIGN Legislation and the UETA*, 56 Bus. Law. 293, 324 (2000).

[297] Robert A. Wittie & Jane K. Winn, *Electronic Records and Signatures Under the Federal E-SIGN Legislation and the UETA*, 56 Bus. Law. 293 (2000).

[298] *Id. See also* Julian Epstein, Essay, *Cleaning up a Mess on the Web: A Comparison of Federal and State Digital Signature Laws*, 5 N.Y.U. J. Legis. & Pub. Pol'y 491 (2001).

[299] Robert Braucher, *Freedom of Contract and the Second Restatement*, 78 Yale L.J. 598 (1969); Nathan M. Crystal, *Codification and the Rise of the Restatement Movement*, 54 Wash. L. Rev. 239 (1979); Charles E. Clark, *The Restatement of Contract Law*, 42 Yale L.J. 643, 655 (1933) (First Restatement); E. Allan Farnsworth, *Ingredients in the Redaction of the Restatement (Second) of Contracts*, 81 Colum. L. Rev. 1 (1981); Gregory E. Maggs, *Ipse Dixit: The Restatement (Second) of Contracts and the Modern Development of Contract Law*, 66 Geo. Wash. L. Rev. 508 (1998); Symposium, *Symposium on the Restatement (Second) of Contracts*, 81 Colum. L. Rev. 1 (1981); Symposium, *The Restatement (Second) of Contracts*, 67 Cornell L. Rev. 631 (1982).

[300] The ALI went on to develop Restatements of the Law of Agency, Conflict of Laws, Employment Law, Foreign Relations, Judgments, The Law Governing Lawyers, Property, Restitution, Security, Suretyship & Guaranties, Torts, Trusts, and Unfair Competition.

Although the Restatement does not have the force of law, courts widely follow its provisions and frequently implement them, though on a piecemeal basis, into state common law.[301] Nevertheless, the black letter "rules" found in the Restatement do not always reflect the majority position among the states.[302] Instead, the Restatement's positions sometimes reflect a more normative or aspirational view of what the rule ought to be, or point in the direction of the trend detected by the drafters of the Restatement in the last quarter of the twentieth century.[303] Developments have not always continued in the trend originally detected at that time.[304] Thus, although the Restatement is a useful resource, it is not as definitive as its title suggests.

[D]   Treatises and Contract Scholarship

[1]   Contracts Treatises

Another important secondary source of contract law is found in the scholarly work of professors, judges, and lawyers. The most important scholarly contributions to contract law are found in the two great multi-volume treatises on contract law written in the first half of the twentieth century by Samuel W. Williston and Arthur Linton Corbin. Both treatises organized and explained contract law to a degree not previously accomplished.[305]

Professor Williston taught Contracts at Harvard Law School from 1890 to 1938. He was the reporter for the first Restatement of Contracts, promulgated in 1932, and was the principal draftsperson of the Uniform Sales Act, the precursor to Article 2 of the Uniform Commercial Code. Williston's "Treatise on Contract Law" was first published in 1920. Since then it has been revised under the editorial leadership first of Walter Jaeger and more recently by Professor Richard Lord.[306]

Professor Corbin, who taught Contracts at Yale from 1903 to 1943, was Williston's competitor, both economically and intellectually. They disagreed on many key components of contract law. Professor Corbin served as a Special Advisor and Reporter for the Remedies portions of the Restatement (First) of Contracts. His even greater treatise was first published between 1950 and 1960. It is currently undergoing its fifth revision under the supervision of Professor Joseph M. Perillo.[307]

There are three other shorter, but still important, treatises on contract law.

---

[301] *E.g.*, Midwest Dredging Co. v. McAninch Corp., 424 N.W.2d 216, 224 (Iowa 1988); AGF, Inc. v. Great Lakes Heat Treating Co., 555 N.E.2d 634, 638–39 (Ohio 1990).

[302] *See* Gregory E. Maggs, *Ipse Dixit: The Restatement (Second) of Contracts and the Modern Development of Contract Law*, 66 Geo. Wash. L. Rev. 508, 510 (1998).

[303] *Id. See generally* E. Allan Farnsworth, *Ingredients in the Redaction of the Restatement (Second) of Contracts*, 81 Colum. L. Rev. 1, 6 (1981).

[304] *See infra* § 3.04 Promissory Estoppel as an Independent Cause of Action.

[305] *See* Theophilus Parsons, Contract Law (1953); William Story, A Treatise on Contract Law Not Under Seal (1844).

[306] Samuel Williston, Treatise on Contract Law (4th ed. 2001).

[307] Arthur Linton Corbin, Corbin on Contracts (Interim ed. 1993) (Joseph M. Perillo, ed.)

Professor E. Allan Farnsworth's[308] treatise, *Contracts*, first published in 1982, currently appears in two forms: a one-volume hornbook used by many law students as an in-depth resource[309] and a three-volume Practitioner's Edition. Another is the one-volume hornbook, *Calamari and Perillo on Contracts* by the late Professors John D. Calamari and Joseph Perillo.[310] The third is Duquesne University President John Edward Murray Jr.'s[311] treatise, *Murray on Contracts*.[312] It is particularly useful for those seeking a general understanding of the relationship between traditional common law rules of contract and modern rules applicable to international transactions under the United Nations Convention on the International Sale of Goods (CISG) and UNIDROIT Principles of International Commercial Contracts.[313]

[2] Contract Theory and Scholarship[314]

The Restatement and these treatises are not the only secondary source of contract law. A rich and abundant source of contract law and theory also exists in the form of more narrowly focused books and law review articles.[315]

Classical formal contract theory and scholarship is characterized by the early work Professor Christopher Columbus Langdell of Harvard Law School, who is said to have first developed the casebook method of legal education in his course on

---

[308] Professor Farnsworth had taught Contracts at Columbia University Law School since 1954. The Reporter for the Restatement (Second) of Contracts, promulgated in 1981, he passed away in 2005.

[309] E. ALLAN FARNSWORTH, CONTRACTS (4th ed. 2004).

[310] JOSEPH M. PERILLO, CALAMARI AND PERILLO ON CONTRACTS (6th ed. 2009).

[311] John Edward Murray Jr. is the Chancellor of Duquesne University and the former Dean of Villanova University Law School. He has taught Contracts at Duquesne, Villanova, and the University of Pittsburgh since 1959.

[312] JOHN EDWARD MURRAY JR., MURRAY ON CONTRACTS (5th ed. 2011).

[313] There are also useful treatises on international law, but few first-year contracts courses will delve sufficiently into this law to make it necessary for students to consult them. *See* JOHN O. HONNOLD, UNIFORM LAW FOR INTERNATIONAL SALES UNDER THE 1980 UNITED NATIONS CONVENTION (3d ed. 1999); PETER SCHLECHTRIEM, UNIFORM SALES LAW: THE UN CONVENTION ON CONTRACTS FOR THE INTERNATIONAL SALE OF GOODS 62 (1986).

[314] Legal Realism: Grant Gilmore, *Legal Realism: Its Cause and Its Cure*, 70 YALE L.J. 1307 (1961); John Henry Schlegel, *American Legal Realism and Empirical Social Sciences: From the Yale Experience*, 28 BUFF. L. REV. 459 (1979); WILLIAM TWINING, KARL LLEWELLYN AND THE REALIST MOVEMENT (2d ed. 1985). Relational Contract Theory: Symposium, *Law, Private Governance and Continuing Relationships*, 1985 WIS. L. REV. 461. Critical Legal Studies: Jay Feinman, *Critical Approaches to Contract Law*, 30 UCLA L. REV. 829 (1983); Duncan Kennedy, *Form and Substance in Private Law Adjudication*, 89 HARV. L. REV. 1685, 1717–1722 (1976); Roberto Unger, *The Critical Legal Studies Movement*, 96 HARV. L. REV. 536, 616–648 (1983); Law and Economics: ROBERT COOTER & THOMAS S. ULEN, LAW AND ECONOMICS (1988); Ronald Coase, *The Problem of Social Cost*, 3 J.L. & ECON. 1 (1960); Charles J. Goetz & Robert E. Scott, *Enforcing Promises: An Examination of the Basis of Contract*, 89 YALE L.J. 1261 (1980); THE ECONOMICS OF CONTRACT LAW (Anthony Kronman and Richard Posner eds. 1979); RICHARD POSNER, ECONOMIC ANALYSIS OF LAW, Ch. 4 (7th ed. 2007).

[315] Brian Leiter, *Rethinking Legal Realism: Toward a Naturalized Jurisprudence*, 76 TEX. L. REV. 267 (1997); Seana Valentine Shiffrin, *The Divergence of Contract and Promise*, 120 HARV. L. REV. 708 (2007).

contract law.[316] A more elaborate taxonomy of contract law was later detailed in Professor Williston's classic contract treatise, first published in 1920,[317] and by Justice Oliver Wendell Holmes Jr., in his great work, The Common Law.[318] These expressions of classical contract doctrine were later summarized, with Professor Williston at the helm, in the American Law Institute's first grand project, The Restatement of Contracts.[319] Classical contract law utilized a fixed set of formal rules into which the changing fact patterns of a dynamic society were forced to fit.[320] Its proponents imagined that rules of contract law could be applied with a degree of certainty thought to be found in the hard sciences. This degree of certainty was, of course, largely an illusion. However, the same illusion is earnestly sought by first-year law students who yearn for a definitive set of formal rules that can be applied predictably to a constantly changing world.

The "modern" period,[321] sometimes characterized as "neoclassical,"[322] challenged many of the premises of the classical doctrine. Led by the great legal realists of the early twentieth century, particularly Arthur Linton Corbin[323] and Karl Llewellyn,[324] these scholars questioned the rigidity of classical contract theory.[325] They viewed contract law as a continually evolving set of guidelines rather than a fixed set of established rules. Their work was assisted by others, particularly Professors Lon Fuller[326] and Grant Gilmore,[327] whose work both recognized the decline of the formalism of the past and paved the way for the continued expansion of the doctrine of promissory estoppel.[328] This era witnessed both the decline of the formalism of the earlier age,[329] and a complete metamorphosis of the law of consideration[330] and its related doctrine, promissory

---

[316] CHRISTOPHER COLUMBUS LANGDELL, A SELECTION OF CASES ON CONTRACT LAW: WITH REFERENCES AND CITATIONS (1871). See Thomas C. Grey, Langdell's Orthodoxy, 45 U. PITT. L. REV. 1 (1983).

[317] SAMUEL WILLISTON, CONTRACT LAW (1920).

[318] OLIVER WENDELL HOLMES JR., THE COMMON LAW (1920).

[319] RESTATEMENT OF CONTRACTS (1932).

[320] See WILLIAM TWINING, KARL LLEWELLYN AND THE REALIST MOVEMENT 10–25 (1985); Charles L. Knapp, Rescuing Reliance: The Perils of Promissory Estoppel, 49 HASTINGS L.J. 1191, 1193–98 (1998).

[321] Charles L. Knapp, Rescuing Reliance: The Perils of Promissory Estoppel, 49 HASTINGS L.J. 1191, 1199 (1998).

[322] See Jay Feinman, Relational Contract Theory in Context, 94 NW. U.L. REV. 737, 738 (2000).

[323] ARTHUR LINTON CORBIN, CORBIN ON CONTRACTS (2001).

[324] See WILLIAM TWINING, KARL LLEWELLYN AND THE REALIST MOVEMENT 26–40 (rev. ed. 1985).

[325] See WILLIAM TWINING, KARL LLEWELLYN AND THE REALIST MOVEMENT (rev. ed. 1985).

[326] See Lon L. Fuller & William R. Perdue Jr., The Reliance Interest in Contract Damages (Part 1), 46 YALE L.J. 52 (1936); Lon L. Fuller & William R. Perdue Jr., The Reliance Interest in Contract Damages (Part 2), 46 YALE L.J. 373 (1937).

[327] GRANT GILMORE, THE DEATH OF CONTRACT (1974).

[328] See Mark Wessman, Should We Fire the Gatekeeper? An Examination of the Doctrine of Consideration, 48 U. MIAMI L. REV. 45, 46–48 (1993).

[329] See, e.g., Michael B. Metzger, The Parol Evidence Rule: Promissory Estoppel's Next Conquest?, 36 VAND. L. REV. 1383 (1983); Olivia W. Karlin & Louis W. Karlin, The California Parol Evidence Rule, 21 SW. U. L. REV. 1361 (1992).

[330] See, e.g., Mark Wessman, Should We Fire the Gatekeeper? An Examination of the Doctrine of Consideration, 48 U. MIAMI L. REV. 45, 45–56 (1993).

estoppel.[331] The two great highlights of this era were the promulgation of the Second Restatement of Contracts[332] and the development and widespread adoption of the Uniform Commercial Code.[333]

However, no sooner had the ink dried on these great works, when a post-modern era began.[334] It was characterized by a variety of schools of contracts scholarship ranging from both poles of the political spectrum, and everywhere in between. Among these schools the most important have been "Law and Economics," "Relational Contract Theory," and "Critical Legal Studies."[335]

The Law and Economics movement uses economic theory to analyze the desirability of legal rules.[336] Economic theorists encourage the development of rules of contracts and other law that will result in the efficient allocation of wealth among members of society.[337] An early example of the application of economic theory to law is found in discussions of the theory of efficient breach.

The theory of efficient breach is a rationale for the availability of expectation damages for breach of contract, based on the supposed allocative efficiency of breach. The theory justifies permitting breach of contract and awarding damages based on the injured party's lost expectations when a third party offers more for the breaching party's performance than the breaching party can obtain by performing according to the terms of his original contract.[338]

Consider, for example, a contract for the sale of a used car for $8,000. If a third party offers to pay $10,000 for the car in question, and the market value of the item is only $8,500, the seller will be able to sell the car to the third party and pay $500 in damages to the disappointed buyer who had agreed to pay only $8,000.[339] The buyer will be able to purchase an equivalent car using the $8,000 he would have paid to the breaching seller together with the $500 in damages recovered on account of the breach and, according to the theory, is no worse off than he would have been if the contract had been performed. The seller, of course, is better off than she would have been if she had performed, because even after paying $500 in

---

[331] *See, e.g.*, Charles L. Knapp, *Reliance in the Revised Restatement: The Proliferation of Promissory Estoppel*, 81 COLUM. L. REV. 52 (1981).

[332] RESTATEMENT (SECOND) OF CONTRACTS (1981).

[333] *See supra* § 1.04[B][1] Uniform Commercial Code.

[334] Charles L. Knapp, *Rescuing Reliance: The Perils of Promissory Estoppel*, 49 HASTINGS L.J. 1191, 1201 (1998).

[335] *See* John E. Murray Jr., *Contract Theories and the Rise of Neoformalism*, 71 FORDHAM L. REV. 869 (2002).

[336] The law and economics movement is customarily traced to two important articles: Ronald Coase, *The Problem of Social Cost*, 3 J.L. & ECON. 1 (1960) and Guido Calabresi, *Some Thoughts on Risk Distribution and the Law of Torts*, 70 YALE L.J. 499 (1961).

[337] RICHARD POSNER, ECONOMIC ANALYSIS OF LAW (6th ed. 2002).

[338] *See* Robert L. Birmingham, *Breach of Contract, Damage Measures, and Economic Efficiency*, 24 RUTGERS L. REV. 273 (1970); John H. Barton, *The Economic Basis of Damages for Breach of Contract*, 1 J. LEGAL STUD. 277 (1972). Nathan B. Oman, *The Failure of Economic Interpretations of the Law of Contract Damages*, 64 WASH & LEE L. REV. 829 (2007).

[339] *See* U.C.C. § 2-712 (2012); *infra* § 12.08[A] Contracts for the Sale of Goods — Breach by the Seller.

damages, she has received more for the car than she would have if she had delivered the car to the original buyer for the $8,000 price. And, the third party is better off than it would have been if the contract had been performed, because it received the car for the value it attributed to the item.[340] Awarding specific performance or punitive damages for breach of this contract would discourage breach, resulting in an inefficient distribution of the goods to the injured buyer who placed a lower value on them than the third party who was willing to pay more. Although the theory is vulnerable to criticism, even among economic theorists,[341] it is probably the single most widely studied application of the economic analysis of contracts in first-year contracts courses in law school.[342]

Virtually every major doctrine in contract law, from offer and acceptance[343] to consideration,[344] excuse,[345] and the law of third-party beneficiaries,[346] has been subjected to one form of economic analysis or the other.[347] However, although economic analysis has played a prevalent role in contract theory and scholarship, it has not, apart from the theory of efficient breach,[348] been very directly influential on courts.

"Relational" contract theory, another important branch of post-modern contract scholarship, is based primarily on the work of Professor Ian Macneil,[349] and his adherents. Professor Macneil's relational contract theory focuses on the failure of both classical and neoclassical approaches to take into account the continuing

---

[340] *See* RICHARD A. POSNER, ECONOMIC ANALYSIS OF LAW 130–31 (6th ed. 2002); Lake River Corp. v. Carborundum Co., 769 F.2d 1284 (7th Cir. 1985) (Posner, J.).

[341] *See, e.g.*, Daniel Friedmann, *The Efficient Breach Fallacy*, 18 J. LEGAL STUDIES 1 (1989).

[342] *See* RANDY BARNETT, CONTRACTS: CASES AND DOCTRINE 186 (2d. ed 1998); JOHN P. DAWSON, WILLIAM BURNETT HARVEY AND STANLEY D. HENDERSON, CONTRACTS, CASES AND COMMENT 31–33 (7th ed. 1998); E. ALLAN FARNSWORTH, WILIAM F. YOUNG & CAROL SANGER, CONTRACTS: CASES AND MATERIALS 7 (6th ed. 2001); LON L. FULLER & MELVIN ARON EISENBERG, BASIC CONTRACT LAW 217–218 (7th ed. 2001); CHARLES L. KNAPP, NATHAN M. CRYSTAL & HARRY G. PRINCE, PROBLEMS IN CONTRACT LAW, CASES AND MATERIALS 1078–85 (4th ed. 1999); JOHN EDWARD MURRAY JR., CONTRACTS: CASES AND MATERIALS 762–66 (5th ed. 2001).

[343] *See* Ian Ayres & Robert Gertner, *Filling Gaps in Incomplete Contracts: An Economic Theory of Default Rules*, 99 YALE L.J. 87, 91–92, 95–107 (1989); Juliet P. Kostritsky, *When Should Contract Law Supply a Liability Rule or Term?: Framing a Principle of Unification for Contracts*, 32 ARIZ. ST. L.J. 1283, 1287–90 (2000).

[344] Roy Kreitner, *The Gift Beyond the Grave: Revisiting the Question of Consideration*, 101 COLUM. L. REV. 1876 (2001).

[345] *E.g.*, Richard A. Posner & Andrew M. Rosenfeld, *Impossibility and Related Doctrines in Contract Law: An Economic Analysis*, 6 J. LEGAL STUD. 81 (1977).

[346] *See* Henry Hansmann & Ugo Mattei, *The Functions of Trust Law: A Comparative Legal and Economic Analysis*, 73 N.Y.U. L. REV. 434, 446 (1998).

[347] Lewis A. Kornhauser, *An Introduction to the Economic Analysis of Contract Remedies*, 57 U. COLO. L. REV. 683 (1986); Eric A. Posner, *Economic Analysis of Contract Law After Three Decades: Success or Failure?*, 112 YALE L.J. 829 (2003).

[348] *E.g.*, Phelps v. Frampton, 170 P.3d 474 (Mont. 2007); McKie v. Huntley, 620 N.W.2d 599, 603 (S.D. 2000) (characterizing efficient breach as a "central feature" of contract law); Allapattah Servs., Inc. v. Exxon Corp., 61 F. Supp. 2d 1326 (S.D. Fla. 1999).

[349] *See, e.g.*, Ian Macneil, *Contracts: Adjustment of Long-Term Economic Relations Under Classical, Neoclassical, and Relational Contract Law*, 72 NW. U.L. REV. 854 (1978).

relationships between parties in many contractual settings.[350]

"Critical Legal Studies,"[351] which many view as an outgrowth of the radicalism of the 1960s, rejects classical and neoclassical contract theory as oppressive mechanisms of a market economy.[352] Although critical legal studies attracted considerable attention in the secondary literature, it has been reported to have been "virtually ignored in the case law."[353]

Influenced in part by the Law and Economics movement, a recent trend toward a new formalism has made its way into contract scholarship.[354] "Neoformalist"[355] scholars are fearful that the apparent flexibility of the neoclassical approach permits unwarranted discretion by judges and courts who are ill-equipped to determine the meaning of a contract with tools other than the express formal terms articulated by the parties.[356]

All of these, and other theoretical approaches to the law, can be found in the wealth of secondary literature about contract law.[357] Strains of these approaches may also be reflected, in varying degrees, in the case law itself, though judges rarely expressly acknowledge their allegiance to these various schools of thought.

---

[350] Symposium, *Law, Private Governance and Continuing Relationships*, 1985 Wis. L. Rev. 461; Jay Feinman, *Relational Contract Theory in Context*, 94 Nw. U.L. Rev. 737 (2000); Ian R. Macneil, The New Social Contract (1980).

[351] *See* Mark Tushnet, *Critical Legal Studies: An Introduction to Its Origins and Underpinnings*, 36 J. Legal Educ. 505 (1987).

[352] Jay M. Friedman, *Critical Approaches to Contract Law*, 30 UCLA L. Rev. 829 (1983); Jody S. Kraus, Essay, *From Langdell to Law and Economics: Two Conceptions of Stare Decisis in Contract Law and Theory*, 94 Va. L. Rev. 157 (2008); Girardeau A. Spann, *A Critical Legal Studies Perspective on Contract Law and Practice*, 1988 Ann. Sur. Am. L. 223.

[353] John Edward Murray Jr., *Contract Theories and the Rise of Neoformalism*, 71 Fordham L. Rev. 869, 875 (2002); Eric A Posner, *Economic Analysis of Contract Law After Three Decades: Success or Failure?*, 112 Yale L.J. 829, 855 (2003); *but see* Ian Ayres, *Valuing Modern Contract Scholarship*, 112 Yale L.J. 881, 895–96 (2003). *See* Lattimer-Stevens Co. v. United Steelworkers, 913 F.2d 1166, 1171 (6th Cir. 1990).

[354] Robert E. Scott, *The Case for Formalism in Relational Contract*, 94 Nw. U.L. Rev. 847 (2000); David Charny, *The New Formalism in Contract*, 66 U. Chi. L. Rev. 842 (1999); Lisa Bernstein, *Formalism in Commercial Law: The Questionable Empirical Basis of Article 2's Incorporation Strategy: A Preliminary Study*, 66 U. Chi. L. Rev. 710 (1999); Omri Ben-Shahar, *The Tentative Case Against Flexibility in Commercial Law*, 66 U. Chi. L. Rev. 781 (1999). *See generally* William J. Woodward Jr., *Neoformalism in a Real World of Forms*, 2001 Wis. L. Rev. 971.

[355] *See generally* Sidney W. DeLong, *"W(h)ither the Reliance Interest?" Placid, Clear-Seeming Words: Some Realism About the New Formalism (with Particular Reference to Promissory Estoppel)*, 38 San Diego L. Rev. 13, 15–16 (2001).

[356] *E.g.*, Lisa Bernstein, *Merchant Law in a Merchant Court: Rethinking the Code's Search for Immanent Business Norms*, 144 U. Pa. L. Rev. 1765 (1996). *See generally* David Charny, *The New Formalism in Contract*, 66 U. Chi. L. Rev. 842 (1999); Robert A. Hillman, *The "New Conservatism" in Contract Law and the Process of Legal Change*, 40 B.C. L. Rev. 879 (1999).

[357] *See* Robert A. Hillman, The Richness of Contract Law (1997); Jay M. Feinman, *The Significance of Contract Theory*, 58 U. Cin. L. Rev. 1293 (1990).

Chapter 2

CONSIDERATION

§ 2.01   ENFORCEABILITY OF PROMISES[1]

A contract is a legally enforceable promise.[2] But, not all promises are enforceable.[3] The principal means our common law uses to distinguish between an enforceable and an unenforceable promise is "consideration." If there is consideration for a promise it is presumed to be enforceable.[4] Absent consideration — or one of its substitutes — the promise is not enforceable.[5]

Consideration is present when the promise was made as part of a "bargain."[6] In this context, "bargain" does not mean "a good deal" or a cheap price. Instead, it means that the promise was made as part of an exchange.[7] The question of whether consideration exists for a promise thus is sometimes said to depend on whether something — almost anything — was given as a "quid pro quo" for the promise.[8]

The consideration doctrine ensures the basic enforceability of promises that are made in the marketplace, where goods, land, and services are traded, or exchanged, for cash or something else. These promises have to be enforceable. Our economy would grind to a screeching halt if promises made as part of an exchange were not enforceable.

However, not all promises are made in the marketplace, and not every promise is part of an exchange. A promise to make a gift,[9] — called a "gratuitous promise," or sometimes an "executory gift" — is, by definition, not made as part of an

---

[1] Randy E. Barnett & Mary E. Becker, *Beyond Reliance: Promissory Estoppel, Contract Formalities, and Misrepresentations*, 15 HOFSTRA L. REV. 443, 450–51 (1987); Melvin A. Eisenberg, *The Principles of Consideration*, 67 CORNELL L. REV. 640, 659–60 (1982); Lon Fuller, *Consideration and Form*, 41 COLUM. L. REV. 799 (1941); Daniel A. Farber & John H. Matheson, *Beyond Promissory Estoppel: Contract Law and the "Invisible Handshake,"* 52 U. CHI. L. REV. 903, 930–47 (1985); E. Allan Farnsworth, *Promises and Paternalism*, 41 WM. & MARY L. REV. 385 (2000); Val Ricks, *The Sophisticated Doctrine of Consideration*, 9 GEO. MASON L. REV. 99 (2000); Mark B. Wessman, *Recent Defenses of Consideration: Commodification and Collaboration*, 41 IND. L. REV. 9 (2008).

[2] RESTATEMENT (SECOND) OF CONTRACTS § 1 (1981). *See* Baehr v. Penn-O-Tex Oil Corp., 104 N.W.2d 661 (Minn. 1960).

[3] OLIVER WENDELL HOLMES, THE COMMON LAW 253 (3d ed. 1991); Randy Barnett, *A Consent Theory of Contract*, 86 COLUM. L. REV. 269 (1986).

[4] Lawyers might say that it is "prima facie" or (on first appearance) enforceable.

[5] *See* RESTATEMENT (SECOND) OF CONTRACTS § 17 (1981).

[6] RESTATEMENT (SECOND) OF CONTRACTS § 71(1) (1981); *See generally* David Gamage & Allon Kedem, *Commodification and Contract Formation: Placing the Consideration Doctrine on Stronger Foundations*, 73 U. CHI. L. REV. 1299 (2006); Daniel Markovits, *Contract and Collaboration*, 113 YALE L. J. 1417 (2004).

[7] RESTATEMENT (SECOND) OF CONTRACTS § 71(2) (1981).

[8] RESTATEMENT (SECOND) OF CONTRACTS § 71 cmt. a (1981).

[9] In the law of property one of the essential elements in making a gift is to express the intention to make the gratuitous transfer presently, and not in the future. Also in the law of property, a gift is not a gift until it is complete, through delivery, at which time the donee becomes the new owner. RESTATEMENT (SECOND) OF PROPERTY § 32.2 (1992). *See* Phillip Mechem, *The Requirement of Delivery in Gifts of Chattels and of Choses in Action Evidenced by Commercial Instruments (Pt. 1)*, 21 U. ILL. L. REV. 341 (1926). Until then, no matter what the old owner has said, she remains the owner free to do with her property whatever she desires. E. Allan Farnsworth, *Promises and Paternalism*, 41 WM. & MARY L. REV. 385, 397–98 (2000). 2 WILLIAM BLACKSTONE, COMMENTARIES ON THE LAWS OF ENGLAND 441 (1766) ("[a true] and proper gift . . . is always accompanied with delivery of possession").

exchange. These promises lack consideration and, unless some other reason for enforcing the promise exists,[10] are not enforceable.

Promises to make gifts commonly occur in two recurring settings: promises to family members and promises to organized charities.[11] In these situations, the person making the promise is usually motivated by a spirit of generosity rather than by whatever she will receive in exchange for her promise.

Although promises to make a gift are not part of an exchange, they are frequently relied on. Family members, confident that their more wealthy relatives will follow through on their commitments, change their plans. Likewise, organized charities start new projects, or expand existing ones, on the faith that charitable pledges made to them will be fulfilled. The plight of a person who changed her position in reliance on a promise cries out for a remedy. As will be seen in the next chapter, promises that are relied upon are enforceable, even where consideration is missing, through the doctrine of promissory estoppel.[12]

Consideration issues sometimes arise in commercial settings. This most frequently happens when the parties to a business deal agree to change the terms of their original bargain. If the modification is one sided, with only one of the parties changing its duties, consideration for the modified promise may be absent. In these situations, courts sometimes relax the consideration doctrine to permit the enforcement of promises that traditionally would not have been enforceable.[13] The doctrine has been relaxed in these settings through legislation.[14] In still other circumstances, promissory estoppel supplies an alternative basis for making the promise enforceable without consideration.[15]

People also sometimes make promises when they feel a sense of moral obligation to compensate someone for a benefit they have previously received.[16] Even though consideration is missing from these promises, courts sometimes still enforce them under the "material benefit" rule.[17] Finally, the law imposes a "quasi-contractual" obligation to make restitution when a person is unjustly enriched at the expense of someone else, even though no promise was ever made. These alternative theories of recovery, promissory estoppel, the material benefit rule, and restitution are explained in the chapter that follows.

---

[10] *See infra* Ch. 3 Promissory Estoppel: Detrimental Reliance.

[11] Dougherty v. Salt, 125 N.E. 94 (N.Y. 1919); Congregation Kadimah Toras-Moshe v. DeLeo, 540 N.E.2d 691 (Mass. 1989); Schnell v. Nell, 1861 Ind. LEXIS 287 (Nov. 25, 1861). *See* Benjamin F. Boyer, *Promissory Estoppel: Principal from Precedents (Pt. 1)*, 50 MICH. L. REV. 639, 644 (1952); E. Allan Farnsworth, *Promises and Paternalism*, 41 WM. & MARY L. REV. 385, 388 (2000).

[12] *See infra* Ch. 3 Promissory Estoppel: Detrimental Reliance.

[13] *See infra* § 2.06 Pre-Existing Legal Duty Rule.

[14] U.C.C. § 2-209 (2012).

[15] *See infra* Ch. 3 Promissory Estoppel: Detrimental Reliance.

[16] E. Allan Farnsworth, *Promises and Paternalism*, 41 WM. & MARY L. REV. 385, 388–89 (2000).

[17] *See infra* § 2.07 Past Consideration and Moral Obligation: The Material Benefit Rule.

§ 2.02   FORMAL ALTERNATIVES TO CONSIDERATION

[A]   Formality and Ritual in Contract Law[18]

Formality and ritual play a significant role in contract law, just as they do in the rest of society.[19] Many of life's most significant occasions, such as birth, graduation, marriage, divorce, and death, are recognized with established rituals designed to signify the importance of the event. Many informal contracts are formalized with the ritual of a signature, or more casually, with a handshake.[20] Even when not required by law, these social constructs play an important part of lay persons' understandings of how agreements are made.

Contract law utilizes a wide variety of rituals to signify the enforceability of a promise. The tradition of the "seal" originally required impressing melted wax with a unique impression. Although the seal was too cumbersome for most informal contracts, where it was used, it left little room for doubt about the parties' intent to be bound. When its ritualistic features were eliminated, it lost its utility. Likewise, the Uniform Written Obligations Act, with its requirement of a signed statement expressing the intent that the contract be legally enforceable, attempts to impose a formal requirement for making a promise legally enforceable in circumstances where the conventional consideration doctrine might not be satisfied. As will be seen, the consideration doctrine itself has some ritualistic features. If the parties adhere to these rituals and make their agreement appear to involve an exchange, their agreement may be enforceable even though there is no real bargain. Sometimes, the appearance or recitation of an exchange is sufficient.

The simple ritual of memorializing a contract in writing and "signing" the written agreement is sometimes critical to the question of whether the agreement will be enforced. The "statue of frauds" requires certain particularly important agreements to be in a signed writing before the agreement can be enforced.[21] In e-commerce transactions, use of a "password," or other means of electronic authentication, now serves as a useful substitute for a more traditional analog signature.[22] These and other rituals have been recognized as useful in contract law in several ways. They have long been recognized as performing certain "cautionary," "evidentiary," "channeling," and "clarification" functions.[23]

---

[18] James B. Ames, *The History of Assumpsit*, 2 Harv. L. Rev. 1 (1888); Lon Fuller, *Consideration and Form*, 41 Colum. L. Rev. 799 (1941); Melvin A. Eisenberg, *Donative Promises*, 47 U. Chi. L. Rev. 1 (1979); Lon Fuller, *Consideration and Form*, 41 Colum. L. Rev. 799 (1941); W.S. Holdsworth, *The Modern History of the Doctrine of Consideration*, 2 B.U.L. Rev. 87 (1922); 3 William S. Holdsworth, History of English Law 441–454 (3d ed. 1927); Duncan Kennedy, *From the Will Theory to the Principle of Private Autonomy: Lon Fuller's "Consideration and Form,"* 100 Colum. L. Rev. 94 (2000); Andrew Kull, *Reconsidering Gratuitous Promises*, 21 J. Legal Stud. 39 (1992).

[19] *See* Morris R. Cohen, *The Basis of Contract*, 46 Harv. L. Rev. 553, 582 (1933).

[20] Rick Smith, Note, *Here's Why Hollywood Should Kiss the Handshake Deal Goodbye*, 23 Loy. L.A. Ent. L. Rev. 503 (2003).

[21] *See infra* Ch. 5 The Statute of Frauds: Is a Writing Required?

[22] *See infra* § 5.08 Electronic Contracting.

[23] Lon Fuller, *Consideration and Form*, 41 Colum. L. Rev. 799 (1941).

All of these mechanisms, from the traditional seal and the statute of frauds to the doctrine of consideration, and even a handshake, serve a cautionary function. To one extent or another, they slow the parties down and give them time to reflect on their decision to enter into the agreement. They give parties more of an opportunity to consider the consequences of their agreement before finalizing their commitment to be bound.

Rituals also perform a valuable evidentiary function. When the enforceability of a promise is challenged in court, the presence of a person's seal or signature provides a large measure of assurance to the court that the promise was a real one. Without this assurance the plaintiff's claim might be nothing more than a flight of fancy, or worse yet, part of a fraudulent scheme. The consideration doctrine's requirement of a bargain, in which the promisor either receives something in exchange for his promise or the promisee incurs a detriment in exchange for the promise, similarly supplies useful evidence that the defendant's promise was real. Otherwise there would be less of a reason for the promisee to supply the promisor with a benefit or for the promisee to suffer some detriment. The presence of a benefit to the promisor or a detriment to the promisee, in apparent exchange for the promise, helps prove that the promise was really made.[24]

The channeling function is a bit more difficult to understand. Adherence to some sort of ritual assists the judicial system in discerning the difference between legally binding promises and those not deserving of government intervention. It also helps members of society to recognize the difference and successfully predict the likely consequences of promises they make.

Finally, scholars have noted that some rituals, and particularly the seal and the statute of frauds, serve a clarification function which helps avoid ambiguity about the terms of the parties' agreement.[25] The necessity of reducing agreements to writing encourages the parties to memorialize more of the details of their transaction in the writing and thus possibly avoid later disputes about their intent.

A significant question in contract law is whether promises should be enforced when they are not accompanied by one of these, or some other, ritual. A further question is whether the more informal doctrine of promissory estoppel provides alternate means of fulfilling the functions served by these rituals, or, in the alternative, whether the promise should be enforced even though the purposes served by these rituals are missing.

[B] The Seal[26]

Before the development of the modern consideration doctrine, promises were enforceable if they were "sealed."[27] The seal involved making an impression on a

---

[24] *See* Lon Fuller, *Consideration and Form*, 41 COLUM. L. REV. 799, 800–04 (1941). *But see* Andrew Kull, *Reconsidering Gratuitous Promises*, 21 J. LEGAL STUD. 39, 51 (1992).

[25] Joseph M. Perillo, *The Statute of Frauds in the Light of the Functions and Dysfunctions of Form*, 23 FORDHAM L. REV. 39, 43–69 (1974).

[26] Robert Braucher, *The Status of the Seal Today*, 9 PRAC. LAW. 97 (1963); E. Allan Farnsworth, *Promises and Paternalism*, 41 WM. & MARY L. REV. 385 (2000); Lon Fuller, *Consideration and Form*,

piece of melted wax which was affixed to the written contract. The sealed writing was then physically delivered to the promisee.[28] When people exchanged promises, each person delivered his own sealed promise to the other. If a promise was made in writing containing a seal, and the promise was not performed, the promisee could bring an action against the promisor under the common law writ of "covenant."[29]

Although modern courts sometimes say that the seal "imports a consideration" or creates a "presumption of consideration," the doctrines are not directly related to one another.[30] As one court said: "[The seal] derives its efficacy from the solemnity of its execution — the acts of sealing and delivery, not upon the idea that the seal imports a consideration, but because it is his solemn act and deed, and is therefore obligatory."[31]

The ritual associated with dripping hot wax onto a written promise and impressing it with a seal was an effective way to ensure both that a promise had been made as well as that it had been carefully considered. Attaching the seal to a promise required deliberate effort. Sealed promises were not made inadvertently or on a momentary impulse.

The seal also made it easy for courts to distinguish promises that were enforceable from those which were not. It also made it easy for people to confidently predict whether a court would enforce the promise. The presumption of enforceability was so strong that a "sealed" promise could not even be defended on the basis of fraud.[32] The seal thus served several important functions that are commonly associated with formal requirements for the enforceability of a promise.[33]

However, as the exclusive means of distinguishing enforceable and unenforceable promises, the seal was far too restrictive. It worked well for particularly important contracts entered into between members of the nobility, but was far too cumbersome for the countless number of routine transactions in the everyday marketplace. This was not a problem in immediate exchanges of goods for cash, but presented a problem when one or both party was going to perform at sometime in the future. The practical necessity for a less ritualistic method of making an enforceable promise, eventually led to the decline of the seal.

---

41 COLUM. L. REV. 799 (1941); Harold D. Hazeltine, *The Formal Contract of Early English Law*, 10 COLUM. L. REV. 608 (1910); Eric Mills Holmes, *Stature and Status of a Promise Under Seal as a Legal Formality*, 29 WILLAMETTE L. REV. 617 (1993) (survey of state treatment of the seal). *See also* 7 J. WIGMORE, EVIDENCE § 2161 (Chadbourn rev. ed. 1978) (history of the seal in England).

[27] *See* Frederick E. Crane, *The Magic of the Private Seal*, 15 COLUM. L. REV. 24 (1915); 3 W.S. HOLDSWORTH, A HISTORY OF ENGLISH LAW 417 (3d ed. Vol. III 1923).

[28] A.W.B. SIMPSON, A HISTORY OF THE COMMON LAW OF CONTRACT 90 (1987). *See* RESTATEMENT (SECOND) OF CONTRACTS § 96 cmt. a (1981).

[29] *Supra* § 1.03 History of Contract Law.

[30] *E.g.*, Venners v. Goldberg, 758 A.2d 567 (Md. Ct. App. 2000).

[31] Walker v. Walker, 1852 N.C. LEXIS 50 (June 1852).

[32] WILLIAM F. WALSH, A TREATISE ON EQUITY 491–92 (1930).

[33] *See infra* § 2.02[A] Formality and Ritual in Contract Law; Lon L. Fuller, *Consideration and Form*, 41 COLUM. L. REV. 779, 800–801 (1941).

This decline occurred in several stages.[34] Originally, the seal had to be impressed upon wax which had been melted and dripped onto the written contract.[35] Later, it was sufficient for the paper itself to be impressed with a seal in the same manner as a notary public or county recorder's office might today emboss its seal on a document to demonstrate its authenticity.[36] Eventually, the simple inclusion of the word "seal" "scrawl" or "scroll" on the document, or including either the words "locus sigilli" (meaning the place of the seal), or even just the preprinted initials "L.S." was enough.[37] The nadir of the seal, however is probably best exemplified by *Appeal of Hacker*, where a 1/8 inch dash following the promisor's written signature was held sufficient as a seal.[38] In other cases, a recitation in the document that it had been sealed was sometimes held sufficient even though there was no other evidence of a seal itself.[39]

The rise of the doctrine of consideration, which made promises enforceable in the absence of a seal, combined with the relaxation of the formal rituals involved in dripping wax onto a document and embossing the wax with a seal, ultimately led to the deterioration of the seal as a means of making a promise enforceable. U.C.C. § 2-203 wipes out the effect of the seal with respect to contracts for the sale of goods.[40] Further, many states have now legislatively eliminated or diminished the effect of a seal with respect to other types of contracts.[41] Other states have eliminated or limited its effect by judicial action.[42]

Despite these changes, the seal still carries some weight in a few states.[43] In some states a sealed contract has a longer statute of limitations period.[44] In others, a seal creates a rebuttable presumption that consideration was supplied.[45] However, with these and a few other minor exceptions, the seal has fallen into disuse and has little modern relevance.[46]

---

[34] *See* Allen v. Sullivan R.R., 1855 N.H. LEXIS 231 (Dec. 1855).

[35] RESTATEMENT (SECOND) OF CONTRACTS § 96 cmt. a (1981).

[36] *E.g.*, Heighway v. Pendleton, 1846 Ohio LEXIS 234 (Dec. 1846).

[37] *E.g.*, Pitts v. Pitchford, 201 So. 2d 563 (Fla. Dist. Ct. App. 1967). *See* RESTATEMENT (SECOND) OF CONTRACTS § 96 cmt. a (1981).

[38] Appeal of Hacker, 15 A. 500 (Pa. 1888).

[39] RESTATEMENT (SECOND) OF CONTRACTS § 100 cmt. b (1981).

[40] U.C.C. § 2-203 & cmt (2010). *See also* U.C.C. § 2A-203 (2010) (lease of goods).

[41] *E.g.*, OHIO REV. CODE ANN. § 5.11 (Anderson 2001). *See* RESTATEMENT (SECOND) OF CONTRACTS § 94, Statutory Note (1981).

[42] *E.g.*, Knott v. Racicot, 812 N.E.2d 1207 (Mass. 2004).

[43] Eric Mills Holmes, *Stature and Status of a Promise Under Seal as a Legal Formality*, 29 WILLAMETTE L. REV. 617 (1993).

[44] *See* RESTATEMENT (SECOND) OF CONTRACTS, Introductory Note to Chapter 4, Topic 3, Contracts Under Seal; Writing as a Statutory Substitute for the Seal (1981).

[45] *E.g.*, CAL. CIV. CODE § 1614 (West 2008).

[46] *See* ARTHUR LINTON CORBIN, 3 CORBIN ON CONTRACTS § 10.2 (2013).

[C]   The Uniform Written Obligations Act[47]

In place of the seal, the National Conference of Commissioners on Uniform State Laws (NCCUSL) and the American Law Institute (ALI)[48] promulgated the Uniform Written Obligations Act. If adopted, it would make a signed written promise enforceable "if the writing also contains an additional express statement, in any form or language, that the signer intends to be legally bound."[49] In effect, the act would have supplanted the seal with a more elaborate express statement that the promisor intended her promise to have binding effect.

It was adopted in only two states,[50] and remains in effect only in Pennsylvania, where it is narrowly construed. Under the Act, if a written promise contains an express statement that the promise was intended to be legally binding, the promise is enforceable without regard to the presence or absence of consideration.[51] This is true even if the critical language appeared in a preprinted standardized form and was not even noticed by the person who signed it.[52]

§ 2.03   CONSIDERATION — A BARGAINED-FOR EXCHANGE[53]

Although consideration has been defined in many ways, it is now customarily regarded as a bargained-for exchange.[54] The human impulse to enforce promises that are part of an exchange is universal.[55] Fortunately, in most cases, exchanges are fairly easy to detect.

Although courts sometimes claim that consideration is present even though there was no exchange, closer examination of the facts of these cases reveals that the promise is enforceable under an alternative theory, which provides a better explanation for its enforceability. This is recognized in Restatement (Second) of Contracts § 17 which specifies that "the formation of a contract requires a bargain . . . [unless a contract is formed] under special rules applicable to formal contracts [regarding the seal] or under the rules stated in [Restatement (Second)]

---

[47] Sherman Steele, *The Uniform Written Obligations Act — A Criticism*, 21 Ill. L. Rev. 185 (1927).

[48] *See supra* § 1.04[B][1] Uniform Commercial Code.

[49] Uniform Written Obligations Act § 1 (1925).

[50] New York has a similar statute. N.Y. Gen. Oblig. Law § 5-1109 (McKinney 2008).

[51] *E.g. In re* Wirth, 14 A.D.3d 572 (N.Y. App. Div. 2005).

[52] Thomas v. First Nat'l Bank of Scranton, 96 A.2d 196 (Pa. Super. Ct. 1953) (pre-printed form releasing bank from liability for failing to stop payment of a check where the bank had a pre-existing duty to follow the customer's directions).

[53] Oliver Wendell Holmes, Jr., The Common Law (1881); Melvin A. Eisenberg, *The Principles of Consideration*, 67 Cornell L. Rev. 640 (1982); Val D. Ricks, *The Sophisticated Doctrine of Consideration*, 9 Geo. Mason L. Rev. 99 (2000).

[54] *See* Restatement (Second) of Contracts § 71 (1981).

[55] Morris. B. Hoffman, *The Neuroeconomic Path of the Law*, 359 Phil. Trans. Royal Soc., Series B, Biological Sciences 1667, 1671 (2004) ("It appears that humans, and indeed all intensely social animals, have a predisposition to follow three central behavioral rules: (i) promises to reciprocate must be kept (contract) . . . .").

§§ 82–94."[56] Thus, the Restatement recognizes that consideration is not the only basis for the enforcement of a promise — the doctrine has several substitutes.

Even though a contract may be formed under several other principles, courts usually first examine the agreement to determine whether there was consideration — whether it was part of an exchange. If the promise is supported by consideration, it is enforceable. Only if consideration is missing must courts bring these other rules to bear on the question.

[A]   The Concept of Exchange[57]

In order to understand consideration it is necessary to understand the concept of an "exchange." Consideration describes a reciprocal exchange between two parties, with each person providing what the other one wants, as part of their agreement in a "bargained-for exchange."[58] This is sometimes described as a *quid pro quo*: "I'll give you what you want if you give me what I want." Stated in a slightly different way, consideration is what each promisor seeks in return for the making of her promise.[59]

Consider an easy example: After deciding to sell his used BMW, Sam invites inquiries from prospective buyers. He eventually decides to sell his car to Barb for $18,000, the price she agrees to pay. Sam promises Barb that he will sell the car to her for $18,000, and Barb promises Sam that she will pay him $18,000 for it. This is a set of two promises involving an obvious bargained-for exchange. Sam and Barb are each making their respective promises in return for *the reciprocal promise* of the other. Both of their promises are supported by consideration because each promise was made in exchange for the other: Sam's promise to sell the car is supported by Barb's promise to pay the agreed price, and Barb's promise to pay is supported by Sam's promise to deliver the car. Their respective promises are consideration for each other's return promise.[60] The same is true in every contract for the sale of goods, because by definition, a "sale" is "the passing of title from the seller to the buyer *for a price*."[61]

It is helpful to imagine that by imposing a requirement of consideration, contract law is saying that before a promise will be enforceable, the promisor must have received something she sought in return for making it — even if what was received was nothing more than the other party's reciprocal promise. Another way of defining consideration, therefore, is to think of it as being "the promisor's price" for her promise.

Now assume that instead of selling his BMW, Sam wants to give it to his good friend Lisa, as a gift. But, Sam wishes to wait until his new Mercedez-Benz arrives

---

[56] RESTATEMENT (SECOND) OF CONTRACTS § 17 (1981).

[57] *See* Jody S. Kraus, Essay, *From Langdell to Law and Economics: Two Conceptions of Stare Decisis in Contract Law and Theory*, 94 VA. L. REV. 157 (2008).

[58] RESTATEMENT (SECOND) OF CONTRACTS § 71(1), (2) (1981).

[59] RESTATEMENT (SECOND) OF CONTRACTS § 71(2) (1981).

[60] *See* RESTATEMENT (SECOND) OF CONTRACTS § 75 (1981).

[61] U.C.C. § 2-106(1) (2002).

before delivering the BMW to her. As a result, Sam says to Lisa, "I'll give you my BMW when the new Benz I have ordered arrives." Lisa expresses her great happiness and says to Sam "I accept — thank you so much" and eagerly awaits the day when she will become the owner of Sam's old car. However, before arrival of the new car, Sam becomes angry with Lisa and backs out of his promise.

There is no consideration for Sam's promise to make the gift. A promise was made, but there is no contract. Even though one might easily conclude that Sam wanted to please his friend Lisa and that he sought her gratitude in return for his promise, Sam's promise nevertheless is gratuitous.[62] Not only is Lisa's gratitude completely amorphous, Sam did not seek it in explicit exchange for his promise. And, even if he had, it would not qualify as consideration — otherwise gratuitous promises might be widely enforceable, a result our legal system does not favor. Sam's promise to give his car to Lisa does not involve a bargained-for exchange, and Lisa has no claim against Sam for breach of contract.

Imagine what would happen to the doctrine of consideration if simple gratitude or "love and affection" were sufficient to make a promise enforceable. Very few promises would be unenforceable, and the property law rule requiring "delivery" to complete a gift would effectively be eliminated. The reasons behind these rules would be frustrated. Neither gratitude nor love and affection can serve as consideration for a promise.[63]

The requirement of an exchange makes it much harder for a dishonest person to falsely claim that he was the beneficiary of a promise.[64] Also, promises to make gifts that we might later regret, due to the bad conduct of the beneficiary, would be enforceable.[65] The unenforceability of gratuitous promises provides an important safety valve for promisors who would otherwise find themselves bound to unworthy recipients of their generosity. Further, we might find ourselves in dire financial straits as a result of having made an improvident promise without having received something in exchange for it. If these promises were enforceable, we might all be more circumspect about making them, and our society would be the poorer as a result of it.[66]

[B]   Consideration Defined as a Benefit or a Detriment

Another, older way of defining consideration was to ask whether the promisee suffered a detriment or the promisor enjoyed some benefit. Although this approach is imprecise and leads to mistakes, courts still sometimes analyze consideration in this way.[67]

---

[62] *See* Carlisle v. T & R Excavating, Inc., 704 N.E.2d 39, 43 (Ohio Ct. App. 1997) (absence of a bargain).

[63] Williams v. Ormsby, 966 N.E.2d 255 (Ohio 2012).

[64] Melvin Aron Eisenberg, *The World of Contract and the World of Gift*, 85 Cal. L. Rev. 821, 828 (1997); Lon L. Fuller, *Consideration and Form*, 41 Colum. L. Rev. 799, 815 (1941).

[65] Melvin Aron Eisenberg, *Donative Promises*, 47 U. Chi. L. Rev. 1, 13–15 (1979).

[66] *See* Charles J. Goetz & Robert E. Scott, *Enforcing Promises: An Examination of the Basis of Contract*, 89 Yale L.J. 1261 (1980).

[67] *E.g.*, NRC Golf Course, LLC v. JMR Golf, LLC, 731 S.E.2d 474 (N.C. Ct. App. 2012).

The famous case of *Hamer v. Sidway*[68] supplies a good example. There, an uncle promised his nephew $5,000[69] if the nephew would abstain from smoking, drinking, swearing, and playing cards or billiards for money until the nephew's 21st birthday.[70] The nephew complied, and the court, finding that the promise had been made in exchange for nephew's restraint, enforced the promise against the uncle's estate.[71]

Significantly, the court expressly rejected the defendant's suggestion that the nephew's avoidance of these vices might be of some benefit to him and therefore should not qualify as a "detriment." The court said: "a valuable consideration . . . may consist either in some right, interest, profit or benefit accruing to one party, or some forbearance, detriment, loss or responsibility given, suffered or undertaken by the other."[72] In other words, it was enough that the nephew had the legal right to use tobacco and to drink liquor[73] and yet refrained from doing so, and that the nephew had abstained from these vices "upon the strength of [the uncle's] promise that for such forbearance he would give him $5,000."[74] Thus, even though the nephew's good behavior might have been good for him in the ordinary sense, he nevertheless suffered the "legal detriment" of abstaining from exercising a legal right.[75] He thus suffered a detriment sufficient to make the uncle's promise binding.

The Restatement (Second) of Contracts conspicuously disclaims the necessity of finding a "benefit to the promisor or detriment to the promisee."[76] Instead, it speaks of a "performance or a return promise" that is "bargained for."[77] However, courts still frequently refer to a benefit to the promisor or a detriment to the promisee to define consideration.[78] The analysis remains useful, though still slightly imprecise, if care is taken in remembering that the benefit or detriment involved in the transaction *must be bargained for.* As the court in *Weavertown Transport Leasing, Inc. v. Moran* explained: "It is not enough . . . that the promisee has suffered a legal detriment . . . . The detriment incurred must be the

---

[68] 27 N.E. 256 (N.Y. 1891).

[69] In 1869, when the promise was made, $5,000 was worth approximately the same as $85,000 in 2012.

[70] These, obviously, were the vices of the day.

[71] You may notice that many cases involving the enforceability of a promise to make a gift, involve an effort to enforce the promise against the "estate" of a promisor who has died. This is no surprise. Even when a promise to make a gift has not been performed, those who make such promises frequently also express their generosity with other gifts. Suing a living donor would almost certainly bring an end to his or her generosity.

[72] Hamer v. Sidway, 27 N.E. 256, 257 (N.Y. 1891).

[73] Apparently, it was a more permissive age in this respect.

[74] *Hamer v. Sidway,* 27 N.E. at 257.

[75] *See also* Davies v. Martel Laboratory Servs., Inc., 545 N.E.2d 475 (Ill. App. Ct. 1989) (promise of a permanent job if plaintiff would work toward an MBA).

[76] Restatement (Second) of Contracts § 79 cmt. b (1981).

[77] Restatement (Second) of Contracts § 71(1) (1981).

[78] *E.g.,* NRC Golf Course, LLC v. JMR Golf, LLC, 731 S.E.2d 474 (N.C. Ct. App. 2012); Minster Farmers Coop. Exch. Co. v. Meyer, 884 N.E.2d 1056 (Ohio 2008). *But see* Sipko v. Koger, Inc., 70 A.3d 512 (N.J. 2013) (no requirement of benefit or detriment).

'quid pro quo', or the 'price' of the promise, and the inducement for which it was made . . . ."[79] Moreover, if a bargain has been made, it is not necessary to identify a specific detriment to the promisee or benefit to the promisor, though they will usually exist.

In analyzing consideration this way, care must be taken to ensure that it is a detriment to *the promisee* or a benefit *to the promisor* that is involved. Serious mistakes are made (mostly on final exams), by first-year law students who find consideration in the detriment incurred by the promisor of having to perform her promise, or in the benefit to the promisee of receiving the benefit of performance. This is backwards! Courts that use this detriment or benefit analysis inquire into whether there was a bargained-for detriment to the promisee or a bargained-for benefit to the promisor.

Courts also sometimes forget to analyze whether the detriment to the promisee or benefit to the promisor was bargained for. A promisee might easily incur a detriment that was not a part of any exchange. Failure to inquire into whether the promisee's detriment was sought by the promisor in exchange for his promise, and was thus part of a bargain, can lead to the mistaken conclusion that consideration is present, even though it is not.

The court in *Prendergast v. Snoeberger*, did a good job of keeping this point firmly in mind.[80] The Snoebergers transferred land to their daughter and her husband — the Prendergasts — as a gift. A deed was delivered and the gift was complete. A few years later, the Prendergasts promised the Snoebergers that they would not transfer the property to anyone else while the Snoebergers were still alive. Later, the Prendergasts wanted to sell the land to finance their escape to a more attractive location, and sued to have their promise not to convey the property to someone else declared unenforceable.[81]

Although their promise was made in apparent recognition of the gift the Snoebergers had previously bestowed on them, the court granted the Prendergasts the relief they sought. The court recognized that although the Snoebergers had suffered the detriment of giving their land away, they had not done so as part of an exchange for the Prendergasts promise. The promise, after all, was made after the gift was complete. And, although the Prendergasts enjoyed a valuable benefit, in the form of the land, they received the land as a gift and not as part of an exchange for their promise to hold on to it until the Snoebergers died. Where there is no exchange, consideration is missing, even though it may be possible to identify some detriment that the promisee suffered, or some benefit that the promisor enjoyed.

---

[79] Weavertown Transport Leasing, Inc. v. Moran, 834 A.2d 1169, 1172 (Pa. Super. Ct. 2003).

[80] Prendergast v. Snoeberger, 796 N.E.2d 588 (Ohio Ct. App. 2003).

[81] My wife and I received a similar gift from her parents. The prospect of suing them under any circumstances, is difficult to imagine.

[C]   Promises as Consideration

The benefit-detriment approach to consideration sometimes raises questions about whether there is consideration in situations where the parties have exchanged nothing more than mutual promises. When, as in *Hamer v. Sidway*,[82] a promise is made in exchange for a performance, there is little difficulty in seeing that the performance of the nephew, in abstaining from engaging in various types of conduct, was a "detriment." Likewise, when a buyer promises to pay the seller at the end of the month for goods that have already been delivered, it is easy to see that the buyer has received a benefit in exchange for his promise — the goods the seller supplied. However, when there is an exchange of reciprocal promises, with each promise made in exchange for the other, it might be more difficult to detect consideration by identifying a benefit to the promisor or a detriment to the promisee. Nevertheless, an exchange has been made, and there is consideration for both promises.

There was a time in the now distant history of contract law when a simple exchange of executory promises did not result in an enforceable agreement. If the promises were "sealed" they were enforceable, but consideration had nothing to do with it. If one of the parties performed, the promise of the other became enforceable, under either the writ of debt, or detinue. But, if the agreement remained wholly "executory," with neither party having yet performed, neither promise could be enforced.

In the late sixteenth century, the law caught on to the practical need to enforce these agreements, though some doubt about the matter arose again late in the nineteenth century. Lawyers and scholars of the time struggled to find a rationale for making exchanges of unperformed promises enforceable. Law students today (and probably some experienced lawyers as well) sometimes make the same mistake and believe that there is no consideration for a promise until the promise made in exchange has been performed. For example, it might seem that Sam's promise to sell his BMW to Barb for $18,000 has no consideration until Barb has actually paid the $18,000 she promised. But, this is wrong. Barb's *promise* to pay supplies the necessary consideration for Sam's promise to sell.

It is the detriment-benefit approach to discussing consideration that leads to the misunderstanding. It might appear that Barb's mere promise cannot be consideration because her promise is a legal detriment only if her promise is legally enforceable. It might also seem that the enforceability of Barb's promise depends on the whether Sam's promise to deliver his car is a legal detriment, but this depends on the enforceability of Barb's promise to pay, which depends on the enforceability of Sam's promise to sell, which depends on Barb's promise . . . . This circular reasoning leads to chaos.[83]

Eventually, scholars found their way out of the tautology. Let's be practical about this: if a pair of executory promises made in exchange for one another, like

---

[82] 27 N.E. 256 (N.Y. 1891).

[83] *See* C.C. Langdell, *Mutual Promises as a Consideration for Each Other*, 14 HARV. L. REV. 496 (1900).

Sam's and Barb's, were not enforceable, the economy would grind to a halt. Promises are exchanged every day in employment contracts, construction deals, business mergers, purchases of inventory and equipment, and loan commitments. These agreements would all be legally meaningless if a promise were not consideration for another promise. The "futures market," among other things, could not exist in such a world. These transactions are at the core of our economy, are supported by consideration, and are enforceable, unless there are other problems with the deal, unrelated to whether consideration is present.

The law achieves this result by taking the position that when one promise is exchanged for another, both promises are supported by consideration *so long as actual performance of each promise would be consideration*.[84] This makes it easy to see that Sam and Barb's BMW deal, involving an exchange of promises,[85] is enforceable. Sam's promise to sell the car is supported by consideration if *performance* of Barb's promise would be consideration for his promise. Payment of $18,000 is an unequivocal detriment to Barb given in exchange for Sam's promise. Likewise, it is an unequivocal benefit to Sam obtained in exchange for his promise. Barb's promise to pay is similarly supported by consideration if Sam's *performance* of his promise would be consideration for her promise. When Sam delivers the car, he has suffered an obvious detriment. Barb's receipt of the car is an obvious benefit.[86] Most importantly, Sam's detriment and Barb's benefit were in express exchange for Barb's promise to pay for the car. Thus, Barb's promise to pay is supported by consideration and is enforceable.[87]

[D]   Performance as Consideration

It is easier to see how a performance operates as consideration. If, at the promisor's request, the promisee performs some act in exchange for the promise, consideration exists and the promise is enforceable.[88] Cases involving rewards, such as where a person makes a promise to pay $10,000 for information leading to the conviction of a criminal, involve the exchange of a performance for the promise of the reward. The person who, in response to the promise of a reward, provided the necessary information, supplied the requested consideration for the promise, and has a legal right to recover the reward.

---

[84] RESTATEMENT (SECOND) OF CONTRACTS § 75 (1981). *See* Val D. Ricks, *The Sophisticated Doctrine of Consideration*, 9 GEO. MASON L. REV. 99 (2000); Samuel Williston, *Consideration in Bilateral Contracts*, 27 HARV. L. REV. 503 (1913); Pearsall v. Alexander, 572 A.2d 113 (D.C. 1990) (exchange of promises to share winnings from lottery tickets).

[85] "Executory" is legal lingo for "unperformed." *See supra* § 1.02[D] Executory Contracts. Learn to use this term, and others like it correctly, and you'll encourage confidence in the other things you say about contract law (such as in your exams). You'll also impress your parents and seem like a drudge to your friend from college (at least those who didn't go to law school).

[86] Even with gasoline at $4.00 per gallon, and higher.

[87] *See* RESTATEMENT (SECOND) OF CONTRACTS § 75 cmt. a (1981).

[88] RESTATEMENT (SECOND) OF CONTRACTS § 72 (1981).

[E]   Forbearance as Consideration

Forbearance from taking action can also operate as consideration.[89] This occurs where the promisee had a legal right to take some action, but abstained from engaging in the activity in exchange for the promise. This is the lesson of *Hamer v. Sidway*,[90] where a nephew abstained from various vices in exchange for his uncle's promise to pay him $5,000 on his 21st birthday. Forbearance, though it consists of inaction, is a type of performance, and thus qualifies as consideration where it is what the promisor sought in exchange for her promise.[91]

Consider another example in a business setting. Assume Twanda loaned Ben $10,000 with Ben promising to pay her back in one year at a fixed rate of 10% interest, for a total of $11,000 due at the end of the year. However, when payment was due, Ben was in financial difficulty. Twanda might bring an immediate lawsuit to collect the $11,000 that is now due, but Ben wants more time to pay. Moreover, Ben's inability to pay suggests that a lawsuit would not result in actual payment, but only in a judgment determining Ben's liability. In cases like this, there is rarely any dispute about the debtor's liability; the only problem is his ability to pay. When this is the source of the problem, a judgment provides little help for the creditor, and may force Ben into bankruptcy.[92] As a result Ben might promise to pay a higher 15% rate of interest and ask Twanda to hold off on her lawsuit for six months while he makes an effort to improve his finances. Here, Twanda might do one of two things: 1) she might agree to hold off suit in exchange for the promise of more interest, or 2) making no promise, she may simply hold off bringing suit. The first of these two alternatives involves an unquestioned bargain: a promise of more time in exchange for a promise of higher interest. The second alternative is the one that presents the problem.

After six months, Ben will either make repayment, or he will not — probably depending on his financial condition at the time. But, if he repays the loan, he might seek to avoid paying the higher rate of interest he promised. If Twanda sues to recover the additional interest,[93] Ben might defend by arguing that his promise to pay the higher rate of interest was not supported by any consideration. Ben could say that what he wanted from Twanda was her commitment not to begin legal proceedings for six months, so that he could be certain of having that much time, rather than merely Twanda's forbearance from bringing suit.

The outcome depends on what Ben sought in return for his promise to pay the

---

[89] RESTATEMENT (SECOND) OF CONTRACTS § 71(3) (1981).

[90] 27 N.E. 256 (N.Y. 1891).

[91] RESTATEMENT (SECOND) OF CONTRACTS § 71(3)(b) (1981).

[92] *See* JEFF FERRIELL & EDWARD J. JANGER, UNDERSTANDING BANKRUPTCY (3d ed. 2012).

[93] Even this simple agreement involves several questions of interpretation: Was the additional rate of interest to be based on the original $10,000 loan, for an additional $250 in interest at the end of the extra six months, or was the additional rate to be based on the $11,000 due at the time the agreement was made, for a total of $275. In addition, there is the question of whether the original rate of 10% interest would continue to accumulate on the unpaid balance, making the total balance due at the end of the six months $11,825. Questions about whether to calculate interest on a daily, weekly, monthly, quarterly, or annual basis provide additional uncertainties about the terms of the parties' agreement. And you thought there wouldn't be math in law school!

higher rate of interest. If Ben's version is correct, that he sought Twanda's commitment to wait, and received her actual forbearance — but no promise, then there is no consideration for his promise to pay the higher rate of interest. Although forbearance at the promisor's request is a valid consideration, if a promise for forbearance was what was sought in exchange for the promise, a promise of forbearance must be supplied.[94] If he sought actual forbearance as consideration for his promise, consideration was present and Ben's promise to pay the extra interest is enforceable. Everything depends on what bargain, if any, was struck. In either event, actual restraint may make the promise enforceable under the parallel doctrine of promissory estoppel.[95]

Other issues arise when forbearance from pursuing a claim in court is the consideration for the promise. Although the claim might be groundless, the consideration doctrine generally avoids becoming embroiled in inquiries over the relative values exchanged by the parties, so long as it is clear that the transaction involved an exchange. However, where forbearance from what turns out to be a completely groundless suit is the consideration given for a promise, courts are sometimes anxious that, by enforcing the promise, they will encourage extortion.[96]

§ 2.04 PROMISES TO MAKE A GIFT[97]

As the foregoing examples illustrate, the law of contracts is primarily focused on commercial transactions that are at the core of our economy. While it might be possible to stretch the doctrine to make gratuitous promises enforceable, perhaps by saying that a person who promises to make a gift does so in order to obtain the gratitude of the beneficiary in exchange, the law has not done this. Unlike promises involved in an exchange, promises to make a gift are not generally enforceable.[98]

---

[94] *E.g.*, Whitten v. Greeley-Shaw, 520 A.2d 1307 (Me. 1987).

[95] RESTATEMENT (SECOND) OF CONTRACTS § 74 cmt. d (1981). *But see* Panasonic Commc'ns. & Sys. Co. v. Dept. of Admin., 691 A.2d 190 (Me. 1997) (no detrimental reliance).

[96] *See infra* § 2.05[C] Settlement of Disputed Claims.

[97] Jane B. Baron, *Gifts, Bargains, and Form*, 64 IND. L.J. 155 (1988–89); Melvin Aron Eisenberg, *The World of Contract and the World of Gift*, 85 CAL. L. REV. 821, 834–35 (1997); Melvin A. Eisenberg, *Donative Promises*, 47 U. CHI. L. REV. 1 (1979); E. Allan Farnsworth, *Promises to Make Gifts*, 43 AM. J. COMP. L. 359 (1995); E. ALLAN FARNSWORTH, CHANGING YOUR MIND: THE LAW OF REGRETTED DECISIONS 133–39 (1998); James D. Gordon III, *A Dialogue About the Doctrine of Consideration*, 75 CORNELL L. REV. 987 (1990); Roy Kreitner, *The Gift Beyond the Grave: Revisiting the Question of Consideration*, 101 COLUM. L. REV. 1876 (2001); Andrew Kull, *Reconsidering Gratuitous Promises*, 21 J. LEGAL STUD. 39 (1992); Melanie B. Leslie, *Enforcing Family Promises: Reliance, Reciprocity, and Relational Contract*, 77 N.C. L. REV. 551 (1999); Richard A. Posner, *Gratuitous Promises in Economics and Law*, 6 J. LEGAL STUD. 411 (1977); Robert A. Prentice, *"Law &" Gratuitous Promises*, 2007 U. ILL. L. REV. 881. *See also* James Andreoni, *Impure Altruism and Donations to Public Goods: A Theory of Warm-Glow Giving*, 100 ECON. J. 464, 464 (1990).

[98] *See* E. Allan Farnsworth, *Promises and Paternalism*, 41 WM. & MARY L. REV. 385, 397 (2000); Robert A. Prentice, *"Law &" Gratuitous Promises*, 2007 U. ILL. L. REV. 881, 938.

[A]   Gift Promises Unenforceable

The unenforceability of a promise to make a gift is illustrated by countless cases involving promises to family members and organized charities.[99] For example, in *Dougherty v. Salt*, an eight-year old's guardian sued the estate of the young boy's aunt to enforce a promise she had made, in the form of a formal promissory note, to pay him $3,000. Even though the text of the note indicated that it had been given for "value received," the circumstances surrounding the aunt's delivery of the note made it clear that it had not been given in exchange for anything and that it was an "unenforceable promise of an executory gift."[100] Likewise, in *Johnson v. Otterbein University*, the court refused to enforce a charitable pledge where the promise was not accompanied by "an act of advantage to Johnson, or . . . a detriment to the institution."[101]

Reasons for the rule against enforcement of promises to make a gift are not always evident from decisions applying the rule. Courts sometimes explain that it would be undesirable to compel a person to make a gift, when his financial circumstances may have changed.[102] Scholars explain that the absence of something provided in exchange for the promise makes it too easy for an unscrupulous person to assert a fraudulent claim that a promise to make a gift has been made and that the reasons for enforcing such promises do not outweigh this difficulty.[103] Moreover, if promises to make a gift were enforceable on grounds of morality, the same grounds could be used to excuse enforceability where the promisor became financially incapable of performing or came to regret his promise due to the bad conduct of the recipient of the promised gift.[104] Others have argued that barring enforcement of promises to make gifts is economically efficient compared to the costs and benefits to society in enforcing them.[105] Still others claim that legal enforceability of gift promises would lead many prospective donors to avoid making such promises at all rather than go to the trouble of spelling out the conditions on which their promises depended.[106] In any event, the rule denying enforcement to these promises is well established.[107]

---

[99] E. Allan Farnsworth, *Promises and Paternalism*, 41 Wm. & Mary L. Rev. 385, 388 (2000).

[100] Dougherty v. Salt, 125 N.E. 94, 95 (N.Y. 1919). *See also* Fischer v. Union Trust Co., 101 N.W. 852 (Mich. 1904); De Mentas v. Estate of Tallas, 764 P.2d 628 (Utah Ct. App. 1988).

[101] Johnson v. Otterbein University, 1885 Ohio LEXIS 231 (Jan. 1885). *See also* Congregation Kadimah Toras-Moshe v. DeLeo, 540 N.E.2d 691 (Mass. 1989); King v. Trustees of Boston Univ., 647 N.E.2d 1196 (Mass. 1995).

[102] *See In re* Barker's Estate, 158 Misc. 803 (N.Y. Sur. Ct. 1936).

[103] Melvin Aron Eisenberg, *The World of Contract and the World of Gift*, 85 Cal. L. Rev. 821, 828 (1997); Lon L. Fuller, *Consideration and Form*, 41 Colum. L. Rev. 799, 815 (1941).

[104] Melvin Aron Eisenberg, *Donative Promises*, 47 U. Chi. L. Rev. 1, 13–15 (1979).

[105] Richard A. Posner, *Gratuitous Promises in Economics and Law*, 6 J. Legal Stud. 411, 411–415 (1977).

[106] Charles J. Goetz & Robert E. Scott, *Enforcing Promises: An Examination of the Basis of Contract*, 89 Yale L.J. 1261 (1980).

[107] *See, e.g.*, Robert A. Prentice, *"Law &" Gratuitous Promises*, 2007 U. Ill. L. Rev. 881.

[B] Conditional Gifts

When the promise to make a gift has strings attached, it is sometimes difficult to tell the difference between an unenforceable promise to make a gift and a bargained-for exchange. There are many conditional gifts that do not involve an exchange. If one of my students has forgotten his wallet, I might promise to give him $6 (the price of the daily "special" at the law school cafeteria), if he will come to my office to get the cash.[108] It should be evident that I am not using my promise of lunch money as part of a bargain to have the student visit my office. Rather, I'm willing to contribute to the cause, but do not want to have to chase the needy student down, to help him out. The condition is not part of an exchange, it merely expresses one of the limits of my generosity.

In other cases, there might at first appear to be nothing more than a conditional gift, but closer examination of the facts reveals that the promisor's generosity is belied by the benefits for the promisor in the transaction. For example, when a real estate developer advertised that those who attended a real estate auction would get a chance to win a new car, the promise was enforceable because the promise was made as an inducement to attend the auction.[109] Attendance at the auction was not merely a condition, it was the very action the promisor hoped to induce by making his promise.

[C] Charitable Pledges[110]

In cases involving promises to organized charities, courts have found ways to make donors' promises enforceable, even though consideration seems to be lacking. One method finds consideration for a donor's promise in the similar promises of other subscribers to contribute to the same charity. Under this approach, for example, a promise by Mark to make a contribution to his alma mater, standing alone, is still an unenforceable promise to make a gift. But, it is clear that if Mark and his classmate Tina exchange promises to one another to each make a contribution to the charity, both of their promises are enforceable. If Mark and Tina each said to one another: "I'll pledge if you will," their promises are supported by consideration and are enforceable.

Courts have sometimes been willing to treat promises by multiple donors, like Mark and Tina, as if they had been made in exchange for one another, even though the contributors have never met nor communicated with one another regarding their promised donations.[111] For example, in *Congregation B'nai Sholom v.*

---

[108] This, of course, is a variation on the famous example, supplied by Professor Williston so many years ago, in what is now politically insensitive terminology, in which a gentleman promises $1 to a "tramp," if the homeless person will walk around the corner with the gentleman to get it. 1 WILLISTON ON CONTRACTS § 112 (3d ed. 1957).

[109] Maughs v. Porter, 161 S.E. 242 (Va. 1931). *See also* Pennsy Supply, Inc. v. Am. Ash Recycling Corp., 895 A.2d 595 (Pa. Super. Ct. 2006).

[110] E. Allan Farnsworth, *Promises and Paternalism*, 41 WM. & MARY L. REV. 385, 403 (2000); Annotation, *Enforceability of Subscription Under Conditional Charitable Pledge*, 97 A.L.R.3d 1054 (1980).

[111] Several years ago, your author wondered if legal concerns were at work behind the scenes when

Martin the court said that "the mutual promise between subscribers of [charitable] pledges for a lawful purpose will constitute a consideration."[112] Thus, when promises are made by a number of donors, as part of an organized drive conducted by the charity, courts engage in the legal fiction[113] that the donors have actually communicated with one another and made their promises in consideration of those made by other donors.

Courts also sometimes enforce promises to charities on a theory of promissory estoppel, where the charity embarked on the building project or scholarship fund for which it had solicited the promised funds.[114] The theory is that the charity reasonably and foreseeably relied on the donor's promise.[115] Of course, unless the promise was for a very large donation, it is unlikely that the charity relied in any meaningful way on each individual pledge. However, the charity has probably relied on the collective value of numerous pledges by embarking on a project that could be financed only by the sum of all of the donations received as part of the drive.

Finally, the Restatement (Second) of Contracts takes the position that a promise to a charity is enforceable without proof of actual reliance, provided that reliance on the promise was reasonably foreseeable by the promisor.[116] However, only a few courts have adopted this view,[117] which is probably more of an expression of how the drafters of the Restatement hoped the law would develop than a true "restatement" of cases that had already been decided.[118]

Yet, despite these many efforts, and despite the many reasons supplied by scholars to make such promises enforceable,[119] promises to make gifts to charities are still sometimes found to be unenforceable due to a lack of consideration.[120]

---

his wife's alma mater suggested that she participate in its fund-raising drive by asking her classmates to "join her" in making a pledge to the college. Asking others to join you in making a contribution is beneficial in other respects, but might also serve to make the pledge legally enforceable.

[112] Congregation B'nai Sholom v. Martin, 173 N.W.2d 504, 510 (Mich. 1969).

[113] A *legal fiction* is "[a]n assumption that something is true even though it may be untrue . . . to alter how a legal rule operates." BLACK'S LAW DICTIONARY (8th ed. 2004). In other contexts we would call it a fantasy.

[114] Danby v. Osteopathic Hosp. Ass'n, 104 A.2d 903 (Del. 1954) (charity relied on donor's promise by commencing construction of a hospital).

[115] Allegheny College v. Nat'l Chautauqua Cty. Bank, 159 N.E. 173 (N.Y. 1927). *See generally* Alfred S. Konefsky, *How to Read, or at Least Not Misread, Cardozo in the* Allegheny College *Case*, 36 BUFF. L. REV. 645 (1987); Leon Lipson, *The* Allegheny College *Case*, 23 YALE L. REP. No. 3, at 11 (1977); Mike Townsend, *Cardozo's* Allegheny College *Opinion: A Case Study in Law as an Art*, 33 HOUS. L. REV. 1103 (1996).

[116] RESTATEMENT (SECOND) OF CONTRACTS § 90(2) (1981).

[117] *See* Md. Nat'l Bank v. United Jewish Appeal Fed., 407 A.2d 1130, 1136 (Md. 1979).

[118] Salsbury v. Nw. Bell Tel. Co., 221 N.W.2d 609, 613 (Iowa 1974). *But see* Md. Nat'l Bank v. United Jewish Appeal Fed., 407 A.2d 1130 (Md. 1979); Arrowsmith v. Mercantile-Safe Deposit and Trust Co., 545 A.2d 674 (Md. 1988).

[119] *See generally* Melvin Aron Eisenberg, *The World of Contract and the World of Gift*, 85 CAL. L. REV. 821 (1997).

[120] *E.g.*, Congregation Kadimah Toras-Moshe v. DeLeo, 540 N.E.2d 691 (Mass. 1989). *See also* Russell G. Donaldson, Annotation, *Lack of Consideration as Barring Enforcement of Promise to Make*

§ 2.05 ADEQUACY OF CONSIDERATION

Given the law's reluctance to enforce promises to make a gift, one might think that contract law would focus on whether the consideration given for a promise was actually worth something. However, the law generally avoids examining the adequacy of consideration given for a promise, unless there was some sort of fraud, oppression, or unconscionability involved in the exchange.[121] As long as there is a real exchange, the parties are free to make enforceable promises in exchange for whatever they desire, regardless of its economic value.

[A]   No Inquiry into Adequacy[122]

As long as the transaction involves a bargain, the law is rarely interested in the amount of value exchanged for the promise.[123] Where consideration exists, the quantity of consideration does not matter. This is illustrated by statements by courts that a mere peppercorn will qualify as consideration, if the parties regard it as such — if the parties were really bargaining for the peppercorn.[124]

This means that the enforceability of the contract between Sam and Barb for the delivery of Sam's used car does not depend on whether the agreed price is even roughly equivalent to the value of the vehicle. What is crucial is whether the agreement involves a real exchange. The law leaves the question of whether the items involved in the exchange are of an equivalent value up to the parties, who are regarded as the best arbiters of value of the property or services involved in the exchange. Thus, the rule that courts will not inquire into the adequacy of consideration, expresses the law's conviction that courts should not take the wisdom of the bargain into account in determining whether it is enforceable.

The fact that objective relative values are usually unimportant is sometimes referred to as "the peppercorn theory of consideration."[125] The law is so unconcerned with the relative values exchanged that a mere peppercorn is

---

Charitable Contribution or Subscription — Modern Cases, 86 A.L.R.4th 241 (1991).

[121] Krell v. Codman, 28 N.E. 578 (Mass. 1891). *See* Note, *The Peppercorn Theory of Consideration and the Doctrine of Fair Exchange in Contact Law*, 35 COLUM. L. REV. 1080 (1935).

[122] Joseph Siprut, Comment, *The Peppercorn Reconsidered: Why a Promise to Sell Blackacre for Nominal Consideration Is Not Binding, but Should Be*, 97 NW. U.L. REV. 1809 (2003); Note, *The Peppercorn Theory of Consideration and the Doctrine of Fair Exchange in Contract Law*, 35 COLUM. L. REV. 1090 (1935).

[123] RESTATEMENT (SECOND) OF CONTRACTS § 79 (1981). *See* Melvin Aron Eisenberg, *The Bargain Principle and Its Limits*, 95 HARV. L. REV. 741, 743–47 (1982); *E.g.*, Schweitzer v. Gibson, 151 N.E. 865 (Ill. 1926); Batsakis v. Demotsis, 226 S.W.2d 673 (Tex. Civ. App. 1949); Westlake v. Adams, 5 C.B. (n.s.) 248, 265, 141 Eng. Rep. 99, 106 (C.P. 1858).

[124] *See* Sfreddo v. Sfreddo, 720 S.E.2d 145 (Va. Ct. App. 2012).

[125] This is a reference to a presumed exchange of something of great value for a peppercorn, of which hundreds or thousands are used to produce rather small amounts of ground pepper. Lon L. Fuller, *Consideration and Form*, 41 COLUM. L. REV. 799, 799 (1941). *See, e.g.*, Williams v. Kansas Dep't of Soc. & Rehab. Serv., 899 P.2d 452, 456 (Kan. 1995) (upholding multi-million dollar trust established with "peppercorn" of $10). *See also* 2 WILLIAM BLACKSTONE, COMMENTARIES ON THE LAWS OF ENGLAND *440 (1766) (asserting that even a peppercorn may be sufficient consideration for a lease).

sufficient to enforce a promise, if the peppercorn is given in exchange for it.[126]

The parties are free to set the terms of the exchange they want to make and contract law will enforce their agreement. As long as a court believes the bargaining process was fair, and that there has been no impermissible overreaching by one of the parties, it will uphold their agreement even if the value one party receives seems to be substantially more than the other gets in return.

This approach not only makes sense, it is critical to the reliability of contractual obligations. If courts were willing to inquire into the relative economic values involved in an exchange, with the threat of refusing to enforce the promise if the values were different, the enforceability of promises generally would be seriously drawn into question. If Barb could back out of her deal to buy Sam's car simply by proving that she had promised to pay more than the car was worth, contracts would be of little societal value.

The court in *Hamer v. Sidway*, involving an uncle's promise to pay $5,000 to his nephew if the nephew refrained from engaging in several bad habits, recognized this problem. In responding to the defendant's argument that there was no consideration for the uncle's promise, because the nephew's abstinence from vice was good for him and not detrimental, the court said that this was "[a] contention, which if well founded, would seem to leave open for controversy in many cases whether that which the promisee did or omitted to do was in fact of such benefit to him as to leave no consideration to support the enforcement of the promisor's agreement."[127]

This is a key point. If a difference in the values exchanged by the parties was a basis for asserting that consideration was missing, every contract could be called into question. Consider an agreement for Karen to sell her house to Phil for $100,000. If Karen had misjudged the value of the house, which was really worth $120,000, and a disparity in value was grounds for avoiding enforceability due to an absence of consideration, Karen could get out of her deal based on her poor judgment in agreeing to sell it for $100,000 in the first place. The same would be true if the market value had changed between the time the contract was made and the time for performance, due to a change in economic circumstances affecting its value. Having agreed to sell for $100,000, Karen would be able to renege even though this is exactly the situation where her promise needs to be enforced. If the enforceability of contracts depended on the ability of the parties to exercise good judgment in determining the value of the agreed exchange, contracts would be of no use.

In this regard, the law's insistence that objective disparities in the values exchanged by the parties do not matter is a key component of the principle of "freedom of contract." Freedom of contract leaves it to the parties to decide for themselves about the relative value of the subject matter of the contract. By agreeing to sell for $100,000, Karen, in the above example, demonstrated the value

---

[126] *See* Thomas v. Thomas, 114 Eng. Rep. 330 (Q.B. 1842); RESTATEMENT (SECOND) OF CONTRACTS § 84 illus. 1 (1981); Joseph Siprut, *The Peppercorn Reconsidered: Why a Promise to Sell Blackacre for Nominal Consideration Is Not Binding, but Should Be*, 97 Nw. U.L. REV. 1809 (2003).

[127] Hamer v. Sidway, 27 N.E. 256, 257 (N.Y. 1891).

she placed on the land. By promising to pay $100,000 for it, Phil demonstrated his belief that it was worth at least that much to him. By enforcing their respective promises, the law seeks to encourage the exchange of value between members of society based on the values placed on the subject matter of the contract by the parties themselves. Permitting parties to exchange land, goods, and services based on their own values is a key component of the operation of our market economy. Thus, permitting a person to get out of a contract because of an objective disparity in the values involved in the exchange would be inconsistent with the operation of a free market system.[128] Whether the transaction was wise, prudent, or beneficial to the parties is up to them and to them alone.

[B]   Nominal Consideration

[1]   Sham Consideration

Although courts are reluctant to inquire into the wisdom of an exchange, where there is a large disparity between the values involved in the exchange, the court might wonder whether it was regarded by the parties as an exchange at all. Parties with a little bit of knowledge about the law might be tempted to make it appear as if the promise was part of an exchange, even where it was nothing more than a promise to make a gift.

This is sometimes evident in cases involving exchanges of unequal sums of cash. For example, in *Schnell v. Nell*[129] the defendant, intending to make a gift, made a written promise to pay $600 to each of three relatives. The promise indicated that it was made in consideration of respective promises by these relatives to pay the defendant a mere 1¢ in return. The court saw through this charade and ruled that although the inadequacy of consideration does not make a promise unenforceable, an exchange of different sums of currency, which has a fixed value, permitted the court to inquire into whether the 1¢ was really the consideration for the promise. The court explained:

> [the doctrine that] inadequacy of consideration will not vitiate an agreement . . . does not apply to a mere exchange of sums of money . . . whose value is exactly fixed, but to the exchange of something of . . . indeterminate value, for money, or perhaps, for some other thing of indeterminate value. In this case, had the one cent mentioned been some particular one cent, a family piece, of ancient, remarkable coin, possessing an indeterminate value, extrinsic from its simple money value, a different view might be taken.[130]

The court went on to explain that the consideration of only a penny was merely nominal and imposed no legal obligation on the promisor. Because the exchange was of two sums of money, without any hint that the $600 represented the accumulated interest on a loan of the 1¢, there was no room for the possibility that the exchange

---

[128] RICHARD POSNER, ECONOMIC ANALYSIS OF LAW 101 (6th ed. 2002).

[129] 1861 Ind. LEXIS 287 (Nov. 25, 1861).

[130] *Schnell v. Nell*, 1861 Ind. LEXIS 287 at *1–*4.

represented the parties' individualistic views of subjective values associated with the respective performances.

However, cases like *Schnell v. Nell* should be contrasted with ones like *Batsakis v. Demotsis*,[131] which also involved an exchange of wildly disparate sums of money. In 1942, in the middle of war-torn Greece, the defendant promised to pay the plaintiff $2,000, plus interest, in a writing that indicated that he had received this amount from the plaintiff. In reality, the plaintiff had loaned the defendant 500,000 Greek Drachmae, which at the time the loan was made, was worth only $25 in U.S. currency. Despite the dramatic difference in the values exchanged, the court enforced the defendant's promise to pay the entire $2,000. "Mere inadequacy of consideration" the court said "will not void a contract."[132]

Unlike the transaction in *Schnell v. Nell*, the loan in *Batsakis* was not intended as a gift. Quite to the contrary, the plaintiff appeared to have made several 500,000 Drachmae loans, but, due to the war, was unlikely to be able to recover from more than a small number of his borrowers. The transaction in *Batsakis v. Demotsis* was a real exchange, with the $25 worth of Greek currency possibly representing the difference between life and death in the midst of war-torn Europe. It is unclear whether the defendant was a generous soul, willing to take a fantastic risk, or an unscrupulous war profiteer, hoping to make an eventual return on his investment. While the loan may have been made under some sort of duress,[133] there was little doubt that it represented a real exchange, and thus satisfied the requirements of the consideration doctrine, despite the disparities involved.

Apart from the stark duress facing the defendant, decisions like *Batsakis* are consistent with those involving "grubstake" contracts in which the promisee gives the promisor what might be viewed as a small sum of money in exchange for the promisor's commitment to give the investor a meaningful share in the results of his endeavors.[134] Both represent true exchanges, even though the values involved in the exchange were significantly different.

Despite this, a gross disparity in the values exchanged may indicate the absence of a real bargain. If so, consideration is lacking. On the other hand, as demonstrated by *Batsakis v. Demotsis*, it may reflect other circumstances not apparent from the face of the transaction. In cases involving family members, where the plaintiff's "love and affection" are sometimes cited by the parties as further motivations for the supposed exchange, questions about the nature of the transaction are more likely to arise than in situations like *Batsakis*, where there is no other reason to suspect that the transaction was intended as a gift.

---

[131] 226 S.W.2d 673 (Tex. Civ. App. 1949).

[132] *Batsakis v. Demotsis*, 226 S.W.2d at 675.

[133] *See* Charles Fried, Contract as Promise 109–111 (1981).

[134] Restatement (Second) of Contracts § 79 illus. 3 (1981). *E.g.*, Embola v. Tuppela, 220 P. 789 (Wash. 1923).

[2]   Contract Modifications

Sham consideration might also be used in an effort to avoid the pre-existing duty rule. The pre-existing duty (or "legal duty") rule bars enforcement of a one-sided modification of an existing contract, if no new consideration is given for one party's agreement to do something beyond what was originally agreed upon. If the only consideration for the revised promise is to perform a duty that already exists — a "pre-existing duty" — there is no real exchange, and no consideration for the modified promise.

This might happen, for example, where a homeowner enters into a contract with a builder, in which the builder promises to build an addition to the homeowner's house, for a predetermined price, and later encounters an unexpected increase in the price of necessary materials. The builder may ask for and receive the homeowner's promises to pay an additional sum, beyond the amount originally agreed upon, for completion of a construction project, even though the builder has a pre-existing legal duty to complete the addition for the original price.[135] It might also occur where a creditor agrees to forgo insisting on payment of an entire sum due, if the debtor pays a smaller amount. In these cases, the homeowner's promise to pay an extra fee, and the creditor's promise to forego suit for the entire original debt, are not supported by consideration, because the promisee has a pre-existing duty to render the return performance.

Well-advised parties might find it easy manufacture consideration and ensure the enforceability of the revised promise. For example, the builder might agree to complete the original project one day earlier than previously promised, or to complete construction of a simple birdhouse in addition to completion of the original structure, as consideration for the owner's promise to pay the extra amount. Likewise, the debtor might agree to pay her creditor the smaller sum, but one day earlier than originally promised or to provide the creditor with a "matchbook" or even a "peppercorn" in exchange for the creditor's agreement to forbear from suing on the balance of the original debt. These examples all involve a new legal duty: finishing a day early, building a birdhouse, or supplying a matchbook, in apparent exchange for the other party's new promise. These examples invite the suggestion that the agreed consideration was a sham, even though the parties unquestionably wanted their modified agreements to be legally binding.

The Restatement (Second) of Contracts recognizes that extremely slight adjustments to the promisee's original duties are sufficient to make a meaningful modification of the other party's duties enforceable.[136] As long as something was supplied in consideration for the modification, even though it might have been minor, the revised promise is enforceable.[137] However, if the modification was not in good faith, it is not enforceable.

---

[135] *See infra* § 2.06 Pre-Existing Legal Duty Rule.

[136] RESTATEMENT (SECOND) OF CONTRACTS § 73 cmt. b & illus. 7 (1981).

[137] *See, e.g.,* Leone v. Precision Plumbing & Heating, 591 P.2d 1002, 1003 (Ariz. Ct. App. 1979).

[C]   Settlement of Disputed Claims

Questions about the enforceability of a promise, due to the insufficiency of consideration, also arise when the consideration for the promise is forbearance from bringing suit on a questionable claim. Suppose that Al threatens to bring suit against Brad in pursuit of a claim that Al knows is invalid. Brad may be unaware that Al's claim is defective. Or Brad may simply realize that paying Al is cheaper than defending against the groundless action, if Al were to sue. In order to avoid suit, Brad might enter into some sort of settlement agreement with Al in which Brad promises to pay money to Al in exchange for Al's forbearance from bringing his claim in court. The main question is whether Brad's promise to pay is enforceable. As explained below, its enforceability it may well depend on whether Al honestly believes in the validity of his claim and whether his belief is reasonable. Even if Al's cause of action is completely invalid, the conflicting societal value in favor of settling disputed claims weighs heavily in favor of enforcement.

The precise legal issue is whether forbearance from pursuit of an invalid claim is consideration to support a return promise to make a payment in settlement of the claim. Here the utility of avoiding inquiries into the relative values exchanged runs directly into the goal of preventing extortion. The conflict is ordinarily resolved in favor of enforcing the settlement agreement, even if the underlying claim turns out to be without merit. Generally, courts insist upon some measure of good faith in contract formation, and forbearing to pursue a claim that the promisor knows is invalid is not consideration for the return promise. However, if the claim's validity is in doubt, forbearance (or a promise to forbear) is sufficient consideration to support a return promise to make pay settlement.[138]

Fiege v. Boehm,[139] decided before the days of prenatal DNA testing, provides a good example. There, the defendant promised to make payments to the plaintiff if she dropped her paternity suit. After the child was born, blood tests revealed that the defendant was not the father. The defendant refused to pay and claimed that there was no consideration for his promise because the paternity claim that the plaintiff had relinquished was groundless and thus entirely without value. The court rejected this defense and ruled that so long as the original claim of paternity was in good faith, and was not "frivolous, vexatious, or unlawful," the defendant's promise was enforceable.[140] The fact that the plaintiff's good faith belief about the identity of her child's father turned out to be mistaken did not matter, so long as her claim was not completely baseless.[141]

---

[138] RESTATEMENT (SECOND) OF CONTRACTS § 74 (1981). Note that the aggrieved party is not barred from a claim based on unjust enrichment or on other quasi-contractual grounds. RESTATEMENT (SECOND) OF CONTRACTS § 90 (1981) provides that "a promise which the promisor should reasonable expect to induce action or forbearance . . . is binding if injustice can be avoided only by enforcement of the promise." The Second Restatement unlike the First, goes on to provide that whatever remedy justice requires can be used. This permits a court to avoid enforcing a promise if using reliance-based or restitutionary-based remedy avoids injustice.

[139] 123 A.2d 316 (Md. 1956).

[140] *Id.* at 322.

[141] *See also* Dyer v. Nat'l By-Prods., Inc., 380 N.W.2d 732 (Iowa 1986) (forebearance from bringing claim for plaintiff's workplace injuries was consideration for employer's promise of lifetime employment,

The Restatement takes the position that so long as the claim was asserted in good faith, the promise is enforceable, even if the promisee's belief in the claim was unreasonable.[142] Likewise, if the validity of the claim was doubtful due to uncertain facts or unresolved questions of law, a contract based on the forbearance from pursuing the doubtful claim can be enforced.[143] Under this standard, the agreement in *Fiege v. Boehm* would have been enforceable even if the plaintiff did not have a belief about whether the defendant was the father of her child, provided there was some factual doubt, at the time the agreement was made, about whether he was the one. Thus, the settlement agreement is enforceable if the validity of the underlying claim was legitimately doubtful, or, even if its invalidity should have been clear, if the promisee had a good faith belief that it was legitimate.[144]

In resolving questions about the enforceability of settlement agreements based on meritless claims, it should be clear that the more fantastic the claim, the lower the likelihood that the plaintiff's belief is in good faith. Thus, even where the enforceability of the agreement depends entirely on the good faith belief of the person who made the claim, the implausibility of the claim will help support the contention that it was not pursued in good faith.[145] Proof of good faith, like proof of all other subjective elements, is often accomplished by efforts to demonstrate the unreasonableness of the belief.[146]

[D] Recitals of Consideration[147]

Sometimes the parties to an otherwise unenforceable promise recite in their written agreement that the promise was supported by consideration, even though it involved no exchange. As in cases involving sham consideration, no bargain is present, but the promisor, by acknowledging the significance of the requirement of consideration, has demonstrated her desire for the promise to have legal consequences. Here, courts adhere to the usual requirement and insist that there actually be an exchange. However, there are two exceptions, option contracts and guarantees, where the law is more lenient and enforces the promise even though consideration is missing.

[1] Recitals Ineffective

In most cases, an unenforceable promise to make a gift is not made enforceable simply by including a recitation that consideration was supplied. Thus, if Dave desires to make a promise to give his land to his daughter Sally enforceable, he might attempt to do so by signing a written promise with the phrase: "for valuable consideration received, I promise to transfer Xanadu to Sally." If Dave

---

even though workers' compensation insurance made plaintiff's negligence claim completely groundless).

[142] RESTATEMENT (SECOND) OF CONTRACTS § 74(1)(b) (1981).

[143] RESTATEMENT (SECOND) OF CONTRACTS § 74(1)(a) (1981).

[144] RESTATEMENT (SECOND) OF CONTRACTS § 74 cmt. b (1981).

[145] *See, e.g.*, RESTATEMENT (SECOND) OF CONTRACTS § 74 cmt. b (1981).

[146] *See* Dyer v. Nat'l By-Prods., Inc., 380 N.W.2d 732 (Iowa 1986).

[147] David Gamage & Allon Kedem, *Commodification and Contract Formation: Placing the Consideration Doctrine on Stronger Foundations*, 73 U. CHI. L. REV. 1299, 1328 (2006).

subsequently dies without delivering a deed, or if he changes his mind about the gift, the court might have to determine whether his promise is enforceable. If the court looks no further than the language of the written agreement, it may conclude that Dave's promise was supported by consideration, even though the precise nature of the agreed exchange was not specified.

If valid, this type of "recital" that the promise was supported by consideration would eviscerate the consideration doctrine, at least for parties who were savvy enough include such a recital. It would make reciting the presence of consideration an effective substitute for a "seal" even though the seal has been abandoned.[148] Because of this, language in a written promise, reciting that consideration is present, is not enough to make the promise enforceable.[149] On the other hand, the recital may create at least a presumption that consideration was present and shift the burden of proof on the question to the person resisting enforcement of the promise. And, as usual, proving a negative may be difficult — if the promisor received anything from the promisee, whatever was supplied might have been given in exchange for the promise.

[2]   Recitals in Option Contracts

Despite the general rule, a recital that consideration was given for a promise may be sufficient to make an option contract enforceable.[150] Option contracts are frequently used in real estate deals. In an option contract, the owner makes an offer to sell the land to a particular buyer, and promises not to revoke the offer, usually for a specific period of time, until the buyer has a chance to investigate the suitability of the property for its purpose and decide whether it wants to go through with the transaction. A promise to keep an offer open, just like any other promise, must normally be supported by consideration.[151] Sometimes, the prospective buyer provides consideration by paying cash for the option.[152] However, the owner may be willing to provide the buyer with an option, effectively taking the land off the market for a while, without receiving any payment.

Because of the importance of option contracts in real estate markets, and because the transaction is still at a preliminary stage, the requirement of consideration has been substantially relaxed for the purposes of enforcing the option. What otherwise might be viewed as sham consideration, of only a few dollars, makes the option enforceable.[153]

---

[148] *See supra* § 2.02[B] The Seal.

[149] RESTATEMENT (SECOND) OF CONTRACTS § 218 cmt. 3 & illus. 3 (1981); TIE Commc'ns., Inc. v. Kopp, 589 A.2d 329 (Conn. 1991).

[150] RESTATEMENT (SECOND) OF CONTRACTS § 87(1)(a) (1981).

[151] *See infra* § 4.09[A] Traditional Option Contracts.

[152] This was done when Capital University Law School, where the author teaches, purchased a new building. In exchange for a cash payment, the owner of the building agreed to remove it from the market in order to give the law school time to study the feasibility of converting the former insurance company headquarters into a law school. The law school paid cash for the owner's promise to keep its offer to sell open and to abstain from selling the building, in the meantime, to any other prospective buyer.

[153] *E.g.*, Honeyfield v. Lambeth, 519 S.W.2d 342 (Mo. Ct. App. 1975).

The Restatement (Second) goes further, and permits a mere recital of consideration to make the option enforceable.[154] Thus, if the owner of land signs a written offer promising to keep the offer open and reciting a "purported consideration" for her promise of the irrevocability of her offer, the promise to keep the offer open is enforceable as long as 1) the terms of the proposed contract are otherwise fair[155] and 2) the option is to be exercised within a reasonable time.[156] Although a few states have adopted the Restatement position,[157] most jurisdictions adhere to the traditional rule that requires either consideration or reasonable reliance to keep an offer open as promised — though these jurisdictions are usually satisfied with what otherwise might be viewed as sham consideration.[158]

In this respect, the Restatement (Second) takes an approach similar to the one adopted by U.C.C. § 2-205 with respect to promises to keep open an offer to sell goods. Section 2-205 makes an offer by a merchant to buy or sell goods irrevocable, without regard to consideration or reliance, so long as the offer was made in a signed writing which contained an express assurance to the offeree that the offer would be held open.[159] And, in many construction settings, a promise by a subcontractor to keep an offer open is irrevocable, even absent consideration, if the general contractor to whom it was made relies on it in making its own offer to the owner of the project.[160]

Likewise, in international transactions, neither consideration, reliance, nor a recital of consideration is necessary to make a promise to keep an offer open enforceable. The United Nations Convention on Contracts for the International Sale of Goods makes a promise to keep an offer open enforceable.[161] Consideration does not enter into the analysis. Moreover, it makes an offer irrevocable, even in the absence of a promise to keep it open, "if it was reasonable for the offeree to rely on the offer as being irrevocable and the offeree acted in reliance on the offer."[162] Both the UNIDROIT Principles of International Commercial Contracts[163] and the Principles of European Contract Law[164] contain the same

---

[154] *See* RESTATEMENT (SECOND) OF CONTRACTS § 87(1)(a) (1981). *E.g.*, Smith v. Wheeler, 210 S.E.2d 702 (Ga. 1974); *In re* Weinsafts Estate, 647 SW.2d 179 (Mo. Ct. App. 1983).

[155] RESTATEMENT (SECOND) OF CONTRACTS § 87(1)(a) (1981).

[156] RESTATEMENT (SECOND) OF CONTRACTS § 87(1)(a) (1981). This rule is not confined to transactions involving real estate, but has its most frequently application in such deals.

[157] *E.g.*, Knott v. Racicot, 812 N.E.2d 1207 (Mass. 2004); 1464-Eight, Ltd. v. Joppich, 154 S.W.3d 101, 102, 104–106, 108–111 (Tex. 2004).

[158] Knott v. Racicot, 812 N.E.2d 1207 (Mass. 2004) (rejecting conclusion presumption of enforceability).

[159] U.C.C. § 2-205 (2012). *See infra* § 4.09[D] Firm Offers Under U.C.C. § 2-205.

[160] Drennan v. Star Paving, Inc., 333 P.2d 757 (Cal. 1958). *See infra* § 4.09[C] Reliance on an Offer. *But see* Fletcher-Harlee Corp. v. Pote Concrete Contractors, Inc., 482 F.3d 247, 249 (3d Cir. 2007) (subcontractor's bid expressly indicated that it was not irrevocable).

[161] CISG Art. 16(2)(a) (1980). *See* JOHN HONNOLD, UNIFORM LAW FOR INTERNATIONAL SALES § 142 (3d ed. 1999).

[162] CISG Art. 16(b)(2) (1980).

[163] PICC Art. 2.1.4 (2004).

rule.

[3] Recitals in Guaranty Contracts

A similar rule applies to guaranty contracts. A guaranty contract is one in which a person (the guarantor or "surety") promises to pay a debt owed by someone else (the principal debtor). Parents frequently make such promises to their children's creditors to assist their adult children in obtaining credit. Likewise, the controlling shareholders of small corporations frequently make such promises to the corporation's creditors to encourage these lenders to extend credit to the business.

If the guarantor makes his or her promise at the time credit is originally extended to the borrower, consideration for the guarantor's promise exists. The consideration for the guarantor's promise to repay the debt in the event of the principal debtor's default is the loan made by the lender to the principal debtor. The fact that the guarantor did not receive the money does not matter — a clear bargain has been made: "Loan money to Junior and I promise to pay if he defaults." The guarantor has received exactly what it bargained for in exchange for its promise: a loan to someone else.

However, consideration is missing if the guarantor's promise is made after the creditor has already made the loan. Thus, if after the loan was made, the creditor becomes anxious about the prospects of receiving payment and asks the borrower to find someone to guarantee the debt, the guarantor's promise might not be part of an exchange. If the borrower defaults, and the guarantor makes its promise in exchange for the creditor's delay in filing suit, there is an exchange, but if the creditor does not yet have the right to sue, and gives nothing else (such as reduction in the rate of interest, or an extended due date), no consideration exists. The loan itself cannot supply the necessary consideration — it is "past consideration" because it has already been made.

In these situations, as with option contracts, the Restatement (Second) of Contracts takes a liberal view. It permits enforcement of the guarantor's promise if the promise is in writing and the writing contains a recital that it was made in exchange for some consideration.[165] Further, the fact that the recited consideration has not been paid does not matter.[166]

However, the Restatement's position on this point has not enjoyed a wide following. Most courts still refuse to enforce a promise in either an option contract or a guaranty contract if the recited consideration has not actually been paid.[167] This approach makes little sense, particularly where the recited amount appears to

---

[164] PECL Art. 2.202 (2002).

[165] Restatement (Second) of Contracts § 88(a) (1981); Joseph Siprut, Comment, *The Peppercorn Reconsidered: Why a Promise to Sell Blackacre for Nominal Consideration Is Not Binding, but Should Be*, 97 Nw. U.L. Rev. 1809 (2003); Mark B. Wessman, *Retraining the Gatekeeper: Further Reflections on the Doctrine of Consideration*, 29 Loy. L.A. L. Rev. 713 (1996); James D. Gordon III, *Consideration and the Commercial-Gift Dichotomy*, 44 Vand. L. Rev. 283 (1991); Melvin Aron Eisenberg, Symposium, *The Principles of Consideration*, 67 Cornell L. Rev. 640 (1982).

[166] 1464-Eight, Ltd. v. Joppich, 154 S.W.3d 101 (Tex. 2004).

[167] *E.g.*, Lewis v. Fletcher, 617 P.2d 834 (Idaho 1980).

be nominal, suggesting nothing more than a sham exchange in any event. If the amount recited to have been given was nothing more than a sham, it should not matter whether it was actually paid. Failure to pay the recited consideration might be relevant to the question of breach, and possibly determinative of whether the promisor is excused from its contractual duties due to a total material breach, but it should not affect the question of whether there was an enforceable promise in the first place. Correspondingly, if the recital was nothing more than a sham, payment of the sham consideration should not operate to magically turn the transaction into a genuine bargain where none was intended.[168]

Some courts attempt to avoid this issue by ruling that the recital of consideration, even if it was not paid, creates an implied promise to supply the specified amount.[169] Other courts take the view that the promisor, having recited that consideration was supplied for his or her promise, should be estopped from denying that consideration was supplied.[170] However, if the promise involved no real exchange, neither of these approaches is sound. The Second Restatement, at least, does not pretend that consideration is present in these cases. Instead, it simply says that these promises should be enforced when the parties have gone to the trouble of expressing their desire that the promise be legally enforceable by reciting that consideration was supplied.

[E]　　Illusory Promises Not Consideration

Ordinarily, where a promise is given in exchange for another promise, both are supported by consideration. Each person's promise supplies the consideration for the promise of the other.[171] The exchange of promises is sufficient if the promise given is what was sought in return by the promisor.[172] As the court explained in *Pearsall v. Alexander*, where two people agreed with one another to share their winnings from lottery tickets they each had purchased, "[b]y exchanging mutual promises to share in the proceeds of winning tickets, adequate consideration was given by both parties. An exchange of promises is consideration, so long as it is bargained-for."[173]

But, if one of the parties' promises is an empty commitment, it is completely without value, there is no exchange for the meaningful promise of the other, and no consideration. An empty or meaningless promise is said to be "illusory" and an illusory promise is not consideration for another person's meaningful promise.[174] When this happens the contract is unenforceable due to a lack of "mutuality of

---

[168] *See* RESTATEMENT (SECOND) OF CONTRACTS § 87 cmt. c (1981).

[169] *E.g.*, Smith v. Wheeler, 210 S.E. 2d 702 (Ga. 1974).

[170] *See* Lawrence v. McCalmont, 43 U.S. 426, 452 (1844) (Story, J.).

[171] RESTATEMENT (SECOND) OF CONTRACTS § 75 (1981).

[172] *E.g.*, Pearsall v. Alexander, 572 A.2d 113, 118 (D.C. 1990) ("[B]y exchanging mutual promises to share in the proceeds of winning tickets, adequate consideration was given by both parties. An exchange of promises is consideration, so long as it is bargained-for").

[173] Pearsall v. Alexander, 572 A.2d 113, 118 (D.C. 1990).

[174] Regensburger v. China Adoption Consultants, Ltd., 138 F.3d 1201 (7th Cir. 1998).

obligation."[175] The mutuality of obligation doctrine is sometimes described somewhat simplistically: "both parties must be bound to a contract, or neither is."[176]

At one time, many promises were regarded as illusory, including those involved in modern requirements and output contracts, as well as in transactions in which one of the parties had a unilateral but limited right to terminate the contract. Fortunately, the law has migrated away from these applications of the mutuality rule and completely illusory promises that do not qualify as consideration are rare.

[1]   Illusory Promises[177]

A promise is illusory if the person who makes the promise retains complete and unfettered discretion over whether to perform. The most obvious example is a promise by a person to do something only if she "wants to."[178] Such a promise is a mere illusion of a promise and is not consideration for a return promise from the other person.[179]

Because situations involving illusory promises always involve two promises, it is sometimes easy to get confused. In these situations, the principal question is whether the meaningful promise made by one of the parties is enforceable. It is not enforceable if the reciprocal promise of the other party is illusory, because an illusory promise is not consideration for the meaningful promise of the first party.

Thus, if Tom promises to sell his car to Phyllis for $15,000 and Phyllis promises to buy it *"if I want to,"* Phyllis's promise is illusory — she'll only buy it if she wants to and retains complete discretion over the decision. Thus, her promise to buy, if you can call it that, is not consideration for Tom's meaningful promise to sell.[180] She might buy it or not, depending entirely on her whim.[181] Since there is no consideration for his promise, Tom's meaningful promise to sell the car is not enforceable. Tom can back out of the deal anytime he wants to, because Phyllis,

---

[175] *E.g.,* Pick Kwik Food Stores, Inc. v. Tenser, 407 So. 2d 216 (Fla. Dist. Ct. App. 1981).

[176] Serpa v. Darling, 810 P.2d 778, 781 (Nev. 1991); Economy Roofing & Insulating Go. v. Zumaris, 538 N.W.2d 641, 650 (Iowa 1995); Dewitt County Public Bldg. Comm'n v. County of De Witt, 469 N.E.2d 689, 695 (Ill. App. Ct. 1984).

[177] Arthur Linton Corbin, *The Effect of Options on Consideration,* 34 Yale L.J. 571 (1925). Val D. Ricks, *In Defense of Mutuality of Obligation: Why "Both Should Be Bound, or Neither,"* 78 Neb. L. Rev. 491 (1999); Michael B. Metzger & Michael J. Phillips, *Promissory Estoppel and Reliance on Illusory Promises,* 44 Sw. L.J. 841 (1990); Herman Oliphant, *Mutuality of Obligation in Bilateral Contracts at Law (pts. 1 & 2),* 25 Colum. L. Rev. 705 (1925), 28 Colum. L. Rev. 997 (1928).

[178] *See, e.g.,* De Los Santos v. Great W. Sugar Co., 348 N.W.2d 842 (Neb. 1984) (carrier's promise to transport as many beets as it could load was the same as, as many as it wanted to, where carrier had made identical commitments to many others and retained complete discretion over whose beets it would load).

[179] Restatement (Second) of Contracts § 77 & cmt. a (1981). *See* Wickham & Burton Coal Co. v. Farmer's Lumber Co., 179 N.W. 417 (Iowa 1920) ("a contract to sell personal property is void for want of mutuality if the quantity to be delivered is conditioned entirely on the will, wish, or want of the buyer"); Harrington v. Harrington, 365 N.W.2d 552, 555 (N.D. 1985) ("a mere illusion").

[180] Restatement (Second) of Contracts § 77 illus. 1 (1981).

[181] Johnson Enter. of Jacksonville, Inc. v. FPL Group, Inc., 162 F.3d 1290, 1311–12 (11th Cir. 1998); NSK Ltd. v. U.S., 115 F.3d 965 (Fed. Cir. 1997).

whose promise was meaningless, did not supply any consideration for it.

As one court explained:

> It is . . . elementary that a contract, which leaves it entirely optional with one of the parties to perform, is not founded on mutual promises. . . . A purported promise that actually promises nothing because it leaves the choice of performance entirely to the offeror is illusory, and an illusory promise is not sufficient consideration to support a contract.[182]

A promise may also be illusory if it is too indefinite to be enforced.[183] If the agreement permits one of the parties to make a crucial decision, such as the quantity of goods to be purchased, or the price, this may make that party's promise as meaningless as a promise to purchase the goods only if that party wants to.[184] However, if the agreement supplies a mechanism providing greater definition to the indefinite terms, in a way which restrains the party's otherwise unfettered discretion, it is consideration for the other party's promise and the deal can be enforced.[185]

Agreements like the one described above between Tom and Phyllis, are rare. More common, are agreements in which one of the parties retains a wide degree, but not completely unrestrained discretion, over her own performance.[186] Where a person has limited her discretion in some meaningful way, her promise is not illusory, and the other party's promise is enforceable. Situations involving limited latitude, where consideration exists, frequently involve exclusive dealing contracts, contracts with unilateral termination provisions, and requirements and output contracts.

[2]   Exclusive Dealing Contracts: Duty to Use Best Effort

An exclusive dealing contract is one in which one party enjoys the exclusive right to sell goods within a particular market. For example, a French wine grower might grant a particular American importer the exclusive rights to receive and distribute the grower's wine in the United States. Or a celebrity might promise to give the exclusive right to use his or her name to the manufacturer of a particular brand. In return, the manufacturer promises to pay the celebrity a fee, or perhaps a commission on every item bearing the celebrity's name that the manufacturer sells: "Air Jordan."

This is essentially what occurred in the famous case of *Wood v. Lucy, Lady Duff-Gordon*,[187] in what might have been the first "celebrity endorsement" of a

---

[182] Board of Educ. v. James Hamilton Constr. Co., 891 P.2d 556, 561 (N.M. Ct. App. 1994).

[183] Lane v. Wahl, 6 P.3d 621 (Wash. Ct. App. 2000).

[184] *E.g.*, Wickham & Burton Coal Co. v. Farmer's Lumber Co., 179 N.W. 417 (Iowa 1920) (an agreement of sale at a certain price of all the coal the buyer "would want to purchase" from the seller was not an enforceable contract).

[185] *See infra* § 4.11 Indefinite Terms and Agreements to Agree.

[186] RESTATEMENT (SECOND) OF CONTRACTS § 79(c) & cmt. f (1981).

[187] 118 N.E. 214 (N.Y. 1917). *Wood v. Lucy, Lady Duff-Gordon* and its "enduring legacy" was the

consumer product. Lucy, a widely celebrated survivor of the Titanic disaster, promised Wood that he would have the exclusive right to sell clothing that she had either designed or endorsed. In return, Wood promised to keep track of his sales and to pay Lucy half of his profits. The problem was that Wood made no express promise to sell a particular quantity of the items bearing her endorsement. Nor did he promise to pay her a set minimum in exchange for the right to use her name. It thus appeared that Wood had unlimited discretion and that he had neither taken any action nor made any promise in exchange for her promise giving him the exclusive right to market items she had endorsed.

When Lucy breached their agreement by permitting others to distribute items she had endorsed, Wood sued. Lucy defended on the grounds that, because Wood had no real obligation to do anything, there was no consideration for her promise. Therefore, she claimed, her promise of exclusivity was unenforceable.

The court rejected her defense. Judge Benjamin Cardozo's well-known opinion held that the contract included an implied promise that Wood would use "reasonable efforts" to market Lucy's designs.[188] Judge Cardozo found this implied promise because the nature of the transaction would not have been rational at all absent some obligation on Wood's part. Lucy promised to give Wood the "exclusive" rights to market products containing her endorsement. Her compensation was to be measured by the results of his efforts alone. He paid no flat fee for the use of her name and set no minimum that he would pay, apart from a percentage of whatever he managed to sell. And, because of the promised right of exclusivity, Lucy stood to earn nothing unless Wood made some efforts. The court would not presume that Lucy intended to place the value of her endorsement completely "at the mercy" of Wood's unrestricted discretion. In these circumstances, the court held that Wood had impliedly promised to "use reasonable efforts to bring profits and revenues into existence."[189]

The imposition of this implied promise supplied the necessary consideration for Lucy's promise of exclusivity. Saddled with a duty to use reasonable efforts, Wood's freedom was restrained. Though he retained wide discretion, and it might be difficult to discern whether his efforts had been reasonable, he did not have complete freedom to do as he liked.

Wood v. Lucy demonstrates that in determining whether a particular promise is

---

subject of a Symposium issue of the Pace Law Review in 2008, consisting of the following artices: James J. Fishman, *The Enduring Legacy of* Wood v. Lucy, Lady Duff-Gordon: *Introduction*, 28 PACE L. REV. 162 (2008); Joseph M. Perillo, *Neutral Standardizing of Contracts*, 28 PACE L. REV. 179 (2008); Peter Linzer, *"Implied," "Inferred," and "Imposed": Default Rules and Adhesion Contracts — the Need for Radical Surgery*, 28 PACE L. REV. 195 (2008); Nicholas R. Weiskopf, Wood v. Lucy: *The Overlap Between Interpretation and Gap-Filling to Achieve Minimum Decencies*, 28 PACE L. REV. 219 (2008); Deborah Zalesne, *Integrating Academic Skills into First Year Curricula: Using* Wood v. Lucy, Lady Duff-Gordon *to Teach the Role of Facts in Legal Reasoning*, 28 PACE L. REV. 271 (2008); Larry A. DiMatteo, *Cardozo, Anti-Formalism, and the Fiction of Noninterventionism*, 28 PACE L. REV. 315 (2008); Meredith R. Miller, *A Picture of the New York Court of Appeals at the Time of* Wood v. Lucy, Lady Duff-Gordon, 28 PACE L. REV. 357 (2008); Monroe H. Freedman, *Cardozo's Opinion in Lady Lucy's Case: "Formative Unconscionability," Impracticality and Judicial Abuse*, 28 PACE L. REV. 395 (2008).

[188] *Wood v. Lucy, Lady Duff-Gordon*, 118 N.E. at 214.

[189] *Wood v. Lucy, Lady Duff-Gordon*, 118 N.E. at 215.

illusory, it is important to always consider both the explicit promises the parties have made as well as the implied promises reasonably inferred from their express commitments. Implied duties, like Wood's implied obligation to make reasonable efforts, can make what otherwise appears to be an illusory or gratuitous promise into one sufficient to support the enforcement of the other party's promises.[190]

In exclusive dealing contracts for the sale of goods, it is no longer necessary for the court to evaluate the economic realities of the transaction to determine if it is appropriate to imply a duty to use reasonable efforts. U.C.C. § 2-306(2) supplies the necessary obligations. Unless the parties to an exclusive dealing contract have agreed otherwise, the seller has a duty to use its "best efforts to supply the goods" and a buyer has a duty to use its "best efforts to promote their [re]sale."[191] This duty, like Wood's duty to make reasonable efforts, is real, and the other party's corresponding duty of exclusivity, is enforceable.

Actually determining whether a party has fulfilled its duty to use its best efforts is more difficult, but if the obligation exists, the duty is not illusory. In proving whether the duty was met, the court might refer to any industry custom, to past conduct between the parties, or to specific efforts that might be outlined in the express agreement.[192]

[3]   Contracts Subject to a Condition[193]

If a promisor's obligation is subject to a condition, and that same party has unfettered control over whether the condition is satisfied, the contract may be unenforceable due to a lack of consideration. In most cases, however, there are likely to be sufficient limitations on the party's discretion to prevent the mutuality doctrine from making the contract unenforceable. And, in many of these cases, the law will imply a duty to take reasonable steps to ensure that the condition is satisfied — this, combined with the restraint on the party's freedom in the event that the condition occurs, supplies the necessary consideration.

[a]   Conditional Promises as Consideration

Conditional promises might appear to be illusory, but usually they are not. A promise is conditional if it is subject to the occurrence of an event, that is not certain to occur.[194] The mere fact that the event on which the promise depends is uncertain to occur, does not mean that the promise involved is meaningless. If it were, all insurance contracts would be unenforceable, because in an insurance

---

[190] *See also* Famous Brands, Inc. v. David Sherman Corp., 814 F.2d 517, 521 (8th Cir. 1987) (implied promise of distributor to use its best efforts to promote the manufacturer's products).

[191] U.C.C. § 2-306(2) (2012).

[192] *See* Alison Grey Anderson, *Conflicts of Interest: Efficiency, Fairness and Corporate Structure*, 25 UCLA L. Rev. 738 (1978); Steven J. Burton, *Breach of Contract and the Common Law Duty to Perform in Good Faith*, 94 Harv. L. Rev. 369 (1980); Charles J. Goetz & Robert E. Scott, *Principles of Relational Contracts*, 67 Va. L. Rev. 1089, 1111–1125 (1981).

[193] *See* Arthur Linton Corbin, *The Effect of Options on Consideration*, 34 Yale. L.J. 571 (1925).

[194] Restatement (Second) of Contracts § 224 (1981). *See* Restatement (Second) of Contracts § 76 cmt. a (1981).

contract the insurer promises to pay the insured only if the event insured against happens. Thus, if Perpetual Life Insurance Co. promises to pay Linda $1 million in the event of her husband's death, the mere fact that the promise depends on her husband's death does not mean that Perpetual Life's promise is illusory. The risk that her husband will die is as real as it gets.[195]

[b]   Promisor in Control of Occurrence of Condition

Conditional promises can be illusory if the promisor is in complete control of the occurrence of the condition. This may give the promisor unfettered discretion over her own obligation and make her promise illusory. If so, it is not consideration for whatever promise was made in return for the conditional promise. Whether the promise is meaningful despite the promisor's control of the condition's occurrence depends on rules regarding "alternative performances."[196]

When a promisor reserves a choice of alternative performances, her promise is consideration if each of the alternatives would have been consideration, in the absence of the choice. Thus, if Miguel promises to sell his car to Rita, and Rita promises to either pay Miguel $10,000 or to paint his house, Rita's alternative performances would each be consideration for Miguel's promise. Thus, even though Rita gets to choose whether to pay the $10,000 or paint Miguel's house, she has limited her freedom in a significant way in exchange for Miguel's promise, making his promise enforceable.

When a promise is subject to a condition and the promisor retains control over occurrence of the condition, forbearance from causing the condition to occur is treated as one of the two alternatives. A frequently cited example is found in *Scott v. Moragues Lumber, Co.*[197] Scott promised to charter a certain ship to Moragues Lumber, subject to the condition that Scott purchase the ship. Although Scott was in complete control over whether he purchased the vessel, forbearance from buying it would have been consideration for Moragues promise. Because buying the boat or forbearance from buying the boat are both good consideration, Moragues's promise was enforceable.[198]

Courts sometimes solve the problem of the promisor's control over the promise by finding an implied promise to make a good faith or reasonable effort to assure occurrence of the condition. A good example is a contract for the purchase of land, in which the buyer's duty is subject to the condition that the buyer qualifies for a mortgage loan. In this situation, the law imposes a duty on the buyer to make a reasonable good faith effort to secure the necessary financing.[199] The buyer's duty to try supplies the necessary consideration for the seller's promise to convey title to the land.

---

[195] *See* RESTATEMENT (SECOND) OF CONTRACTS § 76 cmt. c (1981) (regarding aleatory promises).

[196] RESTATEMENT (SECOND) OF CONTRACTS § 76(2) (1981).

[197] 80 So. 394 (Ala. 1918).

[198] RESTATEMENT (SECOND) OF CONTRACTS § 76 illus. 8 (1981).

[199] *E.g.*, Billman v. Hensel, 391 N.E.2d 671 (Ind. Ct. App. 1979).

[c]   Conditions of Satisfaction

If a promisor's obligation depends on his or her "satisfaction" with the results of the promisee's work, the promisor's duty may appear to be illusory. This type of an agreement might be made in a construction contract, where the owner's duty to pay for the work performed depends on his or her satisfaction with the quality of the work.[200] Or, the buyer of real estate may promise to go through with the deal and pay for the land if she is satisfied with the quality of title tendered by the seller. Likewise, a person who commissions a work of art may make his promise to pay for the completed work expressly subject to his satisfaction with the finished product. In all of these cases, "I'll pay if I'm satisfied" is only slightly more constraining than if the promisor had said, "I'll pay you if I want to." Even though the difference is slight, it is enough to supply the necessary consideration.

In these situations, initial questions may arise over whether the party's satisfaction is limited by a subjective or an objective standard.[201] However, as long as it is limited in some respect, there is consideration for the other person's promise.

Consider, for example, an agreement between Beth and Phil for Phil to be the photographer at Beth's wedding, in which Beth promises to pay Phil if she is satisfied with the pictures he takes. If Phil tries to back out of the agreement, Beth's reservation of the right to pay him only if she is satisfied, raises the question of whether she supplied any consideration for his promise to take the photos. If there is no consideration for his promise, he can back out, without the risk of losing a lawsuit.

In resolving this issue, it will not matter whether Beth's satisfaction is tested by an objective or subjective standard.[202] If Beth must act reasonably in determining whether she is satisfied with the pictures, consideration is supplied by her promise not to act on a whim in rejecting the results. If Beth is entitled to judge the photos by her own personal subjective standards, without regard to the judgment a reasonable person would have made, she is still required to act in good faith in evaluating Phil's work. She may not feign dissatisfaction and refuse to purchase them for some reason unrelated to her personal satisfaction with the quality of the photos.[203] Thus, because Beth's discretion is constrained, either by an obligation to act reasonably, or by a duty to act in good faith, her promise is not illusory and there is consideration for Phil's reciprocal promise to take the photos.

The court's decision in *Mattei v. Hopper*[204] provides another good example. There, the buyer's duty to buy a shopping mall was subject to the condition that the seller enter into leases with tenants who were "satisfactory" to the buyer. The

---

[200] *See* R. D. Hursch, Annotation, *Construction and Effect of Provision in Private Building and Construction Contract That Work Must Be Done to Satisfaction of Owner*, 44 A.L.R.2d 1114 (1955).

[201] *See* Morin Bldg. Prods. Co. v. Baystone Constr., Inc., 717 F.2d 413 (7th Cir. 1983). *See generally infra* § 8.04 Conditions of Satisfaction or Approval.

[202] *See* Storek & Storek, Inc. v. Citicorp Real Estate, Inc., 100 Cal. App. 4th 44 (2002) (explaining the difference between "good faith" and "reasonableness" in the context of a condition of satisfaction).

[203] Mattei v. Hopper, 330 P.2d 625 (Cal. 1958).

[204] *Id.*

buyer did not want to be saddled with bad tenants. Later, when the seller tried to back out of the agreement, it claimed that the condition of the buyer's approval of the tenants was illusory, thus making the seller's promise unenforceable. In rejecting this claim, the court said that the purchaser's mere "expression of dissatisfaction is not conclusive [because] his dissatisfaction must be genuine."[205] By agreeing to purchase the property if he was satisfied with the leases, the purchaser gave up the opportunity to back out of the deal because his own circumstances had changed, or because market conditions had no longer made the purchase a wise transaction. He could back out of the deal if he was dissatisfied with the tenants, but he couldn't falsely claim to be dissatisfied as a pretense for backing out of the deal.

From the foregoing it should be clear that a promise should not be illusory if the promisee's own duty to perform depends on the satisfaction of a third party.[206] Here, although there is discretion, the promisee is not the one who retains the discretion. The promisee's duties are out of his or her hands completely and no one would suggest that placing one's fate in the hands of another was not a detriment, which will support a promise given in exchange. Thus, if Beth promises to pay for Phil's wedding photos, if the photos are satisfactory to Beth's mother, Beth's promise is not illusory and Phil's promise is supported by consideration. Likewise, an owner's promise to pay for a construction project, subject to the satisfaction of the owner's architect, supplies the consideration necessary for the contractor's promise to do the work.

[4]   Unilateral Right to Terminate

Another type of contract which has sometimes been viewed as vulnerable to the claim that there is no mutuality of obligation, and thus no consideration, is one in which one of the parties enjoys a unilateral right to terminate.[207] Distributorship agreements sometimes give the seller the right to unilaterally cancel the buyer's rights to serve as a distributor of the seller's merchandise. The right of one party to unilaterally terminate the contract may make the other party's obligations unenforceable due to a perceived lack of mutuality of obligation.[208] The same problem arises if the contract is for an unstated duration.[209]

However, modern cases have almost completely eliminated this branch of the mutuality doctrine. For example, in *Laclede Gas Co. v. Amoco Oil Co.*, Amoco agreed to supply propane to Laclede for distribution to Laclede's residential customers. The parties anticipated that Laclede's customers would eventually convert their heating systems to natural gas, and thus the contract permitted Laclede to terminate the contract on 30 days' notice. When nationwide oil shortages made it difficult for Amoco to supply the propane, it sought to terminate

---

[205] *Id.* at 628.

[206] Black Lake Pipe Line Co. v. Union Const. Co., Inc., 538 S.W.2d 80, 88 (Tex. 1976).

[207] *See, e.g.*, Miami Coca-Cola Bottling Co. v. Orange Crush Co., 296 F. 693 (5th Cir. 1924).

[208] *E.g.*, Pick Kwik Food Stores, Inc. v. Tenser, 407 So. 2d 216 (Fla. Dist. Ct. App. 1981); Miami Coca-Cola Bottling Co. v. Orange Crush Co., 296 F. 693 (5th Cir. 1924).

[209] *E.g.*, Du Pont de Nemours & Co. v. Claiborne-Reno Co., 64 F.2d 224 (8th Cir. 1933).

the contract. Amoco claimed that its promise to deliver the gas lacked consideration, because of Laclede's right to terminate the contract.[210] The court rejected Amoco's claim and ruled that the Laclede's duty to give 30 days' notice before ending the contract limited Laclede's discretion sufficiently to supply the necessary consideration for Amoco's promise to deliver the propane.

Most courts follow *Laclede* — a unilateral right to terminate does not deprive a contract of consideration, as long as there is some obligation either to provide notice of termination,[211] or to exercise the right to terminate in good faith. Other courts have taken an even more generous approach and regard agreements as enforceable even if they require nothing more than "notice" of termination. Thus, in *Lane v. Wahl*,[212] a multi-year lease was enforceable against the landlord, even though the lessee enjoyed the unilateral right to terminate "at any time," restricted only by his obligation to give "notice in writing to the lessor by certified mail."[213] As one court said: "The alternative of giving notice was not difficult of performance, but it was a sufficient consideration to support the contract."[214] Likewise, if termination is permissible only due to "cause," the mutuality doctrine loses its force, and the contract is enforceable.[215] Even when the contract does not specifically limit the party's right to unilaterally terminate, any implied limitation on its right to do so satisfies the mutuality rule.[216]

Results like these go a long way toward making the mutuality doctrine a dead-letter.[217] Any negligible restraint on the promisee's freedom, such as the duty to act reasonably, or in good faith, or to supply notice of termination, supplies the necessary consideration.

[5] Output and Requirements Contracts[218]

At one time the enforceability of output and requirements contracts was open to question, due to the uncertainty of the quantity involved and the degree of discretion afforded to the parties to determine the amount produced or required. An "output contract" is one in which the quantity is measured by the seller's output. For example, in *Feld v. Henry S. Levy & Sons, Inc.*, the contract required the seller to deliver all of his production of "bread crumbs" to the buyer.[219] A "requirements contract" is similar, except that it measures the quantity by the requirements of the buyer. Thus, in *Eastern Air Lines, Inc. v. Gulf Oil Corp.*, the

---

[210] Laclede Gas Co. v. Amoco Oil Co., 522 F.2d 33 (8th Cir. 1975).

[211] *See, e.g.*, Sedalia Land Co. v. Robinson Brick & Tile Co., 475 P.2d 351 (Colo. Ct. App. 1970); Lindner v. Mid-Continent Petroleum Corp., 252 S.W.2d 631 (Ark. 1952).

[212] 6 P.3d 621 (Wash. Ct. App. 2000).

[213] 6 P.3d at 623. *See also* Walls v. Giuliani, 916 F. Supp. 214 (E.D.N.Y. 1996).

[214] Sylvan Crest Sand & Gravel Co. v. United States, 150 F.2d 642 (2d Cir. 1945).

[215] *E.g.*, Aristocrat Window Co. v. Randell, 206 N.E.2d 545 (Ill. App. Ct. 1965).

[216] RESTATEMENT (SECOND) OF CONTRACTS § 77 cmt. d (1981).

[217] *See* Helle v. Landmark, Inc., 472 N.E.2d 765 (Ohio Ct. App. 1984).

[218] John C. Weistart, *Requirements and Output Contracts: Quantity Variations Under the UCC*, 1973 DUKE L.J. 599.

[219] Feld v. Henry S. Levy & Sons, Inc., 335 N.E. 2d 320 (N.Y. 1975).

airline promised to purchase all of the jet fuel it required from Gulf.[220]

In both of these transactions one of the parties has a measure of discretion: in an output contract the seller has discretion over the quantity it produces; in a requirements contract the buyer determines the quantity it needs. This discretion may make it appear that there is no consideration for the other party's promise to perform — the buyer's promise to purchase all of the seller's output and the seller's promise to deliver the quantity that the buyer requires.

However, these promises are not illusory because they both contain a constraint on the promisee's discretion. With respect to output contracts, by promising to sell all of its output to a particular buyer, the seller has impliedly agreed to refrain from delivering any of the goods that it produces to a different customer. While the seller might possibly reduce its output to zero, any quantity it produces must be sold to the buyer. The buyer in a requirements contract is similarly constrained: although it might reduce the quantity it requires to none, it may not purchase the same goods from another supplier. Instead, it is bound to purchase all of the goods of the type involved that it requires exclusively from the seller.[221] Further, in both these situations, the quantity which may be produced or required is subject to a general requirement of good faith.[222]

Article 2 of the Uniform Commercial Code reinforces this conclusion. Although the Code's text does not expressly dispense with the mutuality rule, the entire text of U.C.C. § 2-306, dealing with output, requirements, and other exclusive dealing contracts, presumes that they are enforceable.[223] Further, the Official Comments to § 2-306 explains that requirements and output contracts do not "lack mutuality of obligation since, under [§ 2-306] the party who will determine quantity is required to operate his plant or conduct his business in good faith and according to commercial standards of fair dealing in the trade so that his output or requirements will approximate a reasonably foreseeable figure."[224]

Apart from the question of whether the contract is supported by consideration, the quantity of goods may be too indefinite for the court to determine whether there has been a breach or to frame an appropriate remedy. U.C.C. § 2-306(1) goes a long way toward solving this problem by measuring the quantity by the good faith output or requirements involved as well as by requiring that the quantity not be "unreasonably disproportionate" to any estimates the parties may have expressed or, in the absence of a stated estimate, to any normal or comparable prior quantity produced or required.[225] However, these issues do not bear directly on the question of consideration.[226]

---

[220] Eastern Air Lines, Inc. v. Gulf Oil Corp., 415 F. Supp. 429 (S.D. Fla. 1975).

[221] *E.g.*, Minn. Lumber Co. v. Whitebreast Coal Co., 43 N.E. 774 (Ill. 1895).

[222] U.C.C. § 2-306(1) (2012).

[223] U.C.C. § 2-306(1) (2012).

[224] U.C.C. § 2-306 cmt. 2 (2012).

[225] U.C.C. § 2-306 (2012). *See* McMichael v. Price, 58 P.2d 549 (Okla. 1936).

[226] *See* U.C.C. § 2-306 cmt. 2 (2012).

[6]   Alternative Performances

A contract calling for alternative performances may lack mutuality if one of the alternatives that a party may select is not consideration.[227] However, if both alternatives impose meaningful obligations, the contract is not illusory. Thus, when Miguel promises to sell his car to Rita, in exchange for Rita's promise to either pay Miguel $10,000 or to paint his house, the fact that Rita has a choice between two alternative performances does not make her commitment illusory. Either performance is meaningful, and thus her promise supplies the necessary consideration for Miguel's promise to deliver the car.

[7]   Mutuality of Obligation in Arbitration Agreements[228]

The mutuality doctrine has recently enjoyed a small resurgence in connection with arbitration clauses. The issue is raised when a contract that contains an arbitration clause gives one of the parties the unilateral unlimited right to revise the underlying contract without obtaining the consent of, or even giving notice to, the other party. Some courts enforce these contracts and their arbitration provisions.[229] However, other courts use the unlimited right to modify the contract to conclude that the entire contract is unenforceable, thus permitting the other party to sidestep the arbitration clause that it contained.[230] This type of unilateral right to modify a contract may also be unconscionable.[231]

§ 2.06   PRE-EXISTING LEGAL DUTY RULE[232]

Under the pre-existing or "legal" duty rule a past promise or a previous performance made by the promisee cannot serve as consideration for a later promise to the promisee.[233] In other words, "past consideration" is no consider-

---

[227] RESTATEMENT (SECOND) OF CONTRACTS § 77 cmt. b & illus. 6 (1981).

[228] Michael L. DeMichele & Richard A. Bales, *Unilateral-Modification Provisions in Employment Arbitration Agreements*, 24 HOFSTRA LAB. & EMP. L.J. 63 (2006); Lindsay K. Griffel, Case Note, *Illusory Promise to Arbitrate Is Not Sufficient Consideration for "Stand-Alone" Arbitration Agreement in Gonzalez v. West Suburban Imports, Inc.*, 6 J. AM. ARB. 65 (2007).

[229] *See, e.g.*, Blair v. Scott Specialty Gases, 283 F.3d 595, 604 (3d Cir. 2002).

[230] *E.g.*, Al-Safin v. Circuit City Stores, Inc., 394 F.3d 1254, 1262 (9th Cir. 2005); Cheek v. United Healthcare of Mid-Atl., Inc., 835 A.2d 656, 657 (Md. 2003).

[231] *See* Al-Safin v. Circuit City Stores, Inc., 394 F.3d 1254, 1262 (9th Cir. 2005).

[232] Harold C. Havighurst, *Consideration, Ethics and Administration*, 42 COLUM. L. REV. 1, 25–30 (1942); Timothy J. Muris, *Opportunistic Behavior and the Law of Contracts*, 65 MINN. L. REV. 521, 546 (1981). *See* Subha Narasimhan, *Modification: The Self-Help Specific Performance Remedy*, 97 YALE L.J. 61 (1987); Richard Nathan, *Grappling with the Pre-Existing Duty Rule: A Proposal for a Statutory Amendment*, 23 AM. BUS. L.J. 509 (1986); Alan Schwartz & Joel Watson, *The Law and Economics of Costly Contracting*, 20 J.L. ECON. & ORG. 2, 24 (2004); KEVIN M. TEEVEN, PROMISES ON PRIOR OBLIGATIONS AT COMMON LAW (1998); Kevin M. Teevan, *Consensual Path to Abolition of Preexisting Duty Rule*, 34 VAL. U. L. REV. 43 (1999); Joel K. Goldstein, *The Legal Duty Rule and Learning About Rules: A Case Study*, 44 ST. LOUIS U. L.J. 1333 (2000).

[233] The RESTATEMENT (SECOND) OF CONTRACTS § 73 (1981) refers to it as the "legal duty" rule. Most cases and commentators tend to call it the "pre-existing duty" rule, though because pre-existing moral duties

ation.

Suppose, for example, that Sam has already entered into a legally binding agreement to sell his car to Barb for $18,000, but that Sam later persuades Barb to promise an additional $500 for the car. If Barb later attempts to back out of her commitment to pay the $500 bonus, Sam will be unable to show that there was any consideration for her promise of the extra amount. His promise to deliver the car cannot serve as the consideration for Barb's revised promise, because at the time she agreed to pay the additional $500, Sam already had a legal duty to deliver the car for only $18,000. This "pre-existing duty" was not incurred in exchange for her promise to pay the higher price.

When courts apply it stringently, the pre-existing duty rule makes one-sided modifications to existing contracts unenforceable. However, courts and legislatures have employed a variety of ways to make such modifications enforceable even though consideration is missing.

The pre-existing duty rule is not really a separate rule of consideration. Instead, it is an application of the rule that recognizes consideration only when there is a true exchange. If a promisee already owes a duty to the promisor to do whatever it was that serves as the supposed consideration for the promise, then the promise is not part of an exchange — consideration is missing.[234] Thus, if the parties attempt to rely on some previous performance or promise by the promisee to serve as the consideration for a new obligation incurred by the promisor, consideration is absent and the promisor's new promise is not enforceable. In other words, past consideration, based on some sort of pre-existing duty, is no consideration.[235]

[A]   Modification of an Existing Contract

As suggested by the foregoing discussion, the pre-existing duty rule has its biggest impact when the parties to an existing contract wish to make a mid-course adjustment to one of the parties' duties. Traditionally, an agreement to modify an existing contract was treated as just like any other agreement which required consideration. If only one of the parties' duties was to be expanded, consideration for the revised duty would be missing and modification might not be enforceable.[236] Thus, in *Lingenfelder v. Wainwright Brewery*[237] an employer's promise to his architect of additional compensation, in exchange for the architect's promise not to back out of the original deal, was unenforceable. The architect made no new promise and incurred no new obligation in exchange for the promise of additional compensation, and he was unable to collect on his employer's revised promise of extra pay.

If both parties undertake additional duties, there will be no problem. Each

---

that do not impose a legal obligation do not invoke the rule, the term "legal duty" is probably more technically precise.

[234] RESTATEMENT (SECOND) OF CONTRACTS § 73 (1981).

[235] Prendergast v. Snoeberger, 796 N.E.2d 588 (Ohio Ct. App. 2003).

[236] *See infra* § 2.06[A] Modification of an Existing Contract.

[237] 15 S.W. 844 (Mo. 1891).

party's promise to incur an additional obligation will serve as the consideration for the other party's reciprocal promise to do something new. Thus, if Cheryl agrees to construct a house for Bill, for a price of $150,000, and they later agree that Cheryl will build an additional room, not included in the original plans, for an additional sum of $25,000, both Cheryl and Bill's promises are enforceable. Cheryl's promise to build the extra room is a new burden, beyond duties under the original deal, and is thus consideration for Bill's promise to pay more money. Bill's promise to pay the extra $25,000 is a new burden as well, and supports Cheryl's promise to take on additional work.

However, circumstances frequently lead the parties to agree to a modification altering only one of the party's duties, and leaving the other party's duties unchanged. Here, consideration for the one-sided modification is lacking. For example, if instead of agreeing to add an extra room to Bill's new house, Cheryl agreed simply to extend the exterior wall another foot, without asking for an increase in the price, the enforceability of her promise to expand the size of the house is doubtful. Since Bill incurred no new obligation in exchange for Cheryl's promise to alter the size of the house, her promise to add the extra foot is not supported by consideration. Absent some other grounds to enforce her promise, it is not binding. If, despite her promise to add the extra space, Cheryl built the house according to the original specifications, Bill might have difficulty enforcing her promise to do the extra work.

[1]   Preventing Coercion

In this context, the pre-existing duty rule is sometimes beneficial. It prevents enforcement of coercive modifications sought by a party who has some sort of overwhelming negotiating leverage over the other party after the original contract has been made. However, as will be seen, strict application of the rule also prevents enforcement of good faith, but one-sided, modifications, where no coercion was involved.

Alaska Packers' Association v. Domenico, supplies a good example of how the traditional rule prevents extortion.[238] The plaintiffs were commercial fishermen who agreed to work on the defendant's fishing boat, off the coast of Alaska. They originally agreed to work for a total salary of $50 plus 2¢ for each fish they caught. Midway through the voyage, when it was too late for the defendant to return to port and find a new crew, the employees went on a wildcat strike and demanded that the employer promise to double their guaranteed amount, increasing their fixed compensation to $100.[239] At the end of the voyage, when the defendant refused to pay the higher sum, the court sided with the defendant, concluding that there was no consideration for the promise of additional pay. The fisherman's "pre-

---

[238] Alaska Packers' Association v. Domenico, 117 F. 99 (9th Cir. 1902). *See* Deborah L. Threedy, *A Fish Story:* Alaska Packers' Association v. Domenico, 2000 Utah L. Rev. 185.

[239] The case was decided in 1902. Adjusted for inflation, the compensation was $2400, instead of $1200, and 50¢ per fish. This still does not seem like a lot of money — depending, of course, on how many fish they might expect to catch and how long the trip would take.

existing duty" to catch fish for the defendant, could not serve as consideration for the defendant's promise of extra pay.[240]

The result in *Alaska Packers* seems right, but for the wrong reason. The fisherman appeared to be taking advantage of their employer's inability to obtain a substitute crew in time for the salmon season off the Alaska coast.[241] The employer's only real alternatives were to give in to the fishermen's demands or to abandon any effort to participate in that year's salmon season. Thus, in *Alaska Packers* the pre-existing duty rule prevented a crew of scurvy fishermen from taking unfair advantage of the monopoly position they held over their employer's business, by virtue of already being out to sea.

Despite this advantage, the pre-existing duty rule cuts too wide a path in preventing the enforcement of good faith modifications. Although it prevents those like the fishermen in *Alaska Packers* from extorting extra pay from their employers, it also prevents enforcement of perfectly reasonable modifications when the parties are under no economic compulsion to give in to unreasonable demands.[242]

Consider the transaction between Cheryl and Bill, in which Cheryl has agreed to construct a house for Bill for one all-inclusive price of $150,000. If Cheryl encounters problems which make performance more difficult than she originally anticipated, she may ask Bill to agree to a price increase. She may even threaten to breach if he doesn't agree to pay the additional sum she needs. Knowing that he can always hire another contractor to finish the work, and sue Cheryl for any additional amount he ends up needing to pay, Bill might call Cheryl's bluff and refuse to agree to the extra amount she demands.

However, this is a risky strategy for Bill. Cheryl can probably finish the work even with the extra payment, for less than another contractor would charge for taking over a partially completed project. Hiring someone else will also probably involve additional delay, which might also be expensive or otherwise inconvenient for Bill, who would probably like to get his house finished and move in. Further, even though Bill could sue Cheryl for any additional amount that he must pay to get someone else to finish the work, Cheryl might be unable to pay the damages Bill could recover. Worse yet, if Bill insists on sticking to the original price, Cheryl might decide to cut corners on the construction project in ways that Bill would be unable to detect, leaving Bill with a poorly constructed home that he'll be dissatisfied with later. Moreover, the additional sum Cheryl seeks might be similar to the amount other contractors would have sought if Bill had chosen them for the project in the first place. Accordingly, Bill might make a rational decision to agree to pay Cheryl the additional sum she needs to get the job done right, even though he has a legal right to resist doing so.

---

[240] *See also* Lingenfelder v. Wainwright Brewery Co., 15 S.W. 844 (Mo. 1891).

[241] The fishermen asserted that their fishing nets were defective. The court gave no credence to this claim. However, if the fishermen held a good faith belief that the nets were defective, this may have supplied the basis for enforcing the employer's promise as a settlement of a good faith dispute over their obligations under the terms, as originally agreed.

[242] *See* United States v. Stump Home Specialities Mfg., 905 F.2d 1117, 1122 (7th Cir. 1990).

In this case, the pre-existing duty rule permits Bill to renege on the promise of extra pay even though he thought it was in his best interests to make the promise. Unless Cheryl agrees to take on additional duties, or to finish the house sooner than she original promised, Bill's promise to pay an additional amount to Cheryl is unenforceable.

In both types of cases — those involving extortion and those involving a good faith mid-course adjustment of the original terms, it might have been easy for the parties to structure the revised deal to ensure that there was consideration for the change. If the contract is at least partly unperformed by both of the parties, they could make the revised contract enforceable by the simple expedient of agreeing to "rescind" their original deal. Each party would promise to release each other from the terms of the original contract, in exchange for a similar return promise of the other. Second, the parties would then enter a new agreement with terms similar to the original contract, but providing for the additional payment the builder seeks because of its increased excavation expense. Thus, to make the modification enforceable, Bill and Cheryl might "tear up" their original contract and then enter into a new contract, containing the increased payment the builder demands.[243]

Proceeding in this way actually involves three contracts: the original one, the contract rescinding the original contract, and the new agreement containing the additional payment. None of these contracts presents problems with whether there is consideration. The original contract, involving Bill's promise to pay for Cheryl's services, is an obvious exchange of money for services. The contract of rescission contains promises from both of the parties to relinquish their rights under the original contract. When given in exchange for each other, these promises supply the necessary consideration: each of the parties could have demanded performance of the terms of the original agreement, but agreed not to. Their final agreement, containing the revised terms, also involves consideration. Having rescinded their original agreement, neither party has a pre-existing duty of any sort to the other. Both are free to contract with each other, or not, as they please. The fact that their new agreement is the same as the original agreement, except for the additional payment, is irrelevant, because neither of them had a pre-existing duty to make the final amended agreement.[244] Having rescinded the original deal, either one of them could have simply walked away.

Using a rescission to ensure that consideration is provided for the modified contract is available only if both parties have obligations remaining to be performed. And, of course, it requires the parties to be sufficiently familiar with the rules concerning consideration to even be aware that the problem exists.[245]

Alternatively, if the parties are aware that their modification is of questionable

---

[243] *See* Schwartzreich v. Bauman-Basch, Inc., 131 N.E. 887 (N.Y. 1921); RESTATEMENT OF CONTRACTS § 406 illus. 1 (1932).

[244] *See* RESTATEMENT (SECOND) OF CONTRACTS § 89 cmt. b (1981). *But see* MacCallum Highlands, Ltd. v. Washington Capital Dus, Inc., 66 F.3d 89 (5th Cir.), *opinion corrected on denial of reconsideration*, 70 F.3d 26 (5th Cir. 1995).

[245] Having said this, it is clear that the parties might tear up their original contract and sign a new one, purely as a means of documenting their new agreement, without giving a moment's thought to whether the maneuver would have an effect on the enforceability of the revised deal.

enforceability, they might try to manufacture consideration by having Cheryl assume some new, but hardly burdensome obligation that would supply the necessary consideration to make Bill's promise of extra pay enforceable. Changing the color paint Cheryl will use, from one hue of white to another, would seem to suffice.

Either method of providing consideration — rescission or a new duty for the revised promise — solves the consideration problem, but does nothing to prevent the type of extortionate modification that was involved in *Alaska Packers*, from being enforced. As Judge Posner pointed out in *United States v. Stump Home Specialities Manufacturing*, the "slight consideration" required by the peppercorn theory "is consistent with coercion."[246] If, in *Alaska Packers*, the court had refused to enforce the employer's promise on the basis of economic duress or bad faith on the part of the fisherman, the case would make more sense. Deciding the case on the basis of a lack of consideration leaves open the possibility that a more savvy crew of anglers will demand the extra pay, but agree to work one extra day, or to go "day sailing" around Alcatraz island at the end of the season, in exchange for the employer's promise of the additional sum.

[2] Modifications Without Consideration

The shortcomings of the pre-existing duty rule have made courts sympathetic to modifications made in the wake of a change of circumstances which led the parties to agree to a modification, even though it might be one-sided and thus lacking in consideration. Likewise, once parties have agreed to a modification, they naturally rely on its terms, leaving the door open for enforcement under promissory estoppel. Further, the U.C.C. completely abandons consideration as a requirement for enforcement of a modification of a contract for the sale or lease of goods, as long as the adjustment was made in good faith. Likewise, in international transactions, where consideration is unnecessary under any circumstances, good faith modifications are enforceable without regard to whether consideration was supplied.

[a] Modification Due to Unanticipated Circumstances

The common law, as reflected in the Restatement (Second) of Contracts, permits enforcement of a modification, even though consideration is lacking, if the modification is "fair and equitable in view of circumstances not anticipated by the parties when the contract was made."[247]

In *Guilford Yacht Club Ass'n, Inc. v. Northeast Dredging, Inc.*,[248] the court permitted enforcement of a one-sided modification on exactly these grounds.[249] The Guilford Yacht Club engaged Northeast Dredging to dredge a channel from

---

[246] United States v. Stump Home Specialties Mfg., 905 F.2d 1117, 1122 (7th Cir. 1990).

[247] RESTATEMENT (SECOND) OF CONTRACTS § 89(a) (1981).

[248] 438 A.2d 478 (Me. 1981).

[249] *See also* Brian Constr. & Dev. Co. v. Brighenti, 405 A.2d 72 (Conn. 1978).

its yacht basin into Guilford Harbor, in order to provide access for members of the yacht club to Long Island Sound. When the work became more difficult than originally anticipated, the yacht club promised to pay Northeast an extra $18,000 for its work. The judge instructed the jury that this promise was enforceable if: "(1) the conditions giving rise to the promise of additional consideration were not anticipated by the parties at the time of the original contract; and (2) those conditions made performance of the original contract unusually difficult."[250] This is similar, though not quite identical, to the rule expressed in the Second Restatement, which does not require the unanticipated circumstances to make performance "unusually difficult."

A similar rule was applied in *Angel v. Murray*.[251] There, a city agreed to pay a refuse collection service a $10,000 bonus because of the unanticipated construction of 400 additional homes in the city which made the original contract more burdensome than the parties had anticipated at the time the contract was made.

Cases like *Guilford Yacht Club* and *Angel v. Murray*, involving modifications made to adjust to unanticipated circumstances, might also be viewed as an example of a settlement agreement made enforceable because of the relinquishment of a claim that the obligations created by the original contract were discharged due to mistake or impossibility. The unanticipated difficulties in dredging the channel to Long Island Sound might possibly have made the original contract unenforceable either due to mistake or change of circumstances.[252] If the original contract was discharged under either theory, the "pre-existing duty" would have been eliminated, and the revised contract, involving a renewed obligation, would be supported by a new consideration.

Under rules regarding the effect of a mistake, the parties to a contract may be excused if the contract was made pursuant to a mutual mistake about a basic assumption on which the contract was made.[253] If there were grounds to excuse the contractor from its duties under the original terms of the contract, an agreement to perform regardless of that excuse is supported by consideration, and is enforceable despite the pre-existing duty. If Northeast Dredging's pre-existing duty was excused due to mutual mistake, a new promise to complete the job supplies a new duty as consideration for the general contractor's promise to pay an extra sum. The same analysis would apply if the parties' original duties were excused due to impossibility, frustration of purpose, or for any other reason.[254]

Even if the unanticipated circumstances did not rise to the level of an excuse, if the party with the pre-existing duty had a good faith belief that its original obligation was excused, consideration can be found in the parties' settlement

---

[250] Guilford Yacht Club Ass'n, Inc. v. Northeast Dredging, Inc., 438 A.2d 478, 481 (Me. 1981).

[251] 322 A.2d 630 (R.I. 1974).

[252] *See infra* Ch. 11 Excuse: Mistake and Change of Circumstances.

[253] *See* RESTATEMENT (SECOND) OF CONTRACTS § 152 (1981); *infra* § 11.02[A] Mutual Mistake.

[254] RESTATEMENT (SECOND) OF CONTRACTS § 261 (1981); *See infra* Ch. 11 Excuse: Mistake and Change of Circumstances.

agreement of the dispute about the validity of the excuse.[255]

Courts apply these rules to circumvent the pre-existing duty rule in situations where it would have prevented enforcement of what appeared to be a legitimate modification.[256] They apply the pre-existing duty rule strictly where the party seeking to enforce the modification acted in bad faith in exacting the promise of additional payment,[257] but find ways to get around the rule when the party seeking enforcement acted in good faith.

[b]   Reliance on a Modification

As with other situations where the consideration doctrine normally applies, foreseeable reliance on a good faith modification makes the modification enforceable despite the absence of consideration. If one of the parties changes its position in reliance on a modification, the modification is likely to be just as enforceable as any other promise on which a promisee has reasonably and foreseeably relied.[258] Here, the elements of promissory estoppel apply to a modification in the same way that they apply to make promises enforceable generally.

A good example is supplied by *Sutherland v. Barclays American/Mortgage Corp.*,[259] where a borrower relied on his lender's promise to permit the borrower to delay her mortgage payments. The court prevented (or "estopped") the lender from asserting the borrower's default, despite the absence of any consideration for the lender's promise to permit the delay. Also, in *Fried v. Fisher*,[260] the court enforced a landlord's promise to release one of two partners from his personal liability on the lease, because the released partner relied on the landlord's promise by leaving the business in the leased premises, and starting a new business elsewhere. And, in the famous decision in *Feinberg v. Pfeiffer Co.*,[261] an employee retired early in reliance on her employer's promise of a pension.

Many cases involving reliance are those in which one of the parties has expressed its willingness to "waive" some term of the contract, usually a condition. A waiver is generally regarded as the intentional relinquishment of a known right.[262] Even though contractual waivers may not require consideration,[263] some

---

[255] *See* Restatement (Second) of Contracts § 74 (1981); *supra* § 2.05[C] Settlement of Disputed Claims.

[256] *See, e.g.*, Quigley v. Wilson, 474 N.W.2d 277, 277–78, 291 (Iowa Ct. App.), *affirmed*, 474 N.W.2d 277 (Iowa 1991).

[257] *See, e.g.*, Alaska Packers v. Domenico, 117 F. 99 (9th Cir. 1902) (applying pre-existing duty rule) and Angel v. Murray, 322 A.2d 630 (R.I. 1974) (not applying pre-existing duty rule). *See also* McCallum Highlands v. Wash. Capital Dus, Inc., 66 F.3d 89, 90, 91, 94, 95 (5th Cir. 1995).

[258] Restatement (Second) of Contracts § 89(c) (1981).

[259] 53 Cal. App. 4th 299 (1997).

[260] 196 A. 39 (Pa. 1938).

[261] 322 S.W.2d 163 (Mo. Ct. App. 1959).

[262] Restatement (Second) of Contracts § 84 cmt. b (1981); Bank v. Truck Ins. Exch., 51 F.3d 736, 739 (7th Cir. 1995). *See* Jessica Wilen Berg, *Understanding Waiver*, 40 Hous. L. Rev. 281 (2003); David V. Snyder, *The Law of Contract and the Concept of Change: Public and Private Attempts to Regulate*

courts insist on either consideration or reliance for a waiver to be found.[264]

[c] Good Faith Modification of Contracts for Goods[265]

Articles 2 and 2A of the Uniform Commercial Code depart from the common law and eliminate the need for consideration when there has been a good faith modification of a contract for the sale or lease of goods.[266] However, unlike the sealed instrument of old, these provisions do not permit the initial creation of an agreement unless there is consideration. The rules only apply to the modification of a contract that is already in place.

In contracts involving a domestic sale of goods, the only question is whether the modification was made in good faith.[267] The requirement of good faith is imposed by the U.C.C.'s general obligation of good faith in the "performance or enforcement" of "[e]very contract or duty."[268] Under revised U.C.C. Article 1, good faith requires "honesty in fact" and "observance of reasonable commercial standards of fair dealing."[269] A modification made on fair terms to accommodate an unanticipated change in circumstances, of the type made enforceable by the Restatement (Second) of Contracts,[270] is undoubtedly enforceable under this standard. On the other hand, a modification exacted through coercion or economic duress would not be enforceable.[271]

[d] Modifications in International Transactions

In international transactions, governed either by the United Nations Convention on Contracts for the International Sale of Goods (CISG), or UNCITRAL's Principles of International Commercial Contracts and Principles of European Contract Law, matters are less complicated. Article 29(1) of the CISG permits a contract to be "modified . . . by the *mere agreement* of the parties."[272] Neither consideration, reliance, nor unanticipated circumstances are required.[273]

Modification, Waiver, and Estoppel, 1999 WIS. L. REV. 607.

[263] *See, e.g., In re* Guardianship of Collins, 327 N.W.2d 230 (Iowa 1982).

[264] *See* Thomason v. Aetna Life Ins. Co., 9 F.3d 645 (7th Cir. 1993).

[265] Robert Hillman, *Policing Contract Modifications Under the UCC: Good Faith and the Doctrine of Economic Duress*, 64 IOWA L. REV. 849 (1979); Richard E. Speidel, *Contract Formation and Modification Under Revised Article 2*, 35 WM. & MARY L. REV. 1305, 1306 (1994).

[266] U.C.C. §§ 2-209(1) (2012). *See also* U.C.C. § 2A-208(1) (2012) (regarding leases of goods).

[267] U.C.C. § 2-209 cmt. 2 (2012).

[268] U.C.C. § 1-304 (2012) (formerly § 1-203).

[269] U.C.C. § 1-201(b)(20) (2012) (formerly § 1-201(19)). The original version of Article 1, which still applies in about twenty states, requires only that non-merchants act with "honesty in fact."

[270] *See* RESTATEMENT (SECOND) OF CONTRACTS § 89(a) (1981).

[271] Roth Steel Products v. Sharon Steel Corp., 705 F.2d 134 (6th Cir. 1983).

[272] CISG Art 29(1) (1980) (emphasis supplied).

[273] *See* Shuttle Packaging v. Tsonakis, 2001 U.S. Dist. LEXIS 21630, at *21 (W.D. Mich. Dec. 17, 2001); ICC Arbitration Case No. 7331 (1994). *See generally* Larry A. DiMatteo, et al., *The Interpretive Turn in International Sales Law: An Analysis of Fifteen Years of CISG Jurisprudence*, 24 NW. J. INT'L

This is consistent with the CISG's general approach, which makes the common law doctrine of consideration irrelevant.[274] Despite this, one American court, apparently concerned that American life would be swamped by a wave of international rule, required consideration to support a modification.[275] It took the view that consideration is properly required under Article 4 of the CISG, which permits a court to apply domestic law to resolve questions of the "validity of the contract."[276] Properly limited, Article 4 should not apply to routine questions of enforceability, but should apply only to unenforceability due to fraud, incompetence, and perhaps unconscionability.[277]

Whether a modification must be made in good faith depends on the interpretation of Article 7(1) of the Convention. It specifies that the *CISG* should be interpreted with a view toward promoting "uniformity . . . and the observance of good faith in international trade."[278] This, however, imposes no express duty on the parties, like the obligation found in U.C.C. § 1-305, to act in good faith.[279] Despite the absence of an express duty of good faith, Article 7(1) makes little sense if no such duty is imposed.[280]

Article 3.2 of the UNIDROIT Principles takes the same approach. It provides that "a contract is concluded, modified or terminated by the mere agreement of the parties, without any further requirements."[281] Article 2.1.18 permits enforcement of a contractual provision requiring a modification to be in writing, but otherwise imposes no restrictions on enforcement of a modification. These provisions makes it clear that the UNIDROIT Principles do not require consideration for a modification to be enforceable.[282] Principles of European Contract Law contain similar provisions.[283]

L. & Bus. 299, 322–23 (2004); Ma del Pilar Perales Viscasillas, *Modification and Termination of the Contract (Art. 29 CISG)*, 25 J.L. & Com. 167, 171–176 (2005); Michael P. Van Alstine, *Consensus, Dissensus, and Contractual Obligation Through the Prism of Uniform International Sales Law*, 37 Va. J. Int'l. L. 1, n.47 (1996).

[274] John E. Murray, Jr., *An Essay on the Formation of Contracts and Related Matters Under the United Nations Convention on Contracts for the International Sale of Goods*, 8 J. L & Com. 11, 48–51 (1988).

[275] Geneva Pharm. Tech. Corp. v. Barr Labs., Inc., 201 F. Supp. 2d 236, 282–83 (S.D.N.Y. 2002).

[276] CISG Art 4(a) (1980).

[277] John O. Honnold, Uniform Law for International Sales §§ 64–68 (3d ed. 1999).

[278] CISG Art. 7(1) (1980).

[279] *See* Robert A. Hillman, *Article 29(2) of the United Nations Convention on Contracts for the Int'l Sale of Goods: A New Effort at Clarifying the Legal Effect of "No Oral Modification" Clauses*, 21 Cornell Int'l L. J. 449, 458 (1988).

[280] Clayton P. Gillette & Steven D. Walt, Sales Law: Domestic and International 82–84 (Foundation Press 1999).

[281] PECL Art. 3.2 (2004).

[282] Sieg Eiselen, *Remarks on the Manner in Which the Unidroit Principles of International Commercial Contracts May Be Used to Interpret or Supplement Article 29 of the CISG*, 14 Pace Int'l L. Rev. 379, 381 (2002); Joachim Zekoll, *The Louisiana Private-Law System: The Best of Both Worlds*, 10 Tul. Eur. & Civ. L.F. 1, 8–9 (1995).

[283] PICC Arts. 2.101(2), 2.106(1) (2002).

[B]   Debt Settlements: Accord and Satisfaction[284]

The pre-existing duty rule also plays a role in agreements to compromise an existing debt. The settlement of a debt is usually referred to as an "accord and satisfaction." The agreement to satisfy the debt through some alternative performance is the "accord"; performance of the accord is the "satisfaction." As with any other contract, an accord and satisfaction of an existing debt requires consideration to be binding. If the debtor's liability on an underlying claim is undisputed and the amount owed has already been determined, the pre-existing duty rule presents difficulties in entering into an enforceable accord and satisfaction. Thus, if Diane owes Carl $5,000 and they reach an agreement that she will pay $4,000 in satisfaction of the claim, there is no consideration for his agreement to accept the lower amount in full satisfaction of the debt. Some new consideration for the accord must be supplied.

If both parties alter their obligations, consideration exists. Thus, if, instead of promising to pay $4,000 in satisfaction of the $5,000 debt, Diane agrees to give Carl her Honda, which is worth only $4,000, consideration is supplied — she had no previous obligation to give Carl the car. Although the car is worth less than the $5,000 debt, the law does not usually inquire into the adequacy of the consideration supplied — it is enough that Diane did something that wasn't part of her pre-existing duty.

Moreover, if Carl's underlying claim is in doubt, resolution of the dispute, with Diane abandoning any claim to a defense that she might have in exchange for Carl's promise to forego suit on a potentially larger claim, the necessary element of exchange is present. As explained below, additional problems persist in dealing with an unperformed or "executory accord" and in distinguishing between an accord and a substituted contract.

[1]   Undisputed Debts[285]

The facts of *Petterson v. Pattberg*,[286] supply a good example of an attempted modification of a contract that had already been fully performed by one of the parties. It involved a loan that had already been made, with the creditor merely

---

[284] Scott J. Burnham, *A Primer on Accord & Satisfaction*, 47 Mont. L. Rev. 1 (1986); Michael D. Floyd, *How Much Satisfaction Should You Expect from an Accord?*, 26 Loy. U. Chi. L.J. 1 (1994); Albert J. Rosenthal, *Discord and Dissatisfaction: Section 1-207 of the Uniform Commercial Code*, 78 Colum. L. Rev. 48 (1978); Jay Winston, Note, *The Evolution of Accord and Satisfaction: Common Law; U.C.C. Section 1-207; U.C.C. Section 3-311*, 28 New Eng. L. Rev. 189 (1993).

[285] Beth A. Eisler, *Oral Modification of Sales Contracts Under the Uniform Commercial Code: The Statute of Frauds Problem*, 58 Wash. U. L. Q. 277 (1980); Robert A. Hillman, *Policing Contract Modifications Under the UCC: Good Faith and the Doctrine of Economic Duress*, 64 Iowa L. Rev. 849 (1979); Robert A. Hillman, *A Study of Uniform Commercial Code Methodology: Contract Modification Under Article Two*, 59 N.C. L. Rev. 335 (1981); John E. Murray, Jr., *The Modification Mystery: Section 2-209 of the Uniform Commercial Code*, 32 Vill. L. Rev. 1 (1987); Mark Roszkowski, *Contract Modification and the Statute of Frauds: Making Sense of Section 2-209 of the Uniform Commercial Code*, 36 Ala. L. Rev. 51 (1984); Richard E. Speidel, *Contract Formation and Modification Under Revised Article 2*, 35 Wm. & Mary L. Rev. 1305 (1994).

[286] 161 N.E. 428 (N.Y. 1928).

waiting for the borrower's promised payments. The creditor offered to modify the contract and to permit the borrower to repay a smaller amount sooner than the original debt was due. Just as in the situation with Diane and Carl, where Diane gives Carl her Honda, the creditor's relinquishment of his right to payment of the entire debt is supported by the borrower's new detriment of making payment *before the larger debt was due.*

This approach works quite well when a creditor is willing to accept a smaller amount in exchange for payment at an earlier date. Unfortunately, when debtors are having financial difficulties, they are more likely to want to pay a smaller sum not earlier, but later than the time the original debt was due. Assume, for example, that Barb has persuaded Sam to sell her his BMW over time, with Barb agreeing to pay the $20,000 price in monthly installment payments over a three-year period. If after six months Barb realizes that she cannot afford the payments, she might persuade Sam to reduce the monthly payments by extending the payments over a five-year period, with interest payable throughout this additional time. In this situation, Barb will be giving something up because she will be paying additional interest over the extended term. This additional detriment supplies the necessary consideration for Sam's promise to permit her to delay payment of the debt.

However, the traditional rule is that payment of a lesser amount does not satisfy a pre-existing obligation to pay a larger amount.[287] Thus, an agreement to accept $4,000 cash in satisfaction of an obligation to pay $5,000 already due, is not enforceable unless the debtor's performance is changed in some other way.

This rule presents a problem in situations involving the attempted reduction or "composition" of a debt. If a smaller sum is paid early, consideration will be found in the premature payment of the obligation not yet due until a later date.[288] If payment of the debt is delayed, with interest to continue to accumulate beyond the original due date, the debtor's obligation to pay interest for a longer time provides the necessary element of exchange.[289] However, if payment of the original debt was due "on demand," or if the time for payments has already passed and no additional interest is due, consideration for the agreement to reduce the amount due is lacking.

Without consideration, the creditor is able to renege on its agreement to accept the lower amount in full satisfaction of the original debt. This result makes debtors' efforts to resolve their financial difficulties by making partial payments to their creditors, in return for an agreement to release them from the unpaid balance, problematical. Many times, of course, the creditors will accept the reduced payment and make no attempt to recover the full amount still due. However, if a creditor changes its mind, and sues to recover the unpaid balance, the lack of consideration for its agreement to forego recovery will cause it not to be enforced. Awareness of the unenforceability of the settlement agreement may even discourage the debtor from agreeing to the modified terms.

---

[287] Foakes v. Beer, 9 App. Cas. 605 (1884). *See* Merton Ferson, *The Rule in* Foakes v. Beer, 31 YALE L.J. 15 (1921); Joseph Gold, *The Present Status of the Rule in* Pinnel's Case, 30 KY. L.J. 72 (1941).

[288] RESTATEMENT (SECOND) OF CONTRACTS § 73 illus. 7 (1981).

[289] *E.g.*, Freeman v. Truitt, 119 So. 2d 765, 770 (Miss. 1960).

If a debtor is obligated to several creditors, the debtor might propose that the creditors enter into an agreement *with one another* to abstain from insisting that the debtor pay the entire sum due to each of them. If multiple creditors enter into such a contract with one another, the necessary consideration is supplied by each creditor's agreement with the others. The debtor will be able to enforce the contract as a third-party beneficiary of the contract between the creditors. Unfortunately, the creditors may be unwilling to agree with one another unless they are able to obtain the consent of everyone to whom the debtor owes money. In these situations it often happens that there is always at least one creditor who is unwilling to agree with the plan proposed by the others. That creditor will, of course, be free to pursue his original claim against the debtor, who may still be unable to afford to pay. Thus, the pre-existing duty rule is a significant barrier to financially troubled debtors' efforts to resolve their situations without resorting to bankruptcy.

[2]   Disputed Debts

When the debt is disputed, resolution of the dispute supplies the necessary consideration for the accord.[290] Thus, if Barb and Sam agree to reduce the amount Barb owes due to an alleged breach of warranty by Sam, their agreement is enforceable. This is consistent with the general rule that a contract settling a disputed claim is enforceable even if the basis for the dispute subsequently turns out to be unfounded. The critical issue is whether the dispute was in good faith. If the dispute is a mere pretense, or if the debtor does not believe in its plausible validity, the accord and satisfaction is not enforceable and the creditor can recover the amount originally due.

[3]   Use of a "Payment in Full" Check as an Accord and Satisfaction[291]

Debtors sometimes attempt to accomplish an accord and satisfaction by ambush, by sending the creditor a check for less than the full amount claimed by the creditor and including a notation on the check that it is intended as "payment in full" for the entire debt. Under conventional rules, delivery of the check is an offer to enter into an accord. If the creditor cashes the check, she manifests her acceptance of the terms of the accord. Payment of the check accomplishes a simultaneous "satisfaction" of the accord and discharges the underlying debt.

There are two principal difficulties in accomplishing an accord and satisfaction through this otherwise convenient mechanism. First, unless the underlying debt is for an undetermined and thus "unliquidated" amount or unless there is otherwise a good faith dispute about the amount of the debt, there is no consideration for the accord. Second, even if the amount of the debt is unliquidated or the subject to dispute, the creditor might easily process the check together with the dozens,

---

[290] Spaulding v. Cahill, 505 A.2d 1186 (Vt. 1985); Cass Const. Co., Inc. v. Brennan, 382 N.W.2d 313 (Neb. 1986).

[291] Patricia B. Fry, *You Can't Have Your Cake and Eat It Too: Accord and Satisfaction Survives the Uniform Commercial Code*, 61 N.D. L. REV. 353 (1985).

hundreds, or even thousands of checks it receives each week, without realizing that it was sent as an offer to enter into a compromise.

In some jurisdictions a creditor could avoid the conclusion that its acceptance of the check implemented an accord and satisfaction by including its own notation on the check to the effect that it was "reserving rights" on the underlying claim despite its deposit of the check.[292] However, most courts held to the contrary and found that an accord and satisfaction had been accomplished despite the creditor's notation purporting to reserve its rights.[293] The issue was resolved by an amendment to what is now U.C.C. § 1-308 making it clear that a "reservation of rights" does not apply to impede what otherwise would be an accord and satisfaction.[294] At the same time, a special provision was added to Article 3 of the U.C.C. specifying the circumstances in which a check or other instrument tendered as full payment can be used to settle a debt.

U.C.C. § 3-311 permits payment by check to settle a claim only if 1) the claim is either unliquidated, or subject to a bona fide dispute, 2) the check is sent in good faith as full satisfaction of the claim, 3) the check is accompanied by a conspicuous statement indicating that it has been tendered in full satisfaction of the claim, and 4) the check is ultimately paid.[295] Even then, § 3-311 permits the creditor to escape from the accord by refunding the amount of the payment within 90 days. This latter provision protects creditors from being tricked into an accord through the use of automated check processing mechanisms which might make it difficult to detect even a "conspicuous" notation that the check was meant to operate as a settlement offer.[296]

Section 3-311 provides several other mechanisms which might result in a successful accord and satisfaction, without the 90-day escape hatch, where the creditor manifests its conscious agreement to the proposed settlement of the dispute. Thus, where the creditor cashes the check with the knowledge that it has been sent as a proposed settlement agreement, there is no reason to permit the creditor to evade the consequences of his initial judgment. Thus, the 90-day period only applies to situations where it is likely that the creditor has processed the check through its usual mechanisms for collecting from its customers and did not know that the check was sent in satisfaction of the claim.[297]

[4]   Effect of Failure to Perform an Accord

When a payment-in-full check is used to implement an accord and satisfaction, the creditor's act of obtaining payment for the check operates both as an acceptance of the offer to enter into an accord and as a satisfaction of the modified

---

[292] *See* AFC Interiors v. DiCello, 544 N.E.2d 869 (Ohio 1989).

[293] *E.g.*, County Fire Door Corp. v. C. F. Wooding Co., 520 A.2d 1028 (Conn. 1987). *See* Vitauts M. Gulbis, Annotation, *Application of UCC § 1-207 to Avoid Discharge of Disputed Claim Upon Qualified Acceptance of Check Tendered as Payment in Full*, 37 A.L.R.4th 358 (1985).

[294] U.C.C. § 1-308(b) (2012) (formerly § 1-207(b)).

[295] U.C.C. § 3-311(a)–(b) (2012).

[296] U.C.C. § 3-311(c)(2) (2012).

[297] *See* U.C.C. § 3-311 cmts. 5–7 (2012).

agreement. Payment of the check fulfills the terms of the accord.

In other circumstances, performance of the modified obligation may not occur until later. The creditor's acceptance of the adjusted terms is an accord, but until performance there is no satisfaction. If the debtor fails to perform the terms of the accord, there is a question about the effect of the accord on the original underlying obligation.

An "executory" accord does not dispose of the original obligation.[298] It merely suspends the underlying debt until the accord is satisfied by performance of the modified obligation.[299] The older common law cases held that the creditor could back out of an executory accord, even if it was supported by consideration.[300] If the debtor breaches the terms of the accord, the suspension of the original obligation is lifted and the creditor can choose to enforce either the accord or the original obligation.[301]

This may not always be an easy choice. The amount due under the original obligation may be more than is due under the terms of the accord, but it will also be subject to plausible dispute. The accord, on the other hand, represents an undisputed and liquidated sum. A judgment on the accord may be easy to obtain without extended litigation.[302] Resolution of the dispute on the underlying claim will be much more likely to involve a trial with all of the additional expenses and uncertainty associated with litigation.

An accord and satisfaction must be distinguished from a "substituted contract" or a "novation."[303] Where the second agreement is intended to completely displace the original contract, there is no mere suspension of the underlying debt. Instead, the second contract completely discharges the original obligation and the creditor's only recourse is to sue on the terms of the new deal.[304] Whether a settlement agreement is an accord or a substitute contract depends upon the intent of the parties to have the new agreement suspend or discharge the original obligation. Although a substitute contract is sometimes referred to as a novation, the latter term is best used to refer to a substitute contract involving a third party.[305]

---

[298] *See* Crown Prod. Co. v. Calif. Food Prod. Corp., 77 Cal. App. 2d 543 (1947).

[299] RESTATEMENT (SECOND) OF CONTRACTS § 281(2) (1981).

[300] *See* McDowell Welding & Pipefitting, Inc. v. United States Gypsum Co., 149 P.3d 173 (Or. Ct. App. 2006); Harold Shepard, *The Executory Accord*, 26 ILL. L. REV. 22 (1931)

[301] RESTATEMENT (SECOND) OF CONTRACTS § 281 (1981). *E.g.*, McDowell Welding & Pipefitting, Inc. v. United States Gypsum Co., 149 P.3d 173 (Or. Ct. App. 2006).

[302] According to Fed. R. Civ. P. 56(c), a party is entitled to summary judgment if "there is no genuine issue as to any material fact and . . . the moving party is entitled to judgment as a matter of law."

[303] RESTATEMENT (SECOND) OF CONTRACTS § 279 (1981).

[304] RESTATEMENT (SECOND) OF CONTRACTS § 281 cmt. e (1981).

[305] Your author was once a party to such a novation. Upon leaving a house he had leased before the lease was over (he bought the house next door), he found new tenants for the owner and persuaded the owner to accept the agreement of the new tenants in complete substitute for his own obligation, from which he was discharged.

§ 2.07   PAST CONSIDERATION AND MORAL OBLIGATION: THE MATERIAL BENEFIT RULE[306]

[A]   Past Consideration Is No Consideration

In most situations, past consideration is no consideration.[307] Promises made in recognition of some past benefit the promisor has received involve no exchange.[308] Although the promise may have been induced by the benefit, the benefit was not the inducement for the promise.[309] Nor was the promisee's detriment induced by the promise. In the absence of an exchange for the promise, consideration is missing and the promise is not usually enforceable on this basis alone.

The well-known case of *Mills v. Wyman*[310] is frequently used to illustrate the general rule that promises made in recognition of past benefits are not enforceable. Mills voluntarily cared for Wyman's adult son when the son became ill while he was away from home. Later, Wyman promised to pay Mills for the son's care. When Wyman reneged on his promise the court held both that Wyman's promise had been made without consideration and that any moral obligation that might exist was not sufficient to make the promise enforceable. The court explained that "the law of society has left most of such obligations to the *interior* forum, as the tribunal of conscience has been aptly called." In other words, the father might have a moral duty to pay — but not a legal one.

A person who makes a promise like this might intend for his promise to be legally binding, and might even go to some length to demonstrate this intent. Nevertheless, if the promise was made in recognition of some past benefit, it could not have been given in exchange for that benefit. The promise is not part of a bargain. Instead, it is merely an afterthought, and is not legally binding.

---

[306] Robert Braucher, *Freedom of Contract and the Second Restatement*, 78 YALE L.J. 598, 605 (1969); Lon L. Fuller, *Consideration and Form*, 41 COLUM. L. REV. 799, 821 (1941); Charles J. Goetz & Robert E. Scott, *Enforcing Promises: An Examination of the Basis of Contract*, 89 YALE L.J. 1261 (1980); Stanley D. Henderson, *Promises Grounded in the Past: The Idea of Unjust Enrichment and the Law of Contract*, 57 VA. L. REV. 1115 (1971); Richard A. Posner, *Gratuitous Promises in Economics and Law*, 6 J. LEGAL STUD. 411, 418–19 (1977); Charles M. Thatcher, *Complementary Promises for Benefits Received: An Illustrated Supplement to Restatement (Second) of Contracts Section 86*, 45 S.D. L. REV. 241 (2000); Steve Thel & Edward Yorio, *The Promissory Basis of Past Consideration*, 78 VA. L. REV. 1045 (1992); Clay B. Tousey III, *Exceptional Circumstances: The Material Benefit Rule in Practice and Theory*, 28 CAMPBELL L. REV. 153 (2006).

[307] Currid v. Meeting House Rest., Inc., 869 A.2d 516 (Pa. Super. Ct. 2005).

[308] Prendergast v. Snoeberger, 796 N.E.2d 588 (Ohio Ct. App. 2003).

[309] *See* Hayes v. Plantations Steel Co., 438 A.2d 1091 (R.I. 1982).

[310] 1825 Mass. LEXIS 44 (Oct. 1825).

[B] Moral Obligation as Grounds for Enforcing a Promise[311]

Despite this modern result, there was an early common law rule that a promise to pay for a past benefit conferred was enforceable due to a moral obligation.[312] However, this earlier rule was incompatible with the doctrine of consideration, and was later repudiated by courts in both England and the United States.[313] Today, with only a few exceptions, promises to pay for past benefits received are not enforceable.[314]

[C] Material Benefit Rule[315]

Despite the general rule, a few cases have enforced promises made by a person who received a material benefit and then promised to pay for it. *Mills v. Wyman*, discussed above, in which such a promise was not enforced, is nearly always paired with the contrasting decision in *Webb v. McGowin*,[316] where the court reached the opposite result. Webb was an employee of McGowin and sustained serious injuries in acting heroically to save McGowin from serious injury. Webb's injuries occurred before the advent of workers' compensation insurance to compensate for workplace injuries. McGowin, however, felt a sense of gratitude toward Webb and later expressed his gratitude by promising to pay Webb a weekly sum for the remainder of Webb's life. McGowin made good on his promise for many years, but, after his death, his estate refused to continue the payments and Webb sued.

The court held that the moral obligation that motivated the McGowin's promise, coupled with the fact that he was saved from death or serious injury, justified

---

[311] Randy Sutton, *Moral or Natural Obligation as Consideration for Contract*, 98 A.L.R.5th 353 (2002).

[312] *See* Val D. Ricks, *The Sophisticated Doctrine of Consideration*, 9 Geo. Mason L. Rev. 99, 118–121 (2000). *See* Kevin M. Teeven, *Conventional Moral Obligation Principle Unduly Limits Qualified Beneficiary Contrary to Case Law*, 86 Marq. L. Rev. 701 (2003); James. B. Ames, *The History of Assumpsit*, 2 Harv. L. Rev. 1, 53 (1888).

[313] *E.g.*, Passante v. McWilliam, 53 Cal. App. 4th 1240, 1245–1247 (1997).

[314] Randy Sutton, Annotation, *Moral or Natural Obligation as Consideration for Contract*, 98 A.L.R.5th 353 (2002). *E.g.*, Leonard v. Gallagher, 235 Cal. App. 2d 362 (1965) (promise by son to pay his mother's debt).

[315] John Dawson, *The Self-Serving Intermeddler*, 87 Harv. L. Rev. 1409 (1974); Melvin A. Eisenberg, *The Principles of Consideration*, 67 Cornell L. Rev. 640, 663–64 (1982); Charles J. Goetz & Robert E. Scott, *Enforcing Promises: An Examination of the Basis of Contract*, 89 Yale L.J. 1261, 1310–11 (1980); William M. Landes & Richard A. Posner, *Salvors, Finders, Good Samaritans, and Other Rescuers: An Economic Study of Law and Altruism*, 7 J. Legal Stud. 83 (1978); Saul Levmore, *Waiting for Rescue: An Essay on the Evolution and Incentive Structure of the Law of Affirmative Obligations*, 72 Va. L. Rev. 879 (1986); Stanley D. Henderson, *Promises Grounded in the Past: The Idea of Unjust Enrichment and the Law of Contracts*, 57 Va. L. Rev. 1115 (1971); Richard A. Posner, *Gratutitous Promises in Economics and Law*, 6 J. Legal Stud. 411, 418–19 (1977); Kevin M. Teeven, *Moral Obligation Promise for Harm Caused*, 39 Gonzaga L. Rev. 349 (2004); Steve Thel & Edward Yorio, *The Promissory Basis of Past Consideration*, 78 Va. L. Rev. 1045 (1993); Clay B. Tousey III, *Exceptional Circumstances: The Material Benefit Rule in Practice and Theory*, 28 Campbell L. Rev. 153 (2006); Geoffrey R. Watson, *In the Tribunal of Conscience:* Mills v. Wyman *Reconsidered*, 71 Tul. L. Rev. 1749 (1997).

[316] 168 So. 196 (Ala. Ct. App. 1935).

enforcing the promise. It said that the case was "clearly distinguishable from [cases] where the consideration is a mere moral obligation or conscientious duty unconnected with receipt by [the] promisor of benefits of a material or pecuniary nature. . . . Here the promisor received a material benefit constituting a valid consideration for this promise."

This passage is misleading to the extent that it characterizes the benefits received by the employer as "consideration." McGowin's promise was made after Webb conferred the benefit on McGowin, and there is no hint in the facts of the case that the benefit was conferred at McGowin's request. Quite to the contrary — Webb jumped out of a window in an emergency effort to save McGowin from injury under circumstances where there was no opportunity for any kind of a bargain. The court characterized it as consideration only because consideration was required to make the promise enforceable. If consideration was what was necessary, then consideration is what the court would call what it had. If a pink elephant had been necessary, the court probably would have said that one existed.

It is significant that McGowin had no legal obligation to pay the employee for his injuries, apart from whatever obligation was created by McGowin's promise. If McGowin had owed an obligation to Webb as a result of his status as an employee, or in restitution for the value of the benefit received, then McGowin's promise could easily have been viewed as having been made in settlement of that obligation. Likewise, if McGowin had made his promise in settlement of any good faith claim that Webb might have believed he held, the promise would have been supported by the consideration of Webb's relinquishment of that claim.[317] But, the court recognized that McGowin owed no duty to Webb apart from his promise and there were no facts suggesting that Webb had asserted a claim. Instead, McGowin's promise was apparently made purely out of a sense of gratitude and moral duty.

The fact that McGowin performed his promise for many years, until his death in old age, is an additional factor present in *Webb v. McGowin* that was missing in *Mills v. Wyman*. McGowin died believing he had an obligation to the employee and his estate stood in his place. In this respect, *Webb v. McGowin* is similar to the decisions in both *Hamer v. Sidway*[318] and *Ricketts v. Scothorn*,[319] discussed previously, in which promises by deceased persons were enforced against their estates where it was clear that the promisors had died without renouncing their promises.[320]

The Restatement (Second) of Contracts takes the position that promises such as these should be enforced when made "in recognition of a benefit previously received by the promisor," but only "to the extent necessary to prevent injustice."[321] It would deny recovery where the benefit, for which the reciprocal promise was made, was conferred as a gift or to the extent that the value of the

---

[317] *See supra* § 2.05[C] Settlement of Disputed Claims.

[318] 27 N.E. 256 (N.Y. 1891).

[319] 77 N.W. 365 (Neb. 1898).

[320] *See supra* § 2.04 Promises to Make a Gift.

[321] RESTATEMENT (SECOND) OF CONTRACTS § 86(1) (1981).

promise was disproportionate to the value of the benefit previously received.[322]

It might be rude to accept a gift, and not, at some time, make a reciprocal gift, but this is not "unjust enrichment." If the benefit for which the promise of reimbursement was made was received as a gift, it seems likely that the promise of reimbursement was intended as a reciprocal gift. A prior close or family relationship between the parties supports the claim that the benefit was meant as nothing more than a gift,[323] but is not controlling.[324] In contrast, an earlier business relationship or contract between the parties, which required payment for any services provided to the promisor, strongly supports the enforceability of the promise.

This aspect of the parties' relationship was dispositive in *Realty Assoc. v. Valley Nat'l Bank*,[325] where a homeowner promised to pay a commission to a real estate broker, who produced a buyer for the promisor's house, after their listing agreement had expired. However, where a prior contractual relationship exists between the parties, the promisor may be liable in any event, either under a contract implied in fact, or in quasi contract, regardless of whether an express promise had ever been made.[326]

[D]   Promises to Pay Obligations Discharged by Operation of Law[327]

The second situation in which a promise for a past benefit is enforceable is more concrete and completely uncontroversial. It arises when some pre-existing obligation is unenforceable due to the operation of law and the original obligor makes a new promise to pay something in recognition of the discharged debt.

For example, if Bob borrowed $1000 from Laura, but failed to repay, Laura might have sued to recover the debt. Her $1000 loan supplies the necessary consideration to make Bob's original promise to pay the debt enforceable. But, sooner or later the statute of limitations on Laura's claim will run out and Laura will be unable to collect the $1000. If, after time runs out, Bob renews his promise to pay the old debt, Bob's new promise is enforceable even though there is no new consideration supplied by Laura for the second promise. The result would be the same regardless of the nature of Laura's original claim against Bob, so long as he had an initial legal duty to pay the original debt.

Situations like these are quite different because they arise in a setting where there had previously been a legally binding obligation. The promise involved is one

---

[322] RESTATEMENT (SECOND) OF CONTRACTS § 86(2) (1981).

[323] *E.g.*, Dementas v. Estate of Tallas, 764 P.2d. 628 (Utah Ct. App. 1988). *See* E. Allan Farnsworth, Essay, *Promises and Paternalism*, 41 WM. & MARY L. REV. 385 (2000).

[324] McMurry v. Magnusson, 849 S.W.2d 619, 623 (Mo. Ct. App. 1993) (enforceable promise to pay for home health care services previously paid for by defendant's sister following auto accident).

[325] 738 P.2d 1121, 1124-25 (Ariz. Ct. App. 1987).

[326] *See* Manwill v. Oyler, 361 P.2d 177 (Utah 1961).

[327] Albert Kocourek, *A Comment on Moral Consideration and the Statute of Limitations*, 18 ILL. L. REV. 538, 549 (1924).

to pay this obligation, even though it is otherwise not enforceable due to expiration of the statute of limitations, discharge in bankruptcy, or incapacity of the obligor at the time of his or her original promise.

[1] Debts Discharged in Bankruptcy

When a debtor gets in over her head financially, the only way out may be to go through bankruptcy.[328] The objective in a bankruptcy proceeding is to fairly and equitably distribute whatever assets the debtor has and then to give the debtor a "fresh start" by discharging any remaining unpaid obligations.[329] Many debtors who have received a discharge later make a new promise to repay the discharged debt in a step known as "reaffirmation."

In most reaffirmations the debtor's promise to pay the discharged debt is supported by consideration. The debtor's promise is commonly exchanged for the creditor's forbearance from repossessing and selling the debtor's car, furniture, or other property that is the collateral for the debt. Although the debtor's obligation to repay the debt is discharged in bankruptcy, the creditor retains its property rights in the collateral and can sell the item to obtain at least a partial satisfaction of the debt. Debtors who wish to keep their property frequently enter into a reaffirmation agreement with the creditor, promising to repay the entire debt.

However, in other situations not involving reaffirmation of a secured debt, consideration may be lacking. The debtor may reaffirm its debt out of a sense of moral obligation or to avoid the disfavor of a family member, employer, or other close associate, who lent the debtor money. In other cases a debtor may reaffirm his or her debts because of the probably false impression that this will somehow improve her credit rating. In these cases, where the debtor is receiving nothing in exchange for her promise, consideration is absent. Nevertheless, these promises are enforceable under the common law of contracts.[330]

Those familiar with bankruptcy practice will recognize that several other formalities must be observed in order for a reaffirmation agreement to be valid.[331] The Bankruptcy Code requires the agreement to be in writing and filed with the bankruptcy court before the bankruptcy case has ended. In most cases the debtor's attorney is expected to file a supporting affidavit expressing his or her judgment that performance of the reaffirmation agreement will not impose an undue hardship on the debtor or on any of the debtor's dependents. And, the debtor is afforded the right to rescind the reaffirmation agreement within sixty days of the time the agreement is filed with the court.[332] These, and other restrictions, go further than the doctrine of consideration in fulfilling the evidentiary, cautionary,

---

[328] Bankruptcy is purely a creature of federal law. *See* 11 U.S.C. §§ 101–1330 (2006). While the law controlling bankruptcy allows for some local variation, it is quite uniform throughout the United States otherwise. *See generally* JEFF FERRIELL & EDWARD J. JANGER, UNDERSTANDING BANKRUPTCY (3d ed. 2012).

[329] *E.g.*, Continental Ill. Bank v. Chicago, Rock Island & Pacific Ry., 294 U.S. 648, 676 (1935).

[330] RESTATEMENT (SECOND) OF CONTRACTS § 83 (1981). *E.g.*, In re Prejean, 994 F.2d 706 (9th Cir. 1993).

[331] 11 U.S.C. § 524(c) (2006).

[332] 11 U.S.C. § 524(c) (2006). *See also* JEFF FERRIELL & EDWARD J. JANGER, UNDERSTANDING BANKRUPTCY § 12.08[B] (3d ed. 2012).

and channeling functions usually associated with the consideration requirement.

[2]   Debts Barred by the Statute of Limitations

A debt may also be unenforceable because the creditor has allowed the statute of limitations to run out without filing suit. A debt barred by the statute of limitations is not extinguished; it is merely unenforceable by way of a legal proceeding. When a debtor who cannot be sued because the statute of limitations has run makes a promise to pay the debt, that new promise is not supported by consideration. But it is, nevertheless, enforceable.[333]

The question is whether the later promise was given in exchange for anything bargained-for at the time the later promise was made. Because enforcement of the debt is barred by the statute of limitations, the debtor who makes a later promise to pay it receives nothing for her renewed promise. Despite the absence of consideration, the promise, like a promise to reaffirm a debt discharged in bankruptcy, is enforceable.[334]

[3]   Obligations Incurred by Minors and Others Suffering from Incapacity

A third type of promise, made in connection with a prior debt, which is enforceable despite the absence of any new consideration, is one made to ratify an obligation incurred while the promisor was incompetent.[335] Contracts made by minors and others suffering from mental incapacity are not enforceable.[336] However, those who suffer from such a legal incapacity frequently continue to enjoy benefits derived from their unenforceable contracts after they become legally competent. The most obvious example is a minor who continues driving the car after reaching her 18th birthday, and, in the eyes of the law at least, becoming an adult. Continued enjoyment of the benefit constitutes a ratification of the debt. Alternatively, upon reaching her majority, or, recovering from some mental impairment, the person may expressly ratify the debt.

Whether the promise is express or implied, it is clear that it lacks consideration. Whatever original bargain was struck is long since past. However, a promise made by a person, in ratification of an earlier contract made while legally incompetent, is always enforceable even though consideration for the new promise is missing. The same is true of any other promise made in recognition of a past duty which has become voidable by operation of law.[337]

---

[333] RESTATEMENT (SECOND) OF CONTRACTS § 82(1) (1981). *E.g.*, First Hawaiian Bank v. Zukerkorn, 633 P.2d 550 (Haw. Ct. App. 1981); Kopp v. Fink, 232 P.2d 161 (Okla. 1951).

[334] RESTATEMENT (SECOND) OF CONTRACTS § 82(1) (1981). *See* Lon L. Fuller, *Consideration and Form*, 41 COLUM. L. REV. 799, 822 (1941).

[335] RESTATEMENT (SECOND) OF CONTRACTS § 85 (1981).

[336] *See infra* § 10.03 Incapacity.

[337] RESTATEMENT (SECOND) OF CONTRACTS § 85 (1981).

[4]   Debts Discharged Due to Failure of a Condition

A fourth situation in which a promise to pay an old obligation is enforceable is when the earlier duty has become unenforceable due to the non-occurrence of a condition on which the duty depended.[338] This rule, in effect, makes waivers of conditions enforceable, in the absence of either consideration or reliance on the waiver.[339]

However, this rule only works when the occurrence of the condition was not a material part of the agreed exchange between the parties.[340] If the condition was a key element of the agreement, it cannot be eliminated in such a cavalier fashion. To rule otherwise would make it too easy to circumvent the normal rule restricting the enforceability of a promise to make a gift. Consider a promise by Aunt Emily to purchase a car from her nephew Steve, for $10,000, to enable him to pay his college tuition. Delivery of the car would be a constructive condition of Aunt Emily's duty to pay Steve the $10,000. If Aunt Emily's promise to "waive" the condition requiring delivery of the car were enforceable, the parties' agreement for the sale of the car could easily be converted into nothing more than a promise by Aunt Emily to make a gift.[341]

On the other hand, an incidental or "ancillary" condition, which is not a material part of the agreed exchange, can be waived without consideration.[342] Thus, if Aunt Emily's promise to buy the car for $10,000 were subject to the condition that Steve have a brake light replaced before he delivered the car, her wavier of the condition regarding replacement of the bulb is enforceable. Most cases involving the waiver of minor conditions of this sort occur in connection with insurance policies, which contain both conditions which are a material part of the agreed exchange, such as the insured's promise to pay the premiums due under the policy, and less critical conditions, such as those relating to timely notice of a claim.[343]

§ 2.08 CONSIDERATION IN GUARANTY CONTRACTS

Guaranty contracts, also known as suretyship contracts, involve a promise by one person to pay or perform the obligation of someone else. These contracts are frequently made by parents who promise to pay debts incurred by one of their children. They are also made by owners of a small corporate businesses, to guaranty payment of a loan to the corporation.

Guaranty contracts always involve at least three parties. First, there is the borrower, who is usually referred to as the "principal debtor" or simply as the "obligor." The second party is the creditor who has made a loan to the principal

---

[338] RESTATEMENT (SECOND) OF CONTRACTS § 84 (1981).

[339] *See infra* § 8.06 Waiver and Estoppel of Conditions.

[340] RESTATEMENT (SECOND) OF CONTRACTS § 84(1)(a) (1981).

[341] RESTATEMENT (SECOND) OF CONTRACTS § 84 cmt. c (1981).

[342] RESTATEMENT (SECOND) OF CONTRACTS § 84 cmt. d (1981); Dark Tobacco Growers' Co-op. Ass'n v. Mason, 263 S.W. 60, 67 (Tenn. 1924). *See* § 3.03 A Consideration Substitute, *supra*.

[343] RESTATEMENT (SECOND) OF CONTRACTS § 84 illus. 4 (1981).

debtor, sometimes referred to as the "obligee." The third person, called the "guarantor," "surety," or sometimes an "accommodation party,"[344] is the one who promises to pay the creditor if the principal debtor defaults.[345] The guaranty arrangement is one of primary and secondary liability, with the obligor having primary liability to satisfy the debt, and the guarantor having secondary liability. In most cases, the surety's duty to come forward arises only if the principal debtor fails to perform is primary obligation as required.[346]

The promise of a surety, like any other promise, must be supported by consideration in order to be enforceable. There is no question that the surety's promise is supported by consideration if her promise was made at the time of the original loan and helped induce the creditor to make the loan. Thus, if City Bank agrees to make a loan to Junior, to enable him to purchase a car only if Mom and Dad agreed to serve as sureties for Junior's debt, the bank's agreement to supply Junior with the loan is the consideration for Mom & Dad's promise to pay. Even though Mom & Dad have not directly "received" anything from the bank, they have made a promise in exchange for the bank's disbursement of funds to Junior. They received exactly what they bargained for — a loan to their child. Similarly, if a lender conditions its willingness to make a loan to a corporation on the controlling shareholder's willingness to promise to repay the loan in the event that her corporation does not, the bank's loan is the consideration for the shareholder's promise to guaranty the corporate debt.

A consideration issue only arises when the surety's promise is made after the loan has already been made. This might happen where the creditor becomes anxious about the principal debtor's ability to pay and asks the principal debtor to identify someone, such as a family member, shareholder, or corporate affiliate, to guarantee the debt. Failing to ensure that there is consideration for the guarantor's promise would be a major source of embarrassment for the bank's loan officers (and possibly the source of a malpractice action against their attorneys, if they were involved in the transaction).

If the debtor is in default at the time the guaranty is obtained, consideration can be found in the creditor's forbearance from bringing an immediate suit against the principal debtor. Even though the creditor's consideration does not run directly to the guarantor, the creditor's forbearance is a detriment given in exchange for the guarantor's promise, and consideration exists. If performance is not then currently due, the promise of the surety can be gratuitous and is not enforceable.

Creditors use various strategies to ensure that there is consideration for the

---

[344] *See* U.C.C. § 3-419 (2012).

[345] Creditors who sense their debtor may not repay them have a powerful incentive to seek a guarantor. The statute of frauds requires that a "promise to answer for the debt or default of another" must be evidenced by a writing to be enforceable. *See infra* § 5.03[C] Contracts to Pay Someone Else's Debt: Suretyship Agreements. The requirement of writing affords sureties protection from unfounded claims that they promised to stand behind someone else's obligation.

[346] Suretyship arrangements occur because many potential debtors cannot obtain credit on their own. The surety, normally a creditworthy individual, steps in to induce the creditor to make the loan to the debtor. A suretyship arrangement can start after a loan has been made but before it goes into default.

guaranty. One mechanism is the inclusion of a broad discretionary default clause in the original loan agreement with the principal debtor. Such provisions are usually referred to as "acceleration at will" clauses. They permit the creditor to unilaterally declare a default and accelerate the debt so that all of the installment payments are immediately due and payable at any time the creditor "deems itself insecure." Such provisions must be implemented in good faith, but are generally enforceable.[347] Thus, if the debtor has good reasons for being concerned about the principal debtor's likelihood of making timely payment, the creditor can deem itself insecure, declare a default, and enter into negotiations with the debtor, and those likely to be willing to guarantee payment of the debt, for a suretyship agreement. Extending the due date of the debt, supplies the necessary consideration for the guarantor's promise to pay.

It is similarly common for suretyship promises, which are required by the statute of frauds to be in writing,[348] to include a recital of some nominal consideration by the obligee. As with other recitals that a nominal consideration has been paid, there is always the possibility that investigation will disclose the payment that was to constitute consideration was never made. However, a surety who can prove that the recited consideration was never paid will almost never win because the courts uniformly hold that a surety is estopped to contest the accuracy of statements of what has been paid.[349]

---

[347] *See* U.C.C. § 1-309 (2012).

[348] It seems intuitive that the statute of frauds should require surety promises to be in writing because they provide a particularly inviting opportunity to inspire false allegations that a promise has been made. *See generally infra* § 5.03[C] Contracts to Pay Someone Else's Debt: Suretyship Agreements.

[349] RESTATEMENT (SECOND) OF CONTRACTS § 88(c) (1981).

Chapter 3

PROMISSORY ESTOPPEL: DETRIMENTAL RELIANCE

§ 3.01   INTRODUCTION TO PROMISSORY ESTOPPEL[1]

As seen in the chapter on consideration,[2] traditional contract doctrine required a promise to be part of a bargain for the promise to be enforceable. Justice Holmes's statement in *Wisconsin & Michigan Railway Co. v. Powers* best illustrates the classical approach to the requirement of a bargain:

> [T]he promise and the detriment are the conventional inducements each for the other. No matter what the actual motive may have been, by the express or implied terms of the supposed contract, the promise and the consideration must purport to be the motive each for the other, in whole or at least in part. It is not enough that the promise induces the detriment or that the detriment induces the promise if the other half is wanting.[3]

In other words, without mutual inducement there is no consideration. And, at least according to classical contract doctrine, without consideration there is no enforceable promise, and no contract.

Despite this traditional approach, the last chapter described several situations where promises were enforced despite the absence of anything resembling an exchange. In addition, as this chapter will explain, promises are sometimes enforceable based on the alternative doctrine of "promissory estoppel." Promissory estoppel makes a promise enforceable where the promisee has reasonably and foreseeably relied on the promise to his detriment. Because of the importance of actions taken by the promisee in reliance on the promise, the doctrine is sometimes and perhaps more aptly referred to as "detrimental reliance."

Promissory estoppel is used in two distinct ways. First, it is used a substitute for consideration where the necessary element of a bargain is missing, but where the promisee has nevertheless changed its position in reliance on the promise. This use occurs in a limited range of circumstances, which include promises among family members, promises to transfer land, gratuitous bailments, charitable subscriptions, waivers of conditions, and promises to supply a pension.[4]

Second, promissory estoppel is also used as an almost tort-like doctrine, where a person has reasonably relied on an incomplete or indefinite agreement. This

---

[1] Patrick Atiyah, *Consideration and Estoppel: The Thawing of the Ice*, 38 Mod. L. Rev. 65 (1975); Randy E. Barnett, *The Death of Reliance*, 46 J. Legal. Educ. 518, 533 (1996); Benjamin F. Boyer, *Promissory Estoppel: Principle from Precedents: Parts I and II*, 50 Mich. L. Rev. 639, 873 (1952); John J. Chung, *Promissory Estoppel and the Protection of Interpersonal Trust*, 56 Clev. St. L. Rev. 37–82 (2008); Daniel A. Farber and John H. Matheson, *Beyond Promissory Estoppel: Contract Law and the "Invisible Handshake,"* 52 U. Chi. L. Rev. 903 (1985); Stanley D. Henderson, *Promissory Estoppel and Traditional Contract Doctrine*, 78 Yale L.J. 343, 376 (1969); Eric Mills Holmes, *Restatement of Promissory Estoppel*, 32 Willamette L. Rev. 263, 275 (1996); Eric Mills Holmes, *The Four Phases of Promissory Estoppel*, 20 Seattle Univ. L. R. 45 (1996); Charles L. Knapp, *Rescuing Reliance: The Perils of Promissory Estoppel*, 49 Hastings L.J. 1191 (1998); Edward Yorio & Steve Thel, *The Promissory Basis of Section 90*, 101 Yale L.J. 111, 120–21 (1991).

[2] *See supra* Ch. 2 Consideration.

[3] 191 U.S. 379, 387 (1903). *See also* Eric Mills Holmes, *Restatement of Promissory Estoppel*, 32 Willamette L. Rev. 263, 275 (1996).

[4] Benjamin F. Boyer, *Promissory Estoppel: Principle from Precedents: Parts I and II*, 50 Mich. L. Rev. 639, 873 (1952).

branch of the doctrine expands contract law to apply to a whole range of situations in which both the classical elements of consideration and mutual assent may be missing. As potentially expansive as this branch of the doctrine may seem, recent cases and scholarship suggest that it may already have reached its zenith as an alternative basis for enforcing promises.

The remainder of this chapter explores the history of promissory estoppel and the circumstances in which it applies today, both as a substitute for consideration and as an independent cause of action.

§ 3.02   ORIGINS OF PROMISSORY ESTOPPEL[5]

Promissory estoppel developed out of the older doctrine of equitable estoppel. It was first used as a substitute for consideration in cases where there was no exchange, but where a person reasonably relied to her detriment on a promise. It later developed into an independent, almost tort-like, cause of action. Although at one time it seemed like it would completely swallow up the doctrine of consideration, it has not developed into the full-blown alternative theory of relief that some once foresaw.[6]

[A]   Equitable Estoppel[7]

No understanding of promissory estoppel is complete without examining the history of the broader general concept of estoppel.[8] Estoppel means to "preclude" or to "prohibit." A person who is subject to an estoppel (or who is "estopped") is precluded from doing something that he otherwise would be free to do.

The law of estoppel is derived from courts of equity that traditionally issued judgments in the form of an order addressed to a particular person. That person was required to obey or face imprisonment for contempt of court.

Early equity cases involving estoppel prevented a person from making a factual assertion that was at odds with his or her earlier misrepresentation of fact.

---

[5] Joel M. Ngugi, *Promissory Estoppel: the Life History of an Ideal Legal Transplant*, 41 U. Rich. L. Rev. 425 (2007); Kevin M. Teeven, *Origins of Promissory Estoppel: Justifiable Reliance and Commercial Uncertainty Before Williston's Restatement*, 34 U. Mem. L. Rev. 499, 533 (2004); Kevin M. Teeven, *A History of Promissory Estoppel: Growth in the Face of Doctrinal Resistance*, 72 Tenn. L. Rev. 1111 (2005).

[6] P. Gregory M. Duhl, *Red Owl's Legacy*, 87 Marq. L. Rev. 297, 309–11 (2003); E. Allan Farnsworth, *Developments in Contract Law During the 1980s: The Top Ten*, 41 Case W. Res. L. Rev. 203, 219–20 (1990); Robert A. Hillman, *Questioning the "New Consensus on Promissory Estoppel: An Empirical and Theoretical Study*, 98 Colum. L. Rev. 580, 615–18 (1998); Charles L. Knapp, *Rescuing Reliance: The Perils of Promissory Estoppel*, 49 Hastings L.J. 1191, 1192 (1998); *But see* David V. Snyder, *Comparative Law in Action: Promissory Estoppel, the Civil Law, and the Mixed Jurisdiction*, 15 Ariz. J. Int'l & Comp. Law 695, 700 (1998).

[7] T. Leigh Anenson, *From Theory to Practice: Analyzing Equitable Estoppel Under a Pluralistic Model of Law*, 11 Lewis & Clark L. Rev. 633 (2007).

[8] The word "estoppel" is derived from the French word "estoupe," which was also the source of the more common English word "stopped." As Lord Coke explains: "it is called an estoppel or conclusion, because a man's own act or acceptance stopeth or cloeth up his mouth to alleage or plead the truth." 2 Coke on Littleton § 667 (1823).

Equitable estoppel, or "estoppel in pais," denies a person the right to plead or prove some fact that is critical to his or her case where doing so would result in an injustice to the other party who had relied to his detriment on that person's conflicting statement of fact.[9] The typical case of equitable estoppel usually involves one person making a statement that something was true and later recanting. If another person relies on the first representation he will be permitted to estop or prevent the person on whom he relied from contradicting the statement that was relied on, regardless of the truth or falsity of the statement.[10]

To understand how equitable estoppel works, assume that a bank receives a check, payable in the amount of $10,000, drawn on the account of a customer who has no history of writing such large checks. Suspicious that the check might have been forged, the bank's head teller calls the customer to inquire about the check's authenticity, and says: "We have just received a $10,000 check with what appears to be your signature, payable to Art Dodger. Did you write the check?" The customer, preoccupied with other matters and thinking the bank was referring to another check that he had written for the same amount, says "Yes, that's my signature; I wrote the check." In response, the bank will undoubtedly pay the check, believing that it is genuine.

Normally a bank is not permitted to charge a customer's account for a check containing a forgery of its customer's signature.[11] However, the customer's statement of fact about his signature will lead the bank to rely.

If the customer sues the bank, due to its improper payment of the check, the bank will be permitted to "estop" the customer from claiming that the signature was forged. Unless the customer can assert that the signature was a forgery, he has no basis to have his account reimbursed for the $10,000. Because the bank's action was reasonable and because the bank changed its position in a significant way in reliance on the customer's statement, equity will intervene and preclude the customer from claiming that the check was forged.[12] Having induced another to believe that one thing was true, the customer is prevented from asserting something different.

Many traditional equitable estoppel cases arose in the context of insurance policies. In *Hetchler v. American Life Insurance Co.*,[13] the plaintiff used equitable estoppel to prevent the insurance company from asserting the expiration date on a life insurance policy where the insurance company had previously misstated the

---

[9] *See* Anfenson v. Banks, 163 N.W. 608 (Iowa 1917). *See also* Stanley D. Henderson, *Promissory Estoppel and Traditional Contract Doctrine*, 78 YALE L.J. 343, 376 (1969).

[10] "Truth" in this context refers to whether an assertion is in accord with objectively determined facts.

[11] *See* U.C.C. § 4-401(a) (2012).

[12] A somewhat more complicated version of this happens every month when banking customers receive their checking account statements, and have the opportunity to examine them for these types of forgeries. Failure to report an unauthorized charge promptly may well lead to the customer being estopped from later trying to have its account recredited for the forged item or for other checks, subsequently forged by the same wrongdoer. *See* U.C.C. § 4-406 (2012).

[13] 254 N.W. 221 (Mich. 1934).

expiration date in a way that led the insured to rely by failing to extend its term before his death. The court explained:

> It is a familiar rule of law that an estoppel arises when one by his acts, representations, or admissions, or by his silence when he ought to speak out, intentionally or through culpable negligence induces another to believe certain facts to exist and such other rightfully relies and acts on such belief, so that he will be prejudiced if the former is permitted to deny the existence of such facts.[14]

The doctrine has also been used in connection with the statute of frauds. If a person falsely represents that he has signed the type of writing necessary to satisfy the statute, he will be estopped from later raising the statute of frauds as a defense to the enforcement of the contract.[15]

Another way of looking at equitable estoppel is to see the doctrine as a way to prevent traps from being sprung on the unwary. One cannot mislead another into believing things are one way and then do an about-face and say, in effect, "gotcha." However, in these early cases, involving "equitable" estoppel, the approach was used only in cases involving misrepresentations of current facts. At the outset, estoppel did not apply to unperformed promises.[16]

[B] The Emergence of Promissory Estoppel[17]

The migration of equitable estoppel into a theory which supported the enforceability of a promise was slow. At the time the transformation took place, the change was only barely perceptible. Its migration can be understood, in part, with reference to the basic elements for a traditional equitable estoppel, based on a misrepresentation of fact.

For an equitable estoppel to arise, several separate elements have to be proven. In *Burdick v. Independent School Dist. No. 52 of Oklahoma County*, the court said there must have been

> 1) a false representation or concealment of facts, 2) made with actual or constructive knowledge of the facts, 3) to a person without knowledge of, or the means of knowing, those facts, 4) with the intent that it be acted upon,

---

[14] *Id.* at 223.

[15] RESTATEMENT OF CONTRACTS § 178 cmt. f (1932).

[16] As far as promises are concerned, if a person making a promise has no present intention of ever performing it, then the fact misrepresented is the present state of the promisor's mind. This will work only in a limited number of cases in which the promisee can show that the promisor never had any intention to perform the promise. This will be very hard to do even in cases where the promisor really never intended to perform.

[17] Benjamin Boyer, *Promissory Estoppel: Principle from Precedents (Pts. 1 & 2)*, 50 MICH. L. REV. 639, 873 (1952); William R. Casto & Val D. Ricks, *"Dear Sister Antillico . . .": The Story of* Kirksey v. Kirksey, 94 GEO. L.J. 321 (2006); Jay M. Feinman, *Promissory Estoppel and Judicial Method*, 97 HARV. L. REV. 678 (1984); Lon L. Fuller, *Consideration and Form*, 41 COLUM. L. REV. 799 (1941); Warren L. Shattuck, *Gratuitous Promises — A New Writ?*, 35 MICH. L. REV. 908 (1937); Eric Mills Holmes, *The Four Phases of Promissory Estoppel*, 20 SEATTLE UNIV. L. R. 45 (1996).

and 5) the person to whom it was made acted in reliance upon it to his detriment.[18]

If any one of these elements was missing, equitable estoppel would not apply. Thus, without the first element — a misrepresentation of fact, the law provided no relief. However, most broken promises do not involve a misrepresentation of fact.

[1]   Misrepresentation of Fact Different from Broken Promise

Because the doctrine of equitable estoppel applied only to misrepresentations of facts and not to broken promises, it took a long time for the courts to develop the doctrine of promissory estoppel. The original doctrine was not available when there had been a promise, but no false representation of fact.

The difficulty in drawing a sharp distinction between a representation of fact, necessary for an equitable estoppel to arise, and a promise, which gives rise to promissory estoppel,[19] made it easy for courts, when they were inclined to do so, to sometimes ignore the difference. In the illustration described above, the insurance agent's false representation that its policy was to permit the policyholder's claim to be filed on the first day after the weekend, if the last day for filing a claim fell on a day when the company was closed, was clearly a misstatement of fact. However, if the agent, instead of making a statement about the insurance company's current rules, had said: "don't worry about it, we'll accept the claim if it's filed the following Monday," it would have been treated as a promise. There's a very narrow difference between "our policy is to accept the claim" and "we will accept the claim." Drawing a legal distinction between these two statements made little sense, given the extraordinary likelihood that the customer would rely, regardless of how it was phrased.

Early promissory estoppel claims arose in similar circumstances. For example, in *Jennings v. Dunning*,[20] the plaintiff submitted an incomplete application for state medical benefits. Her application was initially denied due to her failure to include several required supporting documents. She delayed her appeal of this denial because she was "*assured* on two separate occasions that the rejection of [her initial application] would be reconsidered if additional documents were delivered to [the reviewing agency]."[21] The court estopped the defendant from asserting her delay as a defense because of the injustice that would have resulted due to her reliance on these assurances. Although the court treated the case as involving an equitable estoppel, it is not clear whether the agency, in assuring her that it could submit the additional documents later without prejudicing her rights, had made a promise about the future or a statement of its present intent to permit her this privilege. If it was the former, the court should have used promissory estoppel. If it was the latter, a misrepresentation about its current rules or about

---

[18] 702 P.2d 48, 55 (Okla. 1985).

[19] *See, e.g.*, Cottle Ent., Inc. v. Town of Farmington, 693 A.2d 330, 336 n.6 (Me. 1997).

[20] 440 N.W.2d 671 (Neb. 1989).

[21] *Id.* at 676 (emphasis supplied).

its present intent to adhere to those rules, equitable estoppel would have been apt.

[2]   Promissory Fraud[22]

Cases of "promissory fraud" also helped blur the distinction between a broken promise and a misrepresentation of fact. Muddling the distinction between the two facilitated the emergence of promissory estoppel from cases involving the older doctrine.

Promissory fraud occurs when a person misrepresents his or her intent to perform a promise.[23] When this happens, there is a true misrepresentation of fact. The fact in question is the promisor's current intent to perform.[24] Thus, if I tell you that I intend to give you a ride to school, when I actually plan to leave you waiting on the curb, I have misrepresented my intent. If I *promise* to give you a ride, and intend, at the time I make the promise, to leave you on the curb, I have similarly misrepresented my intent. Thus, where a person intends not to perform, but asserts that he does, he has made a misrepresentation of fact that can serve as the basis for a true equitable estoppel. It was a short step from cases involving promissory fraud, where the promisor lied about his intent to perform, to cases involving what we would now recognize as promissory estoppel, where the promisor did not lie about his intent to perform, but instead, simply changed his mind later and failed to perform. If I promise to drive you to school, intending to do so, but later change my mind or forget, you are still going to be left waiting on the curb, having relied on my promise.

[3]   Reasonable Reliance on an Unenforceable Promise

Another barrier that had to be overcome in order for promissory estoppel to fully develop was equitable estoppel's requirement that the reliance be reasonable. Under equitable estoppel it was not enough for a party to rely on another's misstatement of fact; it was also necessary for her reliance to be reasonable.[25] However, because promises that were not supported by consideration were not enforceable, courts had difficulty reaching the conclusion that a person could "reasonably rely" on such a promise. Reliance would have been reasonable if there was consideration, but if there was consideration for the promise, there would be no need to resort to promissory estoppel. If consideration was missing, it was unreasonable to rely on the promise. This mechanical approach was bound to produce unfair results.

---

[22] Ian Ayres & Gregory Klass, *Promissory Fraud Without Breach*, 2004 WIS. L. REV. 507; Kevin E. Davis, *Promissory Fraud: A Cost-Benefit Analysis*, 2004 WIS. L. REV. 535; Justin Sweet, *Promissory Fraud and the Parol Evidence Rule*, 49 CAL. L. REV. 877 (1961); Note, *The Legal Effect of Promises Made with Intent Not to Perform*, 38 COLUM. L. REV. 1461 (1938).

[23] RESTATEMENT (SECOND) OF TORTS § 530 cmt. c (1977). *E.g.*, Fowler v. Happy Goodman Family, 575 S.W.2d 496 (Tenn. 1978). *See also* Sproul v. Fossi, 548 P.2d 970 (Or. 1976) (reckless disregard for ability to perform as basis for promissory fraud).

[24] *See* Gerhardt v. Harris, 934 P.2d 976 (Kan. 1997).

[25] *E.g.*, Davis v. Davis, 855 P.2d 342, 348 (Wyo. 1993).

Kirksey v. Kirksey[26] illustrates the problem. There, a recently widowed woman received a letter from her deceased husband's brother, offering her a place to live. He instructed her to sell her land and move to land he owned near his home. In reliance on her brother-in-law's promise, she abandoned her land and her other possessions and moved across the country with her children. However, two years later her brother-in-law, apparently tired of his brother's children or otherwise dissatisfied with the arrangement, demanded that she leave. She sued to enforce his promise. The court ruled in favor of the brother-in-law because there was no consideration for his promise. Although moving to his land was a necessary condition of his promise, he was not bargaining with her for her to move. His promise was nothing more than a promise to make a gift of a place to live with the natural condition associated with it that she would have to move to where his property was located in order to have land on which to live. The dissenting judge explained the reason for his dissent, and explained the majority's reasoning:

> The inclination of my mind, is that the loss and inconvenience, which the plaintiff sustained in breaking up, and moving to the defendant's, a distance of sixty miles, is a sufficient consideration to support the promise, to furnish her with a house, and land to cultivate, until she could raise her family. My brothers, however think, that the promise on the part of the defendant, was a mere gratuity, and that an action will not lie for its breach.[27]

At the time, promissory estoppel had not yet emerged from the primal swamp of the common law of equitable estoppel, and the brother-in-law had made no statement of fact on which she had relied. He had unquestionably made a promise, but in the absence of consideration it would have been unreasonable of her to rely on it. Likewise, the plaintiff had not made any substantial improvements to the land; if she had done so, the promise might have been enforceable in equity, to prevent unjust enrichment.

[4]   Reliance Before Consideration Doctrine

Despite this, there had also been a time, before the bargain theory of consideration had crystallized, when a promisee's reliance had been considered to be the basis for enforcing promises in the absence of a seal.[28] Thus, although the law had abandoned these earlier cases, the step from equitable estoppel to promissory estoppel was not entirely without precedent.[29]

---

[26] 8 Ala. 131 (1845). *See* William R. Casto & Val D. Ricks, *"Dear Sister Antillico . . .": The Story of Kirksey v. Kirksey*, 94 GEO. L.J. 321 (2006).

[27] 8 Ala. 131. An unusual feature of the case, is that the court's per curiam decision was written by a judge who dissented from it.

[28] *See* Lon Fuller & Robert Perdue, *The Reliance Interest in Contract Damages, (Pt. 1)*, 46 YALE L.J. 52, 68 (1936).

[29] RESTATEMENT (SECOND) OF CONTRACTS § 90 cmt. a (1981).

[5]   Emergence of Promissory Estoppel

To detect the gradual way in which the law of promissory estoppel developed, it is useful to compare the decision in *Kirksey* with the one more than 50 years later, in *Ricketts v. Scothorn*.[30] Katie Scothorn was a late nineteenth century career woman who held a job as a bookkeeper with a local business. Her grandfather, apparently anxious about the appearance of Katie's employment, wrote out a promissory note to her: "I promise to pay to Katie Scothorn on demand, $2,000, to be at 6 per cent per annum."[31] As he handed her the note, he said to her "I have fixed out something that you have not got to work anymore." Shortly thereafter, apparently in reliance on her grandfather's promise, Katie quit her job.

Later, when Katie brought an action against her grandfather's estate to collect the $2,000, the court ruled in her favor, even though there was no consideration for her grandfather's promise. Although he wanted to make it possible for her to quit her job, he had made it clear that his promise did not depend on her agreement to quit working. The choice was left entirely up to her. Thus, there was no exchange. Instead, the court based its decision on equitable estoppel or "estoppel *in pais*." It said that this equitable estoppel operated "to preclude the defendant from alleging that the note in controversy is lacking in one of the essential elements of a valid contract" — consideration.

There was no question in *Ricketts* but that Katie's reliance was "foreseeable" by her grandfather. Making it possible for her to quit her job was the express reason for his promise. It is not known what circumstances made Katie's action reasonable, but it must be presumed that her grandfather had the financial means to fulfill his promise and perhaps that he had fulfilled similar promises to his other grandchildren.[32] Katie's subsequent decision to go back to work suggests that a modern court might be more reluctant to enforce her grandfather's promise, on the grounds that enforcement might not be necessary to avoid an injustice,[33] but this aspect of the doctrine had not yet been fully developed at that time.

Although Katie's action was brought to enforce her grandfather's promissory note, which was undoubtedly a promise, her grandfather's statement, made when he handed her the note, supplied the court with a thin reed of a statement of fact on which to base its conclusion that equitable estoppel was the proper basis for her claim. Her grandfather said: " 'I have fixed out something that you have not got to work any more.' "[34] This was, strictly speaking, a statement of fact, which could

---

[30] 77 N.W. 365 (Neb. 1898).

[31] This $2,000 would be approximately $56,000 in 2013. At 6% annual interest, it would earn only about $2,800 per year today. The $120 annual income Katie would have earned from her grandfather's note was not much then, and $2,800 in today's economy would not be much more, but it might have been enough in a small town in Nebraska, particularly if she were still living at home. Her job, on the other hand, paid $10 per week, or $520 per year — a little more than $14,500 in today's dollars, or about the federal minimum wage of $14,500 per year at $7.25 per hour for 2,000 hours per year. It's no wonder she went back to work.

[32] In making his promise, Katie's grandfather reportedly said: "None of my grandchildren work and you don't have to." Ricketts v. Scothorn, 77 N.W. 365, 366 (Neb. 1898).

[33] *See* RESTATEMENT (SECOND) OF CONTRACTS § 90(1) (1981).

[34] Ricketts v. Scothorn, 77 N.W. 365, 366 (Neb. 1898).

have formed the basis of an equitable estoppel. Despite this, it is clear that it was grandfather's promise, contained in this promissory note, and not his statement about what he had "fixed out," that provided the basis for the court's decision to enforce the promise.

[6]   Procedural Mechanism of Promissory Estoppel

Ricketts laid the ground work for promissory estoppel to be used as a means of enforcing promises. It also helps explain how promissory estoppel worked in a procedural sense, which is now mostly long forgotten. The plaintiff claims that there has been a breach of contract and alleges the critical elements of mutual assent and consideration. The defendant denies the claim, perhaps admitting that the promise was made and accepted, but denying the plaintiff's claim that it was supported by "consideration." The plaintiff can then reply, raising the issue of his reliance on the promise as a means of preventing or "estopping" the defendant from denying the presence of consideration. The plaintiff's claim of promissory estoppel permits the court to strike the defendant's denial that consideration was present and, *voila*, the necessity of alleging and proving that consideration was present is solved.

§ 3.03   A CONSIDERATION SUBSTITUTE[35]

In the ensuing years, promissory estoppel eventually developed to make a variety of promises enforceable, despite the absence of a bargain. Promissory estoppel is now widely recognized as an alternative basis for making promises enforceable.

The elements of the doctrine are variously stated as involving anywhere from three to five separate elements.[36] These nearly always include the necessity of (1) a promise, (2) the promisor's reasonable expectation that the promise will induce action or forbearance by the promisee, (3) actual reasonable reliance by the promisee, and (4) the necessity of enforcing the promise to avoid injustice.[37] In other words, there must have been reasonable and foreseeable reliance on a promise that results in an injury that justifies a remedy.[38] These elements have been applied in a wide variety of bargain and non-bargain settings.

Nevertheless, the doctrine was originally limited to situations not involving a traditional bargain. It therefore was generally only applied in several distinct

---

[35] Benjamin F. Boyer, *Promissory Estoppel: Principle from Precedents (Pts. 1 & 2)*, 50 MICH. L. REV. 639, 873 (1952); Benjamin F. Boyer, *Promissory Estoppel: Requirements and Limitations of the Doctrine*, 98 U. PA. L. REV. 459 (1950); Melvin Aron Eisenberg, *Donative Promises*, 47 U. CHI. L. REV. 1, 32 (1979); Warren A. Seavey, *Reliance upon Gratuitous Promises or Other Conduct*, 64 HARV. L. REV. 913, 926 (1951); Warren L Shattuck, *Gratuitous Promises — A New Writ?*, 35 MICH. L. REV. 908 (1937).

[36] Jay M. Feinman, *Promissory Estoppel and Judicial Method*, 97 HARV. L. REV. 678, 690 n.56 (1984).

[37] *See* RESTATEMENT (SECOND) OF CONTRACTS § 90(1) (1981).

[38] *E.g.*, Carroll v. Xerox Corp., 294 F.3d 231 (1st Cir. 2002) (three elements); Abbruscato v. Empire Blue Cross and Blue Shield, 274 F.3d 90 (2d Cir. 2001) (four elements); Midwest Energy, Inc. v. Orion Food Sys., Inc., 14 S.W.3d 154 (Mo. Ct. App. 2000) (four elements); Brown v. Branch, 758 N.E.2d 48 (Ind. 2001) (five elements).

categories of cases in which there was no suggestion that the parties had struck any kind of a commercial exchange. These situations involved family gift promises, promises to convey land, gratuitous bailments, and charitable subscriptions.[39] Although these initial settings did not resemble commercial exchanges, the doctrine gradually expanded to encompass business and employment relationships.

The key to these situations was the promisee's reasonable and foreseeable reliance on a promise. Where the promisor had reason to know that the promisee would be reasonably likely to rely on the promise, and the promisee took some affirmative action in reliance on the promise, and was reasonable in doing so, the promise was enforceable.

This was initially accomplished by estopping, or precluding, the promisor from denying that consideration had been supplied for the promise. If the promisor could not deny that there had been consideration, the only impediment to enforcing the promise was removed. Over time, reference to this procedural step was abandoned, and the promise was simply said to be enforceable on the grounds of promissory estoppel alone.[40]

[A]   Family Gift Promises[41]

Promissory estoppel was widely applied to family gift promises, similar to those present in cases like *Kirksey v. Kirksey* and *Ricketts v. Scothorn*.[42] Before *Ricketts v. Scothorn*, courts had sometimes enforced these types of promises by disingenuously claiming that the promisee's actions in reliance on the promise "supplied" the necessary "consideration."[43] After *Ricketts*, courts could approach the problem more directly, without harming the traditional bargain element of the consideration doctrine. Even the venerable decision in *Hamer v. Sidway*,[44] where the court found that a young man's uncle had bargained for his abstinence from various vices, could perhaps have rested more comfortably on the grounds of promissory estoppel than it had on the more frequently cited basis of a true bargain.[45] Decisions since *Ricketts* have routinely enforced family gift promises

---

[39] Benjamin Boyer, *Promissory Estoppel: Principle from Precedents, (Pts. 1 & 2)*, 50 Mich. L. Rev. 639, 873 (1952).

[40] The term "promissory estoppel" is said to have first appeared in Professor Williston's treatise on contract law. *See* Benjamin F. Boyer, *Promissory Estoppel: Requirements and Limitations of the Doctrine*, 98 U. Pa. L. Rev. 459 (1950).

[41] Kevin M. Teeven, *A Legal History of Binding Gratuitous Promises at Common Law: Justifiable Reliance and Moral Obligation*, 43 Duq. L. Rev. 11, 25 (2004).

[42] *See supra* § 3.02[B] The Emergence of Promissory Estoppel. *See also* Seavey v. Drake, 1882 N.H. LEXIS 86 (Dec. 1882).

[43] Devecmon v. Shaw, 14 A. 464 (Md. 1888) (uncle's promise to reimburse his nephew for expenses incurred in a trip to Europe was a sufficient "consideration.").

[44] 27 N.E. 256 (N.Y. 1891).

[45] *See* Blatt v. Univ. of S. Cal., 5 Cal. App. 3d 935, 942–944 (1970); Randy E. Barnett, *The Death of Reliance*, 46 J. Legal. Educ. 518, 533 (1996); Paul T. Wangerin, *Skills Training in "Legal Analysis": A Systematic Approach*, 40 U. Miami L. Rev. 409, 458 (1986). *But see* Charles L. Knapp, *Rescuing Reliance: The Perils of Promissory Estoppel*, 49 Hastings L.J. 1191, 1236 n.221 (1998).

even though an exchange was missing, provided the promisee acted reasonably and foreseeably in reliance on the promise.[46]

Even here, however, a bare promise to a family member is not enforceable without these elements. In *Dewein v. Dewein's Estate*,[47] a brother's promise to take care of his sister, made out of a sense of gratitude and perhaps responsibility for the sacrifices she had made in caring for their parents, was not enforceable where his sister had done nothing in reliance on the promise. But, in *Wright v. Newman*,[48] the defendant's promise to "assume the obligations of fatherhood" and support his companion's child, led the plaintiff to refrain from identifying and seeking support from the child's biological father, and was therefore enforceable on the basis of her detrimental reliance.[49] Thus, the necessary element of reliance might take either the form of affirmation action, or forbearance.

[B]   Promises to Convey Land

Closely related to cases involving promises to family members are those involving a promise to convey an interest in land. Many of these cases involved overtones of enforcing the promise not just to protect the promisee's reliance interest, but also to guard against the risk of unjust enrichment. *Seavey v. Drake*,[50] supplies a good example. There, a father permitted his son to move onto some land that the father owned. He promised to supply the son with a deed, making him the owner of the land. The son took possession of the land, paid the taxes on the land, and made substantial improvements to the land by building a house, a barn, and a stable.[51] When the father failed to deliver the deed, the son sued. The court said that the son's expenditures, which had been induced by his father's promise, constituted "a consideration for the promise," even though it was clear that the father had not entered into a bargain with the son for the construction of the improvements. It was clear to the court that if the promise was not enforced, or some other remedy supplied, the father's beneficiaries would obtain a benefit at the expense of the son, and the son would forfeit all of the expenses he had incurred in making the improvements.[52]

In *Seavey v. Drake*, the son's improvements not only solved the problem of the absence of consideration, they also ensured that the statute of frauds would not be a barrier to the father's oral promise to convey a deed. In similar cases where the promisee relied, but made no improvements to the land, the promise is not usually

---

[46] *E.g.*, Estate of Bucci, 488 P.2d 216 (Colo. Ct. App. 1971) (gratuitous assignment of a right to receive $17,000).

[47] 174 N.E.2d 875 (Ill. App. Ct. 1961).

[48] 467 S.E.2d 533 (Ga. 1996).

[49] *See* Robert A. Hillman, *Questioning the "New Consensus" on Promissory Estoppel: An Empirical and Theoretical Study*, 98 COLUM. L. REV. 580, 603–04 (1998).

[50] 1882 N.H. LEXIS 86 (Dec. 1882).

[51] This was done sometime between 1860 and 1880, at a cost of $3,000. In 2013 dollars, this would be approximately $80,000.

[52] *See also* Greiner v. Greiner, 293 P. 759 (Kan. 1930); Freeman v. Freeman, 1870 N.Y. LEXIS 86 (Oct. 25, 1870).

enforced. For example, in *Boone v. Coe*,[53] the defendant promised to rent land to his sister-in-law and her family, near his home in Texas. Relying on this promise, the plaintiff left her home and businesses in Kentucky and moved across the country. When the defendant reneged, the court held that the promise was unenforceable due to the statute of frauds, because the plaintiff's efforts conferred no benefit on the defendant.

Cases like *Seavey v. Drake* and *Boone v. Coe* seemed to arise with greater frequency in the late nineteenth century and the early part of the twentieth century, when the country was still expanding and plenty of land was available for relatives.[54] Modern examples are more likely to involve neighbors. In *Christy v. Hoke*,[55] the court enforced the defendant's promise to give the plaintiffs an easement across his land in order for them to install a septic system. The plaintiffs relied on the promise of an easement by installing the septic system and building a house. This reliance made the defendant's promise enforceable. A similar promise was enforceable where an owner of adjoining land promised to transfer ownership of a parcel that would facilitate the plaintiff's access to the house he was planning to build.[56] However, in these two more modern examples, the element of a benefit to the promisor, which had been so critical in *Seavey*, was conspicuously missing.

Promissory estoppel is also used in option contracts, most frequently those involving transfers of real estate. For example, in *Ragosta v. Wilder*,[57] the court enforced an owner's written promise to sell his land to the plaintiffs if they showed up at the bank with the price by a certain date, provided that he had not previously sold it to someone else. The plaintiffs incurred expenses to obtain the necessary financing and showed up at the bank, cash in hand, at the designated time. But, the owner refused to go through with the deal. Even though the buyers had only prepared to perform, the court held that they had acted in reliance on the promised sale, and found that the buyers stated a claim for at least some relief.[58]

[C]   Gratuitous Bailments and Agency Relationships

Probably the oldest cases in which the modern doctrine of promissory estoppel can be detected are those in which a person gratuitously undertakes to take care of some property owned by the promisee.[59] *Siegel v. Spear & Co.*[60] is the best known of these older decisions. Spear held a lien on Siegel's furniture and volunteered to store it while Siegel was away for the summer. Spear also volunteered to purchase insurance to cover the furniture, at Siegel's expense. However, Spear failed to

---

[53] 154 S.W. 900 (Ky. 1913).

[54] *See also* Clancy v. Flusky, 58 N.E. 594 (Ill. 1900).

[55] 618 P.2d 1095 (Ariz. Ct. App. 1980).

[56] Larabee v. Booth, 463 N.E.2d 487 (Ind. Ct. App. 1984) (promise to convey adjoining parcel of land to neighbor to permit access to planned house).

[57] 592 A.2d 367 (Vt. 1991).

[58] Restatement (Second) of Contracts § 87 (1981).

[59] Benjamin Boyer, *Promissory Estoppel: Principle from Precedents (Pt. 2)*, 50 Mich. L. Rev. 639, 876 (1952).

[60] 138 N.E. 414 (N.Y. 1923).

purchase the promised insurance, and Siegel's furniture was destroyed in a fire. As a result, Siegel sought to hold Spear liable for his failure to follow through on his promise to have the property insured. Even though Siegel was to have reimbursed Spear for the insurance, the court treated the case as having involved a gratuitous bailment.

Because Spear had failed to perform the terms of the bailment, the court was able to tie the case to a much older line of authority that based liability on the historic distinction between "misfeasance" and "nonfeasance."[61] Misfeasance means defective performance. Nonfeasance refers to nonperformance. In these earlier cases, liability could be found where a person had performed a promise badly — misfeasance — but not where he had failed to perform at all. Because Spear had taken possession of the goods pursuant to the bailment, his complete failure to procure insurance for the furniture permitted the court to treat the case as involving defective performance instead of complete nonperformance.[62]

Later cases dispensed with the distinction between misfeasance and nonfeasance.[63] The modern doctrine of promissory estoppel employs no such distinction. It treats those who perform their promises badly in the same manner as those who fail to perform at all. Thus, promises to obtain insurance are enforceable if they are relied upon, regardless of whether the promisor performed its promise badly, or not at all.[64]

[D]   Charitable Subscriptions[65]

Promissory estoppel made charitable subscriptions (promises to a charity) enforceable without the need for consideration.[66] Promises to a charity, like any other promise to make a gift, lack consideration.[67] Of course, if the donor seeks something in return for his promise, such as the establishment of a chair in the donor's name, or the construction of a particular building, a traditional bargain

---

[61] *See* Thorne v. Deas, 1809 N.Y. LEXIS 164 (Feb. 1809); Comfort v. McCorkle, 268 N.Y.S. 192 (N.Y. Sup. Ct. 1933). *See also* Coggs v. Bernard, 92 Eng. Rep. 107 (K.B. 1703); *supra* § 1.03 History of Contract Law.

[62] *Siegel v. Spear*, 138 N.E. at 415.

[63] *E.g.*, Shoemaker v. Commonwealth Bank, 700 A.2d 1003 (Pa. 1997); East Providence Credit Union v. Geremia, 239 A.2d 725 (R.I. 1968) (secured lender's promise to obtain insurance).

[64] Shoemaker v. Commonwealth Bank, 700 A.2d 1003 (Pa. 1997).

[65] Evelyn Brody, *The Charity in Bankruptcy and Ghosts of Donors Past, Present, and Future*, 29 Seton Hall Legis. J. 471 (2005); Mary Frances Butig, Gordon T. Butler & Lynne M. Murphy, *Pledges to Nonprofit Organizations: Are They Enforceable and Must They Be Enforced?*, 27 U.S.F. L. Rev. 47 (1992); Russell G. Donaldson, Annotation, *Lack of Consideration as Barring Enforcement of Promise to Make Charitable Contribution or Subscription — Modern Cases*, 86 A.L.R.4th 241 (1991). Kevin M. Teeven, *A Legal History of Binding Gratuitous Promises at Common Law: Justifiable Reliance and Moral Obligation*, 43 Duq. L. Rev. 11, 25 (2004).

[66] Keuka College v. Ray, 60 N.E. 325, 326 (N.Y. 1901); Congregation Kadimah Toras-Moshe v. DeLeo, 540 N.E.2d 691 (Mass. 1989) (including promised gift in synagogue's budget was not, by itself, sufficient to constitute reliance). *See* Allegheny College v. Nat'l Chautauqua County Bank, 159 N.E. 173 (N.Y. 1927).

[67] *See* Russell G. Donaldson, Annotation, *Lack of Consideration as Barring Enforcement of Promise to Make Charitable Contribution or Subscription — Modern Cases*, 86 A.L.R.4th 241 (1991).

exists. But normally, no such bargain is made; the donor's promise may be targeted at a particular project, but it is not usually part of a bargain between the donor and the charity.

Despite this reality, courts sometimes stretch the doctrine of consideration to make these gift promises enforceable. One of the best examples is Judge Cardozo's decision in *Allegheny College v. National Chautauqua County Bank*.[68] In *Allegheny College*, Mary Yates Johnston made a written promise: "[i]n consideration of my interest in Christian Education, and in consideration of others subscribing, I hereby subscribe and will pay to the order [of] Allegheny College . . . Five Thousand Dollars." The written promise further indicated that the amount was to fall due 30 days after Mrs. Johnston's death, and it would bear interest until it was paid. The signed writing also specified that "[t]he proceeds of this obligation shall be added to the Endowment of said Institution, or expended in accordance with instructions on the reverse side of this pledge." The other side said: "In loving memory this gift shall be known as the Mary Yates Johnston Memorial Fund, the proceeds from which shall be used to educate students preparing for the ministry."

Thirty months later, and before her death, Mrs. Johnston paid $1,000 of the pledge, even though it was not due until after her death. The college set the sum aside as a scholarship fund for students studying for the ministry. However, seven months after making the $1,000 payment, she repudiated the promise. After her death, the college filed suit to recover the balance from her estate.

The court found that the promise was supported by consideration, which Justice Cardozo described as a "detriment to the promisee sustained by virtue of the promise."[69] He ruled that the college, in accepting the $1,000 payment, had made an implied promise to "do whatever acts were customary or reasonably necessary to maintain the memorial fairly and justly in the spirit of its creation." Thus, a bilateral contract was formed, with Mrs. Johnston promising to pay the remainder of her pledge and the college promising, in exchange, to maintain a memorial in her name.

However, before drawing this conclusion, Cardozo discussed promissory estoppel as a possible basis for the court's decision. He reviewed several earlier New York decisions, referring to them as "signposts on the road" to the state's adoption of promissory estoppel as a basis for enforcing promises. He stated: "Certain, at least, it is that we have adopted the doctrine of promissory estoppel as the equivalent of consideration in connection with our law of charitable subscriptions," and cited several cases as authority for the proposition.

---

[68] 159 N.E. 173 (N.Y. 1927). Further, although the precise holding of the case is that the donor's promise was supported by consideration, the decision is widely cited as authority for promissory estoppel. *See* Bridgeman, *Allegheny College Revisited: Cardozo, Consideration, and Formalism in Context*, 39 U.C. DAVIS L. REV. 149 (2005); Mike Townsend, *Cardozo's* Allegheny College *Opinion: a Case Study in Law as an Art*, 33 HOUS. L. REV. 1103 (1996); Alfred S. Konefsky, *How to Read, or at Least Not Misread, Cardozo in the* Allegheny College *Case*, 36 BUFF. L. REV. 645 (1988); Leon Lipson, *The* Allegheny College *Case*, 23 YALE L. REP. NO. 3, at 11 (1977).

[69] Allegheny College, 59 N.E. at 174 (quoting Wisc. & Mich. Ry. Co. v. Powers, 191 U.S. 379, 386 (1903).

The difficulty was that there was nothing to point to, in the way of reliance, that would have made Mrs. Johnston's promise enforceable under this theory. Nevertheless, a majority of the court agreed with his dictum, that promissory estoppel had already been adopted as a means of making promises to charities enforceable, and later courts cited *Allegheny College* in support of the rule.

Today, promissory estoppel serves as a useful basis for enforcing promises to charities. For example, in *King v. Trustees of Boston University*,[70] the court used it to justify a jury's finding that the great American civil rights leader, Dr. Martin Luther King, had made an enforceable promise to Boston University to donate many of his papers to the University. The University had taken possession of the papers and incurred considerable expense in indexing the papers, making them available to researchers, and providing trained staff members to care for the papers and assist those using them for research. In *In re Howard Marshall Charitable Remainder Annuity Trust*,[71] the court determined that a charitable pledge to Haverford College could have been enforced under the doctrine of promissory estoppel, but that the college had taken no action in reliance on the pledge.

Other courts have taken Restatement (Second) § 90 up on its suggestion that charitable pledges should be enforced without regard to whether there is consideration or reliance.[72] Other courts have rejected this approach and insisted that the pledge be supported by either consideration or some form of reliance.[73]

[E]   Commercial Settings[74]

Courts have sometimes been reluctant to apply promissory estoppel in commercial settings, where a bargain would ordinarily be expected to be found.[75] Despite this hesitancy, promissory estoppel has been used in a variety of business transactions. The most notable of these have been in the context of employment and construction contracts.

Feinberg v. Pfeiffer Co.[76] provides a good illustration of this. In it, the court used promissory estoppel to enforce an employer's promise of a pension.[77] Today,

---

[70] 647 N.E.2d 1196 (Mass. 1995).

[71] 709 So. 2d 662 (La. 1998).

[72] *See* RESTATEMENT (SECOND) OF CONTRACTS § 90(2) (1981); Salsbury v. Nw. Bell Tel. Co., 221 N.W.2d 609 (Iowa 1974).

[73] Md. Nat'l Bank v. United Jewish Appeal Fed., 407 A.2d 1130. 1135–36 (Md. 1979).

[74] Richard Craswell, *Offer, Acceptance, and Efficient Reliance*, 48 STAN. L. REV. 481 (1996); Ofer Grosskopf & Barak Medina, *Regulating Contract Formation: Precontractual Reliance, Sunk Costs, and Market Structure*, 39 CONN. L. REV. 1977 (2007); Alfred S. Konefsky, *Freedom and Interdependence in Twentieth-Century Contract Law: Traynor and Hand and Promissory Estoppel*, 65 U. CIN. L. REV. 1169 (1997); Jean Fleming Powers, *Promissory Estoppel and Wagging the Dog*, 59 ARK. L. REV. 841 (2007); Franklin Schulz, *The Firm Offer Puzzle: A Study of Business Practice in the Construction Industry*, 19 U. CHI. L. REV. 237 (1952).

[75] James Baird Co. v. Gimbel Bros., Inc., 64 F.2d 344 (2d Cir. 1933).

[76] 322 S.W.2d 163 (Mo. Ct. App. 1959).

[77] *See also* Katz v. Danny Dare, Inc., 610 S.W.2d 121 (Mo. Ct. App. 1980); Osborne v. Locke Steel

most such promises are bargained for as part of an employee's compensation package. However, the promise made to Feinberg was supplied near the end of her many years of a long and dedicated service to the company. The promise was not made in exchange for those services, nor for her agreement to retire, at that time, or ever. She remained free to retire or to continue working. The company held a small ceremony honoring her for her many years of loyal service and promised to pay her a pension when and if she decided to retire. She eventually did retire, and a few years later the company, under new management, sought to renege on the promise it had made. The similarity between the Pfeiffer Co.'s promise of a pension to Feinberg, to enable her to retire, and grandpa Ricketts' promise to Katie Scothorn, so that she wouldn't have to work, was hard to ignore. As a result, the court enforced the employer's promise, because of Feinberg's reliance, even though, as an employee at will, the company might have fired her at any time.

In these situations, unlike cases involving pledges to eleemosynary institutions, courts have been more insistent that the promisee incur some meaningful legal detriment in reliance on the promise, even if it was one that resulted in a financial advantage to the employee.[78] Feinberg, of course, took the meaningful step of retiring from her job. In *Hayes v. Plantations Steel Co.*,[79] the plaintiff had already announced his decision to retire when the promise of a pension was made. The court concluded that this made it clear not only that his decision to retire was not consideration for the promise of a pension, but also that he had not relied on the promise in carrying out his decision a week later. Likewise, in *Pitts v. McGraw-Edison*,[80] an employee was forcibly retired and promised a pension. Because he took no action in reliance on the promise of a pension, the employer's promise was not enforceable. However, in *Katz v. Danny Dare, Inc.*,[81] the defendant chose to accept the offer of a pension, rather than be fired, and was able to enforce the promise. There, the court rejected the employer's argument that the employee, as an employee-at-will, had not given up anything to which he was legally entitled, and that he had not relied on the employer's promise.

Promissory estoppel has also found its way into the construction contract bidding process. In the process of preparing a bid for a construction project a general contractor will usually seek bids from various subcontractors to perform discreet portions of the project on the general contractor's behalf. The general contractor uses these bids to calculate the amount of its own general contracting bid to the owner of the project. If one of the subcontractors attempts to back out of its offer, after the general contractor has entered into a deal with the owner of the project, but before the general has managed to get back to the subcontractor to accept, the general contractor is likely to be in a tight spot. It is bound to the terms of its contract with the owner, but may have lost its power to accept the subcontractor's offer.

Chain Co., 218 A.2d 526 (Conn. 1966); Sessions v. S. Cal. Edison Co., 118 P.2d 935 (Cal. Ct. App. 1941).

[78] Vastoler v. Am. Can Co., 700 F.2d 916 (3d Cir. 1983).

[79] 438 A.2d 1091 (R.I. 1982).

[80] 329 F.2d 412 (6th Cir. 1964).

[81] 610 S.W.2d 121 (Mo. Ct. App. 1980).

The general contractor might have paid the subcontractor for its reciprocal promise to keep its offer open, and thus enter into an option contract with the subcontractor, but this is not usually done. Likewise, the general contractor's use of the subcontractor's bid might be viewed as a contract between the parties that the subcontractor will be engaged to do the work, subject to the condition precedent that the contract is awarded to the general contractor by the owner. However, the usual understanding is that the general contractor has made no such commitment to the subcontractor simply by including the subcontractor's bid in the calculation of the general contractor's own offer.[82] In fact, general contractors are usually allowed to renegotiate terms with the subcontractors whose bids they have used after the general construction contract is awarded, or even to select a completely different subcontractor to perform the work, without being held liable to the subcontractor whose bid was used.[83]

The influential decision in *Drennan v. Star Paving Co.*[84] used promissory estoppel in this setting to prevent a subcontractor from revoking its offer, even if there had been no express promise that the offer could be kept open for the time necessary to permit the general contractor to learn whether it had been awarded the general construction contract. Drennan, a general contractor, used the Star Paving Co.'s bid in preparing its general contracting bid on a public school project. After Drennan learned that he had been awarded the job, Star Paving attempted to revoke its subcontracting bid for the paving portion of the job, claiming that it had made a clerical error in computing the amount of its offer. Drennan nevertheless expressed its acceptance of Star Paving's offer, and when Star refused to do the work unless it was paid more, Drennan hired one of Star's competitors to perform the work.

Before *Drennan*, courts had taken the conventional view that an offer was revocable unless there had been a promise supported by consideration to keep the offer open. In this context in particular, courts had expressed an unwillingness to apply promissory estoppel to a "bargain setting."[85]

In *Drennan*, California Chief Justice Traynor ruled that, given the context in which Star Paving's subcontracting bid had been submitted, there was an implied promise that the offer would not be revoked. In reaching this conclusion Traynor relied on decisions that make an offer for a unilateral contract irrevocable after the offeree has begun performance of the act sought.[86] He also held that the general

---

[82] Michael L. Closen & Donald G. Weiland, *The Construction Industry Bidding Cases: Application of Traditional Contract, Promissory Estoppel, and Other Theories to the Relations Between General Contractors and Subcontractors,* 13 J. MARSHALL L. REV. 565, 583 (1980); Franklin Schultz, *The Firm Offer Puzzle: A Study of Business Practice in the Construction Industry,* 19 U. CHI. L. REV. 237 (1952); Thomas J. Stipanowich, *Reconstructing Construction Law: Reality and Reform in a Transactional System,* 1998 WIS. L. REV. 463. *See* Holman Erection Co. v. Orville E. Madsen & Sons, Inc., 330 N.W.2d 693 (Minn. 1983).

[83] *E.g.,* Finney Co. Inc. v. Monarch Constr. Co., 670 S.W.2d 857 (Ky. 1984). *But see* R.S. Bennett & Co. v. Econ. Mech. Indus., Inc., 606 F.2d 182 (7th Cir. 1979).

[84] 333 P.2d 757 (Cal. 1958).

[85] James Baird Co. v. Gimbel Bros., Inc., 64 F.2d 344 (2d Cir. 1933) (L. Hand, J.).

[86] *See infra* § 4.05[B][3] Acceptance by Performance Alone: Unilateral Contracts.

contractor had reasonably relied on this implied promise by basing his own offer on the amount submitted in the subcontractor's bid: "when [the] plaintiff used [the] defendant's offer in computing his own bid, he bound himself to perform in reliance on the defendant's terms."[87] Courts since *Drennan* have been nearly unanimous in adhering to Justice Traynor's original approach.[88]

[F] Promissory Estoppel and the Statute of Frauds[89]

Promissory estoppel has also been used to circumvent the statute of frauds.[90] However, this particular deployment of the doctrine has been particularly controversial. Some jurisdictions have embraced the doctrine. Others have been more skeptical.[91]

For example, in *Brown v. Branch*,[92] the defendant backed out of his promise to give a house to his girlfriend, telling her that "if she moved back to Indiana" that she would always have the house they had lived in on State Route 135. The court ruled that her meager actions of giving up a modest job, ceasing her enrollment in a college business program, and moving back to their home in Indiana did not warrant the type of "unjust and unconscionable injury and loss" that warranted an exception to the statute of frauds. As explained in more detail elsewhere, this skepticism is particularly justified in situations involving contracts required to be in writing because their duration is longer than a year. In those cases an employee's partial performance does little to prove that the employer made a commitment to retain the employee for a definite time.[93]

In contracts for the sale of land, reliance is more likely to be used as a means to circumvent the statute. Buyers of land are less likely to partially perform, without

---

[87] 333 P.2d 757, 760 (Cal. 1958).

[88] RESTATEMENT (SECOND) OF CONTRACTS § 87(2) cmt. e & illus. 6 (1981). *E.g.*, Double AA Builders, Ltd. v. Grand State Constr., L.L.C., 114 P.3d 835 (Ariz. 2005); Alaska Bussell Elec. Co. v. Vern Hickel Constr. Co., 688 P.2d 576 (Alaska 1984). *See generally infra* § 4.09[C] Reliance on an Offer. *See also* Pavel Ent., Inc. v. A.S. Johnson Co., Inc., 674 A.2d 521 (Md. 1996) (insufficient evidence of general contractor's reliance). *But see* Home Elec. Co. v. Underdown Heating & Air Conditioning Co., 358 S.E.2d 539 (N.C. Ct. App. 1987) (declining to use promissory estoppel in this context).

[89] Stephen J. Leacock, *Fingerprints of Equitable Estoppel and Promissory Estoppel on the Statute of Frauds in Contract Law*, 2 WM. & MARY BUS. L. REV. 73 (2011); Gregory E. Maggs, *Ipse Dixit: The Restatement (Second) of Contracts and the Modern Development of Contract Law*, 66 GEO. WASH. L. REV. 508, 523–25 (1998).

[90] *See* RESTATEMENT (SECOND) OF CONTRACTS § 139(1) (1981) ("A promise which the promisor should reasonably expect to induce action or forbearance on the part of the promisee or a third person and which does induce the action or forbearance is enforceable notwithstanding the Statute of Frauds if injustice can be avoided only by enforcement of the promise.").

[91] Robert A. Brazener, Annotation, *Promissory Estoppel as Basis for Avoidance of Statute of Frauds*, 56 A.L.R.3d 1037 (1974).

[92] 758 N.E.2d 48 (Ind. 2001).

[93] *See* Goldstick v. ICM Realty, 788 F.2d 456, 465 (7th Cir. 1986) (Posner, J.); Tanenbaum v. Biscayne Osteopathic Hosp., Inc., 190 So. 2d 777 (Fla. 1966); Stearns v. Emery-Waterhouse Co., 596 A.2d 72 (Me. 1991).

having received a promise that the land will be conveyed.[94]

§ 3.04   PROMISSORY ESTOPPEL AS AN INDEPENDENT CAUSE OF ACTION[95]

Promissory estoppel was originally used merely as a substitute for consideration. In these cases, the promisee's reasonable and foreseeable reliance on the promisor's commitment prevented him from asserting that consideration was lacking.

However, there is another class of cases in which promissory estoppel has been used, not just as a way of getting around the lack of consideration, but as an independent basis for enforcing promises.[96] At times, this branch of the doctrine seems to completely swallow up the classical theory of consideration. These cases developed, for the most part, after these older promissory estoppel cases were formally recognized in § 90 of the First and Second Restatements of Contracts. Today, promissory estoppel is recognized as an independent "doctrine of contract law."[97]

[A]   Promissory Estoppel in the Restatements[98]

In what has been described as "the most important event in twentieth century American contract law,"[99] the drafters of the First Restatement[100] included § 90 as

---

[94] *See* Daigle Com. Group, Inc. v. St. Laurent, 734 A.2d 667 (Me. 1999); Johnson Farms v. McEnroe, 568 N.W.2d 920 (N.D. 1997).

[95] Lucian Ayre Bebchuck & Omri Ben-Sharrar, *Precontractual Reliance*, 30 J. LEGAL STUD. 423 (2001); Mary E. Becker, *Promissory Estoppel Damages*, 16 HOFSTRA L. REV. 131 (1987); Daniel A. Farber & John H. Matheson, *Beyond Promissory Estoppel: Contract Law and the "Invisible Handshake,"* 52 U. CHI. L. REV. 903 (1985); E. Allan Farnsworth, *Precontractual Liability and Preliminary Agreements: Fair Dealing and Failed Negotiations*, 87 COLUM L. REV. 217 (1987); Jay M. Feinman, *Promissory Estoppel and Judicial Method*, 97 HARV. L. REV. 678 (1984); Ofer Grosskopf & Barak Medina, *Regulating Contract Formation: Precontractual Reliance, Sunk Costs, and Market Structure*, 39 CONN. L. REV. 1977 (2007); Charles L. Knapp, *Reliance in the Revised Restatement: The Proliferation of Promissory Estoppel*, 81 COLUM. L. REV. 52 (1981); Michael B. Metzger & Michael J. Phillips, *The Emergency of Promissory Estoppel as an Independent Theory of Recovery*, 35 RUTGERS L. REV. 472, 499 (1983); Kevin M. Teeven, *A History of Promissory Estoppel: Growth in the Face of Doctrinal Resistance*, 72 TENN. L. REV. 1111 (2005).

[96] *See generally* Michael B. Metzger & Michael J. Phillips, *The Emergency of Promissory Estoppel as an Independent Theory of Recovery*, 35 RUTGERS L. REV. 472 (1983); Kevin M. Teeven, *The Advent of Recovery on Market Transactions in the Absence of a Bargain*, 39 AM. BUS. L.J. 289 (2002); Sidney W. DeLong, *The New Requirement of Enforcement Reliance in Commercial Promissory Estoppel: Section 90 as Catch-22*, 1997 WIS. L. REV. 943.

[97] Garwood Packaging, Inc. v. Allen & Co., 378 F.3d 698 (7th Cir. 2004) (Posner, J.).

[98] E. Allan Farnsworth, *Contracts Scholarship in the Age of Analogy*, 85 MICH. L. REV. 1406, 1454–62 (1987); Marco J. Jimenez, *The Many Faces of Promissory Estoppel: An Empirical Analysis Under the Restatement (Second) of Contracts*, 57 UCLA L. REV. 669 (2010); Charles L. Knapp, *Reliance in the Revised Restatement: The Proliferation of Promissory Estoppel*, 81 COLUM. L. REV. 52 (1981); Michael B. Metzger and Michael J. Phillips, *Promissory Estoppel and Reliance on Illusory Promises*, 44 SW. L.J. 841 (1990); Mark Movsesian, *Rediscovering Williston*, 62 WASH & LEE L. REV. 207 (2005); Kevin M. Teeven, *A Legal History of Binding Gratuitous Promises at Common Law: Justifiable Reliance and Moral Obligation*, 43 DUQ. L. REV. 11, 25 (2004).

[99] Peter Linzer, *Section 90 and the First Restatement — The Gilmore Version and the Evidence*

a supplement to its Holmesian definition of consideration as a bargained exchange:

> A promise which the promisor should reasonably expect to induce action or forbearance of a definite and substantial character on the part of the promisee and which does induce such action or forbearance is binding if injustice can be avoided only by enforcement of the promise.[101]

This language requires that there be a promise. The further element requiring that the promise be one that "the promisor should reasonably expect to induce [reliance]" has led most courts to insist that the promise must be "clear and definite." In *Stewart v. Cendant Mobility Services Corp.*,[102] the court said

> [a] fundamental element of promissory estoppel . . . is the existence of a clear and definite promise which a promisor could reasonably have expected to induce reliance. Thus, a promisor is not liable to a promisee who has relied on a promise if, judged by an objective standard, he had no reason to expect any reliance at all.

Indefinite statements of a present intent, which supply no assurances that the defendant's plans will not change, are not enough to invoke the doctrine.

The requirement of a clear and definite promise usually requires that the promise must be express. However, as the decision in *Drennan v. Star Paving Co.* demonstrates,[103] the promise may be implied.[104] In describing promissory estoppel, courts usually refer to the necessity of an "implied or express promise." Nevertheless, the promise must still be definite enough for the promisor to foresee that the promisee will be reasonably likely to rely on it, and courts have been cautious about implied promises that have a tendency to be "broad and vague."[105] Claims of reliance on an implied promise have frequently been made in employment settings, usually based on language disseminated in an employee handbook or company policy manual. In this context, courts have not been enthusiastic about employee claims that the implied promise was clear and definite enough to support a cause of action based on promissory estoppel. Thus, in *Norman v. Tradewinds Airlines, Inc.*,[106] an allegedly implied promise in an employee handbook that employees would not be fired without initial recourse to the employer's system of progressive employee discipline was insufficient to raise a claim of promissory estoppel.[107] Despite the example provided by *Drennan*, some courts have flatly ruled that an

---

from the Time, in A CONTRACTS ANTHOLOGY 338 (Peter Linzer ed., 1995).

[100] A somewhat disputed account of the inclusion of § 90 in the First Restatement can be found in Grant Gilmore, The Death of Contract 59–64 (1974). *See* Peter Linzer, *Section 90 and the First Restatement — The Gilmore Version and the Evidence from the Time*, in A CONTRACTS ANTHOLOGY 338–39 (Peter Linzer ed., 1995); Joseph M Perillo, *Twelve Letters from Arthur L. Corbin to Robert Braucher Annotated*, 50 WASH & LEE L. REV. 755, 768–69 (1993).

[101] RESTATEMENT OF CONTRACTS § 90 (1932).

[102] 837 A.2d 736, 742 (Conn. 2003).

[103] Copeland v. Baskin Robbins U.S.A., 96 Cal. App. 4th 1251, 1261, 1262 n.33 (2002).

[104] *E.g.*, Nappi v. Nappi Distrib., 691 A.2d 1198 (Me. 1997).

[105] *See* C & K Petro. Prods., Inc. v. Equibank, 839 F.2d 188, 192 (3d Cir. 1988).

[106] 286 F. Supp. 2d 575 (M.D.N.C. 2003).

[107] *See also* Galdieri v. Monsanto Co., 245 F. Supp. 2d 636 (E.D. Pa. 2002).

implied promise may not be used in a claim based on promissory estoppel.[108]

There must also, of course, be some reliance on the promise.[109] The Second Restatement makes this explicit. It makes a promise enforceable only if it "does induce . . . action or forbearance."[110] If the promisee does not rely, the promise is not enforceable. In *Blatt v. University of Southern California*,[111] a disappointed law student who was not elected to "Coif" claimed that he had studied harder in law school because of the school's promise that he would be eligible for membership if he earned sufficiently high grades. The court was skeptical about whether any action he took was in reliance on this promise, or was in order to obtain other benefits of scoring well on his exams.

The Second Restatement eliminated the requirement that the reliance be of a "definite and substantial character."[112] It provides:

> A promise which the promisor should reasonably expect to induce action or forbearance on the part of the promisee or a third person and which does induce such action or forbearance is binding only if injustice can be avoided by enforcement of the promise. The remedy granted for breach may be limited as justice requires.[113]

Despite the disappearance of the reference to this phrase from both the title and the text of § 90, courts still require that the promisee's reliance take some definite form.[114] And, despite the elimination of this element from the text of § 90, the requirement lives on both as a factor in determining whether the "injustice can only be avoided by enforcement of the promise" and in cases involving firm offers[115] and guaranty promises,[116] where the Second Restatement explicitly retains the requirement.[117] The mere likelihood of reliance is not enough.

Scholars have noted the distinction between two types of reliance: "performance reliance" and "enforcement reliance."[118] When the promisee realizes that the

---

[108] *See*, C & K Petro. Prods., Inc., v. Equibank, 839 F.2d 188, 192 (3d Cir. 1988); Constar, Inc. v. Nat'l Dist. Ctrs., Inc., 101 F. Supp. 2d 319 (E.D. Pa. 2000).

[109] Sidney W. DeLong, *The New Requirement of Enforcement Reliance in Commercial Promissory Estoppel: Section 90 as Catch-22*, 1997 Wis. L. Rev. 943, 953; Jay M. Feinman, *Promissory Estoppel and Judicial Method*, 97 Harv. L. Rev. 678 (1984); Stanley D. Henderson, *Promissory Estoppel and Traditional Contract Doctrine*, 78 Yale L.J. 343 (1969). *See also* John J. Chung, *Promissory Estoppel and the Protection of Interpersonal Trust*, 56 Clev. St. L. Rev. 37 (2008).

[110] Restatement (Second) of Contracts § 90 cmt. b (1981).

[111] 5 Cal. App. 3d 935 (1970).

[112] Gerald Griffin Reidy, Note, *Definite and Substantial Reliance: Remedying Injustice Under Section 90*, 67 Fordham L. Rev. 1217 (1998).

[113] Restatement (Second) of Contracts § 90 (1981).

[114] *E.g.*, Carroll v. Xerox Corp., 294 F.3d 231 (1st Cir. 2002).

[115] Restatement (Second) of Contracts § 87(2) (1981).

[116] Restatement (Second) of Contracts § 88 (1981).

[117] Charles Knapp, *Reliance in the Revised Restatement: The Proliferation of Promissory Estoppel*, 81 Colum. L. Rev. 52, 58–61 (1981).

[118] Sidney W. DeLong, *The New Requirement of Enforcement Reliance in Commercial Promissory Estoppel: Section 90 as Catch-22*, 1997 Wis. L. Rev. 943, 953.

promise is not legally enforceable, he may still rely on the likelihood of performance. The promisee may be encouraged to rely on the promise due to the promisor's past performance, or on the strength of the personal relationship between the parties. Enforcement reliance, on the other hand, can occur only when the promisee has some reasonable grounds to believe that the promise is legally enforceable, and that some remedy will be available if the promisor does not perform. In these cases, reliance is based not just on the credibility of the promisor, but also on the promisee's belief that the law will provide a remedy if the promisor fails to perform.[119]

The Second Restatement also makes it clear that promissory estoppel may be invoked by a third party who has relied on the defendant's promise where the promisor should reasonably expect its promise to induce reliance by a third person.[120] The illustration supplied by the Restatement refers to a secured creditor's promise to its borrower to release a portion of the collateral to enable the borrower to obtain a loan from another lender. If the lender makes a loan in reliance on the secured creditor's promise of this partial release, the Restatement explains, the new lender will be entitled to enforce the earlier creditor's commitment to provide the release.[121] Other claims by third parties have been permitted where reliance by the third party was clearly contemplated by the promisor, such as a potential franchisee's spouse,[122] a homeowner's association,[123] and the promisor's children, to cite just a few illustrations.[124]

The Second Restatement added language expressly permitting the court to limit the remedy granted for breach "as justice requires." As will be seen, this recognizes that a promise that is enforceable because of the promisee's detrimental reliance may not be enforceable to the full extent of the promisee or third party's lost expectations. Instead, relief may be limited to reimbursement of the expenses the promisee incurred in reliance on the promise.[125]

[B]   Precontractual Liability[126]

Adoption of the original version of § 90 in the First Restatement prompted courts to apply the newly articulated doctrine in ways that had not previously been

---

[119] John J. Chung, *Promissory Estoppel and the Protection of Interpersonal Trust*, 56 CLEV. ST. L. REV. 37 (2008).

[120] *See* RESTATEMENT (SECOND) OF CONTRACTS § 90 cmt. c (1981).

[121] RESTATEMENT (SECOND) OF CONTRACTS § 90 illus. 5 (1981).

[122] Hoffman v. Red Owl Stores, Inc. 133 N.W.2d 267 (Wis. 1965).

[123] Chesus v. Watts, 967 S.W.2d 97 (Mo. Ct. App. 1998).

[124] *See generally* Michael B. Metzger & Michael J. Phillips, *Promissory Estoppel and Third Parties*, 42 Sw. L.J. 931 (1988).

[125] *See infra* § 13.02[A][2] Promises Enforceable Under Promissory Estoppel.

[126] Lucian Ayre Bebchuck & Omri Ben-Sharar, *Precontractual Reliance*, 30 J. LEGAL STUD. 423 (2001); Mary E. Becker, *Promissory Estoppel Damages*, 16 HOFSTRA L. REV. 131 (1987); Daniel A. Farber & John H. Matheson, *Beyond Promissory Estoppel: Contract Law and the "Invisible Handshake,"* 52 U. CHI. L. REV. 903 (1985); E. Allan Farnsworth, *Precontractual Liability and Preliminary Agreements: Fair Dealing and Failed Negotiations*, 87 COLUM. L. REV. 217 (1987); Jay M. Feinman, *Promissory Estoppel and Judicial Method*, 97 HARV. L. REV. 678 (1984); Charles J. Goetz & Robert E. Scott,

imagined. Most significantly, it is sometimes used as a means of enforcing promises made by parties while they are engaged in negotiations leading up to the creation of a contract, even though it is clear that no final agreement has been reached. These "precontractual liability" decisions have a significant impact on the way parties must behave to avoid incurring unintended obligations.

Foremost among these cases is *Hoffman v. Red Owl Stores, Inc.*[127] Over a period of several years Mr. Hoffman was induced to sell his business, move his family, and invest his capital in a variety of business enterprises, with a promise that he would be awarded a Red Owl grocery store franchise at the end of his lengthy path. It was clear, however, that no traditional contract existed between the parties. Neither the precise location of the promised store, nor the terms of the lease, nor other aspects of the transaction had been negotiated at the time that Red Owl decided that Hoffman was not a suitable candidate to operate one of its stores. Despite the absence of a traditional contract, the court awarded relief to Hoffman, and awarded him damages for the expenses he had incurred in reliance on the defendant's encouragement.

The *Hoffman* court explained:

> Originally the doctrine of promissory estoppel was invoked as a substitute for consideration rendering a gratuitous promise enforceable as a contract. If promissory estoppel were to be limited to only those situations where the promise giving rise to the cause of action must be so definite with respect to all details that contract would result were the promise supported by consideration then the defendant's instant promises to Hoffman would not meet this test. However, § 90 does not impose the requirement that the promise giving rise to the cause of action must be so comprehensive in scope as to meet the requirements of an offer that would ripen into a contract if accepted by the promisee.[128]

In this passage the court clearly expands the doctrine of promissory estoppel beyond its original parameters. After *Hoffman*, promissory estoppel was available not only as a substitute for consideration, but also as a substitute for the kind of definite promise that would have been necessary, even if consideration had been present, to hold Red Owl responsible for leading Hoffman to believe that he would be awarded a franchise.

Decisions like *Hoffman* frequently arise in franchise, employment, and merger settings, where the parties are likely to have participated in extended negotiations,

---

Enforcing Promises: An Examination of the Basis of Contract, 89 YALE L.J. 1261 (1980); Robert A. Hillman, *Questioning the "New Consensus" on Promissory Estoppel: An Empirical and Theoretical Study*, 98 COLUM. L. REV. 580 (1998); Michael B. Metzger & Michael J. Phillips, *The Emergence of Promissory Estoppel as an Independent Theory of Recovery*, 35 RUTGERS L. REV. 472, 499 (1983); Jean Fleming Powers, *Promissory Estoppel and Wagging the Dog*, 59 ARK. L. REV. 841 (2007); Alan Schwartz & Robert E. Scott, *Precontractual Liability and Preliminary Agreements*, 120 HARV. L. REV. 661 (2007).

[127] 133 N.W.2d 267 (Wis. 1965). *See* Gregory M. Duhl, *Red Owl's Legacy*, 87 MARQ. L. REV. 297 (2003); Robert E. Scott, Hoffman v. Red Owl Stores *and the Myth of Precontractual Reliance*, 68 OHIO ST. L.J. 71 (2007); William C. Whitford & Stewart Macaulay, Hoffman v. Red Owl Stores: *The Rest of the Story*, 61 HASTINGS L.J. 801 (2010).

[128] 133 N.W.2d at 274.

leading to an increased hope by one of the parties that a deal will be concluded. Where the other party goes too far, and induces the other party to incur meaningful expenses in anticipation of concluding the transaction, liability may be found.

Reliance on this type of encouragement had occurred before *Hoffman v. Red Owl*, in *Goodman v. Dicker*.[129] In *Goodman*, the plaintiff similarly was induced to incur expenses in reliance on the prospect of being awarded a franchise with the defendant's company. Here, however, the defendant gave the plaintiff grounds to invoke equitable estoppel by falsely representing to the defendant that his application for a franchise "had been" approved. However, since *Hoffman*, promissory estoppel has been used as a means of protecting those who have relied on encouraging promises, similar to those made by Red Owl Stores, only to have their hopes dashed when the proposed franchise agreement was never consummated.[130]

More recent decisions in which promissory estoppel has been invoked in an effort to impose liability despite the absence of anything approximating a traditional contract include those involving employment-at-will contracts,[131] shopping center leases,[132] and reporters' promises of confidentiality.[133]

Despite the prominence accorded in first-year Contracts courses to § 90 and to cases like *Hoffman v. Red Owl*, claims of liability based on this expanded version of promissory estoppel have had some spectacular failures.[134] With a few outlying exceptions, employees-at-will have generally failed in pursuing claims of permanent employment by asserting reliance on their employer's promises of a more permanent arrangement, at least in the absence of some definite and unequivocal commitment that more closely approximates a traditional contract.[135] Likewise, courts have generally given effect to conspicuous disclaimers that attempt to make it clear that liability does not attach to representations made by the parties prior to the finalization of a comprehensive agreement.[136] In other cases, the defendant's encouragements have been so vague and indefinite that they do not qualify as promises, or are not sufficiently definite that any reliance on them can be

---

[129] 169 F.2d 684 (D.C. Cir. 1948).

[130] *E.g.*, Midwest Energy, Inc. v. Orion Food Sys., Inc., 14 S.W.3d 154 (Mo. Ct. App. 2000).

[131] Loghry v. Unicover Corp., 927 P.2d 706 (Wyo. 1996); Grouse v. Group Health Plan, Inc., 306 N.W.2d 114 (Minn. 1981). *But see* May v. Harris Mgmt. Corp., 928 So. 2d 140 (La. Ct. App. 2005) (unreasonable to rely on offer of employment at will). *See generally* Tracy A. Bateman, Annotation, *Employer's State-Law Liability for Withdrawing, or Substantially Altering, Job Offer for Indefinite Period Before Employee Actually Commences Employment*, 1 A.L.R.5th 401 (1992).

[132] Wheeler v. White, 398 S.W.2d 93 (Tex. 1965).

[133] *See* Cohen v. Cowles Media Co., 457 N.W.2d 199 (Minn. 1990).

[134] *See* Robert A. Hillman, *Questioning the "New Consensus" on Promissory Estoppel: An Empirical and Theoretical Study*, 98 COLUM. L. REV. 580 (1998); Juliet P. Kostritsky, *The Rise and Fall of Promissory Estoppel or Is Promissory Estoppel Really as Unsuccessful as Scholars Say It Is: A New Look at the Data*, 37 WAKE FOREST L. REV. 531 (2002).

[135] Stearns v. Emery-Waterhouse Co., 596 A.2d 72 (Me. 1991). *See* Sidney W. DeLong, *The New Requirement of Enforcement Reliance in Commercial Promissory Estoppel: Section 90 as Catch-22*, 1997 WIS. L. REV. 943, 1007.

[136] *Id.* at 1007–1011. *E.g.*, Empro Mfg. Co. v. Ball-Co Mfg., Inc., 870 F.2d 423 (7th Cir. 1989) (letter of intent expressly disclaimed legal consequences).

characterized as reasonable.[137] Significantly, in *W.R. Grace & Co. v. Taco Tico Acquisition Corp.*,[138] the court rejected a claim of promissory estoppel based on a letter of intent between the parties where the signed document specifically provided that neither party could rely on representations either of them made before a final deal was concluded.

Despite these failures, some scholars have noted the development of an even newer basis of liability that does not require proof of reliance. These scholars suggest that liability is found whenever there is an "invisible handshake" or a "promise made in furtherance of an economic activity."[139] Still others assert that promissory estoppel, together with a traditional bargain, is but another example of "manifested intent" or what they call a "consent" theory of contract liability.[140] It remains to be seen whether 50 years from now, in any Third Restatement of contracts that has yet to be promulgated, these new theories will receive the same attention that was given to Williston's and Corbin's views about detrimental reliance.[141]

§ 3.05   PROMISSORY ESTOPPEL IN INTERNATIONAL TRANSACTIONS[142]

Because it developed as an outgrowth of the limitations of the consideration doctrine, promissory estoppel did not develop on the European continent, where many modern principles of international contract law were developed. However, the injustice of failing to enforce a promise that has been relied on is widely recognized, and consequently, reasonable reliance provides the basis for enforcing promises in many situations in international trade.

[A]   Reliance Principles in International Sales

Several provisions of the United Nations Convention on the International Sale of Goods recognize the enforceability of promises that have been reasonably relied upon. Most significantly, Article 16(2)(b) makes an offer to enter into a contract irrevocable "if it was reasonable for the offeree to rely on the offer as being irrevocable and the offeree has acted in reliance on the offer."[143] In *Geneva*

---

[137] *E.g.*, Garwood Packaging, Inc. v. Allen & Co., 378 F.3d 698 (7th Cir. 2004).

[138] 454 S.E.2d 789 (Ga. Ct. App. 1995).

[139] Danel A. Farber & John H. Matheson, *Beyond Promissory Estoppel: Contract Law and the "Invisible Handshake,"* 52 U. Chi. L. Rev. 903, 904 (1985). Jay M. Feinman, *The Last Promissory Estoppel Article*, 61 Fordham L. Rev. 303, 304 (1992). *See also* Randy E. Barnett, *The Death of Reliance*, 46 J. Legal Educ. 518 (1996); James Gordley, *Enforcing Promises*, 83 Cal. L. Rev. 547 (1995); Edward Yorio & Steve Thel, *The Promissory Basis of Section 90*, 101 Yale L.J. 111, 113, 152–60 (1991).

[140] *See* Randy Barnett, *A Consent Theory of Contract*, 86 Colum. L. Rev. 269, 291–95 (1986).

[141] Alan Schwartz & Robert E. Scott, *Precontractual Liability and Preliminary Agreements*, 120 Harv. L. Rev. 661 (2007).

[142] David V. Snyder, *Comparative Law in Action: Promissory Estoppel, the Civil Law, and the Mixed Jurisdiction*, 15 Ariz. J. Int'l & Comp. Law 695, 700 (1998) (contending that claims based on promissory estoppel frequently result in damages based on lost expectations).

[143] CISG Art. 16(2)(b) (1980).

Pharmaceuticals Technology Corp. v. Barr Laboratories, Inc.,[144] the court considered whether to apply Article 16(2)(b), and recognized that it represented an international and somewhat "modified version of promissory estoppel that does not require foreseeability or [a] detriment."[145] Although the court ultimately chose not to apply § 16(2)(b), because the parties had not argued its applicability, the court went further and recognized that promissory estoppel claims made outside the area of firm offers could be preempted by the CISG in furtherance of the CISG's goal of uniformity.[146]

Article 29 also recognizes the significance of reliance on an otherwise unenforceable oral modification. Although Article 29 generally enforces contractual provisions requiring modifications to be in writing,[147] at the same time, it recognizes that a party may be "precluded by his conduct from asserting such a provision to the extent that the other party has relied on that conduct."[148] "Preclusion," of course, is synonymous with estoppel.

[B]   Reliance in Other International Transactions[149]

In other international transactions, reliance is also recognized as a basis for enforcing certain promises, though, as mentioned above, neither consideration nor promissory estoppel are generally required for enforcement of a promise under either the UNIDROIT Principles of International Commercial Contracts nor under Principles of European Contract Law. Like the CISG, UNIDROIT Principles recognize that "an offer cannot be revoked . . . if it was reasonable for the offeree to rely on the offer as being irrevocable and the offeree has acted in reliance" on it.[150] Principles of European Commercial Contracts contain a similar provision.[151]

Perhaps more significantly, both sets of principles impose an obligation on the parties to negotiate in good faith. They both acknowledge that the parties are "free to negotiate" and are "not liable for failure to reach an agreement."[152] However, they also make a party responsible for "losses caused to the other party" as a result of negotiating or breaking off negotiations "in bad faith."[153] Both sets of principles specify that beginning or continuing negotiations while intending not to reach an agreement with the other party constitutes bad faith.[154] These obligations can easily form a basis for imposing liability in situations like *Hoffman v. Red Owl*

---

[144] 201 F. Supp. 2d 236 (S.D.N.Y. 2002).

[145] *Id.* at 287.

[146] *Id.*

[147] CISG Art 29(2) (1980).

[148] *Id.*

[149] Nadia E. Nedzel, *A Comparative Study of Good Faith, Fair Dealing, and Precontractual Liability*, 12 Tul. Eur. & Civ. L.F. 97 (1997).

[150] PICC Art. 2.1.4(2)(b) (2004).

[151] PECL Art. 2.02(3)(c) (2002).

[152] PICC Art. 2.1.15 (2004); PECL Art. 2.301(1) (2002).

[153] PICC Art. 2.1.15(2) (2004); PECL Art. 2.301(2) (2002).

[154] PICC Art. 2.1.15(3) (2004). *See* PECL Art. 2.301(3) (2002).

in which American courts have imposed precontractual liability based on principles of reasonable reliance and promissory estoppel.

Chapter 4

MUTUAL ASSENT — CREATING AN AGREEMENT

    [F]   **Letters of Intent**

    [G]   **Good-Faith Negotiation in International Transactions**

§ 4.01 INTRODUCTION TO MUTUAL ASSENT

Mutual assent is one of two key elements of the contract formation process. The other is consideration and its substitutes. Where both mutual assent and consideration are present, a contract has been formed.[1] Mutual assent is normally, though not always, manifested through the process of offer and acceptance.[2] And, although it is mutual assent that is required, courts still usually refer to "offer, acceptance, and consideration" as the basic elements of a contract.[3]

Contractual obligations are based on the parties' expressions of assent. When a court finds "mutual assent," it means that the parties expressed their willingness to be bound to the same terms.[4]

Ordinarily, the first step in determining mutual assent is to analyze the communications between the parties to determine whether there is an offer. If the initial communication was a mere advertisement or some other preliminary stage in the negotiation process, later communications must be examined to determine if any of them is an offer. Once an offer is detected, the next step is to consider to whom it was directed and whether that person accepted. If so, and the resulting agreement involves consideration, a contract has been formed.

Lawyers are familiar with this basic approach of offer, acceptance, and consideration as the basic elements of a contract. The offer-and-acceptance model is often helpful, and frequently must be used in order to communicate rationally with courts and other lawyers about the contract formation process. At the same time, these touchstones are really nothing more than surrogates for the real question of whether the parties have expressed mutual assent to a set of reasonably ascertainable terms.[5] A contract can be made even though it is impossible to isolate the precise moment when it was formed.[6]

---

[1] RESTATEMENT (SECOND) OF CONTRACTS § 17 (1981).

[2] *E.g.*, Fletcher-Harlee Corp. v. Pote Concrete Contractors, Inc., 421 F. Supp. 2d 831, 833 (D.N.J. 2006).

[3] *E.g.*, Syncom Indus., Inc. v. Wood, 920 A.2d 1178, 1187 (N.H. 2007). *See also* D'Oliveira v. Rare Hospitality Intern., Inc., 840 A.2d 538, 540 (R.I. 2004) (where the plaintiff contended that the "contract was established the 'old-fashioned way' through an offer, acceptance and consideration.").

Courts sometimes mistakenly say that four elements are required: mutual assent, offer, acceptance, and consideration. Minster Farmers Coop. Exch. Co. v. Meyer, 884 N.E.2d 1056, 1061 (Ohio 2008). This is wrong. Offer and acceptance are merely one of the mechanisms through which mutual assent is found. *See* Reedy v. The Cincinnati Bengals, Inc., 758 N.E.2d 678, 682 (Ohio Ct. App. 2001) ("there must be a 'meeting of the minds' on the essential terms of the agreement, which is usually demonstrated by an offer and acceptance, and consideration").

[4] RESTATEMENT (SECOND) OF CONTRACTS § 3 (1981).

[5] RESTATEMENT (SECOND) OF CONTRACTS § 3 (1981).

[6] U.C.C. § 2-204(2) (2012).

§ 4.02   OBJECTIVE THEORY OF CONTRACT FORMATION[7]

Mutual assent is sometimes mistakenly understood to mean that both parties must subjectively intend to be bound. Because contract law can be seen as a means of enhancing individual autonomy,[8] which is itself an important principle in our law, searching for subjective commitment has some intuitive appeal. During the nineteenth century, courts sometimes analyzed the contract formation process by attempting to determine whether there had been a "meeting of the minds."[9] Modern decisions still use this archaic phrase, usually without considering its implications.[10]

But, the parties' subjective intent does not usually matter. Instead, contract formation depends on the outward manifestations of the parties' intent and how those manifestations are reasonably understood by the parties.[11] As Judge Learned Hand famously said:

> A contract has, strictly speaking, nothing to do with the [subjective] intent of the parties. A contract is an obligation attached by the mere force of law to certain acts of the parties, usually words, which ordinarily accompany and represent a known intent. If, however, it were proved by twenty bishops that either party when he used the words intended something else than the usual meaning which the law imposes upon them, he would still be held, unless there were some mutual mistake or something else of the sort.[12]

Or, as Professor Corbin explained: "Parties are bound by the reasonable meaning of what they said and not by what they thought."[13]

---

[7] Grant GILMORE, THE DEATH OF CONTRACT 42–44 (1974); Wayne Barnes, *The Objective Theory of Contracts*, 76 U. CIN. L. REV. 1119 (2008); Oliver Wendell Holmes, *The Theory of Legal Interpretation*, 12 HARV. L. REV. 417, 419 (1899); Duncan Kennedy, *From the Will Theory to the Principle of Private Autonomy: Lon Fuller's "Consideration and Form,"* 100 COLUM. L. REV. 94, 131 (2000); Melvin Aron Eisenberg, *Expression Rules in Contract Law and Problems of Offer and Acceptance*, 82 CAL. L. REV. 1127 (1994); Joseph M. Perillo, *The Origins of the Objective Theory of Contract Formation and Interpretation*, 69 FORDHAM L. REV. 427 (2000); Roscoe Pound, *The Role of the Will in Law*, 68 HARV. L. REV. 1, 5 (1954); Lawrence M. Solan, *Contract as Agreement*, 83 NOTRE DAME L. REV. 353 (2007). *See also* Ian R. Macneil, *Contracts: Adjustment of Long-Term Economic Relations Under Classical, Neo-Classical, and Relational Contract Law*, 72 NW. U.L. REV. 854, 884 (1978) (criticizing a purely objective theory of contract formation as expanding the scope of consent beyond the intention of the parties).

[8] *See* Joseph M. Perillo, *The Origins of the Objective Theory of Contract Formation and Interpretation*, 69 FORDHAM L. REV. 427 (2000).

[9] Professor Farnsworth has traced this phrase to the mistaken belief that the word "agreement" was originally derived from the Latin "agregatio mentium." *See* E. Allan Farnsworth, *"Meaning" in the Law of Contracts*, 76 YALE L.J. 939, 943–44 (1967).

[10] *E.g.*, Urban Sites of Chicago, LLC v. Crown Castle USA, 979 N.E.2d 480 (Ill. App. Ct. 2012); Minster Farmers Coop. Exch. Co. v. Meyer, 884 N.E.2d 1056, 1061 (Ohio 2008).

[11] *See* Schaer v. Webster County, 644 N.W.2d 327, 338 (Iowa 2002).

[12] Hotchkiss v. Nat'l City Bank, 200 F. 287, 293 (D.N.Y. 1911).

[13] Arthur L. Corbin, *Offer and Acceptance, and Some of the Resulting Legal Relations*, 26 YALE L.J. 169, 204–06 (1917) (as reprinted and revised by the author in Selected Readings on the Law of Contracts, 170, 197 (1931)).

This objective approach to contract formation is reflected in several sections of the Restatement (Second) of Contracts, which defines a "promise" in terms of "a manifestation of intent";[14] an "agreement" as a "manifestation of mutual assent";[15] and an offer as a "manifestation of willingness to enter into a bargain."[16]

One of the consequences of the objective theory of contract formation is that parties are bound to their agreements regardless of whether they subjectively considered themselves to be "legally" bound. The fact that the parties have not considered the potential legal consequences of their agreement is irrelevant.[17]

A key feature of the objective theory of contract formation is that people are usually bound by agreements they sign, even if they failed to read or understand them. As the court said in *Ray v. William G. Eurice & Bros., Inc.*: "absent fraud, duress, or mutual mistake, . . . one having the capacity to understand a written document who reads and signs it, or without reading it or having it read to him, signs it, is bound by his signature."[18]

Despite this focus on the objective meaning of the parties' outward expressions of intent, subjective intention is not completely irrelevant. For example, if it can be proven that *both* parties subjectively understand that no contract was intended, it is not binding. As the court said in *Kabil Developments Corp. v. Mignot*: "the staunchest 'objectivist' would not let a jury hold two parties to an apparently manifested agreement if neither thought the other meant to assent."[19] When both parties understand that the transaction is a sham or a joke, no contract is formed.[20]

Likewise, if the parties have manifested their intent *not* to be legally bound, their expressed intent will be honored. This rule sometimes applies to agreements found in employee handbooks or university catalogs that expressly disclaim any legal consequences.[21] On the other hand, courts sometimes enforce provisions regarding pension benefits described in employee handbooks, on the theory that they are unilateral contracts that the employee performed by completing performance for the requisite number of years.[22]

---

[14] RESTATEMENT (SECOND) OF CONTRACTS § 2 (1981).

[15] RESTATEMENT (SECOND) OF CONTRACTS § 3 (1981).

[16] RESTATEMENT (SECOND) OF CONTRACTS § 24 (1981).

[17] *See* Stevenson v. United Subcontractors, Inc., 365 Fed. Appx. 752, 754, 2009 U.S. App. LEXIS 27046, at *2 (9th Cir. Dec. 11, 2009).

[18] 93 A.2d 272, 278 (Md. Ct. Spec. App. 1952); MCC-Marble Ceramic Center, Inc. v. Ceramica Nuova D'Agostino, 144 F.3d 1384 (11th Cir. 1998) (party bound to terms of signed contract he did not read that was written in a language he did not understand).

[19] 566 P.2d 505, 509 (Or. 1977).

[20] *E.g.*, New York Trust Co. v. Island Oil & Trans. Corp., 34 F.2d 655 (2d Cir. 1929).

[21] *E.g.*, Ferrera v. A.C. Nielsen, 799 P.2d 458 (Colo. Ct. App. 1990) (conspicuous disclaimer in employee handbook); Bender v. Alderson Broaddus Coll., 575 S.E.2d 112 (W.Va. 2002); Tobias v. Univ. of Texas at Arlington, 824 S.W.2d 201 (Tex. App. 1991). *But see* Sanchez v. Life Care Ctrs. of Am., Inc., 855 P.2d 1256 (Wyo. 1993) (disclaimer in employee handbook insufficiently conspicuous to communicate lack of intent to be bound).

[22] *See, e.g.* McGrath v. R.I. Retirement Bd., 88 F.3d 12, 16–17 (1st Cir. 1996) (collecting cases). *See also* 29 U.S.C. § 1054(g) (2006) (ERISA provision preventing amendments that diminish employees' accrued benefits).

If parties do not regard the agreement as legally binding, there is no contract. This is frequently true of many casual social and family arrangements in which agreements are made for the purpose of convenience without intending them to have legal consequences.[23] So called "gentlemen's agreements" are similarly unenforceable where the parties have somehow expressed their understanding that their agreement, however morally and socially binding, was not meant to have legal consequences.[24] A somewhat disturbing aspect of this rule, as the court ruled in *Cohen v. Cowles Media Co.*, is that a reporter's promise of confidentiality may not be legally binding.[25]

A classic example of the primacy of the parties' objective manifestations is found in *Embry v. Hargadine, McKittrick Dry Goods Co.*[26] Embry was an employee of the Hargadine-McKittrick Dry Goods Company, under a written contract that expired on December 15, 1903. Embry alleged that on December 23, he spoke with Mr. McKittrick, and McKittrick orally agreed to hire him for an additional year. Nevertheless, at the end of the busy holiday season, Embry was laid off.

Resolution of the dispute depended on how their December 23rd conversation was reasonably interpreted. Embry claimed that McKittrick had promised to employ Embry for another year. McKittrick claimed that the conversation had been somewhat different from that claimed by Embry, but that in any event, he had not meant to hire Embry for another year. At trial, the court instructed the jury that it could find a contract only if "both parties *intended* by such conversation to contract with each other."[27]

On appeal, the court ruled that this instruction to the jurors was wrong. The court held that there would have been a contract based on Embry's version of the conversation, even "though McKittrick may not have intended to employ Embry . . . if what McKittrick said would have been taken by a reasonable man to be an employment, and Embry so understood it."[28] Thus, a contract could exist even if McKittrick had not meant to enter into one if a reasonable person could have understood McKittrick's outward manifestations of intent — his words and actions — as an expression of his willingness to enter into a contract, provided, of course, that Embry had in fact understood him to convey this meaning.

Thus, in evaluating whether an agreement exists, it is the outward manifestations of the parties' intent with which the law is primarily concerned.[29] Their intent is

---

[23] Mitzel v. Hauck, 105 N.W.2d 378 (S.D. 1960); Ethan J. Leib, *Friendship & the Law*, 54 UCLA L. REV. 631 (2007).

[24] Hirschkorn v. Severson, 319 N.W.2d 475 (N.D. 1982).

[25] 457 N.W.2d 199, 203 (Minn. 1990), *rev'd on other grounds*, 501 U.S. 663 (1991), *aff'd on remand on different grounds*, 479 N.W.2d 387 (Minn. 1992).

[26] 105 S.W. 777 (Mo. Ct. App. 1907).

[27] *Id.* at 778 (emphasis added).

[28] *Id.* at 779.

[29] *See also* Lucy v. Zehmer, 84 S.E.2d 516 (Va. 1954) (contract for sale of land enforced where the seller secretly intended the transaction as a joke because buyer reasonably understood the seller to have been serious).

relevant only to the extent that it may shed light on how their words and actions are reasonably understood.[30]

Still, subjective intent plays a role. If, in *Hargardine, McKittrick Dry Goods Co.*,[31] Embry had subjectively understood that his employer intended to delay making a decision until later in the year, Embry could not have claimed that a contract existed, even though a reasonable person might have interpreted the exchange otherwise. Thus, in *Keller v. Holderman*[32] an agreement to sell a $15 watch for $300 was not enforceable, because *both parties* understood that it was a joke. The fact that an objective observer, who was not in on the joke, would have interpreted the parties' exchange as serious did not matter.

Likewise, if the other party thought that the offer was serious, but was unreasonable in holding this belief, no contract is formed. This is illustrated by the decision in *Leonard v. Pepsico*,[33] in which a person was unable to accept an advertised proposal to sell a $23 million military Harrier Jet for 15 "Pepsi Points" and $700,000 (the price of 7 million additional "Pepsi Points") because no reasonable person viewing the ad would have understood it as a serious offer.

In evaluating whether a person has a reasonable belief that a proposal is serious, it is not only the words contained in their communications that control. Instead, words are to be interpreted against a wide range of other surrounding circumstances, including the context in which the words were used, the past history of the parties' dealings with one another, and any relevant business norms derived from the customary meaning of the parties' words in a particular geographic region or in the context of a particular trade or business.[34] Any accompanying gestures and inflections that might convey the meaning of their words are also relevant, as these too are part of the parties' outward manifestations of assent.

In international transactions a similar approach applies. CISG Article 8(1) specifies that "statements made by and other conduct of a party are to be interpreted according to his intent where the other party knew or could not have been unaware what that intent was."[35] Otherwise, the words "and conduct of a party are interpreted according to the understanding of a reasonable person . . . in the same circumstances."[36] UNIDROIT's Principles of International Commercial Contracts (PICC)[37] and its Principles of European Contract Law (PECL)[38] contain

---

[30] Kabil Dev. Corp. v. Mignot, 566 P.2d 505 (Or. 1977) (testimony regarding intent to enter into a contract admissible evidence).

[31] 105 S.W. 777 (Mo. Ct. App. 1907).

[32] 1863 Mich. LEXIS 20 (May 12, 1863).

[33] 88 F. Supp. 2d 116 (S.D.N.Y. 1999), *aff'd*, 210 F.3d 88 (2d Cir. 2000).

[34] This is most immediately evident from the definition of "agreement" in U.C.C. § 1-201(b)(3), which means "the bargain of the parties in fact" including not only their language but also terms "inferred from other circumstances, including course of performance, course of dealing, or usage of trade." U.C.C. § 1-201(b)(3) (2012).

[35] CISG Art. 8(1) (1980).

[36] CISG Art. 8(2) (1980).

[37] PICC Arts. 4.1, 4.2, 4.3 (2004).

[38] PECL Art. 5.101 (2002).

language similar to that in the CISG.

§ 4.03 DETERMINING WHETHER AN OFFER HAS BEEN MADE

[A] Offer and Acceptance[39]

The most basic method used to determine whether parties have reached an agreement is to examine the stream of communications between them to evaluate whether they have expressed mutual assent to the same terms.[40] This approach usually begins by determining whether one of the parties made an offer, and if so, whether the other party accepted it.

People usually begin their negotiations with expressions of interest or inquiries that fall short of an offer. These preliminary communications might consist of an advertisement, an inquiry about the price and availability of goods, or a "request for a proposal" (or "RFP"). These communications have no immediate legal consequences, though they may later be used to determine the meaning of any contract that is ultimately formed.[41]

This first manifestation of a commitment to be bound is referred to as an "offer." The person who makes an offer is the "offeror," and the person to whom it is directed is the "offeree."

Once an offer is made, the offeree has a "power of acceptance."[42] If the offeree exercises this power, by manifesting his assent and thus accepting, a contract is formed. The following sections provide a detailed examination of rules governing offer and acceptance.

[B] The Offer

An offer is a communication that objectively manifests a willingness to enter a bargain in a way that justifies another person in believing that his or her assent to the bargain is invited and will conclude it.[43] In other words, if one person says something that would be reasonably interpreted by another as a willingness to enter into a bargain and that the only thing left to be done to conclude the bargain is a simple "yes," an offer has been made. If, pointing to his bike, Miguel says: "Lance, I'll sell you this bicycle for $500 cash today," there is little doubt that the only thing remaining to be done to conclude the deal is for Lance to say "I'll buy it."

---

[39] Jason Scott Johnston, *Communication and Courtship: Cheap Talk Economics and the Law of Contract Formation*, 85 Va. L. Rev. 385 (1999); Avery Katz, *The Strategic Structure of Offer and Acceptance: Game Theory and the Law of Contract Formation*, 89 Mich. L. Rev. 215 (1990); Clark B. Whittier, *The Restatement of Contracts and Mutual Assent*, 17 Cal. L. Rev. 441 (1929); Peter Meijes Tiersma, Comment, *The Language of Offer and Acceptance: Speech Acts and the Question of Intent*, 74 Cal. L. Rev. 189 (1986).

[40] Restatement (Second) of Contracts § 22(1) (1981); PICC Art. 2.1.1 (2004).

[41] *See* Sayer v. Minn. Dept. of Transp., 790 N.W.2d 151 (Minn. 2010).

[42] Restatement (Second) of Contracts § 35 (1981).

[43] Restatement (Second) of Contracts § 24 (1981); PICC Art. 2.1.2 (2004) PECL Art. 2.201(1) (2002).

Because Miguel's intent is definite and unequivocal, and asks for nothing more than a simple expression of agreement from Lance to conclude the agreement, Miguel's statement is an offer.[44] If Miguel said "I might be willing to sell it to you," or "make me an offer to buy it for $500, and I'll decide what I want to do" it would not be an offer. These statements are equivocal, and make it clear that something beyond Lance's expression of assent is necessary to finalize the deal.[45]

[1]   Unequivocal Language[46]

In determining whether a particular communication is an offer courts usually consider whether the language was unequivocal. If the language falls short of expressing a willingness to enter into a binding agreement, or indicates that something other than the offeree's expression of assent is necessary to conclude the deal, there is no offer. Courts usually refer to these preliminary communications as "invitations to negotiate" or an "invitation to make an offer," which have no legal effect.[47]

Consider a basic example involving Sam, who thinks he wants to sell his BMW. If Sam initiates a conversation with Barb by saying, "I want to get at least $20,000 for my car," it would probably be unclear to Barb whether Sam's statement was an offer to sell his BMW to her for $20,000, an invitation to Barb to make an offer herself, or idle chit-chat. If Sam's language is an offer, then Barb can conclude the deal by expressing her assent by saying something like, "Great, I'll take it."[48] However, Sam's statement doesn't even come close to being an offer. At most, it is an invitation to negotiate.[49] Notice that Sam's statement about what he'd like to get for the car contains no words that Barb might reasonably interpret as a commitment to sell the car to her, or anyone else. It contains no words of commitment that she might reasonably interpret as a promise.

Because Sam's statement is at best an invitation to negotiate, any attempt Barb might make to accept will be ineffective. If Barb wants to buy the car, she will have to make an offer that Sam can either accept or reject. Alternatively, Barb might respond by saying something that is also too equivocal to qualify as an offer such as, "I might consider paying $18,000." Her use of the words "might consider" is equivocal and contains nothing expressing a commitment on her part, though it might convey information to Sam about the price she may be willing to pay. Under

---

[44] *See* RESTATEMENT (SECOND) OF CONTRACTS § 32 illus. 1 & 2 (1981).

[45] *See* RESTATEMENT (SECOND) OF CONTRACTS § 26 illus. 4 (1981).

[46] Peter Meijes Tiersma, Comment, *The Language of Offer and Acceptance: Speech Acts and the Question of Intent*, 74 CAL. L. REV. 189 (1986) (regarding the effect of words used in the parties' communications).

[47] *E.g.*, Jeneric/Pentron, Inc. v. Dillon Co., 171 F. Supp. 2d 49, 68 (D. Conn. 2001); RESTATEMENT (SECOND) OF CONTRACTS § 26 (1981).

[48] Because this is a contract for the sale of goods, with a price above the $500 threshold imposed by U.C.C. § 2-201, the statute of frauds may require a writing signed by the party against whom enforcement is sought. However, for the limited purposes of this example it will be useful to set aside any question about whether the agreement must be in writing. *See infra* Ch. 5, The Statute of Frauds: Is a Writing Required?

[49] RESTATEMENT (SECOND) OF CONTRACTS § 26 illus. 4 (1981).

these circumstances, ay attempt by Sam to "accept" would also be premature — there is no offer, and he does not have a "power of acceptance."[50] At this stage of the game, neither party has made a statement that is sufficiently unequivocal to qualify as an offer.

This illustration[51] is analogous to the well-known case of *Owen v. Tunison*[51] in which a prospective buyer inquired, "Will you sell me [certain property] for the sum of $6,000?" The owner replied, "Because of improvements . . . it would not be possible for me to sell it unless I was to receive $16,000 cash." The prospective buyer immediately responded, "[I] accept your offer." When the owner denied that a contract had been made the buyer sued. The court held that the owner's language did not manifest a willingness to sell. In other words, it could not have been reasonably understood as an expression of willingness to enter into a bargain. Instead, it was an invitation to open negotiations.[52] Equivocal language that cannot reasonably be understood as expressing a commitment to be bound is not an offer.

[2]   Reasonable Understanding of the Offeree

Whether language qualifies as an offer must be considered against the backdrop of all of the surrounding circumstances, including any prior relationship between the parties, and any earlier communications between them. An outside observer would be likely to conclude that Sam's expression of his interest in getting $20,000 for his car is not an offer to sell it. However, this conclusion assumes that Barb has no private information about Sam's real intentions other than what appears from the words themselves. In a more realistic situation, Barb's interpretation of Sam's statement would have to be analyzed with reference to the fuller context in which their conversation took place and against the background of their entire relationship. Any prior dealings between them are likely to be helpful in determining the reasonableness of whatever belief Barb has about Sam's intent.

For example, if Sam and Barb have conducted failed negotiations in the past, over a price of $22,000, with Barb expressing her willingness to pay $20,000, Barb might reasonably interpret Sam's statement as an offer. On the other hand, if they have regularly joked with one another about the Barb's purchase of Sam's car, she is probably not justified in regarding even an unequivocal statement of his willingness to sell it to her for $20,000 as an offer. The parties' reasonable interpretation of one another's words depends not just on the language itself, but on the content of any previous communications between them, including any shared community customs.[53]

If it was reasonable for Barb to interpret Sam's statement as an expression of his willingness to sell her the car for $20,000, we would say that Sam had made an offer

---

[50] *See* Fleming Co. of Neb., Inc. v. Michals, 433 N.W.2d 505 (Neb. 1988); Loughlin v. Idora Realty Co., 259 Cal. App. 2d 619 (1968); Henry v. Harker, 122 P. 298 (Or. 1912).

[51] 158 A. 926 (Me. 1932).

[52] *See also* Harvey v. Facey, 62 L.J.-P.C. 127, A.C. 552 (Privy Council 1893) (seller's response to buyer's request for the seller's lowest price, "Lowest cash price for [the property] £900," was not an offer as it did not manifest a willingness to sell).

[53] RESTATEMENT (SECOND) OF CONTRACTS § 26 cmt. a (1981).

to Barb to sell her the car for $20,000, and Barb has a "power of acceptance."[54] Her expression of agreement to the terms of Sam's offer would be an acceptance. Although neither Sam nor Barb used the words "offer" or "acceptance," these words have no magical effect, and their failure to use them does not matter. All that is relevant is whether their communications were reasonably understood as expressions of their mutual assent to the same deal.

[3] No Additional Steps Required

For a statement to be an offer, it must appear that are no barriers other than the offeree's acceptance that stand in the way of concluding an agreement. If further steps must be taken before the other party can accept, no offer has been made.

Consider, for example, whether there would have been an offer in the transaction between Sam and Barb if Sam had initiated the conversation with Barb by saying "I'm going to sell my car for $20,000; if you're interested, make me an offer at that price and I'll consider selling it to you." Here Sam's communication makes it clear that Barb's expression of a commitment to buy the car for $20,000 is not sufficient to finalize the bargain. Instead, it clearly communicates to Barb that Sam retains the right to make a final decision after Barb makes the suggested offer. A communication is not an offer if the recipient should have known that something in addition to his or her own assent was required to conclude the deal.[55]

There might also be other matters that need to be resolved before a deal can be concluded. The absence from Sam's statement of details about the time or place for performance might demonstrate that he believes that there are other matters to be resolved before a deal can be concluded. In more complex business transactions, the parties might agree to certain basic terms but refrain from expressing their final willingness to go through with the deal until these other matters have been resolved.

On the other hand, Sam and Barb may both be largely indifferent to the details of these other aspects of the transaction, so long as the contract is performed at a reasonable time and place. As will be seen, details concerning the time, place, and manner of performance are matters that sometimes can be resolved by the court, even though the parties have failed to agree.[56] In other circumstances they are of critical importance to the parties, and they are not bound until these details are agreed upon.

[4] Words Expressing Commitment

Use of specific words such as "offer," "bid," "propose," "promise," or other words of commitment strongly suggest a willingness to enter into a legally binding agreement. However, the mere presence of the word "offer" is not conclusive if

---

[54] *See* Restatement (Second) of Contracts § 35 (1981).

[55] Restatement (Second) of Contracts § 26 (1981). This same rule is used to prevent formation of a contract, even though the parties have settled on the terms of their agreement, where one of the parties has expressed his intent not to be bound until a later formal written memorial of the agreement is executed. Restatement (Second) of Contracts § 27 (1981). *See infra* § 4.03[C] Preliminary Negotiations.

[56] *See infra* § 4.11[B] Indefinite Agreements for the Sale of Goods.

other language or the context of the communication indicates that it is not intended to express a commitment.

For example, in *Moulton v. Kershaw*,[57] a salt dealer sent an advertising circular that said: "we are authorized to offer Michigan fine salt, in full car-loads of 80–95 bbl., delivered at your city, at 85¢ per bbl." The circular further specified that the seller would be "pleased to receive your order." The plaintiff replied, expressing its intent to "accept." When the seller refused to fill the order, the plaintiff claimed that the circular had been an offer. The absence of a definite quantity term in the circular, combined with the appearance of the communication as an advertisement, led the court to the conclusion that the circular could not have reasonably been interpreted as the seller's offer. Instead, it was merely an invitation by the seller to prospective buyers to submit offers that the seller would accept or reject.

Conversely, the absence of the word "offer" does not mean that the communication is not an offer. If the language of the communication unequivocally communicates that the decision of whether to enter into final agreement is up to the recipient, it is an offer, even though it has not been labeled as such.[58]

[5] Expression of Present Intent

It is sometimes necessary to distinguish between a statement of a *present intent* to do something and a *promise* to take action. The first indicates an intent to follow a plan of action, the second involves a commitment to take the planned action. Contracts are formed by promises, not mere statements of intent.[59]

This distinction was drawn in *Searles v. Trustees of St. Joseph's College*,[60] where a college basketball coach told an injured player's parents that the school intended to pay for their son's medical expenses. The court said a mere statement of present intent, indicating a general willingness to do something, is "insufficient to constitute an offer to enter into a contract."[61] Thus, a person's announcement of his current plans cannot necessarily be interpreted as a commitment to follow through with those plans.[62]

The same is true of predictions and opinions. A mere prediction of future events or an opinion about what is likely to happen in the future, does not rise to the level of an offer. Likewise, an opinion about the quality of land or goods, does not qualify as a warranty.[63]

---

[57] 18 N.W. 172 (Wis. 1884).

[58] *See, e.g.*, Fairmount Glass Works v. Grunden-Martin Woodenware Co., 51 S.W. 196 (Ky. Ct. App. 1899).

[59] My wife knows this distinction well: when I tell her that I "plan" to be home at 6:30, she knows that I'm merely expressing my intent and not making any kind of a commitment.

[60] 695 A.2d 1206 (Me. 1997).

[61] *Id.* at 1211–12.

[62] RESTATEMENT (SECOND) OF CONTRACTS § 2 cmt. e (1981).

[63] RESTATEMENT (SECOND) OF CONTRACTS § 2 cmt. f (1981).

[6] Indefinite Terms

Another important feature of an offer is its inclusion of all of the terms necessary to conclude a binding exchange.[64] A communication that fails to reasonably identify the essential terms of the deal cannot reasonably be interpreted as an expression of a willingness to enter into a contract. Moreover, without enough details about the transaction, a court would find it difficult to determine whether the parties had performed, or to frame a remedy for breach.[65] Thus, to constitute an offer a communication must usually be definite enough to disclose to whom the offer is extended, and to identify the subject matter of the proposed exchange. It is usually also necessary for the offer to include the price and other necessary details such as the time and place for performance. A communication containing all of these details is more likely to be reasonably interpreted as an expression of a willingness to enter into a bargain than one that leaves these details remaining to be resolved.

For example, if Craig, who owns two summer cottages, tells Dorothy, "I'll sell you my summer cottage for $350,000," but does not specify which of his two cottages that he was willing to sell, it will be difficult for a court to determine the terms of the agreement. Likewise, consider the difference between Sam telling Barb "I'll sell you my car, if you want it, for $20,000" and him telling her "I'll sell you my car, if you want it, provided we can settle on a price." The first communication leaves little to be resolved other than the time for performance, which would be construed to be a reasonable time.[66] And, although the U.C.C. permits the court to infer a reasonable price into a contract that has been formed without a resolution of the price,[67] Sam's second communication clearly expresses his intent not to be bound in the absence of an agreement about the price.

In contracts for the sale of goods, U.C.C. § 2-204(3) takes a flexible view about the details that must be included to make an agreement binding. It provides: "[e]ven though one or more terms are left open a contract for sale does not fail for indefiniteness if the parties have intended to make a contract and there is a reasonably certain basis for giving an appropriate remedy."[68] Thus, if the parties have expressed their intention to be bound, the court may enforce their agreement if it contains enough details for the court to frame a remedy.[69] However, the parties must have manifested their intent to be bound; if the lack of details shows that the parties lacked the intent to be bound, there is no contract.

---

[64] RESTATEMENT (SECOND) OF CONTRACTS § 33 (1981) ("reasonably certain"); CISG Art. 14 (1980) ("sufficiently definite"); PICC Art. 2.1.2 (2004) ("sufficiently definite"); PECL Art. 2.103(1) (2002) ("sufficiently defined").

[65] *See* RESTATEMENT (SECOND) OF CONTRACTS § 33(2) (1981) ("The terms of a contract are reasonably certain if they provide a basis for determining the existence of a breach and for giving an appropriate remedy.").

[66] U.C.C. § 2-309(1) (2012).

[67] U.C.C. § 2-305 (2012).

[68] U.C.C. § 2-204(3) (2012).

[69] *See* Mears v. Nationwide Mut. Ins. Co., 91 F.3d 1118 (8th Cir. 1996) (plaintiff won a prize entitling him to "two Mercedes-Benz automobiles" and the court resolved any contractual uncertainty about which model Benz the plaintiff was entitled to as the cheapest models available).

The Restatement takes a similar approach. A communication between the parties is not an offer "unless the terms of the [proposed] contract are reasonably certain."[70] However, the common law provides less leeway than the Code. For example, the common law has been far less forgiving with respect to unresolved price terms than the U.C.C.[71] In cases involving real estate and services, courts are far less willing to set the price, when the parties have not agreed, than they are in cases involving a sale of goods.

In international transactions the rule is the same. The CISG regards a proposal as an offer only "if it is sufficiently definite and indicates the intention of the offeror to be bound in the case of acceptance."[72] UNIDROIT's Principles of International Commercial Contracts uses this same language,[73] and the Principles of European Commercial Contracts specify that a contract is concluded if the parties intended to be bound and "they reach a sufficient agreement"[74] that is "sufficiently defined by the parties so that the contract can be enforced."[75]

[C] Preliminary Negotiations[76]

A contract is created when the parties express their assent to the same terms. People frequently exchange a series of communications while discussing a possible contract. Some of these communications may be offers or acceptances, while others are not. Sellers, of course, need a way to provide information about their goods and services to potential buyers, and advertisements and price quotations serve this function well. However, contract law rarely interprets these initial probes as offers. They do not manifest a definite willingness to deal on the terms included in the broadcast with every potential customer who might see the advertisement and wish to enter into a deal. When the ads are successful and potential buyers appear, negotiations can begin in earnest, and offers are sometimes made. Sometimes these offers are immediately accepted; on other occasions, they lead to further negotiations.

However, even after negotiations begin, it sometimes remains difficult to determine at just what point, if any, one of the parties has made an offer. All human interaction involves some degree of "getting acquainted," and contract negotiations are no exception. The law of contracts permits people, usually sellers, to disseminate information to attract prospective customers without becoming fully committed. This allows people leeway in early negotiations before the point of imminent legal obligation is reached.

---

[70] RESTATEMENT (SECOND) OF CONTRACTS § 33(1) (1981).

[71] *See infra* § 4.11[A] Effect of Missing Terms on Contract Formation.

[72] CISG Art. 14(1) (1980).

[73] PICC Art. 2.1.2 (2004).

[74] PECL Art. 2.101(1) (2002).

[75] PECL Art. 2.103(1) (2002).

[76] Melvin A. Eisenberg, *Expression Rules in Contract Law and Problems of Offer and Acceptance*, 82 CAL. L. REV. 1127 (1994).

[1] Price Quotations

Cases involving price quotations illustrate the difficulty in distinguishing between offers and invitations to negotiate. Sellers frequently advertise their prices. These advertisements are rarely offers. However, prospective customers frequently contact sellers and inquire about the seller's prices. A seller's response might easily express the seller's unequivocal willingness to enter into a transaction with the buyer. On the other hand, it might be nothing more than a more narrowly directed advertisement and thus intended only to supply information to the customer about the prices the seller is generally willing to entertain. The response might even be nothing more than an advertising circular about the nature of the goods available from the seller and the prices that the seller usually charges. In both of these situations the seller's willingness to enter into a contract to sell a specified quantity of the advertised items depends on whether the seller has a sufficient quantity to meet the demand.

Fairmount Glass Works v. Crunden-Marten Woodenware Co.,[77] illustrates the problem. The buyer sent an inquiry to the seller seeking information about the price it wanted for a specific quantity of the seller's glass jars. The seller replied: "Replying to your favor of April 20, we quote you Mason fruit jars, complete, in one-dozen boxes, delivered in East St. Louis, Ill.: Pints $4.50, quarts $5.00, half gallons $6.50, per gross, for immediate acceptance, and shipment not later than May 15, 1895; sixty days' acceptance, or 2 off, cash in ten days." The court recognized that there was a wealth of authority that refused to treat price quotes of this type as offers. Nevertheless, phrase "for immediate acceptance" led the court to conclude that the quote was an offer. The court explained: "We can hardly understand what was meant by the words 'for immediate acceptance,' unless the latter was intended as a proposition to sell at these prices if accepted immediately."[78] Accordingly, the buyer's subsequent unequivocal reply: "Enter order ten car loads as per your quotation. Specifications mailed" was an acceptance.[79]

Despite the holding in *Fairmont Glass Works*, price quotations of this sort are not usually offers. Instead, they are invitations to negotiate or to submit an offer.[80] The law usually treats the word "quote" as a mere invitation to make an offer and not an expression of a commitment to deliver the goods at the quoted price.[81] This demonstrates the role of industry custom or "usage of trade"[82] in deciphering the meaning of communications between actors in the marketplace, while *Fairmont Glass Works* demonstrates how the specific language used by the parties can override the customary meaning of certain terms.

---

[77] 51 S.W. 196 (Ky. 1899).

[78] *Id.* at 197.

[79] *Id. See also* Southworth v. Oliver, 587 P.2d 994 (Or. 1978) (response to request for price of real estate known to be available for sale reasonably construed as an offer).

[80] Kraft Foods N. Am., Inc. v. Banner Eng'g & Sales, Inc., 446 F. Supp. 2d. 551, 568 (E.D. Va. 2006); Dean Foods Co. v. Brancel, 187 F.3d 609, 619 (7th Cir. 1999).

[81] RESTATEMENT (SECOND) OF CONTRACTS § 26 cmt. c & illus. 3 (1981).

[82] U.C.C. § 1-303(c) (2012) (formerly U.C.C. § 1-205).

The fact that the price quote was not sent in response to an inquiry from the buyer does not necessarily transform the quote into an offer. In *Nebraska Seed Co. v. Harsh*,[83] a farmer's letter to a seed dealer, "I have about 1,800 bu. or thereabouts of millet seed of which I am mailing you a sample. . . . I want $2.25 per cwt for this seed f.o.b. Lowell," was not an offer. This language did not communicate the farmer's unequivocal willingness to sell his millet seed to the recipient of the letter at the stated price, but merely informed the recipient that the goods were available. In this respect it was similar to the type of language that might appear "in an advertisement, or circular addressed generally to those engaged in the seed business." A similar result was reached in *Moulton v. Kershaw*,[84] where the seller sent the buyer a notice that it had a quantity of salt available for sale, even though the notice said that the seller was "authorized to offer" the salt for sale at a price of 85 cents per barrel, where it also indicated that the seller "shall be pleased to receive your order."

The fact that the fact that the seller's price quote was sent in reply to an inquiry generated by the seller's advertisement does not resolve the issue. In *Lonergan v. Scolnick*,[85] the seller placed a newspaper ad indicating the availability of a tract of real estate. The ad generated an inquiry from a prospective buyer. In replying to this inquiry the owner sent a "form letter" describing the land in greater detail, giving directions to the land, and stating that his rock-bottom price was $2,500. The court treated the letter as nothing more than a price quote intended to solicit offers and not as a binding commitment on the owner's part to sell the land to the inquiring buyer for a price of $2,500.

In all of these cases courts err on the side of resisting the conclusion that a contract was formed. Moreover, the precise holdings of cases such as these are of limited precedential value because resolution of the issue usually depends on a variety of complex factors that are not limited to the precise language involved. The principal inquiry, in the language of the Restatement, is whether the recipient "had a reasonable belief that his assent to a bargain is invited and will conclude it." In most cases this depends not just on the language contained in the communication, but on industry customs and practices relevant to the transaction, exchanges of information between the parties in the past, and even the format of the communications. The same phrase contained in a newspaper ad might reasonably be construed completely differently if used in a face-to-face conversation. Likewise, words used at the outset of a series of communications might reasonably be construed differently than the same phrase expressed after a previous lengthy discussion.

---

[83] 152 N.W. 310 (Neb. 1915).

[84] 18 N.W. 172 (Wis. 1884).

[85] 129 Cal. App. 2d 179 (1954).

[2]   Advertisements[86]

[a]   Advertisements Not Offers

As these decisions regarding price quotations suggest, advertisements, catalogs, and advertising circulars are not usually offers.[87] Language used in advertisements usually suggests a mere interest in entering into a transaction on the advertised terms. However, it would be unreasonable to believe that the person who circulated the advertisement was willing to expose itself to the potentially unlimited liability that would result if the ad were treated as an offer.[88] If advertisements were considered offers, they could potentially be accepted by anyone *or everyone* who happened to see it.

Reconsider our example involving Sam's desire to sell his used BMW. Assume that Sam placed an ad on the Internet that says:

For sale, 20010 BMW 328xi with only 40,000 miles and all service records.

$22,000. Call Sam at 444–4444.

This ad clearly conveys Sam's interest in selling his car, but the ad is not an offer. Consider the consequences that would result if it were treated as one. If Sam's ad is an offer it has created a power of acceptance in anyone who sees it. If so, and Barb responded to the ad and said: "I'll take the BMW," a contract will be formed. To many people this seems a natural interpretation of Sam's ad and Barb's response. However, the law takes a different and more sensible approach.

Sam's ad is not treated as an expression of Sam's commitment to actually sell his car to whoever responds favorably to the ad. Instead, it is nothing more than an invitation to potential buyers to contact Sam for further discussions that could lead to the sale of the car. Most advertisements are "invitations to negotiate" rather than offers to sell. If the ad were an offer, Sam could end up bound to sell the car to dozens, if not hundreds of prospective buyers, like Barb, who call and say "I accept."

It would be disastrous to bind a seller like Sam to multiple contracts when he or she had only one item to sell. Moreover, treating a dealer's advertisement as an offer would expose it to potentially unlimited liability. In most cases it would be unreasonable for any person who read the ad to believe that by placing it the seller had intended to expose itself to this type of potentially unlimited risk. Accordingly, most advertisements are not offers.[89]

---

[86] Melvin Aron Eisenberg, *Expression Rules in Contract Law and Problems of Offer and Acceptance*, 82 CAL. L. REV. 1127, 1166 (1994); Jay M. Feinman & Stephen R. Brill, *Is an Advertisement an Offer? Why It Is, and Why It Matters*, 58 HASTINGS L.J. 61 (2006); Don F. Vaccaro, Annotation, *Advertisement Addressed to Public Relating to Sale or Purchase of Goods at Specified Price as an Offer the Acceptance of Which Will Consummate a Contract*, 43 A.L.R.3d 1102 (1972).

[87] RESTATEMENT (SECOND) OF CONTRACTS § 26 cmt. b (1981). *But see* Melvin A. Eisenberg, *Expression in Rules in Contract Law and Problems of Offer and Acceptance*, 82 CAL. L. REV. 1127, 1166–72 (1994) (reporting that the majority of modern cases have imposed liability on the advertiser, though frequently for violating a state consumer protection statute, rather than for breach of contract).

[88] *See* Mesaros v. United States, 845 F.2d 1576, 1580 (Fed. Cir. 1988).

[89] *See generally* Donovan v. RRL Corp., 27 P.3d 702 (Cal. 2001).

This result can be seen in cases like *Moulton v. Kershaw*,[90] in which an advertising circular announcing the availability of the goods and the price at which the seller was likely to be willing to sell, was not an offer.[91] The same result is almost certain regardless of the medium in which the advertisement is circulated, whether it is disseminated in a newspaper,[92] a catalog,[93] or price list.[94] The rule was reinforced in *Pepsico v. Leonard*,[95] in which a television ad that jokingly suggested the availability of a Harrier fighter jet in exchange for 7,000,000 "Pepsi Points" was treated as not reasonably understood as an expression of a willingness to be bound, in part because of the rule that advertisements are not normally considered to be offers.[96]

The rule is no different in international sale-of-goods transactions. Article 14 of the CISG indicates that "a proposal other than one addressed to one or more specific persons is to be considered merely as an invitation to make offers."[97] UNIDROIT Principles of Commercial Contracts do not seem to address the issue. However, the Principles of European Contract Law take a different position. They indicate that a professional supplier's proposal to supply goods or services at a specific price "is presumed to be an offer . . . at that price until the stock of goods, or the supplier's capacity to supply the service, is exhausted" even if the proposal appears in a public advertisement or a catalog.[98] European principles treat advertisements as offers, but limit them to the quantity of stock on hand.

[b]   Advertisements Making Definite Offer

Despite the normal rule, some advertisements eliminate the features that prevent them being offers. In *Lefkowitz v. Great Minneapolis Surplus Store*,[99] a store placed a newspaper ad stating that one fur stole would be sold for one dollar to the first person to appear at the store on a particular Saturday. The plaintiff was first to express a desire to purchase the fur stole for the advertised price, but the store refused to sell it to him. The store asserted a previously unmentioned "sales to ladies only" policy that the court refused to let it apply, and also asserted the usual rule that an advertisement was not an offer. In holding for the plaintiff the

---

[90] 18 N.W. 172 (Wis. 1884).

[91] *See also* Neb. Seed Co. v. Harsh, 152 N.W.310 (Neb. 1915) (Advertising circular saying "I have about 1800 bu. of millet seed. I want $2.25 per cwt for this seed f.o.b. Lowell" was not an offer); Rhen Marshall, Inc. v. Purolator Filter Div'n, 318 N.W.2d 284 (Neb. 1982) (advertising circular expressing premiums which would be awarded to customers who ordered specified quantities of merchandise did not constitute an offer).

[92] *E.g.*, Ehrlich v. Willis Music Co., 113 N.E.2d 252, 252 (Ohio Ct. App. 1952) (newspaper ad describing the goods, the price, and the seller's name was merely an invitation to patronize the store).

[93] Litton Microwave Cooking Prods. v. Leviton Mfg. Co., 15 F.3d 790 (8th Cir. 1994).

[94] Audio Visual Assoc., Inc. v. Sharp Elec. Corp., 210 F.3d 254 (4th Cir. 2000); Schumacher & Co. v. Silver Wallpaper & Paint Co., 810 F. Supp. 627, 633 (E.D. Pa. 1992).

[95] 88 F. Supp. 2d 116 (S.D.N.Y. 1999).

[96] *See also* Mesaros v. United States, 845 F.2d 1576 (Fed. Cir. 1988).

[97] CISG Art. 14(2) (1980).

[98] PECL Art. 2.201(3) (2002).

[99] 86 N.W.2d 689 (Minn. 1957).

court determined that the advertisement was quite specific and definite and clearly seemed to be an offer to sell to the first person to appear. Most importantly, the ad's limiting phrase "first-come first-served," eliminated the danger that the seller would have multiple obligations thrust upon it.[100]

The court's decision in *Lefkowitz* demonstrates that an advertisement can operate as an offer if it is sufficiently limited to avoid the problem of potentially unlimited liability.[101] Advertisements of rewards and prizes are usually limited in the same manner as the ad in *Lefkowitz* because the nature of the reward offer, such as for the return of a lost pet, is inherently susceptible to acceptance by only one person. Even where the offer for the reward might be accepted by more than one person, such as one seeking information leading to the arrest and conviction of a criminal, the terms of the reward usually make it clear that the amount offered is the maximum amount available, with the implication that the amount of the reward will have to be shared if more than one person supplies the information leading to the culprit's arrest.

The English decision in *Carlill v. Carbolic Smoke Ball Co.*[102] provides an unusual example of an advertisement that was properly treated as an offer, even though it exposed the offeror to potentially unlimited liability. The advertisement promised a £100 reward to "any person who contracts [the flu] after using the [carbolic smoke ball] three times daily for two weeks according to the printed directions supplied with each ball." Although the ad neither designated a specific offeree nor limited itself to a specific number of potential claimants, the court treated the ad as an offer. By manifesting its willingness to pay a £100 reward to *any person* who qualified, the defendant had effectively assumed the risk of potentially unlimited liability.[103] The manufacturer of the smoke ball promised to pay £100 to anyone who could prove that its claims were wrong and thus expressed indifference to the risk of potentially unlimited liability. It was precisely the manufacturer's willingness to expose itself to this risk that made the advertisement effective.

More modern decisions, such as those in *Izadi v. Machado Ford, Inc.*[104] and *Chang v. First Colonial Savings Bank*,[105] sometimes treat advertisements as offers if they would lead a reasonable person to believe that the proposed deal was available to anyone. In *Izadi*, an auto dealer was bound to the terms of an ad that indicated its willingness to provide a $3,000 minimum trade-in allowance to anyone who "buy[s] a new Ford."[106] In *Chang*, a bank's newspaper ad promising $20,136.12 upon maturity of a $14,000 savings certificate was "clear, definite, and explicit" and

---

[100] *See* Mesaros v. United States, 845 F.2d 1576, 1581 (Fed. Cir. 1988) (distinguishing an advertisement for certain Statue of Liberty coins distributed by the United States Mint that did not contain the limiting language that led to the result in *Lefkowitz*).

[101] Chang v. First Colonial Sav. Bank, 410 S.E.2d 928 (Va. 1991).

[102] 1 Q.B. 256 (1893).

[103] *See also* RESTATEMENT (SECOND) OF CONTRACTS § 26 illus. 2 (1981).

[104] Izadi v. Machado Ford, Inc., 550 So. 2d 1135 (Fla. Dist. Ct. App. 1989).

[105] 410 S.E.2d 928, 930 (Va. 1991).

[106] 550 So. 2d 1135 (Fla. Dist. Ct. App. 1989). Whether the seller was bound was left for later

"left nothing open for negotiation," and thus constituted an offer to anyone who purchased the $14,000 CD.

Information in product advertisements might also provide the basis for a claim of breach of warranty by someone who purchases the advertised item. Probably to encourage the development of commerce, courts traditionally avoided requiring advertisers to back up their claims, which were usually indefinite enough to avoid rising to the level of a warranty. A certain amount of "puffing" is to be expected and permitted. However, a claim for breach of warranty can be based on any "affirmation of fact or promise . . . or description of the goods."[107] Although representations that an item is in "good shape" or of the "highest quality" are unlikely to amount to a warranty,[108] more definite advertisements like "18 miles per gallon on the highway," can form the basis for a claim for breach of warranty.[109]

Modern courts have demonstrated a greater willingness to find that an advertisement might rise to the level of a warranty, provided it is more than a mere opinion. To be a warranty, the ad must be a statement of fact, a definite promise, or a description.[110] The problem of potentially unlimited liability is not a concern in these cases, because liability is limited to the number of items actually sold — no warranty is made to those who do not purchase the goods.

[c]   Effect of Consumer Protection Statues on Advertisements

Advertisements are also regulated to some extent by various governmental agencies, including the Federal Trade Commission, the Food and Drug Administration, and state attorneys general under a variety of federal and state regulatory schemes.[111] For example, many states administer rules prohibiting "bait and switch" advertising schemes by prohibiting businesses from advertising products that are not available in quantities sufficient to meet the anticipated demand.[112] Other statutes regulate "false and misleading advertising."[113] Decisions

---

resolution by a jury. But, the ad was not a mere invitation as a matter of law. *See also* Johnson v. Capital City Ford, Co., 85 So. 2d 75 (La. Ct. App. 1955).

[107] U.C.C. § 2-313(1) (2012). *See generally infra* § 7.02 Express Warranties Concerning Goods.

[108] *E.g.*, Pell City Wood, Inc. v. Forke Bros. Auctioneers, Inc., 474 So. 2d 694 (Ala. 1985) (statement that trucks were in "good condition" and "ready to work tomorrow" not a warranty); *but see* Wat Henry Pontiac v. Bradley, 210 P.2d 348 (Okla. 1949) (car described as in "A-1 shape" and "mechanically perfect" was a warranty).

[109] *See* Royal Bus. Machs., Inc. v. Lorraine Corp., 633 F.2d 34 (7th Cir. 1980) (representation that a copying machine would not cause fires was an affirmation of fact that formed the basis for a claim for breach of warranty).

[110] *E.g.*, Rocky Mtn. Helicopters, Inc. v. Bell Helicopter Textron, Inc., 24 F.3d 125 (10th Cir. 1994); Connick v. Suzuki Motor Co. Ltd., 656 N.E.2d 170 (Ill. App. Ct. 1995).

[111] *See* Jonathan Sheldon & Carolyn L. Carter, Unfair and Deceptive Acts and Practices App. A (6th ed. 2004).

[112] *E.g.*, Ohio Admin. Code. § 109:4-3-03 (2001). The ad in *Izadi v. Machado Ford, Inc.*, 550 So. 2d 1135 (Fla. Dist. Ct. App. 1989), violated a similar Florida statute.

[113] Keith R. Fentonmiller, *Reflections on the Mirror Image Doctrine: Should the Federal Trade*

under these provisions sometimes hold sellers liable, not for breach of contract, but for violation of the relevant consumer protection statute.[114] These rules and statutes should not be confused with common law or statutory rules regarding contract formation.

[D]   Jokes and Hoaxes[115]

Questions occasionally arise about whether a person can become bound to a contract as a result of his or her attempt to play a joke on someone. This is what happened in *Lucy v. Zehmer*.[116] The Zehmers owned a farm that Lucy had previously expressed an interest in buying. They were dining with friends at a tavern when a discussion arose between Mr. Zehmer and Mr. Lucy over whether the Zehmers' farm was for sale and whether Lucy was capable of paying for it. After some give and take the parties seemed to reach an agreement and they wrote the details of the deal on the back of one of the tavern's dinner bills. Mr. Zehmer signed the document and took the further step of having his wife sign, but later refused to convey title to the farm to Lucy, claiming that the entire transaction had been nothing more than a joke.

In concluding that Lucy's belief that the Zehmers had acted in earnest was reasonable, the court considered a variety of factors. It noted that the parties had gone to the trouble of reducing their agreement to written form, containing the signatures of both Mr. and Mrs. Zehmer, and redrafting the text of the original writing so that it clearly represented an agreement of both Mr. and Mrs. Zehmer. The writing contained a provision requiring that title would be satisfactory to the buyer. Moreover, the court found that the price for the land was reasonable. All of these factors made it appear to Lucy that Zehmer was serious. As a result, the court enforced the agreement.

Much the same analysis was employed in *Leonard v. Pepsico*,[117] where there was no contract based on a television advertisement that Pepsico ran containing a facetious "offer" to sell a military "Harrier Jet" — a $23 million aircraft — for 7,000,000 "Pepsi Points" costing only $700,000.[118] Because the plaintiff could not have reasonably understood it as serious, his attempt to accept the "offer" was unavailing.

In *Leonard v. Pepsico*, *Lucy v. Zehmer*, and other similar cases involving alleged jokes, the principal question is whether the joke was reasonably understood as a serious commitment. If the words themselves, or the context in which they are communicated, reveal that one of the parties is not serious, or that he is not yet

---

Commission Regulate False Advertising for Books Promising Wealth, Weight Loss, and Miraculous Cures?, 110 W. Va. L. Rev. 573 (2008).

[114] *E.g.*, Donovan v. RRL Corp., 27 P.3d 702 (Cal. 2001) (applying Cal. Vehicle Code § 11713.1).

[115] Keith A. Rowley, *You Asked for It, You Got It . . . Toy Yoda: Practical Jokes, Prizes and Contract Law*, 3 Nev. L.J. 526 (2003).

[116] 84 S.E.2d 516 (Va. 1954).

[117] 88 F. Supp. 2d 116 (S.D.N.Y. 1999), *aff'd*, 210 F.3d 88 (2d Cir. 2000).

[118] *See* Keith A. Rowley, *You Asked for It, You Got It . . . Toy Yoda: Practical Jokes, Prizes and Contract Law*, 3 Nev. L.J. 526 (2003).

ready to make a commitment to conclude a transaction, the other party may not seize upon the words in an attempt to accept. However, if the words and the surrounding circumstances make it reasonable to conclude that they are in earnest, the fact that they were used in jest does not matter — a contract will be found. In other words, people must be careful what they say if someone else might reasonably take their language to heart.

§ 4.04 ACCEPTANCE

Mutual assent usually depends on the offer and acceptance process. Once an offer has been made, a contract is formed if the offer is accepted.[119] An offer creates a power of acceptance in the hands of the offeree.[120] He or she can act on this power by expressing his or her assent to the offer within the time and in the manner the offer requires.[121]

Whether the offeree's response is an acceptance is governed by the same objective theory of contract formation that is used to determine whether there was an offer in the first place. Thus, as with offers, courts focus on the offeree's outward manifestations of assent, rather than on her secret or otherwise undisclosed subjective intent. Thus, if Sam offers to sell his car to Barb for $16,000, and Barb says "I'll take it," a contract has been formed even though Barb was just kidding. If Sam reasonably understood Barb to be serious, a contract is formed.

Likewise, if Barb responds by saying "I don't want that hunk of junk you drive," Barb has rejected the offer. No deal has been struck, even if Barb was being facetious and really meant to buy the car.

Moreover, if expressions of mutual assent can be detected in the exchange of the parties' communications, a contract can be found even though it is impossible to pin down the precise moment when acceptance occurred.[122] Thus, an acceptance might be expressed through conduct,[123] particularly where the parties have dealt with one another in the past and have developed a mutual understanding of the meaning to be attributed to one another's actions.[124] In rare situations, silence, which is usually ambiguous, may even operate as an acceptance, even though it is impossible to

---

[119] RESTATEMENT (SECOND) OF CONTRACTS § 22(1) (1981); *e.g., In re* Guardianship of Price, 571 N.W.2d 214, 216 (Iowa Ct. App. 1997) ("The only required elements of a binding contract are mutual assent to the contractual terms manifested by an offer and acceptance.").

[120] *See* Wesley Newcomb Hohfeld, *Some Fundamental Legal Conceptions as Applied in Judicial Reasoning*, 23 YALE L.J. 13, 44–54 (1913) (on the distinction between a "power" and a "right" or a "duty"). *See also* Curtis Nyguist, *Teaching Wesley Hohfelds Theory of Legal Relations*, 52 J. LEGAL EDUC. 238 (2002).

[121] RESTATEMENT (SECOND) OF CONTRACTS § 50(1) (1981); CISG Art. 18(1) (1980); PICC Art. 2.1.6(1) (2004); PECL Art. 2.204(1).

[122] RESTATEMENT (SECOND) OF CONTRACTS § 22 (1981); U.C.C. § 2-204(2) (2012).

[123] RESTATEMENT (SECOND) OF CONTRACTS § 53 (1981); CISG Art. 18(1) (1980); PICC Art. 2.1.6(1) (2004); PECL Art. 2.204(1) (2002).

[124] RESTATEMENT (SECOND) OF CONTRACTS § 22 cmt. b (1981); CISG Art. 18(3) (1980); PICC Art. 2.1.6(3) (2004); PECC Art. 2.205(3) (2002).

determine the precise moment that the acceptance occured.[125]

[A] Unequivocal Acceptance

Just as with offers, acceptances must be unequivocal.[126] If the offeree expresses doubt about his or her willingness to enter into the proposed deal, it would not be reasonable for the offeror to understand the response as assent. Thus, if Winkler Builders offers to build an addition to Julie's house for a price of $60,000, and Julie replies: "I might agree to that," she has not accepted. By indicating that she "might" agree, Julie is reserving judgment. Winkler Builders could not justifiably interpret her statement as assent to its offer. On the other hand, if she says, "that's a good price, I want you to build it," Winkler is justified in interpreting her response as an acceptance. If, on the other hand, she says "I want you to build it, but $60,000 is too high a price," her expressed reluctance prevents her response from being an acceptance.

[1] Grumbling Acceptance Effective

Sometimes an offeree communicates her willingness to proceed with the transaction but also expresses some dissatisfaction with the deal. This type of "grumbling acceptance" is every bit as effective an acceptance as a cheerful expression of assent.[127] Thus, if Julie responds to Winkler's offer by saying "I really thought I could find a better price, but all right, I want you to build it," a contract has been formed.[128]

[2] Conditional Acceptance Ineffective

On the other hand, a purported acceptance must not be qualified or otherwise subject to a condition. A response that expresses a willingness to be bound to the terms of the original offer, but which adds additional terms *upon which the offeree's assent depends*, is not an acceptance.[129]

Thus, if in response to Winkler's proposal to construct the room addition to Julie's house for $60,000, Julie replies "I accept, but only if you agree to finish the job within three months," there is no contract. Here, Julie has added a term specifying a time for completion, that Winkler Builders may not be willing to agree to — and she has made her assent conditional ("only if") upon Winkler's agreement to the proposed deadline. Winkler's proposal to do the work for $60,000 may well have contemplated more time in which to finish the work.

---

[125] RESTATEMENT (SECOND) OF CONTRACTS § 69 (1981); CISG Art 18 (1980); Art. 2.1.6 (2004); PECL Arts. 2.204(2) & 2.205(3). *See* infra § 4.05[D] Silence as Acceptance.

[126] RESTATEMENT (SECOND) OF CONTRACTS § 57 (1981).

[127] *E.g.*, Brangier v. Rosenthal, 337 F.2d 952 (9th Cir. 1964); Panhandle Eastern Pipe Line Co. v. Smith, 637 P.2d 1020 (Wyo. 1981).

[128] *See* Price v. Okla. Coll. of Osteopathic Med. and Surgery, 733 P.2d 1357 (Okla. Civ. App. 1986) (offer of employment contract acceptance "under protest").

[129] RESTATEMENT (SECOND) OF CONTRACTS § 59 (1981).

On the other hand, if the additional terms that Julie insists upon go no further than what was already implied in the terms of Winkler's offer, then her response, which merely makes those implied terms explicit, still operates as an acceptance.[130] Thus, if Julie replies "I accept, but only if you agree to finish the job within a reasonable time," a contract has been formed, because Winkler's offer to do the job impliedly promised that the work would be completed within a reasonable time, and Julie's response does nothing more than make this understanding explicit.[131]

At common law, the mere inclusion of additional terms not included in the original offer meant that the response a was not a "mirror image" of the offer, and thus could not be an acceptance. As will be seen, U.C.C. Article 2 makes substantial inroads on this rule in the context of sales of goods.[132]

In transactions still governed by the common law, a mere *request* to change the terms of the offer or to supplement the agreement with additional terms does not prevent an otherwise unequivocal acceptance from creating a contract,[133] unless the acceptance is made conditional on the offeror' s agreement to the proposed change.[134] An unconditional acceptance creates a contract even though it is accompanied by an inquiry about possible changes to the contract's terms.

In international transactions, the rule is somewhat different. A reply that purports to be an acceptance, but that contains "additions, limitations, or other modifications," is both a rejection and a counteroffer.[135] But if it merely contains different or additional terms that do not materially alter the terms contained in the offer, the reply is an acceptance.[136] Unlike U.C.C. § 2-207, the CISG makes it explicit that additional or different terms relating to "price, payment, quality and quantity of the goods, place and time of delivery, extent of one party's liability to the other or the settlement of disputes" are material terms.[137]

In other international transactions the rule is the same. A reply that either states or implies materially different terms is both a rejection and a counteroffer.[138] If the additional or different terms are not material, a contract is formed with the new or different terms as part of the deal.[139] In this latter respect, dealing with terms that are not material, international rules are quite similar to U.C.C. § 2-207, which is explained in detail below.

---

[130] RESTATEMENT (SECOND) OF CONTRACTS § 59 cmt. b (1981).

[131] *See* RESTATEMENT (SECOND) OF CONTRACTS § 59 illus. 3 (1981). *See also* PICC Art. 2.1.11 (2004); PECL Art. 2.208(2) (2002).

[132] *See infra* § 4.10 Mirror-Image Rule and Battle of the Forms Under U.C.C. § 2-207.

[133] RESTATEMENT (SECOND) OF CONTRACTS § 61 (1981).

[134] RESTATEMENT (SECOND) OF CONTRACTS § 59 (1981).

[135] CISG Art. 19(1) (1980).

[136] CISG Art. 19(2) (1980).

[137] CISG Art. 19(3) (1980).

[138] PICC Art. 2.1.11(1). PECL Art. 2.208(1) (2002).

[139] PICC Art. 2.1.11(2) (2004); PECL Art. 2.208(2) (2002).

[B] Who Can Accept?[140]

[1] Acceptance by Person to Whom Offer Is Directed

The offeror "may prescribe as many conditions, or terms . . . as he may wish,"[141] and thus may identify the person or persons who may accept. As a result, an offer may be accepted only by those who are invited to accept it.[142] Thus, when Sam offers to sell his car to Barb by saying "Barb, I'll sell you my car for $20,000," Barb is the only one who may accept. Ben, who was standing in the corner and heard Sam make the offer to Barb, was not invited to enter into a contract to buy the car and may not accept Sam's offer. Likewise, Barb may not assign her power of acceptance to Ben and thus give him the opportunity to accept.[143] Oddly enough, this is true even though Barb might accept Sam's offer and then assign the resulting contract to Ben.[144]

As with other aspects of the contract formation process, the identity of the person or persons who may accept is controlled by the "manifested intention of the offeror . . . ."[145] In this respect, as with other features of an offer, the offeror is the "master of his offer."[146]

This rule recognizes that people are sometimes particular about who they deal with. This is particularly true in transactions involving services, where the parties will have to deal with one another for a period of time after the contract is made. As the court said in *Boston Ice Co. v. Potter*:[147]

> a party has a right to select and determine with whom he will contract, and cannot have another person thrust upon him without his consent. It may be of importance to him who performs the contract, as when he contracts with another to paint a picture, or write a book, or furnish articles of a particular kind, or when he relies upon the character or qualities of an individual, or has, as in this case, reason why he does not wish to deal with a particular party. In all cases, as he may contract with whom he pleases, the sufficiency of his reasons for so doing cannot be inquired into.[148]

And, in cases involving real estate, parties are sometimes discriminating about whom they are willing to deal with, and might be unwilling to transfer their land to

---

[140] Mark Pettit Jr., *Modern Unilateral Contracts*, 63 B.U. L. Rev. 551 (1983).

[141] M.A. Mortenson Co., Inc. v. Timberline Software Corp., 998 P.2d 305, 316 (Wash. 2000).

[142] Restatement (Second) of Contracts § 52 (1981).

[143] Restatement (Second) of Contracts § 52 cmt. a (1981). *E.g.*, Estate of Watts, 162 Cal. App. 3d 1160 (1984) (personal representatives of decedent could not accept offer of settlement following death of offeree because offeree's death terminated the power of acceptance).

[144] Restatement (Second) of Contracts § 52 cmt. a (1981).

[145] Restatement (Second) of Contracts § 29(1) (1981).

[146] *E.g.*, S. Glass & Plastics Co., v. Kemper, 732 S.E.2d 205, 210 (S.C. Ct. App. 2012); Stenzel v. Dell, Inc., 870 A.2d 133 (Me. 2005).

[147] 1877 Mass. LEXIS 200 (June 28, 1877).

[148] 123 Mass. at 4–5. *Cf.* Macke Co. v. Pizza of Gaithersburg, Inc., 270 A.2d 645 (Md. Ct. Spec. App. 1970) (pizza joint resisted delegation of soda-dispensing machine contract to a disreputable provider).

someone outside their family, or to someone who could not be trusted to serve as an appropriate custodian of the land.[149]

[2] Assignability of Offers

Offers are not assignable.[150] Thus, if Craig offers to sell his car to Edie, she cannot transfer Craig's offer to Jack. Edie can, of course, accept Craig's offer, pay for the car, and sell it to Jack. Further, after she has accepted Craig's offer, she may be able to assign the resulting contract to Jack. But, she cannot simply transfer her power of acceptance to Jack.

Option contracts on the other hand, may usually be assigned.[151] An option contract is a contract to keep an offer open.[152] Because an irrevocable offer represents an already concluded contract, the option contract is just as assignable as any other contract. Thus, if Kim makes an offer to Rudy to sell him her house for $200,000 cash, and Rudy pays Kim $500 to keep the offer open for a week, an option contract is formed and Rudy can transfer his right to accept Kim's offer to another person.[153]

[3] Offer to Office Holder

When an offer is made to a person who holds some office, such as president of a corporation, questions sometimes arise about whether the offer has been made to the particular individual or to any person who occupies the position. When an offer is made to an organization, such as a corporation or a partnership,[154] which can act only through agents, it should be clear that the organization can accept through the manifested assent of any authorized agent.[155] However, if the offer is made to a person in his or her individual capacity, that person may not accept for another person, regardless of his or her general authority to act on that other person's behalf.

[4] Offers to Multiple Persons

The fact that an ordinary offer may be accepted only by the person invited to accept does not mean an offer may be made to only one person at a time. Quite to the contrary, a person may direct his offer to a number of people simultaneously, such as where the offer is directed to members of a particular group or to a class

---

[149] At times, of course, sellers may wish to invidiously discriminate against prospective buyers on the basis of their race, gender, ethnic heritage, or sexual orientation. Such discrimination, though sometimes difficult to detect, is immoral and usually illegal.

[150] RESTATEMENT (SECOND) OF CONTRACTS § 52 (1981)

[151] RESTATEMENT (SECOND) OF CONTRACTS § 320 & cmt. a (1981).

[152] § 25 (1981).

[153] *See* RESTATEMENT (SECOND) OF CONTRACTS § 320 illus. 1(1981).

[154] *See* U.C.C. § 1-201(a)(25) (2012) (formerly § 1-201(28)).

[155] RESTATEMENT (SECOND) OF CONTRACTS § 52 cmt. c (1981). *E.g.*, Apostolic Revival Tabernacle v. Charles J. Febel, Inc., 266 N.E.2d 545 (Ill. App. Ct. 1970).

of persons, or even to the public at large.[156] The question of to whom the offer extends (that is, how many people have a power of acceptance) is always a matter of interpretation depending on the words and conduct of the offeror and how they might reasonably have been understood.[157] Offers of rewards and certain auctions illustrate offers that are made to, and can be accepted by, any one of a number of people.

[a] Offers of a Reward

Offers of a reward usually create a power of acceptance in a wide range of people. An advertised offer of a $100 reward to the person who finds and safely returns a lost pet can be accepted by anyone who, with knowledge of the offer, accepts by returning the lost animal.[158] An offer of reward of this type is capable of being accepted by only one person, or perhaps by multiple persons acting together. An offer of a reward for information leading to the arrest and conviction of a criminal is susceptible of being accepted by multiple parties acting independently of one another, with the prize to be shared by those who accept by turning in the fugitive.[159] However, the usual rule is that when one person accepts the offer by supplying the requested information, the power of acceptance created by the offer is terminated.[160]

Even if someone performs the requested act — finds and returns the lost pet — and thus appears to accept the offer of a reward, acceptance does not occur unless the person knew of the reward.[161] Suppose an offer publicizes a $25,000 reward to whoever provides information leading to the arrest of a fugitive. Acceptance of this offer requires action — a mere promise to supply the necessary information is not enough.[162] Of course, a person who turns the culprit in might act for a variety of reasons. A private citizen might supply the information as an act of good citizenship. Or, the fugitive's location might be discovered by a police officer as part of her job. Likewise, a bounty hunter might actually capture the fugitive only because he wished to collect the reward.

[b] Auctions

Some auction sales involve an offer by the seller to a number of prospective buyers, any one of whom might accept, by making the highest bid.[163] In other auctions, the bidders make offers, which the auctioneer, acting on behalf of the

---

[156] RESTATEMENT (SECOND) OF CONTRACTS § 29(2) (1981).

[157] RESTATEMENT (SECOND) OF CONTRACTS § 29(1) (1981).

[158] RESTATEMENT (SECOND) OF CONTRACTS § 29 illus. 1 (1981).

[159] JOSEPH M. PERILLO, 1 CORBIN ON CONTRACTS § 3.10 at 357 (1993) (suggesting pro-rata distribution of the reward).

[160] RESTATEMENT (SECOND) OF CONTRACTS § 29 illus. 1 (1981).

[161] RESTATEMENT (SECOND) OF CONTRACTS § 23 cmt. c (1981). *E.g.*, Slattery v. Wells Fargo Armored Serv. Corp., 366 So. 2d 157 (Fla. Dist. Ct. App. 1979). In most cases, of course, the person who offered the reward will pay it even if no contract was formed.

[162] *See infra* § 4.05[B][3] Acceptance by Performance Alone: Unilateral Contracts.

[163] *See infra* § 4.07 Offer and Acceptance in Auctions.

seller, may accept or reject.

There are two types of auctions: auctions "with reserve" and auctions "without reserve." In most auctions — those conducted "with reserve" — the auctioneer invites offers from potential bidders and may choose to accept or reject the highest bid. The seller's "reserve" refers to the ability of the seller to withdraw the goods from the auction at any time before acceptance of the highest bid. In these auctions, offers are made by the bidders, with any acceptance, by the seller, via the auctioneer.

Auctions "without reserve" operate differently. In these auctions, the seller makes a commitment to sell to whoever submits the highest bid. The seller loses the right to withdraw the goods from the auction once a bid has been made.[164] The seller, therefore, is the offeror. Any bidder may accept the offer by making a qualifying bid. Bidding, therefore, constitutes an exercise of the power of acceptance that the offeror created by placing the goods up for auction. The contract created by a qualifying bid is nevertheless subject to a condition subsequent, and is extinguished if another higher bid is made.[165] Placing the goods up for auction "without reserve" is thus a type of option contract, with the seller unable to revoke the offer if any qualifying bid is made.

[5] Crossed Offers

The rule that a person may not accept an offer of which she is not aware also leads to the conclusion that there is no contract in a situation involving "crossed offers." This occurs when parties simultaneously exchange messages with one another proposing the same deal on the same terms, without knowledge of one another's proposals.[166] Thus, Sam might send a letter to Barb offering to sell her his car for $20,000, without knowing that Barb has sent a letter to him, offering to buy the car for that price. Both parties have manifested their intent to enter into a contract for the sale and purchase of the car for $20,000. But, because each party's offer was written without knowledge of the offer of the other, there is no contract. In most cases like this, of course, the parties will go ahead with the transaction and never realize that they did not have a deal — they may not even realize that their communications were not in response to one another. However, either of them can back out of the transaction without being in breach, if this is done before any further communications ratifying their original proposals.[167]

---

[164] U.C.C. § 2-328(3) (2012). *E.g.*, Pitchfork Ranch Co. v. Bar TL, 615 P.2d 541 (Wyo. 1980).

[165] RESTATEMENT (SECOND) OF CONTRACTS § 28 cmt. d (1981). *E.g.*, Holston v. Pennington, 304 S.E.2d 287 (Va. 1983); Pyles v. Goller, 674 A.2d 35 (Md. Ct. Spec. App. 1996).

[166] RESTATEMENT (SECOND) OF CONTRACTS § 23 cmt. d (1981).

[167] RESTATEMENT (SECOND) OF CONTRACTS § 23 illus. 4 (1981). The same result might be reached because of an absence of consideration. Because neither party's promise was made in exchange for the promise of the other, there was no bargain.

[6] Intent to Accept

The issue of whether a person intends to accept an offer might arise in cases involving the offer of a reward, or some other offer that can be accepted by performance. In these cases, whether a person's actions are motivated by an intent to accept the offer are usually irrelevant.[168]

Most of the time people act with mixed motives. A person who captures a bank robber may do so partially in order to collect any available reward, but also perhaps out of a sense of civic duty, to achieve his or her 15 minutes of fame, or because she achieves a sense of thrill and excitement from whatever danger may be involved. He or she may not even be consciously aware of all of these motives. Courts usually avoid inquiries into the offeree's motives where the offeree has performed the acts necessary to earn a prize or award, and instead treat the offer as having been accepted so long as the offeree knew that the prize or the award was available.

This was illustrated in *Cobaugh v. Klick-Lewis, Inc.*,[169] where a golfer was entitled to a posted prize for hitting a hole-in-one, even though his primary motivation for hitting the ace was the same as every other golfer who has ever stepped up to a tee. Likewise, in *Simmons v. United States*[170] a fisherman who inadvertently caught a "prize" fish while angling for his daily meal was entitled to the award associated with the catch, even though his motive was catching something to eat for lunch.

On the other hand, a person who expressly disclaims an intent to accept the offer of a reward does not accept even though he or she may perform all of the acts requested by the offer.[171]

§ 4.05 MANNER OF ACCEPTANCE

[A] Limited by the Terms of the Offer

A person who makes an offer has control over the terms he proposes.[172] Thus, it is usually said that offeror is the "master of the offer."[173] The offeror has control over the time, place, and manner of acceptance. Accordingly, the only sure way for a person to accept an offer is to follow the instructions specified by the offeror.[174] Thus, if an offer requires acceptance to be provided at a particular time, in a particular place, or in specified manner, the offeree must comply or its purported acceptance is ineffective.[175]

---

[168] RESTATEMENT (SECOND) OF CONTRACTS § 81(2) & cmt. b (1981).

[169] 561 A.2d 1248 (Pa. Super. Ct. 1989).

[170] 308 F.2d 160 (4th Cir. 1962).

[171] *E.g.*, Hewitt v. Anderson, 1880 Cal. LEXIS 435 (Oct. 1880).

[172] Stenzel v. Dell, Inc., 870 A.2d 133 (Me. 2005).

[173] *E.g.*, Discover Bank v. Ray, 162 P.3d 1131, 1133 (Wash. Ct. App. 2007); Wachter Mgmt. Co. v. Dexter & Chaney, Inc., 144 P.3d 747, 755 (Kan. 2006).

[174] RESTATEMENT (SECOND) OF CONTRACTS § 58 (1981).

[175] RESTATEMENT (SECOND) OF CONTRACTS § 60 (1981).

Restrictions on the time, place, or manner of acceptance impose limitations on the offeree's power of acceptance. Thus, if Sam tells Barb that the only way in which she may accept his offer to purchase his car for $20,000 is to present herself at his door, at noon the following day, with a sign around her neck that says "I accept," this is the only way which Barb may accept.[176] Acceptance in some other way, which might otherwise seem reasonable, is ineffective.[177]

Of course, few offerors impose such unusual limits on the manner of acceptance. When an offer requires a specific manner of acceptance, the limitation is usually designed to provide a measure of protection for the offeror in avoiding subsequent disputes about when and whether his offer was accepted. Thus, in *Great Western Sugar Co. v. Lone Star Donut Co.*,[178] where the offer specified that acceptance would not be effective unless it was submitted in writing, an oral acceptance was not sufficient. Similarly, in *Jim L. Shetakis Distributing Co., Inc. v. Centel Communications Co.*,[179] the court ruled that the required manner of acceptance was expressed unambiguously in language contained in the offer that specified that the agreement " 'binds Customer when it is executed by Customer and Centel when it is executed by Centel and delivered to Customer.' " The court reasoned that the offeror "reasonably assumed that it would not be bound unless the . . . sales agreement was 'executed by [the] Customer,' . . . ." as required by the offer.[180]

The ordinary rule for mailed acceptances, is that acceptance is effective when sent, rather than when received.[181] This "mailbox rule" results in formation of a contract through use of the mail before the offeror knows that it has been concluded. Fear of this result might lead a person who makes an offer to specify that any acceptance must be received to become effective. This avoids the possibility that the offeror will be bound to a contract without yet being aware of it.[182]

Restricting the manner of acceptance can also enhance the offeror's ability to revoke his or her offer before it is accepted, by ensuring that the offeror is not bound until he or she learns of the offeree's willingness to go ahead with the deal. If Karen makes an offer to sell her house to Phil, she may wish to have the freedom to consider offers made by other potential buyers until she hears from Phil. However, unless Karen specifies otherwise, the mailbox rule will bind her to a contract with Phil from the moment Phil deposits his acceptance in the mail.[183] By

---

[176] RESTATEMENT (SECOND) OF CONTRACTS § 60 illus. 3 (1981).

[177] RESTATEMENT (SECOND) OF CONTRACTS § 58 illus. 1 (1981). *See generally* W.R. Habeeb, Annotation, *Difference Between Offer and Acceptance as Regards Place of Payment or of Delivery as Variance Preventing Consummation of Contract*, 3 A.L.R.2d 256 (1949).

[178] 721 F.2d 510 (5th Cir. 1983).

[179] 756 P.2d 1186 (Nev. 1988).

[180] *Id.* at 1189.

[181] RESTATEMENT (SECOND) OF CONTRACTS § 63(a) (1981). *E.g.*, Morrison v. Thoelke, 155 So. 2d 889 (Fla. Dist. Ct. App. 1963). *See infra* § 4.06[B] Delayed Communication: Acceptance Effective upon Dispatch.

[182] Electronic communication, which is frequently instantaneous, avoids the problem.

[183] *See infra* § 4.06[B] Delayed Communication: Acceptance Effective upon Dispatch.

carefully restricting the manner of acceptance, Karen can preserve her ability to accept an offer made by someone else while her offer to Phil remains outstanding. She can do so with the knowledge that she can revoke her offer to Phil any time before she has received Phil's acceptance.

Likewise, an offeror might wish to limit acceptance to a method that ensures not only the offeree's willingness to go ahead with the deal, but the offeree's practical ability to perform. Thus, Winkler Builders might offer to complete a room addition for Julie for $60,000, but require as the exclusive manner of expressing her assent that she submit documentation showing that she has received approval for a loan in the amount necessary to pay for the work. Any attempt by Julie to accept, by doing nothing more than agreeing to pay Winkler's price, is ineffective unless she complies with the additional requirements of Winkler's offer that she supply the necessary documentation about her loan.

Here, however, the offeror must be careful to specify that his insistence on this documentation is a part of the manner of acceptance rather than a contractual duty that the offeree must perform after the contract is created.[184] If Winkler carefully specifies that providing the documentation is a condition to formation, no contract exists unless Julie supplies the necessary evidence of her ability to pay. If providing the necessary documentation is not a condition of formation, but a term of the contract, Julie's failure to supply the paperwork does not prevent creation of a contract. Instead, a contract is formed when she expresses her assent to the deal; and her failure to supply evidence of her ability to pay is a breach. If it is a material breach it might excuse Winkler from performing, but if it is a non-material breach, it might merely give him a right to recover damages for any harm he suffered as a result of the breach.

Sellers with limited supply sometimes try to retain control over whether they have entered into an agreement with their customers by including language in their proposals that seeks to prevent formation of a contract until the customer's "acceptance" is approved at the seller's home office. In *International Filter Co. v. Conroe Gin, Ice, & Light Co.*,[185] the seller's proposal indicated that it "becomes a contract when accepted by the purchaser and approved by an executive offer of the [seller], at its [home] office."[186] This limitation on the manner of acceptance made it clear that the seller would not be bound until two things had occurred: (1) the buyer had assented to the deal, and (2) the seller's home office had agreed to the transaction. In effect, it prevented the seller's proposal from operating as an offer.

If the terms of an offer suggest a means of acceptance, but do not make use of the suggested means a condition of formation, the offeree may exercise her power of acceptance in any reasonable manner. Although compliance with the suggested manner of acceptance is effective to conclude an agreement, acceptance through other reasonable means is just as effective.[187]

---

[184] *See* Int'l Filter Co. v. Conroe Gin, Ice & Light Co., 277 S.W. 631 (Tex. Comm'n App. 1925).

[185] I've always wondered about the nature of the buyer's business that led to the designation "Gin, Ice, & Light."

[186] 277 S.W. 631, 631 (Tex. Comm'n App. 1925).

[187] RESTATEMENT (SECOND) OF CONTRACTS § 60 (1981).

U.C.C. Article 2 draws this distinction between a suggested means of acceptance and an exclusive or conditional means of acceptance by specifying that "unless otherwise unambiguously indicated by the language or the circumstances . . . an offer to make a contract shall be construed as inviting acceptance in any reasonable manner and by any reasonable medium in the circumstances."[188] Thus, the offer must make it unambiguously clear that the manner of acceptance specified in the offer is more than a mere suggestion.[189]

Furthermore, an offeror who has carefully designated an exclusive manner of acceptance might subsequently engage in conduct revealing his or her willingness to enter into a contract despite the offeree's failure to conform its acceptance to the method specified in the offer. This happened in *Allied Steel Conveyors, Inc. v. Ford Motor Co.*[190] Ford submitted a purchase order for machinery and its installation in one of Ford's factories. The offer carefully specified that the "purchase order agreement is not binding until accepted [and that] [a]cceptance should be executed on acknowledgment copy which should be returned to buyer."[191] Allied agreed to supply the machine, but never returned the acknowledgment copy. A few weeks later, it showed up at Ford's factory and began installing the machinery.

The court found that even if this language specified an exclusive manner of acceptance, Ford was estopped from asserting Allied's failure to execute and return the acknowledgment copy because Ford had permitted Allied to enter the factory and begin performance of their agreement before the copy was signed and returned.[192] Thus, parties who wish to insist on a particular means of acceptance must act in accordance with their demands. Once the parties begin performance, it is difficult for them to claim that no contract was formed, regardless of what their correspondence says.[193]

[B] Reasonable Manner of Acceptance

If the offer does not unambiguously limit the offeree's power of acceptance, the offeree may accept in any manner reasonable under the circumstances.[194] The offeree may accept by making a return promise or, if invited, by performance. Any reasonable medium in which a return promise is communicated is effective. The means chosen are not limited to the medium in which the offer was conveyed.

---

[188] U.C.C. § 2-206(1)(a) (2012). *See* RESTATEMENT (SECOND) OF CONTRACTS § 30(2) & cmt. b (1981).

[189] *See, e.g.*, Jim L. Shetakis Distrib. Co., v. Centel Comm. Co., 756 P.2d 1186 (Nev. 1988).

[190] 277 F.2d 907 (6th Cir. 1960).

[191] *Id.* at 910. The court might have chosen to rely on Ford's use of the word "should" rather than "must" to draw the conclusion that the specified manner of acceptance was nothing more than a suggestion.

[192] *See also* Empire Mach. Co. v. Litton Bus. Tel. Sys., 566 P.2d 1044 (Ariz. Ct. App. 1977) (offeror waived limited manner of acceptance by cashing buyer's check and retaining the proceeds).

[193] *Id.*

[194] RESTATEMENT (SECOND) OF CONTRACTS § 50(1) & cmt. a (1981).

[1] Acceptance by Return Promise

The most common way to form a contract is for the parties to exchange promises.[195] Thus, if the offeree promises to provide the performance sought in the offer, a contract is formed.[196] The parties can then move on to the performance stage.

Thus, when Sam tells Barb "I'll sell you my car for $20,000," and Barb replies "I'll buy it," the parties have concluded a contract: Sam promised to sell the car to Barb and she promised to pay for it.[197] The fact that neither party has yet performed does not prevent the formation of a contract either due to the absence of an agreement or due to the absence of consideration. The parties' exchange of promises operates as an offer and an acceptance, and the fact that the promises were made in exchange for one another supplies the necessary consideration,[198] even if one of them later fails to perform.[199]

Contracts formed through an exchange of promises are sometimes referred to as "bilateral contracts." The contract is bilateral because it involves two promises, one by each party.[200] The original Restatement of Contracts[201] distinguished between an offer to enter into a bilateral contract, which could be accepted by a return promise, and an offer to enter into a "unilateral contract" in which performance was the only possible manner of acceptance. The current Restatement avoids designating contracts as bilateral or unilateral, but continues to recognize these two different methods of formation.[202]

---

[195] RESTATEMENT (SECOND) OF CONTRACTS § 50(3) & cmt. c (1981).

[196] *See* Comm. Lithographing Co. v. Family Media, Inc., 695 S.W.2d 936, 939 (Mo. Ct. App. 1985) (holding "mutual understanding" is the equivalent of bilateral contract of "a promise for a promise.").

[197] *See* RESTATEMENT (SECOND) OF CONTRACTS § 50(3) & illus. 4 (1981).

[198] RESTATEMENT (SECOND) OF CONTRACTS § 75 (1981). *See supra* § 2.03[C] Promises as Consideration. Law students sometimes misunderstand consideration and conclude that consideration is absent unless one of the parties has at least partially performed. This impression is wrong. The enforceability of an agreement formed through nothing more than an exchange of promises was established in *Slade's Case* in 1602. Slade's Case, 76 Eng. Rep. 1074, 1077 (K.B. 1602). *See supra* § 1.03 History of Contract Law. American law recognized the enforceability of executory promises by the end of the eighteenth century, at the latest. A.W.B. Simpson, *The Horowitz Thesis and the History of Contracts*, 46 U. CHI. L. REV. 533 (1979).

[199] Breach is sometimes referred to as a "failure of consideration." *See* Taliaferro v. Davis, 216 Cal. App. 2d 398 (1963); RESTATEMENT (SECOND) OF CONTRACTS § 237 cmt. a (1981) (stating a preference for the phrase "failure of performance" in order to avoid confusion over whether the contract was supported by consideration when it was made). However, failure of consideration does not mean that the contract was not created. Instead, it means only that one party is in breach. *See* Holm v. Woodworth, 271 So. 2d 167 (Fla. Dist. Ct. App. 1972). Because there is a valid contract, the non-breaching party has the right to recover damages for any harm it has suffered. If the breach is material, the injured party also has the right to suspend or terminate its own performance of the contract due to the failure of a constructive condition. *See infra* § 9.01 The Effect of Breach.

[200] There may, of course, be more than two parties to a contract, but the language of contract law has never conventionally referred to a "multilateral" contract.

[201] RESTATEMENT OF CONTRACTS § 52 (1932).

[202] RESTATEMENT (SECOND) OF CONTRACTS § 45 cmt. a (1981).

In most circumstances, an offeree might accept by making a promise, by performing, or by beginning performance. In these situations performance or the beginning of performance is merely the offeree's manner of expressing his or her intent to enter into the deal proposed by the offeror and thus communicating its promise to perform. Unless the terms of the offer unequivocally require a verbal promise, acceptance may be conveyed either verbally, that is via words,[203] or through conduct that implies a return promise.

[2] Beginning Performance as a Promise

In many cases, the offeror will be indifferent about whether the offeree accepts through words or conduct: either mode of acceptance is reasonable.[204] Thus, when Sam offers to sell his car to Barb for $20,000, Sam will probably find Barb's action of handing him the $20,000 just as effective as a means of acceptance as Barb's promise. If Barb hands him $5000 and says: "here's 1/4 of the price" her part performance is likely to be treated as an acceptance — and an implied commitment to pay the remaining $15,000.

When the terms of an offer make either an express return promise or performance a reasonable method of acceptance, acceptance may be conveyed: (1) by a promise, (2) by the actual commencement of performance, or (3) even by a "tender" of the commencement of performance — such as arriving at the site of the job and proffering a willingness to begin.[205] Beginning performance or tendering the beginning of performance operates just as effectively as an express promise as a means of concluding the agreement. This point cannot be emphasized enough: in this situation, performance serves as a promise, imposing an obligation on the offeree to perform completely.

Regardless of whether acceptance of such an offer is accomplished through an express promise, the beginning of performance, or tender of performance, acceptance exposes the offeree to a claim for breach of contract if the offeree fails to fully perform. Section 62(2) of the Second Restatement makes this clear. In referring to acceptance made by the commencement of performance it specifies that "[s]uch an acceptance *operates as a promise* to render complete performance."[206]

In transactions involving services, beginning performance is a common method of manifesting assent. Thus, if Colleen leaves a voice-mail message for Gary,[207] offering to pay him $5,000 to replace the roof on her house, and Gary shows up and begins work the next day, Gary has accepted.

---

[203] Law students, and many others, frequently use the term "verbal" as a synonym for "oral" and thus use it to refer to spoken words as opposed to written words. However, in its proper sense, communication in the form of "words" is verbal whether those words are conveyed orally or in writing. "Verbal" is derived from the Latin "verbum," meaning "word." THE AMERICAN HERITAGE DICTIONARY OF THE ENGLISH LANGUAGE (1969).

[204] RESTATEMENT (SECOND) OF CONTRACTS § 32 & cmt. a (1981).

[205] RESTATEMENT (SECOND) OF CONTRACTS § 62(1) (1981).

[206] RESTATEMENT (SECOND) OF CONTRACTS § 62(2) (1981).

[207] RESTATEMENT (SECOND) OF CONTRACTS § 62(1) (1981).

[a]   Prompt Shipment of Goods

In contracts for the sale of goods, where the buyer offers to purchase goods for "prompt or current shipment," U.C.C. § 2-206 acknowledges that the seller may accept in any reasonable manner.[208] Acceptance may occur through the seller's promise to deliver the goods or by its prompt actual shipment of them.[209] Somewhat surprisingly, even the seller's shipment of defective goods is an acceptance.[210] Thus, if the buyer sends the seller a purchase order for ten orange gizmos, and the seller responds by shipping seven green widgets, the seller's shipment of the goods is an acceptance — and simultaneously a breach.

Mistakes of this magnitude rarely occur, and are usually quickly corrected. More often, however, the sellers ship defective merchandise, without realizing that the goods are defective. If shipment of defective ("nonconforming") goods were regarded as a counteroffer, the seller could escape responsibility for its shoddy merchandise by contending that its shipment of the defective goods was merely a counteroffer, and that the buyer did not accept. Under the Code's rule, if the buyer orders 10 orange gizmos and the seller promptly ships 10 orange but completely inoperable gizmos, the seller has accepted the buyer's offer to purchase the gizmos and is, at the same time, in breach of warranty. The same result applies if the seller ships 10 green widgets. The seller has accepted, and is simultaneously in breach.

A seller with widgets but no gizmos, who knows widgets are not what the buyer ordered, can avoid formation of a contract by providing the buyer with a timely notice that the widgets were not sent in a mistaken or defective effort to accept the buyer's offer, but, in the words of the U.C.C., "as an accommodation" — in other words, as a counteroffer.[211] Thus, the seller can send items different what was ordered as a counteroffer, but it must clearly indicate that this is what it intends.[212]

[b]   Preparing to Perform

In cases involving services it might be difficult to determine whether performance has actually begun, or whether the offeree has merely begun preparations to perform. Mere preparations are not acceptance.[213] For acceptance to occur in this manner, the offeree must either begin actual performance or "tender" performance.

Assume, for example, that Colleen leaves a voice-mail message for Gary offering to pay him $5,000 to replace the roof on her house, and that Gary shows up and begins work the next day. As explained above, Gary's commencement of work is acceptance of Colleen's offer. And, because Colleen is likely to regard Gary's

---

[208] U.C.C. § 2-206(1)(a) (2012).

[209] U.C.C. § 2-206(1)(b) (2012). *E.g.*, Matrix Int'l Textiles, Inc. v. Jolie Intimates Inc., 7 Misc. 3d 1019(A) (N.Y. Civ. Ct. 2005).

[210] U.C.C. § 2-206(1)(b) (2012). *E.g.*, Dubrofsky v. Messer, 31 U.C.C. Rep. Serv. 907 (Mass. Ct. App. 1981).

[211] U.C.C. § 2-206(1)(b) (2012).

[212] *See* Corinthian Pharmaceutical Sys, Inc. v. Lederle Labs., 724 F. Supp. 605 (S.D. Ind. 1989).

[213] *See* RESTATEMENT (SECOND) OF CONTRACTS § 62 cmt. d (1981).

actions as his promise to finish the job, both of them are bound to a bilateral contract. If Gary quits before he finishes, he will be liable for breach.

But, if Gary merely prepares to begin, by traveling to the store and purchasing nails and shingles for the work, without communicating his intent to Colleen, she may still revoke.[214] Gary's preparations do not qualify as acceptance.[215] While Gary might consider this as the beginning of performance, his actions, objectively viewed, are still equivocal in the sense that the nails and shingles might be suitable for any number of jobs he has been asked to perform.

Moreover, there is no reason for Colleen to know that Gary has made this trip, or any way for her to discern that the materials are those intended to be installed on her roof. Gary's purchase of the necessary materials is not necessarily connected to any particular job, but instead might be nothing more than his effort to keep a ready supply of roofing materials on hand for whenever he needs them.

The distinction between beginning performance and merely preparing to begin was articulated by the decision in *White v. Corlies & Tifft*.[216] White was a builder who was invited to refurbish the offices of Corlies & Tifft. After the parties had settled on the specifications for the work, but before any agreement had been reached that White would be hired to do the work, Corlies & Tifft advised White that he could begin immediately. White then purchased the necessary materials and commenced work in his own shop. The next day, Corlies & Tifft changed its mind, and White sued.

In rejecting the plaintiff's claim, the court drew a sharp distinction between preparing to begin and actually commencing performance; it ruled that White's conduct had not advanced to the second stage. The court explained that the materials White had purchased was "stuff as fit for any other work" and that although he had done some work, nothing he did went beyond what "he would have done for any other like work."[217] The distinction between mere preparations and actual commencement of performance depends on whether the work undertaken is clearly referable to the transaction proposed in the offer.[218]

[3] Acceptance by Performance Alone: Unilateral Contracts[219]

An offer might specify that performance is the only permissible method of acceptance. Offers of rewards are the most obvious example.[220] If Sally posts notice of a $100 reward for the safe return of her cat, she will not be interested in those

---

[214] *See* RESTATEMENT (SECOND) OF CONTRACTS § 62 illus. 1 (1981).

[215] RESTATEMENT (SECOND) OF CONTRACTS § 50 cmt. b (1981).

[216] 1871 N.Y. LEXIS 280 (Nov. 20, 1871).

[217] *Id.* at *6.

[218] RESTATEMENT (SECOND) OF CONTRACTS § 45 cmt. f (1981). *E.g.*, Knight v. Seattle First Nat'l Bank, 589 P.2d 1279 (Wash. Ct. App. 1979); Ever-Tite Roofing Corp. v. Green, 83 So. 2d 449 (La. Ct. App. 1955).

[219] Arthur L. Corbin, *Offer and Acceptance and Some of the Resulting Legal Relations*, 26 YALE L.J. 169 (1917); David G. Epstein & Yvette Joy Liebesman, *Bearded Ladies Walking on the Brooklyn Bridge*, 59 ARK. L. REV. 267 (2006); Mark Pettit Jr., *Modern Unilateral Contracts*, 3 B.U. L. REV. 551 (1983);

who might promise to look for her cat — the $100 will be paid only to someone who finds and returns the lost animal.[221] The only way to accept Sally's offer is to find and return the cat.[222] If Sally's friend Mark promises her that he will look for the cat, or even makes a foolish promise that he will actually find the cat, he has not accepted Sally's offer. Furthermore, if Mark begins looking for the cat, his actions imply no promise to continue looking until he finds the cat or even to continue looking for a reasonable time. He is free to quit at any time.

Apart from offers of a reward, unilateral contracts are also found in option contracts. In an option contract, the seller makes a binding promise to sell her land to a specific buyer if the buyer pays the price by a specific date.[223] To accept, the offeree must tender payment of the price as a means of acceptance.[224] Promising to buy the land, is not sufficient. Other unilateral contracts involve employee benefits, such as pensions, stock options, or bonus offers, which the employee can earn by reaching certain milestones in his or her longevity or performance.[225] Likewise, "letter of credit" transactions, involving a person's promise (commonly a bank) to pay a sum a money if certain specified documents are presented to the bank, all involve a unilateral contract.[226]

Dahl v. Hem Pharmaceuticals Corp.[227] involved a situation a bit more complicated than a conventional reward. Hem Pharmaceuticals was engaged in research to determine the effectiveness of a prescription medicine. It promised Dahl and several others a year's free supply of the new drug if they enrolled and participated

---

Richard E. Speidel, *Contract Formation and Modification Under Revised Article 2*, 35 WM. & MARY L. REV. 1305 (1994); Peter Tiersma, *Reassessing Unilateral Contracts: The Rule of Offer, Acceptance and Promise*, 26 U.C. DAVIS L. REV. 1 (1992); I. Maurice Wormser, *The True Conception of Unilateral Contracts*, 26 YALE L.J. 136 (1916); I. Maurice Wormser, *Book Review*, 3 J. LEGAL ED. 145 (1950) (recanting the position taken 34 years earlier in *The True Conception of Unilateral Contracts*).

[220] RESTATEMENT (SECOND) OF CONTRACTS § 32 cmt. b (1981). Real estate listing contracts are another common example. The owner promises to pay the agent a fee if the agent secures a buyer for the listed property. *E.g.*, Walsenburg Sand & Gravel Co., Inc. v. City Council of Walsenburg, 160 P.3d 297 (Colo. Ct. App. 2007).

[221] *See* Karl Llewellyn, *Our Case-Law of Contract: Offer and Acceptance*, 48 YALE L.J. 779 (1939). Mark B. Wessman, *Is "Contract" the Name of the Game? Promotional Games as Test Cases for Contract Theory*, 34 ARIZ. L. REV. 635 (1992).

[222] Likewise, if, as a stunt, I promise to pay you $10 to pour a glass of water over your head, the only way for you to accept is to get out a glass, fill it up with water, and pour it over your head. Your promise to participate is not enough; nor is getting out the glass and filling it up with water, which are mere preparations to perform. After all, you may simply be getting yourself a glass of water to drink.

[223] Michael J. Cozzillio, *The Option Contract: Irrevocable Not Irrejectable*, 39 CATH. U.L. REV. 491, 505 (1990).

[224] An option contract need not be framed as a unilateral contract. The seller may give the buyer the right to exercise the option by notifying the seller of its intent to exercise the option. *E.g.*, Matrix Prop. Corp. v. TAG Inv., 609 N.W.2d 737 (N.D. 2000).

[225] Mark Pettit Jr., *Modern Unilateral Contracts*, 3 B.U. L. REV. 551, 577 (1983).

[226] *See* Keith A. Rowley, *Anticipatory Repudiation of Letters of Credit*, 56 SMU L. REV. 2235 (2003); Gerald T. McLaughlin, *Exploring Boundaries: A Legal and Structural Analysis of the Independence Principle of Letter of Credit Law*, 119 BANKING L.J. 501 (2002). The nuts and bolts of how letter of credit transactions operate is described in John W. Head, *How Letters of Credit Operate in International Commercial Transactions: An Introduction to the UCP*, 77 J. KAN. B. ASSOC., Mar. 2008, at 16.

[227] 7 F.3d 1399 (9th Cir. 1993).

in a program to test the drug's effectiveness. The participants made no promise to continue with the program until its end. They were free to withdraw from the study at any time. Although they were free to quit, only participation in the program until its conclusion would entitle them to the promised year's free supply of medicine. Nothing short of full performance would suffice, for the obvious reason that the pharmaceutical company would not derive a benefit from the study unless the participants completed the prescribed regimen.

The court characterized the agreement as a "unilateral contract" — one in which completion of the performance sought by the promisor is the only permissible method of acceptance.[228] In such a contract, only one of the parties makes a promise. The offeree may perform or not, as it wishes, but it makes no commitment to do so. As with Sally's invitation to pay $100 for the safe return of her cat, the promisee incurs no express or implied obligation to perform. Instead, the promisee either accepts by fully performing, or fails to accept by failing to completely perform. Part performance is not an acceptance.

This was exactly the situation in *Dahl*. Mr. Dahl and the other participants made no promise to participate in the program all the way to the end. They were free to back out at any time. If they did so, they would lose the right to receive the year's worth of free medicine, but they incurred no liability to the pharmaceutical company for breach of contract. They had made no promise and thus could not breach.[229]

The First Restatement of Contracts used the term "unilateral contract" to describe this type of agreement and distinguished it from a "bilateral contract" which involved an exchange of promises.[230] The Second Restatement avoids this terminology.[231] Instead, the Second Restatement distinguishes between offers that invite acceptance in one of three ways: (1) via a return promise, (2) via performance, or (3) via either performance or a return promise. In cases of doubt, offers are interpreted as inviting the offeree to accept either through a return promise or through performance.[232] What the First Restatement referred to as unilateral contract, the Second Restatement refers to as an offer that unequivocally *does not* invite a "promissory acceptance."[233] An offer that insists on a performance as the only permissible manner of acceptance may not be accepted by a return promise: performance is the only permissible means of acceptance. However, despite the Second Restatement's abandonment of the term "unilateral contract," the label remains in use, as the opinion in *Dahl* and other recent decisions illustrates.[234]

---

[228] *See also* Cook v. Coldwell Banker, 967 S.W.2d 654, 657 (Mo. Ct. App. 1998).

[229] Mark Pettit Jr., *Modern Unilateral Contracts*, 3 B.U. L. REV. 551 (1983). *E.g.*, Cook v. Coldwell Banker, 967 S.W.2d 654, 657 (Mo. Ct. App. 1998); Panto v. Moore Bus. Forms, Inc., 547 A.2d 260 (N.H. 1988) (employer's promise to continue salary, pension, and insurance benefits following possible layoffs might be an enforceable unilateral contract).

[230] RESTATEMENT OF CONTRACTS § 56 (1932).

[231] *See* K.N. Llewellyn, *On Our Case — Law of Contract: Offer and Acceptance*, 48 YALE L.J. 1 (1938); Mark Pettit Jr., *Modern Unilateral Contracts*, 63 B.U. L. REV. 551, 553–54 (1983).

[232] RESTATEMENT (SECOND) OF CONTRACTS § 32 (1981).

[233] *See* RESTATEMENT (SECOND) OF CONTRACTS § 53(3) (1981).

[234] Neb. Beef, Ltd. v. Wells Fargo Bus. Credit, Inc., 470 F.3d 1249 (8th Cir. 2007); Ketcherside v. McLane, 118 S.W.3d 631 (Mo. Ct. App. 2003).

Regardless of what label is applied, there is a difference between an offer that can be accepted by a return promise (the classical bilateral arrangement) and one that can be accepted only by performance (the classical unilateral arrangement). In an offer calling for acceptance by performance and by performance alone, it is clear that a contract is formed only when the offeree manifests her assent to the offer by completing the requested performance.

The distinction between offers that invite performance as the only means of acceptance, and those that invite a promise as a means of acceptance does not mean that in the latter situation, where a bilateral contract is formed, the offeror is uninterested in obtaining the offeree's performance. Quite to the contrary. The offeror who proposes entering into a bilateral contract is just as interested in receiving the offeree's performance as an offeror who makes an offer to enter into a bilateral contract. The difference lies only in the manner in which the contract is created.

[C] Notice of Acceptance

With rare exception,[235] acceptance must be communicated to the offeree. However, the offeree need not receive the acceptance. In most cases, it is sufficient if the offeree makes a reasonable effort to notify the offeror of acceptance.[236]

Thus, if Isaac offers employment to Carmen, and Carmen replies by placing a letter in the mail addressed to Isaac's postal address with the required postage, Carmen has accepted even if, due to some mishap at the post office, her letter is delayed or never arrives.[237] Her acceptance was effective when it was sent.[238] This, of course, presumes that mailing the acceptance was a reasonable method to accept.

Even if the offeree fails to use reasonable diligence to notify the offeror of acceptance, actual notice to the offeror is sufficient, provided it was received before the offer lapsed.[239] Suppose, for example, that Carmen transposes the numbers of Isaac's address when she addresses the envelope containing her acceptance of Isaac's offer.[240] This mistake might cause her letter to be delivered to Isaac's neighbor. But, if the neighbor recognizes that this letter was meant for Isaac and promptly delivers it to him, the fact that Carmen misdirected her acceptance will not prevent formation of a contract. The only difference is that her acceptance is effective only upon its receipt — not when it was dispatched. Of course, if the misdirection delays receipt until after the offer lapses, no contract is formed.

Where the offeree attempts to express his acceptance by beginning to perform, the very act of commencing performance usually conveys notice. For example, if

---

[235] *See infra* § 4.05[D] Silence as Acceptance.

[236] RESTATEMENT (SECOND) OF CONTRACTS § 56 (1981).

[237] RESTATEMENT (SECOND) OF CONTRACTS § 56 cmt. b (1981).

[238] RESTATEMENT (SECOND) OF CONTRACTS § 63 (1981).

[239] RESTATEMENT (SECOND) OF CONTRACTS § 56 (1981).

[240] This happens to your author frequently. He lives at "774" but frequently receives mail sent to "744." He is fortunate to live in a neighborhood with an attentive mail carrier and thoughtful neighbors.

Colleen offers to pay Gary $5,000 to replace the roof on her house, Gary's commencement of work on the roof, in plain view of Colleen and her family, alerts Colleen to Gary's assent to her proposal. Accordingly, an offer that invites acceptance through a promise or performance can sometimes be accepted through the commencement of performance without the necessity of any independent notification to the offeror of the acceptance.[241]

On the other hand, more formal notification is necessary if the offeror requests it,[242] or if the offeree has reason to know that the offeror otherwise is not likely to learn of the commencement of performance.[243] Thus, if Colleen's offer is for Gary to replace the roof on her summer cottage, and Gary knows that Colleen is not in residence at her summer place, his commencement of performance is not sufficient unless he makes a reasonable effort to notify her that he has begun. Quite naturally, a person who wants to avoid questions about whether beginning of performance alone was sufficient will take steps to ensure that the offeror learns of the offeree's intent to accept in addition to beginning performance.[244]

Likewise, the very nature of the offer may reveal that independent notice of acceptance by performance is not necessary.[245] The famous decision in *Carlill v. Carbolic Smoke Ball Co.*[246] provides a good illustration.[247] The defendant was the manufacturer of a flu remedy called the "Carbolic Smoke Ball."[248] It advertised its willingness to pay a £100 prize to anyone who used the Carbolic Smoke Ball according to the manufacturer's instruction, but caught the flu anyway. The plaintiff used the product, but nevertheless caught the flu.

The defendant asserted that the plaintiff, who had otherwise complied with the offer, did not notify the defendant of her intent to use the product and thus had not properly accepted the offer. The court rejected the defendant's claim that it was entitled to notice of acceptance and ruled that notice of acceptance was not necessary. The court explained that any other interpretation of the offer lacked "common sense."[249] The terms of the offer had effectively dispensed with the need for the offeree to convey notice of its acceptance, and permitted performance to operate as an acceptance even though the offeror would not normally learn of it.[250]

---

[241] RESTATEMENT (SECOND) OF CONTRACTS § 54(1) (1981).

[242] RESTATEMENT (SECOND) OF CONTRACTS § 54(1) (1981).

[243] RESTATEMENT (SECOND) OF CONTRACTS § 54(2) (1981).

[244] *See* Bishop v. Eaton, 37 N.E. 665 (Mass. 1894).

[245] RESTATEMENT (SECOND) OF CONTRACTS § 54(2)(c) (1981).

[246] 1893 Q.B. 256 (1892).

[247] The movie *The Paper Chase*, portraying the experiences of a student in his first year of law school, depicts a classroom discussion of the case, led by the archetypical Contracts teacher, Professor Kingsfield.

[248] One law school the author is familiar with named its annual formal dinner-dance, the "Carbolic Smoke Ball," in honor of the case. There is also currently a political news blog that goes by the title ("news unencumbered by the facts"). http://carbolicsmoke.com (last viewed September 24, 2013).

[249] *See generally* A.W.B. Simpson, *Quackery and Contract Law: The Case of the Carbolic Smoke Ball*, 14 J. LEGAL STUD. 345 (1985).

[250] RESTATEMENT (SECOND) OF CONTRACTS § 54 illus. 2 (1981).

A more commercially significant example is an offer by a person to serve as a guarantor for a borrower. Such an offer might invite a creditor to accept by making a loan to the principal debtor, or, more likely, by providing the debtor with goods or services on credit. Such an offer might be made by a parent corporation to a supplier of one of its subsidiaries. The parent would promise to pay for any goods delivered to the subsidiary if the subsidiary fails to pay for them.[251] Thus, if Stampede Burgers, Inc. promises Organic Meats Co. that it will pay for any deliveries of hamburger patties to one of Stampede's subsidiaries in the event that the subsidiary does not pay, there is no need for Organic to notify Stampede that it has accepted the offer by delivering hamburger patties to one of the subsidiaries on credit.

In sales of goods, buyers frequently send the seller a purchase order with the expectation that the seller will ship the goods promptly, without any separate notice of acceptance. If Franklin Manufacturing sends a purchase order to Industrial Supply to purchase a pallet of raw materials for its factory, Franklin might not receive notice of acceptance from Industrial. Instead, Franklin's first notice of the seller's acceptance might be the arrival of the goods. It would make little sense to require a seller to dispatch a separate expression of acceptance when it is likely that the goods themselves will arrive as quickly as any notice that might be sent. On the other hand, modern techniques of electronic contracting over the Internet facilitate prompt and sometimes immediate notice of acceptance, frequently without human intervention.[252]

However, electronic notice is not necessary; the seller can accept by shipping the goods.[253] Dispatching the goods in the direction of the buyer is just as effective as dispatching a letter announcing an intent to ship the goods — maybe better.

Separate notice is still required if shipment will be delayed. If the buyer is not notified of the seller's acceptance "within a reasonable time," the seller may treat the offer as having lapsed.[254] The same rule applies when the seller is in the position of offeror, though when goods are involved, acceptance by performance on the buyer's part would be considerably less common, as transactions involving goods are more usually initiated through an offer made on the part of the buyer.

---

[251] *See* RESTATEMENT (SECOND) OF CONTRACTS § 54 illus. 4 (1981).

[252] Jane K. Winn & Song Yuping, *Can China Promote Electronic Commerce Through Law Reform? Some Preliminary Case Study Evidence*, 20 COLUM. J. ASIAN L. 415 (2007); Sylvia Mercado Kierkegaard, *E-Contract Formation: U.S. and EU Perspectives*, 3 SHIDLER J. L. COM. & TECH. 12 (2007).

[253] U.C.C. § 2-606(1)(b) (2012).

[254] U.C.C. § 2-206(2) (2012). *See* Petersen v. Thompson, 506 P.2d 697 (Or. 1973).

[D] Silence as Acceptance[255]

Silence is inherently equivocal. Therefore, in most cases an offeree's silence is not acceptance.[256] Moreover, an offeror cannot trick the offeree into inadvertently accepting by including language in the offer specifying that silence will operate as an acceptance.[257] Otherwise, unscrupulous sellers would find it far too easy to foist unwanted deals on people who customarily tear up unwanted mail[258] or discard unsolicited spam without even reading the message.

On the other hand, a person who voluntarily accepts the benefit of a valuable service, under circumstances that gave him the opportunity to refuse the services, impliedly consents to pay for the services. This is illustrated by *Day v. Caton*, where the plaintiff built a wall, half of which was installed on the defendant's property.[259] The court instructed the jury that:

> A promise would not be implied from the fact that the plaintiff, with the defendant's knowledge, built the wall and the defendant used it, but it might be implied from the conduct of the parties. If the juries find that the plaintiff undertook and completed the building of the wall with the expectation that the defendant would pay him for it, and the defendant had reason to know that the plaintiff was so acting with that expectation and allowed him so to act without an objection, then the jury might infer a promise on the part of the defendant to pay the plaintiff.[260]

Thus, silent acquiescence in the receipt of a valuable benefit does not imply a promise to pay, but silent acquiescence combined with reason to know of the provider's expectation of payment could give rise to an implied promise.[261]

[1] Unsolicited Merchandise

Unscrupulous sellers sometimes ship goods to buyers who have not ordered them, with the suggestion that the buyer keep the goods and pay for them, or send them back (at the buyer's expense), and thus reject. The common law handled this by treating the offer as accepted if the buyer kept the goods, even if he did not subjectively intend to "accept" the seller's proposal.[262] Under this rule a court is likely to find a contract implied in fact, and treat the offeree's silent acquiescence in

---

[255] Avery Katz, *Transaction Costs and the Legal Mechanics of Exchange: When Should Silence in the Face of an Offer Be Construed as Acceptance?*, 9 J.L. ECON. & ORG. 77 (1993); Melvin Aron Eisenberg, *The Duty to Rescue in Contract Law*, 71 FORDHAM L. REV. 647, 661–64 (2002).

[256] RESTATEMENT (SECOND) OF CONTRACTS § 69 & cmt. a (1981). *See, e.g.*, Vogt v. Madden, 713 P.2d 442 (Idaho Ct. App. 1985) (no acceptance of proposal to renew real estate lease when landlord failed to respond to tenant's proposed terms).

[257] RESTATEMENT (SECOND) OF CONTRACTS § 69 cmt. c (1981).

[258] I have found that it is a good idea to open my mail in the immediate vicinity of the recycling bin in the law school mail room.

[259] 1876 Mass. LEXIS 77 (Feb. 29, 1876).

[260] *Id.* at *2.

[261] RESTATEMENT (SECOND) OF CONTRACTS § 69(1)(a) (1981).

[262] RESTATEMENT (SECOND) OF CONTRACTS § 69(1)(a) (1981).

the receipt and use of valuable goods or services, in circumstances where it knew that payment was expected, as acceptance.

For example, a newspaper carrier, hoping to enlist a new subscriber, might throw a paper onto the porch of a homeowner one day, along with a note stating that he will deliver a paper every day, and call upon the homeowner at the end of the month to collect the price of a month's subscription. The homeowner's inactive silence does not operate as acceptance.[263] However, if the homeowner takes the paper into his house and reads it, his enjoyment of this benefit, with knowledge of the carrier's proposal, operates as acceptance.[264]

While the court system is in little danger of being flooded by claims brought by dishonorable paper carriers,[265] the rule sometimes makes its way into a real dispute. In *Agri Careers, Inc. v. Jepsen*,[266] an employer hired someone who had been referred to it by an employment agency. The referral had been made under circumstances that led the employer to know that the employment agency expected to receive a fee for anyone hired after being referred. The court treated the employer's act of hiring the employee as acceptance of its offer to make referrals.

Silence sometimes operates as an acceptance to a proposal to modify the terms of a pre-existing contract. In *Raasch v. NCR Corp.*,[267] an employee was held to have accepted the employer's proposal to alter their "employment at will" agreement, to add a provision requiring disputes to be resolved through arbitration. The employer's new handbook contained an arbitration provision, and employees knew that their continued employment was subject to the terms contained in the new handbook. The court said that the employee "by not acting in the manner which he personally recognized was the only way to avoid accepting [his employer's new] terms, he knowingly accepted [them]."

Alternatively, even if the offeree's silence is not considered acceptance, a court may nevertheless impose a quasi-contract, or a contract "implied in law," and require the offeree to pay restitution for the value of a benefit that was received.[268] This provides a good alternative rationale for the result in *Agri Careers, Inc. v. Jepsen*. The employer accepted the benefit supplied by the referral of the new employee, with the knowledge that the benefit was supplied with an expectation of payment, and it would have been unjust for the employer to retain the benefit without paying for it.

---

[263] Raasch v. NCR Corp., 254 F. Supp. 2d 847, 867 (S.D. Ohio 2003).

[264] *See also* Day v. Caton, 1876 Mass. LEXIS 77, at *2–5 (Feb. 29, 1876) (one neighbor silently accepted the other's offer to build a party wall if the first would pay half the cost under circumstances in which first neighbor could have so easily objected to the second neighbor's apparent belief that the first neighbor was willing to share the expense).

[265] This outdated image of the young teenager carrying and delivering papers in his parent's neighborhood is stuck in my mind as a result of my own childhood experience. Today's paper carriers are adults, male and female alike. And, despite modern TV ads that continue to depict this archaic image, they all drive cars, not cruiser-style bicycles.

[266] 463 N.W.2d 93 (Iowa Ct. App. 1990).

[267] 254 F. Supp. 2d 847, 866 (S.D. Ohio 2003).

[268] RESTATEMENT (SECOND) OF CONTRACTS § 69(1)(a) (1981); Beacon Homes, Inc. v. Holt, 146 S.E.2d 434 (N.C. 1966); Day v. Caton, 1876 Mass. LEXIS 77 (Feb. 29, 1876).

Dishonest conduct by purveyors of worthless goods, seeking to take advantage of this rule by distributing unordered merchandise to unwary members of the public, has led to governmental regulation of transactions involving the use of the mail to distribute unsolicited merchandise. If the Gizmo Widget Company sends a new kitchen gadget to Rebecca, who examines the item on its arrival and finds it useful even though she had not ordered the item, Rebecca is entitled, under these consumer protection provisions, to treat the item as a gift. She will be entitled to keep it and enjoy the value of whatever benefits it may provide, without being liable either as the result of her acceptance by silence, or in restitution, for the price or value of the item.[269]

[2] Negative Option Agreements

Despite the rule that silence is not an acceptance, the parties can agree that their silence will operate as acceptance. In these circumstances, silence is no longer equivocal.

The most obvious example of silence as acceptance are the ubiquitous music CD, book, wine, or coffee clubs in which the customer enters into an express written agreement that she will take and pay for the seller's "selection of the month" unless the customer takes affirmative action to decline that month's selection.[270] Each month the seller sends its customers an offer, notifying them of the month's selection of music, books, wine, coffee, or beer,[271] accompanied by a postcard for the customers to use to reject the seller's offer. Pursuant to an earlier agreement, the buyer accepts the seller's offer unless the buyer sent the postcard containing its rejection before the deadline. After the deadline has passed, the seller sends the goods — accompanied by an invoice — to the customers who have not returned the rejection.

This marketing method, known as a "negative option plan," is highly susceptible to abuse. This susceptibility has led to government regulation of the amount of time the buyer has in which to exercise its rejection by replying negatively to the seller's proposal.[272]

[3] Effect of Course of Dealing

Silence might also operate as acceptance if the parties' past dealings with one another have led to an understanding that notice of acceptance is not necessary. If the parties have developed a course of dealing that demonstrates their mutual understanding about the meaning of silence, silence may operate as an expression of assent. A classic illustration is supplied by the nineteenth-century decision in *Hobbs v. Massasoit Whip Co.*,[273] in which the court concluded that a buyer's silent

---

[269] 39 U.S.C. § 3009 (2006). Some states have enacted similar legislation. 73 Pa. Stat. Ann. § 2001 (2002). *See generally* Comment, *Unsolicited Merchandise: State and Federal Remedies for a Consumer Problem*, 1970 Duke L.J. 991.

[270] *See, e.g.*, http://www.bomcclub.com/ (last viewed May 22, 2013).

[271] *See* http://www.beermonthclub.com/ (last viewed June 12, 2013).

[272] Use of Negative Option Plans by Sellers in Commerce, 16 C.F.R. § 425.1 (2003).

[273] 33 N.E. 495 (Mass. 1893).

retention of a delivery of "eel skins" operated as an acceptance. The parties had dealt with one another several times in the past, and on each occasion the buyer had received the goods and paid for them. Their course of dealing gave meaning to their silence.[274]

Thus, even though silence normally means nothing, the parties may give it meaning either by entering into an express agreement that specifies the way in which one of the parties' silence is to be interpreted or by acting in a consistent manner over a period of time that demonstrates the meaning that their silence will have.

[E] Means of Communicating Acceptance

Assent may usually be expressed via any reasonable method.[275] The normal methods of communication are usually sufficient: letter, phone call, email, or even text messages. The exception is where the offer expressly limits the mode of acceptance to a particular type of communication. Unless the circumstances indicate otherwise, the mode of communicating the offer is among the reasonable modes of acceptance that the offeree might use to accept.[276] Thus, if an offer is communicated via the mail, the offeree may use the mail or any reasonably similar method of communication, to accept.[277] The same is true of communication by telephone, fax, voicemail, or e-mail.

However, the offeree is not usually limited to the means used to communicate the offer, but may reply in any manner reasonable under the circumstances. Whether a particular mode of communications is reasonable depends on the relative degree of speed and reliability of the method used, any customary business practice in the geographic region or the trade, and any course of dealing established between the parties in their previous dealings.[278] In this regard, the parties are usually afforded a wide degree of flexibility.

Given this latitude, those who plan to insist on one particular method of transacting business are expected to make it unequivocally clear that the usual rules of engaging in commerce do not apply and that some limited mode of communication is required. Those who acquiesce in another means of communication in some transactions will face a difficult time claiming that their assent to later transactions was dependent on the offeree's compliance with the offeror's expressed requirements.

Larger vendors, financial institutions, and other parties sometimes now program their web sites or other computers to automatically make a decision whether to accept or decline a proposed transaction and express assent to the deal.

---

[274] *See also* Am. Bronze Corp. v. Streamway Prods., 456 N.E.2d 1295, 1300 (Ohio Ct. App. 1982) (20-year course of performance of seller's acceptance of buyer's orders by beginning manufacture of the goods without notice to buyer).

[275] RESTATEMENT (SECOND) OF CONTRACTS § 30(2) (1981); U.C.C. § 2-206(1) (2012).

[276] RESTATEMENT (SECOND) OF CONTRACTS § 65 (1981).

[277] RESTATEMENT (SECOND) OF CONTRACTS § 65 cmt. a (1981).

[278] RESTATEMENT (SECOND) OF CONTRACTS § 65 cmt. b (1981).

The Uniform Electronic Transactions Act (UETA) recognizes the validity of automated transactions completed by such electronic agents, and the federal Electronic Signatures in Global and National Commerce Act[279] (E-Sign) upholds agreements by electronic agents made in interstate and foreign commerce.[280] In international transactions, the U.N. Convention on the Use of Electronic Communications in International Contracts[281] provides a similar set of rules.

Electronic Data Interchange (EDI) is a common form of electronic commerce.[282] It is used by businesses to exchange purchase orders, invoices, shipping notices, and other similar documents in a standardized format that facilitates electronic communication in transactions for the sale of goods.[283] EDI was widely used between businesses before the Internet became widely available in the late 1990s. EDI transactions were completed in a highly structured closed network system between businesses who dealt with one another regularly. Although individual sale transactions were conducted electronically, the parties had previously entered into a master agreement, executed by the parties in advance on paper, that governed the EDI transactions.[284]

These transactions stand in stark contrast to those conducted over the Internet, which involves the exchange and storage of digital information in open networks that make it far more difficult for the parties to know who they are really dealing with, and thus make them far more vulnerable to a wide variety of different types of fraud. Whatever these risks, there is nothing about internet communications that prevents them from being used in the contract formation process.

[F] Final Written Contract and "Letters of Intent"[285]

Parties frequently enter into oral negotiations over a complicated deal and settle on a variety of key terms, with the understanding that they will later reduce those terms to a final written document. If a dispute arises before this final document is

---

[279] 15 U.S.C.A. §§ 7001–7031 (2006); Robert A. Hillman & Jeffrey J. Rachlinski, *Standard-Form Contracting in the Electronic Age*, 77 N.Y.U. L. REV. 429 (2002). *See generally supra* § 5.08 Electronic Contracting.

[280] Robert A. Wittie & Jane K. Winn, *Electronic Records & Signatures Under the Federal E-Sign Legislation and UETA*, 56 BUS. LAW. 293, 328 (2000).

[281] U.N. GAOR, 60th Sess., Supp. No. 17 at 65–74, U.N. Doc. A/60/17 (July 15, 2005). The U.N. General Assembly adopted the Convention on November 23, 2005. *See* G.A. Res. 60/21, U.N. Doc. A/RES/60/21 (Nov. 23, 2005). It has been available for adoption by member states since early 2006.

[282] Charles H. Martin, *The Electronic Contracts Convention, the CISG, and New Sources of E-Commerce Law*, 16 TUL. J. INT'L & COMP. L. 467 (2008).

[283] Jean Braucher, *Rent-Seeking and Risk-Fixing in the New Statutory Law of Electronic Commerce: Difficulties in Moving Consumer Protection Online*, 2001 WIS. L. REV. 527; *See* R. J. Robertson Jr., *Electronic Commerce on the Internet and the Statute of Frauds*, 49 S.C. L. REV. 787, 790–96 (1998) (describing the differences between EDI and Internet e-commerce).

[284] Jean Braucher, *Rent-seeking and Risk-fixing in the New Statutory Law of Electronic Commerce: Difficulties in Moving Consumer Protection Online*, 2001 WIS. L. REV. 527, 534.

[285] Daniel C. Draper, *The Broken Commitment: A Modern View of the Mortgage Lender's Remedy*, 59 CORNELL L. REV. 418 (1974); E. Allan Farnsworth, *Precontractual Liability and Preliminary Agreements: Fair Dealing and Failed Negotiations*, 87 COLUM. L. REV. 217 (1987); Charles Knapp, *Enforcing the Contract to Bargain*, 44 N.Y.U. L. REV. 673 (1969); Robert E. Scott, *A Theory of*

signed (or "executed"), one of the parties may claim that a contract was never formed.

The statute of frauds requires some contracts to be in writing,[286] but permits many other contracts to be oral. Even when an agreement is not required to be in writing, the parties frequently find it desirable to reduce their agreement to written form. Putting an agreement in writing helps the parties keep track of what they agreed to do, and will be useful in assisting a court to determine the intent of the parties should a dispute arise. Lawyers frequently refer to the process of reducing a contract to writing as "memorializing" the agreement. The negotiation and memorialization of business agreements constitutes the day-to-day work of many of the country's 1.27 million lawyers.[287]

When the parties anticipate that their agreement will be memorialized in written form, questions sometimes arise over whether the completion of the final written agreement was intended as a condition to the formation of their agreement or whether the deal was already binding and putting it into writing was designed as a mere convenience.

Suppose that utility software developer, Microware, is engaged in negotiations about whether to sell its new program to MegaSoft, a huge purveyor of a popular computer operating system. Microware's owner might conclude a negotiating session with MegaSoft by saying "We agree on all the basic terms of the sale; send me the paperwork and we'll get things finalized." Microware's owner might have intended that the execution of a final written agreement was a condition of the formation of the contract. Under these circumstances, if before a written memorial of their agreement is executed, the parties have a falling out or MegaSoft finds another program that it thinks is better, there is no contract and MegaSoft can get out of the deal. On the other hand, if the "paperwork" was intended not as a condition to the conclusion of a binding agreement, but merely a matter of prudence and convenience, then the parties are bound even before they execute a final document evidencing their agreement.[288]

For example, in *International Castings Group, Inc. v. Premium Standard Farms, Inc.*, the parties exchanged numerous e-mail messages, many of which reflected their intent to reduce their three-year output contract to a more formal written document.[289] When the seller refused to perform, the court ruled that the more formal agreement was intended as a mere memorialization of the agreement that they had already concluded rather than as a condition precedent to the formation of a binding agreement.

Self-enforcing Indefinite Agreements, 103 COLUM. L. REV. 1641 (2003).

[286] *See infra* Ch. 5 The Statute of Frauds: Is a Writing Required?

[287] *See* http://www.americanbar.org/content/dam/aba/migrated/marketresearch/PublicDocuments/2011_national_lawyer_by_state.authcheckdam.pdf (last viewed August 2, 2013). *See also* Tom Paxton, *One Million Lawyers . . . and Other Disasters* (1985 Flying Fish Records, Inc.).

[288] *See generally* E. Allan Farnsworth, *Precontractual Liability and Preliminary Agreements: Fair Dealing and Failed Negotiations*, 87 COLUM. L. REV. 217 (1987); Charles L. Knapp, *Enforcing the Contract to Bargain*, 44 N.Y.U. L. REV. 673, 682–83 (1969).

[289] 358 F. Supp. 2d 863 (W.D. Mo. 2005).

In determining whether execution of a more formal written version of the agreement was intended as a mere formality, courts consider a variety of factors:(1) whether the agreement is one that is usually reduced to written form, (2) the extent of the details remaining to be resolved, (3) the overall size of the transaction, (4) whether the parties had begun preparations for performance before the written version of their agreement was executed, and (5) whether the negotiations between the parties included discussions about the necessity of memorializing the agreement before the parties would be bound.[290]

[G] Assent to Standardized Form Contracts[291]

The contract formation process in situations involving standardized form contracts, or "adhesion contracts," as they are sometimes called, is different from the process involved in other transactions.[292] Customers of insurance companies, auto dealerships, computer software developers, and many other businesses engaged in mass marketing rarely negotiate over the details of the contracts they make. Instead, the seller provides the customer with a preprinted, standardized contract form and gives the customer no opportunity to make adjustments to the terms.

The terms are presented to the customer on a "take it or leave it" basis. Once the customer has selected the product it wishes to purchase, and after the parties' have settled on a price (which, in many cases, is also not subject to negotiation), the parties complete the blanks in a preprinted form agreement containing the few negotiated terms they have discussed, such as quantity, method of payment, and time for performance. Later, when some problem develops, the customer may dispute whether he or she agreed to the all of the preprinted boilerplate terms in the signed documents.

Transactions involving standardized form contracts are commonly regarded as involving a wide disparity in bargaining power between the parties, with the customer lacking any meaningful bargaining power in the transaction other than the power not to enter into the contract at all. Scholars have long disagreed about whether standardized contracts work to the disadvantage of consumers.[293]

---

[290] RESTATEMENT (SECOND) OF CONTRACTS § 27 cmt. c (1981). *E.g.*, Quake Constr., Inc. v. Am. Airlines, Inc., 565 N.E.2d 990, 994 (Ill. 1990); Texaco v. Pennzoil, 729 S.W.2d 768, 819 (Tex. App. 1987).

[291] Robert B. Ahdieh, *The Strategy of Boilerplate*, 104 MICH. L. REV. 1033 (2006); Randy E. Barnett, *Consenting to Form Contracts*, 71 FORDHAM L. REV. 627 (2002); Melvin Aron Eisenberg, *The Limits of Cognition and the Limits of Contract*, 47 STAN. L. REV. 211 (1995); Robert A. Hillman & Jeffrey J. Rachlinski, *Standard-Form Contracting in the Electronic Age*, 77 N.Y.U. L. REV. 429 (2002); Nathan Isaacs, *The Standardizing of Contracts*, 27 YALE L.J. 34 (1917); Friedrich Kessler, *Contracts of Adhesion — Some Thoughts About Freedom of Contract*, 43 COLUM. L. REV. 629 (1943); Russell Korobkin, *Bounded Rationality, Standard Form Contracts, and Unconscionability*, 70 U. CHI. L. REV. 1203 (2003); Arthur Allen Leff, *Unconscionability and the Code — The Emperor's New Clause*, 115 U. PA. L. REV. 485 (1967); W. David Slawson, *The New Meaning of Contract: The Transformation of Contract Law by Standard Forms*, 46 U. PITT. L. REV. 21 (1984); James J. White, *Form Contracts Under Revised Article 2*, 75 WASH. U. L.Q. 315 (1997).

[292] Friedrich Kessler, *Contracts of Adhesion — Some Thoughts About Freedom of Contract*, 43 COLUM. L. REV. 629, 632 (1943).

[293] *Compare* Jeffrey Davis, Revamping Consumer-Credit Contract Law, 68 VA. L. REV. 1333, 1333

However, courts frequently scrutinize standardized form contracts more carefully than agreements that have been carefully negotiated between parties with equal bargaining strength. This scrutiny is usually conducted under one of two doctrines: reasonable expectations and unconscionability. The reasonable expectations doctrine interprets the parties' agreement to conform to the customer's reasonable expectations; the unconscionability doctrine goes further, and denies enforcement to terms of the contract, even if they conform to the parties' reasonable expectations, where the terms are substantively unfair and reflect procedural flaws in the formation process.

[1] Reasonable Expectations[294]

The doctrine of reasonable expectations first developed in connection with insurance policies — the most obvious example of an adhesion contract involving parties of unequal bargaining power. The reasonable expectations doctrine interprets the parties' agreement to conform to the customer's reasonable expectations, even though the documented version of the agreement might conflict with those expectations.

For example, in *C&J Fertilizer, Inc. v. Allied Mutual Insurance Co.*,[295] the plaintiff applied for and purchased a policy to protect it from losses due to "burglary." The terms of the policy defined burglary to exclude not only thefts accomplished by the insured or any of its employees, but also to exclude any burglary that did not result in any "visible marks . . . or physical damage to the exterior of the premises at the place of . . . entry." The insurance company denied the plaintiff's claim, because the burglar was an especially skilled thief who managed to gain entry to the plaintiff's premises without leaving any marks. The court ruled that the policy's exclusion of burglary accomplished by this type of careful entry went beyond the reasonable expectations of the plaintiff, and would not be enforced. The court explained that "[t]he most plaintiff might have reasonably anticipated was a policy requirement of visual evidence . . . indicating the burglary was an 'outside' not an 'inside' job. The exclusion in issue, masking as a definition, makes the insurer's obligation to pay turn on the skill of the burglar, not on the event the parties bargained for: a bona-fide third party burglary resulting in loss of plaintiff's [property]."[296]

Although the reasonable expectations doctrine originated in interpreting insurance policies, it has expanded to apply to other standard form contracts. For

---

(1982) *and* Todd D. Rakoff, *Contracts of Adhesion: An Essay in Reconstruction*, 96 HARV. L. REV. 1173, 1225–29 (1983) *with* Lucian A. Bebchuk & Richard A. Posner, *One-Sided Contracts in Competitive Consumer Markets*, 104 MICH. L. REV. 827, 833–34 (2006) *and* Alan Schwartz & Louis L. Wilde, *Imperfect Information in Markets for Contract Terms: The Examples of Warranties and Security Interests*, 69 VA. L. REV. 1387, 1414–15 (1983).

[294] Roger C. Henderson, *The Doctrine of Reasonable Expectations in Insurance Law After Two Decades*, 51 OHIO ST. L.J. 823 (1990); Stephen J. Ware, Comment, *A Critique of the Reasonable Expectations Doctrine*, 56 U. CHI. L. REV. 1461 (1989).

[295] 227 N.W.2d 169 (Iowa 1975).

[296] *Id.* at 177.

example, in *Broemmer v. Abortion Services of Phoenix*,[297] a patient at an abortion clinic was not bound to a mandatory arbitration clause in the standardized contract that she signed. The court explained that the plaintiff "was under a great deal of emotional stress, had only a high school education, was not experienced in commercial matters, and is still not sure 'what arbitration is.' "[298] As a result, the arbitration agreement fell outside her reasonable expectations and was unenforceable.

Under the Second Restatement's articulation of the doctrine, a party is not bound to terms of a written obligation, despite having signed it, where the other party has reason to know that the party who signed would not have manifested his assent if he knew of the term involved in the dispute.[299] Thus, in *C & J Fertilizer*, the insured was not bound by the definition of burglary contained in the policy, because the insurance company had reason to know that it would not have agreed to the policy if it had understood that it excluded particularly skilled "outside jobs" that left no marks of forced entry on the exterior of the building.[300] Likewise, in *Broemmer* the plaintiff would not have expressed her assent to the contract if she had understood that she was giving up her right to pursue the defendant in court for its negligence.

Other standardized terms of the contract, which are within the scope of the parties' reasonable expectations, are fully enforceable, even if the customer did not read the contract or realize that they were included.[301] Otherwise, standardized form contracts would lose their utility.[302]

[2] Assent to Unconscionable Terms

The unconscionability doctrine, explained in more detail elsewhere,[303] goes beyond the doctrine of reasonable expectations. It prevents enforcement of a contract, or one of its terms, if there was an "absence of meaningful choice on the part of one of the parties together with contract terms which are unreasonably favorable to the other party."[304] It usually involves elements of both procedural and substantive unfairness.[305]

---

[297] 840 P.2d 1013 (Ariz. 1992).

[298] 840 P.2d at 1017.

[299] RESTATEMENT (SECOND) OF CONTRACTS § 211(3) (1981).

[300] *See also* Darner Motor Sales v. Univ. Underwriters, 682 P.2d 388 (Ariz. 1984) ("umbrella" liability policy did not extend coverage as reasonably expected by the insured).

[301] RESTATEMENT (SECOND) OF CONTRACTS § 211(1) (1981).

[302] RESTATEMENT (SECOND) OF CONTRACTS § 211 cmt. b (1981).

[303] *See infra* § 10.05 Unconscionability.

[304] Williams v. Walker-Thomas Furniture Co., 350 F.2d 445, 450 (D.C. Cir. 1965).

[305] *See infra* § 10.05 Unconscionability.

[H] Rolling Contracts[306]

Although it started with the mass marketing of consumer products generally, the development of the personal computer and the wide distribution of computer software brought the question of assent to "rolling contracts" into clear focus. Manufacturers' agreements for many products, particularly computers and computer software, are frequently accompanied by terms that the ultimate user does not learn of until the product has been selected, paid for, brought home, opened, and used.

Agreements that are formed over a period of time, with terms disclosed by a seller in several stages, are referred to as "rolling contracts." A common example is the familiar "shrinkwrap" contract for computer software, in which a customer purchases a software package at a computer store based on the representations and notices on the outside of the package. After paying for the package and taking the software home, the customer unwraps the package and has the opportunity to read and consent to a detailed software license agreement that is either contained in the written documentation accompanying the software or, more recently, displayed on one of the screens that the customer views as part of the process of installing the software on her computer. The customer is usually provided with the opportunity to read and express her consent to the terms of the license by scrolling through many pages of the agreement (or not), and clicking on a button that says "I agree," "I accept," or other similar language. If the customer declines the proffered terms he or she is usually entitled to return the package to the store or to the software developer, and obtain a refund.[307]

A similar process is used to purchase tickets for vacation travel, where the customer frequently does not receive a detailed version of the agreement she has made until after paying the full price of the planned travel.[308] Contracts for insurance policies of various kinds are usually also formed in this manner: the customer pays on one day and receives a copy of the policy, with all of its terms, conditions, and exclusions, at a later time. Many employment contracts are created in much the same way, with assent to many terms regarding salary and duties handled at one time, and the employee being supplied with a detailed employee handbook, which may impose contractual duties or not, later on, when the term of employment begins.

---

[306] Douglas G. Baird, *The Boilerplate Puzzle*, 104 MICH. L. REV. 933 (2006); Randy E. Barnett, *Consenting to Form Contracts*, 71 FORDHAM L. REV. 627, 644 (2002); Jean Braucher, *Cowboy Contracts: The Arizona Supreme Court's Grand Tradition of Transactional Fairness*, 50 ARIZ. L. REV. 191 (2008); Stephen E. Friedman, *Improving the Rolling Contract*, 56 AM. U. L. REV. 1, 50 (2006); Clayton P. Gillette, *Rolling Contracts as an Agency Problem*, 2004 WIS. L. REV. 679; Robert A. Hillman, *Rolling Contracts*, 71 FORDHAM L. REV. 743 (2002); Robert A. Hillman & Jeffrey J. Rachlinski, *Standard-Form Contracting in the Electronic Age*, 77 N.Y.U. L. REV. 429, 439 (2002); Nancy S. Kim, *Clicking and Cringing*, 86 OR. L. REV. 797 (2007); William H. Lawrence, *Rolling Contracts Rolling over Contract Law*, 41 SAN DIEGO L. REV. 1099, 1122 (2004); John E. Murray, Jr., *The Dubious Status of the Rolling Contract Formation Theory*, 50 DUQ. L. REV. 35 (2012); Eric A. Posner, ProCD v. Zeidenberg *and Cognitive Overload in Contractual Bargaining*, 77 U. CHI. L. REV. 1181 (2010).;

[307] *See generally* Robert A. Hillman, *Rolling Contracts*, 71 FORDHAM L. REV. 743, 744 (2002).

[308] Carnival Cruise Lines v. Shute, 499 U.S. 585 (1991).

In most such cases the principal question is whether a customer's general manifestation of intent to purchase the vendor's product operates as a commitment to be bound to all of the terms that might be contained either in the packing containing the goods, or somewhere on the vendor's Internet web site. In this respect, these issues might be more appropriately viewed as relating to questions of interpretation of agreements.[309] However, the significance of decisions about contracts entered into over the Internet, with respect to the contract formation process generally, makes it appropriate to consider them here.[310]

Suppose, for example, that Shawn is interested in purchasing a new project management software package to manage his small but growing construction business. He might conduct a preliminary investigation of the various products available by reading magazine articles and online reviews of the various products. He also might read the information published by the various software vendors on their web sites in which the features and advantages of their programs are touted. Eventually, he is likely to settle on one program and seek to purchase a copy of it for use in his business.

He might purchase the software in one of several ways. He might buy a copy at a computer or office supply store, where he would have the opportunity to examine the box in which a disk containing the program is contained. If it is like most such packaging, the box will describe the general purposes of the software, contain a list of the minimum technological requirements for its use, and describe the features of the program that make it more particularly suited to uses of particular segments of the market than competing products.

Details of the terms of the "license" agreement for the use of the program are probably too lengthy to be included on the outside of the box. Instead, they are probably included somewhere inside the box, either in written form, or as a part of the "documentation" on the CD on which the program itself is stored. Shawn might not have the opportunity to review the details of the license agreement until he is in the process of "installing" the software package on his computer. This, in any event, will occur after he has paid for the copy of the program and returned home.

Alternatively, Shawn might be willing to buy the software online. This might involve entering into an agreement to have a disk containing a copy of the software to be shipped to him for installation on his computer in much the same way as the copy he might have purchased from a "bricks and mortar" store in his hometown. Or, it might be possible to download the program from the developer's web site directly to his computer.

In either case, at some point in the transaction, Shawn will probably have the opportunity to view the terms of the license agreement accompanying the software. This opportunity might occur before Shawn has confirmed his willingness to go through with the purchase, by providing his credit card information, or it might not occur until after he has paid for the software and is in the process of installing the software on his computer. In the first case, the seller's web site might automatically

---

[309] *See infra* Ch. 6 Interpretation of Contracts.

[310] *See* Robert A. Hillman, *Rolling Contracts*, 71 FORDHAM L. REV. 743 (2002).

direct Shawn to a page containing the terms of the license agreement and ask him to click a button or check a box labeled "I agree" to the terms of the software license before asking him to express his final agreement to the purchase. In the latter case, or where Shawn has purchased a copy of the program from a retail vendor, he may not have the opportunity to express his agreement to the terms of the license agreement until after he has paid for his copy of the program and is in the process of installing it on his computer. Here, he will likely have the opportunity to click on "Yes" or "No," or on "I agree" or "I disagree," possibly after being provided with a link to the terms of the license agreement or a text box displaying the first several paragraphs of its terms next to a scroll bar that he might use to view all of the gory details.

Having already concluded that he wishes to deploy the program for use in his business, Shawn may or may not read all the way through the license agreement. Even if he scrolls through the entire agreement, he may or may not understand all of its terms, particularly those relating to "arbitration," "disclaimers of warranties," "limited remedies," "forum selection," or "choice of law." Shawn may come to understand the meaning of the terms only later, if he discovers flaws in the software that make it unsuitable for use in his business, or that cause actual loss to either his data or to his ability to operate his business. Regardless of the manner in which Shawn has purchased the software package, serious questions may arise about his assent to the details of the license agreement.

In *ProCD v. Zeidenberg*,[311] the court addressed the enforceability of a so-called "shrinkwrap license" contained in the terms of a license agreement not fully disclosed to the customer until after he had paid for the software at a retail outlet and returned home to install it on his computer. The software involved in *ProCD* was a database containing the names and addresses of prospective customers for a wide variety of commercial products. Thus, the program was not used simply to store and organize data supplied by a purchaser of the program. Its principal value was the actual data included with the database program. The license agreement included in the package purchased at the retail outlet contained language restricting use of the software. It restricted use of the program and the data it contained to "noncommercial purposes." The defendant wanted to circumvent this restriction, and resold the information in the database to other businesses for their own commercial purposes. Thus, for the minimal purchase price of $150, in violation of the terms of the license accompanying ProCD's software, the defendant attempted to capitalize on the $10 million investment ProCD had made in assembling the data contained in its program.

The court was not impressed with Zeidenberg's entrepreneurial spirit. The court found that Zeidenberg was bound by the "noncommercial purpose" restriction, even though he had not had the opportunity to carefully study the terms of the license restriction before buying a copy of the software. The court said that "[n]otice on the outside, terms on the inside, and a right to return the software for a refund if the terms are unacceptable . . . may be a means of doing business

---

[311] 86 F.3d 1447 (7th Cir. 1996) (J. Easterbrook).

valuable to buyers and sellers alike."[312] In drawing its conclusion that the license restrictions were among the terms of his agreement with ProCD, the court compared this method in which the restricted license agreement was formed with a wide variety of other types of agreements in which money is exchanged before many of the details of the transaction are known, including the purchase of airline tickets, insurance policies, theater tickets, and consumer appliances. The court ultimately held that the licensee had expressed his acceptance of the terms of the restricted license, not by purchasing a copy of the program at the store, but instead "by *using* the software after having an opportunity to read the license at leisure."[313]

The approach taken in *ProCD* was later expanded in *Hill v. Gateway*[314] to a situation involving a purchase of a computer over the telephone. The court held that the buyer of the computer was bound to the detailed terms of the purchase contract, including its binding arbitration clause, even though the customer had not seen them until after he had paid for the machine and unpackaged it at his home. In *Hill* the court emphasized not only the impracticality of requiring telephone transaction order-takers to spell out all of the terms of the agreement before entering into the transaction, but also the binding nature of terms favorable to the consumer, such as those relating to warranties and support, which were not fully disclosed until after payment had been made and the box containing the computer had been delivered.

Language in the Uniform Computer Information Transactions Act (UCITA), which at one time had been destined to become Article 2B of the U.C.C., would have adopted the position taken in these cases, at least with respect to software licensing agreements.[315] There is considerable evidence that the controversy over these provisions was a leading factor in the decision by the National Conference of Commissioners on Uniform State Laws (NCCUSL) to remove UCITA from the U.C.C. It might also have led to NCCUSL's abandonment of efforts to persuade state legislatures to adopt UCITA.[316]

Other courts have been less willing to find customers bound by terms that were not fully disclosed to them before money changed hands. In *Specht v. Netscape Communications*,[317] the court refused to bind a software user to the terms of a software license agreement in which a link to the details of the agreement and a direction to a user to view those terms was located below the edge of the viewable screen that the customer used to express her consent to the terms of the license.

---

[312] 86 F.3d at 1451.

[313] 86 F.3d at 1452 (emphasis in original). *Accord* I. Lan Sys., Inc. v. Netscout Serv. Level Corp., 183 F. Supp. 2d 328 (D. Mass. 2002).

[314] 105 F.3d 1147 (7th Cir. 1997) (J. Easterbrook).

[315] U.C.I.T.A. §§ 201–209 (2002). *See generally* Brian D. McDonald, *The Uniform Computer Information Transactions Act*, 16 Berkeley Tech. L.J. 461 (2001); David A. Szwak, *Uniform Computer Information Transactions Act [U.C.I.T.A.]: The Consumer's Perspective*, 63 La. L. Rev. 27 (2002).

[316] Press Release, National Conference of Commissioners on Uniform State Laws, UCITA Withdrawn from ABA Agenda Without Action (Feb. 10, 2003). *See generally* Brian D. McDonald, *The Uniform Computer Information Transactions Act*, 16 Berkeley Tech. L.J. 461 (2012).

[317] 150 F. Supp. 2d 585 (S.D.N.Y. 2001).

The *Specht* court emphasized that "[v]isitors are not required affirmatively to indicate their assent to the License Agreement, or even to view the license agreement, before proceeding with a download of the software."[318] In *Klocek v. Gateway*,[319] the court explicitly rejected the approach in *Hill* and applied U.C.C. § 2-207(2) to find that an arbitration provision, included in the agreement contained in the box in which the buyer's computer was shipped, was nothing more than a proposal to modify the terms of the contract that had previously been formed between the parties on more general terms.[320] Likewise, in *Casavant v. Norwegian Cruise Line, Ltd.*,[321] the court was unwilling to enforce a forum selection clause contained in a document that the customers did not see until after they have paid, at least where the customers expressed their objections to the terms before embarking on the scheduled cruise.[322]

Cases binding the customer to terms that the customer had a reasonable opportunity to read and consider before making payment are less controversial. In *Forrest v. Verizon Communications, Inc.*,[323] a mobile phone service subscriber who had expressed his assent by clicking the "I agree" button appearing at the end of a "clickwrap" agreement, was found to have consented to the arbitration clause appearing above the button. In addition, in *Caspi v. Microsoft Network, L.L.C.*,[324] the court enforced a forum selection clause in an Internet service provider's subscription agreement that displayed the terms of the agreement and required an expression of assent before any charges were incurred.[325] In *Oltman v. Holland America Line USA, Inc.*,[326] the court enforced a forum selection clause provision in a cruise contract where the customers had a reasonable opportunity to learn of the provision before embarking on their trip. Finally, in *Wachter Management Co. v. Dexter & Chaney, Inc.*, the court regarded the language in a shrink-wrapped package as nothing more than a proposal to modify the contract, which the buyer had done nothing to accept.[327]

These and other decisions dealing with modern methods of contract formation present a variety of issues about the contract formation process. Their ultimate resolution is likely to have an effect on the way mass market dealers conduct their businesses.

---

[318] *Id.* at 588. *See also* Pollstar v. Gigmania Ltd., 170 F. Supp. 2d 974 (E.D. Cal. 2000).

[319] 104 F. Supp. 2d 1332 (D. Kan. 2000).

[320] Kevin W. Grierson, Annotation, *Enforceability of "Clickwrap" or "Shrinkwrap" Agreements Common in Computer Software, Hardware, and Internet Transactions*, 106 A.L.R.5th 309 (2003).

[321] 829 N.E.2d 1171 (Mass. Ct. App. 2005).

[322] 829 N.E.2d at 1182 n.17. *See* Oltman v. Holland Am. Line USA, Inc., 178 P.3d 981 (Wash. 2008) (forum selection clause in cruise contract received after payment enforceable where customers waited until after the cruise to object to its terms).

[323] 805 A.2d 1007 (D.C. 2002).

[324] 732 A.2d 528 (N.J. Super. Ct. Ch. Div. 1999).

[325] *See* Ryan J. Casamiquela, *Contractual Assent and Enforceability in Cyberspace*, 17 Berkeley Tech. L.J. 475 (2002).

[326] 178 P.3d 981 (Wash. 2008).

[327] 144 P.3d 747 (Kan. 2006).

§ 4.06 TIME OF ACCEPTANCE

Acceptance is usually communicated by the offeree through notice of its acceptance to the offeror. Acceptance must be manifested while the offer remains open, or, put another way, while the offeree still holds a "power of acceptance." As explained elsewhere, the offeree's power of acceptance might terminate due to lapse of time, revocation, death of the offeror or other circumstances of which the offeree may be unaware. If acceptance comes too late, it is ineffective to conclude a contract.[328]

[A] Instantaneous Communications: Acceptance Effective upon Receipt

In situations involving simultaneous communication, such as in face-to-face meetings or a telephone conversations, acceptance is effective upon receipt.[329] In these circumstances, the offeror normally learns instantaneously of the offeree's acceptance. In these situations, the parties normally become immediately aware of any failure in the means of communication, such as if the telephone goes dead or a blaring siren drowns out the offeree's voice in a face-to-face meeting.[330] Delay or disruption of the parties' communications in these situations is rare.[331] Disputes about formation of a contract when it happens is rarer still.

[B] Delayed Communication: Acceptance Effective upon Dispatch[332]

Difficulties are more likely to arise where there is some delay in the parties' communication, such as through the use of the mail. The problem becomes acute if offeree's acceptance is sent when the offeree still has a power of acceptance but arrives after his power of acceptance has expired. Thus, if the offer expires at midnight, November 27, and the offeree sends his acceptance on the 26th, but it does not arrive until the 28th, there is a question of whether the acceptance was effective.

Although the rule sometimes creates problems, the common law treats acceptance as effective when it is sent, not when it arrives.[333] Thus, if Phil sends Karen an offer to buy Karen's house, Karen's acceptance is effective when she deposits her acceptance in the mail. If Phil tries to revoke his offer before he has received Karen's response, a contract exists even if Phil uses a more expeditious

---

[328] *See infra* § 4.08 Termination of Offers.

[329] RESTATEMENT (SECOND) OF CONTRACTS § 64 (1981).

[330] RESTATEMENT (SECOND) OF CONTRACTS § 64 cmt. b (1981).

[331] *See* Entores, Ltd. v. Miles Far E. Corp, 2 Q.B. 327 (1955) (contract created over the telephone is complete only when the acceptance is received by the offeror).

[332] Ian Macneil, *Time of Acceptance: Too Many Problems for a Single Rule*, 112 U. PA. L. REV. 947 (1964); Edward S. Stimson, *Effective Time of an Acceptance*, 23 MINN. L. REV. 776 (1939); P.H. Winfield, *Some Aspects of Offer and Acceptance*, 55 L.Q. REV. 499 (1939).

[333] RESTATEMENT (SECOND) OF CONTRACTS § 63 (1981). *E.g.*, Morrison v. Thoelke, 155 So. 2d 889 (Fla. Dist. Ct. App. 1963).

means of communication and makes sure that his revocation arrives before he has received Karen's acceptance.[334]

Likewise, if Karen mails her acceptance, but later changes her mind and calls Phil to reject, she is too late. Her previously sent acceptance already formed a binding agreement, even if Phil learns of her attempt to reject his offer before he receives her previously sent acceptance.

This is exactly what happened in *Morrison v. Thoelke*.[335] The prospective buyers of a tract of land mailed an offer to the owners expressing their willingness to purchase the property. The next day, the owners signed the buyer's offer and deposited their acceptance in the mail. Regretting their precipitous response, they called the buyers by telephone and repudiated the deal. Later, of course, the buyers received the acceptance that the owners had previously sent. They were still interested in going ahead with the transaction and, in an effort to prevent the owners from selling the property to someone else, recorded the contract in the real estate records in the county where the land was located.[336] The court applied the then-well-established rule that an acceptance is effective when sent[337] and held the owners to the acceptance they sent before changing their minds about the deal.

[1]　Reasons for the Dispatch Rule; Criticism

The court in *Morrison v. Thoelke* explained the rule in terms of the necessity of drawing a line somewhere during the course of an exchange of communications between the parties. The court said: "there must be, both in practical and conceptual terms, a point in time when a contract is complete." The court also explained its decision by referring to the nineteenth-century notion that a contract was formed when there was a "meeting of the minds."[338] When the owners dispatched their assent they intended to sell the land to the buyers and thus shared the same intent as the buyers who still wished to purchase the land.

The mailbox rule has been justified on several additional grounds. The Second Restatement asserts that the rule supplies an offeree with a dependable basis for its decision about whether to accept, without the fear that its acceptance will be disappointed by a revocation that is received before the acceptance arrives.[339] This supposedly prevents the offeror's right of revocation from giving the offeror an unfair advantage. The Restatement also justifies the rule, which applies with equal force to situations involving acceptances that never arrive as it does to those in

---

[334] *See, e.g.*, Adams v. Lindsell, 106 Eng. Rep. 250 (K.B. 1818).

[335] 155 So. 2d 889 (Fla. Dist. Ct. App. 1963).

[336] This effectively preserved their rights against those of someone who subsequently entered into another contract with the owners for the purchase of the same land. The mere appearance of the contract in the owner's chain of title would effectively discourage other prospective buyers.

[337] The American version of the rule is derived from the English case of Adams v. Lindsell, 106 Eng. Rep. 250 (K.B. 1818). *See* Ian Macneil, *Time of Acceptance: Too Many Problems for a Single Rule*, 112 U. Pa. L. Rev. 947 (1964).

[338] *See* Reserve Ins. Co. v. Duckett, 238 A.2d 536 (Md. 1968) (recognizing that the dispatch rule is a vestige of the subjective theory of contract formation).

[339] *See* Restatement (Second) of Contracts § 63 cmt. a (1981).

which the offeror attempts to revoke its offer, as promoting the dual interests of "simplicity and clarity."[340]

Others have justified the rule on the grounds of economic efficiency in that it permits the offeree, once it has sent its acceptance, to begin performance immediately. Under this rationale, any other rule would force the offeree to wait to perform until after he or she has received confirmation of the receipt of his or her acceptance. This adds unnecessary transaction costs to the contract formation and performance process. The rule also has been supported as being consistent with the rule that an offeror is the master of the offer and is free, in any event, to require receipt of the acceptance if she is dissatisfied with the uncertainty the rule creates.[341]

On the other hand, the mailbox rule has frequently been criticized as harsh on offerors, who are left facing the uncertainty of being bound to a contract without knowing that it exists. More importantly, it is often viewed as counterintuitive and thus not reflective of the rule that the parties most likely would have chosen had they thought to address the issue.[342] It has also been criticized as inconsistent with the doctrine of consideration, because there can be no real transaction of exchange until the offeror learns that a bargain has been struck. Despite these and other criticisms,[343] the rule persists.

[2] Limitations on the Dispatch Rule

The dispatch rule is subject to several important limits. First, it applies only to situations in which the means of communication used by the parties ordinarily involves some delay. In telephone, teletype, and other modes of communication that are "instantaneous," the rule does not operate.[344]

Second, the means of communication of the acceptance must be one that is authorized by the offer. If the terms of the offer specify a particular exclusive mode of acceptance and the offeree elects to use some other method, his or her acceptance is not effective until it is received.[345]

Likewise, the offeree must send her acceptance properly. A letter that is misaddressed, or that fails to include the proper postage, will not be effective until received.[346] With respect to these limitations, however, an acceptance that is sent within a reasonable time but that uses an improper means of communication or is misdirected is nevertheless effective immediately on dispatch if it is actually

---

[340] RESTATEMENT (SECOND) OF CONTRACTS § 63 cmt. b (1981).

[341] *E.g.,* Worms v. Burgess, 620 P.2d 455, 457 (Okla. Civ. App. 1980).

[342] See Beth A. Eisler, *Default Rules for Contract Formation by Promise and the Need for Revision of the Mailbox Rule,* 79 KY. L.J. 557, 564 (1990–91).

[343] *See* David Marshall Evans, *The Anglo-American Mailing Rule: Some Problems of Offer and Acceptance in Contracts by Correspondence,* 15 INT'L & COMP. L.Q. 553 (1966); Ian Macneil, *Time of Acceptance: Too Many Problems for a Single Rule,* 112 U. PA. L. REV. 947 (1964).

[344] *See* RESTATEMENT (SECOND) OF CONTRACTS § 64 (1981).

[345] RESTATEMENT (SECOND) OF CONTRACTS § 63(a) (1981).

[346] RESTATEMENT (SECOND) OF CONTRACTS § 66 (1981).

received within the time in which a properly sent acceptance would have been received.[347]

[3] Identifying the Time Acceptance Is Sent

A rule that makes a communication effective when it is sent naturally raises the question of what qualifies as having "sent" the letter. Countless cases make it clear that depositing it in a mailbox is sufficient, as this removes the letter from the immediate control of the offeree, even though postal regulations permit the offeree to subsequently retrieve it from the postal service.[348] When other means of communication are used, the principal question is whether the communication has been placed "beyond the offeree's possession."[349] Here, an independent messenger, such as UPS, Federal Express, or some other similar commercial delivery service, is treated the same as the United States Postal Service.[350]

Thus, if Phil has offered to purchase Karen's home, and Karen replies by handing her acceptance to the employee of a bicycle messenger service for delivery to Phil, Karen's acceptance is effective when it is delivered to the independent messenger, even though she might be able to retrieve the acceptance by chasing the messenger down the street or by contacting his employer to return the letter before it has been delivered. The effectiveness of her acceptance depends, of course, on whether transmittal of the acceptance by a bicycle messenger service was an authorized means of communication.

If, on the other hand, Karen hands her acceptance to her own secretary, with instructions to personally deliver it to Phil, her acceptance is not effective until Phil receives it.[351] While it is in the possession of her own secretary, the acceptance is treated as remaining in Karen's possession.[352] Placing it in the interoffice mail basket or in the "out box" in the company mail room probably places it sufficiently outside her immediate control to operate as having been sent,[353] though this remains somewhat uncertain and possibly dependent on how the particular mail room is handled, the responsible individual's position in the company hierarchy,[354] and the applicable chain of command.

---

[347] Your author regularly receives mail even though it is addressed to the wrong street number. He receives this mail because of the courtesy of his neighbor who lives at the address to which it is misdirected. If his neighbor is on vacation, a misdirected acceptance might be delayed beyond the time when it would have been received had it been properly addressed. If so, it would ineffective as an acceptance even if it eventually arrived at the right location.

[348] *See* RESTATEMENT (SECOND) OF CONTRACTS § 63 cmt. e (1981). *E.g.*, Bank of Ipswich v. Harding County Farmers' Mut. Fire & Lightning Ins. Co., 225 N.W. 721 (S.D. 1929).

[349] RESTATEMENT (SECOND) OF CONTRACTS § 63(a) (1981).

[350] RESTATEMENT (SECOND) OF CONTRACTS § 63 cmt. e (1981).

[351] *E.g.*, Pribil v. Ruther, 262 N.W.2d 460 (Neb. 1978).

[352] RESTATEMENT (SECOND) OF CONTRACTS § 63 cmt. e & illus. 11 (1981).

[353] Maclay v. Harvey, 1878 Ill. LEXIS 255 (Sept. 1878) (placing a response in a location where it can be collected by the mail carrier not sufficient to operate as acceptance).

[354] Understandably, there are few opportunities for courts to evaluate the precise lines of demarcation — most of the time when an arguably dispatched acceptance is retrieved, the original offeror never learns that a contract might have been formed.

The dispatch rule is equally effective even if the acceptance never arrives at its intended destination.[355] Thus, a contract is formed even if the offeree is successful in retrieving its acceptance from the mail. However, in such a case, the likelihood of the original offeror learning that the offeree's acceptance had ever been dispatched is slim.[356]

[4] Dispatch Rule in Domestic Sales of Goods

Article 2 of the Uniform Commercial Code, which applies to domestic transactions for the sale of goods, does nothing to modify the dispatch rule. It specifies that title to goods will generally pass from the seller to the buyer "at the time and place at which the seller completes his performance with reference to the physical delivery of the goods."[357] Thus, although Article 2 dispenses with the need to determine the precise moment at which a contract is formed,[358] its position that a buyer becomes owner of the goods as soon as they are shipped seems to adopt the mailbox rule, at least in cases where shipment of the goods is an appropriate means of expressing acceptance.[359]

[5] Time of Acceptance in International Transactions[360]

The CISG applies a different rule to international sale-of-goods transactions. Article 18(2) specifies that "[a]n acceptance is not effective if the indication of assent does not reach the offeror within the time he has fixed or, if no time is fixed, within a reasonable time."[361] At the same time, offers are irrevocable once the offeree has dispatched an acceptance.[362] Thus, dispatch of an acceptance does not conclude a contract, but it does make the offer irrevocable. Nevertheless if the acceptance does not arrive on time, no contract is formed.

In other international transactions, the UNIDROIT Principles of International Commercial Contracts and Principles on European Contract Law adopt the civil law rule that acceptances that are dispatched are not effective until receipt.[363]

---

[355] RESTATEMENT (SECOND) OF CONTRACTS § 63(a) (1981).

[356] *E.g.*, Soldau v. Organon Inc., 860 F.2d 355 (9th Cir. 1988).

[357] U.C.C. § 2-401(2) (2012).

[358] U.C.C. § 2-204 (2012).

[359] *See also* U.C.C. § 1-202(d) (2012) ("A person 'notifies' or 'gives' a notice or notification to another by taking such steps as may be reasonably required to inform the other in ordinary course whether or not such other actually comes to know of it.") (formerly § 1-201(26)).

[360] William S. Dodge, *Teaching The CISG in Contracts*, 50 J. LEGAL EDUC. 72, 81 (2000).

[361] CISG Art. 18(2) (1980).

[362] CISG Art. 16(1) (1980).

[363] PICC Art. 2.1.6(2) (2004); PECL Art. 2.205(1) (2002).

[6] Electronic Commerce[364]

The advent of the Internet, e-mail, and "text messages" raise obvious questions about the scope of the mailbox rule, which, as noted earlier, does not apply to circumstances involving instantaneous communication. Although many people assume that e-mail messages are delivered instantaneously, e-mail messages can take anywhere from several minutes to several hours to be received, or they may never arrive at all. It is entirely possible for there to be a breakdown in the chain of communications between the parties in an exchange of e-mails, which may, after all, occur over a period of several days.[365]

"Instant messaging" communications and "texting," on the other hand, are more similar to face-to-face meetings and telephone conversations where the parties are likely to know immediately if their communication system fails.

The Uniform Electronic Transactions Act (UETA)[366] has been adopted by 47 states and the District of Columbia.[367] UETA, like its federally enacted counterpart, the Electronic Signatures in Global and National Commerce Act (E-SIGN),[368] both treat electronic records as the equivalent of paper documents.[369] However, neither act provides a comprehensive set of rules for dealing with electronic communications — other than treating them as the equivalent of analog methods of concluding contracts.[370]

---

[364] Juanda Lowder Daniel, *Electronic Contracting Under the 2003 Revisions to Article 2 of the Uniform Commercial Code: Clarification or Chaos?*, 20 SANTA CLARA COMPUTER & HIGH TECH. L.J. 319 (2004); Jennifer E. Hill, *The Future of Electronic Contracts in International Sales: Gaps and Natural Remedies under the United Nations Convention on Contracts for the International Sale of Goods*, 2 Nw. J. TECH. & INTELL. PROP. 1 (2003); Robert A. Hillman & Jeffrey J. Rachlinski, *Standard-Form Contracting in the Electronic Age*, 77 N.Y.U. L. REV. 429 (2002); Christina L. Kunz, John E. Ottaviani, Elaine D. Ziff, Juliet M. Moringiello, Kathleen M. Porter & Jennifer C. Debrow, *Browse-Wrap Agreements: Validity of Implied Assent in Electronic Form Agreement* s, 59 BUS. LAW 279, 279–80 (2003); Ronald J. Mann, Essay, *Just One Click: the Reality of Internet Retail Contracting*, 108 COLUM. L. REV. 984 (2008); Charles H. Martin, *The Electronic Contracts Convention, the CISG, and New Sources of E-Commerce Law*, 16 TUL. J. INT'L & COMP. L. 467 (2008); Juliet M. Moringiello, *Signals, Assent and Internet Contracting*, 57 RUTGERS L. REV. 1307 (2005); Valerie Watnick, *The Electronic Formation of Contracts and the Common Law "Mailbox Rule,"* 56 BAYLOR L. REV. 175 (2004).

[365] *See generally* Paul Fasciano, *Internet Electronic Mail: A Last Bastion for the Mailbox Rule*, 25 HOFSTRA L. REV. 971 (1997).

[366] Uniform Electronic Transactions Act (UETA) (1999), 7(A) U.L.A. 252 (2002), also *available at* http://www.uniformlaws.org/shared/docs/electronic%20transactions/ueta_final_99.pdf (last viewed June 13, 2013).

[367] *See* http://uniformlaws.org/LegislativeFactSheet.aspx?title=Electronic%20Transactions%20Act (last viewed June 13, 2013) (still not enacted in New York, Oregon, or Illinois).

[368] Electronic Signatures in Global and National Commerce Act § 101, 15 U.S.C. § 7001 (2006).

[369] Shea C. Meehan, *What Hath Congress Wrought: E-sign, The UETA, and the Question of Preemption*, 37 IDAHO L. REV. 389 (2001); Robert A. Wittie & Jane K Winn, *Electronic Records and Signatures Under the Federal E-Sign Legislation and the UETA*, 56 BUS. LAW. 293 (2000).

[370] UETA § 7 (1999). *See* Daniel R. Murray & Timothy J. Chorvat, *Stepping up to the Next Level: From the UETA to the URE and Beyond*, 37 IDAHO L. REV. 415 (2001).

It also permits contracts to be created through electronic agents.[371] Anyone who has ordered goods through the Internet has probably encountered such an electronic agent — a program that examines the details of the buyer's order, checks the seller's record of its inventory to determine if the goods are available, and automatically accepts the buyer's offer. Large buyers also use electronic agents to order additional items automatically when the buyer's supply of items is reduced to a predesignated level.

UETA also provides rules to determine the time and place of the sending and receipt of electronic messages involved in an electronic transaction.[372] However, apart from treating them as the legal equivalent of other means of communications, it does not deal with effectiveness of unintelligible electronic records. The legal consequences of the record are left to other law.[373]

In international transactions, there is no governing treaty regarding electronic formation of contracts.[374] However, in 2005 UNCITRAL — the International Chamber of Commerce — adopted the Convention on the Use of Electronic Communications in International Contracts (CUECIC), which implements many of the provisions of UNCITRAL's earlier Model Law on Electronic Commerce (MLEC). CUECIC was adopted by the General Assembly of the United Nations later the same year.[375]

Upon becoming effective, CUECIC will apply to "electronic communications in connection with the formation or performance of a contract between parties whose places of business are in different States."[376] It will apply to a wide variety of international transactions, including those for goods, services, and intellectual property. However, it will not apply to transactions with consumers.[377]

The details of its provisions are beyond the scope of this book. However, it generally makes electronic communications the legal equivalent of other means of communication. It contains rules regarding the time of dispatch and receipt, use of electronic agents, and errors in electronic communication.[378] Until it is adopted,

---

[371] UETA § 14 (1999).

[372] UETA § 15 (1999).

[373] UETA § 15 cmt. 1 (1999).

[374] The United Nations Convention on the Use of Electronic Communications in International Contracts, G.A. Res. 60/21, U.N. Doc. A/RES/60/21 (Dec. 9, 2005) (CUECIC), has been signed by 18 nations as of summer, 2013. *See* Status, United Nations Convention on the Use of Electronic Communications in International Contracts, UNCITRAL, 2007, http://www.uncitral.org/uncitral/en/uncitral_texts/electronic_commerce/2005Convention_status.html (last viewed June 13, 2013). By signing the convention these nations, most of which are in Southeast Asia, have only made a commitment to consider its ratification. CUECIC will not become effective until at least three nations ratify it. CUECIC Art. 23.1 (2005). The United States has neither signed nor ratified it, but will probably ratify it, if at all, without the preliminary step of signing it.

[375] Charles H. Martin, *The Electronic Contracts Convention, the CISG, and New Sources of E-Commerce Law*, 16 Tul. J. Int'l & Comp. L. 467 (2008). *See* John D. Gregory, *The Proposed UNCITRAL Convention on Electronic Contracts*, 59 Bus. Law 313, 317 (2003).

[376] CUECIC Art. 1.1 (2005).

[377] CUECIC Art. 2.1(a) (2005).

[378] *See* Charles H. Martin, *The Electronic Contracts Convention, the CISG, and New Sources of*

these matters will be governed by more general rules in other conventions, such as the CISG, by customary international law, and by private agreements between the parties.

[C] Conflicting Communications

The mailbox rule creates several collateral difficulties when one of the parties changes its mind about the transaction and sends a communication that conflicts with an earlier message. This might easily occur, for example, where the offeror makes a better deal with someone else and revokes her offer. Difficulties might also arise if the offeree has second thoughts about a transaction after sending an acceptance, and attempts to reject. Similar problems can occur if the offeree, having rejected an offer, changes his or her mind and sends an acceptance.

[1] Revocation of Offer

Unless the offer is irrevocable, an offeror can revoke her offer any time before acceptance.[379] Thus, a person who makes an offer has considerable leeway any time before the offeree accepts. However, the mailbox rule, which makes acceptances effective upon dispatch, imposes a limit on this freedom. If the offeree sends an acceptance before learning of the offeror's revocation, a contract is formed.

Suppose, for example, that Merlin sends an offer to Agnes proposing to buy her house for $160,000. Afterwards, Merlin finds another house that he prefers and sends Agnes a letter revoking his offer. Merlin's revocation is not effective until Agnes receives it. If Agnes dispatches an acceptance before she receives Merlin's revocation, a contract has been formed.[380]

[2] Rejection and Subsequent Acceptance

Problems can also arise where an offeree rejects but subsequently changes her mind and sends an acceptance. If the rejection arrives first, there is no contract even if the acceptance is sent before the rejection arrives.[381] In this instance, the mailbox rule simply does not apply. This protects the offeror, who is likely to act in reliance on the rejection. The purported acceptance is a counteroffer.[382]

Similarly, if the subsequently sent acceptance overtakes the previously sent rejection and arrives first, the mailbox rule is inapplicable. Instead, a contract is formed upon receipt of the acceptance.[383] But, in this situation, few difficulties are likely to arise, unless the offeree has another change of heart and tries to back out of the deal.

E-Commerce Law, 16 Tul. J. Int'l & Comp. L. 467 (2008).

[379] Restatement (Second) of Contracts § 42 illus. 1 (1981).

[380] Restatement (Second) of Contracts § 42 illus. 2 (1981).

[381] Restatement (Second) of Contracts § 40 cmt. b (1981).

[382] Restatement (Second) of Contracts § 40 (1981).

[383] Restatement (Second) of Contracts § 40 cmt. b & illus. 1 (1981).

Thus, if Kathy sends an offer proposing to purchase Dave's house, and Dave sends a rejection, but later sends an acceptance that overtakes his previously sent rejection, and the acceptance arrives first, it appears that both parties wish to go through with the deal. Kathy may be confused when she receives the rejection, but most of the time, her confusion will be easily resolved through further communication between the parties. In the rare circumstances in which Kathy acts in reliance on the rejection, she will be justified if it was reasonable for her to regard the rejection as a repudiation of the contract.[384]

[3] Acceptance and Subsequent Rejection

A similar situation is where the offeree sends an acceptance but then changes his mind and sends a rejection.

If the rejection overtakes the acceptance and arrives first, holding the parties to a contract may create a problem for the offeror, who might have relied on the rejection and entered into a substitute transaction with someone else.[385] Here, the offeror may enforce the contract that was formed when the offeree's acceptance was dispatched, or, if he or she has relied on the rejection, may estop the offeror from changing his or her mind again and attempting to enforce the contract.[386]

[D] Option Contracts — Acceptance Effective upon Receipt

An option contract is an enforceable agreement to keep an offer open. In an option contract the offeror may not revoke his or her offer.[387] The mailbox rule does not apply to option contracts. An offeree's exercise of an option — an acceptance — is normally effective only when it is received.[388]

For example, in *Salminen v. Frankson*,[389] the parties entered into an option contract giving Salminen 45 days, starting on September 6, to accept Frankson's offer to sell three parcels of land. On October 21, the last day of the option, Salminen deposited notice in the mail that he was accepting Frankson's offer, thus attempting to exercise the option. Frankson did not receive the acceptance until October 23, two days after the option period had expired. The buyer's acceptance came too late. The court explained: "[the] defendant, for valuable consideration, promised to keep her offer open for a specified period of time. She was entitled to know at the end of that period whether or not plaintiff intended to accept the offer. Not having received notice of acceptance at the end of that period, she was entitled to treat the option as expired, which she did."[390] Because Salminen's acceptance was too late, there was no contract.

---

[384] *See infra* § 9.05 Anticipatory Repudiation.

[385] RESTATEMENT (SECOND) OF CONTRACTS § 63 cmt. c & illus. 7 (1981).

[386] RESTATEMENT (SECOND) OF CONTRACTS § 63 cmt. c & illus. 7 (1981).

[387] *See infra* § 4.09[A] Traditional Option Contracts.

[388] RESTATEMENT (SECOND) OF CONTRACTS § 63 (1981). *E.g.*, Musgrove v. Long, 287 S.E.2d 23 (Ga. 1982).

[389] 245 N.W.2d 839, 840 (Minn. 1976).

[390] *Id. But see* McTernan v. LeTendre, 351 N.E.2d 566 (Mass. Ct. App. 1976).

The rule making acceptances of irrevocable offers effective only upon receipt is a default rule. If they want, the parties can agree that the offeree's acceptance will be effective when it is sent, just like it is in other transactions. However, if the option contract does not specify otherwise, acceptance is effective only on the offeror's receipt of the acceptance.

§ 4.07 OFFER AND ACCEPTANCE IN AUCTIONS[391]

Auctions are special arrangements designed to obtain the highest sales price by encouraging competitive bidding among potential buyers. Usually the sale is conducted by a professional auctioneer acting on behalf of the seller. The auctioneer acts as the seller's agent. Typically, the item to be auctioned is displayed or described and the auctioneer solicits bids. The bidding continues until the auctioneer is satisfied that no higher bids will be submitted, at which time he "lets the hammer fall" and concludes the auction by announcing the sale of the auctioned property to the highest bidder.

There are two types of auctions: those "with reserve" and those "without reserve." Identifying the offeror and offeree depends on which kind of auction is involved.

[A] Auctions "With Reserve"

Unless an auction is specified in advance as being "without reserve," the auction is presumed to be "with reserve."[392] In an auction with reserve, the auctioneer (and thus the seller) retains the right to withdraw the property from the auction at any time before completion of the sale. Thus, the auctioneer may terminate the auction without selling the goods, regardless of how many bids have been made or how high the bidding has gone. Effectively, therefore, in an auction with reserve, the auctioneer's acts of displaying the property and "offering" it for sale are a mere invitation to bidders to make offers.[393] There is no contract for the sale of the property until the auctioneer announces that the sale is complete.[394]

[B] Auctions "Without Reserve"

In an auction "without reserve," the situation is reversed: once the auctioneer calls for bids on the property involved, the property cannot be withdrawn from the auction unless no qualified bid is made within a reasonable time.[395] Until the property is "put up," the auction may be cancelled and the property withdrawn.[396] That is, advertisement of the auction is not a binding commitment to sell.[397]

---

[391] David Carl Minneman, Annotation, *Auction Sales Under UCC § 2-328*, 44 A.L.R.4th 110 (1986).

[392] U.C.C. § 2-328(3) (2012).

[393] Restatement (Second) of Contracts § 28(1)(a) & cmt. b (1981).

[394] U.C.C. § 2-328(2) (2012).

[395] U.C.C. § 2-328(3) (2012).

[396] U.C.C. § 2-328 cmt. 2 (2012).

[397] Restatement (Second) of Contracts § 28 cmt. c (1981).

However, once the property is "put up" for auction, the sale must proceed. By putting the property up the auctioneer has effectively made an irrevocable offer to sell the property to the highest bidder, subject only to the condition that there be a qualified bid within a reasonable time.[398]

In an auction "without reserve," bidders are expressing their "acceptances." Each bidder's acceptance concludes a contract, subject only to the condition that no higher qualified bid is made. Thus, each new bid operates to "discharge" the contract created by an earlier bid. If no higher bids are submitted, the auctioneer is obligated to sell the goods to the highest bidder.

[C] Withdrawal of Bids

A curious wrinkle, peculiar to auctions, is that regardless of whether the auction is one "with reserve" or "without reserve," bidders are free to revoke their bids any time before the auctioneer concludes the sale.[399] Moreover, the retraction of the highest bid does not reinstate any previous bid.[400]

Consider, for example, a "no reserve" auction of Fran's car. Because the auction is "without reserve" once the auction begins the car may not be withdrawn unless no one makes a bid within a reasonable time.

If Ben and Dave start bidding on the car, each of their bids will be treated as an acceptance of the auctioneer's offer, with two caveats: (1) they may each withdraw their bids any time before the auctioneer's accepts one of them as the highest bid, and (2) the other bidder might submit a higher bid. Thus, if Ben bids $16,000, but when the auctioneer seems ready to announce the conclusion of the sale, Ben announces that he is retracting his bid, there is no contract. If this happens, Dave's earlier high bid of $15,000 is not revived. Someone must make a new bid, or the auction will fail. Once the auctioneer announces the conclusion of the sale, the highest bidder loses his ability to retract and, as the successful bidder, has a contract to buy the property for the amount of his accepted bid.

§ 4.08 TERMINATION OF OFFERS

Once made, an offer gives the offeree a "power of acceptance."[401] This means that the offeree has the power to conclude the bargain by expressing his assent to the proposed terms.[402]

A contract is formed only if the acceptance occurs before the power of acceptance terminates. If the offeree accepts before the offer terminates, a contract is formed.

---

[398] Restatement (Second) of Contracts § 28(b) & cmt. d (1981).

[399] U.C.C. § 2-328(3) (2012); Restatement (Second) of Contracts § 28(c) (1981).

[400] U.C.C. § 2-328(3) (2012).

[401] Restatement (Second) of Contracts § 35(1) (1981). For general information on termination of offers, see: Wayne Barnes, *The Objective Theory of Contracts*, 76 U. Cin. L. Rev. 1119, 1132 (2008); Val D. Ricks, *The Death of Offers*, 79 Ind. L.J. 667 (2004).

[402] Restatement (Second) of Contracts § 35 cmt. c (1981).

If the offeree tries to accept after the offer terminates, no contract is formed.[403]

An offeree's power of acceptance might be terminated in one of several ways: lapse,[404] revocation,[405] rejection,[406] counteroffer,[407] or death or incapacity of the offeror.[408] The remainder of this section explains each of these events, which prevent formation of a contract unless further communications are exchanged.

[A] Lapse: Expiration of Time for Acceptance

The first way a power of acceptance might terminate is through lapse: expiration of the time for acceptance.[409] As the master of the offer, the offeror has complete discretion to determine how long the offeree has to reply. If the offeror specifies that the offeree has only 10 days, 10 minutes, or 10 seconds to accept, then that is how long the offeree's power of acceptance lasts. Whenever the offer specifies the duration of the offer, the specified time controls.[410]

If the offer does not specify a time for acceptance, the offer lasts for a reasonable time.[411] This is consistent with the more general principle that if the offeror fails to specify the manner of acceptance, then any reasonable manner of acceptance is sufficient.[412]

The exact duration of a reasonable time varies depending on the circumstances. In face-to-face negotiations, an offeree's power of acceptance usually ends when their face-to-face meeting is over.[413] Thus, if when they meet, Sam offers to sell his car to Barb for $16,000 and Barb fails to accept before their conversation ends, she is unable to call Sam the next day and accept. The same is true if their negotiations are conducted over the telephone or some other means of instantaneous communication.

However, the parties may agree to handle things differently. If Sam tells Barb to "think about it and get back to me," the termination of their face-to-face discussion will not terminate Barb's power of acceptance. Likewise, if Barb says "I'll let you know" and Sam does not object, he will probably be treated as extending the time for acceptance beyond the end of their face-to-face meeting. In these situations, Sam's offer lasts for a further reasonable time.

---

[403] RESTATEMENT (SECOND) OF CONTRACTS § 35(2) (1981).

[404] RESTATEMENT (SECOND) OF CONTRACTS § 36(1)(b) (1981).

[405] RESTATEMENT (SECOND) OF CONTRACTS § 36(1)(c) (1981).

[406] RESTATEMENT (SECOND) OF CONTRACTS § 36(1)(a) (1981).

[407] *Id.*

[408] RESTATEMENT (SECOND) OF CONTRACTS § 36(1)(d) (1981).

[409] RESTATEMENT (SECOND) OF CONTRACTS § 36(1)(b) (1981).

[410] RESTATEMENT (SECOND) OF CONTRACTS § 41(1) (1981).

[411] RESTATEMENT (SECOND) OF CONTRACTS § 41(1) & cmt. b (1981). *E.g.*, Vaskie v. West Am. Ins. Co., 556 A.2d 436 (Pa. Super. Ct. 1989).

[412] RESTATEMENT (SECOND) OF CONTRACTS § 41(1) cmt. b (1981).

[413] RESTATEMENT (SECOND) OF CONTRACTS § 41 cmt. d & illus. 4 (1981). *E.g.*, Akers v. J. B. Sedberry, Inc., 286 S.W.2d 617 (Tenn. Ct. App. 1955).

An offer that has lapsed might be subsequently revived. Thus, if two days after their initial face-to-face conversation, Sam calls Barb and says: "do you want the car?," Sam's offer is revived, and Barb may accept.

However not every repetition of an offer operates as a revival. In *Newman v. Schiff*,[414] a notorious tax protestor made an offer during a live TV show that he would pay $100,000 to anyone who called the show and cited any section of the Internal Revenue Code that requires an individual to file a tax return. A tape of the show was aired again, at a later date. The court ruled that the power of acceptance created by his statement was open only for the duration of the show and that it was not revived by a taped rebroadcast of the show by the broadcaster.

The duration of a reasonable time depends on a variety of circumstances related to what the offeree reasonably believes is satisfactory to the offeror.[415] These factors include the past practices of the parties in dealing with one another, any relevant industry custom, and the volatility of the market price of the subject of the proposed agreement.[416] If market prices are relatively stable and there are no other factors indicating a need to act quickly, then a reasonable time will be longer. However, if the market is volatile, with prices changing rapidly, the offeree's time to express its acceptance may be very short.[417]

When communications are exchanged by mail, the normal rule is that an acceptance is timely if it is sent by midnight of the day the offer is received.[418] Otherwise, because of the wide variety of circumstances that might influence the duration of a reasonable time, no hard and fast rules can be established. Instead, it is "determined in the light of the particular circumstances of each case."[419] As in most cases where "reasonableness" is the test, the question of whether the offeree still had a power of acceptance at the time he or she expressed her assent is a question for the jury.[420]

In international transactions the rule is the same, except that acceptance is usually not effective until acceptance is received. Thus, under the CISG, an acceptance must be received "within the time fixed or, if no time is fixed, within a reasonable time."[421] The CISG specifically directs that in calculating a reasonable time "due account" must be "taken of the circumstances of the transaction, including the rapidity of the means of communication employed by the offeror."[422] It further specifies that "an oral offer must be accepted immediately unless the

---

[414] 778 F.2d 460 (8th Cir. 1985).

[415] Family Video Movie Club, Inc. v. Home Folks, Inc., 827 N.E.2d 582 (Ind. Ct. App. 2005).

[416] RESTATEMENT (SECOND) OF CONTRACTS § 41 cmt. b (1981).

[417] RESTATEMENT (SECOND) OF CONTRACTS § 41 cmt. f (1981). *E.g.*, Starkweather v. Gleason, 109 N.E. 635 (Mass. 1915) (stock fluctuating in value).

[418] RESTATEMENT (2d)_§ 41(3) (1981).

[419] Brzezinek v. Covenant Ins. Co., 810 A.2d 306, 310 (Conn. App. Ct. 2002).

[420] *E.g.*, Vaskie v. W. Am. Ins. Co., 556 A.2d 436 (Pa. Super. Ct. 1989).

[421] CISG Art. 18(2) (1980).

[422] *Id.*

circumstances indicate otherwise."[423] UNIDROIT'S Principles of International Commercial Contracts and the Principles of European Contract Law take the same approach.[424]

[B] Revocation by the Offeror[425]

The offeree's power of acceptance also ends when the offeror revokes its offer. This occurs when the offeree learns that the offeror has changed her mind about the deal.

Withdrawing an offer is referred to as a "revocation." Revocation of an offer is effective if it occurs before the offeree has accepted.[426] Thus, if Karen offers to sell her house to Phil, but then notifies Phil that she has sold it to someone else, any later attempt by Phil to accept is ineffective.

[1] Revocation Effective upon Receipt

Revocation is not effective until it is received by the offeree.[427] This is consistent with the principle that the contract formation process depends upon the parties' outward objective manifestations of assent. Revocation terminates the offeree's power of acceptance when it comes into the possession of the offeree or to some person authorized to act on his behalf.[428] However, a revocation or other communication is also received when it is placed in a spot that the recipient has authorized to be used as the place for the delivery of communications. Thus, delivery of a communication to someone's office mailbox ordinarily constitutes receipt, whether it is retrieved from the mailbox, or not.

[2] Indirect Communication of Revocation

Indirect communication of the revocation of an offer is just as effective as direct notice.[429] For example, in *Dickinson v. Dodds*,[430] the offeree learned from a third person that land that had been offered to him for purchase had already been sold to someone else. As a result, his power of acceptance terminated and his subsequent attempt to accept was ineffective. Thus, if Karen offers to sell her house to Phil, but Phil later learns from his friend Joe that Karen has sold the house to someone else, Phil can no longer accept, even though he did not hear about the sale from Karen directly. The same result occurs if Phil learns about the sale in the newspaper.

---

[423] *Id.*

[424] PICC Art. 2.1.7 (2004); PECL Art. 2.206(2) (2002).

[425] Melvin A. Eisenberg, *The Revocation of Offers*, 2004 WIS. L. REV. 271; Charles L. Knapp, *An Offer You Can't Revoke*, 2004 WIS. L. REV. 309.

[426] RESTATEMENT (SECOND) OF CONTRACTS § 42 (1981).

[427] RESTATEMENT (SECOND) OF CONTRACTS § 42 (1981). *E.g.*, Ass'n Local Longshoreman's Union Int'l v. Int'l Longshoreman's Assoc., 940 F. Supp. 779, 783 (E.D. Pa. 1996).

[428] RESTATEMENT (SECOND) OF CONTRACTS § 68 (1981).

[429] RESTATEMENT (SECOND) OF CONTRACTS § 43 (1981).

[430] 2 Ch. D. 463 (1876).

[3] Revocation of Offers Made to the Public

In cases involving offers made to the public, such as an advertisement of a reward, actual receipt by every member of the public who had learned of the offer in the first place may be difficult, if not impossible, to assure. In such cases the offer can be revoked if the offeror publicizes its revocation with the same vigor in which it communicated the offer at the outset.[431]

[4] Revocation Before Deadline for Acceptance

In most cases the offeror is completely free to revoke its offer even if he or she promised to keep the offer open for a specific time. An offeror's express or implied promise to hold an offer open is not generally enforceable. Like most other promises, a promise to keep an offer open must be supported by consideration, or be enforceable due to reasonable reliance, or some other legal rule that makes promises enforceable.[432]

The offeror's ability to revoke an offer any time before acceptance, even if she has supplied a time for acceptance, was dramatically illustrated in *Petterson v. Pattburg*.[433] Pattburg was a creditor of Petterson's and made an offer to accept a smaller sum than the total that was due if the balance was "paid on or before May 31, 1924." This was an offer to enter into a unilateral contract that could be accepted, not by a promise, but only by performance — payment of the specified sum. Petterson appeared at Pattburg's house, knocked on the door, and announced "It is Mr. Petterson. I have come to pay off the mortgage." Pattburg, apparently without opening the door, told Petterson that he had "sold the mortgage," making it clear to Petterson that the offer to compromise the size of debt in exchange for an immediate payment was revoked. Even though Petterson was moments away from tendering payment of the amount sought by Pattburg's offer, and even though he was well within the time limit established by the offer, Pattburg successfully revoked before the final act of actual payment, which was necessary in order for Petterson to accept.

The rule is the same in international transactions. The CISG provides that an offer for the international sale of goods may be revoked if the revocation reaches the offeree before he has dispatched an acceptance.[434] UNIDROIT's Principles and the Principles of European Contract Law contain the same rule.[435]

---

[431] RESTATEMENT (SECOND) OF CONTRACTS § 46 (1981).

[432] An important exception to this rule exists with respect to what are known as "firm offers" for the sale of goods, governed by the U.C.C. U.C.C. § 2-205 provides that a signed written offer from a merchant, which states that it will be held open, is irrevocable for the stated time, not in excess of three months, regardless of whether there is consideration for the promise of irrevocability. U.C.C. § 2-205 (2012). *See infra* § 4.09[D] Firm Offers Under U.C.C. § 2-205.

[433] 161 N.E. 428 (N.Y. 1928).

[434] CISG Art. 16(1) (1980).

[435] PICC Art. 2.1.4(1) (2004); PECL Art. 2.202(1) (2002).

[C] Rejection[436]

An offeree's power of acceptance also terminates when the offeree rejects the offer.[437] Rejection occurs when the offeree communicates his or her intent not to enter into the agreement on the terms proposed by the offeror.[438] As before, it is not the offeree's subjective intent that is important, but rather the communication of that intent to the offeror. Thus, as with revocations, receipt of the rejection is crucial.[439] An offeree who changes his or her mind, and tries to accept after having previously rejected the offer, acts too late.

For example, in *Chaplin v. Consolidated Edison*, the defendant sent a settlement proposal to the plaintiff, offering terms to resolve an employment discrimination suit. The plaintiff's attorney replied saying: "I believed that I could convince [my clients] to accept [your] terms. Unfortunately, that was not the case. After careful consideration they presented objections which have substantial merit."[440] A few weeks later, after an important Court of Appeals decision that affected the law governing the underlying dispute, the plaintiff's lawyer sent another letter to the defendant indicating that his client "had had a 'change of heart' and had decided to accept the [defendant's] offer." In ruling against the employee the court explained: "An offer is extinguished upon rejection. . . . At the time of the plaintiff's purported acceptance, no offer existed."[441]

Of course, not every response by the offeree that does not accept the offer is a rejection. The offeree's initial response may be equivocal. She may seek additional information about the terms of the offer or may inquire about details of the subject matter of the contract. Neither, by itself, is a rejection. For example, when Sam offers to sell his car to Barb, Barb might respond by asking "when would I need to pay you?" or "has it been in any wrecks?" This type of inquiry is not a rejection, because it is not usually understood as an expression of the offeree's unwillingness to go ahead with the deal. Whether a particular response is a rejection depends on the offeror's reasonable understanding of the words used, interpreted against the backdrop of the surrounding circumstances. If only general additional information is sought, the risk is low. However, as we will see, if the request insists on additional terms that the offeree prefers, the communication is a counteroffer. If so, it operates as a rejection and ends the offeree's power to accept.

The offeree might express his or her rejection of the offer as of that particular time, but communicate a willingness to continue considering the offer for a longer period. When Karen offers to sell her house to Phil and tells him that he has a week to decide, Phil might reply "I won't buy it, but I'll get back to you before the end of the week if I change my mind." Here, Phil is conveying his intent to consider the offer open for the entire period Karen specified. Karen cannot reasonably regard

---

[436] Elliot Axelrod, *The Effect of Rejection on the Option Contract*, 6 OKLA. CITY U.L. REV. 415 (1981).

[437] RESTATEMENT (SECOND) OF CONTRACTS § 38(1) (1981).

[438] RESTATEMENT (SECOND) OF CONTRACTS § 38(2) (1981).

[439] RESTATEMENT (SECOND) OF CONTRACTS § 68 (1981).

[440] Chaplin v. Consol. Ed. Co., 537 F. Supp. 1224 (S.D.N.Y. 1982).

[441] *Id.* at 1226.

Phil's statement as a complete rejection of her offer. If she desires to sell the property to someone else, she should unequivocally revoke her offer.[442]

International transactions are treated the same way. In international sale-of-goods transactions, an offer is terminated "when a rejection reaches the offeror."[443] UNIDROIT's Principles of International Commercial Contracts and the Principles of European Contract Law contain identical language. Any other rule would make it impossible for the offeror to enter into negotiations with others.[444]

[D]   Counteroffer

Many of the communications that flow between potential contracting parties are part of negotiations to obtain the best possible deal. If an offeror makes a proposal that the offeree finds unacceptable, the offeree may respond with her own different proposal. When the offeree's reply is itself an offer, but on terms different from those proposed by the offeror, the offeree's power to accept the original offer terminates.[445] As with any offer, the counteroffer gives the original offeror a power of acceptance with respect to the terms of the offeree's counteroffer.

Consider, for example, a simple negotiation between Merle and Agnes for Merle's purchase of Agnes's home. In negotiations over the sale of a home, things usually get started with the seller listing his or her house with a real estate agent. This is a mere advertisement about the seller's interest in selling the home. It usually includes an "asking price" — the price the seller is interested in receiving and is likely to accept.[446] If the asking price is $220,000, Merle might submit a written offer to Agnes indicating his willingness to purchase the house for $205,000 and that Agnes has a week to accept. Merle's offer gives Agnes a power of acceptance — she can conclude the deal by accepting Merle's offer. However, if Agnes responds by proposing to sell the house for $215,000, she rejects Merle's offer. Her counteroffer, of course, it itself an offer, and gives Merle the power to accept Agnes' proposed price.

[1]   Deviant Acceptance as Counteroffer

The traditional rule is that a response contains new or different terms is a counteroffer that rejects the original offer. For example, in *Ardente v. Horan*,[447] a buyer replied to the seller's offer to sell his home with what purported to be an acceptance. However, the buyer's acceptance was accompanied by a letter seeking confirmation that certain furnishings were included in the sale. They made the buyer's acceptance conditional on the seller's willingness to include the furnishings.

---

[442]   RESTATEMENT (SECOND) OF CONTRACTS § 38 cmt. b (1981).

[443]   CISG Art 17 (1980).

[444]   PICC Art. 2.1.5 (2004); PECL Art. 2.203 (2002).

[445]   RESTATEMENT (SECOND) OF CONTRACTS § 39(2) (1981).

[446]   The seller may have a contract with the agent that obligates him or her to accept offers submitted at this price, but prospective buyers do not have the right to enforce it against the seller.

[447]   366 A.2d 162 (R.I. 1976).

As a result, no contract was formed.[448] This rule, that an acceptance must not deviate from the terms of the offer, is frequently referred to as the "mirror image rule."[449]

Despite its name, the mirror image rule does not always require an acceptance to be a true mirror image of the terms of the offer. Some modern cases, no doubt influenced by U.C.C. § 2-207, have softened the harshness of the traditional rule. These courts permit otherwise positive responses as acceptances even if they contain immaterial variations.[450]

[2] Counteroffer While Considering Offer

An offeree might be undecided about accepting the original offer and curious about whether a better deal can be reached, without wanting to lose the opportunity to accept the offer if more favorable terms cannot be obtained. The law accommodates this by permitting parties to make a counteroffer communicating their intent to continue considering the original offer.[451]

For example, when Agnes receives Merle's offer to buy her house for $205,000, she might reply by saying: "I'll consider your offer; in the meantime, I'm willing to sell the house to you for $215,000." This clearly communicates Agnes's willingness to sell the parcel for $215,000 while at the same time avoids indicating her unwillingness to agree to the buyer's $205,000 offer.[452] By communicating that she is keeping the buyer's lower offer under advisement, she prevents the buyer from claiming that he had reasonably relied on her rejection. Such a counteroffer does not extend the time that the offeree has to accept the original offer, but merely preserves the offeree's power to accept until the offer expires or is otherwise terminated.[453]

[3] Acceptance That Defines Implied Terms

Sometimes an offeree's acceptance includes details that seem to be additional, but that are really nothing more than an expression of terms that were implied by the original offer. One party's attempt to specify what the other party implied is not a counteroffer and does not prevent the conclusion of a final agreement.[454] For

---

[448] *See* Princess Cruises, Inc. v. Gen. Elec. Co., 143 F.3d 828 (4th Cir. 1998) (admiralty law).

[449] *E.g.* Sys. Dev. Integration, LLC v. Computer Sciences, Corp., 739 F. Supp. 2d 1063, 1081 (N.D. Ill. 2010); Thomas B. Olson & Associates, P.A. v. Leffert, Jay & Polglaze, P.A., 756 N.W.2d 907, 918 (Minn. Ct. App. 2008)

[450] *E.g.*, Travis v. Tacoma Pub. Sch. Dist. 85 P.3d 959 (Wash. Ct. App. 2004). *See, e.g.*, Poel v. Brunswick-Balke-Collender Co., 110 N.E. 619, 622 (N.Y. 1915); Nomanbhoy Family Ltd. v. McDonald's Corp., 579 F. Supp. 2d 1071 (N.D. Ill. 2008); Montgomery v. English, 902 So. 2d 836 (Fla. Dist. Ct. App. 2005); Gresser v. Hotzler, 604 N.W.2d 379 (Minn. Ct. App. 2000).

[451] RESTATEMENT (SECOND) OF CONTRACTS § 39 cmt. c (1981).

[452] RESTATEMENT (SECOND) OF CONTRACTS § 39 illus. 3 (1981).

[453] RESTATEMENT (SECOND) OF CONTRACTS § 39 cmt. c (1981).

[454] RESTATEMENT (SECOND) OF CONTRACTS § 59 cmt. b (1981). *E.g.*, United States v. Nat'l Optical Stores Co., 407 F.2d 759, 761 (7th Cir. 1969).

example, in *In re Lamarre*,[455] a seller accepted a buyer's offer to purchase property that belonged to the buyer's bankruptcy estate. The acceptance included an express requirement that the sale be approved by the bankruptcy court. Because both parties were aware that the Bankruptcy Code required bankruptcy court approval, obtaining this approval was an implied term of the buyer's offer. Accordingly, the seller's acceptance was unconditional. This is similar to a buyer's inclusion of the requirement that the seller supply "good title," which is usually regarded as an implied term of any contract for the sale of real estate.[456] The same result would be reached if an acceptance required construction work to be completed "within a resonable time" or "in a workmanlike manner."

Similarly, the offeree's acceptance might resolve terms that were left undefined by the offer. For example, in *Valashinas v. Konuito*,[457] the offeree's response included a date for the closing of the transaction, but otherwise contained an expression of his unequivocal willingness to accept. The court explained: "[s]omeone had to fix, or suggest, a closing date, . . . [a]nd plaintiff's notice that he would be ready, on December 31st, to close the transaction, was no more than a suggestion, request or overture."[458] The date was not an additional term that prevented the response from operating as an acceptance — it merely gave greater definition to the terms of the offer.

[4] Acceptance with Suggestions

Depending on how it is expressed, an offeree's response might be an acceptance combined with a suggestion for possible modification to the contract, and not a counteroffer. The offeree might in effect say: "I accept your offer. Now that we have a deal, I propose that we modify it by agreeing to an additional term." This is not a counteroffer. It is an acceptance combined with a proposal for a modification to the contract, or an offer to enter into a separate transaction.

For example, in *Costello v. Pet Inc.*,[459] the court said that "a request for a modification accompanying an acceptance does not prevent the formation of a contract where it is clear that the offeree intended to accept whether or not the modification was accepted." Thus, the common law draws a distinction between an acceptance that *required* agreement to further terms and one that, although expressing assent, *requested* agreement to some further terms.[460]

However, if the offeree's response makes his assent conditional on the offeror's agreement to these further terms, it is a counteroffer, and no contract is formed until the offeror expresses his assent to the new or conflicting terms. Thus, if Phil says, "I'll buy the house for $160,000, but only if you include the appliances for

---

[455] 34 B.R. 264 (Bankr. D. Maine 1983).

[456] RESTATEMENT (SECOND) OF CONTRACTS § 59 illus. 3 (1981). *See* Ryder v. Johnston, 45 So. 181 (Ala. 1907); Nw. Props. Agency v. McGhee, 462 P.2d 249 (Wash. Ct. App. 1969). *See also* U.C.C. § 2-312 (2012) (implied warranty of good title).

[457] 124 N.E.2d 300 (N.Y. 1954).

[458] *Id.* at 303.

[459] 458 N.E.2d 790, 793 (Mass. Ct. App. 1984).

[460] RESTATEMENT (SECOND) OF CONTRACTS § 39(2) & illus. 3 (1981).

another $1,000," there is not yet a contract. Phil has made a counteroffer and thus ended his power of acceptance.

[5] Counteroffer Creates Power of Acceptance

Regardless of whether the offeree's counteroffer operates as a rejection of the terms proposed by the offeror, it places a power of acceptance in the hands of the original offeror. Thus, in *Cook's Pest Control, Inc. v. Rebar*,[461] the customer of a pest control service replied to the service's offer for a renewal of their original contract with a revised offer on different terms, eliminating the service's proposed arbitration provision. The pest control service's conduct in providing services to the customer after receipt of this counteroffer operated as its assent to the revised counterproposal.

[E] Death or Incapacity of the Offeror[462]

The offeror's death or incapacity also terminates the offeree's power of acceptance.[463] Death is rarely ambiguous.[464] Incapacity, on the other hand, is sometimes difficult to detect.[465] Both have the same effect — at least with respect to offers made by the persons whose circumstances have changed.

Oddly, this result is reached even if the offeree is not aware of the offeror's death or incapacity at the time of her attempt to accept.[466] This seems like a vestige of the nineteenth-century subjective approach to contract formation, which focused on whether there was a "meeting of the minds."[467] However, in cases involving an offer to provide a continuing guaranty, courts have sometimes ruled that the offeror's incapacity does not terminate the creditor's ability to accept, by extending credit, unless she has reason to know of the guarantor's incapacity.[468]

Alternatively, the offeror may not become so incapacitated that he or she loses the ability to understand the nature and consequences of the transaction, but may still become impaired in a way that makes him or her unable to control his or her behavior. Individuals who suffer from bipolar disease, which is characterized by manic-depressive behavior, may be in this situation. In the manic stage they might appear to others to be sophisticated business people negotiating a wide variety of complicated deals. This type of incapacity generally impairs a person's ability to

---

[461] 852 So. 2d 730 (Ala. 2002).

[462] Joseph M. Perillo, *The Origins of the Objective Theory of Contract Formation and Interpretation*, 69 FORDHAM L. REV. 427, 464–65 (2000); Val D. Ricks, *The Death of Offers*, 79 IND. L.J. 667 (2004).

[463] RESTATEMENT (SECOND) OF CONTRACTS § 48 (1981).

[464] Benjamin Franklin once said that the only sure things in life were "death and taxes." Will Rogers (a New Deal–era version of "The Daily Show" host Jon Stewart) rejoined that "The difference between the two is that death doesn't worsen every time Congress goes into session."

[465] *See infra* § 10.03 Incapacity.

[466] RESTATEMENT (SECOND) OF CONTRACTS § 49 cmt. a (1981).

[467] RESTATEMENT (SECOND) OF CONTRACTS § 48 cmt. a (1981). *E.g.*, Chain v. Wilhelm, 84 F.2d 138, 140 (4th Cir. 1936).

[468] Swift & Co. v. Smigel, 279 A.2d 895 (N.J. Super. Ct. Ch. Div. 1971), *judgment aff'd*, 289 A.2d 793 (N.J. 1972); Am. Oil Co. v. Wigley's Estate, 169 So. 2d 454 (Miss. 1964).

contract only to the extent that the other party has reason to know of the incapacity, and thus should not terminate the offeree's power of acceptance absent reason to know of the impairment.[469]

Cases involving the death or incapacity of the offeror arise in the context of questions about whether the offeree had accepted before or after the offeror died or became incapacitated. In *Davis v. Jacoby*,[470] the offeror invited his wife's niece and her husband to move to California and care for him and his wife, promising that the niece would inherit their house if they did. The offeree expressed her consent, but the offeror died before the niece actually made the move to California. If the offer was interpreted as inviting acceptance via a promise, a contract had been concluded before the offeror's death. If actual performance was the only permissible method of acceptance, it came too late, and no contract had been created. The court ultimately construed the communications between the parties as inviting a promissory acceptance that had been provided prior to the offeror's demise.

§ 4.09 IRREVOCABLE OFFERS[471]

The common law generally permits a person who has made an offer to revoke it any time before acceptance.[472] In most cases an offer can be revoked even if the offeror made a promise to keep the offer open. Thus, if Karen offers to sell her house to Phil for $200,000[473] and promises to keep the offer open for 48 hours, Karen can nevertheless revoke her offer any time before Phil accepts.[474] Unless supported by consideration, or reasonably relied on, a promise to keep an offer open is no more enforceable than any other gratuitous promise.[475]

Sometimes, offers are kept open for a price, with the offeree agreeing to pay a fee in exchange for the offeror's promise to keep the offer open for a specific time.[476] Alternatively, the offeree might partially perform or foreseeably rely in some other manner on the offeror's promise not to revoke. This type of foreseeable reliance has the same effect as consideration and makes the offer irrevocable. In addition, as explained below, the U.C.C. makes certain offers irrevocable even in the absence of consideration or detrimental reliance.

---

[469] *E.g.*, Faber v. Sweet Style Mfg. Corp., 40 Misc. 2d 212 (N.Y. Sup. Ct. 1963) (manic depressive or "bipolar"). *See also* Ortelere v. Teachers' Retirement Board, 250 N.E.2d 460 (N.Y. 1969) (cerebral arteriosclerosis or hardening of the arteries in the brain).

[470] 34 P.2d 1026 (Cal. 1934).

[471] Melvin A. Eisenberg, *The Revocation of Offers*, 2004 Wis. L. Rev. 271; Charles L. Knapp, *An Offer You Can't Revoke*, 2004 Wis. L. Rev. 309.

[472] Restatement (Second) of Contracts § 42 (1981).

[473] Notice that her asking price keeps going up as the chapter progresses.

[474] Restatement (Second) of Contracts § 42 (1981).

[475] Restatement (Second) of Contracts § 42 illus. 1 (1981). *E.g.*, James Baird Co. v. Gimbel Bros., Inc., 64 F.2d 344 (2d Cir. 1933). *See supra* § 2.04 Promises to Make a Gift.

[476] Restatement (Second) of Contracts § 25 illus. 1 (1981).

[A] Traditional Option Contracts

[1] Consideration for Promise of Irrevocability

The most obvious circumstance in which an offeror is not permitted to revoke its offer is where the offeree has paid for the offeror's promise to keep the offer open. This is a traditional option contract.[477]

Option contracts are frequently used to facilitate the ultimate sale of real estate. A prospective buyer may be seriously interested in purchasing a building, but uncertain whether it will suit her needs.[478] Or, the buyer may wish to avoid making a commitment to buy the property until it can line up deals to purchase adjoining parcels that are necessary for a larger development project. In these circumstances, the seller might be willing to enter into an option contract, effectively taking the property off the market and giving the buyer the right to defer its decision whether to purchase until after she can conduct a careful study of the premises. This permits the buyer to examine the premises carefully, without running the risk that the owner will sell the building to someone else before the buyer's investigation is complete. By making an irrevocable offer the seller exposes himself to the risk that another prospective purchaser might be willing to buy the property. Payment for the option compensates the seller for his willingness to run this risk. Thus, in exchange for $10,000, the seller might offer to sell the building for $5 million, and promise to keep the offer open for a month. The $10,000 fee supplies the necessary consideration making the seller's promise to keep its offer open enforceable. The parties do not yet have a contract for sale of the building, but they have made a contract that the seller's offer to sell will remain open for a month.[479]

[2] Nominal or Recited Consideration for Option Contract

In determining whether an option contract exists, courts adhere strictly to the rule that the amount of consideration is irrelevant, so long as some has been supplied.[480] Thus, even nominal consideration, such as payment of $1.00, in exchange for the promise of irrevocability has been held sufficient to create an enforceable option contract.[481] Moreover, some courts have adopted the Restatement position that a written recital that consideration has been supplied makes a promise to keep an offer open enforceable, as long as the terms of the proposed deal are fair and the offer is to be accepted within a reasonable time.[482]

---

[477] RESTATEMENT (SECOND) OF CONTRACTS § 25 illus. 1 (1981).

[478] *E.g.*, Town of Dandridge v. Patterson, 827 S.W.2d 797, 801 (Tenn. Ct. App. 1991).

[479] *See* RESTATEMENT (SECOND) OF CONTRACTS § 25 (1981). *E.g.*, Driscoll v. Norprop, Inc., 719 N.E.2d 48 (Ohio Ct. App. 1998).

[480] RESTATEMENT (SECOND) OF CONTRACTS § 87 cmt. b (1981).

[481] *E.g.*, Lawrence v. McCalmont, 43 U.S. (2 How.) 426, 452 (1844).

[482] RESTATEMENT (SECOND) OF CONTRACTS § 87(1)(a) (1981); Mack v. Coker, 523 P.2d 1342 (Ariz. Ct. App. 1974). *But* see McLellan v. Charly, 758 N.W.2d 94, 103 (Wis. Ct. App. 2008). *See also* First Nat'l Bankshares v. Geisel, 853 F. Supp. 1344, 1353 n.6 (D. Kan. 1994) (regarding the requirement that the exchange be on fair terms).

[3]   Reliance on Promise of Irrevocability

There are many cases in which an offeree relies to her detriment on a promise of irrevocability, even if the reliance takes the form of nothing more than conducting a careful and perhaps expensive investigation of the property.[483] The buyer of a building, for example, may not be willing to hire architects and engineers to determine whether the building is suitable for the buyer's purpose unless the buyer has some assurances that the property will still be available for purchase when the investigation is concluded. Thus, an enforceable option may induce the creation of a wealth maximizing transaction, even though no real consideration is paid for the option.

[4]   Proof of Promise of Irrevocability

However, there is still a problem of proof. Absent a signed writing, including the promise to keep the offer open, it might be too easy for one of the parties to falsely claim that an option has been provided. Courts have therefore sometimes required the existence of a signed writing containing the promise to keep the offer open as well as a recital that some consideration, however meager, has been paid before enforcing an option contract.[484] This requirement, like the statute of frauds, satisfies the cautionary, evidentiary, and channeling functions of the traditional consideration doctrine.[485] In this respect, the requirement of a written promise, including a recital that consideration has been paid, serves the same functions as the "seal," even though the seal has largely been abandoned.[486] By adhering to the ritual of signing a formal document that recites that consideration has been paid, the parties have demonstrated their deliberate intent that the option be legally binding.[487]

[B]   Beginning Performance[488]

If the offer indicates that performance is the only appropriate means of acceptance, the offer is irrevocable for a reasonable time, when the offeree begins performing.[489] For example, suppose that John tells Rhonda, the owner of Rhonda's Roofing: "Replace my roof by the end of the month and I'll pay you a bonus of $1,000." This offer does not seek a return promise as a means of acceptance of his promise for the bonus, but instead asks for performance. The offer for the bonus is not accepted until completion of the work by the end of the month, but once Rhonda begins work on the new roof, the offer of the bonus may not be revoked.

---

[483] *E.g.*, Drennan v. Star Paving, 333 P.2d 757 (Cal. 1958).

[484] RESTATEMENT (SECOND) OF CONTRACTS § 87(1)(a) (1981).

[485] *See supra* § 2.02[A] Formality and Ritual in Contract Law.

[486] *See supra* § 2.02[B] The Seal.

[487] *See* RESTATEMENT (SECOND) OF CONTRACTS § 87 cmt. b (1981).

[488] David G. Epstein & Yvette Joy Liebesman, *Bearded Ladies Walking on the Brooklyn Bridge*, 59 ARK. L. REV. 267 (2006).

[489] RESTATEMENT (SECOND) OF CONTRACTS § 45 (1981).

Offers of this type, which seek performance as the means of acceptance, have traditionally been regarded as offers to enter into a unilateral contract.[490] Acceptance is accomplished not by a return promise, but, instead, by rendering the performance requested by the offer.[491]

As explained earlier, acceptance of an offer for a unilateral contract is effective only on *completion* of performance.[492] The traditional rule was that until performance is complete, the offer could be revoked.[493]

However, this creates a potential for injustice when performance takes time. In his famous hypothetical, Professor Wormser insisted that an offer by A to pay B $100 if B walked across the Brooklyn Bridge could be revoked anytime before B completed his walk to the other side.[494] The result was harsh, but not as severe as situations in which the offeree has not only acted in reliance on the promise, but had gone further and conferred some valuable benefit on the promisor as a result of his work.

The Second Restatement rejects this approach and treats the beginning of performance as creating an option on the part of the offeree. Section 45(1) provides:

> Where an offer invites an offeree to accept by rendering a performance and does not invite a promissory acceptance, an option contract is created when the offeree tenders or begins the invited performance or tenders a beginning of it.[495]

Offers that invite acceptance by the means of a reciprocal promise can be accepted by the offeree's expression of his or her commitment to perform.[496] If the offer is ambiguous as to whether acceptance may be made by a promise or a performance, then either a promise or performance is a reasonable mode of acceptance.[497] If, on the other hand, the offer unambiguously invites performance as the only method of acceptance, a promise is not sufficient. Then, acceptance is not complete until performance is complete.[498] However, unless the offer clearly specifies otherwise, the beginning of performance results in the creation of an option contract, giving the offeree a reasonable time to complete performance. Tender at the beginning of performance has the same effect. As with other offers,

---

[490] RESTATEMENT OF CONTRACTS § 52 (1932). *See supra* § 4.05[B][3] Acceptance by Performance Alone: Unilateral Contracts.

[491] *E.g.*, BC Tire Corp. v. GTE Directories Corp., 730 P.2d 726, 728 (Wash. Ct. App. 1986) (acceptance effective only on publication of advertisement).

[492] *See supra* § 4.05[B][3] Acceptance by Performance Alone: Unilateral Contracts.

[493] Petterson v. Pattberg, 161 N.E. 428 (N.Y. 1928). *See* Samuel Blinkoff, Note, *Contracts; Acceptance of an Offer for a Unilateral Contract: Effect of Tender*, 14 CORNELL L.Q. 81, 84 (1928).

[494] I. Maurice Wormser, *The True Conception of Unilateral Contracts*, 26 YALE L.J. 136, 136–38 (1916).

[495] RESTATEMENT (SECOND) OF CONTRACTS § 45 (1981).

[496] *See supra* 4.05[B][1] Acceptance by Return Promise.

[497] *See* RESTATEMENT (SECOND) OF CONTRACTS § 32 (1981).

[498] RESTATEMENT (SECOND) OF CONTRACTS § 45(2) (1981). *E.g.*, Dahl v. HEM Pharm. Corp., 7 F.3d 1399 (9th Cir. 1993).

the offeree may accept by completing performance in accordance with the terms of the offer.[499]

[1] Preparing or Beginning

This approach requires a careful distinction between preparing to perform and beginning to perform. Mere preparations are not usually enough to make the offer irrevocable.[500] For work to qualify as partial performance, it must be "unequivocally referable" to the offer, and not preparations that might be in connection with other transactions.

On the other hand, extensive preparations, if they were foreseeable, may be sufficient to make the offer irrevocable on the alternative ground of reasonable reliance on the offer.[501] In *Ragosta v. Wilder*,[502] the offeree relied on an offer to sell the offeror's business by applying for and obtaining the financing necessary to complete the sale. The court rejected the plaintiff's claim that it had gone beyond preparing to perform, but permitted the plaintiff's claim to proceed on a theory of promissory estoppel, because of the expenses the plaintiff incurred in preparing to perform. In doing so, however, the court cautioned that the promise should be enforceable only to the extent "necessary to prevent injustice."[503] This would seem to limit the plaintiff's remedy to recovery of any expenses it incurred, such as in preparing its loan application and paying a loan application or loan commitment fee to obtain the financing necessary to accept the plaintiff's offer.

[2] Notice of Performance

Notice of performance or of the beginning of performance is usually necessary. In most situations the beginning of performance will convey the necessary notice all by itself. For example, in *Brackenbury v. Hodgkin*,[504] the defendant told her daughter and son in law that if they came to live with her, and cared for her the rest of her life, they would become owners of the defendant's land. Mrs. Hodgkin knew right away that that her daughter had arrived and that she was there to stay. No further notice of the beginning of performance was necessary. In situations like this, where the beginning of performance supplies notice, separate notice need not be given.[505]

However, in other more unusual circumstances, such as where performance is rendered in a distant location, performance may not be so "notorious." If the offeree has reason to know that the offeror has no adequate means of learning that

---

[499] *E.g, In re* Harnischfeger Indus., Inc., 270 B.R. 188 (Bankr. D. Del. 2001).

[500] RESTATEMENT (SECOND) OF CONTRACTS § 45 cmt. f (1981); Ragosta v. Wilder, 592 A.2d 367 (Vt. 1991).

[501] *See* RESTATEMENT (SECOND) OF CONTRACTS § 45 cmt. f (1981); RESTATEMENT (SECOND) OF CONTRACTS § 87(2) (1981).

[502] 592 A.2d 367 (Vt. 1991).

[503] *Id.* at 371.

[504] 102 A. 106 (Me. 1917).

[505] RESTATEMENT (SECOND) OF CONTRACTS § 54(1) (1981).

performance has begun, the offer may be revoked.[506]

This result is consistent with the rule of U.C.C. § 2-206(2), which applies to domestic contracts for the sale of goods. A seller might respond to a purchase order simply by beginning manufacture of the goods. This operates as acceptance. However, the buyer is permitted to treat the offer as having lapsed if notice of the acceptance is not sent within a reasonable time.[507] Where the goods are already manufactured, and the seller performs by sending them, the goods are likely to arrive just as quickly as any notice of acceptance that the seller might dispatch.

In international sales, the CISG's rule that acceptance is effective only upon receipt might yield a different result,[508] except that the terms of the offer or the past practices of the parties may permit dispatch of the goods as a means of acceptance.[509] In other international transactions, the rule is the same.[510]

[C] Reliance on an Offer

Even where the offeree's actions have not advanced to the point where they can be characterized as the beginning of performance, preparations to perform may make the offer irrevocable due to promissory estoppel. Section 87(2) of the Second Restatement makes an offer irrevocable if the offeree foreseeably relies on the offer.[511]

Early decisions refused to extend promissory estoppel to situations involving a proposed bargain. In *James Baird v. Gimbel Brothers, Inc.*,[512] a flooring dealer offered to supply all of the linoleum required for a construction project. The offer assured the general contractor to whom it was sent that it would remain open for "prompt acceptance after the general contract has been awarded." The contractor based its own bid on the price quoted by the dealer and was awarded the general contract. Despite these assurances, the dealer withdrew its offer. Even though the general contractor had placed its bid on the dealer's promise to keep his offer open, the court refused to hold the flooring dealer to its commitment. The court held that its promise of irrevocability was nothing more than a gratuitous promise. Because it was not supported by consideration, it was unenforceable.

Later cases recognize the injustice of this result. The situation in *Drennan v. Star Paving*[513] was nearly identical to that involved in *Gimbel Brothers*, except that it involved services, not goods. The defendant, a paving contractor, submitted an offer to the plaintiff to do the paving work on a project for which the plaintiff was preparing his own general contracting bid. However, unlike the offer in *Gimbel Brothers*, the subcontractor's offer in *Drennan* did not contain an express promise

---

[506] Restatement (Second) of Contracts § 54(2) (1981).

[507] U.C.C. § 2-206(2) (2012).

[508] CISG Art. 18(2). *See also* PECL, Art. 2.205 (2002).

[509] CISG Art. 18(3) (1980).

[510] PICC Art. 2.1.6 (2004); PECL Art. 2.205(1) (2002).

[511] Restatement (Second) of Contracts § 87(2) (1981).

[512] 64 F.2d 344 (2d Cir. 1933).

[513] 333 P.2d 757 (Cal. 1958).

that the offer would be kept open. The general contractor nevertheless relied on the sub's offer in computing its own general contracting bid. After the general contractor had been awarded the contract, but before it had accepted the defendant's offer to do the paving work, the defendant revoked its offer, which contained a serious mistake.

Drennan might have paid Star Paving to keep its offer open while Drennan's general contracting bid was being considered. Alternatively, Drennan might have used Star's offer in computing its general contracting bid, in explicit exchange for Star's promise not to revoke its offer.[514] Either step would have supplied the necessary consideration to make a promise by Star to keep its offer open irrevocable.[515] On the facts of the case, however, no such reciprocal exchange was made. Moreover, unlike in *Gimbel Brothers*, Star had not even promised to keep its offer open.

Nevertheless, the California Supreme Court held Star Paving to the terms of its offer. Drawing an analogy to § 45 of the First Restatement and to cases like *Brackenbury v. Hodgkin*,[516] the court found that the construction contract setting of Star Paving's bid gave Star "reason to expect that if its bid proved the lowest it would be used."[517] This, combined with Drennan's actual reliance on Star's offer, resulted in an implied subsidiary promise by Star to keep its offer open pending an award of the general contract. The court said that this subsidiary promise was directly analogous to the subsidiary promise that accompanies an offer to enter into a unilateral contract, that if the requested performance is begun, then the offer may not be revoked until a reasonable time for the completion of the performance has expired.[518]

The court then rejected the ultimate conclusion of the *Gimbel Brothers*[519] court regarding the limited role of promissory estoppel and used it to prevent Star Paving from withdrawing its offer.

The result in *Drennan v. Star Paving* has been followed nearly universally.[520] General contractors who rely on bids submitted by subcontractors are able to prevent subcontractors, whose bids have been relied on, from backing out. Absent circumstances making it clear that the subcontractor retains a right to withdraw its offer,[521] or that the general contractor should have known that the bid contained a mistake,[522] subcontractors are bound by the terms of their offers.

---

[514] *See* Holman Erection Co. v. Orville E. Madsen & Sons, Inc., 330 N.W.2d 693 (Minn. 1983) (listing a subcontractor in a general contracting bid is not an acceptance of the subcontractor's offer).

[515] *Id.* at 759.

[516] 102 A. 106 (Me. 1917).

[517] *Drennan v. Star Paving, Inc.*, 333 P.2d at 759.

[518] *Id. See* RESTATEMENT OF CONTRACTS § 45 cmt. b (1932).

[519] *See also* Pavel Enters., Inc. v. A.S. Johnson, Co., Inc., 674 A.2d 521 (Md. 1996).

[520] *E.g.*, Janke Constr. Co v. Vulcan Mat'l Co., 527 F.2d 772 (7th Cir. 1976). *But see* Home Elec. Co. v. Hall & Underdown Heating & Air Conditioning Co., 358 S.E.2d 539 (N.C. Ct. App. 1987).

[521] *See* Lyon Metal Prods., Inc. v. Hagerman Constr. Corp., 391 N.E.2d 1152 (Ind. Ct. App. 1979).

[522] Gen. Elec. Supply Corp. v. Rep. Const. Corp., 272 P.2d 201 (Or. 1954).

Somewhat surprisingly however, the general contractor is not required to use the subcontractor's bid.[523] It is the contractor's option to use the subcontractor's bid or not.

Suppose, for example, that Rhonda's Roofing submits a subcontracting bid to Winkler Builders[524] to do the roofing work on a construction job on which Winkler is bidding. Under *Drennan*, Winkler's reliance on Rhonda's bid makes it irrevocable. However, despite having used Rhonda's bid in its effort to be awarded the general contract, Winkler can shop around for a lower price from other roofing subcontractors after it has been awarded the general contract.[525] Once it does so, however, it may not go back to the subcontractor and accept the bid.

Thus, on the facts of *Drennan v. Star Paving*, Drennan would have been able to solicit other paving contractors, in an effort to find one willing to do the work at a lower price, without being in breach of any obligation to Star Paving. However, courts usually rule that this type of opportunistic behavior precludes the general contractor from subsequently enforcing the subcontractor's bid, in the event that its efforts to find a cheaper subcontractor are ineffective.[526] Likewise, of course, the subcontractor may seek to prevent reliance, by making it clear that its bid is not an offer.[527]

[D] Firm Offers Under U.C.C. § 2-205

The Uniform Commercial Code has its own solution to the problem of irrevocable offers. It applies to offers to enter into a sale of goods where the resulting agreement will be governed by domestic law. If the transaction is between parties whose countries are signatories to the United Nations Convention on the International Sale of Goods, the CISG governs.

U.C.C. § 2-205 provides:

> An offer by a merchant to buy or sell goods in a signed writing which by its terms gives assurances that it will be held open is not revocable, for lack of consideration, during the time stated or if no time is stated for a reasonable time, but in no event may such period of irrevocability exceed three months.[528]

Thus, offers for the purchase or sale of goods may be irrevocable without consideration, and with no proof of foreseeable reliance on the offer.

---

[523] Michael Gibson, *Promissory Estoppel, Article 2 of the U.C.C., and the Restatement (Third) of Contracts*, 73 Iowa L. Rev. 659, 703 (1988).

[524] As I write this passage, Van Winkle Builders is in my back yard, constructing a garage. Rhonda's Roofing, however, is a fictional character.

[525] *See* Holman Erection Co. v. Orville E. Madsen & Sons, Inc., 330 N.W.2d 693 (Minn. 1983).

[526] Lahr Constr. Corp. v. J. Kozel & Son, Inc., 168 Misc. 2d 759 (N.Y. Sup. Ct. 1996). *See generally* John Edward Murray Jr., Murray on Contracts 141 (5th ed. 2011).

[527] *E.g.*, Fletcher-Harlee Corp. v. Pote Concrete Contractors, Inc., 482 F.3d 247 (3d Cir. 2007). *See* Victor P. Goldberg, *Traynor (Drennan) Versus Hand (Baird): Much Ado About (Almost) Nothing*, 3 J. Legal Analysis 539 (2011).

[528] U.C.C. § 2-205 (2012).

[1] Signed Promise of Irrevocability

Section 2-205 imposes several requirements for an offer to be irrevocable without consideration. First, it must be in writing. A writing includes "printing, typewriting, or any other intentional reduction to tangible form."[529] The Uniform Electronic Transactions Act makes an electronic record sufficient to satisfy this requirement.

Second, the writing must be "signed." A signature "includes any symbol executed or adopted by a party with present intent to adopt or accept a writing."[530] Thus, initials, an "X," or the use of a letterhead form are likely sufficient.[531]

Third, § 2-205 only operates if the offeror is a merchant.[532] The merchant referred to in § 2-205 is the general type of merchant defined in U.C.C. § 2-104(1) and described in the Official Comments as "almost every person in business" who would be familiar with "non-specialized business practices such as answering mail."[533]

The fourth and most important element of U.C.C. § 2-205 is the requirement that the offer "by its terms [it] gives assurance that it will be held open."[534] A simple price quote of the type involved in *Drennan v. Star Paving* is not enough.[535] An offer that indicates: "this offer lapses two weeks from its date," or otherwise merely stipulates a time of lapse, does not contain the necessary assurance. The offer must contain explicit and unequivocal assurances that it will be kept open.

A firm offer, made pursuant to § 2-205, remains irrevocable for the time stated in the offer. If the offer contains the necessary assurances that the offer will remain open, but does not specify a time, then the offer is irrevocable for a reasonable time. However, regardless of whether a time is stated, the maximum period of irrevocability under § 2-205 is three months. To extend the time period beyond three months, apparently, consideration must be supplied.[536]

[2] Preprinted Forms Supplied by the Offeree

Section 2-205 prevents sellers from tricking their customers into inadvertently making a firm offer by supplying them with preprinted purchase order forms containing firm offer language. Under § 2-205, any language purporting to keep an offer open that appears on a form supplied by the offeree must be separately signed by the offeror to make the offer irrevocable. Thus, if Winkler Builders sends a preprinted form to Mills Lumber, asking Mills to use the form in submitting bids,

---

[529] U.C.C. § 1-201(b)(43) (2012) (formerly § 1-201(46)).

[530] U.C.C. § 1-201(b)(37) (2012). This language has recently been changed. Former Article 1 was similar, providing that a signature "included any symbol executed or adopted by a party with present intention to authenticate a writing." Former U.C.C. § 1-201(39) (2000).

[531] U.C.C. § 1-201 cmt. 37 (2012).

[532] U.C.C. § 2-205 (2012).

[533] U.C.C. § 2-104 cmt. 2 (2012).

[534] U.C.C. § 2-205 (2012).

[535] E.A. Coronis Assoc. v. M. Gordon Constr. Co., 216 A.2d 246 (N.J. Super. Ct. Ch. Div. 1966).

[536] U.C.C. § 2-205 (2012).

and the form contains language tracking § 2-205 assuring Winkler that Mills's offer will remain open, Mills's offer remains revocable unless Mills separately signs the particular language containing the assurances that the offer will be kept open.[537] This also prevents buyers from being surprised to learn that they have made a firm offer merely by using the preprinted forms prepared by their suppliers.

[3] Traditional Option Contracts Enforceable

Section 2-205 does nothing to disturb the enforceability of traditional option contracts, where the promise of irrevocability is supported by consideration. If the offeree has paid for the offeror's promise to keep its offer open, there is an enforceable option contract: the offer will remain open for the duration of the agreed time. Moreover, a traditional option contract that is supported by consideration may extend the period of irrevocability beyond the three-month outside limit specified by § 2-205.

[4] Effect of Reliance

Section 2-205 raises difficult questions about the continued vitality of using promissory estoppel to make offers for the sale of goods irrevocable. The issue is whether § 2-205 supersedes the common law in this regard or merely supplements it. Suppose, for example, that Mills Lumber submits a bid to supply the items necessary for Winkler Builders to complete a construction project on which Winkler is bidding. Just like in *Drennan v. Star Paving*, Mills might make no express promise that its offer will remain open. Nevertheless, Winkler is likely to rely on the offer and use it in computing its general contracting bid to the owner of the project. If Mills attempts to revoke, the question of whether promissory estoppel has survived the enactment of § 2-205's firm offer procedure will arise.

U.C.C. § 1-103 speaks to the issue, but only in general terms. It indicates that the common law can be used to supplement the code's provisions unless the common law is "displaced by the particular provisions of [the U.C.C.]"[538] The question, therefore, is whether § 2-205 displaces decisions like *Drennan v. Star Paving*, making § 2-205 the exclusive method of making offers irrevocable in the absence of consideration, in cases involving sales of goods.

Cases addressing the issue reach mixed results.[539] Some decisions expressly reject the use of promissory estoppel in cases involving the sale of goods.[540] However, most courts and commentators take the position that § 2-205 does not prevent the use of promissory estoppel to keep an offer open any more than it prevents the parties from using a traditional option contract in which the promise to keep the offer open is supported by consideration.[541]

---

[537] U.C.C. § 2-205 cmt. 4 (2012).

[538] U.C.C. § 1-103(a) (2012).

[539] Henry Mather, *Firm Offers Under the UCC and the CISG*, 105 DICKINSON L. REV. 31, 39–40 (2000).

[540] Ivey's Plumbing & Elec. Co. v. Petrochem Maint, Inc., 463 F. Supp. 543 (N.D. Miss. 1978). *See also* Michael Gibson, *Promissory Estoppel, Article 2 of the U.C.C., and the Restatement (Third) of Contracts*, 73 IOWA L. REV. 659, 701–03 (1988).

[541] *E.g.*, Jenkins & Boller Co v. Schmidt Iron Works, Inc, 344 N.E.2d 275 (Ill. App. Ct. 1976); E.A.

Still, it would seem odd to permit an offer for the sale of goods to remain open beyond the three-month limit imposed by § 2-205, on a theory of promissory estoppel, where the offer did not meet the code's requirements of a firm offer. Likewise, it is unclear whether an oral assurance that the offer will remain open, beyond expiration of the original time, should be enforceable in the absence of a writing that meets the requirements of § 2-205.

[E]   Irrevocability in International Transactions

[1]   International Sales of Goods

The United Nations Convention on the International Sale of Goods (CISG) adheres generally to principle of the revocability of offers any time before an acceptance is dispatched.[542] Under the CISG an offer is irrevocable "if it indicates . . . that it is irrevocable."[543] The offer may indicate that it is irrevocable either by "stating a fixed time for acceptance or otherwise . . . ."[544] Like U.C.C. § 2-205, therefore, an offer in a transaction governed by the CISG is irrevocable without consideration if the offeror expresses its intent that the offer not be subject to revocation. Unlike § 2-205, the CISG does not require the indication of irrevocability to be in writing.[545] Nor does it impose a time limit on the period of irrevocability.[546]

The CISG also makes an offer irrevocable "if it was reasonable for the offeree to rely on the offer as being irrevocable and the offeree has acted in reliance on the offer."[547] This makes offers like the one in *Drennan v. Star Paving* irrevocable, and might well make offers irrevocable if the offeree invested considerable time or money into investigating whether to accept an offer.[548]

[2]   Irrevocability in Other International Transactions

In other international transactions, the UNIDROIT Principles of International Commercial Contracts and Principles of European Contract Law both generally permit an offer to be revoked any time before an acceptance has been dispatched,[549] but prohibit revocation either if the offer indicates that it will be irrevocable or if it would have been reasonable for the offeree to rely on the offer.[550]

Coronis Assoc. v. M. Gordon Constr. Co., 216 A.2d 246 (N.J. Super. Ct. Ch.. Div. 1966).

[542] CISG Art. 16(1) (1980).

[543] CISG Art. 16(2)(a) (1980).

[544] CISG Art. 16(2)(a) (1980).

[545] Henry Mather, *Firm Offers Under the UCC and the CISG*, 105 Dick. L. Rev. 31, 44 (2000).

[546] *Id.*

[547] CISG Art. 16(2)(b) (1980). *See generally* John O. Honnold, Uniform Law for International Sales Under the 1980 United Nations Convention 160–68 (3d ed. 1999).

[548] *See* John Edward Murray Jr., Murray on Contracts 141 (4th ed. 2001).

[549] PICC Art. 2.1.4(1) (2004); PECL Art. 2.202(1) (2002).

[550] PICC Art. 2.1.4(2) (2004); PECL Art. 2.202(3) (2002). *See generally* Joseph M. Perillo, *UN-IDROIT Principles of International Commercial Contracts: The Black Letter Text and a Review*, 63 Fordham L. Rev. 281, 285 (1994).

§ 4.10 MIRROR-IMAGE RULE AND THE BATTLE OF THE FORMS UNDER U.C.C. § 2-207[551]

In many types of contracts the parties make an effort to memorialize their entire agreement in a single integrated document. For example, in contracts for the sale of land, the parties usually formalize their agreement by executing a single, final, integrated writing containing all of its terms. Complex business transactions, such as those involving the sale of a business,[552] or for the construction of a building,[553] are usually handled the same way: both parties sign a single written agreement containing all of the terms of the parties' agreement. Employment contracts adhere to a similar pattern, though they usually involve a simple basic agreement that is supplemented by the employer's policy manual.[554] Contracts for big-ticket consumer goods, such as for the sale of a car, are handled the same way, with the parties executing a single document containing all of the terms of their deal.

More casual contracts for the sale of goods, on the other hand, involve less formal practices. The parties rarely make an effort to execute a single document containing all of their terms. Instead, they form agreements by exchanging correspondence with one another, frequently using preprinted standardized forms and filling in the blanks with the description, quantity, and price of the goods involved in each separate transaction. When the preprinted details on these forms conflict, problems can arise, especially if the goods turn out to be defective.

These transactions frequently begin with the buyer sending the seller a purchase order, containing the quantity, price, and description of the goods, usually gleaned from the seller's catalog, price list, or web site.[555] The purchase order might also contain a number of preprinted terms about the time and place for delivery, risk of loss, and warranties about the performance of the goods.

Upon receipt of the purchase order the seller expresses its acceptance by sending an acknowledgment of the buyer's order, or, instead, by immediately shipping the goods with an accompanying invoice.[556] The seller's documents usually repeat the price, quantity, and description supplied in the buyer's purchase order.

---

[551] *See* Douglas Baird & Robert Weisberg, *Rules, Standards, and the Battle of the Forms: A Reassessment of § 2-207*, 68 Va. L. Rev. 1217 (1982); Corneill A. Stephens, *Escape from the Battle of the Forms: Keep It Simple, Stupid*, 11 Lewis & Clark L. Rev. 233 (2007); E. Hunter Taylor Jr., *U.C.C. Section 2-207: An Integration of Legal Abstractions and Transactional Reality*, 46 Cin. L. Rev. 419 (1977); Charles M. Thatcher, *Sales Contract Formation and Content — An Annotated Apology for a Proposed Revision of Uniform Commercial Code § 2-207*, 32 S.D. L. Rev. 181 (1987); Gregory M. Travalio, *Clearing the Air After the Battle: Reconciling Fairness and Efficiency in a Formal Approach to U.C.C. Section 2-207*, 33 Case W. Res. L. Rev. 327 (1983).

[552] *E.g.*, Empro Mfg. Co. v. Ball-Co Mfg., Inc., 870 F.2d 423 (7th Cir. 1989) (preliminary "letter of intent" not binding where agreement was subject to execution of a final written contract).

[553] *E.g.*, Flower City Painting Contractors, Inc. v. Gumina Constr., 591 F.2d 162, 163 (2d Cir. 1979).

[554] *E.g.*, Hinson v. Cameron, 742 P.2d 549, 554–55 (Okla. 1987).

[555] Catalogs, price lists, and other advertisements are not usually regarded as offers themselves. *See supra* § 4.03[C][2] Advertisements.

[556] *E.g.*, Hill v. Joseph T. Ryerson & Son, Inc., 268 S.E.2d 296, 307 (W. Va. 1980). An order for prompt or current shipment of goods can normally be accepted either through a prompt promise to ship the goods or through performance, by sending the goods. U.C.C. § 2-206(a)(1) (2012).

Like the buyer's purchase order, the seller's documents frequently also contain a variety of preprinted terms, particularly those regarding warranty disclaimers, limited remedies, or provisions regarding the dispute resolution process.

In other situations, the parties conclude the basic terms of their contract over the telephone, settling on matters such as price, quantity, and a basic description of the goods, and then follow up their conversations with one or more confirming memoranda containing these basic terms and frequently adding a variety of preprinted standardized provisions.[557]

Most of the time, this method of transacting business is convenient and efficient. Once the parties have agreed upon the description, the quantity, the price, and perhaps the terms for payment and delivery, they are usually satisfied that a deal has been concluded. Most agreements are fully performed without the parties noticing that some of the preprinted terms on the forms they have exchanged are different from one another. The goods are delivered, and the buyer pays for them.

However, when the market price of the goods is in flux, or if problems develop with the goods after they have been delivered, variations in the preprinted or "boilerplate" language in their forms might create problems.[558] The common law took one approach; Article 2 of the U.C.C. handles things differently.

As explained earlier in this chapter, the common law treated a purported acceptance that deviated from the terms contained in the original offer as a counteroffer.[559] Under this rule, if Franklin Manufacturing sends a purchase order to Industrial Supply, for the purchase of a new frimulator by December 1, and Industrial Supply responds with an acknowledgment that expresses its commitment to deliver the item, but which adds a term requiring Franklin to submit any dispute that develops to binding arbitration, there would be no contract. Instead, Industrial Supply's response would have been a counteroffer to sell the goods on slightly different terms than those proposed in the offer. To conclude a contract, Franklin Manufacturing would have had to accept the seller's counteroffer. When Industrial Supply delivers the goods, Franklin Manufacturing will mostly likely take and pay for them. Under the common law, this conduct would operate as Franklin's acceptance of Industrial's proposed terms. When a dispute later arose, these terms would govern.

The mirror-image rule sometimes permitted one of the parties to escape from the transaction, even though both parties, if asked, probably would have expressed

---

[557] *E.g.*, Coastal Aviation, Inc. v. Commander Aircraft Co., 937 F. Supp. 1051, 1062 (S.D.N.Y. 1996).

[558] The term "boilerplate" is derived from the late nineteenth-century newspaper practice of using precast or stamped metal for printing presses. Stories were prepared on this boilerplate and distributed to newspapers around the country. Until the mid-twentieth century, thousands of U.S. newspapers received and used this kind of boilerplate from the nation's largest supplier, the Western Newspaper Union. Some companies also sent out press releases as boilerplate so that they had to be printed as written. The term is used today to refer not only to preprinted contract language, that is not meant to be changed, but also to computer programming subroutines that can be inserted in a larger program to perform common recurring functions without the necessity of further editing.

[559] Caldwell v. Heritage House Realty, Inc., 32 S.W.3d 773 (Mo. Ct. App. 2000) (exchange of forms in settlement agreement negotiations); Poel v. Brunswick-Balke-Collender Co., 110 N.E. 619, 622 (N.Y. 1915).

their belief that a contract had been created through their exchange of forms.[560] Despite this, one of the parties may try to get out of the deal if circumstances change in a way that gives it a motive to escape before performance begins.[561] For example, a seller might want to avoid performance where the market value of the goods rose after the forms had been exchanged but before performance began. By avoiding performance the seller could sell the goods to another customer at the higher prevailing market price. Or it might simply try to renegotiate the price with the original buyer. Thus, if the forms exchanged between Industrial Supply and Franklin Manufacturing call for a price of $1,000 per frimulator, but the market value rises to $1,200 per unit before performance has begun, Industrial Supply might want to try to avoid the contract in order to charge the higher price. Alternatively, if the market has declined, or if the project for which it sought the goods fell through and it no longer needed the goods, the buyer might seek to escape from the agreement.

Even when circumstances change, the parties usually want to preserve their ongoing business relationship and, as a result, may resolve the problem without resorting to litigation. However, where the advantages of reneging on the deal are tremendous or where the parties do not have a long-term business relationship, the temptation to seek a way out may be too strong to resist.

The mirror-image rule also created difficulties when problems developed after the goods were delivered. This might occur if the buyer discovered a latent defect in the goods and wanted to return them for a refund or recover consequential damages for breach of warranty. Here the issue would not be whether a contract had been created; delivery by the seller and payment by the buyer puts that question to rest. Instead, the issues are which terms are included in the contract and whether any warranty disclaimers, limited remedies, or dispute resolution procedures, of the type frequently found in seller's acknowledgments, control.

At common law, if the purchase order and acknowledgment did not match, the mirror-image rule prevented formation of the contract until performance began. The result was that a contract was formed according to the terms contained in whichever form was last sent and delivered prior to performance.[562] This was sometimes called the "last-shot rule": whichever party sent the last form before performance commenced prevailed.[563] Because of the recurring pattern of sellers sending acknowledgments to buyers' purchase orders and then sending the goods, this usually resulted in the terms contained in the seller's acknowledgment becoming the terms of the agreement regardless of whether the buyer had read or understood the fine print in the seller's form.

U.C.C. § 2-207 dramatically changed the last-shot effect of the mirror-image rule. However, in doing so it created as many issues as it resolved.

---

[560] *E.g.*, Pack & Process v. Global Paper & Plastics, 1996 U.S. Dist. LEXIS 12774 (D. Del. Aug. 19, 1996).

[561] *E.g.*, Poel v. Brunswick-Balke-Collender Co., 110 N.E. 619 (N.Y. 1915).

[562] *See, e.g.*, Princess Cruises, Inc. v. Gen. Elec. Co., 143 F.3d 828 (4th Cir. 1998) (applying federal admiralty law).

[563] *E.g.*, Garst v. Harris, 58 N.E. 174 (Mass. 1900).

[A] Effect of Deviant Acceptance Under U.C.C. § 2-207(1)

The principal draftsperson of U.C.C. Article 2 harbored a suspicion against standardized form contracts.[564] As a result, § 2-207, rejects the worst aspects of the mirror-image rule and, in doing so, impairs the efficacy of standardized forms to foist unintended terms upon an unwilling party.

Section 2-207(1) provides:

> A definite and seasonable expression of acceptance or a written confirmation which is sent within a reasonable time operates as an acceptance even though it states terms additional to or different from those offered or agreed upon, unless acceptance is made expressly conditional on assent to the additional or different terms.

This overrules the results in cases where the inclusion of different or additional boilerplate terms, in what otherwise purports to be an acceptance, prevents formation of a contract. Most significantly, it impairs the operation of the last-shot rule.[565]

Section 2-207 goes further by addressing situations in which a contract has been formed over the telephone, in a face-to-face conversation, or perhaps over the Internet, without any formal documentation, followed by one of the parties sending "written confirmation" of the deal that contains terms additional to or different from those previously agreed upon. These transactions raise slightly different issues from those involved in a contract concluded through an exchange of forms.

However, § 2-207(1) raises as many questions as it resolves. Some of these questions are put to rest by the remainder of § 2-207, discussed below. Even so, navigation of the language of § 2-207 is usually a significant struggle for first-year law students.

[1] Response to an Offer

Section 2-207(1) is conspicuously silent about offers to enter into a contract. It operates on the presumption that one of the parties has made an offer. It says nothing about the form of an offer, the timing of an offer, or the effect of language in an offer that purports to limit the mode of acceptance. It leaves these issues to the common law and to other relevant sections of the Code. Section 2-207(1) picks up the trail with the effect of a response to an offer.[566]

Thus, in applying § 2-207, one must first find an offer. If the response is a mirror image, a contract is formed on the terms included in both parties' communications. If the response is anything other than a mirror image, § 2-207 must be consulted to determine whether the response is an acceptance.

---

[564] *See* Karl Llewellyn, The Common Law Tradition: Deciding Appeals 370 (1960).

[565] *See, e.g.*, Step-Saver Data Sys., Inc. v. Wyse Tech., 939 F.2d 91, 99 (3d Cir. 1991).

[566] Restatement (Second) of Contracts § 35 (1981).

[2] Acceptance Containing Different or Additional Terms

Section 2-207(1) makes it clear that the mere presence of different or additional terms does not prevent a response from operating as an acceptance. It specifies that a "definite and seasonable expression of acceptance . . . operates as an acceptance even though it contains terms additional to or different from those offered."[567] This language prevents boilerplate terms in a purported acceptance from preventing formation of a contract, merely because they deviate from the terms contained in the offer.

For example, in *C. Itoh & Co. v. Jordan International Co.*,[568] the buyer sent a purchase order for a quantity of steel coils. The seller sent an acknowledgment form repeating all of the terms contained in the buyer's purchase order regarding the description, quantity, and price of the goods. However, the seller's acknowledgment also contained a broad arbitration provision, stipulating that any dispute between the parties would be subject to binding arbitration. In attempting to determine whether the arbitration provision was included in the parties' agreement the court quickly and correctly concluded that, under § 2-207(1) "the *mere presence* of an additional term, such as a provision for arbitration . . . [did] not prevent the formation of a contract."[569] Courts have reached similar results, usually presuming that a contract has been formed in situations involving warranty disclaimers,[570] limited remedies,[571] and forum selection clauses[572] contained in a seller's acknowledgment. The inclusion of these terms does not usually prevent the response from operating as an acceptance.

One maverick decision is *Roto-Lith, Ltd. v. F.P. Bartlett Co.*[573] Roto-Lith sent a purchase order for an adhesive emulsion it planned to use in its manufacturing business. Bartlett's acknowledgment and invoice forms contained a conspicuous disclaimer of the seller's warranties, together with language indicating that Roto-Lith should "notify Seller at once" if these additional terms were not acceptable.[574] The court not only treated Bartlett's warranty disclaimer as a "material alteration" but also completely misinterpreted § 2-207 to make an acceptance containing any such material alteration to be a counteroffer. According to the court, the buyer's acceptance of the goods operated as an expression of its assent to Bartlett's warranty disclaimer.[575]

The *Roto-Lith* result is incompatible with the language of § 2-207, and would have subverted the drafters' intent to supplant the mirror-image rule, if other

---

[567] U.C.C. § 2-207(1) (2012).

[568] 552 F.2d 1228 (7th Cir. 1977).

[569] *Id.* at 1235.

[570] *E.g.*, Rottinghaus v. Howell, 666 P.2d 899 (Wash. Ct. App. 1983).

[571] *E.g.*, Transamerica Oil Corp. v. Lynes, Inc., 723 F.2d 758 (10th Cir. 1983).

[572] *E.g.*, Marlene Indus. Corp. v. Carnac Textiles Inc., 380 N.E.2d 239, 242 (N.Y. 1978) (treating arbitration clause as proposal for addition to the contract).

[573] 297 F.2d 497 (1st Cir. 1962).

[574] *Id.* at 498–99.

[575] *Id.* at 500.

courts had followed it.[576] The decision was so widely criticized that in 1966 the Permanent Editorial Board of the U.C.C. changed the official comments to § 2-207 to include language expressly rejecting the court's decision.[577] Section 2-207(1) is clear that such a provision does not prevent formation of a contract.[578]

[3] Definite and Seasonable Expression of Acceptance

Under § 2-207(1), a deviant acceptance results in the formation of a contract only if it is a "definite and seasonable expression of acceptance."[579] Thus, not every response to an offer results in the formation of a contract.

As under the common law, an outright rejection does not qualify as an "expression of acceptance." Therefore, if the buyer sends a purchase order for 10,000 red bricks, for $1.00 per brick, and the seller responds: "We are unable to fill your order for 10,000 red bricks," there is no contract. Likewise, "we are unable to fill your order for 10,000 red bricks at a price of $1.00 per brick" fails as an expression of acceptance, and no contract is formed.

If the response is not a simple rejection, but instead is a rejection accompanied by a counteroffer, the same result applies. The response, "we are unable to fill your order for 10,000 red bricks, but can supply 10,000 yellow bricks at the price you offer," would undoubtedly be treated as falling short of the "definite expression of acceptance" required by § 2-207(1). Similarly, the seller's response: "We are unable to fill your order for 10,000 red bricks at $1.00 per brick, but can provide them for $1.25 per brick" is similarly an unequivocal rejection of the buyer's offer to pay $1 per brick.

However, problems arise when the response is only an implied rejection. Thus a seller who replies, "We are happy to fill your order for 10,000 red bricks, for a price of $1.25 per brick," injects some uncertainty into the analysis. Under the mirror-image rule this counteroffer would have constituted a rejection of the buyer's proposed price of $1.00 per brick. Section 2-207(1) indicates that the presence of the additional (25¢ more) or different ($1.00 vs. $1.25) term does not prevent formation of a contract, but only if the response is a "definite and seasonable expression of acceptance." However, it seems clear that the seller's response offering to sell "10,000 yellow bricks" would not be an expression of acceptance of an offer to buy "10,000 red bricks" any more than would a response which offered to sell "10,000

---

[576] *See* Ionics, Inc. v. Elmwood Sensors, Inc., 110 F.3d 184, 187 (1st Cir. 1997) (finally formally overruling *Roto-Lith*); Caroline N. Brown, *Restoring Peace in the Battle of the Forms: A Framework for Making Uniform Commercial Code Section 2-207 Work*, 69 N.C. L. Rev. 893, 901 (1991); Harry T. Wellington, *The Nature of Judicial Review*, 91 Yale L.J. 486, 494–95 (1982).

[577] *See* John D. Wladis, *Ending the "Battle of the Forms": A Symposium on the Revision of Section 2-207 of the Uniform Commercial Code*, 49 Bus. Law. 1029, 1033–34 (1994). Furthermore, in the introduction to their treatise on the Uniform Commercial Code, Professor James J. White and Robert S. Summers single out *Roto-Lith* as a prime example of "decisions that other courts should not follow." James J. White & Robert S. Summers, Uniform Commercial Code 11 & n.47 (5th ed. 2000).

[578] Despite the provision's clarity, courts still sometimes misapply § 2-207(1) in a way that resurrects the mirror-image rule. *E.g.*, Montgomery Rubber & Gasket Co. v. Belmont Mach. Co., 308 F. Supp. 2d 1293, 1300 (M.D. Ala. 2004).

[579] U.C.C. § 2-207(1) (2012).

red bandannas."[580] Accordingly, it does not seem that a response that offers to sell the red bricks for $1.25 should be construed as an expression of acceptance of an offer to buy them for $1.00 each.

Unfortunately, the Code's text supplies no test for distinguishing between a "definite and seasonable expression of acceptance," which results in the formation of a contract despite its inclusion of different or additional terms, and a response that is so different from the terms of the offer as not to qualify as an acceptance. Courts and commentators have drawn a distinction between preprinted boilerplate terms and those terms inserted into the parties' forms for each separate transaction. These "dickered,"[581] "bargained,"[582] or "critical" terms usually consist of the description, quantity, price, and payment and delivery terms.

Examples abound. In *Howard Construction Co. v. Jeff-Cole Quarries, Inc.*,[583] the seller's reply contained handwritten changes to the price term proposed by the buyer's purchase order. The court decided that these handwritten changes to the price made the seller's response a counteroffer.[584] In *Alliance Wall Corp. v. Ampat Midwest Corp.*,[585] the parties' communications stated different times for delivery. The buyer insisted on a specific deadline, and the seller was just as adamant about avoiding being pinned down to a specific date. Consequently, the differences in the forms prevented formation a contract.[586] On the other hand, in *Southern Idaho Pipe & Steel Co. v. Cal-Cut Pipe & Supply*,[587] the court treated a buyer's response as an acceptance even though it altered the delivery date proposed by the seller. Thus, the precise line between deviations that prevent formation of a contract and those that do not is sometimes difficult to discern.

The Official Comments to § 2-207 provide only limited guidance. They merely specify several terms that are to be treated as material alterations within the meaning of § 2-207(2). These include terms affecting the seller's warranties, those giving the buyer a right to cancel the contract upon the buyer's failure to make a timely payment,[588] *force majeure* provisions,[589] terms setting a time limit for the

---

[580] Red bandannas can be obtained for approximately $1.25 each; more cheaply if you buy in bulk.

[581] Alliance Wall Corp. v. Ampat Midwest Corp., 477 N.E.2d 1206, 1211 (Ohio Ct. App. 1984). *See* John Edward Murray Jr., *Section 2-207 of the Uniform Commercial Code: Another Word About Incipient Unconscionability*, 39 U. Pitt. L. Rev. 597, 601–03 (1978); N. Stephan Kinsella, *Smashing the Broken Mirror: The Battle of the Forms, UCC 2-207, and Louisiana's Improvements*, 53 La. L. Rev. 1555, 1566 (1993).

[582] *See* James J. White & Robert S. Summers, Uniform Commercial Code § 2–3 at 39–40, 52–53 (6th ed. 2010).

[583] 669 S.W.2d 221, 229 (Mo. Ct. App. 1983).

[584] *See also* United Foods, Inc. v. Hadley-Peoples Mfg. Co., 1994 Tenn. App. LEXIS 277, at *14 (May 20, 1994).

[585] 477 N.E.2d 1206 (Ohio Ct. App. 1984).

[586] *See also* Koehring Co. v. Glowacki, 253 N.W.2d 64 (Wis. 1977) (no contract where purchase order said: "FOB, our truck, your plant, loaded" and confirmation said "as is, where is"); Olefins Trading, Inc. v. Han Yang Chem. Corp., 9 F.3d 282 (3d Cir. 1993).

[587] 567 P.2d 1246 (Idaho 1977).

[588] U.C.C. § 2-207 cmt. 4 (2012).

[589] *See infra* § 11.03[C] Effect of Force Majeure Clauses.

buyer to register complaints about the goods, terms providing for interest charges on overdue payments, and terms limiting the buyer's right of rejection for certain limited defects in the goods.[590] By designating these provisions as candidates for exclusion from the contract under § 2-207(2) the Code presumes that their inclusion did not prevent formation of a contract in the first place under subsection (1).[591]

Thus, deviations in the negotiated terms such as the quantity, description, and price, which usually vary from one contract to the next, usually operate to prevent formation of a contract. However, variations in boilerplate or preprinted terms usually do not automatically prevent a contract from being formed. The only exception to this general pattern, as explained in the next section, is where the offeree's acceptance is expressly conditional on the offeror's assent to the different or additional terms proposed in the offeree's response.

[4] Acceptance Expressly Conditional

As explained above, a definite and seasonable expression of acceptance normally results in the formation of a contract even though it contains boilerplate terms different from or in addition to those in the offer. However, in certain instances an offeree may wish to avoid entering into a contract unless it can be assured that the terms in its "acceptance" are a part of the agreement.

Section 2-207(1) provides offerees with a method to ensure that they will not be bound at all unless the other party agrees to its additional or different terms. Deviant acceptances do not result in the formation of a contract if "acceptance is expressly made conditional on assent to the additional or different terms."[592]

Some responses are unequivocal counteroffers. In *C. Itoh & Co. v. Jordan International Co.*,[593] for example, the seller's response contained the following language:

> Seller's acceptance is, however, expressly conditional on Buyer's assent to the additional or different terms and conditions set forth below and printed on the reverse side. If these terms are not acceptable, Buyer should notify Seller at once.[594]

Even though the mere inclusion of an arbitration clause did not prevent formation of a contract, the arbitration clause, together with this additional language, prevented the seller's acknowledgment from operating as an accep-

---

[590] U.C.C. § 2-207 cmt. 5 (2012).

[591] As explained below, § 2-207(2) permits the incorporation of some nonmaterial additional terms into the contract. Other terms, deemed to be "material alterations" are to be excluded. *See infra* § 4.10[B] Treatment of Different or Additional Terms. Analysis of these terms as candidates for inclusion or exclusion in the contract presumes that a contract has already been formed under § 2-207(1) thus implying that their appearance in a response was not, by itself, enough to prevent the response from constituting a "definite and seasonable expression of acceptance."

[592] U.C.C. § 2-207(1) (2012).

[593] 552 F.2d 1228 (7th Cir. 1977).

[594] *Id.* at 1230.

tance.[595]

On the other hand, in *Idaho Power Co. v. Westinghouse Electric Corp.*,[596] the seller's acknowledgment form contained language purporting to make its acceptance "expressly conditional" on the buyer's assent to the terms contained in its acknowledgment, including its warranty disclaimer. However, the seller proceeded with the transaction and shipped the goods the buyer had ordered without first learning from the buyer whether it agreed to the seller's disclaimer. The court said that "the language used does not clearly reveal that Idaho Power was 'unwilling to proceed with the transaction unless . . . assured of (Westinghouse's) assent to the additional or different terms.' "[597] In *Step-Saver Data Systems, Inc. v. Wyse Technology*,[598] the court went further and required that the offeree's language must "demonstrate an unwillingness to proceed with the transaction unless the additional or different terms are included in the contract."[599]

Parties who wish to ensure that no contract is formed until the other party agrees to their terms should use language that closely tracks the text of § 2-207(1). Similar language is not likely to accomplish the intended result.[600] Those who are really concerned should refuse to begin performance until the other party's express consent is obtained.[601]

[5] Written Confirmations

Section 2-207(1) also applies to a second set of circumstances that is often overlooked. It governs when the parties form their contract informally, such as over the telephone, and one of the parties subsequently sends a written confirmation containing terms additional to or different from those that they discussed.[602] The relevant portion of § 2-207(1) provides that "a written confirmation . . . operates as an acceptance even though it states terms additional to or different from . . . those agreed upon."[603]

At first glance, this language is confusing. On its face, it applies only when the parties' negotiations have already resulted in the formation of a contract. If a contract has already been formed it is difficult to understand how a written confirmation sent by one of the parties could be analyzed as an "acceptance." Under the common law additional or different terms included in the written confirmation

---

[595] *Id.* at 1237.

[596] 596 F.2d 924, 926 (9th Cir. 1979).

[597] *Id.* at 927.

[598] 939 F.2d 91 (3d Cir. 1991).

[599] *Id.* at 101–02.

[600] *See, e.g.*, Manitowoc Marine Group, LLC v. Ameron Int'l Corp., 424 F. Supp. 2d 1119 (E.D. Wis. 2006) (acceptance "subject to" assent to additional terms insufficient to prevent formation); Dorton v. Collins & Aikman Corp. 453 F.2d 1161 (6th Cir. 1972).

[601] Lee. R. Russ, *What Constitutes Acceptance "Expressly Made Conditional" Converting It to Rejection and Counteroffer Under UCC § 2-207(1)*, 22 A.L.R.4th 939 (1983).

[602] *See* U.C.C. § 2-207 cmt. 1 (2012).

[603] U.C.C. § 2-207(1) (2012).

would ordinarily be treated as nothing more than proposals to modify the contract that had previously been formed.

Nevertheless, § 2-207(1) treats a written confirmation, if it is sent within a reasonable time, *as if* it were an acceptance. This treatment operates as a gateway to § 2-207(2), which determines whether these additional terms become a part of the contract even in the absence of the express consent of the other party.[604]

[B]   Treatment of Different or Additional Terms

Section 2-207(2) does not deal with contract formation.[605] It addresses whether *additional* terms, not included in the original offer but present in the offeree's acceptance, are included in the parties' contract. It also addresses whether *additional* terms first introduced in a confirmation sent by one of the parties, following the formation of an oral agreement, are included as part of the deal. Further, although its text does not expressly refer to *different* (conflicting) terms, some courts have ruled that the same rules applicable to additional terms govern the treatment of any terms in the parties' forms that are different from one another.

Section 2-207(2) provides:

> The additional terms are to be construed as proposals for addition to the contract. Between merchants such terms become part of the contract unless:
>
> (a)   the offer expressly limits acceptance to the terms of the offer;
>
> (b)   they materially alter it; or
>
> (c)   notification of objection to them has already been given or is given within a reasonable time after notice of them is received.

[1]   Additional Terms

As explained above, § 2-207(1) permits a contract to be formed as the result of parties' exchange of forms even though the acceptance contains terms in addition to those contained in the offer. Section 2-207(2) addresses the disposition of those terms and whether they become part of the parties' contract or are merely proposals for modification of the contract that must be agreed to separately.

[a]   Proposal to Modify the Contract If Not "Between Merchants"

Under § 2-207(2), the parties' status as merchants plays an important role in determining whether any additional terms stand a chance of becoming a part of the contract. The presumption is that any additional terms contained in the offeree's response are mere proposals for addition to their contract. However, "between

---

[604] *See infra* § 4.10[B] Treatment of Different or Additional Terms.

[605] First-year law students persist in consulting § 2-207(2) to determine whether a contract has been formed. One (or more) of your classmates will make this mistake when you are covering § 2-207(2).

merchants" the additional terms might be added to the contract, unless they are excluded by one of the three provisos of § 2-207(2).

U.C.C. § 2-104(3) specifies that a transaction is "between merchants" if "both parties are chargeable with the knowledge or skill of a merchant."[606] As explained in more detail elsewhere,[607] a merchant is a person who either deals in goods of the kind, or who because of her occupation holds herself out as having knowledge, or skill "peculiar to the *practices* or goods involved in the transaction."[608] A person can also be held to the standard of a merchant if the person employs an agent, broker, or other intermediary who either has or holds himself out as having the necessary knowledge or skill with respect to the transaction.

If either of the parties is a nonmerchant, the transaction is not "between merchants," and any additional terms are treated as nothing more than proposals to modify the contract. In these circumstances the additional term is a mere proposal even if it is unimportant, and even though the other party does not expressly object to its inclusion. The additional term becomes a part of the contract only if agreement to its inclusion is separately expressed. And, because the parties have already formed a contract, and have a duty to perform, performance of the agreement is not, all by itself, sufficient to show agreement to the proposed new terms.

[b]   Inclusion of Additional Term in Transactions "Between Merchants"

On the other hand, if both parties are merchants, the additional terms contained in the offeree's response stands a chance of making it into the contract. The additional term is part of the contract unless one of the three conditions, specified in § 2-207(2)(a)–(c) applies. The nature of these conditions makes it unlikely that any term that matters to the parties will be included among the terms of the deal.

[i]   Offer Expressly Limits Acceptance to Its Own Terms

First, if the original offer expressly limited acceptance to the terms contained in the offer, then the offeree's additional terms are treated as nothing more than proposals to amend the contract.[609]

Thus, an offeror might express its objection to any additional or different terms by expressly limiting acceptance to the terms contained in its offer.[610] Assume that the Franklin Manufacturing sends Industrial Supply Co. a purchase order that conspicuously indicates that Franklin's willingness to enter into a deal depends on Industrial Supply's willingness to be bound to the terms contained in Franklin's offer. If Industrial Supply sends Franklin an acknowledgment containing a limited

---

[606] U.C.C. § 2-104(3) (2012).

[607] *See infra* § 5.06[C] Confirmatory Memorandum in Transacations Between Merchants.

[608] U.C.C. § 2-104(1) (2012) (emphasis added).

[609] U.C.C. § 2-207(2)(a) (2012).

[610] U.C.C. § 2-207(2)(a) (2012).

remedy provision not found in the purchase order, § 2-207(1) will treat Industrial Supply's acknowledgment as an acceptance.[611] However, § 2-207(2) prevents Industrial Supply's additional limited remedy provision from becoming part of the contract. Instead, it treats the term as a proposal for a modification.[612]

[ii]   Additional Term Is a Material Alteration[613]

Even if the offeror has not insisted on an acceptance that is limited to the terms of its offer, any new term in an acceptance that "materially alters" the contract is excluded from the deal.[614] The new term is added to the contract only if agreement to it is obtained through some other mechanism.[615]

The exclusion of material alterations makes it important to distinguish between material and nonmaterial terms included in an offeree's acceptance. Thus, even if Franklin Manufacturing's purchase order says nothing about its unwillingness to contract on terms other than those contained in its purchase order, if Industrial Supply's limited remedy provision is a "material alteration," the limited remedy provision will not be included as part of the contract unless Franklin separately agrees to it.

The Official Comments to § 2-207 indicate that materially altering terms are those that would "result in surprise or hardship if incorporated without express awareness by the other party."[616] The comments mention warranty disclaimers and provisions reducing the time for making complaints about the goods among those which would result in surprise or hardship.[617] Many courts routinely treat arbitration clauses[618] and limited remedy provisions[619] as material alterations.[620] The Official Comments indicate that force majeure clauses, terms providing for interest on overdue payments, or those providing for inspection by a sub purchaser, are usually nonmaterial terms that would be included in the contract

---

[611] *E.g.*, Lockheed Elec. Co. v. Keronix, Inc., 114 Cal. App. 3d 304, 311 (1981).

[612] *Id.* at 311–15. *See also* Brevel Motors Inc. v. Vendo Co., 3 U.C.C. Rep. Serv. 2d 1347 (D.N.J. 1986).

[613] Colin P. Marks, *The Limits of Limiting Liability in the Battle of the Forms: U.C.C. Section 2-207 and the "Material Alteration" Inquiry*, 33 Pepp. L. Rev. 501 (2005).

[614] U.C.C. § 2-207(2)(b) (2012).

[615] *Id.*

[616] U.C.C. § 2-207 cmt. 4 (2012).

[617] *Id. See, e.g.*, Dale R. Horning Co. v. Falconer Glass Indus., Inc., 730 F. Supp. 962 (S.D. Ind. 1990).

[618] *E.g.*, Marlene Indus. Corp. v. Carnac Textiles, Inc., 380 N.E.2d 239 (N.Y. 1978). *Contra* Schulze & Burch Biscuit Co. v. Tree Top, Inc., 831 F.2d 709 (7th Cir. 1987). *See generally* Mark Andrew Cerny, Comment, *A Shield Against Arbitration: U.C.C. Section 2-207's Role in the Enforceability of Arbitration Agreements Included with Delivery of Products*, 51 Ala. L. Rev. 821 (2000).

[619] *E.g.*, Altronics of Bethlehem, Inc. v. Repco, Inc., 957 F.2d 1102, 1107 (3d Cir. 1992) (exclusion of consequential damages a material alteration); Dale R. Horning Co. v. Falconer Glass Indus., Inc., 730 F. Supp. 962 (S.D. Ind. 1990). *Contra* Hydraform Prods. Corp. v. American Steel & Aluminum Corp., 498 A.2d 339 (N.H. 1985) (reasonable limited remedy provision not a material alteration).

[620] *See also* Borden Chem., Inc. v. Jahn Foundry, Corp., 834 N.E.2d 1227 (Mass. Ct. App. 2005) (indemnification provision); Lively v. IJAM, Inc., 114 P.3d 487 (Okla. Civ. App. 2005) (forum selection clause).

absent their exclusion by § 2-207(2)(a) or (c).[621]

Some courts refer to industry standards to determine whether a particular term is a material alteration.[622] Under these decisions, if excluding consequential damages is a standard term in the industry in which Franklin and Industrial Supply participate, including the limitation would not constitute "surprise and hardship" on Franklin and would not be a material alteration. If industry practice demonstrates that prices are established with reference to the buyer's assumption of the risk of consequential damages, then the presumed familiarity of the merchant buyer with those standards precludes any suggestion that a term adhering to trade usage is either a hardship or a surprise.[623]

[iii]   Timely Objection to Additional Terms

Finally, the offeror can always prevent any new or additional terms from being included in the contract by objecting to them within a reasonable time.[624] This notification need not be in writing, though a prudent person will send a written notification to avoid problems proving that objection was made. Thus, if Franklin, upon receipt of Industrial Supply's acknowledgment sends notice back to Industrial Supply that it objects to Industrial's limited remedy provision, that term is kept out of the contract even if it was not a material alteration.

[c]   Additional Terms in Written Confirmation

Section 2-207(2) is also triggered when the parties have entered into an oral agreement and one of the parties has followed it up by sending a written confirmation that contains terms additional to those previously agreed upon. In *Step-Saver Data Systems, Inc. v. Wyse Technology*,[625] the parties formed an agreement for the plaintiff's purchase of the defendant's software program. The defendant subsequently sent copies of its program accompanied by a "box-top license" containing a warranty disclaimer and limited remedy provision. The additional terms contained in the box-top license provided a gateway for the additional terms to become part of this "rolling contract" under § 2-207(2), even though the initial contract had not been formed through an exchange of pre-printed forms.

[d]   Acceptance of Proposal for Modification

A question that naturally arises when the additional terms are regarded merely as proposals to modify the contract is what constitutes acceptance of the proposal to modify. Although this is not expressly addressed by § 2-207(2), it should be clear that mere performance of the contract does not, all by itself, operate as assent to

---

[621] U.C.C. § 2-207 cmt. 5 (2012).

[622] *E.g.*, Valmont Indus., Inc. v. Mitsui & Co. (USA), Inc., 419 F. Supp. 1239 (D. Neb. 1976).

[623] *See* Union Carbide Corp. v. Oscar Mayer Foods Corp., 947 F.2d 1333 (7th Cir. 1991) (J. Posner); Schulze & Burch Biscuit Co v. Tree Top, Inc., 831 F.2d 709 (7th Cir. 1987) (course of dealing).

[624] U.C.C. § 2-207(2)(c) (2012).

[625] 939 F.2d 91 (3d Cir. 1991).

the proposed modification. For example, in *Altronics of Bethlehem, Inc. v. Repco, Inc.*,[626] the seller's invoice contained language purporting to exclude liability for consequential damages. Because exclusion of consequential damages is a material alteration,[627] the term was treated as a proposal for addition to the contract. The buyer's acceptance of and payment for the goods, standing alone, was not an expression of its assent to the proposed modification.[628]

Altronics represents the correct result. Because a contract had already been formed, the buyer had a duty to accept the goods when they arrived. Treating performance of its contractual duties as assent to the seller's additional terms would have left the buyer with an awkward choice between consenting to the additional terms or breaching the contract. Accordingly, assent to the additional terms cannot be implied from performance of the contract alone; it must be express.[629]

[2] Different Terms

At first blush it might seem that § 2-207(2) handles "different terms" in the same way as "additional terms." But, close examination of § 2-207(2) reveals that it is completely silent about the treatment of "different terms." Subsection (1) treats different and additional terms in the same way, in connection with the contract formation process, but subsection (2) is conspicuously silent about whether different terms are included in the contract. The statutory text speaks only to the inclusion or exclusion of "additional terms" contained in what is otherwise a definite expression of acceptance.

Despite this, the Official Comments to § 2-207 refer to the text of the statute as if it treated different and additional terms in the same way. This discrepancy raises the question of whether different terms should be handled with a different approach than additional terms. It might be appropriate to treat terms that affirmatively conflict differently than those that are merely supplemental.[630] Or, the language of § 2-207(2) might be nothing more than a drafting error.

The problem of how different terms are handled is illustrated by *Northrop Corp. v. Litronic Industries.*[631] In response to Northrop's request, Litronic sent Northrop an offer to sell it four customized "printed wire boards." The offer stipulated that the goods would be accompanied by the seller's 90-day warranty to the exclusion of

---

[626] 957 F.2d 1102 (3d Cir. 1992).

[627] Air Prods. & Chems., Inc. v. Fairbanks Morse, Inc., 206 N.W.2d 414 (Wis. 1973); *but see* Hydraform Prods. Corp. v. Am. Steel & Aluminum Corp., 498 A.2d 339 (N.H. 1985) (reasonable limit on consequential damages not a material alteration).

[628] *Altronics of Bethlehem, Inc.*, 957 F.2d at 1108. *See also* Step-Saver Data Sys., Inc. v. Wyse Tech., 939 F.2d 91 (3d Cir. 1991).

[629] *See also* Brown Mach. Inc. v. Hercules, Inc., 770 S.W.2d 416, 421 (Mo. Ct. App. 1989).

[630] *See* John E. Murry Jr., *The Chaos of the "Battle of the Forms": Solutions*, 39 VAND. L. REV. 1307, 1345–65 (1986); John L. Utz, *More on the Battle of the Forms: The Treatment of "Different" Terms Under the Uniform Commercial Code*, 16 U.C.C. L.J. 103 (1983); Douglas G. Baird & Robert Weisberg, *Rules, Standards, and the Battle of the Forms: A Reassessment of Section 2-207*, 68 VA. L. REV. 1217, 1247 (1982).

[631] 29 F.3d 1173 (7th Cir. 1994).

any other warranties. A Northrop representative subsequently called Litronic and "accepted" the offer, indicating that his acceptance would be followed by a formal purchase order. When Northrop's purchase order arrived, it stipulated that the seller would supply a warranty but imposed no limit on the warranty's duration.

The parties' subsequent performance established the existence of a contract even if Northrop's oral acceptance of Litronic's offer did not. The only question was the duration of the warranty. On this point the forms exchanged by the parties diverged: the seller's offer indicated that there was a 90-day warranty, while the buyer's acceptance provided for a warranty but contained no express limit on its duration.

Courts have taken three different approaches to these types of conflicting or "different" terms. The *Northrop* court joined the majority of decisions in taking the view that the conflicting terms knocked each other out.[632] This "knock-out" approach leaves the parties governed by any gap-filling provisions supplied elsewhere in Article 2.[633] In *Northrop*, this provided the buyer with an implied warranty for a reasonable time.[634]

A second approach, discussed but rejected in *Northrop*, is to find that a contract was formed on the terms expressed in the offer, with the deviant term contained in the offeree's acceptance simply dropping out.[635] This would have left Northrop with only a 90-day warranty even though Northrop's request for proposals had advised Litronic that Northrop would be willing to enter into a contract, if at all, only on the terms contained in its purchase order. The difficulty with this view is that it converts the "last-shot" rule of the common law into a "first-shot" rule that preserves the terms contained in the offer and completely eliminates the offeree's terms from the contract.[636]

Judge Posner's opinion acknowledged the existence of a third view, which he favored, but felt constrained by precedent not to apply.[637] This minority view, which is consistent with the official comments to § 2-207, treats different and additional terms in the same way.[638] Under this view the deviant terms become a part of the resulting contract unless they are materially different from one another.[639] This latter approach has the added appeal of avoiding the necessity of drawing the

---

[632] *See also* Gen'l Steel Corp. v. Collins, 196 S.W.3d 18 (Ky. Ct. App. 2006) (buyer crossed out seller's arbitration clause).

[633] *See e.g.*, Ionics v. Elmwood Sensors, Inc., 110 F.3d 184, 189 (1st Cir. 1997) (applying Massachusetts law); Northrop Corp. v. Litronic Indus., 29 F.3d 1173, 1178–79 (7th Cir. 1994).

[634] Northrop Corp. v. Litronic, Indus., 29 F.3d 1173, 1179–80 (7th Cir. 1994).

[635] *E.g.*, Valtrol, Inc. v. Gen. Connectors Corp., 884 F.2d 149, 155 (4th Cir. 1989) (applying South Carolina law); Reaction Molding Tech., Inc. v. Gen. Elec. Co., 588 F. Supp. 1280, 1289 (E.D. Pa. 1984).

[636] Flender Corp. v. Tippins Intern., Inc., 830 A.2d 1279 (Pa. Super. Ct. 2003); Northrop Corp. v. Litronic Indus., 29 F.3d 1173, 1178–79 (7th Cir. 1994).

[637] Northrop Corp., 29 F.3d at 1178–79.

[638] *Id.*

[639] Mead Corp. v. McNally-Pittsburgh Mfg. Corp., 654 F.2d 1197 (6th Cir. 1981) (applying Ohio law); Steiner v. Mobil Oil Corp., 569 P.2d 751 (Cal. 1977).

difficult distinction, also encountered in connection with the parol evidence rule,[640] between terms that are different and those that are additional.[641]

Some have even suggested a fourth alternative in which the court should examine both parties' standard terms and include the one which is most fair.[642] This "best-shot" approach has not received wide acceptance.

As the court in *Northrop* noted, the advantage of the majority knock-out rule is that it adopts a neutral position on a matter over which the parties did not agree.[643] In addition, unlike the traditional mirror-image rule, it prevents the offeree from using boilerplate language to surprise the offeror unfairly.

[C] Contracts Formed Through Conduct

Section 2-207 recognizes that the parties' exchange of correspondence may not result in the formation of a contract. Difficult questions arise when the parties go ahead and perform, despite conflicts in their paperwork that prevent formation of a contract under § 2-207(1). Nevertheless, if the seller delivers the goods and the buyer accepts and pays for them, there is little question that a contract exists. However, if problems develop after performance, disputes are likely to arise over the terms of the contract that the parties' conduct created. Section 2-207(3) provides:

> Conduct by both parties which recognizes the existence of a contract is sufficient to establish a contract for sale although the writings of the parties do not otherwise establish a contract. In such case the terms of the particular contract consist of those terms on which the writings of the parties agree, together with any supplementary terms incorporated under any other provision of this Act.[644]

Under this language, if the exchange of forms between the parties does not result in a contract but performance nevertheless demonstrates that the parties had entered into an agreement of one sort or another, the terms of the agreement are comprised of the terms that match,[645] together with those provided by the gap-filling provisions of Article 2 with respect to price, time, and, of particular significance, warranties and remedies.

In *Alliance Wall Corp. v. Ampat Midwest Corp.*,[646] the forms exchanged by the parties revealed a basic disagreement over the time for performance: the buyer demanded delivery at a specific time, and the seller refused to make a commitment to any definitive deadline. Despite the divergence of their communications regard-

---

[640] *See infra* § 6.05[D] Supplementing a Partially Integrated Contract.

[641] *See* Northrop Corp. v. Litronic Indus., 29 F.3d 1173, 1179–80 (7th Cir. 1994).

[642] Victor P. Goldberg, *The "Battle of the Forms": Fairness, Efficiency, and the Best-Shot Rule*, 76 Or. L. Rev. 155, 166 (1997).

[643] Northrop Corp. v. Litronic Indus., 29 F.3d 1173, 1179–82 (7th Cir. 1994).

[644] U.C.C. § 2-207(3) (2012).

[645] *E.g.*, AgGrow Oils, L.L.C. v. Nat'l Union Fire Ins. Co., 420 F.3d 751, 754–55 (8th Cir. 2005).

[646] 477 N.E.2d 1206 (Ohio Ct. App. 1984).

ing the time for performance, the parties acted as if they had a deal. The seller shipped the goods and the buyer accepted and paid for them when they arrived. This behavior unequivocally demonstrated the existence of a contract for sale even though they had not agreed about the time for delivery. The court applied U.C.C. § 2-207(3) to find that the gap-filling provision of U.C.C. § 2-309,[647] stipulating that in the absence of an agreement delivery shall be made within a "reasonable time," applied. Set against this standard, the seller's performance was timely, even though the buyer had attempted to insist on delivery at an earlier time.

The issue is even more acute when the bargained terms match, but boilerplate language which adds or disclaims a warranty, limits the buyer's remedies, subjects disputes to binding arbitration, or other terms are combined with language making the offeree's response expressly conditional on the offeror's assent to the different or additional terms. As explained above, § 2-207(1) prevents formation of a contract when the reply is an unequivocal counteroffer.[648] In these cases, performance demonstrates the existence of a contract but does not determine which, if any, of the conflicting terms are included in the contract.

Assume, for example, that Franklin Manufacturing submits a purchase order to Industrial Supply. Subsequently, Industrial sends an acknowledgment indicating its agreement to Franklin's quantity, description, price, and delivery terms, but the acknowledgment includes both a provision requiring mandatory arbitration of any disputes arising from the sale and a term making its assent unequivocally conditional on the buyer's agreement to the seller's arbitration clause. At this stage of the exchange, Industrial's express counteroffer prevents formation of a contract. However, if Industrial ships the goods and Franklin accepts them, it is impossible to conclude that a contract between the parties did not exist.

Under the common law, the buyer's acceptance of the goods would have resulted in a contract as well, but with the buyer's actions treated as assent to the terms included in the seller's counteroffer. Section 2-207(3) expressly rejects this result. Instead, it would find the existence of a contract formed by conduct, but without the seller's arbitration clause.

If the additional term contained in the seller's reply is a warranty disclaimer, § 2-207(3) can result in a contract that includes the very warranties that the seller's reply sought to avoid. For example, if the seller's reply is "expressly conditional" on the buyer's assent to the seller's disclaimer of all implied warranties and the parties go ahead and perform without reaching an agreement about the exclusion of warranties, a contact will be concluded under § 2-207(3). That section will exclude the seller's disclaimer. Instead, the gap-filling implied warranty of merchantability will be included in the contract in direct contravention of the seller's attempted disclaimer.[649] Of course, the seller might have avoided the problem by refusing to ship the goods until it obtained the buyer's express consent to the proposed disclaimer, thus preventing formation through conduct.

---

[647] *See infra* § 4.11[B][2] Indefinite Time and Place for Delivery.

[648] *See supra* § 4.10[A][4] Acceptance Expressly Conditional.

[649] *See* Diamond Fruit Growers, Inc. v. Krack Corp., 794 F.2d 1440 (9th Cir. 1986).

[D]   Battle of the Forms in International Transactions[650]

In international sales of goods, Article 2 does not apply. Instead, the contract is likely to be governed by the United Nations Convention on the International Sale of Goods (CISG).[651] The CISG retains the mirror-image rule in a modified form.[652] Article 19(1) provides:

> A reply to an offer which purports to be an acceptance but contains additions, limitations or other modifications is a rejection of the offer and constitutes a counter-offer."[653]

Article 19(2) qualifies the rule:

> However, a reply to an offer which purports to be an acceptance but contains additional or different terms which do not materially alter the terms of the offer constitutes an acceptance, unless the offeror, without undue delay, objects orally to the discrepancy or dispatches a notice to that effect.[654]

Thus, a reply with a nonmaterial deviation still operates as an acceptance, but one with a materially different or materially additional term is not an acceptance.[655] Under Article 19, a reply that mirrors all of the bargained terms but that contains an arbitration clause would probably be treated as a counteroffer because arbitration clauses have been widely regarded as a material alteration.[656] Moreover, Article 19(3) provides a nonexclusive list of terms that are considered material. Additional or different terms dealing with price, payment, quality, quantity, the time and place of delivery, the extent of liability, or the means of settling disputes are all material alterations.[657]

Article 19's resurrection of the mirror-image rule preserves the last-shot rule in cases where the parties have performed the contract before a dispute arises. In cases where the discrepancy is discovered before performance, Article 19(1) permits parties to escape performance when a change in market conditions gives them an

---

[650] Louis F. Del Duca, *Implementation of Contract Formation Statute of Frauds, Parol Evidence, and Battle of Forms CISG Provisions in Civil and Common Law Countries*, 25 J.L. & Com. 133 (2005); Kevin C. Stemp, *A Comparative Analysis of the "Battle of the Forms,"* 15 Transnat'l L. & Contemp. Probs. 243 (2005).

[651] *See supra* § 1.04[B][2] UN Convention on International Sale of Goods.

[652] Henry D. Gabriel, *The Battle of the Forms: A Comparison of the United Nations Convention on Contracts for the International Sale of Goods and the Uniform Commercial Code*, 49 Bus. L. 1053 (1994); William S. Dodge, *Teaching the CISG in Contracts*, 50 J. Legal Educ. 72, 94 (2000); John E. Murray Jr., *An Essay on the Formation of Contracts and Related Matters Under the United Nations Convention on Contracts for the International Sale of Goods*, 8 J.L. & Com. 11 (1988).

[653] CISG Art. 19(1) (1980).

[654] CISG Art. 19(2) (1980).

[655] *See* Henry D. Gabriel, *The Battle of the Forms: A Comparison of the United Nations Convention on Contracts for the International Sale of Goods and the Uniform Commercial Code*, 49 Bus. L. 1053, 1061 (1994).

[656] *See* Filanto, S.p.A. v. Chilewich Int'l Corp., 789 F. Supp. 1229 (S.D.N.Y. 1992).

[657] CISG Art. 19(3) (1980).

incentive to do so.[658]

In other international transactions, the UNIDROIT Principles use a knock-out approach.[659] A term in a standardized form becomes part of the contract between the parties only if both parties' forms are "common in substance."[660] Where the standardized forms do not fully agree, the parties retain the right to declare their intent not to be bound to the contract at all, so long as they act without undue delay.[661] Thus, the UNIDROIT Principles avoid the last-shot rule unless a party unequivocally expresses its intent to be bound only to its own terms.

The Principles of European Contract law follows the same approach of the UNIDROIT Principles. A reply that contains new or different terms that would materially alter the agreement is a rejection and a counteroffer.[662] If the new or different terms are not material alterations, a contract is formed despite the differences between the two forms.[663]

Article 2.209 allows for the possibility that an agreement between the parties has been reached even though the forms they have exchanged do not match. If the parties have reached an agreement otherwise, any "general conditions" or boiler-plate terms in the parties' forms that match are part of the contract. Those that do not match are excluded.

§ 4.11 INDEFINITE TERMS AND AGREEMENTS TO AGREE[664]

It is rarely practical for the parties to consider and agree upon every possible aspect of their transaction. The small size of many agreements would make extensive negotiations over every conceivable issue that might arise between them

---

[658] *See* Henry D. Gabriel, *The Battle of the Forms: A Comparison of the United Nations Convention on Contracts for the International Sale of Goods and the Uniform Commercial Code*, 49 Bus. L. 1053, 1062 (1994); Christine Moccia, Note, *The United Nations Convention on Contracts for the International Sale of Goods and the "Battle of the Forms,"* 13 Fordham Int'l L.J. 649 (1989–90).

[659] Kevin C. Stemp, *A Comparative Analysis of the "Battle of the Forms,"* 15 Transnat'l L. & Contemp. Probs. 243, 286 (2005); Maria del Pilar Perales Viscasillas, *"Battle of the Forms" Under the 1980 United Nations Convention on Contracts for the International Sale of Goods: A Comparison with Section 2-207 UCC and the UNIDROIT Principles*, 10 Pace Int'l L. Rev. 97 (1998); María del Pilar Perales Viscasillas, *The Formation of Contracts & the Principles of European Contract Law*, 13 Pace Int'l L. Rev. 371 (2001)

[660] PICC Art. 2.1.22 (2004).

[661] *Id.*

[662] PECL Article 2.208(1) (2002).

[663] PECL Article 2.208(2) (2002).

[664] Ian Ayres & Robert Gertner, *Filling Gaps in Incomplete Contracts: An Economic Theory of Default Rules*, 99 Yale L.J. 87 (1989); Ian Ayres, *Regulating Opt Out: An Economic Theory of Altering Rules*, 121 Yale L.J. 2032, 2036, 2061–62, 2073 (2012); Randy E. Barnett, *The Sound of Silence: Default Rules and Contractual Consent*, 78 Va. L. Rev. 821 (1992); Richard Craswell, *The "Incomplete Contracts" Literature and Efficient Precautions*, 56 Case W. Res. L. Rev. 151 (2005); George S. Geis, *An Embedded Options Theory of Indefinite Contracts*, 90 Minn. L. Rev. 1664 (2006); Mark P. Gergen, *The Use of Open Terms in Contract*, 92 Colum. L. Rev. 997, 1061–64 (1992); Gillian K. Hadfield, *Judicial Competence and the Interpretation of Incomplete Contracts*, 23 J. Legal Stud. 159 (1994); Oliver Hart & John Moore,

prohibitively expensive. Further, many contracts are created informally with few if any discussions over terms apart from price, quantity, and the time for performance. Commitments are sometimes made without even an agreement as to price.[665] Even in large transactions, with both parties adequately represented, the parties and their lawyers might fail to successfully anticipate every matter upon which an agreement might be useful. As a result, gaps in contracts are inevitable.

Despite this practical reality, the terms of an agreement must be reasonably definite in order for an agreement to be enforced.[666] If the terms are so indefinite that the court would find it impossible to detect a breach, or, even if a breach could be identified, to frame a remedy, no contract can be found. Courts are naturally reluctant to find that a contract exists unless they are able to provide a remedy for its breach. Accordingly, the absence of a reasonably definite agreement sometimes impedes the court's willingness and ability to find that a contract exists.[667]

For example, in *Suffield Development Associates Ltd. Partnership v. Society for Savings*,[668] a loan agreement was too indefinite because neither the amount of the loan nor the amount necessary to finance the project for which it was intended had been settled. Similarly, in *T.O. Stanley Boot Co., Inc. v. Bank of El Paso*,[669] the court refused to enforce a bank's promise to provide a $500,000 line of credit because the parties had not agreed about the due date, the interest rate, or other material terms related to repayment. And, in *Academy Chicago Publishers v. Cheever*,[670] an agreement between a publisher and an author's widow to publish a collection of the author's stories was too indefinite, where the parties had not agreed on the number of pages, the number of stories, or a manner for selection of the stories that would be included. Without these details there was no basis for determining when or whether a breach had occurred.

Although older cases take a more rigid approach, both the Second Restatement of Contracts[671] and the Uniform Commercial Code adopt a flexible standard about the degree of certainty required for the court to find that a contract has been formed. U.C.C. § 2-204 provides:

Foundations of Incomplete Contracts, 66 REV. ECON. STUD. 115 (1999); Avery W. Katz, *Contractual Incompleteness: A Transactional Perspective*, 56 CASE W. RES. L. REV. 169 (2005); Juliet P. Kostritsky, *Taxonomy for Justifying Legal Intervention in an Imperfect World: What to Do When Parties Have Not Achieved Bargains or Have Drafted Incomplete Contracts*, 2004 WIS. L. REV. 323; Alan Schwartz, *Relational Contracts in the Courts: An Analysis of Incomplete Agreements and Judicial Strategies*, 21 J. LEGAL STUD. 271 (1992). See Robert E. Scott, *A Theory of Self-Enforcing Indefinite Agreements*, 103 COLUM. L. REV. 1641 (2003); Robert E. Scott & George G. Triantis, *Incomplete Contracts and the Theory of Contract Design*, 56 CASE W. RES. L. REV. 187 (2005); Omri Ben-Shahar, *"Agreeing to Disagree": Filling Gaps in Deliberately Incomplete Contracts*, 2004 WIS. L. REV. 389.

[665] *E.g.*, Crook v. Cowan, 1870 N.C. LEXIS 237 (June 1870).

[666] RESTATEMENT (SECOND) OF CONTRACTS § 33 (1981).

[667] *E.g.*, Academy Chicago Publ'rs v. Cheever, 578 N.E.2d 981 (Ill. 1991); Klimek v. Perisich, 371 P.2d 956 (Or. 1962).

[668] 708 A.2d 1361 (Conn. 1998).

[669] 847 S.W.2d 218 (Tex. 1992).

[670] 578 N.E.2d 981 (Ill. 1991).

[671] RESTATEMENT (SECOND) OF CONTRACTS § 33 (1981).

Even though one or more terms are left open a contract for sale does not fail for indefiniteness if the parties have intended to make a contract and there is a reasonably certain basis for giving an appropriate remedy.[672]

This formulation presents two issues: first, whether the parties intended to enter into a legally binding agreement; and, second, whether the terms are sufficiently definite to permit the court to frame an appropriate remedy.[673]

The Second Restatement adopts a similar rule recognizing that gaps may reflect the absence of an intent to be bound[674] but that otherwise a contract can be formed if the terms are definite enough to "provide a basis for determining the existence of a breach and for giving an appropriate remedy."[675]

[A]   Effect of Missing Terms on Contract Formation[676]

[1]   Indefinite Terms and the Intent to Be Bound

Gaps are sometimes so profound that they demonstrate the absence of the parties' intent to make a commitment.[677] In these cases there is no contract even if the existing terms are sufficiently definite to permit the court to frame an appropriate remedy. Courts are naturally reluctant to impose an agreement on the parties when they intended not to be bound absent an agreement about the missing terms.[678]

[a]   Agreements to Agree

The question whether gaps in the parties' agreement reflects their intent not to be bound commonly arises when the parties have entered into an "agreement to agree" at some time in the future. Traditionally, such agreements were considered completely unenforceable.[679] For example, in *Joseph Martin, Jr. Delicatessen v.*

---

[672] U.C.C. § 2-204(3) (2012). *See, e.g.*, Channel Home Ctrs., Div. of Grace Retail Corp v. Grossman, 795 F.2d 291 (3d Cir. 1986).

[673] *See* Channel Home Centers, Div. of Grace Retail Corp. v. Grossman, 795 F.2d 291, 298–99 (3d Cir. 1986); Paloukos v. Intermountain Chevrolet Co., 588 P.2d 939, 942 (Idaho 1978); Kleinschmidt Div. of SCM Corp. v. Futuronics Corp., 363 N.E.2d 701, 702 (N.Y. 1977).

[674] Section 33(3) provides: "The fact that one or more terms of a proposed bargain are left open or uncertain may show that a manifestation is not intended to be understood as an offer or as an acceptance." RESTATEMENT (SECOND) OF CONTRACTS § 33(3) (1981).

[675] RESTATEMENT (SECOND) OF CONTRACTS § 33(2) (1981).

[676] Omri Ben-Shahar, *"Agreeing to Disagree": Filling Gaps in Deliberately Incomplete Contracts*, 2004 WIS. L. REV. 389; Richard A. Posner, *The Law and Economics of Contract Interpretation*, 83 TEX. L. REV. 1581, 1587 (2005).

[677] *See generally* Randy Barnett, *The Sound of Silence: Default Rules and Contractual Consent*, 78 VA. L. REV. 821, 869–74 (1992).

[678] Russell Korobkin, *Bounded Rationality, Standard Form Contracts, and Unconscionability*, 70 U. CHI. L. REV. 1203, 1205 (2003).

[679] *E.g.*, Shepard v. Carpenter, 55 N.W. 906 (Minn. 1893). *See generally* Daniel E. Feld, Annotation, *Validity and Enforceability of Provision for Renewal of Lease at Rental to be Fixed by Subsequent Agreement of Parties*, 58 A.L.R.3d 500 (1974).

Schumacher,[680] the parties entered into a commercial real estate lease, specifying that "the Tenant may renew this lease for an additional period of five years at annual rentals to be agreed upon." However, at the time for renewal, the parties were unable to reach an agreement about the rent. The court found that by deferring their agreement about the rent renewal, the parties had, in effect, deferred any commitment to be bound at all. The court might have imposed a contract on the parties, using the market value of the premises as the basis for the rent to be paid.[681] However, the court said that this would impair the parties' freedom to contract by depriving them of the freedom not to contract.[682]

Modern courts have demonstrated a greater willingness to find a contract in situations like the one in *Joseph Martin, Jr. Delicatessen*.[683] This is particularly true in connection with lease renewals where the tenant's option to renew was a key aspect of the agreement, and where the tenant incurred substantial expenses in reliance on its right to renew.[684]

The more indefinite the agreement, of course, the more likely that the parties did not intend to be bound at all.[685] After all, the parties themselves must be able to determine what must be done in order to perform. Their failure to provide themselves with the details they will find necessary to monitor their own performance reflects their intent not to be bound in the first place. Consequently, no contract exists if the basic subject matter of the contract, such as the nature of the goods to be sold[686] or the parcel of land to be conveyed,[687] has not been fixed.

[b]   Letters of Intent

The same problem is encountered in "letters of intent," which are sometimes used by parties who are involved in lengthy and complex negotiations to express terms that they have already agreed about, even though they have not yet agreed to go through with the overall deal.[688] Letters of intent usually contain express language denying the legal enforceability of the terms of the agreement, pending

---

[680] 417 N.E.2d 541 (N.Y. 1981).

[681] Other courts have done precisely that. *See generally* Daniel E. Feld, Annotation, *Validity and Enforceability of Provision for Renewal of Lease at Rental to be Fixed by Subsequent Agreement of the Parties*, 58 A.L.R.3d 500 (1974).

[682] *Joseph Martin, Jr. Delicatessen*, 417 N.E.2d at 543 ("this liberty is no right at all if it is not accompanied by freedom not to contract"). *See also* Boyce v. McMahan, 208 S.E.2d 692 (N.C. 1974); Walker v. Keith, 382 S.W.2d 198 (Ky. Ct. App. 1964).

[683] *E.g.*, Toys, Inc. v. F.M. Burlington Co., 582 A.2d 123 (Vt. 1990); Little Caesar Enter., Inc. v. Bell Canyon Shopping Ctr., 13 P.3d 600 (Utah 2000).

[684] City of Kenai v. Ferguson, 732 P.2d 184 (Alaska 1987); Moolenaar v. Co-Build Co., 354 F. Supp. 980 (D.V.I. 1973).

[685] RESTATEMENT (SECOND) OF CONTRACTS § 33 cmt. c (1981).

[686] *But see* Paloukos v. Intermountain Chevrolet Co., 588 P.2d 939 (Idaho 1978) (agreement for purchase of new auto enforced despite absence of agreement over details concerning the vehicle to be delivered).

[687] *E.g.*, Bland v. Lowery, 327 N.E.2d 477 (Ill. App. Ct. 1975).

[688] *E.g.*, Empro Mfg. Co. v. Ball-Co. Mfg., Inc., 870 F.2d 423 (7th Cir. 1989).

the resolution of remaining issues and subsequent ratification of the agreement.[689]

In many cases, language expressly disclaiming the intent to be bound has been dispositive, preventing formation. Courts reaching this conclusion have emphasized that whether a contract exists does not depend on the actual subjective intent of the parties, but on what they expressed in their communications.[690] This permits the parties to decide for themselves whether legal consequences attach to their preliminary negotiations.[691]

However, preliminary agreements can result in liability if care is not taken to expressly disclaim the intent to be bound. A particularly dramatic example of this occurred in the proposed merger between Pennzoil and Getty Oil, resulting in a $10 billion jury verdict and the eventual bankruptcy of Texaco, which had interfered with the merger.[692]

In *Quake Construction, Inc. v. American Airlines, Inc.*, the court permitted the plaintiff's action to proceed to trial, despite language in the parties' letter of intent giving the defendant the right to "cancel . . . if the parties cannot agree on a fully executed subcontract agreement."[693] The court found that other aspects of the transaction made their intent to be bound ambiguous, thus warranting a trial. In particular, the court focused on the detailed nature of the terms included in the letter of intent, language authorizing immediate commencement of performance, and the implied recognition of the parties that the letter of intent was binding — otherwise "cancellation" would not have been necessary.[694] Thus, where a letter of intent unambiguously demonstrates that it was not intended to be binding, there is no contract. But, if the document is susceptible to any ambiguity on the point, parol evidence is admissible to show the intent to be bound.[695]

Even where a contract is not found, some courts have permitted recovery based on the injured party's reliance expenses.[696] Such liability is imposed for breach of a duty to negotiate in good faith, rather than for breach of the underlying

---

[689] *E.g.*, Dunhill Sec. Corp. v. Microthermal Applications, Inc., 308 F. Supp. 195 (S.D.N.Y. 1969).

[690] Venture Assocs. Corp. v. Zenith Data Sys. Corp., 987 F.2d 429, 432 (7th Cir. 1993); Dresser Indus., Inc. v. Pyrrhus AG, 936 F.2d 921, 926 (7th Cir. 1991); Empro Mfg. Co. v. Ball-Co Mfg., Inc., 870 F.2d 423, 425 (7th Cir. 1989).

[691] Ocean Atl. Dev. Corp. v. Aurora Christian Sch. Inc., 322 F.3d 983 (7th Cir. 2003).

[692] Texaco v. Pennzoil, 729 S.W.2d 768 (Tex. App. 1987) (that's right $10 "billion"). *See generally* Thomas Petzinger Jr., Oil & Honor: The Texaco-Pennzoil Wars (1987).

[693] 565 N.E.2d 990, 993 (Ill. 1990).

[694] *Id.*

[695] *See also* Arcadian Phosphates, Inc. v. Arcadian Corp., 884 F.2d 69, 71–74 (2d Cir. 1989); United Magazine Co. v. Prudential Ins. Co., 877 F. Supp. 1076, 1080 (S.D. Ohio 1995).

[696] Arcadian Phosphates, Inc. v. Arcadian Corp., 884 F.2d 69, 74 (2d Cir. 1989). *See* Omri Ben-Shahar, *Contracts Without Consent: Exploring a New Basis for Contract Liability*, 152 U. Pa. L. Rev. 1829 (2004); Omri Ben-Shahar, *Mutual Assent Versus Gradual Ascent: the Debate over the Right to Retract*, 152 U. Pa. L. Rev. 1947, 1955 (2004); E. Allan Farnsworth, *Precontractual Liability and Preliminary Agreements: Fair Dealing and Failed Negotiations*, 87 Colum. L. Rev. 217 (1987); Jason Scott Johnston, Investment, Information, and Promissory Liability, 152 U. Pa. L. Rev. 1923 (2004); Ronald J. Mann, *Contracts — Only with Consent*, 152 U. Pa. L. Rev. 1873 (2004); Daniel Markovits, *The No-Retraction Principle and the Morality of Negotiations*, 152 U. Pa. L. Rev. 1903 (2004).

contract.[697] Where the parties conclude an agreement on several important terms, but leave other terms open for later resolution, liability might be based on "a mutual commitment to negotiate together in good faith in an effort to reach final agreement."[698] This type of liability due to a failure to continue good-faith negotiations is closely related to the reliance interest liability that results in actions based on promissory estoppel, as in cases like *Hoffman v. Red Owl Stores, Inc.*[699] On the other hand, some courts have criticized this result, which imposes lower damages for bad faith than for an inadvertent breach of a fully completed contract.[700] Even here, however, the agreement may be too indefinite for the court to ascertain whether a duty to bargain in good faith exists, or has been fulfilled.[701]

[2] Indefinite Terms Affecting Enforcement

Sometimes the parties unquestionably intend to be bound, but leave gaps in their agreement that make it difficult for the court to detect a breach.[702] On other occasions the contract may be sufficiently definite to determine whether the parties have performed, but gaps make it difficult for the court to frame an effective remedy.[703] In these circumstances the court may find the agreement too indefinite to enforce.[704]

The terms frequently mentioned as necessary include: parties, price, subject matter of the agreement, consideration, and details regarding time, place, and manner of performance.[705] Most people assume the most important term is the price, but this is not always so. The price can be set by reference to some external standard that is readily accessible.[706] Alternatively, it may be selected by the court, with reference to standards of reasonableness, probably based on the market value of the transaction.[707]

The most important term in a contract is usually the subject matter of the agreement. If the agreement fails to specify what is to be delivered or what is to be

---

[697] *See also* Channel Home Ctrs v. Grossman, 795 F.2d 291 (3d Cir. 1986). *See generally* Charles Knapp, *Enforcing the Contract to Bargain*, 44 N.Y.U. L. REV. 673 (1969).

[698] Teachers Ins. & Annuity Ass'n v. Tribune Co., 670 F. Supp. 491, 498 (S.D.N.Y. 1987). *See also* Budget Mktg., Inc. v. Centronics Corp., 927 F.2d 421, 428 (8th Cir. 1991).

[699] 133 N.W.2d 267, 275 (1965). *See supra* § 3.04 Promissory Estoppel as an Independent Cause of Action.

[700] Venture Assoc., Corp. v. Zenith Data Sys. Corp., 96 F.3d 275, 279 (7th Cir. 1996) ("It would be a paradox to place a lower ceiling on damages for bad faith than on damages for a perfectly innocent breach.").

[701] *E.g.*, Candid Prods., Inc. v. Int'l Skating Union, 530 F. Supp. 1330 (S.D.N.Y. 1982).

[702] RESTATEMENT (SECOND) OF CONTRACTS § 33 cmt. a (1981).

[703] RESTATEMENT (SECOND) OF CONTRACTS § 33 cmt. b (1981).

[704] RESTATEMENT (SECOND) OF CONTRACTS § 33(2) (1981).

[705] *E.g.*, Satellite Dev. Co. v. Bernt, 429 N.W.2d 334 (Neb. 1988); Shull v. Sexton, 390 P.2d 313 (Colo. 1964).

[706] *See* U.C.C. § 2-305(1)(c) (2012).

[707] *But see* Sun Printing & Publ'g Ass'n v. Remington Paper & Power Co., 139 N.E. 470 (N.Y. 1923) (Cardozo, J.).

done, it will be impossible for the court to know whether the parties have performed.

If only one item is involved in a transaction (a car or a house, for example), the quantity will be obvious. However, in many commercial agreements the most significant term, apart from the subject matter of the deal, is the quantity. Under the Uniform Commercial Code, except in cases of requirements and output contracts, no agreement generally exists in the absence of a quantity term.[708] For a contract involving a sale of land, there must be enough of a description to reasonably identify the parcel the parties intend to convey.[709] If services are involved, the scope of the promised work must be supplied.

These are primarily practical problems. If the court is unable to determine what the parties agreed to do, it will be impossible to determine whether one of them is in breach.[710] Likewise, without the details necessary to identify the reasonable expectations of the parties, the court will find it impossible to calculate the amount of damages necessary to compensate for the loss of those expectations.

A good example is supplied by a case from the book industry. In *Academy Chicago Publishers v. Cheever*,[711] the court refused to enforce an agreement calling for the submission of a collection of previously published short stories into a collected anthology. The court found that absent an agreement about the length and content of the proposed book, the method for selecting the stories that would be included, the date for delivery or publication of the manuscript, or other matters relating to its eventual publication, the agreement was too indefinite to permit the court to determine whether the agreement had been kept or broken. Although the court cast its decision in terms of the absence of "a meeting of the minds,"[712] it was clear that the parties had formed the intent to be bound to one another. However, given the breadth and depth of the gaps in their agreement, it was impossible for the court to fill in the gaps to arrive at even a threshold level of performance against which the parties' performance could be measured.

The court in *Cheever* might have attempted to supply a set of minimum terms for the parties, including the number of stories to be submitted and the overall length of the book.[713] However, courts are naturally reluctant to impose terms on the parties that they have not agreed upon. This was particularly true there, where doing so would have involved the court in making decisions that would have affected the publisher's ability to sell the book to Cheever's fans.

Most modern decisions are willing to go further than this in finding terms to fill the gaps left by the parties' agreement. This tendency is even more pronounced where the terms have been left indefinite due to neglect, or where an agreed basis

---

[708] *See, e.g.*, U.C.C. § 2-201(1) (2012).

[709] Sanders v. McNutt, 72 N.E.2d 72 (Ohio 1947) (street address of house sufficient despite absence of town, county, or state).

[710] *See, e.g.*, Koufman v. Int'l Bus. Machs. Corp., 295 F. Supp. 784 (S.D.N.Y. 1969).

[711] 578 N.E.2d 981 (Ill. 1991).

[712] *Id.* at 984.

[713] *Id.*

for resolving a term has failed without the fault of either party. And it is particularly true where there is some objective basis for resolving the indefinite terms. Where the price has not been set, courts frequently resort to the market price.[714] Other terms can be implied by reference to usage of trade, course of dealing, or course of performance as a benchmark for a reasonable term.[715] A long-term course of dealing between the parties increases the likelihood that the court will intervene and provide the necessary definition to permit enforcement.[716] Not surprisingly, where the time for performance is the only matter yet to be resolved, and the parties' intent to be bound is clear, the court is likely to require performance at a reasonable time.[717]

[B]   Indefinite Agreements for the Sale of Goods[718]

Article 2 of the U.C.C. takes a far more liberal approach to the problem of indefinite terms than the common law. The Code's most important provision dealing with the issue is § 2-305, which provides that the parties' failure to settle on a fixed price does not prevent enforcement of a contract for the sale of goods if the parties intended to conclude a contract for sale despite the unresolved price.[719]

Further, the Code explicitly acknowledges that the parties' contract includes any applicable usage of trade, course of dealing, or course of performance.[720] Thus, what appear to be gaps in the parties' contract may be filled in by terms of the agreement supplied by the customary practice either in the industry or between the parties themselves. If the terms are supplied in this manner, the contract is not indefinite.

Where gaps still exist, Article 2 provides a variety of gap-filling terms that can be used to prevent the contract from failing due to uncertainty. It provides gap-fillers for situations where the price, place, time, payment, and in some cases even quantity terms are left open by the parties. The legislative adoption of these gap-filling provisions for contracts involving goods has had a significant impact on the willingness of courts to imply terms into other types of agreements, such as those for construction, employment, and real estate, which otherwise might have been unenforceable because of missing terms.[721]

---

[714] *E.g.*, Alter & Sons, Inc. v. United Eng'r & Constr., Inc., 366 F. Supp. 959 (S.D. Ill. 1973).

[715] *E.g.*, Cobble Hill Nursing Home Inc. v. Henry & Warren Corp., 548 N.E.2d 203 (N.Y. 1989).

[716] *See* Oglebay Norton Co. v. Armco, Inc., 556 N.E.2d 515 (Ohio 1990).

[717] RESTATEMENT (SECOND) OF CONTRACTS § 33 cmt. e (1981). *E.g.*, City of New York v. New York Cent. R. Co., 9 N.E.2d 931, 934 (N.Y. 1937); First Nat'l Bank of Bluefield v. Clark, 447 S.E.2d 558, 563 (W.Va. 1994).

[718] Nellie Eunsoo Choi, Note, *Contracts with Open or Missing Terms Under the Uniform Commercial Code and the Common Law: A Proposal for Unification*, 103 COLUM. L. REV. 50 (2003).

[719] U.C.C. § 2-305(1) (2012).

[720] U.C.C. § 1-201(b)(3) (2012).

[721] *See* RESTATEMENT (SECOND) OF CONTRACTS § 33 (1981).

[1]   Open Price Term — Reasonable Price

As indicated above, U.C.C. § 2-305 recognizes that the parties might conclude a binding contract for the sale of goods without settling on a price.[722] Although the absence of an agreement as to price might reflect the absence of an intent to be bound,[723] the fact that the parties have failed to agree on price or have deferred their negotiations over the price to a later time is not necessarily fatal to the agreement. Section 2-305 specifies that the court can establish a "reasonable price" if:

- the contract is silent regarding price;[724]

- the price is left to be agreed and the parties fail to agree;[725] or

- the parties agree upon an external standard to establish the price and the external standard fails to establish the price.[726]

Thus, where the parties express their commitment to one another, but fail to establish a price, the court may impose a reasonable price.[727] Although it did not involve a sale of goods, if § 2-305 would have applied in *Joseph Martin, Jr., Delicatessen, Inc. v. Schumacher*,[728] it probably would have permitted the court to establish the amount of rent for the renewal term of the lease.

The court is also permitted to impose a reasonable price where the mechanism established by the contract for determining the price fails to operate.[729] This could occur, as it did in *North Central Airlines v. Continental Oil Co.*,[730] where the parties agreed to base the price on a publicly posted price index that is later discontinued.[731] If the parties have agreed to a "reasonable price," the court will have no difficulty in looking to the market to determine the price.[732]

If the contract gives one of the parties discretion to set the price, that discretion must be exercised in good faith.[733] And, if the price is to be established other than by agreement, and fails to be set because of the failure of one of the parties to cooperate, the other has the option to treat the contract as cancelled or to establish a reasonable choice without the other party's participation.[734] Thus, if Industrial Supply and Franklin Manufacturing agree upon a shipment of a specific quantity of frimulators, with Industrial to set the price, and Industrial seeks to avoid the

---

[722] U.C.C. § 2-305 (2012).

[723] U.C.C. § 2-305(4) (2012).

[724] U.C.C. § 2-305(1)(a) (2012).

[725] U.C.C. § 2-305(1)(b) (2012).

[726] U.C.C. § 2-305(1)(c) (2012).

[727] *E.g.*, Alter & Sons, Inc. v. United Eng'rs Constr., Inc., 366 F. Supp. 959 (S.D. Ill. 1973).

[728] 417 N.E.2d 541 (N.Y. 1981).

[729] U.C.C. § 2-305(1) (c) (2012).

[730] 574 F.2d 582 (D.C. Cir. 1978).

[731] *See also* Oglebay Norton Co. v. Armco, Inc., 556 N.E.2d 515 (Ohio 1990).

[732] H.C. Schmieding Produce Co., Inc. v. Cagle, 529 So. 2d 243 (Ala. 1988).

[733] U.C.C. § 2-305(2) (2012).

[734] U.C.C. § 2-305(3) (2012).

contract altogether by refusing to set a price, Franklin will be able to identify the price, and enforce the contract, so long as the price it picks is a reasonable one.

Courts frequently presume that the market value of the goods establishes a reasonable price.[735] However, resorting to the market value is not inevitable. When the court must determine a reasonable price, it may look to several factors to determine the price, including course of performance, course of dealing,[736] usage of trade, as well as market value.[737] Other terms of the contract might also play a role. For example, in *North Central Airlines, Inc. v. Continental Oil Co.*,[738] the court remanded a determination of the reasonable price back to the trial court, which had not fully considered the parties' expressed intention that the seller's raw materials costs should be passed through to the buyer.

Despite all of this, the Code still recognizes that the parties' failure to set a price may reflect their intent not to be bound. Section 2-305(4) provides: "Where, however, the parties intend not to be bound unless the price be fixed or agreed and it is not fixed or agreed there is no contract."[739] As usual, their intent in this regard is determined by their outward manifestations of intent, not their secret or hidden intent.

[2]   Indefinite Time and Place for Delivery

With respect to the time and place for delivery, the parties' failure to include a specific term is far more likely to reflect unspoken assumptions about the terms of the contract than any lack of intent to be bound. These assumptions may be based on past dealings with one another (course of dealing) or industry practices (usage of trade). Or they may be based on the parties' recognition of the gap-filling effect of the Code's provisions. Where the parties' intent to be bound is clear, gap-filling provisions provide the parties with a set of statutory boilerplate terms that are included in their contract unless they agree to the contrary.

[a]   Delivery at Reasonable Time

Tender of delivery of the goods is due at the time the parties have agreed.[740] In the absence of an agreement, delivery is due within a reasonable time.[741] A number of factors will determine what constitutes a reasonable time, including the nature and purpose of the transaction, together with any other extrinsic circumstances,[742] including any relevant usage of trade, course of dealing, or course of

---

[735] *E.g.*, Licklyey v. Max Herbold, Inc., 984 P.2d 697 (Idaho 1999); Havird Oil Co., Inc. v. Marathon Oil Co., Inc., 149 F.3d 283, 290 (4th Cir. 1998).

[736] *See* TCP Indus., Inc. v. Uniroyal, Inc., 661 F.2d 542, 549 (6th Cir. 1981).

[737] *See* Offices Togolais Des Phosphates v. Mulberry Phosphates, Inc., 62 F. Supp. 2d 1316 (M.D. Fla. 1999).

[738] 574 F.2d 582, 593 (D.C. Cir. 1978).

[739] U.C.C. § 2-305(4) (2012). *See* Bethlehem Steel Corp. v. Litton Indus., Inc., 468 A.2d 748 (Pa. Super. Ct. 1983), *aff'd*, 488 A.2d 581 (Pa. 1985).

[740] U.C.C. § 2-309(1) (2012).

[741] *Id.*

[742] U.C.C. § 2-309 cmt. 1 (2012).

performance.[743] Any contemplated circumstances regarding the time necessary for the seller's manufacture or procurement of the goods is also relevant.

Proper tender requires the seller to deliver the goods at a reasonable hour.[744] Thus, attempts to make delivery in the middle of the night, or when the seller otherwise knows quite well that no one will be available to take delivery, are improper. Likewise, the seller must give the buyer a reasonable opportunity to take possession of the goods at the time they are delivered. In most cases, the seller must provide the buyer with any reasonable notification necessary to facilitate the buyer's receipt.[745] Thus, the seller must usually notify the buyer of the time it will tender the goods, so that the buyer knows when to make arrangements to receive them.

[b]   Place for Delivery

The parties to a contract for the sale of goods usually specify where the seller is required to tender delivery of the goods. This is frequently accomplished through an "F.O.B." term specifying tender at the place of shipment or delivery.[746] Or, the place for delivery may be established through any prior course of performance, course of dealing, or usage of trade.[747]

However, if the agreement does not otherwise specify, U.C.C. § 2-308 provides that the place for delivery is the seller's place of business. If the seller has no place of business, such as in a sale between two consumers, the place for delivery is the seller's residence.[748] Thus, in a transaction completed on eBay, unless the parties have agreed otherwise, the seller may fulfill its obligations by tendering the goods at his or her house and require the buyer to make arrangements to obtain them there.

Sometimes the parties plan to have the goods delivered to the buyer at a separate location, such as an independent warehouse on the edge of town. If the contract involves "identified goods" and the parties knew at the time the contract was made that the goods were located at an independent warehouse,[749] then that is the place where delivery is to be made.[750]

---

[743] U.C.C. § 2-309 cmt. 1 (2012).

[744] U.C.C. § 2-503(1)(a) (2002).

[745] U.C.C. § 2-502(1)(a) (2012).

[746] *See* § 4.11[B][2][c] Shipment and Destination Contracts; Mercantile Terms and "Incoterms" *infra*.

[747] *See infra* § 6.04 Customary Practice.

[748] U.C.C. § 2-308(a) (2012).

[749] U.C.C. § 2-308 cmt. 2 (2012).

[750] U.C.C. § 2-308(b) (2012).

[c]   Shipment and Destination Contracts; Mercantile Terms, and "Incoterms"

When the parties are located far apart from one another, in different states or countries, they frequently arrange for the transportation of the goods by an independent shipping company. These railroads, trucking companies, and airlines are referred to as "common carriers" because of their general public duty to transport goods for anyone who agrees to pay the established tariff.[751]

In these cases it might appear as if the contract is indefinite with respect to the place for delivery, but it usually is not. The terms of the contract frequently specify that the price is "F.O.B. seller's location" or "F.O.B. buyer's location." The former is a "shipment contract," in which the seller is required to make a reasonable contract for the carriage of the goods and deliver them to a suitable carrier at the seller's location.[752] For example, in a contract for the sale of frimulators from Industrial Supply to Franklin Manufacturing that indicates that the price is "F.O.B. Industrial Supply loading dock," the seller has the duty to deliver the goods to a carrier at the seller's loading dock, and make a reasonable contract with the carrier for their shipment to Franklin. Any loss or destruction of the goods en route is Franklin's responsibility.

A contract specifying the buyer's location in the F.O.B. term is a "destination contract."[753] In a destination contract the seller is required to ensure that the goods are safely transported to the specified destination. If they are lost or destroyed before they arrive, the seller is responsible.

Merchants also use other mercantile terms, such as "F.A.S.,"[754] "C.I.F." and "C. & F.,"[755] and "ex ship,"[756] as abbreviations for a variety of other terms all dealing with the place of tender and the risk of loss of the goods while they are in transit.[757]

In international transactions these traditional mercantile terms are reflected in "Incoterms," which are published and maintained by the International Chamber of Commerce (ICC).[758] These 13 Incoterms, which fall into four basic categories (E, F, C, and D), work in the same way as mercantile terms — by incorporating them into the terms of their contract, the parties specify the respective rights of the parties and terms regarding the risk of loss to the goods while they are in transit. An "E"-category Incoterm is used when the parties wish to place only limited

---

[751] See generally Phil Nichols, Redefining "Common Carrier": The FCC's Attempt at Deregulation by Redefinition, 1987 DUKE L.J. 501.

[752] See U.C.C. § 2-319(1)(a) (2012).

[753] U.C.C. § 2-319(1)(b) (2012).

[754] U.C.C. § 2-319(2) (2012).

[755] U.C.C. § 2-320 (2012).

[756] U.C.C. § 2-322 (2012).

[757] See generally Seth Gardenswartz, The Risk of Loss in Electronic Transactions: Vintage Law for 21st Century Consumers, 6 VA. J.L. & TECH. 15 (2001).

[758] INCOTERMS 2000: ICC Official Rules for the Interpretation of Trade Terms (ICC Publication No. 560, 1999).

responsibility on the seller to prepare and store the goods for shipment. An "F" Incoterm is a shipment contract that requires the seller not only to prepare the goods for shipment but to place them into the hands of a carrier. A "C"-level Incoterm makes the seller responsible for paying to ship the goods and obtaining insurance on them but otherwise places the risk of loss during their transit on the buyer. Tender occurs at the place of shipment, and if the goods are destroyed and the insurer is bankrupt, the buyer must still pay for the goods. A "D" Incoterm is a destination contract that places considerable responsibility on the seller. Tender occurs, and the risk of loss passes, when the goods arrive at the destination and are tendered there to the buyer.

[3] Time for Payment

Unless the parties make other arrangements, payment is due at the time and place where the buyer will receive the goods.[759] When the parties are in close proximity, with the goods to be delivered directly by the seller or to be picked up by the buyer, payment is due at the time of delivery, unless parties have made other arrangements.

In commercial transactions, when the parties are distant from one another, the goods are likely to be shipped by an independent carrier, such as a trucking company, a railroad, or an airline. Here, more complicated arrangements for payment must sometimes be made — though smaller businesses may pay by credit card, just as many consumers do.

When the goods are to be shipped, buyers frequently give up their right to inspect the goods before payment by agreeing to a "documentary sale." In a documentary sale the seller obtains a bill of lading from the carrier and, while the goods are still in transit, tenders the bill of lading to the buyer together with a demand for payment.[760] When the buyer pays, the seller relinquishes the bill of lading to the buyer. When the goods arrive, the buyer can use the bill of lading to obtain delivery of the goods from the carrier. In these documentary transactions, tender of the documents is the essence of the transaction.[761]

After payment, the buyer still has the right to inspect the goods, and can reject them if they are defective. If the buyer rejects the goods, it will have to recover its payment from the seller.[762] Some protection is afforded to the buyer in this regard by its possession of the goods, which it may retain and sell, if necessary, as collateral for the seller's obligation to refund the price of the rejected goods.[763]

Payment might be made by electronic funds transfer, but payment by check is usually sufficient. However, absent an agreement to the contrary, the seller is

---

[759] U.C.C. § 2-310 (2012).

[760] This demand for payment is frequently in the form of a negotiable draft, governed by Article 3 of the U.C.C.

[761] Ingeborg Schwenzer, *Avoidance of the Contract in Case of Non-Conforming Goods (Article 49(1)(a) CISG)*, 25 J.L. & Com. 437, 440–41 (2005).

[762] *See* U.C.C. § 2-711(1) (2012).

[763] U.C.C. § 2-711(3) (2012).

entitled to insist on cash. However, if the seller refuses to take the buyer's check, the seller will be expected to give the buyer a reasonable extension of time to obtain the necessary currency.[764]

[4] Quantity

Determining the quantity of goods to be delivered is crucial. Without a means for defining the quantity of goods to be sold, it is impossible for a court to determine whether the seller has performed.[765] Likewise, without knowing the agreed quantity, a court is unable to discern whether the buyer has met its corresponding duty to pay.[766] Further, without a set quantity, calculation of damages will similarly be impossible.

Despite the importance of a quantity term, the parties sometimes find it convenient to leave the precise number of items to be delivered unspecified. This frequently happens in farm commodity contracts where the seller, a farmer, is unwilling to make a commitment about the quantity of grain that her farm will produce. Instead, the farmer promises to sell the entire production of the goods from a particular field or from the entire farm to a specific buyer.[767] Likewise, a manufacturer may promise to sell all of a particular product that it produces to a particular buyer, to the exclusion of other customers.

The buyer might also have reasons for wanting to avoid setting a fixed quantity. Thus, a buyer who is unsure of the level of demand from its own customers might agree to purchase the quantity that it "requires" of a particular item from the seller. The contract will leave the precise quantity sought by the buyer to be determined as circumstances develop. For example, a coal-burning, electricity-producing power plant may promise to purchase all of the coal it requires from a particular mine, even though it will not know how much coal it needs until the summer air-conditioning season arrives.[768]

Such arrangements are respectively known as "output" and "requirements" contracts.[769] In an output contract, the seller promises to sell all that it produces to a particular buyer. In a requirements contract, the buyer promises to purchase all of its requirements, or the full extent of the goods of a particular kind that it needs, from a particular seller.

Although the quantity may not be known, U.C.C. § 2-306 provides a mechanism for resolving both the practical problems of detecting a breach and of framing an appropriate remedy. U.C.C. § 2-306(1) measures the quantity involved in these agreements by the good-faith output or requirements involved.[770] It further

---

[764] U.C.C. § 2-511(2) (2012).

[765] U.C.C. § 2-503 (2012).

[766] U.C.C. § 2-507 (2012).

[767] *See* Campbell Soup Co. v. Wentz, 172 F.2d 80 (3d Cir. 1948).

[768] *E.g.*, Mo. Pub. Serv. Co. v. Peabody Coal Co., 583 S.W.2d 721 (Mo. Ct. App. 1979).

[769] Caroline N. Bruckel, *Consideration in Exclusive and Nonexclusive Open Quantity Contracts Under the U.C.C.: A Proposal for a New System of Validation*, 68 MINN. L. REV. 117 (1983).

[770] U.C.C. § 2-306(1) (2012). *E.g.*, Brooklyn Bagel Boys, Inc. v. Earthgrains Refrigerated Dough

requires that the quantity not be "unreasonably disproportionate" to any estimates the parties may have expressed or, in the absence of a stated estimate, to any normal or comparable prior quantity produced or required.[771] Thus, the contract permits a reasonable elasticity in the quantity, but prevents the parties from using some subterfuge to artificially reduce their output or expand their requirements.[772]

The decision in in *Feld v. Henry S. Levy & Sons, Inc.*,[773] supplies a good example of how the duty of good faith operates in an output contract. There, a seller tried to escape its duty to sell its entire output of bread crumbs by ceasing production of the items as a means of limiting its losses. The court found that the unprofitability of the deal would provide an excuse only if the transaction became so unprofitable that continued production would result in "a bankruptcy or genuine imperiling of the very existence of [the seller's] entire business."[774] Because the seller's losses were not so great, it could not avoid its duty to deliver all of its output of the item by ceasing production entirely.

The duty of good faith operates in much the same way to prevent the buyer in a requirements contract from demanding too much. A buyer might be tempted to do this, when the market price of the commodity rises, in an effort to speculate in the market for the goods or to stockpile them as a hedge against the day when the contract expires. Thus, in *Eastern Airlines Inc. v. Gulf Oil Corp.*,[775] where Gulf promised to sell Eastern all of the jet fuel it required for the operation of its airline out of a number of designated airports, the airline would not be permitted to buy more jet fuel than it required as a means of expanding its business to become a seller of jet fuel. Nor would Eastern have been permitted to purchase more fuel than it needed, at the favorable contract price, and place it in storage so that it would have an available supply when the contract expired. These actions would have been in bad faith.

The duty of good faith also prevents the buyer from artificially limiting its needs to avoid the consequences of what has become an unfavorable price term. Thus, a glass manufacturer, who has agreed to purchase all of its requirements of "plastic peanuts" — Styrofoam packaging material — from a particular seller should not be able to switch to using "excelsior" — a packaging material made of wood fibers — to avoid the consequences of the price in its plastic peanuts contract.

Although "good faith" is somewhat amorphous, it is further defined in this context to prevent either party from insisting on a quantity that is "unreasonably disproportionate" to any estimates of quantity that the parties have previously stated. If they have not gone to the trouble to make an estimate, the quantity may

---

Prods., Inc., 212 F.3d 373, 378 (7th Cir. 2000). *See generally* Caroline N. Bruckel, *Consideration in Exclusive and Nonexclusive Open Quantity Contracts Under the U.C.C.: A Proposal for a New System of Validation*, 68 Minn. L. Rev. 117 (1983).

[771] U.C.C. § 2-306 (2012). *See* McMichael v. Price, 58 P.2d 549 (Okla. 1936).

[772] U.C.C. § 2-306 cmt. 1 (2012).

[773] 335 N.E.2d 320 (N.Y. 1975).

[774] *Id.* at 323.

[775] 415 F. Supp. 429 (S.D. Fla. 1975).

not be unreasonably disproportionate to any customary prior output or requirements.[776]

[C] Indefinite Agreements in International Transactions

In international transactions similar principles are used to deal with indefinite terms. The issues in international transactions are the same: whether the parties intended to be bound and whether the terms are too indefinite for the court to detect a breach and provide a remedy.

In international sale-of-goods transactions, the CISG prevents an indefinite proposal from qualifying as an offer.[777] Article 14(1) specifies that a proposal is sufficiently definite if it "indicates the goods and expressly or implicitly fixes or makes provision for determining the quantity and the price."[778]

CISG Articles 31 and 33 provide gap-filling terms regarding the place and time of delivery. In shipment contracts, where the seller has not promised to deliver the goods to a particular destination, the seller performs its obligations when it hands the goods "to the first carrier for transmission to the buyer,"[779] or, if the contract does not involve carriage of the goods, when the seller places the goods at the buyer's disposal, usually at the seller's place of business.[780] Delivery is due, absent some agreement to the contrary, "within a reasonable time after the conclusion of the contract."[781]

If the parties have "validly concluded" a contract but failed to set a price, the CISG specifies that they have impliedly agreed "to the price generally charged at the time of the conclusion of the contract for the goods sold under comparable circumstances in the trade concerned."[782] If the contract does not specify a time for payment, it is due when the seller places the goods or documents relating to the goods at the buyer's disposition.[783] Payment must be made at the seller's place of business or, where applicable, at the place where the goods or documents will be delivered.[784]

Because many international sales involve farm commodities, such as grain, where the price is fixed according to weight, if there is any doubt, the weight is presumed to be based on their "net weight."[785]

Some contracts for the sale of goods permit the buyer to select the goods from the items available from the seller. However, the buyer may not avoid the contract,

---

[776] U.C.C. § 2-306(1) (2012).

[777] CISG Art. 14(1) (1980).

[778] CISG Art. 14(1) (1980).

[779] CISG Art. 31(a) (1980).

[780] CISG Art 31(b)–(c) (1980).

[781] CISG Art. 33(c) (1980).

[782] CISG Art. 55 (1980).

[783] CISG Art. 58 (1980).

[784] CISG Art. 57 (1980).

[785] CISG Art. 56 (1980).

by claiming that it is too indefinite, simply by failing to make a selection. Instead, if the buyer fails to select the goods to be delivered, or to otherwise provide the specifications necessary for performance of the contract, the seller may make the necessary selection or determination.[786]

In resolving any open or otherwise indefinite terms, the CISG, like Article 2, treats any applicable trade usage or previous pattern of conduct as part of the express terms of the agreement.[787]

In other international deals, the UNIDROIT Principles of International Commercial Contracts take a flexible approach. Article 2.1.14 expressly permits formation of a contract with additional terms to be resolved later, as long as there is "an alternative means of rendering the term definite that is reasonable in the circumstances, having regard to the intention of the parties."[788] However, if one of the parties insists that the contract is not concluded until there is agreement on specific topics, no contract is concluded until agreement is reached.[789]

With respect to price, UNIDROIT's Principles of International Commercial Contracts take an approach similar to that in the U.C.C. They do not require that the parties have settled on a price and permit a court to select a price with "reference to the price generally charged at the time of the conclusion of the contract for such performance in comparable circumstances in the trade concerned or, if no such price is available, to a reasonable price."[790] If the duration of an agreement is not specified, it may be ended by either party giving notice a reasonable time in advance.[791] Performance is due at the time fixed for performance or "within a reasonable time after conclusion of the contract."[792]

Usually the parties will agree upon the place for performance, or it will be determinable from the contract in some other way.[793] Otherwise, the place for performance depends on the nature of the obligation. When payment is owed, it is due at the "obligee's place of business." Other obligations are required to be performed at the obligor's "own place of the business."[794]

Principles of European Contract Law require the terms of an agreement to be "sufficiently definite." This is reflected in Article 2.201(1)(b)'s rule that a proposal is not an offer unless it "contains sufficiently definite terms to form a contract."[795]

With respect to price, Article 6.104 indicates that if the parties have neither agreed to a fixed price nor to a method of calculating a price, that they "are to be

---

[786] CISG Art. 65 (1980).

[787] CISG Art. 9 (1980).

[788] PICC Art. 2.1.14 (2004).

[789] PICC Art. 2.1.13 (2004).

[790] PICC Art. 5.1.7(1) (2004).

[791] PICC Art. 5.1.8 (2004).

[792] PICC Art. 6.1.1 (2004).

[793] PICC Art. 6.1.6(1) (2004).

[794] PICC Art. 6.1.6 (2004).

[795] PECL Art. 2.201(1)(b) (2002).

treated as having agreed on a reasonable price."[796] If the parties have left the price to be determined by one of the parties, and the party who has this discretion sets a price that is "grossly unreasonable," then the price is a "reasonable price."[797] The same approach applies if the price is to be fixed by a third person, who sets a grossly unreasonable price.[798]

If the time for performance is not agreed between the parties, performance is due "within a reasonable time after the conclusion of the contract.[799] And, if the contract does not otherwise specify, the place for performance depends on the nature of the performance to be rendered. Payment is to occur at the creditor's location.[800] Other obligations are to be performed at the obligor's location.[801]

Payment of money may be accomplished in any form that is used in the ordinary course of business.[802] If the parties have not specified the currency in which payment is to be made, payment made be made in the currency of the place where payment is to be made at the exchange rate in effect at that place.[803]

§ 4.12 PRECONTRACTUAL LIABILITY[804]

The question of whether parties who are negotiating with one another in pursuit of an agreement have obligations toward one another is particularly acute when one or both of the parties make substantial investments in the anticipated transaction before the parties have concluded a deal. By their very nature, these "sunk costs" cannot be recouped unless the parties go through with the transaction.[805] Thus, if the parties fail to reach an ultimate agreement they will have made a substantial investment with no hope of obtaining a return.

Most of the time, of course, parties do not become bound to one another before reaching a final agreement. The traditional rule was that they could freely negotiate with one another without incurring liability if their negotiations fell through.[806] The

---

[796] PECL Art. 6.104 (2002).

[797] PECL Art. 6.104 (2002).

[798] PECL Art. 6.105 (2002).

[799] PECL Art. 7.102(3) (2002).

[800] PECL Art. 7.101(1)(a) (2002).

[801] PECL Art. 7.101(1)(b) (2002).

[802] PECL Art. 7.107(1) (2002).

[803] PECL Art. 7.108(2) (2002).

[804] Lucian Arye Bebchuk & Omri Ben-Shahar, *Precontractual Reliance*, 30 J. LEGAL STUD. 423 (2001); E. Allan Farnsworth, *Precontractual Liability and Preliminary Agreements: Fair Dealing and Failed Negotiations*, 87 COLUM. L. REV. 217 (1987); Ofer Grosskopf & Barak Medina, *Regulating Contract Formation: Precontractual Reliance, Sunk Costs, and Market Structure*, 39 Conn. L. Rev. 1977 (2007); Alan Schwartz & Robert E. Scott, *Precontractual Liability and Preliminary Agreements*, 120 HARV. L. REV. 661 (2007); Omri Ben-Shahar, *Contracts Without Consent: Exploring a New Basis for Contractual Liability*, 152 U. PENN. L. REV. 1829 (2004).

[805] Alan Schwartz & Robert E. Scott, *Precontractual Liability and Preliminary Agreements*, 120 HARV. L. REV. 661, 663 n.1 (2007).

[806] *See* E. Allan Farnsworth, *Precontractual Liability and Preliminary Agreements: Fair Dealing and Failed Negotiations*, 87 COLUM. L. REV. 217, 221–23 (1987).

traditional rule is illustrated by *R.G. Group, Inc. v. Horn & Hardart Co.*,[807] where several prospective franchisees, whose hopes and dreams were dashed when the franchisor decided not to award them a franchise, sued to recover for expenses they had incurred in pursuit of the franchise. The question was whether the parties' "handshake deal" was enforceable or whether it was contingent upon the execution of a final written agreement. In denying their claims, the court emphasized a key feature of the freedom to contract — the freedom *not* to enter into a binding contract. It explained that:

> The freedom to avoid oral agreements is especially important when business entrepreneurs and corporations engage in substantial and complex dealings. In these circumstances there are often forceful reasons for refusing to make a binding contract unless it is put in writing. The actual drafting of a written instrument will frequently reveal points of disagreement, ambiguity, or omission which must be worked out prior to execution. Details that are unnoticed or passed by in oral discussion will be pinned down when the understanding is reduced to writing. These considerations are not minor; indeed, above a certain level of investment and complexity, requiring written contracts may be the norm in the business world, rather than the exception.[808]

Despite this traditional rule, an increasing number of cases have imposed liability on parties even though they clearly have not yet reached a final agreement. These decisions take several forms. Some courts determine that the parties have concluded a contract, even though they have left additional details to be resolved or expressed their intent to reduce their agreement to a further definitive document. These situations do not involve "precontractual" liability. Other courts find that the preliminary agreement results in an implied duty to bargain in good faith over topics and details not covered by the letter of intent. Still other decisions use promissory estoppel to impose liability for reliance expenses incurred in anticipation of entering into a more formal agreement. The remainder of this section describes all three situations.

[A] Binding Agreement with Formal Written Document to Follow

As more fully discussed elsewhere, the parties sometimes conclude their negotiations but agree that they will subsequently reduce the details of their agreement to a final formal document.[809] As one court explained:

> [This] is a fully binding preliminary agreement, which is created when the parties agree on all the points that require negotiation (including whether to be bound) but agree to memorialize their agreement in a more formal document. Such an agreement is fully binding; it is "preliminary only in form-only in the sense that the parties desire a more elaborate formaliza-

---

[807] R.G. Group, Inc. v. Horn & Hardart Co., 751 F.2d 69 (2d Cir. 1984).

[808] 751 F.2d at 75.

[809] *See supra* § 4.05[F] Final Written Contract and "Letters of Intent".

tion of the agreement." . . . A binding preliminary agreement binds both sides to their ultimate contractual objective in recognition that, "despite the anticipation of further formalities," a contract has been reached. . . . Accordingly, a party may demand performance of the transaction even though the parties fail to produce the "more elaborate formalization of the agreement."[810]

These situations involve a contract, not "precontractual" liability. The parties have concluded their contract; but they have not yet reduced it to its final form.

[B]   Unjust Enrichment

In other settings, the parties may break off negotiations before coming to terms. Where one confers a benefit on another before negotiations end, recovery may be available on a theory of restitution, to prevent unjust enrichment. For example, if while he is engaged in negotiations over the purchase of Agnes's home, Merle supplies Agnes with a down payment, he is entitled to recover the payment in the event that negotiations break down and a deal is never concluded.

Where one party acquires proprietary information or other intellectual property from the other in the course of failed negotiations, a claim might also be brought based on any subsequent misappropriation of those property rights. This might easily occur where the proposed transaction was for the manufacture of a new and innovative product and the manufacturer misappropriates the idea or specifications for the product and manufactures and sells it even though the deal with the innovator did not come to fruition.

Where the enriched party only receives the benefit of the other party's services, rather than property, recovery has been more difficult[811] but not unheard of. In *Earhart v. William Low Co.*,[812] the court awarded compensation for the value of the benefit of land-clearing services that one party provided to the other while they were waiting for financing, upon which any contract between them depended, to become available. Recovery was also permitted in *Precision Testing Laboratories, Ltd v. Kenyon Corp.*, where one of the parties provided extensive technical services in trying to bring the other party's prototype automobile up to the standards necessary to satisfy state pollution standards.[813]

However, most of the time, the parties' negotiations do not result in the conferral of any tangible benefits on one another. Although the parties to failed negotiations frequently incur expenses in connection with their discussions, the law does not impose a general duty to pay for these sunk costs.

---

[810]   Adjustrite Sys., Inc. v. GAB Bus. Servs., Inc., 145 F.3d 543, 548 (2d Cir. 1998) (quoting Teachers Ins. & Annuity Assoc. v. Tribune Co., 670 F. Supp. 491, 498 (S.D.N.Y. 1987)).

[811]   E. Allan Farnsworth, *Precontractual Liability and Preliminary Agreements: Fair Dealing and Failed Negotiations*, 87 COLUM. L. REV. 217, 229–33 (1987).

[812]   600 P.2d 1344 (Cal. 1979).

[813]   644 F. Supp. 1327 (S.D.N.Y. 1986). *See* G. Richard Shell, *Opportunism and Trust in the Negotiation of Commercial Contracts: Toward a New Cause of Action*, 44 VAND. L. REV. 221, 282 (1991).

[C]　Misrepresentation

Precontractual liability is also sometimes found based on misrepresentations that are made in the course of negotiations. A misrepresentation of intent is as much of a misrepresentation of fact as a misrepresentation about the nature of the goods or services involved in the proposed transaction. Thus, a party who represents that he wants to come to terms and conclude a bargain, when he has no such desire, should be liable for the expenses the other party incurs in honestly participating in negotiations over a proposed contract.

The circumstances that might lead a person to brashly lie about his or her intent to enter into a deal are rare. It seems to happen only when continued negotiations over one transaction provide some bargaining advantage in a proposed transaction with someone else. Negotiating simultaneously with two prospective buyers over the terms of a sale is not dishonest — the seller is honestly attempting to obtain the best price possible, and will usually want to let each prospective buyer know that the negotiations are taking place in a competitive setting. However, in the rare circumstance in which a party has a motive to pretend to negotiate with one party in order to gain an advantage in negotiations with someone else, liability for misrepresentation is warranted.[814]

[D]　Promises Made During Negotiations

Parties involved in negotiations with one another sometimes make promises to one another in the course of those negotiations. These promises can give rise to liability, even though a final deal is never concluded.

[1]　Irrevocable Offers

Promises to keep an offer open, discussed in detail elsewhere in this chapter, are an important branch of the law of precontractual liability.[815] As the earlier discussion explained, an offer may be irrevocable on one of several grounds: if it is a traditional option contract, supported by consideration;[816] where there is part performance of an offer that can be accepted by performance,[817] or the offeree otherwise reasonably relies on an express or implied promise that it would remain open; under U.C.C. § 2-205's "firm offer" rule;[818] or, if the promise is governed by the CISG or some other applicable principle of international law.[819]

---

[814] Restatement (Second) of Torts §§ 525, 530 (1977); Markov v. ABC Transfer & Storage Co., 457 P.2d 535, 539–40 (Wash. 1969).

[815] See supra § 4.09 Irrevocable Offers.

[816] See supra § 4.09[A] Traditional Option Contracts.

[817] See supra § 4.09[B] Beginning Performance.

[818] See supra § 4.09[D] Firm Offers Under U.C.C. § 2-205.

[819] See supra § 4.09[E] Irrevocability in International Transactions.

[2] Promissory Estoppel[820]

Other promises made during negotiations can also lead to liability, as a result of the other party's reliance on them, on a more general theory of promissory estoppel. The famous decision in *Hoffman v. Red Owl Stores, Inc.*,[821] which is discussed in detail elsewhere, supplies the rationale for these results.[822] Under *Hoffman*, a person who has been induced to incur expenses based on assurances that the parties will subsequently enter into a contract, may recover for those expenses, even though the details of the promised later contract are too sketchy to enforce fully.[823] Despite *Hoffman's* notoriety, it has been widely criticized[824] and only infrequently followed.[825]

[E] Duty to Bargain in Good Faith

The law has long recognized a duty of good-faith *performance* of contractual obligations. Restatement (Second) of Contracts § 205[826] and U.C.C. § 1-304[827] provide for an obligation of good faith in the performance and enforcement of contracts.[828] The duty of good-faith *performance* of a contract is discussed elsewhere.[829] It applies after a contract has been formed. This section discusses the existence and scope of a precontractual duty to bargain in good faith over the formation of a contract.

Quite apart from a duty of good-faith performance of a contract that has already come into existence, courts sometimes find that parties engaged in negotiations with one another have a duty to negotiate with one another in good faith.[830] Breach of this duty might lead to liability to the other party to the negotiations, permitting recovery for some or all of the expenses that the injured party has incurred during their negotiations.

---

[820] Lucian Arye Bebchuk, Omri Ben-Shahar, *Precontractual Reliance*, 30 J. Legal Stud. 423 (2001). *See also* Daniel A. Farber and John H. Matheson, *Beyond Promissory Estoppel: Contract Law and the "Invisible Handshake,"* 52 U. Chi. L. Rev. 903, 914 (1985).

[821] 133 N.W.2d 267 (Wis. 1965).

[822] *See supra* § 3.04 Promissory Estoppel as an Independent Cause of Action.

[823] Michael B. Metzger & Michael J. Phillips, *The Emergence of Promissory Estoppel as an Independent Theory of Recovery*, 35 Rutgers L. Rev. 472 (1983).

[824] Robert E. Scott, Hoffman v. Red Owl Stores *and the Myth of Precontractual Reliance*, 68 Ohio St. L.J. 71 (2007).

[825] E. Allan Farnsworth, *Precontractual Liability and Preliminary Agreements: Fair Dealing and Failed Negotiations*, 87 Colum. L. Rev. 217, 236–43 (1987); Alan Schwartz & Robert E. Scott, *Precontractual Liability and Preliminary Agreements*, 120 Harv. L. Rev. 661, 670–71 (2007). *See* Beer Capitol Distrib., Inc. v. Guinness Bass Imp. Co., 290 F.3d 877 (7th Cir. 2002).

[826] Restatement (Second) of Contracts § 205 (1981).

[827] U.C.C. § 1-304 (2012) (formerly in § 1-203).

[828] U.C.C. § 1-304 speaks in terms of a duty of "good faith," while the Restatement refers to it as a dual duty of "good faith and fair dealing." The U.C.C. now defines good faith to mean both "honesty in fact" and "the observance of reasonable commercial standards of fair dealing." U.C.C. § 1-201(a)(20) (2012).

[829] *See infra* § 10.06 Duty of Good Faith.

[830] Channel Home Ctrs. v. Grossman, 795 F.2d 291, 299 n.8 (3d Cir. 1986).

The court's decision in *Teachers Insurance and Annuity Association of America v. Tribune Co.*[831] provides an influential framework for the imposition of this duty.[832] There, the parties had engaged in negotiations over the terms of long-term financing to be supplied by Teachers Insurance and Annuity Association (TIAA). As a result of these negotiations, TIAA issued a "commitment letter" containing its commitment to make the loan that the Tribune Co. sought. The commitment remained subject to certain conditions regarding the Tribune's production of certain documents and on the execution of a final formal loan agreement containing details of the transaction. The Tribune Co. signed the commitment letter, which contained express language indicating that it was "a binding agreement between us," but added a notation indicating that it was subject to certain modifications outlined in the cover letter accompanying the executed commitment letter.

Before these details were worked out and loan was consummated, market interest rates dropped. The Tribune, which could borrow from someone else at a more favorable rate, became less interested in paying the interest rate specified in the commitment letter, and refused to continue negotiations over other unresolved aspects of the deal.

After the deal fell through, TIAA sued, alleging that the Tribune Co. had broken off negotiations in bad faith, using the unresolved terms as a subterfuge to get out from under the interest rate contained in the signed commitment letter. The court imposed liability for what it referred to as a "binding preliminary commitment." When the parties agree on several major terms but leave other terms open for further negotiation, they incur an obligation, the court said, "to negotiate the open issues in good faith in an attempt to reach the . . . objective within the agreed framework."[833] This obligation does not, the court said, "commit the parties to their ultimate contractual objective."[834] As long as they make a legitimate effort to close the deal and do not insist on terms that do not conform to the preliminary agreement, they are free to end negotiations without coming to terms.[835]

Similar obligations have been found in cases like *Copeland v. Baskin-Robbins, U.S.A.* and *Channel Home Centers v. Grossman.*[836] In *Copeland v. Baskin Robbins U.S.A.*,[837] the court engaged in a lengthy analysis of the differences between an "agreement to agree," which would not result in any kind of liability, and an "agreement to negotiate," which imposes a duty to continue negotiations in good faith, even though it does not impose an obligation to conclude a final binding

---

[831]   670 F. Supp. 491 (S.D.N.Y 1987).

[832]   Alan Schwartz & Robert E. Scott, *Precontractual Liability and Preliminary Agreements*, 120 Harv. L. Rev. 661, 664 (2007); Robert E. Scott, Hoffman v. Red Owl Stores *and the Myth of Precontractual Reliance*, 68 Ohio St. L.J. 71, 99–100 (2007).

[833]   *Tribune*, 670 F. Supp. at 498.

[834]   *Id.* at 498.

[835]   Adjustrite Sys., Inc. v. GAB Bus. Servs., Inc., 145 F.3d 543, 548 (2d Cir. 1998).

[836]   *E.g.*, Itek Corp. v. Chicago Aerial Indus., 248 A.2d 625 (Del. 1968). *See also* Am. Broad. Co. v. Wolf, 420 N.E.2d 363, 364 (N.Y. 1981).

[837]   96 Cal. App. 4th 1251 (2002).

contract.[838] Likewise, in *Channel Home Centers v. Grossman*,[839] the court found that the owner of a shopping mall, by signing a letter of intent and agreeing to take part of the mall's space off the market while the parties engaged in negotiations to lease it to the plaintiff, had made a commitment to negotiate in good faith over the unresolved terms of the transaction.

The uncertainty of the terms of any agreement that might have been reached had the parties continued their negotiations, combined with the fact that their good-faith negotiations might have failed to lead to a favorable conclusion, will prevent assessment of damages based on the injured party's lost expectations. However, damages based on the injured parties' reliance expenses in connection with the failed discussions might be recoverable.

Other courts have been less sanguine about imposing this obligation unless the parties have manifested their intent to be contractually bound.[840] As one court explained: "The fact that parties commence negotiations looking to a contract, or to the amendment of an existing contract, does not by itself impose any duty on either party not to be unreasonable or not to break off negotiations for any reason or for no reason."[841]

Furthermore, American courts have not adopted the position taken by some European countries that the mere commencement of negotiations imposes a duty to bargain in good faith.[842] This is consistent, of course, with the general difficulty of establishing liability on a theory of reliance in the absence of an expression of intent to be bound.[843]

[F]   Letters of Intent

Cases like *The Tribune Co.* and *Channel Home Centers* are examples of situations in which the parties to negotiations over complex business transactions have reduced their preliminary understandings to a "letter of intent." Letters of intent are useful in transactions where many details must be hammered out between the parties before the deal can be consummated through performance. A letter of intent is particularly likely to be used in connection with large construction projects,[844] joint ventures, partnerships, and franchise agreements,[845] or agreements for the purchase of all of the assets of a business or in a corporate

---

[838] *See also* Channel Home Ctrs., Div. of Grace Retail Corp. v. Grossman, 795 F.2d 291, 293–94, 299 (3d Cir. 1986); Venture Assoc. v. Zenith Data Sys., 987 F.2d 429, 433 (7th Cir. 1993) (duty to bargain in good faith not breached).

[839] 795 F.2d 291 (3d. Cir. 1986).

[840] *E.g.*, Ohio Calculating, Inc. v. CPT Corp., 846 F.2d 497 (8th Cir. 1988); Prenger v. Baumhoer, 939 S.W.2d 23 (Mo. Ct. App. 1997).

[841] Racine & Laramie, Ltd. v. Cal. Dept. of Parks & Rec., 11 Cal. App. 4th 1026 (1992).

[842] Los Angeles Equestrian Ctr., Inc. v. City of Los Angeles, 17 Cal. App. 4th 432, 447 (1993). *See* E. Allan Farnsworth, *Precontractual Liability and Preliminary Agreements: Fair Dealing and Failed Negotiations*, 87 Colum. L. Rev. 217, 239–243 (1987).

[843] *See* Sidney W. DeLong, *The New Requirement of Enforcement Reliance in Commercial Promissory Estoppel: Section 90 as Catch-22*, 1997 Wis. L. Rev. 943.

[844] *E.g.*, Quake Constr., Inc. v. Am. Airlines, Inc., 565 N.E.2d 990 (Ill. 1990).

merger transaction,[846] but they are also used in connection with a wide variety of other business deals.[847]

In one famous case that resulted in a $10 billion judgment for tortious interference with a corporate merger deal, the parties executed an "agreement in principle," which the court examined to determine the parties' intent. Although the preliminary document referred to the later execution and delivery of a more formal written contract, the language it used indicated that these related merely to matters of the timing of various acts that needed to be accomplished and did not make performance "conditional" on the execution of a more formal version of their deal.[848] In other cases, language indicating that their agreement was "subject to" various events, which were still within the control of the parties, has led courts to find that no binding agreement had yet been reached.[849] If the preliminary documents contain a "flat disclaimer" of any legally binding effect, no agreement should be found.[850]

Otherwise, a letter of intent may give rise to several alternative types of liability. The letter of intent may be a fully enforceable contract, with the final written version of the deal operating not as a condition of liability but as a mere ministerial act designed to facilitate performance of a deal that has already been made.[851] If performance begins, on the strength of the letter of intent, even though no contract has been formed, liability for the value of any benefits conferred as a result of the part-performance may be imposed on a theory of unjust enrichment. And, if one of the parties has misrepresented his or her intent, there will be liability in tort for deceit. Likewise, liability may be imposed due to one party's reliance on the representations made in the letter of intent, including liability for breach of an express or implied duty to negotiate in good faith toward the conclusion of a final deal. In other words, unless the parties clearly express their intent not to be bound by the terms of the letter of intent, liability may be found on any of the grounds on which precontractual liability has been based. Such liability may also result if the parties' actions demonstrate the parties' intent to be bound, despite the terms of an express disclaimer.

---

[845] Alan Schwartz & Robert E. Scott, *Precontractual Liability and Preliminary Agreements*, 120 HARV. L. REV. 661, 664–97 (2007).

[846] Budget Mktg., Inc. v. Centronics Corp., 927 F.2d 421 (8th Cir. 1991).

[847] *See* Channel Home Ctrs. v. Grossman, 795 F.2d 291 (3d Cir. 1986) (shopping center lease); Int'l Minerals & Mining Corp. v. Citicorp N. Am., Inc., 736 F. Supp. 587 (D.N.J. 1990) (loan commitment).

[848] Texaco v. Pennzoil, 729 S.W.2d 768, 824 (Tex. App. 1987).

[849] *See* Cochran v. Norkunas, 919 A.2d 700 (Md. 2007); Empro Mfg. Co. v. Ball-Co. Mfg., Inc., 870 F.2d 423 (7th Cir. 1989).

[850] *E.g.*, Feldman v. Allegheny Int'l, Inc., 850 F.2d 1217 (7th Cir. 1988).

[851] *See supra* § 4.05[F] Final Written Contract and "Letters of Intent"; Adjustrite Sys., Inc. v. GAB Bus. Servs., Inc., 145 F.3d 543, 548 (2d Cir. 1998).

[G]   Good-Faith Negotiation in International Transactions[852]

The UNIDROIT Principles of International Commercial Contracts and Principles of European Contract Law recognize that parties who negotiate in good faith are not liable to one another simply because they fail to reach an agreement.[853] However, both sets of international contracting principles make a party who either negotiates in bad faith or who "breaks off negotiations" in bad faith liable for any loss caused to the other party.[854] They both specify that it is in bad faith for a party to begin or continue negotiations when it has already formed the intent not to reach an agreement with the other party.[855] Both sets of principles also impose a duty of confidentiality on the parties, at least where information is exchanged on a confidential basis.[856]

---

[852] Arthur Hartkamp, *The Concept of Good Faith in the UNIDROIT Principles for International Commercial Contracts*, 3 Tul. J. Int'l & Comp L. 65 (1995).

[853] PICC Art. 2.1.15(1) (2004); PECL Art. 2.301(1) (2002).

[854] PICC Art. 2.1.15(2) (2004); PECL Art. 2.301(2) (2002).

[855] PICC Art. 2.1.15(3) (2004); PECL Art. 2.301(3) (2002).

[856] PICC Art. 2.1.16 (2004); PECL Art. 2.302 (2002).

Chapter 5

THE STATUTE OF FRAUDS: IS A WRITING REQUIRED

§ 5.01   INTRODUCTION TO THE STATUTE OF FRAUDS[1]

Although it might be desirable for all contracts to be in writing, the law does not insist on it. Instead, the "statute of frauds" requires written evidence for only a

---

[1] Michael Braunstein, *Remedy, Reason, and the Statute of Frauds: A Critical Economic Analysis,*

limited number of particularly important types of contracts. The major categories are contracts involving real estate, contracts that will take longer than a year to be performed, suretyship agreements, and contracts for the sale of goods with a price of $500 or more. Because not every contract is required to be in writing, determining whether a particular agreement is covered by the statute is a key issue.[2]

Once it has been determined that a contract is "within" the statute of frauds, so that a writing is required, the next critical issue is to determine whether there is a writing that satisfies the statute. Usually, the statute is satisfied by a writing that:

- is signed by the party against whom enforcement is sought (by "the party to be charged");

- demonstrates that a contract has been made; and,

- contains the essential terms of the agreement.[3]

If there is not a sufficient writing, a further inquiry must be made to determine if the conduct of the parties is sufficient to demonstrate the existence of a contract despite the absence of written proof.[4] Such conduct usually consists of part performance or some other reliance. Article 2 of the Uniform Commercial Code, which governs contracts for the sale of goods, employs a particularly elaborate set of exceptions to the statute.[5]

Finally, some consideration must be given to the consequences of the failure to meet the statute's requirements, particularly in cases where there has been some part performance or preparations to perform the unenforceable agreement.[6]

§ 5.02 HISTORY AND PURPOSE OF THE STATUTE OF FRAUDS[7]

For many years, only formal contracts that bore a "seal" could be enforced.[8] When informal promises became generally enforceable, proof that a contract had been formed might depend completely on the testimony of witnesses, usually the parties themselves.

Until adoption of the statute of frauds, English common law did not generally require contracts to be in writing. And, as juries were not subject to the same

---

1989 UTAH L. REV. 383; Morris G. Shanker, *In Defense of the Sales Statute of Frauds and Parole Evidence Rule: A Fair Price of Admission to the Courts*, 100 COM. L.J. 259 (1995); Hugh Evander Willis, *The Statute of Frauds — A Legal Anachronism*, 3 IND. L.J. 427 (1928).

[2] *See infra* § 5.03 : Which Contracts?: The Scope of the Statute of Frauds.

[3] *See* RESTATEMENT (SECOND) OF CONTRACTS § 131 (1981); *infra* § 5.04 Type of Writing Required.

[4] *See infra* § 5.05 The Effect of Part Performance and Reliance.

[5] *See infra* § 5.06 Sale of Goods.

[6] *See infra* § 5.07 Consequences of Failing to Satisfy the Statute.

[7] Joseph Perillo, *The Statue of Frauds in Light of the Functions and Dysfunctions of Form*, 43 FORDHAM L. REV. 39 (1974); Drawford D. Hening, *The Original Drafts of the Statute of Frauds and Their Authors*, 61 U. PA. L. REV. 283 (1913).

[8] *See supra* § 2.02[B] The Seal.

constraints that are imposed today, the absence of written evidence made it too easy for dishonest people to bring false claims that a contract made been made.[9]

The British Parliament adopted the original "Statute of Frauds" in 1677 to stem the tide of contract litigation that had been brought on by the expansion of the writ of assumpsit during the previous century.[10] The statute represented an effort to restrain the flood of groundless suits that plagued seventeenth-century England, by requiring many types of particularly important contracts to be in writing. Without a sufficient writing, the agreement could not be enforced. Thus, the statute of frauds prevents "a contracting party from creating a triable issue concerning the terms of the contract — or for that matter concerning whether a contract even exists — on the basis of his say-so alone."[11] In other words, disreputable charlatans, who might be able to persuade a jury that a contract had been made, were barred from the opportunity to submit their perjured testimony to a jury.

The statute, which applied only applied to a limited set of agreements,[12] was carried in this form from England to the American Colonies, where it remains intact despite its repeal in England.[13] Most states' versions of the statute of frauds bear a close resemblance to the original version adopted more than 300 years ago.[14]

The statute has since been expanded by a multitude of legislative enactments requiring a wide variety of other types of contracts to be in writing in order to be enforced. The most important additional categories are contracts for the sale of goods where the price is $500 or more,[15] contracts for the lease of goods where the total payments to be made by the lessee are $1,000 or more,[16] and security interests in personal property or fixtures.[17] In addition, there are many other, more specialized categories of contracts that fall "within" the statute of frauds.[18] Accordingly, it is a bit of a misnomer to refer to "the" statute of frauds, as if the rule were contained in a single statute. Instead, the statute resides in a multitude of legislative provisions across a vast array of statutory and regulatory rules.

---

[9] *See* Hugh Evander Willis, *The Statute of Frauds — A Legal Anachronism*, 3 IND. L.J. 427, 429–31 (1928).

[10] A.W.B. SIMPSON, A HISTORY OF THE COMMON LAW OF CONTRACT 599 (1987). *See supra* § 1.03 History of Contract Law.

[11] Cloud Corp. v. Hasbro, Inc., 314 F.3d 289, 296 (7th Cir. 2002) (Posner, J.).

[12] A.W.B. SIMPSON, A HISTORY OF THE COMMON LAW OF CONTRACT 600 (1987).

[13] Law Reform Act, 1954, 2 & 3 Eliz. 2, ch. 34. The English version of the statute still applies to suretyship and real estate transactions. *See* Harold Gill Reuschlein, *Recent Statutes, Statutes of Frauds — Part of English Act Repealed*, 68 HARV. L. REV. 383 (1954).

[14] *See generally* RESTATEMENT (SECOND) OF CONTRACTS § 110 (1981). *See, e.g.*, OHIO REV. CODE ANN. § 1335.05 (LexisNexis 2006).

[15] U.C.C. § 2-201(1) (2012). Proposed revisions to Article 2, if adopted, would increase this threshold tenfold, to $5,000. Revised U.C.C. § 2-201(1) (2003). However, these proposed revisions seem destined not to be adopted.

[16] U.C.C. § 2A-201(1) (2012).

[17] U.C.C. § 9-203(b)(3)(A) (2012).

[18] *See* OHIO REV. CODE ANN. § 1335.05 (LexisNexis 2006) (preventing actions against a licensed physician, osteopath, surgeon, or podiatrist on any promise relating to a medical prognosis, unless it is contained in a writing signed by the doctor). *Cf.* Hawkins v. McGee, 146 A. 641 (N.H. 1929).

The statute of frauds is now understood to perform several functions.[19] It still performs an evidentiary function to ensure that there is some evidence other than the self-serving testimony of the plaintiff to support the claim that the promise sued upon was ever made.[20] The evidentiary function of the statute of frauds is regarded as economically efficient, at least to the extent that it limits errors in the fact-finding process.[21] However, as many scholars have pointed out, the statute provides a new avenue for unscrupulous conduct by those who use it in an attempt to avoid performance of an otherwise valid contract.[22]

The statute of frauds, like the historic ritual of the seal[23] and the doctrine of consideration,[24] also serves a cautionary function that some have viewed as paternalistic.[25] By interposing restraints on the enforceability of informal oral contracts, the statute protects people from impulse purchases on a grand scale.[26] Ignoring the question of whether people who make these decisions deserve this protection, there is a considerable risk that the statute also prevents enforcement of some deliberately considered transactions that were simply not reduced to writing. Thus, while the statute might do some good, it carries with it the risk that it will deny enforcement to agreements that should be enforced.

The statute of frauds also serves a "channeling" function.[27] It provides a bright-line test that distinguishes agreements that are enforceable from those that are not. In doing so, the statute facilitates decisions about the enforceability of agreements and, even more importantly, provides the parties with a symbol of enforceability that permits them to understand the likely legal consequences of their actions. The statute's success in fulfilling this latter function accounts for the public misconception that every contract must be in writing.[28] In this respect, the

---

[19] *See generally* Lon Fuller, *Consideration and Form*, 41 COLUM. L. REV. 799, 800–01 (1941); Joseph M. Perillo, *The Statute of Frauds in the Light of the Functions and Dysfunctions of Form*, 43 FORDHAM L. REV. 39 (1974); Jean Fleming Powers, *Rethinking Moral Obligations as a Basis for Contract Recovery*, 54 ME. L. REV. 1, 34 (2002).

[20] *See* Nelson v. Boynton, 1841 Mass. LEXIS 152, *5–*7 (Nov. 1841).

[21] RICHARD A. POSNER, ECONOMIC ANALYSIS OF LAW § 8.4 (6th ed. 2003); Morris G. Shanker, *In Defense of the Sales Statute of Frauds and Parole Evidence Rule: A Fair Price of Admission to the Courts*, 100 COM. L.J. 259, 260, 273–76 (1995).

[22] *See* Francis M Burdick, *A Statute for Promoting Fraud*, 16 COLUM. L. REV. 273, 273–74 (1916); Hugh Evander Willis, *The Statute of Frauds — A Legal Anachronism*, 3 IND. L.J. 427, 429–31 (1928). *See* Task Force, ABA Comm. on the Uniform Commercial Code, *An Appraisal of the March 1, 1990, Preliminary Report of the Uniform Commercial Code Article 2 Study Group*, reprinted in 16 DEL. J. CORP. L. 981, 1038 (1991); *The Statute of Frauds and the Doctrine of Consideration: Report of the English Law Revision Committee*, 15 CANADIAN B. REV. 585, 589 (1937).

[23] *See supra* § 2.02[B] The Seal.

[24] *See supra* § 2.03 Consideration — A Bargained-For Exchange.

[25] George M. Cohen, *The Negligence-Opportunism Tradeoff in Contract Law*, 20 HOFSTRA L. REV. 941, 1002 (1992); ANTHONY T. KRONMAN & RICHARD A. POSNER, THE ECONOMICS OF CONTRACT LAW 253–54 (1979); L. Vold, *The Application of the Statute of Frauds Under the Uniform Sales Act*, 15 MINN. L. REV. 391, 393–95 (1931).

[26] *See* E. Rabel, *The Statute of Frauds and Comparative Legal History*, 63 LAW Q. REV. 174, 178 (1947).

[27] Wior v. Anchor Indus., Inc., 669 N.E.2d 172 (Ind. 1996).

[28] W. David East, *The Statute of Frauds and the Parol Evidence Rule Under the NCCUSL 2000*

statute serves as a mechanism that permits people to know how to make their intentions legally binding when they wish to do so.[29]

The statute also promotes greater certainty about the details of agreements. Faced with the requirement of reducing their agreement to writing, people are more likely to make a complete record of their entire agreement and not just the terms that the statute requires. Putting things in writing also helps limit the ambiguity of the terms of a contract and might also lead the parties to consider other details of their agreement that might otherwise have been overlooked.[30]

Despite these obvious utilitarian functions, serious doubts have been cast on the success of the statute, particularly given the obvious risk that the statute will result in denying enforcement of unwritten agreements that the parties intended to have legal effect.[31] However, for the time being the statute of frauds will remain with us for the foreseeable future.

§ 5.03   WHICH CONTRACTS?: THE SCOPE OF THE STATUTE OF FRAUDS

The statute of frauds applies only to some types of contracts. The first step in analyzing whether a contract satisfies the statute of frauds is to determine whether the statute applies. If the contract is beyond the scope of the statute (or "outside" the statute), no writing is necessary. However, if the contract is "within" the statute, further analysis is necessary to determine whether any writing that exists is sufficient, or whether one of several exceptions permits enforcement in the absence of a writing.

[A]   Contracts for Real Estate

The most important category of contracts that must be in writing are those for the transfer of an interest in real estate.[32] Because agreements to transfer an interest in real estate must frequently be recorded to be enforceable against third parties, the writing requirement has particular utility in connection with agreements to convey land.

The real estate branch of the statute of frauds applies to contracts for every imaginable type of real property right.[33] It applies not just to transfers of title in fee simple absolute, but to mortgages,[34] life estates,[35] easements,[36] time shares,[37]

Annual Meeting Proposed Revision of U.C.C. Article 2, 54 SMU L. Rev. 867, 871 n.10 (2001).

[29] John Kidwell, *Teaching Important Contracts Concepts, Ruminations on Teaching the Statute of Frauds*, 44 St. Louis U. L.J. 1427, 1430 (2000).

[30] Joseph M. Perillo, *The Statute of Frauds in the Light of the Functions and Dysfunctions of Form*, 43 Fordham L. Rev. 39, 56–58 (1974).

[31] *E.g.*, Hugh Evander Willis, *The Statute of Frauds — A Legal Anachronism*, 3 Ind. L.J. 427 (1928); Michael Braunstein, *Remedy, Reason, and the Statute of Frauds: A Critical Economic Analysis*, 1989 Utah L. Rev. 383, 390–403 (1989).

[32] Restatement (Second) of Contracts § 125 (1981).

[33] *E.g.*, *In re* Estate of Conkle, 982 S.W.2d 312 (Mo. Ct. App. 1998) (condominium).

[34] *E.g.*, Armstrong Bus. Servs., Inc. v. AmSouth Bank, 817 So. 2d 665, 674–82 (Ala. 2001).

and long-term leases.[38] The original English statute exempted leases that were for a duration of less than three years from the time of the making of the lease, but many American jurisdictions have limited the exclusion to leases for a period of less than a year.[39]

A mere license, on the other hand, is not an interest in real estate. Contracts for a license to use land are therefore beyond the scope of the statute.[40] This makes the difference between an easement and a license of critical importance.[41] For example, in *Rogel v. Collinson*,[42] an oral promise to permit a neighbor to use a horse trail was not enforceable because the parties had referred to the right involved as an easement. If the right to use the trail had been nothing more than a license, it would have been enforceable despite the failure of the parties to put the agreement in writing.

Finally, although many states have adopted special provisions requiring real estate brokerage contracts to be in writing,[43] such agreements are not within the traditional statute of frauds.

[B]   Contracts That Cannot Be Performed Within a Year[44]

The original statute required contracts to be in writing if they were not capable of being performed within a year of the time the contract was made. This branch of the statute of frauds is a source of considerable confusion.[45] The confusion is caused by the lengths to which courts have gone in construing the statute narrowly.[46]

[1]   Performance Requiring More than a Year

Application of the statute requires an analysis of whether the contract *requires* performance to last beyond a year, measured from the time the contract was made. If performance might be completed within the span of a year, the agreement is

---

[35] *E.g.*, Carley v. Carley, 705 S.W.2d 371 (Tex. App. 1986).

[36] *E.g.*, Singleton v. Haywood Elec. Membership Corp., 565 S.E.2d 234 (N.C. Ct. App. 2002); Moloney v. Weingarten, 118 A.D.2d 836 (N.Y. App. Div. 1986).

[37] Leisure Am. Resorts, Inc. v. Knutilla, 547 So. 2d 424 (Ala. 1989) (applying fraud exception to statute of frauds).

[38] Firth v. Lu, 49 P.3d 117 (Wash. 2002) (lease for more than a year).

[39] RESTATEMENT (SECOND) OF CONTRACTS § 125(4) and cmt. b (1981).

[40] RESTATEMENT (SECOND) OF CONTRACTS § 127 cmt. b (1981). *See* Kitchen v. Kitchen, 641 N.W.2d 245 (Mich. 2002) (irrevocable license within the statute).

[41] This is one of the many issues in which first-year courses in contract law and property overlap.

[42] 765 N.E.2d 255 (Mass. Ct. App. 2002).

[43] *E.g.*, Cal. Civ. Code § 1624(a)(4) (West 2002).

[44] Frank Vickory, *The Erosion of the Employment-at-Will Doctrine and the Statute of Frauds: Time to Amend the Statute*, 30 AM. BUS. L.J. 97 (1992).

[45] *See generally* C.R. Klewin, Inc. v. Flagship Props., Inc., 600 A.2d 772 (Conn. 1991).

[46] *See* Farmer v. Arabian Am. Oil Co., 277 F.2d 46, 51 (2d Cir.), *cert. denied*, 364 U.S. 824 (1960).

beyond the statute and no writing is necessary.[47]

Consider an employment contract between Roland and Alex, requiring Alex to work as a production assistant in Roland's company for eight months. The agreement might or might not be within the statute, depending on when the contract was made and when the eight months of performance was scheduled to begin. If their contract was made on January 1, but Alex was not set to start work until July 1, with performance to run until the end of the following February, the contract would have to be in writing.[48] Performance could not be completed until after more than a year from the time the contract was made. However, if on January 1, Alex agreed to work for an entire year, starting immediately, the contract could be fully performed within a year of the time it was made and would not have to be in writing.[49]

[2]   Likelihood of Performance Beyond a Year

In determining whether the contract can be performed within a year of the time it is made, it is necessary to determine whether completion of the contract before the expiration of a year would be a breach. Thus, if performance *is permitted* to be finished within a year of the time the contract was made, the contract is not within the statute and need not be in writing, no matter how unlikely it seems that the work will be done within a year. The express terms of the contract must be examined to determine if they are consistent with performance being completed within a year of the time the contract was made. Contracts that do not specify a time for performance, but which seem to contemplate that completion will require more than a year, are not generally regarded as falling within the statute. Accordingly, no writing is required.[50] But, there are some decisions to the contrary, such as *Hall v. Hall*,[51] where the court's determination that the contract was likely to take more than a year to be performed made a writing necessary. Despite these decisions, most courts limit the scope of the statute to contracts that are required by their terms to take longer than a year to complete, despite the parties' apparent informal understanding that performance will last for more than a year.

For example, a contract to build a full-scale replica of the Empire State Building would ordinarily not be required to be in writing, despite the strong likelihood that the job would take more than a year to finish.[52] Performance within a year might be unlikely, but it would not be a breach for the contractor to finish in less than a year. The contract would be *legally* capable of performance within a year of its making. If the terms were different, and required the contract to take more than a

---

[47] *See* C.R. Klewin, Inc. v. Flagship Props., Inc., 600 A.2d 772 (Conn. 1991).

[48] *E.g.,* Kass v. Ronnie Jewelry, 371 A.2d 1060 (R.I. 1977) (one-year term to begin four days after formation of the contract).

[49] *See* Co-op Dairy v. Dean, 435 P.2d 470 (Ariz. 1967).

[50] *See* C.R. Klewin, Inc. v. Flagship Props., Inc., 600 A.2d 772 (Conn. 1991).

[51] 309 S.W.2d 12 (Tex. 1957). *See also* Dean v. Myers, 466 So. 2d 952 (Ala. 1985).

[52] *See* Freedman v. Chem. Constr. Corp., 372 N.E.2d 12 (N.Y. 1977). Construction of the Empire State Building took only 410 days.

year to finish, the agreement would be within the statute and a writing would be necessary.

[3] Performance "For Life"

Using this approach, an agreement that requires performance "for life" is not within the statute because the designated life may end within a year, making the contact fully performed.[53] If Comfort Arms Nursing Home makes an agreement to provide care to Betty for the rest of her life, the agreement need not be in writing, regardless of Betty's health, age, or beauty. She might possibly die before the expiration of a year, making full performance possible.[54]

If, on the other hand, the parties agree that Comfort Arms is to care for Betty for a minimum of 18 months, the contract falls within the statute and must be in writing.[55] The fact that Betty's premature death might provide Comfort Arms with an excuse does not take the contract out of the statute. Death might provide the nursing home with a legal excuse for failing to take care of Betty for the full 18 months,[56] but it is not performance.[57]

[4] "Permanent" Employment

Promises of "permanent" employment need not be in writing, as an agreement for a permanent job is regarded as "employment at will," which can be terminated by either party at any time. Thus, because the employment contract could be fully performed at any time within a year of its making, no writing is necessary.[58] On the other hand, if a promise of permanent employment is interpreted as an agreement to retain the employee until the normal retirement age of 65, it is incapable of being performed within a year (at least with respect to an employee who has not yet reached her sixty-fourth birthday at the time the contract was made), and thus within the statute of frauds.[59] However, such contracts are rare.

[5] Effect of Right to Terminate Within a Year

Somewhat more complicated are agreements that specify that performance will last for over a year, but which give one of the parties the right to terminate the contract earlier. These contracts have been viewed in conflicting ways, with some courts treating "termination" as an excuse, similar to death,[60] and others treating

---

[53] RESTATEMENT (SECOND) OF CONTRACTS § 130 cmt. a, illus. 2 (1981). *But see* McInerney v. Charter Golf, Inc., 680 N.E.2d 1347, 1351 (Ill. 1997) (rejecting this traditional result as "hollow and unpersuasive").

[54] RESTATEMENT (SECOND) OF CONTRACTS § 130 cmt. a & illus. 1 (1981).

[55] RESTATEMENT (SECOND) OF CONTRACTS § 130 cmt. b (1981).

[56] *See infra* § 11.03 Change of Circumstances: Impossibility, Impracticability, and Frustration of Purpose.

[57] *E.g.*, Ferrera v. Carpionato Corp., 895 F.2d 818 (1st Cir. 1990).

[58] *E.g.*, Czapla v. Commerz Futures, LLC, 114 F. Supp. 2d 715, 720 (N.D. Ill. 2000). *See* Frank Vickory, *The Erosion of the Employment-at-Will Doctrine and the Statute of Frauds: Time to Amend the Statute*, 30 AM. BUS. L.J. 97, 98–119 (1992).

[59] *See* Wior v. Anchor Indus., Inc., 669 N.E.2d 172 (Ind. 1996).

[60] *E.g.*, French v. Sabey Corp., 951 P.2d 260 (Wash. 1998); Deevy v. Porter, 95 A.2d 596 (N.J. 1953).

termination as a means of alternative performance. If treated the first way, the contract must be in writing. If viewed in the second way, the contract is outside the statute of frauds.[61]

For example, in *Professional Bull Riders, Inc. v. AutoZone, Inc.*,[62] the parties entered into an agreement in which AutoZone promised to provide sponsorship payments to the Bull Riders association from December 29, 2000, until December 31, 2002, but retained a right to terminate the contract at the end of the first year. The court ruled that the sponsor's unilateral right to terminate the contract at the end of a year removed the contract from the statute, making a writing unnecessary. Contracts that are capable of performance within a year of their making, but which are subject to renewal or extension at the option of one of the parties, are likewise treated in different ways, with some courts treating them as within the statute, and other courts dispensing with the necessity of a writing.[63]

[6]   Long Term Contracts for the Sale of Goods

Contracts for the sale of goods are governed by the special statute of frauds in U.C.C. § 2-201. Therefore, they should not be subject to the one-year provision of the more general statute of frauds.[64] It is hard to imagine a realistic contract for the sale of goods, with a price of less than $500, that cannot be performed within a year of its making, but if such a contract were made, it should be enforceable despite the absence of a writing.[65] Such contracts are far more likely to show up on law school and bar exam questions than in the real world.[66] Likewise, a contract for the sale of goods that meets the $500 threshold of § 2-201 is enforceable if the requirements of § 2-201 are satisfied, even if a more detailed writing, required to satisfy the one-year branch of the statute, has not been signed.[67]

[C]   Promises to Pay Someone Else's Debt: Suretyship Agreements[68]

Suretyship contracts must be in writing.[69] A suretyship contract is one in which a person promises "to answer for the debt, default, or miscarriage of another

---

[61] Metz Beverage Co. v. Wyo. Beverages, Inc., 39 P.3d 1051, 1054–57 (Wyo. 2002); Blake v. Voight, 31 N.E. 256 (N.Y. 1892).

[62] 113 P.3d 757 (Colo. 2005).

[63] *Compare* Anderson v. Frye & Bruhn, 124 P. 499 (Wash. 1912) (right of renewal brings the contract within the statute) *with* Ward v. Hasbrouck, 62 N.E. 434 (N.Y. 1902) (full performance may occur without renewal leaving contract beyond the statute), *and* Innovative Networks, Inc. v. Young, 978 F. Supp. 167 (S.D.N.Y. 1997) (unwritten right of renewal, for term beyond a year, unenforceable).

[64] *But see* C.R. Klewin, Inc. v. Flagship Props., Inc., 600 A.2d 772 (Conn. 1991).

[65] Rajala v. Allied Corp., 66 B.R. 582 (D. Kan. 1986); Revised § 2-201(4) & cmt. 8 (2003).

[66] Perhaps a 2-year membership in the "wine of the month club" for a price of $499.94 ($20.81 per bottle).

[67] *E.g.*, Rosenfeld v. Basquiat, 78 F.3d 84 (2d Cir. 1996).

[68] Clarence B. Taylor, *The Statute of Frauds and Misrepresentations as to the Credit of Third Persons: Should California Repeal Its Lord Tenterden's Act*, 16 UCLA L. REV. 603 (1969); John D. Calamari, *The Suretyship Statute of Frauds*, 27 FORDHAM L. REV. 332 (1958); Bernard E. Gegan, *Some*

person."[70] The most familiar suretyship agreement is one that parents sometimes make to pay a debt owed by one of their children. Another common example is an agreement by the controlling shareholder of a small corporation, to pay a debt owed by her company.

[1]   Suretyship Agreements Described[71]

Suretyship agreements necessarily involve at least three parties:

- the original or "principal" debtor;

- the creditor to whom the debt is owed; and

- the surety, who has promised to pay the creditor, if the principal debtor defaults.

Thus, if Louisa promises Commerce Bank that she will repay a loan it made to her son, Miguel, Miguel is the principal debtor, Commerce Bank is the creditor, and the surety (or guarantor) is Louisa.[72] The statute of frauds requires Louisa's agreement, the promise to pay Miguel's debt, to be in writing.

The original English statute of frauds and many modern statutes further specify that the promise of an executor or administrator of an estate to satisfy a debt of the decedent must be in writing.[73] However, this specific provision has been eliminated from some modern versions of the statute in recognition that the broader rule, regarding promises to pay the debt of another generally, covers promises of this sort by executors and administrators of a decedent's estate. The statute does not, of course, apply to promises made by the estate, which will be performed only from the estate's assets.[74]

[a]   Surety for Family Member

As suggested above, suretyship agreements are frequently used to assist family members in obtaining credit. Parents, for example, frequently agree to be sureties to assist their adult children in obtaining loans for tuition payments or to buy a car. Family members might also be willing to serve as sureties to assist a relative in obtaining a loan for a business.

It is in these family transactions where the cautionary function of the statute of frauds plays its most important role. It operates to alert family members, who are usually receiving nothing from the principal debtor, other than love and affection,

---

Exceptions to the Suretyship Statute of Frauds: A Tale of Two Courts, 79 St. John's L. Rev. 319 (2005); Charles C. Marvel, Annotation, *Promise by One Other Than Principal to Indemnify One Agreeing to Become Surety or Guarantor as Within Statute of Frauds*, 13 A.L.R.4th 1153 (1982).

[69] Restatement (Second) of Contracts § 110(1)(b) (1981).

[70] Ohio Rev. Code Ann. § 1335.05 (LexisNexis 2006).

[71] Avery Weiner Katz, *An Economic Analysis of the Guaranty Contract*, 66 U. Chi. L. Rev. 47 (1999).

[72] *See, e.g.*, White v. Household Fin. Corp., 302 N.E.2d 828 (Ind. Ct. App. 1973).

[73] Restatement (Second) of Contracts §§ 110(1)(a), 111, & 111 cmt. a (1981).

[74] Restatement (Second) of Contracts § 111 cmt. a (1981).

that their agreement is a serious commitment that is legally binding.[75]

[b]   Surety for Affiliated Corporation

There are also numerous business settings in which suretyship promises play an important role in facilitating credit. Suretyship contracts are commonly used to assist small businesses in obtaining a loan. Assume that Milburn Corp., as a principal debtor, borrows money from State Bank and that Isaac Investor, who both owns all of the stock of Milburn Corp. and serves as president of the company, promises that he will repay the bank if Milburn Corp. goes bankrupt.[76] By obtaining Isaac's commitment to pay, the bank obtains another source of payment. The personal liability of shareholders, directors, and officers, like Isaac, who control the business, assures the bank that the company will be operated by a highly motivated management team whose members know they will be personally responsible for the business's debts if it fails. The statute of frauds requires Isaac's promise to be in writing.

The same type of agreement might be made by one corporation for another. For example, Isaac Investor might own two separate companies: Milburn Corporation and Pommering Corporation. When State Bank loans funds to Milburn Corp. to help it start up its business operations, it might insist on a guarantee from the more financially stable Pommering Corp., to protect it from Milburn Corp.'s insolvency. In this transaction, Milburn Corp. is still the principal debtor, but Pommering Corp. is the surety, whose suretyship agreement must be in writing. It would not be unusual in this setting for State Bank to seek guarantees from both Isaac Investor, as the owner of both businesses, and from Pommering Corp. If this is done, both Isaac Investor and Pommering Corp. are sureties, whose promises must be in writing.

[c]   Performance Bonds and Professional Sureties

Guarantees are also provided by insurance companies and other firms that are in the business of guaranteeing payment. Such performance "bonds" are frequently used in the construction industry. In a construction setting, a professional surety, operating much like an insurance company, charges a price to a general contractor in exchange for the surety's promise to complete a construction project that the general contractor leaves unfinished. Here, the general contractor is the principal debtor, the owner of the project is the creditor, and the insurance company is the surety.[77] As with other suretyship agreements, the professional surety's promise is required to be written.

Another example that is familiar to nearly all American law students is the guaranteed student loan. Here, a bank or other commercial lender makes a loan to a college student, who is the principal debtor, and a governmental agency,

---

[75] Consideration for the guarantee is usually supplied in these situations by the lender's action of making the loan to the principal debtor. Thus, although the guarantor does not receive anything from the lender, the guarantor's promise is nevertheless supported by consideration.

[76] *See, e.g.*, Tulia Feedlot, Inc. v. United States, 3 Ct. Cl. 364 (1983).

[77] *See, e.g.*, Fed. Ins. Co. v. Sw. Fl. Ret. Ctr., Inc., 708 So. 2d 119 (Fla. 1998).

educational institution, or other reliable financial source serves as guarantor. If the student defaults on his or her loan, the guarantor pays the bank and assumes the risk of collecting from the student.[78]

In these situations the formalities of the transaction leave little doubt that the parties who agree to serve as sureties understand that their promises are legally binding. In other business transactions the statute of frauds plays an important role in distinguishing promises intended to be enforceable from those perhaps not deserving binding legal effect. For example, in *M.J. Pirolli & Sons, Inc. v. Massachusetts Equipment & Supply Co.*, the owner of a general contracting firm repeatedly told his subcontractor's supplier "I'll see that you get paid."[79]

The general contractor's assurances were probably intended to provide assistance in ensuring that the supplier would be paid and not as a legally binding commitment to assume responsibility for the debt if the owner of the project was to become unable to pay. However, where the general contractor's assurances are made to ensure the subcontractor's ability to complete the project, in satisfaction of the general contractor's own business purpose, the promise may be outside the scope of the statute under the "main purpose" test, described below.[80]

[2]   Consideration for Suretyship Promise

Although professional sureties receive compensation for their commitments, many sureties do not. Despite this, consideration for these other sureties' promises is usually present. A father's promise to pay his child's debt is usually made in exchange for the creditor's loan to the child. Thus, although the father, as surety, does not receive the consideration, the critical element of exchange is present, and the surety's promise, apart from any failure to satisfy the statute of frauds, is enforceable.[81] Similarly, a controlling shareholder's promise to pay a bank if a loan to his corporation falls into default is supported by the loan made by the bank in the first place.

If the suretyship promise is made sometime after the loan was originated, consideration may be missing. However, if the surety supplies its promise in exchange for the creditor's agreement to abstain from accelerating the debt owed by the principal debtor, or from bringing an immediate suit to collect or repossess the principal debtor's collateral, the creditor's forbearance from asserting its rights against the principal supplies the necessary exchange. If the principal debtor is not in default, consideration might be supplied by the creditor's agreement to reduce the rate of interest on the loan, to advance additional sums, or to release some of the original collateral.

In addition, the consideration requirement is relaxed in many jurisdictions to

---

[78] Such loans are generally nondischargeable in bankruptcy. 11 U.S.C. § 523(a)(8) (2000). *See generally* JEFF FERRIELL & EDWARD J. JANGER, UNDERSTANDING BANKRUPTCY § 13.03[8] Student Loans, at 504–508 (2007).

[79] 401 N.E.2d 146 (Mass. Ct. App. 1980).

[80] *See* RESTATEMENT (SECOND) OF CONTRACTS § 116 cmt. b, illus. 3 (1981).

[81] *See, e.g.*, Adams v. H & H Meat Prods., Inc., 41 S.W.3d 762, 776–77 (Tex. App. 2001) (promise by buyer's employee to pay for goods delivered to employer).

permit enforcement of a guarantee if the guarantor's signed written promise "recites a purported consideration."[82] Further, statutory rules eliminate the requirement for consideration in some settings, such as those involving an "accommodation party" who signs a negotiable instrument.[83]

Finally, of course, a surety is bound by his or her written promise, even though consideration is missing, if the creditor has acted in reasonable, foreseeable reliance on the promise.[84] A creditor might, in reliance on the surety's promise, refrain from enforcing the principal debtor's obligation without making a binding agreement to do so.[85]

[3]   Principal Debtor or Surety

One of the biggest problems that law students encounter in applying the suretyship branch of the statute of frauds is determining whether the promise was made as a surety to pay a debt owed by someone else or if, instead, the promisor is a principal debtor. Assume that Floyd borrows $20,000 from the bank to finance his business, Floyd's Flowers, Inc. Here, because the loan was made directly to Floyd, he is the principal debtor, not a surety. If the bank instead had loaned the funds directly to Floyd's Flowers, Inc., with Floyd agreeing to personally repay the loan if the corporation did not, the corporation would be the principal debtor and Floyd would be a surety whose promise would have to be in writing. In situations like this, care must be taken to determine the identity of the principal debtor.

Likewise, if Mom and Dad buy a car for Junior on credit, and promise the seller that they will pay for the car, they are principal debtors, not guarantors. The fact that Junior is the owner of the car does not matter. If credit was extended to Mom and Dad, to permit them to make a gift to Junior, Mom and Dad are the borrowers. For example, in *Nakamura v. Fujii*,[86] a college student's parents promised to repay tuition advances made by the plaintiff to maintain their daughter's enrollment in school. The court treated the parents' oral promise as the parents' own primary obligation, with the daughter as a third-party beneficiary of the deal. Viewed in this manner the parents' promise was not an obligation to pay the daughter's original debt. Therefore, the parents' promise was outside the scope of the statute of frauds.

This does not change if Junior buys the car from Mom and Dad, and makes a promise to Mom and Dad that he will make the regular monthly payments they owe to the bank. The bank is a third-party beneficiary of a contract between Junior and his parents. Because Junior's promise is to pay his own debt, for the price of the car, purchased from Mom and Dad, it is not a suretyship contract and does not need to be in writing.

---

[82] RESTATEMENT (SECOND) OF CONTRACTS § 88(a) (1981).

[83] U.C.C. § 3-419(b) (2012) (liability of "accommodation party" to a negotiable instrument "may be enforced . . . whether or not the accommodation party receives consideration"). *See* RESTATEMENT (SECOND) OF CONTRACTS § 88(b) (1981).

[84] RESTATEMENT (SECOND) OF CONTRACTS § 88(c) (1981).

[85] RESTATEMENT (SECOND) OF CONTRACTS § 88 cmt. d (1981).

[86] 253 A.D.2d 387 (N.Y. App. Div. 1998).

[4]   **Leading Object Exception**

Courts have carved out an exception to the statute of frauds if the "leading object" or "main purpose" of the surety's promise was for his own benefit.[87] If the surety's main purpose was to advance his or her own interests, rather than those of the principal debtor, the "gratuitous or sentimental element" present in many suretyship promises is missing and the cautionary purpose of the statute of frauds is less important.[88]

The test for whether the exception applies is whether the consideration for the surety's promise was used or sought by the surety "mainly for his own economic advantage, rather than in order to benefit [the principal debtor]."[89] In evaluating the main purpose, a court will examine the transaction which gave rise to the debt to determine whether the promisor became obligated in order to further its own independent business purposes, or if the promise was primarily made to facilitate a transaction of someone else.

For example, in *Power Entertainment, Inc. v. National Football League Properties, Inc.,*[90] the plaintiff was seeking a license to serve as a distributor of the defendant's football cards. The plaintiff promised to pay a debt owed to the defendant by a former distributor, who had gone bankrupt. The court held that the plaintiff's promise was not within the suretyship branch of the statute of frauds because the plaintiff's main purpose in assuming the debt was to acquire a business opportunity of its own. And, in *Merdes v. Underwood,*[91] the defendant was the controlling shareholder of a corporation. He promised to repay a debt owed by the corporation in order to forestall litigation against the company and to preserve the defendant's own business reputation. Because the main purpose of the promise was to gain a business advantage for the defendant, and not simply to assist the original corporate debtor, the promise to satisfy the debt was enforceable even though it was not in writing.[92]

The leading object or main purpose test, although sometimes elusive, is consistent with the purposes of the statute of frauds. Like consideration, the existence of a tangible benefit to the promisor provides a strong measure of assurance that the promise was made and that it was intended to be enforceable.[93]

[5]   **Promise Made to the Principal Debtor**

Finally, the statute only applies to promises allegedly made directly to the creditor. If the obligor's promise was one made not to the creditor, but to the principal debtor, with the creditor as a third-party beneficiary of the promise, the

---

[87] RESTATEMENT (SECOND) OF CONTRACTS § 116 (1981).

[88] RESTATEMENT (SECOND) OF CONTRACTS § 116 (1981). *E.g.*, Yarbro v. Neil B. McGinnis Equip. Co., 420 P.2d 163 (Ariz. 1966).

[89] RESTATEMENT (SECOND) OF CONTRACTS § 116 (1981).

[90] 151 F.3d 247 (5th Cir. 1998).

[91] 742 P.2d 245 (Alaska 1987).

[92] *See* RESTATEMENT (SECOND) OF CONTRACTS § 116 cmt. b (1981).

[93] *See* White Stag Mfg. Co. v. Wind Surfing, Inc., 679 P.2d 312, 316 (Or. Ct. App. 1984).

statute does not apply. If Fran uses her Lion Bank credit card to pay for her college tuition and then her parents promise Fran that they will pay the bank, there is no suretyship promise. Lion Bank is a third-party beneficiary of a promise made by the parents directly to Fran. Promises made directly to the principal debtor, with the creditor asserting rights as a third-party beneficiary of the contract between the promisor and the debtor, are beyond the statute and need not be in writing.[94] Such promises are not within the literal language of the statute, which requires promises to pay the debt "of another person."[95]

For example, in *Ex parte Ramsay*,[96] a promise by a geographically isolated hospital to pay a doctor's medical school tuition debts, as a means of luring the doctor to agree to work at the hospital, was outside the scope of the statute of frauds and therefore enforceable even though it was not in writing. The hospital made the promise to the doctor, not to his creditors. The hospital's promise was not "to pay the debt of another"; instead, it was a promise to pay a debt owed by the promisee. Likewise, in *Steinberger v. Steinberger*,[97] a father's promise to his daughter to pay her mortgage was enforceable even though it was not in writing. The creditor was a third-party beneficiary of the father's promise.

[D]   Contracts for the Sale or Lease of Goods

The statute of frauds provision of U.C.C. § 2-201 governs contracts for the sale of goods, with the parallel rule of U.C.C. § 2A-201 governing leases of goods. Article 2 applies to all contracts for the sale of goods.[98] Its statute of frauds applies to contracts for the sale of goods with a price of $500 or more.[99] Article 2A, governing leases of goods, requires a writing if the total payments to be made under the original term of the lease, excluding any payments for options to renew the lease, are $1000 or more.[100]

It is the agreed price that triggers the application of the statute, not their market value. Thus a contract for the sale of a boat, which has a fair market value of $20,000, for an agreed price of only $499, does not need to be in writing. However, a contract to sell a worthless painting for $500 is within the statute.

Article 2 has a separate provision regarding modifications to contracts for the sale (but not the lease) of goods. Section 2-209(3) provides: "The requirements of the statute of frauds [in § 2-201] must be satisfied if the contract as modified is

---

[94] *E.g.*, Snyder v. Freeman, 266 S.E.2d 593 (N.C. 1980).

[95] RESTATEMENT (SECOND) OF CONTRACTS § 110(1)(a) (1981); OHIO REV. CODE ANN. § 1335.05 (LexisNexis 2006).

[96] 829 So. 2d 146 (Ala. 2002).

[97] 252 A.D.2d 578 (N.Y. App. Div. 1998).

[98] *See supra* § 1.04[B][1] Uniform Commercial Code.

[99] U.C.C. § 2-201(a) (2012). Recent proposed revisions to § 2-201, if enacted, would raise this threshold to $5,000. Revised U.C.C. § 2-201(a) (2003). *See* W. David East, *Symposium on Revised Article 1 and Proposed Revised Article 2 of the Uniform Commercial Code — The Statute of Frauds and the Parol Evidence Rule Under the NCCUSL 2000 Annual Meeting Proposed Revision of U.C.C.*, 54 SMU L. REV. 867, 877–87 (2001).

[100] U.C.C. § 2A-201 (2012).

within its provisions."[101] This language can be interpreted in a variety of ways,[102] leading to considerable confusion about its proper application.[103]

Most courts ignore the plain text of § 2-209(3) and require any modification of a contract for the sale of goods to be contained in a signed writing, even though the term contained would not have been required to be in the writing had it been contained in the original version of the contract.[104] In *Zemco Mfg., Inc. v. Navistar International Transportation. Corp.*,[105] the court required an agreement extending the duration of a requirements contract to be in writing even though the duration of the original contract would not have needed to be included in the written contract under U.C.C. § 2-201(1). In addition, in *Broeke v. Bellanca Aircraft Corp.*,[106] an oral modification to the terms of a warranty were required to be in writing even though warranty terms generally need not be in writing.

This approach imposes a stricter standard for modifications than for the original contract, implying that there is a greater risk of perjury with respect to modifications than with respect to the original agreement. This may be true, for it seems likely that a jury could more easily be persuaded by perjured testimony that an established contract was modified than perjured testimony that a nonexistent contract had been formed in the first place. Further, the official comments to § 2-209 lend support to this line of cases, indicating that " 'modification' for the future cannot therefore be conjured up by oral testimony."[107]

Other courts take an approach more in line with the text of the statute. These decisions require a writing only for modifications changing the few terms that are required to be in writing, such as quantity, and those that show that a contract has been formed, such as the subject matter of the contract and the identity of the parties.[108] This narrower view is favored by most scholars[109] and is consistent with the text of the statute, which requires only that "the requirements of the statute of frauds section of this Article (Section 2-201) must be satisfied." The literal text of § 2-209 does not impose requirements on a modification beyond those that would have been imposed on the terms of the deal as originally framed.

---

[101]   U.C.C. § 2-209(3) (2012).

[102]   *See* James J. White & Robert S. Summers, Uniform Commercial Code § 2-7 (6th ed. 2010).

[103]   Beth A. Eisler, *Modification of Sales Contracts Under the Uniform Commercial Code: Section 2-209 Reconsidered*, 57 Tenn. L. Rev. 401 (1990); Douglas K. Newell, *Cleaning Up U.C.C. Section 2-209*, 27 Idaho L. Rev. 487 (1990); Robert A. Hillman, *Standards for Revising Article 2 of the U.C.C.: The NOM Clause Model*, 35 Wm. & Mary L. Rev. 1509 (1994).

[104]   Wixon Jewelers, Inc. v. Di-Star, Ltd., 218 F.3d 913 (8th Cir. 2000) (distributorship agreement for diamonds); Green Constr. Co. v. First Indem. of Am. Ins. Co., 735 F. Supp. 1254, 1261 (D.N.J. 1990) (orally modified delivery terms).

[105]   186 F.3d 815, 819 (7th Cir. 1999).

[106]   576 F.2d 582, 584 (5th Cir. 1978).

[107]   U.C.C. § 2-209 cmt. 3 (2012).

[108]   *See* Costco Wholesale Corp. v. World Wide Licensing Corp., 898 P.2d 347, 351 & n.5 (Wash. Ct. App. 1995).

[109]   Michael J. Herbert, *Toward a Unified Theory of Warranty Creation Under Articles 2 and 2A of the Uniform Commercial Code*, 1990 Colum. Bus. L. Rev. 265, 303; John E. Murray Jr., *The Modification Mystery: Section 2-209 of the Uniform Commercial Code*, 32 Vill. L. Rev. 1, 28 (1987).

[E]   Contracts in Consideration of Marriage

The statute of frauds also covers contracts made in consideration of marriage.[110] Although at first blush this might appear to apply to agreements people make to marry one another, the statute does not apply to these agreements, which are almost never in writing.[111] Further, many states have enacted separate statutes making mutual promises to marry unenforceable, even if they are in writing.[112]

Nor does the statute apply to promises that both sets of parents of an engaged couple might make *to one another* concerning gifts to be made to the couple if they get married. Thus, if Mr. and Mrs. Croxton agree with Mr. and Mrs. Hurt that they will each make a $5,000 gift to their children when they marry, the parents' promises to each other supply the necessary consideration. The wedding is not the consideration for the promise; it is merely a condition precedent to their duties to pay the $5000.[113]

Instead, contracts in consideration of marriage are those involving promises to transfer property where part of the consideration for the promise is a promise to marry.[114] For example, in *Byers v. Byers*,[115] a man's promise to support his fiancée's child if she would marry him was required to be in writing. And, in *Tatum v. Tatum*,[116] a promise to leave all of the promisor's property to his spouse, if she would marry him, was required to be in writing. The most common modern example of a contract in consideration of marriage is a prenuptial agreement concerning the couple's property rights after the marriage occurs.[117] Despite this, courts have sometimes held that prenuptial agreements need not be in writing where it is found that the marriage is not the inducement for the promised transfer of property.[118]

Several states have gone further and enacted the Uniform Premarital Agreement Act, which requires any premarital agreement to be in writing. It requires a writing regardless of whether the marriage is the consideration for the agreement.[119]

The statute of frauds also applies to promises by a third person, such as a

---

[110] RESTATEMENT (SECOND) OF CONTRACTS § 110(1)(c) (1981).

[111] RESTATEMENT (SECOND) OF CONTRACTS § 124 cmt a. (1981).

[112] *E.g.*, Albinger v. Harris, 48 P.3d 711, 720 (Mont. 2002).

[113] RESTATEMENT (SECOND) OF CONTRACTS § 124 illus. 5 (1981).

[114] RESTATEMENT (SECOND) OF CONTRACTS § 124 cmt. b (1981); W.M. Moldoff, Annotation, *What Constitutes Promise Made in or upon Consideration of Marriage Within Statute of Frauds*, 75 A.L.R.2d 633 (1961).

[115] 618 P.2d 930 (Okla. 1980).

[116] 606 S.W.2d 31 (Tex. App. 1980).

[117] *E.g.*, Dewberry v. George, 62 P.3d 525 (Wash. Ct. App. 2003) (couple agreed that Dewberry would always be fully employed, that each of their income and property would be held separately, that each would own a home to return to if the marriage failed, and that Dewberry would not get fat).

[118] *E.g.*, Remington v. Remington, 193 P. 550 (Colo. 1920).

[119] *See* Unif. Premarital Agreement Act § 2, 9C U.L.A. 41 (2001). *E.g.*, Hall v. Hall, 222 Cal. App. 3d 578 (1990).

parent, to transfer property in consideration for the marriage of one of his or her offspring. However, promises to make a gift in mere anticipation of an upcoming marriage, or even subject to the condition that the marriage occurs, are not within the statute.[120] For a promise to be within the statute, the marriage must be part of the inducement for the promised transfer.[121]

Postnuptial agreements — those made after the marriage — are not within the statute. The marriage, having already occurred when the agreement was made, could not have been the consideration for the promised transfer.[122] Likewise, cohabitation agreements between unmarried individuals are outside the scope of the traditional statute,[123] though some states have adopted statutes requiring such agreements to be in writing.[124] Of course, if the agreement involves a promise to transfer an interest in real estate, a writing is necessary, regardless of whether it is a "contract in consideration of marriage."[125] Likewise, if the agreement cannot be performed within a year of its making, a writing is necessary.[126]

[F]   Other Contracts Required to Be in Writing

The contracts mentioned above are not the only contracts required to be in writing. The U.C.C. also requires sale or return contracts,[127] letters of credit,[128] and most security agreements[129] to be in writing.[130] Likewise, the U.C.C. used to make contracts for the sale of any kind of personal property, not covered by other more specific rules elsewhere in the U.C.C., unenforceable beyond $5,000 in amount or value of remedy, absent a written memorandum signed by the party against whom enforcement is sought.[131]

In addition, there are a multitude of even more specialized statute-of-frauds

---

[120] Restatement (Second) of Contracts § 124 cmt. c, illus. 5 (1981).

[121] *E.g.*, Larsen v. Johnson, 47 N.W. 615 (Wis. 1890) (consideration was a promise of mutual comfort and support rather than marriage); Steen v. Kirkpatrick, 36 So. 140 (Miss. 1904) (promise to transfer property not in consideration of marriage where promise was made after mutual promises to marry became binding).

[122] *See supra* § 2.06 Pre-Existing Legal Duty Rule.

[123] Morone v. Morone, 413 N.E.2d 1154 (N.Y. 1980).

[124] *E.g.*, Minn. Stat. § 513.075 (1996); Estate of Peterson, 579 N.W.2d 488 (Minn. Ct. App. 1998); Zaremba v. Cliburn, 949 S.W.2d 822 (Tex. App. 1997).

[125] Baron v. Jeffer, 131 A.D.2d 411 (N.Y. App. Div. 1987). *But see* Knauer v. Knauer, 470 A.2d 553 (Pa. Super. Ct. 1983) (agreement between cohabitants to split profits from sale of real estate outside the statute of frauds).

[126] Bereman v. Bereman, 645 P.2d 1155 (Wyo. 1982). *See generally* Tammy L. Lewis, Comment, *Standing in the Shadows: Honoring the Contractual Obligations of Cohabitants for Support*, 15 U. Puget Sound L. Rev. 171, 182 (1991).

[127] U.C.C. § 2-326(3) (2012).

[128] U.C.C. § 5-104 (2012).

[129] U.C.C. § 9-203(b) (2012).

[130] The statute-of-frauds provision for transfers of securities, formerly contained in U.C.C. § 8-319 (1978), has been eliminated. U.C.C. § 8-113 (2012).

[131] See Former U.C.C. § 1-206 (2001). This provision has been eliminated from the most recent set of revisions to Article 1.

provisions throughout the nation, covering a variety of different transactions, including promises by doctors to achieve a particular result for a patient,[132] franchise agreements,[133] agreements to make a loan,[134] and agreements for the sale of a business,[135] to name just a few. Each state's statutes must be carefully examined to determine which types of agreements its legislature requires to be in writing. Rules regarding the type of writing that will satisfy the statute, and exceptions to the statute due to part performance or for other reasons, generally follow the rules outlined below, but may operate differently depending on the statutory language or circumstances inherently involved in the type of contract involved.

[G]   Statute of Frauds in International Transactions[136]

Article 11 of the United Nations Convention on Contracts for the International Sale of Goods (CISG) specifies that contracts within its scope need not be in writing.[137] Article 96, however, permits a "Contracting State" — a country — whose own statutes require contracts of sale to be in writing, to declare that Article 11 does not apply if one of the parties has its place of business in the contracting state.[138] The United States has not made such a declaration. Accordingly, a contract for the sale of goods governed by the CISG need not be in writing, unless the country other than the United States where a party to the contract is located has made a declaration pursuant to Article 96.

In international transactions where UNIDROIT's Principles of International Commercial Contracts apply, there is no general requirement that agreements be reduced to writing, though the parties may, between themselves, agree that modifications to their contract be memorialized.[139] Likewise, Principles of European Commercial Contracts contain no requirement that agreements must be in writing.[140]

---

[132] *E.g.*, Ohio Rev. Code Ann. § 1335.05 (Anderson 2002).

[133] *E.g.*, Ohio Rev. Code Ann. § 1334.06 (Anderson 2002).

[134] *E.g.*, Ala. Code § 8-9-2(7) (Michie 2002).

[135] *E.g.*, Beldengreen v. Ashinsky, 528 N.Y.S.2d 744 (N.Y. Civ. Ct. 1987).

[136] Juan Del Duca, *Implementation of Contract Formation Statute of Frauds, Parol Evidence, and Battle of Forms CISG Provisions in Civil and Common Law Countries*, 25 J.L. & Com. 133 (2005); Janet Walker, *Agreeing to Disagree: Can We Just Have Words? CISG Article 11 and the Model Law Writing Requirement*, 25 J.L. & Com. 153 (2005).

[137] CISG Art. 11 (1980).

[138] CISG Art. 96 (1980).

[139] *See infra* § 5.09[B] Agreements Requiring Modifications in Writing.

[140] María del Pilar Perales Viscasillas, *The Formation of Contracts and the Principles of European Contract Law*, 13 Pace Int'l L. Rev. 371, 374 (2001).

§ 5.04 TYPE OF WRITING REQUIRED[141]

Where the statute of frauds applies, there must be a writing signed by the party against whom enforcement is sought that shows that a contract was formed and that contains all of the essential terms of the agreement.[142] Although there may be problems of proof regarding whether the signatures of the parties are genuine, the more interesting questions of contract law deal with what types of marks qualify as a signature. Apart from this, additional issues deal with the necessary contents of the writing.

[A]   Form of the Writing Irrelevant[143]

One thing at least is clear, the precise form of the writing used to satisfy the statute does not matter. Courts have found a wide variety of types of writings sufficient under the statute, including telegrams,[144] checks,[145] invoices,[146] corporate board minutes,[147] and other notes.[148] In *Southwest Engineering Co. v. Martin Tractor Co.*, a penciled note on a scrap piece of paper satisfied the statute.[149]

Moreover, a sufficient writing may be found in several documents considered together, even though none of them standing alone is sufficient.[150] For example, in *Crabtree v. Elizabeth Arden Sales Corp.*,[151] the court permitted several documents to operate together to satisfy the statute, even though only one of them was signed and even though the documents themselves did not explicitly refer to one another. When multiple documents are combined to form a "composite document," some evidence must be available to show that they are related to one another and to the transaction involved in the dispute.[152] While some courts permit parol evidence to be used to make the necessary connection between them,[153] other courts require

---

[141] Joseph Perillo, *The Statue of Frauds in Light of the Functions and Dysfunctions of Form*, 43 FORDHAM L. REV. 39 (1974).

[142] RESTATEMENT (SECOND) OF CONTRACTS § 131 (1981). *See, e.g.*, Olympia Exp., Inc. v. Linee Aeree Italiane, S.P.A., 509 F.3d 347 (7th Cir. 2007).

[143] Robert L. Misner, *Tape Recordings, Business Transactions via Telephone, and the Statute of Frauds*, 61 IOWA L. REV. 941 (1976).

[144] *E.g.*, Heffernan v. Keith, 127 So. 2d 903, 904 (Fla. Dist. Ct. App. 1961).

[145] Buffaloe v. Hart, 441 S.E.2d 172 (N.C. Ct. App. 1994) (sale of goods); A.B.C. Auto Parts, Inc. v. Moran, 268 N.E.2d 844 (Mass. 1971) (real estate); James J. Derba, Inc. v. Hamilton Service, Inc., 243 N.E.2d 178 (Mass. Ct. App. 1969) (suretyship agreement).

[146] Mid-South Packers, Inc. v. Shoney's, Inc., 761 F.2d 1117 (5th Cir. 1985) (goods).

[147] *E.g.*, DFI Comm., Inc. v. Greenberg, 363 N.E.2d 312, (N.Y. 1977) (contract for more than a year); Tripp v. Pay 'n Pak Stores, Inc., 518 P.2d 1298 (Or. 1974) (transfer of stock under former U.C.C. § 8-319).

[148] *In re* Quad-Cities Constr. Inc., 254 B.R. 459 (Bankr. D. Idaho 2000); Bader Bros. Transfer & Storage, Inc. v. Campbell, 299 So. 2d 114, 115 (Fla. Dist. Ct. App. 1974).

[149] 473 P.2d 18, 22–23 (Kan. 1970).

[150] RESTATEMENT (SECOND) OF CONTRACTS § 132 (1981).

[151] 110 N.E.2d 551, 554 (N.Y. 1953).

[152] RESTATEMENT (SECOND) OF CONTRACTS § 132 (1981).

[153] W.J. Dunn, Annotation, *Admissibility of Parol Evidence to Connect Signed and Unsigned*

the signed writing to expressly refer to the others. And, the signed document must be clearly referable to the transaction in question, without the necessity of resorting to parol testimony.

Further, the writing need not have been signed for the purpose of satisfying the statute of frauds.[154] Nor must the document be delivered to the other party.[155] Thus, a seller's private notes expressing the terms of a deal made over the phone are sufficient to satisfy the statute, if they are signed and contain the necessary information, even though they were never sent to the buyer and even though they were not intended as a formal expression of the terms of the contract.

This is a point that is sometimes forgotten. However, if Sam and Barb enter into an agreement over the phone for the sale of Sam's car for $20,000, and Sam then writes and signs a letter to Barb confirming the terms of their agreement *but never sends it to her*, the statute has still been satisfied. The only difficulty in using private internal notes of this type to satisfy the statute is the requirement that they be "signed."[156]

Further, the statute will have been satisfied even if the writing is lost or destroyed, so long as there is clear and convincing evidence that it once existed.[157] It is not even necessary for the other party to know that the writing exists, so long as proof of its existence is discovered in time to be used in court, either by producing the document or testifying about its existence.[158]

[B]   Contents of the Writing: Essential Terms

Whatever the form of the writing, it must show that a contract was formed, reasonably identify the parties, and describe the essential terms with reasonable certainty.[159] For example, the signed writing in *Olympia Express., Inc. v. Linee Aeree Italiane, S.P.A.*[160] referred only to "mutually determined goals" and did not specify either a quantity or a price. The writing was inadequate to satisfy the statute, even though oral testimony was available to fill in the missing details.

The Restatement's position is that a signed offer satisfies the statute, at least against the person who signed it, but this position is not universal,[161] and is, in any

---

Documents Relied upon as Memorandum to Satisfy Statute of Frauds, 81 A.L.R.2d 991 (1961).

[154] RESTATEMENT (SECOND) OF CONTRACTS § 133 (1981). Crabtree v. Elizabeth Arden Sales Corp., 110 N.E.2d 551, 553 (N.Y. 1953). The sole exception to this is for contracts in consideration of marriage.

[155] RESTATEMENT (SECOND) OF CONTRACTS § 133 cmt. b (1981). *E.g*, Rulon-Miller v. Carhart, 544 A.2d 340, 342. (Me. 1988). *See also* U.C.C. § 2-201 cmt. 6 (2012).

[156] *See* U.C.C. § 1-201(b)(35) (2012) (formerly § 1-201(39)).

[157] RESTATEMENT (SECOND) OF CONTRACTS § 137 (1981).

[158] RESTATEMENT (SECOND) OF CONTRACTS § 133 (1981). *E.g.*, Richardson v. Schaub, 796 P.2d 1304, 1310 (Wyo. 1990).

[159] RESTATEMENT (SECOND) OF CONTRACTS § 131 (1981). *E.g.*, N. Coast Cookies, Inc. v. Sweet Temptations, Inc., 476 N.E.2d 388 (Ohio Ct. App. 1984).

[160] 509 F.3d 347 (7th Cir. 2007).

[161] *Compare* RESTATEMENT (SECOND) OF CONTRACTS § 131(b) (1981), *with* Maderas Tropicales S. de R. L. de C. V. v. S. Crate & Veneer Co., 588 F.2d 971 (5th Cir. 1979) (language of offer revealing that no contract had yet been made was insufficient).

event, not adopted by Article 2 of the U.C.C. with respect to contracts for the sale of goods.[162] Writings showing that the parties conducted negotiations or even settled upon some preliminary terms are not sufficient.[163]

When real estate is involved, courts are sometimes more demanding. It is crucial for the writing to describe the parcel of real estate involved accurately, particularly if specific performance is sought.[164] Some courts require a legal description of the land involved, rather than a mere address.[165] Other states are more liberal and permit more general descriptions that, together with other evidence, reasonably identify the property involved.[166] In *Greer v. Kooiker*,[167] the court required the writing to contain five separate elements: "(1) A statement of the consideration; (2) an adequate description of the parties; (3) an adequate description of the land; (4) the general terms and conditions of the transaction; and (5) subscription [a signature] by the vendor." Despite these rigid requirements, courts generally exhibit a wide degree of latitude in their approach to whether other terms are "essential."[168] Some courts are satisfied with writings that reveal the names of the parties, the subject matter of the contract, and the agreed consideration.[169] Some do not insist that the agreed consideration be included, but instead permit such gaps to be filled in with parol evidence.

Other courts take a more formalistic approach and insist that any term materially affecting the exchange is essential and must be included in the writing.[170] In *Caito v. Juarez*, the court refused to specifically enforce a contract for the sale of real estate where the terms for deferred payment were not included in the signed writing.[171] This is somewhat ironic. It seems that parties should not be able to avoid performing a contract they admit having made, by introducing evidence that the written contract fails to mention some essential term. Before the advent of the "admission" exception to the statute, this was sometimes possible.[172] Taking the statute of frauds this far permits the statute to be used as an

---

[162] U.C.C. § 2-201(1) (2012).

[163] UXB Sand & Gravel v. Rosenfeld Concrete Corp., 641 A.2d 75 (R.I. 1994); *see also* Cal. Natural, Inc. v. Nestle Holdings, Inc., 631 F. Supp. 465 (D.N.J. 1986) (letter of intent expressing absence of binding contract was insufficient to satisfy the statute).

[164] *E.g.*, Moudy v. Manning, 82 S.W.3d 726 (Tex. App. 2002).

[165] *See* Key Design Inc. v. Moser, 983 P.2d 653 (Wash.), opinion amended, 993 P.2d 900 (Wash. 1999); Martin v. Seigel, 212 P.2d 107 (Wash. 1949). *See generally* W. W. Allen, *Annotation, Sufficiency of Description or Designation of Land in Contract or Memorandum of Sale, Under Statute of Frauds*, 23 A.L.R.2d 6 (1952).

[166] *See* Sterling v. Taylor, 113 Cal. App. 4th 931 (2003); Jacobson v. Gulbransen, N.W.2d 84 (S.D. 2001).

[167] 253 N.W.2d 133, 138 (Minn. 1977).

[168] Arthur L. Corbin, 4 Corbin on Contracts § 23.1, 761–67 (1996).

[169] Fruin v. Colonnade One at Old Greenwich Ltd. P'ship, 662 A.2d 129 (Conn. App. Ct. 1995).

[170] *E.g.*, Cohen v. McCutchin, 565 S.W.2d 230 (Tex. 1978); Poel v. Brunswick-Balke-Collender Co. of New York, 110 N.E. 619 (N.Y. 1915).

[171] 795 A.2d 533 (R.I. 2002).

[172] *E.g.*, Key Design Inc. v. Moser, 983 P.2d 653 (Wash. 1999). *See* Peter J. Shedd, *The Judicial Admissions Exception to the Statute of Frauds in Real Estate Transactions*, 19 Real Est. L.J. 232 (1991).

instrument of fraud rather than as a shield against it.[173]

[C]   Signature[174]

To satisfy the statute of frauds a writing must be signed by the party against whom enforcement is sought. The signature of the party seeking enforcement is not needed. For example, if Karen and Phil make an oral agreement for Karen to sell her land to Phil for $100,000, and Phil signs a letter to Karen describing the details of their agreement, the contract can be enforced by Karen against Phil, but not vice versa.[175] However, as explained in a later section, in contracts for the sale of goods between merchants, the contract may sometimes be enforceable against a party whose signature does not appear.[176]

Like the writing itself, the signature may be made in any form, so long as it was made with the intent to authenticate the writing. The signature may consist of a signed or printed name, initials, or even an "X." It may be written, typed, stamped, or copied. Article 2 of the U.C.C. permits any kind of a document, such as an invoice, stationery, or even a memo pad, bearing a preprinted name, to operate as a signature, provided the paper bearing the letterhead was used with the intent to authenticate the document.[177]

The electronic age has raised questions about whether an e-mail signature is sufficient.[178] However, both the Uniform Electronic Transactions Act and the Federal Electronic Signatures Act now make it clear that an electronic signature is sufficient.[179]

[D]   Writing Does Not Prove Assent

Satisfaction of the statute of frauds does not necessarily prove mutual assent. Thus, the presence of a signed writing, sufficient to satisfy the statute, is evidence of an agreement between the parties but is not necessarily a substitute for proof that they actually agreed. A party seeking to enforce a contract that is within the scope of the statute of frauds must clear two distinct hurdles: (1) proving that the

---

[173] *See* Metz Bev. Co. v. Wyo. Bev., Inc., 39 P.3d 1051 (Wyo. 2002); Lakeside Oakland Dev., L.C. v. H & J Beef Co., 644 N.W.2d 765 (Mich. Ct. App. 2002).

[174] John E. Theuman, Annotation, *Satisfaction of Statute of Frauds by E-Mail*, 110 A.L.R.5th 277 (2003).

[175] *E.g.*, Rohlfing v. Tomorrow Realty & Auction Co., Inc., 528 So. 2d 463 (Fla. Dist. Ct. App. 988).

[176] U.C.C. § 2-201(2) (2012). *See infra* § 5.06[C] Confirmatory Memorandum in Transactions Between Merchants.

[177] U.C.C. § 1-201 cmt. 39 (2012); Owen v. Kroger Co., 936 F. Supp. 579 (S.D. Ind. 1996). *But see* Venable v. Hickerson, Phelps, Kirtley & Assoc., Inc., 903 S.W.2d 659 (Mo. Ct. App. 1995) (declining to extend the rule expressed in the U.C.C., permitting letterhead stationery to suffice, to employment contracts).

[178] *See* John E. Theuman, Annotation, *Satisfaction of Statute of Frauds by E-Mail*, 110 A.L.R.5th 277 (2003).

[179] *E.g.*, Int'l Casings Group, Inc. v. Premium Std. Farms, Inc., 358 F. Supp. 2d 863 (W.D. Mo. 2005). *See infra* § 5.08 Electronic Contracting.

agreement was made, and (2) satisfying the requirement of a sufficient writing.[180]

Production of a signed and detailed written contract will usually be sufficient to meet both burdens. In other circumstances there may be a writing sufficient to satisfy the statute, proving that the transaction between the parties was not a complete figment of the plaintiff's imagination, but inadequate to prove that an agreement was actually concluded. Likewise, there may be overwhelming eyewitness evidence of the existence of an agreement, but no writing sufficient to satisfy the statute.

[E]   Precontractual Writings

When the parties have executed one or more documents or e-mail messages before concluding their agreement, the question arises whether these precontractual documents are sufficient. If the purpose of the statute of frauds is to prevent gullible juries from finding promises in circumstances where the alleged contract is a complete figment of the plaintiff's imagination or dishonesty, then any writing that tended to show that the parties had engaged in negotiations about a contract would satisfy the statute. But, if the statute also serves as a hedge against imposing liability where one of the parties misinterpreted the significance of these writings, and any accompanying conversations, they should not be enough.

The issue was before the court in *Monetti, S.P.A. v. Anchor Hocking Corp.*,[181] where the parties exchanged written memos concerning the details of their proposed agreement, before the buyer balked. The seller claimed that their negotiations had resulted in an agreement. The buyer claimed that no contract existed and that the writings involved were not sufficient to show the existence of a contract. Judge Posner ruled that the precontractual writings were sufficient to satisfy the statute. He acknowledged that some decisions held otherwise,[182] but noted that there was authority to the contrary.[183] He further recognized that U.C.C. § 2-201 is drafted in the "present tense" and that "the writing must be sufficient to demonstrate that "a contract for sale *has been made.*' "[184] He nevertheless held that writings executed before a contract is formed can satisfy the statute and that "temporal priority is unnecessary to secure the purposes of the statute."[185] However, not only did the writings in *Monetti* supply extensive details about the transaction, the seller took unilateral action by abandoning its existing distribution network and turning over critical trade secrets to the buyer, in partial performance of the contract. Although the Code's language permitting partial

---

[180] Hinson-Barr, Inc. v. Pinckard, 356 S.E.2d 115, 116 (S.C. 1987).

[181] 931 F.2d 1178 (7th Cir. 1991) (Posner, J.).

[182] Monetti, 931 F.2d at 1182 (*citing* R.S. Bennett & Co. v. Economy Mech. Ind., Inc., 606 F.2d 182, 186 (7th Cir. 1979) (written offer insufficient to satisfy statute of frauds), Micromedia v. Automated Broad. Controls, 799 F.2d 230, 234 (5th Cir. 1986), and Am.Web Press, Inc. v. Harris Corp., 596 F. Supp. 1089, 1093 (D. Colo. 1983)).

[183] Monetti, 931 F.2d at 1182 (*citing* Farrow v. Cahill, 663 F.2d 201, 209 (D.C. Cir. 1980)).

[184] Monetti, 931 F.2d at 1183 (quoting Micromedia v. Automated Broad. Controls, 799 F.2d 230, 345 (5th Cir. 1986) (emphasis in original)).

[185] Monetti, 931 F.2d at 1183.

performance does not speak directly to these types of actions, the court regarded these unilateral actions as "pretty solid evidence that there really was a contract."[186] Thus, although precontractual documents may not be sufficient by themselves to satisfy the statute, they may be sufficient when considered together with action in part performance of the deal.

§ 5.05 THE EFFECT OF PART PERFORMANCE AND RELIANCE

Despite its benefits, the statute of frauds has a potential for abuse.[187] At one time, it was possible for a person to admit the existence of a contract and yet prevent its enforcement by asserting the statute of frauds.[188] Without the development of some exceptions to the statute, unscrupulous parties were able to perform badly, or not at all, and escape liability by asserting the statute of frauds. Accordingly, courts frequently relax the rigor of the statute where there is either part performance or reliance on the oral agreement.[189]

[A]   Part Performance

Part performance has long been recognized as an exception to several branches of the statute of frauds, at least to the extent of the part performance. For example, under U.C.C. § 2-201(3)(c), if a buyer has accepted goods received from the seller, the contract is enforceable, at least to the extent of the quantity that was delivered and accepted, despite the absence of a writing.[190] Likewise, an employee can recover for the value of services he or she has provided in partially performing a contract that he or she claims was to have extended beyond a year, even though nothing was reduced to writing, but he or she may not recover wages for the remainder of the time of the contract.[191] And, an oral agreement for the sale of real estate may be enforceable by a buyer who has paid the price, taken possession, and made improvements to the land.[192]

[1]   Contracts for Real Estate

Specific performance of a contract for the sale of real estate is sometimes available despite the absence of a writing, if the contract is partially performed.[193] The traditional rule requires the part performance to be "unequivocally referable

---

[186] *Id.* at 1183–84.

[187] *E.g.*, Marvin v. Wallis, 119 Eng. Rep. 1035 (Ch. 1856); Hugh Evander Willis, *The Statute of Frauds — A Legal Anachronism (Pt. 2)*, 3 IND. L.J. 528, 541 (1928); *but see* Karl Llewellyn, *What Price Contract? — An Essay in Perspective*, 40 YALE L.J. 704, 747 (1931).

[188] *See* U.C.C. § 2-201 cmt. 7 (2012).

[189] *See, e.g.*, Consol'n Serv., Inc. v. Key Bank Nat'l Ass'n, 185 F.3d 817 (7th Cir. 1999) (Posner, J.).

[190] U.C.C. § 2-201(3)(c) (2012).

[191] RESTATEMENT (SECOND) OF CONTRACTS § 141(1) (1981).

[192] RESTATEMENT (SECOND) OF CONTRACTS § 129 (1981).

[193] Butcher v. Stapley, 23 Eng. Rep. 524 (Ch. 1685); Seavey v. Drake, 1882 N.H. LEXIS 86 (Dec. 1882).

to the contract."[194] To be "unequivocally referable to the contract, the part performance must demonstrate that it was related to the parties' agreement and not to some other transaction. As one court put it "part performance take[s] an alleged contract outside the statute only if [it] cannot be explained in the absence of a contract."[195] Curiously, even though part performance may be enough to warrant specific performance, it is not usually sufficient to permit an award of damages.[196] Thus, while part performance is recognized as sufficient in equity, it was never adopted in actions under the common law to obtain an award of damages.[197]

Specific performance must also be necessary to prevent injustice. Where the buyer has make payment, taken possession, and made improvements to the land, this requirement is usually satisfied and the contract may be enforced, despite the absence of a writing.[198] Where the buyer's performance is less extensive, the statute is not satisfied.

The decision in *Burns v. McCormick*[199] is typical of cases decided in the late nineteenth- and early twentieth-century cases where part performance was insufficient to take an agreement outside of the statute of frauds. The promisor, a widower living on his own, told the plaintiffs that if they moved into his house and took care of him, his home would be theirs when he died. The plaintiffs acted on this promise: they sold their small business, moved in with him, and cared for him until his death. But when the widower died, they discovered that he had taken no action to ensure that they would become owners of his house. There was no written evidence of the promise, and the promisor was deceased. In refusing to enforce the alleged agreement, Justice Cardozo explained that there was nothing about the plaintiff's performance that demonstrated that the widower had made a promise to supply them with any more than the room and board he provided them prior to his death. For part performance to provide a substitute for a writing, "what is done must itself supply the key to what is promised."[200] In Cardozo's view, there was nothing done that made the plaintiff's actions "unequivocally referable to a contract for the sale of land."[201] Despite Cardozo's influence, other decisions, involving similar facts, yielded different though not universally consistent results.[202] In more conventional transactions, where the buyer pays the price and takes possession of the land, the statute is likely to be satisfied.[203]

---

[194] Burns v. McCormick, 135 N.E. 273, 273 (N.Y. 1922); Nicolaides v. Nicolaides, 173 A.D.2d 448 (N.Y. App. Div. 1991); Schwedes v. Romain, 587 P.2d 388, 391 (Mont. 1978).

[195] Owens v. M.E. Schepp, Ltd., 182 P.3d 664, 668 (Ariz. 2008).

[196] *E.g.*, Brassfield v. Allwood, 557 S.W.2d 674, 679 (Mo. Ct. App. 1977). *See also* Collier v. Brooks, 632 So. 2d 149, 155–56 (Fla. Dist. Ct. App. 1994) (contract lasting more than a year).

[197] RESTATEMENT (SECOND) OF CONTRACTS § 129 cmt. c (1981).

[198] *See* Bank of Alton v. Tanaka, 799 P.2d 1029 (Kan. 1990).

[199] 135 N.E. 273 (N.Y. 1922).

[200] *Id.*

[201] *Id.* at 274.

[202] RESTATEMENT (SECOND) OF CONTRACTS § 129 cmt. d & illus. 10 (1981). Tess v. Radley, 107 N.E.2d 677 (Ill. 1952).

[203] *E.g.*, Darby v. Johnson, 477 So. 2d 322 (Ala. 1985).

As indicated above, where the buyer pays the price, takes possession, and makes valuable improvements, specific performance is virtually assured.[204] Some cases permit enforcement where the buyer takes possession and makes improvements, even though he has not paid the price, and even though neither taking possession nor making improvements constituted "performance."[205] Even here, however, possession must be exclusive, and the improvements must not consist of the type of routine repairs a mere tenant would be expected to make.[206]

The buyer's payment of only part of the price is not enough to satisfy the statute.[207] However, the aggrieved buyer is undoubtedly entitled to restitution of the amount he or she has paid, even without other tangible evidence of the contract.[208] In *Cain v. Cross*,[209] there was an alleged oral agreement for the purchase of 806 acres of land for a price of $806,000. The buyer had paid $10,000 down and claimed that the agreement was for payment of $400,000 on delivery of possession, with the balance due at a later time. The court refused to enforce the contract in the absence of either possession or improvements.[210]

Not surprisingly, mere possession of the land combined with payment of what might be nothing more than rent is insufficient to satisfy the statute in favor of a tenant on the land, who alleges that there was a contract for sale.[211] After all, a tenant would normally be expected to have possession and to have paid some rent. Thus, these two factors do nothing to prove that the parties had also made an agreement for the tenant's purchase of the property or, for that matter, to prove the duration of the lease.

Actions taken in preparation for performance, even if in alleged reliance on the contract, are not usually sufficient to satisfy the statute. For example, in *Schwedes v. Romain*, the buyer's action in obtaining financing and offering to pay the price were not enough.[212] These preliminary actions did not constitute part performance. They were mere preparations to perform and not unequivocally referable to the contract. They were not sufficient to demonstrate which land was involved in the deal, and did nothing to prove that the seller had agreed to deliver title.

---

[204] *E.g.*, Vasichek v. Thorsen, 271 N.W.2d 555, 560 (N.D. 1978); Seavey v. Drake, 1882 N.H. LEXIS 86 (Dec. 1882). *See* Restatement (Second) of Contracts § 129 illus. 3 (1981).

[205] David G. Epstein et al., *Reliance on Oral Promises: Statute of Frauds and "Promissory Estoppel*," 42 Tex. Tech L. Rev. 913, 931 (2010).

[206] Kurland v. Stolker, 533 A.2d 1370 (Pa. 1987).

[207] Cain v. Cross, 687 N.E.2d 1141, 1144 (Ill. App. Ct. 1997); Crabill v. Marsh, 1882 Ohio LEXIS 161 (Jan. 1882).

[208] Restatement (Second) of Contracts § 129 illus. 1 (1981). *E.g.*, Pugh v. Gilbreath, 571 P.2d 1241 (Okla. Civ. App. 1977).

[209] 687 N.E.2d 1141 (Ill. App. Ct. 1997).

[210] *Id.*

[211] *See, e.g.*, Gleason v. Gleason, 582 N.E.2d 657 (Ohio Ct. App. 1991); Sutton v. Warner, 12 Cal. App. 4th 415 (1993).

[212] 587 P.2d 388 (Mont. 1978).

[2]   Contracts Not to Be Performed Within a Year

Contracts not to be performed within a year of their making are enforceable by a party who has fully performed.[213] However, some courts permit enforcement in the absence of a writing only if performance occurred before the end of a year.[214] Other courts refuse to enforce the contract, but permit the party who has performed to recover in restitution for the value of any benefit conferred by the part performance.[215] In cases awarding restitution the value of the benefit conferred is frequently similar to the agreed compensation. Sometimes this makes it difficult to tell whether the court is awarding restitution or if it is really enforcing the contract under the guise of providing restitution.[216]

On the other hand, mere partial performance is too equivocal to remove the contract from the statute of frauds.[217] This is particularly true in employment contracts. If Grand Grocery hires Stan to work as a manager, he is likely to show up each day. His presence at the store, for a day, a week, or a month, provides no proof at all that he is anything other than an "employee at will." Stan's service for 10 months provide no proof at all that he was hired for a two-year term.

In *Stearns v. Emery-Waterhouse Co.*,[218] the court vacated a judgment based on an oral promise of long-term employment, even though the plaintiff had given up his job elsewhere and moved to the defendant's location, in reliance on the employer's promise.[219] An employee might leave her job to accept another one involving a promise of employment at will. The mere fact that she has left an existing job does not prove that the new job involved a promise of a definite term of employment.[220] Some courts, on the other hand, have regarded such actions as sufficient to give the employee the opportunity to press her claim of a long-term contract to a jury. For example, in *McIntosh v. Murphy*,[221] the plaintiff sold all of his possessions, left his home in Los Angeles, and moved 2,200 miles to Honolulu to begin employment as the defendant's sales manager, in reliance on the defendant's oral promise of long-term employment. *McIntosh* is, however, unusual. Few cases permit promissory estoppel to be used in this context to satisfy the statute.[222]

Despite this result, part performance is always sufficient to permit the employee

---

[213] RESTATEMENT (SECOND) OF CONTRACTS § 130(2) (1981). *E.g.*, Trimmer v. Short, 492 S.W.2d 179 (Mo. Ct. App. 1973).

[214] *E.g.*, McIntire v. Woodall, 666 A.2d 934 (N.H. 1995); Perlmuter Printing Co. v. Strome, Inc., 436 F. Supp. 409 (N.D. Ohio 1976). *Cf.* RESTATEMENT (SECOND) OF CONTRACTS § 130 cmt. d (1981).

[215] *E.g.*, Meyers v. Waverly Fabrics, 479 N.E.2d 236 (N.Y. 1985); Montgomery v. Futuristic Foods, 66 A.D.2d 64 (N.Y. App. Div. 1978); 4 CAROLINE N. BROWN, CORBIN ON Contracts § 19.15 (Rev. ed. 1997).

[216] *See* Forrer v. Sears Roebuck & Co., 153 N.W.2d 587 (Wis. 1967).

[217] RESTATEMENT (SECOND) OF CONTRACTS § 130 cmt. e (1981); Coca-Cola Co. v. Babyback's Intern., Inc., 841 N.E.2d 557 (Ind. 2006).

[218] 596 A.2d 72 (1991).

[219] *See also* Pollmann v. Belle Plaine Livestock, 567 N.W.2d 405 (Iowa 1997).

[220] *See* Goldstick v. ICM Realty, 788 F.2d 456, 465 (7th Cir. 1986) (recognizing the equivocal nature of part performance of an employment contract).

[221] 469 P.2d 177 (Haw. 1970).

[222] *See also* Coca-Cola Co. v. Babyback's Int'l Inc., 841 N.E.2d 557 (Ind. 2006).

to receive compensation for the work he actually performed. But, this is recovery in restitution, for the value of the benefit he or she conferred, and does not depend on whether the promise of future employment is enforceable. The unperformed or "executory" portion of the contract is not enforceable.

In cases involving part performance, the most difficult question is the effect that the agreed price will have on the plaintiff's right to restitution. An injured provider of services is entitled to recover restitution for the part performance it supplied before the other party's repudiation. If the provider has substantially performed, its recovery is limited to the contract price.[223] But, if it has not yet substantially performed, it may recover for the full value of its work, even though this might put it in a better position than it would have been in if the contract had been performed.[224] In this situation, the contract price is not a limit on the amount it may recover.[225]

Consider a construction contract in which Winkler Builders agrees to build a new major addition to Julie's home, for a price of $100,000, with construction required to occur over an 18-month period. Assume that Winkler spends $80,000 completing only two-thirds of the work in just over a year, before Julie repudiates the deal. If the contract were enforceable, Winkler would be entitled to recover for the full value of its part performance, even though it would have cost an additional $40,000 to finish the job, resulting in a net $20,000 loss.[226] If the contract were not in writing, it would seem odd to use the contract price as a limit on Winkler's right to recover restitution, when the full value of its part performance, unrestrained by the contract price, would have been available had the contract been enforceable.

On the other hand, because the purpose of the statute of frauds is to protect the defendant from fraudulent claims, permitting recovery in restitution beyond the amount alleged to have been promised merely exacerbates any fraud that the plaintiff's performance might have accomplished if restitution is awarded.[227] Thus, some courts have limited the right of restitution in this setting to a pro rata portion of the agreed price.

[B]   Equitable and Promissory Estoppel[228]

Most action taken in reliance on an oral agreement consists of partial performance of the promise. But, parties sometimes rely on the agreement in ways that do not rise to the level of part performance. Reliance that is not partial performance and does not confer a benefit on the defendant, presents more difficult issues. A person's silent acquiescence in the receipt of a valuable performance from the other party provides persuasive evidence that the plaintiff's

---

[223] RESTATEMENT (SECOND) OF CONTRACTS § 373(2) & cmt. b (1981).

[224] RESTATEMENT (SECOND) OF CONTRACTS § 373(1) (1981).

[225] *See infra* § 13.05[A] Loss Contracts — Expectation as a Limit on Restitution.

[226] *See* United States v. Algernon Blair, Inc., 479 F.2d 638 (4th Cir. 1973).

[227] GEORGE E. PALMER, 2 LAW OF RESTITUTION § 6.11 (1978).

[228] *See generally* David G. Epstein et al., *Reliance on Oral Promises: Statute of Frauds and "Promissory Estoppel,"* 42 Tex. TECH L. REV. 913 (2010).

claim rests upon a real transaction — mere preparations for performance are far less probative that a deal was really made. Moreover, mere preparations do nothing to fulfill the cautionary functions of the statute and assist only marginally in serving its channeling functions. Therefore, courts have been mixed in their willingness to permit the use of promissory estoppel as a means of satisfying the statute of frauds. Some courts have recognized the dual doctrines of equitable estoppel and promissory estoppel as means of satisfying the statute. But, the use of promissory estoppel, remains controversial, particularly where the promisee's reliance does not rise to the level of part performance that is unequivocally referable to the alleged agreement.

Equitable estoppel or "estoppel in pais" is the older of the two doctrines. It protects someone who relies on a misrepresentation of fact.[229] Equitable estoppel can be used to satisfy the statute of frauds only when the defendant has made a false representation relating to the necessity or existence of a writing that would satisfy the statute.[230] Thus, equitable estoppel takes the contract out of the statute of frauds where the defendant has falsely represented that there was no need to put their agreement in writing,[231] that the defendant would supply a sufficient writing, or that a writing sufficient to satisfy the statute had already been signed.[232] These are narrow circumstances that do not extend to claims of reliance on a defendant's *promise* to perform.

Breach of a promise does not usually involve a misrepresentation of fact. Many decisions refuse to apply promissory estoppel to satisfy the statute of frauds.[233] This refusal extends from a concern that enforcement will erode the purposes of the statute, and may actually encourage reliance on unwritten agreements. Other cases permit it to be used only where restitution, for the value of the benefit conferred as a result of the promisee's reliance, was either difficult to measure or otherwise inadequate to prevent injustice to the promisee.[234]

The California Supreme Court's decision in *Monarco v. Lo Greco*[235] supplies a good example. Monarco enforced a promise made by the plaintiff's parents that they would leave their estate to her if she remained with them in their home. She relied, living with her parents, working on their farm, and caring for them, for 20

---

[229] *See* Zitelli v. Dermatology Educ. and Res. Found., 633 A.2d 134 (Pa. 1993); East Providence Credit Union v. Geremia, 239 A.2d 725 (R.I. 1968); 3 Eric Mills Holmes, Corbin on Contracts § 8.7 (Rev. ed. 1996).

[230] *See, e.g.,* Bank of Am. v. Pac. Ready-Cut Homes, Inc., 122 Cal. App. 554, 562 (1932); Fiers v. Jacobson, 211 P.2d 968, 972–73 (Mont. 1949). *See generally supra* § 3.02[A] Equitable Estoppel.

[231] Michael B. Metzger, *The Parol Evidence Rule: Promissory Estoppel's Next Conquest*, 36 Vand. L. Rev. 1383, 1425–38 (1983). *See* Federick Innes Fox, Note, *Equitable Estoppel and the Statute of Frauds in California*, 53 Cal. L. Rev. 590, 601 (1965).

[232] Restatement (Second) of Contracts § 139 cmt. b (1981). *See also* Restatement of Contracts § 178 cmt. f (1932); Moore Burger, Inc. v. Phillips Petroleum Co., 492 S.W.2d 934 (Tex. 1972).

[233] *See, e.g.,* Adams v. Petrade Int'l., Inc., 754 S.W.2d 696, 707 (Tex. App. 1988). *E.g.,* Boone v. Coe, 154 S.W. 900 (Ky. Ct. App. 1913). *See generally* Robert A. Brazener, Annotation, *Promissory Estoppel as Basis for Avoidance of Statute of Frauds*, 56 A.L.R.3d 1037 (1974 & Supp. 1991).

[234] *See, e.g.,* Monarco v. Lo Greco, 220 P.2d 737 (Cal. 1950) (promise to leave the family home to a child who returned home and cared for his mother and stepfather for many years).

[235] 220 P.2d 737 (Cal. 1950).

years. The court recognized that its earlier decisions,[236] though purportedly based on equitable estoppel, were really based more on the unconscionable injury that would result from failure to compensate the plaintiffs for the benefits they had conferred than from any real reliance on a misrepresentation about the sufficiency or necessity of a writing.[237] Denying the plaintiff relief would result in the same kind of injustice, even though her parents had made no factual misrepresentation but had just broken their promise. Cases like *Monarco* led away from the distinction between reliance on a misrepresentation of fact and reliance on a promise that had characterized the earlier equitable estoppel decisions. However, these cases still depended on the unjust enrichment of the promisor who had received a benefit as a result of the promisee's reliance.

Later decisions, like the one in *Miller v. Lawlor*,[238] permitted promissory estoppel to be used in the absence of either a misrepresentation or the promisor's receipt of a discernible benefit. In *Miller*, the defendant promised not to build any structure on a particular portion of his land, which adjoined property the plaintiff was interested in acquiring. In reliance on this promise, the plaintiff bought the property and built a residence with a view across the defendant's land. When the defendant proposed to construct a residence obscuring the plaintiff's view, the plaintiff obtained an injunction prohibiting the project from being completed. Although no benefit had been conferred on the defendant, the plaintiff's reasonable and foreseeable reliance on the defendant's promise was enough to satisfy the statute and permit the plaintiff to attempt to persuade the jury that the promise had been made.

By the second half of the twentieth century, scholarly discussion[239] and the promulgation of § 139 of Second Restatement of Contracts, established promissory estoppel as a credible means of satisfying the statute of frauds. Section 139 specifies: "A promise which the promisor should reasonably expect to induce action or forbearance on the part of the promisee or a third person and which does induce the action or forbearance is enforceable notwithstanding the Statute of Frauds if injustice can be avoided only by enforcement of the promise. The remedy granted for breach is to be limited as justice requires."[240]

This language closely adheres to Restatement (Second) § 90, which makes promises enforceable due to promissory estoppel when consideration is missing.[241] However, § 139 recognizes that enforcement of the contract should be limited to

---

[236] *See, e.g.,* Seymour v. Oelrichs, 106 P. 88 (Cal. 1909).

[237] *Monarco,* 220 P.2d at 740–41.

[238] 66 N.W.2d 267 (Iowa 1954). *See generally* Michael B. Metzger, *The Parol Evidence Rule: Promissory Estoppel's Next Conquest?,* 36 VAND. L. REV. 1383, 1422–37 (1983).

[239] Carolyn M. Edwards, *The Statute of Frauds of the Uniform Commercial Code and the Doctrine of Estoppel,* 62 MARQ. L. REV. 205, 222–24 (1978); W.S. McNeill, *Agreements to Reduce to Writing Contracts Within the Statute of Frauds,* 15 VA. L. REV. 553 (1931); Jeffrey G. Steinberg, Note, *Promissory Estoppel as a Means of Defeating the Statute of Frauds,* 44 FORDHAM L. REV. 114 (1975); Lionel Morgan Summers, *The Doctrine of Estoppel Applied to the Statute of Frauds,* 79 U. PA. L. REV. 440 (1931).

[240] RESTATEMENT (SECOND) OF CONTRACTS § 139(1) (1981).

[241] RESTATEMENT (SECOND) OF CONTRACTS § 90 (1981). *See supra* § 3.03 A Consideration Substitute.

circumstances such as the inadequacy of other remedies; the degree, reasonableness and foreseeability of the promisee's reliance; and the corroborative character of the promisee's reliance, which makes enforcement necessary to avoid injustice.[242]

Consistent with these limitations, courts are sometimes reluctant to use promissory estoppel to satisfy the statute of frauds.[243] Although promissory estoppel seems to serve as an adequate hedge against the risk of completely fabricated claims that a contract was made, it does little to advance the cautionary and channeling functions long associated with the statute of frauds.[244]

The advent of § 2-201 of the Uniform Commercial Code has in some respects enhanced the use of promissory estoppel as an exception to the statute. In other respects it has confined it. Section 2-201 supplies an exception for goods to be specially manufactured for the buyer where the seller has relied by either making a substantial beginning in the manufacture of the goods or by making commitments for their procurement,[245] which seems to rest on a principle of reasonable foreseeable reliance similar to that recognized by § 139 of the Second Restatement.[246] However, the narrow scope of the "special manufacture" exception has sometimes been used to confine promissory estoppel as a general exception to the statute of frauds, on the grounds that the text of U.C.C. § 2-201 expressly limits exceptions to the statute to those contained in its text.[247] Thus, the Code's express adoption of an additional exception to the statute has operated to restrict the availability of other unarticulated common law exceptions. The proposed revisions to Article 2 open the door further to the development of promissory estoppel as a further exception to the statute by eliminating the prefatory phrase "except as otherwise provided in this section."[248]

§ 5.06 SALE OF GOODS

Article 2 of the Uniform Commercial Code contains its own statute of frauds.[249] U.C.C. § 2-201 differs from the traditional statute of frauds, both with respect to the nature of the writing required to satisfy the statute, and with respect to the exceptions it provides. It goes a long way toward minimizing the potential for fraudulent use of the statute by parties who might otherwise seek to avoid a

---

[242] RESTATEMENT (SECOND) OF CONTRACTS § 139 (1981).

[243] See Phuong N. Phan, Note, The Waning of Promissory Estoppel, 79 CORNELL L. REV. 1263, 1277 (1994).

[244] See Michael B. Metzger, The Parol Evidence Rule: Promissory Estoppel's Next Conquest?, 36 VAND. L. REV. 1383, 1432–34 (1983).

[245] U.C.C. § 2-201(3)(a) (2012). See infra § 5.06[D] Specially Manufactured Goods.

[246] RESTATEMENT (SECOND) OF CONTRACTS § 139 (1981).

[247] See infra § 5.06[G] Nonstatutory Exceptions.

[248] Revised U.C.C. § 2-201 cmt. 2 (2003). See Linda J. Rusch, Is the Saga of the Uniform Commercial Code Article 2 Revisions Over? A Brief Look at What NCCUSL Finally Approved, 6 DEL. L. REV. 41, 54–55 (2003).

[249] In international sales, governed by the CISG, the agreement need not be in writing. See supra § 5.03[G] Statute of Frauds in International Transactions.

contract despite other facts clearly demonstrating that a contract has been formed.[250]

The basic rule is that "a contract for the sale of goods for the price of $500 or more is not enforceable . . . unless there is some writing sufficient to indicate that a contract for sale has been made between the parties and signed by the party against whom enforcement is sought."[251]

[A]   Price of $500 or More

The statute applies to any contract for the sale of goods with a price of $500 or more.[252] Despite the clear language of the statute, law students persist in referring to the rule as applying to contracts with a price of "over $500." They also make the frequent mistake of believing that the statute applies to any contract with a price of $500 or more, rather than just contracts for the sale of goods.

As with other agreements outside the scope of the statute of frauds, no writing is necessary if the price for the goods is below this threshold.[253] Thus, even though the value of the goods may be thousands of dollars, if the agreed *price* is only $499 the statute does not apply.

In an output contract there is a remote possibility that the seller will not produce a quantity sufficient to raise the price to the $500 threshold. Likewise, there is a finite chance that the buyer's good-faith requirements will leave the price below this margin. However, where the seller's good-faith output or the buyer's good-faith requirements would result in the price falling over the statutory threshold, a writing is required. This is consistent with cases ruling that the statute must be satisfied, even though one of the party's enjoys the right to terminate the contract, in a way that would leave it outside the statute of frauds.

[B]   Writing Signed by the Party Resisting Enforcement

Article 2 requires a writing signed by the party against whom enforcement is sought, which shows that a contract for sale has been made between the parties. Most of the difficulties deal with the contents of the writing rather than its form.

[1]   Writing

The U.C.C. statute of frauds requires written evidence of the contract, which raises the initial question of what qualifies as a "writing." U.C.C. § 1-201(b)(43) defines "written" or "writing" to include any kind of "printing, typewriting, or any

---

[250] *See* U.C.C. § 2-201 cmt. 7 (2012) ("no longer possible to admit the contract in court and still treat the Statute as a defense").

[251] U.C.C. § 2-201(1) (2012).

[252] *Id.*

[253] Recent proposed revisions to Article 2 would have raised the threshold to $5,000. Revised U.C.C. § 2-201(a) (2003). However, these revisions have been abandoned by the Uniform Law Commission and are unlikely to be adopted anywhere. Section 2A-201, governing contracts for the lease of goods, is substantially similar, but with a $1,000 threshold. U.C.C. § 2A-201 (2012).

other intentional reduction to tangible form."[254] While a tape recording might satisfy the requirement of a writing, it has proven difficult to satisfy the further requirement of a "signature" on this type of tangible record.[255]

The modern use of electronic media has raised further questions about what constitutes a writing. The Uniform Electronic Transactions Act (UETA)[256] and the Electronic Signatures in Global and National Commerce Act (E-Sign)[257] solve this problem by making electronic records and signatures equally as effective as their traditional counterparts.[258]

[2]   Sufficient to Show a Contract

Under § 2-201 the required writing need not contain all of the terms of the contract, or even all of its essential terms. Nothing is required regarding price, quality, or the time or place for performance.[259] However, the writing must at least "indicate that a contract for sale has been made between the parties."[260] Moreover, the contract must contain a quantity term; the agreement is not enforceable beyond the quantity expressed in the writing.[261]

The language of § 2-201 suggests that a writing containing an offer is insufficient, as it does not demonstrate that there was ever an agreement to the terms proposed in the offer, and many courts have interpreted the language this way.[262] Other courts have been influenced by the liberal language contained in the Official Comments to § 2-201, indicating that "[a]ll that is required is that the writing afford a basis for believing that the offered oral evidence rests on a real transaction"[263] and have permitted the statute to be satisfied with anything showing that the transaction was more than a figment of the plaintiff's imagination.[264] Decisions reaching this result are true to the liberalizing purpose of § 2-201,[265] without abandoning its evidentiary and cautionary purposes.

---

[254] U.C.C. § 1-201(b)(43) (2012).

[255] Swink & Co., Inc. v. Carroll McEntee & McGinley, Inc., 584 S.W.2d 393 (Ark. 1979).

[256] 7A U.L.A. 225 (1999)

[257] 15 U.S.C. §§ 7001–7006 (2006).

[258] See generally infra § 5.08 Electronic Contracting.

[259] U.C.C. § 2-201 cmt. 1 (2012).

[260] U.C.C. § 2-201(1) (2012).

[261] Id.

[262] E.g., Howard Constr. Co. v. Jeff-Cole Quarries, Inc., 669 S.W.2d 221 (Mo. Ct. App. 1983) (collecting cases).

[263] U.C.C. § 2-201 cmt. 1 (2012).

[264] E.g., Sw. Eng'g Co., Inc. v. Martin Tractor Co., Inc., 473 P.2d 18 (Kan. 1970) (signed price list sufficient).

[265] See generally Monetti, S.P.A. v. Anchor Hocking Corp., 931 F.2d 1178, 1183 (7th Cir. 1991) (Posner, J.).

[3]   Quantity Term

The second sentence of § 2-201(1) indicates that the agreement "is not enforceable . . . beyond the quantity of goods shown in such writing." Most courts applying § 2-201 have interpreted this to mean that in order for a writing to satisfy the statute, it must include a quantity term.[266] This conclusion is supported by the Official Comment to § 2-201, which specifies that the writing "must specify a quantity."[267]

Despite this, a careful and strict reading of § 2-201(1)'s text reveals that it does not require the writing to contain a quantity term.[268] It merely specifies that if the writing used to satisfy the statute includes a quantity term, the contract may not be enforced beyond the quantity included in that writing. In this respect, § 2-201(1) really operates more like the parol evidence rule, and makes any quantity term included in the writing the exclusive evidence of the quantity of goods involved.[269] Nevertheless, most courts routinely apply § 2-201(1) to require the signed writing to include a quantity term.

This insistence is mitigated by courts' liberal approach to what qualifies as a quantity term. For example, in *Upsher-Smith Laboratories, Inc. v. Mylan Laboratories, Inc.*,[270] the court found that a reference to "reasonable quantities" was sufficient. And in *Great Northern Packaging, Inc. v. General Tire & Rubber Co.*,[271] a "blanket order" could be supplemented with parol evidence without violating the statute.

Likewise, a signed writing specifying that the seller will provide all of the buyer's "requirements" or requiring the seller to deliver his or her "output" will usually satisfy the statute.[272] In addition, some courts have been generous in implying the existence of a requirements or output contract from other terms in the writing, such as where the agreement specified that it was a dealership contract for which there was a usage of trade to supply all of the buyer's requirements.[273] Other courts have been less generous, refusing to enforce a contract, even though the writing pointed clearly toward the seller's obligation to deliver all of the buyer's requirements for a specific project.[274] However,

---

[266] *E.g.*, Simmons Foods, Inc. v. Hill's Pet Nutrition, Inc., 270 F.3d 723, 727 (8th Cir. 2001).

[267] U.C.C. § 2-201 cmt. 1 (2012).

[268] JAMES J. WHITE & ROBERT S. SUMMERS, UNIFORM COMMERCIAL CODE 97 n.12 (6th ed. 2010).

[269] Caroline N. Bruckel, *The Weed and the Web: Section 2-201's Corruption of the U.C.C.'s Substantive Provisions — The Quantity Problem*, 1983 U. ILL. L. REV. 811, 816–18. *See also* JAMES J. WHITE & ROBERT S. SUMMERS, 1 UNIFORM COMMERCIAL CODE § 2-4 n.11 (5th ed. 2000); Advent Systems Ltd. v. Unisys Corp., 925 F.2d 670 (3d Cir. 1991) (dictum).

[270] 944 F. Supp. 1411, 1427 n.5 (D. Minn. 1996).

[271] 399 N.W.2d 408 (Mich. Ct. App. 1986).

[272] Brewster Wallcovering Co. v. Blue Mtn. Wallcoverings, Inc., 864 N.E.2d 518 (Mass. Ct. App. 2007); Zemco Mfg., Inc. v. Navistar Int'l Transp. Corp., 186 F.3d 815 (7th Cir. 1999).

[273] *E.g.*, Seaman's Direct Buying Serv., Inc. v. Std. Oil Co., 686 P.2d 1158 (Cal. 1984), *overruled on other grounds*, Freeman & Mills, Inc. v. Belcher Oil Co., 900 P.2d 669 (Cal. 1995).

[274] Cox Caulking & Insulating Co. v. Brockett Distrib. Co., 258 S.E.2d 51 (Ga. Ct. App. 1979). *But see* Port City Const. Co., Inc. v. Henderson, 266 So. 2d 896 (Ala. Civ. App. 1972).

requirements and output contracts should not be unenforceable, due to the absence of a sufficient writing, where there is sufficient documentation to show that there was an agreement to supply all of the buyer's requirements or to deliver all of the seller's output.[275] Parol evidence can then be used to satisfy the demands of U.C.C. § 2-306 for determining the relevant quantities involved and provide a basis for an appropriate remedy.[276]

[4] Signature

[a] Party Against Whom Enforcement Is Sought

Section 2-201(1) requires that the writing be "signed by the party against whom enforcement is sought or by his authorized agent or broker."[277] The key part of this language is the requirement of a signature by the party *against whom enforcement is sought*. The signature of the party seeking to enforce the contract is not required. The writing needs only to contain the signature of the party who is resisting enforcement. This is consistent with more traditional versions of the statute of frauds, which require a signature "by or on behalf of the party to be charged."[278]

For example, if representatives of Industrial Supply and Franklin Manufacturing agree over the phone for Industrial Supply to deliver a piece of equipment to Franklin, and Franklin subsequently attempts to back out of the deal, it will be necessary to produce a writing signed by Franklin. There is no need for Industrial, as the party seeking enforcement of the contract, to have signed the document. Accordingly, Franklin's internal documents may satisfy the statute, even though the documents were neither signed by Industrial nor perhaps even seen by anyone at Industrial Supply.

[b] Party or Its Agent

A signature by the defendant or its agent is sufficient. In the case of a corporation, a sufficient writing will necessarily have been signed by a corporate agent, such as an officer, purchasing agent, or other authorized employee. Further, nothing requires the agent's authority to be in writing.[279]

---

[275] *See supra* § 4.11[B][4] Quantity.

[276] *See* U.C.C. § 2-306 (2012).

[277] U.C.C. § 2-201(1) (2012).

[278] RESTATEMENT (SECOND) OF CONTRACTS § 131 (1981).

[279] *E.g.*, Romani v. Harris, 258 A.2d 187 (Md. 1969). *But see* Comm'n on Ecumenical Mission and Relations of United Presbyterian Church in United States of Am. v. Roger Gray, Ltd., 267 N.E.2d 467 (N.Y. 1971) (agent's authority required to be in writing in connection with contract for transfer of interest in real estate).

[c]   Any Symbol

According to U.C.C. § 1-201(39) a writing is "signed" if it "includes any symbol executed or adopted by a party with present intention to adopt or accept [the] writing."[280] The signature requirement may be satisfied in a variety of ways, including the use of initials, a typewritten name, letterhead stationery, or tape recordings.[281] In *Donovan v. RRL Corp.*,[282] the court even permitted the defendant's advertising brochure containing the seller's name to operate as the necessary signature.

[C]   Confirmatory Memorandum in Transactions Between Merchants[283]

Section 2-201(2) specifies a method of satisfying the statute that is unique to transactions involving goods. Under the "confirmatory memorandum" exception the statute may be satisfied against a merchant who *received* a signed writing, even if he or she has not signed it. Section 2-201(2) provides:

> Between merchants if within a reasonable time a writing in confirmation of the contract and sufficient against the sender is received and the party receiving it has reason to know its contents, it satisfies the requirements of subsection (1) against such party unless written notice of objection to its contents is given within 10 days after it is received.[284]

Thus, if a merchant buyer and a merchant seller[285] conclude a sale over the telephone and the seller sends the buyer a signed writing confirming the sale, the statute is satisfied against the buyer even though he did not sign it. The statute is satisfied in an action against the buyer so long as:

- the seller's writing confirming the contract was sufficient to satisfy the statute in an action against the seller

- the writing was received by the buyer within a reasonable time,[286] and

- the buyer had reason to know the contents of the writing.

- the buyer did not give the seller written notice objecting to the contents of

---

[280] U.C.C. § 1-201(b)(37) (2012) (formerly § 1-201(39)).

[281] Ellis Canning Co. v. Bernstein, 348 F. Supp. 1212, 1228 (D. Colo. 1972).

[282] 27 P.3d 702 (Cal. 2001) (where statute made it illegal to refuse to sell available goods at advertised price).

[283] Randy R. Koenders, Annotation, *Sales: Construction of Statute of Frauds Exception Under UCC § 2-201(2) for Confirmatory Writing Between Merchants*, 82 A.L.R.4th 709 (1990 & Supp. 1994); Charles D. Onafry, Comment, *The Merchant's Exception to the Uniform Commercial Code's Statute of Frauds*, 32 Vill. L. Rev. 133 (1987).

[284] U.C.C. § 2-201(2) (2012). There is no similar provision in Article 2A, with respect to leases of goods. U.C.C. § 2A-201 cmt. (2012).

[285] U.C.C. § 2-104 cmt. 2 (2012).

[286] *See* St. Ansgar Mills, Inc. v. Streit, 613 N.W.2d 289 (Iowa 2000) (reversing trial court's determination, on motion for summary judgment, that confirmation had been sent and received beyond a reasonable time).

the confirmation within 10 days of his receipt of it.

Likewise, if the buyer follows up the phone call by sending a sufficient writing to the seller, and the seller fails to object, the contract is enforceable against the seller, even though the seller did not sign anything.

GPL Treatment, Ltd. v. Louisiana-Pacific Corp.[287] supplies a good example of the operation of the confirmatory memorandum exception. The parties entered into an oral agreement for the purchase and sale of a large quantity of cedar shake shingles.[288] As required by § 2-201(2), both parties were merchants. The seller sent a signed confirmation of the oral agreement to the buyer, who received it promptly. The confirmation requested the buyer to sign it and return it to the seller. The buyer failed to comply with the seller's request, but did nothing to object to the contents of the confirmation. When the market value of cedar shingles declined, the buyer tried to escape from the deal. Because both parties were merchants and the writing sent by the seller would have been sufficient to satisfy the statute of frauds in an action against the seller, the court ruled that the statute was also satisfied as against the buyer, even though there was nothing containing the buyer's signature. The buyer had failed to send a written objection within 10 days of its receipt of the seller's signed confirmation.[289]

[1]   Confirmation

Under § 2-201(2) it is necessary for the writing to have been sent "in confirmation" of the contract and not merely to initiate negotiations that might lead to formation of a contract.[290] Thus, a purchase order sent as the initial offer to enter into a contract has been held insufficient to satisfy the statute against the recipient.[291] Likewise, writings confirming the details of contract negotiations held up to that point are not sufficient.[292]

Further, although the written confirmation must have been received within a *reasonable time*, any written objection to its contents must be sent within 10 days of the confirmation's receipt. Thus, the statute provides considerable flexibility with respect to the sending of the confirmation, but imposes a strict 10-day standard for dispatch of an objection sent by the recipient.

It must be emphasized again, however, that satisfaction of the statute does not prove the existence of a contract. The aggrieved party still must prove the critical element of mutual assent.

---

[287] 914 P.2d 682 (Or. 1996).

[288] Say "cedar shake shingles" quickly three times in a row.

[289] GPL Treatment, Ltd. v. Louisiana-Pacific Corp., 914 P.2d 682 (Or. 1996). *Accord* Bazak Intern. v. Mast Indus., 535 N.E.2d 633 (N.Y. 1989). *But see* Kline Iron & Steel Co., Inc. v. Gray Comm'n. Consultant, Inc., 715 F. Supp. 135 (D.S.C. 1989) (request for signature and return indicated that contract had not yet been formed thus preventing confirmation from satisfying 2-201(2)).

[290] Cent. Ill. Light Co. v. Consol. Coal Co., 349 F.3d 488 (7th Cir. 2003).

[291] Audio Visual Assoc., Inc. v. Sharp Elec. Corp., 210 F.3d 254 (4th Cir. 2000).

[292] Pac. Inland Navigation, Inc. v. Ridel Int'l, Inc., 792 P.2d 443 (Or. Ct. App. 1990).

[2]   Between Merchants

The exception only applies to transactions "between merchants."[293] According to U.C.C. § 2-104, a transaction is between merchants if both parties to the transaction are chargeable with the knowledge or skill of merchants.[294] Thus, it applies only when both the seller and the buyer are merchants.

The definition of merchant includes: (1) a person who deals in goods of the kind; (2) a person who otherwise by his occupation holds himself out as having knowledge or skill peculiar to the practices or the goods involved in the transaction; or (3) a person to whom knowledge or skill peculiar to the practices or goods involved in the transaction may be attributed because of the person's utilization of an agent, broker, or other intermediary who by his occupation holds himself out as having such knowledge or skill.[295] The official comments to U.C.C. § 2-104 elaborate further and indicate that, for the purposes of the confirmatory memorandum provision of the statute of frauds, almost any person in business, who is or ought to be familiar with normal business practices, such as opening mail, is a merchant.[296] Thus, the confirmatory memorandum exception casts a potentially wide swath through the statute of frauds, at least with respect to transactions between businesses.

[3]   Sufficient Against the Sender

For a confirmation to be effective against the recipient, it must be "sufficient against the sender."[297] That is, the writing must contain the sender's signature, must "indicate that a contract for sale has been made between the parties,"[298] and must contain a quantity term. A memo that would not be sufficient to satisfy the statute of frauds in an action brought against the person who sent the memo is not adequate to satisfy the statute in an action against the person who received it.[299]

[4]   Receipt

For a confirmatory memorandum to satisfy the statute against the recipient, there must be proof that the writing was received. As a general matter, evidence that shows that a document was deposited in the mail with a correct address and proper postage raises a presumption that it was delivered to the specified address.

The code is unclear whether "receipt" also requires "receipt of notice" of the

---

[293] U.C.C. § 2-201(2) (2012).

[294] U.C.C. § 2-104(3) (2012). *See generally* Ingrid Michelsen Hillinger, *The Article 2 Merchant Rules: Karl Llewellyn's Attempt to Achieve the Good, the True, the Beautiful in Commercial Law*, 73 GEO. L.J. 1141 (1985).

[295] U.C.C. § 2-104(1) (2012).

[296] U.C.C. § 2-104 cmt. 2 (2012). *See* R.F. Cunningham & Co., Inc. v. Driscoll, 7 Misc. 3d 234 (N.Y. City Ct. 2005) (recognizing split of authority and treating farmer with 37 years of experience as a merchant for purposes of § 2-201(2)).

[297] U.C.C. § 2-201(2) (2012).

[298] U.C.C. § 2-201(1) (2012).

[299] Columbus Trade Exch., Inc. v. AMCA Int'l Corp., 763 F. Supp. 946 (S.D. Ohio 1991).

contents of the confirmation. When an individual receives a document, he or she has notice of its contents, even if he or she fails to open the envelope in which it was sent and read it. A person cannot avoid receiving notice by refusing to open the mail.

In the case of an organization, such as a corporation, a partnership, or some other business or charitable entity, the issue is more problematical. The mere fact that one person in the organization receives a notification does not mean that the organization has received the notice. U.C.C. § 1-201(27) specifies that notice received by an organization is effective "when it is brought to the attention of the individual conducting [the] transaction" to which the notice refers."[300] However, organizations are also required to exercise due diligence in processing their mail. Even if the person conducting the transaction never learns of the organization's receipt of the document, the organization is charged with notice "from the time it would have been brought to [that person's] attention if the organization had exercised due diligence."[301] Due diligence requires organizations to maintain reasonable mailroom procedures "for communicating significant information" to those responsible for conducting the transactions to which those communications refer.[302] The organization must also reasonably comply with its mailroom procedures. Organizations that fail to maintain reasonable mailroom procedures, or fail to follow their own policies, run the risk that they will be held responsible for having received notice of information in documents delivered to the organization, even though the information was never conveyed to anyone with any specific knowledge about the transaction.[303]

[5]   Reason to Know Contents

The confirmatory memorandum exception has one further qualification. The recipient must have "reason to know" the contents of the confirmatory memo. This supplies an extra measure of protection against the dishonest conduct of someone who may send a confirmation of a fictional transaction, when the parties have not yet concluded an oral agreement. When the confirmatory memo comes in the form of an e-mail message, it protects against spurious messages that might otherwise reasonably be regarded as "spam."[304]

[6]   Failure to Object

A confirmatory memorandum satisfies the statute against the recipient only if the recipient fails to object to the contents of the message within 10 days after receiving it.[305] To object, the recipient must send a response before the end of the

---

[300] U.C.C. § 1-201(27) (2012).

[301] *Id.*

[302] *Id.*

[303] *See* Thomson Printing Mach. Co. v. B.F. Goodrich Co., 714 F.2d 744 (7th Cir. 1983).

[304] Bazak Int'l Corp. v. Tarrant Apparel Group, 378 F. Supp. 2d 377 (S.D.N.Y. 2005).

[305] U.C.C. § 2-201(2) (2012).

10th day after receipt. Notice is given when sent, even if the other party never actually receives it.[306]

[D]   Specially Manufactured Goods[307]

U.C.C. section 2-201(3)(a) implements a part-performance exception to the statute of frauds for contracts for the sale of goods. In a contract for sale, no writing is required:

> [i]f the goods are to be specially manufactured for the buyer and are not suitable for sale to others in the ordinary course of the seller's business and the seller, before notice of repudiation is received and under circumstances which reasonably indicate that the goods are for the buyer, has made either a substantial beginning of their manufacture or commitments for their procurement.[308]

Section 2A-201(4)(a) provides a parallel exception for leases of goods.[309]

The special-manufacture exception presumes that a seller will not embark on the manufacture of goods that are not suitable for sale to others unless the seller has made a contract to sell them to the only buyer for whom they are suited. The seller must, of course, also establish that a contract existed; beginning the manufacture of specialized goods satisfies the statute of frauds but does not conclusively establish the existence of a contract for their sale.

The language of § 2-201(3)(a) establishes a four-part test to determine whether the special manufacture exception applies:

(1)   the contract must be for goods which will be specially made for the buyer;

(2)   it must be for goods which will be unsuitable for sale to others in the ordinary course of the seller's business;

(3)   the seller must have substantially begun to manufacture the goods or have made a commitment for their procurement; and

(4)   the manufacture or commitment must have been commenced under circumstances reasonably indicating that the goods are for the buyer and before the seller's receipt of notification of the buyer's repudiation.[310]

The key issues in analyzing § 2-201(3)(a) are whether the goods are "not suitable for sale to others in the ordinary course of the seller's business" and whether the "circumstances reasonably indicate that the goods are for the buyer." This test

---

[306]   *See* U.C.C. § 1-201(26) (2012).

[307]   Thomas R. Malia, Annotation, *Sales: "Specially Manufactured Goods" Statute of Frauds Exception in UCC § 2- 201(3)(a)*, 45 A.L.R.4th 1126 (1986).

[308]   U.C.C. § 2-201(3)(a) (2012).

[309]   U.C.C. § 2A-201 (2012).

[310]   Webcor Packaging Corp. v. AutoZone, Inc., 158 F.3d 354, 356 (6th Cir. 1998); Colo. Carpet Installation, Inc. v. Palermo, 668 P.2d 1384, 1389 (Colo. 1983).

focuses attention on the scope of the market for the goods.[311] Accordingly, where the market for the items is limited to the buyer in question, the exception will likely apply. Thus, contracts for goods bearing the buyer's logo,[312] or built to specifications supplied by the buyer,[313] need not be in writing if the other elements of the exception have been satisfied.

On the other hand, substantially beginning the manufacture of goods for which there is a broader market does not satisfy the statute. The statute is not satisfied in favor of a manufacturer of size-10 paper bags simply because it has ordered a sufficient quantity of brown paper or cut the paper to the size necessary for construction of the bags.[314] However, once the paper has been imprinted with the seller's name and logo, the goods are unsuitable for sale to others in the ordinary course, and the statute has been satisfied. Likewise, the statute has been satisfied if the seller has made arrangements with a third party for the preparation of the goods and sufficient work has been done to make them unsuitable for sale to others.[315]

Where a substantial beginning has been made on only some of the goods, and the rest remain suitable for sale to others, the authorities are in conflict regarding the extent of the enforceability of the contract. The better reasoned decisions hold that the entire contract is enforceable.[316] However, there is also authority for the view that the contract is enforceable only to the extent of the quantity on which a substantial beginning has been made.[317] In addition and more persuasive, are those cases ruling that the manufacture of nothing more than a prototype is insufficient to satisfy the statute.[318] Manufacture of a prototype, which may have been produced by the seller as a means of proving that it was capable of manufacturing the item in question, does nothing to show that the parties made a contract for more extensive production of the item.

[E] Goods Accepted or Payment Made

Part performance, in the form of payment for or acceptance of the goods, also satisfies the statute.[319] Thus, the statute is fulfilled with respect to goods for which payment has been made and accepted by the seller. Likewise, it has been satisfied

---

[311] *See, e.g.,* Impossible Elec. Techniques, Inc. v. Wackenhut Protective Sys., Inc., 669 F.2d 1026 (5th Cir. 1982).

[312] *E.g.,* Smith-Scharff Paper Co. v. P.N. Hirsch & Co. Stores, 754 S.W.2d 928 (Mo. Ct. App. 1988); Flowers Baking Co. of Lynchburg, v. R-P Packaging, Inc., 329 S.E.2d 462 (Va. 1985).

[313] *E.g.,* Kalas v. Cook, 800 A.2d 553 (Conn. App. Ct. 2002) (materials printed with buyer's name).

[314] *See* Colo. Carpet Installation, Inc. v. Palermo, 647 P.2d 686 (Colo. Ct. App. 1982).

[315] Nationwide Papers, Inc. v. Nw. Egg Sales, Inc., 416 P.2d 687 (Wash. 1966).

[316] *E.g.,* Perlmuter Printing Co. v. Strome, Inc., 436 F. Supp. 409 (N.D. Ohio 1976).

[317] *See* EMSG Sys. Div., Inc. v. Miltope Corp., 37 U.C.C. Rep. Serv. 2d 39 (E.D.N.C. 1998).

[318] Chambers Steel Engraving Corp. v. Tambrands, Inc., 895 F.2d 858 (1st Cir. 1990).

[319] U.C.C. § 2-201(3)(c) (2012). *See* Timothy E. Travers, Annotation, *Construction and Application of UCC § 2-201(3)(c) Rendering Contract of Sale Enforceable Notwithstanding Statute of Frauds with Respect to Goods for Which Payment Has Been Made and Accepted or Which Have Been Received and Accepted,* 97 A.L.R.3d 908 (1980).

with respect to goods that have been received and accepted by the buyer. "Acceptance" of goods occurs when the buyer has signified to the seller that he or she will take or retain them, when the buyer does any act inconsistent with the seller's ownership, or when the buyer fails to make an effective rejection.[320] The statute is only satisfied, however, to the extent of the goods that have been accepted or for which payment has been made. Thus, payment for goods delivered to the buyer from January through May satisfies the statute with respect to the deliveries already made, but does not satisfy the statute with respect to deliveries promised for June to November, which have not been made, unless payment was provided in advance.[321] Furthermore, delivery and acceptance of four truckloads of bricks satisfies the statute only with respect to those four truckloads; it does nothing to fulfill the requirement of a writing showing that there was a contract for six additional truckloads.

With respect to satisfying the statute by receipt and acceptance of goods, most disputes have been over whether acceptance has occurred. Most significant are the cases dealing with acceptance by failure to give notice of rejection within a reasonable time under U.C.C. § 2-602(1).[322] Unlike the "special manufacture" exception, it is clear that acceptance satisfies the statute only to the extent of the goods that have been accepted.[323] It does nothing to prove a contract for goods that have not yet been delivered or paid for.

The only difficulty in connection with partial payment has been in connection with partial payment for an individual item, such as where a buyer makes a down payment on a car. Although the text of the statute suggests that the statute can be satisfied only if payment in full has been made, courts have had no difficulty concluding that partial payment provides sufficient evidence of an agreement for "at least one," thus permitting parties to prove the existence of the contract.[324] Thus, part payment takes an "indivisible" contract out of the statute of frauds. However, where performance can be apportioned, part performance satisfies the statute at least with respect to the divisible portion of the contract that has been performed.[325]

Some courts have narrowed the effectiveness of § 2-201(3)(c) by insisting that it can only be used to make the contract enforceable against the party who has *received* part performance and not against a party who has *rendered* part performance. In *Jones v. Wide World of Cars, Inc.*,[326] for example, the buyer transferred funds electronically to the seller, in partial payment for a car. When

---

[320] U.C.C. § 2-606(1) (2012). *See infra* § 9.03 Rejection, Acceptance, and Revocation of Acceptance in Contracts for Goods.

[321] Spiering v. Fairmont Foods Co., 424 F.2d 337 (7th Cir. 1970).

[322] "[Rejection] is ineffective unless the buyer seasonably notifies the seller." U.C.C. § 2-601(1) (2012).

[323] *See infra* § 9.03 Rejection, Acceptance, and Revocation of Acceptance in Contracts for Goods.

[324] *See, e.g.*, Sedmak v. Charlie's Chevrolet, Inc., 622 S.W.2d 694, 698–99 (Mo. Ct. App. 1981). *See generally* Samuel Williston, *The Law of Sales in the Proposed Uniform Commercial Code*, 63 HARV. L. REV. 575 (1950).

[325] *E.g.*, Omega Eng'g, Inc. v. Eastman Kodak Co., 908 F. Supp. 1084 (D. Conn. 1995).

[326] 820 F. Supp. 132 (S.D.N.Y. 1993).

the buyer sought to recover its down payment, the seller refused, asserting that the buyer's part payment satisfied the statute of frauds. The court refused to enforce the contract, saying that the part-performance exception of § 2-201(3) made an oral agreement enforceable against a party who had "accepted" part performance, but did not make the contract enforceable against the party who had supplied the part performance. This result is incompatible with the express language of the statute, which makes an otherwise valid contract enforceable "with respect to goods for which payment has been made and accepted"[327] without reference to which party is seeking to enforce the contract. However, where payment has been received but not accepted, the statute should not be satisfied with respect to an action against the recipient. Thus, if a buyer's check was never cashed, the statute has not been satisfied against the seller.[328]

The corollary provision in U.C.C. Article 2A, regarding leases of goods, is different. Section 2A-201(4)(c) permits the statute to be satisfied only "with respect to goods that have been received and accepted by the lessee."[329] This reflects the drafters' belief that the lessor's receipt and acceptance of rental payments is somehow less reflective of the existence of a real lease agreement than the lessee's acceptance of the goods.[330]

This result is consistent with cases that refuse to permit part performance to satisfy the branch of the statute requiring contracts that take more than a year to perform to be in writing. Six months of rental payments proves nothing about the existence of a longer lease any more than six months of employment proves that a long-term employment contract has been made.[331]

[F]   Admission That a Contract Exists[332]

U.C.C. §§ 2-201(3)(b) and 2A-201(4)(b) permit the statute to be satisfied if the party against whom enforcement is sought admits that the contract for sale or lease was made.[333] However, the contract is enforceable only to the extent of the quantity term included in the admission.[334] The admission exception is satisfied if the party resisting enforcement admits the facts underlying the plaintiff's claim,

---

[327] U.C.C. § 2-201(3)(c) (2012).

[328] *E.g.*, Integrity Material Handling Sys., Inc. v. Deluxe Corp., 722 A.2d 552 (N.J. Super. App. Ch. Div. 1999).

[329] U.C.C. § 2A-201(4)(c) (2012).

[330] *See* U.C.C. § 2A-201 cmt. (2012).

[331] *See supra* § 5.05 The Effect of Part Performance and Reliance.

[332] Peter Shedd, *Statute of Frauds: Judicial Admission Exception — Where Has It Gone? Is It Coming Back?*, 6 WHITTIER L. REV. 1 (1984); Nicholas R. Weiskopf, *In-Court Admissions of Sales Contracts and the Statute of Frauds*, 19 UCC L.J. 195 (1987); Phillip K. Yonge, *The Unheralded Demise of the Statute of Frauds Welsher in Oral Contracts for the Sale of Goods and Investment Securities*, 33 WASH. & LEE L. REV. 1 (1976).

[333] *See generally* Michael J. Herbert, *Procedure and Promise: Rethinking the Admissions Exception to the Statue of Frauds Under U.C.C. Article 2, 2A and 8*, 45 OKLA. L. REV. 203 (1992).

[334] U.C.C. § 2-201(4)(b) (2012); U.C.C. § 2A-201(4)(b) (2012).

even if the defendant resists the conclusion that those facts resulted in a contract.[335]

Most of the important issues relating to the admission exception have been resolved. It does not matter whether the admission was obtained voluntarily or involuntarily.[336] Nor does it matter whether it was made during discovery or during trial.[337] Likewise, the defendant need not make an express admission that a contract has been formed. Instead, it is sufficient if he or she admits facts that would justify the conclusion that the parties had made the contract.[338] An implied admission, however, such as might be inferred from either a demurrer or a motion to dismiss for failure to state a claim, should not operate to satisfy the statute.

Whether the plaintiff should be able to force the defendant to participate in a trial, in the hope that an admission can be obtained in open court, however, is the topic of considerable dispute.[339] Some decisions cut off the litigation discovery process once the defendant has supplied a sworn affidavit denying the existence of a contract.[340] Other decisions permit discovery to continue but stop short of compelling the defendant to participate in a trial if no admission is made in the discovery process.[341] Some courts go further, making the statute of frauds completely unavailable as a basis for preventing a trial.[342] Unfortunately, nothing in the recently approved revisions to Article 2 resolves this conflict.[343]

It should be noted that most courts have expanded the admission exception beyond the scope of Articles 2 and 2A and applied it generally to contracts otherwise required to be evidenced by a writing.[344]

---

[335] E.g., Lewis v. Hughes, 346 A.2d 231 (Md. 1975). See generally Michael J. Herbert, Procedure and Promise: Rethinking the Admissions Exception to the Statue of Frauds under U.C.C. Article 2, 2A and 8, 45 Okla. L. Rev. 203, 210–12 (1992).

[336] Neb. Builders Prods. Co. v. Indus. Erectors, Inc., 478 N.W.2d 257 (Neb. 1992).

[337] Brewster Wallcovering Co. v. Blue Mtn. Wallcoverings, Inc., 864 N.E.2d 518 (Mass. Ct. App. 2007); Roth Steel Prods. v. Sharon Steel Corp., 705 F.2d 134, 142 n. 16 (6th Cir. 1983).

[338] Lewis v. Hughes, 346 A.2d 231 (Md. 1975).

[339] See generally Triangle Mktg., Inc. v. Action Indus., Inc., 630 F. Supp. 1578, 1581–83 (N.D. Ill. 1986). See also M & W Farm Serv. v. Callison, 285 N.W.2d 271, 275–76 (Iowa 1979) (statute of frauds cannot block discovery aimed at extracting an admission).

[340] E.g., DF Activities Corp. v. Brown, 851 F.2d 920, 922–23 (7th Cir. 1988) (Posner, J.). Litigation discovery is the pretrial process of depositions, requests for admissions, requests for the production of documents, and other procedural mechanisms used by the parties to a dispute to obtain information from one another, and sometimes third parties, that might be relevant to the litigation. See Fed. R. Civ. P. 26–37.

[341] E.g., ALA, Inc. v. CCAIR, Inc., 29 F.3d 855, 859–60 (3d Cir. 1994) (applying former U.C.C. § 8-319).

[342] E.g., Garrison v. Piatt, 147 S.E.2d 374 (Ga. Ct. App. 1966).

[343] Revised U.C.C. § 2-201 (2003). See W. David East, The Statute of Frauds and the Parol Evidence Rule Under the NCCUSL 2000 Annual Meeting Proposed Revision of U.C.C. Article 2, 54 SMU L. Rev. 866, 884 (2001).

[344] See Gibson v. Arnold, 288 F.3d 1242, 1246–47 (10th Cir. 2002) (collecting cases).

[G]   Nonstatutory Exceptions[345]

Before the adoption of the U.C.C., common law and equitable exceptions to the statute of frauds mitigated many of the statute's most harmful effects.[346] Inclusion of these exceptions to the Code's statute of frauds has discouraged some courts from employing uncodified common law exceptions, such as equitable and promissory estoppel, which have sometimes been used to circumvent the traditional statute of frauds in cases involving other types of contracts. These courts have sometimes ruled that the specific statutory exceptions contained in U.C.C. §§ 2-201(2) and 2-201(3) have supplanted any common law or equitable exceptions that existed prior to the Code's adoption.[347] These decisions pay heed to the language of U.C.C. § 1-103, which explicitly brings the common law, equity, and even the law merchant into the code unless they have been "displaced by the particular provisions of [the U.C.C.]."[348] But, they contend that the express language in § 2-201(1), providing that a contract for sale is not enforceable "[e]xcept as otherwise *in this section,*" supplants judge-made law outside the bounds of the Code.

Despite this language, most courts addressing the issue have permitted the use of equitable and promissory estoppel to circumvent the Code's requirements.[349] Jurisdictions that have generally recognized promissory estoppel as an exception to the statute of frauds have usually found that the exception survived the enactment of § 2-201.[350] These decisions have not read the text of § 2-201 to completely displace the common law.[351]

---

[345] Francis Timothy Collins, *Contracts — The Availability of Promissory Estoppel to Defeat the Statue of Frauds,* 14 MEMPHIS ST. U.L. REV. 89 (1983); Carolyn M. Edwards, *The Statute of Frauds of the Uniform Commercial Code and the Doctrine of Estoppel,* 62 MARQ. L. REV. 205 (1978); Michael B. Metzger & Michael J. Phillips, *Promissory Estoppel and Section 2-201 of the Uniform Commercial Code,* 26 VILL. L. REV. 63, 69–74 (1980–1981); Lionel Morgan Summers, *The Doctrine of Estoppel Applies to the Statute of Frauds,* 79 U. PA. L. REV. 440 (1931); Note, *The Doctrine of Equitable Estoppel and the Statute of Frauds,* 66 MICH. L. REV. 170 (1967).

[346] *See generally supra* § 5.05 The Effect of Part Performance and Reliance; RESTATEMENT (SECOND) OF CONTRACTS § 139 (1981).

[347] *E.g.,* Futch v. James River-Norwalk, Inc., 722 F. Supp. 1395 (S.D. Miss. 1989). *See* Janine McPeters Murphy, Note, *Promissory Estoppel: Subcontractors' Liability in Construction Bidding Cases,* 63 N.C.L. REV. 387 (1985).

[348] U.C.C. § 1-103(b) (2012). *See generally supra* § 1.04[B][1] Uniform Commercial Code. *See* Robert S. Summers, *General Equitable Principles Under Section 1-103 of the Uniform Commercial Code,* 72 NW. U. L. REV. 906 (1978).

[349] *E.g.,* Allen M. Campbell Co., General Contractors, Inc. v. Virginia Metal Indus., Inc., 708 F.2d 930, 932–33 (4th Cir. 1983); Ralston Purina Co. v. McCollum, 611 S.W.2d 201, 203 (Ark. Ct. App. 1981); R.S. Bennett & Co. v. Economy Mechanical Indus., Inc., 606 F.2d 182 (7th Cir. 1979). *See* Vitauts M. Gulbis, Annotation, *Promissory Estoppel as Basis for Avoidance of UCC Statute of Frauds (U.C.C. § 2-201),* 29 A.L.R.4th 1006 (1984 & Supp. 1991).

[350] *See, e.g.,* R.S. Bennett & Co., Inc. v. Economy Mechanical Industries, Inc., 606 F.2d 182 (7th Cir. 1979) (applying Illinois law); Warder & Lee Elevator, Inc. v. Britten, 274 N.W.2d 339 (Iowa 1979); Decatur Co-op Ass'n v. Urban, 547 P.2d 323 (Kan. 1976).

[351] *E.g.,* Allen M. Campbell Co., Gen. Contractors, Inc. v. Va. Metal Indus., Inc., 708 F.2d 930 (4th Cir. 1983).

B & W Glass, Inc. v. Weather Shield Mfg., Inc.[352] illustrates this approach. After several rounds of negotiations, Weather Shield supplied B & W Glass with an oral price quote for a wide array of custom windows for purchase by B & W in the event that its bid to provide the windows for a construction project was accepted. B & W relied on Weather Shield's price quote in entering into an agreement to supply the windows to the general contractor on the project and advised Weather Shield of its acceptance of the offer. Later, when the parties were attempting to iron out the detailed specifications for the custom windows, Weather Shield determined that it would be unable to meet its commitment and repudiated the contract.[353]

There was no confirmatory memorandum between the parties that would have satisfied the statute under § 2-201(2), and no part performance of the type that would have satisfied § 2-201(3)(a) or (c). Further, Weather Shield consistently denied that a contract had ever been formed, rendering § 2-201(3)(b) inapplicable. The court permitted promissory estoppel to be used as an exception. It reasoned that restricting exceptions to the statute of frauds to those contained in the text of the statute would be inconsistent with the general purpose of the statute: to prevent fraud. Restricting exceptions would also result in a different set of exceptions in contracts for the sale of goods than in contracts for other transactions. The court saw no reason to permit the use of promissory estoppel to enforce a promise by a provider of services and yet to deny its use to enforce an otherwise identical promise by a seller of goods.[354]

§ 5.07   CONSEQUENCES OF FAILING TO SATISFY THE STATUTE

If the statute is not satisfied, the contract may not be enforced. However, where some part performance has been rendered, recovery may still be available in restitution, at least to the extent of the part performance, to prevent unjust enrichment. Decisions permitting recovery on a theory of restitution are sometimes difficult to distinguish from those that rely on part performance as a means of satisfying the statute. In addition, cases permitting recovery to prevent unjust enrichment are also sometimes difficult to distinguish from those that enforce the promise on a theory of promissory estoppel, particularly where the action taken by the plaintiff in reliance on the contract conferred a benefit on the other party.

[A]   Unenforceability

The text of the original statute of frauds specified that "no action shall be brought" on a contract within its bounds.[355] Many modern versions of the statute

---

[352] 829 P.2d 809 (Wyo. 1992).

[353] *Id.* at 811.

[354] *Id.* at 818.

[355] An Act for Prevention of Frauds and Perjuries, Stat 29 Car. II c.3. *See* Crawford. D. Hening, *The Original Drafts of the Statute of Frauds and Their Authors*, 61 PENN. L. REV. 283 (1913).

adhere to this language,[356] though others merely indicate that the contract is "not enforceable." Thus, when a writing is necessary and does not exist, a remedy based on the contract is not available. This usually includes remedies such as money damages and specific performance based on the parties' expectation interest, as well as damages for sums spent in reliance on the agreement.[357] Restitution, however, as a remedy designed to prevent the unjust enrichment that might otherwise occur as a result of part performance, may be available as it is in other situations where a contract is rendered unenforceable by operation of law.[358]

[B]   Restitution for Part Performance[359]

As explained earlier, part performance is frequently recognized as an exception to the statute of frauds, making the contract enforceable.[360] However, where part performance does not make the contract itself enforceable, it may still rise to a right to restitution for the value of any benefit conferred on the party resisting enforcement. Restitution does not seek to implement the contract but, instead, merely attempts to restore the defendant to the pre-contract status quo by depriving it of any benefits it has received, which would be unjustly retained if no remedy were provided.

There are many cases in which the plaintiff has been induced to provide benefits to a family member in exchange for a promise that the family homestead or other valuable real estate will eventually be conveyed. Although many such cases result in enforcement of the promise, due to full performance, others result only in restitution for the value of the benefit conferred.

It is critical that the defendant actually receive a benefit. If the plaintiff incurs expenses but confers no benefit, recovery may be denied. A famous example is supplied by *Boone v. Coe*.[361] There, the defendant promised his Kentucky relatives that if they moved to Texas, he would lease them a tract of land to farm "on the shares." In reliance on this promise the plaintiff moved his family from Kentucky. Upon the family's arrival in Texas, the defendant repudiated his promise. The oral agreement, which could not have been performed within a year of its making, was unenforceable due to the statute of frauds. Although the plaintiff incurred considerable expense in reliance on the defendant's promise, his expenditures conferred no benefit on the defendant, and recovery in restitution was unavailable.

Nevertheless, some courts have expressed a willingness to presume the receipt of a benefit as a result of the plaintiff's part performance. In *Farash v. Sykes*

---

[356] *E.g.*, OHIO REV. CODE ANN. § 1335.05 (LexisNexis 2006).

[357] *See generally infra* § 12.01[B] Expectation, Reliance and Restitution Interests.

[358] *See infra* § 13.07 Restitution When Contract Is Unenforceable.

[359] Lindsey R. Jeanblanc, *Restitution Under the Statute of Frauds: What Constitutes a Legal Benefit*, 26 IND. L.J. 1 (1950); Lindsey R. Jeanblanc, *Restitution Under the Statute of Frauds: Measurement of the Legal Benefit Unjustly Retained*, 15 MO. L. REV. 1 (1950).

[360] *See supra* § 5.05 The Effect of Part Performance and Reliance.

[361] 154 S.W. 900 (Ky. Ct. App. 1913).

Datatronics, Inc.,[362] the plaintiff recovered its expenses in an action based on restitution, even though the defendant received no tangible benefit as a result of the plaintiff's efforts.[363] Decisions like *Farash,* though cast as based on restitution, closely resemble those that permit promissory estoppel to be used as an exception to the statute of frauds but that limit the plaintiff's recovery, as specified by Restatement (2d) § 139, to its reliance expenses in the interests of justice.[364]

§ 5.08 ELECTRONIC CONTRACTING[365]

The statute of frauds has historically enforced contracts formed via electronic means of communication. Nineteenth-century decisions routinely enforced contracts communicated via telegram.[366] However, the common practice of providing the telegraph operator with a signed written version of the message to be sent made this result nearly inevitable.[367] More recent decisions involving the use of telex machines,[368] fax technology,[369] tape recordings,[370] and e-mail[371] have led to mixed results.[372]

These mixed results led to the development of the Uniform Electronic Transactions Act (UETA). Now adopted in 46 states, Puerto Rico, the U.S. Virgin Islands, and the District of Columbia,[373] the act permits the parties to agree to make an

---

[362] 452 N.E.2d 1245 (N.Y. 1983).

[363] *See also* Kearns v. Andree, 139 A. 695 (Conn. 1928).

[364] RESTATEMENT (SECOND) OF CONTRACTS § 139(1) & cmt. d (1981). *E.g.*, Janke Const. Co., Inc. v. Vulcan Materials Co., 386 F. Supp. 687 (W.D. Wis. 1974).

[365] Anthony J. Bellia Jr., *Contracting with Electronic Agents*, 50 EMORY L.J. 1047 (2001); Amelia H. Boss, *The Future of the Uniform Commercial Code Process in an Increasingly International World*, 68 OHIO ST. L.J. 349 (2007); John D. Gregory, *The Proposed UNCITRAL Convention on Electronic Contracts*, 59 BUS. LAW. 313 (2003); R.J. Robertson Jr., *Electronic Commerce on the Internet and the Statute of Frauds*, 49 S.C. L. REV. 787, 798 (1998).

[366] R.J. Robertson Jr., *Electronic Commerce on the Internet and the Statute of Frauds*, 49 S.C. L. REV. 787, 798 (1998). *See, e.g.*, Western Twine Co. v. Wright, 78 N.W. 942, 944 (S.D. 1899).

[367] R.J. Robertson Jr., *Electronic Commerce on the Internet and the Statute of Frauds*, 49 S.C. L. REV. 787, 798–99 (1998).

[368] *E.g.*, Apex Oil Co. v. Vanguard Oil & Serv. Co., 760 F.2d 417, 423 (2d Cir. 1985) (telex satisfied confirmatory memorandum rule of U.C.C. § 2-201(2)).

[369] *See, e.g.*, Parma Tile Mosaic & Marble Co., Inc. v. Estate of Short, 663 N.E.2d 633 (N.Y. 1996) (automatic imprinting of sender's name at the top of each page of a transmitted fax inadequate to satisfy statute of frauds).

[370] Ellis Canning Co. v. Bernstein, 348 F. Supp. 1212 (D. Colo. 1972) (tape recording identifying the parties sufficient to satisfy former U.C.C. § 8-319); Sonders v. Roosevelt, 102 A.D.2d 701 (N.Y. App. Div. 1984), *aff'd mem.*, 476 N.E.2d 996, 996 (N.Y. 1985) (tape recording insufficient).

[371] *E.g.*, Cloud Corp. v. Hasbro, Inc., 314 F.3d 289 (7th Cir. 2002) (sender's name on e-mail constitutes "signature").

[372] R.J. Robertson Jr., *Electronic Commerce on the Internet and the Statute of Frauds*, 49 S.C. L. REV. 787, 801–07 (1998). Deborah L. Wilkerson, Comment, *Electronic Commerce Under the U.C.C. Section 2-201 Statute of Frauds: Are Electronic Messages Enforceable?*, 41 U. KAN. L. REV. 403, 409–19 (1993).

[373] *See* http://uniformlaws.org/Narrative.aspx?title=UETA%20and%20Preemption%20Article .

"electronic signature"[374] contained in a "record"[375] effective as a signed writing.

Their agreement may be implied from the circumstances. In other words, if they voluntarily use email or websites to conduct their transactions, electronic authentication is sufficient to satisfy the statute.

Not to be outdone by the Uniform Law Commission, in 2000 Congress adopted the Electronic Signatures in Global and National Commerce Act (E-Sign), replicating nearly all of UETA's language.[376] E-Sign applies to transactions in interstate commerce, regardless of the parties' agreement to use electronic communications.

Moreover, in 2005, the United Nations General Assembly approved UNCITRAL's Convention on the Use of Electronic Communications in International Contracts,[377] which is patterned after UETA and E-Sign.[378]

§ 5.09 WRITTEN MODIFICATION REQUIRED

Modifications of contracts must sometimes be in writing. A modification may need to be in writing for one of two reasons. First, the statute of frauds may apply. Second, the express terms of the original contract might specify that modifications are not to be enforced unless they are in writing.

[A] Modifications and the Statute of Frauds[379]

The statute of frauds requires certain types of contracts to be in writing.[380] Consistent with the rule that modifications are contracts just like any other, the statute of frauds would seem to apply to a modification to a contract with the same force and effect that it applies to the original agreement.

However, it is not completely clear what it means to say that the statute of frauds applies to modifications. Some jurisdictions require that any material change to a contract must be in writing if the terms of the original contract were within the statute of frauds. Other jurisdictions require the modification to be in writing only if the modification itself is covered by one of the statute's branches. Still other courts hold that the modification needs to be in writing only if the contract "as modified" is within the scope of the statute.

---

[374] UETA § 2(8) (1999).

[375] UETA §§ 7(c) and (d) (1999).

[376] E-Sign § 106(5) and (9), 15 U.S.C. § 7000 (2006).

[377] United Nations Convention on the Use of Electronic Communications in International Contracts, G.A. Res. 60/21, ¶ 12, U.N. GAOR, 60th Sess., Supp. No. 17, U.N. Doc. A/RES/60/21 (November 23, 2005).

[378] Henry D. Gabriel, *United Nations Convention on the Use of Electronic Communications in International Contracts and Compatibility with the American Domestic Law of Electronic Commerce*, 7 LOY. L. & TECH. ANN. 1 (2006–07).

[379] Mark Roszkowski, *Contract Modification and the Statute of Frauds: Making Sense of Section 2-209 of the Uniform Commercial Code*, 36 ALA. L. REV. 51 (1984); Robert A. Hillman, *A Study of Uniform Commercial Code Methodology: Contract Modification under Article Two*, 59 N.C. L. REV. 335 (1981).

[380] *See supra* § 5.03 Which Contracts?: The Scope of the Statute of Frauds

Consider, for example, an 18-month employment contract. Because the contract cannot be performed within a year of its making, it must be in writing in order to be enforced. However, if the parties enter into an oral agreement reducing the term to only 11 months, the necessity of reducing the modification to writing will depend on the approach taken by the jurisdiction in question. If the statute applies to material modifications of any contract that was initially within the scope of the statute, the elimination of seven months of the original term will likely be treated as material and the modification will have to be in writing. In other jurisdictions the oral modification will be enforceable because the modification was for only a seven-month period and the contract as modified is for less than a year. The predominant view is that if the contract as modified is within the statute, there must be a sufficient writing. Thus, if the contract as modified involves a transfer of an interest in real estate or cannot by its terms be completed within a year of its making, the material terms must be in writing.

If the parties to a contract for the transfer of land agree to change the time for performance or the price, the modification is material and must be written. Likewise, the terms of an employment contract, lasting more than a year, are unenforceable unless written.

U.C.C. § 2-209 attempts to resolve the question in cases involving contracts for the sale of goods, but its solution remains troublesome. It requires compliance with the statute of frauds "if the contract as modified is within its provisions."[381] Thus, if the modified contract is one for a sale of goods with a price of $500 or more, the modification needs to be in writing. And, because § 2-201 prevents enforcement of the contract beyond the quantity stated in the writing, any modification of the quantity of goods must be written.

Surprisingly, in cases involving modifications of contracts for the sale of goods, most courts ignore the liberal approach of § 2-201 regarding the contents of the writing. Nothing in § 2-201 requires all of the material terms to be in writing. Most scholars have indicated that a modification that does not change the quantity term need not be written.[382] However, where modifications are concerned, courts have insisted that if the modification is material, and the modified agreement is otherwise within the scope of the statute, then the modification must be in writing.[383]

[B]   Agreements Requiring Modifications in Writing[384]

Even if the statute of frauds does not apply, the parties sometimes create their own requirement that modifications be in writing by including language in their

---

[381] U.C.C. § 2-209(3) (2012).

[382] *See* John E. Murray Jr., *The Modification Mystery: Section 2-209 of the Uniform Commercial Code*, 32 VILL. L. REV. 1, 28 (1987).

[383] *E.g.*, Zemco Mfg., Inc. v. Navistar Int'l Transp. Corp., 186 F.3d 815, 819 (7th Cir. 1999).

[384] Charles L. Knapp, *Rescuing Reliance: The Perils of Promissory Estoppel*, 49 HASTINGS L.J. 1191, 1302–1330 (1998); Frank A. Rothermel, Comment, *Role of Course of Performance and Confirmatory Memoranda in Determining the Scope, Operation and Effect of "No Oral Modification" Clauses*, 48 U. PITT. L. REV. 1239 (1987); Beth A. Eisler, *Modification of Sales Contracts Under the Uniform*

original contract specifying that modifications must be in writing to be enforceable. For example, the contract in *Brookside Farms v. Mama Rizzo's Inc.*[385] provided: "This Agreement may be modified only by a writing signed by the party against whom or against whose successors and assigns enforcement of the modification is sought." Despite language like this, parties frequently make oral modifications without observing their own self-imposed restriction against the practice.

Although these provisions are subject to the same rules as any other term in a contract, aggressive enforcement of an agreement requiring modifications to be in writing can have serious consequences. The problem is particularly acute in construction contracts where the owner authorizes changes to the terms of the original contract at the work site or over the phone and neither party bothers to reduce the modification to written form. In *Universal Builders, Inc. v. Moon Motor Lodge*,[386] the construction contract contained a clause similar to that in *Brookside Farms.* The owner asked the contractor to perform extra work, but the parties never bothered to execute a written modification providing for these "extras."

Confronted with the obvious unfairness of permitting the owner to enjoy the benefit of work it had requested, the court had no difficulty finding that the clause requiring modifications to be in writing had been waived. Likewise, the court found that, either by requesting the extra work or standing idly by without protest while the extra work was accomplished, the owner had impliedly promised to pay the contractor for the reasonable value of its services.

Cases finding that provisions requiring modifications to be in writing have been waived are legion.[387] Further, U.C.C. § 2-209(4) recognizes that a contractual requirement of a signed writing can be waived by an attempted modification that fails to comply with the requirement.[388] The principal questions are first, what constitutes a waiver, and second, whether a waiver of such a "no oral modifications" provision can be reinstated after it has been waived.

In international contracts, where the statute of frauds does not apply,[389] the parties may still enter into an agreement requiring modifications to be in writing.[390] The CISG permits a modification to be made by the "mere agreement"

Commercial Code: Section 2-209 Reconsidered, 57 Tenn. L. Rev. 401 (1990); John Edward Murray Jr., *The Modification Mystery: Section 2-209 of the Uniform Commercial Code*, 32 Vill. L. Rev. 1 (1987).

[385] 873 F. Supp. 1029 (S.D. Tex. 1995).

[386] 244 A.2d 10 (Pa. 1968).

[387] *E.g.*, Chemetron Corp. v. McLouth Steel Corp., 522 F.2d 469, 472 (7th Cir. 1975); Royster-Clark Inc. v. Olsen's Mill, Inc., 714 N.W.2d 530, 535–39 (Wis. 2006) (via course of dealings over 40 years). *But see* Wisc. Knife Works v. Nat'l Metal Crafters, 781 F.2d 1280 (7th Cir. 1986) (requiring reliance).

[388] *See* Beth A. Eisler, *Oral Modification of Sales Contracts Under the Uniform Commercial Code: The Statute of Frauds Problem*, 58 Wash. U. L.Q. 277, 298–302 (1980).

[389] CISG Art. 29(1) (1980). *See supra* § 5.03[G] Statute of Frauds in International Transactions.

[390] Robert A. Hillman, *Article 29(2) of the United Nations Convention on Contracts for the International Sale of Goods: A New Effort at Clarifying the Legal Effect of "No Oral Modifications" Clauses*, 21 Cornell Int'l L. J. 449 (1988); David V. Snyder, *the Law of Contract and the Concept of Change: Public and Private Attempts to Regulate Modification, Waiver, and Estoppel*, 1999 Wis. L. Rev. 607.

of the parties,[391] making it clear that no specific form is required for a modification to be enforceable. Nevertheless, Article 29(2) gives effect to contractual provisions requiring modifications to be in writing.[392] At the same time, it recognizes that "a party may be precluded by his conduct from asserting such a provision to the extent that the other party has relied on that conduct."[393] Thus, even though the parties have agreed that any modifications are required to be written, oral modifications are enforceable if they are relied upon. For example, if, in the face of a "no oral modifications" clause, the parties orally agree to alter the specifications of the goods to be delivered under the contract, and the buyer manufactures the goods in accordance with the oral modification, the modification is enforceable.[394]

The UNIDROIT Principles of International Commercial Contracts contain similar language, making agreements that require modifications to be in writing generally enforceable, but recognizing that a party may be precluded from asserting such a provision where the other party has relied on an oral modification.[395]

The Principles of European Contract Law take a slightly different approach. Under their provisions, a written agreement requiring modifications to be in writing merely establishes a presumption that an oral agreement to modify the contract is not intended to be legally enforceable unless the modification is in writing.[396] Further, as under the CISG and the UNIDROIT Principles, a party may be precluded from asserting a "no oral modifications" clause, by its conduct.[397] PECL goes further, and makes it clear that a party's "statements" — not just its conduct — if relied on, might prevent a party from insisting that the modification be in writing.

---

[391] CISG Art 29(1) (1980).

[392] CISG Art. 29(2) (1980).

[393] *Id.*

[394] *See* JOHN O. HONNOLD, UNIFORM LAW FOR INTERNATIONAL SALES 204 (3d ed. 1999).

[395] PICC Art. 2.1.18 (2004).

[396] PECL Art. 2.106(1) (2002).

[397] PECL Art. 2.106(2) (2002).

Chapter 6

INTERPRETATION OF CONTRACTS

§ 6.01 DETERMINING THE TERMS OF A CONTRACT[1]

The terms of a contract reside primarily in the parties' express language, but are also found in the circumstances surrounding the creation of the contract.[2] These "extrinsic" circumstances include any customary practice followed either in the parties' trade or industry, or geographic area. They also include any private customs developed between the parties during their past dealings with one another.[3]

The process of identifying the terms of a contract and the meaning of those terms can be difficult. Words do not have fixed meanings.[4] However, the parties to a contract must be able to act with confidence about the meaning a court is likely to attribute to their words. Otherwise, they will be unable to evaluate whether their actions conform to their contractual duties.

When a dispute over performance of a contract arises, the court must often intervene to determine the meaning of the terms of a contract. When it does so, its inquiry will usually begin by examining the text of the parties' written contract, or, if the contract is oral, the words they used in forming the contract. This inquiry is an effort to determine the parties' shared intent.[5] When one party's intent about the

---

[1] STEVEN J. BURTON, ELEMENTS OF CONTRACT INTERPRETATION (2009); James W. Bowers, *Murphy's Law and the Elementary Theory of Contract Interpretation: A Response to Schwartz and Scott*, 57 RUTGERS L. REV. 587 (2005); Juliet P. Kostritsky, *Plain Meaning vs. Broad Interpretation: How the Risk of Opportunism Defeats a Unitary Default Rule for Interpretation*, 96 KY. L.J. 43 (2007); Edwin Patterson, *The Interpretation and Construction of Contracts*, 64 COLUM. L. REV. 833 (1964); Keith Rowley, *Contract Construction and Interpretation: From the "Four Corners" to Parol Evidence (and Everything in Between)*, 69 MISS. L.J. 73 (1999); Alan Schwartz & Robert E. Scott, *Contract Theory and the Limits of Contract Law*, 113 YALE L.J. 541 (2003).

[2] U.C.C. § 1-201(b)(3) (2012); RESTATEMENT (SECOND) OF CONTRACTS § 5 (1981).

[3] U.C.C. § 1-303 (2012) (formerly § 1-205).

[4] Pac. Gas & Elec. Co v. G.W. Thomas Drayage & Rigging Co., 442 P.2d 641, 644 (Cal. 1968).

[5] *See infra* § 6.02 Interpreting Express Terms; E. Allan Farnsworth, *"Meaning" in the Law of*

meaning of a term differs from the others, the court must attempt to resolve the difference. Otherwise, the court may be unable to enforce the contract at all.[6]

Courts sometimes must also "construe" the terms of a contract. A court's effort to determine the intent of the parties is properly characterized as "interpretation" of the contract. Other efforts to determine its legal effect, without reference to the intent of the parties, are more accurately referred to as "construction" of the contract.[7] However, courts do not always draw so fine a distinction between these two efforts, and frequently use the terms "interpretation" and "construction" interchangeably.[8] Still, there is a difference between the two. Interpretation involves an honest effort to determine what the parties meant. Construction depends on public policy considerations divorced from whatever the parties may have intended.

Even when the parties have put their agreement in writing, it is not always clear that they intended the written record to serve as the final conclusive evidence of their agreement. In many cases the parties will have made an oral agreement to additional terms that have not been included in the written version of their agreement. The parol evidence rule governs the extent to which the existence of a written version of a contract prevents a court from considering evidence of other terms allegedly agreed upon by the parties, but not included in the writing.[9]

Moreover, contracts are not formed in a vacuum but are nearly always created against a backdrop of industry-wide or geographic customs. These broader customs are known as "usages of trade."[10] Contracts are frequently also made in the context of whatever private customs the parties may have developed between themselves, either in the course of their past dealings[11] or in the course of performance of the very contract whose meaning must be determined.[12] Usage of trade, course of dealing, and course of performance play important roles in determining the terms and meaning of a contract.[13]

Contracts, 76 YALE L.J. 939, 951 (1967); CISG Art. 8 (1980); PICC Art. 4.1(1) (2004); PECL Art. 5.101 (2002).

[6] *See infra* § 6.03 Effect of Misunderstanding.

[7] RESTATEMENT (SECOND) OF CONTRACTS § 200 cmt. c (1981). *See* Robert Braucher, *Interpretation and Legal Effect in the Second Restatement of Contracts*, 81 COLUM. L. REV. 13 (1981); E. Allan Farnsworth, *"Meaning" in the Law of Contracts*, 76 YALE L.J. 939 (1967); Edwin W. Patterson, *The Interpretation and Construction of Contracts*, 64 COLUM. L. REV. 833 (1964); Peter M. Tiersma, *The Ambiguity of Interpretation: Distinguishing Interpretation from Construction*, 73 WASH. U. L. Q. 1095 (1995).

[8] *But see* Am. Med. Intern. v. Scheller, 462 So. 2d 1, 7 (Fla. Dist. Ct. App. 1984).

[9] *See infra* § 6.05 The Parol Evidence Rule.

[10] RESTATEMENT (SECOND) OF CONTRACTS § 222 (1981); U.C.C. § 1-303(c) (2012) (formerly § 1-205(2)); CISG Art. 9(2) (1980); PICC Art. 1.9(2) (2004); PECL Art. 1.105(2) (2002).

[11] RESTATEMENT (SECOND) OF CONTRACTS § 223 (1981); U.C.C. § 1-303(b) (2012) (formerly § 1-205(1)); CISG Art. 9(1) (1980); PICC Art. 1.9(1) (2004); PECL Art. 1.105(1) (2002).

[12] U.C.C. § 2-208(1) (2012).

[13] *See infra* § 6.04 Customary Practice; *infra* § 6.05[F] Evidence of Usage of Trade, Course of Dealing, and Course of Performance.

§ 6.02   INTERPRETING EXPRESS TERMS[14]

In interpreting a contract, the parties' shared intent is paramount.[15] Unfortunately, their intent is not always clear. Further, changes in circumstances provide the parties with incentives to commit perjury or, at a minimum, to shade their memories. Consequently, courts have developed numerous techniques to interpret the parties' words.[16]

[A]   Plain Meaning[17]

Courts frequently try to assess the "plain meaning" of disputed terms.[18] The plain-meaning standard interprets words according to their common meaning, or sometimes based on the meaning attributed to them in a dictionary. As one court explained: "The strongest external sign of agreement between contracting parties is the words they use in their written contract . . . . A court is not authorized to construe a contract in such a way as to modify the plain meaning of its words, under the guise of interpretation."[19] Courts taking this approach are unwilling to consider testimony or other evidence about the parties' intended meaning if the

---

[14] James W. Bowers, *Murphy's Law and the Elementary Theory of Contract Interpretation: A Response to Schwartz and Scott*, 57 RUTGERS L. REV. 587 (2005); Larry A. DiMatteo, *A Theory of Interpretation in the Realm of Idealism*, 5 DEPAUL BUS. & COM. L.J. 17 (2006); Gillian K. Hadfield, *Judicial Competence and the Interpretation of Incomplete Contracts*, 23 J. LEGAL STUD. 159 (1994) (exploring judicial competence and interpretation of incomplete contracts from an analytical perspective); Robert A. Hillman, *The "New Conservatism" in Contract Law and the Process of Legal Change*, 40 B.C. L. REV. 879 (1999); Oliver Wendell Holmes Jr., *The Theory of Legal Interpretation*, 12 HARV. L. REV. 417 (1899); Jiri Janko, Note, *Linguistically Integrated Contractual Interpretation: Incorporating Semiotic Theory of Meaning-Making into Legal Interpretation*, 38 RUTGERS L.J. 601 (2007); Avery Weiner Katz, *The Economics of Form and Substance in Contract Interpretation*, 104 COLUM. L. REV. 496 (2004); Edwin W. Patterson, *The Interpretation and Construction of Contracts*, 64 COLUM. L. REV. 833 (1964); Richard A. Posner, *The Law and Economics of Contract Interpretation*, 83 TEX. L. REV. 1581 (2005); Alan Schwartz & Robert E. Scott, *Contract Theory and the Limits of Contract Law*, 113 YALE L.J. 541 (2003); Eyal Zamir, *The Inverted Hierarchy of Contract Interpretation and Supplementation*, 97 COLUM. L. REV. 1710 (1997).

[15] *E.g.*, Berg v. Hudesman, 801 P.2d 222 (Wash. 1990).

[16] *See* Stephen J. Choi & G. Mitu Gulati, *Contract as Statute*, 104 MICH. L. REV. 1129 (2006) (suggesting that common principles of statutory interpretation be used to interpret boilerplate contract terms).

[17] Owen M. Fiss, *Objectivity and Interpretation*, 34 STAN. L. REV. 739 (1982); Avery Katz, *The Economics of Form and Substance in Contract Interpretation*, 104 COLUM. L. REV. 496 (2004); Juliet P. Kostritsky, *Plain Meaning vs. Broad Interpretation: How the Risk of Opportunism Defeats a Unitary Default Rule for Interpretation*, 96 KY. L.J. 43 (2007); Peter Linzer, *The Comfort of Certainty: Plain Meaning and the Parol Evidence Rule*, 71 FORDHAM L. REV. 799, 839 (2002); Eric A. Posner, *The Parol Evidence Rule, the Plain Meaning Rule, and the Principles of Contractual Interpretation*, 146 U. PA. L. REV. 533 (1998); Steven Shavell, *On the Writing and the Interpretation of Contracts*, 22 J.L. ECON. & ORG. 289 (2005).

[18] *E.g.*, Dawkins v. Walker, 794 So. 2d 333 (Ala. 2001). *See* Edwin W. Patterson, *The Interpretation and Construction of Contracts*, 64 COLUM. L. REV. 833, 838–42 (1964); Keith A. Rowley, *Contract Construction and Interpretation: From the "Four Corners" to Parol Evidence (and Everything in Between)*, 69 MISS. L.J. 73 (1999).

[19] Mellon Bank v. Aetna Bus. Credit, Inc., 619 F.2d 1001, 1009–10 (3d Cir. 1980).

words of the contract are clear.[20] This type of evidence may be considered, only if the "plain" or common meaning cannot be ascertained.[21]

[B]   Contextual Interpretation[22]

Other courts have been fearful that any attempt to determine the plain meaning of a term runs too great a risk of substituting the court's meaning for that intended by the parties.[23] Heavily influenced by Professor Corbin,[24] these courts prefer a contextual approach, which determines the meaning of a term in light of all of the surrounding circumstances, including testimony about the parties' intent.

This extrinsic evidence includes testimony about the purpose of the term.[25] Language in a contract reciting its intended purpose will thus be influential, but not controlling.[26] The history of the parties' negotiations that led to the formation of the contract is also relevant,[27] as is the business context in which the contract was made.

However, there is considerable debate over whether extrinsic evidence can be introduced to demonstrate the existence of an ambiguity in the first place, particularly where the "four corners" of the contract do not reveal an apparent ambiguity. Some courts require that there be a patent ambiguity, on the face of the contract, before evidence of prior negotiations or other extrinsic matters can be considered.[28] Other courts permit use of extrinsic evidence as an aid in determining whether an ambiguity exists.[29]

International law takes a contextual approach. The CISG and UNIDROIT's Principles of International Commercial Contracts focus on the subjective intent of

---

[20] *E.g.*, C & A Constr. Co. v. Benning Constr. Co., 509 S.W.2d 302 (Ark. 1974).

[21] *E.g.*, Trinova Corp. v. Pilkington Bros., P.L.C., 638 N.E.2d 572, 575 (Ohio 1994) (if agreement is complete and unambiguous on its face, parol evidence may not be used in an effort to show a different intent).

[22] Oliver Wendell Holmes Jr., *The Theory of Legal Interpretation*, 12 Harv. L. Rev. 417 (1899); *See* Larry A. DiMatteo, *Reason and Context: A Dual Track Theory of Interpretation*, 109 Penn. St. L. Rev. 397 (2004); Margaret N. Kniffin, *A New Trend in Contract Interpretation: The Search for Reality as Opposed to Virtual Reality*, 74 Or. L. Rev. 643 (1995); Juliet P. Kostritsky, *Plain Meaning vs. Broad Interpretation: How the Risk of Opportunism Defeats a Unitary Default Rule for Interpretation*, 96 Ky. L.J. 43 (2007).

[23] Alyeska Pipeline Serv. Co. v. O'Kelley, 645 P.2d 767, 771 (Alaska 1982); Tigg Corp. v. Dow Corning Corp., 822 F.2d 358, 362 (3d Cir. 1981) (applying U.C.C. § 2-202); Pac. Gas & Elec. Co. v. G.W. Thomas Drayage & Rigging Co., 442 P.2d 641, 645 (Cal. 1968).

[24] Arthur L. Corbin, *The Interpretation of Words and the Parol Evidence Rule*, 50 Cornell L.Q. 161 (1965); Avery Katz, *The Economics of Form and Substance in Contract Interpretation*, 104 Colum. L. Rev. 496, 501 (2004).

[25] Restatement (Second) of Contracts § 202(1) (1981). *E.g.*, Bourke v. Dun & Bradstreet Corp., 159 F.3d 1032, 1039 (7th Cir. 1998); Alvin, Ltd. v. United States Postal Service, 816 F.2d 1562 (Fed. Cir. 1987).

[26] *See* Alaska v. Fairbanks N. Star Borough Sch. Dist., 621 P.2d 1329 (Alaska 1981).

[27] Arnhold v. Ocean Atl. Woodland Corp., 284 F.3d 693, 701–02 (7th Cir. 2001).

[28] Eskimo Pie Corp. v. Whitelawn Dairies, Inc., 284 F. Supp. 987 (S.D.N.Y. 1968).

[29] *E.g.*, P. Gas & Elec. Co. v. G.W. Thomas Drayage & Rigging Co., 442 P.2d 641 (Cal. 1968).

the parties,[30] and the Principles of European Contract Law specify that a contract is to be interpreted according to the common intention of the parties, "even if this differs from the literal meaning of the words."[31]

[C]   Maxims of Construction and Interpretation[32]

In addition to examining the purpose, history, and context in which the contract was made, courts frequently employ a number of interpretation "maxims," or guidelines, in construing ambiguous or unclear language in a contract. While they are sometimes helpful, they are rarely dispositive.[33] Moreover, they are sometimes inconsistent with one another,[34] and are just as contradictory as maxims for life that are sometimes expressed.[35] Nevertheless, it is important to consider them because they are so frequently used.

[1]   Construe Language Consistently Where Possible

Terms in a contract are presumed to be consistent with one another.[36] For example, where a contract for the sale of goods contains both an express warranty and a disclaimer of all express warranties, the court, before finding them in conflict, will attempt to reconcile their meanings.[37] If the disclaimer and the warranty cannot be construed as somehow compatible with one another, public policy

---

[30] CISG Art. 8(1) (1980); PICC Art. 4.1(1). *See* Joseph M. Perillo, *Interpretation of the Contract: Editorial Remarks on the Manner in Which the UNIDROIT Principles May Be Used to Interpret or Supplement CISG Article 8*, in An International Approach to the Interpretation of the United Nations Convention on Contracts for the International Sale of Goods (1980) as Uniform Sales Law 49 (John Felemegas ed. 2007).

[31] PECL Art. 5.101(1) (2002).

[32] Oliver Wendell Holmes Jr., *The Theory of Legal Interpretation*, 12 HARV. L. REV. 417 (1899); KARL LLEWELLYN, THE COMMON LAW TRADITION — DECIDING APPEALS 521–35 (1960) (statutory construction); Karl N. Llewellyn, *Remarks on the Theory of Appellate Decision and the Rules or Canons About How Statutes Are to Be Construed*, 3 VAND. L. REV. 395, 401–06 (1950); Edwin W. Patterson, *The Interpretation and Construction of Contracts*, 64 COLUM. L. REV. 833 (1964); Max Radin, *A Short Way with Statutes*, 56 HARV. L. REV. 388, 423 (1942); Symposium, *A Reevaluation of the Canons of Statutory Interpretation*, 45 VAND. L. REV. 529 (1992); Keith A. Rowley, *Contract Construction and Interpretation: From the "Four Corners" to Parol Evidence (and Everything in Between)*, 69 MISS. L.J. 73, 150 (1999); Roger Young & Stephen Spitz, *SUEM — Spitz's Ultimate Equitable Maxim: In Equity, Good Guys Should Win and Bad Guys Should Lose*, 55 S.C. L. REV. 175, 177 (2003) (listing maxims). *See also* Eugene Volokh, *Lost Maxims of Equity*, 52 J. LEGAL EDUC. 619, 619 (2002) (listing equally humorous maxims).

[33] *E.g.*, Patterson v. Bixby, 364 P.2d 10 (Wash. 1961). *See* Edwin W. Patterson, *The Interpretation and Construction of Contracts*, 64 COLUM. L. REV. 833, 853 (1964).

[34] KARL LLEWELLYN, THE COMMON LAW TRADITION — DECIDING APPEALS 521–535 (1960).

[35] *Compare* "You can't tell a book by its cover" *with* "Where there's smoke, there's fire"; "Better safe than sorry" *with* "Nothing ventured, nothing gained"; "A stitch in time saves nine" *with* "Haste makes waste"; "A penny saved is a penny earned" *with* "You can't take it with you"; "He who hesitates is lost" *with* "Fools rush in"; "Two heads are better than one" *with* "Too many cooks in the kitchen spoil the broth." CARL SAGAN, THE DEMON HAUNTED WORLD 235 (1996).

[36] RESTATEMENT (SECOND) OF CONTRACTS § 202(5) (1981). *See* U.C.C. § 2-208(2) (2012). *E.g.*, Guar. Fin. Serv's, Inc. v. Ryan, 928 F.2d 994, 1000 (11th Cir. 1991).

[37] U.C.C. § 2-316(1) (2012). *See* United States Fibres, Inc. v. Proctor & Schwartz, Inc., 509 F.2d 1043 (6th Cir. 1975).

supports jettisoning the inconsistent disclaimer and preserving the express warranty.[38]

In *United States v. Pielago*,[39] a criminal plea bargain agreement — which is a contract — provided that the government could not use the defendant's testimony against her, but also indicated that it could "use evidence" derived from her information or statements against her." The court found that the more specific provision of the agreement did not contradict, but merely limited the more generic term prohibiting "use."[40] Thus, because the apparently conflicting terms could be reconciled, there was no reason to choose between them.

A corollary rule presumes that the parties intended every portion of their agreement to have legal effect.[41] Thus, where possible, the contract should be interpreted to give effect to every portion of the contract, and where there are two otherwise plausible interpretations of an ambiguous provision, the one that would make another provision of the contract superfluous should be rejected.[42]

[2] Contra Proferentem — Resolve Ambiguity Against the Drafter[43]

Courts commonly assert the maxim *contra proferentem*: ambiguities in a written contract should be construed against the drafter.[44] This approach is commonly used in interpreting insurance contracts[45] and other similar "contracts of adhesion" where one party offers the terms of the agreement to the other on a "take it or leave it" basis, with no opportunity to haggle over specific language.[46] Thus, parties who make an effort to control the terms of a contract by preparing its language may find their efforts used against them if the agreement is ambiguous or was otherwise not drafted with care.[47] *Contra proferentem* is less persuasive

---

[38] U.C.C. § 2-316(1) (2012).

[39] 135 F.3d 703 (11th Cir. 1998).

[40] *Id. See also* Hol-Gar Mfg. Corp. v. United States, 351 F.2d 972 (Ct. Cl. 1965).

[41] RESTATEMENT (SECOND) OF CONTRACTS § 203(a) (1981). *See* Keith A. Rowley, *Contract Construction and Interpretation: From the "Four Corners" to Parol Evidence (and Everything in Between)*, 69 MISS. L.J. 73, 121 (1999).

[42] RESTATEMENT (SECOND) OF CONTRACTS § 203(a) (1981).

[43] Michelle E. Boardman, *Contra Proferentem: The Allure of Ambiguous Boilerplate*, 104 MICH. L. REV. 1105 (2006).

[44] RESTATEMENT (SECOND) OF CONTRACTS § 206 (1981). *E.g.*, Duldulao v. St. Mary of Nazareth Hosp. Ctr., 505 N.E.2d 314 (Ill. 1987); N. Gate Corp. v. Nat'l Food Stores, Inc., 140 N.W.2d 744 (Wis. 1966). *See* Edwin W. Patterson, *The Interpretation of Contracts*, 64 COLUM. L. REV. 833, 835 (1964); Keith A. Rowley, *Contract Construction and Interpretation: From the "Four Corners" to Parol Evidence (and Everything in Between)*, 69 MISS. L.J. 73, 151 (1999).

[45] *E.g.*, YWCA v. Allstate Ins. Co., 275 F.3d 1145 (D.C. Cir. 2002). *See* Keith A. Rowley, *Contract Construction and Interpretation: From the "Four Corners" to Parol Evidence (and Everything in Between)*, 69 MISS. L.J. 73, 171–84 (1999).

[46] Hennessy v. Daniels Law Office, 270 F.3d 551 (8th Cir. 2001) (ambiguity in an offer of judgment agreement was construed against the law firm which drafted its language).

[47] *See* Merrimack Valley Nat'l Bank v. Baird, 363 N.E.2d 688, 690 (Mass. 1977). *But see* Michael B. Rappaport, *The Ambiguity Rule and Insurance Law: Why Insurance Contracts Should Not Be*

when both parties have actively participated in the drafting process, or where they both have expertise in similar transactions.[48]

The same approach is taken in international transactions. UNIDROIT's Principles of International Commercial Contracts provide that "[i]f contract terms supplied by one party are unclear, an interpretation against that party is preferred."[49]

[3] Expressio Unius Est Exclusio Alterius — The Expression of One Excludes Others

Contracts frequently specify a list of items covered by the contract and remain silent about other matters. For example, an agreement between a lender and a borrower might specify the items of the borrower's property that will serve as collateral for the loan, such as: "equipment consisting of tables, chairs, desks, file cabinets, bookshelves, and books," but remain silent about "computers." In such cases applying "expressio unius" means that expressly including some items implies excluding others.[50] Expressly identifying some of the borrower's equipment suggests that the computers, which were not mentioned, were not included as collateral.[51]

A good example is found in *Smart v. Gillette Co. Long Term Disability Plan.*[52] There, an employee's severance agreement provided for a schedule of severance benefits, including severance pay, participation in the employer's health and dental plans, life insurance, a savings plan, and an employee stock ownership plan. The court used expressio unius in reaching its conclusion that the agreement did not include disability insurance coverage, even though the agreement referred generically to "other benefits."[53]

[4] Ejusdem Generis — Of the Same Kind or Class[54]

"Ejusdem generis," which means "of the same kind or class," confines the meaning of general language to the subjects covered by more specific language accompanying the general term.[55] Thus, in the early case of *Insurance Co. v. Seaver,*[56] the Court construed language in an insurance policy preventing the policy from extending to "any death or injury caused by dueling or fighting, or

---

Construed Against the Drafter, 30 GA. L. REV. 171 (1995).

[48] *See* RESTATEMENT (SECOND) OF CONTRACTS § 206 reporter's note (1981); Farmers Auto. Ins. Ass'n v. St. Paul Mercury Ins. Co., 482 F.3d 976 (7th Cir. 2007) (*contra proferentum* not applied where a sophisticated insurance company was in role of the insured).

[49] PICC Art. 4.6 (2004).

[50] *In re* Celotex Corp., 487 F.3d 1320, 1334 (11th Cir. 2007).

[51] Gilchrist Tractor Co. v. Stribling, 192 So. 2d 409, 414–16 (Miss. 1966).

[52] 70 F.3d 173 (1st Cir. 1995).

[53] *Id.*

[54] Keith A. Rowley, *Contract Construction and Interpretation: From the "Four Corners" to Parol Evidence (and Everything in Between),* 69 MISS. L.J. 73, 153–55 (1999).

[55] Sanpete Water Conserv'y Dist. v. Carbon Water Conserv'y Dist., 226 F.3d 1170 (10th Cir. 2000).

[56] 86 U.S. 531 (1873).

other breach of the law on the part of the [insured]" not to encompass participation in a horse race, which was also dangerous, but unlike the specified items, was not itself illegal.

The difficulty in applying ejusdem generis is in determining how broadly or narrowly to classify the list of items. Consider, for example the following list of household items required to be included in the sale of a home: "appliances such as the refrigerator, stove, dishwasher and microwave." If the question is whether the outdoor grill is to be included in the transaction, the list might be classified broadly to refer to any items relating to food and meals. On the other hand, it might just as easily be classified more narrowly to refer to items found only in the kitchen.

[5] Specific Terms Govern General Terms

Courts also usually give greater weight to more specific or precise terms than they do to more general language.[57] For example, in *United States Postal Service v. American Postal Workers Union*,[58] a provision in a collective bargaining contract providing generally for employees' access to a grievance procedure was superseded by a more specific provision denying this right to employees during their probationary period. And, in *Boatmen's National Bank of St. Louis v. Smith*,[59] the court ruled that general language, permitting a borrower to use loan funds for a particular purpose, was superseded by more specific language, specifying one particular stated purpose was the only purpose for which the funds could be used.

Section 2-317 of the Uniform Commercial Code provides a similar rule in connection with warranties provided by sellers of goods. It specifies that "[e]xact or technical specifications displace an inconsistent sample or model [and that a] sample from an existing bulk displaces inconsistent general language of description."[60]

[6] Negotiated Terms Govern Boilerplate Terms

Akin to this approach is the principle that terms over which the parties have expressly negotiated supersede preprinted or boilerplate terms that were not discussed.[61] A related rule treats handwritten terms as controlling printed terms, at least where they cannot be reconciled as consistent with one another.[62]

Likewise, typewritten terms supersede preprinted provisions. For example, in *Mack Investment Co. v. Dominy*,[63] the typewritten payment schedule in a loan agreement superseded the inconsistent schedule on the preprinted portion of the

---

[57] RESTATEMENT (SECOND) OF CONTRACTS § 203(c) (1981).

[58] 922 F.2d 256, 260 (5th Cir. 1991).

[59] 835 F.2d 1200, 1203 (7th Cir. 1987).

[60] U.C.C. § 2-317(a), (b) (2012).

[61] RESTATEMENT (SECOND) OF CONTRACTS § 203(d) & cmt. f (1981).

[62] RESTATEMENT (SECOND) OF CONTRACTS § 203(d) (1981); Hernandez v. Wyeth-Ayerst Labs., 727 N.Y.S.2d 591 (N.Y. Sup. Ct. 2001).

[63] 1 N.W.2d 295 (Neb. 1941).

standardized agreement. The court presumed that the typewritten schedule, which they had taken time to construct, was what the parties had actually intended.[64]

[7]   Construe Contract Consistently with the Public Interest

Finally, courts sometimes indicate that ambiguities should be resolved consistently with the obligation of good faith and in the public interest.[65] For example, in *Washburn v. UNUM Life Insurance Co. of America*,[66] the court construed an ambiguity in a disability insurance policy in a way that permitted disabled employees to perform "active work" temporarily, without losing their long-term disability coverage when they suffer a relapse of their disability.[67] And, in *Seman v. First State Bank*, a construction that favored the continued utility of cashiers' checks was preferred over a construction that would have impaired their utility.[68] Likewise, where ambiguous language is susceptible of two reasonable constructions, the court will favor the construction that renders the contract enforceable.[69]

§ 6.03   EFFECT OF MISUNDERSTANDING[70]

Where the parties use the same word but attribute different meanings to it, there is a misunderstanding.[71] This could easily occur where a word is susceptible to two different meanings. Suppose the parties agree on Monday that their agreement will be performed "next Friday." Literally speaking, the next Friday is four days later, but most people in the United States would interpret "next Friday" to mean Friday in the next occurring week and would use "this Friday" to refer to the Friday occurring later in the same week. If the time for performance is critical, this ambiguity could have disastrous consequences.

On other occasions, the term is not ambiguous, but vague, and thus susceptible to a range of possible meanings. If a court is unable to ascertain the meaning of the contract, it will be unable to determine which party is in breach.[72]

---

[64] *See also* U.C.C. § 3-114 (2012) ("if [a negotiable] instrument contains contradictory terms, typewritten terms prevail over printed terms, handwritten terms prevail over both, and words prevail over numbers").

[65] *E.g.*, Codell Constr. Co. v. Commonwealth, 566 S.W.2d 161 (Ky. Ct. App. 1977). *See* RESTATEMENT (SECOND) OF CONTRACTS § 207 (1981); Edwin W. Patterson, *The Interpretation of Contracts*, 64 COLUM. L. REV. 833, 855 (1964).

[66] 43 F. Supp. 2d 848, 856 (S.D. Ohio 1998).

[67] *Id.*

[68] Seman v. First State Bank, 394 N.W.2d 557 (Minn. Ct. App. 1986).

[69] *E.g.*, Estate of McClain v. McClain, 183 N.E.2d 842 (Ind. Ct. App. 1962).

[70] Melvin Aaron Eisenberg, *Mistake in Contract Law*, 91 CAL. L. REV. 1573 (2003); William F. Young Jr., *Equivocation in the Making of Agreements*, 64 COLUM. L. REV. 619 (1964).

[71] RESTATEMENT (SECOND) OF CONTRACTS § 201 cmt. d (1981).

[72] Hill-Shafer P'ship v. Chilson Family Trust, 799 P.2d 810 (Ariz. 1990).

The Civil War-era case, *Raffles v. Wichelhaus*,[73] supplies a famous example. The parties had agreed to a sale of a quantity of cotton, to be delivered from Bombay, India, to Liverpool, England, with the goods to be transported aboard the ship *"Peerless."* Unknown to the parties, there were two ships named *Peerless* each sailing from Bombay to Liverpool with a load of cotton. The first one set sail in October, while the other did not depart until December. When the first ship arrived in Liverpool, the price of cotton was low in relation to the contract price. Thus, the buyer did not complain when the seller, who had meant the December boat, did not deliver the cotton when the October boat arrived. By the time the December boat made it to Liverpool, the tide of the American Civil War had changed, causing the market price of cotton to rise, but still not enough to make the contract profitable for the buyer.[74] Because it was unclear whether the contract referred to the October *Peerless* or to the December *Peerless*, the court ruled that no contract had been made.[75]

If the parties had meant the same ship, a contract would have been formed based on their shared understanding, regardless of how many ships named *Peerless* there had been.[76] Likewise, if there had been some objective means to resolve the misunderstanding, a contract could have been found. For example, if the seller had known the buyer meant the October boat, but remained silent, the court would have found a contract according to the buyer's intent.[77] Likewise, if the buyer did not know, but had reason to know, that the seller meant the December *Peerless*, a contract would have been found based on the seller's intent.[78]

The misunderstanding in *Raffles v. Wichelhaus* involved a true case of ambiguity, with the term susceptible of two different meanings: the October *Peerless* or the December *Peerless*. Other misunderstandings might result from vague terms, which have a wide spectrum of different possible meanings.[79] Misunderstandings involving true ambiguity are rare; those involving a range of possible meanings are more common. When they arise, efforts are made to construe the contract with reference to an external source, such as usage of trade, course of dealing, or course of performance, to determine whether one of the parties knew or should have known the intent of the other.[80] But, when the court is unable to discern the

---

[73] 159 Eng. Rep. 375 (Exch. 1864).

[74] A.W. Brian Simpson, *Contracts for Cotton to Arrive: The Case of the Two Ships Peerless*, 11 CARDOZO L. REV. 287 (1989).

[75] Raffles v. Wichelhaus, 159 Eng. Rep. 375 (Exch. 1864). *Accord* Oswald v. Allen, 417 F.2d 43 (2d Cir. 1969). *See also* RESTATEMENT (SECOND) OF CONTRACTS § 201(3) cmt. d (1981).

[76] *See* TKO Equip. Co. v. C & G Coal Co., 863 F.2d 541, 545 (7th Cir. 1988) ("If [both parties] wish the symbols 'one Caterpillar D9G tractor' to mean '500 railroad cars full of watermelons,' that's fine — provided [they] share this weird meaning").

[77] RESTATEMENT (SECOND) OF CONTRACTS § 201(2)(a) (1981).

[78] RESTATEMENT (SECOND) OF CONTRACTS § 201(2)(a) (1981). *See* Joyner v. Adams, 361 S.E.2d 902 (N.C. Ct. App. 1987) (remand to determine if one of the parties knew or had reason to know of the intent of the other).

[79] Frigaliment Imp'g Co. v. B.N.S. Int'l Sales Corp., 190 F. Supp. 116, 117 (S.D.N.Y. 1960).

[80] RESTATEMENT (SECOND) OF CONTRACTS § 201(2) (1981).

probable intent, and is thus unable to determine which of the parties is in breach, no contract can be found.

§ 6.04 CUSTOMARY PRACTICE[81]

The parties' contract usually includes any customary practice that arises out of a usage of trade, course of dealing, or course of performance. The Second Restatement refers to any habitual or customary practices as a "usage."[82] Both the Restatement and U.C.C. Article 2 carefully distinguish between a "usage of trade," which refers to the customary practice of others in the industry or the region,[83] and a "course of dealing," which refers to the customary practice between the parties in their previous dealings with one another.[84] Article 2 draws a further distinction between a course of dealing and a "course of performance." The latter is the customary practice of the parties in connection with the particular transaction involved.[85] All of these are relevant to the proper interpretation of a contract[86] and may be used to supplement or qualify a contract.[87]

In international transactions, the CISG,[88] UNIDROIT's Principles of International Contracts,[89] and the Principles of European Commercial Contracts[90] all provide for using applicable usages that they have agreed to or that generally apply, as well as past practices they have followed between themselves.[91]

[A]   Usage of Trade

A *usage of trade* is "any practice or method of dealing having such regularity of observance in a place, vocation, or trade, as to justify an expectation that it will be

---

[81] Lisa Bernstein, *Merchant Law in a Merchant Court: Rethinking the Code's Search for Immanent Business Norms*, 144 U. Pa. L. Rev. 1765 (1996); Richard A. Epstein, *Confusion About Custom: Disentangling Informal Customs from Standard Contractual Provisions*, 66 U. Chi. L. Rev. 821 (1999); Clayton P. Gillette, *The Law Merchant in the Modern Age: Institutional Design and International Usages Under the CISG*, 5 Chi. J. Int'l Law 157 (2004); Amy H. Kastely, *Stock Equipment for the Bargain in Fact: Trade Usage, "Express Terms," and Consistency Under Section 1-205 of the Uniform Commercial Code*, 64 N.C. L. Rev. 777 (1986); Roger W. Kirst, *Usage of Trade and Course of Dealing: Subversion of the UCC Theory*, 1977 U. Ill. L. F. 811; Juliet P. Kostritsky, *Judicial Incorporation of Trade Usages: A Functional Solution to the Opportunism Problem*, 39 Conn. L. Rev. 451 (2006); Joseph H. Levie, *Trade Usage and Custom Under the Common Law and the Uniform Commercial Code*, 40 N.Y.U. L. Rev. 1101 (1965); Eyal Zamir, *The Inverted Hierarchy of Contract Interpretation and Supplementation*, 97 Colum. L. Rev. 1710 (1997).

[82] Restatement (Second) of Contracts § 219 (1981).

[83] U.C.C. § 1-303(c) (2012) (formerly § 1-205(2)); Restatement (Second) of Contracts § 222(1) (1981).

[84] U.C.C. § 1-303(b) (2012) (formerly § 1-205(1)); Restatement (Second) of Contracts § 223(1) (1981).

[85] U.C.C. § 2-208(1) (2012).

[86] Restatement (Second) of Contracts § 220 (1981).

[87] Restatement (Second) of Contracts § 221 (1981).

[88] CISG Art. 9 (1980).

[89] PICC Art. 1.9 (2004).

[90] PECL Art. 1.105 (2002).

[91] Ch. Pamboukis, *The Concept and Function of Usages in the United Nations Convention on the International Sale of Goods*, 25 J.L. & Com. 107 (2005).

observed with respect to the transaction in question."[92] This modern definition should be contrasted with the older common law meaning of a "custom" which could be used to explain or supplement a contract only if the custom was universally followed.[93]

Trade usage is sometimes contained in a trade manual or other document describing industry-wide standards.[94] Accordingly, the customary practice of those engaged in a particular trade or industry, or among those in a particular community, both supplements the express terms of the parties' contract, and may be used to construe its meaning. Older decisions required a custom to be universally followed to qualify as a usage of trade.[95] However, modern cases recognize the existence of a usage of trade to supplement or construe a contract, even where it is not universally followed, as long as it is observed with sufficient regularity to justify an expectation that it will be observed in connection with the contract.[96] It need not even be well known, so long as it was sufficiently definite and widespread that the parties reasonably expected it would be followed.[97]

A usage of trade may be binding even where the parties are not aware of its existence.[98] Thus, newcomers to an industry will be bound.[99] However, care should be taken to ensure that the transaction in question was within the scope of the trade usage and not so far removed from the trade in which it was established for the parties not to have reasonably expected to be bound by it.[100]

[B]   Course of Dealing

A *course of dealing* is a private custom, developed between parties themselves in their past dealings with one another. A course of dealing arises from "a sequence of previous conduct between the parties . . . which is fairly to be regarded as establishing a common basis for understanding for interpreting their expressions and other conduct."[101] A course of dealing is not established simply on the basis of

---

[92] U.C.C. § 1-303(c) (2012) (formerly § 1-205(2)). *See* RESTATEMENT (SECOND) OF CONTRACTS § 222(1) (1981).

[93] *See* Threadgill v. Peabody Coal Co., 526 P.2d 676, 677–78 (Colo. Ct. App. 1974). U.C.C. § 1-303 cmt. 4 (2001) ("not required that a usage of trade be 'ancient or immemorial,' 'universal,' or the like").

[94] U.C.C. § 1-303(c) (2012) (formerly § 1-205(2)).

[95] U.C.C. § 1-303 cmt. 4 (2012); RESTATEMENT (SECOND) OF CONTRACTS § 222 cmt. b (1981); J.H. Levie, *Trade Usage and Custom Under the Common Law and the Uniform Commercial Code*, 40 N.Y.U. L. REV. 1101 (1965). *E.g.*, Fisher v. Congregation B'Nai Yitzhok, 110 A.2d 881 (Pa. Super. Ct. 1955).

[96] Nanakuli Paving & Rock Co. v. Shell Oil Co., 664 F.2d 772, 803 (9th Cir. 1981).

[97] *Id.*

[98] *E.g.*, Marion Coal Co. v. Marc Rich & Co. Int'l, 539 F. Supp. 903, 906 (S.D.N.Y. 1982). *See* Elizabeth Warren, *Trade Usage and Parties in the Trade: An Economic Rationale for an Inflexible Rule*, 42 U. PITT. L. REV. 515 (1981).

[99] Foxco Indus., Ltd. v. Fabric World, Inc., 595 F.2d 976 (5th Cir. 1979); Nanakuli Paving and Rock Co. v. Shell Oil Co., Inc., 664 F.2d 772, 798 n.40 (9th Cir. 1981).

[100] Nanakuli Paving & Rock Co. v. Shell Oil Co., 664 F.2d 772, 790 (9th Cir. 1981).

[101] U.C.C. § 1-303(b) (2012) (formerly § 1-205(1)); RESTATEMENT (SECOND) OF CONTRACTS § 223(1) (1981).

a single previous transaction[102] that is similar, or even identical, to the one involved in the dispute. Thus, evidence about frequency of a pattern of past behavior is necessary to establish a course of dealing between the parties.[103]

[C]   Course of Performance

A "course of performance" is more narrow still, and is based on the parties' behavior in performance of the contract that is being interpreted. A course of performance can be found where the contract "involves repeated occasions for performance by either party with knowledge of the nature of the performance and opportunity for objection to it by the other."[104]

A course of performance thus applies to conduct that occurs after the contract was made. Usage of trade and course of dealing, on the other hand, explicitly refer to customs already in place at the time the parties' contract was formed. For a course of performance to arise, the contract must be one in which there are repeated occasions for performance.[105] Thus, a course of performance could not arise in connection with a contract providing for a single delivery, but must instead arise in the context of a contract providing for or permitting installment deliveries.[106]

§ 6.05   THE PAROL EVIDENCE RULE[107]

The parol evidence rule is designed to preserve the integrity of written contracts.[108] When the parties to a contract have put their agreement in writing and intend that writing to be a complete and final version of their agreement, the rule

---

[102] Kern Oil & Ref. Co. v. Tenneco Oil Co., 792 F.2d 1380 (9th Cir. 1986). *But see* Steinmetz v. Bradbury Co., 618 F.2d 21 (8th Cir. 1980).

[103] Davis v. McDonald's Corp., 44 F. Supp. 2d 1251 (N.D. Fla. 1998).

[104] U.C.C. § 2-208(1) (2012).

[105] *Id.*

[106] U.C.C. § 2-208 cmt. 4 (2012); Nanakuli Paving and Rock Co. v. Shell Oil Co., 664 F.2d 772, 794 (9th Cir. 1981).

[107] Richard F. Broude, *The Consumer and the Parol Evidence Rule: Section 2-202 of the Uniform Commercial Code*, 1970 Duke L.J. 881; Scott J. Burnham, *The Parol Evidence Rule: Don't Be Afraid of the Dark*, 55 Mont. L. Rev. 93 (1994); John D. Calamari & Joseph M. Perillo, *A Plea for a Uniform Parol Evidence Rule and Principles of Contract Interpretation*, 42 Ind. L.J. 333 (1967); Arthur L. Corbin, *The Interpretation of Words and the Parol Evidence Rule*, 50 Cornell L.Q. 161 (1965); Lawrence A. Cunningham, *Toward a Prudential and Credibility-Centered Parol Evidence Rule*, 68 U. Cin. L. Rev. 269 (2000); Juanda Lowder Daniel, *K.I.S.S. the Parol Evidence Rule Goodbye: Simplifying the Concept of Protecting the Parties' Written Agreement*, 57 Syracuse L. Rev. 227 (2007); Edwin McCormick, *The Parol Evidence Rule as a Procedural Device for Control of the Jury*, 41 Yale L.J. 365 (1932); Eric Posner, *The Parol Evidence Rule, the Plain Meaning Rule, and the Principles of Contract Interpretation*, 146 U. Pa. L. Rev. 533 (1998); Justin Sweet, *Contract Making and Parol Evidence: Diagnosis and Treatment of a Sick Rule*, 53 Cornell L. Rev. 1036 (1968); Eyal Zamir, *The Inverted Hierarchy of Contract Interpretation and Supplementation*, 97 Colum. L. Rev. 1710 (1997).

[108] Galmish v. Cicchini, 734 N.E.2d 782, 789 (Ohio 2000). *See* John D. Calamari & Joseph M. Perillo, *A Plea for a Uniform Parol Evidence Rule and Principles of Interpretation*, 42 Ind. L.J. 333 (1967). *But see* 6 Arthur L. Corbin, Corbin on Contracts § 582 (Interim ed. 2008) ("It would have been far better had no such rule ever been stated.").

prevents the jury from considering other evidence that might alter the terms in the writing.[109] The rule prevents either party from introducing evidence of terms, alleged to have been agreed upon, but nevertheless not included in the final written version of the contract.[110]

The parol evidence rule has considerable intuitive appeal.[111] The purpose of reducing agreements to writing is to have a complete and final document to use as a later reference. The rule is based on the several premises: that written evidence is more reliable than oral testimony, that a more recent written document is more reliable than testimony about earlier discussions, and that whatever the parties have put down in writing is a more accurate reflection of the terms of their agreement than their memories. Moreover, preventing the parties from introducing evidence beyond the terms of the written contract limits their opportunity to commit perjury. Even scrupulously honest people have an uncanny ability to perceive events in a manner likely to serve their own interests. Likewise, the rule restricts the ability of juries to rescue sympathetic parties from bad deals.[112] Finally, it reduces the costs imposed on courts and the parties in searching for evidence about the terms of the contract.[113] In sum, the parol evidence rule (1) promotes commercial certainty, (2) permits parties to finalize their agreements, and (3) facilitates parties in performing contractual obligations confidently.

While the parol evidence rule is useful and prevents perjury, it also presents serious dangers. The rule might permit a party to evade promises it made simply because they were inadvertently excluded from the written version of the deal. At worst, it might permit a dishonest party to use false promises deliberately to induce another person to agree to a contract and then capitalize on the exclusion of those terms from the writing in order to back out of its commitments.[114] As a result, the parol evidence rule has been criticized,[115] limited,[116] and sometimes, simply ignored. Some view these qualifications to the rule as desirable ways to ensure the implementation of the intent of the parties.[117] Others view them as undesirable

---

[109] 6 ARTHUR L. CORBIN, CORBIN ON CONTRACTS § 573 (Interim ed. 2008).

[110] *See* Arthur L. Corbin, *The Interpretation of Words and the Parol Evidence Rule*, 50 CORNELL L.Q. 161 (1965); Helen Hadjiyannakis, *The Parol Evidence Rule And Implied Terms: The Sounds of Silence*, 54 FORDHAM L. REV. 35 (1985); Edwin W. Patterson, *The Interpretation and Construction of Contracts*, 64 COLUM. L. REV. 833, 852 (1964); Eric A. Posner, *The Parol Evidence Rule, the Plain Meaning Rule, and the Principles of Contractual Interpretation*, 146 U. PA. L. REV. 533 (1998).

[111] Juanda Lowder Daniel, *K.I.S.S. the Parol Evidence Rule Goodbye: Simplifying the Concept of Protecting the Parties' Written Agreement*, 57 SYRACUSE L. REV. 227, 228 (2007).

[112] *See* Olympia Hotels Corp. v. Johnson Wax Dev. Corp., 908 F.2d 1363, 1373 (7th Cir. 1990) ("Not all parties to contracts want to entrust their fate to the vagaries of juries unversed in the usages of business.") (Posner J.).

[113] Joshua A.T. Fairfield, *The Search Interest in Contract*, 92 IOWA L. REV. 1237, 1265–68 (2007).

[114] These are the same concerns behind criticisms of the statute of frauds, which can be used to perpetrate fraud as easily as it can be used to prevent fraud.

[115] *See* Arthur L. Corbin, *The Interpretation of Words and the Parol Evidence Rule*, 50 CORNELL L.Q. 161 (1965).

[116] *See* Pac. Gas and Elec. Co. v. G.W. Thomas Drayage & Rigging Co., 442 P.2d 641 (Cal. 1968).

[117] *See* Arthur L. Corbin, *The Interpretation of Words and the Parol Evidence Rule*, 50 CORNELL L.Q. 161 (1965); Pac. Gas and Elec. Co. v. G.W. Thomas Drayage & Rigging Co., 442 P.2d 641 (Cal. 1968).

intrusions of courts into the expectations of the parties, which diminish the reliability of written agreements in commerce.[118]

[A]   Meaning of "Parol" Evidence

The parol evidence rule applies with equal force to evidence of oral and written agreements that might be used to vary the terms of a final written contract. Specifically, if the parties have a writing that is supposed to be a complete and final expression of their agreement, then extrinsic evidence of prior or contemporaneous agreements they might have made that would vary or contradict the terms contained in the writing is inadmissible.

[1]   Oral and Written Evidence as Parol

The name of the parol evidence rule, with its reference to "parol," can be misleading. In many other contexts, "parol" means "oral," suggesting that the parol evidence rule excludes only testimony. However, the rule excludes both written and oral evidence of the terms of the parties' agreement that was not included in the final written version of the contract.

[2]   Evidence of Prior and Contemporaneous Agreements Excluded

The parol evidence rule does not exclude all evidence that was not included in the writing. It only excludes evidence of agreements made before or at the same time the writing was executed.[119] The name of the rule is therefore somewhat misleading in its suggestion that all "parol evidence" is excluded from the jury's consideration. Most importantly, the rule has no effect on evidence of oral modifications that the parties may have made after their adoption of the written version of the contract.[120] Thus, if the parties conduct negotiations in January, sign a final written agreement in February, and in March agree to modify their agreement, evidence of terms agreed upon in March may be considered by the jury, even though evidence of terms agreed to in January, but not incorporated into the written memorial signed in February, may not be considered. Likewise, telephone conversations or email messages they exchange, after the written contract was executed, are admissible.[121]

This should be clear from the purpose of the parol evidence rule, which preserves the integrity of written agreements by presuming that everything agreed upon up to that point has been included in the writing. A topic or term not yet discussed by the parties when the writing was adopted could not have been

---

[118] Trident Ctr. v. Conn. Gen'l Life Ins. Co., 847 F.2d 564 (9th Cir. 1988).

[119] U.C.C. § 2-202 (2012); RESTATEMENT (SECOND) OF CONTRACTS § 214 (1981).

[120] *E.g.*, Litman v. Mass. Mut. Life Ins. Co., 739 F.2d 1549, 1558 (11th Cir. 1984). *See* Gregory Scott Crespi, *Clarifying the Boundary Between the Parol Evidence Rule and the Rules Governing Subsequent Oral Modifications*, 34 OHIO N.U.L. REV. 71 (2008).

[121] *E.g.*, Estate of Ryan v. Shuman, 655 S.E.2d 644, 647–48 & 648 n.2 (Ga. Ct. App. 2007); Norris v. Royal Indem. Co., 485 N.E.2d 754 (Ohio Ct. App. 1984); Niebur v. Town of Cicero, 212 F. Supp. 2d 790, 805 (N.D. Ill. 2002); Trad Indus., Ltd. v. Brogan, 805 P.2d 54 (Mont. 1991).

included in the writing. The most a written contract can ever include is terms agreed upon at the time the writing was adopted. Adoption of a written contract as a "final" expression of the terms of the agreement does not prevent the parties from subsequently changing the terms of their agreement, either orally or via a later written agreement, any more than a person's "last will and testament" prevents a person from making a new will. Thus, the parol evidence rule has no place in an analysis of the effectiveness of an alleged subsequent modification of a written contract. The statute of frauds or the terms of the agreement itself may limit the enforceability of an alleged oral modification, but the parol evidence rule does not apply.

[3]   Substantive Rule of Contract Law; Not a Rule of Evidence

Despite its name, the parol evidence rule is a substantive rule of contract law, not a rule of evidence.[122] The rules of evidence reflect policies about the proper means of proving facts in issue; the parol evidence rule reflects a policy about the superseding legal effect of a final written version of an agreement.[123] Treatment of the rule as a substantive rule of contract law has several important consequences. First, it means that the substantive law governing the formation and enforceability of the contract will apply, regardless of which court is resolving the dispute.[124] Likewise, failure to make an objection at the time the offending evidence is introduced does not bar a later effort to prevent the court from considering the evidence.[125]

[B]   Integrated Written Contracts

There is a wide range of potential written evidence of the terms of a contract. This could range from random notes scribbled by one party on a note pad, to a complicated, lengthy, and detailed document, the language of which has been carefully crafted to reflect the precise terms of the parties' agreement.[126] The mere fact that a writing exists does not prevent the court from considering other evidence of the terms of the parties' agreement *unless that was the parties' intent*.[127] Thus, the existence of a detailed but preliminary draft of a contract does not prevent the introduction of evidence of prior negotiations or written terms inconsistent with the draft when the parties did not intend the draft as a final

---

[122] *E.g.*, Abercrombie v. Hayden Corp., 883 P.2d 845 (Or. 1994); Mitchill v. Lath, 160 N.E. 646 (N.Y. 1928).

[123] *See* Charles T. McCormick, *The Parol Evidence Rule as a Procedural Device for the Control of the Jury*, 41 Yale L.J. 365 (1932).

[124] *See* Betz Labs. Inc. v. Hines, 647 F.2d 402 (3d Cir. 1981) (federal court, exercising its diversity jurisdiction, must apply the parol evidence rule of the state whose contract law governs the contact generally); Trident Center v. Conn. Gen'l Life Ins. Co., 847 F.2d 564 (9th Cir. 1988).

[125] *E.g.*, Gajewski v. Bratcher, 221 N.W.2d 614 (N.D. 1974).

[126] Gianni v. R. Russell & Co., 126 A. 791 (Pa. 1924); Thompson v. Libby, 26 N.W. 1 (Minn. 1885).

[127] Hatley v. Stafford, 588 P.2d 603 (Or. 1978).

expression of their agreement.[128] The parol evidence rule applies only when the parties intend a particular writing to serve as a "final expression" of at least some portion of their agreement.

When a writing is intended as such a final expression, it is referred to as "integrated."[129] The term "integrated" is used to refer to the idea that all of the parties' negotiations and preliminary agreements regarding a term have been included or integrated into a final written version of the agreement with the intent that the writing supersedes any contrary prior discussions or agreements.[130]

If the parties intended the writing to serve as a final expression of some, but not all, of the terms agreed upon, it is a "partially integrated" writing.[131] A partially integrated writing is final, but only with respect to the terms actually included in the writing. A partially integrated writing may not be *contradicted* by evidence of any prior or contemporaneous agreements not included in the writing. But, it may be *supplemented* by evidence of additional terms as long as the supplemental terms do not contradict the writing.

A writing intended by the parties as not only final with respect to the terms it includes, but also as complete, is a "fully integrated contract."[132] A fully integrated writing supersedes all prior negotiations and agreements, even if they are consistent with the terms appearing in the writing.[133] Thus, a fully integrated writing may not be contradicted or supplemented by evidence of prior or contemporaneous terms.

[1]   Effect of a Fully Integrated Written Contract

Because it was intended by the parties as both a final and exclusive statement of the terms of their agreement,[134] a fully integrated written contract completely supersedes prior versions of the contract whether oral or written. Likewise, it excludes evidence of additional or "supplemental" terms even if they are consistent with the language in the writing.[135] For example, the fully integrated written contract in *Thompson v. Libby*,[136] for the sale of cut logs, prevented the buyer from introducing evidence that the seller had made a supplemental warranty about the quality of the logs. Likewise, the detailed written contract in *Mitchill v. Lath*,[137] for the purchase and sale of a mansion, excluded testimony offered by the buyer that the seller had also agreed to remove an unsightly shack used as an "ice

---

[128] Cobb-Alvarez v. Union Pac. Corp., 962 F. Supp. 1049, 1055 (N.D. Ill. 1997); Emrich v. Connell, 716 P.2d 863 (Wash. 1986).

[129] RESTATEMENT (SECOND) OF CONTRACTS § 209(1) (1981).

[130] RESTATEMENT (SECOND) OF CONTRACTS § 209 cmt. a (1981).

[131] RESTATEMENT (SECOND) OF CONTRACTS § 210(2) (1981). *See* U.C.C. § 2-202 (2012).

[132] RESTATEMENT (SECOND) OF CONTRACTS § 210(1) (1981). *See* U.C.C. § 2-202(b) (2012).

[133] Masterson v. Sine, 436 P.2d 561 (Cal. 1968).

[134] RESTATEMENT (SECOND) OF CONTRACTS § 210(2) (1981).

[135] U.C.C. § 2-202(b) (2012).

[136] 26 N.W. 1 (Minn. 1885).

[137] 160 N.E. 646 (N.Y. 1928).

house" located on property adjoining the mansion. In both these cases, evidence of the supplemental terms was excluded even though the terms were consistent with those contained in the writings. The written agreements were intended as both final and complete, and thus even evidence of consistent additional terms was excluded.

In contracts for the sale of goods, U.C.C. § 2-202 takes a similar approach. If there is a writing intended by the parties not only as final with respect to the terms it contains, but also "as a complete and exclusive statement of the terms of the agreement," the writing may not be contradicted or even supplemented by evidence of prior or contemporaneous agreements.[138] However, as explained below, the U.C.C. nevertheless permits a final and complete written contract to be explained or supplemented by evidence of a course of dealing, usage of trade, or course of performance.[139]

[2]   Effect of a Partially Integrated Written Contract

Incomplete writings are treated differently. A writing can be final with respect to the terms it contains, but nevertheless not intended by the parties as an exhaustive expression of their entire agreement. Such a writing is only "partially integrated." Parol evidence can be used to explain or supplement a partially integrated writing, but not to contradict it. If the parol evidence does not contradict the terms contained in the writing, the evidence may be considered by the jury.[140]

In *Masterson v. Sine*,[141] a partially integrated written option contract was silent on the question of whether it could be assigned. Because the writing did not address the topic, it was held to be only partially integrated, and the jury was permitted to consider evidence that the parties had agreed that the option could be assigned. In *Brown v. Oliver*,[142] a partially integrated written contract for the sale of a hotel did not bar the introduction of evidence that the parties meant for the furnishings in the hotel to be included as part of the transaction.

Here it should be emphasized that the mere fact that parol evidence may be introduced does not necessarily mean that the jurors will believe it. A jury can consider the testimony but choose not to believe it. Importantly, however, the proponent of the additional term will have the chance to persuade the jury that the parties agreed to the additional term. If the evidence is excluded, the jury will not have the chance to even consider it.

---

[138] U.C.C. § 2-202 (2012). *See also* U.C.C. § 2A-202 (2012).

[139] U.C.C. § 2-202(a) (2012).

[140] *See* U.C.C. § 2-202(b) (2012).

[141] 436 P.2d 561 (Cal. 1968).

[142] 256 P. 1008 (Kan. 1927).

[3] Determining If the Writing Is Integrated[143]

The first and most critical question in any analysis of the parol evidence rule is whether a writing is fully integrated, partially integrated, or completely unintegrated. If it is fully integrated then the writing will be the sole evidence of the terms of the contract. If it is partially integrated, the writing may be supplemented, but not contradicted, by evidence of their prior understandings. If it was completely unintegrated, and not even final with respect to the terms it contained, then the parol evidence rule presents no bar to the jury's consideration of other evidence of the terms of the agreement.[144]

[a] Four Corners of the Contract

Courts take different approaches in making this key threshold decision. The traditional approach is known as the "four-corners test."[145] It calls on the court to examine the writing to determine if it appears complete.[146] If it appears complete, the writing is a fully integrated written contract and all parol evidence or prior agreements is excluded.[147]

Thompson v. Libby[148] supplies a good example of the operation of the four corners test. The parties had both signed a short and simple document reflecting their agreement for the sale of certain logs. Their simple agreement provided:

Agreement

Hastings, Minn., June, 1883

I have this day sold to R.C. Libbey, of Hastings, Minn., all my logs marked "H.C.A.," cut in the winters of 1882 and 1883, for ten dollars a thousand feet, boom scale at Minneapolis, Minnesota, Payments cash as fast as scale bills are produced.

J.H. Thompson

per D.S. Mooers

R.C. Libbey

After the logs were delivered, Libbey complained about their quality and refused to pay. He alleged that Thompson had supplied a warranty of the quality of the wood, even though it was not contained in the writing. The court, in refusing to consider

---

[143] Robert Childres & Stephen J Spitz, *Status in the Law of Contracts*, 47 N.Y.U. L. Rev. 1 (1972); Keith Rowley, *Contract Construction and Interpretation: From the 'Four Corners' to Parol Evidence (and Everything in Between)*, 69 Miss. L.J. 73, 101 (1999).

[144] *See* Emrich v. Connell, 716 P.2d 863, 867 n.1 (Wash. 1986).

[145] Peter Linzer, *The Comfort of Certainty: Plain Meaning and the Parol Evidence Rule*, 71 Fordham L. Rev. 799, 805 (2002); Stephen F. Ross & Daniel Tranen, *The Modern Parol Evidence Rule and Its Implications for New Textualist Statutory Interpretation*, 87 Geo. L.J. 195 (1998).

[146] Air Safety, Inc. v. Teachers Realty Corp., 706 N.E.2d 882 (Ill. 1999).

[147] *See* Tallmadge Bros. v. Iroquois Gas Trans. Sys., 746 A.2d 1277, 1289 (Conn. 2000).

[148] 26 N.W. 1 (Minn. 1885).

the buyer's testimony, ruled that "[t]he only criterion of the completeness of the written contract as a full expression of the agreement of the parties is the writing itself."[149] Because the writing appeared on its face to be complete, it was presumed to be a fully integrated writing, and the buyer's testimony about the seller's warranty was excluded.[150] *Thompson v. Libby* is a good reminder that even a simple basic agreement, without a merger clause, can still constitute a fully integrated written contract.

The four-corners test is most frequently applied when the contract contains an "integration clause," expressing the parties' intent that the writing should be regarded as the final and complete expression of the parties' agrement.[151]

[b]   Extrinsic Evidence

Other courts are willing to conduct a more extensive inquiry into whether the writing was intended as a complete integration.[152] These courts consider evidence beyond the writing itself, in determining whether the parties intended the writing as fully or partially integrated. These courts, however, refuse to consider the disputed parol evidence itself, as part of this threshold determination.[153] They consider other extrinsic circumstances surrounding the making of the contract and the preparation of an execution of the writing, but remain fearful that considering the very evidence in issue would destroy the utility of the parol evidence rule.[154]

[c]   Parol to Show Lack of Integration

Many contemporary courts, heavily influenced by Professor Corbin, are willing to examine any extrinsic evidence, including testimony about the disputed term itself, to determine whether the writing was intended as an exhaustive expression of the parties' agreement. Under this view, if the parties meant to include the term as part of their agreement, but failed to include it in the writing, the writing was not intended as a final and complete expression of the agreement, and the jury should be permitted to consider the evidence in question.[155] Thus, the existence of a parol agreement proves that the writing is not fully integrated.[156]

In considering evidence extrinsic to a writing that appears complete, courts sometimes seek to determine whether the disputed term might "naturally have

---

[149] *Id.* at 2.

[150] *See also* J & B Steel Contractors v. C. Iber & Sons, 642 N.E.2d 1215 (Ill. 1994); Jake C. Byers, Inc. v. J.B.C. Invs., Inc., 834 S.W.2d 806, 812 (Mo. Ct. App. 1992).

[151] *E.g.*, ADR N. Am., L.L.C. v. Agway, Inc., 303 F.3d 653 (6th Cir. 2002).

[152] *See* Tallmadge Bros. v. Iroquois Gas Trans. Sys., 746 A.2d 1277, 1289 (Conn. 2000).

[153] Bussard v. Coll. of St. Thomas, 200 N.W.2d 155 (Minn 1972); Gagne v. Stevens, 696 A.2d 411 (Me. 1997).

[154] Samuel Williston, 3 Williston on Contracts § 633 (1936).

[155] Arthur Linton Corbin, 6 Corbin on Contracts § 582 (Interim ed. 2008).

[156] Stephen F. Ross & Daniel Tranen, *The Modern Parol Evidence Rule and Its Implications for New Textualist Statutory Interpretation*, 87 Geo. L.J. 195, 205 (1998). *See* Trident Center v. Conn. Gen'l Life Ins. Co., 847 F.2d 564 (9th Cir. 1988).

been omitted" from the writing.[157] If the term "might naturally have been omitted," the writing is only partially integrated, and the jury may consider the parol evidence. Otherwise, the evidence is excluded even if it does not contradict the writing. Thus, in *Lee v. Joseph E. Seagram & Sons*,[158] the court found that an agreement to provide a second distributorship might naturally have been omitted from an otherwise apparently complete written first distributorship contract.

The U.C.C. takes slightly different approach. Instead of inquiring whether the term "might naturally have been omitted," the Official Comments to U.C.C. § 2-202 indicate that the court should inquire into whether the disputed term "would certainly have been included."[159] Under this test, courts have greater leeway to conclude that the writing is not fully integrated.

If there is separate consideration for the parol promise, this is a strong indication that the writing was not intended as a complete expression of their agreement.[160] For example, a written contract between Ray and Agnes for the sale of a racehorse for $10,000 would not preclude evidence of a separate oral agreement for Ray to rent space in his stable for the horse and provide it with daily care for an agreed additional price of $300 per month.[161] The fact that there is separate consideration for the promise to stable and care for the horse demonstrates that this collateral promise is outside the scope of the contract for sale, and does not contradict it any way.[162] However, of course, there may be no separate consideration — the plaintiff may contend that the collateral promise is enforceable under the doctrine of promissory estoppel, and that entering into the written contract was the action that the plaintiff took in reliance on the promise.[163]

Finally, although most courts no longer confine their inquiry to the four corners of the document, the form of the document remains relevant. Thus, the sophistication of the parties,[164] the length of the agreement, and the degree of detail included in the writing are significant considerations. The opportunity of the parties to make revisions to the writing should also be considered.[165] Nevertheless, more basic writings, such as those sent in confirmation of terms negotiated over the telephone, might also be regarded as fully integrated writings.[166]

---

[157] RESTATEMENT (SECOND) OF CONTRACTS § 216(2)(b) (1981).

[158] 552 F.2d 447 (2d Cir. 1977).

[159] U.C.C. § 2-202 cmt. 3 (2012).

[160] RESTATEMENT (SECOND) OF CONTRACTS § 216(2)(a) (1981); Rowe v. Allely, 507 N.W.2d 293, 296 (Neb. 1993).

[161] RESTATEMENT (SECOND) OF CONTRACTS § 216 illus. 3 (1981).

[162] John Edward Murry Jr., *The Parol Evidence Process and Standardized Agreements Under the Restatement (Second) of Contracts*, 123 U. PA. L. REV. 1342 (1975).

[163] *E.g.*, Lee v. Joseph E. Seagram & Sons, Inc., 552 F.2d 447 (2d Cir. 1977).

[164] *See* Tallmadge Bros. v. Iroquois Gas Trans. Sys., L.P., 746 A.2d 1277 (Conn. 2000).

[165] Gianni v. R. Russell & Co., 126 A. 791 (Pa. 1924); Acme Markets v. Dawson Enters., 251 A.2d 839 (Md. 1969).

[166] *See* Step-Saver Data Sys., Inc. v. Wyse Tech., 939 F.2d 91 (3d Cir. 1991).

[4]   Effect of a "Merger Clause"

Many written contracts contain an express term specifying that the writing is the final and complete expression of their agreement. Language to this effect is referred to as a "merger" or "integration" clause, referring to the supposed merger of all of the terms agreed upon into a single writing, as if the writing were a one-lane highway into which all traffic (promises) had been funneled. The presence of a properly drafted merger clause creates a presumption that the contract is fully integrated.[167]

However, merger clauses are not always conclusive.[168] First, the text of the clause must be examined to determine its likely intent. Poorly drafted merger clauses might help persuade the court that the writing is only partially integrated, such as where the clause merely prohibits evidence of conflicting terms.

Moreover, if the clause was included as a result of fraud, bad faith, unconscionability, or mistake,[169] parol may be admitted to supplement the contract, notwithstanding the merger provision. And, not surprisingly, a merger clause in a standardized form contract, that one of the parties may have neither read nor understood, is vulnerable to attack as not necessarily reflecting the intent of the parties.[170]

The Uniform Commercial Code does not refer to the conclusive or presumptive effect of a merger clause. Cases applying U.C.C. § 2-202, however, have routinely enforced these provisions[171] unless they are unconscionable.[172] Likewise, the United Nations Convention on Contracts for the International Sale of Goods (CISG), which rejects the parol evidence rule generally,[173] is silent on the enforceability of a merger clause. Although the case law interpreting the CISG is sparse, it is anticipated that it will enforce an otherwise valid merger clause, in accordance with the intent of the parties.[174]

[5]   Role of the Court

At least one aspect of the parol evidence rule is clear: the threshold determination of whether a written contract is fully integrated, partially integrated, or completely unintegrated is for the court, not the jury, to make. It is

---

[167] *Ex parte* Palm Harbor Homes, Inc., 798 So. 2d 656 (Ala. 2001).

[168] RESTATEMENT (SECOND) OF CONTRACTS § 216 cmt. 3 (1981); Masterson v. Sine, 436 P.2d 561 (Cal. 1968).

[169] Smith v. Cent. Soya of Athens, Inc., 604 F. Supp. 518, 526 (E.D.N.C. 1985).

[170] Sierra Diesel Injection Serv., Inc. v. Burroughs Corp., Inc. 656 F. Supp. 426 (D. Nev. 1987); Eberhardt v. Comerica Bank, 171 B.R. 239, 243 (Bankr. E.D. Mich. 1994).

[171] *See, e.g.*, Seibel v. Layne & Bowler, Inc. 641 P.2d 668 (Or. Ct. App. 1982).

[172] Kerry L. Macintosh, *When Are Merger Clauses Unconscionable?*, 64 DENV. U.L. REV. 529 (1988).

[173] CISG Art. 8(1) (1980). *E.g.*, MCC-Marble Ceramic Center, Inc. v. Ceramica Nuova D'Agostino, S.P.A., 144 F.3d 1384 (11th Cir. 1998). *But see* Beijing Metals & Minerals Export/Import Corp. v. Am. Bus. Ctr., Inc., 993 F.2d 1178, 1183 n.9 (5th Cir. 1993) (applying parol evidence rule).

[174] Ronald A. Brand & Harry M. Fletchner, *Arbitration and Contract Formation in International Trade: First Interpretations of the U.N. Sales Convention*, 112 J.L. & COM. 239, 252 (1993).

a question of law.[175] Thus, in reaching a preliminary decision on whether the writing was intended by the parties as final and complete, the court will consider extrinsic evidence, sometimes including the very parol evidence whose admissibility is in question. The question for the court is not whether the parties agreed to the supposed term, but rather whether the writing was integrated.[176] If the court resolves the question of integration in favor of the proponent of the additional term, and the term is supplemental, not contradictory, the jury will have the opportunity to consider the evidence and make its own decision about whether the term was part of the agreement.

[C]   Collateral Contracts

A *collateral contract* is an agreement that is separate and distinct from the integrated written contract. Evidence of a collateral contract is admissible, as long as it does not contradict the main final written contract. Unfortunately, the term "collateral contract" is used in several different and sometimes conflicting ways.

One way it is used is to refer to a completely separate agreement between the same parties as the main agreement, but dealing with a separate subject, and involving separate consideration. The parol evidence rule does not permit the existence of one contract to prevent evidence that there is another contract, side by side with the main agreement that is in final written form. For example, the fact that Sam and Barb have agreed in writing that Sam will sell his BMW to Barb for $15,000, does not prevent Barb from introducing evidence that they had a separate oral agreement for Sam to paint Barb's house, for a price of $5000. These are two separate agreements, dealing with two separate subjects, each with independent consideration. Nothing about the painting services to be supplied by Sam contradicts the written contract for the sale of the BMW. Accordingly, the written contract for the sale of the car does not impede the ability of the parties to attempt to prove the existence of the contract to have Barb's house painted. This is true even if the agreement for the sale of the car includes a merger clause.[177]

But, "collateral agreement" is sometimes also used to refer to a subsidiary promise, somehow related to the main written contract, that is without separate consideration. Thus, if Barb claims that she agreed to buy Sam's BMW only because Sam agreed to replace the tires, a question will arise whether she should be able to testify about this promise. There is no separate consideration for Sam's alleged promise to install new tires on the car before delivering it to Barb, and the promise of new tires does not contradict the written contract in any way.

In this situation, involving a contract for the sale of goods (both the car and the tires) the court's inquiry will be whether Sam's promise to put new tires on the car is one that "certainly would have been included" in the writing, if the promise had been made. If the court believes that the promise of new tires is so closely related

---

[175] Luria Bros. & Co. v. Pielet Bros. Scrap Iron & Metal, Inc., 600 F.2d 103, 109 (7th Cir. 1979); Hatley v. Stafford, 588 P.2d 603 (Or. 1978). *See* Charles McCormick, Handbook of the Law of Evidence 237 (1954).

[176] Hatley v. Stafford, 588 P.2d 603 (Or. 1978).

[177] Restatement (Second) of Contracts § 216(2)(a) & cmt. c (1981).

to the contract for the sale of the car that it would certainly have been included in the writing if the promise had been made, the evidence is inadmissible.

Common law expressions of the issue use a slightly different and more restrictive test: whether the promise "might naturally be omitted from the writing."[178] Thus, in *Mitchill v. Lath*,[179] the court decided that a seller's oral promise to remove an unsightly "ice house" (a shed used to store ice in the days before refrigeration), from property across the road was not admissible. The court determined that the promise concerning removal of the ice house was "sufficiently connected with the principal transaction as to part and parcel of it."[180]

[D]   Supplementing a Partially Integrated Contract

If the court has determined that a written contract is final but not necessarily complete, that is, that it is partially but not fully integrated, a second preliminary determination must be made before permitting the jury to consider the evidence: the court must also determine whether the term is consistent with the language of the written contract.[181] Thus, if the term is consistent, the evidence will be admitted as an additional or supplemental term, and the jury will be allowed to consider the veracity of the proponent of the supposed provision. However, if the term contradicts the language of the writing, the proposed evidence of it will be excluded.

Determining whether a particular term contradicts or merely supplements a written contract has proven difficult. Two tests have emerged. One permits the introduction of parol evidence that does not specifically contradict or negate an express provision of the contract.[182] The other is more restrictive, preventing admissibility if there is an "absence of reasonable harmony" between the written contract and the supposed parol agreement.[183]

In *Hunt Foods & Industries v. Doliner*,[184] the defendant sought to introduce evidence that a written and apparently unconditional stock option was subject to a condition that had not been included in the written version of the contract. The court ruled that because the written contract was silent on the question of conditions on the plaintiff's right to exercise the option, the writing did not expressly negate the existence of the condition, and the jury was permitted to consider whether the condition had been agreed upon.

The court in *Luria Brothers & Co. v. Pielet Brothers Scrap Iron & Metal, Inc.*[185] was more restrictive. The court decided that a parol condition excusing the seller from delivering a specific quantity of scrap metal was not "in reasonable

---

[178] RESTATEMENT (SECOND) OF CONTRACTS § 216(2)(b) (1981).

[179] 160 N.E. 646 (N.Y. 1928).

[180] *Id.* at 647. *See also* Masterson v. Sine, 436 P.2d 561 (Cal. 1968).

[181] RESTATEMENT (SECOND) OF CONTRACTS § 216 (1981); U.C.C. § 2-202(a) (2012).

[182] Hunt Foods & Indus., Inc. v. Doliner, 26 A.D.2d 41 (N.Y. 1966).

[183] Luria Bros. & Co. v. Pielet Bros. Scrap Iron & Metal, Inc., 600 F.2d 103 (7th Cir. 1979).

[184] 26 A.D.2d 41 (N.Y. 1966).

[185] 600 F.2d 103 (7th Cir. 1979).

harmony" with the unconditional language of the seller's obligations in the written contract. Most courts have taken the more restrictive "reasonable harmony" approach used in *Luria Brothers*.[186]

[E]   Resolving Ambiguity and "Plain Meaning"[187]

Parol evidence is naturally admissible to resolve ambiguities in an integrated written contract.[188] Here, as with seemingly every aspect of the parol evidence rule, two views predominate. One holds that although words may lack a "fixed meaning," they do have a "plain meaning" that can ordinarily be discerned,[189] and that this plain meaning prevents any ambiguity. The competing view holds that, in interpreting contracts, the meaning intended by the parties should prevail regardless of any fixed, plain, or standard meaning familiar to the court,[190] and that the court should consider this evidence in the process of identifying whether the contract is ambiguous.

The latter view, is reflected by the California Supreme Court's decision in *Pacific Gas & Electric. v. G.W. Thomas Drayage & Rigging Co.*[191] The written agreement required the defendant to perform certain work for the plaintiff " 'at [its] own risk and expense' and to 'indemnify' plaintiff 'against all loss, damage, expense and liability resulting from injury to property, arising out of or in any way connected with the performance of this contract.' "[192] The defendant contended that the parties meant this language to apply only to require the defendant to pay for damage to property owned by a third party, and thus that it did not require the defendant to pay for harm done to the plaintiff's property.

Chief Justice Traynor took the view that words used in a contract could not have a plain meaning apart from the meaning attributed to the words by the parties to the contract in question. The court ruled that parol evidence is admissible if it is relevant "to prove a meaning to which the language of the instrument is reasonably

---

[186] *E.g.*, ARB, Inc. v. E-Sys., Inc. 663 F.2d 189 (D.C. Cir. 1980); Alaska N. Dev., Inc. v. Alyeska Pipeline Serv. Co., 666 P.2d 33 (Alaska 1983).

[187] Arthur L. Corbin, *The Interpretation of Words and the Parol Evidence Rule*, 50 CORNELL L.Q. 161 (1965); Susan Martin Davidson, *Yes, Judge Kozinski, There Is a Parol Evidence Rule in California — The Lessons of a Pyrrhic Victory*, 25 SW. U. L. REV. 1 (1995); Olivia W. Karlin & Louis W. Karlin, *The California Parol Evidence Rule*, 21 SW. U. L. REV. 1361 (1992); Stephen L. Lubben, *Chief Justice Traynor's Contract Jurisprudence and the Free Law Dilemma: Naziism, the Judiciary, and California's Contract Law*, 7 S. CAL. INTERDISCIPLINARY L. J. (1998); Richard A. Posner, *The Law and Economics of Contract Interpretation*, 83 TEX. L. REV. 1581 (2005); Harry G. Prince, *Contract Interpretation in California: Plain Meaning, Parol Evidence and Use of the "Just Result" Principle*, 31 LOY. L.A. L. REV. 557 (1998); Ferdinand S. Tino, Annotation, *The Parol Evidence Rule and Admissibility of Extrinsic Evidence to Establish or Clarify Ambiguity in Written Contract*, 40 A.L.R.3d 1384 (1971).

[188] Arthur L. Corbin, *The Interpretation of Words and the Parol Evidence Rule*, 50 CORNELL L.Q. 161 (1965).

[189] *E.g.*, Aultman Hosp. Ass'n v. Cmty. Mut. Ins. Co., 544 N.E.2d 920, 923 (Ohio 1989); Brantley Venture Partners II, L.P. v. Dauphin Deposit, 7 F. Supp. 2d 936 (N.D. Ohio 1998).

[190] Taylor v. State Farm Mut. Auto. Ins. Co., 854 P.2d 1134 (Ariz. 1993).

[191] 442 P.2d 641 (Cal. 1968).

[192] *Id.* at 642.

susceptible."[193] Traynor's opinion emphasized that adherence to any supposed "plain meaning" of the written contract, without reference to extrinsic evidence, might fail to effectuate the intent of the parties. Worse yet, it ran the risk of substituting the trial judge's understanding of the term, limited only by the bounds of her own linguistic background. This contextual approach,[194] which sometimes even permits the use of parol evidence to demonstrate the existence of an ambiguity,[195] as well as to resolve it, has been predominant in recent decisions, but has not been without its critics.

Twenty years after *Pacific Gas and Electric* (*PG&E* as the company is known),[196] in *Trident Center v. Connecticut General Life Insurance Co.*,[197] the United States Court of Appeals for the Ninth Circuit criticized *PG&E* for casting serious doubt on the vitality of the parol evidence rule.[198] The *PG&E* court's permissive approach would place the meaning of all written contracts in doubt. If followed, the court was worried that Justice Traynor's approach in *PG&E* not only impairs the enforceability of written contracts, but also, "chips away at the foundation of our legal system" because it gives "credence to the idea that words are inadequate to express concepts."[199] Judge Kozinski would have preferred a more restrictive "textualist" approach similar to that sometimes advanced by the United States Supreme Court in interpreting federal legislation.[200]

For example, in *Steuart v. McChesney*,[201] the language of the contract gave the plaintiff a "right of first refusal" on a parcel of land, for a "value equivalent to the market value as maintained by the [county tax assessor]."[202] When the defendant placed the property on the market, bids were received far in excess of the value as determined by the county tax assessor, and the defendant sought to have the agreement construed as requiring the plaintiff to pay either the amount tendered by a third-party buyer, or the market value as determined by an independent appraisal. The court recognized the dangers inherent in any assumption that words have any fixed or absolute meaning apart from that intended by the parties, but chose to adhere to the "plain" or apparent meaning of the written contract.

Several reasons are usually advanced for adhering to the plain meaning of a written contract. Interpreting the document according to its plain meaning is said to minimize the ability of the court to rewrite the contract to mean something other

---

[193] *Id.* at 644.

[194] *E.g.*, C.R. Anthony Co. v. Loretto Mall Partners, 817 P.2d 238 (N.M. 1991).

[195] *E.g.*, Robert Indus., Inc. v. Spence, 291 N.E.2d 407 (Mass. 1973).

[196] Its customers sometimes write utility checks payable to "Pigs, Goats, and Elephants."

[197] 847 F.2d 564 (9th Cir. 1988).

[198] *See* Olivia W. Karlin & Louis W. Karlin, *The California Parol Evidence Rule*, 21 Sw. U. L. Rev. 1361 (1992); Susan J. Martin-Davidson, *Yes, Judge Kozinski, There Is a Parol Evidence Rule in California — The Lessons of a Pyrrhic Victory*, 25 Sw. U. L. Rev. 1 (1995).

[199] Trident Ctr., 847 F.2d at 569.

[200] *See* Stephen F. Ross & Daniel Tranen, *The Modern Parol Evidence Rule and Its Implications for New Textualist Statutory Interpretation*, 87 Geo. L.J. 195 (1998).

[201] 444 A.2d 659 (Pa. 1982).

[202] *Id.* at 660.

than what it says.[203] However, the plain-meaning approach is vulnerable to the criticism that it may rewrite the intent of the parties if that intent was poorly articulated in the written record.[204] Thus, the plain-meaning approach may detract from the principle of freedom of contract by imposing the general meaning of a term in place of that intended by the parties.

Further, parties who have taken the time to reduce their agreement to writing should be presumed to have drafted it carefully, to have selected their words with care, and courts should not assume otherwise.[205] However, this assumption is not always justified, particularly in the context of standard form contracts, which may have been well-crafted by one of the parties but not fully understood or even read by the other. Thus, the plain-meaning rule may be more appropriate in the context of written contracts that have been carefully negotiated by well represented, sophisticated parties.[206] The strongest rationale in favor of the plain-meaning approach is that it enhances the parties' ability to rely on the text of the written contract.[207]

In determining the "plain" or standard meaning of terms or resolving an ambiguity, evidence of usage of trade, course of dealing, or course of performance will also be useful.[208] However, despite some earlier decisions to the contrary,[209] the court need not determine that the written contract is ambiguous to resort to these sources.[210]

Courts sometimes draw a distinction between patent and latent ambiguities. A patent ambiguity is one that appears on the face of the contract itself.[211] A latent ambiguity is one that becomes apparent only when extrinsic evidence is taken into account.[212] In determining whether the contract contains a latent ambiguity, some courts refuse to consider self-serving declarations from the parties about their intent. These courts restrict the range of extrinsic evidence to more objective evidence, such as the testimony of third parties or evidence about a relevant usage of trade.[213]

---

[203] *Id.* at 662.

[204] *See* Sun Oil Co. v. Madeley, 626 S.W.2d 726 (Tex. 1981).

[205] Steuart v. McChesney, 444 A.2d 659 (Pa. 1982).

[206] *See* Gulf Oil Corp. v. Am. La. Pipe Co., 282 F.2d 401 (6th Cir. 1960).

[207] Steuart v. McChesney, 444 A.2d 659 (Pa. 1982); David Charney, *Hypothetical Bargains: The Normative Structure of Contract Interpretation*, 89 MICH. L. REV. 1815 (1991).

[208] U.C.C. § 2-202(a) & cmt. 2 (2012).

[209] *E.g.*, Mathieson Alkali Works v. Va. Banner Coal Corp., 136 S.E. 673 (Va. 1927).

[210] Columbia Nitrogen Corp. v. Royster Co., 451 F.2d 3 (4th Cir. 1971).

[211] Crown Mgmt. Corp. v. Goodman, 452 So. 2d 49, 52 (Fla. Dist. Ct. App. 1984).

[212] Bohler-Uddeholm Am., Inc. v. Ellwood Group, Inc., 247 F.3d 79 (3d Cir. 2001).

[213] *E.g.*, AM Int'l, Inv. v. Graphic Mgmt., Assoc., Inc., 44 F.3d 572 (7th Cir. 1995).

[F]   Evidence of Usage of Trade, Course of Dealing, and Course of Performance[214]

In contracts for the sale of goods, evidence of usage of trade, course of dealing, and course of performance may be used to supplement or explain a partially or a fully integrated written contract. U.C.C. § 2-202 provides that a final written contract may be "explained or supplemented" with a course of dealing, a usage of trade, a course of performance,[215] or with evidence of consistent additional terms.[216] Evidence of consistent additional terms, however, is expressly prohibited if the writing was intended not just as final but also as complete and exclusive.[217] But, this qualification does not limit evidence of a usage of trade, a course of dealing, or a course of performance to supplement the fully integrated contract.[218] Although the Restatement and many cases take the same approach with respect to usages of trade,[219] other decisions permit consideration of evidence of trade usage, course of performance, and course of dealing, only if the written text is ambiguous or silent.[220]

However, consistent with the hierarchy established in U.C.C. §§ 1-205 and 2-208,[221] neither course of dealing, usage of trade,[222] nor course of performance[223] may contradict the express terms of the contract. So, where industry or private customary practice is consistent with the express terms of a fully integrated written contract, these customs may be used to supplement its terms.[224] Where the integrated writing contradicts such customs, the final writing will control. U.C.C. § 2-202(a) thus operates on the presumption that existing trade practices were taken for granted when the document was executed.[225]

This rule raises again the difficult question of when usage of trade, course of dealing, or course of performance are "consistent" with the terms of the contract, or when they "contradict" its terms. Courts, again, have taken divergent views. The contract in *Columbia Nitrogen Corp. v. Royster Co.*[226] had an express price-

---

[214] Juliet P. Kostritsky, *Judicial Incorporation of Trade Usages: A Functional Solution to the Opportunism Problem*, 39 CONN. L. REV. 451 (2006); Ch. Pamboukis, *The Concept and Function of Usages in the United Nations Convention on the International Sale of Goods*, 25 J.L. & COM. 107 (2005).

[215] U.C.C. § 2-202(a) (2012). *See also* U.C.C. § 2A-202(a) (2012).

[216] U.C.C. § 2-202(b) (2012).

[217] U.C.C. § 2-202(b) (2012).

[218] U.C.C. § 2-202(a) (2012). *E.g.*, Carter Baron Drilling v. Badger Oil Corp., 581 F. Supp. 592, 595 (D. Colo. 1984); Columbia Nitrogen Corp. v. Royster Co., 451 F.2d 3 (4th Cir. 1971).

[219] RESTATEMENT (SECOND) OF CONTRACTS § 222 cmt. b (1981).

[220] Affiliated FM Ins. Co. v. Const. Reinsurance Corp., 626 N.E.2d 878 (Mass. 1994).

[221] *See infra* § 6.04 Customary Practice. Roger W. Kirst, *Usage of Trade and Course of Dealing: Subversion of the U.C.C. Theory*, 1977 U. ILL. L.F. 811; Eyal Zamir, *The Inverted Hierarchy of Contract Interpretation and Supplementation*, 97 COLUM. L. REV. 1710 (1997).

[222] U.C.C. § 1-303(e) (2012) (formerly § 1-205(4)).

[223] U.C.C. § 2-208(2) (2012).

[224] *E.g.*, Nanakuli Paving & Rock Co. v. Shell Oil Co., 664 F.2d 772 (9th Cir. 1981).

[225] U.C.C. § 2-202 cmt. 2 (2012).

[226] 451 F.2d 3 (4th Cir. 1971).

escalation clause, protecting the seller in a rising market. The contract was silent about how to handle the declining market faced by the parties as a result of weather conditions. Finding nothing in the contract inconsistent with an industry custom permitting relief, the court admitted the evidence.[227] The court adopted the standard expressed in the Official Comments to U.C.C. § 2-202 requiring these customs to be "carefully negated" by the written contract.[228] Other cases, like those determining whether parol evidence may be used to supplement a final written contract,[229] have precluded evidence of a usage of trade or course of dealing that is not in reasonable harmony with the express terms of the contract.[230] Cases applying the common law parol evidence rule, heavily influenced by U.C.C. § 2-202, have taken a similar approach.[231]

§ 6.06 EXCEPTIONS TO THE PAROL EVIDENCE RULE[232]

Although the parol evidence rule precludes evidence used to contradict or supplement a fully integrated written contract, it does not prevent the parties from introducing evidence to show that the formation of the contract was subject to some condition that was not expressed in the writing.[233] Nor does it prohibit evidence that the parties made a separate or "collateral" contract. Likewise, it does not restrict evidence showing that the contract was invalid due to illegality, fraud, duress, mistake, or the absence of consideration.[234] Finally, parol may sometimes be introduced to "reform" an integrated contract due to a "scrivener's error." This is sometimes referred to as a "mistake in integration."[235] These exceptions are more fully explained, below.

[A] Conditional Formation[236]

The parol evidence rule does not exclude evidence that the contract simply did not exist. Evidence of a parol condition, upon which formation of the contract depends, proves that the writing was not an integrated contract. Thus, the parol evidence rule does not prohibit one of the parties from introducing testimony or

---

[227] *Id.*

[228] *Id.* at 10, quoting U.C.C. § 2-202 cmt. 2 (2012). *See also* Nanakuli Paving & Rock Co. v. Shell Oil Co., 664 F.2d 772 (9th Cir. 1981) (usage of trade permitted to qualify, but not "totally negate" express terms).

[229] *E.g.*, Luria Bros. & Co. v. Pielet Bros. Scrap Iron & Metal, Inc., 600 F.2d 103 (7th Cir. 1979).

[230] S. Concrete Serv's, Inc. v. Mableton Contractors, Inc., 407 F. Supp. 581 (N.D. Ga. 1975), *aff'd per curiam*, 569 F.2d 1154 (5th Cir. 1978).

[231] Carter Baron Drilling v. Badger Oil Corp., 581 F. Supp. 592 (D. Colo. 1984).

[232] Juanda Lowder Daniel, *K.I.S.S. the Parol Evidence Rule Goodbye: Simplifying the Concept of Protecting the Parties' Written Agreement*, 57 SYRACUSE L. REV. 227 (2007).

[233] RESTATEMENT (SECOND) OF CONTRACTS § 217 (1981).

[234] RESTATEMENT (SECOND) OF CONTRACTS § 214(d) (1981).

[235] RESTATEMENT (SECOND) OF CONTRACTS § 214(e) (1981).

[236] R.E.H., Annotation, *Admissibility of Parol Evidence to Show That a Bill or Note Was Conditional, or Given for a Special Purpose*, 105 A.L.R. 1346 (1936).

other evidence to show that there was no agreement in the first place.[237]

For example, if the parties to a written contract for the purchase of a business agree that the entire deal is subject to approval of other members of the buyer's family, evidence of the condition is admissible.[238] Either party may prove that no contract was formed because of the existence of the condition and its failure to occur.[239] Likewise, parol is admissible to prove that a promissory note, which on its face appears to be unconditional, was subject to a condition not evident on the face of the instrument.[240]

This exception to the parol evidence rule, however, must be applied carefully. It does not permit evidence to show that one of the parties' obligations to perform was subject to a condition not contained in the contract. To be admissible the condition must be one that affects the existence of the contract, not simply one of the duties undertaken by the parties.[241]

[B]   Invalid Contract: Illegality, Fraud, Duress, Mistake, Lack of Consideration[242]

The parol evidence rule does not prohibit evidence that the contract is invalid due to illegality, fraud, duress, mistake, or the absence of consideration. Thus, the existence of an apparently integrated written contract will not preclude evidence showing that the contract was executed simply as a joke or as a sham to cover up for the parties' illegal activities.[243] Nor will it restrict evidence showing that the contract was illegal or for an illegal purpose.[244]

Similarly, parol evidence may be used to prove that the contract was procured by fraud.[245] This exception is justified on the theory that the parol evidence is introduced not to enforce a parol term, but instead to show that because of the fraud, the contract is voidable.[246] In applying this exception some courts attempt to distinguish between terms extrinsic to the writing and those which are intrinsic or

---

[237] Palatine Nat'l Bank v. Olson, 366 N.W.2d 726 (Minn. Ct. App. 1985). This exception is generally regarded as having originated in the English case, *Pym v. Campbell*, 6 El. & Bl. 370 (Q.B. 1856).

[238] *E.g.*, Wickenheiser v. Ramm Vending Promotion, Inc., 560 So. 2d 350 (Fla. Dist. Ct. App. 1990). *See generally* Arthur L. Corbin, *Conditional Delivery of Written Contracts*, 36 Yale L.J. 443, 458 (1927).

[239] Restatement (Second) of Contracts § 217 illus. 5 (1981).

[240] FPI Dev., Inc. v. Nakashima, 231 Cal. App. 3d 367 (1991).

[241] Union Elec. Co. v. Fundways, Ltd., 886 S.W.2d 169 (Mo. Ct. App. 1994). *Contra* Restatement (Second) of Contracts § 217 (1981); W. Commerce Bank v. Gillespie, 775 P.2d 737 (N.M. 1989).

[242] Ralph C. Anzivino, *The Fraud in the Inducement Exception to the Economic Loss Doctrine*, 90 Marq. L. Rev. 921, 937 (2007); Ian Ayres & Gregory Klass, *Promissory Fraud Without Breach*, 2004 Wis. L. Rev. 507; Kevin E. Davis, *Promissory Fraud: A Cost-Benefit Analysis*, 2004 Wis. L. Rev. 535; Kevin Davis, *Licensing Lies: Merger Clauses, the Parol Evidence Rule and Pre-Contractual Misrepresentations*, 33 Val. U. L. Rev. 485 (1999).

[243] Jinro Am., Inc. v. Secure Invs., Inc., 266 F.3d 993, 1000 (9th Cir. 2001).

[244] Horbach v. Coyle, 2 F.2d 702 (8th Cir. 1924).

[245] *E.g.*, Galmish v. Cicchini, 734 N.E.2d 782, 789 (Ohio 2000).

[246] *See* Sabo v. Delman, 143 N.E.2d 906 (N.Y. 1957).

vary directly from the terms of the writing.[247] If the extrinsic evidence directly contradicts the express terms of the contract, it is not admissible.[248] However, if evidence of representations that fraudulently induced the agreement pertains to a matter extrinsic to the writing, the evidence is admissible to prove that the contract is not enforceable due to the fraud.[249]

A tort action to recover for deceit will, of course, completely circumvent the parol evidence rule.[250] The rule is a rule of contract law, not a rule of torts. However, an action for fraud or deceit will encounter other significant barriers due to the necessity of proving that the defendant's misrepresentations were made with the intent to deceive.[251]

A conventional integration clause stipulating that the written contract is the entire agreement between the parties will not usually affect a claim of fraud.[252] However, conspicuous language indicating that a party has not relied on representations not contained in the writing may preclude an action for fraud or other misrepresentation based on a claim of such reliance.[253] Because reliance is an element of any claim of fraud, language in the written contract disclaiming any reliance on representations outside of those included in the writing, may preclude assertions that this type of reliance occurred. As usual, however, this may depend on whether the disclaimer was a negotiated term or simply included as boilerplate language buried in the bowels of the fine print.

Likewise, parol is admissible to prove that the contract was formed under duress. Parol evidence may also be used to show that the contract was made pursuant to a mistake.[254] And, a party may introduce evidence to contradict a recital in the written contract that there was consideration for the defendant's promise.[255]

[C]   Reformation Due to Mistake in Integration

Sometimes the written record of the contract simply does not accurately reflect its terms. Terms may have been inadvertently included or excluded from the writing. In either case, parol evidence is admissible to show that the writing was executed by mistake and to reform the writing to reflect the parties' actual intent. If the parties executed the writing pursuant to a mutual mistake that it contained all of the terms of their agreement, evidence showing that the writing did not

---

[247] Justin Sweet, *Promissory Fraud and the Parol Evidence Rule*, 49 CAL. L. REV. 877 (1961). *E.g.*, Sherrodd, Inc. v. Morrison-Knudsen Co., 815 P.2d 1135 (Mont. 1991).

[248] *E.g.*, Maust v. Bank One Columbus, N.A., 614 N.E.2d 765 (Ohio Ct. App. 1992).

[249] *See* Taylor v. State Farm Mut. Auto. Ins. Co., 854 P.2d 1134 (Ariz. 1993).

[250] Envtl. Sys. Inc. v. Rexham Corp. 624 So. 2d 1379 (Ala. 1993); Bros. v. Morrone-O'Keefe Dev. Co., 2003 Ohio App. LEXIS 6366 (Dec. 23, 2003).

[251] *See, e.g.*, Page Keeton, *Fraud, the Necessity for an Intent to Deceive*, 5 UCLA L. REV. 583 (1958).

[252] Keller v. A.O. Smith Harvestore Prods., Inc. 819 P.2d 69, 73 (Colo. 1991).

[253] *E.g.*, Danann Realty Corp. v. Harris, 157 N.E.2d 597 (N.Y. 1959).

[254] RESTATEMENT (SECOND) OF CONTRACTS § 214(d) (1981).

[255] RESTATEMENT (SECOND) OF CONTRACTS § 218(1) (1981).

contain their entire agreement should be allowed.

In such cases, the writing can be "reformed" to reflect the agreed terms. Thus, in *Hoffman v. Chapman*,[256] parol evidence was admissible to reform a deed that mistakenly described a second parcel of property, not intended by the parties to have been conveyed.[257] Reformation is available, however, only where the mistake was mutual, and where there is "clear and convincing" evidence of the mistake.[258] However, reformation may not be available where one of the parties has reasonably relied on its language.[259]

§ 6.07 PAROL EVIDENCE IN INTERNATIONAL TRANSACTIONS[260]

Although "lex mercatoria" (the law merchant)[261] generally recognizes the relevance of a written contract to determine the parties' intent, it does not generally apply the parol evidence rule. Thus, neither the CISG, the UNIDROIT Principles, nor the Principles of European Contract Law contain a parol evidence rule.

Article 11 of the CISG permits a contract to be proven "by any means, including witnesses."[262] As a result, several American courts have refused to apply the parol evidence rule to disputes governed by the CISG.[263] Significantly, the Advisory Council of the United Nations Convention on Contracts for the International Sale of Goods has agreed that neither the common law parol evidence rule nor the plain-meaning rule is part of the CISG.[264] On the other hand, a contractual merger clause, expressing the parties' intent that a signed writing contains their entire agreement, may be enforceable, at least to the extent that it prevents a party from

---

[256] 34 A.2d 438 (Md. 1943).

[257] *See generally* George E. Palmer, *Reformation and the Parol Evidence Rule*, 65 Mich. L. Rev. 833 (1967).

[258] *E.g.*, Parrish v. City of Carbondale, 378 N.E.2d 243 (Ill. App. Ct. 1978).

[259] *See* The Travelers Ins. Co. v. Bailey, 197 A.2d 813 (Vt. 1964).

[260] Karen Halverson Cross, *Parol Evidence Under the CISG: The "Homeward Trend" Reconsidered*, 68 Ohio St. L.J. 133 (2007); Larry A. DiMatteo, *An International Contract Law Formula: The Informality of International Business Transactions Plus the Internalization of Contract Law Equal Unexpected Contractual Liability*, 23 Syracuse J. Int'l L. & Com. 67, 103 (1997); Clayton P. Gillette, *The Law Merchant in the Modern Age: Institutional Design and International Usages Under the CISG*, 5 Chi J. Int'l Law 157 (2004); Marlyse McQuillen, Note, *The Development of a Federal CISG Common Law in U.S. Courts: Patterns of Interpretation and Citation*, 61 U. Miami L. Rev. 509, 520–23 (2007); Alberto Luis Zuppi, *The Parol Evidence Rule: A Comparative Study of the Common Law, the Civil Law Tradition, and Lex Mercatoria*, 35 Ga. J. Int'l & Comp. L. 233 (2007).

[261] *See supra* § 1.04[A][3] The Law Merchant.

[262] CISG Art. 11 (1980).

[263] *E.g.*, MCC-Marble Ceramic Ctr., Inc. v. Ceramica Nuova D'Agostino, S.P.A., 144 F.3d 1384 (11th Cir. 1998); Mitchell Aircraft Spares, Inc. v. European Aircraft Service AB, 23 F. Supp. 2d 915 (N.D. Ill. 1998); Calzaturificio Claudia s.n.c. v. Olivieri Footwear Ltd., 1998 U.S. Dist. LEXIS 4586 (S.D.N.Y. Apr. 7, 1998). *See* Peter J. Calleo, Note, *The Inapplicability of the Parol Evidence Rule to the United Nations Convention on Contracts for the International Sale of Goods*, 28 Hofstra L. Rev. 799 (2000).

[264] Advisory Council of the United Nations Convention on Contracts for the International Sale of Goods, Opinion No. 3, Parol Evidence Rule, Plain Meaning Rule, Contractual Merger Clause and the CISG, Oct. 23, 2004.

relying on promises and agreements not included in the writing. If intended, such a clause may also bar evidence of otherwise relevant usages of trade.[265]

UNIDROIT's Principles of International Commercial Contracts takes the same approach. It contains nothing resembling the parol evidence rule. Article 1.2 permits a contract to be "proved by any means, including witnesses."[266] Likewise, Article 4.3 requires the court to give regard to:

all the circumstances, including,

  (a) preliminary negotiations between the parties;

  (b) practices which the parties have established between themselves;

  (c) the conduct of the parties subsequent to the conclusion of the contract;

  (d) the nature and purpose of the contract;

  (e) the meaning commonly given to terms and expressions in the trade concerned; [and]

  (f) usages.[267]

Despite the absence of a parol evidence rule, the UNIDROIT Principles give effect to a merger clause: "A contract in writing which contains a clause indicating that the writing completely embodies the terms on which the parties have agreed cannot be contradicted or supplemented by evidence of prior statements or agreements. However, such statements or agreements may be used to interpret the writing."[268]

The Principles of European Commercial Contracts take much the same approach, permitting the court to consider all evidence relevant to the creation of the contract.[269] The parties are likewise bound by "any usage to which they have agreed and by any practice they have established between themselves"[270] as well as by "a usage which would be considered generally applicable by persons in the same situation as the parties [unless] the application of such usage would be unreasonable."[271] But, an "individually negotiated merger clause" prohibits the court from considering "any prior statements, undertakings or agreements which are not embodied in the writing."[272]

---

[265] *Id.*

[266] PICC Art 1.2 (2004).

[267] PICC Art 4.2 (2004).

[268] PICC Art. 2.1.17 (2004).

[269] PECL Art. 2.101(2) (2002).

[270] PECL Art. 1.105(1) (2002).

[271] PECL Art. 1.105(2) (2002).

[272] PECL Art. 2.105(1) (2002).

Chapter 7

WARRANTIES

§ 7.01 INTRODUCTION TO WARRANTIES[1]

[A]   Transactions Involving Warranties

The historic rule regarding a buyer's protection, dating to the early seventeenth century, was "caveat emptor" — let the buyer beware.[2] Buyers simply assumed the risk regarding the quality of goods they purchased, and the seller was not responsible for defects in their quality.[3] Over the last six decades, the doctrine of caveat emptor has been abandoned. Today, buyers of goods enjoy wide warranty protection.[4]

Primarily due to the marketing efforts of the manufacturers of branded goods, warranties are most commonly associated with contracts for the sale of goods. Domestic contracts for the sale of goods are governed by Article 2 of the U.C.C.[5] When Sam buys a new car from an auto dealership, it will probably be accompanied by an express warranty from the manufacturer in addition to whatever protection he might also have as a result of his contract with the dealership. The same is likely true if he buys a new toaster from a local department

---

[1] Debra L. Goetz, Kathryn L. Moore, Douglas E. Perry, David S. Raab & Jeffery S. Ross, *Special Project, Article Two Warranties in Commercial Transactions: an Update*, 72 CORNELL L. REV. 1159, 1186–87 (1987).

[2] *E.g.*, Chandelor v. Lopus, 79 Eng. Rep. 3 (Ct. Exch. 1603); Seixas v. Wood, 2 Cai. 48 (N.Y. 1804).

[3] *See* Walton H. Hamilton, *The Ancient Maxim Caveat Emptor*, 40 YALE L.J. 1133 (1931).

[4] Timothy J. Sullivan, *Innovation in the Law of Warranty: The Burden of Reform*, 32 HASTINGS L.J. 341 (1980).

[5] *See supra* § 1.04[B][1] Uniform Commercial Code.

store. The manufacturer's express warranty will be supplied in a booklet or sheet of paper accompanying the goods.

"Warranties" are commonly included in a wide variety of other transactions, including construction contracts, contracts for the sale of land, residential leases, and contracts for the assignment of accounts receivables and other valuable rights of collection.[6] Thus, a home builder might guarantee that its work will be "free from defects in workmanship and materials." The seller of undeveloped land might supply a warranty that the buyer of the land will receive "good and marketable title."[7] And a merchant, selling the right to collect the accounts owed by his customers to a finance company, might supply the factor with a warranty that the accounts will be "collectible" by the buyer, as a degree of protection against the risk that the customers will be unable or unwilling to pay.

Likewise, warranties relating to goods are not limited to transactions involving new items. Because an express warranty arises from any statement of fact or description supplied by the seller, a warranty might arise from informal statements made by the seller. For example, when Sam sells his old BMW to Barb, he may supply her with a warranty in connection with the car, simply by telling Barb that "the car has never been in a wreck."

There are also several implied warranties, such as the warranty in some sale of goods transactions, that the goods are of "merchantable" quality. Similarly, a residential landlord might be liable for an implied warranty that the leased premises are "habitable." These and other implied warranties are more fully explained below.

[B]   Sources of Warranty Law

Because of the prevalent use of warranties in contracts for the sale of goods, most discussions of warranties focus on the warranty provisions in U.C.C. Article 2. It provides for three types of warranties relating to the quality of the goods: express warranties,[8] the implied warranty of merchantability,[9] and the implied warranty of fitness for particular purpose.[10] It also provides for an implied warranty of good title.[11] In addition, written warranties of consumer products are regulated by the federal Magnuson-Moss Warranty Act.[12] As will be seen, this federal law primarily regulates the manner in which written consumer product warranties are disclosed to the public, but it does little to regulate the content of warranties.[13]

---

[6] U.C.C. § 2-314(2) (2012).

[7] The contract might therefore require a "warranty deed." See generally ROBERT KRATOVIL, REAL ESTATE LAW § 98 (2d ed. 1952).

[8] U.C.C. § 2-313 (2012). See infra § 7.02 Express Warranties Concerning Goods.

[9] U.C.C. § 2-314 (2012). See infra § 7.03 Implied Warranty of Merchantability.

[10] U.C.C. § 2-315 (2012). See infra § 7.04 Implied Warranty of Fitness for Particular Purpose.

[11] U.C.C. § 2-312 (2012). See infra § 7.05 Implied Warranty of Good Title.

[12] 15 U.S.C. §§ 2301–2312 (2006).

[13] See infra § 7.07[B][5] Federal Magnuson-Moss Warranty Act.

In international transactions involving the sale of goods, the United Nations Convention on the International Sale of Goods (CISG) occupies some of the territory. However, the CISG's treatment of warranties is far less comprehensive than the U.C.C.'s.

Warranties are also based on the common law. This is particularly true in connection with the implied warranty of habitability that has been imposed in leases of residential real estate[14] and in purchases of newly constructed homes.[15]

§ 7.02 EXPRESS WARRANTIES CONCERNING GOODS

In a contract for the sale of goods an express warranty might arise in any one of several ways. U.C.C. § 2-313 specifies that a warranty arises from any of the following that is a "part of the basis of the bargain":[16]

- a seller's affirmation of fact about the goods;
- a seller's promise about the goods;
- a seller's description of the goods;
- a sample of the goods; or
- a model of the goods.

Thus, the seller does not need to use the words "warranty" or "guarantee," or even specifically intend to make a warranty in order for one to exist.[17] Express warranties can even be made inadvertently without the specific intent to confer legal rights on the buyer, such as where the seller describes the goods or shows the buyer a model or sample of the goods. Moreover, even though Article 2 only applies to contracts for the sale of goods, the common law cases frequently apply these standards to transactions outside the scope of Article 2 where a person has made an affirmation of fact, a promise, a description, or a model as part of an effort to complete a sale of real estate, services, or some other product.

[A] Affirmations of Fact[18]

An express warranty arises from any affirmation of fact or promise the seller makes about the goods.[19] However, language amounting to nothing more than the seller's opinion about the goods, or consisting merely of the seller's

---

[14] *E.g.*, Javins v. First Nat'l Realty Corp., 428 F.2d 1071 (D.C. Cir. 1970).

[15] *E.g.*, Caceci v. Di Canio Constr. Corp., 526 N.E.2d 266 (N.Y. 1988).

[16] U.C.C. § 2-313 (2012). U.C.C. § 2A-210, applicable to express warranties made by a lessor of goods, is nearly identical to § 2-313. Similarities between transactions for the sale of goods, and those for the lease of goods, justified substantially similar treatment of warranties in both transactions. U.C.C. § 2A-201 cmt. (2012).

[17] U.C.C. § 2-313 cmt. 3 (2012).

[18] Charles Pierson, Comment, *Does "Puff" Create an Express Warranty of Merchantability? Where the Hornbooks Go Wrong*, 36 Duq. L. Rev. 887 (1998).

[19] U.C.C. § 2-313(1)(a) (2012).

recommendation of the goods, is not a warranty. Affirmations of fact and promises create warranties; opinions do not.[20]

If, as part of his effort to persuade Barb to buy his car, Sam tells her that "it's a great car and runs like a dream" or that "it gets good mileage," his characterizations will probably not rise to the level of a warranty. The seller's opinions are treated as meaningless "puffing" or "sales talk." On the other hand, if he tells her that the car is a "1980 model,"[21] "has been driven only 20,000 miles," or that it gets "35 miles to the gallon on the highway," he has made a warranty that the car conforms to these descriptions.[22]

Whether a particular statement is a fact or an opinion frequently depends on its specificity.[23] Vague, general statements, such as those made in *Guiggey v. Bombardier*, that a used snowmobile "runs nice," that the original owner "took real good care of [it]," and that "[the snowmobile] will go good" were not sufficiently specific to constitute affirmations of fact.[24] These sort of generic statements are regarded as mere "puffing."[25]

Disparities in the relative degree of expertise and sophistication between buyer and seller also affect whether a seller's representations are treated as opinion or fact.[26] Thus, in *Royal Business Machines Inc. v. Lorraine Corp.*,[27] the court indicated that the "decisive test" in distinguishing a statement of fact from an opinion is "whether the seller asserts a fact of which the buyer is ignorant or merely states an opinion or judgment *on a matter of which the seller has no special knowledge and on which the buyer may be expected also to have an opinion and to exercise his judgment.*"[28]

In some cases this leads to an analysis of the reasonableness of the buyer's reliance, even though § 2-313 purports to discard "reliance" as a factor.[29] A stark example of this is found in *Price Bros. Co. v. Philadelphia Gear Corp.*[30] There, the court held that exaggerated factual claims in the seller's promotional literature did

---

[20] U.C.C. § 2-313 cmt. 8 (2012).

[21] Goodwin v. Durant Bank & Trust Co., 952 P.2d 41 (Okla. 1998).

[22] *But see* Jones v. Kellner, 451 N.E.2d 548 (Ohio Ct. App. 1982) ("mechanically A-1" was a warranty).

[23] Debra L. Goetz, Kathryn L. Moore, Douglas E. Perry, David S. Raab & Jeffery S. Ross, *Special Project, Article Two Warranties in Commercial Transactions: An Update*, 72 CORNELL L. REV. 1159, 1186 (1987).

[24] Guiggey v. Bombardier, 615 A.2d 1169 (Me. 1992).

[25] David A. Hoffman, *The Best Puffery Article Ever*, 91 IOWA L. REV. 1395 (2006); Ivan L. Preston, *Puffery and Other 'Loophole' Claims: How the Law's "Don't Ask, Don't Tell" Policy Condones Fraudulent Falsity in Advertising*, 18 J.L. & COM. 49 (1998).

[26] Debra L. Goetz, Kathryn L. Moore, Douglas E. Perry, David S. Raab & Jeffery S. Ross, *Special Project, Article Two Warranties in Commercial Transactions: An Update*, 72 CORNELL L. REV. 1159, 1186–87 (1987).

[27] 633 F.2d 34 (7th Cir. 1980).

[28] *Id.* at 41 (emphasis added). *See also* Overstreet v. Norden Labs., Inc., 669 F.2d 1286, 1290–91 (6th Cir. 1982).

[29] U.C.C. § 2-313 cmt. 3 (2012); *e.g.*, Lutz Farms v. Asgrow Seed Co., 948 F.2d 638 (10th Cir. 1991).

[30] 649 F.2d 416 (6th Cir. 1981).

not give rise to an express warranty. The court cited the unreasonableness of the sophisticated buyer's reliance on the seller's literature. It explained that the performance specifications enumerated by the buyer were persuasive indications that the buyer had carefully considered its needs and that it had ordered the goods with those specific needs in mind. The court ruled that this level of "specificity [was] antithetical to any finding that [the buyer had] relied on nonspecific, precontract statements" in the seller's sales literature.[31] In *Royal Business Machines* the court indicated that the buyer's experiences with the seller's goods, based on earlier deliveries of the same items, could prevent him from reasonably relying on representations that had previously proven untrue.[32]

[B]   Relate to the Goods

The promise or affirmation of fact must also "relate to the goods" involved in the sale.[33] Courts have sometimes drawn a very sharp line between promises that relate to the goods themselves, and those that relate to ancillary aspects of the transaction. In *Royal Business Machines* the seller's representations that "replacement parts" for a copying machine "were readily available," and that the "cost of supplies" was "no more than 1/2 cent per copy" were not express warranties because they were not representations about the copying machine itself but about parts and supplies for the machine.[34]

Decisions like *Royal Business Machines*, refusing to find liability based on statements about related goods, miss the mark. The seller's representations about the availability of replacement parts and the cost of supplies were, in reality, statements about the reliability of the goods and the expense of their operation. The seller used these statements in an effort to induce the buyer to purchase the goods, and thus undoubtedly believed that they related to the goods. The requirement that the seller's promises and representations "relate to the goods" should be nothing more than a requirement that the statements be somehow related to the transaction involving the goods made as part of an inducement to the buyer to make the purchase.

A warranty can also be based on a seller's promise about the goods. Older cases had limited warranties to situations where the seller had used language that appeared in the form of a promise, or that specifically used the words "warranty" or "guaranty." These decisions are specifically overruled by U.C.C. § 2-313, which makes it clear that the seller need not even intend to supply a warranty, much less use language in the form of a promise.[35] Thus, any seller's promise that "relates to the good" and that is "a part of the basis of the bargain" gives rise to a warranty regardless of whether the words "promise," "warranty," or "guarantee" are used.

Sellers frequently make promises about the action they will take to correct or

---

[31] *Id.* at 422.

[32] *Royal Business Machines*, 633 F.2d at 44–45.

[33] U.C.C. § 2-313 (2012).

[34] *Royal Business Machines*, 633 F.2d at 42–44.

[35] U.C.C. § 2-313(2) (2012).

repair any malfunctions that develop after the goods have been delivered to the buyer. In this respect, a seller's agreement to supply the buyer with a particular remedy in connection with goods is also a warranty under both Article 2 and federal Magnuson-Moss Warranty Act.[36] However, a mere service contract, which does not arise from a sale of goods, is not a warranty,[37] though it may still confer legal rights.

[C]   Description of the Goods

Express warranties are also created by the seller's description of the goods. If the seller's description is part of the basis of the bargain, there is a warranty that the goods will comply with it.[38] Thus, the seller's characterization of a crane as a "15–20 ton crane" resulted in a warranty that the crane could lift at least 15 tons.[39] Likewise, in *Malul v. Capital Cabinets, Inc.*,[40] there was a breach of warranty where kitchen cabinets were described as including "French doors" when the goods delivered by the seller did not include any "French"-style doors.

In some cases, the seller's description of the goods includes an explicit statement about the function the goods will perform. Goods described as "snow throwers," for example, must be capable of "throwing snow" to conform to the warranty created by the description. A description of the goods as a "new red Streamstar automobile" is more problematic with regard to any warranted functionality. This description undoubtedly creates a warranty that the car is new,[41] that its color is red, that it is a "Streamstar" model, and that it is an automobile. However, the effect of its description as an "automobile" is unclear. The description of the goods as an automobile might amount to an express warranty of the merchantability of the car; that it is fit for the ordinary purpose of an automobile and is thus suitable for transportation.[42] If the brakes fail, or the engine repeatedly stalls, it probably does not conform to its description as an automobile.

In *Taylor v. Alfama*,[43] the seller's description of a car as having a "rebuilt engine" and "in mint condition" resulted in an express warranty that the car perform as one would ordinarily expect a car with a rebuilt engine and in mint condition would perform. An extreme example, probably reaching the wrong

---

[36] *See* 15 U.S.C. § 2301(6)(B) (2006).

[37] *E.g., In re* Breast Implant Prod. Liab. Litig., 503 S.E.2d 445 (S.C. 1998); Cook v. Downing, 891 P.2d 611 (Okla. Ct. App. 1994) (dentist was not a "merchant," and "dentures" were not "goods" under the U.C.C.).

[38] U.C.C. § 2-313(1)(b) (2012).

[39] Standard Stevedoring Co. v. Jaffe, 302 S.W.2d 829 (Tenn. Ct. App. 1956) (applying the Uniform Sales Act, the precursor to U.C.C. Article 2).

[40] 740 N.Y.S.2d 828 (N.Y. Civ. Ct. 2002).

[41] Frank Griffin Volkswagen, Inc. v. Smith, 610 So. 2d 597 (Fla. Dist. Ct. App. 1992); Rivers v. BMW of North America, Inc., 449 S.E.2d 337 (Ga. Ct. App. 1994) (description of car as "new" was warranty that it had not been repainted to repair damage caused by acid rain).

[42] *See* Guiggey v. Bombardier, 615 A.2d 1169 (Me. 1992).

[43] 481 A.2d 1059 (Vt. 1984).

result, is provided by *Moore v. Puget Sound Plywood, Inc.*,[44] where a description of the goods as "laminated siding" created an express warranty that the siding would last for the lifetime of the house.

In other cases, there may be some question regarding the meaning of the seller's description. In *Besicorp Group, Inc. v. Thermo Electron Corp.*,[45] the court found it necessary to determine what was meant by the seller's description of the goods as a "turnkey" energy system.[46] The court found that this term meant that the "seller must complete all the work, and assume all the risk that was necessary to turn the finished product over to the buyer."[47]

The Official Comments to U.C.C. § 2-313 make it clear that the description of the goods might be found in technical specifications,[48] or blueprints accompanying the goods, or as a result of past deliveries made by the seller.[49] Evidence of an applicable usage of trade or course of performance is relevant in ascertaining the precise meaning of the description. In this respect, there is considerable overlap between express warranties created as a result of the seller's description, and the implied warranty of merchantability that the goods, among other things, will "pass without objection in the trade under the contract description."[50]

[D]   Sample or Model

A seller's demonstration of a sample or a model of the goods creates an express warranty that the goods will conform to the characteristics of the sample or model.[51] Samples are drawn from the goods to be sold. Thus, a seller of grain might provide the buyer with a sample from the bulk of grain that will be sold. Models, on the other hand, are mere exemplars, not part of the bulk that will be delivered.[52] Because samples are drawn from the goods that are the subject matter of the sale, a sample is generally regarded as more definitive of the quality expected to be delivered than a model.[53]

Most of the time a sample or model is part of the basis of the bargain simply because the seller used it during the negotiations that led to the sale.[54] Here, though, some inquiry into the parties' purpose in displaying the item must be made

---

[44] 332 N.W.2d 212 (Neb. 1983).

[45] 981 F. Supp. 86 (N.D.N.Y. 1997).

[46] *See also* Malul v. Capital Cabinets, Inc., 740 N.Y.S.2d 828 (N.Y. Civ. Ct. 2002) ("French Doors').

[47] *See also* USM Corp., 546 N.E.2d at 893–94, 893 n.9 (Mass. Ct. App. 1989).

[48] *E.g.*, Ricwill, Inc. v. S.L. Pappas & Co., 599 So. 2d 1126 (Ala. 1992).

[49] U.C.C. § 2-314 cmt. 5 (2012). *See* Duffin v. Idaho Crop Improvement Ass'n, 895 P.2d 1195, 1203–04 (Idaho 1995).

[50] U.C.C. § 2-314(2)(a) (2012).

[51] U.C.C. § 2-313(1)(c) (2012).

[52] U.C.C. § 2-313 cmt. 6 (2012). *See* Barton v. Tra-Mo, Inc., 686 P.2d 423, 425 (Or. Ct. App. 1984).

[53] U.C.C. § 2-313 cmt. 6 (2012). *See* Import Traders, Inc. v. Frederick Mfg. Corp., 457 N.Y.S. 742 (N.Y. City Civ. Ct. 1983) (model, used only as an illustration did not create an express warranty); Amtel, Inc. v. Arnold Indus., Inc., 31 U.C.C. Rep. Serv. 48 (D. Conn. 1980).

[54] *E.g.*, Barton v. Tra-Mo, Inc., 686 P.2d 423, 425 (Or. Ct. App. 1984).

because it might have been used as an example of size or color rather than quality.[55]

Sometimes, on the other hand, a sample is a critical component of the sale. In *Glyptal, Inc. v. Englehard Corp.*, the buyer tested the seller's sample of "cadmium 20" by incorporating it into its paint formulation to determine if the finished product conformed to the buyer's product specifications. However, where the seller's sample is supplied after the buyer has made a commitment to purchase the goods, it is difficult for the buyer to claim that the sample or model served as a basis of the bargain.[56] Samples or models provided after the contract has been formed are less likely to result in the creation of a warranty than the seller's promises, unless they are supplied as a means of assuring the buyer as to the quality of the goods.[57]

As with express warranties generally, the seller's use of a sample or model creates an express warranty despite any effort the seller might make to disclaim all express and implied warranties. In *Materials Marketing Corp. v. Spencer*,[58] the seller provided the buyer with a sample of ceramic tile to be used by the buyer in lining his swimming pool. The tiles contained in the seller's second shipment failed to match either the sample or the tiles contained in the first shipment. The seller's disclaimer of express warranties was ineffective to negate its warranty that the tiles would conform to the seller's sample.

[E]   Basis of the Bargain[59]

Before the U.C.C., the Uniform Sales Act required reliance on the seller's representations to establish an express warranty.[60] Nevertheless, most courts found reliance if the seller's representation was one that would "naturally induce a buyer to purchase the goods."[61]

---

[55] *See, e.g.*, Thrall v. Renno, 695 S.W.2d 84 (Tex. App. 1985).

[56] Indus. Graphics, Inc. v. Asahi Corp., 485 F. Supp. 793 (D. Minn. 1980).

[57] *See* U.C.C. § 2-313 cmt. 7 (2012).

[58] 40 S.W.3d 172 (Tex. Ct. App. 2012).

[59] Robert S. Adler, *The Last Best Argument for Eliminating Reliance from Express Warranties: "Real-World" Consumers Don't Read Warranties*, 45 S.C. L. REV. 429, 444–45 (1994); Charles A. Heckman, *"Reliance" or "Common Honesty of Speech": The History and Interpretation of Section 2-313 of the Uniform Commercial Code*, 38 CASE W. RES. L. REV. 1 (1988); Sidney Kwestel, *Freedom from Reliance: A Contract Approach to Express Warranty*, 26 SUFFOLK U. L. REV. 959, 997–1000 (1992); John E. Murray Jr., *The Revision of Article 2: Romancing the Prism*, 35 WM. & MARY L. REV. 1447, 1486–90 (1994); Donald J. Smythe, Essay, *The Scope of a Bargain and the Value of a Promise*, 60 S.C. L. REV. 203 (2008); Matthew A. Victor, *Express Warranties Under the UCC — Reliance Revisited*, 25 NEW ENG. L. REV. 477 (1990); Note, *"Basis of the Bargain" — What Role Reliance?*, 34 U. PITT. L. REV. 145 (1972).

[60] UNIF. SALES ACT § 12 (1906). *See* SAMUEL WILLISTON, THE LAW GOVERNING SALES OF GOODS AT COMMON LAW AND UNDER THE UNIFORM SALES ACT 366 (2d ed. 1924). *See* Indust-Ri-Chem Lab., Inc. v. Park-Pak Co., Inc., 602 S.W.2d 282, 293 (Tex. Ct. App. 1980).

[61] *See* SAMUEL WILLISTON, 1 WILLISTON ON CONTRACTS § 206 (1936). *E.g.*, Turner v. Central Hardware Co., 186 S.W.2d 603 (Mo. 1945).

The term "reliance" is conspicuously missing from U.C.C. § 2-313.[62] Instead, the U.C.C. specifies that an express warranty exists if the seller's affirmations of fact, promises, descriptions, samples or models are "part of the basis of the bargain."[63] The Official Comments to § 2-313 indicate that the seller's affirmations about the goods "during a bargain are regarded as part of the description of the goods; hence no particular reliance on such statements need be shown."[64] The U.C.C. therefore presumes that the seller's statements are part of the basis of the bargain "unless good reason is shown to the contrary."[65]

Although reliance need not be proven, some courts give sellers the opportunity to demonstrate that the buyer did not rely,[66] or that the buyer disbelieved the seller's representations.[67] Under these decisions, reliance is not a part of the plaintiff's prima facie case, but the absence of reliance operates as a defense. Thus, if Sam, in persuading Barb to buy his car, tells her that the car only has 30,000 miles on it, but Barb believes that Sam is lying and buys the car anyway, Barb may have no claim for breach of warranty when she is able to confirm that the car has many more miles on it.

A few courts have found a reliance requirement implicit in § 2-313. In *Wendt v. Beardmore Suburban Chevrolet, Inc.*,[68] the court ruled that "since an express warranty must have been 'made part of the basis of the bargain,' it is essential that the plaintiffs prove reliance upon the warranty."[69] In addition, in *Indust-Ri-Chem Laboratory, Inc. v. Park-Pak Co.*,[70] the court required the buyer to prove actual reliance after the seller introduced evidence indicating that the buyer had not relied.[71]

Courts usually require the buyer to have at least been aware of the representations that form the basis of the buyer's claim.[72] Courts also sometimes rule that no express warranty arises from representations made after the

---

[62] *See generally* John E. Murray Jr., *"Basis of the Bargain": Transcending Classical Concepts*, 66 MINN. L. REV. 283 (1982).

[63] U.C.C. § 2-313(1)(a)–(c) (2012).

[64] U.C.C. § 2-313 cmt. 3 (2012).

[65] U.C.C. § 2-313 cmt. 8 (2012).

[66] *E.g.*, Torres v. Nw. Eng'g Co., 949 P.2d 1004, 1015 (Haw. Ct. App. 1997); Indust-Ri-Chem Lab., Inc. v. Park-Pak Co., 602 S.W.2d 282, 293 (Tex. Ct. App. 1980). *See generally* William E. Boyd, *Representing Consumers — The Uniform Commercial Code and Beyond*, 9 ARIZ. L. REV. 372, 385 (1968).

[67] Frank J. Wozniak, Annotation, *Purchaser's Disbelief in, or Nonreliance upon, Express Warranties Made by Seller in Contract for Sale of Business as Precluding Action for Breach of Express Warranties*, 7 A.L.R.5th 841 (1992).

[68] 366 N.W.2d 424 (Neb. 1985).

[69] *Id.* at 424. *See also* Royal Bus. Mach. v. Lorraine Corp., 633 F.2d 34, 44 n.7 (7th Cir. 1980); Overstreet v. Norden Labs., Inc., 669 F.2d 1286 (6th Cir. 1982).

[70] 602 S.W.2d 282 (Tex. Civ. App. 1980).

[71] *Id.* at 293. *See* John E. Murray Jr., *"Basis of the Bargain": Transcending Classical Concepts*, 66 MINN. L. REV. 283, 294–95 (1982) (criticizing *Indust-Ri-Chem Laboratory*).

[72] *E.g.*, Thomas v. Amway Corp., 488 A.2d 716 (R.I. 1985); Massey-Ferguson, Inc. v. Laird, 432 So. 2d 1259, 1261 (Ala. 1983); Perfetti v. McGhan Med., 662 P.2d 646 (N.M. Ct. App.), *cert. denied*, 662 P.2d 645 (N.M. 1983).

agreement has been made.[73] However, the official comments to U.C.C. § 2-313 reject this conclusion, and treat these warranties as modifications to the contract.[74] Most decisions have thus held that statements made after the contract has been concluded may become a part of the basis of the bargain.[75]

§ 7.03   IMPLIED WARRANTY OF MERCHANTABILITY[76]

U.C.C. § 2-314 imposes an implied warranty of merchantability — that goods will be fit for their ordinary purpose — if the seller is a merchant with respect to goods of that kind.[77] Thus, the implied warranty of merchantability does not apply in every sale of goods; it only arises when the seller is a merchant with respect to the goods involved in the sale. Likewise, there is an implied warranty of merchantability in transactions, such as those that might occur in restaurants, involving the serving of food or drink for value, regardless of whether the items are to be consumed on the premises or taken away.[78]

The main issues that arise under § 2-314 are: first, whether the seller is not just a merchant in the more general sense, but a "merchant *with respect to goods of the kind*" involved in the sale; second, the precise standards imposed by the warranty that the goods will be of "merchantable quality"; and third, the steps necessary to effectively disclaim the warranty. The first two of these issues are discussed in the remainder of this section. Questions concerning disclaimers of implied warranties are raised later in this chapter.[79]

[A]   Seller a Merchant with Respect to Goods of the Kind

Although Article 2 of the U.C.C. applies to every domestic sale of goods, the implied warranty of merchantability does not arise in every sale. It applies only when the seller is a merchant with respect to goods of the kind that are involved in the transaction.[80] Thus, if Sam sells his private car to Barb, he is not acting as a merchant. Moreover, if Sam is a plumber and sells his work van to Barb, he will not supply her with an implied warranty of merchantability, even though he is a

---

[73] *E.g.*, Global Truck & Equip. Co., Inc. v. Palmer Mach. Works, Inc., 628 F. Supp. 641 (N.D. Miss. 1986); Pake v. Byrd, 286 S.E.2d 588 (N.C. Ct. App. 1982).

[74] U.C.C. § 2-313 cmt. 7 (2012).

[75] *E.g.*, Glyptal, Inc. v. Engelhard Corp., 801 F. Supp. 887, 897 n.8 (D. Mass. 1992). *See also* Russell Donaldson, Annotation, *Affirmations or Representations Made After Sale Is Closed as Basis of Warranty Under UCC § 2-313(1)(a)*, 47 A.L.R.4th 200 (1986). This is compatible with the position staked out by proposed revisions to U.C.C. Article 2. *See* Revised U.C.C. § 2-313 cmt. 9 (2003).

[76] Dawn R. Swink, J. Brad Reich, *Caveat Vendor: Potential Progeny, Paternity, and Product Liability Online*, 2007 B.Y.U. L. Rev. 857.

[77] U.C.C. § 2-314(1) (2012).

[78] *Id.*

[79] *See infra* § 7.07[B] Disclaimer of Implied Warranties.

[80] U.C.C. § 2-213(1) (2012).

merchant in the general sense of U.C.C. § 2-104,[81] because he is not a merchant with respect to that type of goods, though he may make an implied warranty of merchantability in connection with plumbing supplies that he sells. If, on the other hand, Sam is an auto dealer selling a car from his inventory, he is a merchant with respect to goods of the kind and will supply a warranty of merchantability in connection with the sale to Barb.

It is critical to recognize that not everyone who is a "merchant" in the general sense is a "merchant with respect to goods of [the] kind" who makes an implied warranty of merchantability. A merchant, according to § 2-104(1), is:

> a person who deals in goods of the kind or otherwise by his occupation holds himself out as having knowledge or skill peculiar to the practices or goods involved in the transaction or to whom such knowledge or skill may be attributed by his employment of an agent or broker or other intermediary who by his occupation holds himself out as having such knowledge or skill.

The Official Comments to U.C.C. § 2-104 provide valuable assistance in distinguishing between someone who is a merchant for most purposes and a person who is a merchant with respect to goods of the kind, for the purposes of the implied warranty of merchantability. There are three different contexts in which the definition of a merchant is important.

The first is in the context of U.C.C. §§ 2-201, 2-205, 2-207, and 2-209, all dealing generally with the contract formation process and where, as the comments indicate, a person's familiarity with general business practices justifies his or her treatment as a merchant.[82]

The second is in the context dealt with here, U.C.C. § 2-314 and the implied warranty of merchantability. The comments specify that a person is only a merchant with respect to goods of a particular kind if he or she has "professional status as to particular kinds of goods."[83] Responsibility for the quality of goods sold is imposed only on those who by their professional status have particular expertise with respect to the goods in question, or who, by holding themselves out as having such expertise, ought to bear the same responsibility as someone with that expertise.[84]

The code recognizes a third category of rules regarding merchants,[85] such as those involving the standard for "good faith" on the part of a merchant,[86] and a merchant's responsibilities in connection with rejected goods,[87] the risk of loss,[88]

---

[81] U.C.C. § 2-104 (2012).

[82] U.C.C. § 2-104 cmt. 2 (2012).

[83] *Id.*

[84] The rules in §§ 2-402(2) and 2-403(2) regarding retention of goods by a merchant seller and the effect of entrustment of goods use "merchant" in the same limited sense. *Id.*

[85] U.C.C. § 2-104 cmt. 2 (2012).

[86] *See* U.C.C. § 2-103(1)(b) (2012).

[87] U.C.C. §§ 2-603, 2-605 (2012).

[88] U.C.C. § 2-509 (2012).

and adequate assurance of future performance.[89] In these contexts, the more generalized sense of the definition of a merchant controls.

Manufacturers,[90] distributors,[91] and retailers[92] who sell goods of the kind on a regular basis are almost always found to be "merchants with respect to goods of the kind" as required by U.C.C. § 2-314. Thus, liability is imposed on sellers who have expertise in connection with the goods, who represent themselves as having such expertise, or whose business enterprise justifies holding them responsible for the quality of the goods they distribute, regardless of any actual or projected expertise.

When the goods are sold from the seller's stock of inventory,[93] the seller is nearly always a merchant even if the seller lacked any particular expertise in connection with the goods. Where the goods were used primarily as equipment in the operation of the seller's business, the warranty of merchantability is rarely imposed. Isolated sales of goods do not result in a seller being treated as a merchant with respect to goods of the kind, even if the seller has considerable expertise in the use and operation of the goods.[94]

In *Fred J. Moore, Inc. v. Schinmann*,[95] a farmer who grew mint to make mint oil and who made a one-time sale of mint roots to another mint farmer, was a dealer in mint oil but not in mint roots. Thus, he was not a merchant with respect to mint roots and did not make an implied warranty that the mint roots were merchantable. Similarly, in *Kates Millinery v. Benay-Albee Corp.*,[96] a manufacturer of novelty hats who sold a pressing machine used in manufacturing the hats to another manufacturer was not "a merchant with respect to goods of that kind." The seller may have been a merchant with respect to hats, but was not a merchant with respect to hat-making equipment.[97]

On the other hand, in *Nutting v. Ford Motor Co.*,[98] the owner of a fleet of automobiles, who regularly sold its entire fleet after a year's use to a used car dealer, was a merchant with respect to goods of the kind and was responsible for the merchantability of the vehicles.[99] And, in *Miller v. Badgley*,[100] a seller who owned

---

[89] U.C.C. § 2-609 (2012).

[90] *E.g.*, Knapp Shoes, Inc. v. Sylvania Shoe Mfg. Corp., 640 N.E.2d 1101, 1103 n.3 (Mass. 1994); Valley Iron & Steel Co. v. Thorin, 562 P.2d 1212 (Or. 1977) (first-time manufacture of goods).

[91] *E.g.*, Rogers Wholesalers v. M.J. Indus. (*In re* Rogers Wholesalers), 37 B.R. 18, 20 (Bankr. D. Mass. 1983).

[92] *E.g.*, Commonwealth v. Johnson Insulation, 682 N.E.2d 1323, 1327 n.5 (Mass. 1997).

[93] *Cf.* U.C.C. § 9-102(a)(48) (2012).

[94] *In re* Jackson Television, Ltd., 21 B.R. 790, 793 n.1 (Bankr. E.D. Tenn. 1990); Cohen v. Hathaway, 595 F. Supp. 579 (D. Mass. 1984).

[95] 700 P.2d 754, 757 (Wash. App. 1985).

[96] 450 N.Y.S.2d 975, 976–77 (N.Y. Civ. Ct. 1982).

[97] *See also* McGregor v. Dimou, 422 N.Y.S.2d 806, 809 (N.Y. Civ. Ct. 1979) (body shop that sold a used car was not a merchant of used cars despite having made the occasional sale); Bevard v. Ajax Mfg. Co., 473 F. Supp. 35, 37–38 (E.D. Mich. 1979) (seller of a used press through a used equipment dealer not a merchant despite past occasional sales).

[98] 584 N.Y.S.2d 653, 657 (N.Y. App. Div. 1992).

[99] *See also* Ferragamo v. Mass. Bay Transp. Auth., 481 N.E.2d 477 (Mass. 1985).

a boat-building company and who held himself out to the buyer as having professional knowledge and skill in this field could not deny his status as a "merchant with respect to goods of that kind" merely because he sold the sailboat in question privately instead of selling it via the corporate entity through which he normally dealt.

[B] Meaning of "Merchantability"[101]

A seller who is a merchant with respect to the goods makes an implied warranty that the goods are of "merchantable" quality. To be merchantable, the goods need not be perfect. Nor must they be suitable for every imaginable purpose for which the buyer may use them. U.C.C. § 2-314(2) spells out the criteria for merchantability. It requires that the goods must at least:

(a) pass without objection in the trade under the contract description; and

(b) in the case of fungible goods, be of fair average quality within the description; and

(c) be fit for the ordinary purposes for which such goods are used; and

(d) run, within the variations permitted by the agreement, of even kind, quality and quantity within each unit and among all units involved; and

(e) be adequately contained, packaged, and labeled as the agreement may require; and

(f) conform to the promises or affirmations of fact made on the container or label, if any.

[1] Fit for the Ordinary Purpose

The most important standard in this laundry list is that the goods must be "fit for the ordinary purposes for which such goods are used."[102] Thus, they must be capable of performing the ordinary tasks for which they were designed and purchased.[103]

Most claims that goods are not fit for their ordinary purpose involve defects in the design[104] or manufacture[105] of the goods. Many of these claims also involve personal injuries. caused by the defect. When personal injury is involved the plaintiff usually also asserts a claim for negligence in the design or manufacture of the goods and for strict liability in tort for an unreasonably dangerous or

---

[100] 753 P.2d 530 (Wash. Ct. App. 1988).

[101] Franklin E. Crawford, Note, *Fit for Its Ordinary Purpose? Tobacco, Fast Food, and the Implied Warranty of Merchantability*, 63 Ohio St. L.J. 1165 (2002).

[102] U.C.C. § 2-314(2)(c) (2012).

[103] *See* Saratoga Spa & Bath Inc. v. Beeche Sys. Corp., 656 N.Y.S.2d 787 (N.Y. App. Div. 1997); Pronti v. DML of Elmira, Inc., 103 A.D.2d 916 (N.Y. App. Div. 1984) (furniture not perfect, but still suitable for its intended purposes).

[104] *E.g.*, Wasylow v. Glock, Inc., 975 F. Supp. 370 (D. Mass. 1996) (defective gun design).

[105] *E.g.*, Chambers v. Osteonics Corp., 109 F.3d 1243 (7th Cir. 1997) (defective artificial hip).

"defective" product under § 402A of the Restatement (Second) of Torts. In cases involving personal injuries courts frequently equate the fitness of the goods for their ordinary purpose under U.C.C. § 2-314 with the test for whether they are "defective" under § 402A.[106] In *Commonwealth v. Johnson Insulation*,[107] the court explained that "liability under this implied warranty is congruent in nearly all respects with the principles expressed in Restatement (Second) of Torts § 402A."[108]

Many other claims for breach of the warranty of merchantability involve so-called "lemon" automobiles, and are based on design or manufacturing defects.[109] However, not every manufacturing defect renders the goods unfit for their ordinary purpose. In *Taterka v. Ford Motor Co.*,[110] an improperly installed taillight assembly gasket did not make the car unmerchantable. The rust caused by the defective gasket developed over the time it took to drive the car 75,000 miles. The court explained that "where a car can provide safe, reliable transportation it is generally considered merchantable."[111] The defective gasket was unquestionably a defect, but it was not one that made the car unfit for its ordinary purpose of providing transportation.[112]

Recently, personal injury plaintiffs have attempted to use the implied warranty of merchantability as the basis for claims against sellers of cigarettes,[113] guns,[114] and alcohol.[115] Cases alleging that cigarettes are unmerchantable reach mixed results,[116] with most decisions finding that cigarettes are not unmerchantable

---

[106] *E.g.*, Ford Motor Co. v. Gen. Acc. Ins. Co., 779 A.2d 362, 370 (Md. 2001); Commonwealth v. Johnson Insulation, 682 N.E.2d 1323 (Mass. 1997).

[107] 682 N.E.2d 1323 (Mass. 1997).

[108] *Id.* at 1326.

[109] *E.g.*, Fredrick v. Dreyer, 257 N.W.2d 835 (S.D. 1977). Many states have separate statutes dealing specifically with defectively designed or manufactured automobiles. These so-called "lemon laws" usually permit the buyer to rescind the transaction and obtain a refund of the price of a new automobile if its defects cannot be remedied after a specified number of attempts. *See, e.g.*, Ohio Rev. Code Ann. § 1345.71-75 (Anderson 2006). *See generally infra* § 1402[D] Failure of Remedy to Achieve its Essential Purpose.

[110] 271 N.W.2d 653 (Wis. 1978).

[111] *Id.* at 655.

[112] This decision has made me wonder about my 1995 Ford Windstar minivan, which was delivered with a faulty head gasket. The engine performed fine for 65,000 miles before the gasket failed and the engine needed to be replaced. Because Ford Motor Co. replaced the engine at its own expense, the "merchantability" of the vehicle was never tested by a court. Later, the brakes failed. I now own a Honda.

[113] *E.g.*, Semowich v. R.J. Reynolds Tobacco Co., 8 U.C.C. Rep. Serv. 2d 976 (N.D.N.Y. 1988).

[114] *E.g.*, Wasylow v. Glock, Inc., 975 F. Supp. 370 (D. Mass. 1996); Rhodes v. R.G. Indus., Inc., 325 S.E.2d 465, 467 (Ga. Ct. App. 1984). *See* Debra Burke, Joanne Hopper & B.J. Dunlap, *Women, Guns, and the Uniform Commercial Code*, 33 Willamette L. Rev. 219 (1997); Jean Macchiaroli Eggen, *Gun Torts: Defining a Cause of Action for Victims in Suits Against Gun Manufacturers*, 81 N.C. L. Rev. 115 (2002).

[115] *E.g.*, Morris v. Adolph Coors Co., 735 S.W.2d 578 (Tex. Ct. App. 1987) (beer not unmerchantable simply because it impairs the ability to drive an automobile); *see* Wayne J. Carroll, *One Last Attempt at Liability for "Vice" Products: A Different Ending to the "Willie Story" Story*, 99 Com. L.J. 108 (1994).

[116] *See* Johnson v. Brown & Williamson Tobacco Corp., 122 F. Supp. 2d 194 (D. Mass. 2000).

simply because they cause cancer.[117] The problem with attaching liability to cigarettes, guns, and alcohol is that many other consumer products, such as cream cheese, motorcycles, and sugar, might be highly vulnerable to the same claim.[118]

[2] Pass Without Objection in the Trade Under the Description

To be merchantable, goods must also "pass without objection in the trade under the contract description."[119] This explicitly incorporates a usage of trade standard for the merchantability of goods.[120] This can be helpful in attempting to determine whether the goods meet the general standard of merchantability. For example, in *Royal Typewriter Co. v. Xerographic Supplies Corp.*,[121] the court referred to industry-wide safety standards to evaluate the merchantability of a copying machine that proved to be a fire hazard. Without an industry standard to use as a basis for comparison, evaluating the quality of the goods may be more subjective.

[3] Fungible Goods — Fair Average Quality Within the Description

This trade standard is frequently read together with the test for fungible goods,[122] which also must be of "fair average quality within the description."[123] Goods are "fungible" when any single unit, either by its very nature or due to usage of trade, is the equivalent of any other unit.[124] Thus, Extra Fancy Premium "Granny Smith" apples are fungible because one bushel of Extra Fancy Premium Granny Smith apples is expected to be of the same fair average quality as the next such bushel.

To be merchantable, the goods must be of "fair average quality" within the description. Deviations might exist without impairing the merchantability of the apples as "Extra Fancy Premium Granny Smith" apples. To be merchantable under this standard, the goods must be around the "middle belt of quality, not the least or the worse that can be understood in the particular trade by the

---

[117] Green v. The Am. Tobacco Co., 409 F.2d 1166 (5th Cir. 1969) (adopting the dissenting opinion of Simpson J., at 391 F.2d at 110), *cert. denied*, 397 U.S. 911 (1970). *See generally*, Franklin E. Crawford, Note, *Fit for Its Ordinary Purpose? Tobacco, Fast Food, and the Implied Warranty of Merchantability*, 63 Ohio St. L.J. 1165 (2002).

[118] Brad Reich, *Getting the Skinny: Fast Food Fat-Based Litigation Is Not a Legal Threat to Business, But It Should Be*, 23 Hofstra Lab. & Emp. L.J. 345 (2006); John Alan Cohan, *Obesity, Public Policy, and Tort Claims Against Fast-Food Companies*, 12 Widener L.J. 103, 110–11 (2003); Jonathan S. Goldman, *Take That Tobacco Settlement and Supersize It!: The Deep Frying of the Fast Food Industry?*, 13 Temp. Pol. & Civ. Rts. L. Rev. 113 (2003).

[119] U.C.C. § 2-314(2)(a) (2012).

[120] U.C.C. § 2-314 cmt. 2 (2012).

[121] 719 F.2d 1092 (11th Cir. 1983).

[122] U.C.C. § 2-314 cmt. 7 (2012); T. J. Stevenson & Co. v. 81,193 Bags of Flour, 629 F.2d 338, 351–53 (5th Cir. 1980) (insect-infested flour was not merchantable).

[123] U.C.C. § 2-314(2)(b) (2012).

[124] U.C.C. § 1-201(b)(18) (2012) (formerly § 1-201(17)).

designation."[125] Under this standard, a "fair percentage" of the lowest quality within the description is permissible.[126]

When applying this standard the price charged can provide some guidance as to the quality required.[127] If the price of the goods is somewhat lower than the market price for goods that fit within the description, it might reasonably be expected that a greater percentage of the goods would fit into the lower range of quality to be expected. On the other hand, if the price is at the higher end of the scale, a smaller than usual percentage of items within the lower range might be required.

[4] Adequately Contained, Packaged, and Labeled

To be merchantable, goods must also be "adequately contained, packaged, and labeled."[128] This requirement has proven particularly significant in personal injury cases involving inadequate safety warnings.[129] However, decisions involving safety warnings are nearly always based in part on strict liability in tort for an unreasonably defective product.[130] They may also involve federal warning label standards and questions of federal preemption.[131]

The requirement of adequate packaging has also led to liability for goods that have broken during shipment,[132] or, in one well known case, involving injuries suffered by a shattered wine glass at a restaurant.[133] The wine was unmerchantable, because the container — the glass — was defective.

[5] Conform to Promises or Facts Stated on the Label

Merchantability also requires the goods to "conform to the promise or affirmations of fact made on the container or label."[134] This makes the implied warranty of merchantability similar to express warranties based on the seller's

---

[125] U.C.C. § 2-314 cmt. 7 (2012).

[126] *Id.*

[127] *Id.*

[128] U.C.C. § 2-314(12)(e) (2012).

[129] *E.g.*, Stephens v. G.D. Searle & Co., 602 F. Supp. 379 (E.D. Mich. 1985). *See generally* Candada J. Moore, Note, *The Duty to Warn Within the Implied Warranty of Merchantability:* Reid v. Eckerds Drugs, Inc., 41 Ohio St. L.J. 747 (1980).

[130] *See* Lisa L. Locke, Note, *Products Liability and Home-Exercise Equipment: A Failure to Warn and Instruct May Be Hazardous to Your Health*, 22 Suffolk U. L. Rev. 779 (1988); Wolfe v. Ford Motor Co., 434 N.E.2d 1008, 1011 (Mass. 1982) (standard of liability for defective product the same as for breach of warranty of merchantability). *But see* Plas-Tex, Inc. v. U.S. Steel Corp., 772 S.W.2d 442 (Tex. 1989) (explaining the difference under Texas law).

[131] *E.g.*, Arnold v. Dow Chem. Co., 91 Cal. App. 4th 698 (2001) (state law preempted regarding warning, but not with respect to allegation of defective product design).

[132] *E.g.*, Standard Brands Chem. Indus, Inc. v. Pilot Freight Carriers, Inc., 1971 N.Y. Misc. LEXIS 1756 (Mar. 18, 1971).

[133] Shaffer v. Victoria Station, Inc., 588 P.2d 233, 234 (Wash. 1978). *See also* Keaton v. A.B.C. Drug Co., 467 S.E.2d 558 (Ga. 1996) (bleach on shelf in store, without cap on bottle); Hadley v. Hillcrest Dairy, Inc. 171 N.E.2d 293 (Mass. 1961) (shattering milk bottle).

[134] U.C.C. § 2-314(2)(f) (2012).

promises or affirmations of fact. In *Native American Arts, Inc. v. Bundy-Howard, Inc.*,[135] goods were unmerchantable because they were not made by Native Americans, though the label indicated that they were. This nonconformity would have also been a breach of the express warranty that the goods match the seller's description. Significantly, however, the implied warranty of merchantability does not require that the buyer relied on, or even read or saw, the label.

In this respect, the implied warranty of merchantability is broader than express warranties arising from promises or affirmations of fact made by the seller, which give rise to liability only if they are "part of the basis of the bargain."[136] Thus, even a buyer who does not read the label is entitled to relief if the goods do not conform to the promises or representations of fact contained on the package or label, as long as the implied warranty of merchantability has not been effectively disclaimed.[137]

§ 7.04 IMPLIED WARRANTY OF FITNESS FOR PARTICULAR PURPOSE

When goods are fit for their ordinary purpose, but not fit for the buyer's particular purpose, the implied warranty of fitness for particular purpose of U.C.C. § 2-315 might apply.[138] For example, a "Mini Cooper" automobile might be suitable for its ordinary purpose of providing transportation, but not be suitable for towing a boat. Sellers are not ordinarily responsible for ensuring that goods are suitable for a buyer's particular purpose, unless the seller is aware of the buyer's purpose and selects goods for the buyer.

Section 2-315 provides:

> Where the seller at the time of contracting has reason to know any particular purpose for which the goods are required and that the buyer is relying on the seller's skill or judgment to select or furnish suitable goods, there is unless excluded or modified under the next section an implied warranty that the goods shall be fit for such purpose.[139]

Thus, the buyer has a measure of protection when the goods are not fit for the buyer's idiosyncratic use, even though they might be suitable for their ordinary purpose. However, this protection exists only when the buyer relies on the seller's skill or judgment to select or furnish the goods, and even then only if the seller had reason to know of both the buyer's particular purpose and that the buyer was relying on the seller's skill or judgment in selecting the goods.[140]

Unlike the implied warranty of merchantability, the implied warranty of fitness

---

[135] 2002 U.S. Dist. LEXIS 12682 (N.D. Ill. July 11, 2002).

[136] U.C.C. § 2-313 (2012). *See supra* § 7.02[A] Affirmations of Fact.

[137] *E.g.*, Eichenberger v. Wilhelm, 244 N.W.2d 691 (N.D. 1976).

[138] Article 2A provides a similar implied warranty of fitness for particular purpose in U.C.C. § 2A-213 (2012).

[139] U.C.C. § 2-315 (2012).

[140] U.C.C. § 2-315 cmt. 1 (2012).

for particular purpose does not depend on the seller's status as a merchant. As a practical matter, however, it is rare to find cases in which the buyer relied on the skill or judgment of a seller who was not, in fact, a merchant with respect to the goods involved.

[A]   Buyer's Particular Purpose[141]

The implied warranty of fitness for particular purpose applies when the goods are unfit for a specialized or "particular" purpose intended by the buyer, rather than when the goods are unfit for their ordinary purpose. It applies when the buyer's purpose is "peculiar to the nature of the [buyer's] business" or other activity for which the goods were purchased.[142] The buyer's purpose need not be unusual or bizarre in any way, but must be distinct from the ordinary use. Thus, use of a window air conditioner to cool a bedroom is the ordinary purpose; using the same unit to cool a 2,000-seat auditorium would be a particular purpose.[143]

Goods might be of merchantable quality and perfectly suitable for their usual purpose, but still not be fit for the buyer's particular purpose. Boots are made for walking, but are not suitable for playing tennis or running a marathon. In *Lewis v. Mobile Oil Corp.*,[144] a buyer who operated a sawmill converted his equipment from mechanical to hydraulic operation and purchased oil recommended to him by the seller. The recommended oil was plain mineral oil, without any chemical additives. The absence of any additives caused Lewis's equipment to run poorly and to frequently break down, resulting in lost profits. Although the plain mineral oil was suitable for its ordinary purpose, it was not suitable for use in the buyer's hydraulic equipment.[145]

Where a seller has recommended goods to the buyer, either for their ordinary purpose or for a more idiosyncratic use, the seller is likely to have also made an express warranty about goods. It is difficult to imagine a situation in which the seller has reason to know that the buyer is relying on the seller's judgment in selecting the goods in which the seller does not make some affirmative statement of fact or other representation that the goods will suit the buyer's purpose. If, after the buyer explains that she needs an air conditioning unit to cool a 3,000-square-foot auditorium full of people, the seller displays a unit and says "this will do the job," the seller has made an express warranty that the goods are suitable for the buyer's purpose. Any express warranties made by the seller will provide the buyer with a sufficient avenue for relief, subject only to the difficulties of proof including the potential effect of the parol evidence rule.[146]

---

[141] C. Clifford Allen, III, Annotation, *What Constitutes "Particular Purpose" Within Meaning of UCC § 2-315 Dealing with Implied Warranty of Fitness*, 83 A.L.R.3d 669 (1978).

[142] U.C.C. § 2-315 cmt. 2 (2012).

[143] *See* Fiddler's Inn, Inc. v. Andrews Distrib. Co., 612 S.W.2d 166 (Tenn. Ct. App. 1980).

[144] 438 F.2d 500 (8th Cir. 1971).

[145] *See also* Int'l Paper Co. v. Farrar, 700 P.2d 642 (N.M. 1985) (cardboard boxes, suitable for other purposes, were unfit for transporting tomatoes).

[146] *See supra* § 6.05 The Parol Evidence Rule.

[B]   Reliance on Seller's Skill or Judgment

The implied warranty of fitness for particular purpose applies only if the buyer acts in reliance on the seller's skill or judgment to either select or furnish goods that are suitable for the buyer's particular purpose.[147] Thus, unlike either express warranties or the implied warranty of merchantability, the warranty of fitness for particular purpose is made only where the buyer actually relies on the seller's judgment in selecting or recommending the goods for the buyer's intended use.[148] The buyer must allege and prove its actual reliance as part of its prima facie case.[149]

Where the buyer has more expertise than the seller[150] or relies on the judgment of a third party, there is no implied warranty of fitness for particular purpose.[151] For example, in *Presto v. Sandoz Pharmaceuticals Corp.*, the buyer of prescription medicine purchased the drug not in reliance on the judgment of the seller, but in reliance on the recommendation of the doctor who prescribed the medicine.[152]

Likewise, buyers who depend upon their own judgment to select goods suitable for their intended task do not enjoy this warranty protection.[153] In *Royal Business Machines, Inc. v. Lorraine Corp.*,[154] the buyer purchased several copying machines from the seller over a year-and-a-half period. In remanding for a second trial the court expressed its skepticism about whether the buyer, who acquired a large measure of expertise with respect to the goods during the parties' relationship, did not eventually make its own judgment with respect to the suitability of the goods for its purpose. The court said: "[w]e view it as most unlikely that a dealer who now concedes himself to be an expert in the field of plain paper copiers did not at some point, as his experience with the machines increased, rely on his own judgment in making purchases."[155]

Similarly, there is no warranty of fitness for particular purpose when the buyer provides the seller with the specifications for the goods, and the seller manufactures them to meet the buyer's specifications.[156] In *Commonwealth. v. Johnson Insulation*,[157] the buyer's specification of a particular brand and type of insulation prevented the seller from becoming liable for an implied warranty of fitness for particular purpose when the asbestos insulation delivered by the seller

---

[147] U.C.C. § 2-315 (2012).

[148] U.C.C. § 2-315 cmt. 1 (2012).

[149] *See* Indus. Hard Chrome Ltd. v. Hetran, Inc., 64 F. Supp. 2d 741 (N.D. Ill. 1999).

[150] *E.g.*, Sylvia Coal Co. v. Mercury Coal & Coke Co., 156 S.E.2d 1 (W.V. 1967).

[151] Beard Plumbing and Heating, Inc. v. Thompson Plastics, Inc., 152 F.3d 313 (4th Cir. 1998) (reliance on remote merchant, not on seller); O'Keefe Elevator Co., Inc. v. Second Ave. Props., Ltd., 343 N.W.2d 54 (Neb. 1984).

[152] 487 S.E.2d 70 (Ga. Ct. App. 1997).

[153] E.g., Carpenter v. Land O'Lakes, Inc., 976 F. Supp. 968 (D. Or. 1997).

[154] 633 F.2d 34 (7th Cir. 1980).

[155] *Id.* at 46.

[156] U.C.C. § 2-315 cmt. 5 (2012).

[157] 682 N.E.2d 1323, 1327 (Mass. 1997).

turned out to be harmful. The seller did nothing more than supply the asbestos insulation ordered by the buyer.[158] Of course, there may well be an implied warranty of merchantability in situations like these, making the implied warranty of fitness for particular purpose superfluous.[159]

[C]   Seller's Reason to Know

An implied warranty of fitness for particular arises only when the seller has reason to know of the buyer's reliance on the seller's skill or judgment regarding the goods.[160] This is easily satisfied where the seller recommends the goods to the buyer after learning of the buyer's intended use.[161] Thus, in *Neilson Business Equipment Center, Inc. v. Monteleone*,[162] the seller knew that the buyer intended to use the computer system involved in the buyer's medical practice. The court found an implied warranty of fitness for particular purpose even though the buyer did not formally advise the seller of his reliance or even that the goods would be used in his medical practice. It was enough that the seller had reason to know the buyer's purpose and that the buyer was relying on the seller's judgment in selecting an appropriate system for that use.

On the other hand, if the buyer does nothing that reveals its intended use, the seller is not responsible when the goods turn out to be unsuitable for the buyer's particular purpose. In *Diamond Surface, Inc. v. State Cement Plant Commission*,[163] the buyer planned to use the seller's cement for a process known as "slip paving" but never advised the seller that this was the intended purpose of the cement. There was no implied warranty that the cement would be suitable for this particular paving process.[164]

§ 7.05   IMPLIED WARRANTY OF GOOD TITLE

In addition to implied warranties regarding the quality of goods, the U.C.C. implies several warranties relating to the seller's ownership of the goods, and ensuring that the goods do not infringe someone's intellectual property rights. Buyers are thereby protected against the risk that some third party may claim a property right in the goods purchased, or that the buyer may not use or resell the goods without becoming responsible for breach of someone's patent, copyright, or trademark on the goods.

---

[158] *See also* Lewis and Sims, Inc. v. Key Indus., Inc., 557 P.2d 1318 (Wash. Ct. App. 1976) (seller supplied goods conforming to buyer's specifications).

[159] Commonwealth. v. Johnson Insulation, 682 N.E.2d 1323, 1327–28 (Mass. 1997).

[160] U.C.C. § 2-315 (2012).

[161] *E.g.*, L.B. Trucking Co. v. Townsend Grain and Feed Co., 163 B.R. 709 (Bankr. D. Del. 1994).

[162] 524 A.2d 1172 (Del. 1987).

[163] 583 N.W.2d 155 (S.D. 1998).

[164] *See also* Wisc. Elec. Power Co. v. Zallea Bros., Inc., 606 F.2d 697 (7th Cir. 1979); Bergquist v. Mackay Engines, Inc., 538 N.W.2d 655, 658 (Iowa Ct. App. 1995).

[A]   Warranty of Good Title

Article 2 of the U.C.C. provides for an implied warranty of good title in every contract for the sale of goods[165] unless the warranty is effectively disclaimed. U.C.C. § 2-312(1) provides:

> Subject to subsection (2) there is in a contract for sale a warranty by the seller that,
>
> (a)   the title conveyed shall be good, and its transfer rightful; and
>
> (b)   the goods shall be delivered free from any security interest or other lien or encumbrance of which the buyer at the time of contracting has no knowledge.

Thus, if Sam steals a BMW from Orson, and then sells it to Barb, Sam is liable to Barb for breach of his warranty of good title.[166] When Orson recovers the car from Barb, Barb will have a valid claim against Sam for breach of his implied warranty of good title. However, Barb will probably find the utility of this claim fairly limited, either because Sam is in jail, has absconded, or has no assets to pay her judgment against him.

This warranty is made by every seller, regardless of his or her status as a merchant, and is breached if the buyer loses the goods to someone with a claim of superior title. This will occur only rarely, such as where the goods were stolen prior to their sale to the buyer, making the seller's title absolutely void.[167] If the seller obtained the goods through fraud, his or her own title is merely "voidable," not void. A seller whose title is voidable has the power to convey good title to a good-faith purchaser for value. Thus, the buyer's title will be good, so long as he or she was not aware of the seller's own fraud in obtaining the goods.

For example, if a wholesaler uses a false financial statement to persuade a manufacturer of goods to deliver goods to the wholesaler on credit even though the manufacturer is insolvent, the wholesaler's title will be voidable. The manufacturer will be able to reclaim the goods under U.C.C. § 2-702.[168] However, if the wholesaler has sold them to a retailer and the retailer in good faith gives value for the goods, the retailer obtains good title to them.[169]

Even if the buyer obtains good title, the seller may still be in breach of its implied warranty of good title. The Official Comments to U.C.C. § 2-312 specify that the buyer must not "be exposed to a lawsuit in order to protect" his or her good title.[170] Thus, if there is a cloud on the buyer's title making it necessary for the buyer to

---

[165] U.C.C. § 2-312 (2012). A similar warranty is provided in leases of goods by U.C.C. § 2A-211.

[166] U.C.C. § 2-403 specifies that a person with "voidable" title can convey good title to a good-faith purchaser for value, like Barb. U.C.C. § 2-403(1) (2012). Here, however, Sam's title would be completely "void," not merely voidable. As a result, Barb would obtain only the void title that Sam had, or, in other words, no title.

[167] *E.g.*, Doyle v. Harben, 660 S.W.2d 586 (Tex. Ct. App. 1983).

[168] U.C.C. § 2-702 (2012).

[169] U.C.C. § 2-403(1) (2012).

[170] U.C.C. § 2-312 cmt. 1 (2012).

defend his or her ownership, the seller is responsible for the expenses the buyer incurs in making a defense.[171]

The seller's implied warranty of good title is also implicated when the goods are sold still subject to a security interest in favor of one of the seller's creditors. This will not happen often. Under Article 9, a buyer in the ordinary course of business takes goods free from a security interest created by the seller so long as the buyer did not know that the sale was a violation of the secured creditor's rights.[172] However, in the unusual circumstance of a person selling an item of used business equipment, the buyer's title will remain subject to a security interest previously granted to the seller's creditor. If the seller is bankrupt, the creditor may seek recourse from the buyer. When this occurs, the buyer will have a claim in the bankruptcy proceeding for the seller's breach of the warranty of good title. However, unless there are substantial assets in the seller's bankruptcy estate, the claim may be practically worthless.

[B]　　Warranty Against Infringement

U.C.C. § 2-312(3) also provides for an implied warranty to protect the buyer against claims of third parties for patent, trademark, or copyright infringement.[173] Unlike the warranty of good title, however, the warranty against infringement is made only by a "seller who is a merchant regularly dealing in goods of the kind."[174] Thus, if a retailer is forced to cease selling goods bearing a trademarked logo because his merchant seller did not have permission to use the logo, the retailer is able to recover from the seller for his loss. On the other hand, though, a buyer who purchases used manufacturing equipment from someone who does not regularly sell similar goods buys them at her own risk that their use infringes someone's intellectual property rights. Such a buyer may wish to negotiate for an express warranty against infringement.

[C]　　Disclaimer or Exclusion of Warranty of Good Title or Against Infringement

The implied warranty of good title can be disclaimed or excluded, usually by specific language in the contract eliminating or modifying the seller's obligation to convey good title.[175] Thus, the parties are free to allocate the risk of ownership or infringement between themselves.

It can also be impliedly disclaimed through circumstances that give the buyer reason to know that the seller does not claim to have good title himself, or that the seller is purporting only to sell whatever rights the seller may have.[176] Likewise, forced sales, such as those conducted by a sheriff, or a foreclosing secured creditor,

---

[171] *E.g.*, Maroone Chevrolet, Inc. v. Nordstrom, 587 So. 2d 514 (Fla. Dist. Ct. App. 1991).

[172] U.C.C. § 9-320(a) (2012).

[173] U.C.C. § 2-312(3) (2012).

[174] *Id. See* U.C.C. § 2-312 cmt. 3 (2012).

[175] U.C.C. § 2-312(2) (2012).

[176] *Id.*

do not result in an implied warranty of good title. Such sales convey only the title held by the debtor, and impose no responsibility on the person conducting the sale for the purpose of satisfying a debt.[177]

Similarly, a sale made by the executor of a decedent's estate carries no implication that the seller's title is good.[178] The executor of an estate likely has no idea whether the decedent owned the items in his or her possession. Buyers from an estate should realize this and thus obtain no claim against the executor or the estate if it is subsequently discovered that the decedent did not own all of the items that were included in the estate sale.

§ 7.06　IMPLIED WARRANTY OF HABITABILITY[179]

For many years the doctrine of caveat emptor[180] applied to contracts for the sale of new homes. Absent an express warranty from the seller, the buyer enjoyed no protection from the risk of faulty workmanship or the incorporation of defective materials in a new home.[181] While the seller's fraud, including its intentional concealment of construction defects, would give rise to liability,[182] this provided no protection where the builder was, due to negligence or simple ignorance, unaware of the flaws.[183] Likewise, liability for negligent construction provided no relief for purely economic loss, where the defect did not lead to property damage or personal injury.[184]

Following the lead supplied by courts in England,[185] by the mid-1970s many American courts had developed a theory of an implied warranty of habitability in contracts for the purchase and construction of new residential real estate.[186] Similar

---

[177]　U.C.C. § 2-312 cmt. 5 (2012).

[178]　*Id.*

[179]　Leo Bearman Jr., *Caveat Emptor in Sales of Realty — Recent Assaults upon the Rule*, 14 VAND. L. REV. 541 (1961); Roger A. Cunningham, *The New Implied and Statutory Warranties of Habitability in Residential Leases: From Contract to Status*, 16 URB. L. ANN. 3 (1979); Timothy Davis, *The Illusive Warranty of Workmanlike Performance: Constructing a Conceptual Framework*, 72 NEB. L. REV. 981 (1993); Ernest F. Roberts, *The Case of the Unwary House Buyer: The Housing Merchant Did It*, 52 CORNELL L.Q. 835 (1967); Jeff Sovern, *Toward a Theory of Warranties in Sales of New Homes: Housing the Implied Warranty Advocates, Law and Economic Mavens, and Consumer Psychologists Under One Roof*, 1993 WIS. L. REV. 13, 15–21.

[180]　*See generally* Walton H. Hamilton, *The Ancient Maxim Caveat Emptor*, 40 YALE L.J. 1133 (1931).

[181]　Jeff Sovern, *Toward a Theory of Warranties in Sales of New Homes: Housing the Implied Warranty Advocates, Law and Economic Mavens, and Consumer Psychologists Under One Roof*, 1993 WIS. L. REV. 13, 16.

[182]　*E.g.*, Barnhouse v. City of Pinole, 133 Cal. App. 3d 171, 186–188 (1982).

[183]　*E.g.*, Hughes v. Stusser, 415 P.2d 89 (Wash. 1966).

[184]　*E.g.*, Atherton Condominium Apartment-Owners Assoc. Bd. of Dir. v. Blume Dev. Co., 799 P.2d 250 (Wash. 1990).

[185]　*See, e.g.*, Perry v. Sharon Dev. Co., 4 All E.R. 390 (C.A. 1937).

[186]　*E.g.*, McDonald v. Mianecki, 398 A.2d 1283 (N.J. 1979); Vanderschrier v. Aaron, 140 N.E.2d 819, 821 (Ohio Ct. App. 1957). *But see* P.B.R. Enters., Inc. v. Perren, 253 S.E.2d 765, 767 (Ga. 1979); Bruce Farms, Inc. v. Coupe, 247 S.E.2d 400 (Va. 1978) (adhering to caveat emptor).

protection has been extended in some states by statute.[187] Thus, depending on the circumstances, a buyer who purchases a newly constructed home may have a claim against the seller for breach of warranty, even in the absence of fraud or any express warranty supplied by the seller.

However, the implied warranty of habitability is not as broad as the implied warranty of merchantability, made with respect to goods. Habitability does not usually extend to require every aspect of a newly constructed home to be fit for its ordinary purpose.[188] Rather, it is usually limited to ensure that the house is safe, sanitary, and otherwise fit for human habitation,[189] and protects against conditions that are dangerous, hazardous, or detrimental to the life, health or safety of the residents.[190] Some courts define habitability as substantial compliance with all building and housing codes.[191] Thus, a breach of the warranty would occur by the construction of a foundation that will not support the weight of the building, or the failure to install an adequate septic system,[192] but would not extend to a poorly constructed patio[193] or an inoperable "media room."

Where the warranty has been recognized, it applies to only newly constructed homes; it does not generally apply to renovations of existing structures.[194] Thus, if Crash Construction Co. builds and sells a new home to Jim and Joan, and it contains structural defects that make it uninhabitable, Crash is liable. But, if Jim and Joan hire Crash to install a new room onto their existing house, the warranty does not apply. They will have to find some express warranty or fraudulent misrepresentation by Crash Construction as a source of relief.[195] Fortunately, many home renovation contracts frequently extend some express warranty protection to the homeowner, in the form of a promise to perform the contracted services in a "workmanlike manner."[196] In addition, many states have consumer protection statutes that protect homeowners from defective remodeling work.

Likewise, the warranty of habitability is not made by those who construct a home for use as their residence and subsequently sell it to someone else.[197] Thus, if Crash Construction builds a house for Bob and Linda to use as their home, and the couple

---

[187] *E.g.*, N.Y. Gen. Bus. Law § 777-a (McKinney 1996); Fumarelli v. Marsam Dev. Inc., 680 N.Y.S.2d 440 (N.Y. 1998); Va. Code Ann. § 55–70.1 (LexisNexis 2008 Supp.).

[188] *See, e.g.*, Aronsohn v. Mandara, 484 A.2d 675 (N.J. 1984) (defective patio in home renovation contract not covered by the warranty of habitability).

[189] *E.g.*, Stuart v. Coldwell Banker Commercial Group, 745 P.2d 1284, 1289 (Wash. 1987). *See* Frona M. Powell & Jane P. Mallor, *The Case for an Implied Warranty of Quality in Sales of Commercial Real Estate*, 68 Wash. U. L. Q. 305, 314 (1990).

[190] *E.g.*, Albrecht v. Clifford, 767 N.E.2d 42 (Mass. 2002). *See generally* Timothy Davis, *The Illusive Warranty of Workmanlike Performance: Constructing a Conceptual Framework*, 72 Neb. L. Rev. 981 (1993).

[191] Carpenter v. Donohoe, 388 P.2d 399 (Colo. 1964).

[192] Becker v. Graber Builders, Inc., 561 S.E.2d 905 (N.C. Ct. App. 2002).

[193] Aronsohn v. Mandara, 484 A.2d 675 (N.J. 1984).

[194] *But see* Andreychack v. Lent, 607 A.2d 1346 (N.J. App. Div. 1992).

[195] U.C.C. § 2-314(2) (2012).

[196] *See, e.g.*, C.P. Robbins & Assocs. v. Stevens, 301 So. 2d 196 (Ala. Civ. App. 1984).

[197] *E.g.*, Everts v. Parkinson, 555 S.E.2d 667 (N.C. Ct. App. 2001); William K. Jones, *Economic*

subsequently sells the house to Frank and Dorothy, the new buyers have no cause of action against Bob and Linda on a theory of implied warranty of habitability due to defects arising from Crash's poor performance. In this respect, it is similar to the implied warranty of merchantability, which is made only by sellers who qualify as "merchants with respect to the goods."[198]

If Frank and Dorothy attempt to recover from Crash, they are likely to encounter difficulties because they do not have a direct contractual relationship with Crash. Crash had a contract with Bob and Linda, the original purchasers of the house, but not with Frank and Dorothy. Thus, Frank and Dorothy are not in "privity of contract" with Crash.

Privity of contract is a significant issue in connection with the implied warranty of habitability. The "privity" doctrine generally prevents suits for breach of contract by persons who were not parties to the contract in question, unless the plaintiff was an intended "third-party beneficiary" of the contract or an assignee of one of original parties' rights.[199] Privity of contract is an issue in cases like these where a person buys the house from the original homeowner, but has no contract with the builder who constructed it for that original owner.[200] It is also an issue when an owner attempts to recover from a subcontractor who has performed construction services for the builder-vendor of the house. The homeowner's contract is with the builder, not with the subcontractors who were hired by the builder to assist in the construction of the home.

Some jurisdictions have abandoned the privity requirement and permit owners to recover from subcontractors and other suppliers, on a variety of theories. Some courts have simply eliminated the privity requirement.[201] Some courts treat the subsequent buyer as a third-party beneficiary of the contract between the subcontractor and the builder-vendor.[202] Others permit recovery on a theory of negligence, where privity of contract is no barrier.[203] However, where the loss is purely economic, and involves no personal injury or catastrophic harm to property, courts that have not abandoned the privity requirement deny recovery for negligence.[204] Further, some states have enacted a statutory warranty law that

---

Losses Caused by Construction Deficiencies: The Competing Regimes of Contract and Tort, 59 U. CIN. L. REV. 1051, 1061 (1991).

[198]   U.C.C. § 2-314(2) (2012).

[199]   *See supra* § 16.01[C] Privity of Contract.

[200]   *E.g.*, Boackle v. Bedwell Const. Co., Inc., 770 So. 2d 1076 (Ala. 2000); Crowder v. Vandendeale, 564 S.W.2d 879 (Mo. 1978).

[201]   *E.g.*, Sewell v. Gregory, 371 S.E.2d 82 (W. Va. 1988); Moxley v. Laramie Builders, Inc., 600 P.2d 733 (Wyo. 1979). *Cf.* Real Estate Mktg., Inc. v. Franz, 885 S.W.2d 921 (Ky. 1994); Arvai v. Shaw, 345 S.E.2d 715 (S.C. 1986). *See generally* William K. Jones, *Economic Losses Caused by Construction Deficiencies: The Competing Regimes of Contract and Tort*, 59 U. CIN. L. REV. 1051, 1077–83 (1991); Joseph C. Brown Jr., Comment, *The Implied Warranty of Habitability Doctrine in Residential Real Property Conveyances: Policy-Backed Change Proposals*, 62 WASH. L. REV. 743 (1987).

[202]   *See* Keel v. Titan Constr. Corp., 639 P.2d 1228 (Okla. 1981); Syndoulos Lutheran Church v. A.R.C. Indus., 662 P.2d 109 (Alaska 1983); Lin v. Gatehouse Constr. Co., 616 N.E.2d 519 (Ohio Ct. App. 1992).

[203]   *E.g.*, Cosmopolitan Homes, Inc. v. Weller, 663 P.2d 1041 (Colo. 1983); Brown v. Fowler, 279 N.W.2d 907 (S.D. 1979).

[204]   William K. Jones, *Economic Losses Caused by Construction Deficiencies: The Competing*

expends protection to subsequent purchasers.[205]

In some circumstances, liability has even been extended to lenders.[206] Lenders who finance the construction or purchase of a new home are not usually responsible for defects caused by the builder.[207] However, if a construction lender — a lender who finances the construction of a home or an entire subdivision — participates in the construction project in a "joint venture" or partnership with a builder or developer, the buyer may be able to recover from the lender as a result of its "active participation" in the construction of the defective home.[208] Other states impose liability only if the lender was "substantially involved" in the construction process.[209]

Unlike implied warranties relating to goods, the implied warranty of habitability cannot generally be disclaimed by a builder.[210] In this respect, it seems more like it is based on principles of tort than contract.

In both construction and other contexts, courts have sometimes imposed an implied warranty of workmanlike performance.[211] This warranty, unlike the warranty of merchantability or habitability, focuses on the process of performance rather than the quality of the end product.[212] Likewise, the implied warranty of workmanlike performance extends protection beyond conditions that make a residential structure unsafe. Thus, in *Aronsohn v. Mandara*,[213] where the defendant constructed an outdoor patio poorly, the court recognized that the warranty of habitability did not apply, but that the plaintiff still might recover for harm to the patio caused by unworkmanlike performance in its construction. Further, unlike the implied warranty of habitability, the implied warranty of workmanlike performance is not strictly limited to construction contracts. It has been applied to termite inspection services,[214] transportation services,[215] and management services.[216] It has not, however, generally been applied to professional services, where a fault-

---

Regimes of Contract and Tort, 59 U. Cin. L. Rev. 1051, 1083–89 (1991); Melvin A. Eisenberg, *Third Party Beneficiaries*, 92 Colum. L. Rev. 1358, 1404 (1992).

[205] *E.g.*, Fumarelli v. Marsam Dev. Inc., 680 N.Y.S.2d 440 (N.Y. 1998); Randy Suttom, Annotation, *Validity, Construction, and Application of New Home Warranty Acts*, 101 A.L.R.5th 447 (2002).

[206] Margaret N. Fox, Note, *Commodo Caveo: "Lender Beware" — An Analysis of Lender Liability for Construction Defects Under the Implied Warranty of Habitability*, 59 S.C. L. Rev. 493 (2008).

[207] Jeffrey T. Walter, Annotation, *Financing Agency's Liability to Purchaser of New Home or Structure for Consequences of Construction Defects*, 20 A.L.R.5th 499, 507–08 (1994).

[208] Connor v. Great W. Sav. & Loan Ass'n, 447 P.2d 609 (Cal. 1968).

[209] Kirkman v. Parex, Inc., 632 S.E.2d 854 (S.C. 2006).

[210] Albrecht v. Clifford, 767 N.E.2d 42, 47 (Mass. 2002); Centex Homes v. Buecher, 955 S.W.2d 266 (Tex. 2002). *See* Frona M. Powell, *Disclaimers of Implied Warranty in the Sale of New Homes*, 34 Vill. L. Rev. 1123 (1989).

[211] *See* Timothy Davis, *The Illusive Warranty of Workmanlike Performance: Constructing a Conceptual Framework*, 72 Neb. L. Rev. 981 (1993).

[212] *Id.* at 1012–13.

[213] 484 A.2d 675 (N.J. 1984).

[214] Davis v. New England Pest Control Co., 576 A.2d 1240 (R.I. 1990).

[215] Leonard & Harral Packing Co. v. Ward, 971 S.W.2d 671 (Tex. 1998).

[216] Zenda Grain & Supply Co. v. Farmland Indus., Inc., 894 P.2d 881 (Kan. 1995).

based negligence standard has prevailed. Moreover, unlike the warranty of habitability, the implied warranty of workmanlike performance can be effectively disclaimed.[217] In this respect, it is more like the implied warranty of merchantability that applies when goods are involved.

Some courts have been more restrictive and have limited the implied warranty of workmanlike performance of services to situations where public policy and the absence of alternative avenues of relief make the imposition of an implied warranty necessary. For example, in *Rocky Mountain Helicopters, Inc. v. Lubbock County Hospital District*,[218] the court refused to impose an implied warranty of workmanlike performance to services performed incidental to helicopter maintenance, where an action for negligent performance of those services was available.

§ 7.07 WARRANTY DISCLAIMERS[219]

Sellers sometimes attempt to limit the buyer's warranty protection to whatever rights are supplied in a formal express written warranty. Not surprisingly, it is impossible for a seller to make an express warranty and at the same time attempt to disclaim its existence. Accordingly, subject to restraints imposed by the parol evidence rule, attempted disclaimers of express warranties are ineffective.[220]

The implied warranties of merchantability and fitness for particular purpose, on the other hand, may usually be disclaimed.[221] Article 2 not only permits their disclaimer but provides "safe harbor" language that a seller can use to be more confident of the enforceability of the disclaimer.[222] Despite this, if a written express warranty is made with respect to a consumer product, the federal Magnuson-Moss Warranty Act restricts the warrantor's ability to disclaim its implied warranties.[223]

Any opportunity for the buyer to inspect the goods before the sale may also exclude any warranties regarding defects that the buyer's inspection would have revealed.[224] In addition, quite apart from disclaimers of the seller's warranties, the seller may attempt to protect itself from liability for breach of warranty with a limited remedy clause, such as those commonly used in connection with automobiles that restrict the buyer to repair or replacement of any defective parts.[225]

---

[217] Associated Builders, Inc. v. Oczkowski, 801 A.2d 1008, 1012 (Me. 2002); Centex Homes v. Buecher, 955 S.W.2d 266 (Tex. 2002) (disclaimer of warranty of workmanlike performance permissible only where contract supplies sufficient details of the manner and quality of work required to be performed).

[218] 987 S.W.2d 50 (Tex. 1998).

[219] George L. Priest, *A Theory of the Consumer Product Warranty*, 90 YALE L.J. 1297 (1981). *See also* Stephen E. Friedman, *Text and Circumstance: Warranty Disclaimers in a World of Rolling Contracts*, 46 ARIZ. L. REV. 677 (2004).

[220] *See infra* § 7.07[A] Disclaimers of Express Warranties.

[221] *See infra* § 7.07[B] Disclaimers of Implied Warranties.

[222] *See infra* § 7.07[B][1] Disclaimer Language.

[223] *See infra* § 7.07[B][5] Federal Magnuson-Moss Warranty Act.

[224] *See infra* § 7.07[B][3] Warranty Exclusion Through Buyer's Opportunity to Inspect.

[225] *See infra* § 7.07[C] Limited Remedies.

[A]   Disclaimers of Express Warranties[226]

A seller might attempt to disclaim its express warranty without realizing that it had made the warranty in the first place. In order to incur warranty liability a seller need not use the term "warranty" or "guarantee" or even subjectively realize that its descriptions, promises, or other representations amount to a warranty.[227] Thus, a seller who has described the goods or provided the buyer with a sample or model without realizing that this has resulted in a warranty might attempt to disclaim any express warranties. When this happens, the court will first attempt to construe the language of the disclaimer in a way that is consistent with the warranty.[228] However, where the two cannot be reconciled, the attempted disclaimer is discarded.[229]

Despite this general rule, if there is a final written contract, the parol evidence rule may make a disclaimer of express warranties effective. The parol evidence rule[230] prohibits the introduction of evidence of a prior or contemporaneous promise to contradict the terms of a written contract that is intended as a final expression of the parties' agreement.[231] If the writing was intended as both a final and complete expression of the parties' agreement, evidence of additional prior or contemporaneous terms is prohibited, even if the terms are consistent with those included in the writing.[232] Accordingly, a final and complete written contract that expressly disclaims that the seller made any express warranties other than those contained in the writing can be effective to prevent the introduction of evidence about the seller's representations that otherwise might have resulted in a warranty.

Consider what might happen when Sam goes to purchase his new car. When Sam starts examining a new model a sales agent might tell him that "it gets 35 miles to the gallon on the highway." This is a factual representation that constitutes an express warranty under U.C.C. § 2-313. However, when Sam signs a contract to buy the car, the written agreement may stipulate that "there are no express warranties beyond those contained in this written contract" and "buyer has not relied on any statements made by the seller's agent, except those contained herein." It might also contain a "merger" or "integration" clause, specifying that "this writing contains the entire agreement between the parties." In the face of this language, Sam may have a difficult time asserting the express warranty made by the sales agent about the car's mileage, unless he is able to use it in an effort to show that the seller committed fraud.

---

[226] Thomas J. Holdych & George Ferrell, *Individual Negotiation of Warranty Disclaimers: An Economic Analysis of an Assumedly Market Enhancing Rule*, 13 U. Puget Sound L. Rev. 237 (1990); Michael J. Phillips, *Unconscionability and Article 2 Implied Warranty Disclaimers*, 62 Chi.-Kent L. Rev. 199 (1985).

[227] U.C.C. § 2-313(2) (2012).

[228] U.C.C. § 2-316(1) (2012).

[229] *Id.*

[230] *See generally supra* § 6.05 The Parol Evidence Rule.

[231] U.C.C. § 2-202 (2012).

[232] *Id.*

A final and exclusive written contract that disclaims express warranties, and that disclaims the authority of the seller's sales agent to create warranties not contained in the writing, will prevent oral representations about the quality or characteristics of the goods from creating an express warranty. In *Bushendorf v. Freightliner Corp.*,[233] a salesperson's oral representations that a tractor-trailer engine was a "425 horsepower engine" were inadmissible to prove breach of warranty in the face of a written contract that contained an integration clause. The clause specified that the writing was a final expression of the parties' agreement and that it did not include promises or representations not contained in the writing.[234]

However, where the written contract is not intended to be an exclusive expression of the parties' agreement, the seller's use of a sample creates an express warranty despite the seller's efforts to make an effective disclaimer. In *Alimenta (U.S.A.), Inc. v. Anheuser-Busch Co.*,[235] peanut samples supplied by the seller were part of the basis of the bargain, and thus there was an express warranty that the peanuts would conform to the sample, even though the written contract did not refer to the sample. The court ruled that the written contract was not a complete and exclusive statement of the parties' agreement, and the sample did not contradict anything contained in the writing.

Moreover, the parol evidence rule does not exclude evidence of the seller's fraud. Thus, the buyer can introduce evidence of the seller's representations to show that the seller knew they were false and made them with the intent to deceive the buyer.[236] In *Wagner v. Rao*,[237] the buyer was permitted to introduce evidence that the seller's oral representations about a used Mercedes-Benz automobile were intentionally false, despite the seller's use of written language indicating that the goods were sold "as is" in a writing containing a clause indicating that the written contract was a complete and exclusive statement of the terms of their agreement.[238] In this and other respects, the parol evidence rule operates with regard to warranties in the same way it operates in connection with other oral representations not contained in the written version of the contract.[239]

[B]   Disclaimers of Implied Warranties

The U.C.C. permits sellers to disclaim the implied warranties of merchantability and fitness for a particular purpose through the use of certain prescribed language,

---

[233] 13 F.3d 1024, 1027 (7th Cir. 1993).

[234] *See also* Schneider v. Miller, 597 N.E.2d 175 (Ohio Ct. App. 1991); Jordan v. Doonan Truck & Equip., Inc., 552 P.2d 881 (Kan. 1976); Tracy v. Vinton Motors, Inc., 296 A.2d 269, 271 (Vt. 1972) (express disclaimer of other warranties barred evidence of seller's oral representations to prove express warranty).

[235] 803 F.2d 1160 (11th Cir. 1986).

[236] *E.g.*, Wagner v. Rao, 885 P.2d 174 (Ariz. Ct. App. 1994). *See supra* § 6.06[B] Invalid Contract: Illegality, Fraud, Duress, Mistake, Lack of Consideration.

[237] 885 P.2d 174 (Ariz. Ct. App. 1994).

[238] *See also* RESTATEMENT (SECOND) OF CONTRACTS § 164(1) (1981).

[239] *See generally supra* § 6.05 The Parol Evidence Rule.

through the buyer's inspection, or, more rarely, by custom. However, it should be noted that a seller's efforts to disclaim implied warranties are heavily regulated both by federal[240] and state consumer protection legislation.

In addition, a limited remedy provision, restricting the remedies a buyer can obtain for breach of the seller's warranty, can have much the same effect as a warranty disclaimer. Limited remedy provisions are discussed in another chapter[241] and are also subject to an array of federal and state consumer protection rules.

[1]   Disclaimer Language

The most common method of disclaiming implied warranties is through language in the agreement eliminating the seller's responsibility for anything other than its express warranties. U.C.C. § 2-316 specifies that both the implied warranty of merchantability and the implied warranty of fitness for particular purpose can be disclaimed through the use of several key terms or phrases.

The implied warranty of merchantability is disclaimed if the word "merchantability" is included in the disclaimer.[242] Oddly, the express language of the code seems to permit an oral disclaimer of the implied warranty of merchantability, as long as the word "merchantability" is used. However, the difficulties of proof would make it foolish for a seller to plan on this. Sellers prefer written disclaimers.

The implied warranty of fitness for a particular purpose is disclaimed by conspicuous written language indicating that "[t]here are no warranties which extend beyond the description on the face hereof."[243] To disclaim the warranty of fitness in a lease of goods, U.C.C. Article 2A sanctions the sentence: "There is no warranty that the goods will be fit for a particular purpose."[244] The implied warranty of fitness for particular purpose, unlike merchantability, can be disclaimed only in writing.[245]

After reading U.C.C. § 2-316(2) one might conclude that it provided the only mechanism for effectively disclaiming the implied warranties of merchantability and fitness for particular purpose. However, a careful examination of its text reveals that it is "[s]ubject to subsection (3)."[246] U.C.C. § 2-216(3) allows for disclaimers of both warranties through the use of other language and through means other than a conspicuous written disclaimer.

U.C.C. § 2-316(3) permits the exclusion of "all implied warranties" through the use of language such as " 'as is,' 'with all faults,' or other language that in common

---

[240] *See infra* § 7.07[B][5] Federal Magnuson-Moss Warranty Act.

[241] *See infra* § 14.02 Limited Remedies.

[242] U.C.C. §§ 2-316(2), 2A-214(2) (2012).

[243] U.C.C. § 2-316(2) (2012).

[244] U.C.C. § 2A-214(2) (2012).

[245] U.C.C. § 2-316(2) (2012).

[246] U.C.C. § 2-316(2) (2012). U.C.C. § 2A-214(2) is drafted in similar fashion, with all of subsection (2) expressly subject to the qualifying language of subsection (3). U.C.C. § 2A-214(2) (2012).

understanding calls the buyer's attention to the exclusion of warranties and makes plain that there is no implied warranty."[247] Anyone who has wandered around a used car lot probably recognizes that "as is" is commonly used in connection with the sale of used cars to disclaim the seller's responsibility for the quality of the car.

[2]   Conspicuous[248]

Regardless of the language used, the disclaimer must be conspicuous. Section 2-316(2) explicitly requires written disclaimers employing the term "merchantability" to be conspicuous. It also requires disclaimers of the implied warranty of fitness for particular purpose to be in a conspicuous writing.[249] Although one might read § 2-316(3) to permit an inconspicuous disclaimer of these implied warranties,[250] courts have consistently demanded that disclaimers be conspicuous.[251] Whether a particular disclaimer is conspicuous is a question of law to be resolved by the court, not by the jury.[252]

The U.C.C. defines "conspicuous." It provides that language is conspicuous "when it is so written that a reasonable person against whom it is to operate ought to have noticed it."[253] The Code goes on to indicate that "a printed heading in capitals is conspicuous" and that "[l]anguage in the body of a form is 'conspicuous' if it is in large or other type or color."[254]

A disclaimer that was never received by or otherwise made available to the buyer for review is not conspicuous.[255] Likewise, a disclaimer in the body of the text of a contract, but not set apart in any way that would draw attention to it, is usually inconspicuous.[256] *In Lumber Mutual Insurance Co. v. Clarklift of Detroit,*

---

[247] U.C.C. § 2-316(3) (2012).

[248] Cheryl R. Eisen, *Don't Confuse Us with the Facts?: The Relevance of the Buyer's Knowledge of a Written Exclusion of an Implied Warranty Which Is Inconspicuous as a Matter of Law*, 15 Seton Hall Legis. J. 297 (1991); Stephen E. Friedman, *Text and Circumstance: Warranty Disclaimers in a World of Rolling Contracts*, 46 Ariz. L. Rev. 677 (2004); Bernard F. Kistler Jr., *U.C.C. Article Two Warranty Disclaimers and the Conspicuousness Requirement of Section 2-316*, 43 Mercer L. Rev. 943 (1992).

[249] U.C.C. § 2-316(2) (2012).

[250] *See* William H. Danne Jr., Annotation, *Construction and Effect of UCC § 2-316(2) Providing That Implied Warranty Disclaimer Must Be "Conspicuous,"* 73 A.L.R.3d 248, 254 (1976).

[251] *E.g.*, White v. First Fed. Sav. & Loan Assoc. of Atlanta, 280 S.E.2d 398, 399–401 (Ga. Ct. App. 1981); R.J. Robertson Jr., *A Modest Proposal Regarding the Enforceability of "As Is" Disclaimers of Implied Warranties: What the Buyer Doesn't Know Shouldn't Hurt*, 99 Com. L.J. 1, 29–31 (1994). *Cf.* Gaylord v. Lawler Mobile Homes, Inc., 477 So. 2d 382, 383 (Ala. 1985); Janet L. Richards, *"As Is" Provisions — What Do They Really Mean?*, 41 Ala. L. Rev. 435, 450–54 (1990).

[252] U.C.C. § 1-201(b)(10) (2012). *E.g.*, Carpenter v. Mobile World, Inc., 551 N.E.2d 724 (Ill. App. Ct. 1990).

[253] U.C.C. § 1-201(b)(10) (2012).

[254] U.C.C. § 1-201(b)(10) (2012).

[255] Materials Mktg Corp. v. Spencer, 40 S.W.3d 172 (Tex. Ct. App. 2001).

[256] Bailey v. Tucker Equip. Sales, Inc., 510 S.E.2d 904 (Ga. Ct. App. 1999) ("as is" in body of agreement); Providence & Worcester R. Co. v. Sargent & Greenleaf, Inc., 802 F. Supp. 680 (D.R.I. 1992); Lacks v. Bottled Gas Corp., 205 S.E.2d 671 (Va. 1974).

Inc.,[257] however, the court treated such a disclaimer as effective because of the buyer's degree of sophistication.[258] The court explained that the primary focus in determining whether the requirement was met was "whether a reasonable person ought to have noticed it, taking into account the guideline language of § 1-201(10), as well as any other circumstances that protect the buyer from surprise."[259] Even though the "as is" disclaimer language was the same size and style as the other language in the contract, the buyer was a sophisticated party and the invoice provided to the buyer contained an abbreviated listing of product information in capital letters, among which was the "as is" disclaimer language. Under these circumstances, the seller was entitled to summary dismissal of the buyer's warranty claim.

The mere appearance of the disclaimer in large type is not always sufficient. In *Massey-Ferguson, Inc. v. Utley*,[260] an express warranty clause with a heading in capital letters that excluded all implied warranties was not conspicuous because it was on the back of the contract form and was referred to by words in only ordinary type on the front. Otherwise conspicuous disclaimers, appearing on the back of a two-page form contract, have usually received more favorable treatment if conspicuous language appears on the front directing the buyer's attention to the back of the form.[261]

[3] Warranty Exclusion Through Buyer's Opportunity to Inspect

Implied warranties are excluded when the buyer inspects either the goods or a sample or model, at least with respect to defects that the inspection ought to have revealed.[262] In *Hays v. General Electric Co.*,[263] the buyer's testing procedures, which revealed that the seller's motors were susceptible to overheating, effectively disclaimed the implied warranty of merchantability with respect to motors ordered after the tests were conducted, but did not impair the warranty with respect to items purchased before the testing occurred. And in *Sobiech v. International Staple and Machine Co., Inc.*,[264] the experimental nature of the goods themselves, when combined with the buyer's unquestioned awareness of potential problems with them, were sufficient to eliminate any implied warranty. Implied warranties against defects that an inspection would have revealed are also disclaimed if the buyer refuses to inspect the goods after the seller has expressly demanded that the

---

[257] Lumber Mut. Ins. Co. v. Clarklift of Detroit, Inc., 569 N.W.2d 681 (Mich. Ct. App. 1997). *See also* Am. Elec. Power Co. v. Westinghouse Elec. Corp., 418 F. Supp. 435 (S.D.N.Y. 1976).

[258] *See also* Ellmer v. Del. Mini-Computer Sys., Inc., 665 S.W.2d 158 (Tex. Civ. App. 1983); Dugan & Meyers Const. Co., Inc. v. Worthington Pump Corp. (USA), 746 F.2d 1166, 1178 (6th Cir. 1984).

[259] Lumber Mut. Ins. Co., 569 N.W.2d at 742.

[260] 439 S.W.2d 57 (Ky. 1969).

[261] *E.g.*, Childers & Venters, Inc. v. Sowards, 460 S.W.2d 343 (Ky. 1970).

[262] U.C.C. § 2-316(3)(b) (2012).

[263] 151 F. Supp. 2d 1001 (N.D. Ill. 2001).

[264] 867 F.2d 778 (2nd Cir. 1989).

buyer conduct an inspection.[265] In *Tarulli v. Birds in Paradise*,[266] the buyer of a pet cockatoo assumed the risk of illnesses afflicting the bird that would have been revealed from a veterinary examination that the seller demanded the buyer conduct before agreeing to purchase the animal. Thus, implied warranties can be excluded either by a buyer's inspection or the opportunity to inspect the goods.

However, implied warranties are excluded in this manner only where the buyer has examined the goods "as fully as [it] desired" and not simply because the buyer "took a look" at the goods before entering into the transaction.[267] Significantly, proposed revisions to U.C.C. Article 2, that are unlikely to ever be adopted, moved the requirement that the seller demand that the buyer make an inspection from the comments to the statutory language, removing any doubt whether such a demand is required.[268]

The buyer's failure to inspect, following an appropriate demand, does exclude the seller's liability for defects that the inspection would not have revealed.[269] This qualification brings the level of the buyer's expertise into the picture.[270] A buyer with expertise in connection with the goods is expected to discover more defects than a lay or casual buyer. And, in some situations, the buyer may have greater expertise with respect to the goods than the seller, even if the seller qualifies, for the purposes of the implied warranty of merchantability, as a merchant with respect to goods of the kind.

Consistent with the law of contract formation generally, the inspection contemplated by U.C.C. § 2-316 is one that occurs before the contract was made. The seller is not protected from warranty liability by an inspection at the time of the seller's delivery of the goods, after the contract was entered into.[271] However, the buyer's failure to detect and report a defect in an inspection conducted at the time of delivery may impair the buyer's right to subsequently revoke acceptance of the goods, even though a warranty applies.[272]

Despite all of this, testing and inspections do not exclude any express warranties that the seller has made with respect to the goods,[273] though the buyer's examination and awareness of any defects in the goods may rebut his or her contention that the seller's express warranty was a part of the basis of the bargain.[274]

---

[265] U.C.C. § 2-316 cmt. 8 (2012); *e.g.*, Cato Equip. Co., Inc. v. Matthews, 372 S.E.2d 872, (N.C. Ct. App. 1988); Murray v. Kleen Leen, Inc. 354 N.E.2d 415 (Ill. App. Ct. 1976).

[266] 417 N.Y.S.2d 854 (N.Y. City Civ. Ct. 1979).

[267] *E.g.*, Banco Del Estado v. Navistar Int'l Transp. Corp., 954 F. Supp. 1275 (N.D. Ill. 1997).

[268] Revised U.C.C. § 2-316(3)(b) (2003).

[269] *E.g.*, Loden v. Drake, 881 P.2d 467 (Colo. Ct. App. 1994).

[270] U.C.C. § 2-316 cmt. 8 (2012).

[271] U.C.C. § 2-316 cmt. 8 (2012). *See, e.g.*, Seattle Flight Serv., Inc. v. City of Auburn, 604 P.2d 975, 978 (Wash. Ct. App. 1979).

[272] U.C.C. § 2-607(2) (2012).

[273] James River Equip., Co. v. Beadle County Equip., Inc., 646 N.W.2d 265, 270 (S.D. 2002); Gen. Elec. Co. v. United States Dynamics, Inc., 403 F.2d 933, 935 (1st Cir. 1968).

[274] *See supra* § 7.02[E] Basis of the Bargain.

[4]   Exclusion Through Course of Dealing, Usage of Trade, or Course of Performance

Implied warranties can also be excluded or modified through a course of dealing, a course of performance, or a usage of trade.[275] Thus, the parties conduct, either as participants in an industry or in dealing with one another, can demonstrate their intent to place the risk of certain defects on the buyer.

However, the parties' conduct can be a two-edged sword. A usage of trade, course of dealing, or course of performance may assist the buyer in establishing that the seller's attempts to disclaim responsibility for the merchantability of its goods were ineffective. In *Oregon Bank v. Nautilus Crane & Equipment Corp.*,[276] the court denied summary judgment and permitted the plaintiff to attempt to prove that its otherwise effective disclaimer had been waived through a course of performance or a usage of industry trade establishing the seller's responsibility for defects in the goods.

[5]   Federal Magnuson-Moss Warranty Act

Warranties and disclaimers in contracts for the sale of consumer products are regulated by the Magnuson-Moss Warranty — Federal Trade Commission Improvement Act.[277] The Magnuson-Moss Warranty Act is the source of the "full" and "limited" warranty designations used in connection with manufacturer's express written warranties on many consumer products.[278] The act and its accompanying regulations[279] are also the source of the disclosure requirements imposed on manufacturers and others who choose to make an express warranty on a consumer product, such as those requiring "clear identification of the names and addresses of the warrantors,"[280] and "the step-by-step procedure that the consumer should take in order to obtain performance [from the warrantor]," among others.[281]

The Magnuson-Moss Warranty Act prohibits a person who makes an express written warranty, or who enters into a service contract with respect to the goods, from disclaiming or modifying any implied warranties that arise under state law.[282] However, the warrantor may limit the duration of any implied warranties to the duration of the express written warranty, provided the limitation is "conscionable and is set forth in clear and unmistakable language and prominently displayed on

---

[275] U.C.C. § 2-316(3)(c) (2012).

[276] 683 P.2d 95 (Or. Ct. App. 1984).

[277] Act of Jan 4, 1985, Pub. L. No. 93-637, 88 Stat. 2183 (1975), codified at 15 U.S.C. §§ 2301–2312 (2006) (hereinafter Magnuson-Moss Warranty Act).

[278] 15 U.S.C. § 2303(a) (2006).

[279] 16 C.F.R. 700.1–703.8 (2003).

[280] 15 U.S.C. § 2302(a)(1) (2006).

[281] *See generally* Roberta A. Riegert, *An Overview of the Magnuson-Moss Warranty Act and the Successful Consumer-Plaintiff's Right to Attorney's Fees*, 95 Com. L.J. 469 (1990).

[282] 15 U.S.C. § 2308 (2006).

the face of the warranty."[283]

The Act applies only to goods that are "normally used for personal, family, or household purposes." It does not impose any warranties, but rather applies only when a manufacturer, seller, or other person decides to make a "written warranty," either in the form of a representation or promise relating to the quality of the goods[284] or in the form of a promise to supply a refund, repair, replacement, or other remedy should the goods fail to meet their specifications.[285]

The most important feature of the Magnuson-Moss Warranty Act is its provision for the recovery of attorneys' fees,[286] which are not normally available for breach of a contract for the sale of goods. The right to recover attorney fees is important because, absent personal injury, the amount involved in disputes over most consumer products makes recourse to litigation extremely unlikely. Few consumers will spend thousands of dollars to pursue a claim for breach of warranty in the sale of a $39.95 toaster oven. Exposing sellers to the risk of having to pay the buyer's attorneys' fees, combined with the risk of having to defend against a class action, is thought to give sellers an incentive to voluntarily honor the warranties they supply in cases where the desire for a good reputation for quality products does not accomplish the task on its own.

[C]   Limited Remedies[287]

Article 2 provides a wide array of remedies for breach of warranty. Many of them are procedural. The "perfect tender rule" of § 2-601 permits a disappointed buyer to reject goods if they fail to conform to the specifications of the contract "in any respect."[288] Even after the buyer has accepted goods tendered by the seller, the buyer may "revoke acceptance" if the failure of the goods to conform to the seller's warranty "substantially impairs" the value of the goods to the buyer.[289] Others permit the recovery of money damages.[290]

However, these remedies may be expanded or limited by agreement.[291] Resorting to an agreed remedy is optional unless the parties have expressly

---

[283] 15 U.S.C. § 2308(b) (2006).

[284] 15 U.S.C. § 2301(6)(b) (2006).

[285] 15 U.S.C. § 2301(6)(b) (2006).

[286] 15 U.S.C. § 2310(d)(2) (2006).

[287] John Eddy, *On the "Essential" Purpose of Limited Remedies: The Metaphysics of UCC Section 2-719(2)*, 65 CAL. L. REV. 23 (1977); Manning Gilbert Warren III & Michelle Rowe, *The Effect of Warranty Disclaimers on Revocation of Acceptance Under the Uniform Commercial Code*, 37 ALA. L. REV. 307 (1986); David Frisch, *Buyer's Remedies and Warranty Disclaimers: The Case for Mistake and the Indeterminacy of U.C.C. Section 1-103*, 43 ARK. L. REV. 291 (1990).

[288] U.C.C. § 2-601 (2012). *See infra* § 9.02[A][2] Breach in Single Delivery Contracts: The Perfect Tender Rule.

[289] U.C.C. § 2-608 (2012). *See infra* § 9.03[C] Revocation of Acceptance.

[290] U.C.C. § 2-714 (2012). *See infra* § 12.08[A] Contracts for the Sale of Goods — Breach by the Seller.

[291] U.C.C. § 2-719 (2012).

agreed that the remedy provided for in the contract is the exclusive remedy.[292] And, as explained in more detail elsewhere, an agreed remedy provision may be unenforceable if it is unconscionable,[293] or if it has "failed of its essential purpose."[294] Limited remedy provisions, and restrictions on their enforceability, are explained elsewhere.[295]

§ 7.08   DEFENSES TO WARRANTY CLAIMS

Claims for breach of warranty are subject to several important defenses. Some, such as the buyer's failure to give adequate notice of the breach, or the buyer's assumption of the risk, are based on the buyer's conduct. Others, such as the statute of limitations and the absence of privity, are based on legal constraints.

[A]   Failure to Give Notice[296]

The buyer's right to reject goods, due to a breach of warranty or otherwise, depends on the buyer giving seasonable notice of its rejection.[297] Likewise, because the seller ordinarily has the right to attempt to cure a defective delivery,[298] the buyer must explain the defect that led her to reject the goods.[299] The buyer's failure to specify the reasons for rejection, or otherwise to alert the seller to any defects that she could reasonably detect, precludes her from relying on an "unstated defect to justify rejection or to establish breach."[300] This requirement facilitates the seller's effort to fix the problem by curing the defect and prevents the buyer from rejecting the goods as part of a bad faith effort to take advantage of a declining market value for the goods involved.[301]

Likewise, when the buyer has accepted defective goods, the buyer "must within a reasonable time after he discovers or should have discovered any breach notify the seller of breach *or be barred from any remedy*."[302] Because of the devastating impact of failure to give timely notice, the most difficult issue in connection with this requirement is what constitutes a "reasonable time."[303]

---

[292] U.C.C. § 2-719(1)(b) (2012).

[293] U.C.C. § 2-719(3) (2012).

[294] U.C.C. § 2-719(2) (2012).

[295] *See infra* § 14.02 Limited Remedies.

[296] John C. Reitz, *Against Notice: A Proposal to Restrict the Notice of Claims Rule in UCC § 2-607(3)(a)*, 73 Cornell L. Rev. 534 (1988).

[297] U.C.C. § 2-602(1) (2012).

[298] *See infra* § 9.04[A] Seller's Right to Cure.

[299] U.C.C. § 2-605(1) (2012).

[300] *Id.* Traders, Inc. v. Trust Co. Bank, 720 F. Supp. 1100, 1111 (S.D.N.Y. 1989). *See generally* Lawrence R. Eno, *Price Movement and Unstated Objections to the Defective Performance of Sales Contracts*, 44 Yale L.J. 782 (1935) (analyzing pre-code cases).

[301] *See, e.g.*, Oda Nursery, Inc. v. Garcia Tree & Lawn, Inc., 708 P.2d 1039 (N.M. 1985).

[302] U.C.C. § 2-607(3)(a) (2012) (emphasis added).

[303] Jane Massey Draper, Annotation, *Sufficiency and Timeliness of Buyer's Notice Under UCC § 2-607(3)(a) of Seller's Breach of Warranty*, 89 A.L.R.5th 319 (2001).

Courts have been quite unforgiving toward buyers who have delayed giving notice beyond a reasonable time. For example, in *Hebron v. American Isuzu Motors, Inc.*,[304] the plaintiff's truck rolled over following a defensive driving maneuver, causing the plaintiff serious personal injuries. Two years later the defendant sued the manufacturer, alleging that a design defect made the car susceptible to rolling over. This suit was the plaintiff's first notice to the manufacturer of her claim that the goods were unmerchantable. The court dismissed the plaintiff's claim because his delay in reporting the incident deprived the defendant of the opportunity to investigate the accident.[305]

In determining whether the buyer's notice was sent within a reasonable time, courts consider the purposes of the rule: giving the seller an opportunity to cure and permitting the seller to gather any evidence that might be necessary should litigation ensue.[306] The rule also discourages doubtful claims and, like the statute of limitations, permits sellers to close their books with respect to past and apparently satisfactory transactions.

[B]   Defenses Based on the Buyer's Conduct[307]

The buyer's own conduct in connection with the goods themselves may supply the seller with a defense to the buyer's breach-of-warranty claim. In actions based on negligence or strict product liability in tort, the plaintiff's conduct provides a defense if it amounts to either contributory negligence or assumption of the risk.[308] However, the U.C.C. contains no reference to either contributory negligence or to assumption of the risk.

Instead, U.C.C. § 2-714, specifies that a buyer who has "accepted goods and given notification . . . may recover as damages for any non-conformity . . . the loss *resulting in the ordinary course of events from the seller's breach.*"[309] It further specifies that the buyer may recover consequential damages[310] *"resulting from the seller's breach . . . which could not reasonably be prevented* by cover *or otherwise;* and injury to person or property *proximately resulting* from any breach of warranty."[311] The U.C.C., therefore, treats issues of contributory negligence and assumption of the risk as questions of causation.[312] If the plaintiff's own conduct was the proximate cause of his or her harm, the defendant is not liable.

---

[304] 60 F.3d 1095 (4th Cir. 1995).

[305] *Id.* at 1098.

[306] *E.g.*, Standard Alliance Indus., Inc. v. Black Clawson Co., 587 F.2d 813, 826 (6th Cir. 1978). *See generally* JAMES J. WHITE & ROBERT S. SUMMERS, UNIFORM COMMERCIAL CODE § 11-10, 417 (5th ed. 2000).

[307] Keith R. Fentonmiller, *Reflections on the Mirror Image Doctrine: Should the Federal Trade Commission Regulate False Advertising for Books Promising Wealth, Weight Loss, and Miraculous Cures?*, 110 W. VA. L. REV. 573 (2008).

[308] RESTATEMENT (SECOND) OF TORTS § 402A cmt. n (1965).

[309] U.C.C. § 2-714(1) (2012) (emphasis added).

[310] U.C.C. § 2-714(3) (2012).

[311] U.C.C. § 2-715(2) (2012) (emphasis added).

[312] *See* U.C.C. § 2-314 cmt. 13 (2012); Sullivan Indus., Inc. v. Double Seal Glass Co., 480 N.W.2d 623, 633 (Mich. Ct. App. 1991).

The Official Comments to U.C.C. § 2-715 suggest that the buyer might assume the risk that the goods are defective by failing to discover a defect that should have been discovered by a reasonable inspection of the goods.[313] However, most courts have held that the buyer's failure to inspect does not break the chain of proximate cause that makes the seller liable.[314] This is consistent with decisions holding that contributory negligence is no defense to an action for either breach of warranty[315] or strict product liability.[316]

Assumption of the risk, on the other hand, is a defense to both claims of breach of warranty[317] and strict liability in tort.[318] Thus, a buyer who voluntarily assumes a known risk, such as by continuing to use the goods after a defect is discovered, is unable to recover[319] either because his own conduct was the proximate cause of the harm[320] or because the buyer's continued use of the goods was a failure to mitigate damages under U.C.C. § 2-715(2)(b).[321]

Likewise, a buyer who misuses the goods may not recover, due either to her assumption of the risk,[322] or because her misuse was the proximate cause of the harm.[323] For example, in *Steele v. Encore Mfg. Co.*,[324] the buyer could not recover for breach of an alleged implied warranty of merchantability because he failed to follow the manufacturer's instructions for proper use of an air compressor.

Likewise, the plaintiff's use of the goods despite an open and obvious defect constitutes a defense.[325] If Sam buys a new car from a dealership but continues to drive it after he realizes that the brakes are not working, he has little reason to complain when he has an accident because he was unable to stop.

Not surprisingly, principles of comparative fault are frequently used in allocating responsibility between the parties in a breach of warranty action, just as

---

[313] U.C.C. § 2-715 cmt. 5 (2012).

[314] *See* Upjohn Co. v. Rachelle Labs., Inc., 661 F.2d 1105 (6th Cir. 1981); *but see* S.G. Supply Co. v. Greenwood Int'l, Inc., 769 F. Supp. 1430, 1441 n.15 (N.D. Ill. 1991) (indicating failure to inspect could have impact on buyer's damages).

[315] *E.g.*, Duff v. Bonner Bldg. Supply., Inc., 666 P.2d 650 (Idaho 1983).

[316] RESTATEMENT (SECOND) OF TORTS § 402A cmt. n (1965).

[317] *E.g.*, E.L. Kellett, Annotation, *Contributory Negligence or Assumption of Risk as Defense to Action for Personal Injury, Death, or Property Damage Resulting from Alleged Breach of Implied Warranty*, 4 A.L.R.3d 501 (1965).

[318] RESTATEMENT (SECOND) OF TORTS § 402A cmt. n (1965). *See, e.g.*, Williams v. Brown Mfg. Co., 261 N.E.2d 305 (Ill. 1970).

[319] *E.g.*, Broce-O'Dell Concrete Prods, Inc. v. Mel Jarvis Constr. Co., 634 P.2d 1142 (Kan. 1981).

[320] *See* Piotrowski v. Southworth Prods. Corp., 15 F.3d 748 (8th Cir. 1994).

[321] *E.g.*, Chatfield v. Sherwin-Williams Co., 266 N.W.2d 171 (Minn. 1978).

[322] *See* Traylor v. Husqvarna Motor, 988 F.2d 729 (7th Cir. 1993); Herrick v. Monsanto Co., 874 F.2d 594, 598 (8th Cir. 1998).

[323] *See, e.g.*, Wood v. Bass Pro Shops, Inc., 462 S.E.2d 101, 103 (Va. 1995) (rejecting assumption of the risk as a defense to breach of warranty, but permitting "unforeseeable misuse" as a defense); Fleck v. Titan Tire Corp., 77 F. Supp. 2d 605 (E.D. Mich. 2001).

[324] 579 N.W.2d 563 (Neb. Ct. App. 1998).

[325] Wood v. Bass Pro Shops, Inc., 462 S.E.2d 101, 103 (Va. 1995); Brockett v. Harrell Bros., Inc., 143 S.E.2d 897 (Va. 1965).

they are in allocating the loss in actions based on negligence and strict product liability in tort. This is particularly true where personal injuries are involved,[326] but is nearly inevitable in cases involving purely economic loss.[327] Thus, the court might determine that the seller's breach of warranty was partially responsible for the buyer's harm, but that the buyer's misconduct was also a contributing factor. The court, as it would in a negligence action, would limit the buyer's recovery to the extent that the buyer's own conduct was a contributing factor to his or her injuries. However, statutory limitations on the scope of a state's comparative fault statute might prevent the court from implementing principles of comparative negligence in an action based on breach of warranty. Courts have not yet fully worked out exactly how this might affect an action based on claims of negligence, strict liability in tort, and breach of warranty.[328]

[C] Absence of Privity[329]

In the past, many actions for breach of warranty were absolutely barred unless the claim was made by the buyer of the goods directly against his or her seller. If the parties to the dispute were not the parties to the contract, there was a lack of "privity" between the parties, and the action could not be maintained.[330] Actions in tort, on the other hand, like those brought to recover for an unreasonably dangerous product, under § 402A of the Restatement (Second) of Torts, could be maintained against remote sellers with whom the injured plaintiff had no direct contractual relationship. Thus, recovery in tort was frequently the preferred cause of action where the plaintiffs suffered personal injury or property damage.

Still, an action in tort may not be available, either because the traditionally shorter two-year statute of limitations has run or because the plaintiff's damages consist purely of economic loss, with no personal injuries or property damage caused as a result of the breach of the seller's warranty. In such cases, recourse may be available only in an action based on contract, and the doctrine of privity of contract may prove to be a barrier.

Privity issues are usually divided into two categories: horizontal privity and vertical privity. Questions of horizontal privity deal with the rights of bystanders to the transaction who did not buy the goods but who might be affected by them.

---

[326] *E.g.*, Larsen v. Pacesetter Sys. Inc., 837 P.2d 1273 (Haw. 1992); Cipollone v. Liggett Group, Inc., 893 F.2d 541 (3d Cir. 1990), *rev'd in part on other grounds*, 505 U.S. 504 (1992).

[327] Signal Oil and Gas Co. v. Universal Oil Prods., 572 S.W.2d 320 (Tex. 1978) (property damage and economic loss).

[328] *See*, e.g., Correia v. Firestone Tire & Rubber Co., 446 N.E.2d 1033 (Mass. 1983).

[329] Wayne K. Lewis, *Toward a Theory of Strict "Claim" Liability: Warranty Relief for Advertising Representations*, 47 Ohio St. L.J. 671 (1986); William Prosser, *The Fall of the Citadel*, 50 Minn. L. Rev. 791 (1966); William L. Prosser, *The Assault upon the Citadel (Strict Liability to the Consumer)*, 69 Yale L.J. 1099 (1960); Curtis R. Reitz, *Manufacturers' Warranties of Consumer Goods*, 75 Wash. U. L. Q. 357 (1997); Richard E. Speidel, *Warranty Theory, Economic Loss, and the Privity Requirement: Once More into the Void*, 67 B.U. L. Rev. 9 (1987); James J. White, *Retail Sellers and the Enforcement of Manufacturer Warranties: An Application of the Uniform Commercial Code to Consumer Product Distribution Systems*, 32 Wayne L. Rev. 1045 (1986).

[330] *See* William Prosser, *The Fall of the Citadel (Strict Liability to the Consumer)*, 50 Minn. L. Rev. 791 (1966) (among the greatest law review articles ever written).

Thus, an injury to a member of the buyer's family or a household guest raises a question of horizontal privity. As will be seen, U.C.C. § 2-318 provides a detailed set of rules about the ability of a bystander to recover.[331]

Questions of vertical privity deal with the ability of a buyer somewhere within the chain of distribution of the goods to sue a remote seller with whom the buyer did not directly deal.[332] Thus, when a consumer buyer asserts rights as a beneficiary of the warranty made by the manufacturer to the retailer, there is a question of vertical privity. As will be seen, the modern practice of manufacturers making express warranties directly to the ultimate consumers of their products has had a significant impact on consumers' ability to recover from remote sellers in the chain of distribution.

Furthermore, in situations involving personal injury or property damage, enterprise liability for defective products under § 402A of the Restatement (Second) of Torts has made the privity doctrine largely irrelevant. In cases involving direct economic loss, due to the lost value of the goods themselves or involving consequential economic harm such as lost profits due to the defective performance of the goods, questions of both horizontal and vertical privity raise fundamental questions about the differences between contract and tort.

[1]   Horizontal Privity[333]

Questions of horizontal privity arise when someone other than the buyer, such as a family member, house guest, or even a passerby, is harmed by the goods.[334] U.C.C. § 2-318 provides three alternative rules for who, other than the immediate buyer, might bring a claim against the seller despite the absence of horizontal privity. *Alternative A* permits a claim to be brought by any "natural person who is in the family or household of the buyer, or who is a guest in his home if it is reasonable to expect that such person may use, consume or be affected by the goods and who is injured in person by breach of the warranty."[335] This provision extends the warranty's protection only to those who are closely associated with the buyer. Significantly, it only provides protection for those who suffer personal injury as a result of the breach of warranty. *Alternative A* does not permit a third party to recover for either property damage or economic loss. Thus, a house guest who is burned by a defective coffee pot can recover for her injuries. But, a family

---

[331] *See infra* § 7.08[C][1] Horizontal Privity.

[332] *See infra* § 7.08[C][2] Vertical Privity.

[333] Christopher C. Little, Comment, *Suing Upstream: Commercial Reality and Recovery for Economic Loss in Breach of Warranty Actions by Non-Privity Consumers*, 42 Wake Forest L. Rev. 831 (2007); Richard E. Speidel, *Warranty Theory, Economic Loss, and the Privity Requirement: Once More into the Void*, 67 B.U. L. Rev. 9 (1987); William L. Stallworth, *An Analysis of Warranty Claims Instituted by Non Privity Plaintiffs in Jurisdictions That Have Adopted Uniform Commercial Code Section 2-318 (Alternatives B & C)*, 27 Akron L. Rev. 197 (1993); William L. Stallworth, *An Analysis of Warranty Claims Instituted by Non Privity Plaintiffs in Jurisdictions That Have Adopted Uniform Commercial Code Section 2-318 (Alternatives A)*, 20 Pepp. L. Rev. 1215 (1993).

[334] *See generally* William L. Stallworth, *An Analysis of Warranty Claims Instituted by Non Privity Plaintiffs in Jurisdictions That Have Adopted Uniform Commercial Code Section 2-318 (Alternatives B & C)*, 27 Akron L. Rev. 197 (1993).

[335] U.C.C. § 2-318 *Alternative A* (2012).

member who misses an important business opportunity because the telephone failed to ring has no claim for the economic loss he suffered as a result of the failure of the goods to conform to the seller's express or implied warranties. Under *Alternative A*, more remote bystanders are not protected by the seller's warranty, even though they might reasonably be expected to use or be affected by the goods.[336]

The buyer herself, as an immediate party to the contract, is in privity with the seller and may recover for either personal injury, property damage, or purely economic loss caused by the seller's breach, limited only by the restriction imposed by U.C.C. § 2-715(2) that the buyer's consequential damages must be foreseeable to the seller at the time the contract was made.[337]

Alternative B is less restrictive. It extends protection to "*any* natural person who may reasonably be expected to use, consume, or be affected by the goods and who is injured in person by the breach of the warranty."[338] The plaintiff might be a neighbor who has borrowed the defective goods, or a passerby affected by the product. Or, the plaintiff might be an employee of the buyer, injured while using the goods on his employer's behalf.[339] Most importantly, however, *Alternative B*, like *Alternative A*, extends protection to those other than the buyer only to plaintiffs who suffer personal injury. Remote parties who suffer property damage or economic loss alone may not recover.

Alternative C is the most liberal of the three alternative provisions. It extends a warranty's protection to "*any person* who may reasonably be expected to use, consume or be affected by the goods and who *is injured* by the breach."[340] This alternative not only permits business entities to recover, but allows recovery for those who suffer property damage or even economic loss as a result of the breach of the seller's warranty.

The most difficult question, particularly with respect to *Alternatives A* and *B*, is whether § 9-318 imposes a ceiling or establishes a floor for actions by those not in horizontal privity with the defendant. *Alternative A*, for example, clearly permits a houseguest who has suffered a personal injury to recover as a beneficiary of the seller's warranty. The language of *Alternative A*, however, does not explicitly either permit or prohibit a neighbor, injured while borrowing the debtor's car, from bringing suit. Nor does it prohibit a family member from recovering for physical damage to her property. Decisions have gone in both directions, with some

---

[336] Crews v. W.A. Brown & Son, Inc., 416 S.E.2d 924 (N.C. Ct. App. 1992) (warranty did not extend to members of the buyer's church, who were neither members of the buyer's family, nor guests in her home at the time their injury occurred).

[337] *See infra* § 12.04 Limits on Damages: Foreseeability.

[338] U.C.C. § 2-318 *Alternative B* (2012).

[339] *E.g.*, Pust v. Union Supply Co., 561 P.2d 355 (Colo. Ct. App. 1977). *Cf.* Lauren Fallick, Comment, *Are Employees "A" O.K.?: An Analysis of Jurisdictions Extending or Denying Warranty Coverage to a Purchaser's Employees Under Uniform Commercial Code Section 2-318, Alternative A*, 29 Nova L. Rev. 721 (2005) (analyzing liability under Alternative A).

[340] U.C.C. § 2-318 *Alternative C* (2012).

cases concluding that the rules in § 2-318 establish a ceiling[341] and others concluding that they merely impose a floor.[342] It should be noted in this regard that *Alternative C* permits the seller to expressly limit the scope of the warranty's protection, at least with respect to the rights of nonprivity plaintiffs who have suffered only property damage or economic loss.[343]

[2] Vertical Privity[344]

Questions of vertical privity deal with the rights of a buyer or other plaintiff to recover from a seller further up in the chain of distribution of the goods than the buyer's immediate seller. Questions of vertical privity are critical when the seller is no longer in business, is bankrupt, or has effectively disclaimed or limited its warranty liability. Thus, if the buyer of a defective laptop computer cannot recover from his immediate seller, a question of vertical privity arises if the buyer seeks recovery from the regional distributor or manufacturer of the item. Unlike questions of horizontal privity, addressed by U.C.C. § 2-318, the U.C.C. is neutral with respect to a buyer's ability to recover from a remote seller, as a beneficiary of whatever warranty that seller may have made to its immediate buyer.[345]

Where personal injuries are involved, the availability of a claim based on strict product liability makes questions of vertical privity less important, except in cases where the statute of limitations has run on the plaintiff's tort claim but has not yet expired under U.C.C. § 2-725.[346] Here, courts are divided, with most jurisdictions permitting recovery when personal injuries are involved,[347] and with others preserving the privity barrier to a contract recovery.[348]

When the loss is purely economic, many courts have dropped the privity barrier, at least where the loss is to the value of the goods themselves.[349] When the plaintiff seeks recovery for consequential damages or "secondary" economic loss, courts have been more restrictive.[350] However, some courts have permitted recovery by

---

[341] *E.g.*, Crews v. W.A. Brown & Son, Inc., 416 S.E.2d 924 (N.C. Ct. App. 1992).

[342] *E.g.*, Whitaker v. Lian Feng Mach. Co., 509 N.E.2d 591 (Ill. App. Ct. 1987).

[343] U.C.C. § 2-318 *Alternative C* (2012).

[344] Donald F. Clifford, *Express Warranty Liability of Remote Sellers: One Purchase, Two Relationships*, 75 Wash. U. L. Q. 413, 421 (1997); Harry M. Flechtner, *Enforcing Manufacturers' Warranties, "Pass Through" Warranties, and the Like: Can the Buyer Get a Refund?*, 50 Rutgers L. Rev. 397 (1998); Curtis R. Reitz, *Manufacturers' Warranties of Consumer Goods*, 75 Wash. U. L. Q. 357 (1997).

[345] *See* U.C.C. § 2-318 cmt. 3 (2012).

[346] *See infra* § 7.08[D] Statute of Limitations.

[347] *E.g.*, Lonzrick v. Republic Steel Corp., 218 N.E.2d 185 (Ohio 1966); Reid v. Volkswagen of Am., Inc., 512 F.2d 1294 (6th Cir. 1975).

[348] *E.g.*, Seekings v. Jimmy GMC of Tucson, Inc., 638 P.2d 210 (Ariz. 1981) (permitting recovery in tort but not in contract).

[349] *E.g.*, Spagnol Enterprises, Inc. v. Digital Equip. Corp., 568 A.2d 948 (Pa. Super. Ct. 1990); *cf.* Vermont Plastics, Inc. v. Brine, Inc., 824 F. Supp. 444 (D. Vt. 1993).

[350] Tomka v. Hoechst Celanese Corp., 528 N.W.2d 103 (Iowa 1995); Prof'l Lens Plan, Inc. v. Polaris Leasing Corp., 675 P.2d 887 (Kan. 1985). *Contra, e.g.*, Sullivan Indus., Inc. v. Double Seal Glass Co., 480 N.W.2d 623 (Mich. Ct. App. 1991).

simply eliminating vertical privity as a bar to an action for breach of warranty. In *Elden v. Simmons*,[351] the court permitted a remote purchaser of a house to pursue an action against the manufacturer of the bricks used in the construction of the structure. And, in *Israel Phoenix Assurance Co., Ltd. v. SMS Sutton, Inc.*,[352] the court permitted the owner of a car to bring a breach of warranty action against the supplier of a new cylinder, even though the plaintiff had not purchased the cylinder from the defendant, but from one of the defendant's customers.

Other courts have denied recovery, unless the remote buyer establishes that it was a third-party beneficiary of the warranty provided by the manufacturer to its distributor, from whom the buyer acquired the goods. Thus, in *Tex Enterprises, Inc. v. Brockway Standard, Inc.*,[353] the buyer of cans sued both its distributor and the manufacturer to recover for harm caused to the buyer's product, a sealant, which hardened due to rust inhibitor in the cans. The Washington Supreme Court dismissed the warranty action against the manufacturer, but remanded to permit the plaintiff to attempt to establish that it was an intended third-party beneficiary of any warranties made by the manufacturer to the distributor.[354]

Remote buyers are nearly always able to recover from a manufacturer or other nonvertical privity defendant for breach of an express warranty made directly to the buyer, even for purely economic loss.[355] Buyers are entitled to recover because the manufacturer's warranty runs directly to the retail buyer, creating a contract between the parties and thus establishing privity of contract, even though there is no direct consideration between the parties.[356] Recovery is available either under the type of written express warranty provided by manufacturers directly to the ultimate consumer,[357] or as a result of advertising claims[358] that are express warranties under the standards expressed in U.C.C. § 2-313.[359]

[D]   Statute of Limitations

The statute of limitations for sales of goods is four years, commencing at the time the cause of action accrued.[360] The Code specifically authorizes agreements reducing this time period to not less than one year.[361]

---

[351] 631 P.2d 739 (Okla. 1981).

[352] 787 F. Supp. 102 (W.D. Pa. 1992).

[353] 66 P.3d 625 (Wash. 2003).

[354] *See also* Bobb Forest Prods., Inc. v. Morbark Indus., Inc., 783 N.E.2d 560, 576 (Ohio Ct. App. 2002).

[355] *E.g.*, Spring Motors Distribs., Inc. v. Ford Motor Co., 489 A.2d 660 (N.J. 1985).

[356] *E.g.*, Gochey v. Bombardier, Inc., 572 A.2d 921, 924 (Vt. 1990).

[357] *Id.*

[358] *E.g.*, Randy Knitwear, Inc. v. Am. Cyanamid Co., 181 N.E.2d 399 (N.Y. 1962); Prairie Prodd., Inc. v. Agchem Division-Pennwalt Corp., 514 N.E.2d 1299 (Ind. Ct. App. 1987). *See* Wayne K. Lewis, *Toward a Theory of Strict "Claim" Liability: Warranty Relief for Advertising Representations*, 47 Ohio St. L.J. 671 (1986).

[359] *See supra* § 7.02 Express Warranties Concerning Goods.

[360] U.C.C. § 2-725(1) (2012).

[361] *Id.*

The most difficult issue is determining when a cause of action accrues. Section 2-725(2) specifies that a cause of action accrues "when the breach occurs," regardless of whether the injured party is aware of the breach.[362] A breach of warranty occurs "when tender of delivery is made."[363] The law thus ordinarily presumes that a warranty is nothing more than a representation of the quality of the goods at the time they are delivered.[364] Such warranties are breached, if at all, if the goods do not conform to the terms of the contract at the time they are delivered. Their deficiencies, however, may not be discovered by the buyer within four years of delivery.[365]

This is quite different from the rule in tort where a cause of action is generally regarded as accruing when the defect causes some harm.[366] In some cases involving harm that is difficult to detect, the cause of action does not accrue until the harm is or should have been discovered.[367]

This "discovery rule" applies to contracts for the sale of goods only when the seller's warranty explicitly extends to the future performance of the goods.[368] In these situations the buyer's discovery of the breach is necessarily delayed. The cause of action does not accrue until the buyer either discovers the breach or should have discovered it.[369]

Thus, whether the statute begins to run at the time the goods are tendered, or at the time the plaintiff should have discovered the harm, depends in the first instance on whether the plaintiff's claim is sounded in contract or tort.[370] Claims for personal injury or property damage, based on either negligence or strict liability in tort for injury caused by a defective product, are likely to be characterized as arising in tort. If the claim is sounded in contract for breach of warranty,[371] the court must determine whether the warranty "explicitly extends to future performance."[372] In a combined action to recover for personal injury, property damage, and economic loss, the plaintiff's claims may well be separated, with the buyer's personal injury and property damage claims governed by the discovery rule and what is usually a two-year statute of limitations in tort, and the claims for economic loss governed by the time-of-tender rule and subject to the

---

[362] U.C.C. § 2-725(2) (2012).

[363] *Id. See* Sarah Howard Jenkins, *Contracting Out of Article 2: Minimizing the Obligation of Performance & Liability for Breach*, 40 Loy. L.A. L. Rev. 401, 415–17 (2006).

[364] Max E. Klinger, *The Concept of Warranty Duration: A Tangled Web*, 89 Dick. L. Rev. 935, 939 (1985).

[365] *See* Nationwide Ins. Co. v. Gen. Motors Corp., 625 A.2d 1172, 1174 (Pa. 1993).

[366] White v. Schnoebelen, 18 A.2d 185 (N.H. 1941).

[367] *See e.g.*, Franklin v. Albert, 411 N.E.2d 458 (Mass. 1980). *See generally* David A. Soneshein, *A Discovery Rule in Medical Malpractice: Massachusetts Joins the Fold*, 3 Western New Eng. L. Rev. 433 (1981).

[368] U.C.C. § 2-725(2) (2012).

[369] *Id.*

[370] *See generally* Lynn LoPucki, *Statute of Limitations in Warranty*, 21 U. Fla. L. Rev. 336 (1969).

[371] *See* Mendel v. Pittsburgh Plate Glass Co., 253 N.E.2d 207 (N.Y. 1969) (action for personal injury based on breach of warranty).

[372] U.C.C. § 2-725(2) (2012).

four-year limitations period of U.C.C. § 2-725. Warranty and product liability claims arising from injuries due to exposure to asbestos present a good example, with claims for economic loss ordinarily governed by the time of tender rule and claims for personal injury governed by the discovery rule.[373]

In one sense every warranty extends to the future performance of the goods. Nonconforming goods may not fail or cause any harm as a result of their nonconformity until long after they have been tendered. For example, the generator purchased in 1977 in *City of Cohoes v. Kestner Engineers*[374] did not cause the buyer any harm until it blew up in 1989, even though it had been defective from the time of delivery. Accordingly, the buyer's cause of action for breach of its express warranty was precluded by the code's four-year statute of limitations.[375] Likewise, the seller's express warranty in *Orlando v. Novurania of America, Inc.*, stating that a used boat had "not been repaired," accrued at the time the goods were tendered, and an action for breach of that warranty could not be maintained more than four years after the time of tender.[376]

Whether to apply the time-of-tender rule or the discovery rule was particularly important in connection with claims based on Y2K bugs in computer software. Where they existed, Y2K bugs were present at the time the software was tendered. However, due to their inherent nature, these bugs would not manifest themselves until midnight January 1, 2000, when software limited to utilizing dates beginning with "19" or presuming a twentieth-century date and using only two digits for the year would crash.[377]

The implied warranty of merchantability — that the goods are fit for their ordinary purpose — is normally one that can be breached only at the time the goods are tendered. Thus, in *Coady v. Marvin Lumber and Cedar Co.*,[378] the buyer's cause of action for breach of the seller's implied warranty of the merchantability of new windows accrued at the time the windows were delivered. However, a cause of action for breach of the seller's express 10-year warranty, promising to repair or replace defective windows, did not accrue until the buyer should have discovered a defect.[379]

On the other hand, *Nationwide Insurance Co. v. General Motors Corp.*[380] supplies a good example of a warranty that "expressly extends" to future

---

[373] *See generally* Alex J. Grant, Note, *When Does the Clock Start Ticking?: Applying the Statute of Limitations in Asbestos Property Damage Actions*, 80 Cornell L. Rev. 695 (1995). *See* David G. Owen, *Special Defenses in Modern Products Liability Law*, 70 Mo. L. Rev. 1, 28 (2005).

[374] 640 N.Y.S.2d 917 (N.Y. App. Div. 1996).

[375] *Id.*

[376] Orlando v. Novurania of America, Inc., 162 F. Supp. 2d 220 (S.D.N.Y. 2001). *See also* Murphy v. Spelts-Schultz Lumber Co. of Grand Island, 481 N.W.2d 422 (Neb. 1992) (future performance rule did not apply to warranty on "wood trusses" incorporated into a home).

[377] David S. Godkin & Marc E. Betinsky, *1999 Defenses in Year 2000 Litigation: New Technology, Old Theories*, 5 B.U. J. Sci. & Tech. L. 2 (1999).

[378] 167 F. Supp. 2d 166 (D. Mass. 2001).

[379] *Id.*

[380] 625 A.2d 1172, 1175 (Pa. 1993).

performance, thus delaying the accrual of the buyer's cause of action until he discovered or should have discovered the breach. There, the manufacturer's warranty promised that it would repair or replace any defective part for the first 12 months or 12,000 miles. The court ruled that the only logical interpretation of this language extended the seller's promised performance until the time a repair was needed sometime during the 12-month or 12,000-mile period. The court ruled that the manufacturer's promise to "repair or replace" could not be breached until the manufacturer failed to perform the promised repair.[381] Accordingly, the cause of action accrued at the time the promised repair was not made, without regard to the time the goods were tendered.[382]

Some courts have been more restrictive, not treating this common language as an explicit promise of future performance because it does not promise that the goods will perform in a particular way in the future.[383] However, this analysis leads to the absurd result that the buyer would have no cause of action for breach of what is normally referred to as a "seven-year, 70,000-mile warranty" if the defect in the goods first manifested itself more than four years after the seller's tender of the goods.[384]

Some courts have ruled that a warranty explicitly extends to future performance where the nature of the goods themselves implies a promise of future performance. Thus, a contract for the sale of a burial vault, which was promised to give "satisfactory service at all times" was a warranty explicitly extending to future performance.[385] Likewise, a contract for the sale of a special coating, designed and installed only to extend the life of the windows to which it was applied, implied an understanding that the seller's warranty extended to the future performance of the goods.[386]

Thus, in evaluating whether the statute of frauds has expired on a claim arising from a defect in goods, courts must consider differences between claims based on contract and tort as well as the meaning of § 2-725(2)'s language applying the discovery rule to promises of future performance.

---

[381] *Id.* at 1176.

[382] *See generally* Alice M. Wright, Annotation, *What Constitutes Warranty Explicitly Extending to "Future Performance" for Purposes of UCC § 2-725(2),* 81 A.L.R.5th 483 (2000).

[383] *See, e.g.,* Tittle v. Steel City Oldsmobile GMC Truck, Inc., 544 So. 2d 883 (Ala. 1989); Voth v. Chrysler Motor Corp., 545 P.2d 371 (Kan. 1976).

[384] Nationwide Ins. Co. v. Gen. Motors Corp., 625 A.2d 1172, 1176 n.7 (Pa. 1993). *See also* Poli v. DaimlerChrysler Corp., 793 A.2d 104 (N.J. Super. Ct. 2002).

[385] Mittasch v. Seal Lock Burial Vault, Inc., 344 N.Y.S.2d 101 (N.Y. App. Div. 1973).

[386] Imperia v. Marvin Windows of New York, Inc., 747 N.Y.S.2d 35 (N.Y. App. Div. 2002).

§ 7.09   WARRANTIES IN INTERNATIONAL TRANSACTIONS

[A]   Express and Implied Warranties in International Sales of Goods

In international sale-of-goods transactions, other than those involving buyers who are consumers, the United Nations Convention on the International Sale of Goods (CISG) nearly always applies. CISG Article 35(1) specifies that "[t]he seller must deliver goods which are of the quantity, quality and description required by the contract and which are contained or packaged in the manner required by the contract."[387] This language acknowledges that the seller's description of the goods is a warranty that the goods will conform to the description. Because the CISG does not include a parol evidence rule, descriptions made by the seller before entering into a final written contract are presumably part of the agreement, unless the written contract, through an integration clause or otherwise, expressly excludes such descriptions from the deal.

Article 35(2) further specifies that goods do not conform to a contract unless they:

(a)   are fit for the purposes for which goods of the same description would ordinarily be used;

(b)   are fit for any particular purpose expressly or impliedly made known to the seller at the time of the conclusion of the contract, except where the circumstances show that the buyer did not rely, or that it was unreasonable for him to rely, on the seller's skill and judgment;

(c)   possess the qualities of goods which the seller has held out to the buyer as a sample or model;

(d)   are contained or packaged in the manner usual for such goods or, where there is no such manner, in a manner adequate to preserve and protect the goods.[388]

This language combines elements of the U.C.C.'s provisions on express and implied warranties. Article 35(2)(c) and (d)'s requirements that the goods possess the qualities that match any sample or model is similar to the requirement of U.C.C. § 2-313(1)(c) regarding the source of express warranties.[389] Article 35(2)(a)'s requirement that the goods be "fit for the purposes for which goods of the same description would ordinarily be used" is similar to the language in U.C.C. § 2-314 regarding the implied warranty of merchantability. Article 35(2)(d), requiring the goods to be contained or packaged in an appropriate manner, is similar to language in U.C.C. § 2-314(e) regarding adequate packaging. Likewise, the language in Article 35(2)(b) is similar to that in U.C.C. § 2-315 regarding the fitness of the goods for the buyer's particular purpose. Although fine distinctions might be drawn between the language of Article 35 and that contained in the U.C.C.'s

---

[387] CISG Art 35(1) (1980).

[388] CISG Art 35(2) (1980).

[389] *See* CISG Art 35(2)(c) and (d) (1980); U.C.C. § 2-213(1)(c) (2012).

warranty provisions, doing so would be antithetical to the underlying purposes of both sets of rules.

[B]   Disclaimers of Warranties in International Sales of Goods

The CISG is silent regarding disclaimers of warranties. However, several of its provisions make it clear that they can be disclaimed. CISG Article 6 broadly permits the parties to abrogate any part of the CISG by express agreement.[390] Article 35(2) indicates that its implied warranty provisions apply "[e]xcept where the parties have agreed otherwise."[391] And, Article 35(3) specifies that the seller is not responsible for a nonconformity based on the implied warranties contained in Article 35(2) "if at the time of the conclusion of the contract the buyer knew or could not have been unaware of such lack of conformity."[392] Conspicuous language in the contract indicating that the goods were sold "as is," which would be an effective disclaimer under U.C.C. § 2-316(3)(a), would seem to be effective under this provision — as would other similar language that called the buyer's attention to the lack of any warranties. Hidden disclaimers, buried in the contract's boilerplate terms, are arguably ineffective, even though the CISG contains no specific requirement that the disclaimer be conspicuous, on the grounds that the parties did not agree to the disclaimer.

---

[390] CISG Art. 6 (1980).

[391] CISG Art 35(2) (1980).

[392] CISG Art 35(3) (1980).

Chapter 8

CONDITIONS

A condition is an event, which is uncertain to occur, upon which a duty depends.[1] Conditions are used to directly or indirectly allocate the risks involved in the transaction, and to control the sequence of performance.[2] This chapter will explain how conditions operate, how to distinguish between a condition and a promise, and how different types of conditions affect the parties' respective obligations.

§ 8.01 MEANING AND EFFECT OF CONDITIONS

All contracts consist of at least one promise. Bilateral contracts[3] involve at least two promises — one by each party. Most of the time the promises in a contract are subject to some sort of limitation or condition on which one or both of the parties' promises to perform depend.

These terms are conditions. Sometimes the conditions are expressly stated, as in insurance policies that characteristically make the insurance company's promise to pay conditional on the occurrence of some harm or loss to the insured, or only if the insured reports the incident to the insurance company within a specific time after the incident occurs.

Other times, conditions are imposed through the operation of law, in the form of a "constructive" condition. For example, in a simple contract for the sale of goods, involving the buyer's promise to pay for the goods and the seller's promise to deliver them, the buyer's promise to pay is subject to a constructive condition that the seller tender delivery of the goods.[4] In other contracts, the imposition of these constructive conditions is more complex and depends on the nature of the contract and on both the customary practice and the risks inherently involved in requiring one party to perform in advance of the other. The remainder of this section will explain exactly what conditions are and how they operate to facilitate or limit the promises contained in a contract.

---

[1] Restatement (Second) of Contracts § 224 (1981).

[2] Arthur L. Corbin, *Conditions in the Law of Contracts*, 28 Yale L.J. 739 (1919); Robert Childres, *Conditions in the Law of Contracts*, 45 N.Y.U. L. Rev. 33 (1970).

[3] *See supra* § 1.02[C] Bilateral and Unilateral Contracts.

[4] U.C.C. § 2-507 (2012).

[A]   What Is a Condition?

Chances are good that, like your author, you learned about conditions as a child. The author's parents would not permit him to watch television after dinner unless he had already done his homework.[5] Similarly, when his family had brussels sprouts for dinner, eating some of them was a condition of having dessert.[6] If the adults who raised you had rules, they probably had conditions like these that were imposed with varying degrees of rigor while you were growing up.[7]

In the law of contracts, a condition is a term that limits or qualifies a promise. More precisely, a condition is "an event, not certain to occur, which must occur, unless its non-occurrence is excused, before performance under a contract becomes due."[8] A condition can be thought of as the first part of an "if-then" statement, such as "if X, then Y." "X," just like finishing homework or eating brussels sprouts, is the condition. When a condition is imposed on a promise, the condition must occur before the performance of the promise becomes due. Moreover, because occurrence of the condition is uncertain, the promisor's duty to perform its promise is equally uncertain.

[B]   Use of Conditions to Facilitate Performance

Conditions facilitate performance of a contract in a variety of ways. They might be used in a simple way, such as to fix the sequence of the parties' respective performances. They are also used to permit the parties to avoid risks associated with the transaction. Likewise, they might be used to establish procedural mechanisms, such as notice and proof of loss, designed to alert the parties that their performance is due, or to otherwise structure the timing of performance. They might also be used, in a creative fashion, to establish alternative performances when future events are uncertain.

[1]   Establishing the Sequence of Performance

Conditions are particularly useful in establishing the order of the parties' performances. Thus, a construction contract might specify that the owner's duty to pay is expressly conditional on the contractor's completion of the construction project. In a more complicated construction project, the contract might specify that the contractor's obligation to continue its work is subject to the express condition

---

[5] As a consequence of his desire to watch television, and other consequences attached to failure to finish his homework, your author always completed his homework — usually before dinner. Work first, play later.

[6] Your author was fond of dessert, but not enough to persuade him to eat brussels sprouts. If eating brussels sprouts had been a condition of being able to watch TV, he may have grown to like them — or, he may have spent even more time reading, and less time watching TV.

[7] If your parents did not have rules, law school and law practice may prove to be a considerable challenge for you.

[8] *E.g.*, Merritt Hill Vineyards v. Windy Heights Vineyard, 460 N.E.2d 1077, 1081 (N.Y. 1984). *See* RESTATEMENT (SECOND) OF CONTRACTS § 224 (1981); Arthur L. Corbin, *Conditions in the Law of Contracts*, 28 YALE L.J. 739 (1919).

that the owner makes a series of scheduled "progress payments" at various stages in the completion of the work.[9]

[2]   Excusing Performance

Conditions are also used to protect the parties from taking risks they would prefer to avoid. These types of conditions permit a party to escape from its duty to perform by providing it with an excuse not to perform. Thus, a catering firm might insist on customers making a 20% down payment just to get their event on the caterer's schedule, and perhaps an additional payment of the balance, a week before the event. The first down payment protects the caterer against the risk that the customer will cancel the event after it is too late for the caterer to locate another job for the date in question. The second payment protects the caterer against the risk that the customer will cancel after the caterer has purchased the food for the event.

In a completely different setting, a buyer's duty to perform a contract to purchase real estate might be made expressly conditional on the buyer's ability to qualify for a mortgage loan in an amount sufficient to pay the price of the land. Or, the buyer might insist on a term that makes her duty to go through with the purchase subject to the condition that she succeeds in selling her existing home. This type of condition protects the buyer from liability if she is unable to perform due to the unavailability of a loan, inability to sell her existing house, or both.[10] Similarly, the seller of a house may want the protection of a term that conditions his duty to deliver title to his old house on the completion of the construction of his new house. This would protect the seller from the necessity of moving into an apartment if completion of the new house is delayed until after the time set for the closing on the deal for the sale of his existing home.[11]

[3]   Procedural Conditions

Conditions can also be used to establish procedural obligations that a party must satisfy in order to enjoy the benefits of the other party's performance. Insurance policies are usually laden with these types of conditions. A typical homeowner's insurance policy might specify that the homeowner must give the insurer prompt notice of a fire as a condition to receiving payment for damage the fire caused. Such a policy might also specify that the insurance company's duty to pay is conditioned on the homeowner's preservation of the damaged property until the insurance company has an opportunity to inspect the damage. This provides the insurance company with an opportunity to determine both whether the damage really occurred and whether it was caused by an event covered by the policy (and not by

---

[9] *E.g.*, Palmer v. Watson Constr. Co., 121 N.W.2d 62 (Minn. 1963); Loyal Erectors, Inc. v. Hamilton & Son, Inc., 312 A.2d 748 (Me. 1973). While writing this passage, your author was looking out the window toward his partially completed garage, knowing that his final payment would not become due until the builder finished installing the roof, which had been installed incorrectly once before, and then removed.

[10] *E.g.*, Highland Inns Corp. v. Am. Landmark Corp., 650 S.W.2d 667 (Mo. Ct. App. 1983).

[11] *E.g.*, Chirichella v. Erwin, 310 A.2d 555 (Md. 1973).

the intentional acts of the policy holder).[12] Finally, insurance policies also nearly always provide that timely payment of the premiums is a condition of the company's duty to pay. This condition does not just facilitate performance; it is central to the insurer's reasons for issuing the policy.

[4] Alternative Performances

Conditions may also be used to provide for alternative performances, with the parties' duties depending on how an uncertain future event develops. An old but particularly vivid example of this occurred in *Gray v. Gardner*, involving a contract for the sale of whale oil.[13] The whale oil had previously been delivered to the buyer, who had already paid 60¢ per gallon for it. The contract provided for the buyer to pay an additional 25¢ per gallon, but the buyer's duty to pay this extra amount was expressly conditional on the total quantity of whale oil that arrived in the Nantucket and New Bedford, Massachusetts, harbors by a specific date. If the quantity of oil received in these ports was greater than the set amount, the buyer's promise to pay the extra 25¢ was "void." By making the promise to pay the higher price subject to a condition, which depended on the total supply of oil on the market that year, the parties were able to establish a set of alternative performances for their contract, based on whether oil production was high or low for the year.[14]

Regardless of whether conditions are used simply to establish the sequence of performance, to allocate certain risks between the parties, or to provide procedures for the orderly performance of the contract, the failure of a condition to occur can have potentially devastating consequences for the parties' ability to obtain what they sought from the deal.

[5] Ensuring Satisfaction

Conditions are also sometimes used to ensure that one of the parties is fully satisfied with the other party's performance. These types of conditions are particularly useful when the recipient might want to exercise some sort of subjective judgment about the other party's performance, especially where personal services are involved. For example, newlyweds may wish to pay their wedding photographer only if they are satisfied with the photos of their wedding. Or, a landowner may wish to pay an architect for the design of a new home only if the landowner is satisfied with the plans.

These types of conditions are subject to special rules because they present the risk that the party whose "satisfaction" is necessary will feign dissatisfaction in order to get out of the contract for some other reason — such as where the

---

[12] *See, e.g.*, Howard v. Fed. Crop Ins. Corp., 540 F.2d 695 (4th Cir. 1976).

[13] Gray v. Gardner, 1821 Mass. LEXIS 16 (Mar. 1821). Those who have trouble envisioning whale ships arriving in Nantucket harbor, might imagine tankers of crude petroleum arriving at a refinery near a foggy port.

[14] *See also* Clark v. West, 86 N.E. 1 (N.Y. 1908) (unconditional promise to pay author of a text on the law of "corporations" $2 per page combined with promise to pay an additional $4 per page if the author would abstain from the use of intoxicating liquors during the production of the book).

newlyweds decide that they prefer the photos taken by their friends, rather than the "staged" scenes taken by the professional photographer; or where the landowner finds a less expensive architect.

[C] Consequences of Failure of a Condition

When performance of a promise is subject to a condition, nonoccurrence of the condition has two distinct consequences. First, performance of the duty upon which the condition depends is not due until the condition occurs. Thus, nonoccurrence of the condition will delay, or "suspend," the promisor's duty to perform,[15] until the condition has been satisfied. Second, if due to the passage of time, or otherwise, a condition never occurs, the duty which is dependent on the condition is discharged.[16] However, the simple nonoccurrence of a condition does not give rise to a claim for damages unless the party responsible for making the condition occur has also *promised* to make it happen.[17]

[1] Suspension of a Duty

Sometimes, nonoccurrence of a condition suspends a duty, temporarily. This can occur regardless of whether the condition is an express condition or a constructive condition. For example, assume that Winkler Builders promises to build a garage for Julie for a promised price of $20,000. Winkler's substantial performance of its promise to build the garage is a constructive condition of Julie's duty to pay.[18] If Winkler delays installing the roof, Julie has the right to delay payment until the job is substantially complete.

[2] Discharge of a Duty

In other circumstances, nonoccurrence of a condition completely discharges a duty. For example, in *Luttinger v. Rosen*, the buyer promised to purchase a tract of land, subject to an express condition that the buyer could obtain "first mortgage financing on [the] premises from a bank or other lending institution in an amount of $45,000 for a term of not less than twenty (20) years and at an interest rate which does not exceed 8½ percent per annum."[19] The buyers tried, but failed, to obtain the necessary financing. Because the condition was not satisfied, the buyer's duty to purchase the land never matured. Thus, their failure to go ahead with the sale was not a breach. As one court put it: "[w]here the performance of either party or the validity of the contract itself is conditioned upon the occurrence of some event, the contractual obligation does not arise if that event does not occur."[20]

Thus, complete failure of the condition excuses the duty entirely.[21] For example,

---

[15] RESTATEMENT (SECOND) OF CONTRACTS § 225(1) & cmt. a (1981).

[16] RESTATEMENT (SECOND) OF CONTRACTS § 225(2) & cmt. a (1981).

[17] RESTATEMENT (SECOND) OF CONTRACTS § 225(3) (1981).

[18] *See infra* § 8.03[B] Express, Implied, and Constructive Conditions.

[19] Luttinger v. Rosen, 316 A.2d 757 (Conn. 1972).

[20] Cauff, Lippman & Co. v. Apogee Fin. Group, Inc., 807 F. Supp. 1007, 1022 (S.D.N.Y. 1992).

[21] RESTATEMENT (SECOND) OF CONTRACTS § 225(2) (1981).

in *Irving v. Town of Clinton*,[22] the town of Clinton, Maine, entered into an agreement with a snow-plowing contractor to plow snow from the town's streets. The agreement was made expressly conditional on approval by the voters at the annual town meeting. The voters failed to approve the deal, and the town's duty to pay the contractor was discharged by the nonoccurrence of the express condition on which the town's promise depended. Similarly, if Phil agrees to buy Karen's house, but makes his promise subject to the condition that he obtain a mortgage loan, Phil's duty is discharged if he is unable, despite his reasonable good-faith effort, to obtain the necessary financing.

Inman v. Clyde Hall Drilling Co.[23] supplies a particularly dramatic example of the consequences of the nonoccurrence of a condition. The employment contract between the parties required employees to provide formal written notice of any grievance within 30 days of the incident upon which the grievance was based. After the plaintiff was fired, he failed to give formal written notice of his objection to his firing. Instead, within the 30-day period, he filed a lawsuit against the employer. The employer resisted, on the basis that the plaintiff had failed to fulfill the condition expressed in the contract. The court ruled the condition had not been satisfied, even though the employer had been served with notice of the lawsuit within the 30-day period. The court explained that it could not ignore other terms of the contract, which further required employees to wait six months before filing suit, and thus unquestionably required the employee to provide separate notice of his grievance. This condition had not been fulfilled, and the employee's suit was dismissed without any factual inquiry into the basis for the employee's claim.[24]

Questions sometimes arise over whether an express condition must be strictly performed or whether the doctrine of substantial performance, which applies to promises, also applies to conditions. Most courts still rule that express conditions cannot be "substantially performed."

Oppenheimer & Co. v. Oppenheim, Appel, Dixon & Co. supplies a good example of this rule. It involved a contract for the sublease of a parcel of commercial real estate.[25] The sublease was subject to the condition that the plaintiff — the original tenant and sub lessor — supply the subtenant with the landlord's written consent to the modifications to the premises the subtenant wished to make. Written consent had to be provided by a specific deadline. Although oral notice of the owner's approval was given within the time frame established by the condition, the plaintiff did not deliver the required written approval until 23 days after the established deadline. The court refused to consider whether the express condition had been substantially performed through the oral notice, when the condition required written notice.

---

[22] 711 A.2d 141, 141–42 (Me. 1998).

[23] 369 P.2d 498 (Alaska 1962).

[24] Because of the procedural posture of the case, *Inman v. Clyde Hall Drilling Co.* also supplies an excellent example of how, what might otherwise have been a complicated factual dispute over the merits of the plaintiff's case, was dismissed before a word of testimony had been given, because of the failure of a condition to be satisfied.

[25] Oppenheimer & Co. v. Oppenheim, Appel, Dixon & Co., 660 N.E.2d 415 (N.Y. 1995). *See* Peter A. Alces, *On Discovering Doctrine: "Justice" in Contract Agreement*, 83 Wash. U. L. Q. 471, 488–90 (2005).

In holding that the defendant's duty was discharged due to the failure of the condition to occur, the *Oppenheimer* court drew a sharp distinction between express and constructive conditions.[26] It held that "[e]xpress conditions must be literally performed, whereas constructive conditions, which ordinarily arise from language of promise, are subject to the precept that substantial compliance is sufficient."[27] In doing so, it followed the rule in the Second Restatement of Contracts, that "there is no mitigating standard of materiality or substantiality applicable to the nonoccurrence of [an express condition.]"[28] To rule otherwise, the court said, would "frustrate the clearly expressed intention of the parties."[29] Thus, although constructive conditions, which are imposed as a matter of law based on promises contained in the contract, may be substantially performed, express conditions must be fully performed. Failure of an express condition excuses the promisor from duties upon which the condition depends.[30]

Finally, it should be clear that failure of a pure condition does not give rise to a claim for damages, or for any other remedy.[31] The plaintiff in *Oppenheimer* did not *promise* to obtain the owner's written approval of the defendant's proposed alterations and was not in a position to ensure that the owner's approval could be obtained. Thus, the mere fact that the condition failed to occur was not a breach that gave rise to a cause of action for damages.

§ 8.02 DISTINGUISHING CONDITIONS FROM PROMISES

A promise is an expression of an intention to act or to refrain from acting in a specified way, made in a way that justifies another person in understanding that a commitment has been made.[32] A condition is an event that must occur before at least one of the party's performances becomes due.[33] Promises are at the heart of contract formation; conditions are at the heart of contract performance. Promises form the basis of the parties' respective duties. Conditions limit those promises, and thus limit the duties that those promises create. Promises create duties; pure conditions do not.

Rather, as explained in the immediately preceding section, the failure of a condition to occur excuses the promisor from the duty created by her promise. Although conditions may be waived or otherwise excused, their failure can nevertheless disrupt performance of the contract. They operate to provide an orderly path for the performance of the parties' respective obligations under the

---

[26] *See infra* § 8.03[B] Express, Implied, and Constructive Conditions.

[27] *Oppenheimer & Co.*, 660 N.E.2d at 418.

[28] *Id.* (quoting RESTATEMENT (SECOND) OF CONTRACTS § 237 cmt. d (1981)).

[29] *Id.* at 420.

[30] *But see* Robert Childres, *Conditions in the Law of Contracts*, 45 N.Y.U. L. REV. 33 (1970) (contending that conditions should be capable of substantial performance).

[31] RESTATEMENT (SECOND) OF CONTRACTS § 225(3) (1981).

[32] RESTATEMENT (SECOND) OF CONTRACTS § 2 (1981).

[33] RESTATEMENT (SECOND) OF CONTRACTS § 224 (1981).

terms of the contract and perhaps to permit the parties to avoid performance if a condition fails to occur.

Many agreements involve no express conditions. In an agreement between Orson and Barb, for the sale and purchase of Orson's house, the agreement may simply contain Orson's promise to deliver title and possession of the house and Barb's promise to pay $250,000 at the agreed time for closing. Performances of their respective promises are subject to "constructive conditions" derived from these promises, but the contract contains no express conditions. Because of the constructive conditions, Barb is excused from paying the price if Orson doesn't deliver a deed, and Orson is excused from delivering a deed if Barb fails to pay the $250,000, but otherwise their respective performances are "unconditional."

Contracts for the sale of a home, like the one between Orson and Barb, sometimes contain elaborate express conditions. It is common, for example, for the buyer's promise to pay to be subject to an express condition that the buyer be able to obtain a mortgage loan in an amount sufficient to pay all or a large portion of the price. If such a condition is included in their contract, and if Barb is unable to qualify for a loan, she is not required to pay for the house. Orson, of course, is also excused from performance because, even though Barb's duty to pay is excused, her payment is still a constructive condition of Orson's duty to convey good title. Performance will not occur, but Barb is not in breach and owes no damages to Orson on account of her nonperformance.[34]

[A]   Construction as Promise Preferred[35]

In most situations it is easy to tell the difference between a promise and a condition: the contract's language will unmistakably make the term a condition. Thus, although no particular language is required to create a condition, terms and phrases such as "on the condition that," "unless," "subject to," "provided that," or even a simple "if" are commonly used to indicate a condition.[36]

However, where the language is ambiguous, differences between the consequences of breach of a promise and failure of a condition may make it necessary for a court to determine whether a term was a promise or a condition. If a promise is broken, the breach gives the injured party the right to a remedy. Failure of a condition, on the other hand, excuses the other party from its duty to perform its own obligations, and may result in one party forfeiting the benefits of the contract as well as whatever part performance he or she may have already rendered.

For example, a term in an auto insurance policy requiring the policy owner to give notice to the insurance company within 10 days of the occurrence of an

---

[34] Note that Barb may be in breach if, in bad faith, she causes the condition to fail to occur by not applying for the loan. *E.g.*, Lach v. Cahill, 85 A.2d 481 (Conn. 1951).

[35] *See* Robert C. Childres and Bruce Dennis Sales, *Restatement 2d and the Law of Conditions in Contracts*, 44 Miss. L.J. 591 (1973); Hugh Evander Willis, *Promissory and Non-Promissory Conditions*, 16 Ind. L.J. 349 (1941).

[36] Restatement (Second) of Contracts § 226 cmt. a (1981); *See* Oppenheimer & Co. v. Oppenheim, Appel, Dixon & Co., 660 N.E.2d 415, 418 (N.Y. 1995); Glaholm v. Hays, 133 Eng. Rep. 743 (C.P. 1841).

accident is usually phrased to leave no doubt that it is a condition. A policyholder who fails to give the required notice is not responsible for damages due to breach; instead, she merely loses the right to recover for her loss.

Furthermore, the general rule is that an express condition, unlike a promise, may not be "substantially performed."[37] In other words, near completion of the condition is not enough. Thus, the consequences of the failure of a condition can be harsh.

Because of the potentially harsh consequences of the failure of a condition, ambiguous language is usually construed as a promise rather than as a condition.[38] A good example is found in *Rohauer v. Little.*[39] The written agreement for the sale of real estate provided that an abstract of title or title insurance commitment "shall be furnished [to] the purchaser on or before July 10, 1981." When the seller failed to provide either by the stated deadline, the buyer backed out of the deal. The court noted that this language was similar to provisions that other courts had construed as a promise, rather than as a condition precedent. The court explained that, where possible, "it is preferable to construe [a] provision as a promise [and] avoid the potentially harsh effects . . . that can result by" treating it as an express condition.[40] Because the language was not unequivocally stated as a condition, the court held that the term was a promise, and permitted the seller to attempt to show that it had substantially performed.[41]

Some terms, such as a borrower's promise to repay a loan, are simple promises. Others, such as one requiring an insured to give timely notice of an accident, are pure conditions. Still other terms serve both as a promise and as a condition — these are "promissory conditions." Promissory conditions are conditions that a party promises to fulfill.[42] Thus, if a contract for the sale of land makes the buyer's payment of the price a condition of the seller's duty to deliver a deed, and also imposes a duty on the buyer to pay the price, it is a promissory condition. Failure to comply with promissory conditions has two effects: it excuses the other party from its obligation to perform its own duties, and, at the same time gives the other party the right to recover a remedy for breach.[43] Thus, if the buyer fails to pay the price for the land, the seller is both excused from delivering a deed, and has a right to recover damages from the buyer for breach of his promise.

---

[37] *See* Robert Childres, *Conditions in the Law of Contracts*, 45 N.Y.U. L. Rev. 33 (1970).

[38] Restatement (Second) of Contracts § 227(1) (1981).

[39] 736 P.2d 403, 409 (Colo. 1987).

[40] *Id.*

[41] *See also* Howard v. Fed. Crop Ins. Corp., 540 F.2d 695 (4th Cir. 1976) (clear designation of one term as a condition led to interpretation of another term, without a similarly clear designation, as a promise).

[42] Connecticut General Life Ins. Co. v. Chicago Title & Trust Co., 714 F.2d 48, 52 (7th Cir. 1983); Internatio-Rotterdam, Inc. v. River Brand Rice Mills, Inc., 259 F.2d 137 (2d Cir. 1958).

[43] Restatement (Second) of Contracts § 227(1)(c) (1981). *See* Robert A. Hillman, *An Analysis of the Cessation of Contractual Relations*, 68 Cornell L. Rev. 617, 655–57 (1983); Hugh Evander Willis, *Promissory and Non-Promissory Conditions*, 16 Ind. L.J. 349 (1941).

[B]   Time for Performance

Terms that set the time for performance might be construed either as conditions or promises. If the time for performance of a promise operates as a condition, delay in performance results in the release of the other party from the contract. If the term merely establishes the time parameters for the other party's performance, it may only give rise to a right to recover damages due to the delay.

This is sometimes an issue when the term indicates that one party's duty to pay arises when it receives payment from someone else. This type of "pay-when-paid" clause is frequently used in construction contracts.[44] The contract between a subcontractor and the general contractor (the "general") on a construction project might provide for the subcontractor to be paid by the general "when the general receives payment from the owner." If the owner pays the general, the general will have the funds necessary to pay the subcontractor, and, in most cases, everything is fine.

A problem arises if the owner defaults by failing to pay the general contractor. If the owner discharges its debts in bankruptcy, the problem becomes particularly acute. If the term is construed as a condition, the general contractor is excused from paying the subcontractor. This, in effect, places the risk of the owner's solvency on the subcontractor, even though it is in a weak position to evaluate or bear this risk. If the parties intended to shift the risk of nonpayment in this fashion, then treating the term as a condition fulfills their intent. However, it seems unlikely that a subcontractor would be willing to assume this kind of a risk, especially without the prior opportunity to evaluate the creditworthiness of the owner. As the court said in *Peacock Construction Co. v. Modern Air Conditioning, Inc.*,[45] "small contractors, who must have payment for their work to remain in business, will not ordinarily assume the risk of the owner's failure to pay the general contractor."[46]

As a result, courts usually construe these terms as promises dealing with the reasonable time for performance, not as conditions.[47] As with most other terms of a contract, the parties are free to draft their contract to place the risk of the owner's performance wherever they choose[48]

Thus, where the parties have agreed that payment is due only if the other party receives payment from someone else, rather than "when" payment is received from the third person, the court will enforce the agreement according to its terms.[49]

---

[44] Margie Alsbrook, Comment, *Contracting Away an Honest Day's Pay: An Examination of Conditional Payment Clauses in Construction Contracts*, 58 ARK. L. REV. 353 (2005); William M. Hill & Donna M. Evans, *Pay When Paid Provisions: Still a Conundrum*, 18 CONSTR. LAW. 16 (1998).

[45] 353 So. 2d 840 (Fla. 1977).

[46] *Id.* at 842.

[47] *See* RESTATEMENT (SECOND) OF CONTRACTS § 227 illus. 1–3 (1981). *E.g.*, Main Elec., Ltd. v. Printz Serv's Corp., 980 P.2d 522 (Colo. 1999); OBS Co., Inc. v. Pace Const. Corp., 558 So. 2d 404 (Fla. 1990).

[48] *E.g.*, Mascioni v. I.B. Miller, Inc., 184 N.E. 473 (N.Y. 1933) (jury determination that risk assumed by subcontractor); Gilbane Bldg. Co. v. Brisk Waterproofing Co., Inc., 585 A.2d 248 (Md. Ct. App. 1991).

[49] MidAmerica Constr. Mgmt., Inc. v. Mastec N. Am., Inc., 436 F.3d 1257 (10th Cir. 2006).

However, where the risk is customarily borne by one of the parties, such as a general contractor in a construction setting, the parties are required to express their intention unambiguously if it is contrary to what is customary in these transactions.[50]

Pay-when-paid clauses are also used in contracts for the sale of goods in which the buyer promises to pay for the goods as soon as it receives payment from its own customer.[51] Unless there is some reason to believe that the seller intended to assume the credit risk of dealing with the buyer's customer, the term regarding the timing of payment is rarely construed as a condition. Instead, payment is due at a reasonable time, with the time the buyer expected to receive payment as the extent of the reasonable time.

§ 8.03   CLASSIFYING CONDITIONS

Conditions are classified in two ways. The first classification deals with the manner in which conditions operate and distinguishes among conditions precedent, conditions subsequent, and concurrent conditions. The second classification is based on the manner in which conditions arise, and distinguishes between express conditions, implied conditions, and constructive conditions. These distinctions also have an effect on how the condition applies.

[A]   Conditions Precedent, Conditions Subsequent, and Concurrent Conditions[52]

[1]   Conditions Precedent

Most conditions are conditions precedent. A condition precedent is an event that must occur *before* a duty to perform a promise matures. As the court in *Schmidt v. J.C. Robinson Seed Co.*,[53] explained: "[a condition precedent is] a condition which must be performed before the parties' agreement becomes a binding contract or a condition which must be fulfilled before a duty to perform an existing contract arises."[54]

Thus, if the condition does not occur, the duty that is subject to the condition never becomes due. If a buyer's promise to purchase land is subject to the condition that the buyer obtains a commitment for a mortgage loan, obtaining the loan is a condition precedent to the buyer's obligation to go through with the purchase. If the buyer is unable to obtain the loan, she has no duty to buy the land.

---

[50] Koch v. Const. Tech., Inc., 924 S.W.2d 68 (Tenn. 1996); Peacock Const. Co., Inc. v. Modern Air Conditioning, Inc., 353 So. 2d 840 (Fla. 1977); Thos. J. Dyer Co. v. Bishop Int'l Eng. Co., 303 F.2d 655 (6th Cir. 1962).

[51] Ewell v. Landing, 85 A.2d 475 (Md. 1952). *See also* Bank of Am. Nat. Trust & Sav. Ass'n v. Engleman, 225 P.2d 597 (Cal. Ct. App. 1950).

[52] OLIVER WENDELL HOLMES JR., THE COMMON LAW 316–318 (1991); Bertram Harnett & John Thornton, *The Insurance Condition Subsequent: A Needle in a Semantic Haystack*, 17 FORDHAM L. REV. 220 (1948).

[53] 370 N.W.2d 103 (Neb. 1985).

[54] *Id.* at 107.

Backing out of the deal is not a breach. Likewise, if an insurance company's duty to pay for a loss is conditioned on its receipt of timely notice of the loss, and the insured does not supply the necessary notice, the insurance company does not have to pay.

[2]   Conditions Subsequent

A condition subsequent is an event which excuses a duty that has already matured.[55] In the language of the Second Restatement of Contracts, the occurrence of a condition subsequent "terminates a duty."[56] As one court explained, a condition subsequent is a condition "which by its express terms provides for an ipso facto cancellation on the happening or non-occurrence of a stipulated event or condition."[57]

The distinction between a condition precedent and a condition subsequent rarely matters. In either event, the occurrence or nonoccurrence of the condition affects the promisor's duty. However, where evidence of the occurrence of the condition is scant, or simply nonexistent, characterization of a condition as a condition precedent or as a condition subsequent affects the resolution of the dispute because of differences in which party has the burden of pleading and proof.

The burden of pleading and proof that a condition precedent has occurred rests with the party seeking to enforce the promise.[58] The burden of proof regarding the occurrence of a condition subsequent, on the other hand, rests with the person seeking to avoid its duty.[59] However, some courts reject this technical distinction and place the burden on the party who asserts that the condition has occurred, regardless of its characterization as a condition precedent or subsequent.[60]

[3]   Concurrent Conditions

When conditions are "concurrent," both parties' performances must occur simultaneously. Concurrent conditions usually exist when the parties have promised simultaneous performance. If one party fails to perform its promise, the other party is excused from its duty to perform.

Contracts for the sale of goods frequently require simultaneous performance, with each party's performance operating as a constructive condition of the other party's duty to perform. Unless the parties have agreed otherwise, the seller's duty to deliver the goods is conditional on the buyer's payment (or "tender") of the

---

[55] *See* Cambria Sav. & Loan Assoc. v. Estate of Gross, 439 A.2d 1236 (Pa. Super. Ct. 1982).

[56] RESTATEMENT (SECOND) OF CONTRACTS § 230 (1981). The Second Restatement completely avoids use of the terms "condition precedent" and "condition subsequent." RESTATEMENT (SECOND) OF CONTRACTS § 230 cmt. a (1981). Instead, it refers to "conditions" and "events that terminate a duty." At least one court has dismissed the new language as merely "semantic." Redux, Ltd. v. Commercial Union Ins. Co., 1995 U.S. Dist. LEXIS 2545 at *10 n.7 (D. Kan. Feb. 7, 1995). *See also* Howard v. Youngman, 81 S.W.3d 101, 110 n.2 (Mo. Ct. App. 2002).

[57] Berger v. McBride & Son Builders, Inc., 447 S.W.2d 18, 19 (Mo. Ct. App. 1969).

[58] Griffin v. Am. Gen. Life and Accident Ins. Co., 752 So. 2d 621 (Fla. Dist. Ct. App. 1999).

[59] *E.g.*, Lindenbaum v. Royco Prop. Corp., 165 A.D.2d 254 (N.Y. App. Div. 1991).

[60] *See, e.g.*, Sam's Style Shop v. Cosmos Broad. Corp., 694 F.2d 998 (5th Cir. 1982).

price.[61] Likewise, the buyer's duty to tender the price is conditional on the seller's tender of the goods.[62] Thus, in a contract between Jeannie and Marco in which Jeannie promises to sell her bicycle to Marco for $100, Jeannie's duty to deliver the bike is subject to the condition that Marco pay the $100. Likewise, Marco's promise to pay is conditional on Jeannie's delivery of the bike.

[B]   Express, Implied, and Constructive Conditions[63]

Conditions can also be classified as express, implied, or constructive conditions, based on the source of the condition. Conditions might be derived from the agreement of the parties themselves or might be imposed as a matter of law.

[1]   Express Conditions

An express condition is one that is spelled out in the terms of the agreement. Express conditions are frequently created through explicit language indicating that the term is an "express condition" or a "condition precedent."[64] Other characteristic language might make a promise "subject to," "provided that," or simply "if" an event occurs.[65]

[2]   Implied Conditions

"Implied conditions" are also found in the parties' agreement, but not in its express language. Instead, they are based on the parties' conduct. An *implied condition* is a true condition that is derived from the intent of the parties as determined by their conduct, the context of the transaction, and the implied meaning of other language in the agreement, rather than by terms creating an express condition.[66] For example, a construction contract between Betty and Hank might specify that Betty will build the home to conform to a set of detailed architectural drawings supplied by Hank. If Hank fails to supply the drawings necessary for Betty to begin construction, the court will likely rule that their agreement included an implied condition that Hank supply the necessary drawings.

In addition, rules regarding excuse due to impossibility, explained elsewhere,[67] are sometimes expressed in terms of implied conditions. For example, in the classic English impossibility case of *Taylor v. Caldwell*,[68] the owner of a theater was excused from providing the theater for a series of concerts because the theater had

---

[61] U.C.C. § 2-507(1) (2012).

[62] U.C.C. § 2-511(1) (2012).

[63] Clinton W. Francis, *The Structure of Judicial Administration and the Development of Contract Law in Seventeenth-Century England*, 83 COLUM. L. REV. 35 (1983); Edwin W. Patterson, *Constructive Conditions in Contracts*, 42 COLUM. L. REV. 903 (1942).

[64] RESTATEMENT (SECOND) OF CONTRACTS § 226 cmt. a (1981).

[65] Fulton County v. Collum Properties, Inc., 388 S.E.2d 916, 918 (Ga. Ct. App. 1989).

[66] *See* Dorn v. Stanhope Steel, Inc., 534 A.2d 798 (Pa. Super. Ct. 1987).

[67] *See infra* § 11.03[A][1] Origins of the Doctrine: Impossibility.

[68] 3 B. & S. 826, 122 Eng. Rep. 309 (K.B. 1863).

burned down. The court's rationale was that the continued existence of the theater was an "implied condition" of the parties' agreement.

Courts also sometimes refer to the duty of good faith and fair dealing as an implied or constructive condition.[69] For example, in *Zobel & Dahl Construction v. Crotty*, the court said that "every contract contains an implied condition that each party will not unjustifiably hinder the other from performing."[70] Thus, if one party acts in bad faith to impede the other party's performance, the implied condition fails, and the other party is excused from its obligations under the contract.

This implied "condition" is also sometimes referred to as an implied "covenant" of good faith and fair dealing. Breach of the covenant of good faith is treated as a failure of a constructive condition, and a material breach, which justifies the other party in suspending or terminating its performance. Because it is also a breach, it gives the other party the right to recover damages for breach of the covenant.

[3]   Constructive Conditions

Express and implied conditions are different from "constructive conditions," which courts sometimes also refer to as "implied conditions." Constructive conditions are imposed by the court to ensure that there is a structured basis for determining the order of performance and to prevent injustice. Although they are imposed by the court, they are derived from the promises made by the parties and the circumstances surrounding the transaction.

Constructive conditions arise in bilateral contracts — those in which the parties have made reciprocal promises to one another. Thus, in a simple contract in which Sam agrees to sell his BMW to Barb for $15,000, Sam and Barb have both made promises: Sam promised to deliver the car and Barb promised to pay the price. Although the contract does not use language that expressly makes their respective duties conditional on the performance of the other, the law does so. Thus, Sam's delivery of the car is a condition — a constructive condition — of Barb's duty to pay the price, and Barb's payment of the price is a constructive condition of Sam's duty to deliver the car. Because their performances are due simultaneously, these constructive conditions are also concurrent conditions.

Although today it might seem obvious that Sam's and Barb's duties are contingent on each other's performance, this has not always been true. Before the late eighteenth century, promises in bilateral contracts were usually regarded as independent of one another.[71] Unless the contract expressly made one party's performance conditional on the performance of the other, a party could not refuse to perform simply because the other party was in breach.[72] If the parties were careful enough to make their duties expressly conditional on one another, this did not present a problem, but as the enforceability of informal contracts expanded, parties were not always careful to draft their agreements — if they reduced them

---

[69] Red River Wings, Inc. v. Hoot, Inc., 751 N.W.2d 206, 227 (N.D. 2008).

[70] Zobel & Dahl Construction v. Crotty, 356 N.W.2d 42, 45 (Minn. 1984).

[71] *See* Arthur L. Corbin, *Discharge of Contracts*, 22 Yale L.J. 513, 517–18 (1913).

[72] Nichols v. Raynbred, Hob. 88, 80 Eng. Rep. 238 (K.B. 1615).

to writing at all — to provide this type of protection against the other party's breach.

At one time, promises made between two parties were viewed as completely "independent" of one another, even though they had been made as part of an exchange. In *Nichols v. Raynbred*,[73] the seller of a cow was able to sue to recover the price due from the buyer without proving that he had delivered the cow. The buyer could have made his promise to pay the price expressly conditional on the seller's delivery of the cow, but if this condition was not made an express part of the promise, the court would not alter the agreement on the buyer's behalf.

This approach made some marginal sense with respect to promises that were enforceable under the seal,[74] but it was impractical in a commercial economy where promises were viewed by the parties as dependent on one another. The 1773 English case, *Kingston v. Preston*,[75] is one of the earliest examples of a court finding a constructive condition to establish the order of performance. It still provides a good illustration of how a court might examine the parties' promises and the context of the agreement to determine the order of performance in a contract. A textile merchant entered into an agreement to sell his business to one of his employees. Because the employee could not afford to pay cash, the merchant agreed to permit the buyer to defer payment. To reduce the risk that the buyer would never be able to pay, the buyer promised to provide "satisfactory" collateral for the debt. The buyer was unable to perform his promise to provide collateral but sued the seller anyway for breach of his promise to transfer ownership of the business.

Today, we would immediately realize that the seller was not obligated to transfer the business until the buyer supplied the promised collateral. In the early eighteenth century this was not yet so clear. Unless the parties had taken care to make their promises expressly dependent on one another, they were regarded as completely "independent," with each party bound to perform his promise irrespective of whether the other had performed. Lord Mansfield, who understood the practical commercial realities of the transaction, ruled that permitting the buyer to prevail even though he had not yet provided the promised collateral "would be the greatest injustice."[76] Accordingly, he treated performance of the buyer's promise to provide collateral as a condition precedent to the seller's duty to transfer title to the business's assets. Without this protection the seller would have been required to transfer the business on unsecured credit — exactly what he had tried to avoid by insisting on security for the debt.

The law now recognizes that the parties' promises in bilateral agreements are usually dependent on one another so that a material breach by one party excuses the other party from performing. Thus, substantial performance of each party's promise is a condition of the other party's duty to continue to perform. If one party

---

[73] Hob. 88, 8 Eng. Rep. 238 (K.B. 1615).

[74] *See* Anonymous, Y.B. 15 Henry VII, fol. 10b pl. 17 (1500).

[75] 2 Doug. 689, 99 Eng. Rep. 437 (K.B. 1773).

[76] *Id.* at 438. (This is from an advocate's description of the case in *Jones v. Barkley*, 99 Eng. Rep. 434, 437 (K.B. 1781)).

commits a material breach (that is, fails to substantially perform), the other party may suspend its own performance. If the breach is not cured, the nonbreaching party can cancel the contract due to a material breach. The relationship between the doctrine of substantial performance and the law of constructive conditions is explored in more detail in another chapter.[77]

§ 8.04   CONDITIONS REQUIRING SATISFACTION OR APPROVAL[78]

Contracts sometimes make one party's duty conditional on one of the parties' personal satisfaction with the other party's performance. This type of an agreement might be made in a contract for architectural drawings, where the customer's duty to pay for the design work performed depends on his or her satisfaction with the results. They are also sometimes included in construction contracts,[79] though they are more useful in contracts involving performances that will be of limited value to the buyer unless he or she is personally satisfied with the result, such as a family portrait, or a set of wedding photos.

Conditions of satisfaction are handled in one of two ways, depending on whether the contract involves a matter of personal taste or aesthetics, or deals instead with questions of functional utility.[80] In cases involving aesthetic considerations, courts are more inclined to use a subjective standard, which merely requires the promisor to act in good faith.[81] This standard prevents the promisor from using his or her dissatisfaction as a pretext for trying to avoid the contract on some other grounds,[82] but permits him to avoid performing his promise if he is honestly dissatisfied. As long as a promisor was honestly dissatisfied with the results, the condition based on his satisfaction had failed to occur, and his duty to pay did not mature.[83]

Performances that lend themselves to objective evaluation, such as whether a machine functions properly, or a building is structurally sound, depend on whether a reasonable person would have been satisfied with the work.[84] However, even

---

[77] *See infra* Ch. 9 Performance and Breach.

[78] James Brook, *Conditions of Personal Satisfaction in the Law of Contracts*, 27 N.Y.L. SCH. L. REV. 103 (1981); Larry A. DiMatteo, *The Norms of Contract: The Fairness Inquiry and the "Law of Satisfaction — A Nonunified Theory*, 24 HOFSTRA L. REV. 349 (1995).

[79] *See* R. D. Hursch, Annotation, *Construction and Effect of Provision in Private Building and Construction Contract That Work Must Be Done to Satisfaction of Owner*, 44 A.L.R.2d 1114 (1955).

[80] *E.g.*, Hutton v. Monograms Plus, Inc., 604 N.E.2d 200 (Ohio Ct. App. 1992); Haymore v. Levinson, 328 P.2d 307 (Utah 1958) (construction contract treated as involving functional utility and thus "satisfactory completion" evaluated by an objective standard of reasonableness).

[81] *See, e.g.*, Mattei v. Hopper, 330 P.2d 625, (Cal. 1958); Omni Group, Inc. v. Seattle-First Nat'l Bank, 645 P.2d 727, 729 (Wash. Ct. App. 1982). Whether a party acted in good faith is normally a question for the jury. McCabe/Marra Co. v. City of Dover, 652 N.E.2d 236, 245 (Ohio Ct. App. 1995).

[82] *See, e.g.*, Locke v. Warner Bros., Inc., 57 Cal. App. 4th 354 (1997); Fursmidt v. Hotel Abbey Holding Corp., 10 A.D.2d 447 (N.Y. App. Div. 1960); Kree Inst. of Electrolysis, Inc. v. Fageros, 478 S.W.2d 569 (Tex. App. 1972).

[83] *E.g.*, Stone Mtn. Prop., Ltd. v. Helmer, 229 S.E.2d 779, 783 (Ga. Ct. App. 1976).

[84] RESTATEMENT (SECOND) OF CONTRACTS § 228 (1981). *See* Morin Bldg. Prods. Co. v. Baystone Constr., Inc., 717 F.2d 413 (7th Cir. 1983). *See generally* Larry A. DiMatteo, *The Norms of Contract: The*

where the functional or commercial utility is involved, if the factors affecting whether a reasonable person would be satisfied are multifaceted, the complexity of the determination may justify the conclusion that the parties intended to use a subjective standard.[85] Likewise, the parties are always free to make their agreement expressly depend on a subjective standard of satisfaction, though in cases involving functional or commercial utility, they may need to demonstrate that they consciously bargained over this standard. Boilerplate language may not do the job.[86]

Difficulties arise when a person decides that the work is not satisfactory but nevertheless retains the benefits of the other party's work.[87] For example, if Mike promises to restore a piece of Cheryl's furniture, with payment being conditioned on Cheryl's personal satisfaction with the result, the restored item will still belong to Cheryl even if she is dissatisfied with the results of Mike's efforts. This creates a risk that Cheryl will dishonestly pretend to be dissatisfied as a means of obtaining the benefit of Mike's work without having to pay for it. A court might guard against this risk by evaluating Cheryl's judgment according to objective criteria. The usual concern about causing forfeiture is likely to lead a court to construe the contract to require the promisor to act not just in good faith but also reasonably in determining whether he or she is satisfied.[88] Another approach, which provides some measure of protection against dishonesty, is to find that the condition of satisfaction was not satisfied, but permit recovery in restitution to prevent unjust enrichment.

When a promisor's duty depends on the satisfaction of a third party, the concern over whether a person might pretend to be dissatisfied as a pretext for getting out of the contract is less pronounced. Accordingly, these cases are more likely to employ a subjective standard of simple good faith.[89] For example, a construction contract might provide that "final payment is subject to a licensed architect's certificate that the building has been constructed in accordance with the plans and specifications." So long as the architect does not act fraudulently, or otherwise in bad faith, his or her approval of the work is a condition of the owner's duty to pay.[90] From the point of view of a court that is called upon to enforce this arrangement, it is possible to police the decision by requiring the architect to make a good-faith evaluation of whether to issue the certificate honestly and in accordance with professional standards.[91]

Fairness Inquiry and the "Law of Satisfaction" — A Nonunified Theory, 24 HOFSTRA L. REV. 349, 399–410 (1995); Steven Petrikis, Note, *Conditions of Personal Satisfaction Under the Uniform Commercial Code: Is There Room for Unreasonableness*, 42 U. PITT. L. REV. 375 (1981).

[85] *See, e.g.*, Mattei v. Hopper, 330 P.2d 625, (Cal. 1958).

[86] *See* Morin Building Prods. Co. v. Baystone Constr., Inc. 717 F.2d 413 (7th Cir. 1983).

[87] Outside the realm of contract law it is clear that a perfectly formed lemon chiffon cake tastes no better than one that is tilted to one side.

[88] *See* RESTATEMENT (SECOND) OF CONTRACTS § 228 cmt. b (1981).

[89] *See* RESTATEMENT (SECOND) OF CONTRACTS § 227 cmt. c & illus. 5 (1981).

[90] *See, e.g.*, Laurel Race Course, Inc. v. Regal Const. Co., Inc., 333 A.2d 319 (Md. 1975); Maurer v. Sch. Dist. No. 1, 152 N.W. 999 (Mich. 1915).

[91] *See* Loyal Erectors, Inc. v. Hamilton & Son, Inc., 312 A.2d 748 (Me. 1973).

§ 8.05 EXCUSE OF CONDITIONS

When a condition fails to occur, the party whose duty depends on its occurrence is discharged from its contractual duties, unless the condition is excused.[92] Conditions may be excused for a variety of reasons. Ancillary conditions, which were not a material part of the agreed exchange, may be excused due to their impossibility of performance.[93] A condition may also be excused if its occurrence is hindered by one of the parties, if the promisor repudiates its obligations under the contract, or if the party whose duty is subject to the condition waives the condition or is otherwise estopped from asserting its failure. Finally, conditions are sometimes excused or limited to avoid forfeiture that otherwise might occur.

[A]   Impossibility of Ancillary Conditions[94]

Unanticipated circumstances sometimes prevent conditions from being fulfilled. If circumstances beyond the control of the parties make performance of a condition impossiblé or impracticable, the condition may be excused. Not surprisingly, impossibility is no excuse if the circumstances that prevented occurrence of the condition were precisely the circumstances that led the parties to impose the condition in the first place. Thus, if the occurrence of the condition was a material part of the agreed exchange, its failure cannot be excused.[95]

However, ancillary conditions can be excused. For example, if a casualty insurance policy requires the insured to give notice of an insured accident within 14 days of the accident, and the insured is rendered unconscious as a result of the accident, the condition on the insurance company's duty to pay for the insured's injuries is excused.[96] The condition requiring notice is not a material part of the agreed exchange — the insurance company did not enter into the contract for the purpose of obtaining notice about the casualty suffered by the insured. Rather, notice was designed merely to facilitate the main purpose of the contract, to protect the insured from the casualty loss. The insurance company entered into the contract to receive payment of premiums. Timely payment is a condition of the insurance company's duty to pay. Payment of the premiums is a material part of the agreed exchange, and the insured's financial difficulty in paying the premiums does not supply an excuse.

---

[92] RESTATEMENT (SECOND) OF CONTRACTS § 225 & cmt. b (1981).

[93] RESTATEMENT (SECOND) OF CONTRACTS § 271 (1981).

[94] William Hughes Mulligan, *Does War Excuse the Payment of Life Insurance Premiums*, 17 FORDHAM L. REV. 63 (1948).

[95] RESTATEMENT (SECOND) OF CONTRACTS § 271 (1981).

[96] *E.g.*, Royal-Globe Ins. Co. v. Craven, 585 N.E.2d 315 (Mass. 1992) (24-hour notice excused where insured was unconscious for more than 24 hours after accident covered by the policy); McCoy v. New York Life Ins. Co., 258 N.W. 320 (Iowa 1935) (notice excused where notice of disability under terms of disability policy was impossible). *See* RESTATEMENT (SECOND) OF CONTRACTS § 271 illus. 2 (1981).

[B]　　Interference with Occurrence of the Condition

Conditions are sometimes impeded by one of the parties. When this happens, the condition is excused.[97] A common illustration of this type of hindrance is the failure of the buyer of a parcel of real estate to apply for a mortgage loan when the buyer's duty to go through with the deal is expressly subject to his ability to obtain a loan.[98] A dramatic example of hindrance occurred during the Great Depression, in *Foreman State Trust & Savings Bank v. Tauber.*[99] There, a prenuptial agreement provided for a sizeable payment of money to the wife, but only if she survived her husband. The husband later murdered his wife, thus preventing the condition that she survives him from occurring. The court enforced the promise for the benefit of the wife's estate, even though she did not outlive him.

Cases like *Tauber* involve a negative obligation to refrain from conduct that would interfere with satisfying the condition. Other cases, involving a party's failure to take some action upon which occurrence of the condition depends, such as applying for a loan or a governmental permit, involve an affirmative obligation to act in good faith.[100]

This duty of good faith can apply with equal vigor in cases involving constructive conditions. In *Sullivan v. Bullock*,[101] a homeowner who had been uncooperative with a builder was liable for the profit the builder would have made from full performance, even though the builder did not substantially perform. The homeowner impeded the builder's access to the house, interfering with his ability to perform. In permitting the builder to recover, the court said that "[i]mplied in every contract is a condition to cooperate" and that "in construction contracts, the duty to cooperate encompasses allowing access to the premises to enable the contractor to perform the work."[102] People who get in the way of the other party's efforts to perform cannot complain about the other party's failure to fulfill its obligations.

[C]　　Repudiation[103]

Where a person repudiates the contract, conditions on that party's duties that are within the control of the other party are excused.[104] In these circumstances it would be absurd to insist that the other party continue to prepare for performance by taking steps to satisfy all of the conditions necessary to trigger the repudiating

---

[97] RESTATEMENT (SECOND) OF CONTRACTS § 245 (1981).

[98] RESTATEMENT (SECOND) OF CONTRACTS § 245 illus. 3 (1981). *See* Lach v. Cahill, 85 A.2d 481 (Conn. 1951) (buyer did not apply for mortgage loan); Vanadium Corp. v. Fid. & Deposit Co., 159 F.2d 105 (2d Cir. 1947) (party's failure to seek required governmental approval).

[99] 180 N.E. 827 (Ill. 1932).

[100] *E.g.*, Bellevue Coll. v. Greater Omaha Realty Co., 348 N.W.2d 837 (Neb. 1984).

[101] 864 P.2d 184 (Idaho. Ct. App. 1993).

[102] *See also* Bell v. Elder, 782 P.2d 545 (Utah Ct. App. 1989) (buyer's failure to pay a fee for installation of water hookup excused seller's duty to ensure availability of water to the premises).

[103] John P. Dawson, *Waiver of Conditions Precedent on a Repudiation*, 96 L.Q. REV. 239 (1980).

[104] *See* RESTATEMENT (SECOND) OF CONTRACTS § 255 (1981).

party's duty to perform. The law does not generally require useless conduct.

Excuse of a condition due to repudiation could easily occur in the context of an insurance policy. If the insurance company repudiates its obligation to satisfy a claim, the insured is excused from the condition that it supplies the company with formal written notice of the claim.[105] There would, after all, be little reason for the insured to give formal notice to the insurance company of a claim that, due to the repudiation, the policyholder already knows will be denied. Likewise, if a buyer's duty to pay for land is conditioned on obtaining a mortgage loan, the condition is excused if the seller repudiates the contract. There is no reason for the buyer to apply for a loan when the seller has already announced its intent not to perform.

However, in order for a repudiation to excuse occurrence of a condition, the repudiation must have contributed to the nonoccurrence of the condition. If the condition would have failed regardless of the repudiation, the condition is not excused.[106] Repudiation operates only to excuse a condition if the repudiation interferes with occurrence of the condition.

Conditions excused by repudiation are revived if the repudiation is retracted. Repudiations may be retracted if the other party has not indicated that he regards the repudiation as final or materially changed his position in reliance on the repudiation.[107] Thus, the repudiating party may not retract its repudiation after it is too late for the other party to take steps to cause conditions to occur on which performance of the contract depends.

[D]　　　Waiver and Estoppel of Conditions[108]

Conditions can also be waived. If a person who has made a conditional promise waives the condition, his or her duty no longer depends on whether the condition has occurred. Similarly, a person who makes a conditional promise may, as a result of his or her conduct, be "estopped" from asserting the nonoccurrence of the condition.

Waiver and estoppel are closely related overlapping doctrines that are frequently confused with one another. This confusion occurs because the words "waiver" and "estoppel" are frequently used interchangeably, without taking care to distinguish between their somewhat different elements. Further, courts sometimes say that there is no real difference between the doctrines, and that the concepts are completely interchangeable.[109] Thus, although careful courts insist that differences between the two doctrines be followed,[110] others fail to draw sharp lines between them.

---

[105] RESTATEMENT (SECOND) OF CONTRACTS § 255 illus. 1 (1981).

[106] *See* RESTATEMENT (SECOND) OF CONTRACTS § 255 illus. 2 (1981).

[107] RESTATEMENT (SECOND) OF CONTRACTS § 256 (1981); U.C.C. § 2-610 (2012).

[108] *See* John S. Ewart, *"Waiver" in Insurance Law*, 13 IOWA L. REV. 129 (1928); Robert E. Keeton, *Insurance Law Rights at Variance with Policy Provisions*, 83 HARV. L. REV. 961 (1970).

[109] Hanover Ins. Co. v. Fireman's Fund Ins. Co., 586 A.2d 567, 573 (Conn. 1991).

[110] *E.g.*, Thomason v. Aetna Life Ins. Co., 9 F.3d 645 (7th Cir. 1993).

The most critical questions concerning waiver and estoppel involve whether the promisee must have acted in reliance on the promisor's alleged waiver and the extent to which a term that was a material part of the agreed exchange can be waived. Another critical issue is whether a condition that has been waived can be reinstated. This also frequently depends on the nature and extent of the reliance on the waiver.

[1]   Time of Waiver

Whether an alleged waiver or estoppel is effective may depend on the sequence of events and whether the alleged waiver occurs before or after the time for satisfying the condition. If the waiver occurs after the time for the condition to occur has passed, the waiver is sometimes called an "election." In these instances, the obligor is said to have made an "election to forgo some advantage he might have insisted on."[111] Cases involving an election tend not to require any element of reliance on the part of the promisee. As will be seen, this type of waiver is not possible when the condition involved was a material part of the agreed exchange between the parties.

Where the waiver is based on words or conduct that occur at a time when the condition might still be satisfied, courts tend to use principles of estoppel, and require the promisee to have relied for the condition to be excused. This requirement is easily met where the promisee, acting in reliance on the promisor's words or conduct, ceases its efforts to cause the condition to occur. In these circumstances, the condition can usually be revived, following notice, provided that the actions taken in reliance can still be undone. Sometimes, of course, the toothpaste simply cannot be put back into the tube.[112]

[2]   Waiver of a Condition

A *waiver* is an "intentional relinquishment of a known right."[113] However, this simple definition is misleading. As will be seen, conditions are sometimes inadvertently waived. This supports the conclusion that a waiver, at least in this context, need not be intentional. It is sufficient if the obligor knows or has reason to know of the essential facts related to the condition. Likewise, a condition is not, strictly speaking, a "right." Despite these drawbacks, the definition is commonly used to describe a waiver.

Courts have explained the notion of a waiver as resting on "an idea no more complicated than that any competent adult can abandon a legal right and if he does so then he has lost it forever."[114] Constitutional rights are waived in this fashion in

---

[111] Lafayette Car Wash, Inc. v. Boes, 282 N.E.2d 837 (Ind. 1972).

[112] *See infra* § 8.05[D][4] Reinstatement of Conditions.

[113] *E.g.*, VanDyke Const. Co. v. Stillwater Mining Co., 78 P.3d 844, 847 (Mont. 2003); Cole Taylor Bank v. Truck Ins. Exch., 51 F.3d 736 (7th Cir. 1995) (Posner, J.). *See* RESTATEMENT (SECOND) OF CONTRACTS § 84 cmt. b (1981). Your author was once paid $10,000 as an expert witness, to testify to this effect. He was paid for many hours of preparation to testify as to other matters, but his proposed testimony was ruled inadmissible.

[114] McElroy v. B.F. Goodrich Co., 73 F.3d 722, 724 (7th Cir. 1996).

police station interrogation rooms every day. It would seem that contractual rights should be subject to waiver with no less difficulty.[115]

In *Clark v. West*,[116] a well-known publisher of law books entered into a contract with a law professor for the production of a book on corporate law. Their contract contained a condition that provided for alternative performances. The publisher made an unconditional promise to pay $2 per page, together with a promise to pay an additional $4 per page on the condition that the author would abstain from drinking alcohol while he was working on the book. The author did not abstain. But, the publisher had full knowledge of the author's continued drinking, and repeatedly promised that he[117] would nevertheless pay the additional $4 per page. Thus, in *Clark v. West*, the publisher knew that he could insist on performance of the condition, knew that the condition had not been satisfied, but renounced his insistence on the condition. This is a classic waiver.

Express waivers of the type involved in *Clark v. West* are not unusual. They frequently occur when the contract is subject to an express condition that is designed to protect the promisor from a risk that it decides is not important.

For example, if Alice and Tom enter into an agreement for the purchase of Tom's house, Alice might insist that the contract be subject to the condition that she sells her existing house before being obligated to go through with the deal with Tom. Alice might become unconcerned about selling her existing house if it turns out that it is in high demand, with lots of prospective buyers lining up to make offers to purchase it. The likelihood of her being able to sell her existing house might lead her to have a diminished concern about being stuck with two houses and two mortgage payments if she goes ahead with the purchase of Tom's house. Thus, she might just tell Tom that she will close on the deal with him, even though her current house has not yet been sold. Because of the waiver, she will be unable to resist performance of the contract by asserting the condition.

Waiver of a condition may also be implied through conduct that demonstrates a promisor's intent to perform despite the failure of the condition. For example, in *Standard Supply Co. v. Reliance Insurance Co.*,[118] the plaintiff's fire insurance policy was subject to a condition that the premises remain occupied either by the owner or a tenant. Prior to its renewal of the policy, the insurance company conducted an inspection of the building and discovered that it was unoccupied. Despite notice that it was vacant, the insurance company renewed the policy. The building subsequently burned, and the insurer tried to evade paying for the loss because the structure had been unoccupied. The court ruled that these facts would have justified the jury in determining that the condition had been waived.

An important limitation on waiver is that only ancillary conditions may be waived. The doctrine of waiver may not apply to a condition that was a material

---

[115] Cole Taylor Bank v. Truck Ins. Exch., 51 F.3d 736, 739 (7th Cir. 1995).

[116] 86 N.E. 1 (N.Y. 1908).

[117] At this time, the publisher was Mr. West, the former owner and operator of the West Publishing Co., when it was a sole proprietorship.

[118] 272 S.E.2d 394 (N.C. Ct. App. 1980).

part of the agreed exchange.[119] As Judge Posner has explained: "[u]nless the right waived is a minor one . . . why would someone give it up in exchange for nothing?"[120] Cases involving constructive conditions, derived from the promises exchanged between the parties, present the most obvious example of conditions that cannot be waived. In a contract between Sam and Barb for the sale of Sam's car for $15,000, Barb's performance of her promise to pay the $15,000 price is a constructive condition of Sam's promise to tender delivery of his car.[121] Moreover, payment of the price is a material part of the agreed exchange. Therefore, there could be no "waiver" of the constructive condition that Barb pay the price. In other words, "one cannot waive himself into a duty to make a gift."[122]

In *Rose v. Mitsubishi International Corp.*,[123] the buyer promised to pay for the seller's land, subject to the condition that the seller supply clear and marketable title. The court distinguished between a material condition, like the seller's promise to supply clear and marketable title, which could not be waived, and an ancillary condition, such as a time for the delivery of title, which in most cases will be nothing more than a matter of convenience for the parties.

The court in *Clark v. West* emphasized this point.[124] In holding that the condition of the author's abstinence could be waived, the court explained the ancillary nature of the condition by noting that it was "not a contract to write books in order that the [author] shall keep sober, but a contract containing a stipulation that he shall keep sober so that he may write satisfactory books."[125] In other words, the condition regarding the author's abstinence from liquor was designed to facilitate the author's promise to fulfill the fundamental purpose of the contract — completion of the book — and thus was one that could be waived.

[3]   Estoppel Against Conditions

An obligor might also be "estopped" or precluded from asserting the nonoccurrence of a condition. An obligor is estopped if the promisee relies on a misrepresentation of fact, a promise, or conduct by the obligor in connection with the condition. The most obvious example of estoppel due to reliance occurs when the promisee ceases its efforts to ensure satisfaction of the condition in reliance on the obligor's promise that it will perform regardless of any failure of condition.

Some of the earliest estoppel cases were based on "estoppel in pais" or "equitable estoppel."[126] Equitable estoppel is based on one person's reliance on

---

[119] RESTATEMENT (SECOND) OF CONTRACTS § 84(1) (1981). *See, e.g.*, Rose v. Mitsubishi Int'l Corp., 423 F. Supp. 1162, 1166–67 (E.D. Pa. 1976).

[120] Cole Taylor Bank v. Truck Ins. Exch., 51 F.3d 736, 739 (7th Cir. 1995).

[121] U.C.C. § 2-511(1) (2012).

[122] Nat'l Util. Serv. Inc. v. Whirlpool Corp., 325 F.2d 779, 781 (2d Cir. 1963); 8 CATHERINE M.A. MCCAULIFF, CORBIN ON CONTRACTS § 40.2 (Rev'd ed. 1999). *See supra* § 2.04 Promises to Make a Gift.

[123] 423 F. Supp. 1162 (E.D. Pa. 1976).

[124] Clark v. West, 86 N.E. at 3.

[125] *Id.* at 3–4.

[126] *See, e.g.*, Am. Nat'l Bank v. A.G. Sommerville, Inc., 216 P. 376 (Cal. 1923).

another person's misrepresentation of a fact.[127] Equitable "[e]stoppel bars asserting the truth by one whose misleading conduct has induced another to act to his detriment in reliance on what is untrue."[128]

For example, if Bud mails his premium payment to his insurance company and then calls to inquire whether the payment was received, he is likely to rely on what the company tells him. If the insurance company mistakenly tells him that the payment was received and thus that the condition of payment had been satisfied, the company will be estopped from later claiming that the payment had never arrived. If, in response to Bud's inquiry, the company had told him that the payment had not been received, he probably would have scurried around to find out what happened to his check and to make sure that the company received the necessary payment. By providing him with false information about its receipt of the payment, the insurance company has dissuaded him from taking further action to satisfy the condition. Bud must still eventually pay the premiums — he will not receive coverage for free — but the insurance company cannot assert nonpayment as a basis for denying coverage. Equitable estoppel effectively precludes a person who has made a mistake about critical facts "from speaking the truth in his own behalf."[129]

Promissory estoppel, on the other hand, arises not as a result of reliance on a misrepresentation of fact, but due to reliance on a promise. Thus, equitable estoppel arises when a person relies on a statement of how things presently exist, while promissory estoppel arises when a person relies on a promise of what will be done in the future.[130] The importance of this distinction, which once was critical,[131] has less modern significance, given the law's broad recognition of promissory estoppel.

The key element of both equitable and promissory estoppel is reliance. A promisee's reliance on either the promisor's statement of fact, or on his or her express or implied promise to excuse a condition, may prevent a promisor from insisting on strict compliance with it.

[4]　　　Reinstatement of Conditions

A further issue relevant to waiver and estoppel is the extent to which a condition, once excused, can be reinstated. Reinstatement is possible only with respect to waivers that occur before the time for the occurrence of the condition has passed. Once the time for its occurrence has passed, it is impossible for the condition to be satisfied.[132]

---

[127] Leigh Anenson, *From Theory to Practice: Analyzing Equitable Estoppel Under a Pluralistic Model of Law*, 11 LEWIS & CLARK L. REV. 633 (2007); 2 JOHN NORTON POMERY, EQUITY JURISPRUDENCE § 805 (2d ed. 1892).

[128] Berry v. Bd. of Trs., 663 A.2d 14, 18 n.8 (Me. 1995).

[129] Shaffer v. Hines, 573 S.W.2d 420, 422 (Mo. Ct. App. 1978).

[130] *Id.*

[131] *See, e.g.*, Prescott v. Jones, 41 A. 352 (N.H. 1898).

[132] *See* RESTATEMENT (SECOND) OF CONTRACTS § 84(2)(a) & cmt. f (1981).

Parties to a contract frequently tolerate minor deviations from the terms of a contract, but when they believe that their tolerance is being taken for granted or abused their attitude of tolerance may change. Likewise, circumstances might change in a way that makes it more difficult to put up with the other party's indifference to the condition. Moreover, the parties may have a different attitude about the relative importance of a condition while performance of the contract continues, than they do after the relationship has broken down and they are headed toward litigation.[133] When one party attempts to insist on future strict compliance with a condition, the issue is whether a condition that has been waived can be reinstated.

Most courts take the position that a condition can be reinstated unless the other party has changed its position in some material and permanent way, in reliance on the waiver.[134] In *Daniels v. Philadelphia Fair Housing Commission*, a landlord successfully retracted its waiver of the tenant's duty to make utility payments by giving notice to the tenant that she would be required to reassume this duty with respect to future months.[135]

Thus, if Sue has been making late rent payments to her landlord, and the landlord has been consistently accepting the late payments without objection, the landlord is estopped from suddenly changing its attitude and attempting to evict Sue due to her failure to pay the rent on time. However, unless Sue has made significant changes in her life in reliance on the landlord's acquiescence in her persistently late payment, her landlord can reinstate the condition of timely payment by sending her notice, and giving her a reasonable time to make the necessary adjustment.[136]

However, if the other party has changed its position in some permanent way in reliance on the waiver, the condition may not unilaterally be reinstated. For example, in *Wolff v. McCrossan*,[137] a landlord was prohibited from retracting his waiver of several conditions that had been imposed on the tenant's right to exercise an option to purchase the property. One of these conditions established a deadline for the tenant to exercise the option. The landlord was unable to reinstate the deadline because the landlord had waived the condition and the tenant had failed to meet the deadline in reliance on the landlord's waiver.

---

[133] *See* Lisa Bernstein, *Merchant Law in a Merchant Court: Rethinking the Code's Search for Immanent Business Norms*, 144 U. PA. L. REV. 1765, 1796 (1996).

[134] RESTATEMENT (SECOND) OF CONTRACTS § 84(2)(a) (1981); U.C.C. § 2-209(5) (2012).

[135] Daniels v. Philadelphia Fair Housing Commission, 513 A.2d 501 (Pa. 1986). *See also* Storek & Storek, Inc. v. Citicorp Real Estate, Inc., 100 Cal. App. 4th 44 (2002); Max 327, Inc. v. City of Portland, 838 P.2d 631, 633 (Or. Ct. App. 1992).

[136] *See, e.g.*, Porter v. Harrington, 159 N.E. 530 (Mass. 1928) (late installment payments in a land sale contract).

[137] 210 N.W.2d 41 (Minn. 1973).

[5]   Waiver, Estoppel, and Modification Compared

The similar doctrines of waiver, election, and estoppel should be compared to the more formal mechanism for altering the terms of a contract: a modification. A modification of a contract is itself a contract. Thus, a modification, like any other contract, requires mutual assent. Waivers can occur through the unilateral conduct of one of the parties, though estoppel usually requires some action by the promisee in reliance on the waiver.

Likewise, the traditional common law rule required a modification to be supported by consideration.[138] Article 2 of the Uniform Commercial Code dispenses with the requirement of consideration for the modification of a contract for the sale of goods.[139] However, the requirement still applies, though in a watered-down fashion, with respect to contracts not governed by these portions of the U.C.C.[140] Consideration is not necessary for either waiver or estoppel, and although reliance is the key to estoppel, an express waiver may occur even though the promisee has not relied on it.[141]

Absent some sort of permanent material change in position, a waiver may usually be retracted. However, because a modification is based on a mutual agreement between the parties, a modification may not be unilaterally retracted by one party, without the manifested assent of the other.

[6]   Effect of "Anti-Waiver" Provisions

Just as written contracts sometimes require modifications to be in writing,[142] they also sometimes provide that conditions are not subject to waiver and that conduct of one of the parties that might otherwise give rise to a waiver may not be so construed. Not surprisingly, most decisions make these nonwaiver provisions just as vulnerable to waiver as any other term of a contract.[143] Thus, a party who expressly waives a condition, or who acts as if the condition will not be enforced, may be treated as having waived the provision in the contract that purports to deny effect to such a waiver. It is difficult for parties to use boilerplate language to deprive meaningful words or conduct of their significance.[144]

[E]   Excuse Avoiding Forfeiture

Requiring strict adherence to a condition can have devastating effects. The owner of an insurance policy can lose both his house and the benefits of his fire insurance policy if he fails to strictly comply with conditions in his homeowner's

---

[138] *See supra* § 2.06[A] Modification of an Existing Contract.

[139] U.C.C. § 2-209(1) (2012). *See* U.C.C. § 2A-208(1) (2012) (lease of goods).

[140] RESTATEMENT (SECOND) OF CONTRACTS §§ 73 & 89 (1981).

[141] *E.g.*, Wachovia Bank & Trust Co. v. Rubish, 293 S.E.2d 749 (N.C.), *reh'g denied* ,302 S.E.2d 884 (N.C. 1982).

[142] *See supra* § 5.09[B] Agreements Requiring Modifications in Writing.

[143] *E.g.*, Universal Builders v. Moon Motor Lodge, 244 A.2d 10, 15 (Pa. 1968); Moe v. John Deere Co., 516 N.W.2d 332 (S.D. 1994).

[144] *See* GRANT GILMORE, SECURITY INTERESTS IN PERSONAL PROPERTY 1214 (1964).

policy. Likewise, a builder who completes a project one day late, when payment is subject to the condition of timely completion, might forego its right to payment for the value of all of the labor and materials that have been incorporated into the job if strict compliance with the condition of timely completion is insisted upon.[145] However, "equity abhors forfeitures and will seize upon slight circumstances indicating a waiver to avoid or prevent them."[146] Accordingly, conditions may be excused when strict adherence to their requirements would result in a disproportionate forfeiture.[147]

The most obvious example of a disproportionate forfeiture can be found in cases involving installment land sale contracts. When interest rates are high,[148] sellers sometimes have difficulty finding buyers who can qualify for a mortgage loan. Sellers are therefore likely to be willing to sell their property via a land sale contract, with the buyer making regular monthly installment payments to the seller and the seller obligated to deliver title when the entire balance of the purchase price has been paid.[149]

Depending on the language in the contract, the seller's duty to deliver title may be subject to the condition precedent that the buyer makes all monthly principal and interest payments on a timely basis. If applied strictly, this might mean that the seller could keep all of the payments it has previously received, and yet refuse to convey title to the land, even after years and years of timely monthly payments. Thus, the buyer would lose not only his or her right to receive title to the land, but also all of the payments previously made. The seller, on the other hand, would get to keep both the payments and the land. Any judge faced with such an obviously disproportionate forfeiture of both land and money is likely to bend over backwards to find a way to excuse the failure of the condition of timely payment.[150]

Cases such as *J.N.A. Realty Corp v. Cross Bay Chelsea, Inc.*,[151] which is frequently used to illustrate the point, are only slightly less compelling. There, a commercial real estate lease gave the tenant, a restaurateur, an option to renew the 10-year lease for an additional 24-year term, subject to the condition that the tenant notify the landlord of its intent to renew "in writing by registered or certified mail six (6) months prior to the last day of the term" of the original lease.

---

[145] *See* RESTATEMENT (SECOND) OF CONTRACTS § 229 illus. 3 (1981).

[146] Berry v. Crawford, 373 S.W.2d 129 (Ark. 1963). *See also* Conn. Light and Power Co. v. Lighthouse Landings, Inc., 900 A.2d 1242, 1252 n.15 (Conn. 2006).

[147] RESTATEMENT (SECOND) OF CONTRACTS § 229 (1981). *See* Hoosier Energy Rural Elec. Coop. v. Amoco Tax Leasing IV Corp., 34 F.3d 1310, 1320 (7th Cir. 1994).

[148] After several decades of low interest rates, it may be difficult to imagine a world with high interest rates. Nevertheless, in the early 1980s, mortgage interest rates were sky-high. They climbed nearly to 16%. Your author once financed the purchase of a home at an annual interest rate of 12% and was happy to get it. Needless to say, he refinanced quickly when rates came down.

[149] If the seller still owes money on his own mortgage, he agrees to keep the payments current with his own lender. This arrangement is known as a "wraparound mortgage." James L. Isham, Annotation, *Validity and Effect of "Wraparound" Mortgages Whereby Purchaser Incorporates into Agreed Payments to Grantor Latter's Obligation on Initial Mortgage*, 36 A.L.R.4th 144 (1985).

[150] *See* Sharp v. Holthusen, 616 P.2d 374 (Mont. 1980) (balloon payment delayed due to unanticipated difficulty in obtaining health department and third-party lender approval of well water).

[151] 366 N.E.2d 1313, 1315 (N.Y. 1977).

The lease was subsequently assigned to a new tenant who, through inadvertent neglect, failed to give the landlord the requisite written notice of its intent to renew.

The court was sensitive to the tenant's plight. If the condition of timely notice was strictly applied, the tenant would lose not only the amounts it had paid for the assignment of the lease, but also the value of both the improvements it had made to the premises and the goodwill it had established with its customers at that location.[152] However, the court was also concerned that the landlord might have taken some action in reliance on its failure to receive timely notice of the tenant's intent to renew. If, for example, the landlord had entered into another contract to lease the premises to another tenant, it might have been held liable, as a result of the court's decision, for breach of that second lease. Accordingly, the court reversed the trial court's decision, excusing the condition, and remanded the dispute back to the trial judge for a new trial to resolve any issues about the harm to the landlord that might result if the condition were enforced.

Cases involving claims of excuse of a condition due to forfeiture require the court to balance the competing interests of the parties and the relative harm to each of them if the condition is either strictly enforced or excused. Thus, in another case involving a tenant's failure to provide timely notice of renewal, the court considered (1) whether the failure to give notice was due to simple negligence or as the result of gross or willful neglect, (2) whether the delay was slight, and (3) whether the impact of relief from the condition on the party seeking strict enforcement was significant.[153]

Other courts have been less willing to provide relief. Unless the contract is ambiguous, or there is some reason to believe that the tenant might have relied on something the landlord said or did to delay providing notice, courts are naturally reluctant to rewrite the parties' agreement. For example, in *Soho Development Corp. v. Dean & DeLuca*,[154] the court distinguished *J.N.A. Realty* because, unlike the earlier case, the landlord in *Soho Development* had regularly informed the tenant of its obligations under the lease. And, in *Guy Dean's Lake Shore Marina, Inc. v. Ramey*,[155] the court simply would not adopt the rule of *J.N.A. Realty* permitting the risk of forfeiture to excuse a condition.[156] In other cases, such as option contracts, permitting excusing a condition of timely notice may permit an unscrupulous party to gamble on fluctuations in a volatile market, to the other party's disadvantage.[157]

---

[152] It is commonly said that the three most important factors in the success of a restaurant (or any retail business) are (1) location, (2) location, and (3) location.

[153] *See* R & R of Conn., Inc. v. Stiegler, 493 A.2d 293 (Conn. Ct. App. 1985).

[154] 131 A.D.2d 385 (N.Y. App. Div. 1987).

[155] 518 N.W.2d 129 (Neb. 1994).

[156] *See also* United Props. Ltd. v. Walgreen Props., Inc., 82 P.3d 535 (N.M. Ct. App. 2003) (citing risk of instability in real estate markets if conditions were excused due to inadvertence).

[157] *E.g.*, Livesey v. Copps Corp. 280 N.W.2d 339 (Wis.Ct. App. 1979); Taylor v. Eagle Ridge Dev's, LLC, 29 S.W.3d 767 (Ark. Ct. App. 2000).

§ 8.06 CONDITIONS IN INTERNATIONAL TRANSACTIONS

Like Article 2 of the U.C.C., the CISG does not contain any provisions dealing with conditions. Instead, it leaves them largely to other law. CISG Article 7 specifies, in this regard, that "matters governed by [the CISG] which are not expressly settled in it are to be settled in conformity with the general principles on which it is based or, in the absence of such principles, in conformity with the law applicable by virtue of the rules of private international law."[158] This language calls for applying the CISG's underlying principles and rule of private international law only with respect to matters that are *governed by* the CISG, though not expressly resolved by it. This leaves open broad areas of the law, possibly including the law relating to the treatment of conditions, to be governed by other sources.

Despite this, the CISG provides some guidance about the law of conditions. Article 8 indicates that the terms of the contract are to be based on the expressed intent of the parties, "according to the understanding that a reasonable person . . . would have had in the same circumstances."[159] Thus, questions about whether a term was intended as a promise or a condition are to be resolved based on the manifested intent of the parties as reasonably understood by persons in similar circumstances.

Likewise, the CISG makes performance by the seller and the buyer concurrent constructive conditions of one another's duties. Article 53 requires the buyer to pay the price for the goods, and take delivery of them, as required by the contract.[160] Unless the contract specifies otherwise, payment is to be made "when the seller places either the goods or documents controlling their disposition at the buyer's disposal."[161] Thus, absent any contrary agreement, payment and delivery are concurrent conditions of one another. Of course, in many situations involving international sales, payment will be due when documents, such as a bill of lading, relating to the goods and governing their disposition are tendered. Thus, the price will be paid in exchange for documents rather than for the goods themselves.

In addition, in parallel with domestic law governing the doctrines of substantial performance and material breach, the parties have the right to terminate the contract if the other party's failure to perform "amounts to a fundamental breach of contract."[162] This suggests that the CISG applies rules regarding constructive conditions similar to those deployed by domestic common law principles.

Although the CISG does not contain any specific provisions regarding the avoidance of conditions, it liberally permits modifications based on nothing more than the agreement of the parties.[163] It includes several provisions that mirror common law rules regarding the effect of waiver, reliance, impossibility, hindrance, and the avoidance of forfeitures.

---

[158] CISG Art. 7(2) (1980).

[159] CISG Art. 8(2) (1980).

[160] CISG Art. 53 (1980).

[161] CISG Art. 58(1) (1980).

[162] CISG Arts. 49(1) & 64(1)(a) (1980).

[163] CISG Art. 29(1) (1980).

UNIDROIT Principles of International Commercial Contracts (PICC) and the Principles of European Contract Law (PECL), like U.C.C. Article 2 and the CISG, contain no express rules governing conditions. However, both specify that the contract must be interpreted according to the intention of the parties.[164]

PICC treats the parties' obligations as concurrent "[t]o the extent that . . . performances . . . can be rendered simultaneously . . . unless the circumstances indicate otherwise."[165] However, if the performance of one of the parties "requires a period of time, that party is bound to render its performance first."[166] PECL contains similar language.[167] This is consistent with domestic law regarding implied conditions and the order of performance.[168] Consistent with domestic law regarding constructive conditions, PICC and PECL also permit an aggrieved party to suspend[169] or terminate performance[170] in response to a "fundamental" nonperformance.[171]

With respect to the avoidance of conditions, both PICC and PECL impose obligations on the parties to act in good faith.[172] PICC is more explicit in imposing an obligation to "co-operate with the other party when such co-operation may reasonably be expected for the performance of that party's obligations."[173] Both sets of rules provide for modifications of contracts that make ample room for the concept of waiver and estoppel.[174]

---

[164] PICC Art. 4.1(1) (2004); PECL Art. 5.101(1) (2002).

[165] PICC Art. 6.1.4(1) (2004).

[166] PICC Art. 6.1.4(2) (2004).

[167] PECL Art. 7.104 (2002).

[168] *See supra* § 8.03[B][2] Implied Conditions.

[169] PICC Art. 7.1.3 (2004)(1); PECL Art. 9.201 (2002).

[170] PICC Art. 7.3.1 (2004); PECL Art. 9.301 (2002).

[171] Damien Nyer, *Withholding Performance for Breach in International Transactions: An Exercise in Equations, Proportions or Coercion?*, 18 Pace Int'l L. Rev. 29 (2006).

[172] PICC Art. 5.1.2(c) (2004); PECL Art. 6.102(c) (2002).

[173] PICC Art. 5.1.3 (2004).

[174] *See* PICC Art. 2.1.18 (2004) (regarding reliance on an oral modification); PECL Art. 2.106(2) (2002).

Chapter 9

PERFORMANCE AND BREACH

§ 9.01   THE EFFECT OF BREACH: MATERIAL BREACH, SUBSTANTIAL PERFORMANCE, AND CONSTRUCTIVE CONDITIONS[1]

The legal effect of full performance of a contract is simple: it "discharges" the parties' contractual duties.[2] If Sam promises to sell his car to Barb and delivers the car as promised at the agreed time for performance, Sam's duty under the contract for sale is discharged. When Betty pays Sam the agreed price, her duty is similarly discharged. Likewise, a builder's full and final completion of a construction project, according to the specifications of the contract, discharges its contractual duties.[3] Full performance is the opposite of breach, and thus a party who has fully performed is not liable for breach.

Nonperformance of a contractual duty is a breach unless the nonperformance is excused.[4] Breach of contract, when it occurs, has two potential consequences. First, breach always entitles the injured party to a remedy,[5] usually money damages.[6] This critical point must not be lost in discussions about the other consequences of a breach, which may depend on whether the breach is material, whether the breach is cured, and whether the injured party elects to treat it as a total or a partial

---

[1] Amy B. Cohen, *Reviving* Jacob & Youngs, Inc. v. Kent: *Material Breach Doctrine Reconsidered,* 42 VILL. L. REV. 65 (1997); Robert A. Hillman, *Keeping the Deal Together After Material Breach — Common Law Mitigation Rules, the UCC, and the Restatement (Second) of Contracts,* 47 U. COLO. L. REV. 553 (1976); William H. Lawrence, *Cure After Breach of Contract Under the Restatement (Second),* 70 MINN. L. REV. 713 (1986); William Patterson, *Constructive Conditions in Contracts,* 42 COLUM. L. REV. 903 (1942).

[2] RESTATEMENT (SECOND) OF CONTRACTS § 235(1) (1981).

[3] RESTATEMENT (SECOND) OF CONTRACTS § 235 illus. 1 (1981).

[4] RESTATEMENT (SECOND) OF CONTRACTS § 235 & cmt. b (1981).

[5] RESTATEMENT (SECOND) OF CONTRACTS § 236 cmt. b (1981). *See infra* Chs. 12–15.

[6] *See infra* § 12.01 Introduction to Contract Remedies.

breach. Any breach, no matter how trivial, can result in an award of damages or an appropriate equitable remedy.

Second, depending on the relative seriousness of the breach, the injured party may also be entitled to temporarily suspend its own performance or sometimes even terminate or "rescind" the contract.[7] Because every breach entitles the injured party to some remedy, most of the difficult issues relating to the effect of breach deal with this second question: the extent to which the injured party is permitted to suspend or terminate performance of its own duties under the contract. As will be seen, the injured party's rights depend first on whether the breach was material or nonmaterial, on whether the breaching party cures the breach, and on whether the injured party elects to treat the breach as a total material breach or merely as a partial breach.

[A]   Material Breach and Substantial Performance

Not every breach of contract is significant enough to constitute a "material breach." Whether a particular breach is material depends on the following factors:[8]

(1)   the extent of the harm to the injured party,[9]

(2)   the adequacy of monetary damages to compensate for the injured party's loss,[10]

(3)   the ability and willingness of the breaching party to implement a cure,[11]

(4)   the good faith of the breaching party,[12] and,

(5)   the extent to which the breaching party will suffer a forfeiture if the breach is treated as material.[13]

Although every breach gives the injured party the right to a remedy,[14] only a material breach justifies the injured party in suspending or terminating performance of its own contractual duties. A party who improperly suspends

---

[7] The right to terminate the contract is sometimes referred to as a right to "rescind" due to breach. This is, of course, different from a mutually agreed upon rescission by the parties.

[8] RESTATEMENT (SECOND) OF CONTRACTS § 241 (1981). *See also* Eric G. Andersen, *A New Look at Material Breach in the Law of Contracts*, 21 U.C. DAVIS. L. REV. 1073 (1988).

[9] RESTATEMENT (SECOND) OF CONTRACTS § 241(a) (1981).

[10] RESTATEMENT (SECOND) OF CONTRACTS § 241(b) (1981).

[11] RESTATEMENT (SECOND) OF CONTRACTS § 241(d) (1981).

[12] RESTATEMENT (SECOND) OF CONTRACTS § 241(e) (1981).

[13] RESTATEMENT (SECOND) OF CONTRACTS § 241(c) (1981). *See, e.g.*, Sackett v. Spindler, 248 Cal. App. 2d 220, 229–230 (1967) (factors to consider in determining whether a failure to fully perform constitutes a material breach of the contract include: "(1) The extent to which the injured party will obtain the substantial benefit which he could have reasonably anticipated; (2) the extent to which the injured party may be adequately compensated in damages for lack of complete performance; (3) the extent to which the party failing to perform has already partly performed or made preparations for performance; (4) the greater or less hardship on the party failing to perform in terminating the contract; (5) the willful, negligent, or innocent behavior of the party failing to perform; and (6) the greater or less uncertainty that the party failing to perform will perform the remainder of the contract.").

[14] RESTATEMENT (SECOND) OF CONTRACTS § 236 cmt. b (1981).

performance, in the mistaken belief that the other party has committed a material breach, may itself be in material breach. Thus, it is important to be able to distinguish between a material breach and a non-material breach.

Many cases involving claims of material breach involve construction contracts. Whether a particular defect is material depends, as it does in other cases, on several factors, most of which are related to the extent of harm caused to the injured party. In *Jacob & Young, Inc. v. Kent*,[15] involving use of the wrong band of pipe in the construction of a home, it was easy to conclude that the contractor's breach, which had no effect on the structural integrity, durability, or appearance of the house, was not a material breach. In *Plante v. Jacobs*,[16] a contract to construct a house for the defendant was substantially performed even though the contractor failed to install items such as kitchen cabinets, gutters, and closet rods, and even though an interior wall between the living room and kitchen was misplaced by one foot, which narrowed the size of the living room. Accordingly, the court permitted the breaching party to recover the balance of the price remaining due, offset by the amounts necessary to complete the unfinished features of the house. Most of the defects were easily repaired, and the misplacement of the wall had no effect on the market value of the house or its utility to the buyers.

Structural defects, which deprive the building of its utility, are unquestionably material. However, cosmetic defects that impair only the appearance of the work may also qualify as a material breach. This is made clear by the facts in *O.W. Grun Roofing & Construction Co v. Cope*,[17] where a new russet-colored roof was tainted with yellow streaks. The only way to correct the problem was to replace the roof with new shingles. The court explained that it was "not prepared to hold that a contractor who tenders a performance so deficient that it can be remedied only by completely redoing the work . . . has substantially performed."[18]

Unfortunately, there is no easy mathematical formula for determining whether a particular breach is material. As the court explained in *Plante v. Jacobs*, "no mathematical rule relating to the percentage of the price, the cost of completion, or of completeness can be laid down to determine substantial performance [or material breach] of a building contract."[19] Instead, the court compared the defective performance with the contemplated purposes and disappointed expectations of the injured party.

The lack of precision involved in determining whether a particular breach is material should lead parties to act with a degree of caution in deciding whether to suspend performance when the other party breaches. Before taking such precipitous action, a party should at least notify the other party of the nature of the defect and identify how failure to implement a timely cure of the breach will impair the injured party's expectations. In some cases, making a demand for adequate

---

[15] 129 N.E. 889 (N.Y. 1921).

[16] 103 N.W.2d 296 (Wis. 1960).

[17] 529 S.W.2d 258 (Tex. Civ. App. 1975).

[18] *Id.* at 263.

[19] Plante v. Jacobs, 103 N.W.2d at 298.

assurances of future performance[20] may provide an adequate interim solution to the problem that avoids the risks associated with suspending performance of one's own obligations.

Sometimes performance is not defective; it is simply late. Whether a delay is material depends in the first instance on whether "time is of the essence." Delay in performance is frequently easily compensable with money damages, as in the case of delay in performance of a contract for the sale of land where delay can be compensated for with damages based on the rental value of the premises.[21] However, delay may cause serious harm, particularly where the injured party is relying on timely performance to enable it to perform its own obligations with other parties.

If the contract explicitly provides that time is of the essence, courts are far more likely to treat delay as a material breach.[22] However, the mere presence of a boilerplate provision stating that "time is of the essence" will not prevent a court from considering the usual factors used to determine whether a particular delay is material.[23] A short delay with no apparent harm to the nonbreaching party should not be treated as material, despite the presence of language purporting to make delay important.[24]

Delay in making payment may or may not be a material breach, depending on the size and importance of the payment and the extent of the delay. Questions concerning whether a delay in payment is a material breach most frequently arise in the context of an executory accord.[25] An "accord" is a contract under which a creditor or other obligee agrees to accept a substituted performance in satisfaction of some other duty. If the substituted duty is not performed, the original duty is revived.[26] When the substituted duty is a promise to pay a sum of money, and payment is delayed, the creditor may claim that the delay prevents performance of the accord and that the original duty to pay a larger amount is revived.

For example, in *Associated Builders Inc. v. Coggins*,[27] a dispute developed over payment for construction services that had been supplied to Coggins. In settlement of the dispute, Coggins agreed to make two $25,000 cash payments. Under their agreement, timely payment would relieve Coggins of any obligation to pay an

---

[20] *See infra* § 9.06 Prospective Inability to Perform.

[21] RESTATEMENT (SECOND) OF CONTRACTS § 242 cmt. c (1981). *See, e.g.*, Worcester Heritage Soc'y Inc. v. Trussell, 577 N.E.2d 1009 (Mass. Ct. App. 1991) (delay in completion of renovations to historic structure).

[22] *See* Elda Arnhold & Byzantio, L.L.C. v. Ocean Atl. Woodland Corp., 284 F.3d 693 (7th Cir. 2002) ("drop dead clause" in settlement agreement enforced where parties intended even a single day's delay to operate as a material breach).

[23] RESTATEMENT (SECOND) OF CONTRACTS § 242(c) & cmt. d (1981). *See* Pederson v. McGuire, 333 N.W.2d 823 (S.D. 1983).

[24] RESTATEMENT (SECOND) OF CONTRACTS § 242 cmt. d (1981). *E.g.*, Found. Dev. Corp. v. Loehmann's, Inc., 788 P.2d 1189 (Ariz. 1990) (inadvertent 2-day delay in making payment not material regardless of clause stating that timely payment was a condition).

[25] *See supra* § 2.06[B] Debt Settlements: Accord and Satisfaction.

[26] Frank Felix Assoc., Ltd. v. Austin Drugs, Inc., 111 F.3d 284 (2d Cir. 1997); Assoc'd Builders, Inc. v. Coggins, 722 A.2d 1278 (Me. 1999).

[27] 722 A.2d 1279 (Me. 1999).

additional $20,000 that Associated claimed it was owed. When Coggins sent the second $25,000 payment three days after it was due, Associated claimed that the delay was a material breach of the settlement agreement (the "accord"), which prevented the payment from satisfying the underlying obligation. According to Associated, the delay revived Coggins's liability to pay the larger sum. The court applied § 241 of the Second Restatement, which treats delay as a one of several factors in determining whether breach is material, and concluded that because the 3-day delay did not harm the creditor in any significant way, Coggins had substantially performed the accord. The original duty to pay more was satisfied. Thus, if payment is late, and the delay is short and causes no harm, the delay is not material.[28]

Delay in a progress payment in a construction contract is more likely to be at least a partial material breach. Without receipt of the owner's progress payment, the builder will probably find it difficult to pay the laborers and suppliers upon whom it depends to continue work. If payment is delayed beyond a reasonable time, the harm to the builder will cause the partial breach to ripen into a total breach, permitting the builder to terminate the project completely and sue for total material breach. One court explained that a "slight deviation either in time or amount of progress payments should not justify rescission or abandonment," but there is a material breach where the delay is "extended and unreasonable."[29]

The breaching party's culpability may also be relevant in determining whether a particular breach is material. In *Jacob & Youngs, Inc. v. Kent*, Judge Cardozo announced that the substantial performance doctrine could not be invoked by a person who was in "willful" default. His view was that "the willful transgressor must accept the penalty of his own transgression."[30] While modern decisions still sometimes articulate this view,[31] other courts have adopted the position taken by the Second Restatement of Contracts that the breaching party's adherence to standards of good faith and fair dealing are not dispositive, but are simply one factor to consider[32] in determining whether the substantial performance doctrine may be invoked.[33]

---

[28] *See also* Edward Waters Coll., Inc. v. Johnson, 707 So. 2d 801, 802 (Fla. Dist. Ct. App. 1998) (1-day delay not material where time was not "of the essence" and creditor suffered no hardship as a result); A.E. Giroux, Inc. v. Contract Servs. Assocs., Div. of Premium Corp. of Am., Inc., 299 N.W.2d 20, 20–21 (Mich. Ct. App. 1980) (1-day delay was substantial performance in absence of material damage to the recipient).

[29] United States v. W. Cas. & Sur. Co., 498 F.2d 335, 339 (9th Cir. 1974). *See also* Turner Concrete Steel Co. v. Chester Constr. & Contracting Co., 114 A. 780, 782 (Pa. 1921).

[30] Jacob & Youngs, Inc. v. Kent, 129 N.E. at 893.

[31] Murray's Iron Works, Inc. v. Boyce, 158 Cal. App. 4th 1279 (2008); Curtis Constr. Co., Inc. v. Am. Steel Span, Inc., 707 N.W.2d 68, (N.D. 2005); Huntsville & Madison Cty. R.R. Auth. v. Ala. Indus. R.R. Inc., 505 So. 2d 341 (Ala. 1987).

[32] RESTATEMENT (SECOND) OF CONTRACTS § 241(e) & cmt. f (1981).

[33] Vincenzi v. Cerro, 442 A.2d 1352 (Conn. 1982); Hadden v. Consol. Edison Co. of N.Y., Inc., 312 N.E.2d 445 (N.Y. 1974).

[B]　　　Rights of Injured Party After Material Breach

An aggrieved party's rights depend on whether a breach is material. While any breach, no matter how small, entitles the aggrieved party to money damages, only a material breach justifies the injured party in suspending or terminating its own performance. A material breach gives the injured party several options.

- The injured party may elect to treat the breach as a partial breach, continue performance, and seek money damages for the harm caused by the breach;[34]

- The injured party might suspend its own performance and give the breaching party the opportunity to cure the breach

- Alternatively, if the breach is serious enough to constitute a total material breach, the injured party may terminate or "cancel" the contract and recover damages for the entire remaining performance due from the breaching party.[35]

These options apply only if the breach is material. If the breach is non-material, the injured party may recover damages for the breach, but may not suspend or terminate performance of its own contractual duties. If it does so, it will be in breach and its actions may justify the other party in suspending or terminating the contract.

Consider a construction contract in which Barbara agrees to build a new house for Orson according to a detailed set of specifications. If Barbara's work suffers from several minor defects, Orson is entitled to damages based on the amount necessary to correct the defects, but possibly limited to the difference in value between the house as it was built and the house as it would have been built if Barbara had followed all of the specifications.[36]

If Orson discovers a serious defect midway through completion of the project, Orson might decide to notify Barbara of the breach and demand that she cure it, but nevertheless continue making any scheduled progress payments without suspending his own performance. Or, Orson may suspend any progress payments he has promised to make, and possibly order Barbara to stop performing until she cures the defects. If the breach is sufficiently serious, Orson may cancel the contract, order Barbara off the premises, cease making any payments and sue Barbara for a total material breach.

Construction projects of the type between Barbara and Orson frequently provide for periodic progress payments to the builder due at several separate stages of the project. Assume that Orson has promised to pay Barbara a total of $100,000, with a $10,000 progress payment due on July 1, when work on the foundation was to be completed. Assume that upon Barbara's completion of the foundation, Orson discovers that the concrete blocks that comprise the foundation

---

[34] RESTATEMENT (SECOND) OF CONTRACTS § 236 cmt. b (1981).

[35] RESTATEMENT (SECOND) OF CONTRACTS § 236(1) & cmt. b (1981).

[36] *See infra* § 12.08[D] Construction Contracts: Breach by the Builder — Cost of Performance or Difference in Value.

walls are not properly aligned, affecting the structural integrity of the project. This is likely to be a material breach and Orson will likely be permitted to refuse to make the progress payment that would otherwise be due.

Because the defect is one that can be cured by relaying the foundation, Orson may not be entitled to cancel the contract immediately. Instead, he will be required to provide Barbara with notice of the defect and a reasonable opportunity to cure. If Barbara cures the defect within a reasonable time, she will be entitled to receipt of the progress payment that had been due on July 1 and may resume work on the project. If Barbara fails to cure the misaligned foundation wall, Orson will be entitled to terminate the contract completely, refuse to permit her to continue work, and sue her for any damages he suffers as a result of the likely delay in completion of the job.

K & G Construction Co. v. Harris[37] provides a good example of how a breach occurring in the middle of performance affects the respective rights and responsibilities of the parties. The parties agreed to certain excavation work to be done in connection with the plaintiff's housing development. One of the contractor's bulldozers damaged a building that had already been completed, causing several thousand dollars of damage and making the building unusable. When the contractor refused to pay for the necessary repairs, the owner retaliated by refusing to make a progress payment that was due for work the contractor had already completed. In response, the contractor not only refused to pay for the damage to the building, but also refused to continue work on the project.

The court had no difficulty finding that the damage to the already completed building was a material breach. The harm caused by the errant bulldozer was "more than double" the amount of the progress payment then owed to the contractor. Accordingly, it found that the owner was justified in suspending the progress payment and that the contractor's refusal to continue work was therefore unjustified. Because it was improper, the refusal to continue was a repudiation of the contract, which justified the owner in terminating the contract and hiring a substitute excavation contractor to complete the work. As a result, the contractor ended up liable not just for the harm its bulldozer operator had done to the plaintiff's building, but also for the additional expense the plaintiff incurred in hiring someone else to finish the excavation work required for his construction project. As the court explained: "[i]f the refusal to pay an installment is justified on the owner's part, the contractor is not justified in abandoning work by reason of that refusal. His abandonment of the work will itself be a wrongful repudiation that goes to the essence, even if the defects in performance did not."[38]

If the builder's breach had been something more trivial, such as showing up for work a half-hour late one day, this would not, by itself, have permitted the owner to suspend performance. This would carry too great a risk that the owner would use a minor breach as a pretext for attempting to terminate the contract, and perhaps take advantage of changes in market conditions for construction services.

---

[37] 164 A.2d 451 (Md. 1960).

[38] *Id.* (quoting Corbin on Contracts).

This modern approach to the effect of breach, reflected in the Second Restatement, is slightly different from the traditional approach taken by earlier common law. These older rules were inflexible. They made no room for "cure" by a party who had committed a material breach. Under the earlier common law cases, no distinction was drawn between a curable and a noncurable breach, although the ease of implementing a cure was relevant in determining whether the breach was material in the first place. Instead, there was simply a question of whether the breach was material or nonmaterial. Material breach permitted the injured party to "rescind" the contract and terminate performance of its own duties to perform. The injured party could, of course, elect to merely suspend performance, but had no obligation to provide the breaching party with an opportunity to cure. The Second Restatement gives a materially breaching party the opportunity to implement a cure before permitting the injured party to cancel the contract.

[C]   Constructive Conditions and Substantial Performance[39]

These rules concerning material breach are directly related to rules discussed earlier about substantial performance and constructive conditions.[40] In a bilateral contract each party's duty of performance is conditioned on the other party's substantial performance of its reciprocal contractual obligations.[41] Each party's duty to perform is said to be "dependent" on the other party's performance of its reciprocal duties.

For example, in a contract for the sale of Sam's BMW to Barb, Barb's contractual duty to pay the price is conditioned on Sam's delivery of the car.[42] Likewise, Sam's duty to deliver the car is conditioned on Barb's payment of the price.[43] Each party's obligations are dependent on the performance of the other's. They are "concurrent constructive conditions" of one another. Thus, in contracts for the sale of goods, governed by Article 2 of the Uniform Commercial Code, a breach "of the whole contract" by the buyer permits the seller to "cancel" the contract.[44] If the seller's failure to deliver a conforming tender "goes to the whole contract," the buyer is afforded a similar right.[45] The references to a breach of "the whole contract" are synonymous with the common law concept of total material breach.

In a contract for real estate, the same is true. The seller's duty to convey good title is conditioned on the buyer's payment of the agreed price, and the buyer's duty to pay is conditioned on the seller's delivery of a deed. If one party fails to

---

[39] *See* RICHARD DANZIG, THE CAPABILITY PROBLEM IN CONTRACT LAW 111 (1978); Amy B. Cohen, *Reviving Jacob & Youngs v. Kent: Material Breach Doctrine Reconsidered*, 42 VILL. L. REV. 65 (1997).

[40] *See supra* § 8.03[B] Express, Implied, and Constructive Conditions.

[41] RESTATEMENT (SECOND) OF CONTRACTS § 237 (1981).

[42] U.C.C. § 2-511 (2012).

[43] U.C.C. § 2-507 (2012).

[44] U.C.C. § 2-703(f) (2012).

[45] U.C.C. § 2-711(1) (2012).

perform, the other party is entitled not just to damages, but also to refuse to perform its own contractual duties.

In construction and other service contracts, where there is a total failure to perform, the law of constructive conditions works in the same way: a builder's complete failure to perform its contract to build excuses the owner from his or her promise to pay. If the parties agreed that payment was to be made in advance, the owner's failure to make the promised payment excuses the builder from its duty to perform. Where one party's breach is complete and total, there is little difficulty in finding that the other party is released from its reciprocal duties under the contract. The law's early recognition that reciprocal duties were usually dependent on one another was an important step in the development and modernization of contract law.[46]

However, this important development was accompanied by a serious potential flaw. Carried too far, treating reciprocal promises as dependent or conditional on one another might permit a party to exploit an insignificant breach to escape performance of its contractual obligations when circumstances unrelated to the breach have given the party a motive to try to do so. Consider, for example, the situation that might exist if Alice enters into a contract to purchase a beachfront condominium from Dave, with the closing scheduled for 10:00 a.m. on December 12. If Alice finds an alternative condo in a more desirable location and for a lower price, she may seek to exploit any minor shortcoming in Dave's performance as an excuse to evade her contract with him. If Dave is held up in traffic on December 12, and calls at 9:55 a.m. to announce that he will be five minutes late for the closing, Alice should not be permitted to pounce on this otherwise reasonable delay to avoid going through with the deal.

Concern over this type of exploitation quickly led to the doctrine of substantial performance. A party may not evade its contractual duties by asserting the failure of a constructive condition based on a trivial deviation from the other party's contractual obligations.[47] A party may assert a breach by the other party as a justification for its own nonperformance only if the other party's breach was material. Today, the doctrine is frequently illustrated by Judge Cardozo's opinion in *Jacob & Youngs, Inc. v. Kent.*[48]

There, the parties entered into a written contract for the construction of an elaborate home. The contract specified that the builder would use "Reading"-brand pipe to complete the plumbing in the house. When the house was complete, and after the owner had lived in it for several months, he discovered that the builder had used "Cohoes"-brand pipe instead of the "Reading" pipe stipulated in the contract. Relying on the law of constructive conditions, the owner asserted that he was under no duty to make the final $3,500 payment on the overall $77,000 price until the builder fully performed its promise to build the house according to the agreed specifications.

---

[46] Kingston v. Preston, 2 Doug. 689, 99 Eng. Rep. 437 (K.B. 1773). *See supra* § 8.03[B] Express, Implied, and Constructive Conditions.

[47] *See* Boone v. Eyre, 1 H. Bl. 273 (1777).

[48] 129 N.E. 889 (N.Y. 1921). *See* RICHARD DANZIG, THE CAPABILITY PROBLEM IN CONTRACT LAW 111 (1978).

Judge Cardozo recognized that applying established contract law would have produced a very unfair result, partly because the owner had been occupying the house for more than six months when the dispute arose, but mostly because there was no discernable difference in quality between Reading pipe and Cohoes pipe.[49] If the owner's claim of failure of the condition precedent had been accepted, no further inquiry would have been necessary. The owner's duty to pay the $3,500 balance would have never have become due, and the result would have amounted to a partial forfeiture by the builder.

This was exactly the result reached in the trial court where the builder's evidence, showing that the characteristics of Cohoes pipe were identical to those of Reading pipe, was excluded. In requiring a new trial, where this evidence would be admitted, Judge Cardozo prevented this undesirable result by firmly establishing the doctrine of "substantial performance" into the law of constructive conditions. Judge Cardozo reasoned that the evidence would have helped establish that "the defect was insignificant in its relation to the project."[50] In other words, the builder had substantially done what was necessary to satisfy the condition precedent to the owner's obligation to pay. That is, the house was complete in nearly every respect. The only defect was the builder's use of the wrong brand of pipe. Accordingly, the court concluded that the constructive condition of completion of the house was satisfied and the owner was obligated to pay. The defect could be compensated for with damages caused by the builder's failure to use the specified pipe.

Jacob & Youngs, Inc. v. Kent established that substantial performance of a contractual duty satisfies any "constructive condition" derived from that duty to the other party's obligations to perform. The owner's duty to make the final payment was subject to the constructive condition of the builder's performance of its duty to complete the house according to the agreed specifications. Substantial performance of the builder's duty satisfied this constructive condition.

However, the substantial performance doctrine does not lead to a conclusion that a party can fail to perform parts of a contract with impunity. Judge Cardozo also recognized that permitting a party who had itself failed to fully perform to nevertheless obtain the other party's reciprocal performance was fraught with potential difficulty. Taken to an extreme, the doctrine of substantial performance might remove the protections the parties had bargained for in establishing the order of performance of their respective duties. The substantial performance doctrine was limited in two important ways.

First, and most importantly, the doctrine of substantial performance is limited by its own terms. It applies only when the breach involved is not serious. A material breach justifies the other party in. suspending performance. And, an uncured material breach continues to operate as a failure of a constructive

---

[49] A careful reading of the case leaves one with the strong impression that the owner must have kept searching for some deviation from the specifications to justify refusing to make the final payment. The owner had been living in the house for approximately six months when the dispute over the pipe arose, and the issue over making final payment came to a head (so to speak).

[50] Jacob & Youngs, Inc. v. Kent, 129 N.E. at 890.

condition to the other party's duty to perform.[51] If the contractor in *Jacob & Youngs, Inc. v. Kent* had used oatmeal instead of cement to hold the structure together, making the building structurally unsound, the defect would undoubtedly have been a material breach and the builder would not have been entitled to receive the owner's final payment. The builder also would have been liable for other damages caused by the breach, probably the cost of demolishing the defective building and rebuilding it with cement.

Second, a person who has only substantially performed a promise has, by definition, not fully performed and is thus liable for damages caused as a result of its breach. In *Jacob & Youngs, Inc. v. Kent*, the homeowner retained a claim for damages against the defaulting builder based on its failure to fully perform by using the designated brand of pipe. The homeowner could recover for the loss in value he suffered as a result of the builder's failure to use Reading pipe.[52] In other cases, where the cost of repairing the faulty performance was not so grossly disproportionate to the additional value to be obtained, an owner would be entitled to damages based on the cost of repair.[53]

[D]   Divisibility of Contracts[54]

The potentially devastating effect of a material breach in permitting the other party to suspend or terminate its duty to perform may be mitigated by the doctrine of divisible contracts. It applies when the parties have agreed to a succession of performances that can be easily separated into discrete divisible parts. A party's material breach of one divisible portion of the contract may not operate to discharge the injured party from continuing to perform in connection with other divisible portions of the contract.[55]

Consider, for example, a contract between Barb and Sam for the sale of Sam's house and Sam's car to Barb for $150,000 and $7,000, respectively. Barb's failure to tender the $7,000 price for the car should not permit Sam to suspend or terminate his obligation to tender a deed for the house, provided, of course, that Barb tenders the $150,000 purchase price for the house at the time and place scheduled for performance.

Whether the contract is divisible into discrete separate portions depends on the intent of the parties. Their intent can usually indicated by whether the performances can be apportioned and whether the apportioned performances were regarded by the parties as the agreed equivalents for one another.

The famous case of *Tipton v. Feitner*[56] involved the sale of a combination of both a number of "dressed" (slaughtered) hogs and live hogs. There was one price for

---

[51] RESTATEMENT (SECOND) OF CONTRACTS § 237 (1981).

[52] Jacob & Youngs, Inc. v. Kent, 129 N.E. at 891.

[53] *E.g.*, Plante v. Jacobs, 103 N.W.2d 296 (1960) (awarding cost of performance for some defects and difference in value for others).

[54] Carl E. McGowan, *The Divisibility of Employment Contracts*, 21 IOWA L. REV. 50 (1935).

[55] RESTATEMENT (SECOND) OF CONTRACTS § 233 (1981).

[56] 1859 N.Y. LEXIS 211 (Dec. 1859).

the dressed hogs, which were set for immediate delivery, and another price for the live hogs, which were to be delivered at a later time. The contract was easily divided into two portions: dressed hogs and live hogs. Likewise, there was no question but that the separate prices for each set of hogs articulated in the contract had been viewed by the parties as equivalent exchanges.[57]

The same is true in the deal between Sam and Barb for the sale of Sam's house and his car. The house and the car are clearly separate from one another, and the parties appear to have intended the $150,000 price to be the agreed equivalent for the house, with the $7,000 intended as the agreed equivalent for the car. In these circumstances a court would have no trouble treating the contract as divisible.

Carrig v. Gilbert-Varker Corp.[58] provides a modern example of a contract that can be apportioned. The contract required the builder to construct 35 houses. The builder completed only 20 of them before abandoning the project. The court explained: "where the contract consists of several and distinct items to be furnished [with] the consideration to be apportioned to each item according to its value and as a separate unit rather than as a part of the whole, then the contract is severable or divisible."[59]

In determining whether the contract is divisible, courts consider two key factors:[60] (1) whether the parties' performances are separable into corresponding pairs of performances, and (2) whether the parts of each pair of performances were regarded as agreed equivalents.[61] These tests might be fairly easy to satisfy in cases like *Carrig* where the total price might be divided into a "price per house." Apportionment is more difficult where the total performance is regarded as greater than the sum of its parts.

Carrig is thus distinguishable from a contract for the sale of a matched set of dining room furniture: a table, eight matching chairs, and a china cabinet for a price of $10,000. While the individual pieces might be physically separated, it is impossible to determine which portion of the price should be attributable to the table, the chairs, and the cabinet. The difficulty is compounded in this case by the likelihood that the matched set is worth more as a unit than the sum of its parts if sold separately.

If material breach of one part of the contract substantially impairs the overall purpose of the contract, the contract cannot be apportioned. This is typically true in contracts involving several stages of an overall project, like the construction of a single building, where each stage consists of preparation for the next.[62]

---

[57] *See also* Gill v. Johnstown Lumber Co., 25 A. 120 (Pa. 1892) (contract to transport four million feet of logs calling for payment of one dollar per thousand feet for oak logs and 75¢ per thousand feet for all other logs).

[58] 50 N.E.2d 59 (Mass. 1943).

[59] *Id.* at 63. RESTATEMENT (SECOND) OF CONTRACTS § 240 (1981) (example of "agreed equivalents").

[60] RESTATEMENT (SECOND) OF CONTRACTS § 183 (1981).

[61] Thunderstik Lodge, Inc. v. Reuer, 613 N.W.2d 44 (S.D. 2000).

[62] RESTATEMENT (SECOND) OF CONTRACTS § 240 illus. 7 (1981). *See also* Pa. Exch. Bank v. United States, 170 F. Supp. 629 (Ct. Cl. 1959) (preliminary stages were merely incidental preparations for subsequent stages of performance).

[E] Restitution for Part Performance

A party who is in material breach may be entitled to compensation for its part performance prior to the breach. It cannot, of course, recover for breach of contract, because the other party is not in breach. However, this does not mean that the breaching party has not conferred a significant benefit on the injured party. Even though the injured party has a right to recover from the breaching party for damages suffered as a result of the breach, the breaching party has an offsetting right to recover on a theory of restitution for the value of the benefit it conveyed.

This is illustrated by the decision in *Plante v. Jacobs*.[63] A contractor breached its duty to construct a home by leaving substantial portions of the plumbing, electrical, heating, tile, flooring, and decorating work undone. Although he did not substantially perform and was in material breach, the court permitted him to recover, on a theory of quantum meruit, for the value of the work he had done.[64]

If, on the contrary, the defects in the contractor's performance were sufficiently serious that various aspects of the project would have to be done over to make the building suitable for occupancy, the completed work might not have conferred a substantial benefit to the owner, and no recovery in restitution would be available.[65]

[F] Fundamental Breach in International Transactions[66]

In international contracts for the sale of goods, the CISG permits an injured buyer or seller to avoid the contract[67] if there is a "fundamental breach." The concept of fundamental breach is similar to the common law concept of total material breach. A breach is fundamental if:

> it results in such detriment to the other party as substantially to deprive him of what he is entitled to expect under the contract, unless the party in breach did not foresee and a reasonable person of the same kind in the same circumstance would not have foreseen such a remedy.[68]

In other international transactions, UNIDROIT Principles use the same continental European concept of fundamental breach to permit an injured party to

---

[63] 103 N.W.2d 296 (Wis. 1960).

[64] *See also* Kreyer v. Driscoll, 159 N.W.2d 680 (Wis. 1968).

[65] *E.g.*, O.W. Grun Roofing & Constr. Co. v. Cope, 529 S.W.2d 258 (Tex. Civ. App. 1974) (new roof had to be replaced because of material defects in its appearance that could not otherwise be repaired).

[66] Damien Nyer, *Withholding Performance for Breach in International Transactions: An Exercise in Equations, Proportions or Coercion?*, 18 PACE INT'L L. REV. 29 (2006); Franco Ferrari, *Fundamental Breach of Contract Under the UN Sales Convention — 25 Years of Article 25 CISG*, 25 J.L. & COM. 489 (2006).

[67] CISG Arts. 49 (buyer's right) & 64 (seller's right) (1980).

[68] CISG Art. 25 (1980).

"terminate" the contract.[69] The factors used to determine whether a particular failure to perform is fundamental are similar to those used by the common law to evaluate whether there has been a material breach. They are whether:

(a) the nonperformance substantially deprives the aggrieved party of what it was entitled to expect under the contract unless the other party did not foresee and could not reasonably have foreseen such result;

(b) strict compliance with the obligation which has not been performed is of essence under the contract;

(c) the non-performance is intentional or reckless;

(d) the non-performance gives the aggrieved party reason to believe that it cannot rely on the other party's future performance; and

(e) the non-performing party will suffer disproportionate loss as a result of the preparation or performance if the contract is terminated.[70]

In the case of delayed performance, the aggrieved party may terminate the contract if delay is fundamental or, even if it is not, if the other party fails to perform before the time permitted under the "Nachfrist" time extension period expires.[71] If there is a delay that does not justify termination, the injured party may withhold its own performance until the other party either tenders performance (in the case of contracts calling for simultaneous performance) or until the other party has performed (in the case of contracts calling for the other party to perform first).[72]

The Principles of European Commercial Contracts contain similar rules. A party may terminate the contract if the other party's nonperformance is fundamental.[73] Under these slightly different principles a breach is fundamental if "strict compliance . . . is the essence of the contract," if "the nonperformance substantially deprives the aggrieved party of what it was entitled to expect [and that result was foreseeable]," or if "the nonperformance is intentional and gives the aggrieved party reason to believe that it cannot rely on the other party's future perfor-mance."[74]

As under the UNIDROIT Principles, delayed performance justifies termination if the delay is fundamental, or where the aggrieved party has complied with the Nachfrist procedure by notifying the other party of an additional reasonable period

---

[69] PICC Art. 7.3.1 (2004).

[70] PICC Art. 7.3.1(2) (2004).

[71] PICC Art. 7.3.1 (2004). *See* PICC Art. 7.1.5 (2004). "Nachfrist" is a concept borrowed from German law. In the CISG and the UNIDROIT Principles, it permits the aggrieved party to extend the period in which the other party may perform. CISG Art. 47 & 63 (1980); PICC Art. 7.1 (2004). *See generally* Peter A. Pilounis, *The Remedies of Specific Performance, Price Reduction and Additional Time (Nachfrist) Under the CISG: Are These Worthwhile Changes or Additions to English Sales Law?*, 12 Pace Int'l L. Rev. 1, 42 (2000).

[72] PICC Art. 7.1.3 (2004).

[73] PECL Art. 9.301(1) (2002).

[74] PECL Art. 8.103 (2002).

of time to perform and the other party has failed to do so.[75]

§ 9.02 PERFORMANCE AND BREACH IN CONTRACTS FOR GOODS

Domestic contracts for the sale of goods are governed by Article 2 of the Uniform Commercial Code. Under Article 2, the seller has a duty to make a conforming tender of the goods, and the buyer has a duty to pay for them. Both the goods and the manner of their tender must conform to the contract. The effect of a breach — or "nonconforming tender" — depends on whether the contract calls for a single delivery or deliveries in installments. In contracts calling for delivery of goods in a single installment the injured party may reject defective goods even if the defect is minor. However, where delivery may be made in installments, the buyer's right to refuse delivery — or "reject" — depends on whether the defect has a material effect on the buyer. The buyer has a duty to accept a conforming tender, usually after inspecting the goods. If the buyer rejects, the seller usually enjoys the opportunity to cure the defect with a conforming tender — and sometimes has extra time to do so. If the buyer accepts, he or she has a duty to pay for the goods. However, as will be seen, the buyer might subsequently "revoke acceptance" if he or she discovers a serious latent defect. In international sales, the parties have similar rights and obligations.

[A]   Seller's Duty to Tender Delivery

The parties' basic duties under the Uniform Commercial Code are simple: the seller's duty is "to transfer and deliver [the goods];"[76] the buyer's duty is to "accept and pay in accordance with the contract."[77] In international sales these duties are no different.[78] In most cases, the buyer has the right to inspect the goods before accepting them, but not necessarily before paying the price. Although these duties are simply stated, they can be considerably more complex, depending on the nature and details of the contract.

[1]   Tender by Seller

In domestic sales, "tender of delivery" requires the seller to "put and hold confirming goods at the buyer's disposition and give the buyer any notification reasonably necessary to enable him to take delivery."[79] The precise time, manner, and place for tender depends on the terms of the contract,[80] but if the contract is silent about these matters, it should occur at a reasonable time[81] and at the seller's

---

[75] PECL Arts. 9.301(2) & 8.106(3) (2002).

[76] U.C.C. § 2-301 (2012).

[77] *Id.*

[78] CISG Art. 30 (Obligations of the Seller) & 53 (Obligations of the Buyer) (1980).

[79] U.C.C. § 2-503(1) (2012).

[80] U.C.C. § 2-503(1) (2012).

[81] U.C.C. § 2-309 (2012). *See supra* § 4.11[B][2][a] Delivery at Reasonable Time.

location.[82] If the goods are to be shipped by an independent carrier, tender might occur either when the goods are placed in the hands of a carrier, or when the carrier tenders them at the specified destination, depending on the terms of the contract.[83] In these cases, the seller must also tender any documents — such as a bill of lading — that are necessary for the buyer to take possession.[84] When the goods are in storage in an independent warehouse, and are to be "delivered [to the buyer] without being moved" out of the warehouse, tender occurs when the seller tenders the documents necessary for the buyer to obtain the goods from the warehouse or otherwise obtains the warehouse's acknowledgment of the buyer's right to possession of the goods.[85]

In international sales, tender is far more likely to occur through a documentary transaction, with the seller making arrangements for the goods to be transported to the buyer's location — or possibly directly to the buyer's customer in a "drop shipment" — by an independent carrier, such as an airline or shipping line. In these cases, the parties are likely to be uneasy about the prospects for the other's performance: the distance between them is far and, if enforcement is necessary, it might have to be pursued in a foreign country. Fortunately, international merchants and their banks long ago developed a solution to these risks.

When goods are to be shipped a long distance, in either a domestic or an international sale, the transaction is usually accomplished through a documentary sale. The details of the transaction are complex, but the basic format is simple. It usually involves at least five parties: (1) the seller, (2) the buyer, (3) a common carrier such as an airline or shipping company, (4) the seller's bank, and (5) the buyer's bank. Other carriers may also be involved if the goods are to be transported via multiple means of transportation involving more than one company. Likewise, there may be intermediary banks involved if the seller's bank and the buyer's bank do not already have a business relationship with one another.

Suppose, for example, that an American air conditioner manufacturer wishes to purchase compressors, for use in their air conditioners, from an Italian supplier.[86] The contract specifies that the compressors will be sent "FOB, NY" — the buyer's place of business, with the seller to arrange for their transportation. Under the CISG, the seller "must make such contracts as are necessary for carriage to the place fixed by means of transportation appropriate in the circumstances and according to the usual terms for such transportation."[87] When the seller delivers the goods to the carrier, the carrier will give the seller a "bill of lading," which operates as an acknowledgment of its receipt of the goods and as a contract for their transportation. The seller will convey this bill of lading, together with a

---

[82] U.C.C. § 2-309 (2012). *See supra* § 4.11[B][2][b] Place for Delivery.

[83] U.C.C. § 503(2) (2012). *See supra* § 4.11[B][2][c] Shipment and Destination Contracts; Mercantile Terms and "Incoterms."

[84] U.C.C. § 2-503(3), (5) (2012). This is usually referred to as a "documentary sale."

[85] U.C.C. § 2-503(4) (2012).

[86] *See* Delchi Carrier SpA v. Rotorex Corp., 71 F.3d 1024 (2d Cir. 1995).

[87] CISG Art. 32(2) (1980). *See* U.C.C. § 2-504 (2012).

"draft," which orders the buyer to pay the price of the goods,[88] to its bank. The seller's bank, in turn, conveys the bill of lading and draft to the buyer's bank, sometimes through one or more intermediary banks, together with any customs or inspections certificates relating to the goods. The buyer's bank probably anticipates receiving these documents, and may have made a prior commitment to advance funds to pay the price of the goods, in the form of a "letter of credit," which obligates the bank to pay if the documents presented to it conform to the requirements of the bank's commitment. Assuming that everything is in order, the buyer's bank will pay the amount specified in the seller's draft, deliver the bill of lading to the buyer, and make arrangements to recover the amount it paid, from its customer, the buyer. When the goods arrive, the buyer will have already received possession of the bill of lading, which entitles the buyer to receive the goods from the carrier.[89]

[2]   Breach in Single Delivery Contracts: The Perfect Tender Rule[90]

In contracts calling for a single delivery of goods, the perfect tender rule applies.[91] It permits a buyer to reject goods if they are defective in any way, even if the seller has substantially performed.[92] The perfect tender rule was firmly established in the United States by 1885[93] and is now codified in U.C.C. § 2-601.

U.C.C. § 2-601 gives the buyer three alternatives if the goods or the manner of the seller's tender of delivery "fail *in any respect* to conform to the contract." The buyer may reject the whole, accept the whole, or accept any commercial unit or units and reject the rest.[94] Thus, the buyer may reject the entire delivery if there is *any* defect either in the goods themselves or in the manner of the seller's tender of delivery. Most significantly, the defect need not be material.[95] In other words,

---

[88] A draft is similar to a check, and is governed by the same body of law as checks. A check is a banking customer's order, instructing the bank to pay money to the designated payee. The customer has funds on deposit with the bank, and the bank has a contractual duty to pay this amount to whomever the customer instructs it to pay. Similarly, under the terms of the contract for sale, a buyer owes money to the seller — the price of the goods. Thus, the seller uses a draft to instruct, or "order," the buyer to pay the sum of money owed, to whomever the seller directs — usually the seller's bank.

[89] If this seems too complicated or counterintuitive, don't worry. Few first-year courses in contract law delve into these matters, which are usually reserved for an upper-level course, if your law school has one, in the law of Sales or International Commerce. For a more detailed description of how these transactions operate, see RALPH H. FOLSOM, 1 INTERNATIONAL BUSINESS TRANSACTIONS § 6.2 (2012 ed.).

[90] George L. Priest, *Breach and Remedy for Tender of Non-Conforming Goods Under the Uniform Commercial Code: An Economic Approach*, 91 HARV. L. REV. 960 (1978); William H. Lawrence, *The Prematurely Reported Demise of the Perfect Tender Rule*, 35 KAN. L. REV. 557 (1987); Michael A. Schmitt & David Frisch, *The Perfect Tender Rule — An "Acceptable" Interpretation*, 13 U. TOL. L. REV. 1375 (1982).

[91] Bowes v. Shand, [1877] 2 Q.B.D 1112.

[92] Mitsubishi Goshi Kaisha v. J. Aron & Co., 16 F.2d 185, 186 (2d Cir. 1926).

[93] *See* Norrington v. Wright, 115 U.S. 188 (1885); John Honnold, *Buyer's Right of Rejection*, 97 U. PA. L. REV. 457 (1949).

[94] U.C.C. § 2-601 (2012).

[95] *See, e.g.*, Moulton Cavity & Mold, Inc. v. Lyn-Flex Indus., Inc., 396 A.2d 1024, 1027–28 (Me. 1979).

under U.C.C. Article 2, the doctrine of substantial performance does not apply in single-delivery contracts for the sale of goods.[96]

An historic example that illustrates the provenance of this rule is found in *Filley v. Pope*.[97] There, the buyer was excused from its obligation to accept a delivery of scrap iron, not because of a defect in the iron itself, but because it was shipped to the buyer's location in New Orleans *from* Leith, rather than *from* Glasgow, Scotland, as specified in the contract. More recently, in *Raimirez v. Autosport*,[98] the buyer of a camper van was justified in rejecting delivery because of minor defects in the paint, the absence of electric and sewer hookups, and wet seat cushions. None of these defects were serious, and all of them could have been readily cured. Nevertheless, the buyer was justified in rejecting the camper van.

The perfect tender rule seems harsh and has been criticized[99] because it permits buyers to use a minor defect as a pretense to attempt to escape an otherwise unprofitable deal.[100] However, it has been justified as providing greater certainty than a rule permitting rejection only for defects that are material.[101] It protects a buyer from having to make a subtle judgment about whether the breach is serious. Instead, a buyer need only decide if the goods fail to conform to the specifications of the contract.

The potentially harsh impact of the rule is mitigated in several ways. First, the terms of the contract may be sufficiently flexible to restrain the buyer's ability to reject goods due to a minor imperfection. For example, goods conform to the implied warranty of merchantability, despite minor defects, so long as they "pass without objection in the trade under the contract description,"[102] or, "in the case of fungible goods, if they are of fair average quality within the description."[103] With respect to express warranties, variations permitted by usage of trade or course of dealing may supply considerable leeway in determining whether the goods or the tender are conforming. If variations in the quality of the goods are not sufficient to make them unmerchantable, or if variations are permitted by any applicable usage of trade or course of dealing, the buyer may not reject them.

Second, a breaching seller usually enjoys the right to cure a defective tender.[104]

---

[96] *E.g.*, Printing Ctr. of Tex., Inc. v. Supermind Publ'g Co., 669 S.W.2d 779 (Tex. App. 1984).

[97] 115 U.S. 213 (1885).

[98] 440 A.2d 1345 (N.J. 1982).

[99] *See* John A. Sebert Jr., *Rejection, Revocation, and Cure Under Article 2 of the Uniform Commercial Code: Some Modest Proposals*, 84 Nw. U. L. Rev. 375 (1990).

[100] *See* Lawrence R. Eno, *Price Movement and Unstated Objections to the Defective Performance of a Sales Contract*, 44 Yale L.J. 782, 801 (1935).

[101] *See* William H. Lawrence, *The Prematurely Reported Demise of the Perfect Tender Rule*, 35 Kan. L. Rev. 557 (1987); William H. Lawrence, *Appropriate Standards for a Buyer's Refusal to Keep Goods Tendered by a Seller*, 35 Wm. & Mary L. Rev. 1635 (1994).

[102] U.C.C. § 2-314(2)(a) (2012).

[103] U.C.C. § 2-314(2)(b) (2012).

[104] U.C.C. § 2-508 (2012); *See* William H. Lawrence, *Cure After Breach of Contract Under the Restatement (Second) of Contracts: An Analytical Comparison with the Uniform Commercial Code*, 70 Minn. L. Rev. 713 (1986).

Thus, upon the buyer's rejection, the seller usually has an additional reasonable time to tender conforming goods.[105] Rejection by the buyer, therefore, does not put an end to the contract.

Third, the perfect tender rule applies only to single-delivery contracts. In contracts calling for delivery in multiple installments, the buyer may reject only if defects substantially impair the value of the goods to the buyer.[106]

Fourth, in order to reject, buyers must scrupulously comply with the requirement of giving timely notice of their intent to reject.[107] Failure to give timely and unequivocal notice of rejection deprives the buyer of its right to reject. In addition, the buyer's failure to specify the grounds for its rejection adequately may make a timely attempt to reject ineffective. These limitations deprive buyers of a large part of their incentive to take opportunistic advantage of a minor defect by rejecting goods that, despite some flaw, are suitable for the buyer's needs.[108]

Occasionally a court refuses to apply the perfect tender rule. In *D.P. Technology Corp. v. Sherwood Tool, Inc.*,[109] the court ruled that late delivery did not justify the buyer in rejecting goods unless the delay was substantial.[110] However, despite decisions like *Sherwood Tool*, courts are more likely to find some other basis to soften the blow of the rule than they are to deny it outright.

[3] Breach in Installment Contracts[111]

The buyer's right to reject is considerably more limited in contracts that permit the goods to be delivered in multiple installments. In installment contracts the perfect tender rule does not apply.[112] Instead, the buyer may reject a defective installment only if the defect "substantially impairs the value of that installment."[113] The buyer may not cancel the entire contract unless one or more defective installments substantially impair the value of the entire contract.[114]

[a] Rejection of Single Installment

The inapplicability of the perfect tender rule to contracts calling for delivery in more than one installment makes it important to be able to distinguish between single-delivery contracts and those permitting or requiring deliveries in installments. U.C.C. § 2-612 specifies that "[a]n 'installment contract' is one which

---

[105] *See infra* § 9.04 Breaching Party's Right to Cure.

[106] U.C.C. § 2-612 (2012). *See infra* § 9.03[B] Rejection or Acceptance.

[107] U.C.C. § 2-602 (2012). *See infra* § 9.03[B][1] Manner of Rejection.

[108] U.C.C. § 2-605 (2012). *See infra* § 9.03[B][1] Manner of Rejection.

[109] 751 F. Supp. 1038 (D. Conn. 1990).

[110] *See also* Clark v. Zaid, Inc., 282 A.2d 483 (Md. 1971).

[111] Elizabeth H. Patterson, *UCC Section 2-612(3): Breach of an Installment Contract and a Hobson's Choice for the Aggrieved Party*, 48 Ohio St. L.J. 177 (1987).

[112] U.C.C. § 2-601 is expressly "[s]ubject to the provisions of [Article 2] on breach in installment contracts." U.C.C. § 2-601 (2012).

[113] U.C.C. § 2-612(2) (2012).

[114] U.C.C. § 2-612(3) (2012).

requires or authorizes the delivery of goods in separate lots to be separately accepted."[115] In many cases the contract will provide expressly for installment deliveries.[116] In other cases the contract may be silent, but other circumstances may indicate that installment deliveries are contemplated. In this regard, U.C.C. § 2-307 further specifies that:

> Unless otherwise agreed all goods called for by a contract for sale must be tendered in a single delivery and payment is due only on such tender but where the circumstances give either party the right to make or demand delivery in lots the price if it can be apportioned may be demanded for each lot.[117]

Under this language, cases like *Kelly Construction Co. v. Hackensack Brick Co.*,[118] where it is impractical for the buyer to take delivery of all the goods at one time, are treated as permitting deliveries to be made in installments.[119] The contract need not specify that it is one for installment deliveries so long as the circumstances indicate that installment deliveries were contemplated and thus tacitly approved.[120] In an installment delivery contract a minor defect in some of the goods, or a shortfall in the quantity of an individual installment that does not impair the value of the entire installment, does not warrant rejection of the entire delivery.

Whether a defect substantially impairs the installment is similar to the question under the common law of whether a breach is material.[121] On the one hand, bricks that are the wrong size or color, and therefore cannot be used with other bricks as part of the same construction project, can be rejected. On the other hand, if all but a few of the bricks (or pallets) can be used without undue burden or expense, the buyer must usually accept and pay for them. If the buyer rejects them, even though the defect does not substantially impair the value of the installment, the buyer is in breach. If the buyer breaches by wrongfully rejecting an installment, the seller is entitled to exercise its own rights, including possibly the right to cancel the contract.[122]

As in single-delivery contracts, the buyer's right to reject an individual installment is tempered by the seller's right to cure.[123] If defects in an individual delivery are serious enough to substantially impair the value of the delivery to the buyer, the

---

[115] U.C.C. § 2-612(1) (2012). Section 2-612(1) further specifies that the parties may not avoid the application of § 2-612 through language indicating that " 'each delivery is a separate contract' or its equivalent."

[116] *E.g.*, McDonnell Douglas Corp. v. United States, 182 F.3d 1319, 1322 (Fed. Cir. 1999) (8 Navy stealth fighters with a price of more than $4 billion).

[117] U.C.C. § 2-307 (2012).

[118] 103 A. 417 (N.J. 1918).

[119] *See* U.C.C. § 2-307 cmt. 3 (2012). By their very nature, bricks can be laid only one course at a time.

[120] *See, e.g.*, Extrusion Painting, Inc. v. Awnings Unltd., Inc., 37 F. Supp. 2d 985 (E.D. Mich. 1999).

[121] *See* RESTATEMENT (SECOND) OF CONTRACTS § 241 (1981). *See supra* § 9.01[A] Material Breach and Substantial Performance.

[122] U.C.C. § 2-703 (2012).

[123] *See, e.g.*, Midwest Mobile Diagnostic Imaging, L.L.C. v. Dynamics Corp. of Am., 965 F. Supp. 1003, 1010 (W.D. Mich. 1997); Graulich Caterer, Inc. v. Hans Holterbosch, Inc., 243 A.2d 253 (N.J. 1968).

seller nevertheless has a right to cure the defect. Unlike the right to cure in single-delivery contracts, here the right to cure is absolute.[124] It does not depend, as it does under § 2-508, on whether the deadline for performance has not yet passed or whether the seller had reason to believe the buyer would accept.[125] If the seller gives adequate assurance that it will cure, the buyer may not reject.[126] Cure might involve replacement of the defective goods or an appropriate adjustment in the price.[127] The buyer must, of course, give the seller timely notice of the substantially impairing defect, and the seller must give notice of its intent to cure.[128]

[b]   Breach of the Whole

A defect in a single installment does not justify cancellation of the entire contract unless the defect "substantially impairs the value of the whole contract."[129] The cumulative effect of repeated defects in several installments may be serious enough to give the buyer the right to cancel the entire contract. For example, in *Graulich Caterer, Inc. v. Hans Holterbosch, Inc.*,[130] the seller's deliveries of German-style food to accompany German beer (Lowenbrau) at the 1964 World's Fair[131] did not conform to the samples that the seller had previously provided. The first delivery was unappetizing, and the buyer complained. When the second delivery, of more than 2,000 units, was similarly defective, the seller cancelled the contract and refused to accept subsequent deliveries. The recurrence of the defects, along with the failure of the seller to correct the deficiencies,[132] justified the seller in cancelling the contract. The defects substantially impaired the value of the contract to the buyer, whose customers complained and did not return.

Even though most cases involving substantial impairment of the contract involve multiple failed attempts to deliver conforming goods, defects in a single installment may be serious enough to impair the value of the entire deal. In *Midwest Mobile Diagnostic Imaging, L.L.C. v. Dynamics Corp.*,[133] the seller's failure to make timely delivery of one of four magnetic resonance imaging (MRI)

---

[124] *See* William H. Lawrence, *Appropriate Standards for a Buyer's Refusal to Keep Goods Tendered by a Seller*, 35 Wm. & Mary L. Rev. 1635, 1687–89 (1994).

[125] Midwest Mobile Diagnostic Imaging, L.L.C. v. Dynamics Corp. of Am., 965 F. Supp. 1003, 1010–11 (W.D. Mich. 1997). *But see* Arkla Energy Res. v. Roye Realty & Dev., Inc., 9 F.3d 855 (10th Cir. 1993).

[126] U.C.C. § 2-612(2) (2012).

[127] Cont'l Forest Prods., Inc. v. White Lumber Sales, Inc., 474 P.2d 1 (Or. 1970).

[128] U.C.C. § 2-508 (2012). *See infra* § 9.04 Breaching Party's Right to Cure.

[129] U.C.C. § 2-612(3) (2012).

[130] 243 A.2d 253 (N.J. 1968).

[131] Your author attended the fair in 1964, but has no recollection of the food served at the Lowenbrau Pavilion — or of the beer. He was only 10 years old.

[132] This was one of the first attempts to use microwave ovens to prepare previously frozen food. After the disappointing results, the buyer quit using the microwave ovens and prepared the food with traditional cooking equipment.

[133] 965 F. Supp. 1003 (W.D. Mich. 1997).

trailers seriously harmed the buyer's ability to fulfill commitments it had made to its customers, thereby justifying cancellation. Similarly, in *Hubbard v. UTZ Quality Foods, Inc.*,[134] a defective shipment of potatoes substantially impaired the value of the entire contract, which contained detailed specifications regarding the color and other quality standards for all of the potatoes to be delivered. However, a delay that has no serious effect on the buyer's operations does not substantially impair the value of the contract and thus does not permit the buyer to cancel.[135]

On the other hand, courts have generally ruled that the buyer's failure to make timely payment for an installment that has been delivered is a defect that substantially impairs the value of the contract to the seller.[136] Missed payments are likely to have an adverse effect on the seller's cash flow and thus impede its operations.[137] Moreover, requiring the seller to make further deliveries after the buyer has failed to pay for deliveries already made materially changes the credit terms of the contract in a way not contemplated by the parties. This exposes the seller to the risk of never receiving payment for multiple deliveries.[138] However, the fact that past payments have been made late, rather than not at all, does not ordinarily permit the seller to discontinue future shipments.[139]

Cases involving missed payments and defective installment deliveries raise the question of how an aggrieved party's right to demand adequate assurances of future performance[140] affects its right to cancel under § 2-612. In *Cassidy Podell Lynch, Inc. v. Snyder General Corp.*,[141] the seller did not have the right to cancel due to a missed payment, because the seller failed to invoke its right to demand adequate assurance of future performance under U.C.C. § 2-609. However, this approach was rejected in *Cherwell-Ralli, Inc. v. Rytman Grain Co., Inc.*,[142] where the court noted that, although demanding adequate assurance might be prudent as part of an effort to avoid overreacting to what might not be a material breach, demanding assurance of future performance is not necessary where a defective installment substantially impairs the value of the entire contract.

[B]   Payment and the Buyer's Right to Inspect

The buyer has a duty to pay for goods it accepts.[143] Tender of payment is a condition of the seller's duty to tender delivery[144] and is due, absent an agreement

---

[134] 903 F. Supp. 444 (W.D.N.Y. 1995).

[135] *See, e.g.*, Emanuel Law Outlines, Inc. v. Multi-State Legal Studies, Inc., 899 F. Supp. 1081 (S.D.N.Y. 1995).

[136] *E.g.*, L&M Ent., Inc. v. BEI Sensors & Sys. Co., 231 F.3d 1284, 1287–88 (10th Cir. 2000).

[137] *See* Plotnick v. Pa. Smelting & Ref. Co., 194 F.2d 859, 862 (3d Cir. 1952) (decided under the Uniform Sales Act, the predecessor to Article 2 of the U.C.C.).

[138] *E.g.*, L&M Ent., Inc. v. BEI Sensors & Sys. Co., 231 F.3d 1284 (10th Cir. 2000).

[139] *E.g.*, Cassidy Podell Lynch, Inc. v. Snyder Gen. Corp., 944 F.2d 1131 (3d Cir. 1991).

[140] *See infra* § 9.06 Prospective Inability to Perform.

[141] 944 F.2d 1131 (3d Cir. 1991).

[142] 433 A.2d 984 (Conn. 1980).

[143] U.C.C. § 2-709(a) (2012).CISG Art. 53 (1980). *See infra* § 9.03[B][2] Buyer's Acceptance.

[144] U.C.C. § 2-511(a) (2012); CISG Art. 53 (1980).

to the contrary, at the time and place that the buyer is to receive the goods.[145] If nothing is said about the place or method of delivery, delivery, and thus payment, is due at the seller's place of business.[146] In a shipment contract, tender occurs when the seller delivers the goods to a carrier for transportation to the buyer, but payment is not due until the buyer receives them.

In most such contracts the parties have agreed that payment will be made against documents. If so, the buyer's duty to pay arises when the documents — a bill of lading, paperwork regarding inspections and customs duties, and any other documents involved in the transaction — are tendered to the buyer or the buyer's agent.

The buyer usually has a right to inspect the goods before making payment.[147] If this inspection reveals a defect, the buyer can reject the goods.[148] But, in a documentary sale, where the buyer must pay for the goods upon the seller's tender of the relevant documents, the buyer only has the right to inspect the documents, not the goods, prior to payment.[149] This does not prejudice the buyer's right to reject if the goods are nonconforming, but places the buyer in the uncomfortable situation of having taken possession of and paying for goods before inspecting them.[150]

[C] Fundamental Breach in International Sales of Goods[151]

Rather than apply the perfect tender rule of the U.C.C., the CISG applies the doctrine of fundamental breach.[152] The CISG specifies that the buyer may "declare the contract avoided" if the seller's failure to perform "amounts to a fundamental breach of the contract."[153] A fundamental breach is one that "results in such detriment to the [buyer] as substantially to deprive him of what he is entitled to expect under the contract."[154] Thus, the CISG adopts a material breach approach to contracts for the sale of goods, regardless of whether the contract is a single-delivery contract or an installment-delivery contract.

In cases of nondelivery, the buyer may avoid the contract if the seller fails to deliver the goods within whatever reasonable "Nachfrist" time the buyer

---

[145] U.C.C. § 2-310(a) (2012); CISG Art. 57(1) (1980).

[146] U.C.C. § 2-308(a) (2012); CISG Art. 57(1)(a) (1980).

[147] U.C.C. § 2-513(1) (2012); CISG Art. 58(3) (1980).

[148] *See infra* § 9.03[B] Rejection or Acceptance.

[149] U.C.C. § 2-513(3)(b) (2012); CISG Art. 58 (1980).

[150] In this situation, the buyer retains a security interest in the goods and can use them as collateral to secure recovery of the price he or she has already paid. U.C.C. § 2-711(3) (2012).

[151] Damien Nyer, *Withholding Performance for Breach in International Transactions: An Exercise in Equations, Proportions or Coercion?*, 18 Pace Int'l L. Rev. 29 (2006).

[152] CISG Art. 25 (1980).

[153] CISG Art. 49(1)(a) (1980).

[154] CISG Art. 25 (1980). A breach is not fundamental if this degree of harm was not foreseeable by the breaching party.

establishes for the seller to deliver the goods after they were due.[155]

Similar to the rule in U.C.C. § 2-608(2), the buyer loses his or her right to avoid the contract if he or she does not declare the contract avoided within a reasonable time after learning of the seller's late delivery, or, with respect to defects in the quality of the goods, within a reasonable time after the buyer ought to have known of the defect.[156]

§ 9.03   REJECTION, ACCEPTANCE, AND REVOCATION OF ACCEPTANCE IN CONTRACTS FOR GOODS[157]

A buyer who discovers that goods are defective must decide whether to send them back or to keep them. By rightfully rejecting defective goods, a buyer avoids his or her obligation to pay the price. If the buyer accepts goods despite a defect, he or she has a duty to pay. Consistent with his or her obligation to mitigate damages, however, the buyer retains a right to recover damages for harm caused by the seller's breach.[158] Thus, the buyer's rights vary depending on the response to the seller's delivery.

[A]   Consequences of the Buyer's Acceptance

Under the perfect tender rule, when the contract calls for a single delivery, the seller may reject the goods if they are defective in any respect.[159] In contracts permitting deliveries in installments, the buyer may reject an individual installment only if the defects in the delivery substantially impair the value of that installment.[160]

A buyer who accepts goods must pay the price.[161] If the goods are defective, and the buyer rejects them, he or she need not pay. Once the buyer accepts, his or her ability to revoke acceptance and return the goods depends on whether any defect discovered is one that substantially impairs the value of the goods.[162] This is particularly important in single-delivery contracts where the buyer loses the benefits of the perfect tender rule by accepting. Finally, the buyer has a duty to pay the price for goods he or she accepted, even if the goods are defective in some respect. Nevertheless, the buyer retains the right to recover damages from the

---

[155] CISG Art. 49(1)(b) (1980).

[156] CISG Art. 49(2) (1980).

[157] John A. Sebert Jr., *Rejection, Revocation, and Cure Under Article 2 of the Uniform Commercial Code: Some Modest Proposals*, 84 Nw. U. L. Rev. 375 (1990); Gregory Travalio, *The UCC's Three "R's": Rejection, Revocation and (the Seller's) Right to Cure*, 53 U. Cin. L. Rev. 931 (1984); Douglas J. Whaley, *Tender, Acceptance, Rejection and Revocation, The UCC's TARR Baby*, 22 Drake L. Rev. 1 (1974).

[158] *See* Intervale Steel Corp. v. Borg & Beck Div., Borg-Warner Corp., 578 F. Supp. 1081, 1086–87 (E.D. Mich. 1984).

[159] *See supra* § 9.03[B] Rejection or Acceptance.

[160] *See supra* § 9.03[C] Rejection of Acceptance.

[161] U.C.C. § 2-607(1) (2012).

[162] U.C.C. § 2-607(2) (2012). *See* William H. Lawrence & William H. Henning, Understanding Sales and Leases of Goods (1996).

seller based on the difference in value of the goods as warranted and as delivered.[163] These differences in the buyer's rights, once the threshold of the buyer's acceptance of the goods is crossed, make it important to understand some of the procedural aspects of rightful rejection. Otherwise, the buyer might impair his or her own rights by inadvertently accepting the goods.

[B]   Rejection or Acceptance[164]

Because of the consequences of acceptance, it is important to understand what constitutes acceptance. As will be seen, although the buyer can expressly accept the goods, acceptance most often occurs through the buyer's failure to effectively reject them.[165]

[1]   Manner of Rejection

To reject, a buyer must take affirmative action. The buyer must "seasonably notify the seller" of rejection.[166] The notice must be given "within a reasonable time after . . . delivery or tender."[167] Thus, a buyer who wishes to reject may neither delay nor equivocate. A buyer who waits too long to complain about a defect in the goods, or who merely grumbles about the quality of the goods without unequivocally rejecting them, has accepted them.[168]

As elsewhere in the law, what constitutes a reasonable time varies depending on the situation. It is likely to depend on the nature of the goods and the complexity of any inspection or testing that must be done to determine whether the goods are defective. Where defects are easily discovered, the buyer must act quickly. In *Miron v. Yonkers Raceway, Inc.*,[169] the buyer of a racehorse failed to have the horse's legs examined immediately upon delivery of the horse and was found to have accepted by failing to discover the defect and reject the horse within a day of its delivery.

On the other hand, where elaborate testing must be conducted to detect any defects, more time is permitted. Likewise, the time for the buyer's rejection may be extended by a seller's promises to cure a reported defect.[170] Not surprisingly,

---

[163] U.C.C. § 2-714 (2012). *See infra* § 12.08[A] Contracts for the Sale of Goods — Breach by the Seller.

[164] Douglas J. Whaley, *Tender, Acceptance, Rejection and Revocation, The UCC's TARR Baby*, 22 Drake L. Rev. 1 (1974).

[165] In this context, "acceptance" and "rejection" have nothing to do with the contract formation process. Quite to the contrary, once acceptance or rejection of the goods is an issue, a contract has already been formed. In this context the Code refers to acceptance and rejection *of the goods* rather than of an offer to enter into a contract.

[166] U.C.C. § 2-602(1) (2012).

[167] *Id.*

[168] *See, e.g.*, Van Dorn Co. v. Future Chem. & Oil Corp., 753 F.2d 565, 575 (7th Cir. 1985).

[169] 400 F.2d 112 (2d Cir. 1968).

[170] Jones v. Abriani, 350 N.E.2d 635, 643 (Ind. Ct. App. 1976); Steinmetz v. Robertus, 637 P.2d 31 (Mont. 1981) (buyer's cooperation with seller in attempting to "work the bugs out" would not be permitted to prejudice buyer's right to reject when efforts were ineffective).

where the contract specifies a time for the buyer's inspection, failure to reject within the specified time operates as acceptance of the goods.[171]

The potential prejudicial effect on the seller due to a delay is also an important factor. Further, the buyer's notice of rejection must make it clear to the seller that the goods are unacceptable. Merely supplying notice of a defect or problem with the goods is not sufficient, by itself, as notice of rejection.

In addition, a buyer must specify the grounds for its rejection.[172] If the buyer fails to advise the seller of the exact nature of the defect, the seller cannot know what is necessary to effectuate a cure. Thus, if the buyer rejects a shipment of bricks because they are the wrong color and the wrong size, but notifies the seller only that the size was nonconforming, the seller might attempt to cure with a replacement shipment of bricks that are still the wrong color. By failing to specify both grounds for its rejection, the buyer has waived its complaint about the color.[173]

However, this type of waiver does not apply to defects that the seller could not have cured even if it had been appraised of the nature of the problem.[174] Nor does it apply to defects that were not ascertainable by a reasonable inspection.[175]

Despite these limitations, rejection is not the buyer's only remedy. A buyer who fails to properly reject defective goods may still recover damages, so long as it gave general notice of the defect pursuant to U.C.C. § 2-607(3)(a). Thus, a buyer who gives timely notice of a problem with the goods, but who fails to make clear his or her intent to reject them, is not be barred from recovering damages.[176] If the buyer simply notifies the seller that the transaction is troublesome, his or her general right to damages — though not its right to reject — is preserved.[177]

[2]   Buyer's Acceptance

Acceptance of goods can occur in several ways.[178] Most of the time acceptance of the goods occurs through nothing more than the buyer's failure to effectively reject them. They are accepted if the buyer fails to reject.[179] Thus, inaction by the buyer

---

[171] Nw. Airlines v. Aeroservice Inc., 168 F. Supp. 2d 1052, 1054 (D. Minn. 2001).

[172] *See* U.C.C. § 2-605(1) (2012).

[173] *E.g.*, Texpor Traders, Inc. v. Trust Co. Bank, 720 F. Supp. 1100, 1111 (S.D.N.Y. 1989).

[174] U.C.C. § 2-605(1)(a) (2012). In transactions between merchants, the buyer waives any defect it does not specify after the seller makes a written request for a full and final statement of the defects, even if the defects were ones the seller could not have cured. U.C.C. § 2-605(1)(b) (2012).

[175] U.C.C. § 2-605(1) (2012).

[176] Cliffstar Corp. v. Elmar Indus., Inc., 678 N.Y.S.2d 222 (N.Y. App. Div. 1998).

[177] Computer Strategies v. Commodore Bus. Machs., 483 N.Y.S.2d 716 (N.Y. App. Div. 1984).

[178] Acceptance of the goods, following delivery, is different from "acceptance" of an offer during the contract formation process. In this context, "acceptance" refers to the buyer's retention of the goods after their delivery. In the context of the contract formation process, "acceptance" refers to a manifestation of intent to enter into a legally binding agreement. *See supra* § 4.04 Acceptance; Gillen v. Atlanta Systems, Inc., 997 F.2d 280, 284 n.1 (7th Cir. 1993).

[179] U.C.C. § 2-606(1)(b) (2012).

is the equivalent of acceptance. In *Northwest Airlines, Inc. v. Aeroservice, Inc.*,[180] the buyer accepted aircraft components simply by remaining silent beyond the 10-day period specified in the contract as the reasonable time for the buyer's inspection.[181] However, acceptance does not occur through inaction until the buyer has had a reasonable opportunity to inspect the goods.[182]

The buyer also accepts if it engages in "any act inconsistent with the seller's ownership."[183] For example, in *Lorenzo Banfi di Banfi Renzo & Co. v. Davis Congress Shops, Inc.*,[184] the buyer exercised ownership over defective shoes shipped by the manufacturer by both placing them in its inventory and reselling some of them to its own customers. And, in *Delorise Brown, M.D., Inc. v. Allio*,[185] the buyer accepted a defective computer system by modifying it. In both of these cases, the court treated the buyer's actions as an exercise of ownership rights over the goods that constituted acceptance.

The buyer's continued use of the goods after giving notice purporting to reject them has caused some difficulty.[186] Some courts treat continued use of the goods at its face value and prevent the buyer from subsequently claiming that it did not accept.[187] Other courts recognize that an aggrieved buyer may have little financial choice other than continuing to use the goods,[188] and permit the buyer to maintain its posture of rejection, despite continued use of the goods, so long as the use is reasonable.[189] In reaching this conclusion, courts frequently emphasize the practical considerations confronting the buyer who may need the goods and whose resources may be exhausted as a result of the transaction with the breaching seller.[190] However, a rejecting buyer who continues to use the goods may be liable to the seller, on a theory of restitution, for the value of its use.[191] These courts

---

[180] 168 F. Supp. 2d 1052 (D. Minn. 2001).

[181] *See also* Fablok Mills, Inc. v. Cocker Mach. & Foundry Co., 310 A.2d 491 (N.J. Super. Ct. App. Div. 1973) (buyer notified seller of problems, but did not express its intent to reject due to the defects).

[182] *Id.*

[183] U.C.C. § 2-606(1)(c) (2012).

[184] 568 F. Supp. 432 (N.D. Ill. 1983).

[185] 620 N.E.2d 1020 (Ohio Ct. App. 1993).

[186] John R. Bates, *Continued Use of Goods After Rejection or Revocation of Acceptance: The UCC Rule Revealed, Reviewed and Revised*, 25 RUTGERS L.J. 1 (1993); Carolyn F. Lazaris, Note, *Article 2: Revocation of Acceptance — Should a Seller Be Granted a Setoff for the Buyer's Use of the Goods?*, 30 NEW ENG. L. REV. 1073 (1996); R.J. Robertson Jr., *Rights and Obligations of Buyers with Respect to Goods in Their Possession After Rightful Rejection or Justifiable Revocation of Acceptance*, 60 IND. L.J. 663 (1985).

[187] *E.g.*, Bryant v. Prenger, 717 S.W.2d 242, 244 (Mo. Ct. App. 1986); Wendt v. Beardmore Suburban Chevrolet, Inc., 366 N.W.2d 424 (Neb. 1985).

[188] *See, e.g.*, Liarikos v. Mello, 639 N.E.2d 716 (Mass. 1994); Computerized Radiological Servs. v. Syntex Corp., 595 F. Supp. 1495 (E.D.N.Y. 1984) (continued use was the only reasonable method of mitigating damages due to difficulty in obtaining cover for a defective X-ray machine for one year).

[189] McCullough v. Bill Swad Chrysler-Plymouth, Inc., 449 N.E.2d 1289 (Ohio 1983); Aluminum Line Prods. Co. v. Rolls-Royce Motors, Inc., 649 N.E.2d 887 (Ohio Ct. App. 1994).

[190] *See Ex parte* Stem, 571 So. 2d 1112, 1114 (Ala. 1990).

[191] *E.g.*, Erling v. Homera, Inc., 298 N.W.2d 478 (N.D. 1980). *See also* Revised U.C.C. § 2-608(4)(b) (2003) (reasonable use permitted, with liability for value of use).

apply the same rule to buyers who continue using the goods after revoking acceptance under U.C.C. § 2-608.[192]

The buyer might also expressly accept by advising the seller of its intent to retain the goods. Thus, the buyer accepts if it "signifies to the seller that the goods are conforming or that he will take or retain them in spite of their nonconformity."[193] Even if the goods are not conforming, if the buyer expresses its intention to accept or to keep the goods, the buyer has accepted.

[C]   Revocation of Acceptance[194]

Once the buyer has accepted, his or her right to return the goods is more limited. The buyer may still "revoke acceptance" of the goods, but only if the defect substantially impairs their value to him or her.[195] Revocation of acceptance due to a substantially impairing defect, under U.C.C. § 2-608, is the equivalent of rescission due to material breach under the common law.[196] Even when a defect substantially impairs the value of the goods, the buyer may revoke acceptance only if the buyer originally accepted the goods on the reasonable assumption that the defect would be cured.[197] Alternatively, if the buyer accepted the goods without discovering the defect, he or she retains the right to revoke acceptance if acceptance was induced by the difficulty of discovering the defect or by the seller's assurances.[198]

[1]   Substantial Impairment

Although the perfect tender rule permits goods involved in a single-delivery contract to be rejected because of only a slight defect, once accepted, the goods may not be returned unless the defect is serious. In this respect, the standard for revocation of acceptance is similar to the standard for rejection in an installment contract. Both situations require a defect that "substantially impairs" the value of the goods.

In the context of revocation of acceptance, § 2-608 appears to use a subjective standard for determining whether the defect is serious enough to justify the buyer's refusal to keep the goods or to pay for them. It permits revocation of

---

[192] *See infra* § 9.03[C] Revocation of Acceptance.

[193] U.C.C. § 2-606(1)(a) (2012).

[194] Peter G. Dillon & Alvin C. Harrell, *Revocation of Acceptance Under UCC Section 2-608 as a Remedy in a Consumer Sales Transaction Involving Conflicting Oral Quality Representations and Standardized Quality Warranty Disclaimer Language*, 25 OKLA. CITY U. L. REV. 269 (2000); George L. Priest, *Breach and Remedy for the Tender of Nonconforming Goods Under the Uniform Commercial Code: An Economic Approach*, 91 HARV. L. REV. 960, 984 (1978).

[195] U.C.C. § 2-608(1) (2012). *See generally* Lee R. Russ, Annotation, *What Constitutes "Substantial Impairment" Entitling Buyer to Revoke His Acceptance of Goods Under UCC § 2-608(1)*, 38 A.L.R.5th 191 (1996).

[196] *E.g.*, Cissell Mfg. Co. v. Park, 36 P.3d 85 (Colo. Ct. App. 2001).

[197] U.C.C. § 2-608(1)(a) (2012).

[198] U.C.C. § 2-608(1)(b) (2012).

acceptance where the "non-conformity substantially impairs [the] value *to him.*"[199] Thus, the buyer's individual circumstances are taken into account in determining whether the buyer may return the goods without liability for paying the price. Section 2-612, on the other hand, regarding rejection of goods in an installment contract, appears to use an objective standard.[200]

The considerations relevant to determining whether a defect substantially impairs the value of the goods to the buyer are similar to those in common law cases dealing with whether a breach is material.[201] They include: (1) the nature of the defects, (2) the cost and length of any time required for repair of the goods, (3) whether past repair attempts have been successful, (4) the buyer's ability to use the goods while repairs are attempted, (5) the extent of inconvenience and consequential harm suffered by the buyer due to the nonconformities, and (6) the availability and cost of alternative goods pending repair.[202]

In cases involving new automobiles, some courts have applied a "shaken faith" doctrine to determine whether the buyer is entitled to revoke acceptance. The question is not simply a matter of determining whether the defect makes the car dangerous or unreliable, but rather whether the defect "shakes the buyer's faith or undermines his confidence in the reliability and integrity" of the vehicle.[203] The doctrine is based on the premises that once a buyer's confidence in the goods is destroyed, it cannot be restored.

[2]   Revocation of Acceptance Permitted

Revocation of acceptance is not permitted in every situation involving a defect that substantially impairs the value of the goods to the buyer. Revocation of acceptance due to a substantially impairing defect is permitted in three situations. First, the buyer may revoke acceptance where he or she accepted the goods on the reasonable assumption that the seller would cure the defect and the seller has failed to implement a cure within a reasonable time.[204] For example, in *Fortin v. Ox-Bow Marina, Inc.*,[205] the court allowed the buyer to revoke acceptance of a boat accepted four months earlier when the seller had provided repeated assurances that it would repair the reported defects.[206] Likewise, where the

---

[199] U.C.C. § 2-608(1) (2012) (emphasis supplied).

[200] *See* Keen v. Modern Trailer Sales, Inc., 578 P.2d 668 (Colo. Ct. App. 1978).

[201] *See* RESTATEMENT (SECOND) OF CONTRACTS § 237 cmt. b (1981); *supra* § 9.01[A] Material Breach and Substantial Performance.

[202] *See* Palmucci v. Brunswick Corp., 710 A.2d 1045 (N.J. Super. Ct. App. Div. 1998).

[203] Abele v. Bayliner Marine Corp., 11 F. Supp. 2d 955 (N.D. Ohio 1997); Inniss v. Methot Buick-Opel, Inc., 506 A.2d 212, 219 (Me. 1986). *But see* Belfour v. Schaumberg Auto, 713 N.E.2d 1233, 1238 (Ill. App. Ct. 1999) (rejecting buyer's assertion that seller could not "cure" buyer's psychological loss of confidence in the seller's product).

[204] U.C.C. § 2-608(1)(a) (2012). *See* N. Am. Lighting, Inc. v. Hopkins Mfg. Corp., 37 F.3d 1253 (7th Cir. 1994); Toshiba Mach. Co. v. SPM Flow Control, Inc., 180 S.W.3d 761 (Tex. App. 2005).

[205] 557 N.E.2d 1157 (Mass. 1990).

[206] *See also* Jackson v. Rocky Mtn. Datsun, Inc., 693 P.2d 391 (Colo. Ct. App. 1984); CMI Corp. v. Leemar Steel Co., Inc., 733 F.2d 1410 (10th Cir. 1984).

seller's efforts to cure defects are not successful, the buyer may revoke his or her acceptance and obtain a refund.

An extreme example is supplied in *Waddell v. L.V.R.V. Inc.*,[207] where the seller's repeated efforts over an 18-month period were inadequate to correct various problems in a new recreational vehicle, including engine overheating and air conditioning, heating, and electrical system malfunctions. The nonconformities impaired the value of the RV, and the buyers were deprived of the benefit of their bargain. Their delay in asserting the right to revoke acceptance for the year and a half that the seller took in attempting to remedy the problems did not prevent the buyers from exercising their right. Their time to revoke acceptance was tolled while the seller retained possession of the RV and attempted to make repairs.

Second, the buyer may have accepted defective goods because of the difficulty of discovering the defect prior to acceptance.[208] In *Colonial Dodge, Inc. v. Miller*,[209] the court permitted revocation of acceptance due to a missing spare tire, where its absence was difficult to detect because of its hidden location under a fastened panel.[210] And, in *Blommer Chocolate Co. v. Bongards Creameries, Inc.*,[211] the buyer was entitled to revoke acceptance of "whey," a by-product of milk, due to the presence of salmonella bacteria in the goods. Salmonella, as the parties agreed, is particularly difficult to detect. Likewise, in *Atlan Industries, Inc. v. O.E.M., Inc.*,[212] the buyer's revocation of acceptance was justified where the buyer accepted the goods based on test samples selected from the goods, and subsequently discovered that the items tested were unrepresentative of the items subsequently delivered.

Third, the buyer might revoke acceptance where the buyer failed to discover the defect, not because of the difficulty of its detection, but because of the seller's assurances about the quality of the goods.[213] It does not matter whether the assurances were provided by the seller in good faith, or otherwise.[214]

[3]   Notice and Timing of Revocation of Acceptance[215]

As with rejection, revocation of acceptance requires timely and unequivocal notice. The buyer must revoke acceptance within a reasonable time after discovering either the defect or the grounds for revoking acceptance. In many cases, the buyer's decision to revoke acceptance will be based not on the discovery

---

[207] 125 P.3d 1160 (Nev. 2006).

[208] U.C.C. § 2-605(1)(b) (2012). *See* S & R Metals, Inc. v. C. Itoh & Co., 859 F.2d 814 (9th Cir. 1988).

[209] 362 N.W.2d 704 (Mich. 1984).

[210] One might sensibly question the court's conclusion that a missing spare tire was a sufficiently serious defect to substantially impair the value of the car. On the other hand, being stuck in the middle of nowhere, without a spare tire, is a potentially life-endangering situation.

[211] 644 F. Supp. 234 (N.D. Ill. 1986).

[212] 555 F. Supp. 184 (W.D. Okla. 1983).

[213] U.C.C. § 2-608(1)(b) (2012). *See* N. Am. Lighting, Inc. v. Hopkins Mfg. Corp., 37 F.3d 1253 (7th Cir. 1994); Toshiba Mach. Co. v. SPM Flow Control, Inc., 180 S.W.3d 761 (Tex. App. 2005).

[214] U.C.C. § 2-608 cmt. 3 (2012).

[215] Fleming James, *Products Liability*, 34 TEX. L. REV. 192, 197 (1955).

of a latent defect, but on the seller's failure to implement an effective cure.[216] In such cases, the time for revoking acceptance extends beyond the time for giving notification of breach under U.C.C. § 2-607(3)(a).[217]

Likewise, the buyer must revoke acceptance before any substantial change in the condition of the goods — apart from changes that were caused by the very defect that impairs their value.[218] The buyer's use or fabrication of the goods might prevent it from revoking acceptance if this results in a substantial change in the condition of the goods. In *Intervale Steel Corp. v. Borg & Beck Div., Borg-Warner*,[219] the buyer's action in fabricating scrap steel parts prevented it from revoking acceptance. And, in *Trinkle v. Schumacker Co.*,[220] the buyer was prevented from revoking acceptance when the defect in the seller's fabric, which otherwise would have justified revocation of acceptance, was not discoverable until after the buyer had cut the fabric into shades.[221] However, if the change in the condition of the goods was a result of the very defect that led the buyer to revoke acceptance, this limitation does not apply. Thus, the destruction of an automobile, resulting from defective brakes would not prevent revocation of acceptance even though the value of the vehicle had been destroyed.

As with rejection, the buyer's notice of revocation of acceptance must do more than advise the seller that there is a problem with the transaction. Mere notice of breach or a request for a cure, while sufficient to preserve the buyer's general right to damages, is not notice of revocation of acceptance.[222] As with notice of rejection, notice of revocation of acceptance must make it clear that the buyer does not intend to keep the goods.[223]

§ 9.04 BREACHING PARTY'S RIGHT TO CURE[224]

A key issue in cases involving nonperformance is the extent to which the breaching party must be given the opportunity to cure the breach. Thus, a seller delivering nonconforming goods might seek to repair the defect or replace the defective goods with items that conform to the contract's specifications. Likewise, in a construction contract, a builder might attempt to repair defects in its performance

---

[216] U.C.C. § 2-608 cmt. 4 (2012).

[217] *See, e.g.*, Magnum Press Automation, Inc. v. Thomas & Betts Corp., 758 N.E.2d 507, 511 (Ill. App. Ct. 2001); Fortin v. Ox-Bow Marina, Inc., 557 N.E.2d 1157 (Mass. 1990).

[218] U.C.C. § 2-608 (2012).

[219] 578 F. Supp. 1081 (E.D. Mich. 1984).

[220] 301 N.W.2d 255 (Wis. 1980).

[221] *But see* Alimenta (U.S.A.), Inc. v. Anheuser-Busch Co., Inc., 803 F.2d 1160 (11th Cir. 1986) (revocation permitted despite substantial change in condition where change did not affect the value of the goods).

[222] U.C.C. § 2-608 cmt. 5 (2012).

[223] *E.g.*, Malul v. Capital Cabinets, Inc., 740 N.Y.S.2d 828 (N.Y. City Civ. Ct. 2002).

[224] William H. Lawrence, *Cure After Breach of Contract Under the Restatement (Second) of Contracts: An Analytical Comparison with the Uniform Commercial Code*, 70 MINN. L. REV. 713 (1986); Michael A. Schmitt & David Frisch, *The Perfect Tender Rule — An "Acceptable" Interpretation*, 13 U. TOL. L. REV. 1375 (1982).

in an effort to maintain the parties' contractual relationship and avoid the necessity of paying damages or having the contract terminated. Here, the issue is whether the injured party must accommodate the breaching party's efforts to perform the contract. The issue, in effect, is whether the injured party must mitigate its harm by continuing to deal with the breaching party.[225]

[A]   Seller's Right to Cure[226]

In contracts for the sale of goods, the seller's right to cure is somewhat different depending on whether the contract is a domestic transaction, governed by U.C.C. Article 2, or an international deal, governed by the CISG. Both Article 2 and the CISG give sellers the opportunity to cure a defective tender, but impose different limits on the right.

[1]   Cure in Domestic Sales

Rightful rejection by the buyer does not necessarily result in cancellation of the contract. Quite to the contrary, because in most circumstances the seller has a right to cure a defective tender by delivering conforming goods.[227] The seller might also cure by repairing the goods, or, in some cases, by permitting an adjustment in the price. If the seller cures, it remains responsible for any damages caused by its initial nonconforming tender, but is otherwise entitled to enforce the contract.

The seller's right to cure arises in two situations. The first is when the "time for performance has not yet expired."[228] Accordingly, a seller who delivers defective goods, but delivers them early, has a second chance to deliver conforming goods by "seasonably notifying the buyer of his intention to cure."[229]

The second circumstance in which the seller is permitted to cure is more surprising. Section 2-508(2) provides: "Where the buyer rejects a non-conforming tender which the seller had reasonable grounds to believe would be acceptable with or without a money allowance the seller may if he seasonably notifies the buyer have a *further reasonable time* to substitute a conforming tender."[230] This is a true second chance for a breaching seller. It applies even if the seller knew that the goods were nonconforming, so long as the seller had "reasonable grounds to believe" the goods would be acceptable to the buyer.

---

[225] *See infra* § 12.05 Limits on Damages: Mitigation.

[226] E. Allan Farnsworth, *The Problems of Nonperformance in Contract*, 17 New Eng. L. Rev. 2 (1982); Howard Foss, *The Seller's Right to Cure When the Buyer Revokes Acceptance: Erase the Line in the Sand*, 16 S. Ill. U. L.J. 3 (1991); William H. Lawrence, *Cure in Contract for the Sale of Goods: Looking Beyond Section 2-508*, 21 UCC L.J. 333 (1989); John A. Sebert Jr., *Rejection, Revocation, and Cure Under Article 2 of the Uniform Commercial Code: Some Modest Proposals*, 84 Nw. U. L. Rev. 375 (1990).

[227] *See generally* Alan Schwartz, *Cure and Revocation for Quality Defects: The Utility of Bargains*, 16 B.C. Indus. & Com. L. Rev. 543 (1975).

[228] U.C.C. § 2-508 (2012).

[229] *Id.*

[230] U.C.C. § 2-508(2) (2012).

In *Bartus v. Ricardi*,[231] the buyer signed a contract to purchase an Acousticon model A-600 hearing aid. The seller delivered a "modified and improved" model A-665, expecting it to be acceptable to the buyer. The buyer rejected the A-665, complaining of noise and headaches. The buyer subsequently refused to take delivery of either another A-665 or an A-660 deciding, that he did not want any hearing aid from the seller. The court ruled that the buyer was in breach. The seller had every reason to expect that its new and improved model A-665 would be acceptable to the buyer and thus the buyer had no choice but to give the seller an opportunity to cure by delivering the promised model A-660.

Section 2-508 does not give the seller an unlimited time to cure, or an unlimited number of opportunities to deliver the goods required by the contract. For example, in *Ramirez v Autosport*,[232] the new camper van delivered to the buyers was defective in several respects. The paint was scratched, neither the electric nor the sewer hookups were installed, and the hubcaps were missing. Under the perfect tender rule the buyers were justified in rejecting the RV, which did not conform to the specifications of the contract and was not ready for delivery. The buyers subsequently returned to the seller's dealership and were advised that the camper van was ready for delivery, only to find that workers were still repairing the scratched paint and that the windows had been left open, allowing some of the interior cushions to become wet. Two weeks later, when they were again told that the van would be ready for delivery, the seller was unable to deliver the camper van and, after waiting for several hours, the buyers "left in disgust." The court found that although the seller had a right to cure, its failure to do so within a reasonable time justified the buyer in terminating the contract.

The seller's right to cure only applies after rejection. It does not usually extend to situations involving a buyer's revocation of acceptance due to a substantially impairing defect.[233] Of course, a buyer who accepts the goods because of the seller's assurances that a cure will be forthcoming implicitly gives the seller an opportunity to cure and may revoke acceptance if the promised cure is not forthcoming.[234]

[2]   Cure in International Sales

The United Nations Convention on the International Sale of Goods contains two provisions on a seller's right to cure. Article 37 gives the seller a virtually unlimited right to cure prior to the date for performance. Thus, if the seller has made an early delivery of defective goods, the CISG permits the seller to make a new tender of conforming goods, "provided that the exercise of this right does not cause

---

[231] 284 N.Y.S.2d 222 (N.Y. City Ct. 1967).

[232] 440 A.2d 1345 (N.J. 1982).

[233] *E.g.*, Am. Honda Motor Co. v. Boyd, 475 So. 2d 835, 840 (Ala. 1985); U.S. Roofing, Inc. v. Credit Alliance Corp., 228 Cal. App. 3d 1431 (1991). *See also* Bonebrake v. Cox, 499 F.2d 951, 957 (8th Cir. 1974). *But see* Fitzner Pontiac-Buick-Cadillac, Inc. v. Smith, 523 So. 2d 324, 327–28 (Miss. 1988); Oberg v. Phillips, 615 P.2d 1022, 1026 (Okla. Ct. App. 1980).

[234] U.C.C. § 2-608 (2012). *See* Champion Ford Sales, Inc. v. Levine, 433 A.2d 1218, 1222 (Md. Ct. Spec. App. 1981).

the buyer unreasonable inconvenience or unreasonable expense."[235] The right to cure exists even if the defect is a serious one, which would otherwise constitute a "fundamental breach" and give the buyer a right to avoid the contract.

Article 48 gives the seller a similar, but more limited, right to cure "after the date for delivery."[236] This right depends on whether the seller's conforming tender can be accomplished "without unreasonable delay" and without causing the buyer either "unreasonable inconvenience" or "uncertainty of reimbursement by the seller of expenses advanced by the buyer."[237]

Regardless of whether the seller cures before or after the time for delivery, the buyer retains the right to recover for any damages it suffers as a result of the seller's initial defective delivery.[238] Thus, the buyer does not waive its right to damages for the seller's initial breach simply because it afforded the seller the opportunity to cure. The seller's cure thus mitigates the buyer's damages; it does not eliminate them.

[B]   Common Law Right to Cure

The common law also gives breaching parties the right to cure. Section 241 of the Second Restatement of Contracts indicates that in determining whether a failure to perform is material, one of the factors that should be considered is "the likelihood that the party failing to perform . . . will cure his failure, taking account of all the circumstances including any reasonable assurances."[239] Section 237, dealing with constructive conditions, further explains that "it is a condition of each party's remaining duties to render performances to be exchanged . . . that there be *no uncured* material failure by the other party [to perform]."[240] Thus, a breach that cannot be cured is more likely to give rise to a claim of total breach.[241]

[C]   Cure in International Transactions

In international transactions, the parties enjoy a similar right to cure. As explained above, the CISG gives sellers a limited right to cure a defective tender of goods.[242] In other transactions, the UNIDROIT Principles permit a nonperforming party to cure any failure to perform, but only if it gives notice, without undue delay, of both its intent to cure and the proposed manner and time of the cure.[243] This right exists only if "cure is appropriate in the circumstances" and the "aggrieved party has no legitimate interest in refusing" to permit a

---

[235] CISG Art. 37 (1980).

[236] CISG Art. 48(1) (1980).

[237] CISG Art. 48(1) (1980).

[238] CISG Art. 37 & 48 (1980).

[239] RESTATEMENT (SECOND) OF CONTRACTS § 241(d) (1981).

[240] RESTATEMENT (SECOND) OF CONTRACTS § 237 (1981) (emphasis added).

[241] *See* RESTATEMENT (SECOND) OF CONTRACTS § 241 cmt. b. (1981).

[242] *See supra* § 9.04[C] Cure in International Transactions.

[243] PICC Art. 7.1.4(1)(a) (2004).

cure.[244] This right to cure evaporates if it is not implemented promptly,[245] but the mere fact that the aggrieved party has previously given notice of termination does not, of itself, prevent cure.[246] However, the aggrieved party is permitted to withhold performance while it waits for the cure to be implemented.[247] If the aggrieved party suffers some harm, such as from a delay while the breaching party cures, the aggrieved party is entitled to compensation for this harm.[248]

The Principles of European Contract Law provide a similar set of rights. They give a nonperforming party the right to "make a new and conforming tender" in two situations: (1) "where the time for performance has not yet arrived," or (2) where any "delay would not [be a] fundamental breach."[249]

§ 9.05 ANTICIPATORY REPUDIATION[250]

Breach of a contract occurs when a party fails to perform. As explained earlier,[251] if the breach is total, the aggrieved party is entitled to terminate the contract, cease performance of its own obligations,[252] and bring an immediate action for breach of the entire contract.[253]

However, breach cannot be certain to occur until the time for performance. If one of the parties announces its intent not to perform, or takes action that would make performance impossible, before the deadline for performance, there has not yet been a real breach. Instead, an "anticipatory repudiation" or "repudiation" has occurred.[254] As will be seen, in most situations, the aggrieved party is entitled to treat repudiation the same as a breach.

Repudiation occurs when a party renounces its contractual duty before the time fixed for performance. It requires "a definite and unequivocal manifestation" that a person "will not render the promised performance when the time fixed for it in the

---

[244] PICC Art. 7.1.4(1)(b)–(c) (2004).

[245] PICC Art. 7.1.4(1)(d) (2004).

[246] PICC Art. 7.1.4(2) (2004).

[247] PICC Art. 7.1.4(4) (2004).

[248] PICC Art. 7.1.4(5) (2004).

[249] PECL Art. 8.104 (2002).

[250] Eric G. Andersen, *A New Look at Material Breach in the Law of Contracts*, 21 U.C. DAVIS. L. REV. 1073 (1988); Henry Winthrop Ballantine, *Anticipatory Breach and the Enforcement of Contractual Duties*, 22 MICH. L. REV. 329 (1924); Robert A. Hillman, *Keeping the Deal Together After Material Breach — Common Law Mitigation Rules, the UCC, and the Restatement (Second) of Contracts*, 47 U. COLO. L. REV. 553 (1976); Keith A. Rowley, *A Brief History of Anticipatory Repudiation in American Contract Law*, 69 U. CIN. L. REV. 565 (2001); Alexander J. Triantis & George G. Triantis, *Timing Problems in Contract Breach Decisions*, 41 J. L. & ECON. 163 (1998); Samuel Williston, *Repudiation of Contracts (Pt. 2)*, 14 HARV. L. REV. 421 (1901).

[251] *See supra* § 9.01[A] Material Breach and Substantial Performance.

[252] RESTATEMENT (SECOND) OF CONTRACTS § 237 (1981).

[253] RESTATEMENT (SECOND) OF CONTRACTS § 243 (1981).

[254] RESTATEMENT (SECOND) OF CONTRACTS § 250 (1981). A repudiation is sometimes mischaracterized as an "anticipatory breach."

contract arrives."[255] Although repudiation is not, strictly speaking, a breach, it has the same effect as a material breach.[256] It permits the aggrieved party to suspend performance, and if the repudiation is not retracted within a reasonable time to terminate the contract, cease performance of its own duties, and bring an immediate action to recover damages.[257]

Although it seems obvious that a promise to breach should be treated the same as a breach, the doctrine of anticipatory repudiation was not firmly established until the mid-nineteenth century, in the case of *Hochster v. De La Tour*.[258] In April 1852, the defendant employed the plaintiff as a courier for a period of three months. However, the plaintiff's service was not scheduled to begin until June 1. On May 11, the defendant repudiated the contract by informing the plaintiff that his services would not be required. The plaintiff immediately brought suit, even though the time for him to begin work for the defendant had not arrived.

Before *Hochster*, the plaintiff would not have been able to bring an immediate action to enforce the contract.[259] Worse yet, he would have been required to hold himself available to begin working for the defendant until the time for performance, passing up other opportunities for alternative employment that might have presented themselves. This was not only wasteful of the plaintiff's time, it also made it difficult for the plaintiff to take immediate steps to mitigate his damages. *Hochster* changed all this by establishing the aggrieved party's right to respond to a repudiation by bringing suit immediately to recover damages for total breach.

[A] Manner of Repudiation

Repudiation can occur in several ways. It usually consists of a statement by one of the parties indicating its inability or unwillingness to perform. A repudiation can also occur if a party voluntarily takes action that would make breach apparently inevitable. In either case, the threatened or anticipated breach must be a breach that, if it occurred, would constitute a total material breach.

As will be seen, it is sometimes difficult for an aggrieved party to determine whether the other party has repudiated. Moreover, a party that overreacts to a possible repudiation may find itself in breach. To guard against this, the law provides a mechanism for a party who has good reason to doubt the other party's future performance to make a demand for adequate assurance that the performance is forthcoming. Should the other party not provide adequate

---

[255] Wholesale Sand & Gravel, Inc. v. Decker, 630 A.2d 710 (Me. 1993).

[256] *See* RESTATEMENT (SECOND) OF CONTRACTS § 253 (1981). *See generally* Thomas H. Jackson, *Anticipatory Repudiation and the Temporal Element of Contract Law: An Economic Inquiry into Contract Damages in Cases of Prospective Nonperformance*, 31 STAN. L. REV. 69 (1978).

[257] RESTATEMENT (SECOND) OF CONTRACTS § 253 (1981). *See* U.C.C. § 2-610 (2012). Apart from its inclusion in the Uniform Commercial Code, the doctrine has still not been adopted in Massachusetts. *See* Spence v. Berkshire Life Ins. Co., 561 F. Supp. 2d 126 (D. Mass. 2008).

[258] 118 Eng. Rep. 922 (Q.B. 1853). *See* Keith A. Rowley, *A Brief History of Anticipatory Repudiation in American Contract Law*, 69 U. CIN. L. REV. 565, 573 (2001).

[259] Larry T. Garvin, *Adequate Assurance of Performance: of Risk, Duress, and Cognition*, 69 U. COLO. L. REV. 71, 77 (1998).

assurances, the aggrieved party can proceed on the assumption there has been a repudiation.[260]

The remainder of this section discusses anticipatory repudiation. The section that follows explains the circumstances that permit a party to demand adequate assurance of future performance and the type of assurances necessary to avoid a repudiation.[261]

[1]   Threat of Material Breach

To constitute a repudiation, the threatened breach must be one that would qualify as a material breach.[262] Threat of a partial breach is not a repudiation.[263] Thus, in determining whether a threatened or impending breach is a repudiation, the aggrieved party must consider the gravity of the anticipated action. Normally, a threat to delay performance for a short time that will not substantially impair the value of the contract and will not constitute a total material breach if it occurs, is not a repudiation.[264] However, if the threatened delay would be a material breach, the threat is a repudiation.[265]

[2]   Definite and Unequivocal[266]

Repudiation most commonly occurs, as it did in the famous case *Hochster v. De La Tour*,[267] with one party announcing its intent not to perform. In *Hochster*, the defendant's repudiation was definite. When the repudiation is more equivocal, the injured party is faced with a difficult choice. If the employer had said "I think my plans might change — I'm not sure whether I'll need you in June," the employee might have immediately sought another job. If he took another job and the original employer's plans went ahead, the employee would have been the one in breach.[268] However, if the employer's plans changed and the plaintiff in the meantime passed up comparable employment, there is a risk that the employee would have failed to mitigate his damages.

To minimize this risk, courts frequently insist that a repudiation be "definite and unequivocal."[269] A party's expression of doubt about its ability to perform is not

---

[260] RESTATEMENT (SECOND) OF CONTRACTS § 251 (1981).

[261] *See infra* § 9.06 Prospective Inability to Perform.

[262] RESTATEMENT (SECOND) OF CONTRACTS § 250(a) (1981).

[263] RESTATEMENT (SECOND) OF CONTRACTS § 250 cmt. d (1981).

[264] RESTATEMENT (SECOND) OF CONTRACTS § 250 illus. 8 (1981).

[265] *E.g.*, Thermo Electron Corp. v. Schiavone Constr. Co., 958 F.2d 1158, 1164 (1st Cir. 1992).

[266] Arthur Rosett, *Partial, Qualified, and Equivocal Repudiation of Contract*, 81 COLUM. L. REV. 93 (1981).

[267] 118 Eng. Rep. 922 (Q.B. 1853).

[268] *See, e.g.*, Truman L. Flatt & Sons Co. v. Schupf, 649 N.E.2d 990 (Ill. App. Ct.), *cert. denied*, 657 N.E.2d 640 (Ill. 1995).

[269] *E.g.*, Harrell v. Sea Colony, Inc., 370 A.2d 119 (Md. Ct. Spec. App. 1977); Whlsl. Sand & Gravel, Inc. v. Decker, 630 A.2d 710 (Me. 1993); Tenavision, Inc. v. Neuman, 379 N.E.2d 1166, 1168 (N.Y. 1979).

enough.[270] In *Harrell v. Sea Colony, Inc.*,[271] the buyer of a condominium apartment sent the seller a letter requesting that he be released from his contract to buy the unit and seeking the return of his deposit. In response, the seller sold the unit in question to another buyer, but did not consent to the request. When the buyer sued not only to recover the deposit, but also to obtain damages based on the difference between the contract price and the market value of the unit, the seller asserted that his resale of the unit was justified by the buyer's letter seeking to be released from the contract. The court held that the buyer had not repudiated but merely asked to be released from the contract, and that his request was not sufficiently definite to constitute a repudiation.

The court in *McCloskey & Co. v. Minweld Steel Co.*[272] reached the same result in a construction contract. The defendant subcontractor sent a letter to the general contractor seeking the general contractor's assistance in obtaining the materials necessary for it to commence work on time. Nothing in the defendant's letter indicated that it had "definitely abandoned all hope" of performing without the assistance it sought.[273]

There is reason to believe that this traditional standard has been relaxed. In contracts for the sale of goods, governed by Article 2 of the U.C.C., a less demanding standard applies. Although § 2-610 does not define repudiation, its official comments indicate that a "[r]epudiation can result from action which reasonably indicates a rejection of the continuing obligation."[274]

The Second Restatement of Contracts also takes a liberal approach. It specifies only that the obligor's statement "must be sufficiently positive to be reasonably interpreted to mean that the party will not or cannot perform."[275] Still, statements of mere doubt about the ability to perform or requests for modifications to the terms of the contract, absent a refusal to perform, fall short of the standard necessary to be treated as a repudiation. However, equivocal threats and statements of doubt will usually give rise to a right to demand adequate assurance of future performance,[276] and can ripen into a repudiation if sufficient assurances are not provided.[277]

Courts have sometimes suggested that a good-faith denial of the existence of a contract is not a repudiation.[278] However, most courts treat denial of liability and

---

[270] RESTATEMENT (SECOND) OF CONTRACTS § 250 cmt. b (1981). *See* Drake v. Wickwire, 795 P.2d 195 (Alaska 1990) (attorney who advised client to declare a repudiation and terminate performance held liable for malpractice).

[271] 370 A.2d 119 (Md. Ct. Spec. App. 1977).

[272] 220 F.2d 101 (3d Cir. 1955).

[273] *Id.* at 104.

[274] U.C.C. § 2-610 cmt. 2 (2012).

[275] RESTATEMENT (SECOND) OF CONTRACTS § 250 cmt. b. (1981).

[276] *See infra* § 9.06 Prospective Inability to Perform.

[277] *See* RESTATEMENT (SECOND) OF CONTRACTS § 251 (1981).

[278] *See, e.g.*, N.Y. Life Ins. Co. v. Viglas, 297 U.S. 672, 676–78 (1936).

refusal to perform is a repudiation even if the denial is reasonable and in good faith.[279]

[3] Performance Impossible

Repudiation also occurs when one party takes voluntary action that appears to make its performance impossible.[280] If the seller of real estate resells the property to another buyer before the time for performance, the original buyer is entitled to treat the seller's action as a repudiation.[281] In this situation, even though there is a possibility that the seller will be able to buy the property back in time to perform its obligation to the original buyer, this possibility is so remote, and depends in any event on the willingness of the second buyer to reconvey the property, that treating the sale of the land to someone else justifies treating the seller's action as a repudiation.

On the other hand, the mere financial difficulty, or even outright insolvency, of a party is not usually a repudiation. Insolvency takes several forms, and may not impede performance. However, it may be grounds for demanding adequate assurances of performance.[282] Insolvency can occur either because the party's liabilities exceed its assets[283] or because it is unable to pay its debts when they fall due.[284] Of course, mere rumors of a party's insolvency or other financial difficulty may not even be enough to warrant a demand for adequate assurances of performance, much less a repudiation.

Circumstances involuntarily foisted on a party that are not a result of its voluntary action are not usually treated as a repudiation.[285] However, circumstances such as labor strike or some physical calamity, that threaten the party's ability to perform may justify a demand for adequate assurance of performance and may become a repudiation if the necessary assurances are not supplied.[286]

[B] Effect of Repudiation[287]

The doctrine of anticipatory repudiation has several important consequences. First, it permits the injured party to bring an immediate action to recover damages

---

[279] RESTATEMENT (SECOND) OF CONTRACTS § 250 cmt. d (1981); Chamberlin v. Puckett Constr., 921 P.2d 1237 (Mont. 1996); Thermo Electron Corp. v. Schiavone Constr. Co., 958 F.2d 1158 (1st Cir. 1992). *See also* ARTHUR LINTON CORBIN, 9 CORBIN ON CONTRACTS § 973 (Interim ed. 2002).

[280] RESTATEMENT (SECOND) OF CONTRACTS § 250(b) (1981).

[281] RESTATEMENT (SECOND) OF CONTRACTS § 250 illus. 5 (1981).

[282] RESTATEMENT (SECOND) OF CONTRACTS § 252(1) (1981).

[283] *See* 11 U.S.C. § 101(32) (2006). This is the "balance sheet" or "legal" test for insolvency.

[284] *See* 11 U.S.C. § 303(h)(1) (2006). This is the "equitable" definition of insolvency.

[285] RESTATEMENT (SECOND) OF CONTRACTS § 250 cmt. c (1981).

[286] *See infra* § 9.06 Prospective Inability to Perform.

[287] Celia R. Taylor, *Self-Help in Contract Law: An Exploration and Proposal*, 33 WAKE FOREST L. REV. 839 (1998).

for total breach.[288] Second, it permits the aggrieved party to treat the contract as terminated and discharges it from any obligations it has under the contract.[289] Likewise, repudiation excuses most conditions on which the repudiating party's duties depended.[290] However, as will be seen, the aggrieved party is entitled to wait for performance and urge the other party to retract its threatened breach.[291] Retraction is permitted any time before the repudiating party's performance is due,[292] provided that the aggrieved party has not taken action to cancel the contract or otherwise materially changed its position because of the repudiation.[293]

[C]   Repudiation in Contracts for Goods[294]

The law of anticipatory repudiation under Article 2 of the U.C.C., for domestic contracts involving the sale of goods, is substantially the same as under the common law applicable to other types of contracts. Repudiation permits the aggrieved party to immediately resort to a remedy,[295] but only if the repudiation is of "a performance not yet due the loss of which will *substantially impair the value of the contract to the other.*"[296] Thus, U.C.C. § 2-610 employs the same language found elsewhere in the code to refer to what the common law would characterize as a total material breach.[297] The Official Comments to § 2-610 indicate that the value of the contract is substantially impaired if the ultimate tender the aggrieved party must wait to receive will result in "material inconvenience or injustice."[298]

The Code does not otherwise attempt to define repudiation. The common law traditionally required a "definite and unequivocal" repudiation. The Official Comments to U.C.C. § 2-610 impose a similar standard: "anticipatory repudiation centers upon an overt communication of intention . . . which . . . demonstrates a clear determination not to continue with performance."[299] Elsewhere, however, the Official Comments indicate that "[r]epudiation can result from action which *reasonably indicates* a rejection of the continuing obligation."[300] Thus, as under the common law, repudiation of a contract for the sale of goods can consist of a

---

[288] Restatement (Second) of Contracts § 253(1) (1981); U.C.C. § 2-609(b) (2012).

[289] Restatement (Second) of Contracts § 253(2) (1981); U.C.C. § 2-609(c) (2012).

[290] Restatement (Second) of Contracts § 255 (1981).

[291] U.C.C. § 2-610(a) (2012).

[292] U.C.C. § 2-611(1) (2012).

[293] Restatement (Second) of Contracts § 256 (1981); U.C.C. § 2-611(1) (2012).

[294] Thomas H. Jackson, *"Anticipatory Repudiation" and the Temporal Element of Contract Law: An Economic Inquiry into Contract Damages in Cases of Prospective Nonperformance*, 31 Stan. L. Rev. 69 (1978); George I. Wallach, *Anticipatory Repudiation and the UCC*, 13 UCC L.J. 48 (1980).

[295] U.C.C. § 2-610(b) (2012).

[296] U.C.C. § 2-610 (2012) (emphasis supplied).

[297] *See* Truman L. Flatt & Sons Co. v. Schupf, 649 N.E.2d 990, 995 (Ill. App. Ct.), *appeal denied*, 657 N.E.2d 640 (Ill. 1995). *See generally* Keith A. Rowley, *A Brief History of Anticipatory Repudiation in American Contract Law*, 69 U. Cin. L. Rev. 565, 617–18 (2012).

[298] U.C.C. § 2-610 cmt. 3 (2012).

[299] U.C.C. § 2-610 cmt. 1 (2012).

[300] *Id.*

statement expressing a refusal to perform,[301] or conduct that makes the likelihood of performance seem remote.

Article 2 explicitly provides for a third type of anticipatory repudiation. A party's failure to provide adequate assurances when required to do so under U.C.C. § 2-609 is treated as a repudiation.[302] As further explained later in this chapter,[303] Article 2 requires a party to provide adequate assurances of future performance where the other party has reasonable grounds for insecurity and makes a proper demand for assurances that performance will be supplied.[304]

In international sale-of-goods transactions, under the CISG, a party may suspend its own performance when "it becomes apparent that the other party will not perform a substantial part of his obligations."[305] It becomes apparent that the other party will not perform if there is "a serious deficiency in his ability to perform or in his creditworthiness."[306] The other party's conduct in preparing to perform or in actual performance might also reveal that it will not perform a substantial portion of its duties.[307] Notice of suspension is required.[308] Further, the party suspending performance must resume performance if the other party supplies it with adequate assurance of its performance.[309]

In addition, Article 72 of the CISG provides that: "If prior to the date for performance of the contract it is clear that one of the parties will commit a fundamental breach of contract, the other party may declare the contract avoided.[310] Thus, the CISG distinguishes between circumstances that, on the one hand, make it "apparent" that the other party will not perform a "substantial part of his obligations" and those that, on the other hand, make it "clear" that the party will "commit a fundamental breach." The first permits suspension of the other party's reciprocal duties; the latter, like anticipatory repudiation, permits complete avoidance, or termination of the contract.

The most important issues under this language are when "it is clear" that a breach is forthcoming and whether the anticipated breach is "fundamental."[311] These issues are likely to be resolved consistently with decisions under the common law and the U.C.C. regarding whether the repudiation has been "definite and unequivocal" and whether the threatened breach was "material."

In other international transactions, rules on repudiation resemble those under

---

[301] *See, e.g.*, Am. Bronze Corp. v. Streamway Prods., 456 N.E.2d 1295 (Ohio Ct. App. 1982) (seller announced its refusal to perform).

[302] *See* U.C.C. § 2-609 (2012).

[303] *See infra* § 9.06 Prospective Inability to Perform.

[304] U.C.C. § 2-609 (2012).

[305] CISG Art. 71(1) (1980).

[306] CISG Art. 71(1)(a) (1980).

[307] CISG Art. 71(1)(b) (1980).

[308] CISG Art. 71(3)(1980).

[309] *Id.*

[310] CISG Art. 72(1) (1980).

[311] *See, e.g.*, Magellan Intern. Corp. v. Salzgitter Handel GmbH, 76 F. Supp. 2d 919 (N.D. Ill. 1999).

the CISG. Article 7.3.3 of the UNIDROIT Principles of International Commercial Contracts permit termination when it is "clear" that there will be a "fundamental non-performance."[312] A mere "reasonable belief" that a fundamental nonperformance will occur justifies suspension and a demand for adequate assurances of performance.[313] If the necessary assurances are not supplied, the aggrieved party then may terminate.[314] Article 8.105 of the Principles of European Contract Law provide a similar rule.[315]

§ 9.06 PROSPECTIVE INABILITY TO PERFORM[316]

As the foregoing discussion of the law of anticipatory repudiation suggests, it is sometimes difficult for a party to know whether the other party has repudiated. Moreover, the other party's expressions of doubt about its ability to perform, or circumstances that make the likelihood of performance uncertain, might not rise to the level of definiteness to constitute a repudiation. These uncertainties leave a party who is concerned about receiving the other performance with a difficult choice. It could suspend or terminate its own performance, and run the risk that its action will be premature and be held liable for breach. Or, it could continue to perform and run the risk that it is pouring money into a contract that has already run aground.[317] A cautious party who continues to perform may find itself unable to recover for the expenses it incurred, either because the other party is judgment-proof or because its conduct will be treated as a failure to properly mitigate damages.[318]

This was the situation confronting the seller in *Pittsburgh-Des Moines Steel Co. v. Brookhaven Manor Water Co.*[319] The seller of a million-gallon water tank grew anxious about the buyer's ability to pay and demanded that the funds necessary to pay the $175,000 price be placed in escrow while the water tank was being constructed, even though the terms of the contract did not require payment to be made until 30 days after work on the water tank had been completed. When the

---

[312] PICL Art. 7.3.3 (2004).

[313] PICL Art. 7.3.4 (2004).

[314] *Id.*

[315] PECL Art. 8.105 (2002).

[316] Richard Craswell, *Insecurity, Repudiation, and Cure*, 19 J. LEGAL STUD. 399 (1990); Gregory S. Crespi, *The Adequate Assurances Doctrine After U.C.C. § 2-609: A Test of the Efficiency of the Common Law*, 38 VILL. L. REV. 179, 182–83 (1993); Larry T. Garvin, *Adequate Assurance of Performance: of Risk, Duress, and Cognition*, 69 U. COLO. L. REV. 71 (1998); Robert A. Hillman, *Keeping the Deal Together After Material Breach — Common Law Mitigation Rules, the UCC, and the Restatement (Second) of Contracts*, 47 U. COLO. L. REV. 553 (1976); R.J. Robertson Jr., *The Right to Demand Adequate Assurance of Due Performance: Uniform Commercial Code Section 2-609 and Restatement (Second) of Contracts Section 251*, 38 DRAKE L. REV. 305 (1988–89); Arthur I. Rosett, *Contract Performance: Promises, Conditions, and the Obligation to Communicate*, 22 UCLA L. REV. 1083 (1975); James J. White, *Eight Cases and Section 251*, 67 CORNELL L. REV. 841 (1982).

[317] Larry T. Garvin, *Adequate Assurance of Performance: of Risk, Duress, and Cognition*, 69 U. COLO. L. REV. 71, 87–88 (1998).

[318] *See* Rockingham County v. Luten Bridge Co., 35 F.2d 301 (4th Cir. 1929).

[319] 532 F.2d 572 (7th Cir. 1976).

seller failed to receive the assurances it had sought, it suspended its own performance and was subsequently held to have itself repudiated the contract. The seller's repudiation gave the buyer the right to obtain a remedy for breach.[320]

The common law provided little recourse for a party with legitimate concerns about the other party's willingness or ability to perform.[321] Unless the other party repudiated,[322] a party worried about the likelihood of receiving a return performance had few good alternatives. And, expressions of its own reluctance to continue to perform might themselves rise to the level of a repudiation.

Article 2 of the Uniform Commercial Code helps parties avoid this dilemma by establishing the right of a party, who has good reason to doubt the ability of the other party to perform, to demand adequate assurances of performance and to treat the other party's failure to provide sufficient assurances as a repudiation.[323] The relevant portion of U.C.C. § 2-609 provides:

> When reasonable grounds for insecurity arise with respect to the performance of either party the other may in writing demand adequate assurance of due performance and until he receives such assurance may if commercially reasonable suspend any performance for which he has not already received the agreed return.[324]

Section 2-609(4) further provides:

> After receipt of a justified demand failure to provide within a reasonable time not exceeding thirty days such assurance of due performance as is adequate under the circumstances of the particular case is a repudiation of the contract.[325]

Encouraged by § 2-609 and the Second Restatement,[326] many states have incorporated the right to demand adequate assurance of future performance into the common law of contracts generally,[327] though some jurisdictions still rigidly limit its use to situations within the scope of Article 2.[328]

The Code's language raises two critical issues. The first is what constitutes

---

[320] *See also* Scott v. Crown, 765 P.2d 1043 (Colo. Ct. App. 1988) (seller demanded assurances of performance and refused to make delivery of grain under second contract where it became uncertain of buyer's ability to pay for goods that had already been delivered, for which payment was not yet due).

[321] *See, e.g.,* Mincks Agri Ctr., Inc. v. Bell Farms, Inc., 611 N.W.2d 270, 281–82 (Iowa 2000).

[322] *See supra* § 9.05[A] Manner of Repudiation.

[323] *See generally* R.J. Robertson Jr., *The Right to Demand Adequate Assurance of Due Performance: Uniform Commercial Code Section 2-609 and Restatement (Second) of Contracts Section 251,* 38 Drake L. Rev. 305 (1988–89); Larry T. Garvin, *Adequate Assurance of Performance: of Risk, Duress, and Cognition,* 69 U. Colo. L. Rev. 71 (1998).

[324] U.C.C. § 2-609(1) (2012).

[325] U.C.C. § 2-609(4) (2012).

[326] *See* Restatement (Second) of Contracts § 251 (1981).

[327] *E.g.,* Norcon Power Partners v. Niagara Mohawk Power Corp., 705 N.E.2d 656 (N.Y. 1998); Keith A. Rowley, *A Brief History of Anticipatory Repudiation in American Contract Law,* 69 U. Cin. L. Rev. 565, 625, n.336 (2001).

[328] U.C.C. § 2A-401 (2012).

"reasonable grounds for insecurity"; the second is what assurances are "adequate."

[A]   Reasonable Grounds for Insecurity

There must be reasonable grounds for insecurity to justify a party's demand for adequate assurances of performance. A party who makes a premature demand for adequate assurances of performance, in circumstances that are not reasonable grounds for insecurity, may find itself in breach if it unjustifiably suspends performance in response to the other party's failure to provide the demanded assurances.[329] On the other hand, it is clear that statements or conduct that would not be sufficiently definite and unequivocal to qualify as a repudiation create the type of reasonable grounds for insecurity that justify making a demand for adequate assurances of performance under § 2-609.

Most situations involving grounds for insecurity are likely to occur between merchants. When both parties are merchants, the code expressly provides that the "reasonableness of grounds for insecurity . . . shall be determined according to commercial standards."[330] It depends on the other party's words and actions, as well as any course of dealing or course of performance between the parties, as well as the nature of the contract involved and the industry in which the transaction occurs.[331]

The Official Comments to U.C.C. § 2-609 are instructive in determining what constitutes reasonable grounds for insecurity. A buyer who discovers that the seller is delivering defective items to its other customers has reasonable grounds for insecurity, unless the terms of the contract would have required the buyer to make payment before inspecting the goods.[332] Likewise, rumors of a buyer's declining financial situation from normally reliable sources are likely to give a seller reasonable grounds for insecurity.[333]

On the other hand, information that the buyer had not yet received a loan it might need to make subsequent payment for the goods was not reasonable grounds for insecurity in *Pittsburgh-Des Moines Steel Co. v. Brookhaven Manor Water Co.*,[334] where there were no other grounds to question the buyer's financial stability, and there was no reason to believe that the buyer's financial circumstances had changed since the contract was formed.[335] And, in *Cherwell-Ralli, Inc. v. Rytman Grain Co.*,[336] the buyer's demand for adequate assurances was not warranted simply because a delivery truck driver, not employed by the

---

[329] *See, e.g.*, Pittsburgh-Des Moines Steel Co. v. Brookhaven Manor Water Co., 532 F.2d 572 (7th Cir. 1976).

[330] U.C.C. § 2-609(2) (2012).

[331] Hornell Brewing Co. v. Spry, 664 N.Y.S.2d 698 (N.Y. Sup. Ct. 1997).

[332] U.C.C. § 2-609 cmt. 3 (2012). *See, e.g.*, Creusot-Loire Int'l, Inc. v. Coppus Eng'g Corp., 585 F. Supp. 45 (S.D.N.Y. 1983).

[333] U.C.C. § 2-609 cmt. 4 (2012). *See, e.g.*, Scott v. Crown, 765 P.2d 1043 (Colo. Ct. App. 1988); Turntables, Inc. v. Gestetner, 382 N.Y.S.2d 798 (N.Y. App. Div. 1976).

[334] 532 F.2d 572 (7th Cir. 1976).

[335] *Compare* Hornell Brewing Co. v. Spry, 664 N.Y.S.2d 698 (N.Y. Sup. Ct. 1997).

[336] 433 A.2d 984 (Conn. 1980).

seller, suggested that further shipments would not be made.[337]

Thus, under § 2-609, a party might find itself confronting a dilemma similar to the one imposed by § 2-610 and the doctrine of anticipatory repudiation.[338] The party must evaluate the circumstances that give rise to its uncertainty to determine whether it has sufficient grounds to demand adequate assurances of performance. If it misjudges the gravity of the situation and suspends performance when the level of assurances it demands are not forthcoming, its suspension of performance will be a repudiation.

[B]   Demand for Adequate Assurance of Performance

A party with reasonable grounds for insecurity may "in writing demand adequate assurance of due performance."[339] Despite the Code's clear language, courts have not always insisted that the demand be given in writing, at least where the demand for assurances was sufficiently clear and unequivocal.[340]

Further, the party seeking relief must unequivocally demand adequate assurances of performance. Mere requests for information[341] or for a meeting[342] are not sufficient. Instead, the aggrieved party must make its demand in a clear and direct manner, indicating that it is either suspending performance until assurances are provided or that it will treat the other party's failure to provide the necessary assurances as a repudiation.

After an appropriate demand for assurances is made, the next concern is whether the assurances supplied by the other party are adequate. What constitutes adequate assurances varies, depending on the circumstances that give rise to the insecurity about performance.[343] The aggrieved party must be cautious in the level of assurances that it insists upon. If it requires more assurances than § 2-609 requires, continued suspension of its own performance will constitute a breach.

Moreover, courts have sometimes been skeptical of demands for assurances that seek more than the contract requires, even though the Official Comments to U.C.C. § 2-609 suggest that such a demand is permissible.[344] In *Pittsburgh-Des*

---

[337] *See also In re* Coast Trading Co., Inc., 26 B.R. 737 (Bankr. D. Or. 1982) (inability of seller to obtain items for delivery to buyer from its usual supplier was not reasonable grounds for insecurity where seller was known to have access to other suppliers who could provide the goods necessary for fulfillment of the contract).

[338] Deanna Wise, Comment, *Proposed Amendments to Article 2 of the Uniform Commercial Code: The Tangled Web of Anticipatory Repudiation and the Right to Demand Assurances*, 40 U. KAN. L. REV. 287, 299 (1991).

[339] U.C.C. § 2-609(1) (2012).

[340] *E.g.*, Atwood-Kellogg, Inc. v. Nickeson Farms, 602 N.W.2d 749 (S.D. 1999); AMF, Inc. v. McDonald's Corp., 536 F.2d 1167 (7th Cir. 1976). *But see* Bodine v. Sewer, Inc. v. E. Ill. Precast, Inc., 493 N.E.2d 705 (Ill. App. Ct. 1987) (writing required).

[341] SPS Indus., Inc. v. Atl. Steel Co., 366 S.E.2d 410 (Ga. Ct. App. 1988).

[342] Penberthy Electromelt Int'l, Inc. v. U.S. Gypsum Co., 686 P.2d 1138 (Wash. Ct. App. 1984).

[343] U.C.C. § 2-609 cmt. 4 (2012).

[344] U.C.C. § 2-609 cmt. 4 (2012) ("security . . . or a satisfactory explanation").

Moines Steel Co. v. Brookhaven Manor Water Co.,[345] the court ruled that the aggrieved party was not permitted to demand that the price be placed in escrow[346] or that the buyer's principal shareholder provide a personal guarantee of payment, neither of which were required in the contract. However, in *Creusot-Loire International, Inc. v. Coppus Engineering Corp.*,[347] the court held that it was not unreasonable for the plaintiff to demand a letter of credit as an adequate assurance of performance.[348]

In no event is the aggrieved party to demand more than would be necessary to adequately assure performance. Thus, the aggrieved party should not be able to exploit even reasonable grounds for insecurity to obtain concessions beyond those required to provide adequate assurance that the terms of the contract will be performed when due.

In some cases, verbal assurances that past difficulties will not recur may be sufficient.[349] However, a history of failing to live up to past assurances that past problems will be corrected may warrant a demand for more concrete assurances, in the form of a bond, funds placed in escrow, or some other action that ensures performance.[350] Likewise, assurances that future deliveries will not suffer from defects discovered in a past installment may not be sufficient unless the seller takes action to cure defects in an earlier delivery.[351]

When properly demanded, any necessary assurances must be supplied within a reasonable time, which in contracts for the sale of goods may not exceed 30 days.[352] Unlike § 2-609, the Restatement imposes no similar 30-day limit. What is a reasonable time for providing assurances within the 30-day maximum limit depends on the circumstances warranting the demand for adequate assurances and the circumstances facing the aggrieved party if assurances of future performance are not provided.

[C]   Consequences of Failure to Provide Adequate Assurances

The consequences of a party's failure to provide timely and adequate assurances of future performance are clear. The aggrieved party may treat an inadequate response as a repudiation.[353]

The aggrieved party's rights following a repudiation are specified by U.C.C. § 2-

---

[345] 532 F.2d 572 (7th Cir. 1976).

[346] *But see* Kunian v. Dev. Corp. of Am., 334 A.2d 427 (Conn. 1973).

[347] 585 F. Supp. 45 (S.D.N.Y. 1983).

[348] *See also* Scott v. Crown, 765 P.2d 1043 (Colo. Ct. App. 1988).

[349] U.C.C. § 2-609 cmt. 4 (2012).

[350] *E.g.*, LNS Inv. Co., Inc. v. Phillips 66 Co., 731 F. Supp. 1484 (D. Kan. 1990).

[351] U.C.C. § 2-609 cmt. 4 (2012).

[352] U.C.C. § 2-609(4) (2012).

[353] U.C.C. § 2-609(4) (2012); Restatement (Second) of Contracts § 251(b) & cmt. e (1981).

610.[354] Thus, the right to suspend performance ripens into the right to terminate the contract and to resort to the usual remedies for breach.[355] Although the aggrieved party might urge retraction of the repudiation, presumably by continuing to seek adequate assurances of performance, it has no obligation to do so. And, although it might exercise its right to "await performance" for a commercially reasonable time,[356] this seems both unlikely and imprudent following a demand for adequate assurances of future performance.

[D]   Prospective Inability to Perform in International Transactions[357]

In international sale-of-goods transactions, CISG Article 71 permits a party to "suspend the performance of his obligations" if it "becomes apparent that the other party will not perform a substantial part of his obligations"[358] due to either (1) a "serious deficiency in his ability to perform," or (2) "his conduct in preparing to perform or in performing."[359] Suspension is seemingly permitted even if the anticipated breach would not be a fundamental breach of the type that would permit termination. However, if the CISG is read together with the UNIDROIT Principles, it may be necessary for the threatened breach to be "fundamental."

The CISG requires a party who suspends performance to give immediate "notice of suspension to the other party."[360] If, following suspension, the other party provides "adequate assurance of performance," suspension must be abated, and performance must continue.[361]

The UNIDROIT Principles of International Commercial Contracts are similar. They permit a party who "reasonably believes that there will be a fundamental nonperformance" to "demand adequate assurance of due performance" and to "withhold its own performance" while awaiting the necessary assurances.[362] If adequate assurances are not provided "within a reasonable time," the party with the right to demand the assurances can "terminate the contract."[363]

The Principles of European Contract Law are virtually identical, except that they permit continued suspension only "so long as such reasonable belief [that there will be a fundamental breach] continues."[364] This recognizes that the aggrieved party may obtain information, other than assurances from the other

---

[354] *See supra* § 9.05 Anticipatory Repudiation.

[355] U.C.C. § 2-609(4) (2012); RESTATEMENT (SECOND) OF CONTRACTS § 251(b) (1981).

[356] U.C.C. § 2-610(a) (2012).

[357] John P. McMahon, *Coping with Nonconforming Tender and Insecurity Under UCC Article 2 and the CISG*, 39 U.C.C. L.J. 533 (2007).

[358] CISG Art 71(1) (1980).

[359] CISG Art. 71(1)(a), (b) (1980).

[360] CISG Art. 71(3) (1980).

[361] CISG Art. 71(3) (1980).

[362] PICC Art. 7.3.4 (2004).

[363] PICC Art. 7.3.4 (2004).

[364] PECL Art. 8.105(1) (2002).

party, that would lead it to believe that the other party will perform. If, after a reasonable time, the necessary assurances are not provided, notice of termination must be given "without delay."[365]

---

[365] PECL Art. 8.015(2) (2002).

Chapter 10

DEFENSES

§ 10.01   TYPES OF CONTRACT DEFENSES[1]

In an action for breach of contract, the plaintiff bears the burden of alleging and proving that the contract was made, that the defendant is in breach, and that the plaintiff was harmed as a result of the breach. The defendant can resist the plaintiff's claim in one of three ways.

First, the defendant might simply deny one or more of the plaintiff's allegations, thereby seeking to prove that the allegations in the plaintiff's complaint are false, such as by denying that an agreement was ever reached. In some cases, the plaintiff's ability to prove its claim depends on the credibility of the witnesses to the events that led to the dispute.[2] The process of proof might occur very quickly if the evidence is clear and overwhelming, but might take many months of discovery followed by a lengthy trial.

Second, the defendant might "demur" to the plaintiff's complaint, thereby contending that the law does not provide relief, even if the plaintiff proves the facts it alleges. In most states this often takes the form of a motion to dismiss the plaintiff's complaint for failure to state a claim upon which relief can be granted.[3] This strategy was tried unsuccessfully in the well-known "moral consideration" case of *Webb v. McGowin,*[4] where the defendant's demurrer was initially sustained but later overruled.[5] If successful, this strategy is very efficient, because it permits resolution of the dispute without a lengthy trial. However, it will only work if the facts the plaintiff alleges provide no legal basis for relief.

A third strategy is to prove additional facts which establish an affirmative defense to the plaintiff's claim. Thus, even if the plaintiff shows that there was a contract between the parties, and that the defendant failed to perform, the defendant's additional facts deprive the plaintiff's claim of any legal effect. This chapter, and the chapter that follows, explore the doctrines that provide a basis for raising this type of defense.

§ 10.02   CONTRACTS CONTRARY TO PUBLIC POLICY; ILLEGAL CONTRACTS[6]

There are limits to our freedom of contract, just as there are limits to our right to free speech. The public policy in favor of freedom of contract is sometimes

---

[1] Miriam Cherry, *A Tyrannosaurus-Rex Aptly Named "Sue": Using a Disputed Dinosaur to Teach Contract Defenses*, 81 N.D. L. Rev. 295 (2005).

[2] *E.g.*, Shieldkret v. Park Place Entm't Corp., 2002 U.S. Dist. LEXIS 1032 (E.D.N.Y. Jan. 23, 2002).

[3] F.R.C.P. 12(b)(6).

[4] 168 So. 196 (Ala. Ct. App. 1935).

[5] *See supra* § 2.07 Past Consideration and Moral Obligation: The Material Benefit Rule.

[6] Harlan M. Blake, *Employee Agreements Not to Compete*, 73 Harv. L. Rev. 625 (1960); Judith Areen, *Baby M Reconsidered*, 76 Geo. L.J. 1741 (1988); Walter Gellhorn, *Contracts and Public Policy*, 35 Colum. L. Rev. 679 (1935); Juliet P. Kostritsky, *Illegal Contracts and Efficient Deterrence: A Study in Modern Contract Theory*, 74 Iowa L. Rev. 115, 116–17 (1988); Gerald T. McLaughlin, *Letters of Credit and Illegal Contracts: The Limits of the Independence Principle*, 48 Ohio St. L.J. 1197 (1989); Richard Posner, *The Ethics and Economics of Enforcing Contracts of Surrogate Motherhood*, 5 J. Contemp.

overshadowed by competing policies dealing with the subject matter of the contract.[7] Courts are naturally reluctant to become involved in enforcing agreements that detract from the public welfare, and would prefer to deter bad behavior.[8] Thus, agreements to commit a crime are illegal and unenforceable, as are agreements to commit a tort.[9] Contracts involving sensitive family matters are likewise sometimes subject to careful public scrutiny that may result in the agreement being unenforceable.

In analyzing whether a contract or a term in a contract violates public policy, it is necessary to identify the public policy involved. It must be something more specific than to "do good and avoid evil."[10] The public policy might be facilitating competition and free trade, preserving family relationships, or ensuring public safety. Without at least this type of identification of the public policy concern, too many contracts would be susceptible to the charge that they violate public policy.[11]

In some cases, the legislature will have declared the contract illegal or unenforceable. If so, the court need not engage in any difficult analysis. As one court explained: "a party to an illegal contract cannot ask a court of law to help him carry out his illegal object . . . . For no court should be required to serve as paymaster of the wages of crime, or referee between thieves."[12]

However, where there is no specific legal proscription, courts must weigh the public policy involved against the competing public interest in the enforcement of private agreements.[13] In considering the public interest in enforcement of the agreement courts must take into account the parties' expectations, the extent of any forfeiture that would result if enforcement is denied, and whether there is any special public interest in enforcement of the contract or the term in question.[14] The court must weigh these factors against the relative strength of the public policy that the contract offends, the likelihood that refusing to enforce the agreement will advance the public policy, the nature of the misconduct involved in the contract, the extent to which it was deliberate misconduct, and the nexus between the misconduct and the offensive contractual term.[15] Of course, how these factors weigh against one another varies considerably, depending on the contract and the public policy involved in the calculus.

HEALTH L. & POLY. 21 (1989); George A. Strong, *The Enforceability of Illegal Contracts*, 12 HASTINGS L.J. 347 (1961); John W. Wade, *Benefits Obtained Under Illegal Transactions — Reasons for and Against Allowing Restitution*, 25 TEX. L. REV. 31 (1946).

[7] *See generally* Sternaman v. Metro. Life Ins. Co., 62 N.E. 763, 764 (N.Y. 1902).

[8] RESTATEMENT (SECOND) OF CONTRACTS, Introductory Note to Chapter 8, Unenforceability on Grounds of Public Policy §§ 178–190 (1981).

[9] RESTATEMENT (SECOND) OF CONTRACTS § 291(1981).

[10] 1 Peter 3:10–12

[11] *See* Wagenseller v. Scottsdale Mem. Hosp., 710 P.2d 1025, 1033 (Ariz. 1985) (expressions of public policy not contained solely in statutory and constitutional law).

[12] Stone v. Freeman, 82 N.E.2d 571, 572–73 (N.Y. 1948).

[13] RESTATEMENT (SECOND) OF CONTRACTS § 178(1) (1981).

[14] RESTATEMENT (SECOND) OF CONTRACTS § 178(2) (1981).

[15] RESTATEMENT (SECOND) OF CONTRACTS § 178(3) (1981).

[A] Contracts That Violate Public Policy[16]

[1] Contracts for an Illegal Purpose

If the ultimate purpose of an agreement is to commit a crime, the agreement is illegal and void.[17] For example, an agreement by an athlete to shave points in a game, in return for a promised payment, is illegal in most states, and would be unenforceable. An agreement to tortiously injure someone is similarly illegal and unenforceable.[18] However, most questions about the legality of a contract are not so obvious.

Even where the contract itself is not illegal, if the contract was entered into in order to circumvent a legal proscription, the contract is void. For example, in *Trees v. Kersey*,[19] a joint venture between two builders was void where it had been entered into in an effort to facilitate the unlicensed builder's ability to bid on public works in violation of a state licensing law.

Likewise, where the subject matter of the contract indicates that it is in furtherance of some illegal purpose, it is void. For example, in *Bovard v. American Horse Enterprises, Inc.*, the court held that a contract for the manufacture of drug paraphernalia was void, even though manufacture and sale of these materials was not a crime.[20] The court acknowledged that determining whether a particular contract violates public policy "necessarily involves a degree of subjectivity." It recognized that the uncertainty involved in such a determination should lead a court to allow the "parties the widest latitude" and that before concluding that a contract is against public policy that the court should "carefully inquire into the nature of the conduct, the nature of the public harm which may be involved, and the moral quality of the conduct of the parties in light of the prevailing standards of the community. . . ."[21] The court found that the public policy against manufacturing drug paraphernalia was strongly implied in the statutory prohibition against use of illicit drugs. *Bovard* thus illustrates one of the ways that a court might detect a public policy that makes a contract unenforceable.

[2] Contracts in Restraint of Trade[22]

Both state and federal laws prohibit contracts that restrain trade. For example, price-fixing agreements between competitors are not only void,[23] they are felonies.[24] Agreements between competitors not to compete within each other's

---

[16] Walter Gellhorn, *Contracts and Public Policy*, 35 Colum. L. Rev. 679 (1935); Juliet P. Kostrisky, *Illegal Contracts and Efficient Deterrence: A Study in Modern Contract Theory*, 74 Iowa L. Rev. 115 (1988); George A. Strong, *The Enforceability of Illegal Contracts*, 12 Hastings L.J. 347, 347 (1961).

[17] Nature's 10 Jewelers v. Gunderson, 648 N.W.2d 804 (S.D. 2002).

[18] Restatement (Second) of Contracts § 192 (1981).

[19] 56 P.3d 765 (Idaho 2002).

[20] 201 Cal. App. 3d 832 (1988).

[21] *Id.* at 839–841 (quoting Moran v. Harris, 131 Cal. App. 3d (1982).

[22] Harlan M. Blake, *Employee Agreements Not to Compete*, 73 Harv. L. Rev. 625 (1960); Griffin Toronjo Pivateau, *Putting the Blue Pencil Down: An Argument for Specificity in Noncompete*

geographic territories similarly violate the law and are unenforceable.[25] Collusive agreements between bidders at an auction are also void.[26] In all of these agreements, the main purpose of the contract is to limit competition.[27] It is no surprise that the law of contracts, with its principal goal of promoting the freedom of contract, refuses to enforce agreements that are designed to restrict freedom of contract.

However, agreements limiting competition are legal if they are connected ("ancillary") to a contract with an otherwise legitimate purpose. They are enforceable if they impose reasonable restraints that are narrowly tailored to serve the legitimate purpose of the underlying agreement.

Covenants not to compete are common in contracts for the sale of a business and in some employment contracts. For example, the buyer of a business might insist that the seller agree not to enter into the same trade or business in the same geographic region as the buyer, for a long enough period for the buyer to establish itself in the industry. Likewise, an employer may insist on an employee's agreement not to compete with the employer for a reasonable time after the employee leaves the employer's business. Covenants not to compete are also frequently used in franchise contracts.[28]

Restraint of trade is not the primary object of any of these transactions. In the sale of a business the primary purpose of the transaction is the completion of the sale. The covenant not to compete merely facilitates this purpose.[29] Likewise, in an employment contract, the covenant helps ensure that the employee does not take unfair advantage of training or other benefits he has obtained from his employer,[30] or misappropriate his employer's trade secrets. In these situations, the covenant not to compete is enforceable, as long as it is reasonable. Its reasonableness depends on whether its geographic scope and duration are narrowly tailored to fulfill the main purpose of the underlying contract.[31]

Agreements, 86 NEB. L. REV. 672 (2008); Kenneth R. Swift, *Void Agreements, Knocked-Out Terms, and Blue Pencils: Judicial and Legislative Handling of Unreasonable Terms in Noncompete Agreements*, 24 HOFSTRA LAB. & EMP. L.J. 223 (2008); Robert M. Wilcox, *Enforcing Lawyer Non-Competition Agreements While Maintaining the Profession: The Role of Conflict of Interest Principles*, 84 MINN. L. REV. 915 (2000).

[23] RESTATEMENT (SECOND) OF CONTRACTS § 186 illus. 1 (1981).

[24] Sherman Act, 15 U.S.C. §§ 1–7 (2006); Ariz. v. Maricopa County Med. Soc'y, 457 U.S. 332 (1982).

[25] RESTATEMENT (SECOND) OF CONTRACTS § 187 illus. 2 (1981). *See generally* Robert Bork, *The Rule of Reason and the Per Se Concept: Price Fixing and Market Division*, 74 YALE L.J. 775 (1965).

[26] RESTATEMENT (SECOND) OF CONTRACTS § 187 illus. 3 (1981).

[27] RESTATEMENT (SECOND) OF CONTRACTS § 187 (1981).

[28] *See* Robert W. Emerson, *Franchising Covenants Against Competition*, 80 IOWA L. REV. 1049 (1995).

[29] *E.g.*, Fine Foods, Inc. v. Dahlin, 523 A.2d 1228 (Vt. 1987); Karpinski v. Ingrasci, 268 N.E.2d 751 (N.Y. 1971).

[30] *See* Donahue v. Permacel Tape Corp., 127 N.E.2d 235, 240 (Ind. 1955); Data Mgmt., Inc. v. Greene, 757 P.2d 62 (Alaska 1988); Morgan's Home Equip. v. Martucci, 136 A.2d 838 (Pa. 1957).

[31] Hopper v. All Pet Animal Clinic, 861 P.2d 531, 543–46 (Wyo. 1993). *See* RESTATEMENT (SECOND) OF CONTRACTS § 188 (1981).

For example, in *Fine Foods, Inc. v. Dahlin*,[32] the defendant sold his Brattleboro, Vermont, restaurant and agreed, as a part of the sale, not to engage in the restaurant business for five years anywhere within 25 miles of Brattleboro. A few months later he began working as the maitre d' at another restaurant in Brattleboro, in violation of the terms of the covenant not to compete. The court enforced the agreement, despite its concern for "the right of individuals to freely engage in desirable commercial activity." The court found that neither the duration nor the geographic scope of the covenant imposed an undue restriction on the defendant, who was free to work in the restaurant business outside the 25-mile radius of Brattleboro at any time.

In *Valley Medical Specialists v. Farber*,[33] on the other hand, a similar covenant was used in an employment contract between a medical practice and a physician. It prevented the doctor from practicing medicine anywhere else within 5 miles of any of his employer's locations three years after he left. The court held that the restriction was unreasonable. It explained that "[t]he restriction cannot be greater than necessary to protect [the employer's] legitimate interests." The legitimate purpose of the restriction was to "give the employer a reasonable amount of time to overcome the former employee's loss, usually by hiring a replacement and giving that replacement time to establish a working relationship [with his or her patients]." But, the restriction was too broad because patients of the type Farber had been seeing in his pulmonology practice typically required contact with the treating physician once every six months, and thus a 6-month period would give patients the opportunity to decide whether to continue seeing Farber's replacement. The court was also concerned that the restriction did not permit an exception for emergency medical treatment and was not limited to pulmonology. The court's decision was also based, in part, on "the sensitive and personal nature of the doctor-patient relationship," which might be harmed if Farber's patients were prevented from seeing a physician with whom they had established a relationship.[34] Thus, the public's interest in the ready availability of the services involved, was also important.

If a restrictive covenant is unreasonable, either because it is too broad in geographic scope or because its duration is too long, the court might simply eliminate the covenant from the contract.[35] Alternatively, it might use the "blue-pencil" rule[36] to strike the offensive portion of the clause.[37] Thus, if an overly broad clause prevents competition in "Columbus or elsewhere in Franklin County," the

---

[32] 523 A.2d 1228 (Vt. 1986).

[33] 982 P.2d 1277 (Ariz. 1999).

[34] *See* Seena L. Kafker, *Golden Handcuffs: Enforceability of Noncompetition Clauses in Professional Partnership Agreements of Accountants, Physicians, and Attorneys*, 31 Am. Bus. L.J. 31 (1993).

[35] *E.g.*, Brockley v. Lozier Corp., 488 N.W.2d 556, 563–64 (Neb. 1992); Rollins Protective Serv. Co. v. Palermo, 287 S.E.2d 546, 549 (Ga. 1982).

[36] Because copying machines would not generally reproduce the color blue, proofreaders often use a blue pencil to strike out mistakes. Students who qualify for their school's law review will quickly learn about this tradition in a very practical way.

[37] *See* RESTATEMENT OF CONTRACTS § 518 (1932). *E.g.*, Licocci v. Cardinal Assoc., Inc., 432 N.E.2d 446, 452 (Ind. Ct. App. 1982), *vacated on other grounds*, 445 N.E.2d 556 (Ind. 1983).

court might simply strike the language "or elsewhere in Franklin County" to limit the geographic scope of the clause to extend only to the Columbus city limits. When the phrasing of the clause does not lend itself to this type of revision, the court might redraft the clause entirely to make it reasonable.[38]

Eliminating the offensive clause entirely discourages parties from attempting to draft overly broad restrictions, but at the expense of completely disrupting the transaction. Revising the provision preserves the parties' reasonable expectations, but might encourage parties to draft intentionally broad rules knowing that most of them will be voluntarily complied with and that the worst that will happen if the covenant is challenged is that it will be adjusted by the court.

In situations involving professional services, such as those provided by doctors or lawyers, covenants not to compete are sometimes subjected to greater restrictions. For example, the Model Rules of Professional Conduct prohibit lawyers from entering into an agreement not to compete with one another, even in an employment contract.[39] Accordingly, most courts have refused to enforce restrictive covenants included in agreements between lawyers.[40] Although reasonable ancillary covenants not to compete are generally held enforceable against doctors,[41] courts sometimes refuse to enforce them because of their effect on members of the public whose access to medical services might be limited.[42]

[3]   Violations of Public Licensing Laws

State and local governments have a wide variety of licensing statutes. Lawyers, doctors, and other professionals are required to hold a valid professional license. Construction contractors are also usually required to hold a state or local license. Likewise, restaurants are nearly always required to hold valid food service and liquor licenses. And, nearly every person in business is required to hold a local business license. If a person lacks the necessary license, his agreements may be unenforceable.

The enforceability of the contract depends on the purpose of the licensing law. If the licensing requirement's purpose is to protect the public, a contract made in violation of the licensing law is illegal and unenforceable. Thus, lawyers and doctors practicing without a valid license are unable to collect their fees.[43]

---

[38] RESTATEMENT (SECOND) OF CONTRACTS § 182, Reporter's Note (1981).

[39] MODEL R. PROF. CONDUCT 5.6 (1983). *See* Dwyer v. Jung, 336 A.2d 498 (N.J. Super), *aff'd*, 348 A.2d 208 (N.J. App. Div. 1975). *But see* Miller v. Foulston, Siefkin, Powers & Eberhardt, 790 P.2d 404 (Kan. 1990) (regarding retirement).

[40] *E.g.*, Cohen v. Lord, Day & Lord, 550 N.E.2d 410 (N.Y. 1989). *But see* Howard v. Babcock, 863 P.2d 150 (Cal. 1990).

[41] *E.g.*, Karlin v. Weinberg, 390 A.2d 1161 (N.J. 1978).

[42] *See* Valley Medical Specialists v. Farber, 982 P.2d 1277 (Ariz. 1999); Nalle Clinic Co. v. Parker, 399 S.E.2d 363 (N.C. Ct. App. 1991). *See generally* Michael G. Getty, *Enforceability of Noncompetition Covenants in Physician Employment Contracts*, 7 J. Legal Med. 235 (1986); Ferdinand S. Tinio, Annotation, *Validity and Construction of Contractual Restrictions on Right of Medical Practitioner to Practice, Incident to Employment Agreement*, 62 A.L.R.3d 1014 (1975).

[43] *E.g.*, Lozoff v. Shore Heights, Ltd., 362 N.E.2d 1047 (Ill. 1977) (unlicensed lawyer unable to collect fees from client); Tovar v. Paxton Community Memorial Hosp., 330 N.E.2d 247 (Ill. App. Ct. 1975)

Unlicensed builders are treated the same way.[44] On the other hand, if the purpose of the licensing law is merely to generate revenue for the state or the city, the lack of a license will not impair the contract's enforcement.[45]

Even where the purpose of the licensing law is regulatory, courts frequently permit enforcement of the contract where there has been substantial compliance with the licensing requirement and the underlying purposes of the licensing law have been fulfilled. In *McNairy v. Sugar Creek Resort, Inc.*,[46] a grading contractor who began work for a golf course while his application for a license was pending was permitted to recover for work he had done before the license was issued. The contractor was qualified to obtain a license, and the license was granted before the work was completed. If the contractor had not substantially complied, the contract would have been unenforceable.[47]

Furthermore, courts sometimes award restitution for the value of the benefit conferred by the unlicensed party to prevent a complete forfeiture.[48] Other courts deny recovery in restitution on the grounds that this would frustrate the purpose of the licensing requirement.[49] These conflicting results often depend as much on the precise language of the state licensing statute as on the court's view of the competing policies involved.[50]

[4]   Contracts Affecting Family Relationships[51]

Agreements dealing with family and other close personal relationships are sometimes unenforceable. Adoption and surrogacy agreements,[52] prenuptial[53] and postnuptial[54] agreements, and cohabitation agreements between unmarried individuals are all examples of agreements that may violate public policies.[55] Decisions about these types of relationships frequently provide good examples of

---

(refusing to enforce unlicensed doctor's employment contract).

[44] *E.g.*, Cevern v. Ferbish, 666 A.2d 17 (D.C. 1995).

[45] *See* RESTATEMENT (SECOND) OF CONTRACTS § 181 illus. 1 (1981). *E.g.*, S. Ctr. Plumbing & Heating Supply Co. v. Charles, 234 N.E.2d 358 (Ill. App. Ct. 1967). *See generally* Juliet P. Kostritsky, *Illegal Contracts and Efficient Deterrence: A Study in Modern Contract Theory*, 74 IOWA L. REV. 115 (1988).

[46] 576 So. 2d 185 (Ala. 1991).

[47] *E.g.*, Gross v. Bayshore Land Co., 710 P.2d 1007 (Alaska 1985).

[48] Gene Taylor & Sons Plumbing Co. v. Corondolet Realty Trust, 611 S.W.2d 572 (Tenn. 1981); Trees v. Kersey, 56 P.3d 765 (Idaho 2002).

[49] *E.g.*, Bryan Builders Supply v. Midyette, 162 S.E.2d 507 (N.C. 1969); Millington v. Rapoport, 469 N.Y.S.2d 787 (N.Y. App. Div. 1983).

[50] *E.g.*, Gene Taylor & Sons Plumbing Co. v. Corondolet Realty Trust, 611 S.W.2d 572 (Tenn. 1981).

[51] Judith T. Younger, *Perspectives on Antenuptial Agreements*, 40 RUTGERS L. REV. 1059 (1988); J. Thomas Oldham & David S. Candill, *A Reconnaissance of Public Policy Restrictions upon Enforcement of Contracts Between Cohabitants*, 18 FAM. L.Q. 91 (1981); Harry Prince, *Public Policy Limitations on Cohabitation Agreements: Unruly Horse or Circus Pony?*, 70 MINN. L. REV. 163 (1985).

[52] *E.g.*, R.R. v. M.H., 689 N.E.2d 790 (Mass. 1998).

[53] *E.g.*, *In re* Marriage of DiFatta, 714 N.E.2d 1092 (Ill. App. Ct. 1999); *In re* Marriage of Spiegal, 553 N.W.3d 309 (Iowa 1997).

[54] *See, e.g.*, Borelli v. Brusseau, 12 Cal. App. 4th 647 (1993).

[55] *E.g.*, Wilcox v. Trautz, 693 N.E.2d 141 (Mass. 1998); Marvin v. Marvin, 557 P.2d 106 (Cal. 1976).

the conflict between the general policy promoting freedom of contract and more specific policies promoting the family as the most basic organizational unit of society.

Surrogacy contracts provide a good example. These agreements provide for a woman — the surrogate — to serve as the gestator of an unborn child, and to relinquish all parental rights to the child, upon its birth. She performs these services in exchange for a cash payment and medical care while she is pregnant. The father's spouse subsequently adopts the child. While an increasing number of states have adopted statutes specifically regulating such agreements, in other states they are governed only by whatever regulations the state has regarding more traditional adoptions.

The widely reported decision in the *Baby M*[56] case supplies a good example of how courts approach these transactions. After the birth of the child, the surrogate challenged the enforceability of the surrogacy contract, claiming that it violated both the state's adoption laws and the public policy that custody decisions should be based on the "best interests of the child." She also claimed that the contract exploited the surrogate, was inconsistent with basic principles of human dignity, and that its enforcement would undermine traditional family values.[57]

The New Jersey Supreme Court held that the surrogacy contract violated both the New Jersey adoption statute and the public policy of the state.[58] The court emphasized that the statutory prohibition against paying for the adoption of a child reflected a "strong" public policy and that "baby selling" involved an inherent potential for the exploitation of the surrogate at the potential expense of the child.[59] The court also found that the surrogate's promise to relinquish her parental rights was not a sufficient reason for the court to terminate her rights against her wishes. In addition to finding that the contract contradicted state statutes governing adoption and termination of parental rights, it found that the contract violated the basic public policy that the best interests of the child should determine questions of custody, regardless of any agreement the child's parents may have made. Likewise, the court said, the contract was inconsistent with the public policy that presumed that children should normally be brought up by their natural parents.[60] The court also questioned the trial court's determination that the surrogate mother had made a voluntary and fully informed decision when she entered into the contract.[61]

Since *Baby M*, many states have enacted legislation directly addressing

---

[56] In the Matter of Baby "M," A Pseudonym for an Actual Person, 525 A.2d 1128 (N.J. Super. Ct. Ch. Div. 1987), *reversed by*, 537 A.2d 1227 (N.J. 1988).

[57] *Id.* at 1157.

[58] In the Matter of Baby "M," A Pseudonym for an Actual Person, 537 A.2d 1227 (N.J. 1988).

[59] *Id. at* 1242.

[60] *Id.* at 1247.

[61] *Id.* at 1248. *See* Judith Areen, Baby M *Reconsidered*, 76 Geo. L.J. 1741 (1988); Richard A. Posner, *The Ethics and Economics of Enforcing Contracts of Surrogate Motherhood*, 5 J. Contemp. Health L. & Pol'y 21 (1989).

surrogacy contracts.[62] Courts addressing these agreements usually recognize the conflict between legislative and more general public policies regarding family life on the one hand, and the more general policy promoting the enforceability of private agreements on the other hand. They frequently express concern that the surrogate has not been adequately informed about the risks involved in the contract.

Where questions of family relationships are involved, concerns that the decision to enter into the contract was fully informed and that the terms are fair are more pronounced than in situations involving more conventional commercial transactions.[63] For example, prenuptial agreements are usually valid only if the terms of the agreement are fair and reasonable and if the agreement was entered into following full disclosure between the parties of their assets and sources of income.[64] Examples of other agreements likely to be affected by public policies regarding family relationships are those regarding cohabitation,[65] the disposition of frozen embryos,[66] agreements for the donation of bone marrow or other human organs,[67] and agreements by "sperm donors relinquishing parental rights,[68] among others.

[5]   Gambling Contracts

Despite the prevalence of state-supported gambling, in the form of licensed casinos, race tracks, charity bingo, and state-operated lotteries, the traditional American view has been that gambling contracts are illegal.[69] The general rule is that an agreement is an illegal wager if consideration was paid for a *chance* to win a prize.[70] The main consequence of making wagering contracts illegal is that

---

[62] *E.g.*, Ariz. Rev. Stat. § 25-218(A) (LexisNexis 2008) (making surrogacy contracts unenforceable); Wash. Rev. Code Ann. §§ 26.26.230, 26.26.240 (LexisNexis 2006) (unenforceable if surrogate will be paid); Va. Code Ann. §§ 29-159(B), 20-160(B) (2004) (permitting enforcement of surrogacy contracts, with judicial approval if the intended mother is infertile).

[63] *See* R.R. v. M.H., 689 N.E.2d 790 (Mass. 1998); Johnson v. Calvert, 851 P.2d 776 (Cal.), *cert. denied*, 510 U.S. 874, *cert. dismissed sub nom.*, Baby Boy J. v. Johnson, 510 U.S. 938 (1993) (involving gestational surrogacy with the surrogate implanted with a fertilized zygote from the biological parents).

[64] *E.g.*, Matter of Marriage of Matson, 730 P.2d 668 (Wash. 1986).

[65] *E.g.*, Marvin v. Marvin, 557 P.2d 106 (Cal. 1976); Watts v. Watts, 405 N.W.2d 303 (Wis. 1987).

[66] *E.g.*, Roman v. Roman, 193 S.W.3d 40 (Tex. Ct. App. 2006); Litowitz v. Litowitz, 48 P.3d 261 (Wash. 2002); Kass v. Kass, 696 N.E.2d 174 (N.Y. 1998); Paul Walter, *His, Hers, or Theirs — Custody, Control, and Contracts: Allocating Decisional Authority over Frozen Embryos*, 29 Seton Hall L. Rev. 937 (1999).

[67] *E.g.*, Wilson v. Adkins, 941 S.W.2d 440 (Ark. Ct. App. 1997). *See generally* Sean R. Fitzgibbons, *Cadaveric Organ Donation and Consent: A Comparative Analysis of the United States, Japan, Singapore, and China*, 6 Ilsa J. Int'l & Comp. L. 73 (1999).

[68] *E.g.*, Lamaritata v. Lucas, 823 So. 2d 316 (Fla. Dist. Ct. App. 2002) (enforcing agreement under state "sperm donor" statute); LaChapelle v. Mitten, 607 N.W.2d 151 (Minn. Ct. App. 2000).

[69] Mark Pettit Jr., *Freedom, Freedom of Contract, and the "Rise and Fall,"* 79 B.U. L. Rev. 263, 319–20 (1999); Michael P. Sullivan, Annotation, *Private Contests and Lotteries: Entrants' Rights and Remedies*, 64 A.L.R.4th 1021, 1029 (1988 & Supp. 2000); James L. Buchwalter, Annotation, *Right to Recover Money Lent for Gambling Purposes*, 74 A.L.R.5th 369 (1999).

[70] *E.g.*, FCC v. Am. Broad. Co., 347 U.S. 284, 290 (1954). Despite this, student organizations across the country frequently conduct illegal raffles.

gambling debts cannot be enforced.[71] Thus, checks or money orders written to satisfy gambling debts are not enforceable, even if the state in which the wager was made would have enforced the obligation.[72]

[6]   Limited Remedies and Liability Waivers

Agreements limiting or waiving liability may also be unenforceable. Thus, agreements that release a person from responsibility for his or her own negligence are subject to heightened scrutiny. These "liability waivers" are frequently encountered in agreements between sponsors of physical activities and participants in those activities, such as skiing, skydiving, or bicycle racing, where there is an inherent risk of injury to the participants.[73] Liability waivers of this type are generally enforceable provided that the agreement is clear and conspicuous,[74] the participant fully appreciates the risks involved in the activity,[75] and the waiver does not exculpate the defendant from reckless or grossly negligent conduct.[76] Courts tend to review the language of liability waivers with a careful eye, imposing liability where the waiver's language fails to directly address the circumstances which led to the plaintiff's injury.[77]

Courts are also reluctant to enforce liability waivers in contracts involving performance of a public duty.[78] Accordingly, waivers are less likely to be enforceable when the party seeking its protection is providing a service that is a practical necessity that is not otherwise readily available,[79] such as medical treatment,[80] transportation by a common carrier,[81] and bailment in a warehouse.[82]

---

[71] See, e.g., Metro. Creditors Serv. v. Sadri, 15 Cal. App. 4th 1821 (1993); Boardwalk Regency Corp. v. Travelers Exp. Co., Inc., 745 F. Supp. 1266 (E.D. Mich. 1990).

[72] Casanova Club v. Bisharat, 458 A.2d 1 (Conn. 1983).

[73] See Chadwick v. Colt Ross Outfitters, Inc., 100 P.3d 465 (Colo. 2004) (back-country hunting trip); Moore v. Hartley Motors, Inc., 36 P.3d 628 (Alaska 2001) (ATV training course); Okura v. U.S. Cycling Fed'n, 186 Cal. App. 3d 1462, 1465–69 (1986) (bicycle racing) (your author has both drafted and signed liability waivers for bicycling events). See http://www.goba.com/pdfs/2013/regform.pdf (last viewed Dec. 10, 2012).

[74] See Geczi v. Lifetime Fitness, 973 N.E.2d 801 (Ohio Ct. App. 2012); Yauger v. Skiing Enters., Inc., 557 N.W.2d 60 (Wis. 1996).

[75] See Reardon v. Windswept Farm, LLC, 905 A.2d 1156 (Conn. 2006) (horse-riding student was not well-equipped to evaluate whether she and the horse were well-suited to one another); Lloyd v. Sugarloaf Mtn. Corp., 833 A.2d 1 (Me. 2003) (release must spell out risks); Renaud v. 200 Convention Ctr. Ltd., 728 P.2d 445 (Nev. 1986).

[76] E.g., Chauvlier v. Booth Creek Ski Holdings, Inc., 35 P.3d 383 (Wash. Ct. App. 2001); Murphy v. N. Am. River Runners, Inc., 412 S.E.2d 504 (W.Va. 1991).

[77] See Laeroc Waikiki Parkside, LLC v. K.S.K. (Oahu) Ltd., 166 P.3d 961, 981 (Haw. 2007); Yauger v. Skiing Enters., Inc., 557 N.W.2d 60 (Wis. 1996).

[78] See Tunkl v. Regents of Univ. of Cal., 383 P.2d 441 (Cal. 1963); B & B Livery, Inc. v. Riehl, 960 P.2d 134, 137 (Colo. 1998); Pelletier v. Alameda Yacht Harbor, 188 Cal. App. 3d 1551 (1986).

[79] Tunkl v. Regents of Univ. of Cal., 383 P.2d 441, 445 (Cal. 1963). See generally Blake Morant, Contracts Limiting Liability: A Paradox with Tacit Solutions, 69 TUL. L. REV. 715, 740 (1995); Mary Ann Connell & Frederick G. Savage, Releases: Is There Still a Place for Their Use by Colleges and Universities?, 29 J.C. & U.L. 579 (2003).

[80] E.g., Tunkl v. Regents of the Univ. of Cal., 383 P.2d 441 (Cal. 1963).

Likewise, although the Uniform Commercial Code generally adheres to the principle of freedom of contract,[83] it nevertheless specifies that statutory "obligations of good faith, diligence, reasonableness and care" may not be disclaimed by agreement.[84] However, the Code permits the parties to determine by agreement the standards by which performance of these duties will be measured, subject only to the requirement that the standards not be "manifestly unreasonable."[85]

Provisions in contracts for the sale of goods that limit the remedies available to the parties for breach are likewise subject to judicial scrutiny. U.C.C. § 2-719 generally permits the parties to provide for remedies in substitution for the remedies otherwise provided by the code for breach of a contract for the sale of goods.[86] However, such a substituted remedy is not enforceable if it is "unconscionable,"[87] and any attempt to exclude consequential damages for personal injuries caused by defective consumer goods is presumed to be unconscionable.[88] Likewise, if a limited remedy "fails of its essential purpose," the injured party is permitted to ignore the limited remedy provision and seek recourse through the Code's usual remedies.[89] Liquidated damage provisions are subject to similar restraints and are not enforceable if they are penalties.[90]

[B] Effect of Illegality

The effect of illegality varies. Some agreements, such as those to commit a crime, are simply void. Other agreements, such as those that violate regulatory licensing statutes, are merely voidable, and thus unenforceable by the party who would benefit from the contract's illegal provisions. When some portion of the contract is illegal, it can usually be severed from the rest of the contract, which remains enforceable. Finally, courts sometimes award damages in restitution for the value of any benefits conferred in partial or full performance of an illegal contract, even though the contract itself is unenforceable.

---

[81] U.C.C. § 7-309 (2012).

[82] U.C.C. § 7-204 (2012).

[83] U.C.C. § 1-302(a) (2012) (formerly § 1-102(3)).

[84] *Id.*

[85] *Id.*

[86] U.C.C. § 2-719(1)(a) (2012).

[87] U.C.C. § 2-719(3) (2012).

[88] *Id.*

[89] U.C.C. § 2-719(2) (2012). *See generally infra* § 14.02 Limited Remedies.

[90] *See infra* § 14.03 Liquidated Damages.

[1]   Void or Voidable

An important distinction is drawn between contracts which are "void ab initio" (or "null and void") and those which are merely "voidable" at the election of one of the parties.[91] A void contract is really no contract at all.[92] If the contract is completely void, it cannot be enforced by either party and has no effect on their legal relationships with one another or with others. Contracts are completely void due to a conflict with public policy only where they are completely illegal, such as an agreement to commit a crime. Bribery is a good example of this: the contract itself is the crime.

A voidable contract, on the other hand, is one that is merely unenforceable at the election of one of the parties.[93] Most of the time agreements that conflict with public policy are not void but merely voidable: the party burdened by the illegal contract or term has the power to avoid his or her own liability on the contract, but retains the right to affirm the contract and enforce it against the other party.[94] Thus, a homeowner retains the right to enforce a contract against an unlicensed contractor even though the contract may be unenforceable against the homeowner. The party sought to be protected by the regulatory license enjoys the advantage of the law requiring the license, but will not suffer as a result of the rule.

[2]   Severability of Illegal Terms

When a contract is generally enforceable, but contains illegal terms, the court may sever the unenforceable provisions from the rest of the contract. This is similar to the approach taken by U.C.C. § 2-302 regarding unconscionable contract provisions.[95]

The same approach is used by both U.C.C. § 2-718 and the common law in dealing with agreed damages provisions that are determined to be unenforceable penalties.[96] The punitive provision is eliminated from the contract, and the aggrieved party is free to seek recourse as it would have if the provision had not been included in the contract in the first place.[97]

This same blue-pencil approach is sometimes taken in dealing with overly broad covenants not to compete.[98] Modern courts sometimes take a more flexible approach, not merely eliminating the offensive provision, but reformulating the terms of the agreement to deprive them of their illegal effect. Reflecting this approach, U.C.C. § 2-302 authorizes the court to "*limit the application* of any

---

[91] *See* RESTATEMENT (SECOND) OF CONTRACTS § 7 (1981). *See generally supra* § 1.02[F] Void, Voidable, and Unenforceable Contracts.

[92] *See* RESTATEMENT (SECOND) OF CONTRACTS § 7 cmt. a (1981).

[93] Black Hills Invs., Inc. v. Albertson's, Inc., 146 Cal. App. 4th 883 (2007).

[94] Ockey v. Lehmer, 189 P.3d 51, 57 (Utah 2008).

[95] *See infra* § 10.05 Unconscionability.

[96] *See infra* § 14.03[B] Penalty; or Enforceable Liquidated Damages.

[97] U.C.C. § 2-718 (2012).

[98] *See supra* § 10.02[A][2] Contracts in Restraint of Trade.

unconscionable clause as to avoid any unconscionable result."[99] This approach can be observed where courts treat covenants not to compete by redrafting the terms of the agreement to prevent competition in a more limited geographic area or for a shorter time than specified in the contract.[100]

[3]   Restitution for Benefits Conferred[101]

Restitution for the value of benefits conferred under an illegal contract is not usually available.[102] Instead, the court usually leaves the parties where it finds them, thus permitting them to retain whatever benefits they may have received under the unenforceable agreement.[103] Thus, in *Hartman v. Harris*,[104] an art dealer was unable to recover restitution from his son and his son's agent for breach of an agreement to share the proceeds from the sale of a stolen statue. And, in *Harry Berenter, Inc. v. Berman*,[105] an unlicensed contractor was prohibited from pursuing recovery either under the contract or in restitution for improvements it had made to the defendant's home. The owner retained the benefits of the builder's work, without having to pay for them.

Nevertheless, restitution is sometimes available where violation of the statute was unintentional or inadvertent.[106] For example, in *Pelletier v. Johnson*,[107] a vinyl siding installer was permitted to recover for the reasonable value of his work despite his violation of a state "Home Solicitations and Referral Sales Act," where the homeowner received the value of the contractor's services and the contractor had neither defrauded the homeowner nor knowingly violated the statute.

Permitting recovery frustrates the purpose of the public policy that underlies the refusal to enforce the contract. Accordingly, recovery in restitution sometimes depends on the importance of the public policy involved.[108] Likewise, courts sometimes also award restitution when the parties are not equally in the wrong. Thus, if the party seeking restitution is not "in pari delicto" (equally at fault) with the party from whom restitution is sought, a remedy is available. When both have participated in some wrongdoing, the court will leave the parties where it found them. This probably explains the result in *Hartman v. Harris*, described above, in connection with the agreement to share the proceeds from the sale of a stolen work

---

[99] U.C.C. § 2-302 (2012) (emphasis supplied).

[100] *See* Valley Med. Specialists v. Farber, 982 P.2d 1277, 1286 (Ariz. 1999).

[101] John W. Wade, *Restitution of Benefits Acquired Through Illegal Transactions*, 95 U. Pa. L. Rev. 261 (1947); John W. Wade, *Benefits Obtained Under Illegal Transactions — Reasons for and Against Allowing Restitution*, 25 Tex. L. Rev. 31 (1946); Percy H. Winfield, *Public Policy in the English Common Law*, 42 Harv. L. Rev. 76 (1928).

[102] Restatement (Second) of Contracts § 197 (1981).

[103] Restatement (Second) of Contracts § 197 cmt. a (1981).

[104] 810 F. Supp. 82, 86 (S.D.N.Y. 1992).

[105] 265 A.2d 759 (Md. 1970).

[106] Restatement (Second) of Contracts § 198 (1981).

[107] 937 P.2d 668, 669, 672 (Ariz. Ct. App. 1996).

[108] Restatement (Second) of Contracts § 199 (1981).

of art.[109]

A related issue is whether the injured party can obtain restitution for payments made before the contract was avoided. In *Fausnight v. Perkins*, for example, a homeowner made payments to an unlicensed contractor, who partially completed renovations to the homeowner's house. Even though the contractor could not recover for the full value of his work, the court prevented the homeowner from recovering payments it had already made to the contractor, indicating that "allowing the recovery of such payments is not necessary to effectuate the policy of licensing statutes."[110] However, some courts permit the recovery as a preventive measure, designed to discourage those who might otherwise seek to enter into agreements that violate the law.[111]

[C]   Illegality in International Agreements

The CISG does not address the issue of illegality. Any basis for illegality of an international sales contract is thus governed by domestic law or other international treaties. Likewise, UNIDROIT Principles are silent about issues of illegality of the transaction.[112] Any question about the legality of an international agreement is governed by domestic law or more specific international treaties, such as of the European Economic Community relating to contracts in restraint of trade, or other standards of private international law that are far beyond the scope of this book.

§ 10.03   INCAPACITY

Contracts are based on consent. Thus, to enter into a legally binding contract, a person must have the legal and mental capacity necessary to express his or her consent to an agreement.[113] Thus, the law protects those who are deemed incapable of adequately protecting their own interests. Minors, those with permanent mental impairments, or those who are suffering from serious mental illnesses are the principal beneficiaries of this protection.[114] Others, who may be quite capable of protecting themselves in ordinary situations, might be temporarily impaired due to the effects of drugs or alcohol.[115]

Contracts entered into by people suffering from these incapacities are usually voidable at their election. Where the agreement is merely voidable, and not utterly void, it can still be enforced by the person who lacked capacity, and it might be subsequently ratified through language or conduct that demonstrates the party's

---

[109] RESTATEMENT (SECOND) OF CONTRACTS § 198(b) & cmt. b (1981).

[110] Fausnight v. Perkins, 994 So. 2d 912 (Ala. 2008). *See* Maurice T. Brunner, Annotation, *Recovery Back of Money Paid to Unlicensed Person Required by Law to Have Occupational or Business License or Permit to Make Contract*, 74 A.L.R.3d 637 (1976).

[111] *E.g.*, Ransburg v. Haase, 586 N.E.2d 1295, 1300 (Ill. App. Ct. 1992).

[112] PICC Art. 3.1(b) (2004); PECL Art. 4.101 (2002).

[113] RESTATEMENT (SECOND) OF CONTRACTS § 12(1) (1981).

[114] RESTATEMENT (SECOND) OF CONTRACTS § 12(2) (1981).

[115] RESTATEMENT (SECOND) OF CONTRACTS § 12(2)(d) (1981).

willingness to go ahead with the agreement, after the circumstances that caused his or her incapacities have been resolved.

[A] Minors[116]

The most common cases where a lack of capacity arises involve "minors," — or "infants," as they are sometimes called — persons who have not yet reached the legal age of contractual capacity.[117] In the United States, those under 18 are regarded as too immature to enter into a contract.[118] The policy underlying this rule is to protect children from adults who may take advantage of their immaturity.[119]

At one time, contracts with minors were void, and could not be enforced by either party.[120] Today, however, they are merely "voidable."[121] The agreement may be enforced by the minor, but not by the adult. Further, the minor may ratify the contract after reaching his or her majority,[122] but the adult does not have this option.

There is nothing strictly illegal about an adult making a contract with a minor, and such agreements may be completely fair and above board. If the minor decides to perform the agreement, then it will stand as made between the parties. However, as a general rule, "[i]nfants are not liable on any of their contracts, except for necessaries. With [this] exception, all other contracts of infants, whether executory or executed, may be avoided or ratified at the election of the infant."[123]

[1] Obligation to Pay Restitution

One of the recurring problems involving the contracts of minors is the extent to which a minor who disaffirms a contract is liable in restitution for the value of the benefits he has received. Assume, for example, that 15-year old Bart buys a car

---

[116] *See* Juanda Lowder Daniel, *Virtually Mature: Examining the Policy of Minors' Incapacity to Contract Through the Cyberscope*, 43 GONZ. L. REV. 239 (2008); Anthony Kronman, *Paternalism and the Law of Contracts*, 92 YALE L.J. 763, 795 (1984); Larry A. DiMatteo, *Deconstructing the Myth of the "Infancy Law Doctrine": From Incapacity to Accountability*, 21 OHIO N.U.L. REV. 481 (1995); Michael J. Navin, *The Contracts of Minors Viewed from the Perspective of Fair Exchange*, 50 N.C. L. REV. 517 (1972) (Professor Navin was the co-author of the first edition of *Understanding Contracts*).

[117] RESTATEMENT (SECOND) OF CONTRACTS § 14 (1981). *See* Robert G. Edge, *Voidability of Minor's Contracts: A Feudal Doctrine in a Modern Economy*, 1 GA. L. REV. 205 (1967).

[118] RESTATEMENT (SECOND) OF CONTRACTS § 14 (1981). *See generally In re* Estate of Duran, 66 P.3d 326 (N.M. 2003).

[119] *See, e.g.,* Jones v. Dressel, 623 P.2d 370, 373 (Colo. 1981).

[120] RESTATEMENT (SECOND) OF CONTRACTS § 14 cmt. b (1981). *See generally* Dodson v. Shrader, 824 S.W.2d 545 (Tenn. 1992).

[121] RESTATEMENT (SECOND) OF CONTRACTS § 14 (1981).

[122] RESTATEMENT (SECOND) OF CONTRACTS § 7 & illus. 1 (1981). *E.g.,* Zelnick v. Adams, 606 S.E.2d 843 (Va. 2005).

[123] H & S Homes, L.L.C. v. McDonald, 823 So. 2d 627, 630 (Ala. 2001). *But see* Douglass v. Pflueger Hawaii, Inc., 135 P.3d 129 (Haw. 2006) (arbitration clause in minor's employment contract enforceable because of state statute permitting employment of minors age 16 or older).

from an automobile dealer for $8000.[124] But, just before his 18th birthday, Bart disaffirms the agreement and seeks return of the $8000 he paid for it. The question is what obligation Bart has to give the car back, and pay the seller for the value he has used since purchasing the car.[125]

There is no doubt that Bart must give back the car.[126] A question remains whether he is responsible for the loss in value of the car due to wear and tear, or destruction, before he disaffirms. The car might have been driven many miles or even been in an accident. It may be little more than a crumpled pile of metal, plastic, wire, and glass. In these situations, the minor may disaffirm the contract without liability for the loss in value of the car before disaffirmance. The risk of this loss is one of the risks an adult automobile dealer assumes when dealing with someone who is not yet of legal age.[127] Thus, given a choice between protecting the minor, and providing full satisfaction to the adult who has dealt with the minor, the law usually chooses to protect the minor.[128] The adult, after all, could have protected himself or herself in the first place by refraining from entering in the agreement with the minor. As the court said in *Keser v. Chagnon*: "[H]e who deals with a minor does so at his own peril . . . ."[129] In other words, at least in this situation: let the seller beware. Adults must take care in determining the age of persons with whom they contract.

[2]   Ratification After Age of Majority

A person who ratifies a contract after reaching her age of majority is responsible for the contract just as any other adult would be. Once a person becomes an adult, the protection provided to minors is no longer necessary.

No binding decision by an infant regarding his contracts with adults can be made until he becomes an adult.[130] Upon reaching majority, a minor has a reasonable time to disaffirm the contract.[131] If he disaffirms the contract, he is

---

[124] It would seem that sophisticated merchants selling expensive machines like cars would take steps to ensure that they were dealing with an adult. Such is not always the case, however. *E.g.*, Central Bucks Aero, Inc. v. Smith, 310 A.2d 283 (Pa. Super. Ct. 1973) (wrecked airplane returned to seller).

[125] *See, e.g.*, Kiefer v. Fred Howe Motors, Inc., 158 N.W.2d 288 (Wis. 1968).

[126] *See* Gillis v. Whitley's Discount Auto Sales, Inc., 319 S.E.2d 661 (N.C. Ct. App. 1984).

[127] *E.g.*, Halbman v. Lemke, 298 N.W.2d 562 (Wis. 1980); Johnson Motors, Inc. v. Coleman, 232 So. 2d 716 (Miss. 1970). *See generally* Michael J. Navin, *The Contracts of Minors Viewed from the Perspective of Fair Exchange*, 50 N.C. L. REV. 517 (1972) (Professor Navin was a co-author of the first edition of this book. He passed away a few weeks before the manuscript for the first edition was submitted to the publisher and thus never saw the results of his work.). *But see, e.g.*, Dodson v. Shrader, 824 S.W.2d 545 (Tenn. 1992); W. E. Shipley, Annotation, *Infant's Liability for Use or Depreciation of Subject Matter, in Action to Recover Purchase Price upon His Disaffirmance of Contract to Purchase Goods*, 12 A.L.R.3d 1174 (1967).

[128] *See* Kiefer v. Fred Howe Motors, Inc., 158 N.W.2d 288 (Wis. 1968).

[129] 410 P.2d 637, 640 (Colo. 1966).

[130] *See* Poli v. Nat'l Bank of Detroit, 93 N.W.2d 925, 926 (Mich. 1950). *See also* Cassella v. Tiberio, 87 N.E.2d 377, 378 (Ohio Ct. App. 1947).

[131] *See* Milicic v. The Basketball Mktg. Co., 857 A.2d 689 (Pa. Super. Ct. 2004); *In re* Estate of Duran, 66 P.3d 326 (N.M. 2003); Hawkins v. Peart, 37 P.3d 1062, 1066 (Utah 2001); Lewis v. CEDU Educ. Servs., Inc., 15 P.3d 1147, 1150, n.3 (Idaho 2000) ("the contract of a minor, if made whilst he is an unmarried

entitled to the return of whatever he paid, and is relieved from any unperformed duties. If he ratifies, or fails to disaffirm within a reasonable time, the agreement is treated the same as any other contract and his former infancy is irrelevant.

Ratification might occur in a formal manner, such as where the minor executes a new agreement, ratifying the obligation he made before becoming an adult.[132]

Most of the time, however, ratification occurs more casually. If the minor retains the benefits of a contract beyond a reasonable time after she becomes an adult, her continued use of the benefits of the contract operates as ratification.[133] Thus, if Sam sold his car to Barb while Barb was still 17, Barb's continued use of the car for a reasonable time after her eighteenth birthday operates as her ratification of the promise to pay for it. But, she probably has beyond the stroke of midnight on her eighteenth birthday to act. If she disaffirms within a reasonable time, she can still avoid the contract.[134] The extent of a reasonable time, as always, is difficult to pin down. Compare, for example, *Bobby Floars Toyota, Inc. v. Smith*,[135] where the minor ratified by continuing to use an auto for 10 months after his eighteenth birthday,[136] with *Adams v. Barcomb*,[137] where continued use of a car for two months after becoming an adult was not a sufficient expression of intent to ratify the contract, and the buyer was still permitted to disaffirm.

[3] Misrepresentation of Age

When minors misrepresent their age, the issue is more clouded. It is easy to imagine a 17-year-old using forged documents to purchase a car and, upon reaching the age of majority, attempting to disaffirm. This type of misrepresentation is a particular problem with minors who have an older appearance and use a forged or altered driver's license to confirm the impression.[138]

The purpose of preventing adults from enforcing agreements against minors is to protect children from overreaching adults. However, when a scheming teenager fraudulently induces an innocent adult to enter into an agreement, the only

---

minor, may be disaffirmed by the minor himself, either before his majority or within a reasonable time afterwards").

[132] 352 P.2d 259 (Colo. 1960). *See also* Robertson v. Robertson, 229 So. 2d 642 (Fla. Dist. Ct. App. 1969) (promise by son to repay educational loans).

[133] *Compare* Bobby Floars Toyota, Inc. v. Smith, 269 S.E.2d 320 (N.C. Ct. App. 1980) (retention of auto for 10 months after majority birthday constituted ratification), *with* Adams v. Barcomb, 216 A.2d 648 (Vt. 1966) (continued use of auto for two months was not sufficient to demonstrate intent to ratify). *See also In re* Score Bd., Inc., 238 B.R. 585, 592 (D.N.J. 1999) (NBA star Kobe Bryant ratified marketing agreement entered into when he was a minor).

[134] RESTATEMENT (SECOND) OF CONTRACTS §§ 380–81 (1981).

[135] 269 S.E.2d 320 (N.C. Ct. App. 1980).

[136] This was when the age of majority was 18.

[137] 216 A.2d 648 (Vt. 1966).

[138] For example, although I am confident that he did not misrepresent his age, former Ohio State University basketball player Greg Oden, who played professional basketball for a time with the Portland Trailblazers, looked like he was in his early thirties when he was only an 18-year-old freshman at Ohio State. *See* http://www.gregoden.com/gallery.php (last viewed January 2, 2013).

overreaching is by the disreputable minor.[139] This makes it inappropriate to blindly apply the rule that the contracts of minors can be avoided. Although some courts adhere to the rule permitting the minor to disaffirm,[140] others use estoppel to prevent the minor from disaffirming the contract.[141]

As with any estoppel, the other party must reasonably rely on the misrepresentation and cannot hide behind falsified documents that the minor's youthful appearance belies. Lenders who usually obtain credit reports on prospective borrowers should be expected to follow these same procedures in every case and cannot claim to rely on a falsified driver's license, when a routine credit check would have revealed the minor's true age.

[4] Liability for Necessities of Life

The rule permitting minors to avoid contracts can be a double-edged sword. On one hand, it protects minors from overreaching adults. On the other hand, it makes it very difficult for minors to make contracts to purchase goods and services they want or need. Because not all infants are in the same position, contract law aims at ensuring that minors can obtain the necessities of life, despite their lack of capacity.

If a minor makes a contract to purchase a necessity of life, the minor is liable in restitution for the value of the goods or services that he received.[142] Here again, liability is based on quasi-contract, and not on the enforceability of the minor's promise.

The only difficult question that may arise is whether the goods or services supplied to the minor are "necessaries." Necessaries usually include food, shelter, clothing, and medical treatment.[143] Employment has sometimes also been regarded as a necessity,[144] and where a minor needs an automobile to travel to a job that the minor needs in order to survive, an automobile might also qualify. The issue is primarily a question of fact.[145]

Housing may or may not be a necessity, depending on whether the minor is able

---

[139] *See* Zouch *ex dem.* Abbot & Hallet v. Parsons, 97 Eng. Rep. 1103 (1765) (Lord Mansfield) (permitting a minor who has misrepresented his age to disaffirm would turn the defense of infancy into a "weapon of injustice").

[140] *See* Nicholas v. People, 973 P.2d 1213 (Colo. 1999); Gillis v. Whitley's Discount Auto Sales, Inc., 319 S.E.2d 661 (N.C. Ct. App. 1984).

[141] Haydocy Pontiac, Inc. v. Lee, 250 N.E.2d 898 (Ohio Ct. App. 1969); Nichols v. English, 154 S.E.2d 239 (Ga. 1967). *See generally*, A.D. Kaufman, Annotation, *Infant's Misrepresentations as to His Age as Estopping Him from Disaffirming His Voidable Transaction*, 29 A.L.R.3d 1270 (1970).

[142] RESTATEMENT (SECOND) OF CONTRACTS § 12 cmt. f (1981). *See, e.g.*, Schmidt v. Prince George's Hosp., 784 A.2d 1112 (Md. 2001) (emergency medical treatment provided to minor).

[143] John D. Hodson, Annotation, *Infant's Liability for Medical, Dental, or Hospital Services*, 53 A.L.R.4th 1249 (1987).

[144] *E.g.*, Gastonia Personnel Corp. v. Rogers, 172 S.E.2d 19 (N.C. 1970) (minor liable for employment agency fee).

[145] Slaney v. Westwood Auto, Inc., 322 N.E.2d 768 (Mass. 1975).

to live with his or her parents, or another responsible adult, such as a guardian.[146] Thus, a precocious 17-year-old who moves out of his parents' home, but has the option of returning to live with them, is not liable in restitution to his landlord, while a 17-year-old whose parents will not permit him to return home, is liable for the value of the benefit he received.[147]

Closely related to the rule that allows recovery from minors for necessities is the rule that permits recovery from minors who have been "emancipated." Emancipated minors are those who live on their own separately from their parents and who are responsible for sustaining themselves.[148] It requires no stretch of the imagination to consider the plight of teenage parents trying to support a child and needing to be able to enter into binding agreements in order to survive.

Courts have taken opposing views on this issue, with some courts treating emancipation as an indication of the minor's capacity to contract,[149] and others adhering to the traditional distinction between contracts for the necessities of life and other agreements.[150] However, most courts treat emancipated minors as adults as far as their ability to make binding contracts is concerned.[151]

[5]   Liability Waivers for Minors

The incapacity of minors is particularly important in connection with liability waivers that facilitate children's participation in sports activities and school events. Event sponsors and their insurers frequently attempt to limit their potential liability by warning participants of the dangers involved in these events and seeking an agreement exculpating them from liability for negligence that might result in an injury to the participants. It is impossible to obtain effective consent from a minor. Further, in most states, parents and guardians are unable to enter into a contract that prevents the child from recovering for injuries sustained, due to the negligence of an event's sponsor, without court approval.[152]

[B]   Mental Incapacity[153]

The law also protects persons who are mentally ill or otherwise cognitively impaired.[154] Just as with infants, contracts with those suffering from a mental

---

[146] Rivera v. Reading House Auth., 819 F. Supp. 1323 (E.D. Pa. 1993).

[147] Webster St. P'ship, Ltd. v. Sheridan, 368 N.W.2d 439 (Neb. 1985).

[148] King v. Braden, 418 N.W.2d 739, 741 (Minn. Ct. App. 1988) (married minor in U.S. military, emancipated by court order).

[149] Lay v. Suggs, 559 So. 2d 740 (Fla. Dist. Ct. App. 1990) (state statute treating married minors as emancipated); *In re* Greer, 184 So. 2d 104 (La. Ct. App. 1966).

[150] E.g., Mitchell By and Through Fee v. Mitchell, 963 S.W.2d 222 (Ky. Ct. App. 1998).

[151] The relatively recent reduction in the age of majority from 21 to 18 has lessened the prevalence of cases involving emancipated minors, because many infants previously considered to be emancipated were older than 18 but less than 21. *See generally* Carol Sanger & Eleanor W. Willemsen, *Minor Changes: Emancipating Children in Modern Times*, 25 U. Mich. J.L. Reform 239 (1992).

[152] *E.g.,* Cooper v. Aspen Skiing, 48 P.3d 1229 (Colo. 2002). *But see* Zivich v. Mentor Soccer Club, 696 N.E.2d 201 (Ohio 1998).

[153] George J. Alexander & Thomas S. Szasz, *From Contract to Status Via Psychiatry*, 13 Santa

impairment are voidable at the option of the person suffering from the incapacity.

The other party, who suffers from no impairment, may not use the impaired person's incapacity as grounds for avoiding the contract. As one court explained: "[T]he rule requiring guardians for incompetent persons is for their protection. 'Its purpose is not to burden nor hinder them in enforcing their rights; nor to confer any privilege or advantage on persons who claim adversely to them or who may be trying to take advantage of them.' "[155] If the person lacks capacity to enter into a contract, his agreements are voidable at his the election.[156] And, as with contracts made by minors, the person suffering from the mental impairment can ratify the agreement after reacquiring his mental capacity.[157]

However, unlike situations involving minors, who become competent on their eighteenth birthday, it may be difficult to determine the exact moment when a person suffering from a mental disability reacquired his or her mental abilities.

[1] Adjudication of Incompetence

A person whose mental impairment renders him completely unable to manage his affairs can be adjudicated as mentally incompetent by a court. A guardian is appointed to manage the person's affairs.

Agreements made by a person who has been adjudicated as incompetent are not merely voidable; they are void.[158] Thus, their agreements may not subsequently be ratified after the person is released from the guardianship, though, of course, a new contract on similar terms could then be made.[159]

The policy against enforcing contracts made by those who have been adjudicated as incompetent is so strong that it applies even though the incompetent person may have enjoyed a "lucid interval" at the time the contract was made.[160] But, contracts made after the person has completely regained his mental faculties and the guardianship has been abandoned, are fully enforceable.[161]

CLARA L. REV. 537 (1973); Alexander M. Meikeljohn, *Contractual and Donative Capacity*, 39 CASE. W. RES. L. REV. 307 (1988–89); Henry Weihofen, *Mental Incompetency to Contract or Convey*, 39 S. CAL. L. REV. 211 (1966).

[154] RESTATEMENT (SECOND) OF CONTRACTS § 15 (1981). *E.g.*, Blackhurst v. Transamerica Ins. Co., 699 P.2d 688, 695 (Utah 1985) ("The civil law protects incompetents by providing safeguards for those who lack capacity to bind themselves in contract.").

[155] Blackhurst v. Transamerica Ins. Co., 699 P.2d 688 (Utah 1985).

[156] Weaver v. St. Joseph of the Pines, Inc., 652 S.E.2d 701 (N.C. Ct. App. 2007).

[157] *E.g.*, Apfelbat v. Nat'l Bank Wyandotte-Taylor, 404 N.W.2d 725 (Mich. Ct. App. 1975); Wood v. Newell, 182 N.W. 965 (Minn. 1921).

[158] *E.g.*, 755 Ill. Comp. Stat. 5/11a-22(b) (West 2008).

[159] RESTATEMENT (SECOND) OF CONTRACTS § 13 (1981). *E.g.*, SunTrust Bank, Middle Ga. N.A. v. Harper, 551 S.E.2d 419 (Ga. Ct. App. 2001).

[160] RESTATEMENT (SECOND) OF CONTRACTS § 13 cmt a (1981).

[161] *E.g.* United Pac. Ins. Co. v. Buchanan, 765 P.2d 23 (Wash. Ct. App. 1988).

[2]   Cognitive and Volitional Tests[162]

Many people who suffer from a mental disability are never adjudicated as incompetent and placed under the care of a guardian. Accordingly, questions sometimes arise about the enforceability of a contract entered into by a person who is actually suffering from a mental illness or defect, even though he has not yet been adjudicated as incompetent.

In these situations, there is a real tension between protecting persons who are incompetent and respecting individual autonomy.[163] As one court explained: "There must be stability in contractual relations and protection of the expectations of parties who bargain in good faith. On the other hand, it is also desirable to protect persons who may understand the nature of the transaction but who, due to mental illness, cannot control their conduct."[164]

These conflicting policies were long balanced by a traditional rule that prevented enforcement of a contract against a person who, because of a mental disease or disability, was incapable of understanding the nature and consequences of the transaction at the time it was made.[165] For example, in *Hauer v. Union State Bank*,[166] the impaired party suffered brain damage in a motorcycle accident. Although she had been released from guardianship, she remained unable to remember, to read, to write, and to spell. She was, according to testimony introduced in the trial, malleable, gullible, and "unable to make reasoned decisions."[167] In these circumstances, the jury was justified in concluding that she was incompetent when she entered into a loan and security agreement with the bank. However, this traditional "cognitive" standard is quite strict and might not protect those with mental illnesses that do not completely impair their cognitive skills, but that nevertheless affect their ability to control their behavior in other respects.

More recent decisions, reflecting our greater understanding of mental disease, adopt a more flexible "volitional" standard, based on the ability of a person to "act in a reasonable manner in relation to the transaction."[168] Here, however, unlike the more traditional cognitive standard, the volitional test makes a contract voidable by the impaired person only where the other party to the transaction "has reason to know" of the condition that has affected the impaired person's behavior.[169]

---

[162] Milton D. Green, *Public Policies Underlying the Law of Mental Incompetency*, 38 Mich. L. Rev. 1189 (1940); Kenny Hegland, *Teaching Elder Law in Contracts*, 30 Stetson L. Rev. 1319 (2001); Wendy Chung Rossiter, Comment, *No Protection for the Elderly: The Inadequacy of the Capacity Doctrine in Avoiding Unfair Contracts Involving Seniors*, 78 Or. L. Rev. 807 (1999).

[163] *E.g.*, Ortelere v. Teachers' Ret. Bd., 250 N.E.2d 460 (N.Y. 1969).

[164] *Id.* at 465.

[165] Restatement (Second) of Contracts § 15(1)(a) (1981).

[166] 532 N.W.2d 456 (Wis. 1995).

[167] *Id.* at 461.

[168] Restatement (Second) of Contracts § 15(1)(b) (1981).

[169] *E.g.*, Krasner v. Berk, 319 N.E.2d 897 (Mass. 1974); Farnum v. Silvano, 540 N.E.2d 202 (Mass. Ct. App. 1989).

The more modern 2-part test has sometimes been used by individuals who are suffering from bipolar disease that is typified by manic-depressive episodes. During the manic stage, these individuals often appear quite competent. Although they are completely unable to control their behavior, the other party to the transaction usually has no reason to know that they are suffering from a mental disease.[170] Unless the other party has reason to know of the impairment, relief is not available.[171] This protects the reliance and expectation interests of third parties who may deal with the impaired person without having any reason to realize that the person is ill.[172]

[3]   Intoxication[173]

Courts have little sympathy for the defense of "contracting under the influence."[174] Even though compulsive alcoholism and other drug use are forms of mental illness, they are often viewed as self-induced.[175] Moreover, it is not always obvious to the other party to the transaction that a person who is consuming these substances is impaired.[176] Accordingly, relief is limited to situations where the person is incapable of understanding the transaction and the other party to the contract has reason to know that the affected party is impaired.[177]

[C]   Incapacity in International Transactions

The CISG[178] expressly sidesteps issues related to lack of capacity. However, because the CISG does not apply to transactions with consumers, it is unlikely that it will govern a dispute involving a minor. It may apply to a dispute involving a sale to a mentally incompetent sole proprietor of a business, but this is expected to be a rare occasion. If it occurs, questions of the sole proprietor's incapacity are left to the applicable domestic law of the country whose law otherwise governs the dispute.[179]

Like the CISG, neither the UNIDROIT Principles nor the Principles of

---

[170] *Id.*

[171] Fingerhut v. Kralyn Enters., Inc., 337 N.Y.S.2d 394 (N.Y. Sup. Ct. 1971).

[172] *See* George J. Alexander & Thomas S. Szasz, *From Contract to Status Via Psychiatry*, 13 SANTA CLARA L. REV. 537 (1973).

[173] Jeffrey C. Hallam, Comment, *Rolling the Dice: Should Intoxicated Gamblers Recover Their Losses?*, 85 NW. U. L. REV. 240 (1990).

[174] *E.g.*, Fitts v. Griffin, 304 F. Supp. 2d 1337 (M.D. Ala. 2004); Miller v. Rhode Island Hosp., 625 A.2d 778 (R.I. 1993).

[175] *See* Kukulski v. Bolda, 116 N.E.2d 384 (Ill. 1953) (plaintiff could not obtain specific performance of the contract where plaintiff was aware that defendant was too intoxicated to comprehend the nature of the transaction when the contract was executed).

[176] Hickey v. Griggs, 738 P.2d 899, 901 (N.M. 1987).

[177] RESTATEMENT (SECOND) OF CONTRACTS § 16 (1981). *E.g.*, Williamson v. Matthews, 379 So. 2d 1245 (Ala. 1980).

[178] *Infra* § 10.05 Unconscionability.

[179] Michael Joachim Bonell, *The CISG, European Contract Law and the Development of a World Contract Law*, 56 AM. J. COMP. L. 1, 3 (2008).

European Commercial Contracts address questions of lack of capacity.[180] Issues of the parties' capacity to enter into a contract are thus governed, as they are in international contracts for the sale of goods, by the applicable domestic law.

§ 10.04   OBTAINING ASSENT IMPROPERLY: FRAUD, DURESS, AND UNDUE INFLUENCE[181]

[A]   Improper Persuasion[182]

Parties sometimes use heavy-handed negotiation tactics. Several doctrines mitigate the effect of any bad behavior the parties have engaged in. The root question is whether one party's negotiating tactics have impaired the other party's consent to the transaction to warrant the law's refusal to enforce the agreement.

In evaluating grounds for permitting a person to escape from a contract due to the bad behavior of the other, consideration must be given to the fundamental premise of our law that individuals are free to consent to whatever agreements they wish. But, contract law also assumes that people deal with each other in what are known as "arms-length" settings.[183] This means that both parties are expected, and indeed encouraged, to behave in ways that maximize their individual self-interests.[184] Plainly stated, sellers try to sell at the highest price they can induce the buyer to pay, and buyers try to get sellers to sell at the lowest price they can persuade the seller to accept.

The long-standing common law principle of caveat emptor ("let the buyer beware") required buyers to be primarily responsible for assuring that they receive a fair deal when they give their assent. Buyers, and sellers too, for that matter, should not expect that their counterparts will act in ways that diminish the value of their own positions. As Judge Posner has said: "Contract law does not require parties to behave altruistically toward each other; it does not proceed on

---

[180] PICC Art. 3.1(a) (2004); PECL Art. 4.101 (2002).

[181] John P. Dawson, *Economic Duress — An Essay in Perspective*, 45 MICH. L. REV. 253 (1947); Fleming James Jr. & Oscar S. Gray, *Misrepresentation (Pts. I & II)*, 37 MD. L. REV. 286, 488 (1977–78); Robert Hale, *Bargaining, Duress, and Economic Liberty*, 43 COLUM. L. REV. 603 (1943); W. Page Keeton, *Fraud: Misrepresentation of Opinion*, 21 MINN. L. REV. 643 (1937); Juliet P. Kostritsky, *Stepping Out of the Morass of Duress Cases: A Suggested Policy Guide*, 53 ALB. L. REV. 581 (1989); Anthony T. Kronman, *Paternalism and the Law of Contracts*, 92 YALE L.J. 763 (1983); Anthony T. Kronman, *Mistake, Disclosure, Information and the Law of Contracts*, 7 J. LEGAL STUD. 1 (1978).

[182] Grace M. Giesel, *A Realistic Proposal for the Contract Duress Doctrine*, 107 W. VA. L. REV. 443 (2005); Julie Kostritsky, *Stepping Out of the Morass of Duress Cases: A Suggested Policy Guide*, 53 ALBANY L. REV. 583, 589 (1989); Hamish Stewart, *A Formal Approach to Contractual Duress*, 47 U. TORONTO L.J. 175 (1997); Sian E. Provost, Note, *A Defense of a Rights-Based Approach to Identifying Coercion in Contract Law*, 73 TEX. L. REV. 629 (1995).

[183] *See* Laidlaw v. Organ, 15 U.S. 178 (1817) ("even if the vendor had been entitled to the disclosure, he waived it by not insisting on an answer to his question . . . . There was . . . no circumvention or maneuver practiced by the vendee, unless *rising earlier in the morning, and obtaining by superior diligence and alertness that* intelligence by which the price of commodities was regulated, be such.").

[184] *See* ADAM SMITH, THE WEALTH OF NATIONS 22 (5th ed. London 1789).

the philosophy that I am my brother's keeper."[185] Thus, buyers ought to be diligent in inspecting the goods or the land they are considering purchasing. Buyers are both expected and entitled to do this. Despite this "look out for yourself" flavor of contract law, the bargaining process is not the equivalent of "anything goes" warfare, and this section examines the lines between permissible and impermissible negotiating tactics.

[B]   Fraud, Misrepresentation, and Nondisclosure[186]

People sometimes lie. More frequently, even where they have no dishonest intent, they have an uncanny ability to perceive the world in terms favorable to their own interests. On other occasions, even well intentioned, careful people make mistakes. When one party intentionally, negligently, or innocently misrepresents facts, the other may enter into an agreement in reliance on the misrepresentation. A person's false representations of important facts may result in liability for breach of warranty,[187] or, in limited circumstances, may permit one of the parties to avoid the contract due to mistake[188] or misrepresentation. Thus, a person who consented to the terms of a contract in reliance on the other party's factual misrepresentations may rescind the agreement when the true facts are discovered. Rescission is also permitted when the other party has made no affirmative misrepresentation of fact, but has failed to disclose critical factual details relevant to the other party's decision to enter into the contract.[189]

[1]   Relationship Between the Tort of "Deceit" and Misrepresentation in Contract[190]

There is a close connection between rules of contract law that permit a party to escape from a contract made in reliance on a factual misrepresentation, and the tort known as "deceit," or, more commonly, "fraud."[191] In the law of torts, damages

---

[185] The Original Great Am. Chocolate Chip Cookie Co. v. River Valley Cookies, Ltd., 970 F.2d 273, 280 (7th Cir. 1992) (Posner, J.).

[186] Randy Barnett, *Rational Bargaining Theory and Contract: Default Rules, Hypothetical Consent, the Duty to Disclose, and Fraud*, 15 Harv. J.L. & Pub. Pol'y 783 (1992); Richard Craswell, *Taking Information Seriously: Misrepresentation and Nondisclosure in Contract Law and Elsewhere*, 92 Va. L. Rev. 565 (2006); Sheldon Gardner & Robert Kuehl, *Acquiring an Historical Understanding of Duties to Disclose, Fraud, and Warranties*, 104 Com. L.J. 168 (1999); Ofer Grosskopf & Barak Medina, *A Revised Economic Theory of Disclosure Duties and Break-Up Fees in Contract Law*, 13 Stan. J.L. Bus. & Fin. 148 (2007); Robert Keeton, *Fraud, Concealment and Non-Disclosure*, 15 Tex. L. Rev. 1 (1936); Anthony Kronman, *Disclosure, Information, and the Law of Contracts*, 7 J. Legal Stud. 1 (1978); Michelle Oberman, *Sex, Lies, and the Duty to Disclose*, 47 Ariz. L. Rev. 871 (2005); Alan M. Weinberger, *Let the Buyer Be Well Informed? — Doubting the Demise of Caveat Emptor*, 55 Md. L. Rev. 387 (1996); Christopher T. Wonnell, *The Structure of a General Theory of Nondisclosure*, 41 Case W. Res. L. Rev. 329 (1991).

[187] *See supra* Ch. 7 Warranties.

[188] *See infra* § 11.02 Mistake.

[189] Restatement (Second) of Contracts § 164 (1981). *See supra* § 11.02[C] Relationship of Mistake to Warranty, Misrepresentation, and Fraud.

[190] Ian Ayres & Gregory Klass, *Promissory Fraud Without Breach*, 2004 Wis. L. Rev. 507.

[191] *See generally* Restatement (Second) of Torts § 525 (1977).

are available for a misrepresentation only when a number of difficult elements are proven. The plaintiff must prove that: (1) the defendant made a statement of fact (not opinion); (2) the statement was material; (3) the statement was false; (4) the defendant knew it was false;[192] (5) the defendant intended to induce reliance on the statement; (6) the plaintiff actually relied on the statement; (7) his or her reliance was reasonable; and (8) the plaintiff suffered some actual pecuniary loss as a result of its reliance.[193] Further, where malice can be proven, punitive damages can be awarded.[194] These daunting elements are difficult to prove.

In contract law, a false representation might be used by the party injured by it in several ways. First, it might be used as grounds for the recovery of damages due to breach of warranty.[195] Second, the misrepresentation might also be used in an effort to avoid the contract entirely through rescission.[196] However, the standards for establishing a claim for damages or rescission due to a misrepresentation are far less burdensome than when damages are sought for the tort of deceit. In particular, in a contract action, the elements of knowledge of the falsity of the representation and intent to deceive are not normally required. And, as explained in connection with the law of express warranties, the strict common law requirement of reliance has been eliminated, at least in connection with contracts for the sale or lease of goods under the Uniform Commercial Code.[197]

[2]   Voidability Due to Misrepresentation

A "misrepresentation" is "an assertion that is not in accord with the facts."[198] When a party relies on a material or fraudulent misrepresentation of fact, the resulting contract is voidable.[199]

[a]   Fraud in the Factum and Fraud in the Inducement

The law has long divided intentional fraud into two types. The most heinous type of fraud is "fraud in the factum."[200] "Factum" comes from Latin and means "making or doing." Thus, this type of fraud is often described as "fraud in the

---

[192] Early requirements included establishing an intent to deceive. Later, recklessly or negligently making a false statement became sufficient. This is the difference between the torts of fraud and misrepresentation.

[193] *See generally*, Fleming James Jr. & Oscar S. Gray, *Misrepresentation (Pts. I & II)*, 37 Mᴅ. L. Rᴇᴠ. 286, 488 (1977–78); Page Keeton, *Fraud: The Necessity for an Intent to Deceive*, 5 UCLA L. Rᴇᴠ. 583 (1958); Rᴇsᴛᴀᴛᴇᴍᴇɴᴛ (Sᴇᴄᴏɴᴅ) ᴏꜰ Tᴏʀᴛs § 549 (1977).

[194] Rᴇsᴛᴀᴛᴇᴍᴇɴᴛ (Sᴇᴄᴏɴᴅ) ᴏꜰ Tᴏʀᴛs § 549 (1977).

[195] *See supra* Ch. 7 Warranties.

[196] Rᴇsᴛᴀᴛᴇᴍᴇɴᴛ (Sᴇᴄᴏɴᴅ) ᴏꜰ Cᴏɴᴛʀᴀᴄᴛs § 164 (1981). *See* Fleming James Jr. & Oscar S. Gray, *Misrepresentation (Pts. I & II)*, 37 Mᴅ. L. Rᴇᴠ. 286, 488 (1977–78).

[197] *See supra* § 7.02[E] Basis of the Bargain.

[198] Rᴇsᴛᴀᴛᴇᴍᴇɴᴛ (Sᴇᴄᴏɴᴅ) ᴏꜰ Cᴏɴᴛʀᴀᴄᴛs § 159 (1981).

[199] Rᴇsᴛᴀᴛᴇᴍᴇɴᴛ (Sᴇᴄᴏɴᴅ) ᴏꜰ Cᴏɴᴛʀᴀᴄᴛs § 162 (1981).

[200] Rᴇsᴛᴀᴛᴇᴍᴇɴᴛ (Sᴇᴄᴏɴᴅ) ᴏꜰ Cᴏɴᴛʀᴀᴄᴛs § 163 cmt. a (1981).

execution." It is also sometimes called "real" fraud or "essential" fraud.[201]

Fraud in the factum occurs when an unscrupulous person tricks someone else into signing a meaningful agreement by making it appear that he or she is signing a completely different document, such as an innocuous letter. When the fraud prevents the injured victim from understanding the nature of the document he or she had signed, the fraud operates to prevent formation of a contract.[202] However, this type of fraud rarely occurs.

The second and more common type of fraud is "fraud in the inducement." This occurs when one party makes an intentionally false material statement that causes the other party to assent to a proposed agreement.

[b] Misrepresentation of Fact

Here, as in the law of warranty,[203] it is critical that there be a misrepresentation of fact rather than a mere opinion.[204] Thus, a seller's recommendation of a vehicle as a "good car" does not give rise to claim for misrepresentation. Whether a car is good or bad is a matter of opinion, not fact.

Despite this, a false representation of an opinion, particularly if it is an "expert" opinion, provides a basis for relief.[205] In *Vokes v. Arthur Murray, Inc.*,[206] a dance studio's false representations about a customer's skill and potential as a dancer provided grounds for rescission of her agreement to pay for more than 2,000 hours of dance instruction.[207] And, in *Rodi v. Southern New England School of Law*,[208] the court permitted the plaintiff to maintain his cause of action against the law school that had admitted him, based on his allegation that the school had misrepresented its opinion about the school's prospects for obtaining accreditation from the American Bar Association. Thus, while opinions are not normally actionable, if an expert expresses a high opinion, when his or her opinion is in reality low, relief will be provided.

---

[201] *See* U.C.C. § 3-305 cmt. 1 (2012).

[202] RESTATEMENT (SECOND) OF CONTRACTS § 163 (1981). The distinction between these two types of fraud will weigh more heavily if you take an elective course in Commercial Paper. *See* U.C.C. § 3-305(a)(1)(iii) & cmt. 1 (2012).

[203] *See supra* § 7.02[A] Affirmations of Fact.

[204] RESTATEMENT (SECOND) OF CONTRACTS § 159 & cmt. c (1981).

[205] *See* RESTATEMENT (SECOND) OF CONTRACTS § 168 (1981).

[206] 212 So. 2d 906 (Fla. Dist. Ct. App. 1968). *See also* Syester v. Banta, 133 N.W.2d 666 (Iowa 1965).

[207] To put this in context, many law schools require approximately 90 hours of semester credit for graduation. At 15 hours of classroom instruction per credit hour, this would result in 1,335 hours of classroom instruction compared to the 2,302 hours of dance lessons Vokes agreed to buy. The price of slightly over $31,000 in 1961, would be approximately $230,000 in 2013, adjusted for inflation. With this many lessons, and modest talent, Vokes should have been dancing with the stars.

[208] 389 F.3d 5 (1st Cir. 2004).

[c]   Intentional or Reckless Misrepresentation

To constitute the tort of deceit, a misrepresentation must usually be intentionally false and intended to deceive.[209] Thus, common law fraud involves an element of intent or "scienter."[210]

Reckless misrepresentations might not be intentionally false, but they are still treated as involving intentional fraud, such as where someone is consciously aware of his own ignorance about some critical fact but makes a representation about it anyway.[211] For example, if, in attempting to sell her house to Phil, Karen represents that the basement floor never gets wet, even though she has never been to the basement and has no remote idea about whether the basement remains dry, she is acting recklessly with the facts. If the basement gets wet when it rains, her inaccurate statement will be treated the same as if she had known this all along.

[d]   Fraudulent Misrepresentation

In contract, a false representation supplies grounds for rescission, if the misrepresentation was either "fraudulent" or "material." A misrepresentation is fraudulent if the person who made the false assertion:

- knew that it was false;

- believed that it was false;

- did not have the confidence he or she stated or implied in the truth of the statement; or

- did not have the basis that he or she stated or implied in the truth of the assertion.[212]

These situations all involve a degree of culpability on the part of the person who has made the false representation.

[e]   Material Misrepresentations

However, not all misrepresentations are intentional or even reckless. Some may be merely negligent or even the result of a carefully considered honest mistake. These misrepresentations are also grounds for rescission of the contract if they were "material." A false representation is material if it is "likely to induce a reasonable person to manifest his assent" to an agreement,[213] or if the person who has made the false representation knows that it will in fact be likely to induce assent on the part of the other party involved.[214]

For example, if Sam had originally purchased his BMW from an unscrupulous

---

[209] RESTATEMENT (SECOND) OF CONTRACTS § 162 cmt. a (1981).

[210] RESTATEMENT (SECOND) OF CONTRACTS § 162 cmt. b (1981).

[211] RESTATEMENT (SECOND) OF CONTRACTS § 162(1)(c) (1981).

[212] RESTATEMENT (SECOND) OF CONTRACTS § 162(1) (1981).

[213] RESTATEMENT (SECOND) OF CONTRACTS § 162(2) (1981).

[214] *Id.*

used car dealer who criminally turned the odometer back before selling to Sam, Sam may honestly believe that the car only has 65,000 miles on it, even though it really has been driven 165,000 miles.[215] If the car otherwise appears to be in good shape, and he tells Barb that it only has 65,000 miles on it, his misrepresentation is likely to have an impact on Barb's willingness to buy the car for Sam's proposed price. Here, it is clear that an innocent false statement has the same potential to mislead as a deliberate lie. And, when the car needs regular repairs because of the extra 100,000 miles, the repairs will not be less expensive for Barb because of Sam's innocence and naiveté.

In this situation, Barb probably has a claim against Sam for breach of warranty. Alternatively, she may want to forego her right to recover damages and merely rescind the transaction, returning the car to Sam and recovering whatever she paid for it. Even though Sam's representation was not fraudulent, it was almost certainly "material" because of the likelihood that the mileage on the car would induce someone like Barb to agree to buy it.

Most cases like this involve misrepresentations that are material because they would have mattered to any reasonable person. For example, in *Halpert v. Rosenthal*,[216] the seller was liable for its completely innocent representation that his house was free of termites. The buyer's claim was permitted to go forward, without the necessity of proving that the seller knew, or even should have known, that the house had been infested. This is the type of manifestation that would have mattered to any reasonable person without regard to his or her personal characteristics, interests, or idiosyncracies.[217] Similarly, in *Cousineau v. Walker*,[218] a buyer of land was permitted to rescind a transaction due to the seller's innocent but nevertheless material misrepresentation that the land he had agreed to purchase contained a substantial quantity of gravel, which could be removed for sale for use in a nearby highway construction project. The only reason to purchase the property for the price involved was to extract the gravel that the seller believed was located on the land. When it turned out that the land was nearly devoid of gravel, the buyer was permitted to rescind.

Even where the false representation might not matter to a reasonable person, it might make a difference to a person based on his or her particular interests. Imagine, for example, a situation in which Bill owns a banjo that he falsely believes was once owned by "John Hartford," an accomplished but not widely known bluegrass musician.[219] Because of Hartford's relative obscurity, a reasonable person might be more interested in the quality of the instrument itself and might not care whether it had once been owned by Hartford. But, if Bill knows that Sally is an enthusiastic fan of John Hartford, he may tell Sally that Hartford had owned the banjo in the anticipation that this information will induce Sally to buy it. If so,

---

[215] Your author once owned a 12-year-old car with only 73,000 miles on it. He lives only 1 mile from his law school. For three years in a row, he rode more miles on his bicycle than in his car.

[216] 267 A.2d 730 (R.I. 1970).

[217] *See* RESTATEMENT (SECOND) OF CONTRACTS § 162 cmt. c (1981).

[218] 613 P.2d 608 (Alaska 1980).

[219] Hartford wrote a once popular song titled "Gentle on My Mind," which performer Glen Campbell made famous. Here, I realize, I'm showing my age (and musical preferences).

his misrepresentation is material, and Sally will be able to use it as grounds to avoid the contract, even though a reasonable person interested in a high-quality instrument, but lacking Sally's idiosyncratic interest, would not have cared.

In addition, misrepresentations of fact are likely to give rise to a claim for damages for breach of warranty, even where the defect is not material and does not permit the misled party to rescind. Here, damages will be based on the difference in value of the property if it has lived up to the seller's representations and the value of the property in the condition it is in.[220]

[f] Reasonable Reliance

Not every fraudulent or material misrepresentation justifies rescission of a contract. For the misrepresentation to make the contract voidable, it must have been reasonably relied on by the party seeking to escape from the contract.[221] Thus, there must be actual reliance on the misrepresentation, and that reliance must have been reasonable under the circumstances.

This standard is similar to the standard for "revocation of acceptance" in a contract for the sale of goods, where the buyer discovers a latent defect in the goods that substantially impairs their value under U.C.C. § 2-615.[222] This remedy is the U.C.C.'s version of rescission due to material breach. Where the material breach is founded on a breach of warranty, it may be difficult to discern the difference between a claim for equitable rescission and a claim that the buyer is entitled to revoke acceptance of the goods under U.C.C. § 2-615.

[3] Nondisclosure[223]

In some circumstances, a contract may be rescinded due to the failure of a party to disclose a material fact. Silence about a material fact or efforts to conceal a material fact operate as fraudulent or material misrepresentation person involved has a duty to speak.[224] A homeowner, who paints over water damage on his walls or ceiling, is just as guilty of fraud as a homeowner who lies about whether his roof

---

[220] U.C.C. § 2-714 (2012).

[221] RESTATEMENT (SECOND) OF CONTRACTS § 164 (1981).

[222] See supra § 9.03[C] Revocation of Acceptance.

[223] Richard Craswell, *Taking Information Seriously: Misrepresentation and Nondisclosure in Contract Law and Elsewhere*, 92 VA. L. REV. 565 (2006); Melvin A. Eisenberg, *Disclosure in Contract Law*, 91 CAL. L. REV. 1645 (2003); Sheldon Gardner and Robert Kuehl, *Acquiring an Historical Understanding of Duties to Disclose, Fraud, and Warranties*, 104 COM. L.J. 168 (1999); Kimberly D. Krawiec & Kathryn Zeiler, *Common-Law Disclosure Duties and the Sin of Omission: Testing the Meta-Theories*, 91 VA. L. REV. 1795 (2005); Michael H. Rubin, *The Ethics of Negotiations: Are There Any?*, 56 LA. L. REV. 447, 462 (1995); Janet Kiholm Smith & Richard L. Smith, *Contract Law, Mutual Mistake, and Incentives to Produce and Disclose Information*, 19 J. LEGAL STUD. 467 (1990); Alan Strudler, *Moral Complexity in the Law of Nondisclosure*, 45 UCLA L. REV. 337 (1997); Alan M. Weinberger, *Let the Buyer Be Well Informed? — Doubting the Demise of Caveat Emptor*, 55 MD. L. REV. 387 (1996).

[224] See Anthony Kronman, *Disclosure, Information, and the Law of Contracts*, 7 J. LEGAL STUD. 1 (1978); E.T. Tsai, Annotation, *Duty of Vendor of Real Estate to Give Purchaser Information as to Termite Infestation*, 22 A.L.R.3d 972 (1968); Christopher T. Wonnell, *The Structure of a General Theory of Nondisclosure*, 41 CASE W. RES. L. REV. 329 (1991).

leaks.[225] For example, in *Kracl v. Loseke*,[226] sellers of a home covered visible appearance of termite damage by placing sheetrock on the basement ceiling and by covering the floor joists where the damage appeared as part of their effort to "spruce up" the house prior to sale. Although it involved no affirmative statement, this is garden-variety fraud.

Likewise, a party who is aware of information that the other party might reasonably be expected to wish to know, may be liable for failing to disclose the information, even if he or she takes no steps to conceal the facts. For example, in *Stambovsky v. Ackley*,[227] the buyer was entitled to rescind due to the seller's failure to disclose that the house had a reputation of being haunted by "poltergeists."

The precise parameters of the duty to disclose information about a transaction are unclear. However, it is limited to only a few situations.

The first is where disclosure is necessary to correct an earlier statement. This may be necessary if circumstances change in a way that makes an earlier accurate statement, no longer true.[228] Thus, if a person becomes insolvent, previous statements he has made about his financial condition must be corrected. Failure to supply an update will make agreements based on the earlier uncorrected information voidable, if the nondisclosure is fraudulent or material.[229] If a person acquires information that reveals that an earlier representation he has made is false, he has a duty to correct the mistake.[230] Similarly, a person must disclose any fact which he knows would correct a mistake that the other party is making about the contents of the written version of the parties' agreement.[231]

Second, a person has a duty to reveal facts when he knows that the disclosure will correct a mistake of the other party about one of the other party's basic assumptions about the deal. However, the duty to speak applies only if the nondisclosure is not in good faith.[232] The most obvious example of this is where one party realizes that the other party's offer is based on a unilateral mistake. On the other hand, parties are not expected to make disclosures to adjust for the other party's inexperience or bad judgment. Nor are people required to reveal the results of their research where the underlying information is equally accessible to anyone who looks for it.[233]

Third, there is a duty to disclose material information about the transaction

---

[225] RESTATEMENT (SECOND) OF CONTRACTS § 160 (1981).

[226] 461 N.W.2d 67 (Neb. 1990).

[227] 572 N.Y.S. 2d 672 (N.Y. App. Div. 1991).

[228] RESTATEMENT (SECOND) OF CONTRACTS § 161(a) & cmt. c (1981).

[229] RESTATEMENT (SECOND) OF CONTRACTS § 161 illus. 1 (1981); Bursey v. Clement, 387 A.2d 346 (N.H. 1978).

[230] RESTATEMENT (SECOND) OF CONTRACTS § 161 (1981).

[231] RESTATEMENT (SECOND) OF CONTRACTS § 161(c) (1981).

[232] RESTATEMENT (SECOND) OF CONTRACTS § 161(b) (1981).

[233] *See* Laidlaw v. Organ, 15 U.S. 178 (1817). *See* Anthony Kronman, *Mistake, Disclosure, Information, and the Law of Contracts*, 7 J. LEGAL STUD. 1 (1978).

when the parties have a confidential or fiduciary relationship with one another.[234] Fiduciary relationships, of the type that result in a duty to disclose, include those between an attorney and his or her client,[235] a trustee and the beneficiary of the trust, or in other circumstances where one party has placed his or her trust or confidence in another. While friendships are usually not enough to result in such a relationship, other close relationships may be, particularly where there is a disparity in age, experience, or expertise between the parties that leads one of them to place particular trust or confidence in the other.

[a]   Material Nondisclosure

The right to rescind arises only when nondisclosure was fraudulent or dealt with a material fact. Termite infestations and water damage are among the items of information that have been held to be material in sales of residential real estate.[236] Nearly any fact that has a "quantifiable effect on the market value of the premises"[237] could form the basis of an action for rescission due to material nondisclosure.[238]

[4]   Effect of a "No-Reliance" Clause[239]

The parties to a contract sometimes include a provision in their contract specifying that they have relied only on their own inspections and judgment and not on the representations supplied by the other party. These sorts of provisions are similar to warranty disclaimers that specify that the buyer is purchasing the property on an "as is" basis.[240] The Restatement denies enforcement of these disclaimers.[241] Although U.C.C. § 2-316 prevents enforcement of a disclaimer that contradicts an express warranty, the warranty is subject to the effect of the parol evidence rule.[242] Despite the Restatement's position, where a disclaimer of reliance has been freely negotiated and was not itself induced by a misrepresentation, a court is likely to enforce it.

For example, in *LaFazia v. Howe*,[243] the sellers of a small restaurant made false

---

[234] RESTATEMENT (SECOND) OF CONTRACTS § 161(d) (1981).

[235] *E.g.* Miller v. Sears, 636 P.2d 1183 (Alaska 1981).

[236] Hill v. Jones, 725 P.2d 1115 (Ariz. 1986); Weintraub v. Krobatsch, 317 A.2d 68 (N.J. 1974) (cockroaches); Marchand v. Presutti, 509 A.2d 1092 (Conn. Ct. App. 1986) (flooding).

[237] Reed v. King, 145 Cal. App. 3d 261 (1983) (seller's failure to disclose murders that had occurred in the house, which had "quantifiable effect on market value of the premises," could form the basis of an action for rescission due to material nondisclosure). *See also* Stambovsky v. Ackley, 572 N.Y.S.2d 672 (N.Y. App. Div. 1991) (rescission for failure to disclose presence of "poltergeists").

[238] Hill v. Jones, 725 P.2d 1115 (Ariz. Ct. App. 1986) (past termite infestation); Reed v. King, 145 Cal. App. 3d 261 (1983) (house was site of multiple murder).

[239] Kevin Davis, *Licensing Lies: Merger Clauses, the Parol Evidence Rule and Pre-Contractual Misrepresentations*, 33 VAL. U. L. REV. 485 (1999).

[240] *See supra* § 7.07 Warranty Disclaimers.

[241] RESTATEMENT (SECOND) OF CONTRACTS § 196 (1981).

[242] U.C.C. § 2-316(1) (2012).

[243] 575 A.2d 182 (R.I. 1990).

representations to the buyers about the restaurant's financial condition. The written contract specified that "the Buyers rely on their own judgment as to the past, present or prospective volume of business or profits of the business of the Seller and does not rely on any representations of the Seller with respect to the same." In preventing the buyer from pursuing its claim of misrepresentation, the court emphasized that the provision was "not a general but a specific disclaimer" and because of the provision ruled that the plaintiff's alleged reliance on the seller's representations about the profitability of the business was not justifiable. Likewise, in *Dannan Realty Corp. v. Harris*,[244] the court enforced a specific clause indicating that the seller had made no representations other than those contained in the written version of their agreement to prevent the buyer from maintaining an action for damages due to fraudulent oral misrepresentations about the property.

Other courts have restricted claims of fraud even where the "no-reliance" clause was more of a general boilerplate provision than the more narrowly defined specific disclaimer contained in *LaFazia*. Still other courts have permitted such a clause to prevent actions based on innocent or negligent misrepresentations, but prevented them from forestalling actions based on intentional fraud.[245] Despite the reluctance of some courts to disregard boilerplate language disclaiming reliance on parol representations, some courts are willing to enforce them. In *Rissman v. Rissman*, Judge Posner said "the fact that the language has been used before does not make it less binding when used again. Phrases become boilerplate when many parties find that the language serves their ends."[246] This, the court said, was a reason to enforce the provision rather than a reason to disregard it.

In one sense, a person who seeks to get out of a transaction by asserting the effect of a false representation after signing an agreement that stipulates that he did not rely on the other party's representations is himself a liar. In making his claim for relief from the contract he says: "I lied when I told you I wasn't relying on your prior statements."[247] Thus, parties may include written terms specifying the extent to which they have relied on one another's representations. On the other hand, dishonest persons should not be permitted to bury language seeking to exculpate themselves from responsibility for their own affirmatively bad conduct.[248]

---

[244] *See also* Danann Realty Corp. v. Harris, 157 N.E.2d 597 (N.Y. 1959).

[245] *E.g.*, Wilkinson v. Carpenter, 554 P.2d 512 (Or. 1976).

[246] Rissman v. Rissman, 213 F.3d 381, 395 (7th Cir. 2000).

[247] *Id.* at 383.

[248] *E.g.*, Rio Grande Jewelers Supply, Inc. v. Data Gen. Corp., 689 P.2d 1269 (N.M. 1984); Snyder v. Lovercheck, 992 P.2d 1079 (Wyo. 1999).

[C]   Improper Threats[249]

Contractual duties are based on the consent of the parties.[250] Thus, if one of the party's manifestation of assent was not freely given, one of the necessary components of a contract is absent. Agreements obtained through duress are not enforceable.[251]

A contract is voidable due to duress when one of the parties induces the other to express his consent with an improper threat.[252] The essential question is whether the threat deprived the other party of his or her ability to consent to the agreement.[253]

The law recognizes several types of duress. Physical duress — the proverbial "gun to the head" — renders the victim's expression of assent ineffective and thus makes the contract void.[254] Extortion and other threats may so intimidate a person that he or she has no reasonable alternative other than to consent. In these situations, there is no physical compulsion and the contract is not rendered void. Instead, it is voidable at the election of the victim of the improper threat.[255]

The significance of the distinction between "void" and "voidable" is that if the contract is merely voidable, the party suffering from the duress can subsequently ratify the agreement by expressing his or her consent or accepting the benefits of the contract once the effects of the improper threat have been reduced or eliminated.[256]

Originally the defense of duress was available only in connection with threats of bodily harm or criminal prosecution.[257] In early English courts,[258] as well as in the early American jurisdictions, the threat involved had to have been serious enough to compel a person of "ordinary courage" to yield to it.[259] For example, in

---

[249] John P. Dawson, *Economic Duress — An Essay in Perspective*, 45 Mich. L. Rev. 253 (1947); Grace M. Giesel, *A Realistic Proposal for the Contract Duress Doctrine*, 107 W. Va. L. Rev. 443 (2005); Julie Kostritsky, *Stepping Out of the Morass of Duress Cases: A Suggested Policy Guide*, 53 Albany L. Rev. 583 (1989).

[250] *See supra* Ch. 4 Mutual Assent — Creating an Agreement.

[251] Restatement (Second) of Contracts § 174 (1981).

[252] Restatement (Second) of Contracts § 175 (1981).

[253] *See* Gallaher Drug Co. v. Robinson, 232 N.E.2d 668, 670 (Ohio Mun. Ct. 1965) ("The question in each case must be whether the person threatened was deprived of his freedom of will, and that is a question of fact, in the determination of which regard should be had to the nature of the threats, the sex, age, and condition of life of the party, and the attending circumstances.").

[254] Restatement (Second) of Contracts § 174 (1981); United States v. Bond, 586 A.2d 734, 738–40 (Md. 1991).

[255] Cumberland & Ohio Co. of Texas, Inc. v. First Am. Nat'l Bank, 936 F.2d 846 (6th Cir. 1991).

[256] Restatement (Second) of Contracts § 175 (1981). *E.g.*, Hyman v. Ford Motor Co., 142 F. Supp. 2d 735 (D.S.C. 2001).

[257] These were known as "duress per minas" and "duress of imprisonment." Rubenstein v. Rubenstein, 120 A.2d 11, 14 (N.J. 1956).

[258] 8 Holdsworth, History of English Law 51 (3d ed. 1924).

[259] *See* Brown v. Pierce, 74 U.S. 205 (1869).

Tallmadge v. Robinson,[260] the court explained that the historical standard depended on the "effect upon the mind of a man of ordinary firmness and courage."[261] This standard was hard to meet.

Modern courts take a more relaxed approach, which depends on whether one party made an improper threat that left the other party with "no reasonable alternative" other than to consent to the proposed agreement.[262] In *Tallmadge*, the court said that the modern test seeks to determine the effect of the threat "upon the particular person toward whom such conduct is directed, and in determining such effect the age, sex, health, and mental condition of the person affected, the relationship of the parties and all the surrounding circumstances . . . ."[263] Other formulations of the rule permit relief where "the victim [had] no choice but to agree to the other party's terms or face serious financial hardship . . . if the threat were to be carried out."[264]

[1] Physical Duress

The proverbial (perhaps even literal) "gun to the head" is, of course, duress. Threatening to assault or batter the other party or someone related to the other person in order to obtain their assent is also duress.[265] Almost any threat to commit an act that is in violation of the criminal law will constitute duress. In *Trane Co. v. Bond*, the court explained that "in addition to actual physical compulsion, a threat of imminent physical violence is exerted upon the victim of such magnitude as to cause a reasonable person, in the circumstances, to fear loss of life, or serious physical injury, or actual imprisonment for refusal to sign the document."[266] Because this type of duress prevents a person from exercising his or her "free will," it renders the contract completely void.[267] Fortunately, this type of duress is rare. And, when it occurs, it rarely generates any legal controversy.

[2] Extortion

Another, more common type of duress is extortion or "blackmail." Extortion occurs when one person demands payment from another by threatening to disclose evidence of a crime or other embarrassing information. In *Tallmadge v. Robinson*,[268] the defendant succumbed to a threat to provide false testimony that the defendant's father had committed incest. Even if the party seeking relief from the contract has committed a crime, threatened prosecution constitutes duress. On the other hand, a threat to institute civil proceedings is not duress because it is

---

[260] 109 N.E.2d 496, 499 (Ohio 1952). *See generally* John P. Dawson, *Economic Duress — An Essay in Perspective*, 45 Mich. L. Rev. 253 (1947).

[261] *Id.* at 499.

[262] Restatement (Second) of Contracts § 175(1) (1981).

[263] Tallmadge v. Robinson, 109 N.E.2d at 500.

[264] Totem Marine Tug & Barge, Inc. v. Alyeska Pipeline Serv. Co., 584 P.2d 15, 22 (Alaska 1978).

[265] Rubenstein v. Rubenstein, 120 A.2d 11 (N.J. 1956).

[266] Trane Co. v. Bond, 586 A.2d 734, 740 (Md. 1991).

[267] *E.g.*, Fairbanks v. Snow, 13 N.E. 596 (Mass. 1887).

[268] 109 N.E.2d 496 (Ohio 1952).

lawful to pursue legally available civil remedies.[269] However, a threat to file a law suit that would be an "abuse of process" is an improper threat that would constitute duress.

One area that presents problems is where a party threatens to disclose information to a prosecutor that could lead to criminal charges being brought against the other party. This kind of threat usually constitutes duress because it is improper for a private party to attempt to use the criminal law for personal gain.[270] Thus, in *Berger v. Berger*,[271] a threat to report the defendant to the IRS was a sufficient threat to constitute duress. Every citizen has an obligation to report information that another may have committed a crime to the authorities. Not only does making such a threat involve duress that can vitiate consent, it can also result in criminal charges being brought against the person who made the threat. As indicated earlier, the essence of blackmail is to demand payment from another for silence, which is exactly what someone threatening to go to a prosecutor does.

Likewise, in *Germantown Manufacturing Co. v. Rawlinson*,[272] an employee's obligation on two promissory notes was unenforceable when she was threatened with the arrest of her husband for embezzlement. The court described the threat as "the epitome of duress."[273] Thus, the threat of criminal prosecution is widely regarded as duress.[274] Not surprisingly, an attorney who makes this type of a threat to gain an advantage in a civil suit is in violation of the Model Rules of Professional Conduct: "A lawyer shall not present, participate in presenting, or threaten to present criminal charges solely to obtain an advantage in a civil matter."[275]

[3]　　Threats to Take Other Legal Action

Apart from extortion, threats to take action that is otherwise legal do not normally constitute duress. Thus, good-faith threats to file a lawsuit do not normally constitute duress.[276] When a creditor says: "pay me what you owe me, or I'll sue," the threat is not improper and any resulting settlement agreement is not voidable due to duress. However, a threat made in bad faith will qualify if it meets the other requirements for avoidance of the contract.

Some threats are unquestionably permitted. Hard bargains nearly always involve the parties' threats to take their business elsewhere if the other party does not agree to the first party's demands. If Barb could get out of her promise to buy Sam's car for $20,000 simply because Sam had threatened not to sell it to her for a

---

[269] Cont'l Cas. Co. v. Huizar, 740 S.W.2d 429 (Tex. 1987); Dunham v. Griswold, 3 N.E. 76 (N.Y. 1885).

[270] RESTATEMENT (SECOND) OF CONTRACTS § 176(1)(b) & cmt. c (1981).

[271] 466 So. 2d 1149 (Fla. Dist. Ct. App. 1985).

[272] 491 A.2d 138 (Pa. Super. Ct. 1985).

[273] *Id.* at 145.

[274] RESTATEMENT (SECOND) OF CONTRACTS § 176(1)(b) (1981).

[275] MODEL CODE OF PROF'L RESPONSIBILITY DR 7-105 (1980).

[276] RESTATEMENT (SECOND) OF CONTRACTS § 176(1)(c) & cmt. d (1981).

lower price, nearly every contract would be vulnerable to avoidance due to duress.[277]

The difficulty is in distinguishing between a proper threat and an improper threat. Here, the Second Restatement of Contracts provides guidance. A threat to commit a crime or a tort, a threat of a criminal prosecution, and a bad-faith threat to bring a civil action are improper.[278]

Other, less onerous threats may or may not be improper, depending on their effect on the agreed exchange. A threat is improper if the threatened act would "harm the recipient and would not significantly benefit the party making the threat."[279] Thus an employer's threat to make it difficult for the employee to obtain alternative employment, unless the employee signs a release of potential claims against the employer, is improper. If the employee has no alternative but to acquiesce to the employer's demand, the improper threat makes the release voidable by the employee.[280]

In these cases, the difficulty for an employee is not in showing that the threat was improper, but in establishing the necessary degree of compulsion that deprived him or her of any reasonable alternative. Thus, in *Blubaugh v. Turner*,[281] a threatened loss of the opportunity to receive outplacement counseling and $4,560 in separation pay was not enough to show that the employee "would face such immediate financial ruin that he could not seek remedy to provide redress for alleged wrongful termination" if he failed to sign the settlement. But, the employer's threat in *Maust v. Bank One Columbus, N.A.*[282] to "financially ruin" the employee if he did not sign a release was improper where the employee believed that the employer, because of its contacts in the community, was in a position to make good on its threat.

The Second Restatement also indicates that a threat is improper if "the effectiveness of the threat . . . is significantly increased by prior unfair dealing by the party making the threat."[283] For example, in *Andreini v. Hultgren*,[284] a surgeon who assured a patient that she would enjoy a full recovery from her condition, but waited until just before surgery to ask her to sign a complete waiver of her claims against him, was improper. And, in the well-known decision in *Austin Instrument, Inc. v. Loral Corp.*,[285] a component manufacturer's threat to stop delivery of goods the buyer needed to fulfill its own obligations to the United States Navy, which would have prevented the buyer from securing additional

---

[277] *E.g.*, Boud v. SDNCO, Inc., 54 P.3d 1131, 1137–38 (Utah 2002).

[278] RESTATEMENT (SECOND) OF CONTRACTS § 176(1)(a)–(c) (1981).

[279] RESTATEMENT (SECOND) OF CONTRACTS § 176(2)(a) (1981).

[280] RESTATEMENT (SECOND) OF CONTRACTS § 176 illus. 12 (1981). *See* Jay M. Zitter, Annotation, *What Constitutes Duress by Employer or Former Employer Vitiating Employee's Release of Employer from Claims Arising Out of Employment*, 30 A.L.R.4th 294 (1984).

[281] 842 P.2d 1072 (Wyo. 1992).

[282] 614 N.E.2d 765, 768–69 (Ohio Ct. App. 1992).

[283] RESTATEMENT (SECOND) OF CONTRACTS § 176(2)(b) (1981).

[284] 860 P.2d 916, 920–22 (Utah 1993).

[285] 272 N.E.2d 533 (N.Y. 1971).

contracts with the government, constituted "economic duress."

It is also improper to use a power for illegitimate purposes.[286] Thus, a public utility could not threaten to cut off a customer's supply of the necessary service in order to gain an advantage in contract negotiations over some other matter.[287]

[4] Economic Duress[288]

Economic duress is a particular type of unfair bargaining tactic that uses financial pressure to induce an agreement. Some types of economic pressure are permissible — and even desirable. Other economic pressure makes the agreement unenforceable.

[a] Hard Bargaining Distinguished

The owner of property can refuse to sell, even though he or she knows that the buyer is desperate to make a deal. The mere threat of the loss of the bargain is not duress.[289] In general, the parties are "free to drive whatever bargain the market [will] bear."[290]

Likewise, employers have the right to insist on terms they view as favorable to their interests. Even the threat of the loss of employment, if the employee does not agree to the employer's terms, is not duress where the employer does not go further and threaten to poison the well and make it difficult for the employee to obtain alternative employment elsewhere.

For example, in *Quigley v. KMPG Peat Marwick, LLP*,[291] an employee was bound by the terms of the arbitration agreement he signed as part of his employment contract, even though the term was offered on a "take-it-or-leave-it" basis. If every refusal to negotiate over individual terms constituted duress, every bargain would be vulnerable to attack. It follows that parties are generally free to deal only on terms that they prefer, even if this means that the other party has little choice but to accept them in order to go through with a deal. Such is the competitive marketplace. On the other hand, if one party's plight is the result of the other's actions, relief may be available.[292]

---

[286] RESTATEMENT (SECOND) OF CONTRACTS § 176 (1981).

[287] RESTATEMENT (SECOND) OF CONTRACTS § 176 illus. 16 (1981).

[288] P.S. Atiyah, *Economic Duress and the "Overborne Will*," 98 L.Q. REV. 197 (1982); Clare Dalton, *An Essay in the Deconstruction of a Doctrine*, 94 YALE L.J. 997, 1024–39 (1985); John Dalzell, *Duress by Economic Pressure*, 20 N.C. L. REV. 237 (1942); John P. Dawson, *Economic Duress — An Essay in Perspective*, 45 MICH. L. REV. 253 (1947); Robert Hale, *Bargaining, Duress, and Economic Liberty*, 43 COLUM. L. REV. 603 (1943).

[289] *E.g.*, Boud v. SDNCO, Inc., 54 P.3d 1131, 1137–38 (Utah 2002).

[290] Cabot Corp. v. AVX Corp., 863 N.E.2d 503, 512 (Mass. 2007).

[291] 749 A.2d 405 (N.J. Super. Ct. App. Div. 2000).

[292] RESTATEMENT (SECOND) OF CONTRACTS § 176 illus. 13 (1981).

[b]   Threat to Breach

Economic duress is a particular problem in connection with modifications of an existing contract. Here, the prevailing standard, just as in other cases of duress, is whether the agreement was induced by an improper threat that left the other party with no reasonable alternative other than to assent to the proposed modification. Economic duress occurs when a party takes unfair advantage of changed economic circumstances, which give the other party no practical alternative but to give in to demands to modify the contract. The principal difficullty in these cases is with threats by one of the parties to breach if the other party does not consent to the proposed modification. In some circumstances a person seeks modification of the contract due to changed circumstances that make his performance more difficult than originally anticipated. In other situations, the modification is sought only to take advantage of the other party's weakness. In either circumstance, the core principle of freedom of contract may conflict with concerns for fairness, particularly when circumstances give one of the parties' superior bargaining power over the other.

Although it was decided on the grounds of no consideration,[293] *Alaska Packers' Association v. Domenico*[294] is a good example of economic duress.[295] There, employees demanded a raise after their employer's commercial fishing boat was hundreds of miles away from port and unable to return to hire a different crew. Their employer submitted to their demands and promised extra pay. There was no physical duress, and no mutiny,[296] but their threat to strike left their employer with only two alternatives: give in to the fishermen's demands or abandon the entire Alaskan salmon season. The speculative nature of the damages the employer would have suffered made recourse to this remedy uncertain at best, and the absence of a courthouse in the middle of the ocean made the equitable remedy of an injunction prohibiting them from working for anyone else unrealistic.[297]

However, relying on the absence of consideration for the modification is a poor way to prevent enforcement of modifications extracted by duress. The consideration doctrine throws the baby out with the bath water. It makes perfectly reasonable modifications unenforceable even though they were made in good faith and without any economic pressure or duress. At the same time, it permits enforcement of coercive modifications if the parties have been sufficiently well represented to adjust each party's duties to provide at least the appearance of an exchange. If, for example, the fishermen in *Alaska Packers'* had agreed to go "day sailing" around Alcatraz Island upon their return to San Francisco in exchange for their employer's promise of extra pay, there would have been consideration for the employer's promise.

---

[293] *See supra* § 2.06 Pre-Existing Legal Duty Rule.

[294] 117 F. 99 (9th Cir. 1902).

[295] *See* Selmer Co. v. Blakeslee-Midwest Co., 704 F.2d 924, 927 (7th Cir. 1983).

[296] *See* Stilk v. Myrick, 170 Eng. Rep. 1168 (Ct. Common Pleas 1809).

[297] Selmer Co. v. Blakeslee-Midwest Co., 704 F.2d 924, 928 (7th Cir. 1983) (characterizing the fisherman in *Alaska Packers'* as having made "an attempt to exploit the [employer's] lack of an adequate legal remedy").

In *Austin Instrument, Inc. v. Loral Corp.*,[298] the court addressed the problem directly. Austin Instrument agreed to sell certain precision gear components for use by Loral in the manufacture of "radar sets" for the United States Navy. The deal was made as part of the country's military ramp up in the early years of the disastrous Vietnam conflict.[299] Before Austin had completed delivery of the gear components, Loral entered into a second contract to supply additional radar sets to the Navy. When it sought to buy additional gear components for the second installment of radar sets, Austin demanded that Loral pay a higher price and threatened not to deliver *any* of the goods unless Loral complied.[300]

In refusing to enforce Loral's promise to pay the higher price, the court said that Austin's threat to breach the first contract "deprived Loral of its free will."[301] It left Loral with "no reasonable alternative" other than consenting to the increased price.[302] Austin had taken unfair advantage of the importance of Loral's relationship with the government. Significantly as well, Loral demonstrated that cover was impossible — it could not have obtained a sufficient number of gear sets from the limited number of vendors approved by the government to meet its obligations to the Navy. Moreover, asking for a time extension from the Navy would have harmed Loral's relationship with the government in ways that could not have been measured.

In *Austin Instrument, Inc.*, these factors, which made Loral's legal remedy inadequate, were critical. One party's threat to breach has no sting if the victim can easily obtain a substitute for the goods or services that were to have been provided. For economic duress to make the contract voidable, the victim must have no other reasonable alternative. Thus, if "cover" is a reasonable alternative, it will be hard to make a claim of duress. If, as in *Austin Instrument, Inc.*, a substitute could not be obtained in time to avoid serious and irremediable harm, however, a substitute will not suffice.

The victim's financial difficulties often play a role in its sense of desperation. Here, courts disagree about whether taking advantage of another party's financial distress is enough to constitute duress when the distress was caused by circumstances other than the misconduct of the party exerting the pressure. In *Centric Corp. v. Morrison-Knudsen Co.*,[303] the court rejected the claim that

---

[298] 272 N.E.2d 533 (N.Y. 1971).

[299] *Cf.* United States v. Iraq (2002–2012).

[300] Note that there was consideration: In exchange for the modification to the price for the first installment of gear sets, Austin promised to supply a second installment of gear sets.

[301] Austin Instrument, Inc., 272 N.E.2d at 536. *See also* Brock v. Entre Computer Centers, Inc., 933 F.2d 1253, 1260 (4th Cir. 1991) (a party asserting economic duress "must establish that a wrongful threat was made which was of such character as to *destroy the free agency* of the party to whom the threat was directed.") (emphasis added). *See generally* Meredity R. Miller, *Revisiting* Austin v. Loral: *A Study in Economic Duress, Contract Modification and Framing*, 2 Hastings Bus. L.J. 357 (2006).

[302] Restatement (Second) of Contracts § 176(2) (1981). *See* Mach. Hauling, Inc. v. Steel of W. Va., 384 S.E.2d 139, 142 (W. Va. 1989) ("Where the plaintiff is forced into a transaction as a result of unlawful threats or wrongful, oppressive, or unconscionable conduct on the part of the defendant which leaves the plaintiff no *reasonable alternative but to acquiesce*, the plaintiff may void the transaction and recover any economic loss.") (emphasis added).

[303] 731 P.2d 411 (Okla. 1986).

exploitation of another party's financial hardship could not serve as the basis for a claim of duress, absent evidence that the hardship was attributable to the party who allegedly exerted the overbearing pressure. The court said:

> [H]ard bargaining, efficient breaches, and reasonable settlements of good faith disputes are acceptable, even desirable, in our economic system. However, the minimum standards are not limited to precepts of rationality and self-interest — they include equitable notions of fairness and propriety which preclude the wrongful exploitation of business exigencies to obtain disproportionate exchanges of value which, in turn, undermine the freedom to contract and the proper functioning of the system.[304]

Other courts have permitted one party to take advantage of another's financial distress, as long as the financial hardship was the result of circumstances other than that party's own conduct. In *Selmer Co v. Blakeslee-Midwest*[305] a subcontractor agreed to accept an immediate payment of only $67,000 in settlement of its claim for $120,000 originally promised to it by the general contractor. The subcontractor agreed to this reduced amount because of its pressing need for cash, presumably to pay its own suppliers, employees, and creditors. In responding to the subcontractor's claim that this settlement was procured through duress, and that it therefore should be entitled to recover the balance due on the $120,000 claim, the court said: "The mere stress of business conditions will not constitute duress where the defendant was not responsible for the conditions."[306]

[D] Undue Influence

Undue pressure does not always take the form of an improper threat. Sometimes it is reflected in unrelenting efforts to persuade. When the person who is the target of unrelenting pressure is unusually vulnerable to its effects, the contract may be voidable due to "undue influence."[307]

Recall that a basic assumption of contract law is that each party is free to maximize his or her own position.[308] We describe this as acting "at arm's length," and there is nothing improper about a party refusing to deal unless the other meets her price. Even if the reluctant party knows of a great need or desire on the part of the other to make a deal, it is proper to insist on getting one's price or

---

[304] *Id.* at 413–14.

[305] 704 F.2d 924 (7th Cir. 1983).

[306] *Id.* at 928 (quoting Johnson, Drake & Piper, Inc. v. United States, 531 F.2d 1037, 1042 (Ct. Cl. 1976) (per curiam)). *See also* Spradling v. Blackburn, 919 F. Supp. 969 (S.D. W. Va. 1996).

[307] RESTATEMENT (SECOND) OF CONTRACTS § 177 (1981). *See* Orwick v. Moldawer, 822 A.2d 506, 509 (Md. Ct. Spec. App. 2003) ("Generally, undue influence amounts to physical or moral coercion that forces a testator to follow another's judgment instead of his own.") (quoting Moore v. Smith, 321 Md. 347, 353, 582 A.2d 1237 (1990)); Rice v. Office of Servicemembers' Group Life Ins., 260 F.3d 1240, 1250 (Okla. 2001); Tinsley v. General Motors Corp., 227 F.3d 700, 704 (Mich. 2000) (undue influence is generally defined as "influence that is sufficient to overpower volition, destroy free agency, and impel the grantor to act against the grantor's inclination and free will").

[308] *See, e.g.*, Kakaes v. George Washington Univ., 790 A.2d 581, 584–585 (D.C. 2002) ("We agree . . . that individuals usually benefit when left free to maximize their own interests in negotiating the terms of a contract.").

refuse to make a deal. Arm's length transactions often work to the advantage of one party and the disadvantage of the other. That is the nature of a system that permits parties the freedom to make or to refuse to make contracts.

Sometimes, however, the arm's-length assumption may either be inappropriate or it may be substantially weakened due to one of the party's unusual susceptibility to overbearing pressure. In the first instance, it is wrong to assume that the parties are dealing on an arm's-length basis when there is a fiduciary or other confidential relationship between the parties such that one has a duty to put the interests of another ahead of his or her own. Common illustrations of fiduciary duties are the relationships between a trustee and his beneficiaries, and attorneys and their clients. One can also think of adults having a duty to minors and parents to their children as quasi-fiduciary obligations. The music and sports industries provide many illustrations because agents have a duty to act in their client's best interests in dealing with others.

Anytime that a court determines that someone with fiduciary or quasi-fiduciary obligation has entered into a contract on unfair terms with the person to whom the duty is owed, the contract is voidable at the request of the beneficiary.[309] Reaching this result does not normally require any showing that there was wrongdoing by the fiduciary, but only that the result of the parties bargain was unfair.

However, not every close relationship involves a fiduciary duty. However, even absent a close and trusting relationship, unscrupulous people sometimes take unfair advantage of a vulnerable person's weakened resistance to pressure. When the parties enjoy a close and trusting relationship or one party is under the domination of the other, the law provides relief from the oppressive party's overbearing and unfair persuasive methods.[310]

Two separate elements must be proven. First, the party seeking to avoid the contract must have either been "under the domination" of the party engaged in the overbearing pressure or involved in a sufficiently close relationship with that person so that he or she is justified in believing that the person will not engage in conduct which is inconsistent with his or her welfare.[311] Second, the party exercising the influence must engage in some type of "unfair persuasion."[312]

Many undue influence cases involve transfers of family wealth. Thus, M.L. ("Luther") Leathers, who was 90 years old, in a weakened mental state, and bedridden, was vulnerable to the "dominion" of his nephew and his nephew's wife, who persuaded him to make a gift to them. His agreement to transfer his property to them was unenforceable because of their over overbearing pressure on him in his vulnerable condition.[313] And, in *Eldridge v. May*,[314] siblings who trusted one another to look after each other's interests had a confidential relationship that

---

[309] RESTATEMENT (SECOND) OF CONTRACTS § 173 (1981).

[310] RESTATEMENT (SECOND) OF CONTRACTS § 177 (1981).

[311] RESTATEMENT (SECOND) OF CONTRACTS § 177 cmt. a (1981).

[312] RESTATEMENT (SECOND) OF CONTRACTS § 177 cmt. b (1981).

[313] Turner v. Leathers, 232 S.W.2d 269 (Tenn. 1950).

[314] 150 A. 378 (Me. 1930).

resulted in reversal of a transaction even though "it could not have been impeached if no confidential relation had existed."

Close friendships, on the other hand, are not normally regarded as sufficient to establish the type of trusting relationship that will automatically permit a contract to be avoided due to undue influence. There must have been conduct that would have deprived the victim of the pressure of his or her ability to exercise "free will."[315] Other relationships that are frequently mentioned as normally creating this type of relationship are principal and agent,[316] guardian and ward, physician and patient, nurse and invalid, and other relationships in which one is in a position of dominion or influence over another.

The relationship between a borrower and his or her creditor does not, by itself, establish the type of fiduciary or confidential relationship that justifies the borrower in believing that the creditor will act in the borrower's best interests.[317] Likewise, the relationship between a builder and the owner of a construction project, even though frequently friendly and trustful, is not normally the kind of relationship that would justify one in believing that the other will lay down his or her own self-interest to benefit the other.[318]

Improper and undue influence can also occur where one party is subject to the domination of another. The weaker party in this type of relationship is sometimes unusually vulnerable to overbearing persuasive tactics due to stress from external causes, such as, for example, a recent serious illness or death in the immediate family.[319] Other examples of externally caused stress can include losing a job or having a long-standing relationship end. Where unusual stress or pressure has affected the decision-making capacity of a party, and that was known, or should have been known, to the other party, a court may decide that the assent manifested was not genuine and that the contract is voidable by the victim of the undue influence.

The decision in *Odorizzi v. Bloomfield School District*[320] is frequently used to illustrate this principle. Odorizzi was a school teacher who was arrested on charges of illegal sexual activity.[321] His supervisors persuaded him to resign in a meeting at his home, immediately after his return from 40 sleepless hours undergoing

---

[315] *In re* Copelan, 553 S.E.2d 278 (Ga. Ct. App. 2001). *See also* Newell v. High Lawn Memorial Park Co., 264 S.E.2d 454 (W. Va. 1980).

[316] *E.g.*, McNeill v. Dobson-Bainbridge Realty Co., 195 S.W.2d 626 (Tenn. 1946).

[317] *E.g.*, Umbaugh Pole Bldg. Co., Inc. v. Scott, 390 N.E.2d 320 (Ohio 1979).

[318] Davis v. Carpenter, 274 S.E.2d 567 (Ga. 1981). *But see In re* Harris, 49 P.3d 710 (Okla. 2002) (deposit of funds with contractor for disbursement to subcontractors created trust fund and imposed fiduciary relationship for purposes of determining whether debt was nondischargeable in bankruptcy).

[319] *See* Butler v. O'Brien, 133 N.E.2d 274, 279 (Ill. 1956) ("we have observed that a mind wearied and debilitated by long-continued and serious illness is susceptible to undue influence and liable to be imposed upon by fraud and misrepresentation; that the feebler the mind of the testator, no matter from what cause, whether from sickness or otherwise, the less evidence will be required to invalidate the will of such person.").

[320] 246 Cal. App. 2d 123 (1966).

[321] *See* Curtis Nyquist, Patrick Ruiz, & Frank Smith, *Using Students as Discussion Leaders on Sexual Orientation and Gender Identity Issues in First-Year Courses*, 49 J. LEGAL EDUC. 535 (1999).

interrogation at the police station. In sustaining his claim of undue influence, the court identified the factors that are associated with what the court characterized as "overpersuasion":

> (1) discussion of the transaction at an unusual or inappropriate time, (2) consummation of the transaction in an unusual place, (3) insistent demand that the business be finished at once, (4) extreme emphasis on untoward consequences of delay, (5) the use of multiple persuaders by the dominant side against a single servient party, (6) absence of third-party advisers to the servient party, and (7) statements that there is no time to consult financial advisers or attorneys.[322]

Where these tactics are employed by someone in a confidential or domination relationship, with the person whose consent is thereby obtained, the agreement may be avoided and the parties returned to the status quo through rescission of the agreement and restitution of any benefits that have been exchanged as a result of the improperly obtained agreement.

[E]   Unfair Bargaining in International Contracts

In international sale-of-goods transactions, as explained in more detail below,[323] the CISG avoids questions related to the validity of the contract.[324] Thus, issues regarding fraud, duress, and undue influence are not within its scope. Accordingly, these issues are left to domestic law.[325]

UNIDROIT Principles of International Commercial Contracts and the Principles of European Contract Law both address the issues. Article 3.8 of the UNIDROIT Principles permits a party to "avoid the contract when it has been led to conclude the contract by the other party's fraudulent representation."[326] Article 3.8 does not define what constitutes a "fraudulent representation," but it does specifically refer to "language or practices" as fraudulent nondisclosures that, "according to reasonable commercial standards of fair dealing, the [other] party should have disclosed."[327] This language does not specifically require reliance, but requires the party seeking relief to show that the fraudulent misrepresentation or nondisclosure "led [it] to conclude the contract." Although it does not specifically require the misrepresentation to have been intentionally or recklessly false, the requirement of a "fraudulent" rather than a negligent or innocent misrepresentation fairly implies that some element of intent is necessary.

The Principles of European Contract Law take a similar approach.[328] However, they specifically provide that a representation or nondisclosure is fraudulent only if

---

[322] Odorizzi v. Bloomfield School District, 246 Cal. App. 2d 123, 132–133 (1966).

[323] *Infra* § 10.05 Unconscionability.

[324] CISG Art. 4 & 4(a) (1980).

[325] Michael Joachim Bonell, *The CISG, European Contract Law and the Development of a World Contract Law*, 56 Am. J. Comp. L. 1, 3 (2008).

[326] PICC Art. 3.8 (2004).

[327] *Id.*

[328] PECL Art. 4.107(1) (2002).

it was "intended to deceive."[329] They further specify that in determining whether a party has a duty to disclose particular information, the court should consider "(a) whether the party had special expertise; (b) the cost to it of acquiring the relevant information; (c) whether the other party could reasonably acquire the information for itself; and (d) the apparent importance of the information to the other party."[330]

Article 3.9 of the UNIDROIT Principles similarly permits avoidance when a party "has been led to conclude the contract by the other party's unjustified threat."[331] The threat must be "so imminent and serious as to leave the [threatened party] no reasonable alternative.[332] Article 3.9 further specifies that the contract may be avoided if the threat is "wrongful in itself" or if "it is wrongful to use [the threat] as a means to obtain the conclusion of the contract."[333] The Principles of European Commercial Contracts include nearly identical language.[334]

The UNIDROIT Principles also permit relief where one party has "taken unfair advantage of the [other] party's dependence, economic distress or urgent needs, or . . . improvidence."[335] European Commercial Contract Principles provide a similar rule that refers to a party who was "dependent on or had a relationship of trust with the other party."[336] Both would thus provide relief in circumstances similar two those where undue influence is grounds for avoidance of a contract.

§ 10.05   UNCONSCIONABILITY[337]

The unconscionability doctrine makes contracts unenforceable due to a combination of procedural and substantive problems where neither flaws in the bargaining process nor defects in substantive terms alone, are sufficient to make the contract unenforceable.

The doctrine is drawn from the traditional practice of courts of equity in balancing the respective hardships that would be suffered by the parties if equitable

---

[329] PECL Art. 4.107(2) (2002).

[330] PECL Art. 4.107(3) (2002).

[331] PICC Art. 3.9 (2004).

[332] *Id.*

[333] *Id.*

[334] PECL Art. 4.108 (2002).

[335] PICC Art. 3.10 (2004).

[336] PECL Art. 4.109(1)(a) (2002).

[337] Brian Bix, *Epstein, Craswell, Economics, Unconscionability, and Morality*, 19 Q. L. REV. 715 (2000); Richard Craswell, *Property Rules and Liability Rules in Unconscionability and Related Doctrines*, 60 U. CHI. L. REV. 1 (1993); Clare Dalton, *An Essay in the Deconstruction of a Doctrine*, 94 YALE L.J. 997, 1024–39 (1985); Richard A. Epstein, *Unconscionability: A Critical Reappraisal*, 18 J.L. & ECON. 293 (1975); James Gordley, *Equality in Exchange*, 69 CALIF. L. REV. 1587 (1981); Jeffrey L. Harrison, *Class, Personality, Contract, and Unconscionability*, 35 WM. & MARY L. REV. 445 (1994); Arthur Allen Leff, *Unconscionability and the Code — The Emperor's New Clause*, 115 U. PA. L. REV. 485 (1967); Robert A. Hillman, *Debunking Some Myths About Unconscionability: A New Framework for U.C.C. Section 2-302*, 67 CORNELL L. REV. 1 (1981); Russell Korobkin, *Bounded Rationality, Standard Form Contracts, and Unconscionability*, 70 U. CHI. L. REV. 1203, 1230–31 (2003); Seana Valentine Shiffrin, *Paternalism, Unconscionability Doctrine, and Accommodation*, 29 PHIL. & PUB. AFF. 205 (2000).

relief were granted or denied.[338] Equitable relief, such as specific performance, was unavailable if the contract was unduly burdensome or oppressive,[339] particularly if one of the parties suffered from an inferior bargaining position at the time the contract was made.[340] The doctrine sometimes sounded as if it was based on a lack of capacity, where the terms were "such as no man in his senses and not under delusion would make on the one hand, and as no honest and fair man would accept on the other."[341]

Today, the doctrine is enshrined in U.C.C. § 2-302, which explicitly permits courts to determine that a contract or a clause in a contract is unconscionable.[342] However, § 2-302 does not attempt to define unconscionability. The official comments to § 2-302 provide some guidance, indicating that the principle behind § 2-302 is "one of the prevention of oppression and unfair surprise."[343]

An early and widely cited application of the principle is found in *Williams v. Walker-Thomas Furniture Co.*[344] Over a period of five years, Williams signed a series of contracts with the Walker-Thomas Furniture Co. to purchase various home appliances and items of household furniture. Williams agreed to make regular monthly installment payments for the items she purchased and would own the items outright when the stream of payments was complete. If she defaulted, the furniture store could repossess the items and resell them.

However, Walker-Thomas was not content with the right to repossess the items that Williams had not yet paid for. The contract included a "cross-collateralization" clause. This provision permitted Walker-Thomas to repossess *any* of the items it had sold to Williams on credit, until the full price of *all* of the items she had bought was paid in full. Thus, if she had purchased eight items over a five-year period, with a total price of $1,000, and failed to make a final $25 payment to pay off the debt owed on the final item, Walker-Thomas could repossess all eight items.

The economic effect of this cross-collateralization clause was potentially devastating to Williams. If she missed a single payment, she could lose all of the furniture and appliances she had ever purchased from Walker-Thomas. Worse yet, because of a combination of the depreciated value of the items due to normal wear and tear, the costs of repossession and sale, and the limited market for used goods, Walker-Thomas was unlikely to obtain much of a real financial return from its repossession of the items from Williams. The most likely effect of the clause was to

---

[338] *See infra* § 15.04 Balancing the Equities: Practicality and Fairness. *See* Dando B. Cellini & Barry L. Wertz, Comment, *Unconscionable Contract Provisions: A History of Unenforceability from Roman Law to the U.C.C.*, 42 Tul. L. Rev. 193 (1967).

[339] *See, e.g.*, Wollums v. Horsley, 20 S.W. 781 (Ky. Ct. App. 1892).

[340] McKinnon v. Benedict, 157 N.W.2d 665 (Wis. 1968). *See generally* Arthur Allen Leff, *Unconscionability and the Code — The Emperor's New Clause*, 115 U. Pa. L. Rev. 485, 532 (1967); Emily Sherwin, *Law and Equity in Contract*, 50 Md. L. Rev. 253, 254–55 (1991).

[341] Earl of Chesterfield v. Janssen, 28 Eng. Rep. 82, 100 (Ch. Ct. 1850).

[342] U.C.C. § 2-302 (2012).

[343] U.C.C. § 2-302 cmt. 1 (2012). *See also* Restatement (Second) of Contracts § 202 (1981).

[344] 350 F.2d 445 (D.C. Cir. 1965). *See* Robert H. Skilton & Orrin L. Helstad, *Protection of the Installment Buyer of Goods Under the Uniform Commercial Code*, 65 Mich. L. Rev. 1465, 1476–81 (1967).

threaten Williams with being wiped out completely — providing her with a powerful incentive to make timely payments.

The court, taking a cue both from several older unconscionability cases,[345] as well as from U.C.C. § 2-302, which had not yet gone into effect, found that the provision was unconscionable. In reaching this conclusion the court said: "Unconscionability has generally been recognized to include an absence of meaningful choice on the part of one of the parties together with contract terms which are unreasonably favorable to the other party."[346] This passage has become the defining expression of the unconscionability doctrine.

As defined in *Williams v. Walker-Thomas Furniture Co.* and most modern decisions, the unconscionability doctrine has two prongs.[347] One is procedural; the other is substantive. A contract is procedurally unconscionable when one of the parties lacked a meaningful choice in entering into the contract. The contract is substantively unconscionable when its terms are oppressively one-sided. These two prongs fit neatly into the purpose of the unconscionability doctrine, articulated by § 2-302, of preventing both oppression (from one-sided terms) and unfair surprise (due to an absence of meaningful choice).[348]

The procedural flaws in the formation of the Walker-Thomas Furniture company contract, standing alone, were not enough to establish a claim of fraud, duress, or even undue influence. Walker-Thomas did not lie to Williams about the cross-collateralization clause. Nor did it make any improper threat to induce her to enter into the agreement against her will. Likewise, it did not use overly aggressive means of persuasion or take unfair advantage of any relationship of trust or confidence with Williams. However, it used an obscure provision in a "standardized form contract" and had given Williams no opportunity to bargain over the language or effect of the offensive term. Instead, the contract had been presented to her on a "take-it-or-leave-it" basis. As such, it was a "contract of adhesion."[349]

Likewise, the cross-collateralization clause was not itself illegal.[350] The legislature had not proscribed provisions of the type included in the contract, and the clause did not violate any established common law rule that would have rendered it

---

[345] Williams v. Walker-Thomas Furniture Co., 350 F.2d 445, 448 n.2 (D.C. 1965).

[346] *Id.* at 450.

[347] Peter A. Alces, *Guerilla Terms*, 56 EMORY L.J. 1511 (2007); Daniel D. Barnhizer, *Inequality of Bargaining Power*, 76 U. COLO. L. REV. 139 (2005); Arthur A. Leff, *Unconscionability and the Code — The Emperor's New Clause*, 115 U. PA. L. REV. 485 (1967).

[348] *E.g.*, DiMizio v. Romo, 756 N.E.2d 1018 (Ind. Ct. App. 2001). *See* Arthur A. Leff, *Unconscionability and the Code — The Emperor's New Clause*, 115 U. PA. L. REV. 485 (1967). Unfortunately, courts have not consistently applied this glib connection between "oppression" and "one-sided terms," on the one hand, and "unfair surprise" and the "absence of meaningful choice," on the other, as respectively reflecting the substantive and procedural aspects of unconscionability.

[349] *See supra* § 1.02[E] Adhesion Contracts.

[350] Today, the *Walker-Thomas* cross-collateralization clause would violate the Federal Trade Commission's Credit Practice Rules, which make it an unfair credit practice for a creditor to obtain a nonpurchase money security interest in many types of household goods. *See* 16 C.F.R. §§ 444.1–444.5 (2003). It would also violate state statutes specifically directed at cross-collateralization clauses. *See* D.C. Code 28-3805(a) (2003).

void. Nevertheless, the combination of a contract formation process that might have left Williams either unsure about the meaning of the contract or unable to bargain for more favorable terms, together with the potentially devastating impact of the terms themselves, justified the court in striking down the clause.

Since *Williams v. Walker-Thomas Furniture Co.*, many courts have recognized this two-pronged aspect of unconscionability.[351] For example, in *Armendariz v. Foundation Health Psychcare Services, Inc.*,[352] the California Supreme Court found that a mandatory pre-employment arbitration clause in an employment contract was unconscionable. The adhesive nature of the contract alone was sufficient to satisfy the procedural prong. Despite the public policy considerations frequently cited in favor of arbitration and other alternative dispute resolution methods, the court concluded that arbitration gave the employer a one-sided advantage with no reasonable justification, thus satisfying the substantive prong.[353] The court explained that its unconscionability analysis involved a sliding-scale approach: "the more substantively oppressive the contract term, the less evidence of procedural unconscionability is required to come to the conclusion that the term is unenforceable, and vice versa."[354]

Procedural unconscionability is sometimes found, as it was in *Armendariz*, based on the adhesive nature of the contract. However, the mere fact that the contract was offered without the opportunity to vary its terms is not usually enough, standing alone, to make the contract procedurally unconscionable.

Courts usually insist on more, such as a lack of knowledge or voluntariness on the part of the party disadvantaged by the contract, inconspicuous or small print, complex legalistic language, or a disparity in the sophistication or bargaining power of the parties, frequently combined with a lack of opportunity to study the contract or to inquire about its terms.[355] These factors explain why some businesses frequently ask consumers to separately initial certain provisions of a standardized contract, thus apparently demonstrating the consumer's understanding that the initialed term was included in the contract and manifesting their assent to its provisions. This assists the party who drafted the contract in proving that the other party was not a victim of "unfair surprise."

A wide variety of terms have been found to be substantively unconscionable, depending on the nature of the underlying transaction and the extent of the procedural flaws in the formation of the contract. As explained elsewhere, a term in a contract for the sale of goods that excludes liability for personal injuries is

---

[351] *See* Adler v. Fred Lind Manor, 103 P.3d 773 (Wash. 2004).

[352] 6 P.3d 669, 767 (Cal. 2000).

[353] *See* Doctor's Assoc., Inc. v. Casarotto, 517 U.S. 681 (1996) (unconscionability available as a defense to enforceability of arbitration provision so long as state law does not "single-out" arbitration clauses as unconscionable).

[354] *Id.* at 767–68. *See also* Funding Systems Leasing Corp. v. King Louie Int'l, Inc., 597 S.W.2d 624 (Mo. Ct. App. 1979) (adopting sliding scale analysis).

[355] *See* East Ford, Inc. v. Taylor, 826 So. 2d 709, 714 (Miss. 2002). *See also* Burch v. Second Judicial Dist. Court of State ex rel. County of Washoe, 49 P.3d 647 (Nev. 2002); Williams v. Walker-Thomas Furniture Co., 350 F.2d 445, 449 (D.C. Cir. 1965). *See* Daniel D. Barnhizer, *Inequality of Bargaining Power*, 76 U. Colo. L. Rev. 139 (2005).

presumed to be unconscionable.[356] And, although a different analysis is usually used to determine whether "liquidated damages" are unreasonably high, unconscionability analysis is sometimes used to determine whether liquidated damages are too low.[357] Likewise, attempts to disclaim warranties may be unconscionable, without regard to the requirements of U.C.C. § 2-316, which expressly governs the manner in which warranties may be disclaimed.[358]

The unconscionability doctrine has had its biggest impact in cases involving consumers. Consumers are far more likely than merchants to suffer from the type of disparity in bargaining power or lack of sophistication that would warrant a finding of procedural unconscionability. Not surprisingly, therefore, courts have been skeptical of claims of unconscionability pursued by merchants or other professionals.[359]

Commercial entities are generally held to a more exacting standard than consumers, either because of a greater expectation that they will read and understand the terms of agreements they make, or because commercial entities are given far greater latitude in their ability to allocate the risks associated with the transaction between themselves.[360] Unlike consumers, commercial enterprises are likely to have had a greater opportunity to diversify their risks and thus to protect themselves against the harm that would result from a single bad deal. In *Continental Airlines v. Goodyear Tire & Rubber Co.*, the court noted that the unconscionability doctrine "makes little sense in the context of two large, legally sophisticated companies . . . ."[361] Likewise, businesses are more likely to have engaged the assistance of counsel in conducting negotiations for a business transaction. It makes little sense when the party seeking relief engaged the assistance of counsel in connection with the formation of the contract.[362]

Despite this, merchants have sometimes been successful in claiming that a contract was unconscionable. This has usually occurred based on a serious procedural flaw in the bargaining process rather than due to the court's objection to the parties' allocations of risks between themselves as too one-sided.[363]

In *A & M Produce Co. v. FMC Corp.*,[364] a limited-remedy provision excluding liability for consequential economic loss in a contract for the sale of agricultural equipment was held unconscionable. The court emphasized both the disparity in

---

[356] U.C.C. § 2-719(3) (2012). *See infra* § 14.02[C] Unconscionability of Limited Remedies.

[357] RESTATEMENT (SECOND) OF CONTRACTS § 356 cmt. a (1981).

[358] *E.g.*, Evans v. Graham Ford, Inc., 442 N.E.2d 777 (Ohio Ct. App. 1981). *See* John A. Menchaca, II, Note, *Unconscionability and as Is Disclaimers in Sales Contracts*, 16 OKLA. CITY U. L. REV. 345 (1991).

[359] *E.g.*, Beanstalk Group, Inc. v. A.M. Gen. Corp., 283 F.3d 856, 865 (7th Cir. 2002).

[360] *E.g.*, Zapatha v. Dairy Mart, 408 N.E.2d 1370 (Mass. 1980).

[361] Continental Airlines v. Goodyear Tire & Rubber Co., 819 F.2d 1519, 1527 (9th Cir. 1987) (contract for sale of an airplane).

[362] Cryogenic Equip., Inc. v. S. Nitrogen, Inc., 490 F.2d 696, 699 (8th Cir. 1974) (negotiators included a knowledgeable commercial lawyer with 18 years experience).

[363] *See* Jane P. Mallor, *Unconscionability in Contracts Between Merchants*, 40 Sw. L.J. 1065 (1986).

[364] 135 Cal. App. 3d 473 (1982).

bargaining power between the parties and the inconspicuous appearance of the offensive clause on the back of the form contract. The court also noted the oppressive nature of the provision, which shifted entirely to the buyer the risk of harm to the buyer's business resulting from defects in the seller's product. Many cases involving determinations that a commercial contract was unconscionable involved a liability waiver like the one in *A & M Produce.*

In evaluating claims of unconscionability pursued by merchants, stereotypes about shrewd, sophisticated business men and women should be avoided. Although the buyer in *A & M Produce* was a sizeable local business entity, undoubtedly with some business acumen, not every merchant is educated, sophisticated, or even literate. The retail merchant in *Johnson v. Mobil Oil Co.*[365] had not completed high school before taking over his filling station business. Modern courts sometimes recognize that a person may be theoretically and technically a merchant but functionally a consumer in terms of his or her education, experience, and business acumen.[366]

On the other hand, the doctrine of unconscionability might cut too wide a swath through the economy if it is permitted to be used by parties who find a sudden interest in emphasizing their own lack of sophistication in an attempt to extricate themselves from a bad business deal. If it is too easy for parties to escape from contracts they should not have been made in the first place, others will become more reluctant to deal at all, and the wheels of commerce will grind more slowly in general.

The CISG is silent about the unconscionability doctrine. Article 4 of the CISG, which limits the convention's scope to issues governing contract formation and those pertaining to the rights and obligations of the immediate parties arising from the contract, might be interpreted to exclude the issue of unenforceability from the scope of the CISG.[367] This conclusion is buttressed by the language of Article 4(a) which specifies that the convention "is not concerned with . . . the validity of the contract or any of its provisions . . . ."[368]

As with other issues of validity, this leaves open the possibility that the domestic law of unconscionability may apply to contracts for the international sale of goods that are otherwise governed by the CISG. This, of course, detracts considerably from the goal of uniformity expressed in Article 7(a), as different countries may take an entirely different approach to the issue.[369]

In other international agreements, the unconscionability doctrine has taken hold.

---

[365] 415 F. Supp. 264 (E.D. Mich. 1976).

[366] *See, e.g.*, Moscatiello v. Pittsburgh Contractors Equip. Co., 595 A.2d 1190 (Pa. Super. Ct. 1991). *See generally* Larry T. Garvin, *Small Business and the False Dichotomies of Contract Law*, 40 WAKE FOREST L. REV. 295 (2005).

[367] Helen Elizabeth Hartnell, *Rousing the Sleeping Dog: The Validity Exception to the Convention on Contracts for the International Sale of Goods*, 18 YALE J. INT'L L. 1, 80–87 (1993).

[368] CISG Art. 4(a) (1980).

[369] *See* A.H. Angelo & E.P. Ellinger, *Unconscionable Contracts: A Comparative Study of the Approaches in England, France, Germany, and the United States*, 14 LOYOLA L.A. INT'L & COMP. L. REV. 455 (1992).

The UNIDROIT Principles expressly provide that "[a] party may avoid the contract or an individual term of it if, at the time of the conclusion of the contract, the contract or term unjustifiably gave the other party an excessive advantage."[370] In determining whether the contract or one of its terms may be avoided, the court is directed to give regard to whether one party has "taken unfair advantage" of the other's "dependence, economic distress or urgent needs, or of its improvidence, ignorance, inexperience or lack of bargaining skills."[371] The court should also consider "the nature and purpose of the contract."[372] Unlike domestic law, which usually avoids efforts to adjust the contract — other than eliminating an offensive provision — the UNIDROIT Principles expressly acknowledge the court's authority to "adapt the contract or term in order to make it accord with reasonable commercial standards of fair dealing."[373]

The Principles of European Commercial Contracts contain similar provisions, permitting avoidance of either the entire contract or one of its terms if one of the parties suffered from a weakness in bargaining power due to "a relationship of trust," "economic distress," "urgent needs," or was "improvident, ignorant, inexperienced or lacking in bargaining skill"[374] and the other party "took advantage of the first party's situation in a way which was grossly unfair or took an excessive benefit."[375] This language is reminiscent of the traditional unconscionability doctrine's reference to procedural and substantive unconscionability.

PECC Article 4.110 speaks directly to the enforceability of adhesion contracts. It permits a party to avoid a term that "has not been individually negotiated if, contrary to the requirements of good faith and fair dealing, it causes a significant imbalance in the parties' rights and obligations arising under the contract to the detriment of [the party seeking relief]."[376] However, this right does not extend to terms that define "the main subject matter of the contract" unless the term is not in "plain and intelligible language."[377] Nor does it extend to the basic question of the "adequacy in value of one party's obligations compared to the value of the obligations of the other party."[378] This latter language would seem to preclude a determination that the price was unconscionably high.

§ 10.06 DUTY OF GOOD FAITH[379]

Closely related to the doctrine of unconscionability is the implied duty of good faith in the performance of a contract. One party's failure to perform in good faith

---

[370] PICC Art. 3.10(1) (2004).

[371] PICC Art. 3.10(1)(a) (2004).

[372] PICC Art. 3.10(1)(b) (2004).

[373] PICC Art. 3.10(2) (2004).

[374] PECL Art. 4.109(1)(a) (2002).

[375] PECL Art. 4.109(1)(b) (2002).

[376] PECL Art. 4.110(1) (2002).

[377] PECL Art. 4.110(2)(a) (2002).

[378] PECL Art. 4.110(2)(b) (2002).

[379] Steven J. Burton, *Breach of Contract and the Common Law Duty to Perform in Good Faith*, 94

can supply the other party with a defense. In other circumstances, breach of the implied duty of good faith gives rise to a cause of action for breach.

The duty of good faith is derived from cases that impose an implied duty on the parties to do nothing to interfere with the other parties' performance of their contractual obligations.[380] For example, in *Pattterson v. Meyerhofer*,[381] the parties had a contract for the sale of land that the seller had not yet acquired. The buyer interefered in the seller's efforts to purchase the land at a foreclosure sale auction. The court said: "[b]y entering into the contract to purchase from the plaintiff property which she knew he would have to buy at the foreclosure sale in order to convey it to her, the defendant impliedly agreed that she would do nothing to prevent him from acquiring the property at such sale."[382] This was derived, the court said from "an implied undertaking on the part of each party that he [sic] will not intentionally and purposely do anything to prevent the other party from carrying out the agreement on his part."[383] This traditional rule is commonly applied to prevent a party from interfering with the efforts of the other party to satisfy a condition on which the first party's duty of performance depends.[384]

The affirmative duty of good faith performance was first articulated in *Kirke La Shelle Co. v. Paul Armstrong Co.*,[385] where the owner of the rights to a play impaired the value of a license he had granted for a public performance of the play, by granting someone else a license to make a film of the play. The court said:

> In every contract there is an implied covenant that neither party shall do anything which will have the effect of destroying or injuring the right of the other party to receive the fruits of the contract, which means that in every contract there is an implied obligation of good faith and fair dealing.

Later cases echoed this passage and the duty is now a fixture in both the Uniform Commercial Code[386] and the Second Restatement of Contracts.[387]

HARV. L. REV. 369 (1980); Harold Dubroff, *The Implied Covenant of Good Faith in Contract Interpretation and Gap-Filling: Reviling a Revered Relic*, 80 ST. JOHN's L. REV. 559 (2006); E. Allan Farnsworth, *Good Faith Performance and Commercial Reasonableness Under the Uniform Commercial Code*, 30 U. CHI. L. REV. 666 (1963); Thomas A. Diamond & Howard Foss, *Proposed Standards for Evaluating When the Covenant of Good Faith and Fair Dealing Has Been Violated: A Framework for Resolving the Mystery*, 47 HASTINGS L.J. 585 (1996); Emily M.S. Houh, *The Doctrine of Good Faith in Contract Law: A (Nearly) Empty Vessel?*, 2005 UTAH L. REV. 1; Timothy J. Muris, *Opportunistic Behavior and the Law of Contracts*, 65 MINN. L. REV. 521 (1981); Robert S. Summers, *The General Duty of Good Faith — Its Recognition and Conceptualization*, 67 CORNELL L. REV. 810 (1982); Robert S. Summers, *"Good Faith" in General Contract Law and the Sales Provisions of the Uniform Commercial Code*, 54 VA. L. REV. 195 (1968).

[380] RESTATEMENT (SECOND) OF CONTRACTS § 315 (1981). *See* U.C.C. § 2-609 (2012).

[381] 97 N.E. 472 (N.Y. 1912).

[382] Pattterson v. Meyerhofer, 97 N.E. at 473.

[383] *Id.*

[384] RESTATEMENT (SECOND) OF CONTRACTS § 245 (1981). *See supra* § 8.05[B] Interference with Occurrence of the Condition.

[385] 188 N.E. 163, 167 (N.Y. 1933).

[386] U.C.C. § 1-304 (2012) (formerly § 1-203). Section 1-304 provides: "Every contract or duty within [the Uniform Commercial Code] imposes an obligation of good faith in its performance and enforcement."

[A] Meaning of the Duty of Good Faith Performance

The nature of duty of good faith is expressed in many different ways. For many years, U.C.C. Article 1 defined good faith as nothing more than "honesty in fact,"[388] which has sometimes been characterized as "pure of heart, but empty of head" — not requiring reasonable behavior, but at least preventing dishonesty. Article 2 defined it differently with respect to merchants, for whom the obligation meant both "honesty in fact" and "the observance of reasonable commercial standards of fair dealing."[389] Revised U.C.C. Article 1 now uses this two-pronged definition for everyone.[390] The Second Restatement of Contracts approves of the U.C.C. definition[391] and recognizes that the meaning of the obligation varies, depending on the context.[392]

The duty is most frequently explained in terms of the types of behavior it prevents rather than the type of conduct it requires. Thus, it prevents a

> lack of diligence, willfully rendering only substantial performance, . . . abusing the power to specify terms or to determine compliance, . . . interfering with or failing to cooperate in the other party's performance, pretending to dispute or arbitrarily disputing, adopting overreaching or "weaseling" interpretations or constructions of contract language, taking advantage of the other party's weaknesses to get a favorable readjustment or settlement of a dispute, abusing the right to adequate assurances of performance, refusing for ulterior reasons to accept the other party's slightly defective performance, willfully failing to mitigate the other party's damages and abusing a privilege to terminate contractual relations.[393]

The high-water mark for the obligation of good faith performance may well be the decision in *KMC, Inc. v. Irving Trust Co.*,[394] which held that a bank's duty of good faith to one of its borrowers prevented it from exercising its contractual right to cut off the supply of funds to its borrower and demand payment of the debt, until the borrower had an opportunity to refinance.

Other courts have taken a more restrictive view, permitting parties to exercise their contractual rights so long as they do not take opportunistic advantage of the

---

[387] RESTATEMENT (SECOND) OF CONTRACTS § 205 (1981). Section 205 imposes a duty of "good faith and fair dealing."

[388] Former U.C.C. § 1-201(19) (2000).

[389] Former U.C.C. § 2-103(b) (2012).

[390] U.C.C. § 1-201(b)(20) (2012). As of the beginning of 2013, nearly every state had adopted revised Article 1, but some of them retained the "honesty in fact" standard for parties who are not merchants.

[391] RESTATEMENT (SECOND) OF CONTRACTS § 205 cmt. a (1981).

[392] *Id.*

[393] Robert S. Summers, *"Good faith" in General Contract Law and the Sales Provisions of the Uniform Commercial Code*, 54 VA. L. REV. 195, 216–17 (1968). *See also* RESTATEMENT (SECOND) OF CONTRACTS § 205 cmt. a & d (1981).

[394] 757 F.2d 752, 769–63 (6th Cir. 1986).

other party's vulnerability.[395] For example, in *Market Street Associates v. Frey*,[396] the parties had entered into a sale and leaseback transaction of real estate used as a shopping center. The contract gave the tenant the right to buy the property back at a favorable price in the event that the owner was unwilling to provide financing to make improvements to the mall. The tenant asked the owner to provide financing, but neglected to remind the owner that, under the terms of the contract, its failure to provide the requested financing gave the tenant the right to repurchase the property for less than its market value. The evidence supported two versions of the facts. One version, favorable to the tenant, was that the owner, a sophisticated national pension fund, had simply failed to read and understand the terms of the contract and was thus bound to perform the contract as agreed. The other version, favorable to the owner, was that the tenant did not want the owner to provide the requested financing, but used its request for financing to trick the owner into denying the request, so that it could accomplish its real objective of buying the property for less than its fair market value. The latter version of the facts amounted to bad faith: "opportunistic behavior" that could not have been contemplated at the time the contract was drafted.

Courts such as those in *Market Street Associates* do not require parties to behave altruistically toward one another, or as fiduciaries, but merely require that they not take opportunistic advantage of gaps in the contract or circumstances that might not have been contemplated when the contract was formed. The precise meaning of the duty is, in any event, best understood in the context of the circumstances in which it is most frequently invoked.

In international transactions, Article 7 of the CISG provides only that its provisions should be interpreted in a way that promotes "the observance of good faith in international trade."[397] Unlike the U.C.C., it imposes no affirmative duty on the parties to act in good faith.[398] However, several other provisions of the CISG impose duties that are sufficiently similar to the duty of good faith that it may fairly be interpreted to generally impose a broad duty of good faith performance, similar to the duty imposed by the U.C.C.[399] The UNIDROIT Principles on International Commercial Contracts, on the other hand, affirmatively require parties to "act in accordance with good faith and fair dealing in international trade."[400] As in the

---

[395] Kham & Nate's Shoes No. 2, Inc. v. First Bank of Whiting, 908 F.2d 1351 (7th Cir. 1990) (Easterbrook, J.).

[396] 941 F.2d 588 (7th Cir. 1991) (Posner, J.). *See* Todd D. Rakoff, *Good Faith in Contract Performance:* Market Street Assoc. Ltd. Partnership v. Frey, 120 Harv. L. Rev. 1187 (2007).

[397] CISG Art. 7(1) (1980). *See* Lisa Spagnolo, *Opening Pandora's Box: Good Faith and Precontractual Liability in the CISG*, 21 Temp. Int'l & Comp. L.J. 261 (2007).

[398] Paul J. Powers, *Defining the Undefinable: Good Faith and the United Nations Convention on the Contracts for the International Sale of Goods*, 18 J.L. & Com. 333 (1999).

[399] Michael Bridge, *A Law for International Sale of Goods*, 37 Hong Kong L. J. 17, 27–29 (2007); Disa Sim, *The Scope and Application of Good Faith in the Vienna Convention on Contracts for the International Sale of Goods* 19, 21, in Review of the Convention on Contracts for the International Sale of Goods 2002–2003, 21 (Pace Int'l L. Rev. ed. 2004); Christopher Sheaffer, Note, *The Failure of the United Nations Convention on Contracts for the International Sale of Goods and a Proposal for a New Uniform Global Code in International Sales Law*, 15 Cardozo J. Int'l & Comp. L. 461, 470–72 (2007).

[400] PICC Art. 1.7(1) (2004). *See* E.A. Farnsworth, *The Eason-Weinmann Colloquium on Interna-*

Uniform Commercial Code, this duty may not be disclaimed.[401] The Principles of European Contract Law take the same approach.[402]

[B]   Duty to Use "Reasonable" or "Best" Efforts[403]

Similar to the duty of good faith is the duty, which applies in some situations, that a party will make an effort to accomplish some task related to the contract. The duty to use one's "reasonable" or "best efforts" frequently applies in exclusive dealing contracts, such as where one party has the exclusive right to sell goods designed or manufactured by the other party in a particular market.

The classic example of this duty is found in *Wood v. Lucy, Lady Duff-Gordon*,[404] where the court held that the exclusive distributor of designer clothing had an implied duty to "use reasonable efforts" to market items designed by the defendant. Although the contract was silent about the distributor's obligation in this regard, the only compensation that the designer was to receive was a percentage of the distributor's revenue. In this circumstance, the entire transaction would be pointless unless the parties had reasonably understood that the distributor was required to use reasonable efforts to sell the items that it had the exclusive right to sell.

This duty to exercise "reasonable efforts" has been embraced by the Uniform Commercial Code as a duty to use "best efforts" in any "agreement by either the seller or the buyer for exclusive dealing in the kind of goods" involved in the transaction, by the seller to supply the goods and by the buyer to promote their sale.[405] Thus, if Manufacturing Supply enters into a contract giving Commercial Distributors the exclusive right to distribute the frimulators made by Manufacturing Supply in a particular geographic region, Commercial Distributors must use its best efforts to promote the sale of the frimulators within its exclusive geographic territory.

---

tional and Comparative Law: Duties of Good Faith and Fair Dealing Under the UNIDROIT Principles, Relevant International Conventions, and National Laws, 3 Tul. J. Int'l & Comp. L. 47, 59–61 (1995); Richard E. Speidel, *The Characteristics and Challenges of Relational Contracts*, 94 Nw. U. L. Rev. 823, 841–43 (2000).

[401] PICC Art. 1.7(2) (2004).

[402] PECL Art. 1.201 (2002). *See generally* E. Allan Farnsworth, *Duties of Good Faith and Fair Dealing Under the UNIDROIT Principles, Relevant International Conventions, and National Laws*, 3 Tul. J. Int'l & Comp. L. 47, 52 (1995).

[403] *See* Harold Dubroff, *The Implied Covenant of Good Faith in Contract Interpretation and Gap-Filling: Reviling a Revered Relic*, 80 St. John's L. Rev. 559 (2006); Daniel J. Coplan, *When Is "Best Efforts" Really "Best Efforts": An Analysis of the Obligation to Exploit in Entertainment Licensing Agreements and an Overview of How the Term "Best Efforts" Has Been Construed in Litigation*, 31 Sw. U. L. Rev. 725, 726 (2002); E. Allan Farnsworth, *On Trying to Keep One's Promises: The Duty of Best Efforts in Contract Law*, 46 U. Pitt. L. Rev. 1 (1984); Charles J. Goetz & Robert E. Scott, *Principles of Relational Contracts*, 67 Va. L. Rev. 1089, 1119 (1981) ("A search for the meaning of a best efforts obligation in terms of traditional legal doctrine is not very illuminating."); Victor P. Goldberg, *In Search of Best Efforts: Reinterpreting* Bloor v. Falstaff, 44 St. Louis U. L.J. 1465 (2000); Zachary Miller, Note, *Best Efforts?: Differing Judicial Interpretations of a Familiar Term*, 48 Ariz. L. Rev. 615 (2006).

[404] 118 N.E. 214 (N.Y. 1917).

[405] U.C.C. § 2-306(2) (2012).

Sometimes this duty is made an explicit part of the deal. In *Bloor v. Falstaff Brewing Corp.*,[406] the defendant purchased the plaintiff's brewery and promised to pay the plaintiff a royalty of 50 cents for each barrel of the plaintiff's brand of beer that it sold. The defendant also promised to "use its best efforts to promote and maintain a high volume of sales" of the plaintiff's brand (Ballantine Beer). This promise limited the defendant's discretion to make marketing decisions about which brands of beer to promote. It required the defendant not only "to treat the Ballantine brands as well as its own" but to take additional steps to maintain the "high volume of sales" that the contract required. The defendant was not required to drive itself into bankruptcy in an effort to maintain these levels, but it could not let the plaintiff's brands languish in favor of its own brands, on which it owed no royalty.[407]

[C] Duty of Good Faith in Specific Circumstances

The duty of good faith performance is most commonly an issue in situations where one of the parties enjoys some level of discretion in the performance of its obligations.

[1] Requirements and Output Contracts[408]

The most obvious example of this is in requirements and output contracts, where one of the parties retains discretion over the quantity of goods or services that will be exchanged. The quantity of goods to be produced or purchased is measured by the "actual output or requirements as may occur in good faith."[409] A seller's attempts to artificially restrict its output to avoid losses that will be suffered if it continues to manufacture and deliver the goods at the agreed price violates its duty to act in good faith.[410] Likewise, the buyer, in a requirements contract at a favorable price, cannot insist on deliveries of more good than it requires for normal operations, in order to resell the commodity at the higher market price, or to stockpile it as a hedge against the day when its requirements contract expires.[411]

---

[406] 601 F.2d 609 (2d Cir. 1979) (for those who are interested, the lower court's opinion, contains an excellent history of the beer industry, all the way "back to Domesday Book and beyond" at 454 F. Supp. 258 (S.D.N.Y. 1978)).

[407] *See also* Feld v. Henry S. Levy & Sons, Inc., 335 N.E.2d 320 (1975) (exclusive dealing contract requiring producer of "bread crumbs" to sell all of its output to the buyer); Victor P. Goldberg, *In Search of Best Efforts: Reinterpreting* Bloor v. Falstaff, 44 St. Louis U. L.J. 1465 (2000); Todd D. Rakof, *Good Faith in Contract Performance:* Market Street Associates Ltd. Partnership v. Frey, 120 Harv. L. Rev. 1187 (2007).

[408] James Lockhart, Annotation, *Establishment and Construction of Requirements Contracts Under § 2-306(1) of Uniform Commercial Code*, 94 A.L.R.5th 247 (2001); Victor P. Goldberg, *Discretion in Long-Term Open Quantity Contracts: Reining in Good Faith*, 35 U.C. Davis L. Rev. 319 (2002).

[409] U.C.C. § 2-306(1) (2012); Restatement (Second) of Contracts § 33 illus. 10 (1981). *See supra* § 2.05[E][5], Output and Requirements Contracts; *supra* § 4.11[B][4] Quantity.

[410] *E.g.*, Feld v. Henry S. Levy & Sons, Inc., 335 N.E.2d 320 (N.Y. 1975).

[411] *See* Orange and Rockland Utilities, Inc. v. Amerada Hess Corp., 59 A.D.2d 110 (N.Y. App. Div. 1977). Empire Gas Corp. v. Am. Bakeries Co., 840 F.2d 1333 (7th Cir. 1988). *See generally* John C.

[2]   Discretion to Set Price

The duty of good faith also applies to a party that has the unilateral right to set the price. U.C.C. § 2-316 recognizes that a contract is enforceable even though the parties have left the price to be determined by one of the parties.[412] But, it limits the parties' discretion: "A price to be fixed by the seller or by the buyer means a price for him [sic] to fix in good faith."[413] Thus, the price must be set in accordance with commercial standards of fair dealing in the trade.[414]

In cases involving consumers, the price must not be higher than the reasonable expectations of the parties. For example, in *Best v. United States National Bank*,[415] a customer's checking account contract gave the bank the discretion to set the fee for any checks that its customers wrote without having adequate funds in their account to cover the checks ("NSF" checks, meaning "not sufficient funds"). The plaintiff successfully challenged the bank's fee by showing that the bank's charges for other services were based on the bank's costs, together with an allowance for overhead and the bank's ordinary profit margin. This method of establishing other fees provided a basis for the customer's reasonable expectations about how fees for NSF checks would be calculated. Failing to establish fees in a manner consistent with the customer's reasonable expectations violated the bank's duty of good faith. Cases like this must be read in conjunction with decisions like *Maxwell v. Fidelity Financial Services*[416] and *People v. Two Wheel Corp.*,[417] which deal with whether the high price of goods alone, in the absence of any procedural irregularities, is enough to make a contract unconscionable.[418]

[3]   Unilateral Termination

The duty of good faith also limits the potentially harsh consequences of agreements that permit one or both of the parties to unilaterally terminate the contract. Rights to unilaterally terminate are sometimes used in loan agreements that permit the creditor to "accelerate" the time for payment, either "at will" or under circumstances that lead the creditor to "deem itself insecure." Similar unilateral termination rights also appear in franchise contracts and distributorship agreements, where they must also be must also be exercised in good faith.

In loan agreements, most courts require the creditor's decision to accelerate the debt to be "reasonable" and not due to the creditor's unreasonable fears or arbitrary whims.[419] However, other courts apply a subjective test, which depends

---

Weistart, *Requirements and Output Contracts: Quantity Variations Under the UCC*, 1973 DUKE L.J. 599.

[412] U.C.C. § 2-305(1) (2012).

[413] U.C.C. § 2-316(2) (2012).

[414] U.C.C. § 2-103 (2012). *See* Auto-Chlor System of Minn., Inc. v. Johnson Diversey, 328 F. Supp. 2d 980 (D. Minn. 2004).

[415] 739 P.2d 554 (Or. 1987). *See* James J. White, *NSF Fees*, 68 Ohio St. L.J. 185 (2007).

[416] 907 P.2d 51 (Ariz. 1995).

[417] 525 N.E.2d 692 (N.Y. 1988).

[418] *See supra* § 10.05 Unconscionability.

[419] Kupka v. Morey, 541 P.2d 740, 747 (Alaska 1975).

on whether the creditor was genuinely concerned about the prospects for payment rather than on the reasonable likelihood of default.[420]

Contracts for the sale of goods without a specified duration last for a "reasonable time" but otherwise may be terminated at any time by either party.[421] U.C.C. § 2-309 further provides that the general duties of "good faith and sound commercial practice" usually require reasonable notification of the unilateral termination of an agreement, to permit the other party to make alternative arrangements.[422] But, the duty to supply notice does not otherwise alter the right to unilaterally terminate for either a good reason or no reason at all.[423]

This is a particular problem in franchise agreements,[424] where the franchisor's reasons for terminating the franchise may be subtle, regardless of whether it is for sound business reasons or due to some sort of illegal discrimination.[425] Some courts have held that unilateral termination may be prohibited at least until the franchisee has had a reasonable opportunity to recoup its capital investment.[426] However, most courts have held that where the contract expressly supplies one or both of the parties the right to unilaterally terminate, the duty of good faith does not impose a substantive limit on this right.[427]

[4]   Contract Modifications

Modifications to existing contracts are another area where good faith plays a key role. For many years the preexisting duty rule was the principal limit on one-sided modifications. However, the preexisting duty rule disposed of many good-faith modifications along with those procured through duress.[428] Today, modifications of contracts for the sale or lease of goods are enforceable, even in the absence of consideration, subject only to the requirement that they were not procured through duress or other bad-faith conduct.[429] In cases governed by the common law, the requirement that the modification be "fair and equitable in view of circumstances not anticipated by the parties when the contract was made" goes a long way toward achieving the same goals of preventing bad-faith modifications that the U.C.C. seeks to achieve.[430]

---

[420] *E.g.*, Watseka First Nat'l Bank v. Ruda, 552 N.E.2d 775 (Ill. 1990).

[421] U.C.C. § 2-309 (2012).

[422] U.C.C. § 2-309 cmt. 8 (2012).

[423] Corenswet, Inc. v. Amana Refrigeration, Inc., 594 F.2d 129 (5th Cir. 1979); Bak-A-Lum Corp. v. Alcoa Bldg. Prods., Inc. 351 A.2d 349 (N.J. 1976).

[424] *See* Walter Gellhorn, *Limitations on Contract Termination Rights — Franchise Cancellations*, 1967 Duke L.J. 465, 474.

[425] Robert W. Emerson, *Franchise Terminations: Legal Rights and Practical Effects When Franchisees Claim the Franchisor Discriminates*, 35 Am. Bus. L.J. 559 (1998).

[426] Clausen & Sons Inc. v. Theodore Hamm Brewing Co., 395 F.2d 388 (8th Cir. 1968).

[427] United Airlines, Inc. v. Good Taste, Inc., 982 P.2d 1259 (Alaska 1999).

[428] United States v. Stump Home Specialties Mfg., 905 F.2d 1117, 1122 (7th Cir. 1990) (Posner, J.).

[429] *See* U.C.C. § 2-209 (2012); Robert A. Hillman, *Policing Contract Modifications Under the UCC: Good Faith and the Doctrine of Economic Duress*, 64 Iowa L. Rev. 849 (1979).

[430] Restatement (Second) of Contracts § 89 (1981).

[5] Employment at Will[431]

The duty of good faith plays a lesser role in "employment at will" agreements. Employers are usually permitted to fire employees who have not been promised employment for any particular term or subject to any express limitations, for any reason or no reason.[432] In most jurisdictions, an employee's only basis for a claim of breach of the duty of good faith was that he or she was discharged in violation of some affirmative public policy, such as those prohibiting discrimination on the basis of age, gender, race, sexual orientation, or religion,[433] or those providing protection to so-called "whistle blowers."[434]

[6] Lender Liability[435]

The duty of good faith plays a similar role in the law that applies to installment payment obligations, such as commercial lines of credit, installment sales contracts, and promissory notes. Many of these obligations call for regular monthly installment payments, with a set date for the full principal debt to be finally paid. Nevertheless, the agreement frequently gives the creditor the right to "accelerate" the debt, and require immediate payment of the outstanding principal balance, if the creditor "deems itself insecure" or determines, in its discretion, that the prospects of payment are diminished. Acceleration at will is limited by U.C.C. § 1-309, which prevents exercise of the clause only if the creditor "in good faith believes that the prospect of payment or performance is impaired."[436]

The express terms of some of these obligations make them payable "on demand." If so, the creditor is permitted to require payment according to the terms of the contract whenever it decides to make the necessary demand. However, the duty of good faith may prevent a demand for payment that is made solely to cause harm to the debtor.[437]

The court's decision in *K.M.C. Co., Inc. v. Irving Trust Co.*[438] sent fears throughout the banking community. There, a bank exercised its contractual right

---

[431] *See* Richard Epstein, *In Defense of the Contract at Will*, 51 U. CHI. L. REV. 947 (1984); Peter Linzer, *The Decline of Assent: At-Will Employment as a Case Study of the Breakdown of Private Law Theory*, 20 GA. L. REV. 323 (1986); Glen Weissenberger, *Remedies for Employer's Wrongful Discharge of an Employee Subject to Employment of an Indefinite Duration*, 21 IND. L. REV. 547 (1988); Note, *Protecting At-Will Employees Against Wrongful Discharge: The Duty to Search Only in Good Faith*, 93 HARV. L. REV. 1816 (1980).

[432] *E.g.*, Cromeens, Holloman, Sibert, Inc. v. AB Volvo, 349 F.3d 376 (7th Cir. 2003).

[433] *E.g.*, Cimochowski v. Hartford Public Schools, 802 A.2d 800 (Conn. 2002).

[434] *E.g.*, Sheets v. Teddy's Frosted Foods, Inc., 427 A.2d 385 (Conn. 1980).

[435] DENNIS M. PATTERSON, GOOD FAITH AND LENDER LIABILITY (1990); William H. Lawrence & Robert D. Wilson, *Good Faith in Calling Demand Notes and in Refusing to Extend Additional Financing*, 63 IND. L.J. 825 (1988); Dennis M. Patterson, *Good Faith, Lender Liability and Discretionary Acceleration: Of Llewellyn, Wittgenstein, and the Uniform Commercial Code*, 68 TEX. L. REV. 169 (1989).

[436] U.C.C. § 1-309 (2003) (former § 1-208).

[437] *See, e.g.*, K.M.C. Co., Inc. v. Irving Trust Co., 757 F.2d 752 (6th Cir. 1985); Corey R. Chivers, Note, *"Contracting Around" the Good Faith Covenant to Avoid Lender Liability*, 1991 COLUM. BUS. L. REV. 359, 386.

[438] 757 F.2d 752, 759–63 (6th Cir. 1986).

to terminate a line of credit, without giving the debtor time to attempt to obtain an alternate source of financing. Although the bank's decision appeared to have been precipitated by a personal falling out between the borrower and bank officer responsible for the decision, banks became fearful that they would be held liable for taking action that otherwise appeared to be well within the terms of their contract with the borrower. Other courts have taken a more restrictive view, permitting parties to exercise their contractual rights so long as they do not take opportunistic advantage of the other party's vulnerability.[439]

[7] Percentage Leases[440]

Claims based on bad-faith conduct have also been prevalent in commercial lease agreements where the rent owed to the landlord is based on a percentage of the tenant's gross revenue. Tenants who take affirmative steps to divert business away from the premises, for the sole purpose of minimizing amounts due under the lease, are likely to run afoul of their duty to act in good faith.[441] However, where the tenant's actions were taken for other sound business purposes, they are not violations of the covenant of good faith even though they resulted in a reduction of the business's gross receipts.[442]

[8] Insurance Contracts

As a final example, insurance companies have long been vulnerable to the claim that their failure to settle or satisfy a claim has been in "bad faith."[443] This liability originated in cases involving actions brought by third parties on account of an insurer's failure to settle a claim against one of its insureds.[444] It gradually expanded to cover actions brought directly by the insured.[445] The gravamen of the action, which lies in tort, is a bad-faith refusal to honor a valid claim.

In all of these situations, efforts to inflict harm on the other party out of spite, or for some other reason, are incompatible with the obligation of good faith.[446] Where the action that is alleged to have been taken in bad faith is motivated by

---

[439] *See* Kham & Nate's Shoes No. 2, Inc. v. First Bank of Whiting, 908 F.2d 1351 (7th Cir. 1990) (J. Easterbrook); *See also Speeches from the Federalist Society Fifth Annual Lawyers Convention: Individual Responsibility and the Law*, 77 CORNELL L. REV. 955, 1111 (1992) (asked to comment on the rise of lender liability suits, Judge Easterbrook said: "Not in the Seventh Circuit.").

[440] Richard Thigpen, *Good Faith Performance Under Percentage Leases*, 51 MISS. L.J. 315 (1981).

[441] *E.g.*, Goldberg 168-05 Corp. v. Levy, 9 N.Y.S.2d 304 (N.Y. Sup. Ct. 1938).

[442] Spanish Oaks, Inc. v. Hy-Vee, Inc., 655 N.W.2d 390, 402–03 (Neb. 2003). *See generally*, STEVEN J. BURTON & ERIC G. ANDERSEN, CONTRACTUAL GOOD FAITH § 2.3.3 (1995).

[443] *See* Roger C. Henderson, *The Tort of Bad Faith in First-Party Insurance Transactions After Two Decades*, 37 ARIZ. L. REV. 1153 (1995).

[444] *E.g.*, Comunale v. Traders & Gen. Ins. Co., 328 P.2d 198 (Cal. 1958); Motorists Mut. Ins. Co. v. Said, 590 N.E.2d 1228, 1232 (Ohio 1992).

[445] *E.g.*, Gruenberg v. Aetna Ins. Co., 510 P.2d 1032 (Cal. 1973); Zoppo v. Homestead Ins. Co., 644 N.E.2d 397 (Ohio 1994).

[446] *E.g.*, Stop & Shop, Inc. v. Ganem, 200 N.E.2d 248, 253 (Mass. 1964) ("[w]e assume . . . that [the parties' interests] could be protected against certain acts . . . for spite or to inflict harm"); K.M.C. Co., Inc. v. Irving Trust Co., 757 F.2d 752 (6th Cir. 1985).

commercially reasonable business judgment, it will not be treated as in bad faith, unless it was designed to take unfair "advantage of gaps in a contract in order to exploit the vulnerabilities that arise when contractual performance is sequential rather than simultaneous."[447] Whether action to take advantage of other vulnerabilities constitutes bad faith, particularly where the parties had a reasonable opportunity to allocate the risk of changed circumstances, remains unclear.

[D] Good Faith in International Contracts[448]

In international sales of goods, the role of good faith is unclear. CISG Article 7(1) provides that "[i]n the interpretation of [the CISG], regard is to be had to its international character and to the need to promote uniformity in its application and the observance of good faith in international trade."[449] This language conspicuously avoids imposing any affirmative duty of good faith in international sale-of-goods transactions of the type that is imposed by the U.C.C. in domestic transactions within the United States.[450] Rather, it merely specifies that the treaty itself should be interpreted with a view toward promoting good faith in international trade. However, other provisions of the CISG impose obligations that, fairly construed, amount to a duty to act in good faith.[451]

In other international transactions, the UNIDROIT Principles of International Commercial Contracts imposes an affirmative duty of good faith that is similar to the duty imposed by the U.C.C. UNIDROIT Principles. Article 1.7 provides that "[e]ach party must act in accordance with good faith and fair dealing in international trade."[452] This duty may not be excluded or limited.[453] Article 1.201 of the Principles of European Contract Law contains nearly identical language.[454] Nevertheless, the role of this duty, particularly to questions of precontractual liability, is uncertain.

---

[447] See The Original Great Am. Chocolate Chip Cookie Co. v. River Valley Cookies, Ltd., 970 F.2d 273, 280 (7th Cir. 1992).

[448] E. Allan Farnsworth, *Duties of Good Faith and Fair Dealing Under the UNIDROIT Principles, Relevant International Conventions, and National Laws*, 3 TUL. J. INT'L & COMP. L. 47 (1995); Freidrich Kessler & Edith Fine, *Culpa in Contrahendo, Bargaining in Good Faith, and Freedom of Contract: A Comparative Study*, 77 HARV. L. REV. 401 (1964); Alexander S. Komarov, *Internationality, Uniformity and Observance of Good Faith as Criteria in Interpretation of CISG: Some Remarks on Article 7(1)*, 25 J.L. & COM. 75 (2005).

[449] CISG Art. 7(1) (1980).

[450] U.C.C. § 1-304 (2012).

[451] See Michael Bridge, *A Law for International Sale of Goods*, 37 HONG KONG L. J. 17, 27–29 (2007).

[452] PICC Art. 1.7(1) (2004).

[453] PICC Art. 1.7(2) (2004).

[454] PECL Art. 1.201 (2002). See Harry Flechtner, *Comparing the General Good Faith Provisions of the PECL and the UCC: Appearance and Reality*, 13 PACE INT'L L. REV. 295 (2001).

Chapter 11

EXCUSE: MISTAKE AND CHANGE OF CIRCUMSTANCES

[B]   Change of Circumstances in International Transactions

§ 11.01   EXCUSE FROM CONTRACTUAL DUTIES[1]

The law of contracts sometimes excuses parties for their failure to perform. If nonperformance is excused, there is no breach, and damages are not available. However, restitution may be provided for any benefits conferred by one party on another before the circumstances warranting the excuse came to light. Relief is provided in two basic situations: mistake and change of circumstances.

Excuse due to mistake is available when one or both of the parties enter into the contract due to some mistaken belief about a key fact relevant to the transaction. Excuse is more likely to be available when both parties are mistaken — when it is a "mutual mistake", than when there is a "unilateral mistake" by only one of the parties.

Excuse is also available when circumstances change in a way that makes performance impossible — such as where a party whose physical ability to perform is critical to performance becomes disabled or dies, after the contract has been made. Destruction of the property that is the subject matter of the deal might also make performance impossible, and provides the parties with an excuse. Circumstances might also arise which frustrate the underlying fundamental purpose of the contract. Finally, the parties might also be excused when a change in circumstances makes performance far more difficult — or "impracticable" — than when the contract was made.

Despite their similarities, both doctrines are narrow. Expanding them to permit greater relief would make escape from the legitimate and reasonable expectations of the parties too easy.[2] If carried too far, both doctrines would disrupt the utility of contracts as a mechanism for giving parties a reliable way to guard against the risks of unknown facts and an uncertain future.

§ 11.02   MISTAKE[3]

The parties to a contract are excused from performing if the agreement was entered into due to some shared or "mutual" mistake that was a basic assumption of their contract.[4] Relief due to mistake is based on underlying principles of

---

[1] Dionysios P. Flambouras, *The Doctrines of Impossibility of Performance and Clausula Rebus Sic Stantibus in the 1980 Convention on Contracts for the International Sale of Goods and the Principles of European Contract Law — A Comparative Analysis*, 13 PACE INT'L L. REV. 261 (2001); Nancy Kim, *Mistakes, Changed Circumstances and Intent*, 56 U. KAN. L. REV. 473 (2008); Andrew Kull, *Mistake, Frustration, and the Windfall Principle of Contract Remedies*, 43 HASTINGS L.J. 1 (1991).

[2] Melvin Aron Eisenberg, *Probability and Chance in Contract Law*, 45 UCLA L. REV. 1005, 1037 (1998).

[3] Melvin Aron Eisenberg, *Mistake in Contract Law*, 91 CAL. L. REV. 1573 (2003); Roland R. Foulke, *Mistake in the Formation and Performance of a Contract*, 11 COLUM. L. REV. 197 (1911); Frona M. Powell, *Mistake of Fact in the Sale of Real Property*, 40 DRAKE L. REV. 91 (1991); Eric Rasmusen & Ian Ayres, *Mutual and Unilateral Mistake in Contract Law*, 22 J. LEGAL STUD. 309 (1993).

[4] RESTATEMENT (SECOND) OF CONTRACTS § 152(1) (1981). *See* Val D. Ricks, *American Mutual Mistake:*

contract formation. If the parties entered into a contract only because of a shared mistake about existing facts, their assent to the contract was faulty and their agreement should not be enforced.

On the other hand, freedom to contract is a core principle of our contract law,[5] and most of the time those who make otherwise enforceable promises are not protected from their failure to fully investigate the relevant facts before making a binding commitment.

Most contracts involve exchanges of property, and there are two fairly predictable patterns of mistakes. The first is where a seller discovers some condition that makes the property far more valuable than previously believed. The possibilities are endless: oil or gold is discovered on the land that is being sold, a Renoir hides under a nondescript painting, or the value of stock quadruples due to previously unreleased information about the company. Even if neither party was aware of the hidden condition until after the contract was made, the sellers are still likely to be upset because they will be losing a large benefit once the contract is performed.

The second common mistake is where a buyer discovers conditions that make the property far less valuable than previously believed. The possibilities here are also endless: the house is infested with termites, the engine in the 1995 Windstar automobile has a defective head gasket, or the product on which the value of a company is based is discovered to be dangerous. If it turns out that the sellers had prior knowledge in these situations, the question is often one of fraud or misrepresentation.[6] But even if the sellers had no previous knowledge, buyers are still likely to feel victimized because they are going to lose substantially once the contract is performed.

Of course, sometimes parties assume the risk that they have made some fundamental mistake about the transaction. The classic mistake case, *Wood v. Boynton*,[7] illustrates this. Wood found an attractive stone, but wasn't sure what kind of stone it was or if it had any value. She took it to Boynton, who was a jeweler. He wasn't sure what it was either, and they both speculated that it might be a topaz. With both of them unsure of its character, Wood sold it to Boyton for $1. Later, when it was discovered that it was an uncut diamond, worth $700, Wood sued to rescind the transaction and to recover the rock.

In rejecting Wood's effort to reclaim the diamond, the court said that she had "[chosen] to sell it without further investigation as to its intrinsic value to a person who was guilty of no fraud or unfairness." In other words "she made a bad bargain."[8] Wood sold the stone even though she was consciously aware of her own ignorance about its value or character. Moreover, Boynton might possibly have

---

Half-Civilian Mongrel, Consideration Reincarnate, 58 LA. L. REV. 663 (1998).

[5] A corollary to this idea is that individuals are free to make mistakes and that they should not expect to be rescued when they do.

[6] *See, e.g.*, Smith v. Zimbalist, 38 P.2d 170 (Cal. Ct. App. 1934) (description of two violins as a "Stradivarius" and a "Guarnerius"). *See* Andrew Kull, *Mistake, Frustration, and the Windfall Principle of Contract Remedies*, 43 HASTINGS L.J. 1 (1991).

[7] 25 N.W. 42 (Wis. 1885).

[8] *Id.* at 44. Adjusted for inflation, the amounts would be $20 and $15,000, respectively, today.

encountered many customers like Wood who had found a rock of unknown identity. It was probably in his best interest, for the purposes of customer relations, if nothing else, to buy such items if there was any chance that they might later prove to have value. Although the deal turned out well for him, he also assumed a risk — that he had wasted a dollar on a worthless pebble.[9]

A second difficulty with providing relief due to mistake is that when a party's expectations are disappointed, it may be too easy to assert that the contract was entered into because of a mutual mistake. The parties to a contract are free to set the value of their exchange, but contracts are frequently breached when one of the parties realizes that it made a bad deal. Contract law would be in shambles if every disappointed dealmaker could escape liability by showing that his or her "assent" was predicated on an erroneous assumption affecting the value of the transaction.

Still, there are times when a genuine mistake has been made. In *Beachcomber Coins, Inc. v. Bosket*,[10] the parties exchanged what seemed like a rare 1916 Denver mint dime that was later discovered to have been a counterfeit. Both parties believed it was authentic at the time of the sale and did not enter into the transaction with the belief that the true facts about the coin were uncertain or unknown. As a result, the court permitted the buyer to rescind the contract and recover the $500 he had paid for the worthless fake. However, while relief for mistake is sometimes available, it is narrowly confined to preserve the efficacy of contracts generally.

[A]   Mutual Mistake

The parties to a contract are excused when they entered into the contract due to a mutual mistake of fact as to a basic assumption on which the contract was made that has material effect on the performances due under the contract, so long as the party seeking relief from the contract did not assume the risk of the mistake when the contract was made.[11] Thus, for mistake to provide the grounds for relief, the mistake first must be a mistake of fact and not just a poor judgment. Second, the mistake must be about some fundamental assumption on which the contract was based, rather than about a peripheral matter. Third, the mistake must have a material effect on the agreed exchange. Finally, the party seeking relief must not have assumed the risk that he had made the very mistake that he claims is the basis for relief.[12]

---

[9] *See also* City of Everett v. Estate of Sumstad, 631 P.2d 366 (Wash. 1981) (no relief to seller after its estate auction sale of a locked safe, without the key, later found to contain more than $30,000).

[10] 400 A.2d 78 (N.J. Super Ct. 1979). Today, a 1916 Denver mint dime has a retail value of approximately $500–$6,000, depending on its condition.

[11] Restatement (Second) of Contracts § 152(1) (1981).

[12] Restatement (Second) of Contracts § 152 (1981). *E.g.*, Atlas Corp. v. United States, 895 F.2d 745, 750 (Fed. Cir. 1990).

[1] Mistake of Fact[13]

A mistake is "a belief that is not in accord with the facts,"[14] or "an erroneous belief."[15] Relief due to mistake is available only when the parties are mistaken about some existing fact, not when they have made a bad prediction about the future.[16] When relief due to mistake is sought, the mistake usually involves some misapprehension about the condition of real estate[17] or the nature or characteristics of goods that are the subject of a sale.

Parties might also be relieved when they have a mistaken belief about how the law applies to their transaction, such as where they believe that property zoned for residential purposes only, is zoned for commercial use.[18] Today, courts draw no distinction between mistakes of law and mistakes of other facts.[19] Either can provide a basis for excuse.[20]

On the other hand, parties who make a mistaken *judgment* are not entitled to relief. If Barb agrees to buy Sam's rear-wheel-drive BMW under the mistaken belief that it handles well in the snow, she will hardly have cause for relief.[21] As one court explained, "if the mistake resulted from a miscalculation as to the economic climate, to undo the contract would fly in the face of the very reason for having contracts in the first place."[22]

Another important type of mutual mistake sometimes occurs in the drafting of a written memorial of a contract. A "scrivener's error" is "a clerical error, or an error resulting from a minor mistake or inadvertence, especially in writing or copying something."[23] Where such a mistake has occurred, a court of equity will permit "reformation" of the mistake "to reflect the true agreement of the parties on which there was a meeting of the minds."[24] Thus, if Sam and Barb agree that

---

[13] Robert L. Birmingham, *A Rose by Any Other Word: Mutual Mistake in* Sherwood v. Walker, 21 U.C. DAVIS. L. REV. 197 (1987).

[14] RESTATEMENT (SECOND) OF CONTRACTS § 151 (1981); Lenawee Cty. Bd. of Health v. Messerly, 331 N.W.2d 203 (Mich. 1982). Professor Eisenberg has described these types of mistakes as "shared mistaken factual assumptions." Melvin Aron Eisenberg, *Mistake in Contract Law*, 91 CAL. L. REV. 1573, 1620 (2003).

[15] RESTATEMENT (SECOND) OF CONTRACTS § 151 cmt a (1981).

[16] *See* Ryan v. Ryan, 640 S.E.2d 64, 68 (W. Va. 2006); Hansen v. Little Bear Inn. Co., 9 P.3d 960, 964 (Wyo. 2000).

[17] Lenawee Cty. Bd. of Health v. Messerly, 331 N.W.2d 203 (Mich. 1982).

[18] *E.g.*, Gartner v. Eikill, 319 N.W.2d 397 (Minn. 1982); Dover Pool & Racquet Club v. Brooking, 322 N.E.2d 168 (Mass. 1975).

[19] *E.g.*, Barkhausen v. Cont'l Ill. Nat'l Bank & Trust Co., 120 N.E.2d 649 (Ill. 1954); Reggio v. Warren, 93 N.E. 805, 807 (Mass. 1911).

[20] RESTATEMENT (SECOND) OF CONTRACTS § 151 cmt. b (1981).

[21] Professor Eisenberg has characterized this as an "evaluative" mistake. Melvin Aron Eisenberg, *Mistake in Contract Law*, 91 CAL. L. REV. 1573, 1581–82 (2003).

[22] S.T.S. Transp. Serv., Inc. v. Volvo White Truck Corp., 766 F.2d 1089, 1093 (7th Cir. 1985).

[23] Schaffner v. 514 W. Grant Place Condo. Ass'n, Inc., 756 N.E.2d 854, 863 (Ill. App. Ct. 2001). *See also* JP Morgan Chase Bank, N.A. v. Qualls, 866 N.E.2d 71 (Ohio Ct. App. 2007).

[24] Am. President Lines, Ltd. v. United States, 821 F.2d 1571, 1582 (Fed. Cir. 1987). *See also*

Barb will pay $20,000.00 for Sam's car, but they inadvertently add a zero (0) before the decimal point when they wrote out their agreement, Barb will be entitled to relief from the mistake to avoid paying the $200,000.00 reflected in the written record of their agreement.[25]

A mutual mistake of this type is an important exception to the parol evidence rule.[26] To prevent parties from taking unfair advantage of this exception, proof of the mistake must usually be "clear and convincing,"[27] or in some jurisdictions, "beyond a reasonable doubt."[28]

Many scrivener's errors arise in contracts for the sale of real estate that contain mistaken descriptions of the land involved in the dispute. In *Hoffman v. Chapman*,[29] the parties agreed upon the sale of "Lot 4," a 96' by 150' portion of a housing development, containing only one house. However, the deed they received misdescribed the parcel in a way that would have resulted in the transfer of twice as much land, including a second dwelling. It was clear that this was not what was intended, and the court permitted reformation of the written contract. These types of errors also frequently occur in insurance contracts,[30] construction contracts,[31] and mortgages,[32] though the doctrine is certainly not limited to these types of agreements.

[2]   Basic Assumption of the Contract

For relief to be granted the mistaken belief must concern a basic assumption of the contract.[33] Early decisions tried to distinguish between mistakes about "the very nature of the thing" and mistakes about the "quality" or value of the thing. In *Sherwood v. Walker*,[34] the court granted relief to the seller of a cow because the parties had been mistaken about whether it was a breeding cow or a "barren" cow. The court viewed this not as a mere matter of quality, but a mistake that went to the very nature of the animal involved in the deal. Modern decisions make no

---

Wheeler-Dealer, Ltd. v. Christ, 885 N.E.2d 350 (Ill. App. Ct. 2008). *See generally* George E. Palmer, *Reformation and the Parol Evidence Rule*, 65 Mich. L. Rev. 833 (1967).

[25] Restatement (Second) of Contracts § 155 (1981).

[26] *E.g.*, Wheeler-Dealer, Ltd. v. Christ, 885 N.E.2d 350 (Ill. Ct. 2008). *See supra* § 6.06[C] Reformation Due to Mistake in Integration.

[27] Restatement (Second) of Contracts § 155 cmt. c (1981). *Eg.*, Bown v. Loveland, 678 P.2d 292 (Utah 1984); Wesley v. Schaller Subaru, Inc., 893 A.2d 389 (Conn. 2006); Thompson v. Estate of Coffield, 894 P.2d 1065 (Okla. 1995).

[28] The Travelers Ins. Co. v. Bailey, 197 A.2d 813 (Vt. 1964).

[29] 34 A.2d 438 (Md. Ct. App. 1943).

[30] The Travelers Ins. Co. v. Bailey, 197 A.2d 813 (Vt. 1964) (annuity agreement to pay $500 per year for 10 years reflected in writing as agreement to pay $500 per month for 100 months minimum, or $5,000 vs. $50,000).

[31] Hous. Auth. of Coll. Park v. Macro Hous., Inc., 340 A.2d 216 (Md. 1975) (agreement to delete portion of contract calling for installation of appliances in housing units).

[32] *E.g.*, Davenport v. Beck, 576 P.2d 1199 (Okla. Ct. App. 1977).

[33] Restatement (Second) of Contracts § 152 (1981).

[34] 33 N.W. 919 (Mich. 1887). *See* Norman Otto Stockmeyer, *To Err Is Human, to Moo, Bovine: The Rose of Aberlone Story*, 24 Thomas M. Cooley L. Rev. 491 (2007).

attempt to distinguish between the nature of the thing involved and its "quality."[35] Instead, they apply the Second Restatement test, which depends on whether the mistake concerned something that was a fundamental or "basic assumption" of the contract.[36]

In many cases it is easy to determine that the mistake related to the parties' basic assumptions. If the parties execute a contract to rent a building without being aware that the building has already burned, their agreement will probably be excused due to mistake. Likewise, if the contract depends on the health of a particular individual and the person has already been injured or has died at the time the contract was made, the parties will be excused.[37] Thus, the basic fact about which they were mistaken may be one which was not even discussed, even though it was foundational to the creation of the contract.

Mistaken assumptions about market value are not mistakes that relate to a basic assumption of the contract.[38] Instead, they are matters of judgment for which relief is not usually available. For example, if Barb agrees to buy Sam's BMW, because she mistakenly believes that it will prove to be a valuable "classic car," and it turns out to be a dud, her inaccurate prediction is not the basis for relief. Many contracts are gambles about the future. The bet is not off just because it turns out to be a bad one. The same is true about misjudgments about the current market value of the subject matter of the contract. If a contract could be avoided because of a mistaken belief about the market value of a commodity, many contracts would be upset. In other cases, whether the parties were mistaken about a basic assumption is sometimes difficult to discern. In these cases, this element of the rule tends to depend on whether the party seeking relief has assumed the risk of the mistake.

[3]   Material Effect on the Exchange

Even though many, many mistakes can happen, only errors that have a "material" effect on the transaction provide the basis for an excuse. If an error does not have a material effect on the exchange, it is disregarded.[39]

The test for materiality is objective.[40] Unless a reasonable person would consider the effect of the mistake significant in the making of the contract, the existence of an otherwise identifiable mistake will be considered irrelevant. When the effect of the mistake on the values exchanged in the transaction is only slight,

---

[35] Lenawee Cty. Bd. of Health v. Messerly, 331 N.W.2d 203, 209 (Mich. 1982).

[36] *Id.* at 209. *See* Clayton X-Ray Co. v. Evenson, 826 S.W.2d 45 (Mo. Ct. App. 1992); Restatement (Second) of Contracts § 152(1) (1981). *See also* Andrew Kull, *Mistake, Frustration, and the Windfall Principle of Contract Remedies*, 43 Hastings L.J. 1, 12 (1991); Frona M. Powell, *Mistake in the Sale of Real Property*, 40 Drake L. Rev. 91, 98–99 (1991).

[37] Restatement (Second) of Contracts § 152 cmt. b & illus. 6 (1981).

[38] Restatement (Second) of Contracts § 152 cmt. b (1981).

[39] *See, e.g.*, Restatement (Second) of Contracts § 151 illus. 6 (1981).

[40] *See* People v. Pirnia, 113 Cal. App. 4th 120, 121 (2003) ("In assessing materiality, an objective test is preferable."). *See* NSY, Inc. v. Sunoco, 218 F. Supp. 2d 708, 712–13 (E.D. Pa. 2002) ("[M]ateriality is applied as an objective test of the significance of a fact to the transactions under consideration.").

relief is not available. But if it completely frustrates the purpose of the contract, makes performance impossible, or seriously impairs the equivalencies of the values that are exchanged, and the other elements are satisfied, the mistake permits the party harmed by the mistake to avoid the contract.[41]

[4]   Assumption of the Risk

Questions about whether a person has assumed the risk of a mistake are at the heart of the analysis. A party who has assumed the risk of a mistake cannot assert the mistake as grounds to escape the contract.[42]

An important category of cases in which the risk of a mistake has been assumed comprises those in which the parties have entered into the contract despite their conscious awareness that they were facing an unknown set of circumstances. *City of Everett v. Estate of Sumstad*[43] provides a dramatic example. Among the items sold at an estate auction was a safe. It was sold even though it contained a locked compartment, the key to which had not been found. Because it was an estate auction, the owner of the safe was not available to provide information about what, if anything, might be found in the locked compartment. The auctioneer sold "the safe and its contents" to the buyer, who found that the compartment contained more than $32,000 in cash. The court held that the sale of the safe, under these circumstances, "reflected a mutual assent to the sale of the unknown contents of the [safe]."[44] The seller — the decedent's estate — demonstrated its willingness to sell the safe and its contents despite the administrator's awareness that he was ignorant about its contents.

Cases like these involve "conscious uncertainty" or "conscious ignorance."[45] When a person agrees to sell something despite being consciously ignorant of its nature, he has demonstrated indifference to the true facts. He has therefore assumed the risk that it might be more valuable than believed, or that the item is something completely different than imagined. An economic analysis of the transaction suggests that the seller has calculated the risk that he might be mistaken as to its value, and added the value of that risk into the price. This analysis regards the buyer as having made a similar calculation in determining the price he was willing to pay. Thus, in entering into the contract the parties have considered the risks and potential benefits of the transaction, including the risk associated with their own uncertainty, and have transferred these risks and benefits from the seller to the buyer.

This analysis is now usually applied to the classic decision in *Sherwood v.*

---

[41] Val D. Ricks, *American Mutual Mistake: Half-Civilian Mongrel, Consideration Reincarnate*, 58 LA. L. REV. 663, 669–70 (1998); Andrew Kull, *Mistake, Frustration, and the Windfall Principle of Contract Remedies*, 43 HASTINGS L.J. 1, 9–11 (1991); GEORGE E. PALMER, MISTAKE AND UNJUST ENRICHMENT 35–39 (1962).

[42] RESTATEMENT (SECOND) OF CONTRACTS § 154 (1981).

[43] 631 P.2d 366 (Wash. 1981).

[44] *Id.* at 367.

[45] RESTATEMENT (SECOND) OF CONTRACTS § 154 cmt. c (1981); Melvin Aron Eisenberg, *Mistake in Contract Law*, 91 CAL. L. REV. 1573, 1630 (2003).

Walker,[46] described above.[47] Neither the buyer nor the seller could have known whether the cow in *Sherwood v. Walker* was still capable of bearing calves. The seller presumed she was not, and the buyer did not know but was willing to take the chance. In one sense the parties were not mistaken — they both understood the risk they were facing.[48]

Assumption of the risk is also frequently an issue when one party to a settlement agreement in a personal injury action seeks release from the agreement on the basis that the agreement was made pursuant to a "mistake" about the extent of his or her injuries. Here, the public policy in favor of settling disputes runs head on into the doctrine of mistake.[49]

Williams v. Glash[50] provides a good illustration of this type of mistake. In an effort to settle a dispute arising from an auto accident, the defendant's insurance company wrote the plaintiff a check for $889.46, as compensation for damage to the plaintiff's car. Not yet realizing that she had suffered any physical injuries from the accident, the plaintiff checked a box marked "No" on a form supplied to her by the defendant's insurer, indicating that no one had been physically injured in the accident. She then indorsed a settlement check below language that said: "The undersigned payee accepts the amount of this payment in full settlement of all claims for damages to property and for bodily injury whether known or unknown which the payee claims against any insured." After the check had been deposited and finally paid, the plaintiff discovered that she was suffering from temporomandibular joint syndrome ("TMJ"), which caused her to suffer from head and neck pain. She sought to rescind the release on the grounds of mutual mistake.

The court acknowledged the existence of a " 'modern trend' of setting aside releases when the injury later sued for was unknown at the time of the signing" and proceeded to permit the plaintiff to attempt to prove her claim of mutual mistake. The question was whether the plaintiff, despite the clear language of the release, had "intentionally assumed the risk of unknown injuries."

It was significant that not only did the plaintiff claim not to have known of her injuries, but also that the parties did not discuss or bargain for any settlement of any possible unknown injuries. Likewise, because the amount the plaintiff received was precisely the amount of the property damage to her car, it was clear that she had received no separate consideration for any possible unknown personal injuries. Furthermore, the defendant's insurance company had even coded the check to indicate that it was solely for property damage and not for any claimed or possible personal injuries. Under these circumstances, the court concluded that there was a genuine issue of material fact regarding the parties' intent that the release does

---

[46] 33 N.W. 919 (Mich. 1887).

[47] *See* Melvin Aron Eisenberg, *Mistake in Contract Law*, 91 Cal. L. Rev. 1573, 1634 (2003).

[48] Restatement (Second) of Contracts § 154(b) (1981). *E.g.*, Estate of Nelson v. Rice, 12 P.3d 238 (Ariz. Ct. App. 2000) (no relief for estate from sale of $1,000,000 painting for $60).

[49] *See* Michael A. DiSabatino, Annotation, *Modern Status of Rules as to Avoidance of Release of Personal Injury Claim on Ground of Mistake as to Nature and Extent of Injuries*, 13 A.L.R.4th 686 (1982) (collecting cases).

[50] 789 S.W.2d 261 (Tex. 1990).

not cover personal injuries, which precluded summary judgment against the plaintiff.[51] *Williams v. Glash* reflects the weight of authority, which treats dispute settlement agreements much like any other case involving a mutual mistake.[52]

In some cases the parties have expressly manifested their allocation of the risk of any mistakes. Used cars are frequently sold on an "as is" basis. If so, the buyer assumes any risk of mistake about the quality of the car.[53] Contracts for the sale of real estate also sometimes include language indicating that the sale is made on an "as is" basis or that the buyer is relying exclusively on its own inspection of the property without regard to any undiscovered defects or conditions. Executors of decedents' estates and bankruptcy trustees, who have not lived in the houses they are selling and have no reason to be aware of problems with the property, frequently sell real estate on as "as is" basis.[54] Thus, if Karen, as executor of her father's will, sells her parent's house to Phil on an "as is" basis, and Phil later discovers that the house was, at the time of the sale, infested with termites, Phil will not be able to assert that there was a mutual mistake that should provide him with relief.[55] Language of this type is treated as an express allocation of the risk of any mistake to the buyer, although this might depend on whether the term was specifically negotiated between the parties,[56] or, if it was boilerplate language, whether it was conspicuous.[57]

[B]   Unilateral Mistake[58]

A "unilateral mistake" occurs when only one of the parties is mistaken.[59] Relief is not usually available in cases of unilateral mistake, unless there was some sort of

---

[51] *Id.* at 264. *See also* LeBlanc v. Friedman, 781 N.E.2d 1283, 287 (Mass. 2002) (medical malpractice claim).

[52] *See generally* Michael A. DiSabatino, Annotation, *Modern Status of Rules as to Avoidance of Release of Personal Injury Claim on Ground of Mistake as to Nature and Extent of Injuries*, 13 A.L.R.4th 686, 691 (1982).

[53] RESTATEMENT (SECOND) OF CONTRACTS § 154(a) & cmt. b (1981). *E.g.*, Schneider v. Miller, 597 N.E.2d 175 (Ohio Ct. App. 1991). *See also* U.C.C. § 2-316(3)(a) (2012); *supra* § 7.07 Warranty Disclaimers.

[54] Your author, who had not lived in the structure for many years and was unfamiliar with its defects, sold his parent's house "as is" when he served as the executor of his mother's estate. The buyers employed an independent engineering firm to inspect the house, and several minor repairs were made prior to the sale.

[55] *E.g.*, Stewart v. Thrasher, 610 N.E.2d 799 (Ill. App. Ct. 1993); Copland v. Nathaniel, 624 N.Y.S.2d 514 (Sup. Ct. 1995).

[56] *E.g.*, Shore Builders, Inc. v. Dogwood, Inc., 616 F. Supp. 1004 (D. Del. 1985).

[57] Cohen v. North Ridge Farms, Inc., 712 F. Supp. 1265 (E.D. Ky. 1989).

[58] Melvin A. Eisenberg, *Disclosure in Contract Law*, 91 CAL. L. REV. 1645 (2003); Wendell F. Grimes & Barry J. Walker, *Unilateral Mistakes in Construction Bids: Methods of Proof and Theories of Recovery — A Modern Approach*, 5 B.C. IND. & COM. L. REV. 213 (1964); Ernest M. Jones, *The Law of Mistaken Bids*, 48 U. CIN. L. REV. 43 (1979); Anthony T. Kronman, *Mistake, Disclosure, Information, and the Law of Contracts*, 7 J. LEGAL STUD. 1 (1978); Edwin W. Patterson, *Equitable Relief for Unilateral Mistake*, 28 COLUM. L. REV. 859 (1928); Janet K. Smith & Richard L. Smith, Contract Law, *Mutual Mistake, and Incentives to Produce and Disclose Information*, 19 J. LEGAL STUD. 467 (1990).

[59] RESTATEMENT (SECOND) OF CONTRACTS § 153 (1981). *E.g.*, Drennan v. Star Paving Co., 333 P.2d 757 (Cal. 1958).

overreaching or bad faith by the other party.[60] Mistaken buyers or sellers are generally just out of luck. A seller who underestimates the value of her property will usually have to perform even though she learns of her error before transferring ownership to the buyer. Likewise, a buyer who overestimates the value of his purchase will usually be required to perform, or pay damages, even though he discovers his error before taking ownership from the seller. As a practical matter, this result is all but required in order to maintain a free enterprise system in which the participants enjoy freedom to make their own contracts — and their own mistakes.

The construction contract bidding process sometimes leads to claims for relief based on a unilateral mistake. To understand how a unilateral mistake might be made, it is helpful to understand how the construction industry operates. In both large and small construction projects a "general contractor" takes responsibility for the overall project. For a set price, the general contractor agrees to build a structure that is "complete in accordance with the [owner's] specifications." However, most general contractors do not have a full range of skilled laborers, such as plumbers, electricians, painters, masons, and so on, in their full-time employ. Unable to do all of the detailed work themselves, general contractors usually rely on specialists for various parts of the job, referred to as subcontractors.

Before submitting its bid to the owner of a construction project, a general contractor usually solicits bids from subcontractors for discrete portions of the work, such as excavation, electric, plumbing, and "heating, ventilation, and air conditioning" ("HVAC"). The general contractor then chooses the subcontractors' bids it wishes to use for the project and compiles an overall bid that is submitted to the owner. Sometimes the individual bids of the subcontractors are disclosed in the overall bid, and sometimes they are not.[61]

The process of haggling with subcontractors is hectic and often continues right up until the deadline for general contractors to submit their bids. This process sometimes results in a variety of mistakes: subcontractors make mistakes in calculating their subcontracting bids, and general contractors make mistakes in calculating their general contracting bids. When the owner accepts a bid from a general contractor that contains a significant error, the question arises whether the general contractor can obtain relief from the mistake. The mistakes can be so large that the accepted bid may be significantly lower in price than the next highest bid, and the question is whether the accepting owner should have realized that the "low bid" contained an error.[62]

Resolution of these disputes usually depends on what the accepting party should have known. Unless the mistake was such that it should have been obvious, a

---

[60] RESTATEMENT (SECOND) OF CONTRACTS § 153 (1981).

[61] The owner has a contract only with the general contractor, not with the subcontractors, and thus does not need to know, when the bid is accepted, which subcontractors will do these parts of the work.

[62] An offeree cannot validly accept an "offer" known to have been made in jest or one known to be the product of a mistake, because the offeree knows that the offeror is not serious about entering a contract on the terms contained in the offer. *See supra* § 4.03[D] Jokes and Hoaxes; RESTATEMENT (SECOND) OF CONTRACTS § 153(b) & cmt. e (1981).

general contractor is usually out of luck if the owner has accepted its erroneous bid. Likewise, a subcontractor who has submitted a mistaken bid is usually bound to it.

The well known promissory estoppel decision in *Drennan v. Star Paving Co.*[63] supplies a good example. Star Paving submitted a subcontracting bid for the paving work on a school construction project, not realizing that its bid had been miscalculated. Star Paving's effort to escape the consequences of its mistake was rejected because the general contractor, who relied on it in submitting its own bid, "had no reason to know that [Star Paving] had made a mistake."[64]

Thus, when one party has submitted a mistaken offer, no contract will result from an acceptance of the offer if the other party had reason to know of the mistake.[65] In *Drennan*, the disparity between Star Paving's mistaken bid and the bids of other subcontractors who had submitted bids for the same work was not so great that Drennan should have realized it was mistaken. In other cases, where the disparity was larger, the offeree has not been permitted to "snap-up" an offer that it should have known was based on a mistake.[66]

On the other hand, relief is sometimes provided where there has been a clerical or mathematical mistake and the mistake was discovered before the other party had relied on it in any substantial way. In *Elsinore Union Elementary School District v. Kastorff*,[67] a contractor had submitted a mistaken bid by failing to carry over the amount of a subcontracting bid to the column it used to calculate its "total" bid. The contractor reported its mistake the morning after its bid had been approved by the school board, but before the board had taken any real action in reliance on the accuracy of the bid. In providing relief, the court said that he should not be denied relief "from an unfair, inequitable, and unintended bargain."[68] Likewise, in *S.T.S. Transport Service Inc. v. Volvo White Truck Corp.*,[69] the court said clerical and mathematical errors are "difficult to prevent, and . . . no useful social purpose is served by enforcing the mistaken term." In granting relief the court noted that there was no incentive for parties to make such mistakes, nor any difficulty in distinguishing between mathematical or clerical mistakes on the one hand, and mistakes of judgment on the other.[70] Further, in *Wil-Fred's Inc. v.*

---

[63] 333 P.2d 757 (Cal. 1958).

[64] *Id.* at 761.

[65] RESTATEMENT (SECOND) OF CONTRACTS § 153(b) (1981). *See* Ernest M. Jones, *The Law of Mistaken Bids*, 48 U. CIN. L. REV. 43(1979); Benedict F. Lubell, *Unilateral Palpable and Impalpable Mistake in Construction Contracts*, 16 MINN. L. REV. 137 (1932).

[66] *See, e.g.*, United States v. Braunstein, 75 F. Supp. 137 (S.D.N.Y. 1947); Laidlaw v. Organ, 15 U.S. 178 (1817). *See* Andrew Kull, *Unilateral Mistake: The Baseball Card Case*, 70 WASH U. L. Q. 57, 62 & n.8 (1992). *See generally* Anthony T. Kronman, *Mistake, Disclosure, Information, and the Law of Contracts*, 7 J. LEGAL STUD. 1 (1979).

[67] 353 P.2d 713 (Cal. 1960).

[68] *See also* Lemoge Elec. v. County of San Mateo, 297 P.2d 638 (Cal. 1956); M.F. Kemper Constr. Co. v. City of Los Angeles, 235 P.2d 7 (Cal. 1951).

[69] 766 F.2d 1089 (7th Cir. 1985).

[70] *But see* White v. Berrenda Mesa Water Dist., 7 Cal. App. 3d 894 (1970) ("mixed mistake" of fact and judgment).

Metropolitan Sanitary District,[71] the court clouded the distinction between a clerical mistake and an error in judgment by providing relief to a contractor whose otherwise reliable subcontractor has misinterpreted the owner's specifications. As in these other cases, the error was discovered after a contract had been formed, but before the other party had taken any concrete action in reliance on it.

[C] Relationship of Mistake to Warranty, Misrepresentation, and Fraud

Circumstances that might lead to a claim of mistake sometimes also provide the basis of a claim for breach of warranty, misrepresentation, or even intentional fraud. Thus, any discussion of mistake must consider its relationship to these other rules.

Warranties may be express or implied.[72] Express warranties usually arise from descriptions, promises, or statements of fact concerning the nature or quality of real estate or goods. An implied warranty may arise from the circumstances surrounding the transaction. Goods sold by a person who is in the business of selling goods of that kind are likely to be accompanied by an implied warranty that the goods will be of "merchantable" quality and will be fit for the ordinary purpose of similar goods.[73] Similarly, residential real estate may be accompanied by an implied warranty that it is "habitable."[74] If the land or goods do not conform to the warranties supplied by the seller, the buyer may rescind the contract due to the seller's material breach of its warranty.

Warranty claims might alternatively be characterized as based on an innocent, negligent, or even a fraudulent misrepresentation of a material fact. If the buyer reasonably relied on the misrepresentation, he or she will usually be entitled to relief from the contract.

Likewise, if the seller intentionally lied about the quality of the goods, or the condition of the land or its structures, the buyer may rescind the contract due to the seller's fraud. And, in the proper circumstances, the seller's failure to reveal a material fact concerning the property may similarly lead to a claim for fraud.

Consider the example of the purchase of a new house, which had been constructed with termite-infested lumber. At one time, the law might have allocated this risk to the buyer under the doctrine of "caveat emptor": "let the buyer beware."[75] Caveat emptor imposes on buyers the responsibility to take whatever steps are necessary to inform themselves of the value or condition of the subject matter of the contract. If there has been a mistake that harms a buyer who was supposed to look out for himself, probably only fraudulent conduct by the seller will enable the buyer to escape from having to perform. A legal system like

---

[71] 372 N.E.2d 946 (Ill. App. Ct. 1978).

[72] U.C.C. § 2-313 (2012). *See supra* § 7.02 Express Warranties Concerning Goods.

[73] U.C.C. § 2-314 (2012). *See supra* § 7.03 Implied Warranty of Merchantability.

[74] *See supra* § 7.06 Implied Warranty of Habitability.

[75] *See* Seibert v. Mock, 510 N.E.2d 1373, 1375 (Ind. Ct. App. 1987).

ours that values autonomy often leaves parties to suffer the consequences of their own carelessness.

However, this doctrine of personal responsibility has suffered a serious decline. Upon discovering the termite infestation, the buyer might sue to rescind the transaction alleging that the parties had made a mutual mistake that the house was constructed of sound building materials.[76] The buyer might also claim that the seller was in breach of its implied warranty that the structure was habitable or an express warranty if the seller had made factual representations about the quality of materials used to construct the house or about the structural integrity of the house.[77] If the buyer believed that the seller knew that some of the lumber had been infested, but failed to disclose the fact, the buyer might include a cause of action for fraud.[78]

§ 11.03   CHANGE OF CIRCUMSTANCES: IMPOSSIBILITY, IMPRACTICABILITY, AND FRUSTRATION OF PURPOSE[79]

The previous section explained how the law treats mistaken factual assumptions about existing circumstances. This section deals with the effect of inaccurate predictions about the future.

The future, of course, is uncertain. Changes affect market conditions and can cause the supply of goods and services to increase or diminish. Other events can cause demand to expand or contract. Prices rise and fall in response to the events. People make agreements that can go a long way to protect against these changes in market conditions.

For example, a farmer might agree to deliver her sunflower seed crop in the future at a fixed price, in order to reduce the risk of a decline in the crop's market value due to an increase in supply or a decline in demand. The seller achieves a predictable price and the buyer obtains a certain source of supply. Thus, the contract provides each party with a strong measure of protection against an otherwise uncertain future.

Unfortunately, their contract does not protect the parties from every possible contingency. In making the contract, each party also takes a chance that the future will change in a way that will lead one of them to regret having made the contract.

---

[76] *E.g.* Davey v. Brownson, 478 P.2d 258 (Wash. Ct. App. 1970).

[77] Hinson v. Jefferson, 215 S.E.2d 102 (N.C. 1975).

[78] *See* Copland v. Nathaniel, 624 N.Y.S.2d 514 (Sup. Ct. 1995); Lester v. Bird, 408 S.E.2d 147 (Ga. Ct. App. 1991).

[79] John P. Dawson, *Judicial Revision of Frustrated Contracts: The United States,* 64 B.U. L. Rev. 1 (1984); James Gordley, *Impossibility and Changed and Unforeseen Circumstances,* 52 Am. J. Comp. L. 513 (2004); Sheldon W. Halpern, *Application of the Doctrine of Commercial Impracticability: Searching for "The Wisdom of Solomon,"* 135 U. Pa. L. Rev. 1123 (1987); John E. Murray, *A Postscript: Ruminations and Presentations About Impracticability and Mistake,* 1 J.L. & Com. 60 (1981); Richard A. Posner & Andrew M. Rosenfield, *Impossibility and Related Doctrines in Contract Law: An Economic Analysis,* 6 J. Legal Stud. 83 (1977); Donald J. Smythe, *Bounded Rationality, the Doctrine of Impracticability, and the Governance of Relational Contracts,* 13 S. Cal. Interdisc. L. J. 227 (2004).

The farmer runs the risk that supply of sunflower seeds will diminish causing the market value of the crop to rise. If this happens, the contract with the buyer prevents the farmer from taking advantage of the increased value of her crop. Likewise, the buyer runs the risk that demand will fall in relation to the available supply and that the market value of the crop will fall below the agreed price. Despite these possibilities, the enforceability of their contract permits these parties to act on the basis of their tolerance for risk and their guess about the likelihood that the market will rise or fall, to set a price that takes these factors into account. Contract law thus plays a critical role in the ability of individuals to plan for the future.

Circumstances can also change in other more dramatic ways. Wars break out; buildings burn; and tragically, people unexpectedly die.[80] When really bad or unexpected things happen, questions arise about whether parties should be held to contracts that were made with the assumption that these events would not occur.

Contract law provides a limited escape hatch when circumstances change in a way that is inconsistent with the basic assumptions the parties shared at the time the contract was made. Contract law originally limited this escape to situations in which the change of circumstances had made performance literally impossible. This approach limited relief to situations where unanticipated events resulted in the destruction of the subject matter of the contract,[81] or the death or disability of a person whose physical ability to perform was indispensable to the performance of the contract.[82] The law later expanded to provide relief where performance had not become completely impossible, but where the contemplated purpose of the contract was frustrated due to an unanticipated turn of events.[83] The doctrine later expanded even further to situations where the change in circumstances had not made performance impossible nor completely frustrated the purpose of the contract, but where the burden of performing had changed in a way that was beyond the risks assumed by the parties when the contract was made.[84] Performance in this kind of situation is said to have become "commercially impracticable."

These doctrines must be carefully constrained if contracts are to retain their meaning and utility. If every change of circumstance that made performance more difficult, expensive, or disadvantageous provided an excuse, contracts would become meaningless. Thus, as with the doctrine of excuse due to mistake, limits must be imposed. The remainder of this section will examine the rules dealing with changes in circumstance, the limitations imposed on the availability of the doctrines, and what alternative remedies the law provides when the performance of a contract is excused due to unanticipated events.

---

[80] *See supra* Preface.

[81] RESTATEMENT (SECOND) OF CONTRACTS § 263 (1981). *Eg.*, Taylor v. Caldwell, 122 Eng. Rep. 309 (K.B. 1863).

[82] RESTATEMENT (SECOND) OF CONTRACTS § 262 (1981).

[83] RESTATEMENT (SECOND) OF CONTRACTS § 265 (1981). *Eg.*, Krell v. Henry, 2 K.B. 740 (C.A. 1903).

[84] RESTATEMENT (SECOND) OF CONTRACTS § 261 (1981); Mineral Park Land Co. v. Howard, 156 P. 458 (Cal. 1916).

[A]   Impossibility and Impracticability[85]

The modern doctrine of excuse due to commercial impracticability had its origins in decisions that excused the parties from performance when performance became literally impossible, usually due to the death of one of the parties whose continued existence was essential to performance, or due to the physical destruction of the subject matter of the contract — such as a unique work of art or a building. Later, the doctrine was expanded to permit excuse when unanticipated events frustrated the purpose of the contract. Today, performance may be excused when unanticipated circumstances make performance considerably more difficult than the parities could have imagined when they made their original deal.

[1]   Origins of the Doctrine: Impossibility[86]

At early English common law performance of a contract was not excused due to a change of circumstances, unless the parties had provided for the contingency by making their duties expressly conditional. Thus, in the seventeenth century case of *Paradine v. Jane*,[87] the court refused to excuse a tenant from his duty to pay rent despite his ouster by an invading army. In reaching this seemingly harsh decision the court emphasized that the tenant "might have provided against [the invasion] by his contract." In other words, the parties should have considered the possibility that an invading army would disrupt performance and included language excusing the tenant if an invasion were to occur.

The United States Supreme Court recognized this principle in *Dermott v. Jones*,[88] where, referring to *Paradine v. Jane* and other similar cases, it explained:

> The principle which controlled the decisions referred to rests upon a solid foundation of reason and justice. It regards the sanctity of contracts. It requires parties to do what they have agreed to do. If unexpected impediments lie in the way, and a loss must ensue, it leaves the loss where the contract places it. If the parties have made no provision for a dispensation, the rule of law gives none. It does not allow a contract fairly made to be annulled, and it does not permit it to be interpolated what the parties themselves have not stipulated.[89]

---

[85] Michelle White, *Contract Breach and Contract Discharge Due to Impossibility: A Unified Theory*, 17 J. Legal Stud. 353 (1988); Richard A. Posner & Andrew Rosenfield, *Impossibility and Related Doctrines in Contract Law: An Economic Analysis*, 6 J. Legal Stud. 83 (1977).

[86] David J. Ibbetson, *Fault and Absolute Liability in Pre-Modern Contract Law*, 18 Leg. Hist. 1 (1997); W. Buckland, *Cause and Frustration in Roman and Common Law*, 46 Harv. L. Rev. 1281 (1933); Marcia J. Speziale, *The Turn of the Twentieth Century as the Dawn of Contract "Interpretation": Reflections in Theories of Impossibility*, 17 Duq. L. Rev. 555 (1978–79); John D. Wladis, *Impracticability as Risk Allocation: The Effect of Changed Circumstances upon Contract Obligations for the Sale of Goods*, 22 Ga. L. Rev. 503 (1988); John D. Wladis, *Common Law and Uncommon Events: The Development of the Doctrine of Impossibility of Performance in English Contract Law*, 75 Geo. L.J. 1575 (1987).

[87] 82 Eng. Rep. 897 (1647).

[88] 69 U.S. 1, 8 (1864).

[89] *Id.* at 8.

Decisions like *Paradine v. Jane* and *Dermott v. Jones* had the advantage of making the obligations imposed by contracts reliable. However, they overlooked the practical reality that people are utterly incapable of foreseeing every future contingency that might affect their plans. Our ability to anticipate future events is just not that good.

However, even these early decisions recognized that the death of a person whose continued existence was indispensable to the performance of the contract was grounds for relief.[90] Contracts for personal services are excused by the death of the person whose services were to be performed.[91] Thus it was said that "if an author undertakes to compose a work, and dies before completing it, his executors are discharged from this contract: for the undertaking is merely personal in its nature, and, by the intervention of the contractor's death, has become impossible to be performed."[92] However, this principle was limited to services that were "personal" in nature, and that therefore could only have been performed or supervised by the person who had died or become incapacitated.[93]

Suppose, for example, that "Team Velo" hires star bicycle racer Taylor Phinney to become its leader. After making a substantial investment in hiring other members of the team to assist Phinney in winning races, he is seriously injured in a hunting accident and cannot complete the season. Because no one else can perform on Phinney's behalf, he will be excused.[94]

Assume, on the other hand, that Julie hired a large construction firm operated by Ron and Sal to re-grade her driveway and cover it with gravel, but that Ron died before the work was done. In this case, neither Ron's estate nor Sal is discharged from the duty to finish the work. There is nothing about the services involved to suggest that performance requires either Ron's or Sal's personal involvement.[95]

The early common law also recognized that destruction of the subject matter of the contract might serve as an excuse.[96] The modern origins of the doctrine of impossibility excusing performance are usually traced to just such a case: *Taylor v. Caldwell*.[97] The defendant promised to make his theater available to the plaintiffs for a series of four concerts, with the plaintiffs to pay £100 at the end of each day of the series. Before the concerts were scheduled to take place, the theater was destroyed in a fire. The plaintiffs sued to recover the expenses they had incurred in preparations for the concerts, which could no longer be held.

Despite the unconditional nature of the defendant's promise, the court ruled that

---

[90] William v. Floyd, 82 Eng. Rep. 95 (K.B. 1629).

[91] RESTATEMENT (SECOND) OF CONTRACTS § 262 (1981).

[92] Hyde v. Dean of Windsor, 78 Eng. Rep. 798 (Q.B. 1597).

[93] The principle has been extended to situations where the services were to be rendered personally to the recipient, whose death would also operate as an excuse. *E.g.*, Harrison v. Conlan, 1865 Mass. LEXIS 41 (Jan. 1865).

[94] *See* CNA & Am. Cas. v. Arlyn Phoenix, 678 So. 2d 378 (Fla Dist. Ct. App. 1996).

[95] RESTATEMENT (SECOND) OF CONTRACTS § 262 illus. 9 (1981).

[96] *E.g.*, Williams v. Lloyd, 82 Eng. Rep. 95 (K.B. 1629).

[97] 3 B. & S. 826, 122 Eng. Rep. 309 (K.B. 1863).

his duty to provide the theater had been excused. The court ruled that the parties must have known that the contract could not be fulfilled unless the theater continued to exist at the time for the performance. According to the court, the parties "must have contemplated [the] continuing existence [of the theater] as the foundation of what was to be done." The court presumed that if the parties had thought about the matter that they would have included in their contract an express condition that would excuse the parties from their contract in the event of the destruction of the theater without the fault of either party.

The court treated the continued existence of the theater as an implied condition of the contract. Although the contract was not made expressly conditional on the continued existence of the theater, the court ruled that its existence was a basic underlying assumption of the parties at the time the contract was made. Destruction of the theater caused the condition to fail and, as with any other failure of a condition precedent, excused the parties from their duties.[98]

Early decisions following *Caldwell* excused the parties from their contract only if performance had become truly *impossible*. This was consistent with previous decisions that excused the parties due to the death of an indispensable party[99] or due to the destruction of the specific goods that were the subject matter of the contract.[100] The doctrine now also applies to situations where performance has become impossible due to intervening governmental regulation.[101]

[2]   Commercial Impracticability[102]

The impossibility doctrine was gradually expanded to cover situations where a change of circumstances had made performance not literally impossible, but unduly burdensome. The modern doctrine of "commercial impracticability" originated in *Mineral Park Land Co. v. Howard*,[103] which involved a contract for hauling gravel from the plaintiff's land for construction of the defendant's bridge. The gravel unexpectedly became submerged. Its removal was still possible, but only at considerable additional expense. The court excused the parties from

---

[98] *See supra* § 8.01[C] Consequences of Failure of a Condition.

[99] *See* Restatement (Second) of Contracts § 262 (1981).

[100] *See* Restatement (Second) of Contracts § 263 (1981).

[101] *See* Restatement (Second) of Contracts § 264 (1981).

[102] Robert L. Birmingham, *Why Is There* Taylor v. Caldwell? *Three Propositions About Impracticability*, 23 U.S.F. L. Rev. (1989); Christopher J. Bruce, *An Economic Analysis of the Impossibility Doctrine*, 11 J. Legal Stud. 311 (1982); John P. Dawson, *Judicial Revision of Frustrated Contracts: The United States*, 64 B.U. L. Rev. 1 (1984); Sheldon W. Halpern, *Application of the Doctrine of Commercial Impracticability: Searching for "The Wisdom of Solomon,"* 135 U. Pa. L. Rev. 1123 (1987); Richard A. Posner & Andrew M. Rosenfeld, *Impossibility and Related Doctrines in Contract Law: An Economic Analysis*, 6 J. Legal Stud. 83 (1977); Harry G. Prince, *Commercial Impracticability: A Textual and Economic Analysis of Section 2-615 of the Uniform Commercial Code*, 19 Ind. L. Rev. 457 (1986); Michelle J. White, *Contract Breach and Contract Discharge Due to Impossibility: A Unified Theory*, 17 J. Legal Stud. 353, 360–74 (1988); John D. Wladis, *Impracticability as Risk Allocation: The Effect of Changed Circumstances upon Obligations for the Sale of Goods*, 22 Ga. L. Rev. 503 (1988); John D. Wladis, *Impracticability as Risk Allocation: The Effect of Changed Circumstances upon Contract Obligations for the Sale of Goods*, 22 Ga. L. Rev. 503 (1988).

[103] 156 P. 458 (Cal. 1916).

performance, saying that "a thing is impossible in legal contemplation when it is not practicable; and a thing is impracticable when it can only be done at an excessive and unreasonable cost."[104]

This expanded rule provides relief when a party's performance becomes impracticable due to the occurrence of an event or other contingency, the nonoccurrence of which was a basic assumption on which the contract was made, unless the disrupting event was caused by the party seeking relief or unless that party assumed the risk that the event would occur.[105]

[a] Basic Assumption of the Contract

The decision in *Taylor v. Caldwell* was based on a finding that the continued existence of the theater had been an "implied condition." Modern decisions no longer use this rationale.[106] Instead, excuse due to changed circumstances depends on whether the nonoccurrence of the disruptive event was a "basic assumption" on which the contract was made.[107]

In similar circumstances today, a court would consider whether the continued existence of the theater was a basic assumption on which the contract was made. In contracts made by farmers to sell their crops, the continued existence of the crop is a basic assumption of the contract. If the crop is destroyed in a storm, the farmer is excused from his promise to sell the crop upon harvest.[108]

But, in a contract to sell agricultural commodities, a distinction is drawn between a contract to sell the crops grown on a particular farm and a contract to sell a specified quantity of crops without identifying where the crops will be grown.[109] If farmer Jimmy Jordan[110] promises to sell his entire crop of potatoes and blight destroys the crop, he will be excused. If he promises to sell 1,000 bushels of potatoes, without specifying whether the potatoes will come from his crop or from a potato broker, he will not be excused. Although the circumstances surrounding the creation of the contract will usually be admissible to show whether the parties understood that Jordan would deliver the potatoes from his crop,[111] courts have sometimes been reluctant to consider parol evidence on the question of whether it was a contract to sell the potatoes from his field or one to sell potatoes grown anywhere.[112]

---

[104] *Id.* at 460.

[105] *Compare* U.C.C. § 2-615 (2012) *with* RESTATEMENT (SECOND) OF CONTRACTS § 261 (1981).

[106] *See* William Herbert Page, *The Development of the Doctrine of Impossibility of Performance*, 18 MICH. L. REV. 589 (1920).

[107] *See* U.C.C. § 2-615 (2012); RESTATEMENT (SECOND) OF CONTRACTS § 261 (1981); RESTATEMENT (SECOND) OF CONTRACTS, Introductory Note to Chapter 11, 310–11 (1981).

[108] RESTATEMENT (SECOND) OF CONTRACTS § 263 illus. 7 (1981).

[109] *E.g.*, ConAgra, Inc. v. Bartlett P'ship, 540 N.W.2d 333, 337–38 (Neb. 1995) (collecting cases); Elliot J. Katz, Annotation, *Construction and Effect of UCC Sec. 2-613 Governing Casualty to Goods Identified to a Contract, Without Fault of Buyer or Seller*, 51 A.L.R.4th 537 (1987).

[110] My uncle, who used to be a potato farmer.

[111] *See, e.g.*, Unke v. Thorpe, 59 N.W.2d 419 (S.D. 1953).

[112] Bunge Corp. v. Recker, 519 F.2d 449 (8th Cir. 1975).

Cases involving the death or incapacity of a person who is indispensable to the performance of the contract are treated in the same way. The question is whether the ability of a particular individual to perform was a basic assumption that the parties made when they entered into the contract.[113] Relief is most likely to be granted in cases involving someone with unique or specialized services, or where the recipient selected the person because of his confidence in the skill, judgment, or abilities of the person who has become unavailable.[114]

If the blues band "The Ultrasonics" hires Dave as its guitar player, but Dave injures his hand and can no longer play, he is excused from performing his contract. He was hired for his personal skill, ability, and style, as well as how well his talents fit in with those of other members of the band. On the other hand, work to be done by a large roofing company is unlikely to depend on the personal attention of any particular employee or owner of the business. If one of them falls ill, (or just falls), nothing about the services involved suggests that performance is impossible or even more difficult.[115]

The principal question in these cases is whether the deceased or injured person was necessary for performance of the contract. In *In re Estate of Roccamonte*,[116] the court ruled that the promisor's commitment to provide "lifetime support" to his female cohabitant was enforceable against his estate where the facts showed that the parties intended the obligation to remain intact if he died first, so his continued existence was not a basic assumption of the contract. A party was not relieved from performance on account of the illness of his attorney in *Monteiro v. American Home Assurance. Co.*,[117] where the court determined that any reasonable attorney could have provided the representation the buyer needed in connection with the performance of his or her duties. However, this does not mean that the death or other unavailability of a person who is not a party to the contract is never an excuse. In *International House of Talent v. Alabama*,[118] the court excused the popular Country and Western band (not the state) from its contract with a talent agency, because of the departure of the president of the agency, whose personal services had been a basic assumption of the contract.

The intervening event that makes performance impracticable can be either legislation or other governmental action that either makes performance illegal or that saddles the parties with additional regulatory burdens not contemplated when the contract was made.[119] If the necessity of compliance with a governmental rule

---

[113] RESTATEMENT (SECOND) OF CONTRACTS § 262 (1981).

[114] *E.g.*, Wasserman Theatrical Enter., Inc. v. Harris, 77 A.2d 329 (Conn. 1950) (death of character actor Walter Houston); CNA & Am. Cas. v. Arlyn Phoenix, 678 So. 2d 378 (Fla. Dist. Ct. App. 1996) (death of actor River Phoenix). With grief and a sense of tremendous irony, Professor Ferriell found himself reviewing this footnote only two days after learning of the untimely death of Professor Mike Navin, co-author of the first edition of this book. *See supra* Preface.

[115] RESTATEMENT (SECOND) OF CONTRACTS § 262 illus. 9 (1981).

[116] 787 A.2d 198, 207 (N.J. Super. Ct. 2001), *affirmed as modified*, 808 A.2d 838 (N.J. 2002).

[117] 416 A.2d 1189 (Conn. 1979).

[118] 712 S.W.2d 78, 88 (Tenn. 1986) (the Country and Western band "Alabama," not the state).

[119] RESTATEMENT (SECOND) OF CONTRACTS § 264 (1981); Baily v. De Crespigny, 4 Q.B. 180 (L.R. 1869) ("Lex non cogit ad impossibilia").

or regulation makes performance impossible or impracticable, performance is excused.[120]

A dramatic example of this occurred in *The Isle of Mull*,[121] when a contract for the charter of a ship was disrupted by the British Admiralty when it requisitioned the ship for use in World War I. The owner of the vessel was excused from making the ship available for the agreed charter.

Government action sometimes makes an agreement illegal. In *Centex v. Dalton*,[122] a contract between a bank and a consultant was excused when the Federal Home Loan Bank Board took over the bank and implemented regulations prohibiting payment to the consultant. Likewise, during the Cold War, a contract for the shipment of a printing press was excused when the United States government refused to grant a license for its shipment to buyers in the Soviet Union.[123] And, in *Florida Power & Light Co. v. Westinghouse Electric Corp.*,[124] the builder of a nuclear power plant was excused from its obligation to dispose of spent nuclear fuel after the federal government unexpectedly discontinued its program for reprocessing spent fuel and no other commercial reprocessing or off-site storage facilities were available.

It still must be shown that the nonoccurrence of the governmental action was a basic assumption of the contract and that the party seeking relief had not assumed the risk that it would occur. For example, in *Lloyd v. Murphy*,[125] a lessee was not excused from his duty to pay rent on the land her rented for use as an auto dealership, even though wartime restrictions on the sale of new automobiles had frustrated one of the main purposes of the lease. The lease had been executed in early 1941, in anticipation of America's involvement in World War II. The lessee had not only anticipated America's involvement in the war, with its inevitable restrictions on auto sales, but planned to take advantage of an expected increased demand for cars in the months leading up to the war. As the court explained: "If [the supervening event] was foreseeable there should have been provision for it in the contract, and the absence of such a provision gives rise to the inference that the risk was assumed."[126] By entering into the lease under these circumstances, the tenant had assumed the risk that car sales would be restricted.

---

[120] RESTATEMENT (SECOND) OF CONTRACTS § 264 (1981).

[121] Isles S.S. Co. v. Gans S.S. Line, 278 F. 131 (4th Cir. 1921).

[122] 840 S.W.2d 952 (Tex. 1992).

[123] Amtorg Trading Corp. v. Miehle Printing Press & Mfg. Co., 206 F.2d 103 (2d Cir. 1953). *See also* Acme Moving & Storage Corp. v. Bower, 306 A.2d 545 (Md. 1973).

[124] 826 F.2d 239 (4th Cir. 1987).

[125] 153 P.2d 47 (Cal. 1944).

[126] *Id.* at 50.

[b]   Performance Becomes Impracticable[127]

Not only must the intervening event be unexpected, it must also make performance either impossible, or at least "impracticable." Section 2-615 of the Uniform Commercial Code speaks in terms of "commercial impracticability,"[128] while the Second Restatement articulates the test simply as "impracticable."[129]

No excuse is available if performance merely becomes more expensive, more burdensome, or unprofitable. A change in market conditions that makes the contract less advantageous, or even unprofitable, will not suffice.[130] In a well known series of cases, occasioned by the temporary closing of the Suez Canal in 1956, courts held that, although the rerouting of vessels around the Cape of Good Hope (the southern tip of Africa) was more expensive, the variation in the cost of performance was not sufficient to make performance unduly burdensome or commercially impracticable.[131] Courts reached the same result in cases arising during the inflation caused by the OPEC oil crisis of the early 1970s. The increase in the worldwide price of oil made many contracts unprofitable. In the cases decided during the 1970s, the resulting hardships were not generally regarded as sufficiently burdensome to serve as an excuse.[132] Something more devastating is usually required.

For example, excuse was warranted in *Opera Company of Boston, Inc. v. Wolf Trap Foundation*[133] when a thunderstorm resulted in a widespread electrical outage. The defendant cancelled the plaintiff's scheduled performance when it became clear that the power could not be restored until after the performance would have been over.

A related issue is whether performance must be "objectively" or "subjectively" impracticable. Thus, there is a difference between a duty that cannot be performed by anyone and one that the party seeking relief will have great difficulty performing, even though someone else might not find it unduly burdensome. Relief

---

[127] Harold J. Berman, *Excuse for Nonperformance in Light of Contract Practice in International Trade*, 63 COLUM. L. REV. 1413 (1963); Robert L. Birmingham, *A Second Look at the Suez Canal Cases: Excuse for Nonperformance of Contractual Obligations in Light of Economic Theory*, 20 HASTINGS L.J. 1393 (1969); Jennifer S. Martin, *Adapting U.C.C. § 2-615 Excuse for Civilian-Military Contractors in Wartime*, 61 FLA. L. REV. 99 (2009).

[128] U.C.C. § 2-615 (2012).

[129] RESTATEMENT (SECOND) OF CONTRACTS § 261 (1981). The standard of "commercial impracticability" in U.C.C. § 2-615 is commonly used in transactions other than those involving the sale of goods. *E.g.*, Asphalt Int'l, Inc. v. Enter. Shipping Corp., 667 F.2d 261, 265–66 (2d Cir. 1981) (repair of a chartered vessel); Transatlantic Fin. Corp. v. United States, 363 F.2d 312, 314–15 (D.C. Cir. 1966) (transportation contract).

[130] *See* Karl Wendt Farm Equip. Co. v. Int'l Harvester Co., 931 F.2d 1112 (6th Cir. 1991); Dills v. Town of Enfield, 557 A.2d 517 (Conn. 1989) (difficulty in obtaining financing insufficient for excuse).

[131] *E.g.*, Transatl. Fin'g Corp. v. United States, 363 F.2d 312 (D.C. Cir. 1966). *See* Robert L. Birmingham, *A Second Look at the Suez Canal Cases: Excuse for Nonperformance of Contractual Obligations in the Light of Economic Theory*, 20 HASTINGS L.J. 1393 (1969).

[132] *E.g.*, E. Airlines v. Gulf Oil Corp., 415 F. Supp. 429 (S.D. Fla. 1975).

[133] 817 F.2d 1094 (4th Cir. 1987).

is generally provided only when performance is objectively impracticable.[134]

[c]   Circumstances Beyond the Control of the Parties

A further requirement is that the event must have been beyond the control of the party seeking relief from the contract. If the party adversely affected by the supervening event either caused it to occur, or failed to take advantage of the opportunity to prevent it, that party will have no excuse.[135] For example, if the owner of the theater in *Taylor v. Caldwell* had set the fire, he would not be entitled to relief.

Cases involving suicide or other self-inflicted injuries are particularly troublesome given the complex psychological factors that lead a person to engage in self-destructive behavior. The court in *Handicapped Children's Education Board v. Lukaszewski*[136] was unwilling to release a person from performance when the medical condition that caused her inability to perform was a result of her insistence on driving 50 miles each day to work rather than moving closer to her job. However, in *CNA & American Casualty v. Arlyn ["River"] Phoenix*,[137] the court was unwilling to become embroiled in the question of whether the uses of tobacco, alcohol, or illicit drugs were the type of self-inflicted injuries that would prevent a party from being relieved from his or her contractual duties.

[d]   Assumption of the Risk[138]

Most importantly, as with the law of excuse due to mutual mistake, a party may not be excused by the occurrence of risks assumed by the party seeking relief. If parties to a contract could escape their obligations when performance became difficult, whether due to the loss of a job, the birth of a child, or a decline in the popularity of their product, contracts would become virtually meaningless. Entering into a contract always involves the assumption of some risk about uncertain future events. Here the question is whether the events that have made performance more burdensome were within the scope of the risks assumed by the party seeking relief.

In some cases the contract will clearly indicate who bears the risk of loss. Where the contract is silent, the court must examine the circumstances to determine whether the party seeking relief assumed the risk that the intervening event would occur. In *Lloyd v. Murphy*,[139] the court held that an auto dealership, which opened

---

[134] RESTATEMENT (SECOND) OF CONTRACTS § 261 cmt. e (1981). *E.g.*, Seaboard Lumber Co. v. United States, 308 F.3d 1283, 1294 (Fed. Cir. 2002).

[135] RESTATEMENT (SECOND) OF CONTRACTS § 261 cmt. d (1981).

[136] 332 N.W.2d 774 (Wis. 1983).

[137] 678 So. 2d 378 (Fla. Dist. Ct. App. 1996).

[138] Victor P. Goldberg, *Impossibility and Related Excuses*, 144 J. INSTL. & THERET. ECON. 100 (1988); RICHARD POSNER, ECONOMIC ANALYSIS OF LAW 104 (6th ed. 2002); Richard A. Posner & Andrew M. Rosenfeld, *Impossibility and Related Doctrines in Contract Law: An Economic Analysis*, 6 J. LEGAL STUD. 83 (1977).

[139] 153 P.2d 47 (Cal. 1944).

its doors in the fall of 1941, assumed the risk that the government would restrict the sale of new automobiles if the country became involved in World War II. The defendant opened its auto dealership to take advantage of the increase in demand for automobiles due to the widespread public anticipation that the United States would enter the war, and was in no position to claim that government restrictions on the sale of automobiles, imposed shortly after the bombing of Pearl Harbor, was an unanticipated event that should result in an excuse.

In construction contracts, a sharp dividing line is drawn between contracts for new construction and those for renovation of existing structures. In cases where a building under construction is wholly or partially destroyed before substantial performance of the work, the risk of loss is usually placed on the builder.[140] The loss of the partially completed structure provides the builder no excuse. However, where the premises are destroyed while undergoing renovation, the risk of loss lies with the owner, who is presumed to have had the building insured against loss in any event.[141] The parties are free to allocate the risk of loss however they see fit. This is usually accomplished with language in the contract requiring one of the parties to acquire insurance protecting against such a loss.

An economic analysis of excuse would place the risk on the party in the best position to either guard against the loss or obtain insurance.[142] This may explain the results in the construction cases where the builder is in the best position to insure against loss in the case of new construction, and the owner in cases involving renovation.

Not surprisingly, a person who promises to do something that he knows might be technologically impossible, is not excused when technological barriers prove to be insurmountable. In *United States v. Wegematic*,[143] the defendant agreed to supply a "general-purpose electronic digital computing system" to the government that would transcend the capabilities of other similar devices of the time (1956). When engineering difficulties made it impossible to deliver the computer on time, the defendant sought to avoid liability for the $100 per day liquidated damages provision in the contract, on the grounds of impracticability. The seller had gambled on its ability to produce the technological breakthroughs that it promised, and thus assumed the risk that the those breakthroughs would be more difficult to achieve than it had imagined when it made the contract.

Assumption of the risk usually cuts against relief in fixed-price, long-term supply contracts. In *Northern Indiana Public Service Co. v. Carbon County Coal Co.*[144] (or "*NIPSCO*"), Judge Posner found that a coal-burning power plant had assumed the risk that electricity could be purchased from other suppliers more

---

[140] RESTATEMENT (SECOND) OF CONTRACTS § 263 illus. 4 (1981). *See, e.g.*, Tompkins v. Dudley, 1862 N.Y. LEXIS 132 (Sept. 1862). *But see* Butterfield v. Byron, 27 N.E. 667 (Mass. 1891).

[141] RESTATEMENT (SECOND) OF CONTRACTS § 263 illus. 3 (1981). *Eg.*, Carroll v. Bowersock, 164 P. 143 (Kan. 1917).

[142] *See generally* Richard Posner & Andrew M. Rosenfield, *Impossibility and Related Doctrines in Contract Law: An Economic Analysis*, 6 J. LEGAL STUD. 83, 90 (1977).

[143] 360 F.2d 674 (2d Cir. 1966).

[144] 799 F.2d 265 (7th Cir. 1986).

cheaply than it could be produced in the buyer's power plant by agreeing to a fixed-price, long-term requirements contract with the plaintiff's coal company. He reasoned that the principal purpose of the contract had been to allocate the risk of the cost of producing electricity between the parties, and that providing relief to the buyer would nullify that purpose. The *NIPSCO* decision is consistent with an array of decisions dealing with long-term "take or pay" contracts between producers of natural gas and pipeline companies who distribute the gas.[145] However, it stands in sharp contrast to a decision such as *Aluminum Co. of America v. Essex Group, Inc.*,[146] where the court went so far as to order an equitable adjustment to the terms of the contract in light of what the court characterized as a "mistake" in the manner in which the long-term price was to be calculated.

The foreseeability of a supervening event is frequently relevant to whether a party assumed the risk that it would occur. Older cases required that the supervening event be "unforseen."[147] Article 2 of the U.C.C. suggests that this remains the appropriate standard.[148] However, courts have sometimes denied relief if the event was "reasonably foreseeable"[149] on the theory that the parties had assumed the risk of all foreseeable events.[150] Commentators, on the other hand, have rejected using "unforeseeability" as being too harsh a standard even though it may be a relevant consideration.[151] Most modern decisions turn on whether the event was unexpected rather than whether it was foreseeable.[152]

[3] Casualty to Identified Goods

The traditional rule excusing performance of a contract for the sale of specific goods, when the goods are destroyed before the time of performance, is codified in U.C.C. § 2-613. It excuses the parties when the goods are destroyed without the fault of either party, before the risk of loss has passed to the buyer.

However, § 2-613 applies only to a narrow range of circumstances: "[w]here the contract requires for its performance goods identified when the contract is made." Thus, it does not apply to every contract for the sale of goods, but only where the goods involved are selected by the parties at the very moment the contract is

---

[145] J. Michael Medina, Gregory A. McKenzie & Bruce M. Daniel, *Take or Litigate: Enforcing the Plain Meaning of the Take-Or-Pay Clause in Natural Gas Contracts*, 40 Ark. L. Rev. 185 (1986); E. Allan Farnsworth, *Developments in Contract Law During the 1980's: The Top Ten*, 41 Case W. Res. L. Rev. 203, 213–16 (1990).

[146] 499 F. Supp. 53, 76 (W.D. Pa. 1980).

[147] *E.g.*, Louisville & N.R.R. v. Mottley, 219 U.S. 467 (1911).

[148] *See* U.C.C. § 2-615 cmt. 1 (2012) ("unforeseen supervening circumstances").

[149] *E.g.*, E. Airlines v. Gulf Oil Corp., 415 F. Supp. 429 (S.D. Fla. 1965); Gold v. Salem Lutheran Home Ass'n, 347 P.2d 687, 689 (Cal. 1959). *See* Subha Narasimhan, *Of Expectations, Incomplete Contracting, and the Bargain Principle*, 74 Cal. L. Rev. 1123, 1125 n.7 (1986).

[150] *See also* Bende & Sons, Inc. v. Crown Rec., Inc., 548 F. Supp. 1018 (E.D.N.Y. 1982).

[151] *See* E. Allan Farnsworth, *Disputes over Omission in Contracts*, 68 Colum. L. Rev. 860, 887 (1968); Opera Co. v. Wolf Trap Found., 817 F.2d 1094, 1102 (4th Cir. 1987).

[152] *See* Gerhard Wagner, *Essay in Defense of the Impossibility Defense*, 27 Loy. U. Chi. L.J. 55, 86 (1995). *E.g.*, Aluminum Co. of Am. v. Essex Group, Inc., 499 F. Supp. 53, 76 (W.D. Pa. 1980).

formed. This usually only occurs in cases involving unique items or where the seller does not have a ready supply of similar goods available for sale.

For example, performance of a contract for the sale of a specific work of art is excused if lightning strikes the seller's gallery before the painting is delivered. However, if the buyer agrees to purchase one of several hundred prints of the same painting, and the print that has been *subsequently* earmarked for delivery to the buyer is destroyed, the seller must rely on the general doctrine of commercial impracticability found in U.C.C. § 2-615, and not on U.C.C. § 2-613, which only applies when the specific item necessary for performance has been selected or "identified" *at the time the contract was made.* The difference is between: "I'll buy *that* one" and "I'll buy one *like* that one." In the former situation, the specific item was identified at the time the contract was formed, and its loss or destruction prior to delivery will be excused, even if other similar items are available to the seller.[153] In the latter circumstance, identification of the specific item to be delivered to the buyer was left for later. Destruction of the item subsequently selected is not grounds for relief under U.C.C. § 2-613, though it might provide a basis for relief under the broader ground of general commercial impracticability.[154] Most of the time, of course, buyers are indifferent about the serial number of consumer items that are otherwise indistinguishable from other items of the same make and model.

In contracts involving farm products and other commodities, U.C.C. § 2-613 applies if the contract is to sell a specific crop that has been damaged, but does not apply if the contract is for the sale of a specific quantity of goods without regard to their source.[155]

Section 2-613 also requires that the casualty occur before the risk of loss has passed to the buyer. If the goods are destroyed after the risk has passed, then under the rules established in U.C.C. § 2-509, the contract is not avoided and the buyer must pay the price.[156]

[B]   Frustration of Purpose[157]

In some cases supervening events do not make performance impossible or even more difficult, but instead merely frustrate the purpose of one of the parties. The early decision in *Krell v. Henry*[158] illustrates the principle. The contract was for occupancy of an apartment on Pall Mall in London, overlooking the coronation parade route for King Edward VII. When the King became ill, the parade was cancelled. The owner of the apartment had already received one-third of the

---

[153] *E.g.*, Emery v. Weed, 494 A.2d 438 (Pa. Super. Ct. 1985).

[154] U.C.C. § 2-615 (2012).

[155] Bunge v. Recker, 519 F.2d 449 (8th Cir. 1975).

[156] *See* U.C.C. § 2-509 (2012).

[157] Arthur Anderson, *Frustration of Contract — A Rejected Doctrine*, 3 DePaul L. Rev. 1 (1953); T. Ward Chapman, Comment, *Contracts — Frustration of Purpose*, 59 Mich. L. Rev. 98 (1960); Andrew Kull, *Mistake, Frustration, and the Windfall Principle of Contract Remedies*, 43 Hastings L.J. 1, 42–52 (1991); Nicholas R. Weiskopf, *Frustration of Contractual Purpose — Doctrine or Myth?*, 70 St. John's L. Rev. 239 (1996).

[158] 2 K.B. 740 (Ct. App. 1903).

agreed price of £75 and sued to recover the balance due. The court ruled that the coronation parade was the basic foundation of the contract and that its cancellation discharged the parties from the contract.

Performance was neither impossible nor unduly burdensome. The defendant could have occupied the apartment, sat on the balcony, and looked out over Pall Mall at the time originally scheduled for the parade. However, the street below would have been devoid of anything other than the usual daily traffic, so performance would have been pointless. Thus, where an unanticipated event has substantially frustrated the principal purpose of the contract, performance is excused.[159]

The elements of frustration of purpose are nearly identical to those for impracticability. Excuse is warranted only when the purpose of the contract has been frustrated because of an event which the parties had assumed would not occur. The frustrating event might have been foreseeable, or even foreseen, so long as its occurrence was unexpected.

In addition, the unexpected event must substantially frustrate the principal purpose of the contract.[160] In *Chase Precast Corp. v. John J. Paonessa Co., Inc.*,[161] the purpose of a contract for the purchase of highway median barriers was frustrated when public outcry over the appearance of the barriers led the government to cancel its plans to use them. Likewise, in *Washington State Hop Producers, Inc. v. Goschie Farms, Inc.*,[162] a contract for the sale of governmental marketing allotments for hops was frustrated when the United States Department of Agriculture cancelled its allotment program and permitted hop growers to market their hops without a governmentally approved allotment. In these and other frustration-of-purpose cases, both parties shared the same underlying ultimate purpose for the contract. When unanticipated events made performance pointless, the parties were excused.

In some situations one party's underlying purpose will be of no consequence to the other. In *Scottsdale Road General Partners v. Kuhn Farm Machinery*,[163] the defendant contracted with a hotel to host a trade show and convention. The plaintiff had hoped to attract a significant number of European dealers, whose attendance was critical to the success of the meeting. Concerns about the safety of international travel in the wake of Iraq's 1991 invasion of Kuwait, coupled with the fears of international terrorism, dissuaded most European dealers from attending. In denying relief to the defendant, the court emphasized that it had failed to establish that the parties shared a common understanding that the defendant's principal purpose in entering the contract was for the attendance of its European dealers. Thus, although the parties need not have the same purpose, the purpose that has been frustrated must have been contemplated by the other party as part of the principal design of the party seeking relief. Frustration of a hidden, secret,

---

[159] RESTATEMENT (SECOND) OF CONTRACTS § 265 (1981).

[160] *Id.*

[161] 566 N.E.2d 603 (Mass. 1991).

[162] 773 P.2d 70 (Wash. 1989).

[163] 909 P.2d 408 (Ariz. Ct. App. 1995).

or otherwise undisclosed purpose is not enough.

As with impracticability, the intervening event must have been beyond the control of the party seeking an excuse, and the risk of the occurrence of the event must not have been assumed by the party seeking relief. As with impracticability, assumption of the risk is a critical element. Further, although foreseeability of the risk does not dispose of the issue of whether the nonoccurrence of the event was a basic assumption, the foreseeability of a potentially frustrating event is highly relevant to the question of whether the risk was assumed by the party seeking relief. The fact that the lease for the auto dealership in *Lloyd v. Murphy*[164] was entered into when America's entry into World War II was both foreseeable and anticipated helped persuade the court that the lessee had assumed the risk that the sale of autos would soon be restricted.

[C]   Effect of "Force Majeure" Clauses

Parties sometimes include language in their agreements excusing the parties if unanticipated events occur. These "force majeure" clauses may provide broader relief than the legal doctrines of impossibility, impracticability or frustration of purpose.

A good example is found in *Austin Co. v. United States*,[165] where a contract for the development of a digital data recording system provided:

> The Contractor shall not be liable for any excess costs if any failure to perform the contract arises out of causes beyond the control and without the fault or negligence of the Contractor. Such causes include, but are not restricted to, acts of God or of the public enemy, acts of the Government, fires, floods, epidemics, quarantine restrictions, strikes, freight embargoes, unusually severe weather, and defaults of subcontractors due to any of such causes.

Language of this type removes any uncertainty about the effect of the specified occurrences, some of which, such as "strikes," are generally not regarded as an excuse under commercial impracticability.

The principal difficulty with force majeure clauses is in deciding whether an event that is not specifically mentioned is within the scope of the clause.[166] The interpretive rule of "ejusdem generis" provides that general words in a contract are interpreted to refer to matters of the same kind or class as those referred to in the particular examples included in the language involved.[167] In *Austin*, the general language referring to "acts of God" was thus interpreted to refer to extrinsic contingencies and not to the inherent difficulties that made performance of the

---

[164] 153 P.2d 47 (Cal. 1944).

[165] 314 F.2d 518 (Ct. Cl. 1963).

[166] Noralyn O. Harlow, Annotation, *Construction and Effect of "Changed Conditions" Clause in Public Works or Construction Contract with State or Its Subdivision*, 56 A.L.R.4th 1042 (1987).

[167] *See supra* § 6.02[C][4] Ejusdem Generis — Of the Same Kind or Class.

contract technologically impossible.[168] Ultimately, however, this is a matter of interpretation, and is thus governed by the myriad of rules that are involved in interpreting the meaning of contractual language.[169]

[D]   Risk of Loss in Contracts for Goods

Excuse due to a change in circumstances, such as destruction of the subject matter of the contract, depends upon whether the party seeking relief has contractually assumed the risk of the loss. In many cases, the parties will have expressly or impliedly agreed which party has the risk of loss. In other cases, the U.C.C. provides default rules governing this issue.

[1]   Risk of Loss in Domestic Sales

Article 2 of the U.C.C. contains several rules allocating the risk of loss between the parties that apply in varying circumstances, depending on how delivery of the goods is to be accomplished. If the contract "requires or authorizes the seller to ship the goods" via an independent "carrier," the risk of loss during transit rests upon either the buyer or the seller, depending on whether it is a "shipment" contract or a "destination" contract.[170] In a shipment contract, where the seller is obligated merely to tender the goods to the carrier, the risk of loss is on the buyer while they are in transit.[171] A shipment contract is usually indicated by terms such as "F.O.B. Seller's Loading Dock" or other similar language indicating that the price is based on the buyer paying for transportation of the goods from the designated location.[172] In a destination contract, the seller is responsible for the goods until they arrive at the specified destination.[173] If they are destroyed en route, the seller must bear the loss. Usually, of course, the carrier will have insurance, but if the carrier doesn't have insurance, or the insurer is insolvent, it will be important to determine where the risk of loss lies. Even when the carrier is fully insured, it will be important to know whether the buyer or seller should file the claim.

In other circumstances, the goods may be in storage at an independent warehouse. The parties might agree that they are to be delivered to the buyer "without being moved."[174] This is sometimes accomplished through the use of "documents of title," such as a warehouse receipt[175] or a delivery order.[176] In these

---

[168] *See also* Kama Rippa Music, Inc. v. Schekeryk, 510 F.2d 837 (2d Cir. 1975); Charles J. Goetz & Robert E. Scott, *The Limits of Expanded Choice: An Analysis Between Express and Implied Contract Terms*, 73 Calif. L. Rev. 261 (1985).

[169] *See supra* § 6.02 Interpreting Express Terms.

[170] *See generally* U.C.C. § 2-504 cmt. 1 (2012); *supra* § 4.11[B][2][c] Shipment and Destination Contracts; Mercantile Terms, and "Incoterms."

[171] U.C.C. § 2-509(1)(a) (2012). *E.g.*, Wilson v. Brawn of Calif., Inc., 132 Cal. App. 4th 549 (2005).

[172] *See supra* § 4.11[B][2][c] Shipment and Destination Contracts; Mercantile Terms and "Incoterms."

[173] U.C.C. § 2-509(1)(b) (2012).

[174] U.C.C. § 2-509(2) (2012).

[175] *See* U.C.C. § 1-201(a) (42) (2012).

cases, the risk of destruction of the goods shifts from the seller to the buyer when the seller delivers the necessary document to the buyer, or when the warehouse acknowledges the buyer's right to possession of the goods.[177]

In other situations, the goods will be delivered directly to the buyer, without the involvement of a third-party carrier or an independent warehouse. In these cases, one of two rules applies. If the seller is a merchant, the risk passes to the buyer only upon its receipt of the goods.[178] If the seller is not a merchant, the risk passes when the seller tenders delivery,[179] regardless of whether the buyer receives them at that time.

In all of these situations, breach by one of the parties may adjust the allocation of the risk. When defects in the goods give the buyer a right to reject them,[180] the risk of their destruction remains on the seller until the goods are accepted by the buyer[181] or until the seller effectuates a cure.[182] If the buyer initially accepts the goods, but later justifiably revokes its acceptance, the buyer may treat the risk of loss as if it had remained on the seller to the extent of any deficiency in its insurance coverage.[183] Similarly, if the buyer repudiates the contract before the risk has passed, with respect to goods that have already been identified to the contract, the seller may regard the risk as having shifted to the buyer to the extent of any deficiency in the seller's insurance, but only for a reasonable time after the repudiation.[184]

[2]   Risk of Loss in International Sales[185]

Like the U.C.C., the United Nations Convention on the International Sale of Goods contains rules governing the risk of loss of goods that play a role when the goods are destroyed. In international transactions the risk of loss of goods while in transit may be greater than in purely domestic transactions, not just because of the greater distances involved, but because of uncertain political and security conditions in foreign countries involved either in the transaction itself, or in the transportation of the goods from the seller to the buyer.

Like U.C.C. § 2-509, the CISG places the risk of loss of the goods during their carriage on the seller or the buyer depending on whether the contract is a

---

[176] *See* U.C.C. § 7-102(a)(5) (2012).

[177] *See* U.C.C. § 2-509(2) (2012).

[178] U.C.C. § 2-509(3) (2012).

[179] *Id.*

[180] *See supra* § 9.02 Performance and Breach in Contracts for Goods.

[181] *See supra* § 9.03[B] Rejection or Acceptance.

[182] *See supra* § 9.04 Breaching Party's Right to Cure.

[183] U.C.C. § 2-509(2) (2012).

[184] U.C.C. § 2-509(3) (2012).

[185] J. Bermand & M. Ladd, *Risk of Loss or Damages in Documentary Transactions Under the Convention on the International Sale of Goods*, 21 Cornell Int'l. L.J. 423 (1988); Johan Erauw, *CISG Articles 66–70: The Risk of Loss and Passing It*, 25 J.L. & Com. 203 (2005).

shipment[186] or a destination contract.[187] It further provides for the situation that occurs more commonly in international transactions, when goods are sold while they are "in transit."[188] Thus, the seller may make a contract for the sale of goods that are already headed for the United States. In this situation, the risk passes to the buyer at the time the contract is made.[189]

The residual rule, in other cases, shifts the risk from the seller to the buyer "when he takes over the goods."[190] In most cases the buyer will take the goods over at the seller's place of business. If the parties agree that the buyer will take the goods at some other place, the risk passes to the buyer "when delivery is due and the buyer is aware of the fact that the goods are placed at his disposal at that place."[191] Of course, this can only occur with respect to goods after they have been identified to the contract. Goods that are yet to be manufactured by the seller cannot be identified until after their manufacture is completed, and the risk cannot pass until manufacture and identification occurs.[192]

§ 11.04 REMEDIES FOR CHANGE OF CIRCUMSTANCES

If performance becomes impossible after the contract has been partially performed, some remedy in addition to excuse is warranted. Otherwise, the party who has partially performed will suffer the loss of the expenses it incurred, and the party who has received this performance will be unjustly enriched.

Consider a simple example involving Sam's agreement to sell his BMW to Barb for $17,000. If Barb paid Sam a $3,000 down payment and the car is destroyed before the car is delivered, Barb will want her money back. If Sam used the down payment to make $2,000 worth of agreed, repairs Sam will want to keep at least this amount to cover his expenses.

[A]   Apportionment of Divisible Contracts[193]

In some cases involving multiple performances, the contract may be logically divided into severable portions. If so, a proportionate amount of the price will be allocated to the completed part of the contract. Thus, the contract may be enforced to the extent that a divisible portion has been completed, with performance of the remainder of the contract excused. For example, if a builder has completed work on two of five identical houses, that were to be built for a total price of $500,000, and a flood diverts a river onto the land destroying the two completed houses, it will be easy for a court to apportion the price and require the owner of the land to

---

[186] CISG Art. 67(1) (1980).

[187] CISG Art. 67(1) (1980).

[188] CISG Art. 68 (1980).

[189] *Id.*

[190] CISG Art. 69(1) (1980).

[191] CISG Art. 69 (1988).

[192] CISG Art. 69(3) (1980).

[193] Phillip P. Weiss, Comment, *Apportioning Loss After Discharge of a Burdensome Contract: A Statutory Solution*, 69 YALE L.J. 1054 (1960).

pay $200,000 for the two completed houses and excuse both parties from their remaining obligations.[194]

Where apportionment is possible, the court will excuse the parties from the unperformed part of the contract, but leave the portion of the contract that had already been performed, intact. This is similar to the apportionment that might occur when there has been a material breach of a divisible contract.[195]

[B]   Restitution for Part Performance

When a contract cannot be apportioned, the problem of how to handle part performance is more difficult to resolve. Consider a situation where the buyer makes a down payment for goods to be manufactured by the seller. Apportionment is not an option if performance becomes impossible after the seller has made some progress on the goods, but none of them are ready to be delivered.

The issue arose in several English coronation parade cases, like *Krell v. Henry*.[196] In *Krell*, the defendant had paid one-third of the £75 price for the right to occupy the plaintiff's apartments overlooking the route of the King's coronation on Pall Mall.[197] Performance was excused when the parade was cancelled due to the King's illness. When the plaintiff sued to recover the balance due, the defendant counterclaimed for the recovery of his £25 down payment. The defendant withdrew his claim to recover the down payment, but the court nevertheless indicated, in dictum, that "subsequent impossibility does not affect rights already acquired." This suggested that reimbursement of the down payment would not have been available.

This suggestion was later adopted in *Chandler v. Webster*,[198] another coronation parade case. There, the tenant was unable to recover amounts paid before the parade was cancelled, and was liable for sums that had become due before cancellation. Thus, sums paid or due before June 24, 1902 (the day the parade was cancelled) remained due, despite the excuse. Rent due not until after the parade was cancelled were excused. In accordance with the terms of the contract, the court left the loss where it had fallen at the time the intervening event occurred.

The injustice of this result is apparent. The tenant in one apartment may have made payment in full while the tenant in another apartment may have promised only to make payment on the morning of the parade, without any real difference in the degree of risk the parties intended to assume. The first tenant would have lost his entire payment while the second would have been liable for nothing, based on the justification of enforcing an agreement that the court had already determined was to be excused.

Today, courts require restitution for the value of any benefits conferred before

---

[194] *E.g.*, Gill v. Johnstown Lumber Co., 25 A. 120 (Pa. 1892). *See also* CISG Art. 50 (1988).

[195] *See supra* § 9.01[D] Divisibility of Contracts.

[196] 2 K.B. 740 (Ct. App. 1903).

[197] Given inflation, this would have been approximately £5,600 or about $14,000 at exchange rates prevailing in 2009. This was an expensive daily rental.

[198] 1 K.B. 493 (1904).

the occurrence of the disrupting event, but adjust the amount that may be recovered to compensate the other party for expenses it had already incurred in beginning performance, before the disrupting event.[199]

The problem of providing full restitution without regard to amounts that have already been spent in reliance on the contract is frequently illustrated by another English case, *Fibrosa Spolka Akcyjna v. Fairbairn Lawson Combe Barbour Ltd.*[200] The plaintiff was a Polish textile company who ordered a piece of textile machinery from an English manufacturer, making a £1,000 down payment. Six weeks after the down payment was made, Germany invaded Poland, and Britain declared war on Germany. Performance of the contract became impossible. The buyer sued to recover its down payment and the seller refused because it had begun work that would be wasted if the item was not to be delivered to the buyer. The House of Lords ultimately permitted the buyer to recover the entire £1,000 without deduction for amounts already spent by the seller.

The result in *Fibrosa* seems unfair. Any measure of the defendant's unjust enrichment would have to take into account sums the defendant had already spent that it could not recoup. Further, the formation of the contract, when war was imminent, indicated that the down payment had been made to partially protect the defendant from the risk that the outbreak of war would leave it unable to perform after incurring considerable start-up expenses.[201] Down payments are frequently required to protect a party, like the seller in *Fibrosa*, from the risk of exactly this type of loss. Significantly, since *Fibrosa*, the United Kingdom has passed legislation that permits the recovery of money paid, subject to offset for expenses incurred in partial performance before the contract was excused.[202]

With a few notable exceptions,[203] American courts have never been satisfied with the rule of *Chandler v. Webster* that the loss should rest wherever it falls. Instead, they have tended to award restitution for the value of benefits conferred through part performance.[204]

In *Carroll v. Bowersock*,[205] the court drew a sharp distinction between work incorporated into the partially completed structure and work done in preparation for performance. A contractor agreed to build a new steel-reinforced concrete floor in the defendant's warehouse. At the time the entire building burned, the

---

[199] RESTATEMENT (SECOND) OF CONTRACTS § 272 (1981).

[200] [1943] A.C. 32 (H.L. 1942).

[201] Andrew Kull, *Mistake, Frustration, and the Windfall Principle of Contract Remedies*, 43 HASTINGS L.J. 1 (1991).

[202] Law Reform (Frustrated Contracts) Act, 1943, 6 & 7 Geo. 6, ch. 40. *See* R.G. McElroy & Glanville Williams, *The Coronation Cases — I*, 4 MOD. L. REV. 241 (1941); *The Coronation Cases — II*, 5 MOD. L. REV. 1 (1941).

[203] *E.g.*, Krause v. Board of Trustees, 70 N.E. 264 (Ind. 1904); Ala. Football, Inc. v. Wright, 452 F. Supp. 182 (N.D. Tex. 1977), *aff'd*, 607 F.2d 1004 (5th Cir. 1979) (no recovery of "signing bonus" when football league failed to materialize).

[204] *See* RESTATEMENT (SECOND) OF CONTRACTS § 377 (1981); Annotation, *Who Must Bear the Loss from Destruction of or Damage to Building During Performance of Building Contract, Without Fault of Either Party*, 53 A.L.R. 103, 116–28 (1928). *E.g.*, Butterfield v. Byron, 27 N.E. 667 (Mass. 1891).

[205] 164 P. 143 (Kan. 1917).

contractor had installed footers to support the new floor, constructed wooden forms in which to pour concrete for the posts that would support the floor, and placed steel reinforcing rods into the forms.

The court awarded the contractor restitution for the value of the benefit of his work that had already been incorporated into the building, such as the concrete footers that had already been poured, but denied recovery for either the work performed in constructing the wooden forms, or for the value of the materials used to construct them. The court explained that the forms had not been incorporated into the work. Likewise, the steel rods had not yet been permanently attached to the building and could still have been removed by the contractor had the fire not occurred. Accordingly, no benefit had been conferred upon the owner, and he was not liable for them.[206] Protection is thus afforded to protect against unjust enrichment, but not to compensate for expenditures incurred in reliance on the contract that did not result in a benefit conferred on the other party.[207]

[C]   Abatement of the Price and the Effect of Insurance[208]

In contracts for the sale of real estate, where part of the property is destroyed before performance, issues arise over whether the price should be reduced to the extent of the loss. The rule varies considerably, depending upon the jurisdiction. In most states, the risk of loss rests on the buyer, who is treated as the owner of the property as soon as the contract is executed, even if the buyer does not yet have possession. In a few states, the risk remains with the seller until title is transferred.[209] However, in a growing number of states, the loss rests upon whoever has the right to possession at the time of the loss, regardless of who has legal title.[210]

When one of the parties is insured against the risk of loss, questions arise concerning the extent to which the insurance should be used to cover the loss. This question frequently arises in contracts for the sale of real estate where a building on the land is destroyed between the time the contract is made and the time title is transferred. The risk of loss usually rests on the buyer who must perform the contract, despite the loss of the building and any frustration of purpose which its loss may have caused.

This result is mitigated in many jurisdictions by giving the buyer the protection

---

[206] *See* 2 GEORGE PALMER, LAW OF RESTITUTION § 7.8 at 148–50 (1978).

[207] RESTATEMENT (SECOND) OF CONTRACTS § 272 cmt b. (1981). *See* Quagliana v. Exquisite Home Builders, Inc, 538 P.2d 301, 307 (Utah 1975); *but see* N. Corp. v. Chugach Elec. Ass'n, 518 P.2d 76 (Alaska), *modified on rehearing*, 523 P.2d 1243 (Alaska 1974), *on appeal from trial on remand*, 562 P.2d 1053 (Alaska 1977).

[208] Randy R. Koenders, Annotation, *Risk of Loss by Casualty Pending Contract for Conveyance of Real Property Modern Cases*, 85 A.L.R.4th 233 (2001).

[209] *See, e.g.*, Skelly Oil Co. v. Ashmore, 365 S.W.2d 582, 588–89 (Mo. 1963).

[210] *See, e.g.*, Lucenti v. Cayuga Apartments, 399 N.E.2d 918, 923–24 (N.Y. 1979). UNIFORM VENDOR AND PURCHASER RISK ACT § 1, 14 U.L.A. 471 (1968).

of any insurance on the premises that may be carried by the seller.[211] Thus, if the buyer has promised to pay $300,000 for a parcel of land, and a building located on the land burns down, through the fault of neither, the buyer is entitled to reduce the price by the amount of the seller's insurance coverage. If the seller's policy pays $200,000 for the loss, the buyer may obtain specific performance by paying only the remaining $100,000. In this way the seller obtains the entire value of its $300,000 expectation under the terms of the contract: $200,000 from its insurer and $100,000 from the buyer. The buyer obtains the land for $100,000 of its own funds and can use the remainder of the money it would have used to pay for the land to rebuild. Of course, the risk that the seller's insurance coverage is not sufficient to pay for restoring the destroyed building is on the buyer.

[D]   Adjustment of the Contract[212]

One further possible solution to the problem of commercial impracticability remains. The court might make an equitable adjustment to the contract to accommodate the changed circumstances. This is what the court did in an infamous mutual mistake case, *Aluminum Co. of America v. Essex Group, Inc.*[213] The plaintiff, the Aluminum Company of America (ALCOA), entered into a long-term contract to supply aluminum to Essex. The price for ALCOA's aluminum was based on a complicated formula, devised for the parties by economist Alan Greenspan, who later served from 1987 to 2006 as Chairman of the Federal Reserve Bank. The price changed based on increases in the Wholesale Price Index for Industrial Commodities and changes in the average hourly labor rates paid to ALCOA employees at the factory where the aluminum to be supplied to Essex was manufactured. The formula was designed to ensure that ALCOA earned an average net income of approximately 4 cents per pound.

Unfortunately, the price-fixing policies of OPEC, together with unanticipated pollution control measures, resulted in an increase in ALCOA's electricity costs. Smelting bauxite to produce aluminum requires massive amounts of electricity, and ALCOA's production costs far outstripped the increases anticipated by the formula incorporated into the contract. Because of the losses it was experiencing from these unanticipated market conditions, ALCOA sought relief from the contract on the grounds that the parties had made a mutual mistake about the effects of the price adjustment clause.

Despite the language in the comments to U.C.C. § 2-615, which indicates that "[i]ncreased cost alone does not excuse performance," the court found that the

---

[211] *E.g.*, Skelly Oil Co. v. Ashmore, 365 S.W.2d 582 (Mo. 1963).

[212] John P. Dawson, *Judicial Revision of Frustrated Contracts: The United States*, 64 B.U. L. Rev. 1 (1984); Jeffrey L. Harrison, *A Case for Loss Sharing*, 56 S. Cal. L. Rev. 573 (1983); Thomas R. Hurst, *Inflation, Deflation and Long Term Contractual Relationships Under UCC Section 2-615*, 95 Com. L.J. 290 (1990); Larry A. DiMatteo, *Equity's Modification of Contract: An Analysis of the Twentieth Century's Equitable Reformation of Contract Law*, 33 New Eng. L. Rev. 265 (1999); Jeffrey L. Harrison, *A Case for Loss Sharing*, 56 S. Cal. L. Rev. 573 (1983); Ian MacNeil, *Contracts: Adjustment of Long-Term Economic Relations Under Classical Neoclassical, and Relations Contract Law*, 72 Nw. U.L. Rev. 854 (1978); William F. Young, *Half Measures*, 81 Colum. L. Rev. 19 (1981).

[213] 499 F. Supp. 53 (W.D. Pa. 1980).

extraordinary increase in ALCOA's production costs, and the unanticipated circumstances that led to the increase, warranted relief. However, rather than simply excusing ALCOA from the contract, Federal District Judge Teitelbaum made an equitable adjustment to the price term of the contract designed to achieve a profit for ALCOA of 1% per pound for aluminum delivered to Essex under the terms of the contract, the minimum profit that the contract's formula was designed to achieve. The price under Judge Teitelbaum's revised formula was limited only by the absolute maximum cap of 65 cents per pound, which had been included as an absolute ceiling in the original contract.

Before the decision in *ALCOA*, this type of equitable adjustment of the terms of the contract had not been thought possible. Until *ALCOA*, courts were permitted either to enforce the contract according to its terms, or to excuse performance altogether due to impracticability, but not to rewrite the agreement to create something in between these possibilities. The notion of an adjustment to the contract on terms selected by the court was nearly unimaginable.

Significantly, the new price structure imposed by the court was never implemented by the parties, who settled while Judge Teitelbaum's groundbreaking decision was on appeal. It has generated considerable debate among courts and scholars about the appropriate role of the judiciary in attempting to resolve claims that a contract has become commercially impracticable.[214] Despite its groundbreaking approach, the *ALCOA* decision has not been widely followed.[215]

§ 11.05 MISTAKE AND CHANGE OF CIRCUMSTANCE IN INTERNATIONAL TRANSACTIONS[216]

International transactions involving the sale of goods are governed by the CISG, which contains no express provision for mutual mistake, but directly addresses excuse due to an unanticipated change in circumstances. UNIDROIT's Principles of International Commercial Contracts and Principles of European Contract Law provide guidance on both the effect of a mutual mistake and change of circumstances.

[A]   Mistake in International Transactions

The CISG does not directly address mutual mistake.[217] However, CISG Article 79 provides an exemption to the duty of performance due to an "impediment," and

---

[214] *See generally* Robert A. Hillman, *Court Adjustment of Long-Term Contracts: An Analysis Under Modern Contract Law*, 1987 DUKE L.J. 1; Ian Macneil, *Contracts: Adjustment of Long-Term Economic Relations Under Classical, Neo-Classical and Relational Contract Law*, 72 Nw. U. L. REV. 854 (1978).

[215] *See* Beaver Creek Coal v. Nev. Power, 968 F.2d 19 (10th Cir. 1992).

[216] Dionysios P. Flambouras, *The Doctrine of Impossibility of Performance and Clausula Rebus Sic Standibus in the 1980 Vienna Convention on International Sales and the Principles of European Contract Law — A Comparative Analysis*, 13 PACE INT. L. REV. 261 (2001); Carla Spivack, *Of Shrinking Sweatsuits and Poison Vine Wax: A Comparison of Basis for Excuse Under U.C.C. § 2-615 and CISG Article 79*, 27 U. PA. J. INT'L ECON. L. 757 (2006).

[217] *See Id.*

might apply to a mistake regarding an "existing impossibility" due to the prior destruction of the goods, as it does to a subsequent event that impedes performance.[218] More importantly, cases involving a mistake due to the buyer's misdescription of the goods are expressly governed by rules regarding express warranties just as they are under U.C.C. § 2-314.[219]

UNIDROIT's Principles of International Commercial Contracts provide for relief from mutual mistake under rules very similar to those applicable under our common law. UNIDROIT's rule regarding unilateral mistake is quite liberal, permitting avoidance of the contract if the other party had not yet acted in reliance on the mistake at the time it was discovered.[220] If the contract is avoided due to mistake, "either party may claim restitution of whatever it has supplied under the contract."[221] But, a party who "knew or ought to have known of the ground for avoidance" must still pay damages based on the other party's lost expectations.[222]

The Principles of European Contract Law address the problem of both unilateral and mutual mistake in more detail. Relief for unilateral mistake is available if the other party supplied the information that led to the mistake, or knew or should have known of the mistake and in bad faith failed to draw the mistaken party's attention to its error.[223] In either event, relief depends on whether the other party knew or ought to have known that the mistake was sufficiently important that the mistaken party would not have made the contract, or would have insisted on fundamentally different terms, if it had not made the mistake.[224] The Principles provide wide latitude to the court to prevent avoidance if, "in the circumstances [the party's] mistake was inexcusable" or if the party assumed the risk of the mistake or should bear the risk of the mistake.[225]

Mutual mistake is governed by similar rules. Avoidance due to a mutual mistake is permitted only if the mistake is material in the sense that the contract would not have been made, or would only have been made on fundamentally different terms,[226] if the mistake had not been made, and if the risk of the mistake was not assumed by the party who made it.[227] Likewise, relief is unavailable if the mistake was "inexcusable."[228]

---

[218] Dionysios P. Flambouras, *The Doctrines of Impossibility of Performance and Causula Rebus Sic Stantibus in the 1980 Convention on Contracts for the International Sale of Goods and the Principles of European Contract Law — A Comparative Analysis*, 13 Pace Int'l L. Rev. 261, 268 (2001).

[219] Helen Elizabeth Hartnell, *Rousing the Sleeping Dog: The Validity Exception to the Convention on Contracts for the International Sale of Goods*, 18 Yale J. Int'l L. 1, 72–77 (1993).

[220] PICC Art 3.5(1)(a) (2004).

[221] PICC Art. 3.17(2) (2004).

[222] PICC Art. 3.18 (2004).

[223] PECL Art 4.103(1)(a)(i)–(ii) (2002).

[224] PECL Art 4.103(1)(b) (2002).

[225] PECL Art. 4.103(2) (2002).

[226] PECL Art. 4.103(1)(b) (2002).

[227] PECL Art. 4.103(2)(b) (2002).

[228] PECL Art. 4.103(2)(a) (2002).

[B]   Change of Circumstances in International Transactions[229]

In international contracts for the sale of goods, the CISG provides for an "exemption" from liability under circumstances similar to those in which a party may be excused under U.C.C. § 2-615.[230] Under CISG Article 79, a party is exempted from a duty under a contract for the sale of goods if its failure was due to an "impediment" and (1) the impediment was beyond the party's control; (2) the party could not reasonably be expected to have taken the impediment into account at the time "of the conclusion of the contract"; and (3) the party could not reasonably be expected to avoid or overcome the impediment or its consequences.[231] The party seeking exemption from its obligations must give notice of the impediment within a reasonable time after it knew or should have known of it.[232] Temporary impediments, on the other hand, provide an excuse only for the limited duration of the impediment.[233]

The UNIDROIT Principles provide for similar rules, permitting different degrees of excuse due either to "force majeure"[234] or "hardship."[235] Force majeure is similar to the common law's older principle relieving the parties from the contract entirely, but only due to strict impossibility.[236] "Hardship," on the other hand, is similar to our doctrine of impracticability, but differs in that it does not provide a complete excuse. Instead, it authorizes the court to "adapt" the contract to accommodate for the hardship,[237] in much the same way the court attempted to correct for the mistake in the *ALCOA* case discussed above.[238] The "disadvantaged party," if it acts "without undue delay," has the right to "request renegotiations."[239] If the parties are unable to reach an agreement within a reasonable time, the parties may ask the court to terminate the contract or "adapt the contract with a view to restoring its equilibrium."[240]

The Principles of European Contract Law take a similar approach. Parties

---

[229] Joseph M. Perillo, *Force Majeure and Hardship Under the UNIDROIT Principles of International Commercial Contracts*, 5 Tul. J. Int'l & Comp. L. 5 (1997); Carla Spivack, *Of Shrinking Sweatsuits and Poison Vine Wax: A Comparison of Basis for Excuse Under U.C.C. § 2-615 and CISG Article 79*, 27 U. Pa. J. Int'l Econ. L. 757 (2006).

[230] Dionysios P. Flambouras, *The Doctrines of Impossibility of Performance and Causula Rebus Sic Stantibus in the 1980 Convention on Contracts for the International Sale of Goods and the Principles of European Contract Law — A Comparative Analysis*, 13 Pace Int'l L. Rev. 261 (2001).

[231] CISG Art. 79(1) (1980).

[232] CISG Art. 79(4) (1980).

[233] CISG Art. 79(3) (1980).

[234] PICC Art. 7.1.7 (2004).

[235] PICC Arts. 6.2.1–6.3 (2004).

[236] Dietrich Maskow, *Hardship and Force Majeure*, 40 Am. J. Comp. L. 657–74 (1992).

[237] Joseph M. Perillo, *Force Majeure and Hardship Under the UNIDROIT Principles of International Commercial Contracts*, 5 Tul. J. Int'l & Comp. L. 5, 25 (1997).

[238] Aluminum Co. of Am. v. Essex Group, Inc., 499 F. Supp. 53 (W.D. Pa. 1980).

[239] PICC Art. 6.2.3 (2004).

[240] PICC Art. 6.2.3(4) (2004).

generally remain obligated to perform their agreements "even if performance has become more onerous because of a change of circumstances."[241] But, if a change of circumstances makes performance "excessively onerous," the parties have a duty to "enter into negotiations with a view to adapting the contract or terminating it."[242] They may not suspend performance during the course of these negotiations, but, if their efforts to reach an agreement fail, they can seek relief from the court.[243] The European Contract Principles contain a parallel provision that permits a party's nonperformance to be excused "if it proves that [its nonperformance] is due to an impediment beyond its control and that it could not reasonably have been expected to take the impediment into account [when the contract was made] or to have avoided or overcome the impediment or its consequences."[244]

---

[241] PECL Art. 6.111(1) (2002).

[242] PECL Art. 6.111(2) (2002).

[243] PECL Art. 6.111(3) (2002).

[244] PECL Art. 8.108(1) (2002).

Chapter 12

REMEDIES: EXPECTATION DAMAGES

§ 12.01   INTRODUCTION TO CONTRACT REMEDIES[1]

[A]   Remedies in General

Most contracts are performed. Parties perform their agreements for the same reasons they made them in the first place: to obtain the benefits of the return promise from the other party. Even when they have already received what they bargained for, parties perform their agreements to maintain their own reputation in the community, and because they believe that it is the right thing to do. Most contracts would likely be performed even if there were no formal legal remedies for breach of contract.

Still, circumstances change and motivations vary, and parties sometimes fail to follow through with their commitments. When one party breaches, the other is likely to be interested in obtaining a remedy. Likewise, a party considering breaking its promise is likely to be curious about the consequences of its actions. Moreover, prudent people consider these matters before even entering into a contract, and might even address the issue while drafting the contract. Therefore, a good understanding of the law of contract remedies facilitates parties' threshold decisions of whether to enter into a contract in the first place and what terms to bargain for.[2]

The normal remedy for breach of contract is money damages.[3] The amount should be sufficient to place the aggrieved party in as good a position as it would have been in if the contract had been performed.[4] However, damages are

---

[1] David W. Barnes & Deborah Zalesne, *A Unifying Theory of Contract Damage Rules*, 55 Syracuse L. Rev. 495 (2005); E. Allan Farnsworth, *Legal Remedies for Breach of Contract*, 70 Colum. L. Rev. 1145, 1147 (1970); Robert Cooter & Melvin A. Eisenberg, *Damages for Breach of Contract*, 73 Calif. L. Rev. 1432 (1985); Lon L. Fuller & William R. Perdue, *The Reliance Interest in Contract Damages (Pts. 1 & 2)*, 46 Yale L.J. 42, 373 (1936–37); Avery W. Katz, *Remedies for Breach of Contract Under the CISG*, 25 Int'l Rev. L. & Econ. 378, 384 (2006); Ellen Peters, *Remedies for Breach of Contract Relating to the Sale of Goods Under the Uniform Commercial Code: A Roadmap for Article Two*, 73 Yale L.J. 199 (1963); David H. Vernon, *Expectancy Damages for Breach of Contract: A Primer and Critique*, 1976 Wash. U. L.Q. 179; Edward Yorio, *In Defense of Money Damages for Breach of Contract*, 82 Colum. L. Rev. 1365 (1982).

[2] This factor is so important that many law school Contracts courses begin with remedies.

[3] Restatement (Second) of Contracts § 345(a) (1981).

[4] Restatement (Second) of Contracts § 344(a) (1981); U.C.C. § 1-106(1) (2012). *See* Oxy USA, Inc. v. Babbitt, 268 F.3d 1001, 1007 (10th Cir. 2001).

sometimes limited to amounts spent in "reliance" on the contract.[5] Reliance damages place the injured party back into the position it would have been in before the contract was made.[6] In still other circumstances, damages may be based in restitution, to prevent unjust enrichment.[7]

Alternative remedies include equitable relief,[8] usually in the form of a court order of "specific performance" requiring the breaching party to perform, or an "injunction" that is aimed at preventing breach.[9] A defendant who violates this type of court order is guilty of contempt and is thus vulnerable to criminal sanctions, theoretically including jail. In other situations, the court might provide declaratory relief specifying the relative rights of the parties, with or without an accompanying award of damages.[10]

Sometimes, the parties' agree about a remedy in advance. The contract might contain an agreed or "liquidated" damages provision,[11] or an agreement limiting the injured party's remedy.[12] Further, they might agree about the method by which their rights and remedies are to be adjudicated, such as through mediation or arbitration.[13]

[B] Expectation, Reliance, and Restitution Interests[14]

In framing a remedy, courts try to satisfy one of three remedial interests: expectation, reliance, or restitution.[15] These interests generally reflect views about the appropriate societal role of contract enforcement generally.[16]

---

[5] *See, e.g.,* Sullivan v. O'Connor, 296 N.E.2d 183 (Mass. 1973); Security Store & Mfg. Co. v. Am. Ry. Express Co., 51 S.W.2d 572 (Mo. Ct. App. 1932). *See generally infra* § 13.02 Damages Based on the Reliance Interest; Lon Fuller & William Perdue, *The Reliance Interest in Contract Damages (Pts. 1 & 2)*, 46 YALE L.J. 52, 373 (1936, 1937).

[6] RESTATEMENT (SECOND) OF CONTRACTS § 344(b) (1981).

[7] RESTATEMENT (SECOND) OF CONTRACTS § 345 cmt. c (1981).

[8] *See infra* Chapter 15 Equitable Remedies.

[9] RESTATEMENT (SECOND) OF CONTRACTS § 345(b) (1981).

[10] RESTATEMENT (SECOND) OF CONTRACTS § 345(e) & cmt. d (1981).

[11] *See infra* § 14.03 Liquidated Damages.

[12] *See infra* § 14.02 Limited Remedies.

[13] Moses H. Cone Mem'l Hosp. v. Mercury Constr. Corp., 460 U.S. 1, 24–25 (1983) (emphasizing the liberal federal policy in favor of the enforceability of arbitration agreements). *See also* Shearson/American Express v. McMahon, 482 U.S. 220 (1987). *See generally* E. Allan Farnsworth, *Punitive Damages in Arbitration*, 20 STETSON L. REV. 395 (1991).

[14] Robert L. Birmingham, *Notes on the Reliance Interest*, 60 WASH L. REV. 217 (1985); Richard Craswell, *Against Fuller and Perdue*, 67 U. CHI. L. REV. 99 (2000); Lon L. Fuller & William R. Perdue, *The Reliance Interest in Contract Damages (Pts. 1 & 2)*, 46 YALE L.J. 42, 373 (1936–37); Avery Katz, *Reflections on Fuller and Perdue's the Reliance Interest in Contract Damages: A Positive Economic Framework*, 21 U. MICH. J.L. REF. 541 (1988); Jim Lietzel, *Reliance and Contract Breach*, 52 LAW & CONTEMP. PROB. 87 (1989).

[15] Lon Fuller & William Perdue, *The Reliance Interest in Contract Damages (Pt. 1)*, 46 YALE L.J. 52, 373 (1936) (the starting point in any discussion of contract damages).

[16] P.S. ATIYAH, PROMISES, MORALS, AND LAW (1981); CHARLES FRIED, CONTRACT AS PROMISE: A THEORY OF CONTRACTUAL OBLIGATION 17–27 (1981); Robert Birmingham, *Notes on the Reliance Interest*, 60 WASH. L.

The expectation interest is satisfied by awarding damages in an amount sufficient to place that party in as good a position as it would have been in had the contract been performed,[17] or, as is frequently said, to give the aggrieved party "the benefit of its bargain."[18] When it is difficult to calculate the amount necessary to compensate for lost expectations, a different approach is used. The injured party recovers the expenses it incurred in reliance on the contract.[19] This places it back into the position it would have been in, if the contract had never been made.

Alternatively, the law might simply seek to prevent the breaching party from being unjustly enriched. This is done by awarding damages based on restitution, not only to the aggrieved party, but also possibly to the party in breach where necessary to prevent the aggrieved party from unjustly benefiting from the contract.

The distinctions among these three interests can be best understood in the context of a simple example. Assume that after entering into a contract for the purchase of a house, for $200,000, that 1) the buyer gave the seller a $5,000 down payment; 2) spent $400 to have the house appraised in connection with her loan application; and 3) paid her lawyer $600 to attend the closing. When the seller refused to perform, the buyer purchased another equivalent house for $210,000, and incurred another $1,000 in appraisal and legal fees.

If the contract had been performed, the buyer would have purchased the original house after spending a total of $201,000: $200,000 for the house, $400 in appraisal fees, and $600 in attorneys' fees. She has already spent $6,000 of this amount, consisting of the $5,000 down payment and the $1,000 in fees. On the other hand, because of the seller's breach, the buyer has saved the $195,000 balance of the price. She now must pay $210,000, or $10,000 extra, for a different house, together with an additional $1,000 in appraisal and attorneys' fees in connection with the second transaction, for a total of $211,000. Accordingly, her expectation damages, necessary to place her in the position she would have been in if the contract had been performed, will be $16,000. This sum includes return of the $5,000 down payment, recovery of the $400 appraisal fee and the $600 in attorneys' fees wasted in connection with the first house. It also includes the $10,000 extra it cost to purchase an equivalent house with the same market value as house involved in the broken contract.

The buyer's reliance expenses include only the $5,000 down payment and the

---

REV. 217 (1985); Lon L. Fuller & William R. Perdue Jr., *The Reliance Interest in Contract Damages (Pts. 1–2)*, 46 YALE L.J. 52, 373 (1936–37); Michael B. Kelly, *The Phantom Reliance Interest in Contract Damages*, 1992 WIS. L. REV. 1755; Mark Pettit Jr., *Private Advantage and Public Powers: Reexamining the Expectation and Reliance Interests in Contract Damages*, 38 HASTINGS L.J. 417, 444–53 (1986); W. David Slawson, *The Role of Reliance in Contract Damages*, 76 CORNELL L. REV. 197 (1990) (supporting the expectation measure); STEPHEN A. SMITH, CONTRACT THEORY 41-163 (2004); Christopher T. Wonnell, *Expectation, Reliance, and the Two Contractual Wrongs*, 38 SAN DIEGO L. REV. 53 (2001).

[17] RESTATEMENT (SECOND) OF CONTRACTS § 344(a) (1981); U.C.C. § 1-305(a) (2012) (formerly § 1-106(1)); Allapattah Serv., Inc. v. Exxon Corp., 61 F. Supp. 2d 1326 (S.D. Fla. 1999). *See* Melvin A. Eisenberg, *Actual and Virtual Specific Performance, the Theory of Efficient Breach, and the Indifference Principle in Contract Law*, 93 CAL. L. REV. 975, 979 (2005).

[18] RESTATEMENT (SECOND) OF CONTRACTS § 344(a) cmt. a (1981).

[19] RESTATEMENT (SECOND) OF CONTRACTS § 344(b) (1981).

$1,000 in appraisal and legal fees. Recovery of $6,000 places her back in the position she would have been in if the contract with the breaching seller had never been made.

If the buyer recovers in restitution for the value of the benefit conferred on the breaching party, she will recover only her $5,000 down payment. Recovery of the down payment prevents the breaching seller from being unjustly enriched by his breach. The $400 appraisal fee and the $600 in attorneys' fees were wasted, but their expenditure did not confer a benefit on the breaching party. Restitution seeks only to prevent unjust enrichment, and thus these expenditures are not recoverable under this theory.

From this example, it should be clear that the buyer's expectation recovery includes elements of both reliance and restitution. In most cases, expectation is the more desirable recovery. However, depending on the circumstances, reliance or restitution might be more attractive to the aggrieved buyer. This is particularly true if the value of her lost expectation is difficult to prove,[20] or if performance of the contract might have resulted in a financial loss.[21]

§ 12.02   DAMAGES BASED ON THE INJURED PARTY'S EXPECTATIONS[22]

The most common type of remedy for breach of contract is an award of money damages, usually based on the injured party's lost expectations. Money damages are designed primarily to compensate the injured party for the harm it suffered as a result of the breach. Punitive damages are available only when the breach of contract is accompanied by an intentional tort. Where the injured party is unable to prove that it suffered any loss as a result of the breach, it is limited to nominal damages only.

[A]   Expectation Damages[23]

Expectation damages are designed to put the injured party in as good a position as it would have been in if the contract had been performed.[24] This measure of damages compensates the aggrieved party for any value it lost directly as a result

---

[20] *See infra* § 12.06 Limits on Damages: Reasonable Certainty.

[21] *See infra* § 13.05[A] Loss Contracts — Expectation as a Limit on Restitution.

[22] David W. Barnes & Deborah Zalesne, *A Unifying Theory of Contract Damage Rules*, 55 Syracuse L. Rev. 495 (2005); E. Allan Farnsworth, *Legal Remedies for Breach of Contract*, 70 Colum. L. Rev. 1145, 1147 (1970).

[23] David W. Barnes, *The Net Expectation Interest in Contract Damages*, 48 Emory L.J. 1137 (1999). *See* David W. Barnes, *The Meaning of Value in Contract Damages and Contract Theory*, 46 Am. U. L. Rev. 1, 4 (1996); Robert Birmingham, *Breach of Contract, Damage Measures, and Economic Efficiency*, 24 Rutgers L. Rev. 273 (1970); Robert Cooter & Melvin A. Eisenberg, *Damages for Breach of Contract*, 73 Cal. L. Rev. 1432 (1985); Peter Linzer, *On the Amorality of Contract Remedies — Efficiency, Equity, and the Second Restatement*, 81 Colum. L. Rev. 111 (1981); David Vernon, *Expectancy Damages for Breach of Contract: A Primer and a Critique*, 1976 Wash. U.L.Q. 179.

[24] Restatement (Second) of Contracts § 344(a) (1981); U.C.C. § 1-106 (2012); CISG Art. 74 (1980); PICC Art. 7.4.2 (2004); PECL Art. 9.502 (2002).

of the breach.[25] This is usually measured by the difference in value between what was promised and what was received,[26] the additional expense of obtaining a replacement,[27] or its value.[28]

In addition, the injured party is entitled to recover for any other loss, such as incidental or consequential damages caused by the breach.[29] Incidental damages usually consist of expenditures routinely incurred by the parties in the wake of a breach, such as the costs associated with inspecting the defective performance, the costs of storing any defective goods, costs associated with efforts to obtain a substitute, and any insurance or interest expenses that the injured party incurs.[30] These expenses do not always occur, but they are common enough that the injured party does not need to prove that they were foreseeable by the breaching party.

Injured parties also sometimes suffer consequential damages, as a result of lost opportunities caused by the breach. They sometimes suffer property damage or personal injury, particularly in the case of defective and dangerous products.

The consequential damages suffered by businesses are usually different from those in consumer transactions. In cases involving businesses, consequential damages usually consist of lost profits. This might occur for example, when the owner of land fails to go through with its promise to lease property to a tenant,[31] or where the seller of goods fails to deliver them to its customer. It might also occur when a trucking company or railroad delays delivering goods.[32] They might also consist of liability imposed on the buyer as a result of defects in the goods when the buyer ends up liable to others for these defects. In cases involving consumers, consequential damages may consist of lost income, personal injury, or property damage.

Damages are recoverable only for harm caused by the breach.[33] They are subject to three important additional limitations: damages must be foreseeable,[34] they must be proven with reasonable certainty,[35] and they must not have been preventable by the injured party through its own reasonable steps to mitigate the

---

[25] RESTATEMENT (SECOND) OF CONTRACTS § 347(a) (1981).

[26] *See* U.C.C. § 2-714(2) (2012); Hawkins v. McGee, 146 A. 641 (N.H. 1929).

[27] *See* U.C.C. § 2-712 (2012); Laredo Hides Co., Inc. v. H & H Meat Prods. Co., Inc., 513 S.W.2d 210 (Tex. Ct. App. 1974); *cf.* Louise Caroline Nursing Home, Inc. v. Dix Constr. Co., 285 N.E.2d 904 (Mass. 1972) (cost of completion).

[28] *See* U.C.C. § 2-713 (2012); Acme Mills & Elevator Co. v. Johnson, 133 S.W. 784 (Ky. Ct. App. 1911); Tongish v. Thomas, 840 P.2d 471 (Kan. 1992).

[29] RESTATEMENT (SECOND) OF CONTRACTS § 347(b) (1981).

[30] RESTATEMENT (SECOND) OF CONTRACTS § 347 cmt. c (1981). *Compare* U.C.C. § 2-710 (2012), *with* U.C.C. § 2-715(1) (2012). *See infra* § 12.08[A] Contracts for the Sale of Goods — Breach by the Seller; *infra* § 12.08[B] Contracts for the Sale of Goods — Breach by the Buyer.

[31] *See, e.g.,* Fera v. Village Plaza, Inc., 242 N.W.2d 372 (Mich. 1976).

[32] Hadley v. Baxendale, 156 Eng. Rep. 145 (Ct. Exch. 1854).

[33] RESTATEMENT (SECOND) OF CONTRACTS § 347 cmt. e (1981). *See* Krauss v. Greenbarg, 137 F.2d 569 (3d Cir. 1943); *infra* § 12.03 Causation.

[34] *See infra* § 12.04 Limits on Damages: Foreseeability.

[35] *See infra* § 12.06 Limits on Damages: Reasonable Certainty.

harm, such as through obtaining a substitute or repairing the defects.[36] Further, the breaching party is permitted to reduce the damages it must pay by the amount of any costs or losses avoided by the injured party as a result of the breach.[37]

[B]   Punitive Damages[38]

Punitive or "exemplary" damages are incompatible with the basic goal of compensating the injured party for its lost expectations.[39] Therefore, punitive damages are unavailable for a simple breach of contract,[40] even if the breach is intentional,[41] unless the breaching party's conduct rose to the level of an intentional tort.[42]

The standard for awarding punitive damages is limited to cases involving "willful and wanton" misconduct. For example, in *Miller v. Byrne*,[43] the court permitted the jury to consider an award of punitive damages where the defendant insurer and an attorney had allegedly failed to inform its client of a settlement offer in reckless disregard of the consequences.

It is rare to see punitive damages awarded in a case based primarily on breach of a warranty for the sale of goods. But, in *Hibschman Pontiac, Inc. v. Batchelor*,[44] the court found the necessary degree of "malice, fraud, gross negligence or oppressive conduct" when a car dealership failed to repair the plaintiff's automobile after repeated promises to do so. The court explained:

> Paint was bubbled, the radio never worked properly, the hood and bumper were twisted and misaligned, the universal joints failed, the transmission linkage was improperly adjusted, the timing chain was defective causing improper tune-up and the carburetor was defective, among other things. Batchelor took the car to the defendant with a list of defects on numerous

---

[36] *See* U.C.C. § 2-715(2)(a) (2012); CISG Art. 75 (1980); *infra* § 12.05 Limits on Damages: Mitigation.

[37] RESTATEMENT (SECOND) OF CONTRACTS § 347(c) (1981).

[38] Frank J. Cavico Jr., *Punitive Damages for Breach of Contract — A Principled Approach*, 22 ST. MARY'S L.J. 357 (1990); C.Y. Cyrus Chu & Chen-Ying Huang, *On the Definition and Efficiency of Punitive Damages*, 24 INT'L REV. LAW & ECON. 241 (2004); William S. Dodge, *The Case for Punitive Damages in Contracts*, 48 DUKE L.J. 629 (1999); E. Allan Farnsworth, *Legal Remedies for Breach of Contract*, 70 COLUM. L. REV. 1145, 1147 (1970); Marc Galanter, *Contract in Court; Or Almost Everything You May or May Not Want to Know About Contract Litigation*, 2001 WIS. L. REV. 577, 603–06; Steven B. Katz, *The California Tort of Bad Faith Breach, the Dissent in* Seaman's v. Standard Oil, *and the Role of Punitive Damages in Contract Doctrine*, 60 S. CAL. L. REV. 509 (1987); A. Mitchell Polinsky & Steven Shavell, *Punitive Damages: An Economic Analysis*, 111 HARV. L. REV. 869, 936–39 (1998).

[39] *See* RESTATEMENT (SECOND) OF CONTRACTS § 355 (1981). *E.g.*, White v. Benkowski, 155 N.W.2d 74 (Wis. 1967).

[40] *See* Patricia H. Marschall, *Willfulness: A Crucial Factor in Choosing Remedies for Breach of Contract*, 24 ARIZ. L. REV. 733 (1982).

[41] *E.g.*, Allapattah Serv., Inc. v. Exxon Corp., 61 F. Supp. 2d 1326 (S.D. Fla. 1999).

[42] RESTATEMENT (SECOND) OF CONTRACTS § 355 (1981). *See generally* Barry Perlstein, *Crossing the Contract-Tort Boundary: An Economic Argument for the Imposition of Extracompensatory Damages for Opportunistic Breach of Contract*, 58 BROOKLYN L. REV. 877 (1992).

[43] 916 P.2d 566, 580 (Colo. Ct. App. 1995).

[44] 362 N.E.2d 845 (Ind. 1977).

occasions and picked up the car when told it was "all ready to go." It was reasonable to infer that the defendant's service manager represented repairs to have been made when he knew that the work had not been done.[45]

But even here, the court found that an independent tort had been committed. Without a tort, separate from a breach of warranty, most courts refuse to award punitive damages unless the defendants conduct amounted to a separate tort.[46]

Because punitive damages are available only when the defendant's conduct amounts to a separate tort, the U.C.C. makes no reference to the availability of punitive damages. The CISG, on the other hand, seems to expressly prohibit the recoverability of punitive damages with language preventing damages that "exceed the loss which the party in breach foresaw or ought to have foreseen at the time of the conclusion of the contract."[47] Similarly, neither UNIDROIT's Principles of International Commercial Contracts, nor the Principles of European Contract Law make any mention of the availability of punitive damages for breach of contract. Punitive damages are generally not available under these international regimes.[48]

[C]   Nominal Damages

Consistent with the expectation principle, only nominal damages are available where the aggrieved party is unable to establish any loss as a result of a breach.[49] Where nominal damages are awarded, they are usually only token in nature and usually consist of a dollar.[50]

For example, in *Freund v. Washington Square Press, Inc.*,[51] the amount of royalties the plaintiff would have realized from the publication of a book could not be ascertained "with adequate certainty" and, as a consequence, the plaintiff was limited to nominal damages consisting of six cents. Nevertheless, in some cases, an award of purely nominal damages may still be significant. The award will establish the defendant's wrongdoing and may assist in the recovery of court costs[52] or

---

[45] *Id.* at 848.

[46] *Id.* at 846–47. *See generally* E. Allan Farnsworth, *Punitive Damages in Arbitration*, 20 STETSON L. REV. 395 (1991).

[47] CISG Art. 74 (1980). *See* Amy A. Kirby, *Punitive Damages in Contract Actions: The Tension Between the United Nations Convention on Contracts for the International Sale of Goods and U.S. Law*, 16 J.L. & COM. 215 (1997). *But see* Peter Schlechtriem, *The Borderline of Tort and Contract — Opening a New Frontier?*, 21 CORNELL INT'L L.J. 467, 474 (1988).

[48] *But see* Aaron J. Polak, *Punitive Damages in Commercial Contract Arbitration — Still an Issue After All These Years*, 10 OHIO ST. J. ON DISP. RESOL. 41 (1994); Sarah L. Rubright, Comment, *The Struggle of Punitive Damages in Arbitration: How to Get What You Want out of an Arbitration Agreement*, 5 J. AM. ARB. 373 (2006).

[49] RESTATEMENT (SECOND) OF CONTRACTS § 346(2) (1981). *E.g.*, Larson v. City of Fergus Falls, 229 F.3d 692 (8th Cir. 2000); ESPN, Inc. v. Office of the Comm'r of Baseball, 76 F. Supp. 2d 416, 421 (S.D.N.Y. 1999). *See also* Chronister Oil Co. v. Unocal Ref. & Mktg., 34 F.3d 462, 466 (7th Cir. 1994) (Posner, J.).

[50] *See, e.g.*, Johnson Ent. of Jacksonville, Inc. v. FPL Group, Inc., 162 F.3d 1290 (11th Cir. 1998); Freund v. Wash. Square Press, Inc., 314 N.E.2d 419 (N.Y. 1974).

[51] 314 N.E.2d 419 (N.Y. 1974).

[52] Johnson Ent. of Jacksonville, Inc. v. FPL Group, Inc., 162 F.3d 1290, 1330 (11th Cir. 1998).

attorneys' fees.[53] A judgment involving an award of nominal damages might also vindicate the aggrieved party's rights or sense of right, in the same way as an action for declaratory relief.

[D]   Economic Analysis of Contract Damages[54]

Early in its development, the "Law and Economics" movement[55] turned its attention to the law of contract damages. Economic analysis of contract damages rules have suggested the theory of "efficient breach."[56] Under this theory, a breach of contract is desirable if a party can gain a profit through breach even after paying damages to compensate the other party for its disappointment.[57] As one court recently said: "if it is more efficient for a party to breach a contract and pay expectancy damages in order to enter a superior contract, courts will not interfere by requiring the breaching party to pay more than was due under their contract."[58]

Thus, according to the theory of efficient breach, it is desirable for the seller of goods with a contract to sell them at a price of $10,000 to breach if the seller can resell the goods for $15,000, while satisfying the injured buyer's lost expectation by paying it only $2,000 in damages. The theory claims that the injured buyer is no worse off than it would have been had the contact been performed, and after paying damages, the seller will have made an additional profit of $3,000 by reselling the goods. The theory suggests that an additional advantage for society is that the second buyer will have obtained the goods at the price at which he valued them.[59] The seller is better off, the second buyer is better off, and the injured buyer, having been compensated for its loss, is no worse off than if the contract had been performed. Courts have thus sometimes recognized that "certain breaches, such as those where the breaching party's gains exceed the injured party's losses,

---

[53] MindGames, Inc. v. W. Publ'g Co., 218 F.3d 652 (7th Cir. 2000).

[54] Robert Birmingham, *Breach of Contract, Damage Measures, and Economic Efficiency*, 24 RUTGERS L. REV. 237 (1970); Melvin A. Eisenberg, *Actual and Virtual Specific Performance, the Theory of Efficient Breach, and the Indifference Principle in Contract Law*, 93 CAL. L. REV. 975 (2005); Jay Friedman, *The Efficient Breach Fallacy*, 18 J. LEGAL STUD. 1 (1989); Victor P. Goldberg, *An Economic Analysis of the Lost-Volume Retails Seller*, 57 S. CAL. L. REV. 283 (1984); Louis Kornhauser, *An Introduction to the Economic Analysis of Contract Remedies*, 57 U. COLO. L. REV. 683 (1986); Ian R. Macneil, *Efficient Breach of Contract: Circles in the Sky*, 68 VA. L. REV. 947 (1982); Eric A. Posner, *Economic Analysis of Contract Law After Three Decades: Success or Failure?*, 112 YALE L.J. 829 (2003); RICHARD POSNER, ECONOMIC ANALYSIS OF LAW Ch. 4 (6th ed. 2002); Sam Rea, *Efficiency Implications of Penalties and Liquidated Damages*, 13 J. LEGAL STUD. 147 (1984).

[55] *See supra* § 1.04[D][2] Contract Theory and Scholarship.

[56] Daniel Markovits & Alan Schwartz, *The Myth of Efficient Breach: New Defenses of the Expectation Interest*, 97 VA. L. REV. 1939, 1948 (2011).

[57] *See* Robert L. Birmingham, *Breach of Contract, Damage Measures, and Economic Efficiency*, 24 RUTGERS L. REV. 273 (1970); Charles J. Goetz & Robert E. Scott, *Liquidated Damages, Penalties, and the Just Compensation Principle: Some Notes on an Enforcement Model and a Theory of Efficient Breach*, 77 COLUM. L. REV. 553 (1977).

[58] Arrowhead School Dist. No. 75, Park County v. Klyap, 79 P.3d 250, 256 (Mont. 2003). *See also* Grupo Televisa, S.A. v. Telemundo Commc'ns Group, Inc., 485 F.3d 1233, 1245–46 (11th Cir. 2007); Allapattah Serv., Inc. v. Exxon Corp., 61 F. Supp. 2d 1326 (S.D. Fla. 1999).

[59] RICHARD A. POSNER, ECONOMIC ANALYSIS OF LAW 133 (6th ed. 2002).

are thought to be desirable."[60]

Other economic theorists have criticized this basic approach as failing to take into account the real-world transaction costs associated with entering into the breached contract and in dealing with the aftermath of the breach.[61] They have argued in favor of awarding specific performance. They contend that compelling delivery of the goods would shift the gains associated with the contract to the injured party without allocating the goods in an inefficient manner.[62] Thus, in the above example, if specific performance were available, the seller would be compelled to renegotiate the contract with the buyer, in order to take advantage of the opportunity to resell the goods to the alternative buyer, who valued them more highly. Or the buyer might compel performance, and resell them herself to the alternative buyer. Still others question the entire premise of the economic theorists and dispute whether allocative efficiency is a proper goal of contract law.[63] Not surprisingly, although courts have sometimes paid lip service to a rudimentary theory of efficient breach,[64] few have embraced economic analysis of contract remedies on a wholesale basis.[65]

§ 12.03 CAUSATION

A person who breaks her promise is not responsible for all of the bad luck suffered by the other party. The breaching party is responsible only for the harm caused by her breach.[66] In contract, however, causation does not occupy the central role it holds in the law of torts.

In contracts, causation is seemingly relegated to a somewhat secondary role, with the foreseeability doctrine of *Hadley v. Baxendale*[67] taking precedence. Thus, many remote damages are not recoverable even if they were proximately caused by the breach. If the damages were not foreseeable to the breaching party at the time the contract was made, they are not recoverable. Therefore, with respect to unforeseeable harm, the question of causation never becomes important.

Despite the appearance that causation is unimportant, a breaching party is never responsible for harm that its breach did not cause. The injured party must prove

---

[60] Giampapa v. Am. Family Mut. Ins. Co., 64 P.3d 230, 252 (Colo. 2003). *See also* McKie v. Huntley, 620 N.W.2d 599 (S.D. 2000).

[61] *E.g.*, See Melvin A. Eisenberg, *Actual and Virtual Specific Performance, the Theory of Efficient Breach, and the Indifference Principle in Contract Law*, 93 CAL. L. REV. 975, 997–1016 (2005); Daniel A. Farber, *Reassessing the Economic Efficiency of Compensatory Damages for Breach of Contract*, 66 VA. L. REV. 1443, 1448 (1980); Daniel Friedman, *The Efficient Breach Fallacy*, 18 J. LEGAL STUD. 1 (1989).

[62] *E.g.*, Alan Schwartz, *The Case for Specific Performance*, 89 YALE L.J. 271 (1979).

[63] *E.g.*, Patricia H. Marschall, *Willfulness: A Crucial Factor in Choosing Remedies for Breach*, 24 ARIZ. L. REV. 733, 761 (1982).

[64] *E.g.*, Reiver v. Murdoch & Walsh, P.A., 625 F. Supp. 998, 1015 (D. Del. 1985).

[65] *E.g.*, Patton v. Mid-Continent Sys., 841 F.2d 742 (7th Cir. 1988).

[66] Florafax Int'l, Inc. v. GTE Mkt. Res., Inc., 933 P.2d 282, 292 (Okla. 1997).

[67] 156 Eng. Rep. 145 (Ct. Exch. 1854). *See generally infra* § 12.04 Limits on Damages: Foreseeability.

that the defendant's breach caused its injury.[68] Where the plaintiff's harm was caused by a multiplicity of factors, courts require that the injured party prove that the defendant's breach was at least a "substantial factor" in causing the harm.[69]

For example, in *Redgrave v. Boston Symphony Orchestra*,[70] the defendant cancelled an appearance by the plaintiff, actor Vanessa Redgrave, "in the wake of protests over Redgrave's participation [in one of the symphony's productions] because of her support of the Palestine Liberation Organization."[71] The court affirmed the trial judge's judgment for the defendant, notwithstanding the jury's verdict in Redgrave's favor, in part because the plaintiff was unable to prove that her career had suffered as result of the symphony's actions rather than because of her political views.[72] In the court's view the jury's conclusion that the actor's career had declined because of the defendant's breach was based on " 'conjecture and speculation' [rather] than on a sufficient factual basis."[73]

Causation also plays a supporting role in the law of contract damages under the doctrines of mitigation and certainty. The mitigation doctrine prevents an injured party from recovering damages for harm that the injured party itself could have prevented, through its own reasonable conduct, after the breach. The mitigation principle is analogous to the "contributory negligence" principle in torts. The injured party's so-called "duty" to mitigate prevents the injured party from recovering for the "avoidable consequences" of a breach.[74]

The rule that damages must be "reasonably certain"[75] also brings questions of causation into the picture.[76] The certainty rule is most frequently applicable in connection with lost profits. The injured party must prove that its lost profits were caused by the breach, and not simply the result of a poor business plan or other circumstances unrelated to the broken contract.[77] Likewise, the extent of the loss must be provable with reasonable certainty, and not be a matter of speculation.[78] Without such a rule, the breaching party might end up liable, not just for the consequences of its breach, but also for the failed hopes and dreams of its disappointed contracting partner.

In transactions for the sale of goods, both the U.C.C. and the CISG require the injured party to prove that its damages were caused by the breach. U.C.C. § 2-715(2) refers to the injured party's ability to recover for "consequential damages

---

[68] RESTATEMENT (SECOND) OF CONTRACTS § 347 cmt. e (1981).

[69] Parke State Bank v. Akers, 659 N.E.2d 1031 (Ind. 1995); Indep. Mech. Contractors, Inc. v. Gordon T. Burke & Sons, 635 A.2d 487 (N.H. 1993).

[70] 855 F.2d 888 (1st Cir. 1988).

[71] *Id.* at 890.

[72] *Id.* at 898–99.

[73] *Id.* at 899.

[74] *See infra* § 12.05 Limits on Damages: Mitigation.

[75] RESTATEMENT (SECOND) OF CONTRACTS § 352 (1981).

[76] *See infra* § 12.06 Limits on Damages: Reasonable Certainty.

[77] Chicago Coliseum Club v. Dempsey, 1932 Ill. App. LEXIS 805, *8–*11 (Mar. 1932); Kenford Co. v. Erie County, 493 N.E.2d 234, 235 (N.Y. 1986).

[78] Fera v. Vill. Plaza, Inc., 242 N.W.2d 372, 375–76 (Mich. 1976).

resulting from the seller's breach," and CISG Article 74 permits the injured party to recover only for losses "suffered . . . as a consequence of the breach."[79]

In international transactions other than those governed by the CISG, the UNIDROIT Principles of International Commercial Contracts permit the injured party to recover only for "harm sustained as a result of the non-performance."[80] Similarly, the Principles of European Contract Law permit the aggrieved party to recover only for "loss caused by the other party's non-performance."[81]

§ 12.04   LIMITS ON DAMAGES: FORESEEABILITY[82]

The most important limit on damages for breach of contract is the requirement that the harm occurring as a result of the breach must have been foreseeable by the party in breach, at the time the contract was made.[83] Thus, breaching parties are not responsible for consequences that they should not have foreseen.

The foreseeability doctrine originated in the nineteenth-century case, *Hadley v. Baxendale*,[84] a decision that was once characterized as "the fixed star in the jurisprudential firmament."[85] In *Hadley*, the owner of a flour mill was unable to recover the profits it lost while inoperable due to a railroad's delay in delivering a critical part.

In an opinion that is still widely cited today,[86] the *Hadley v. Baxendale* court established two rules for the recovery of damages for breach of contract. First, the injured party may recover all damages that occurred in the ordinary course of things, as a result of the breach. These are known as general or "direct" damages. Damages for the direct harm that a party suffers as the result of a breach are recoverable without proof that the harm was foreseeable by the breaching party at the time the contract was made. For example, a buyer of goods does not need to

---

[79]   CISG Art. 74 (1980).

[80]   PICC Art. 7.4.2(1) (2004).

[81]   PECL Art. 9.501(1) (2002).

[82]   Ian Ayres & Robert Gertner, *Filling Gaps in Incomplete Contracts: An Economic Theory of Default Rules*, 99 YALE L.J. 87, 101–18 (1989); Thomas A. Diamond & Howard Foss, *Consequential Damages for Commercial Loss: An Alternative to* Hadley v. Baxendale, 63 FORDHAM L. REV. 665 (1994); Melvin A. Eisenberg, *The Principle of* Hadley v. Baxendale, 80 CAL. L. REV. 563 (1992); Richard Epstein, *Beyond Foreseeability: Consequential Damages in the Law of Contract*, 18 J. LEGAL STUD. 105 (1989); Larry T. Garvin, *Disproportionality and the Law of Consequential Damages: Default Theory and Cognitive Reality*, 59 OHIO ST. L.J. 339 (1998); Jason S. Johnston, *Strategic Bargaining and the Economic Theory of Contract Default Rules*, 100 YALE L.J. 615 (1990).

[83]   RESTATEMENT (SECOND) OF CONTRACTS § 351(1) (1981).

[84]   156 Eng. Rep. 145 (Ct. Exch. 1854). *See* George S. Geis, *Empirically Assessing* Hadley v. Baxendale, 32 FLA. ST. U. L. REV. 897 (2005).

[85]   GRANT GILMORE, THE DEATH OF CONTRACT 83 (1974). *But see* Barry E. Adler, *The Questionable Ascent of* Hadley v. Baxendale, 51 STAN. L. REV. 1547 (1999).

[86]   *E.g.*, Sunnyland Farms, Inc. v. Cent. N. M. Elec. Co-op., Inc., 301 P.3d 387 (N.M. 2013); CR-RSC Tower I, LLC v. RSC Tower I, LLC, 56 A.3d 170, 195 (Md. 2012); Tractebel Energy Mktg, Inc. v. AEP Power Mktg, Inc., 487 F.3d 89, 109 (2d Cir. 2007) ("Every lawyer will recall from his or her first-year contracts class the paradigmatic example of Hadley v. Baxendale"); Totaro, Duffy, Cannova & Co. v. Lane, Middleton & Co., 921 A.2d 1100 (N.J. 2007).

prove that the seller should have known that its failure to deliver them would deprive the buyer of their value. Consequently, U.C.C. § 2-713 permits an aggrieved buyer to recover the difference between the market value of the goods and their contract price, without regard to whether the seller had "reason to know" of this loss.

Recovery for indirect harm (or "special damages") is a different matter. The injured party can recover for harm that did not occur in the ordinary course of things, but instead as a result of the particular requirements or circumstances of the injured party, only if these special circumstances were foreseeable by the breaching party *at the time the contract was made*.[87] In *Hadley* itself, this prevented the mill owner from recovering damages for the profits it lost due to the inoperability of the mill while the transportation of the critical component was delayed.

Some indirect losses are more foreseeable than others. This was recognized many years afterwards in *Victoria Laundry (Windsor), Ltd. v. Newman Industries, Ltd.*,[88] where the seller of a boiler was late delivering it to a commercial laundry. The court permitted the laundry to recover for lost revenues that would routinely have been earned through use of the new boiler, because the seller knew that the boiler was to be used in the buyer's business. As a result, the seller could not claim to be surprised that its late delivery caused the buyer to lose some general revenues. The court explained:

> [n]o commercial concern commonly purchases for the purposes of its business a very large and expensive structure like this a boiler 19 feet high and costing over 2000 *l.* — with any other motive, and no supplier, let alone an engineering company, which has promised delivery of such an article by a particular date, with knowledge that it was to be put into use immediately on delivery, can reasonably contend that it could not foresee that loss of business . . . would be liable to result to the purchaser from a long delay.[89]

Despite this, the court prevented the laundry from recovering for indirect losses from certain particularly lucrative dying contracts that were beyond the scope of what the laundry would have earned using the boiler in the ordinary course and of which the seller had been unaware.[90] With respect to these particularly lucrative contracts the court said "in order that the plaintiffs should recover specifically and as such, the profits expected on these contracts, the defendants would have had to know, at the time their agreement with the plaintiffs, of the prospect and terms of such contract."[91]

Thus, although there must be proof of the foreseeability of all special damages, some special damages, like the routine profits that the buyer expected to generate in *Victoria Laundry*, are easily proven to have been foreseeable by the breaching

---

[87] Totaro, Duffy, Cannova & Co. v. Lane, Middleton & Co., 921 A.2d 1100, 1104–05 (N.J. 2007).

[88] 1 All E.R. 997 (K.B. 1949).

[89] Victoria Laundry (Windsor), Ltd. v. Newman Industries, Ltd., 1 All E.R. 997, 1003 (K.B. 1949).

[90] Victoria Laundry (Windsor), Ltd. v. Newman Industries, Ltd., 1 All E.R. 997, 1005 (K.B. 1949).

[91] *Id.*

party. The foreseeability of other special damages, resulting from harm beyond what would frequently be suffered, might be more difficult to prove in the absence of evidence that the risk of the harm was directly communicated to the breaching party at the time the contract was created.

[A] Test of Foreseeability

The test of foreseeability originally articulated in *Hadley v. Baxendale* was narrow. Baron Alderson would have permitted recovery only if the harm could "reasonably be supposed to have been in the contemplation of the parties . . . as the probable result" of a breach, or "if the consequential circumstances under which the contract was made *were communicated* by the plaintiffs to the defendant, and thus known to both parties."[92] As later cases demonstrate, the injured party's harm may be foreseeable by the breaching party as a result of general business or other information acquired through means other than direct communication from the injured party.

There was a period when courts applied the narrow "tacit agreement" test of foreseeability, discussed below.[93] However, modern courts apply an objective "reason to foresee" test based on facts that the breaching party knew or should have known. Article 2 of the U.C.C. utilizes a similar "reason to know" standard.[94]

[1] Reason to Foresee

Modern cases permit the injured party to recover special or consequential damages only when the breaching party had "reason to foresee" the harm "as a probable result of the breach."[95] Thus, it is an objective test based primarily on what the breaching party should have realized from the facts that it knew or should have known, and not a subjective test of what the breaching party actually considered.[96]

This test has been expressed in several ways in addition to the "reason to foresee" standard of the Restatement (Second) of Contracts.[97] One English court, in attempting to set the outer limits of foreseeability, indicated that the injured party's harm was foreseeable if it was "not unlikely" to occur.[98] In *Hector Martinez & Co. v. Southern Pacific. Transportation. Co.*, the court indicated that the injured party's harm was foreseeable if "it was not so remote as to make it

---

[92] Hadley v. Baxendale, 156 Eng. Rep. 145 (Ex. 1854).

[93] *Infra* § 12.04[A][3] Tacit Agreement Test.

[94] *Infra* § 12.04[B] Foreseeability in Sales of Goods. *E.g.*, Cricket Alley Corp. v. Data Terminal Sys., Inc., 732 P.2d 719 (Kan. 1987).

[95] RESTATEMENT (SECOND) OF CONTRACTS § 351 (1981).

[96] *E.g.*, Prutch v. Ford Motor Co., 618 P.2d 657 (Colo. 1980) (defendant liable "for consequences that may not have been actually foreseen but which were foreseeable").

[97] Thomas A. Diamond & Howard Foss, *Consequential Damages for Commercial Loss: An Alternative to* Hadley v. Baxendale, 63 FORDHAM L. REV. 665, 669–70 (1994).

[98] Koufos v. C Czarnikow, Ltd. [The Heron II], [1969] A.C. 350 (H.L. 1967).

unforeseeable to a reasonable man at the time of contracting."[99]

The test is applied as of the time the parties entered into the contract, not at some later time during performance of the contract or at the time of the breach. Thus, information first acquired by the breaching party after performance has begun, or at any time after formation, should not affect an analysis of whether the injured party's harm was foreseeable. On the other hand, the limits imposed by the parol evidence rule do not apply to prevent the injured party from introducing evidence of the parties' precontract negotiations to prove that the injured party's harm was foreseeable at the time the contract was made.[100]

Further, it is the nature of the harm that must be foreseeable, not the extent of the harm. If it is foreseeable to a breaching seller that the buyer will lose profits as a result of the seller's breach, the full extent of the loss need not be foreseeable. As one court explained: "[i]t is not necessary that the specific injury or amount of harm be foreseen, but only that a reasonable person in [the seller's] position would foresee that in the usual course of events, damages would follow from its breach."[101] Thus, if ordinary market forces result in a loss of unforeseeable magnitude, the seller is liable. On the other hand, if the loss occurs as a result of unusual and unforeseeable market conditions that made it possible for the buyer to obtain an unanticipated profit from the goods, recovery for the extraordinary profit is not available.

Moreover, it is necessary only that the breaching party has reason to foresee the nature of the harm that is likely to result from a breach, rather than the circumstances that precipitated the breach.[102] Thus, if a seller has reason to know that delay in delivering goods to the buyer will cause the buyer to lose profits, and the goods are delayed because the ship carrying them to the buyer is overtaken by pirates, the fact that the theft of the goods itself was unforeseeable does not matter.[103]

[2]   Foreseeability of Lost Profits

Many cases involving foreseeability, including *Hadley v. Baxendale* itself, involve claims for lost profits from collateral contracts that the injured party would have made if the main contract had been performed. These cases nearly always involve the claim of a recipient of goods, land, or services, who claims that its profits were diminished as a result of the provider's breach.[104] Thus, the lost revenue that would ordinarily have been generated from the use of goods that were to have been delivered was foreseeable to a manufacturer who knew that the goods involved in the transaction were to be used in the buyer's business

---

[99] Hector Martinez & Co. v. Southern Pacific. Transportation. Co., 606 F.2d 106, 110 (5th Cir. 1979), *cert. denied*, 446 U.S. 982 (1980).

[100] RESTATEMENT (SECOND) OF CONTRACTS § 351 cmt. b (1981).

[101] Barnard v. Compugraphic Corp., 667 P.2d 117, 120 (Wash. Ct. App. 1983). *See* Roy Ryden Anderson, *Incidental and Consequential Damages*, 7 J.L. & COM. 327, 364 (1987).

[102] E. ALLAN FARNSWORTH, CONTRACTS 795 (4th ed. 2004).

[103] Spang Indus. v. Aetna Cas. & Sur. Co., 512 F.2d 365 (2d Cir. 1975).

[104] *E.g.*, Florafax Int'l, Inc. v. GTE Mkt. Res., Inc., 933 P.2d 282 (Okla. 1997).

operations.[105] But, absent notice of the circumstances that made timely delivery critical to a particular contract, with unusually high profits, the extra profits were not recoverable.[106] Likewise, buyers who are known to purchase the goods either for resale or to use as components in goods they are manufacturing can recover the profits ordinarily generated from such a resale as foreseeable consequential damages.

However, in most cases, substitute goods are available to the buyer. The lost profits on any contract for resale are not foreseeable unless the seller had reason to know of the circumstances that would make it difficult to obtain a substitute.[107] The same is true in connection with the breach of a contract to make a loan. Lost profits are foreseeable only if the unavailability of the loan from another lender was foreseeable at the time the loan agreement was made.[108]

In evaluating the foreseeability of lost profits, it is useful to distinguish between several types of lost profits.[109] A buyer's loss of the direct profits that it would have earned from sales of undelivered or defective goods is readily foreseeable by a seller who has reason to know that the buyer is purchasing the goods for the purpose of resale.[110]

In some cases, a buyer may also lose sales of other items — what has sometimes been called "secondary profits" — because of reduced business caused by buyers reduced purchase of the seller's goods. This might easily occur, for example, in connection with a gasoline station, that might sell fewer car washes because of the seller's failure to deliver promised fuel.[111] However, these lost secondary profits are likely to occur only in connection with the buyer's main product line. A gas station will likely lose sales of milk if it has no gas; it is far less likely to lose sales of gas or beer if its milk supplier fails to make a delivery. Thus, lost secondary profits are more likely to be foreseeable in connection with a seller's failure to deliver the products that are the primary source of the buyer's sales than in connection with undelivered or defective secondary products.

An aggrieved buyer might also lose goodwill, or future business, if its reputation declines, particularly as a result of its receipt and resale of defective goods. For example, prominent American toy manufacturers seem likely to lose business generally, as a result of consumer fears about toys with lead paint, in the wake of the delivery of some products with lead paint. The buyer is likely to lose profits from sales of perfectly safe toys because customers are wary about the quality of the buyer's goods, long after defective and dangerous items have been removed

---

[105] *E.g.*, Lewis v. Mobil Oil Corp., 438 F.2d 500 (8th Cir. 1971).

[106] *See also* Victoria Laundry (Windsor) Ltd. v. Newman Indus., Ltd., [1949] 1 All E.R. 997 (K.B.).

[107] Czarnikow-Rionda Co. v. Fed. Sugar Ref. Co., 173 N.E. 913 (N.Y. 1930).

[108] RESTATEMENT (SECOND) OF CONTRACTS § 351 cmt. e (1981). *E.g.*, Stacy v. Merch. Bank, 482 A.2d 61 (Vt. 1984).

[109] *See* Roy Ryden Anderson, *Incidental and Consequential Damages*, 7 J.L. & COM. 327 (1987).

[110] AM/PM Franchise Ass'n v. Atl. Richfield Co., 584 A.2d 915, 921–23 (Pa. 1990); Kunststoffwerk Alfred Huber v. R. J. Dick, Inc., 621 F.2d 560, 563 (3rd Cir. 1980). *See* RESTATEMENT (SECOND) OF CONTRACTS § 351 cmt. b (1981).

[111] *See* AM/PM Franchise Ass'n v. Atl. Richfield Co., 584 A.2d 915, 923–25 (Pa. 1990).

from the shelves. While it may be difficult to calculate the amount of this harm with reasonable certainty, the harm is usually foreseeable by suppliers who know that the buyer is selling branded goods.

Buyers are also likely to lose profits from use of a seller's goods or services in their own business operations. Lost profits are foreseeable if the seller had reason to know that its failure to deliver conforming goods in a timely manner would disrupt the buyer's business.[112] However, recovery of lost profits is frequently more difficult in these cases than in cases involving a purchase of goods for resale.[113] This is not due to the unforeseeability of the loss, but rather because of greater difficulties in proving that the seller's breach was the cause of the buyer's loss, rather than other factors affecting the buyer's operations or from the buyer's failure to mitigate.

[3]   Tacit Agreement Test

At one time foreseeability was governed by the more restrictive "tacit agreement" test. Frequently attributed to Justice Holmes' 100-year-old decision in *Globe Refining Co. v. Landa Cotton Oil Co.*,[114] the tacit agreement test imposed liability only if it "may fairly be presumed he would have assented to if they had been presented to his mind."[115] What Holmes meant by this test was that it was not enough for the plaintiff to show that the defendant knew or should have known of the harm that the plaintiff would suffer as a result of a specific breach. The plaintiff had to go beyond this and prove that the defendant at least tacitly agreed to assume responsibility for the loss.[116] Today, the tacit agreement test is discredited.[117] It was explicitly rejected by the Uniform Commercial Code.[118] It applies in only two states, and even then only in disputes not governed by the U.C.C.[119]

Despite the rejection of the tacit agreement test, some cases reflect a reluctance to conclude that damages are foreseeable if they are grossly disproportionate to the consideration received by the breaching party in connection with the contract.[120] However, despite its appeal, the disproportionality between the value of the contract to the breaching party and the amount of damages caused by its

---

[112] Lewis v. Mobil Oil Corp., 438 F.2d 500, 510–11 (8th Cir. 1971).

[113] RESTATEMENT (SECOND) OF CONTRACTS § 351 cmt. b (1981); Roy Ryden Anderson, *Incidental and Consequential Damages*, 7 J.L. & COM. 327, 405 (1987).

[114] 190 U.S. 540 (1903).

[115] *Id.* at 543.

[116] *E.g.*, Reynolds Health Care Services, Inc. v. HMNH, Inc., 217 S.W.3d 797 (Ark. 2005); Morrow v. First Nat'l Bank of Hot Springs, 550 S.W.2d 429 (Ark. 1977).

[117] RESTATEMENT (SECOND) OF CONTRACTS § 351 cmt. 1 (1981). *E.g.*, R.I. Lampus Co. v. Neville Cement Prods. Corp., 378 A.2d 288, 291–93 (Pa. 1977).

[118] U.C.C. § 2-715 cmt. 2 (2012).

[119] Kenford Co. v. County of Erie, 537 N.E.2d 176 (N.Y. 1989); Morrow v. First Nat'l Bank of Hot Springs, 550 S.W.2d 429 (Ark. 1977).

[120] RESTATEMENT (SECOND) OF CONTRACTS § 351 cmt. f (1981). *E.g.*, Kerr S.S. Co. v. Radio Corp. of Am., 157 N.E. 140 (N.Y. 1927) (Cardozo, J.).

breach has not yet made it into the mainstream of foreseeability analysis.[121]

[B] Foreseeability in Sales of Goods[122]

Article 2 of the Uniform Commercial Code adopted the foreseeability standard of *Hadley v. Baxendale* in its provision regarding the recovery of a buyer's consequential damages. U.C.C. § 2-715(2) provides:

Consequential damages resulting from the seller's breach include:

(a) any loss resulting from general or particular requirements and needs of which the seller at the time of contracting had reason to know and which could not reasonably be prevented by cover or otherwise.

(b) injury to person or property proximately resulting from any breach of warranty.[123]

Thus, the U.C.C. speaks of foreseeability in terms of "reason to know."[124] Despite the disparity in language, the U.C.C.'s "reason to know" standard is generally regarded as the same objective test of foreseeability established by *Hadley v. Baxendale*.[125] Thus, in *Wullschleger & Co., Inc. v. Jenny Fashions, Inc.*, a fabric merchant had reason to know that defects in fabric delivered to a garment manufacturer would result in lost profits due to the buyer's inability to use the goods for "circle skirts," even though the goods were suitable for other types of skirts that the buyer also manufactured.[126]

[C] Foreseeability in International Transactions[127]

The United Nations Convention on the International Sale of Goods (CISG) takes a slightly different approach to foreseeability. CISG Article 74 makes the breaching party liable for damages which it "forsesaw or ought to have foreseen as a *possible* consequence of the breach."[128] The foreseeability test in *Hadley* and

---

[121] *E.g.*, M.M. Silta, Inc. v. Cleveland Cliffs, Inc., 572 F.3d 532, 536 (8th Cir. 2009). *See generally* Larry T. Garvin, *Disproportionality and the Law of Consequential Damages: Default Theory and Cognitive Reality*, 59 Ohio St. L.J. 339 (1998).

[122] Peter Linzer, Hadley v. Baxendale *and the Seamless Web of Law*, 11 Tex. Wesleyan L. Rev. 225 (2005).

[123] U.C.C. § 2-715(2) (2012). *See also* U.C.C. § 2A-520(2) (2012) (lease of goods).

[124] Proposed revisions to Article 2 use similar language in establishing a standard for a seller's recovery of consequential damages. It provides: "Consequential damages resulting from the buyer's breach include any loss resulting from the general or particular requirements and needs of which the buyer at the time of contracting had reason to know and which could not reasonably be prevented by resale or otherwise." Revised U.C.C. § 2-710(2) (2003).

[125] *E.g.*, Cricket Alley Corp. v. Data Terminal Sys., Inc., 732 P.2d 719 (Kan. 1987); Hendricks & Assoc., Inc. v. Daewoo Corp., 923 F.2d 209, 213–14 (1st Cir. 1991).

[126] Wullschleger & Co., Inc. v. Jenny Fashions, Inc., 618 F. Supp. 373 (S.D.N.Y. 1985).

[127] John Y. Gotanda, *Recovering Lost Profits in International Disputes*, 36 Geo. J. Int'l L. 61, 68–70 (2004).

[128] CISG Art. 74 (1980) (emphasis added).

U.C.C. § 2-715(2) impose liability for the *probable* consequences of a breach.[129] Some have suggested that the CISG expands the range of damages beyond what has traditionally been available.[130] Despite this, most cases have read this language as the equivalent of the rule in *Hadley*.[131]

UNIDROIT's Principles of International Commercial Contracts and Commission on European Contract Law's Principles of European Contract Law take a more traditional approach based on the probability of harm rather than the mere possibility. Article 7.4.4 of the UNIDROIT Principles imposes liability "only for the harm which [the non-performing party] foresaw or could reasonable have foreseen at the time of the [formation] of the contract as being likely to result from its non-performance."[132] The European Contract Law Principles use nearly identical language, but permit recovery of damages that were not foreseeable if "the non-performance was intentional or grossly negligent."[133]

[D]   Limit on Recovery for Emotional Distress[134]

Damages for emotional distress are not usually available for breach of contract, even if they are foreseeable.[135] This is true even though the probability of emotional distress, as a result of many types of breach, is entirely foreseeable within the *Hadley* standard.[136] Anyone who has suffered through the turmoil of home renovation will understand the distress that might be associated with the prospect of a contractor walking off the job, or worse yet, doing shoddy work.[137]

---

[129] RESTATEMENT (SECOND) OF CONTRACTS § 351(1) (1981). *See* The Heron II, 1967 All E.R. 686 (House of Lords 1967) ("not unlikely" to result).

[130] Arthur G. Murphey, *Consequential Damages in Contracts for the International Sale of Goods and the Legacy of* Hadley, 23 GEO. WASH. J. INT'L L. & ECON. 415, 474 (1989).

[131] Delchi Carrier Spa v. Rotorex, Corp., 71 F.3d 1024, 1030 (2d Cir. 1995). *See* E. Allan Farnsworth, *Damages and Specific Relief*, 27 AM. J. COMP. L. 247, 253 (1979); John Y. Gotanda, *Awarding Damages Under the United Nations Convention on the International Sale of Goods: A Matter of Interpretation*, 37 GEO. J. INT'L L. 95 (2005); John Edward Murray Jr., *Ten Years of the United Nations Sales Convention: The Neglect of CISG: A Workable Solution*, 17 J. L. & COM. 365 (1998).

[132] PICC Art. 7.4.4 (2004).

[133] PECL Art. 9.503 (2002).

[134] Ralph C. Anzivino, *The Fraud in the Inducement Exception to the Economic Loss Doctrine*, 90 MARQ. L. REV. 921 (2007), Peter A. Bell, *The Bell Tolls: Toward Full Tort Recovery for Psychic Injury*, 36 U. FLA. L. REV. 333 (1984); Ronnie Cohen & Shannon O'Byrne, *Cry Me a River: Recovery of Mental Distress Damages in a Breach of Contract Action — A North American Perspective*, 42 AM. BUS. L.J. 97 (2005); Richard N. Pearson, *Liability for Negligently Inflicted Psychic Harm: A Response to Professor Bell*, 36 U. FLA. L. REV. 413 (1984); Douglas J. Whaley, *Paying for the Agony, The Recovery of Emotional Distress Damages in Contract Actions*, 26 SUFFOLK L. REV. 935 (1992).

[135] *See generally* Charlotte K. Goldberg, *Emotional Distress Damages and Breach of Contract: A New Approach*, 20 U.C. DAVIS L. REV. 57 (1986).

[136] *See* Gaglidari v. Denny's Rests., 815 P.2d 1362, 1373 (Wash. 1991) (wrongful discharge from employment). *See also* Levin v. Halston Ltd., 91 Misc. 2d 601 (N.Y. Civ. Ct. 1977) (damages for emotional distress denied for breach of contract to deliver custom-made wedding dress).

[137] *E.g.*, Erlich v. Menezes, 981 P.2d 978 (Cal. 1999) (negligent construction resulting to no personal injury); B & M Homes, Inc. v. Hogan, 376 So. 2d 667 (Ala. 1979); Hancock v. Northcutt, 808 P.2d 251 (Alaska 1991); Young v. Abalene Pest Control Serv., 444 A.2d 514, 516 (N.H. 1982) (termite inspector's failure to discover colony of carpenter ants); Ronnie Cohen & Shannon O'Byrne, *Cry Me a River:*

Likewise, anyone who has experienced a round of corporate downsizing will be well aware of the emotional turmoil experienced in the wake of the loss of a job.[138] Nevertheless, recovery is not usually available in these types of cases for emotional distress.[139]

In denying recovery for emotional distress, many courts cite the risk of fabricated or exaggerated claims of emotional distress,[140] and thus the potential for overcompensation. Although concern is also expressed for the absence of a market standard that can be used to measure the value of emotional distress,[141] this has not been an impediment in cases involving torts with foreseeable emotional distress.[142]

Despite these concerns, damages for emotional distress have been awarded in contracts where the likelihood of such harm is particularly acute.[143] Disputes with funeral directors over the handling of a deceased loved one's remains predominate as examples of the types of cases where breach would be likely to result in emotional distress.[144] Damages for emotional distress have also been awarded in cases involving physical harm, such as the type that might result from breach of a contract to perform cosmetic surgery,[145] to perform a cesarean birth,[146] or otherwise in connection with medical services.[147] They have likewise been available for failure to properly convey a message concerning the health of a family member.[148] And, consistent with the availability of punitive damages in such cases, damages for emotional distress are sometimes awarded in cases involving bad faith, particularly where the plaintiff's emotional distress was foreseeable by the breaching party.[149]

Recovery of Mental Distress Damages in a Breach of Contract Action — A North American Perspective, 42 Am. Bus. L.J. 97 (2005); Michael G. Walsh, Annotation, *Recovery for Mental Anguish or Emotional Distress, Absent Independent Physical Injury, Consequent upon Breach of Contract or Warranty in Connection with Construction of Home or Other Building*, 7 A.L.R.4th 1178 (1981).

[138] *E.g.*, Valentine v. Gen'l Am. Credit, Inc., 362 N.W.2d 628 (Mich. 1984) (no recovery for emotional distress following wrongful discharge from employment).

[139] *E.g.*, Gaglidari v. Denny's Rests., 815 P.2d 1362, 1373 (Wash. 1991). *But see* B & M Homes v. Hogan, 376 So. 2d 667 (Ala. 1979) (emotional distress damages awarded for breach of construction contract for new home).

[140] *E.g.*, Garvis v. Employers Mut. Cas. Co., 497 N.W.2d 254, 257 n.3 (Minn. 1993).

[141] Valentine v. Gen'l Am. Credit, Inc., 362 N.W.2d 628, 631 (Mich. 1984).

[142] Peter A. Bell, *The Bell Tolls: Toward Full Tort Recovery for Psychic Injury*, 36 U. Fla. L. Rev. 333 (1984); Richard N. Perason, *Liability for Negligently Inflicted Psychic Harm: A Response to Professor Bell*, 36 U. Fla. L. Rev. 413 (1984); Douglas J. Whaley, *Paying for the Agony, the Recovery of Emotional Distress Damages in Contract Actions*, 26 Suffolk L. Rev. 935 (1992).

[143] Restatement (Second) of Contracts § 353 (1981). *See* Deitsch v. Music, Co. 453 N.E.2d 1302 (Ohio Mun. Ct. 1983). *See* Joseph P. Tomain, *Contract Compensation in Nonmarket Transactions*, 46 U. Pitt. L. Rev. 867 (1985).

[144] *E.g.*, Lamm v. Shingleton, 55 S.E.2d 810 (N.C. 1949); Flores v. Baca, 871 P.2d 962 (N.M. 1994).

[145] *E.g.*, Sullivan v. O'Connor, 296 N.E.2d 183 (Mass. 1973).

[146] Stewart v. Rudner, 84 N.W.2d 816 (Mich. 1957).

[147] *E.g.*, Oswald v. LeGrand, 453 N.W.2d 634 (Iowa 1990).

[148] *E.g.*, Avery v. Arnold Home, Inc., 169 N.W.2d 135 (Mich. Ct. App. 1969).

[149] Giampapa v. Am. Family Mut. Ins. Co., 64 P.3d 230 (Colo. 2003).

Another class of cases in which damages for mental distress have been awarded are those in which the plaintiff suffered some sort of public humiliation as a result of the breach.[150] Although it has long been said that damages for emotional distress will be awarded in cases involving public humiliation or eviction of hotel guests, passengers on public transportation, or ticket holders to entertainment events, few cases involving these situations have recently arisen.[151] In part, however, this is due more to the rise of civil rights actions and other tort claims for which these damages are more readily available.

In cases where the principal purpose of the contract is to protect a person's privacy interests, awarding damages for emotional distress may be the only possible measure of damages.[152] However, some courts have refused to award damages in these cases in the absence of an independent tort, such as the negligent or intentional infliction of emotional distress, or invasion of the plaintiff's right of privacy.[153] Because of this, in cases where damages for emotional distress are awarded, it is sometimes difficult to discern whether liability for emotional harm is available due to breach of contract, or as a result of the tort.[154]

§ 12.05   LIMITS ON DAMAGES: MITIGATION[155]

An injured party may not recover damages for losses or other harm that it could have reasonably avoided, even though avoiding these losses might require the injured party to take some additional affirmative steps,[156] and incur additional expenses. This is frequently called the "duty to mitigate." However, referring to this limit on the recovery of damages as a "duty" is misleading. Breach of a duty gives the other party a right to recover damages from the party who violated its duty. Failure to mitigate damages confers no such right. Instead, it merely prevents the injured party from recovering damages that would not have occurred if the injured party had taken steps to mitigate its harm.

In this respect, the duty to mitigate is little more than an application of the principle that the injured party can recover damages only for those harms caused by the breach. Harm that the injured party could have avoided, through its own reasonable actions, was not caused by the breach, but by the injured party's failure to take steps to avoid the loss.

---

[150] *E.g.*, Trimble v. City & County of Denver, 697 P.2d 716 (Colo. 1985).

[151] *See* Gillespie v. Brooklyn H.R. Co., 70 N.E. 857 (N.Y. 1904) (pubic transportation); Frewen v. Page, 131 N.E. 475 (Mass. 1921) (hotel guest); Aaron v. Ward, 96 N.E. 736 (N.Y. 1911) (entertainment).

[152] Lamm v. Shingleton, 55 S.E.2d 810, 813 (N.C. 1949).

[153] Deli v. Univ. of Minn., 578 N.W.2d 779 (Minn. Ct. App. 1998).

[154] Deli v. Univ. of Minn., 578 N.W.2d 779 (Minn. Ct. App. 1998).

[155] R.F. Chase, Annotation, *Landlord's Duty on Tenant's Failure to Occupy, or Abandonment of Premises, to Mitigate Damages by Accepting or Procuring Another Tenant*, 21 A.L.R.3d 534 (1968); Robert Hillman, *Keeping the Deal Together After Material Breach — Common Law Mitigation Rules, the UCC, and the Restatement (Second) of Contracts*, 47 U. Colo. L. Rev. 553 (1976); Charles J. Goetz & Robert E. Scott, *The Mitigation Principle: Toward a General Theory of Contractual Obligation*, 69 Va. L. Rev. 967 (1983); Clive M. Schmitthoff, *The Duty to Mitigate*, 1961 J. Bus. L. 361; Christopher T. Wonnell, *The Abstract Character of Contract Law*, 22 Conn. L. Rev. 437, 489 (1990).

[156] Restatement (Second) of Contracts § 350 (1981).

This universally accepted rule[157] encourages the aggrieved party to minimize waste and is thus consistent with principles of economic efficiency.[158] The duty to mitigate is incorporated into many of the U.C.C.'s specific provisions. The most obvious of these is U.C.C. § 2-715, which permits an injured buyer to recover for consequential damages only if the harm "could not reasonably be prevented by cover or otherwise."[159]

The United Nations Convention on the International Sale of Goods (CISG) also incorporates the mitigation principle into its damages formulas. However, it also contains a general rule requiring an injured party to "take such measures as are reasonable in the circumstances to mitigate the loss, including loss of profit, resulting from the breach."[160] A party that fails to mitigate may have its damages reduced by the amount of the loss that it could have avoided by taking these steps.[161]

The Principles of International Commercial Contracts (PICC) and the Principles of European Contract Law (PECL) both recognize that the injured party's damages are subject to mitigation. PICC provides that the injured party's "full compensation for harm sustained as a result of non-performance" should take "into account any gain to the aggrieved party resulting from its avoidance of cost or harm."[162] They also specify that the breaching party is not liable for harm that "could have been reduced by the [aggrieved] party's taking reasonable steps."[163] PECL's language is nearly identical.[164]

The mitigation principle has both affirmative and passive aspects.[165] The passive or "negative" aspect requires the injured party to avoid conduct that will aggravate its own harm. An obvious example is provided by the well-known decision in *Rockingham County v. Luten Bridge Co.*[166] The aggrieved construction company was prevented from recovering expenses it had incurred in continuing performance after it received notification of the other party's repudiation of the contract. The court said that the injured party "[had a] duty to do nothing to increase the damages flowing [from the breach]."[167] Thus, it was limited to recovering the expenses it had incurred up to the time of the repudiation, together with the profit

---

[157] *E.g.*, Air et Chaleur, S.A. v. Janeway, 757 F.2d 489, 494 (2d Cir. 1985).

[158] *See generally* Charles J. Goetz & Robert E. Scott, *The Mitigation Principle: Toward a General Theory of Contractual Obligation*, 69 Va. L. Rev. 967 (1983).

[159] *E.g.*, U.C.C. § 2-715(2). *See infra* § 12.08[A] Contracts for the Sale of Goods — Breach by the Seller.

[160] CISG Art. 77 (1980).

[161] CISG Art. 77 (1980).

[162] PICC Art. 7.4.2 (2004).

[163] PICC Art. 7.4.8 (2004).

[164] PECL Art. 9.505 (2002).

[165] Charles J. Goetz & Robert E. Scott, *The Mitigation Principle: Toward a General Theory of Contractual Obligation*, 69 Va. L. Rev. 967, 973 n.18 (1983).

[166] 35 F.2d 301 (4th Cir. 1929). *See* Barak Richman, Jordi Weinstock & Jason Mehta, *A Bridge, a Tax Revolt, and the Struggle to Industrialize: The Story and Legacy of* Rockingham County v. Luten Bridge Co., 84 N.C. L. Rev. 1841 (2006).

[167] Rockingham County, 35 F.2d at 307.

it would have made had there been no breach. This puts the injured builder in the position it would have been in, if the contract, had been performed, with an adjustment for the expenses it could have avoided after learning of the other party's repudiation.[168]

U.C.C. § 2-704(2) might appear to be an exception to this rule, but it is not. It applies when the buyer repudiates while the seller is still in the process of manufacturing goods for delivery to the buyer. It permits the seller to choose between completing manufacture of unfinished goods or selling the items for scrap or salvage. The seller has not failed to mitigate, if it makes this choice "in the exercise of reasonable commercial judgment for the purposes of avoiding loss."[169] Therefore, so long as the breaching seller's decision to complete the manufacture of the unfinished goods has been part of a commercially reasonable effort to minimize eventual loss (such as through resale), the seller is able to recover for its additional expenses even though, with the subsequent advantages of hindsight, it might have been better to stop the manufacturing process and sell the partially manufactured goods for their scrap value.[170] A similar approach is taken in construction contracts, where an aggrieved owner makes an unsuccessful attempt to repair defective work rather than starting over.[171]

Mitigation frequently also requires the injured party to avoid harm by making proactive efforts to avoid a loss. For example, a buyer of goods that fails to make an effort to purchase substitute goods and thus "cover" under U.C.C. § 2-712[172] is unable to obtain consequential damages for any harm that could have been prevented.[173] Likewise, a wrongfully discharged employee must take reasonable steps to find another similar job.[174] On the other hand, it is still the subject of debate whether an aggrieved landlord is required to make a reasonable effort to re-let premises left vacant by a defaulting tenant.[175]

The affirmative aspect of mitigation permits the aggrieved party to recover for expenses it incurs in the effort to mitigate. Thus, an injured buyer of goods can recover for expenses it incurs in attempting to locate substitute goods, even if those

---

[168] *See also* Clark v. Marsiglia, 1845 N.Y. LEXIS 68 (July 1845).

[169] U.C.C. § 2-704(2) (2012). *E.g.*, Young v. Frank's Nursery & Crafts, Inc., 569 N.E.2d 1034 (Ohio 1991). *But see* Madsen v. Murrey & Sons, Co. 743 P.2d 1212, 1215 (Utah 1987) (inappropriately second-guessing the seller's judgment not to complete manufacture of 100 pool tables built to the buyer's specifications to include pinball-machine like electronic components).

[170] *See* U.C.C. § 2-704 cmt. 2 (2012).

[171] *See* Marchesseault v. Jackson, 611 A.2d 95, 98 (Me. 1992).

[172] U.C.C. § 2-712 (2012). *See infra* § 12.08[A] Contracts for the Sale of Goods — Breach by the Seller.

[173] U.C.C. § 2-715(2)(a) (2012).

[174] Lee v. Scotia Prince Cruises Ltd., 828 A.2d 210 (Me. 2003).

[175] *Compare* Sommer v. Kridel, 378 A.2d 767 (N.J. 1977) *and* Austin Hill Country Realty, Inc. v. Palisades Plaza, Inc., 948 S.W.2d 293 (Tex. 1997) (recognizing duty to mitigate) *with* Holy Properties Limited, L.P. v. Kenneth Cole Productions, Inc., 661 N.E.2d 694 (N.Y. 1995) (adhering to traditional rule imposing no duty in commercial leases). *See generally* Christopher Vaeth, Annotation, *Landlord's Duty, on Tenant's Failure to Occupy, or Abandonment of Premises, to Mitigate Damages by Accepting or Procuring Another Tenant*, 75 A.L.R.5th 1 (2000).

efforts fail. Likewise, a wrongfully discharged employee can recover for his or her expenses in seeking substitute employment.[176]

[A]   Mitigation in Employment Contracts[177]

The mitigation principle applies with equal force in employment contracts. To recover for her lost salary, a wrongfully discharged employee must make reasonable efforts to pursue alternative employment of a substantially similar character.[178] Sums spent in seeking alternative employment are recoverable.[179] Amounts that the employee could have earned in a job of similar character are deducted from the damages if the substitute work is refused. On the other hand, the employee does not have to accept employment of a different or inferior character.

This point is illustrated by the well-known decision in *Parker v. Twentieth Century-Fox Film Corp.*[180] The plaintiff, better known as the actor Shirley MacLaine, was discharged from her contract to star in a movie musical *Bloomer Girl.* She later turned down the lead in the Western drama *Big Country, Big Man* and sued to recover the salary she had been promised for appearing in *Bloomer Girl.* The court determined that playing the female lead in a dramatic Western was inferior as a matter of law to her lead role in the musical review for which she had been originally engaged. MacLaine, the court ruled, was entitled to the $750,000 salary she had been promised.[181] As those familiar with her career know, several years later MacLaine played the "different and inferior" lead female role in the Western drama *Two Mules for Sister Sara,* co-starring Clint Eastwood.

While the differences between the two types of roles would not seem to warrant the California court's conclusion, other differences, such as MacLaine's discretionary rights over both the script and the director in *Bloomer Girl,* as well as the strong likelihood that the movie was loosely based on the life of a Civil War-era women's rights activist,[182] may justify the result.[183]

In cases involving other discharged employees courts have ruled that alternative employment as a teacher is not an adequate substitute for a job as a

---

[176] *See* RESTATEMENT (SECOND) OF CONTRACTS §§ 350(2) & 347 cmt. c (1981).

[177] Mary Joe Frug, *Re-Reading Contracts: A Feminist Analysis of a Contracts Casebook,* 34 AM. U. L. REV. 1065, 1114–25 (1985); Victor P. Goldberg, *Bloomer Girl Revisited or How to Frame an Unmade Picture,* 1998 WIS. L REV. 1051; Richard J. Gonzalez, *Satisfying the Duty to Mitigate in Employment Cases: A Survey and Guide,* 69 MISS. L.J. 749 (1999).

[178] Lee v. Scotia Prince Cruises Ltd., 828 A.2d 210 (Me. 2003).

[179] *E.g.,* Mr. Eddie, Inc. v. Ginsberg, 430 S.W.2d 5 (Tex. Civ. App. 1968). *See* RESTATEMENT (SECOND) OF CONTRACTS § 347 cmt. c & illus. 3 (1981).

[180] 474 P.2d 689 (Cal. 1970).

[181] These were 1966 dollars. Adjusted for inflation, her salary would have been approximately $5 1/4 million in 2012.

[182] *See* Mary Joe Frug, *Re-Reading Contracts: A Feminist Analysis of a Contracts Casebook,* 34 AM. U.L. REV. 1065, 1114–25 (1985).

[183] *See also* Victor P. Goldberg, *Bloomer Girl Revisited or How to Frame an Unmade Picture,* 1998 WIS. L. REV. 1051 (regarding the "pay-or-play" clause in the *Bloomer Girl* contract).

school principal, even though the salary is the same.[184] Likewise, working as a kitchen manager in a restaurant, which involves physical labor, is different and inferior to work as a general restaurant manager, which involves different duties.[185]

Wrongfully discharged employees are also required to make a reasonably diligent effort to secure another job. For example, a college teacher who delayed her effort to find a new teaching position, and who even then did little more than check the local classified ads, without seeking the assistance of an employment agency or submitting her résumé to available trade journals, was precluded from receiving her lost wages, even though the employer had not proven the availability of alternative employment.[186] A discharged employee who makes no reasonable effort to secure alternative employment cannot recover his or her lost wages, even if he or she removed herself from the labor market for personal reasons.[187] However, an employee is not required to look for or accept even substantially similar employment in a geographically distant location.[188]

Amounts the employee could have earned are deducted only if the alternative available employment was incompatible with performance under the contract in question. In *Soules v. Independent School District No. 518*,[189] a teacher who was wrongfully discharged from her part-time position, and subsequently turned down a full-time teaching job for less pay, lost only one-half of the salary from the alternative job, because only half of it was incompatible with her half-time position with the school district that fired her.[190]

Amounts an employee actually earned are deducted from his or her damages, provided that the person could not have reasonably held both jobs simultaneously.[191] Such earnings are deducted even if the alternative employment requires duties different from or inferior to those in the contract with the defendant.[192] After all, dollars actually received are perfect substitutes from those promised by the breaching employer. Thus, an employee who takes a different or inferior job must deduct her earnings from the damages she can recover in her "wrongful discharge" suit against her former employer.[193]

Government benefits, such as unemployment compensation and social security

---

[184] *E.g.*, Williams v. Albemarle City Bd. of Educ., 508 F.2d 1242 (4th Cir. 1974).

[185] Feges v. Perkins Rests., Inc., 483 N.W.2d 701, 709 (Minn. 1992).

[186] Sellers v. Delgado Coll., 902 F.2d 1189 (5th Cir. 1990).

[187] Miller v. Marsh, 766 F.2d 490 (11th Cir. 1985). *But see* Thorkildson v. Ins. Co. of N. Am., Co., 631 F. Supp. 372 (D. Minn. 1986).

[188] Hadra v. Herman Blum Consulting Eng'rs, 632 F.2d 1242, 1246 (5th Cir. 1980); Hubbard Broad., Inc. v. Loescher, 291 N.W.2d 216 (Minn. 1980); Punkar v. King Plastic Corp., 290 So. 2d 505 (Fla. Dist. Ct. App. 1974); William H. Danne Jr., Annotation, *Nature of Alternative Employment Which Employee Must Accept to Minimize Damages for Wrongful Discharge*, 44 A.L.R.3d 629 (1972).

[189] 258 N.W.2d 103 (Minn. 1977).

[190] *See also* Marshall v. Mardels, Inc., 1978 U.S. Dist. LEXIS 16565 (E.D.N.Y. July 17, 1978).

[191] *E.g.*, Marshall Sch. Dist. v. Hill, 939 S.W.2d 319 (Ark. Ct. App. 1997).

[192] S. Keswick, Inc. v. Whetherholt, 293 So. 2d 109 (Fla. Dist. Ct. App. 1974).

[193] *Id.*; Marshall Sch. Dist. v. Hill, 939 S.W.2d 319 (Ark. Ct. App. 1997).

benefits, have received disparate treatment.[194] Some courts have reduced the injured employee's damages by the amount of any unemployment compensation benefits the employee received.[195] However, Social Security disability[196] and retirement benefits[197] have been treated differently because, unlike unemployment benefits, the employer's contribution to Social Security is not affected by the number of claims made by its employees.[198] The distinction has also been based on the greater likelihood of a windfall to the employee if amounts received as unemployment compensation are not deducted from the recovery.[199]

Employers also have a duty to mitigate their damages, by taking reasonable steps to seek and employ someone to provide the services that were to have been performed by the breaching employee. The fact that the substitute had better qualifications than the breaching employee does not impair the employer's ability to recover for the additional salary that had to be paid to the substitute, where the employer has taken reasonable steps to hire someone with qualifications that are comparable to those of the employee who left.[200]

[B]   Lost Volume Transactions

Substitutes mitigate the harm caused by a breach. Sometimes, however, what appears to be a "substitute" is not. Instead, it is an additional transaction that the innocent party would have entered into even if the other party had not breached. The harm to the injured party is the loss of profit that results from the "lost volume" that the injured party experiences as a result of the breach.[201] A second transaction does not replace this lost volume.

A common example of this occurs in the construction industry. The profit made by a contractor on a second construction project, entered into after one customer's breach, is usually not a substitute for the profit lost on the broken deal. In most situations, the contractor could have performed both jobs and earned a profit on each of them simply by hiring a second crew.[202] Unless they are incapable of expanding, most service providers are lost-volume suppliers. If one of the customers repudiates, the breach reduces the volume of the provider's business, thus reducing its profits. Therefore, the supplier's damages should be based on the lost profit on the broken deal, without any deduction for revenues earned on

---

[194] See generally John G. Fleming, The Collateral Source Rule and Contract Damages, 71 Calif. L. Rev. 56 (1983).

[195] Corl v. Huron Castings, Inc., 544 N.W.2d 278 (Mich. 1996). Accord Masterson v. Boliden-Allis, Inc., 865 P.2d 1031 (Kan. Ct. App. 1993).

[196] Seibel v. Liberty Homes, Inc., 752 P.2d 291 (Or. 1988).

[197] Filter v. City of Vernonia, 770 P.2d 83 (Or. 1989); State ex rel. Stacy v. Batavia Local Sch. Dist. Bd. of Educ., 829 N.E.2d 298 (Ohio 2005).

[198] Filter v. City of Vernonia, 770 P.2d 83 (Or. 1989).

[199] Id.; Dehnart v. Waukesha Brewing Co., 124 N.W.2d 664 (Wis. 1962).

[200] E.g., Handicapped Children's Educ. Bd. v. Lukaszewski, 332 N.W.2d 774 (Wis. 1983).

[201] See Robert J. Harris, A Radical Restatement of the Law of Seller's Damages: Sales Act and Commercial Code Results Compared, 18 Stan. L. Rev. 66 (1985).

[202] See, e.g., Kearsarge Computer v. Acme Staple Co., 366 A.2d 467 (N.H. 1976).

additional transactions that the supplier entered into.

Individual employees, on the other hand, are usually not lost-volume suppliers of their own personal services. Unlike a contractor, employees are not usually in a position to provide an unlimited supply of personal services. There are, after all, only 24 hours in a day. Consequently, an employee's new job is usually treated as substitute employment, unless the new job is one that the discharged employee could have taken regardless of the employer's breach.[203]

Using the actor Shirley MacLaine's situation in *Parker v. Twentieth Century Fox* as an example, it should be clear that Screen Actors Guild scale earnings she might receive as a guest on a late-night talk show would not detract from her recovery from the movie studio for its breach of her contract to star in *Bloomer Girl*. But, any payment she received for appearing in a Broadway play during the time that *Bloomer Girl* was scheduled to be in production would cut into the damages she could recover. She can appear on *The Daily Show* while simultaneously shooting a movie, but she probably cannot appear in a Broadway play while filming scenes in a movie in Los Angeles.[204] Likewise, a part-time job during a different shift, or on weekends, during what would have been the employee's own time, would not be considered substitute employment.[205]

Sellers of goods are usually more like a construction firm than an individual employee. Those who are in the business of selling goods usually have access to additional inventory, and could have sold additional items and earned additional profits, even if a particular customer backs out of a deal. Thus, if the seller "resells" an item that the original buyer refused to take, this second sale is not really a substitute for deal with the breaching buyer. Instead, it is an additional transaction that the seller could have made despite the first buyer's breach.

Because of their lost-volume status, sellers of readily available goods are usually entitled to recover the profit they would have made if the buyer had gone through with the deal. Thus, U.C.C. § 2-708(2) permits an aggrieved seller to recover the profit it would have made on a sale of goods in any case where "resale" of the goods is not really a substitute transaction.[206]

Those who are not in the business of selling goods of the kind, on the other hand, do not usually qualify as lost-volume sellers. These sellers generally lack a readily available source of similar goods. Thus, while a bicycle shop might be a lost-volume seller, a recreational bicyclist, selling one of his used bikes, is not. For

---

[203] *See* Jetz Serv. Co. v. Salina Props., 865 P.2d 1051, 1055 (Kan. Ct. App. 1993).

[204] Obviously, if the movie were being filmed in New York, it might be possible for the actress to work on both jobs simultaneously. Your author once spent a semester commuting between Champaign, Illinois, and San Jose, California, while teaching at both the University of Illinois College of Law and the University of Santa Clara School of Law. Fortunately, the classes did not meet simultaneously. He has frequently taught during the same semester, at both his home school, Capital University Law School, and the Moritz College of Law at Ohio State, only a few miles away.

[205] *E.g.*, Gianetti v. Norwalk Hosp., 779 A.2d 847 (Conn. Ct. App. 2001) (discharged surgeon capable of entering into additional "moonlighting" employment).

[206] U.C.C. § 2-708(2) (2012). *See infra* § 12.08[B] Contracts for the Sale of goods — Breach by the Buyer.

these sellers, any subsequent sale of the goods involved in a contract for sale is a true substitute. Accordingly, the price obtained for the goods is a substitute for the price not paid by the breaching buyer.

In the case of both lost-volume suppliers of goods and lost-volume providers of services, the injured party must usually prove (1) it had the capacity to enter into an additional transaction,[207] (2) that it would have entered into an additional transaction if the breach had not occurred, and (3) that this additional transaction would have resulted in a profit.[208] If the supplier would not have entered into an additional sale if the customer had fully performed, the supplier has not suffered lost volume as a result of the breach. If the supplier would have entered into another transaction but would not have made a profit on it, the customer's breach has similarly, not caused the supplier any harm.

[C]　Expenses Incurred in Mitigation

An injured party is also entitled to recover the reasonable expenses it incurs in the efforts it takes to mitigate.[209] These might include, for example, reasonable expenses incurred in an effort to seek alternative employment,[210] interest charges,[211] or relocation expenses.[212]

In this regard, U.C.C. § 2-704(2) permits an aggrieved seller to make a commercially reasonable choice between completing manufacture of the goods or selling for scrap any partially completed items when the seller learns of the buyer's repudiation, while the manufacturing process is underway, but before it is completed.[213]

The injured party does not, however, have free reign to incur any expenses under the guise of mitigation. It may not recover unreasonable or excessive costs,[214] nor may it recover capital expenditures designed to permanently improve its property.[215] Yet, considerable leeway is given to an injured party who incurs expenses in a good-faith effort to minimize its own harm, even where such expenditures turn out, with the benefit of reflective hindsight, to have been wasted.[216] Further, in evaluating the reasonableness of the injured party's expenses, the court will consider whether the injured party's judgment in incurring

---

[207] *E.g.*, Eneractive Group, Inc. v. Carefree of Colo., 1993 U.S. App. LEXIS 13499 (7th Cir. June 3, 1993); Ragen Corp. v. Kearney & Trecker Corp., 912 F.2d 619 (3d Cir. 1990).

[208] *See* Rodriguez v. Learjet, Inc., 946 P.2d 1010, 1015 (Kan. Ct. App. 1997); *infra* § 12.08[B] Contracts for the Sale of Goods — Breach by the Buyer.

[209] RESTATEMENT (SECOND) OF CONTRACTS § 347 cmt. c (1981).

[210] Mr. Eddie, Inc. v. Ginsberg, 430 S.W.2d 5 (Tex. Ct. App. 1968).

[211] Goodpasture, Inc. v. M/V Pollux, 688 F.2d 1003 (5th Cir. 1982).

[212] O'Toole v. Northrop Grumman Corp., 305 F.3d 1222 (10th Cir. 2002).

[213] *See infra* § 12.08[B] Contracts for the Sale of Goods — Breach by the Buyer.

[214] Lasalle Talman Bank, F.S.B. v. United States, 1999 U.S. Claims LEXIS 239 (Sept. 30, 1999).

[215] Kallman v. Tandy Corp., 2000 U.S. Dist. LEXIS 3068 (N.D. Ill. Mar. 9, 2000).

[216] Santiago v. Sea-Land Serv., 366 F. Supp. 1309 (D.P.R. 1973); Automated Donut Sys., Inc. v. Consol. Rail Corp., 424 N.E.2d 265 (Mass. Ct. App. 1981).

the expense, was exercised in a time of crisis brought on by the other party's breach.[217]

[D]   Mitigation in International Transactions[218]

Article 77 of the CISG requires injured buyers in international sale-of-goods transactions to "take such measures as are reasonable in the circumstances to mitigate the loss."[219] If the injured party fails to mitigate, the breaching party may "claim a reduction in the damages in the amount by which the loss should have been mitigated."[220]

The mitigation principle is reflected elsewhere in the CISG, such as in Article 75, which permits an injured buyer to recover the difference between the contract price and the price of substitute goods, only if the buyer purchased the replacements "in a reasonable manner and within a reasonable time after avoidance."[221]

Both the UNIDROIT's Principles of International Commercial Contracts (PICC) and its Principles of European Contract Law (PECL) impose the same general rule. PICC Article 7.4.7 specifies that when the aggrieved party's harm is "due in part to an act or omission of the aggrieved party . . . the amount of damages shall be reduced to the extent that [the aggrieved party's acts or omissions] have contributed to the harm."[222] Article 7.4.8(1) buttresses this rule by providing that "[t]he non-performing party is not liable for harm suffered by the aggrieved party to the extent that the harm could have been reduced by the latter party's taking reasonable steps."[223] At the same time, it permits the aggrieved party to "recover any expenses reasonably incurred in attempting to reduce the harm."[224] PECL contains similar provisions.[225]

§ 12.06   LIMITS ON DAMAGES: REASONABLE CERTAINTY[226]

Damages are recoverable only if they are "reasonably certain."[227] Damages are reasonably certain only if both the fact and the amount of the loss can be adequately

---

[217] *E.g.*, W.D.I.A. Corp. v. McGraw-Hill, Inc., 34 F. Supp. 2d 612 (S.D. Ohio 1998).

[218] Helmut Koziol, *Reduction in Damages According to Article 77 CISG*, 25 J.L. & COM. 385 (2005); Chang-Sop Shin, *Declaration of Price Reduction Under the CISG Article 50 Price Reduction Remedy*, 25 J.L. & COM. 349 (2005); Eyal Zamir, *The Missing Interest: Restoration of the Contractual Equivalence*, 93 VA. L. REV. 59, 76 (2007).

[219] CISG Art. 77 (1980).

[220] CISG Art. 77 (1980).

[221] CISG Art. 75 (1980).

[222] PICC Art. 7.4.7 (2004).

[223] PICC Art. 7.4.8(a) (2004).

[224] PICC Art. 7.4.8(b) (2004).

[225] *See* PECL Arts. 9.504 & 9.505 (2002).

[226] RESTATEMENT (SECOND) OF CONTRACTS § 352 (1981). *See generally* Sha-Shana N.L. Crichton, *Distinguishing Between Direct and Consequential Damages Under New York Law in Breach of*

proven.[228] This limit is particularly important in connection with claims of a buyer or recipient's consequential damages consisting of "lost profits." Even if lost profits are foreseeable, it may be difficult to prove that profits were lost because of the defendant's breach. This is particularly true where the overall success of the aggrieved party's business was either in question to begin with, or subject to a wide variety of speculative contingencies. And, even when it is clear that the plaintiff lost some profit because of the defendant's breach, proving the extent of its losses may be difficult, if not impossible.

In the well-known case of *Chicago Coliseum Club v. Dempsey*,[229] lost profits were not recoverable from the world heavyweight boxing champ, Jack Dempsey, for breach of his agreement to participate in a title fight. The profits to be earned from the spectacle depended on a wide variety of factors, including the ability of the promoters, the weather on the night of the fight, the reputation of the fighters, the extent of publicity, and other imponderables.[230]

Modern cases continue to apply the rule. In *ESPN Inc. v. Office of the Commissioner of Baseball*,[231] the court prevented Major League Baseball from introducing evidence about its belief that it had lost profits where it was unable to point to any specific lost opportunity, sponsor, or decline in ticket sales in the wake of ESPN's breach of an agreement to televise several September baseball games in order to broadcast several NFL football games being played at the same time. The court explained that the plaintiff had done nothing other than make "vague assertions that it was 'hurt.' "[232] And, in *Florafax International., Inc. v. GTE Market Resources, Inc.*, the court said:

> In order for damages to be recoverable for breach of contract they must be clearly ascertainable, in both their nature and origin, and it must be made to appear that they are the natural and proximate consequence of the breach and not speculative or contingent. . . . It is not necessary, however, for the recovery of lost profits shown to have been caused by a breach of contract, that the profits be established with absolute certainty and barring any possibility of failure, but it s only required that it be established with reasonable certainty that profits would have been made had the contract not been breached.[233]

Services Contract Cases, 45 How. L.J. 597 (2002); Michael T. Gibson, *Reliance Damages in the Law of Sales Under Article 2 of the Uniform Commercial Code*, 29 Ariz. St. L.J. 909 (1997); Matthew Milikowsky, Note, *A Not Intractable Problem: Reasonable Certainty*, Tractebel, *and the Problem of Damages for Anticipatory Breach of a Long-Term Contract in a Thin Market*, 108 Colum. L. Rev. 452 (2008).

[227] Restatement (Second) of Contracts § 352 (1981).

[228] *See generally* Roger I. Abrams, Donald Welsch & Bruce Jonas, *Stillborn Enterprises: Calculating Expectation Damages Using Forensic Economics*, 57 Ohio St. L.J. 809 (1996); Bernadette J. Bollas, Note, *The New Business Rule and the Denial of Lost Profits*, 48 Ohio St. L.J. 855 (1987).

[229] 1932 Ill. App. LEXIS 805 (Mar. 1932).

[230] Chicago Coliseum Club v. Dempsey, 1932 Ill. App. LEXIS 805, *8–*11 (Mar. 1932).

[231] 76 F. Supp. 2d 416 (S.D.N.Y. 1999).

[232] *Id.* at 421.

[233] Florafax International., Inc. v. GTE Market Resources, Inc., 933 P.2d 282, 296 (Okla. 1997). *See*

Where the plaintiff has a sufficient track record on which to base its claims regarding future profitability, damages are recoverable, even though circumstances might arise that would make the plaintiff's venture completely unprofitable. In *Rombola v. Cosindas*,[234] for example, the future profitability of a race horse was proven with reasonable certainty where the horse had a track record of having won 40% of its past races the last two years in a row and winning similar amounts in both years.[235] Further, the success of others might provide a sufficient basis for recovery. For example, in *Fera v. Village Plaza*,[236] expert testimony from those familiar with the plaintiff's industry and market supplied a sufficiently reliable basis to permit the question of lost profits to be considered by the jury. And, in *Contemporary Mission, Inc. v. Famous Music, Corp.*, the court ruled that the plaintiff should have been permitted to introduce evidence about the eventual success of music recordings that had reached the same level as the plaintiff's, before the defendant had unjustifiably withdrawn it from the market.[237]

Some courts distinguish between the fact and amount of loss and provide considerably greater leeway in permitting the plaintiff to prove the extent of its lost profits, once it has crossed the threshold of reasonably certainty with respect to the fact of lost profits.[238] However, other courts adhere to the traditional rule and subject both the fact and amount of the plaintiff's lost profits to the reasonable certainty rule.[239] Still other courts seem to simply ignore the difference.[240]

[A]   Lost Profits of New Businesses

Concern about other factors affecting the profitability of an enterprise is particularly acute when a new business is involved. Not only do many new businesses fail, but they lack a track record on which the amount of lost profits can be based. This led to an early rule flatly prohibiting a new business from recovering for lost profits.[241] Most courts now take a more liberal approach, rejecting the per se legal rule against recovery of lost profits, but still requiring that the fact and amount of such profits be proven with reasonable certainty.[242] However, some courts still impose a more rigorous standard of proof for lost profits claimed by new businesses than for those claimed by more established

---

also Ashland Mgmt. Inc. v. Janien, 624 N.E.2d 1007 (N.Y. 1993).

[234] 220 N.E.2d 919 (Mass. 1966).

[235] Rombola v. Cosindas, 220 N.E.2d 919 (Mass. 1966).

[236] 242 N.W.2d 372 (Mich. 1976).

[237] Contemporary Mission, Inc. v. Famous Music, Corp., 557 F.2d 918 (2d Cir. 1977).

[238] *E.g.*, Mid-America Tablewares, Inc. v. Mogi Trading Co., 100 F.3d 1353, 1367 (7th Cir. 1996); Florafax Int'l, Inc. v. GTE Market Res., Inc., 933 P.2d 282, 296 (Okla. 1997); Locke v. United States, 283 F.2d 521 (Ct. Cl. 1960); ROBERT L. DUNN, RECOVERY OF DAMAGES FOR LOST PROFITS § 1.6 (5th ed. 1998).

[239] *E.g.*, City of Gahanna v. Eastgate Props., Inc., 521 N.E.2d 814, 817–18 (Ohio 1988).

[240] Andrew F. Halaby, *No Summary Judgment for You! One State's (Unjustified) Treatment of Contract Claims for Lost Profits*, 7 U. MIAMI BUS. L. REV. 57, 61–62 (1998).

[241] *E.g.*, Evergreen Amusement Corp. v. Milstead, 112 A.2d 901 (Md. 1955).

[242] *E.g.*, Fera v. Vill. Plaza, Inc., 242 N.W.2d 372 (1976); Drews Co. v. Ledwith-Wolfe Assoc., 371 S.E.2d 532 (S.C. 1988).

concerns.[243] And a few states still adhere to the new business rule, preventing a new business from even attempting to prove its lost profits.[244]

Another approach to lost profits, but one that is used only rarely, is to award the injured party the value of its lost opportunity for a profit. In cases involving contests, where one of the contestants is wrongfully deprived of the opportunity to compete, recovery has been completely denied because the contestant could not prove, with the requisite degree of certainty, that he or she would have won.[245] Despite this, there is little question that the opportunity to participate in the competition has some value, regardless of the uncertainty of taking home the ultimate prize. If a value can be placed on the opportunity to compete, this value should be awarded as a measure of the injured party's loss.[246]

[B]   Reasonable Certainty in Sales of Goods

Article 2 of the U.C.C. is silent about the necessity of proving lost profits with reasonable certainty. The code makes no reference to the rule. However, it generally applies common law principles except when they are expressly "displaced by the particular provisions of [the code]."[247] Similarly, U.C.C. § 1-106(1) specifies that the Code's remedies "shall be liberally administered," but that "neither consequential or special . . . damages may be had except as specifically provided in [the code] or by other rule of law."[248] The Code's official comments indicate that it rejects the suggestion that damages must be "calculable with mathematical accuracy,"[249] but nothing addresses the common law requirement of proof of lost profits with reasonable certainty. Cases decided under the Code unfailingly apply the rule in contracts for the sale of goods.[250]

[C]   Reasonable Certainty in International Transactions[251]

In international sales of goods, the CISG does not specifically mention a rule requiring lost profits or other damages to be proven with reasonable certainty, but the principle is a well known feature of lex mercatoria — the "law merchant."[252]

---

[243] *E.g.*, Kenford Co. v. Erie County, 493 N.E.2d 234 (N.Y. 1986) (rejecting claim for 20 years of lost profits from management contract for contemplated domed stadium in Buffalo).

[244] RSB Laboratory Servs., Inc. v. BSI Corp., 847 A.2d 599 (N.J. Super. Ct. 2004).

[245] *E.g.*, W. Union Tel. Co. v. Crall, 18 P. 719 (Kan. 1888) (disqualification from horse race).

[246] Chaplain v. HIcks [1911] 2 K.B. 897 (Ct. App.); Van Gulik v. Res. Devel. Council, 695 P.2d 1071 (Alaska 1985); Air Tech. Corp. v. Gen. Elec. Co., 199 N.E.2d 538 (Mass. 1964); Wachtel v. Nat'l Alfalfa Journal Co., 176 N.W. 801 (Iowa 1921).

[247] U.C.C. § 1-103 (2012).

[248] U.C.C. § 1-106(1) (2012).

[249] U.C.C. § 1-106 cmt. 1 (2012).

[250] E.g., RIJ Pharm. Corp. v. Ivax Pharm., Inc., 322 F. Supp. 2d 406, (S.D.N.Y. 2004); HGI Assocs., Inc. v. Wetmore Printing Co., 427 F.3d 867 (11th Cir. 2005).

[251] John Y. Gotanda, *Recovering Lost Profits in International Disputes*, 36 GEO. J. INT'L L. 61 (2004).

[252] Sieg Eiselen, *Measuring Damages for Breach of Contract: Remarks on the Manner in Which the UNIDROIT Principles of International Commercial Contracts May Be Used to Interpret or Supple-*

This is reflected in Article 7.4.3 of UNIDROIT's Principles of International Commercial Contracts, which addresses the issue directly: "Compensation is due only for harm, including future harm, that is established with a reasonable degree of certainty."[253] Further, Article 9.501 of the Principles of European Contract Law permits recovery only for "future loss which is reasonably likely to occur."[254]

§ 12.07   LIMITS ON DAMAGES: ATTORNEYS' FEES AND LITIGATION COSTS; INTEREST

Because of the amounts involved, and the difficulty of proof, many claims for breach of contract are not worth bringing unless the injured party is able to recover the attorney fees and other litigation expenses that it incurs in the course of establishing its right to other relief. Likewise, the value of a recovery can seriously be diminished, due to the passage of time, unless interest on the injured party's damages is also recoverable.

[A]   Attorneys' Fees and Litigation Costs[255]

The general rule in the United States is that attorneys' fees and the other costs of litigation are not recoverable for breach of contract. Exceptions exist if the contract expressly makes attorneys' fees and litigation costs available,[256] or if there is an express legislative authorization[257] for their recovery.[258] Where the contract permits their recovery, the amount is limited to reasonable costs and attorneys' fees, consistent with limits on the recoverability of agreed damages generally.[259]

While an English style "loser pays" rule is frequently suggested as a means of restricting frivolous personal injury litigation,[260] this approach has not caught on in

---

ment Article 74 of the CISG, in An International Approach to the Interpretation of the United Nations Convention on Contracts for the International Sale of Goods 215 (John Felemegas ed. 2007).

[253] PICC Art. 7.4.3 (2004).

[254] PECL Art. 9.501(2) (2002).

[255] Jarno Vanto, *Attorneys' Fees as Damages in International Commercial Litigation*, 15 PACE INT'L L. REV. 203 (2003).

[256] *See generally* DAN B. DOBBS, LAW OF REMEDIES § 3.10(3) (2d ed. 1993).

[257] Many state and federal statutes now provide for the recovery of such fees. *See, e.g.*, Ohio Rev. Code. Ann. § 1345.09 (Anderson 2002) (for unconscionable, unfair, or deceptive consumer sales practices); 17 U.S.C. § 505 (2000) (for copyright violations); 42 U.S.C. § 1988 (2000) (federal civil rights actions). For a collection of statutes authorizing recovery of attorneys' fees see 3 Mary Francis Derfner & Arthur D. Wolf, Court Awarded Attorney Fees (Shirley rev. 2001).

[258] *See* Alyeska Pipeline Serv. Co. v. Wilderness Soc'y, 421 U.S. 240 (1975).

[259] *See, e.g.*, Equitable Lumber Corp. v. IPA Land Dev. Corp., 344 N.E.2d 391 (N.Y. 1976). *But compare* Northwoods Condo. Owners' Assn. v. Arnold, 770 N.E.2d 627 (Ohio Ct. App. 2002) (agreement for attorneys' fees unenforceable in adhesion contract) *with* Vermeer of S. Ohio, Inc.v. Argo Constr. Co., 700 N.E.2d 1 (Ohio Ct. App. 2001) (acknowledging exception permitting enforcement of fee-shifting agreements "that are the product of a 'free and understanding negotiation,' . . . between 'parties of equal bargaining power and similar sophistication' ").

[260] *See generally* Geoffrey Woodroffe, *Loser Pays and Conditional Fees — An English Solution?*, 37 WASHBURN L.J. 345, 349–51 (1998); Alyeska Pipeline Serv. Co. v. Wilderness Soc'y, 421 U.S. 240 (1975).

the United States, despite its prevalence in British Commonwealth jurisdictions and on the European continent.[261] Critics of fee-shifting contend that it would discourage meritorious suits and restrict access to justice.[262] Proponents claim it would stem the tide of nuisance suits.

The United Nations Convention on the International Sale of Goods (CISG) does not change this rule. The few American cases that have addressed the issue have ruled that the foreseeable losses that are recoverable under CISG Article 74 do not include attorneys' fees.[263] However, other cases permit their recovery.[264]

Neither the UNIDROIT Principles of International Commercial Contracts nor the Principles of European Contract Law, which are largely restatements of continental European "lex mercatoria" principles, make any mention of the recoverability of attorneys' fees. Despite this, costs of arbitration and attorneys' fees are generally regarded as recoverable in international commercial arbitration.[265]

[B]   Interest[266]

It has frequently been said that "justice delayed, is justice denied."[267] Although usually cited in connection with individuals' civil rights, the maxim is also true in connection with awards of money damages. If an injured party cannot recover interest on the amount of damages due, the ravages of inflation can quickly dissipate the value of an award of damages. Further, delayed payment does not place the injured party in as good a position as it would have been in, if the contract had been performed.[268]

Despite this, the availability of prejudgment interest is controversial. At one

---

[261] *See generally* Werner Pfennigstorf, *The European Experience with Attorney Fee Shifting*, 47 L. & Contemp. Probs. 37 (1984).

[262] Thomas D. Rowe Jr., *The Legal Theory of Attorney Fee Shifting: A Critical Overview*, 1982 Duke L.J. 651; John F. Vargo, *The American Rule on Attorney Fee Allocation: The Injured Person's Access to Justice*, 42 Am. U. L. Rev. 1567 (1993).

[263] Zapata Hermanos Sucesores, S.A. v. Hearthside Baking Co., 313 F.3d 385 (7th Cir. 2002) (Posner, J.); Harry M. Flechtner, *Recovering Attorneys' Fees as Damages Under the U.N. Sales Convention (CISG): The Role of Case Law in the New Int'l Practice, with Comments on* Zapata Hermanos v. Hearthside Baking, 22 Nw. J. Int'l L. & Bus. 121 (2002); Jarno Vanto, *Attorneys' Fees as Damages in International Commercial Litigation*, 15 Pace Int'l L. Rev. 203 (2003).

[264] John Felemegas, *An Interpretation of Article 74 CISG by the U.S. Court of Appeals*, 15 Pace Int'l L. Rev. 91, 99–128 (2003) (discussing authorities); Marlyse McQuillen, Note, *The Development of a Federal CISG Common Law in U.S. Courts: Patterns of Interpretation and Citation*, 61 U. Miami L. Rev. 509, 533 (2007).

[265] Emmanuel Gaillard, *Use of General Principles of International Law in International Long-Term Contracts*, 27 Int'l Bus. Law. 214, 216 (1999); John Gotonda, *Awarding Costs and Attorneys' Fees in International Commercial Arbitrations*, 21 Mich. J. Int'l L. 1 (1997).

[266] Michael S. Knoll, *A Primer on Prejudgment Interest*, 75 Tex. L. Rev. 293 (1996); Thomas J. Olmstead, *Compound Pre-Judgment Interests as an Element of Just Compensation*, 47 Ark. L. Rev. 937 (1994).

[267] The statement is frequently attributed to William Gladstone. *See* Geo. Walter Brewing Co. v. Henseleit, 132 N.W. 631, 632 (Wis. 1911).

[268] *See* Procter & Gamble Distrib. Co. v. Sherman, 2 F.2d 165, 166 (S.D.N.Y. 1924) (L. Hand, J.).

time, interest was both sinful and illegal as "usury."[269] However, modern attitudes have changed appreciably, and aggrieved parties are frequently able to recover interest on their claims to compensate for the delay between the accrual of their cause of action and a final judgment liquidating their right to damages.

Many contracts provide for interest, and courts usually enforce these agreements. Loan agreements, of course, nearly always provide for the payment of interest. The practice is so prevalent that the Internal Revenue Service (IRS) frequently regards an interest-free loan as a gift that is subject to gift tax, based on the amount of market interest that would ordinarily have been changed in an arms-length transaction between unrelated parties. The interest that a debtor promises to pay on the amount of the loan is simply part of the consideration the creditor is entitled to in exchange for the borrower's use of the money. As such, its recoverability is not remotely controversial, so long as the rate does not violate any remaining statutory usury limits that would make the rate of interest illegal.

Many other contracts, such as those for the sale of goods and the delivery of services, contain language obligating the customer to pay interest on sums not paid when due.[270] Thus, it is not uncommon to find language in even a simple construction contract requiring the customer to pay interest at the rate of 1.5% per month on amounts remaining unpaid one month after completion of the work. These agreements are generally enforceable. Further, when the injured party's breach consists of nothing more than a failure to pay a set sum of money, interest is generally recoverable "from the time for performance."[271]

There is greater disagreement over the recoverability of interest on "unliquidated" sums of the type that might be owed in tort cases or in contract disputes involving breach by a seller of goods or a provider of services.[272] In these cases the amount due is usually in considerably greater controversy, and jurisdictions disagree about the recoverability of prejudgment interest. In some states, prejudgment interest is recoverable on unliquidated sums to the same extent that it is due on liquidated amounts.[273] In other states, and sometimes by statute, prejudgment interest is available only on sums that are either fixed by contract or "readily ascertainable."[274]

Where prejudgment interest is awarded, the rate of interest must be determined. It may be provided for by contract, so long as the rate is not usurious, or sometimes by statute. When neither of these sources of an appropriate interest rate is available, courts have discretion over the rate to be applied, with a goal of providing the injured party with "just compensation" for the amount it would have received "had it been paid when performance was due."[275]

---

[269] *See* William H. Loyd, *Penalties and Forfeitures*, 29 Harv. L. Rev. 117–119 (1915).

[270] Restatement (Second) of Contracts § 354 cmt. c (1981).

[271] Restatement (Second) of Contracts § 354(1) (1981).

[272] *See* Phoenix Eng'g and Supply Inc. v. Univ'l Elec. Co., Inc., 104 F.3d 1137 (9th Cir. 1997).

[273] *E.g.*, Royal Elec. Constr. v. Ohio State Univ., 652 N.E.2d 687, 692 (Ohio 1995).

[274] *E.g.*, Cal. Civ. Code § 3287 (West 1997).

[275] Restatement (Second) of Contracts § 354(2) (1981).

Postjudgment interest is also usually available, and is far less controversial — most states have statutes that provide for it.[276] Such statutes usually permit the continued accumulation of interest at the contract rate, if the contract provides for the payment of interest.[277] Otherwise, the statutory rate applies.[278]

§ 12.08   REMEDIES IN SPECIFIC TYPES OF CONTRACTS[279]

Expectation damages can be calculated for any type of contract based on a simple generic formula, subject to the limitations discussed above, that prevent recovery for harm that was not foreseeable, that could have been mitigated, and for losses that are not reasonably certain. This basic formula is spelled out in Restatement § 347:

- lost value (direct loss)

- plus other loss (indirect loss, including incidental and consequential damages)

- minus costs or other losses that the injured party avoided as a result of not rendering its own performance.[280]

Although this broad formula works well in any situation, the law provides a variety of more narrowly tailored formulas that are customarily applied in specific situations to which they are adapted. However, these more precise formulas are nothing more than specific applications of this broader approach, and can easily be fit into the parameters of the more general rule.

[A]   Contracts for the Sale of Goods — Breach by the Seller

The buyer's remedies for breach of a contract for the domestic sale of goods are outlined in U.C.C. § 2-711. Some of them are procedural remedies that are related to the law of constructive conditions, such as the right to reject or revoke acceptance of nonconforming goods[281] and the right to cancel the contract due to the seller's breach.[282] In addition, an aggrieved buyer is permitted to recover money damages. The amount includes recovery of any down payment on the price,

---

[276] *E.g.*, N.Y. Civ. Prac. Law §§ 5003, 5004 (McKinney 2007); Ohio Rev. Code §§ 1343.01–03 (LexisNexis 2006).

[277] *E.g.*, Ohio Rev. Code § 1343.03 (LexisNexis 2006).

[278] *E.g.*, N.Y. Civ. Prac. Law § 5004 (McKinney 2007) (9%); Ohio Rev. Code Ann. § 1343.03 (federal short-term rate) (LexisNexis 2006).

[279] John Sebert, *Remedies Under Article Two of the Uniform Commercial Code: An Agenda for Review*, 130 U. Pa. L. Rev. 360 (1981).

[280] Restatement (Second) of Contracts § 347 (1981). *See* E. Allan Farnsworth, *Legal Remedies for Breach of Contract*, 70 Colum. L. Rev. 1145 (1970).

[281] *See supra* § 9.03 Rejection, Acceptance, and Revocation of Acceptance in Contracts for Goods.

[282] U.C.C. § 2-711(1) (2012).

plus the difference between the contract price and either the cost of cover or the market value of the goods.

If the seller repudiates or the buyer either rightfully rejects or rightfully revokes acceptance, the buyer may to recover restitution of any portion of the price that he or she has paid.[283] Thus, if Barb pays $3,000 to Sam as a down payment on her contract to buy his car and Sam backs out of the deal, Barb can get her $3,000 back. If Sam delivers the car, but it is defective, Barb must decide whether to accept or reject the vehicle. If she rejects it, and Sam does not cure the defect, Barb can again recover the entire $3,000 down payment, regardless of the value of the car. But, if Barb accepts the car despite the defect, she is entitled to deduct whatever damages she has suffered from the $17,000 remaining due on the original $20,000 price. The CISG provides a similar right,[284] and explicitly permits the buyer to recover interest, dating from the time the down payment was made.[285]

The injured buyer is also able to recover her direct loss with damages based on the difference between either the cost of obtaining a reasonable substitute or the market value of the goods minus the contract price. Most buyers, of course, will "cover" by purchasing substitute goods. Their direct loss is measured by the "cost of cover" minus the contract price.[286] If the contract price was $1,000 and substitute goods cost $1,200, the buyer's direct loss is the $200 difference. Of course, if the buyer procures a substitute for less than the contract price, it has suffered no damages as a result of its cover, though incidental or consequential damages will also be available, if they exist. In such a case, the innocent buyer need not account to the breaching seller for any such gain.[287] The CISG provides for a similar remedy.[288]

In obtaining cover the buyer must act in good faith, without unreasonable delay, and must obtain a reasonable substitute for the undelivered or defective goods.[289] These obligations are consistent with the injured party's duty to mitigate. Thus, the buyer may not pile damages on by procuring alternative goods at the highest available price. Nor may the buyer speculate on the market at the seller's risk, waiting in the hope that the market will decline in the anticipation of passing any rise in the cost of a substitute to the breaching seller should the buyer's hopes fail to materialize. However, the fact that in hindsight it can be seen that a better or less expensive substitute was available does not necessarily mean that the cover was improper.[290] The press of time and the avoidance of consequential damages may make purchasing better goods, at a higher price, reasonable.

---

[283] U.C.C. § 2-711(1) (2012).

[284] CISG Art. 81(2) (1980).

[285] CISG Art. 84(1) (1980).

[286] U.C.C. § 2-712 (2012).

[287] *E.g.*, Claise v. Bernardi, 413 N.E.2d 609, 612 (Ind. Ct. App. 1980).

[288] CISG Art. 74 (1980). *See* Jeffrey S. Sutton, Comment, *Measuring Damages Under the United Nations Convention on the International Sale of Goods*, 50 Ohio St. L.J. 747 (1989) (In 2003, Sutton was confirmed as Judge on the United States Court of Appeals for the Sixth Circuit).

[289] U.C.C. § 2-712(1) (2012).

[290] U.C.C. § 2-712 cmt. 2 (2012).

When the buyer has failed to try to cover,[291] or if the buyer has acquired substitute goods in violation of § 2-712's restrictions, the buyer may recover the difference between the market value of the goods and the contract price.[292] The relevant market is the one at the place where the goods were to be tendered.[293]

When the seller repudiates before the scheduled time for delivery, calculating damages based on their market value is more complicated. The difficulty arises from uncertainty over the appropriate time to measure their market value. If the market is stable, of course, this will not be a problem. But, if the market fluctuates between the time of the repudiation and the time delivery was due, both technical and theoretical questions exist.[294]

The technical difficulties arise from the language of U.C.C. § 2-713(1), which specifies that the market price must be determined as of the "time when the buyer learned of the breach."[295] This phrase works perfectly well in cases of nondelivery or where the buyer refuses to keep defective goods, but it is poorly adapted to cases involving repudiation. In cases involving repudiation, three separate interpretations have emerged.[296]

The phrase might be interpreted broadly to include the time the buyer learned of the repudiation. Many courts have interpreted it in this uncomplicated way.[297] Yet, this interpretation is at odds with two separate provisions of the U.C.C.

U.C.C. § 2-723(1) specifies that the market should be measured at the time the buyer "learned of the repudiation" in cases that come to trial before the time for performance is due.[298] Use of the phrase "learned of the repudiation" elsewhere in the U.C.C. demonstrates that the drafters knew how to deploy this concept when they intended. The absence of the phrase from § 2-713 suggests that the drafters did not mean that the time the buyer "learned of the repudiation" was the same thing as the time the buyer "learned of the breach."

Further, measuring the market at the time the buyer learns of the seller's repudiation detracts from the rights accorded to buyers by U.C.C. § 2-610. It gives an aggrieved party the specific right to "await performance by the repudiating party . . . for a commercially reasonable time."[299] Measuring the buyer's damages based on the market value of the goods at the time the buyer learned of the repudiation detracts from the buyer's right to wait for a commercially reasonable

---

[291] See Panhandle Agri-Service, Inc. v. Becker, 644 P.2d 413 (Kan. 1982).

[292] E.g. Egerer v. CSR West, LLC, 67 P.3d 1128 (Wash. Ct. App. 2003).

[293] U.C.C. § 2-713(2) (2012).

[294] See, e.g., Mo. Furnace Co. v. Cochran, 8 Fed. 463 (W.D. Pa. 1881).

[295] U.C.C. § 2-713(1) (2012).

[296] See generally Thomas H. Jackson, Anticipatory Repudiation and the Temporal Element of Contract Law: An Economic Inquiry into Contract Damages in Cases of Prospective Nonperformance, 31 Stan. L. Rev. 69 (1978).

[297] E.g., Trinidad Bean & Elevator Co. v. Frosh, 494 N.W.2d 347 (Neb. Ct. App. 1992).

[298] U.C.C. § 2-723(1) (2012).

[299] U.C.C. § 2-610 (2012).

time before resorting to a remedy.[300] This right to wait has led most courts to interpret § 2-713 to mean that the market should be measured a commercially reasonable time after the buyer learned of the seller's repudiation.[301]

A third group of courts have been influenced by the conspicuous absence of language in the Official Comments to U.C.C. § 2-713 of any expressed intent to alter the pre-Code law. These courts apply § 2-713(1) literally and measure the market at the time performance was due, without regard to when the buyer learned of the seller's intent not to perform.[302]

Under the CISG, the time for measuring the market is specified as "the difference between the price fixed by the contract and the current price at the time of avoidance." If the aggrieved buyer avoids the contract only "after taking over the goods," the market is measured as of the time the buyer takes over the goods, rather than the time of avoidance.[303]

Sometimes a buyer decides to keep goods even though they are defective. For example, the buyer of a new car is unlikely to refuse delivery just because the cigarette lighter does not work.[304] Likewise, a buyer might determine that it makes more sense to perform its own repairs on defective components delivered by one of its suppliers rather than delay its production schedule while waiting for an alternative supplier to deliver conforming goods.[305]

A buyer who accepts defective goods is required to pay for them.[306] But, this does not prevent the buyer from recovering damages for breach of warranty, due to the defect.[307] Thus, if the seller's tender was late,[308] the buyer may recover any losses it has suffered in the ordinary course of events[309] due to the delay, together with any incidental or consequential damages recoverable under U.C.C. § 2-715.[310] However, if the buyer suffers no damages as a result of the delay, the buyer is liable for the price, without any offset.[311]

If the buyer accepts the goods despite a breach of warranty,[312] damages are

---

[300] *See* Cosden Oil & Chem. Co. v. Karl O. Helm Aktiengesellschaft, 736 F.2d 1064 (5th Cir. 1984).

[301] *See, e.g.*, Oloffson v. Coomer, 296 N.E.2d 871 (Ill. App. Ct. 1973); John A. Sebert Jr., *Remedies Under Article Two of the Uniform Commercial Code: An Agenda for Review*, 130 U. Pa. L. Rev. 360, 376 (1981).

[302] *E.g.*, Roth Steel Prods. v. Sharon Steel Corp., 705 F.2d 134, 156 (6th Cir. 1983).

[303] CISG Art. 76(1) (1980).

[304] These common devices have been replaced with "power ports" used primarily to operate cell phones, GPS (global positioning system) navigation receivers, and two-way radios.

[305] *See, e.g.*, Cambridge Tech., Inc. v. Argyle Indus., Inc., 807 A.2d 125 (Md. Ct. App. 2002).

[306] U.C.C. § 2-607(1) (2012).

[307] Roy R. Anderson, *Buyer's Damages for Breach in Regard to Accepted Goods*, 57 Miss. L.J. 317 (1987).

[308] Fertico Belgium S.A. v. Phosphate Chem. Export Ass'n, Inc., 510 N.E.2d 334 (N.Y. 1987).

[309] U.C.C. § 2-714(1) (2012).

[310] U.C.C. § 2-714(3) (2012)

[311] *E.g.*, Conn. Inv. Casting Corp. v. Made-Rite Tool Co., 416 N.E.2d 966 (Mass. 1981).

[312] *See supra* Chapter 7 Warranties.

based on the difference in value between the goods as warranted and as accepted.[313] In many cases, where the defects are minor, the cost of obtaining repairs will be less expensive.[314] For example, if a $500 repair will bring defective goods up to the value they would have had if they had been as warranted, $500 is the appropriate measure of the difference in value remedy under § 2-714.[315]

Where repairs are more costly, the buyer will usually be better off rejecting the goods and obtaining a substitute rather than resorting to obtaining compensation for the cost of repairs. Where this is not possible, repair may be the only recourse to avoid other consequential harm.[316]

Buyers are also entitled to any incidental damages that they may incur.[317] U.C.C. § 2-715(1) does not define incidental damages, but nevertheless provides a list of useful illustrations of the types of damages that are recoverable under this category.[318] They include expenses incurred in inspecting the goods, in receiving the goods, or in transporting or caring for the goods following their rejection.[319] The buyer may also suffer incidental damages in the course of attempting to purchase substitute goods, such as a broker's fee or other similar expenses.[320] These illustrations demonstrate that incidental damages are usually the out-of-pocket expenses the buyer incurs in the course of attempting to mitigate its harm, either by repairing the defective goods, protecting the defective goods from harm, or in efforts to obtain substitute goods. Thus, any expenses the buyer incurs in fulfilling its obligations with respect to rejected goods will be recoverable as incidental damages.

Delchi Carrier Spa v. Rotorex Corp.,[321] decided under the CISG, supplies a good example of a buyer's incidental damages. When the air-conditioning compressors delivered by the seller were defective, the buyer rejected them and took steps to obtain substitute compressors for the portable room air-conditioning units it was in the process of manufacturing. It incurred recoverable incidental expenses in attempting to repair the defects in the seller's compressors, in expediting shipment of compressors that it had previously ordered from another supplier, and in handling and storing the defective compressors that the seller had delivered. Although the CISG does not draw a distinction between consequential

---

[313] U.C.C. § 2-714(2) (2012).

[314] *E.g.*, Davis Indus. Sales, Inc. v. Workman Constr. Co., Inc., 856 S.W.2d 355 (Mo. Ct. App. 1993); Taylor v. Alfama, 481 A.2d 1059 (Vt. 1984).

[315] *See* Manouchehri v. Heim, 941 P.2d 978, 981 (N.M. Ct. App. 1997).

[316] Cont'l Sand & Gravel, Inc. v. K & K Sand & Gravel, Inc., 755 F.2d 87 (7th Cir. 1985) (cost of repairs exceeded purchase price of goods).

[317] U.C.C. § 2-715(1) (2012). *See* Roy R. Anderson, *Incidental and Consequential Damages*, 7 J.L. & Commerce 327 (1987).

[318] Roy R. Anderson, *Incidental and Consequential Damages*, 7 J. L. & Com. 327, 333 (1987).

[319] U.C.C. § 2-714(1) (2012). *See* Petroleo Brasileiro, S. A. Petrobras v. Ameropan Oil Co., 372 F. Supp. 503, 508 (E.D.N.Y. 1974).

[320] U.C.C. § 2-714(1) (2012). *See* Nobs Chemical, U.S.A., Inc. v. Koppers Co., Inc., 616 F.2d 212, 216 (5th Cir. 1980) (collecting cases). See also John S. Herbrand, Annotation, *Buyer's Incidental and Consequential Damages from Seller's Breach Under UCC § 2-715*, 96 A.L.R.3d 299 (1979).

[321] 71 F.3d 1024 (2d Cir. 1995).

and incidental damages, these are all items that are recoverable under this category.[322]

Unlike consequential damages, a buyer's recovery for incidental damages need not be foreseeable.[323] They are recoverable as long as they are reasonable.[324] The requirement that these damages be "reasonable" is probably a sufficient hedge against the likelihood that the buyer could recover incidental damages for harm that could not have been contemplated at the time the contract was made.[325]

The CISG does not specifically mention incidental damages. However, courts that have considered the issue have awarded them as part of the aggrieved party's expectation damages. *Delchi Carrier Spa v. Rotorex Corp.*, mentioned above, required these damages to be reasonably foreseeable, in order to be recoverable under the CISG.[326]

Incidental damages under U.C.C. § 2-715(1) should be distinguished from "incidental reliance expense," available as a portion of damages based on the reliance interest rather than on the injured party's lost expectations.[327]

Aggrieved buyers are also entitled to recover for any consequential damages caused by the seller's breach. Consequential damages frequently consist of lost profits suffered as a result of the inability of the buyer to resell the goods to others,[328] or from its inability to otherwise use the goods in connection with its dealings with third parties.[329] They also include loss of goodwill, if it can be proven with reasonable certainty.[330] And, of course, they also might consist of damage to other property caused by a defect in the goods[331] or for personal injuries caused by defective goods.[332]

Consequential damages other than those for personal injury and property damage, are only recoverable if, at the time the contract was made, the breaching party had reason to know of the buyer's "general or particular requirements and needs" that led to the consequential harm.[333] And, they are not recoverable if the

---

[322] *See* William S. Dodge, *Teaching the CISG in Contracts*, 50 J. LEGAL EDUC. 72, 93–94 (2000).

[323] U.C.C. § 2-715(1) (2012).

[324] WILLIAM H. HENNING & GEORGE I. WALLACH, THE LAW OF SALES UNDER THE UNIFORM COMMERCIAL CODE ¶ 10.04 (1992).

[325] *But see* Delchi Carrier SpA v. Rotorex Corp., 71 F.3d 1024 (2d Cir. 2005) (determining whether certain incidental damages were foreseeable).

[326] Delchi Carrier Spa v. Rotorex Corp., 71 F.3d 1024 (2d Cir. 1995). *See* Eric C. Schneider, *Measuring Damages Under the CISG*, 9 PACE INT'L L. REV. 223 (1997).

[327] *See infra* § 13.02[B] Types of Reliance Damages: Essential and Incidental Reliance.

[328] *E.g.*, Delano Growers' Co-op. Winery v. Supreme Wine Co., Inc., 473 N.E.2d 1066 (Mass. 1985).

[329] *E.g.*, Fertico Belgium S.A. v. Phosphate Chem. Export Assoc., 510 N.E.2d 334 (N.Y. 1987); Manouchehri v. Heim, 941 P.2d 978, 982 (N.M. Ct. App. 1997).

[330] AM/PM Franchise Ass'n v. Atl. Richfield Co., 584 A.2d 915 (Pa. 1990).

[331] *E.g.*, Fed. Ins. Co. v. Vill. of Westmont, 649 N.E.2d 986 (Ill. App. Ct. 1995) (property damage due to defective water meter). *See also* Chase Manhattan Bank, N.A. v. T & N PLC, 905 F. Supp. 107 (S.D.N.Y. 1995) (asbestos).

[332] *E.g.*, Denny v. Ford Motor Co., 662 N.E.2d 730 (N.Y. 1995).

[333] U.C.C. § 2-715(2)(a). *See supra* § 12.04[B] Foreseeability in Sales of Goods.

buyer could have avoided the loss by obtaining substitute goods or taking other reasonable actions to prevent the loss.[334] Further, as with other damages, they are recoverable only if they were caused by the breach and are ascertainable with reasonable certainty. The CISG imposes similar restrictions.[335]

[B]   Contracts for the Sale of Goods — Breach by the Buyer

When the buyer is in breach, the injured seller has an array of procedural remedies as well as an assortment of money damage formulas from which to select. Likewise, in the right circumstances the seller may be able to compel specific performance and require the buyer to pay the price of the goods.

The seller's procedural rights, derived from the law of constructive conditions and the seller's duty to mitigate, include the right to identify goods to the contract, to either complete their manufacture and resell them or to cease production and recoup their salvage value, and to stop delivery of goods that have already been identified and are in transit to the breaching buyer. These actions only impair the seller's right to recover damages if it acts unreasonably or in bad faith in exercising its rights.

When buyers back out of a deal, sellers usually attempt to resell the goods.[336] If they are successful, their direct damages depend on the resale price.[337] If the resale price is lower than the contract price, the seller is entitled to recover the difference from the buyer, together with any incidental damages, but minus any expenses saved as a result of the breach.[338] Thus, if Barb repudiates her agreement to pay Sam $20,000 for his used BMW, and Sam subsequently sells the car to Rosa for $18,500, Sam is entitled to the $1,500 difference. However, where the resale price is for more than the contract price, the seller is not required to account to the buyer for amounts gained on the resale.[339] If Sam is able to persuade Rosa to pay him $21,000 for the car, he has no duty to pay the bonus to Barb. The CISG provides a similar remedy.[340]

The resale transaction must be conducted in good faith and in a commercially reasonable manner.[341] This requires the seller to advertise the availability of the goods, though it does not require any particular manner of promoting their sale. The manner in which other such goods are normally advertised in the trade or industry is a good guide to whether the seller's advertising efforts are

---

[334] U.C.C. § 2-715(2)(a). *See infra* § 12.05 Limits on Damages: Mitigation.

[335] CISG Art. 74 & 77 (1980). *See* Delchi Carrier SpA v. Rotorex, 71 F.3d 1024 (2d Cir. 1995).

[336] U.C.C. § 2-706(1) (2012).

[337] Roy R. Anderson, *Plunging the Depths of the Seller's Resale Remedy Under the Uniform Commercial Code*, 50 J. Air L. & Com. 411 (1985).

[338] Id.

[339] U.C.C. § 2-706(6) (2012).

[340] CISG Art. 75 (1980).

[341] U.C.C. § 2-706(1) (2012). E.g., Coast Trading Co. v. Cudahy Co., 592 F.2d 1074, 1080–81 (9th Cir. 1979).

commercially reasonable. In international sales, Article 75 of the CISG, like § 2-706 permits the aggrieved buyer to resell the goods and recover the difference between "the contract price and the price in the substitute transaction."[342]

The seller's failure to resell the goods, or its failure to conduct the resale in a commercially reasonable manner, does not deprive the seller of all remedies.[343] Instead, a seller who neglects to resell, or who resells without complying with U.C.C. § 2-706, will find its damages limited to the difference between the market value of the goods and the contract price under § 2-708(1).[344] Thus, if Barb repudiates her agreement to purchase Sam's car for the agreed price of $20,000, and Sam subsequently resells the car to his brother-in-law Emmet for only $12,000, the sale might have been unreasonable. If so, Sam's damages will be limited to the difference between the $20,000 contract price and the market value of the car. If the market value is $18,000, Sam will recover $2,000, together with any incidental damages he has suffered. If the market value was $20,000 or higher, his only damages will be the incidental damages available under U.C.C. § 2-710. Limiting the seller to damages based on the market value restrains sellers from attempting to punish the buyer for its breach by unreasonably reselling the goods at a bargain basement price.

The difference between the contract price and either the market value or the resale price of the goods does not always put an injured seller in as good a position as performance.[345] If the seller could have sold multiple units of the same item, and made a profit on each transaction, the normal formulas do not give the seller the benefit of its bargain. In these situations, involving "lost volume sellers" U.C.C. § 2-708(2) permits the seller to recover "the profit (including reasonable overhead) which the seller would have made from full performance by the buyer."[346]

The principle is illustrated by the widely known decision in *Neri v. Retail Marine*.[347] There, the buyer backed out of a contract to purchase a boat from Retail Marine's boat dealership. Retail Marine sold the boat to another customer for the same price Neri had agreed to pay. Although this might have appeared to be a "resale" with damages recoverable under U.C.C. § 2-706, the court ruled that the second sale was not a "substitute" for the transaction with Neri.[348] It reasoned that if Neri had gone through with his purchase, Retail Marine would have sold

---

[342] CISG Art. 74 (1980). The CISG is organized differently than the U.C.C. Article 74 is drafted broadly to permit the aggrieved party to recover the difference between the contract price and the price in the substitute transaction. With respect to aggrieved sellers, this is the market price minus the resale price. With respect to aggrieved buyers, it is the price of cover minus the contract price.

[343] See Coast Trading Co. v. Cudahy Co., 592 F.2d 1074 (9th Cir. 1979) (seller resold, but not in good faith). The 2003 revisions to Article 2 expressly provide that the seller's failure to resell does not automatically bar the seller from all remedies. Revised U.C.C. § 2-706(7) (2003).

[344] U.C.C. § 2-706 cmt. 2 (2012). *See, e.g.*, Apex Oil Co. v. Belcher Co. of New York, Inc., 855 F.2d 997 (2d Cir. 1988).

[345] Robert E. Scott, *The Case for Market Damages: Revisiting the Lost-Profits Puzzle*, 57 U. Chi. L. Rev. 1155 (1990).

[346] U.C.C. § 2-708(2) (2012).

[347] 285 N.E.2d 311 (N.Y. 1972).

[348] *Id.* at 315.

two boats, and earned a profit on each of them. Because of the loss in the volume of total sales caused by Neri's breach, Retail Marine was a "lost-volume seller," and entitled to recover the profit it would have made on the sale to Neri if the contract had been performed.

The principal difficulty in applying U.C.C. § 2-708(2) is identifying the lost volume sellers to which it applies. The Code's official comments indicate that § 2-708(2)'s lost profit recovery is available to those who sell "standard priced goods . . . ." However, not all sellers of standard priced goods have access to additional sources of supply, and not every seller who could have made an additional sale would have made a profit on the additional sale. Those who are selling below cost might enter into additional transactions, but every sale they make brings them closer to the brink of bankruptcy. As explained earlier, a seller is entitled to recover for a lost profit on a contract only if (1) it had the capacity for an additional sale,[349] (2) it would have chosen to make the additional sale if the earlier contract had not been breached, and (3) the additional transaction would have resulted in a profit.[350]

Calculating a seller's lost profit usually involves deducting the costs the seller saved as a result of the buyer's breach from the contract price, in much the same way as in a construction contract. The Code expressly permits the seller to retain, as part of its profit on the deal, a reasonable overhead attributable to the seller's fixed costs associated with the transaction, which were not saved as a result of the breach.[351] Furthermore, Language in § 2-708(2) indicating that this lost profit must make include a "due credit for payments or proceeds of resale" has been consistently interpreted to apply only in situations where the goods involved in the sale were sold for their scrap value.[352]

In international sale transactions, the CISG expressly permits the injured party to recover any "loss of profit" it suffers as a result of the breach.[353] Unlike the U.C.C., however, it does not contain a special provision recognizing that the difference between the contract price and either the resale price or the market value may be insufficient to compensate for a lost-volume seller's lost profit. Cases decided under the CISG have recognized that seller's might suffer such a loss and have applied the same analysis used in connection with § 2-708(2) to reach the same results.[354]

In some cases, the seller is entitled to recover the full contract price. The most obvious situation is where the buyer has accepted the goods.[355] Even if the buyer

---

[349] *E.g.*, Eneractive Group, Inc. v. Carefree of Colo., 1993 U.S. App. LEXIS 13499 (7th Cir. June 3, 1993); Ragen Corp. v. Kearney & Trecker Corp., 912 F.2d 619 (3d Cir. 1990).

[350] *See* Rodriguez v. Learjet, Inc., 946 P.2d 1010, 1015 (Kan. Ct. App. 1997); *infra* § 12.08[B] Contracts for the Sale of Goods — Breach by the Buyer.

[351] U.C.C. § 2-708(2) (2012); Nobs Chem. U.S.A., Inc. v. Koppers Co., 616 F.2d 212 (5th Cir. 1980).

[352] *E.g.*, R.E. Davis Chem. Corp. v. Diasonics, Inc., 826 F.2d 678, 674 (7th Cir. 1987).

[353] CISG Art. 74 (1980).

[354] Djakhongir Saidov, *Methods of Limiting Damages Under the Vienna Convention on Contracts for the International Sale of Goods*, 14 PACE INT'L L. REV. 307, 318–26 (2002).

[355] U.C.C. § 2-709(1)(a) (2012).

wrongfully rejects the goods, the seller is entitled to the contract price if the goods cannot be resold or if the circumstances indicate that any reasonable effort to resell them would be futile.[356] Goods printed with the buyer's logo are a good example.[357] An action to recover the entire price is also available when the goods have been destroyed, without the seller's fault, within a commercially reasonable time after the risk of loss has passed to the buyer.[358]

The CISG also permits the seller to recover the price. Consistent with the broader availability of specific performance under CISG, Article 62 provides that "the seller may require the buyer to pay the price, take delivery, or perform his other obligations," except in cases where the seller has already resorted to a different remedy.[359] This broad rule permitting the seller to recover the price may be limited by Article 28, which generally prevents specific performance where it would not be permitted under the domestic law of the jurisdiction in which the court presides.[360] However, because Article 28's limit expressly refers to "specific performance," rather than to the seller's ability to recover the price, it might only properly apply to cases involving breach by the seller.[361]

In addition to obtaining the foregoing damages under §§ 2-706, 2-708, or 2-709, aggrieved sellers are always entitled to incidental damages caused by the breach.[362] A seller's incidental damages usually consist of any commercially reasonable charges, expenses, or commissions incurred in exercising its right to stop delivery, or in the transportation, care, or custody of the goods following the buyer's breach.[363] Thus, in *Neri v. Retail Marine*, the injured seller was entitled to recover, in addition to its lost profit, for the costs it incurred in storing, insuring, and caring for the goods prior to their resale. None of these costs would have been incurred had the buyer taken delivery of the boat as promised.[364]

Similar expenses incurred in the seller's effort to resell the goods are likewise recoverable as incidental damages.[365] However, the seller's litigation costs do not qualify for recovery.[366]

On the other hand, Article 2 is conspicuously silent about a seller's ability to recover consequential damages. This has led most courts to deny sellers any recovery for damages resulting from any harm to a transaction with a third party,

---

[356] U.C.C. § 2-709(1)(b) (2012).

[357] *E.g.*, Foxco Indus., Ltd. v. Fabric World, Inc., 595 F.2d 976 (5th Cir. 1979) (specially manufactured fabric).

[358] U.C.C. § 2-709(1)(a) (2012).

[359] CISG Art. 62 (1980).

[360] CISG Art. 28 (1980).

[361] *See* Amy H. Kastely, *The Right to Require Performance*, 63 WASH L. REV. 607, 634 (1988).

[362] *See* U.C.C. §§ 2-706, 2-708 (2012).

[363] U.C.C. § 2-710 (2012).

[364] Neri v. Retail Marine, 285 N.E.2d 311 (N.Y. 1972).

[365] Lee Oldsmobile, Inc. v. Kaiden, 363 A.2d 270 (Md. Ct. App. 1976).

[366] Bill's Coal Co., Inc. v. Bd. of Pub. Utils. of Springfield, Mo., 887 F.2d 242, 246 (10th Cir. 1987).

such as loss of a volume discount.[367] Interest expense incurred between the time for performance and the time of resale has been denied when it was characterized as an item of consequential damages.[368] These items have been awarded, however, when characterized as incidental damages instead.[369]

The 2003 revision of Article 2 specifically addresses the issue and permits sellers to recover consequential damages, subject to the usual restrictions concerning foreseeability and avoidability of the consequential harm.[370] However, in a "consumer contract" between a "merchant seller and a consumer buyer,"[371] the seller may not recover consequential damages from the buyer.[372] Although the 2003 revisions are unlikely to be adopted, their recognition that sellers may suffer lost profits should aid courts in awarding them in appropriate circumstances.

The CISG makes no specific mention of a seller's consequential damages, but generally permits an aggrieved party to recover for any loss it suffers as a result of the other party's breach.[373] Its broad language permits the seller to recover any consequential damages it has suffered due to the breach subject to the usual limits of foreseeability, mitigation, and reasonable certainty.

[C]   Damages for Breach of Contract for Real Estate[374]

Damages for breach of a contract for the sale of real estate are similar to those in contracts for the sale of goods, except of course that real estate transactions are not governed by the U.C.C. In addition, specific performance is more commonly available in contracts for the sale of land, though it is not always practical, and not always desired by the injured party.

The buyer's damages for breach of a contract for the sale or lease of real estate are nearly identical to those available to aggrieved buyers of goods. Buyers of land (and other property) are injured when the value of the property they had the right to purchase is higher than the contract price. Thus, they are usually able to recover their down payment together with market value of the land minus the contract price.[375] This, together with any incidental and consequential damages caused by the breach, will place the injured buyer in as good a position as it would have been if, if the contract had been performed. The buyer's incidental damages are likely to include title examination fees, inspection fees, and sometimes increased costs of financing or construction.[376] Expenses incurred in an effort to mitigate the buyer's

---

[367] Afram Export Corp. v. Metallurgiki Halyps, S.A. 772 F.2d 1358 (7th Cir. 1985).

[368] Nobs Chem., U.S.A., Inc., v. Koppers Co., Inc., 616 F.2d 212 (5th Cir. 1980).

[369] Neri v. Retail Marine, 285 N.E.2d 311 (N.Y. 1972) (finance charges).

[370] Revised U.C.C. § 2-710(2) (2003).

[371] Revised U.C.C. § 2-103(d) (2003).

[372] Revised U.C.C. § 2-710(3) (2003).

[373] CISG Art. 74 (1980).

[374] Lawrence V. Berkovich, *To Pay or to Convey?: A Theory of Remedies for Breach of Real Estate Contracts*, 1995 ANN. SURV. AM. L. 319.

[375] *E.g.*, Wilt v. Waterfield, 273 S.W.2d 290, 296 (Mo. 1954).

[376] RICHARD POWELL, POWELL ON REAL PROPERTY § 81.04 (Matthew Bender 2002).

losses are usually recoverable as incidental damages.[377] Consequential damages, such as profits the buyer anticipated earning through use of the land, are available, but subject to the usual limitations based on the foreseeability of the harm, the buyer's ability to avoid the consequential loss, and the ability of the buyer to prove any lost profits with reasonable certainty.

Where the seller's breach consists of a good-faith failure to deliver good title due to a previously unknown defect in the seller's chain of ownership, some courts still adhere to the "English Rule" established by *Flureau v. Thornhill*.[378] The English Rule developed in recognition of the difficulty of determining the status of a seller's title.[379] It limits damages to the buyer's reliance expenses incurred in connection with the sale.[380] However, the rule has been criticized both in England and the United States, and a growing number of jurisdictions now follow the "American Rule," which permits recovery based on the market value of good title.[381]

Where the seller or lessor delays performance, the buyer should be able to recover the lost value of the property during the delay, usually measured by the rental value.[382] This amount may be subject to offset by the amount of the buyer's savings, or interest earned on the funds that would otherwise have been used to complete the purchase.[383]

When the buyer is in breach, the seller or lessor can recover damages measured by the difference between the contract price and the market value of the land.[384] The seller may also recover any incidental damages, such as those associated with maintenance of the property or taxes levied after the time for performance.[385] Consequential damages are also available to the seller if, at the time the contract was made, the buyer had reason to know of the harm which gave rise to the damages.[386]

In some states the seller is permitted to retain any down payment made by the buyer, up to approximately 10% of the total purchase price.[387] Permitting the seller to retain the down payment is vulnerable to the criticism that this is out of step with the prevailing approach to damages for breach of contract, based on the aggrieved party's lost expectations.[388] Nevertheless, the rule operates somewhat

---

[377] *E.g.*, Hutchison v. Pyburn, 567 S.W.2d 762 (Tenn. Ct. App. 1977) (moving expenses).

[378] 96 Eng. Rep. 635 (C.P. 1776).

[379] A.J. Oakley, *Pecuniary Compensation for Failure to Complete a Contract for the Sale of Land*, 39 Cambridge L.J. 59 (1980).

[380] *See, e.g.*, Beard v. S/E Joint Venture, 581 A.2d 1275 (Md. 1989).

[381] *See* Donovan v. Bachstadt, 453 A.2d 160 (N.J. 1982) (abandoning the English rule in favor of the American rule).

[382] *E.g.*, Gorzelsky v. Leckey, 586 A.2d 952 (Pa. Super. Ct. 1991); Shelter Corp. of Canada, Ltd. v. Bozin, 468 So. 2d 1094 (Fla. Dist. Ct. App. 1985).

[383] *E.g.*, Hirschfeld v. Borchard Affiliations, Inc., 190 N.Y.S.2d 588 (N.Y. Sup. Ct. 1959).

[384] *E.g.*, Gilmartin Bros., Inc. v. Kern, 916 S.W.2d 324 (Mo. Ct. App. 1995).

[385] Richard Powell, Powell on Real Property § 81.04[2][c] (Matthew Bender 2002).

[386] *See* Turner v. Benson, 672 S.W.2d 752 (Tenn. 1984).

[387] *See* Maxton Builders, Inc. v. Lo Galbo, 502 N.E.2d 184 (N.Y. 1986).

[388] Freedman v. Rector, Wardens & Vestrymen, 230 P.2d 629 (Cal. 1951); Joseph M. Perillo,

like a liquidated damages provision. Further, it is compatible with a similar rule in U.C.C. § 2-718, which in some cases permits the seller to retain as much as 20% of the purchase price, even if no actual damages are proven.[389]

[D]   Construction Contracts: Breach by the Builder — Cost of Performance or Difference in Value[390]

When the contractor or other provider of services breaches, the usual remedy is damages equal to the cost of having the project performed or corrected by someone else.[391] This is comparable to a buyer's rights to recover the cost of obtaining a substitute. In most cases this is cheaper than paying the difference in value between the work as promised and as performed, and will more effectively prevent consequential harm that might otherwise occur as a result of the provider's breach.

For example, if Rhonda's Roofing agrees to install a new roof on Howard's house for $5,000, but performs badly, requiring $1,000 in repairs, Howard can recover the extra $1,000 necessary to repair the defective work. If he has not yet paid Rhonda, Howard might simply deduct the $1,000 expense from the unpaid balance due. In either event, Howard will have obtained his new roof for $5,000 of his own funds, as he agreed.

This $1,000 worth of repairs is usually lower than the difference in value between a house with a new roof and one with a defective roof. Moreover, it is far cheaper than the potential consequential harm to the house and its contents that might occur as a result of having a leaky roof. Accordingly, in construction contracts, the cost of performance is usually the most efficient method of fulfilling the injured party's lost expectations.

Incomplete performance is handled the same way. If Rhonda completes only 90% of the roof and it costs Howard $1,000 to have someone finish the job, Howard can recover the $1,000 as damages resulting from the breach. Alternatively, if Howard has not paid anything to Rhonda, he might just deduct the $1,000 from the unpaid portion of the price.

In either event, the breaching contractor receives part payment for its part performance. This is similar to the right of a breaching seller to receive payment for goods accepted by the buyer, subject to the obligation to pay offsetting

Restitution in the Second Restatement of Contracts, 81 COLUM. L. REV. 37 (1981).

   [389] U.C.C. § 2-718(2)(b) (2012) ($500 maximum).

   [390] Carol Chomsky, *Of Soil Pits and Swimming Pools: Reconsidering the Measure of Damages for Construction Contracts*, 75 MINN. L. REV. 1445 (1991); Juanda Lowder Daniel, *Avoiding Economic Waste in Contract Damages: Myths, Misunderstanding, and Malcontent*, 85 NEB. L. REV. 875 (2007); John P. Luddington, Annotation, *Modern Status of Rule as to Whether Cost of Correction or Difference in Value of Structures Is Proper Measure of Damages for Breach of Construction Contract*, 41 A.L.R.4th 131 (1985); Judith L. Maute, Peevyhouse v. Garland Coal & Mining Co., *Revisited: The Ballad of Willie and Lucille*, 89 NW. U. L. REV. 1341 (1995); Timothy J. Muris, *Cost of Completion or Diminution in Market Value: The Relevance of Subjective Value*, 12 J. LEGAL STUD. 379 (1983); RICHARD A. POSNER, ECONOMIC ANALYSIS OF LAW 134 (6th ed. 2002).

   [391] RESTATEMENT (SECOND) OF CONTRACTS § 348(2)(a) (1981). *See, e.g.*, Am. Standard, Inc. v. Schectman, 439 N.Y.S.2d 529, 532 (N.Y. App. Div.), *appeal denied*, 427 N.E.2d 512 (N.Y. 1981).

damages, to the buyer for any shortfall or defect in the goods.

Naturally, if the work is completed or repaired for less than the unpaid portion of the contract price, the recipient cannot recover the full cost to complete. In *Louise Caroline Nursing Home, Inc. v. Dix Construction Co.*,[392] the owner was able to complete construction of a building for less than the amount specified in the contract, even after hiring a substitute builder to finish the job. As a result, the owner was not entitled to any recovery from the original builder, who had failed to finish the project. The building was actually cheaper as a result of the breach than it would have been had the contract been performed.

Sometimes the cost of completing a construction project is far higher than the value of the completed work. For example, if the water pipes in a new house are poorly installed, portions of the house might have to be dismantled to correct the deficient work. Without repairs, the pipes might burst and cause extensive damage to the home. In situations like these, the homeowner is likely to use the recovery to complete the repairs rather than run the risk of damage to his or her home.

In other cases, making the repairs is a less attractive option. If a brick patio is installed without a layer of limestone gravel underneath the bricks, the consequences are not so devastating. If the cost of correcting the deficient work is awarded there is a risk of either overcompensating the injured party, who might decide to pocket the damages based on the cost of completion rather than correcting the deficient work. In one such case, involving $4,000,000 necessary to repair a ship to make it worth $2,000,000, the court said: "[c]ommon sense and reality tell us that [the plaintiff] will not so spend the money [to make the repairs]."[393]

Most homeowners would probably repair the defective water pipes, for fear of subsequent damage to their home if the pipes were to break. On the other hand, many homeowners would probably put any money received to replace the brick patio in the bank, or use it for an unexpected vacation, rather than paying to lift all the bricks, properly install the gravel, and relay the brick patio. Businesses are even more likely to use funds they recover for other purposes.[394]

Where the disparity between the cost of completion and the difference in value is high, courts are reluctant to award damages based on the cost of performance. The law, however, is not well settled about the circumstances in which the injured party should be restricted to the difference in value, which is sometimes only nominal.

The well-known case of *Jacob & Youngs, Inc. v. Kent*[395] provides a good illustration of cases limiting the injured party to the difference in value. The builder constructed a house using "Cohoes"-brand pipe in breach of the terms of

---

[392] 285 N.E.2d 904 (Mass. 1972).

[393] E.S.S. Lines, Inc. v. United States, 112. F. Supp. 167 (Ct. Cl. 1953).

[394] *See* E.S.S. Lines, Inc. v. United States, 112 F. Supp. 167 (Ct. Cl. 1953); Melvin Aron Eisenberg, *Actual and Virtual Specific Performance, the Theory of Efficient Breach, and the Indifference Principle in Contract Law*, 93 CAL. L. REV. 975, 1050 (2005).

[395] 129 N.E. 889 (N.Y. 1921).

the contract which specified that "Reading"-brand pipe should be used. Cohoes pipe had all of the same performance characteristics and durability as Reading pipe. The two brands of pipe were identical in every respect, except for the manufacturer's label.

The court, finding that the contract had been substantially performed, limited the owner's recovery to the difference in value between the house as promised and its value as constructed. Not surprisingly, this amounted to zero. The court explained that the cost of performance would have been grossly out of proportion to the benefit to be achieved by completing the corrective work.[396] Rational homeowners, if awarded the cost of demolishing the completed house and rebuilding it with the stipulated brand of pipe, would simply pocket the award and thus be overcompensated for the breach. The purpose of the contract was to construct a sturdy and durable residence. That purpose had been achieved despite substitution of the brands of pipe. Actually replacing the pipe, which would have necessitated destruction of the mansion, would have resulted in both physical and economic waste.[397]

If the main purpose of the construction project in *Jacob & Young, Inc. v. Kent* had been to showcase the performance characteristics and durability of Reading pipe, a different result might have been reached.[398] Use of the Reading brand of pipe would have been the main purpose of the contract and not merely "ancillary." Likewise, where the owner has a personal or aesthetic interest in the promised performance, cost of performance may be available even if completing the work as promised would result in some economic waste.

Homeowners frequently undertake construction projects designed to appeal to their individual taste or preferences, without regard to the impact the work will have on the market value of their property.[399] Cost of performance damages are usually awarded in situations where the owner has a recognizable aesthetic interest, even though the breach has little or no impact on the market value of the structure.[400] Here, satisfying the owner's aesthetic interest is a main purpose of the contract, and failing to perform cannot be regarded as incidental or ancillary to the principal purpose of the contract.[401] For example, consider the case of a homeowner who hires a painter to paint the house blue. If the painter breaches by

---

[396] *Id.* at 891.

[397] RESTATEMENT (SECOND) OF CONTRACTS § 348 cmt. c (1981). See Carol Chomsky, *Of Spoil Pits and Swimming Pools: Reconsidering the Measure of Damages for Construction Contracts*, 74 MINN. L. REV. 1445, 1454–60 (1991) (regarding use of the term "economic waste"); Alan Schwartz, *Market Damages, Efficient Contracting, and the Economic Waste Fallacy*, 108 COLUM. L. REV. 1610 (2008).

[398] *See* Timothy J. Muris, *Cost of Completion or Diminution in Market Value: The Relevance of Subjective Value*, 12 J. LEGAL STUD. 379 (1983). *See also* American Standard, Inc. v. Schectman, 80 A.D.2d 318 (N.Y. App. Div. 1981).

[399] *E.g.*, Advanced, Inc. v. Wilks, 711 P.2d 524 (Alaska 1985).

[400] *E.g.*, Fox v. Webb, 105 So. 2d 75 (Ala. 1958). *See* Carol Chomsky, *Of Spoil Pits and Swimming Pools: Reconsidering the Measure of Damages for Construction Contracts*, 74 MINN. L. REV. 1445, 1456 (1991).

[401] City Sch. Dist. of Elmira v. McLane Constr. Co., 85 A.D.2d 749 (N.Y. App. Div. 1981); Kangas v. Trust, 441 N.E.2d 1271 (Ill. App. Ct. 1982).

painting the house white, the homeowner would be entitled to recover the cost of covering the white paint with a coat (or two) of blue. No one would suggest that the homeowner would be unable to recover the cost of performance even if the market value of the house was actually increased by the painter's having painted the house white.[402] Likewise, cost of performance may also be warranted if deficient performance would leave the premises in an unsafe or unusable condition, even where the defects have only a marginal impact on the market value of the property.

Some cases following *Jacob & Young* have indicated that the rule limits the recipient to the difference in value where the breach was limited to an incidental aspect of the contract.[403] Chief among these is *Peevyhouse v. Garland Coal & Mining Co.*,[404] where the court determined that cost of performance would not be awarded for a strip-mining company's failure to restore the grade of leased land, after removal of the coal deposits, which had been the principal purpose of the lease. *Peevyhouse* is a notorious and widely criticized decision,[405] which was decided at the same time as a bribery scandal in the same court.[406] Judicial misconduct aside, however, breach of an incidental term of the contract does not justify cost of performance damages that are grossly disproportionate to the loss in market value caused by the breach.[407]

Commentators have sometimes suggested that efforts by courts to avoid "economic waste" and decisions about whether a particular breach was incidental to the essential purpose of the contract are little more than reflections of the disparity in normative values between the court and the injured party. This seems almost certainly to have been true in *Peevyhouse*.

In other cases it may instead be an unarticulated application of the foreseeability standard of *Hadley v. Baxendale*. Cost of performance would ordinarily not be available under the foreseeability standard, where the breaching party did not, at the time the contact was made, have reason to know that the other party could only be made whole with damages based on the cost of performance.[408] For example, it seems unlikely that the contractor in *Jacob & Young* would have had reason to know that the homeowner had an aesthetic interest in the brand of

---

[402] Gory Assoc'd Indus., Inc. v. Jupiter Roofing & Sheet Metal, Inc., 358 So. 2d 93, 94–95 (Fla. Dist. Ct. App. 1978); City Sch. Dist. of Elmira v. McLane Constr. Co., 85 A.D.2d 749 (N.Y. App. Div. 1981).

[403] Carol Chomsky, *Of Spoil Pits and Swimming Pools: Reconsidering the Measure of Damages for Construction Contracts*, 74 Minn. L. Rev. 1445, 1458–59 (1991).

[404] 382 P.2d 109 (Okla. 1962).

[405] Stewart Macaulay, *An Empirical View of Contract*, 1985 Wis. L. Rev. 465, 470; Judith L. Maute, Peevyhouse v. Garland Coal & Mining Co. *Revisited: The Ballad of Willie and Lucille*, 89 Nw. U. L. Rev. 1341, 1428 (1995); Robert Cooter & Thomas Ulen, Law and Economics 611 (1988); E. Allan Farnsworth, *Legal Remedies for Breach of Contract*, 70 Colum. L. Rev. 1145, 1175 (1970); Peter Linzer, On the *Amorality of Contract Remedies: Efficiency, Equity and the Second Restatement*, 81 Colum. L. Rev. 111, 134–38 (1981).

[406] Judith L. Maute, Peevyhouse v. Garland Coal & Mining Co. *Revisited: The Ballad of Willie and Lucille*, 89 Nw. U. L. Rev. 1341, 1455–71 (1995).

[407] *E.g*, Hitchcock v. Peter Kiewit & Sons, Co., 479 F.2d 1257 (10th Cir. 1973).

[408] *E.g.*, P.G. Lake, Inc. v. Sheffield, 438 S.W.2d 952, 957 (Tex. Civ. App. 1969).

pipe used in the construction of his home that related to anything other than the functional utility of the pipe.

Finally, courts sometimes cite the wilful nature of the defendant's breach as a justification for the cost of performance remedy.[409] However, consideration of the breaching party's purpose is incompatible with the customary goal of contract damages of fulfilling the injured party's expectations. Emphasizing the willful nature of the breach seems more appropriate in situations where breach is to be actively discouraged by the award of punitive damages. On the other hand, it might be an appropriate means of compelling disgorgement of the profit the breaching party made as a result of its intentional breach.[410] Where the difference in value would compensate the defendant for its lost expectations, awarding cost of performance would deter rather than encourage what might be an economically efficient breach.

[E]   Construction Contracts: Breach by the Customer

Where the owner or other recipient of construction or other services is in breach, the builder or other service provider can recover damages based on one of two alternative formulas, each of which should provide full compensation for the direct value lost due to the breach.[411] First, the builder might recover the unpaid portion of the contract price minus any costs or other losses that were avoided as a result of the breach.[412] Thus, if Winkler Builders was hired to construct a fence at Beth's house for a price of $2,000, and Beth repudiates, Winkler can recover the $2,000 price minus whatever expenses he has avoided as a result of her breach. If work had not yet begun but would have cost $1,600 to complete, Winkler is entitled to the contract price of $2,000 minus the $1,600 expenses saved. This results in Winkler's recovery of the $400 profit it would have made on the transaction. If Winkler had already begun and spent $1,000, with work costing another $600 remaining to be done at the time of Beth's breach, Winkler could recover a total of $1,400. This is the sum of the $2,000 price minus the $600 in expenses that Winkler saved.

Alternatively, the supplier's damages can be based on the cost of any part performance it rendered before the breach plus the profit that would have been earned if the contract had been fully performed.[413] Assume again, in the fence construction contract between Winkler Builders and Beth, that Winkler had spent

---

[409] *E.g.*, Groves v. John Wunder Corp., 286 N.W. 235 (Minn. 1939); American Standard, Inc. v. Schectman, 80 A.D.2d 318, 321–324 (N.Y. App. Div. 1981); John P. Ludington, Annotation, *Modern Status of Rule as to Whether Cost of Correction or Difference in Value of Structures Is Proper Measure of Damages for Breach of Construction Contract*, 1 A.L.R.4th 131 (1985).

[410] E. Allan Farnsworth, *Your Loss or My Gain? The Dilemma of the Disgorgement Principle in Breach of Contract*, 94 YALE L.J. 1339 (1985).

[411] *See* Petropoulos v. Lubienski, 152 A.2d 801 (Md. 1959).

[412] RESTATEMENT (SECOND) OF CONTRACTS § 347 illus. 6 (1981). E.g., Burns v. Gould, 374 A.2d 193, 221 (Conn. 1977). *See generally* Edwin W. Patterson, *Builder's Measure of Recovery for Breach of Contract*, 31 COLUM. L. REV. 1286 (1931).

[413] Aiello Constr. Inc. v. Nationwide Tractor Trailer Training and Placement Corp., 413 A.2d 85 (R.I. 1980); Warner v. McLay, 103 A. 113 (Conn. 1918).

$1,000 before Beth's breach, and it would have earned a $400 profit on the deal upon full performance. Winkler can recover the $1,000 it has already spent, plus the $400 anticipated profit, for a total recovery, just as before, of $1,400.

These two formulas, contract price minus expenses saved and expenses incurred plus profit are algebraic equivalents. In mathematical terms: (Contract Price − Expense Saved) = (Expense Incurred + Profit).

Many service providers, like many sellers of goods, provide services to multiple customers simultaneously.[414] Thus, the fact that they enter into another contract with another customer, following one customer's breach, does not mean that the contract with the subsequent customer is a substitute transaction that mitigates the profits lost on the deal with first customer. In this way, suppliers of services are much like lost-volume sellers, who could have entered into numerous contracts with many customers and made a profit on each deal. Contracts entered into with additional customers do not necessarily mitigate the lost profit on the deal with a breaching customer.[415] This profit should include any reasonable overhead normally attributed to the transaction.[416] Fixed overhead costs are not usually avoided as a result of the breach, and thus do not represent any savings for the injured builder.[417]

As with lost volume sellers of goods, the mere fact that the service provider could have entered into another transaction does not mean that it would have, or that it would have made a profit on the additional deal. For example, a trucking company can nearly always enter into an additional transaction to transport goods.[418] However, if performing an additional contract would require the company to purchase an additional truck and hire an additional driver, the trucking company probably would not enter into the additional transaction. It is unlikely that the revenue it would gain from the additional transaction would be sufficient to cover the additional costs that it would incur in performing.

Moreover, if expenditures incurred in part performance of a contract have some salvage value (and thus have not really been fully spent), the salvage value is deducted from the recovery to avoid overcompensation.[419] Still using the example involving Beth's fence, if $200 of the $1,000 of Winkler's expenses incurred can be salvaged, such as materials purchased but not yet installed and therefore usable on another fencing job, Winkler's recovery is reduced by this amount to only

---

[414] Bitterroot Intern. Sys. Ltd. v. W. Star Trucks, Inc., 153 P.3d 627 (Mont. 2007); *In re* El Paso Refinery, L.P., 196 B.R. 58 (Bankr. W.D. Tex. 1996).

[415] Bitterroot Intern. Sys. Ltd. v. W. Star Trucks, Inc., 153 P.3d 627 (Mont. 2007); Wired Music, Inc. v. Clark, 168 N.E.2d 736 (Ill. App. Ct. 1960).

[416] Vitex Mfg. Corp. v. Caribtex, Corp. 377 F.2d 795 (3d Cir. 1967); Teradyne, Inc. v. Teledyne Industries, Inc., 676 F.2d 865 (1st Cir. 1982).

[417] *See generally* S.R. Shapiro, Annotation, *Overhead Expense as Recoverable Element of Damages*, 3 A.L.R.3d 689 (1965); H. Kent Munson, *Fixed Overhead Expenses: The Gremlins of Lost Profits Damage*, 56 J. Mo. B. 104 (2000).

[418] Bitterroot Intern. Sys. Ltd. v. W. Star Trucks, Inc., 153 P.3d 627 (Mont. 2007).

[419] RESTATEMENT (SECOND) OF CONTRACTS § 347 illus. 7 (1981). *E.g.*, Indus. Circuits Co. v. Terminal Comm., Inc., 216 S.E.2d 919, 924–26 (N.C. Ct. App. 1975).

$1,200.[420] In effect, it has not incurred $1,000 in expenses, but only $800.

Builders and others who provide services sometimes underestimate their costs and enter into a losing contract that will cost more to complete than the contractor agreed to charge. Consider a situation in which Winkler Construction agrees to build Beth's fence for $2,000 even though full performance will ultimately cost Winkler $2,100. If Beth breaches after Winkler has spent $1,000, then full performance (which would have cost another $1,100 and earned the right to receive only $2,000) would have resulted in a $100 net loss to Winkler. Winkler should be reluctant to ask to be placed in the position he would have been in if the contract been performed. By charging too low a price, performance would have caused Winkler to suffer a $100 loss. He will hope to take advantage of the other party's breach to avoid this loss.

This illustration raises the question whether the contractor can sue to recover all of the expenses it incurred in part performance, even though full performance would have resulted in a loss. If successful in recovering all of its reliance expenses, the injured party will be able to shift the consequences of its bad judgment, in bidding too little on the job, to the breaching party. This would place the injured party in a position better than the one it would have been in if the contract had been fully performed.

However, the breaching owner may be able to avoid paying all of the injured contractor's expenses. If Winkler agreed to finish the fence for a price of $2,000, has already spent $1,000, and would find it necessary to spend $1,100 to finish the job, Winkler's recovery should be limited to $900, through application of one of the two standard expectation formulas. The first formula, contract price ($2,000), minus expenses saved ($1,100), yields a total recovery of $900. The second formula, expenses incurred ($1,000), plus the negative profit ($100), yields the same amount, $900. This will place Winkler in exactly the position he would have been in had the contract been performed — a $100 loss. Alternatively, Winkler's recovery of his reliance expenses of $1,000 would fully reimburse him for the expenses he had incurred and thus protect him from the $100 loss he would have suffered if the contract has been performed. By limiting the contractor to recovering only $900, he will experience the same $100 loss. Of course, the burden of proof in showing that the contract could only have been performed at a loss will be on the breaching party.

[F]   Employment Contracts

Employment contracts are similar to other service contracts, except that they are regulated by state and federal law restricting an employer's ability to discriminate against employees on the basis of race, age, gender, disability, or other immutable characteristics. Furthermore, in many states most employment contracts are subject to termination at any time, with or without notice, under the "employment at will" doctrine, so long as the termination does not violate the

---

[420] Those disturbed by the prospect of a lawsuit brought to recover such a small amount of money should simply alter the facts to imagine the construction of a small building for $2,000,000 instead of a fence for $2,000.

employee's statutory rights.[421] If the terms of the contract permit either party to unilaterally terminate the contract "at will" or with some sort of limited advance notice, termination does not usually lead to substantial damage claims. As a result, actions for breach of employment contracts are usually limited to those with a specific duration, or those in which termination by the employer must otherwise be justified by good cause.[422]

Breach by an employee usually entitles the employer to recover any additional salary that must be paid to a replacement.[423] If the employer takes reasonable steps to hire a substitute with comparable qualifications, the salary paid to a better qualified person, who is more valuable to the employer, may also be recovered.[424] In addition, the employer can recover any incidental expenses it incurs associated with its efforts to locate and train a replacement,[425] plus any foreseeable consequential damages[426] such as lost profits, provided that they can be proven with reasonable certainty.[427] Courts are frequently skeptical of claims for profits allegedly lost due to an employee's abandonment of his or her responsibilities, and refuse to allow their recovery[428] unless the employee had unique skills that the parties reasonably believed could not be adequately performed by someone else.[429]

In the proper circumstances, an injunction may be available to restrain the breaching employee from accepting alternative employment in the same line of work, but specific performance is not available.[430] This is particularly true where the contract contains a restrictive covenant that prohibits the employee from working for one of the employer's competitors.[431] These "no compete" clauses are generally enforceable, provided they are ancillary to the main purpose of the contract and are reasonably limited in time and geographic scope.[432]

When the tables are turned and an employee is wrongfully discharged, immediate recovery can be obtained not just for the portion of the contract already performed, but for the balance of the remaining term. The value of the wages are

---

[421] *E.g.*, Kulch v. Structural Fibers, Inc., 677 N.E.2d 308 (Ohio 1997).

[422] *See* Wright v. Honda of Am., Mfg., 653 N.E.2d 381, 384 (Ohio 1995).

[423] Roth v. Speck, 126 A.2d 153 (D.C. Mun. Ct. App. 1956); Handicapped Children's Educ. Bd. v. Lukaszewski, 332 N.W.2d 774 (Wis. 1983).

[424] Handicapped Children's Educ. Bd. v. Lukaszewski, 332 N.W.2d 774 (Wis. 1983).

[425] Med+Plus Neck & Back Pain Ctr. v. Noffsinger, 726 N.E.2d 687 (Ill. App. Ct. 2000); John Jay Esthetic Salon, Inc. v. Woods, 435 So. 2d 1051 (La. Ct. App. 1983).

[426] *E.g.*, Johnson v. Bovee, 574 P.2d 513, 514 (Colo. Ct. App. 1978); ARTHUR LINTON CORBIN, 11 CORBIN ON CONTRACTS § 1095 (Interim Ed. 2002).

[427] *Id.* at 693 (expressing disfavor of recovery of lost profits); Royal's Reconditioning Corp., Inc. v. Royal, 689 N.E.2d 237 (Ill. App. Ct. 1997); Arabesque Studios, Inc. v. Academy of Fine Arts Int'l, Inc., 529 S.W.2d 564 (Tex. Ct. App. 1975) (lost profits proved with reasonable certainty).

[428] *E.g.*, Valentine Dolls, Inc. v. McMillan, 202 N.Y.S.2d 620 (N.Y. Sup. Ct. 1960).

[429] *E.g.*, Eckles v. Sharman, 548 F.2d 905, 910 (10th Cir. 1977); Triangle Waist Co. v. Todd, 154 N.Y.S. 542 (N.Y. App. Div. 1915).

[430] *See infra* Chapter 15 Equitable Remedies.

[431] RESTATEMENT (SECOND) OF CONTRACTS § 188(2)(b) (1981).

[432] RESTATEMENT (SECOND) OF CONTRACTS § 188 cmt. g (1981).

discounted to their present value.[433]

The aggrieved employee is expected to make a reasonable effort to pursue alternative employment in mitigation of his or her loss.[434] Earnings the employee could have earned, if a reasonable effort had been made, will be deducted from the damages owed by the employer.[435] However, the employee need not accept alternative employment that is different or inferior. Nor must the employee accept an offer of reinstatement if the offer is conditioned on a waiver of the employee's rights due to the wrongful discharge[436] or is otherwise on terms different from those involved in the contract in question.[437]

Damages for harm to the employee's reputation are more difficult to recover, even though discharged employees are likely to feel the sting of this harm long after they have secured a new job. These damages are frequently regarded as too speculative to permit recovery.[438] However, some courts are willing to permit the recovery of these damages where the claim is more specific than a loss of reputation generally, and seek recovery for loss of a concrete opportunity for a specific job.[439]

Finally, where the employee has been discharged in violation of his or her statutory rights against illegal discrimination, the employee is usually entitled to reinstatement, attorneys' fees, and, in some cases, punitive damages.[440]

---

[433] *E.g.*, Battaglia v. Clinical Perfusionists, Inc., 658 A.2d 680 (Md. Ct. App. 1995); Ochoa v. Interbrew America, Inc., 999 F.2d 626 (2d Cir. 1993). Thus, if the employee's salary was payable in equal monthly installments over a three-year period, the total salary should be reduced to compensate for the fact that the employee will be receiving the salary early, in dollars.

[434] *See supra* § 12.05[A] Mitigation in Employment Contracts.

[435] RESTATEMENT (SECOND) OF CONTRACTS § 350(1) (1981). *E.g.*, Soules v. Indep. Sch. Dist. No. 518, 258 N.W.2d 103 (Minn. 1977); Ballard v. El Dorado Tire Co., 512 F.2d 901 (5th Cir. 1975).

[436] *E.g.*, Schwarze v. Solo Cup Co., 445 N.E.2d 872, 876 (Ill. App. Ct. 1983).

[437] Parker v. Twentieth Century-Fox Film Corp., 474 P.2d 689 (Cal. 1970).

[438] *E.g.*, Rice v. Cmty. Health Ass'n, 203 F.3d 283 (4th Cir. 2000). *See generally* Joel E. Smith, Annotation, *Recovery by Writer, Artist, or Entertainer for Loss of Publicity or Reputation Resulting from Breach of Contract*, 96 A.L.R.3d 437 (1979).

[439] Redgrave v. Boston Symphony Orchestra, Inc., 855 F.2d 888 (1st Cir. 1988).

[440] *See, e.g.*, Simpson v. Sheahan, 104 F.3d 998 (7th Cir. 1997).

Chapter 13

RELIANCE AND RESTITUTION

§ 13.01 RELIANCE AND RESTITUTION AS ALTERNATIVES[1]

Damages for breach of contract are not always based on the injured party's lost expectations.[2] They can also be based on either the plaintiff's reliance or restitution

---

[1] Robert Childres & Jack Garamella, *The Law of Restitution and the Reliance Interest in Contract*, 64 N.W.U. L. REV. 433 (1969); Melvin A. Eisenberg, *The Bargain Principle and Its Limits*, 95 HARV. L. REV. 741 (1982); E. Allan Farnsworth, *Remedies for Breach of Contract*, 70 COLUM. L. REV. 1145 (1970); Lon L. Fuller & William R. Perdue Jr., *The Reliance Interest in Contract Damages (Pts. I & II)*, 46 YALE L.J. 52 (1936); Stewart Macaulay, *The Reliance Interest and the World Outside the Law Schools' Doors*,

interest.

Damages based on the plaintiff's reliance interest are calculated based on what would be necessary to restore the injured party to the position it was in before the contract was made — to the pre-contract status quo.[3] They are measured by the position the injured party would have been in if the contract had never been made. In this respect, damages based on an injured party's reliance interest are usually easy to calculate. They usually consist of nothing more than the out-of-pocket expenses the injured party incurred in reliance on the contract.

The goal of restitution, on the other hand, is to prevent unjust enrichment.[4] Damages in restitution are measured by the value of the benefit conferred by one part to the contract, on the other.[5] Restitution is available both as a remedy for breach,[6] and to prevent unjust enrichment when the parties have rendered part performance pursuant to an unenforceable contract.[7] It is also used as a remedy for a breaching party who has partially performed before committing a breach.[8] Finally, restitution is also used in situations where there is no contract at all, but where it would be unjust for a person to retain a benefit he or she had received without providing compensation.[9] This last category of situations where restitution may be available is vast, and much of it is far beyond the scope of a first-year course in contract law.[10]

Actions to recover in restitution are characterized as based either in quasi-contract or as a contract implied-in-law.[11] A quasi-contract (meaning "like a contract") is not really a contract at all, because it is not based on the agreement of the parties. Instead, quasi-contract is based on the injustice of permitting a person to retain a benefit received at the expense of another.[12] Actions based on quasi-contract are frequently mischaracterized as arising under "quantum meruit,"

1991 WIS. L. REV. 247; Aaron R. Petty, *The Reliance Interest in Restitution*, 32 S. ILL. U. L.J. 365 (2008).

[2] *See supra* § 12.02 Damages Based on the Injured Party's Expectations.

[3] Lon L. Fuller & William R. Perdue Jr., *The Reliance Interest in Contract Damages (Pt. 1)*, 46 YALE L.J. 52, 54 (1936) (if you are only going to read one law review article about contract remedies, this is the one to read). *See* Robert Birmingham, *Notes on the Reliance Interest*, 60 WASH. L. REV. 217, 217 (1985).

[4] Andrew Kull, *Disgorgement for Breach, the "Restitution Interest," and the Restatement of Contracts*, 79 TEX. L. REV. 2021, 2029 n.21 (2001). Lon L. Fuller & William R. Perdue Jr., *The Reliance Interest in Contract Damages (Pt. 1)*, 46 YALE L.J. 52, 54 (1936). *See also* Joseph M. Perillo, *Restitution in a Contractual Context and the Restatement (Third) of Restitution & Unjust Enrichment*, 68 WASH & LEE. L. REV. 1007 (2011)

[5] RESTATEMENT (SECOND) OF CONTRACTS § 371 (1981).

[6] *See infra* § 13.05 Restitution as an Alternative Remedy for Breach.

[7] *See infra* § 13.07 Restitution When Contract Is Unenforceable.

[8] *See infra* § 13.06 Restitution for the Breaching Party.

[9] *See, e.g.,* Cotnam v. Wisdom, 104 S.W. 164 (Ark. 1907) (unconscious emergency room patient responsible for value of treatment provided). *See infra* § 13.08 Restitution Where No Contact Exists: Quasi-Contract.

[10] *See* RESTATEMENT OF RESTITUTION (1937); GEORGE E. PALMER, LAW OF RESTITUTION (1978).

[11] Andrew Kull, *Restitution as a Remedy for Breach of Contract*, 67 S. CAL. L. REV. 1465 (1995); Douglas Laycock, *The Scope and Significance of Restitution*, 67 TEX. L. REV. 1277 (1989).

[12] *E.g., In re* MBA, 51 B.R. 966, 974 (Bankr. E.D. Va. 1985).

which means "as much as [the claimant] deserves."[13] At early common law this was a subspecies of general assumpsit, used to recover for work or labor done by a person with the expectation of payment.[14]

In many cases, the facts make it difficult to distinguish reliance from restitution. There is frequently a strong correlation between the plaintiff's out-of-pocket expenses and the benefit received by the defendant. Where the injured party's out of pocket expenses have all been incurred in providing a benefit to the party in breach, reliance and restitution may be the same.[15] Thus, if a buyer of land makes a $10,000 down payment, and the seller refuses to perform, the injured buyer's out-of-pocket $10,000 expense is the same amount as the $10,000 benefit the seller received. The difference between reliance and restitution may be hard to discern because courts sometimes use the cost to one party of conferring a benefit on the other as a means of measuring the value of the benefit received by the other.[16]

§ 13.02   DAMAGES BASED ON THE RELIANCE INTEREST[17]

Where expectation damages are not fully recoverable, damages based on the injured party's reliance interest are a useful alternative. Unlike expectation damages, reliance expenses are nearly always easy to calculate.[18] Much of the time, the injured parties need only produce the cancelled checks or receipts for their expenditures.[19]

---

[13] *See* Maglica v. Maglica, 66 Cal. App. 4th 442 (1998).

[14] Doug Rendelman, *Quantum Meruit for the Subcontractor: Has Restitution Jumped off Dawson's Dock?*, 79 Tex. L. Rev. 2055 (2001); F.B. Ames, *The History of Assumpsit*, 2 Harv. L. Rev. 1 (1888); Restatement (Second) of Contracts § 4 cmt. b (1981); John W. Wade, *Restitution for Benefits Conferred Without Request*, 19 Vand. L. Rev. 1183 (1966).

[15] *See, e.g.*, Farash v. Sykes Datatronics, Inc., 452 N.E.2d 1245 (N.Y. 1983).

[16] *See* W. H. Fuller Co. v. Seater, 595 N.W.2d 96, 99–100 (Wis. Ct. App. 1999).

[17] David W. Barbes, *"W(h)ither the Reliance Interest?" Remedies for Imperfect Transactions in Contracts and Torts*, 38 San Diego L. Rev. 193 (2001); Lon L. Fuller & William R. Perdue Jr., *The Reliance Interest in Contract Damages (Pt. I)*, 46 Yale L.J. 52 (1936); Michael T. Gibson, *Reliance Damages in the Law of Sales Under Article 2 of the Uniform Commercial Code*, 29 Ariz. St. L.J. 909 (1997); Robert E. Hudec, *Restating the "Reliance Interest,"* 67 Cornell. L. Rev. 704 (1982); Charles L. Knapp, *Reliance in the Revised Restatement: The Proliferation of Promissory Estoppel*, 81 Colum. L. Rev. 52 (1981); Stewart Macaulay, *The Reliance Interest and the World Outside the Law Schools' Doors*, 1991 Wis. L. Rev. 247; W. David Slawson, *The Role of Reliance in Contract Damages*, 76 Cornell L. Rev. 131 (1990); Comment, *Once More into the Breach: Promissory Estoppel and Traditional Damages Doctrine*, 37 U. Chi. L. Rev. 559, 566 (1970).

[18] *See* Mary E. Becker, *Promissory Estoppel Damages*, 16 Hofstra L. Rev. 131 (1987); Kevin M. Teeven, *The Advent of Recovery on Market Transactions in the Absence of a Bargain*, 39 Am. Bus. L. J. 289 (2002).

[19] All of us used to receive our cancelled checks back from our bank. Today, these are rarely available. Instead, the bank may only be able to supply an "image" of the cancelled check — the original is usually destroyed — sometimes by the bank in which it was initially deposited.

[A]   Circumstances Favoring Reliance Damages

Reliance is used as an alternative to expectation damages in several situations. First, it is commonly used when calculating the value of injured party's lost expectation is difficult, such as where the fact or amount of its lost profits is speculative. Reliance is also sometimes used when the promise is not part of an exchange, but is enforceable only because of the injured party's reliance on the promise — under the doctrine of promissory estoppel. Reliance might also be used where there is some public policy against full enforcement of the promise, even though it might be part of a traditional bargain.

[1]   Expectation Damages Speculative or Uncertain

Damages based on the injured party's reliance interest are most often sought where a full recovery, based on the party's lost expectations, is speculative or otherwise difficult to prove. Lost profits are sometimes particularly difficult to prove.

In *Chicago Coliseum Club v. Dempsey*,[20] the defendant backed out of his agreement to participate in a boxing match for the world heavyweight title. The court was unwilling to award any lost revenue to the plaintiff for amounts it would have earned from promoting the fight because these sums were too speculative. No one could tell how many tickets would have been sold for the fight or how much it would have cost to put on the show. Instead, the court limited the plaintiff's recovery to the expenses it had incurred in reliance on the contract between the time the contract was made and before the defendant repudiated his obligations.[21]

In other circumstances, the injured party may be reluctant to seek recovery based on its lost expectations. The injured party may fear that, having entered into a losing contract, recovery based on the value of the injured party's lost expectations would place it in the unfortunate position of being saddled with the financial loss that it would have suffered if the contract had been fully performed.[22] As Judge Learned Hand said in *Albert & Son v. Armstrong Rubber Co.*:

> It is often very hard to learn what the value of the performance would have been; and it is a common expedient, and a just one, in such situations to put the peril of the answer upon that party who by his wrong has made the issue relevant to the rights of the other. On principle therefore the proper solution would seem to be that the promisee may recover his outlay in preparation for the performance, subject to the privilege of the promisor to reduce it by as much as he can show that the promisee would have lost if the contract had been performed.[23]

---

[20] 1932 Ill. App. LEXIS 805 (Mar. 1932). *See also* Security Store & Mfg. Co. v. Am. Ry. Exp., 51 S.W.2d 572 (Mo. Ct. App. 1932). *See supra* § 12.06 Limits on Damages: Reasonable Certainty.

[21] *See also* Hollywood Fantasy Corp. v. Gabor, 151 F.3d 203, 214–16 (5th Cir. 1998); Wartzman v. Hightower Prods., Ltd., 456 A.2d 82 (Md. Ct. App. 1983).

[22] *See, e.g.*, Mistletoe Express Serv. v. Locke, 762 S.W.2d 637 (Tex. Ct. App. 1988); RESTATEMENT (SECOND) OF CONTRACTS § 349 cmt. a (1981).

[23] Albert & Son v. Armstrong Rubber Co., 178 F.2d 182, 189 (2d Cir. 1949). *See also* Wartzman v.

In other words, the plaintiff can recover its reliance expenses; if the plaintiff would have spent more than he would have earned from performance, it is up to the defendant, whose breach caused the problem in the first place, to prove it.[24]

For example, if Rhonda's Roofing has agreed to install a new roof on Patrick's house for a price of $3,000, and spent $1,800 in completing the first half of the project, before Patrick repudiates, Rhonda may prefer to recover the $1,800 she has already spent rather than attempt to recover using the normal expectation formula of contract price minus expenses saved.[25] Recovery in expectation would yield Rhonda only $1,200. If finishing the job would have cost Rhonda another $1,800, the normal expectation formula (contract price minus expenses saved), would have saddled her with the $600 loss she would have suffered had the contract been fully performed. By switching to a recovery based on reliance, Rhonda may be able to avoid this anticipated loss. If there are difficulties in proving the amount it would have cost to finish the project, the burden of proving that amount is on the defendant.

[2]   Promises Enforceable Under Promissory Estoppel[26]

In addition, if the promise is not supported by consideration, or is otherwise not part of a traditional bargain, but is enforceable on a theory of promissory estoppel, damages might be limited to the amounts the injured party spent in reliance on the defendant's promise.[27]

As explained in more detail elsewhere, promissory estoppel is used in several different ways.[28] It is sometimes used as nothing more than a substitute for consideration, where the element of an exchange is missing from the transaction. In those cases, the plaintiff may recover damages, just as in any other case involving a breach of contract, as compensation for its lost expectations.

However, promissory estoppel is also sometimes used as a tort-like cause of action, where there is not an enforceable traditional contract. In these situations, damages can be limited to the expenses incurred in reliance on the promise.[29]

Hightower Prods., Ltd., 456 A.2d 82 (Md. Ct. Spec. App. 1983).

[24] RESTATEMENT (SECOND) OF CONTRACTS § 349 (1981).

[25] *See supra* § 12.08[E] Construction Contracts: Breach by the Customer.

[26] Benjamin F. Boyer, *Promisorry Estoppel: Requirements and Limitations of the Doctrine*, 98 U. PA. L REV. 459, 497 (1950); Lucian Arye Bebchuck & Omri Ben-Sharar, *Precontractual Reliance*, 30 J. LEGAL STUD. 423 (2001); Mary E. Becker, *Promissory Estoppel Damages*, 16 HOFSTRA L. REV. 131 (1987); E. Allan Farnsworth, *Pre-Contractual Liability and Preliminary Agreements: Fair Dealing and Failed Negotiations*, 87 COLUM. L. REV. 217 (1987); Eric Mills Holmes, *Restatement of Promissory Estoppel*, 32 WILLAMETTE L. REV. 263 (1996); William D. Metzger & David Phillips, *The Emergency of Promissory Estoppel as an Independent Theory of Recovery*, 35 RUTGERS L. REV. 472 (1983); Edward Yorio & Steve Thel, *The Promissory Basis of Section 90*, 101 YALE L.J. 111 (1991).

[27] Walser v. Toyota Motor Sales, U.S.A., Inc., 43 F.3d 396 (8th Cir. 1994); RESTATEMENT (SECOND) OF CONTRACTS § 349 cmt. b (1981).

[28] *See supra* Chapter 3 Promissory Estoppel: Detrimental Reliance.

[29] RESTATEMENT (SECOND) OF CONTRACTS § 90 cmt. d (1981). *See* Hi-Pac, Ltd. v. Avoset Corp., 26 F. Supp. 2d 1230 n.5 (D. Haw. 1997); Hoffman v. Red Owl Stores, Inc. 133 N.W.2d 267 (Wis. 1965); Wheeler

Many promissory estoppel cases award expectation damages without considering whether a different measure of damages should be used.[30] Other decisions limit recovery to the injured party's reliance expenses, as a matter within the discretion of the court.[31] Support for this result may be found in Restatement (Second) § 90, which permits the remedy to be "limited as justice requires."[32]

Decisions limiting damages to reliance expenses may reflect nothing more than the presence of unarticulated reasons for denying recovery of the injured party's lost expectations, such as where they are too difficult to calculate,[33] or where the loss was not foreseeable.[34] Thus, cases limiting damages to reliance expenses should be carefully scrutinized to determine whether expectation damages would have been available, even if the plaintiff had succeeded on the more traditional ground of breach of contract. Such decisions may simply breathe new life into the now discounted rule prohibiting the recovery of lost profits for a new business.[35]

On the other hand, these decisions may represent a more fundamental distinction between traditional breach of contract claims and those resting upon the more modern basis of promissory estoppel. Where the transaction was not a conventional bargain, damages based on the injured party's lost expectations may not be warranted. Or, it may be that the plaintiff's remedy should be more limited, because of a more basic underlying skepticism about claims based solely on promissory estoppel, where the injured party's expectations are more inchoate. This may be particularly true in cases like *Hoffman v. Red Owl*[36] and *Walster v. Toyota Motor Sales, U.S.A., Inc.*,[37] where liability was found even though the parties stopped short of entering into the final formal contract to which their negotiations were leading.

Some support for this approach can be found in cases that use promissory estoppel to navigate around the statute of frauds, while at the same time limiting the plaintiff's recovery to its reliance expenses or the value of the benefit conferred on the breaching party as a result of those expenses.[38] The use of promissory

---

v. White, 398 S.W.2d 93 (Tex. 1965); Goodman v. Dicker, 169 F.2d 684 (D.C. Cir. 1948); Charles L. Knapp, *Reliance in the Revised Restatement: The Proliferation of Promissory Estoppel*, 81 COLUM. L. REV. 52 (1981).

[30] Mary E. Becker, *Promissory Estoppel Damages*, 16 HOFSTRA L. REV. 131 (1987); David V. Snyder, *Comparative Law in Action: Promissory Estoppel, the Civil Law, and the Mixed Jurisdiction*, 15 ARIZ. J. INT'L & COMP. L. 695, 700 (1998); Edward Yorio & Steve Thel, *The Promissory Basis of Section 90*, 101 YALE L.J. 111 (1991).

[31] Walser v. Toyota Motor Sales, U.S.A., Inc., 43 F.3d 396 (8th Cir. 1994); Cyberchron Corp. v. Calldata Sys. Dev., Inc., 47 F.3d 39 (2d Cir. 1995).

[32] RESTATEMENT (SECOND) § 90 (1981).

[33] *See, e.g.*, Copeland v. Baskin-Robbins U.S.A., 96 Cal. App. 4th 1251, 1262–63 (2002).

[34] Mary E. Becker, *Promissory Estoppel Damages*, 16 HOFSTRA L. REV. 131 (1987).

[35] *See, e.g.*, Walser v. Toyota Motor Sales, U.S.A., Inc., 43 F.3d 396 (8th Cir. 1994). *See supra* § 12.06 Limits on Damages: Reasonable Certainty.

[36] 133 N.W.2d 267 (Wis. 1965).

[37] 43 F.3d 396 (8th Cir. 1994).

[38] *E.g.*, Montanaro Bros. Builders, Inc. v. Snow, 460 A.2d 1297 (Conn. 1983); Chevalier v. Lane's, Inc., 213 S.W.2d 530 (Tex. 1948). *See* Robert A. Brazener, Annotation, *Promissory Estoppel as a Basis for*

estoppel as an exception to the statute of frauds remains somewhat controversial.[39] Concern for its misuse might be mitigated by limiting the remedy to reliance or restitution.

Early commentators, in rejecting any such distinction, took the highly formalistic view that if a promise was binding, it should be enforced in the same manner, regardless of the basis for it being enforceable.[40] More recently, scholars have justified awarding full expectation damages as the best way of ensuring the injured party's recovery of all of its reliance expenses, including intangibles such as lost opportunities.[41] A few cases have permitted such recoveries, explaining that the extent of damages is within the equitable discretion of the court.[42]

[3]   Public Policy to Limit Damages

In other circumstances, there may be a public policy that limits the availability of damages based on the injured party's expectations, but where some limited degree of enforceability is still desired. A good example is provided by *Sullivan v. O'Connor*.[43] There, the court limited the liability of a plastic surgeon for breach of a promise to achieve a particular result for a patient, out of a fear that doctors would otherwise be reluctant to provide reassuring and therapeutic statements to their patients.[44]

The now outdated rule of *Flureau v. Thornhill*,[45] which limited a buyer's damages to its reliance expenses, when a seller of land was unable to deliver good title due to a previously unknown flaw in the seller's chain of title, provides a similar example. The concern in *Flureau*, and in American cases that followed it,[46] was that exposure to liability for expectation damages would discourage real estate deals, particularly before modern recording statutes were developed, when there was no adequate system for keeping track of interests in land. With too much at stake, and no way to guard against the risk of latent defects in the seller's chain of title, parties would be discouraged from entering into what otherwise might be

---

Avoidance of Statute of Frauds, 56 A.L.R.3d 1037 (1974); Phuong N. Pham, Note, *The Waning of Promissory Estoppel*, 79 CORNELL L. REV. 1263 (1994).

[39] *See, e.g.*, Olympic Holding Co. v. Ace Ltd., 909 N.E.2d 93, 101–05 (Ohio 2009); Stearns v. Emery-Waterhouse Co., 596 A.2d 72 (Me. 1991); David G. Epstein, Ryan D. Starbird & Joshua C. Vincent, *Reliance on Oral Promises: Statute of Frauds and "Promissory Estoppel,"* 42 TEX. TECH. L. REV. 913, 935 (2010).

[40] Samuel Williston, 4 A.L.I. Proc. 103–04 (Appendix) (1926), *reprinted in* PETER LINZER, A CONTRACTS ANTHOLOGY 339–49 (2d ed. 1995).

[41] *See* Melvin A. Eisenberg, *Donative Promises*, 47 U. CHI. L. REV. 1, 29 (1979); Comment, *Once More into the Breach: Promissory Estoppel and Traditional Damages Doctrine*, 37 U. CHI. L. REV. 559, 566 (1970).

[42] *See also* Walters v. Marathon Oil Co., 642 F.2d 1098 (7th Cir. 1981).

[43] 296 N.E.2d 183 (Mass. 1973).

[44] *Cf.* Shaheen v. Knight, 11 Pa. D & C. 2d 41 (Lycoming Cty Pa. Ct. Common Pleas 1957) (no expectation recovery for breach of contract to perform a successful sterilization procedure).

[45] 96 Eng. Rep. 635 (K.B. 1776).

[46] *E.g.*, Beard v. S/E Joint Venture, 581 A.2d 1275 (Md. 1990).

wealth-maximizing transactions.[47]

In some situations, the prospect of a full expectation recovery might discourage otherwise desirable transactions between members of society.[48] Damages might still be awarded in these cases, based on expenses the injured party incurs in reliance on the contract.

[B]   Types of Reliance Damages: Essential and Incidental Reliance[49]

Although courts rarely do so,[50] it is sometimes useful to distinguish between essential reliance expenses and incidental reliance expenses.[51] The distinction was first brought to light in the groundbreaking article by Professor Lon Fuller and his student, William Perdue, on reliance damages.[52] Essential reliance expenses are those that the injured party incurs in either preparing to perform the contract, or in actual performance of the contract.[53] They are essential in the sense that the injured party must incur them in order to perform his or her own contractual duties. Incidental reliance expenses, on the other hand, are those incurred in pursuit of collateral transactions, usually with other people.[54] The distinction is particularly useful in connection with whether the plaintiff must prove that the expenses were foreseeable by the defendant at the time the contract was made.[55]

The facts of *Security Store & Manufacturing Co. v. American Railway Express Co.*[56] are frequently used to illustrate the distinction between essential and incidental reliance expenses. There, the defendant failed to deliver all of the parts of a new type of furnace from the plaintiff's headquarters in Kansas City, Missouri, to Atlantic City, New Jersey, where the plaintiff had planned to display the new furnace at a trade show. The plaintiff did not claim any lost profits, which would

---

[47] DANIEL B. DOBBS, LAW OF REMEDIES § 12.11(1)at 822–25 (2d ed. 1993).

[48] *See* U.C.C. § 4A-305 & cmt. 2 (2012) (electronic funds transfers).

[49] Lon L. Fuller & William R. Perdue Jr., *The Reliance Interest in Contract Damages*, 46 YALE L.J. 52, 77–79 (Pt. 1) (1936); Robert E. Hudec, *Restating the "Reliance Interest,"* 67 CORNELL L. REV. 704, 724–26 (1982); Stewart Macaulay, *The Reliance Interest and the World Outside the Law Schools' Doors*, 1991 WIS. L. REV. 247, 268.

[50] The distinction is used far more frequently by the United States Court of Claims, than by courts applying state law. *E.g.*, Am. Capital Corp. v. United States, 2005 U.S. Claims LEXIS 16 (Fed. Cl. Jan. 19, 2005).

[51] RESTATEMENT (SECOND) OF CONTRACTS § 349 cmt. a (1981). *See generally* Christopher W. Frost, *Reconsidering the Reliance Interest*, 44 ST. LOUIS U. L.J. 1361, 1365 n.27 (2000);

[52] Lon L. Fuller & William R. Perdue, *The Reliance Interest in Contract Damages (Pt. 1)*, 46 YALE L.J. 52, 78 (1936) (if you read only one of the articles cited in this book, this is the one to read — even though it is old). *See also* Stewart Macaulay, *The Reliance Interest and the World Outside the Law Schools' Doors*, 1991 WIS. L. REV. 247, 268. *But see* Robert E. Hudec, *Restating the "Reliance Interest,"* 67 CORNELL L. REV. 704, 724–26 (1982) (questioning this terminology).

[53] RESTATEMENT (SECOND) OF CONTRACTS § 349 cmt. a (1981).

[54] *Id.* They are sometimes called "collateral" reliance expenses. *E.g.*, Am. Capital Corp. v. United States, 63 Fed. Cl. 637 (2005).

[55] *See* Robert Hudec, *Restating the "Reliance Interest,"* 67 CORNELL L. REV. at 724–725 (1982).

[56] 51 S.W.2d 572 (Mo. Ct. App. 1932).

have been extraordinarily difficult to prove with any reasonable certainty — particularly since it was a prototype of a new product. Instead, the plaintiff sought only to recover the expenses it incurred in reliance on the contract, to restore it to the status quo that existed before the contract was made. The first of these expenses was the $147 the plaintiff paid to the defendant to transport the furnace to the location of the trade show. The plaintiff made a contract for the carriage of the furnace and thus had a contractual duty to pay for the defendant's services. This amount was thus recoverable as an essential reliance expense.

The plaintiff intended to transport the furnace exhibit to Atlantic City to display it at a trade show, with the anticipation of making sales that would result in profits. In reliance on the defendant's promise to deliver the exhibit to Atlantic City in time for the show, the defendant incurred other expenses. These included the price of a booth at the trade show, round-trip travel and lodging expenses of the employees who would set up and demonstrate the furnace, and the cost of returning the exhibit back to the plaintiff's Kansas City headquarters. All of these expenses, together with the wages of the two employees during the show, were incidental reliance expenses. They were all incurred by the plaintiff in reliance on the contract and in pursuit of the opportunity to display the new furnace at the Atlantic City show and make sales to prospective customers. Because of the defendant's breach, all of these expenses were wasted. Because they were foreseeable by the defendant at the time the contract was made, they were recoverable, even though they were merely incidental, and were not required to have been incurred as a part of the injured party's contractual obligations to the defendant.

The essential reliance expenses were inherently foreseeable by the breaching party at the time the contract was made. The defendant could not have failed to know that the plaintiff would pay the price the defendant charged as the carriage fee for hauling the furnace to Atlantic City. However, the other expenses, which were incurred only because of the plaintiff's plan to display the furnace at the trade show, were not *inherently* foreseeable by the defendant. Therefore, under the foreseeability rule of *Hadley v. Baxendale*, the defendant should be liable for them only if it had some other reason to know that they would be incurred. The plaintiff must prove that the breaching party had information that gave it reason to know of the likelihood that these expenses would be incurred. Thus, the difference between essential reliance expenses and incidental reliance expenses helps in determining which expenses the breaching party must prove were foreseeable by the breaching party. Essential reliance expenses — those that must be incurred — are inherently foreseeable, and thus are recoverable without separate proof on the question of foreseeability. Incidental reliance expenses, on the other hand — which might be incurred in some transactions, but not in others — require independent proof that the breaching party had reason to know that they were at stake. In this respect, the difference between essential and incidental reliance expenses is similar to the difference between general and special expectation damages, in the context of foreseeability analysis under *Hadley v. Baxendale* and its progeny.

Finally, "incidental reliance expenses" should not be confused with "incidental damages" of the type recoverable under U.C.C. §§ 2-710 and 2-715(1).[57] These two types of damages share a name but represent completely different concepts. Incidental damages are almost always expenses incurred in mitigation of the harm the injured party would otherwise incur. Expenses incurred after the injured party learns of the defendant's breach or repudiation are not "in reliance" on the contract. Thus, they are not recoverable as incidental reliance expenses, though they may be recoverable as reasonable mitigation expenses.

[C]   Lost Opportunity for Profit as Reliance Expense

Entering into one contract frequently involves giving up the opportunity to enter into another one. For example, a real estate investor who decides to enter into a contract to purchase an apartment building might pass up the opportunity to purchase another building somewhere else. If the first deal falls through, the opportunity to buy the second building may have already been snapped up by another investor. Thus, by entering into the first contract, the investor lost the opportunity to make a profit from buying the other building.

The value of this lost opportunity for profit is sometimes recoverable as a reliance expense.[58] The principal difficulty with permitting recovery for such lost opportunities as a reliance expense is that doing so expands reliance to closely resemble expectation damages. Expanding reliance damages to include recovery for the value of lost opportunities blurs the distinction between reliance and expectation.[59]

Further, without careful attention to the difference between gross profit and net profit there is a considerable danger of awarding the plaintiff two recoveries for the same loss. Such a double recovery occurs if the court awards the plaintiff damages for the expenses it incurred in pursuit of a profit combined with the gross revenue that the plaintiff would have earned if the venture had been successful.

A simple example makes this clear. Assume that a promoter enters into a contract with the owner of a 10,000-seat theater for an upcoming concert. After entering into the agreement for use of the theater, and paying the theater owner $20,000, the promoter incurs additional expenses of $50,000 in advertising the show, hiring security guards, and printing tickets and programs. The promoter anticipates paying an additional $150,000 to the performers. If the show sells out, the promoter anticipates earning $250,000 in gross revenue by selling 10,000 tickets at $25 each. Because the promoter has already spent $70,000 and will incur another $150,000 expense if the concert is held, the promoter will receive a net $30,000 profit. If the theater owner reneges and the concert cannot be held, the promoter is entitled to recover damages for breach.

A full expectation recovery would permit the promoter to recover the $70,000 in

---

[57] *See supra* § 12.08[A] Contracts for the Sale of Goods — Breach by the Seller; *supra* § 12.08[B] Contracts for the Sale of Goods — Breach by the Buyer.

[58] Dialist Co. v. Pulford, 399 A.2d 1374, 1382 (Md. Ct. Spec. App. 1979).

[59] Michael B. Kelly, *The Phantom Reliance Interest in Contract Damages*, 1992 Wis. L. Rev. 1755, 1769; Mark Pettit Jr., *Private Advantage and Public Power: Reexamining the Expectation and Reliance Interest in Contract Damages*, 38 Hastings L.J. 417 (1987).

expenses it had incurred plus the $30,000 net profits it would have earned from putting on the show. Alternatively, the promoter could recover the entire gross revenue of $250,000, less the $150,000 expense saved as a result of the breach due to not having to pay the band.[60] Either method permits the promoter to recover a total of $100,000.

A double recovery would result if the promoter sought to recover the gross revenue of $250,000, minus the $150,000 expenses saved, *plus* the $70,000 expenses incurred in preparing for the show. Including sums for reliance expenses incurred in the pursuit of the gross revenue, together with gross revenue that would have been received, provides a windfall to the plaintiff beyond what it would have obtained if the contract had been performed.[61]

The principal advantage of seeking reliance damages is to avoid the uncertainty associated with attempting to recover lost profits. Expanding reliance to include the value of lost opportunities results in losing this advantage. Further, it does so at the risk of being unable to recover expenses incurred before the contract was made, which were not truly incurred "in reliance" on the contract.[62] However, if these hazards are avoided, the value of lost opportunities may be recovered as a type of reliance expense.[63]

§ 13.03 LIMITATIONS ON RELIANCE DAMAGES

Like expectation damages, recoveries based on reliance expenses are subject to several limitations. Some courts prohibit recovery of expenses incurred before the promise was made, even if they were incurred in pursuit of the goal that was the purpose of the promise. Further, as with expectation damages, reliance expenses cannot be recovered if they are beyond what was foreseeable by the breaching party at the time the promise was made. Moreover, the mitigation principle applies with the same force to damages based on reliance as it does to damages based on lost expectations: the injured party may not recover for expenses that could have been avoided or recouped. Likewise, the extent of the reliance expense must be proven with reasonable certainty. Finally, if the aggrieved party would have suffered a net loss, the aggrieved party is unable to use the coincidence of the broken promise to shift this loss to the breaching party.

---

[60] For the moment, ignore the fact that the promoter may also be liable to the performers. For the purposes of this example, assume that the performers were able to earn the same amount at another concert on the same night in a different town.

[61] *See* Eric G. Anderson, *The Reliance Interest and Damages for Breach of Contract*, 53 Md. L. R. 1 (1994); E. Allan Farnsworth, *Legal Remedies for Breach of Contract*, 70 Colum. L. Rev. 1145, 1170–74 (1970).

[62] *See infra* § 13.03[A] Pre-Contract Expenses.

[63] *See* Walters v. Marathon Oil Co., 642 F.2d 1098 (7th Cir. 1981).

[A]   Pre-Contract Expenses[64]

A recurring, and sometimes perplexing issue, in actions to recover reliance expense, concerns the recoverability of expenses incurred by the injured party before the contract was made.[65] For example, in *Chicago Coliseum Club v. Dempsey*,[66] the plaintiff made some initial investments in pursuit of a proposed prize fight between contender Harry Wills and world heavyweight champion Jack Dempsey, before obtaining Dempsey's agreement to participate in the fight. The Chicago Coliseum Club anticipated that ticket sales and radio broadcast rights for the fight would have generated enough revenue to cover these pre-contract expenses as well as those that had not been incurred until after Dempsey signed. Nevertheless, the court denied recovery for these pre-contract expenses because they had not been incurred *in reliance* on Dempsey's promise to fight. Instead, it said that "the plaintiff speculated as to the result of his efforts to procure the [contract with Dempsey]."[67]

The result in *Dempsey* is frequently contrasted with the outcome in the English case, *Anglia Television Ltd v. Reed.*[68] When Reed backed out of an agreement to appear in a television movie, and the production company was unable to find a substitute, Anglia Television successfully recovered the expenses it incurred before entering into the contract with Reed in addition to those incurred thereafter. The court reasoned that the pre-contract expenses had been foreseeable to Reed at the time the contract was made and were thus recoverable even though they had not been incurred in reliance on his promise.[69]

An award of all of the plaintiff's expenses poses the risk that the plaintiff will receive a windfall. The production might not have earned enough money to cover all of the plaintiff's expenses. In other words, it might have resulted in a financial loss. However, the defendant will have the opportunity to prove that this would have been the result. If the defendant is successful, it can limit the plaintiff's ability

---

[64] Lucian Arye Bebchuk & Omri Ben-Shahar, *Precontractual Reliance*, 30 J. Legal Stud. 423, 457 (2001); Gregory S. Crespi, *Recovering Pre-Contractual Expenditures as an Element of Reliance Damages*, 49 SMU L. Rev. 43 (1995); Ofer Grosskopf & Barak Medina, *Regulating Contract Formation: Precontractual Reliance, Sunk Costs, and Market Structure*, 39 Conn. L. Rev. 1977 (2007); Robert E. Scott, Hoffman v. Red Owl Stores *and the Myth of Precontractual Reliance*, 68 Ohio St. L.J. 71 (2007).

[65] *See* Mitchell L. Engler and Susan B. Heyman, *The Missing Elements of Contract Damages*, 84 Temp. L. Rev. 119 (2011); Gregory S. Crespi, *Recovering Pre-Contractual Expenditures as an Element of Reliance Damages*, 49 SMU L. Rev. 43 (1995).

[66] 1932 Ill. App. LEXIS 805 (Mar. 1932).

[67] *Id.* at *3–*5. *See also* Drysdale v. Woerth, 153 F. Supp. 2d 678 (E.D. Pa. 2001); Skanchy v. Calcados Ortope SA, 952 P.2d 1071 (Utah Ct. App. 1998).

[68] 3 All. E.R. 690 (Ct. App. Civ. Div. 1971). The defendant, American actor Robert Reed, later played the role of the father, Mike Brady, on the early 1970s television sitcom "The Brady Bunch." As a young actor he played a New York City criminal defense lawyer in the TV drama "The Defenders," co-starring E.G. Marshall. Reed died in 1992.

[69] *See also* Security Store & Mfg Co. v. Am. Ry. Express Co., 51 S.W.2d 572 (Mo. Ct. App. 1932) (permitting recovery of pre-contract expenses against a common carrier, who, because of its common law duty to agree to the proposed contract for carriage of the goods, could not have refused to enter into the contract).

to recover for all of its expenses.[70] Awarding the plaintiff all of its expenses, regardless of whether they were incurred before or after the contract was made, effectively creates a rebuttable presumption that the venture would have resulted in a profit.[71]

[B]   Foreseeability of Reliance Expenses

Like all contract damages, reliance expenses are not recoverable unless the breaching party had reason to know that the loss would occur as a consequence of a breach. Thus, seeking to recover reliance damages, instead of those based on the injured party's expectations, will not insulate the injured party from the requirement that damages must be foreseeable in order to be recovered.[72]

The distinction between essential and incidental reliance expenses[73] is particularly useful in connection with analyzing the foreseeability of reliance damages. Because essential reliance expenses are those the injured party was obligated to incur in order to perform, they are inherently foreseeable.[74] The breaching party always has reason to know that the other party will incur the expenses it must in order to perform.[75]

Incidental reliance expenses, on the other hand, are those beyond what is required for performance. They are incurred in connection with collateral transactions. For example, a wholesaler expecting to receive goods from the manufacturer might incur expenses in an effort to market the goods to its customers. Likewise, a manufacturer might alter its factory to prepare for the delivery of new equipment. Or, as in *Chicago Coliseum Club v. Dempsey*, the promoter of an event is likely to incur expenses designed to enhance the quality of the anticipated performance.

The breaching party may or may not have reason to know of these collateral transactions. Thus, foreseeability of these incidental reliance expenses should not be presumed. Instead, the injured party must show that the breaching party had reason to know that these expenses would be incurred, even if the precise amount of the expense could not have been fully contemplated.

---

[70] *E.g.*, Mistletoe Express Service v. Locke, 762 S.W.2d 637 (Tex. App. 1988); L. Albert & Son v. Armstrong Rubber Co., 178 F.2d 182 (2d Cir. 1949) ("the proper solution would seem to be that the promisee may recover his outlay in preparation for the performance, subject to the privilege of the promisor to reduce it by as much as he can show that the promisee would have lost, if the contract had been performed.")

[71] Melvin Aron Eisenberg, *Probability and Chance in Contract Law*, 45 UCLA L. REV. 1005, 1058 (1998); Gregory S. Crespi, *Recovering Pre-Contractual Expenditures as an Element of Reliance Damages*, 49 SMU L. REV. 43 (1995); D. W. McLauchlan, *Damages for Pre-Contract Expenditure*, 11 N.Z.U. L.R. 346, 351–54 (1985).

[72] *See* W. David Slawson, *The Role of Reliance in Contract Damages*, 76 CORNELL L. REV. 197, 220 (1990).

[73] *See supra* § 13.02[B] Types of Reliance Damages: Essential and Incidental Reliance.

[74] Albert & Son v. Armstrong Rubber Co., 178 F.2d 182, 189–90 (2d Cir. 1949).

[75] Robert E. Hudec, *Restating the "Reliance Interest,"* 67 CORNELL L. REV. 704, 724 (1982) (referring to "direct" and "consequential" reliance expenses).

In many cases, proof of the foreseeability of incidental reliance expenses should be easy. If the breaching party has entered into similar transactions in the past, it is likely to be familiar with the plans that its contracting partners usually make in anticipation of performance. In some cases, the breaching party may have participated in implementing those plans. The mere fact that foreseeability must be proven does not mean the injured party's expenses may not be recovered.

[C] Mitigation of Reliance Expenses

The mitigation doctrine, which prevents an aggrieved party from recovering for losses it could have reasonably avoided, applies with equal force to actions to recover reliance expenses. Reliance expenses are recoverable by the plaintiff only if they were wasted and if the loss could not have been avoided. If loss or waste of the expense can be avoided, either by diverting the investment to some other activity or by selling any items purchased for their salvage value, the plaintiff should not be permitted to recover the expense as part of its reliance damages.

Likewise, the injured party may not usually recover for expenses it incurred after it learned of the defendant's repudiation of its promise.[76] These expenses cannot be said to have been incurred "in reliance" on the contract, though they may be separately recoverable as reasonable mitigation expenses.[77]

[D] Reasonable Certainty

As with expectation damages, reliance expenses are recoverable only if they can be proven with reasonable certainty. In most cases, proof of the plaintiff's reliance expenses will be easy. The injured party simply needs to produce its canceled checks and receipts and demonstrate that its expenses were incurred in reliance on the contract. Recall, in this regard, that actions to recover reliance expenses are often pursued precisely because of the relative ease of proving the amount of the plaintiff's expenses, rather than trying to prove the amount of any lost profits.[78]

Despite this, some types of reliance expenses may be difficult to prove. One example of this, discussed above, is opportunity costs for the value of opportunities passed up by the plaintiff in reliance on the defendant's promise.[79] Although these are sometimes recoverable, the difficulty of proving these and other highly intangible forms of reliance justifies the general rule awarding contract damages on the injured party's lost expectations.[80]

---

[76] Chicago Coliseum Club v. Dempsey, 1932 Ill. App. LEXIS 805 (Mar. 1932).

[77] Kenford Co., Inc. v. Erie County, 108 A.D.2d 132 (N.Y. App. Div. 1985).

[78] See supra § 12.06 Limits on Damages: Reasonable Certainty.

[79] See supra § 13.02[C] Lost Opportunity for Profit as Reliance Expense.

[80] W. David Slawson, *The Role of Reliance in Contract Damages*, 76 CORNELL L. REV. 197, 219–20 (1990).

[E]   Loss Contracts — Expectation as Limit on Reliance Damages

As discussed earlier, the breaching party should be afforded the opportunity to prove that the value of the injured party's expectation was less than its reliance expense.[81] This would limit the injured party's recovery.[82] If performance of the contract would have resulted in a loss, the defendant's breach should not result in rescuing the plaintiff from the loss he or she would have received had the contract been performed.

Consider an agreement by Winkler Construction to build a garden shed for Julie for $1,500. If Julie repudiates the contract after Winkler has spent $1,200 and finished two-thirds of the work necessary to finish the shed, with $600 remaining to be spent to finish it, Winkler should not be able to recover all of its reliance expenses. If the contract had been performed, Winkler would have received only $1,500, after spending $1,800, resulting in a $300 loss. Permitting Winkler to recover the entire $1,200 reliance expense would allow it to avoid this anticipated loss for no good reason. Julie's breach should not result in her being saddled with the loss Winkler had agreed to bear.

In other cases, the amount the injured party would have earned as a result of performance is not so clear. In cases like *Chicago Coliseum Club v. Dempsey*,[83] the amount of revenue the Coliseum Club would have earned from a fight between Dempsey and Wills was speculative. It may have turned out that the expenses incurred in promoting the fight would have outstripped the money that would have been earned from ticket sales and other revenue sources. In such a case the plaintiff is likely to seek recovery of its reliance expenses because of the difficulty of proving the amount of profit that would have resulted from performance. Recovery will usually be permitted.[84] However, the defendant is permitted to attempt to prove that the plaintiff would have suffered a loss on the deal and limit the plaintiff's recovery, just as in the case of the contractor who charged too small a price for the garden shed.

However, it will be just as difficult for the defendant to prove how much the injured party would have earned from performance, as it would have been for the plaintiff to prove its lost profits — and maybe more so. Permitting the defendant to limit the plaintiff's ability to recover its reliance expenses shifts the burden of proving the amount that would have been earned from the fight to the defendant. If the defendant can meet that burden, and prove that the plaintiff would have suffered a loss, then the loss should be borne by the plaintiff.[85]

---

[81] RESTATEMENT (SECOND) OF CONTRACTS § 349 (1981).

[82] *See supra* § 13.03[A] Pre-Contract Expenses.

[83] 1932 Ill. App. LEXIS 805 (Mar. 1932).

[84] *See* Michael B. Kelly, *The Phantom Reliance Interest in Contract Damages*, 1992 WIS. L. REV. 1755, 1802; Christopher T. Wonnell, *Expectation, Reliance, and the Two Contractual Wrongs*, 38 SAN DIEGO L. REV. 53 (2001).

[85] *E.g.*, Doering Equip. Co. v. John Deere Co., 815 N.E.2d 234 (Mass. Ct. App. 2004).

§ 13.04 RESTITUTION — PREVENTING UNJUST ENRICHMENT[86]

Instead of seeking recovery for its lost expectations, an injured party will sometimes be satisfied with rescission of the contract and the return of whatever benefits he or she has conferred on the breaching party. Rescission and restitution are usually available as alternative remedies for breach of contract. In other situations, recovery of a plaintiff's lost expectations may be unavailable because the contract is unenforceable, and restitution of benefits the parties have conferred on one another is the only available grounds for relief. Or, the breaching party may seek recovery of whatever benefits it has conferred prior to its own breach. Finally, one of the parties may have conferred a benefit on the other under some other circumstances where it would be unjust to permit the recipient to retain the benefit without compensation. In all of these situations, recovery is available in restitution, to prevent one of the parties from being unjustly enriched at the expense of the other.

Because the purpose of restitution is to prevent unjust enrichment, the measure of restitution is usually the value of the benefit in the hands of the defendant. If the benefit was in the form of a cash payment, return of an equivalent amount, with any necessary adjustment for the time value of the money, is the appropriate remedy.[87] In cases involving the delivery of specific property, specific restitution, or return of the property transferred, may be available.[88] However, some circumstances do not lend themselves to specific restitution. These situations include those where a benefit was conferred by providing services; where the property transferred has changed in some material way; or where the rights of third parties, such as a good-faith purchaser for value would be impaired if specific restitution were awarded.[89]

In these cases the value of the benefit conferred can be measured in one of several ways. First, it might be measured by the amount it would have cost the defendant to acquire the benefit from someone else.[90] Thus, if the benefit involved is the installation of a new roof on the defendant's home, the value of the benefit could be measured by the price the defendant would have had to have paid to obtain the new roof from someone other than the plaintiff. Courts sometimes used the price normally charged by the plaintiff for conferring the benefit, as an alternative means of establishing the value of the benefit conferred. To the extent that the contract price is admissible proof of the value of the benefit conferred, a restitution

---

[86] Eric G. Anderson, *The Restoration Interest and Damages for Breach of Contract*, 53 Md. L. Rev. 1, 106 (1994); Mark P. Gergen, *Restitution as a Bridge over Troubled Contractual Waters*, 71 Fordham L. Rev. 709 (2002); Saul Levmore, *Explaining Restitution*, 71 Va. L. Rev. 65 (1985); George E. Palmer, Law of Restitution (1978); Joseph M. Perillo, *Restitution in the Second Restatement of Contracts*, 81 Colum. L. Rev. 37 (1981); Chaim Saiman, *Restating Restitution: A Case of Contemporary Common Law Conceptualism*, 52 Vill. L. Rev. 487 (2007).

[87] *E.g.*, CBS, Inc. v. Merrick, 716 F.2d 1292, 1296 (9th Cir. 1983).

[88] Restatement (Second) of Contracts § 372 (1981).

[89] *See* Restatement (Second) of Contracts § 372 cmt. b (1981).

[90] Restatement (Second) of Contracts § 371(a) (1981).

remedy may bear a strong resemblance to enforcement of the contract through an award of expectation damages.[91]

Alternatively, the court might use the increase in the value of the defendant's property as a method of establishing the value of the benefit conferred.[92] Thus, in the example of the new roof, the court might award the plaintiff the difference between the house as it was before the roof was installed and its value with the new roof. In normal circumstances, the first alternative will be less.[93] Sometimes, perhaps confusing reliance with restitution, courts use the cost to the plaintiff of conferring the benefit as a measure of the value of the benefit in the hands of the defendant.[94] When this happens, it looks a great deal like reliance rather than restitution.[95] Nevertheless, as a means of calculating the value of the benefit conferred, it has the advantage of being easy to prove.

Other courts have drawn a sharp distinction between reliance and restitution, and denied recovery for reliance expenses that did not result in the defendant receiving a benefit. For example, in *Santoro v. Mack*,[96] the plaintiff's oral agreement to purchase land from the defendant was unenforceable under the statute of frauds. The plaintiff nevertheless sought to recover for the fees he had paid to an architect to prepare a set of plans for a building to be constructed on the land. However, because these plans conferred no benefit on the defendant, recovery in restitution was denied.[97]

Even more difficult, with respect to the use of reliance expenses as means of measuring restitution, are cases in which one of the parties has incurred an expense before some unanticipated event discharged the parties' duties because performance became impossible.[98] Most cases permit recovery only to the extent of the conferred on the other party.

For example, in *Carroll v. Bowersock*,[99] a contractor sued to recover for his part performance of a contract to replace the floor in the defendant's warehouse with a new floor of reinforced concrete. After the plaintiff began work, the building burned to the ground. Destruction of the building discharged the parties from their duties under the contract. The contractor was permitted to recover for all of the work it completed before the fire. However, this recovery did not include amounts for the cost of labor or materials in constructing wooden "forms" that were to have been used in pouring the new concrete floors.

---

[91] *E.g.*, Pinches v. Swedish Evangelical Lutheran Church, 10 A. 264 (Conn. 1887).

[92] RESTATEMENT (SECOND) OF CONTRACTS § 371(b) (1981).

[93] RESTATEMENT (SECOND) OF CONTRACTS § 371 cmt. b (1981).

[94] Farash v. Sykes Datatronics, Inc., 452 N.E.2d 1245 (N.Y. 1983).

[95] *See* Aaron R. Petty, *The Reliance Interest in Restitution*, 32 S. ILL. U. L.J. 365 (2008).

[96] 145 A. 273 (Conn. 1929).

[97] *See also* Boone v. Coe, 154 S.W. 900 (Ky. Ct. App. 1913). *But see* Arthur L. Corbin, *Quasi Contractual Obligations*, 21 YALE L.J. 533, 550 (1912).

[98] *See supra* § 11.03 Change of Circumstances: Impossibility, Impracticability, and Frustration of Purpose.

[99] 164 P. 143 (Kan. 1917).

The court reasoned that the forms were not to be incorporated in the structure and thus conferred no benefit on the defendant before the fire excused performance. The court also denied recovery for the cost of labor or materials in laying steel reinforcing rods, which would have been incorporated into the structure once the concrete was poured, but which had not yet been permanently installed at the time the fire occurred. According to the court, efforts to put the steel reinforcing rods in place conferred no benefit on the defendant because they had not been incorporated into the structure before the fire destroyed the building.[100]

Few courts have been as conservative as *Carroll v. Bowersock* in their evaluation of whether a benefit has been conferred. However, most have adhered to the distinction between expenses that conferred a benefit and those that did not.[101]

Some scholars have argued that when performance of a contract is disrupted, and the contract is rendered unenforceable, restitution should be awarded based not only on the amount of the defendant's enrichment, but also on the reliance expenses incurred by the plaintiff in preparing to perform.[102] Few cases, however, have permitted such awards.[103]

§ 13.05 RESTITUTION AS AN ALTERNATIVE REMEDY FOR BREACH[104]

Restitution is available as an alternative remedy for total material breach.[105] Restitution permits recovery of whatever benefits the injured party has conferred on the party in breach. The injured party may prefer restitution as a means of justifying its own return of property or other benefits received from the party in breach that, because of their defects, have no use.[106] Restitution may also be sought either because of the difficulty in proving the injured party's lost expectation or to avoid the consequences of having entered into a losing deal.[107]

Recovery in restitution is fundamentally different from an action to recover

---

[100] *Id.* at 145.

[101] *E.g.*, Novecon, Ltd. v. Bulgarian-Am. Ent. Fund, 967 F. Supp. 1382 (D.D.C. 1997), *aff'd*, 190 F.3d 556 (D.C. Cir. 1999); Far W. Fed. Bank, S.B. v. Office of Thrift Supervision-Director, 119 F.3d 1358 (9th Cir. 1997).

[102] *See* John P. Dawson, *Restitution Without Enrichment*, 61 B.U.L. Rev. 563 (1981); Jeffrey L Harrison, *A Case for Loss Sharing*, 56 S. Cal. L. Rev. 573 (1983).

[103] *See* Joseph M. Perillo, *Restitution in the Second Restatement of Contracts*, 81 Colum. L. Rev. 37 (1981); William F. Young, *Half Measures*, 81 Colum. L. Rev. 19 (1981).

[104] John P. Dawson, *Restitution or Damages*, 20 Ohio St. L.J. 175 (1959); Barnard E. Gegan, *In Defense of Restitution: A Comment on Mather*, 57 S. Cal. L. Rev. 723 (1984); Andrew Kull, *Restitution as a Remedy for Breach of Contract*, 67 S. Cal. L. Rev. 1465 (1994); Henry Mather, *Restitution as a Remedy for Breach of Contract: The Case of the Partially Performing Seller*, 92 Yale L.J. 14 (1982); George E. Palmer, *The Contract Price as a Limit on Restitution for the Defendant's Breach*, 20 Ohio St. L.J. 264 (1950); Joseph M. Perillo *Restitution in a Contractual Context*, 73 Colum. L. Rev. 1208 (1973).

[105] Restatement (Second) of Contracts § 373 (1981).

[106] George E. Palmer, The Law of Restitution 368 (1978).

[107] *Id.*

expectation or reliance damages. An action seeking recovery of expectation or reliance damages is a means of *enforcing* the contract. Restitution, on the other hand, ignores the contract, and seeks recovery of benefits conferred and unjustly retained. This distinction has led some jurisdictions to limit recovery of restitution when there is an otherwise enforceable express contract between the parties, unless there are grounds for rescission due to material breach.[108] Courts in these states have reasoned that the terms of the parties' agreement determine the parties' rights, and, in the absence of fraud, bad faith, or illegality, the contract must be used to resolve those rights.[109]

On another front, several scholars have recognized that the remedy for breach, long characterized as restitution to prevent unjust enrichment, is really designed to fulfill a "restoration" interest by restoring the plaintiff to the pre-contract status quo.[110] Disgorgement of benefits received from the contract, which may be greater or lesser than the amount necessary to simply restore the plaintiff to his or her former position, is quite different.[111]

Most jurisdictions permit recovery of restitution as an alternative remedy for breach of contract.[112] This is sometimes explained on the theory that the injured party has the right to renounce the contract, effectively rescinding it, because of the other party's repudiation or total material breach. Although the injured party may not use restitution to obtain a double recovery, for both its lost expectations and the benefits conferred on the party in breach,[113] pursuit of alternative claims, for either remedy, is permitted.

Restitution, like rescission, is available only when there has been either a repudiation or an uncured material breach that justifies the injured party in terminating the contract.[114] Courts explain that the breach must be "essential"[115] or that there must be a "total breach"[116] in order for rescission and restitution to

---

[108] *E.g.*, Aetna Life Ins. Co. v. Satterlee, 475 N.W.2d 569, 573 (S.D. 1991); Truly v. Austin, 744 S.W.2d 934 (Tex. 1988).

[109] *E.g.*, Wolfer Enter., Inc. v. Overbrook Dev. Corp., 724 N.E.2d 1251 (Ohio Ct. App. 1999).

[110] *See* Joseph M. Perillo, *Restitution in a Contractual Context and the Restatement (Third) of Restitution & Unjust Enrichment*, 68 Wash & Lee. L. Rev. 1007 (2011); Melvin Aron Eisenberg, *The Disgorgement Interest in Contract Law*, 105 Mich. L. Rev. 559 (2006); E. Allan Farnsworth, *Your Loss or My Gain? The Dilemma of the Disgorgement Principle in Breach of Contract*, 94 Yale L.J. 1339 (1985); James Stevens Rogers, *Restitution for Wrongs and the Restatement (Third) of the Law of Restitution and Unjust Enrichment*, 42 Wake Forest L. Rev. 55 (2007). *See also* 3 Dan B. Dobbs, Law of Remedies § 12.7(4), at 171 (2d ed. 1993).

[111] *Id. See also* Andrew Kull, *Disgorgement for Breach, the "Restitution Interest" and the Restatement of Contracts*, 79 Texas L. Rev. 2021 (2001); Joseph M. Perillo, *Restitution in a Contractual Context*, 73 Colum. L. Rev. 1208 (1973) (restitution aims as restoration of both parties to the pre-contract status quo).

[112] Restatement (Second) of Contracts § 373 (1981).

[113] Restatement (Second) of Contracts § 378 cmt. a (1981).

[114] Restatement (Second) of Contracts § 373(1) (1981).

[115] George E. Palmer, The Law of Restitution 409 (1978).

[116] Restatement (Second) of Contracts § 373(1) (1981).

be available as a remedy.[117] Expectation damages are available for partial breach, but restitution is not.

In determining whether there has been a total breach, the primary question is whether the breach has effectively defeated the essential purpose of the contract.[118] Thus, if Cathy's Construction Co. enters into a contract to build a house for Dave and builds it so badly that it is unsafe to occupy, the purpose of the contract is completely frustrated and the breach is total. Dave is entitled to rescind the contract and recover everything he has paid.[119] However, rescission and restitution would not be available if the only problem was that repairs were necessary to the siding. For example, in *Rubinstein v. Mester*,[120] rescission and restitution were not available where the difference between an interior decorator's "estimate" and the final charge was only 1.4% over the original estimate, and performance was otherwise in compliance with the terms of the agreement.

Traditionally, restitution is available as a remedy for breach only if the injured party elects to "rescind" the contract. "Rescission" is an unfortunate term. It is also used in the completely different context of a mutual agreement between the parties to cancel their contract. Rescission and restitution as a remedy for breach should not be confused with the parties' decision to rescind or abandon their contract *by agreement*.[121] Article 2 of the Uniform Commercial Code avoids this problem by referring to the injured party's right to "cancel" the contract where the breach "goes to the whole contract."[122]

The injured party must give notice of its election to rescind or cancel the contract, and tender back to the breaching party all of the benefits it has received from the party in breach. In equity, however, actual tender was not required as long as the injured party remained ready and able to tender back the benefits it received, perhaps through an offset against the amount it was able to recover from the party in breach.[123] The requirement of rescission meant, among other things, that an injured party who continues performing the contract, following a breach, had effectively abandoned its right to rescind.[124] When this happens, other remedies, based on enforcement of the contract, remain available.

---

[117] *See supra* § 9.01 The Effect of Breach.

[118] *E.g.*, Fed. Land Bank of Wichita v. Krug, 856 P.2d 111 (Kan. 1993); Folkers v. Sw. Leasing, 431 N.W.2d 177 (Iowa Ct. App. 1988). *See* George E. Palmer, The Law of Restitution 410 (1978 & Supp. 2002).

[119] Eliker v. Chief Indus., Inc., 498 N.W.2d 564 (Neb. 1993).

[120] 362 So. 2d 986 (Fla. Dist. Ct. App. 1978).

[121] *See* Restatement (Second) of Contracts § 283(1) (1981) ("an agreement under which each party agrees to discharge all of the other party's remaining duties of performance under an existing contract.").

[122] U.C.C. § 2-711(1) (2012). *See also* U.C.C. § 2-703 (2012).

[123] Restatement (Second) of Contracts § 384 (1981).

[124] *E.g.*, Accusoft Corp. v. Palo, 237 F.3d 31, 55–56 (1st Cir. 2001).

[A]   Loss Contracts — Expectation as a Limit on Restitution[125]

In most contracts, performance results in a gain for both parties — otherwise they would not have made the deal. However, sometimes, due to bad judgment or misfortune, full performance of the contract would have led one of the parties to suffer a loss.[126] When this happens, the aggrieved party might try to avoid the consequences of this anticipated loss by suing to recover in restitution for the value of any benefit it conferred on the defendant before the breach.

A simple but uncommon example might occur if a buyer makes an advance payment for goods that are worth less than the agreed price. Most of the time, a seller in this position is eager to perform. However, if the seller becomes unable to perform, the buyer would naturally prefer return of its down payment over a recovery based on the market value of the goods. A buyer who makes full advance payment of the $15,000 price of a car worth only $14,000 will prefer the return of his $15,000 payment over damages calculated by subtracting $15,000 from the $14,000 market value, which would result in nothing. In this easy case, U.C.C. § 2-711 permits the buyer to recover "so much of the price as has been paid,"[127] despite the loss. Of course, when the contract price is higher than the value of the car, sellers usually perform.

Construction cases in which the recipient commits a material breach or repudiates the contract, after partial performance by the provider, are more difficult. Assume that Joventy hires Winkler Builders to construct a fence around her yard for a price of $2,000. After Winkler has finished two-thirds of the work, at an expense of $1,500, with another $750 to spend to complete the work, Joventy repudiates the contract. Winkler might seek restitution rather than expectation. Expectation damages entitle Winkler to the $250 loss he would have suffered if Joventy had not repudiated and he had fully performed. Depending on how the value of the benefit of his work is calculated, recovery in restitution might protect him from this loss. Somewhat surprisingly, most cases permit the aggrieved party — in this case, Winkler Builders — to recover in restitution for the value of the benefit conferred, without regard to the loss it would have suffered if the contract had been fully performed.[128]

This ability of a party to use restitution to recover the full value of the benefit it has conferred, even though it made a contract to confer the benefit at a loss, flies in the face of the fundamental goal of the law of contract damages, which is to place

---

[125] George E. Palmer, *The Contract Price as a Limit on Restitution for the Defendant's Breach*, 20 Ohio St. L.J. (1959).

[126] A classic comedy, with an ending scene that involves such a contract, is *Trading Places* starring former "Saturday Night Live" cast members Eddie Murphy and Dan Aykroyd. Sometime during the semester you are studying contract damages would be a good time to watch the film.

[127] U.C.C. § 2-711 (2012). *See also* Bush v. Canfield, 1818 Conn. LEXIS 19 (June 1818).

[128] United States v. Algernon Blair, Inc., 479 F.2d 638 (4th Cir. 1973). *See also* United States v. W. States Mech. Contractors, Inc., 834 F.2d 1533 (10th Cir. 1987); Mobil Oil Exploration & Prod'g S.E., Inc. v. United States, 530 U.S. 604 (2000); Edwin W. Patterson, *Builder's Measure of Recovery for Breach of Contract*, 31 Colum. L. Rev. 1286 (1941).

the injured party in as good a position as performance.[129] This result, although frequently criticized,[130] is often justified on the principle that a party who has breached the contract should not be entitled to seek refuge in the broken deal.[131]

As explained elsewhere,[132] the principal exception to this rule is where the injured party has substantially performed by one party and the only performance remaining due by the other party is paying the price.[133] For example, in *Oliver v. Campbell*,[134] an attorney who substantially performed the services agreed upon with his client before being discharged was limited to the agreed $750 fee, even though his services were worth $5,000. Where there has been complete or at least substantial performance, the injured party cannot sidestep the contract price and recover for the greater value of the benefit conferred, simply by switching theories. The court articulated the traditional rule: "The remedy of restitution in money is not available to one who has fully performed his part of a contract, if the only part of the agreed exchange for such performance that has not been rendered by the defendant is a sum of money constituting a liquidated debt."[135]

Some decisions prorate the contract price based on the percentage of the contract performed before the breach.[136] This is the usual practice where the contract is "divisible" and, as explained in the next section, can therefore be apportioned into discrete segments. However, in *Kehoe v. Rutherford*,[137] the court prorated the contract price even though the contract was not divisible. The contractor was limited to the "unit price" contained in a contract to grade 4,000 feet of a city street even though the contractor would have charged a higher unit price for a smaller job.

[B] Divisibility

The problem of whether to permit recovery for the value of the benefit conferred in excess of the value of performance can be avoided if a divisible portion

---

[129] Lon L. Fuller & William R. Perdue Jr., *The Reliance Interest in Contract Damages (Pt. 1)*, 46 YALE L.J. 42, 71–80 (1936); Andrew Kull, *Disgorgement for Breach, the "Restitution Interest" and the Restatement of Contracts*, 79 TEXAS L. REV. 2021, 2041 n.49 (2001); George E. Palmer, *The Contract Price as a Limit on Restitution for Defendant's Breach*, 20 OHIO ST. L.J. 264 (1959).

[130] Robert Childres & Jack Garamella, *The Law of Restitution and the Reliance Interest in Contract*, 64 NW. L. REV. 433, 440–41 (1969); Henry Mather, *Restitution as a Remedy for Breach of Contract: The Case of the Partially Performing Seller*, 92 YALE L.J. 14 (1982); Joseph M. Perillo, *Restitution in the Second Restatement of Contracts*, 81 COLUM. L. REV. 37, 44–45 (1981).

[131] Bausch & Lomb Inc. v. Bressler, 977 F.2d 720 (2d Cir. 1992). *See* Bernard E. Gegan, *In Defense of Restitution: A Comment on Mather, Restitution as a Remedy for Breach of Contract: The Case of the Partially Performing Seller*, 57 S. CAL. L. REV. 723 (1984); RESTATEMENT (SECOND) OF CONTRACTS § 373 cmt. d (1981).

[132] *See supra* § 12.08[E] Construction Contracts: Breach by the Customer.

[133] RESTATEMENT (SECOND) OF CONTRACTS § 373(1) (1981).

[134] 273 P.2d 15 (Cal. 1954).

[135] *Id.* at 20.

[136] *See generally* Henry Mather, *Restitution as a Remedy for Breach of Contract: The Case of the Partially Performing Seller*, 92 YALE L.J. 14, 19 (1982).

[137] 27 A. 912 (N.J. Super. Ct. 1893).

of the contract has been substantially performed. In such cases, the injured party is limited to the apportioned price of the completed portion of the contract.[138] Thus, a builder who completes six of eight identical houses may recover three-fourths of the contract price.[139]

Divisibility helps insulate the injured party from the consequences of having entered into a losing deal. If the price for constructing all eight houses was $800,000, and the cost of completing each structure was $110,000, the contractor would have suffered an $80,000 loss upon full performance. Permitting the contractor to recover three-fourths of the $800,000 price, or $600,000, leaves the contractor with only a $60,000 loss.

This approach only works if the contract is "divisible" — that is, if it is capable of being apportioned. A contract is divisible only if it involves "corresponding pairs of part performances" that are "properly regarded as agreed equivalents" of one another.[140] Thus, in a contract to build a house for $200,000, completion of three-fourths of house would not be a divisible portion of the contract, even if the agreement provides for four equal progress payments.[141] Because three-fourths of a house is not worth 75% of a completed house, and is not anywhere near 75% as useful as a fully completed house, the payment schedule does not reflect the parties' understanding that the project is divisible into four divisible equal parts.

§ 13.06 RESTITUTION FOR THE BREACHING PARTY[142]

At one time, the common law prevented a breaching party from recovering anything.[143] Courts were reluctant to permit a breaching party to gain any advantage from its own misconduct.[144] Nevertheless, courts long ago realized that permitting restitution for the party in breach not only prevents the innocent party from enjoying a windfall, it also prevents forfeitures.[145] Thus, restitution is usually available to the breaching party for the value of the benefit of any part performance it provided before its breach.[146] This recovery is not directly on the contract,

---

[138] *See, e.g.*, Shapiro Eng'g Corp. v. Francis O. Day Co., 137 A.2d 695 (Md. 1958) (loss construction firm would have suffered on second divisible portion of the contract not subtracted from price due for completion of the first portion of the contract).

[139] *E.g.*, Dibol & Plank v. E.H. Minott, 1859 Iowa Sup. LEXIS 100 (Dec. 1859).

[140] *See* RESTATEMENT (SECOND) OF CONTRACTS § 240 (1981).

[141] *See* RESTATEMENT (SECOND) OF CONTRACTS § 240 cmt. e illus. 7 (1981).

[142] Robert L. Birmingham *Breach of Contract, Damage Measures, and Economic Efficiency*, 24 RUTGERS L. REV. 273, 286–92 (1970); Arthur L. Corbin, *The Right of a Defaulting Vendee to the Restitution of Installments Paid*, 40 YALE L.J. 1013, 1013 (1931); Robert J. Nordstrom & Irwin F. Woodland, *Recovery by Building Contractor in Default*, 20 OHIO ST. L. J. 193 (1959); 1 GEORGE E. PALMER, THE LAW OF RESTITUTION 5.1–5.5 (1978); Joseph M. Perillo, *Restitution in the Second Restatement of Contracts*, 81 COLUM. L. REV. 37, 50 (1981).

[143] Arthur L. Corbin, *The Right of a Defaulting Vendee to the Restitution of Installments Paid*, 40 YALE L.J. 1013, 1014 (1931). *E.g.*, Ketchum v. Evertson, 1816 N.Y. LEXIS 109 (Aug. 1816); Stark v. Parker, 1824 Mass. LEXIS 28 (Mar. 1824).

[144] *See* Lawrence v. Miller, 1881 N.Y. LEXIS 190, *16 (Oct. 4, 1881).

[145] Britton v. Turner, 1834 N.H. LEXIS 48 (July 1834).

[146] RESTATEMENT (SECOND) OF CONTRACTS § 374 (1981). *But see* Albre Marble & Tile Co. v. Goverman,

because the breaching party cannot establish a key element of an action for breach of contract: breach. Instead, recovery is based on liability for the value of the benefit conferred on the other party. Absent the ability to recover in restitution, the breaching party could sustain a considerable forfeiture, and the innocent party would receive a windfall.[147]

The danger of forfeiture and a corresponding windfall is most easily illustrated in the context of a construction contract which provides for payment upon completion of the work. If, for example, a paving contractor completes two-thirds of a sidewalk and then quits work, the homeowner will receive a substantial windfall unless he or she is required to pay for the completed portion of the walk. Thus, the breaching contractor is entitled to compensation for the work it has completed, even though it did not finish, and is in breach.[148]

A breaching contractor is normally entitled to restitution for benefits conferred by his or her part performance,[149] even if he or she has not substantially performed.[150] Although some cases deny restitution without substantial performance,[151] these often subtly expand the circumstances in which part performance is regarded as "substantial."[152]

Of course, in cases where there truly has been substantial performance, recovery in restitution is not necessary. A party who has substantially performed is entitled to enforce the contract, and have its damages diminished only by whatever damages the other party suffered as a result of any nonmaterial breach.[153] Quite naturally, if the breach was so serious that the innocent party was effectively deprived of any benefit of its bargain, and received no material from part performance, recovery is denied. This is more likely to occur where performance is seriously defective, rather than simply incomplete.

A common circumstance in which a breaching party seeks recovery in restitution involves a breaching buyer of real estate who has made a substantial down payment but then fails to pay the remainder of the price. For example, a buyer of land might make a 5% or 10% down payment, find herself unable to complete the transaction, and then sue to recover the payment made. The potential unfairness of permitting the seller to retain the down payment is exacerbated when the seller promptly

---

233 N.E.2d 533 (Mass. 1968); Mech. Piping Serv. Inc. v. Jayeff Constr. Corp., 626 N.Y.S.2d 547 (N.Y. App. Div. 1995).

[147] Arthur L. Corbin, *The Right of a Defaulting Vendee to the Restitution of Installments Paid*, 40 YALE L.J. 1013, 1013 (1931).

[148] *See also* Britton v. Turner, 1834 N.H. LEXIS 48 (July 1834).

[149] *E.g.*, Pinches v. Swedish Evangelical Lutheran Church, 10 A. 264 (Conn. 1887). *See* Robert J. Nordstrom & Irwin F. Woodland, *Recovery by Building Contractor in Default*, 20 OHIO ST. L.J. 193 (1959).

[150] *E.g.*, Levan v. Richter, 504 N.Ed 1373 (Ill. App. Ct. 1987).

[151] *E.g.*, Steel Storage & Elevator Constr. v. Stock, 121 N.E.786 (N.Y. 1919); Albre Marble & Tile Co. v. Goverman, 233 N.E.2d 533 (Mass. 1969).

[152] 1 GEORGE E. PALMER, THE LAW OF RESTITUTION 667–78 (1978).

[153] *See, e.g.*, Kelley v. Hance, 142 A. 683 (Conn. 1928) (characterizing the decision in *Pinches v. Swedish Evangelical Lutheran Church*, 10 A. 264 (Conn. 1887), as having been based not on quasi-contract, but for recovery of the remainder of the price after substantial performance).

resells the property involved for the same or even a higher price.

Recognizing that the seller may have incurred some expenses in getting ready to perform, or in reselling the property,[154] some courts deny the buyer the right to recover small amounts paid as "earnest money."[155] Other courts follow this practice at least where the contract provides that the 10% down payment may be retained by the seller as "liquidated damages"[156] Even here, however, the amount must pass muster as an enforceable liquidated damages provision.[157] Still other courts permit the buyer to recover the down payment, subject to the injured party's ability to prove it was harmed by the buyer's breach.[158]

More devastating are cases involving long-term land sale contracts where the buyer has made numerous installment payments, taken possession of the land, and made improvements on the property before defaulting.[159] Unless the seller is required to refund some or all of the installment payments, the seller will enjoy a substantial windfall, keeping both the payments and title to the improved land. Modern decisions permit recovery of the amounts paid, offset by the amount of the seller's damages, if there are any.[160]

If the breaching buyer has taken possession of the property, and made substantial improvements before breaching, the buyer may also be entitled to restitution for the value of these improvements, at least up to the enhanced value of the land.[161] However, many courts deny restitution for the value of these improvements because they may foist an unwelcome benefit on the seller and might create the potential for abuse by buyers who are unable to locate another customer for the land with the improvements.[162]

Some courts insist on denying any recovery for the breaching buyer, whether or not the contract contains a clause providing for forfeiture of the sums paid,[163] even though this will result in a forfeiture, and even though the forfeiture is the greatest

---

[154] Your author hopes you will never find yourself, as he has, saddled with real estate that is difficult to sell.

[155] *E.g.*, Ottenstein v. W. Reserve Acad., 374 N.E.2d 427 (Ohio Ct. App. 1977).

[156] *See* Maxton Builders, Inc. v. Lo Galbo, 502 N.E.2d 184, 188, 189 n.3 (N.Y. 1986); Vines v. Orchard Hills, Inc., 435 A.2d 1022 (Conn. 1980).

[157] *See infra* § 14.03 Liquidated Damages.

[158] *E.g.*, Freedman v. Rector, Wardens & Vestrymen of St. Matthias Parish, 230 P.2d 629 (Cal. 1951).

[159] *See, e.g.*, Flath v. Bauman, 722 S.W.2d 125 (Mo. Ct. App. 1986) (27% of price paid).

[160] *E.g.*, Caplan v. Schroeder, 364 P.2d 321 (Cal. 1961); Arthur L. Corbin, *The Right of a Defaulting Vendee to Restitution of Installments Paid*, 40 YALE L.J. 1013 (1931); Grant S. Nelson & Dale A. Whitman, *Installment Land Contracts — The National Scene Revisited*, 1985 BYU L. REV. 1, 20–24.

[161] Anderson v. DeLisle, 352 N.W.2d 794 (Minn. Ct. App. 1984). *But see* Brakke v. Hilgers, 374 N.W.2d 553 (Minn. Ct. App. 1985) (denying restitution for improvements and distinguishing *Anderson*).

[162] *E.g.*, Salamon v. Terra, 477 N.E.2d 1029 (Mass. 1985).

[163] Kaufman Hotel & Rest. Co. v. Thomas, 190 A.2d 434 (Pa. 1963); Flath v. Bauman, 722 S.W.2d 125, 130 (Mo. Ct. App. 1986); Baker v. Taylor & Co., 237 S.W.2d 471 (Ark. 1951) (no forfeiture clause); James O. Pearson Jr., Annotation, *Modern Status of Defaulting Vendee's Right to Recover Contractual Payments Withheld by Vendor as Forfeited*, 4 A.L.R.4th 993 (1981).

for the plaintiff who has performed the most.[164]

In contracts for the sale of goods, U.C.C. § 2-718(2) expressly permits a breaching buyer to recover the amount of any payment it has made, subject to the seller's right to retain the amount specified by any otherwise enforceable liquidated damages provision,[165] or, in the absence of such a term, the amount of the seller's actual damages.[166]

Section 2-718(2) also permits the seller to retain a breaching buyer's down payment, even in the absence of liquidated or actual damages, of up to 20% of the value of the buyer's total performance, or $500, whichever is less. This statutory damages provision undoubtedly compensates an aggrieved seller for a variety of incidental and consequential damages suffered as a result of the buyer's breach. This effectively compensates the seller for damages it suffers due to delay, expenses associated with resale, or for a lost profit on the transaction, without the necessity of proving the amount of its loss. This provision thus serves the same function as a term, sometimes found in real estate contracts, permitting the seller to retain a small amount of earnest money or, up to a 10% down payment, as liquidated damages.[167]

Some decisions persist in preventing recovery by a party whose breach was "willful."[168] However, the modern trend is to disregard the defaulting plaintiff's culpability in determining whether it is entitled to restitution.[169] Moreover, even those decisions that deny recovery limit the circumstances of willful breach to those involving an intentional and material deviation from the terms of the contract[170] or where the breaching party is also guilty of a tort.[171] Section 36 of the Third Restatement of Restitution & Unjust Enrichment, denies restitution to a breaching party only if the "default involves fraud or other inequitable conduct."[172]

Even though restitution may be awarded to the breaching party, the injured party is naturally entitled to offset the amount it pays in restitution by the amount of damages it has suffered as a result of the breach. Thus, a breaching buyer's right to recover its down payment is reduced by the amount of damages suffered by the innocent seller.[173] Similarly, an aggrieved employer may deduct from any wages due the employee the costs of finding a replacement, though this right is frequently subject to restrictions imposed by labor and employment law to prevent employers from taking unfair advantage of their right to offset. It will also be able to deduct

---

[164] *See* Freedman v. Rector, 230 P.2d 629, 632 (Cal. 1951).

[165] U.C.C. § 2-718(2) (2012).

[166] U.C.C. § 2-718(3) (2012). *E.g.*, Neri v. Retail Marine Corp., 285 N.E.2d 311 (N.Y. Ct. App. 1972).

[167] U.C.C. § 2-719(2) (2012).

[168] *E.g.*, Roundup Cattle Feeders v. Horpestad, 603 P.2d 1044 (Mont. 1979).

[169] Lancellotti v. Thomas, 491 A.2d 117 (Pa. Super. Ct. 1985); Ducolon Mech., Inc. v. Shinstine/Forness, Inc., 893 P.2d 1127, 1130 n.3 (Wash. Ct. App. 1995).

[170] *See* RESTATEMENT (SECOND) OF CONTRACTS § 374 cmt. b (1981).

[171] *But see* Freedman v. Rector, 230 P.2d 629, 632 (Cal. 1951).

[172] RESTATEMENT (THIRD) OF RESTITUTION & UNJUST ENRICHMENT § 36(40 (2011)

[173] U.C.C. § 2-718(2) (2012).

any reasonably certain lost profits together with any other foreseeable consequential losses suffered because of a delay in completion of the project to which the departing employee was assigned.[174] Obviously, where the injured party's damages are substantial its offsetting recovery may completely swallow up the breaching party's right in restitution.[175]

§ 13.07 RESTITUTION WHEN CONTRACT IS UNENFORCEABLE

Restitution is also used as a remedy for the value of benefits conferred in partial performance of a contract that is unenforceable due to incapacity, mistake, or even some sort of wrongdoing such as fraud or duress.[176] When used in this manner, restitution is an independent theory of liability, rather than a mere remedy. Thus, when a minor purchases a car for cash, and later seeks to disaffirm the contract, the minor is entitled to restitution of the price he or she paid for the vehicle.[177] In such a case, the minor will be required to supply restitution of the benefits of the contract remaining in his or her possession, even if this consists of nothing more than a mangled mass of twisted metal, glass, and plastic.[178]

Restitution is similarly available for the value of benefits conferred when a voidable contract is disaffirmed because of mental incapacity,[179] mistake,[180] misrepresentation,[181] duress,[182] undue influence,[183] or abuse of a fiduciary relationship.[184] It is also available when a contract is rendered unenforceable due to impossibility, impracticability, or frustration of purpose.[185]

For example, in *Louisville & Nashville R.R. Co. v. Crowe*,[186] the defendant's promise to provide the plaintiff with a lifetime railway pass, given in exchange for a right of way that the plaintiff transferred to the railroad, was rendered illegal by a federal statute. Between the time the contract was made, and the time it was declared illegal, the railroad had already been built over the land on which the right of way had been granted, making specific restitution — taking the easement away from the railroad — highly impractical. Instead, the railroad was required to provide restitution for the value of the right of way it received under the contract,

---

[174] *See* Britton v. Turner, 1834 N.H. LEXIS 48 (July 1834).

[175] *E.g.*, Denver Ventures, Inc. v. Arlington Lane Corp., 754 P.2d 785 (Colo. Ct. App. 1988).

[176] RESTATEMENT (SECOND) OF CONTRACTS § 376 (1981); RESTATEMENT (THIRD) OF RESTITUTION & UNJUST ENRICHMENT §§ 31–35 (2011)

[177] *E.g.*, Kiefer v. Fred Howe Motors, Inc., 158 N.W.2d 288 (Wis. 1968).

[178] *See* Halbman v. Lemke, 298 N.W.2d 562 (Wis. 1980).

[179] *See supra* § 10.03[A] Minors.

[180] *See supra* § 11.02[A] Mutual Mistake.

[181] *See supra* § 10.04 Obtaining Assent Improperly: Fraud, Duress, and Undue Influence.

[182] *See supra* § 10.04[C] Improper Threats.

[183] *See supra* § 10.04[D] Undue Influence.

[184] RESTATEMENT (SECOND) § 376 (1981).

[185] *See supra* Ch. 11 Excuse: Mistake and Change of Circumstances.

[186] 160 S.W. 759 (Ky. 1913).

with an adjustment made for the value already received by the plaintiff, before his lifetime pass was declared illegal.

In some situations the defendant may have spent some of the benefit it received in partially performing its own obligations under the contract. This could easily occur if a buyer makes a down payment for goods that will be specially manufactured for the buyer and completion of the goods is disrupted due to an intervening event that makes the contract unenforceable.[187] This is what happened in *Fibrosa Spolka Akcyjna v. Fiarbairn Lawson Comb Barbour, Ltd.*[188] The buyer, who was located in Poland, made a down payment of £1,000, and the seller, located in England, began work. When World War II made performance impossible, the buyer sued to recover its down payment. The court granted restitution for the full £1,000, effectively penalizing the seller, who had already spent much of the sum beginning to perform.[189]

Proper resolution of the dispute would have permitted restitution but with an offset for any unsalvageable expenses incurred by the seller in reliance on the contract. This would have prevented unjust enrichment of the seller who was enriched, not by the amount it received, but by the amount it retained after performance of the contract was frustrated.[190]

Restitution is sometimes also used to prevent unjust enrichment when there has been part performance of an oral agreement that is unenforceable under the statute of frauds.[191] In many cases, part performance satisfies the statute of frauds.[192] In other cases, where the statute is not satisfied by the part performance, recovery in restitution is still possible, and does not violate the statute of frauds. Where it applies, the statute of frauds prevents *enforcement* of the promise. A claim in quasi-contract is not an action to enforce a promise. Quite to the contrary, it simply prevents any unjust enrichment that might occur as a result of the benefits the parties conveyed on one another as a result of their part performance of the unenforceable agreement.[193] Although recovery in reliance is generally prohibited by the statute of frauds, actions to recover in restitution for the value of benefits conferred occasionally muddy the distinction between reliance and restitution. This occurs where the court uses the plaintiff's reliance expenses as a method of calculating the value of the benefit conferred on the defendant.[194] Despite this use of reliance expenses as a proxy for the value of the benefit conferred, the theory on which recovery is supplied is restitution.

---

[187] *See supra* § 11.03 Change of Circumstances: Impossibility, Impracticability, and Frustration of Purpose.

[188] 1 K.B. 12 (1942)

[189] *See* Andrew Kull, *Rationalizing Restitution*, 83 Calif. L. Rev. 1191, 1209 n.53 (1995).

[190] Restatement (Third) of Restitution & Unjust Enrichment § 34(2)(b) (2011).

[191] Restatement (Second) of Contracts § 375 (1981).

[192] *See supra* § 5.05 The Effect of Part Performance and Reliance.

[193] *See* Grappo v. Alitalia Linee Aeree Italiane, 56 F.3d 427, 433 (2d Cir. 1995).

[194] *See* Farash v. Sykes Datatronics, Inc., 452 N.E.2d 1245 (N.Y. 1983).

§ 13.08   RESTITUTION WHERE NO CONTRACT EXISTS: QUASI-CONTRACT[195]

Although the full extent of the law of restitution is far beyond the scope of this chapter,[196] some explanation of recovery in quasi-contract is useful in order to put restitution as a remedy in contract disputes in perspective. An action in "quasi-contract" to recover for the value of the benefit conferred is frequently available to prevent unjust enrichment, even though no contract has been formed.[197]

One of the common circumstances where this occurs is where a benefit is conferred at the defendant's request, under circumstances in which the parties expect that compensation will be provided.[198] However, in many of these cases, resort to quasi-contract is not necessary. Where liability is based on the assent of the parties an implied-in-fact contract can be enforced even though its terms may be uncertain.[199] In these situations, it is sometimes difficult to distinguish between a contract implied in fact, with the price determined by reference to the customary price, and a quasi-contract or contract "implied in law," with the value of the benefit conferred determined by referring to the ordinary or customary charge for a similar benefit.[200] Recoveries under either theory are likely to be similar, and courts are not always careful to distinguish between the two grounds for relief.

Restitution is sometimes available when the benefit is conferred without request. In *Cotnam v. Wisdom*,[201] Wisdom provided emergency medical treatment to a patient while the patient remained unconscious, following an accident. There was, of course, no contract, as the unconscious patient was unable to consent to the treatment he received, or to agree to pay for the plaintiff's services. Despite Wisdom's efforts, the patient died. The court permitted the plaintiff to recover on a theory of quasi-contract for the reasonable value of the services supplied. Thus, recovery for the value of the benefit conferred is available when emergency services are provided by a person who is ordinarily compensated for those services. The court explained that this "quasi-contract" was not a true contract "but a mere fiction of law creating a contract where none existed in order that there might be a remedy for this right."[202]

---

[195] John P. Dawson, *The Self-Serving Intermeddler*, 87 Harv. L. Rev. 1409, 1445–46 (1974); John P. Dawson, *Restitution Without Enrichment*, 61 B.U. L. Rev. 563, 620 (1981); Andrew Kull, *Rationalizing Restitution*, 83 Cal. L. Rev. 1191, 1196 (1995); Douglas Laycock, *The Scope and Significance of Restitution*, 67 Texas L. Rev. 1277 (1989); Saul Levmore, *Explaining Restitution*, 71 Va. L. Rev. 65, 88–89 (1985); Emily Sherwin, *Restitution and Equity: An Analysis of the Principle of Unjust Enrichment*, 79 Texas L. Rev. 2083, 2088–89 (2001); John W. Wade, *Restitution for Benefits Conferred Without Request*, 19 Vand. L. Rev. 1183 (1966); Christopher T. Wonnell, *Replacing the Unity Principle of Unjust Enrichment*, 45 Emory L.J. 153 (1996).

[196] *See* Restatement (Third) of Restitution and Unjust Enrichment (2011). Douglas Laycock, *Restoring Restitution to the Canon*, 110 Mich. L. Rev. 929 (2012).

[197] Maglica v. Maglica, 66 Cal. App. 4th 442 (1998).

[198] 2 George E. Palmer, The Law of Restitution 358 (1979).

[199] *See, e.g.*, Seaview Ass'n of Fire Island, N.Y., Inc. v. Williams, 510 N.E.2d 793 (N.Y. 1987).

[200] *E.g.*, Martin v. Campanaro, 156 F.2d 127 (2d Cir. 1946).

[201] 104 S.W. 164 (Ark. 1907).

[202] *See also In re* Estate of Crisan, 107 N.W.2d 907 (Mich. 1961).

A person who provides someone else with any of the necessities of life, such as food, shelter, or clothing, can recover restitution for the value of these benefits from the recipient's spouse or a parent where the benefits satisfied the spouse or parent's duty to provide support to the person who received the assistance directly.[203] And, a person who pays for the funeral expenses of another usually has a right of restitution from the decedent's estate.[204] Most of these decisions are justified by the obvious societal benefits gained by imposing liability on those who receive these necessary emergency services, and the obvious fear that those who provide them will be reluctant to do so if they have no right to be paid.

Despite these results, family members are usually unable to recover. Benefits they provide are presumed to have been intended as gifts.[205] However, this presumption can be overcome by evidence that the recipient knew or should have known that the benefit was provided with the expectation of payment.[206]

As the cases denying recovery to family members suggest, recovery in restitution is not available to "volunteers." Nor is restitution available to "officious intermeddlers" who foist unnecessary services upon unwilling recipients.[207] It should not be surprising that restitution is unavailable to someone who has conferred a benefit intending it as a gift. If recovery could be obtained, the holiday season would bankrupt those of us with generous friends and relatives. However, retention of a gift without compensation is not unjust, even though the failure to make a reciprocal gesture may be rude. As the court said in *Glenn v. Savag*, "the law will never permit a friendly act . . . to be converted into a pecuniary demand."[208]

Likewise, restitution is not available to those who provide services without request, at least in the absence of a serious emergency.[209] Thus, builders may not generate revenue by wandering around the neighborhood making unsolicited repairs.[210]

On the other hand, a person who voluntarily acquiesces in the receipt of a benefit, with the understanding that payment is expected, is liable in restitution for the value of the benefit conferred.[211] In *Schott v. Westinghouse Electric Corp.*,[212] an employee who deposited a cost-savings proposal, as part of a company-sponsored program encouraging employees to submit suggestions with the possibility of the

---

[203] *E.g.*, Greenspan v. Slate, 97 A.2d 390 (N.J. 1953).

[204] *In re* Estate of MacFarline, 14 P.3d 551 (Okla. 2000).

[205] *See In re* Estate of Lutz, 620 N.W.2d 589 (N.D. 2000).

[206] Estate of Cleveland v. Gorden, 837 S.W.2d 68 (Tenn. Ct. App. 1992).

[207] *See generally*, 2 George E. Palmer, The Law of Restitution Ch. 10 (1978).

[208] 13 P. 442, 448 (Or. 1887).

[209] Feingold v. Pucello, 654 A.2d 1093 (Pa. Super. Ct. 1995) (no restitution for value of the services of an attorney who, with the hope of being hired, investigated an accident and did other preliminary work before obtaining an agreement to represent the victim of the accident).

[210] Daniel B. Dobbs, The Law of Remedies § 4.9 (1993).

[211] *See, e.g,* GFR Leasing Corp. v. Transp. Equip. Specialists, Inc., 737 So. 2d 628 (Fla. Dist. Ct. App. 1999); Po River Water & Sewer Co. v. Indian Acres Club of Thornburg, Inc., 495 S.E.2d 479 (Va. 1998).

[212] 259 A.2d 443 (Pa. 1969).

receipt of a cash award, was not a mere volunteer. And, building contractors who comply with change orders and deviations from a written contract's specifications are routinely awarded compensation for their extra work, though recovery might be awarded either on the theory that the customer's request gave rise to a contract implied in fact,[213] or because there is a right to restitution in quasi-contract. Recovery is usually permitted even if the contract requires such modifications to the contract to be in writing.[214]

However, where the benefit is conferred voluntarily, without any express or implied suggestion that payment is expected, recovery is not allowed. If Phil volunteers to take his elderly neighbor, Chloe, to the grocery store once a week, Chloe owes Phil no duty to pay him for the benefit she received as a result. Phil is simply acting as a good Samaritan and has no right to restitution. In *Martin v. Little, Brown & Co.*[215] an individual who volunteered to supply information to a publisher about the plagiarism of one of its author's works was not permitted to recover. The court held that the "whistle blower" had acted merely as a volunteer and had done nothing to suggest that he was willing to supply the information only in exchange for payment or reward.

Lastly, situations involving the receipt of unordered merchandise through the mail are now governed by federal law. Although use of such goods would have constituted acceptance by silence under the common law,[216] federal consumer protection law now permits a person who receives unordered merchandise through the mail to treat the items as a gift.[217]

---

[213] *E.g,* Ganley v. G & W Ltd., 409 A.2d 761 (Md. Ct. Spec. App. 1980).

[214] *E.g.,* Weichert Co. v. Realtors v. Ryan, 608 A.2d 280 (N.J. 1992).

[215] 450 A.2d 984 (Pa. Super. Ct. 1981).

[216] *E.g.,* Pace v. Sagebrush Sales, Co., 560 P.2d 789 (Ariz. 1977). *See generally supra* § 4.05[D] Silence as Acceptance.

[217] 39 U.S.C. § 3009 (2006).

Chapter 14

AGREED REMEDIES

§ 14.01 INTRODUCTION TO AGREED REMEDIES

Many contracts include terms that spell out the remedies that will be available if one of the parties fails to perform. Some contracts stipulate the form of the remedy and place a limit on or entirely exclude money damages. These are usually called "limited remedy" provisions.

A common example is a provision in a new automobile "warranty" limiting the buyer's remedies for any defect in the car to repair or replacement of any defective parts. Most of the time, these repairs solve the problem. The loose wire is reattached or the defective component is replaced. On these occasions, the limited remedy of repair or replacement of defective parts puts the injured party in as good a position as it would have been in if the auto had not suffered from any defects, except, of course, for the time and annoyance involved in taking the car to a dealership to have the problem repaired.[1]

Sometimes, however, the defect is hard to diagnose or difficult to repair. On other occasions the defect does not surface until it causes an accident resulting in serious personal injury to the buyer or someone else. When this happens, legal issues arise about the enforceability of the seller's attempt to limit its liability to repair or replacement of the part that caused the accident.

Other agreed remedy provisions specify the amount of damages recoverable by the injured party, or specify a formula to be used in calculating the amount of damages. These types of clauses are usually referred to as "liquidated damages" provisions. They attempt to quantify or "liquidate" the amount the breaching party is required to pay as a consequence of its breach. Liquidated damages clauses carry the potential to undercompensate an injured party who has failed to fully consider all of the adverse consequences of a breach. Alternatively, they might overcompensate the injured party with a windfall that greatly exceeds the harm caused by the breach.

§ 14.02 LIMITED REMEDIES

A limited remedy provision is one that imposes a barrier on the types of remedies the injured party may receive or on the types of harm for which a remedy may be available. These limits reflect the parties' allocation of the risks associated with the contract, and are usually fully enforceable.[2] However, circumstances may arise which render the limitation unenforceable and permit the injured party to pursue other legal remedies.

[A]   Types of Limited Remedies

Many modern contracts include a clause providing for a specific remedy from one or both of the parties in the event of a breach. The manufacturer's warranty supplied with most new cars is a good example. Limited remedy provisions accompanying warranties on consumer electronic products are another good example. The limited remedy provision accompanying a recently purchased DVD player provides:

> REPAIR OR REPLACEMENT AS PROVIDED UNDER THIS WARRANTY IS THE EXCLUSIVE REMEDY OF THE CONSUMER. [THE SELLER] SHALL NOT BE LIABLE FOR ANY INCIDENTAL OR CONSEQUENTIAL DAMAGES FOR BREACH OF ANY EXPRESS OR IMPLIED WARRANTY ON THIS PRODUCT.

This language, together with terms in the manufacturer's warranty that promises to repair or replace defective parts in the DVD, limits the buyer's

---

[1] Reimbursement for these expenses would probably be recoverable as incidental damages under U.C.C. §§ 2-714 and 2-715(1), but they are excluded by the limited remedy.

[2] *See, e.g.,* JOM, Inc. v. Adell Plastics, Inc., 151 F.3d 15, 28 (1st Cir. 1998); Rainbow Country Rentals & Retail, Inc. v. Ameritech Pub., Inc., 706 N.W.2d 95 (Wis. 2005). *See* Charles J. Goetz & Robert E. Scott, *Liquidated Damages, Penalties and the Just Compensation Principle: Some Notes on an Enforcement Model and a Theory of Efficient Breach,* 77 COLUM. L. REV. 554, 590 (1977).

remedies in two important ways. First, it restrains the buyer from seeking remedies other than the promised repair or replacement of any defective parts. It prevents the buyer from attempting to recover damages that otherwise would be available based on the difference in value between a DVD player that performs as promised by the seller and the defective DVD player the seller delivered.[3] It also prevents the buyer from attempting to revoke its acceptance of the DVD player due to a substantially impairing defect in the goods and obtain a refund of the price.[4] Third, it denies the plaintiff the right to receive any remedy at all for any incidental or consequential damages that might occur as a result of the breach.[5] Thus, if the DVD player fails to operate when the buyer attempts to use it to play or project a program for an important business presentation, the buyer may not recover the lost profits or other business losses it suffers in the wake of the failure of the machine to live up to the seller's warranty.

Many cases involving limited remedy provisions, like this one, involve goods. Where goods are involved, U.C.C. § 2-719 governs. It permits the parties to agree to specific remedies either in addition to those supplied by the U.C.C. generally, or as a complete substitute for what the Code provides.[6]

Section 2-719 specifically authorizes use of a term limiting a buyer's remedies to return of the goods with restitution of the price, to repair, or to replacement of any defective goods or their components.[7] Thus, the limited remedy provision quoted above accompanying the new DVD player is generally enforceable.

In many cases involving the limited remedy of repair, defective goods are promptly and efficiently repaired by the seller. Thus, the limited remedy of repair operates much like the right of the seller to effectuate a cure under U.C.C. § 2-508[8] to preserve the contractual relationship between the parties and to resolve the dispute consistently with the general legal goal of contract remedies law of placing the injured party in as good a position as performance.[9]

Limiting the buyer's remedy to repair or replacement of defective parts is not likely to satisfy a buyer who has lost profits because of a product's shortcomings. Additionally, some product defects can have more dire consequences: defective brakes could cause an accident; a defective toaster oven could catch fire and destroy a house; a defective smoke detector could result in the death of an entire family. Repair or replacement of the defective parts in the brakes, the toaster, or the smoke detector will be cold comfort to a buyer who suffers these devastating losses. As will be seen, the law limits the enforceability of these types of limited remedy provisions.

---

[3] U.C.C. § 2-714 (2012).

[4] U.C.C. § 2-608 (2012).

[5] U.C.C. § 2-715(2) (2012).

[6] U.C.C. § 2-719(1)(a) (2012).

[7] U.C.C. § 2-719(1)(a) (2012).

[8] U.C.C. § 2-508 (2012). *See supra* § 9.04[A] Seller's Right to Cure.

[9] U.C.C. § 1-305 (2012) (formerly § 1-106).

[B]   Optional If Not Exclusive

The first important restraint on limited remedy provisions is found in U.C.C. § 2-719. It makes remedies specified in a contract for the sale of goods optional unless they are "expressly agreed to be exclusive."[10] A seller who wants to limit the remedies available to its customers must make it plain that the remedies contained in the agreement are the only ones available and are not just additional options to those that the customer could otherwise obtain. Not surprisingly, the boilerplate language in most consumer product warranties specifies that the limited remedy is exclusive. If language to this effect is missing, the limited remedy will be treated as nothing more than an optional remedy available at the buyer's choice[11] unless an applicable usage of trade or course of dealing supplies the necessary exclusivity.[12] If the language is ambiguous as to the exclusivity of remedy, the ambiguity will usually be construed against the breaching seller.[13]

[C]   Unconscionability of Limited Remedies

Just like any other term in a contract, an unconscionable limited remedy is unenforceable.[14] In general, a term is unconscionable if it is unreasonably one-sided and the party disfavored by the one-sided term had no meaningful choice at the time the contract was made. Unconscionability usually involves a two-pronged test to determine whether the term of the contract in question is substantively unfair and whether the contract formation procedure was flawed.[15]

Apart from this traditional unconscionability analysis, a limited remedy provision is unconscionable if it fails to provide a "minimum adequate remedy" for the seller's breach.[16] The normal standard for contract remedies seeks to place the injured party in as good a position as performance.[17] But, this does not mean that a minimum adequate remedy must put the injured party in as good a position as performance. If this were required, then all limited remedy provisions would be completely unenforceable simply because they impose a limit on the available remedies. Section 2-719 permits the parties to limit remedies by allocating the risks associated with the transaction within the limits of the unconscionability doctrine.

Despite the general ability of the parties to allocate risks, a provision that

---

[10] U.C.C. § 2-719(1)(b) (2012).

[11] *See* Booth Real Estate & Ins. Agency v. Sprague Heating & Elec., 599 N.E.2d 325 (Ohio Ct. App. 1991). *But see* Dow Corning Corp. v. Capitol Aviation, Inc., 411 F.2d 622 (7th Cir. 1969) (exclusivity implied).

[12] Figgie Int'l, Inc. v. Destileria Serralles, Inc., 190 F.3d 252, 256 (4th Cir. 1999). *See also* CogniTest Corp. v. Riverside Pub. Co., 107 F.3d 493 (7th Cir. 1997) (exclusivity implied).

[13] *See* Gaynor Elec. Co. v. Hollander, 618 A.2d 532 (Conn. Ct. App. 1993); Ford Motor Co. v. Reid, 465 S.W.2d 80 (Ark. 1971). *See supra* § 6.02[C][2] Contra Proferentum — Resolve Ambiguity Against the Drafter.

[14] U.C.C. § 2-302 (2012); Restatement (Second) of Contracts § 208 (1981).

[15] *See supra* § 10.05 Unconscionability.

[16] U.C.C. § 2-719 cmt. 1 (2012).

[17] U.C.C. § 1-305 (2012) (formerly § 1-106).

effectively deprives an injured party of any remedy is presumably unenforceable.[18] Nevertheless, sellers' efforts to limit their liability to repairing or replacing defective items and avoiding liability for consequential damages are generally valid if there are no flaws in the bargaining process that led to the contract.

The U.C.C. pays particular attention to the seller's efforts to limit or exclude liability for consequential damages. In contracts for consumer goods,[19] a provision excluding liability for consequential damages arising from personal injury is presumed to be unconscionable.[20] Thus, automobile dealers may not avoid the potentially disastrous consequences of selling defectively manufactured cars through the simple expedient of including exculpatory language in the contracts they make with their customers.[21] Despite the suggestion in U.C.C. § 2-719(3) that an exclusion of damages for personal injury is only "prima facie" unconscionable, overcoming the presumption appears impossible. Even if such an exclusion were found to be otherwise enforceable, liability in tort for manufacture or sale of an unreasonably defective product under § 402A of the Restatement (Second) of Torts would likely render the exclusion irrelevant.[22]

In cases involving property damage,[23] economic loss, or even personal injury where the goods were purchased for a business purpose,[24] the presumption does not apply.[25] However, the inapplicability of the presumption provides no safe harbor from attack on grounds of unconscionability, particularly where the clause excluding consequential damages is inconspicuous or where there are other factors demonstrating an absence of meaningful choice.[26]

Courts recognize that contractual provisions limiting remedies and excluding consequential damages shift the risk of a limited remedy's failure from the seller to the buyer. Accordingly, they look at the circumstances surrounding the creation of the contract to determine whether it would be unconscionable to enforce the parties' agreed allocation of risk.[27] Courts are more likely to find an exclusion of consequential damages unconscionable in situations where the buyer is a consumer, where there is a disparity in bargaining power between the parties, or where the consequential damages clause appears in a preprinted form contract.[28] Conversely, if the exclusion was freely negotiated between sophisticated parties or otherwise represents a conscious effort to allocate the foreseeable risks associated

---

[18] *See, e.g.*, Wilson Trading Corp. v. David Ferguson, Ltd., 244 N.E.2d 685 (N.Y. 1968).

[19] *See* U.C.C. § 9-102(a)(23) (2012) ("goods that are used or bought for use primarily for personal, family, or household purposes").

[20] U.C.C. § 2-719(3) (2012).

[21] *See, e.g.*, Henningsen v. Bloomfield Motors, 161 A.2d 69 (N.J. 1960).

[22] *See* RESTATEMENT (SECOND) OF TORTS § 402A cmt. m (1965).

[23] *E.g.*, Gladden v. Cadillac Motor Car Div., Gen. Motors Corp., 416 A.2d 394, 403 (N.J. 1980); Bond v. Nibco, Inc., 623 A.2d 731, 739 (Md. 1993).

[24] *E.g.*, Schlenz v. John Deere Co., 511 F. Supp. 224 (D. Mont. 1981).

[25] U.C.C. § 2-719(3) (2012).

[26] *E.g.*, A & M Produce Co. v. FMC Corp., 135 Cal. App. 3d 473 (1982).

[27] Chatlos Sys. Inc. v. Nat'l Cash Register Corp., 635 F.2d 1081, 1087 (3d Cir. 1980).

[28] Pierce v. Catalina Yachts, Inc., 2 P.3d 618 (Alaska 2000).

with the transaction, the court is far less likely to strike down this type of the exclusion.[29] Normally, however, language excluding consequential damages other than those for personal injury from consumer goods is enforceable as an allocation of the risks associated with the goods.

As an added measure of protection, most courts have required limited remedy provisions to be "conspicuous." Although the Code does not expressly require this, courts have realized that a limited remedy provision can have much the same effect as a disclaimer of warranties. Because warranty disclaimers must be conspicuous, limited remedy provisions are usually subjected to the same requirement.[30] Where consumer goods are involved, the requirements of the federal Magnuson-Moss Warranty Act[31] also requires limited remedy provisions to be disclosed "on the face of the warranty."[32]

[D]   Failure of Limited Remedy to Achieve Its Essential Purpose

Even where an agreed remedy is not unconscionable, it is unenforceable if it "fails of its essential purpose."[33] Here, the focus is on the effect of the clause rather than on procedural flaws in the contract formation process.

Disputes about the alleged failure of the essential purpose of a limited remedy usually involve a seller's inability to successfully repair defective goods after a reasonable number of attempts.[34] Most of these cases involve cars. In *Goddard v. General Motors Corp.*,[35] the warranty expressly limited the buyer's remedy to repair and replacement of any defective parts. The plaintiff's car was beset with a variety of defects, making it nearly impossible for the seller to keep up with the necessary repairs. During the first 10 months of ownership, the car's starter, fuel pump, water pump, transmission (twice), electrical system, and thermostat all failed and had to be replaced. As a result, the car was always in the shop for promised repairs. This effectively deprived the buyer of the basic benefit of his bargain and prevented the limited remedy of repair and replacement from fulfilling its essential purpose. Accordingly, the buyer was not bound by the limited remedy and was permitted to pursue an action to obtain other remedies under the Code.[36]

When a limited remedy fails of its essential purpose, an additional question that

---

[29] Schurtz v. BMW of N. Am., Inc., 814 P.2d 1108, 1112–13 (Utah 1991).

[30] *E.g.*, Ins. Co. of N. Am. v. Automatic Sprinkler Corp. of Am., 423 N.E.2d 151 (Ohio 1981).

[31] Magnuson-Moss Warranty — Federal Trade Commission Improvement Act, Act of 1975, Pub. L. No. 93-637, 99 Stat. 2183, 15 U.S.C. §§ 2301–2312 (2006).

[32] 15 U.S.C. § 2304 (2006).

[33] U.C.C. § 2-719(2) (2012); Jonathan A. Eddy, *On the "Essential" Purposes of Limited Remedies: The Metaphysics of U.C.C. Section 2-719(2)*, 65 Cal. L. Rev. 28 (1977); Roy Ryden Anderson, *Essential Purpose and Essential Failure of Purpose: A Look at Section 2-719 of the Uniform Commercial Code*, 31 Sw. L.J. 759 (1977).

[34] Riley v. Ford Motor Co., 442 F.2d 670 (5th Cir. 1971).

[35] 396 N.E.2d 761 (Ohio 1979).

[36] Funk v. Montgomery AMC/Jeep/Renault, 586 N.E.2d 1113 (Ohio Ct. App. 1990). *See also* Atwell v. Beckwith Machinery Co, 872 A.2d 1216 (Pa. Super. Ct. 2005).

frequently arises is whether any contractual limit on consequential damages is enforceable. Courts have taken conflicting views.[37] One group of cases takes what is known as the "dependent" view and reads § 2-719(2)'s reference to remedies "provided in [the U.C.C.]" as overriding a contract's consequential damage exclusion.[38] This approach to § 2-719 makes an exclusion of consequential damages dependent on whether a limited remedy fails of its essential purpose.[39] Other courts take an "independent" view that, because §§ 2-719(2) and (3) are separate subsections with separate language and separate standards, the failure of a limited remedy has no effect on a clause excluding consequential damages.[40]

Finally, some states have enacted "lemon" laws that directly address the inability of a manufacturer to repair a defective automobile.[41] These statutes, though not necessarily tied directly to U.C.C. § 2-719, have the effect of quantifying the number of attempts a manufacturer has to correct a defect before being obligated to refund the price of the car. Such statutes usually only apply to "new cars"[42] and provide the manufacturer with a greater number of opportunities to repair defects that are merely annoying but not particularly dangerous before being obligated to refund the purchaser's price. Lemon laws usually impose the obligation to supply a refund on the automobile manufacturer and not on the individual dealer who sold the car directly to the consumer.

[E]   Federal Magnuson-Moss Warranty Act

Limited remedy provisions are also regulated by the Federal Magnuson-Moss Warranty Act.[43] It applies to goods "normally used for personal, family, or household purposes."[44] The act does not require a seller to supply a warranty, but does require specified disclosures to be made if a warranty is provided.[45] In addition, it prevents sellers who make express warranties from attempting to disclaim the implied warranty of merchantability or the implied warranty of fitness for particular purpose.[46] The act also imposes certain minimum standards for express written warranties[47] and requires warranties which do not meet these

---

[37] Rheem Mfg. Co. v. Phelps Heating & Air Conditioning, Inc., 746 N.E.2d 941 (Ind. 2001); Int'l Fin. Serv., Inc. v. Franz, 534 N.W.2d 261 (Minn. 1995); Lewis Refrigeration Co. v. Sawyer Fruit Vegetable and Cold Storage Co., 709 F.2d 427 (6th Cir. 1983).

[38] *See, e.g.* Middletown Concrete Prod. v. Black Clawson Co., 802 F. Supp. 1135, 1151 (D. Del. 1992) (collecting cases).

[39] *See* Adams v. J.I. Case Co., 261 N.E.2d 1, 8 (Ill. App. Ct. 1970).

[40] *See* Waters v. Massey-Ferguson, Inc., 775 F.2d 587, 592–93 (4th Cir. 1985) (collecting cases); Int'l Fin. Serv. Inc. v. Franz, 534 N.W.2d 261 (Minn. 1995).

[41] *E.g,* Ohio Rev. Code §§ 1345.71–1345.78 (Anderson 2002).

[42] *E.g.,* Ohio Rev. Code § 1345.73 (Anderson 2002).

[43] Act of 1975, Pub. L. No. 93-637, 99 Stat. 2183, 15 U.S.C. §§ 2301–2312 (2006).

[44] 15 U.S.C. § 2301(1) (2006).

[45] 15 U.S.C. §§ 2302–2303 (2006).

[46] 15 U.S.C. § 2308 (2006).

[47] 15 U.S.C. § 2304 (2006).

minimum standards to be labeled as "limited."[48]

With respect to limited remedy provisions, the act has little impact other than to require that the warrantor must "remedy such consumer product within a reasonable time and without charge in the case of a defect, malfunction, or failure to conform with [the] written warranty."[49] The customary limited remedy of repair or replacement of the product will suffice. Moreover, the rare manufacturer who supplies a "full" warranty must conspicuously disclose any limitation or exclusion of consequential damages on the face of the warranty.[50]

§ 14.03 LIQUIDATED DAMAGES[51]

Contracts sometimes specify an amount of money to be paid as damages for any breach.[52] When the amount specified is significantly different from the amount of actual damages, or where it is difficult to prove the amount of actual damages suffered by the injured party, the enforceability of the agreed damages clause may be questioned. When this happens, the issue is whether the agreed amount is enforceable as a "liquidated damages" provision, or unenforceable because it is a "penalty."

[A]   History of Liquidated Damages: The Penal Bond[53]

At one time, parties sometimes used a "penal bond" to ensure performance of a contract.[54] These bonds were separate "sealed" promises that were enforceable in an action in "covenant" for the payment of a fixed sum of money.[55] This ancillary agreement would specify that the obligation to pay the amount of the bond could be fully discharged by fully performing the primary contract. Thus, the bond would require payment of a fixed sum, subject to a condition that was tied to performance of the main contract that could result in discharge of the bond. For example, the bond might provide: "I promise to pay $10,000, unless I perform my contract to construct a house for Mr. Jones by December 15, 2015." If the house was

---

[48] 15 U.S.C. § 2303(a)(2) (2006).

[49] 15 U.S.C. § 2304(a)(1) (2006).

[50] 15 U.S.C. § 2304(a)(4) (2006).

[51] Charles J. Goetz & Robert E. Scott, *Liquidated Damages, Penalties and the Just Compensation Principle*, 77 COLUM. L. REV. 553 (1977); Alan Schwartz, *The Myth That Promisees Prefer Supracompensatory Remedies: An Analysis of Contracting for Damage Measures*, 100 YALE L.J. 376 (1990); Tess Wilkinson-Ryan, *Do Liquidated Damages Encourage Breach? A Psychological Experiment*, 108 MICH. L. REV. 633, 636 (2010).

[52] Kenneth W. Clarkson, Roger LeRoy Miller & Timothy J. Muris, *Liquidated Damages v. Penalties: Sense or Nonsense?*, 1978 WIS. L. REV. 351; Larry A. DiMatteo, *A Theory of Efficient Penalty: Eliminating the Law of Liquidated Damages*, 38 AM. BUS. L.J. 633 (2001); Charles A. Goetz & Robert E. Scott, *Liquidated Damages, Penalties and the Just Compensation Principle: Some Notes on an Enforcement Model and a Theory of Efficient Breach*, 77 COLUM. L. REV. 554 (1977); Ian R. Macneil, *Power of Contact and Agreed Remedies*, 47 CORNELL L. REV. 495 (1962).

[53] William H. Lloyd, *Penalties and Forfeitures*, 29 HARV. L. REV. 117 (1915).

[54] Curtis Nyquist, *A Contract Tale from the Crypt*, 30 HOU. L. REV. 1205, 1232–33 (1993); A.W.B. Simpson, *The Penal Bond with Conditional Defeasance*, 82 L.Q. REV. 392, 393 (1966).

[55] *See supra* § 1.03 History of Contract Law.

completed by December 15, 2015, the promisor was released from his duty to pay the $10,000. If not, the promisee could enforce the bond.

At one time, these bonds were strictly enforced.[56] Their enforceability made them an effective way of imposing a penalty for breach of a contract. The threat of this penalty discouraged breach.

The principal difficulty with these bonds was their potential for a forfeiture, particularly when the underlying contract was substantially though not completely performed.[57] Assume, for example, that Winkler Construction Co. makes a sealed promise to pay $100,000, but will be excused from paying if it constructs the mansion it is under contract to build, using only Reading-brand pipe.[58] If Winkler completes the mansion but uses one section of Cohoes-brand pipe instead of Reading, the ancillary promise to pay the $100,000 will not be discharged. The contractor would be required to pay the full $100,000, even though the only damages that would have been available for breach of the construction contract would have been the difference in value between a mansion constructed with Reading pipe and one constructed with Cohoes pipe.[59] The contractor would liable for paying $100,000 even though the harm caused by the breach was insignificant, and this might mean that the owner would receive the house essentially for free. A better example of a forfeiture would be hard to imagine.

The punitive effect of these bonds led courts of equity to be unwilling to enforce them.[60] Although performance bonds are still used, they now operate to ensure a guaranteed source of funds for payment of the actual damages rather than to coerce performance.[61]

---

[56] *E.g.*, Leasing Serv. Corp. v. Justice, 673 F.2d 70 (2d Cir. 1982). *See* WILLIAM SHAKESPEARE, THE MERCHANT OF VENICE, act 4, sc. 1; A.W.B. Simpson, *The Penal Bond with Conditional Defeasance*, 82 L.Q. REV. 392, 411–12 (1966) (explaining that "[t]he law governing bonds is tough law" and that such conditional bonds were almost always enforced"); Charles J. Goetz & Robert E. Scott, *Liquidated Damages, Penalties and the Just Compensation Principle: Some Notes on an Enforcement Model and a Theory of Efficient Breach*, 77 COLUM. L. REV. 554, 554 (1977); THEODORE SEDGWICK, A TREATISE ON THE MEASURE OF DAMAGES 394 (New York, J.S. Voorhies 2d ed. 1852).

[57] Martin D. Beglieter, *Anti-Contest Clauses: When You Care Enough to Send the Final Threat*, 26 ARIZ. ST. L.J. 629, 654–55 (1994).

[58] *See* Jacob & Youngs, Inc. v. Kent, 129 N.E. 889 (N.Y. 1921).

[59] *Id.* at 890.

[60] A.W.B. SIMPSON, A HISTORY OF THE COMMON LAW OF CONTRACT 118 (1975). *See* Wasserman's Inc. v. Twp. of Middletown, 645 A.2d 100, 105 (N.J. 1994). *See generally* RESTATEMENT (SECOND) OF CONTRACTS § 356(2) (1981).

[61] AMERICAN BAR ASSOCIATION, PERFORMANCE BONDS (1997).

[B] Penalty; or Enforceable Liquidated Damages[62]

Although penal bonds are no commonly longer used,[63] modern contracts frequently specify an amount of damages owed in the event of a breach. These agreed or "liquidated" damages provisions are enforceable if they represent a legitimate effort to predict the extent of the harm that will be caused by a breach. They are not enforceable if they constitute a penalty intended to discourage one of the parties from breaching. The principal difficulty is distinguishing between an enforceable liquidated damages provision and an unenforceable penalty.

Courts use a three-part test to distinguish between an enforceable liquidated damages clause and an unenforceable penalty: (1) the purpose of the clause; (2) the difficulty of proof of the amount of actual damages; and (3) the proportionality of the agreed sum to the actual or anticipated harm.[64]

[1] Purpose of the Agreed Damages Provision

Most courts still usually say that the purpose of the clause is a critical factor in determining the enforceability of an agreed remedy.[65] However, they are naturally reluctant to trust the self-serving statements of the parties about a clause's purpose. Not surprisingly, agreements usually refer to the term as a "liquidated damages" provision, probably hoping that this beneficial characterization of the provision will enhance its enforceability. Agreements sometimes go so far as to use language indicating that the agreed amount is "intended as liquidated damages and not as a penalty." Although some courts have refused to enforce a provision simply because it was labeled in the contract as a "penalty,"[66] they are not often fooled by the simple expedient of its characterization as a "liquidated damages" clause.[67] Thus, in determining the purpose of the clause, the parties' own characterization of the provision is not likely to control.[68] Instead, its purpose is more often determined with reference to the other two prongs of the test: the relative degree of anticipated or actual difficulty in determining the actual damages, and whether the stipulated amount is grossly disproportionate to the

---

[62] Jack Graves, *Penalty Clauses and the CISG*, 30 J.L. & COM. 153 (2012); William S. Harwood, Comment, *Liquidated Damages: A Comparison of the Common Law and the Uniform Commercial Code*, 45 FORDHAM L. REV. 1349, 1349 (1977).

[63] *See* Gerald T. McLaughlin, *Standby Letters of Credit and Penalty Clauses: An Unexpected Synergy*, 43 OHIO ST. L. J. 1, 6 (1982).

[64] *E.g*, Wassenaar v. Panos, 331 N.W.2d 357, 363 (Wis. 1983).

[65] *See* Wassenaar v. Panos, 331 NW.2d 357, 363 (Wis. 1983); Wasserman's Inc. v. Twp. of Middletown, 645 A.2d 100, 106 (N.J. 1994).

[66] *E.g.*, Easton Telecom Serv., L.L.C. v. Corecomm Internet Group, Inc., 216 F. Supp. 2d 695 (N.D. Ohio 2002).

[67] *E.g.*, Wasserman's Inc. v. Twp. of Middletown, 645 A.2d 100, 109 (N.J. 1994); Fretwell v. Prot. Alarm Co., 764 P.2d 149 (Okla. 1988).

[68] Wasserman's Inc. v. Twp. of Middletown, 645 A.2d 100, 107 (N.J. 1994); Westhaven Assoc., Ltd v. CC. of Madison, Inc., 652 N.W.2d 819, 824–25 (Wis. Ct. App. 2002) (discussing evidentiary value of parties' stated intent); Kenneth W. Clarkson, Roger LeRoy Miller & Timothy J. Muris, *Liquidated Damages v. Penalties: Sense or Nonsense?*, 1978 WIS. L. REV. 351, 353.

actual or anticipated harm.[69]

[2]   Difficulty of Determining Actual Damages

The relative degree of difficulty in determining the injured party's actual damages sheds light on the likely enforceability of an agreed damages clause.[70] If the damages caused by a breach are easily calculable, the agreed amount is less likely to be enforced.[71] However, where the actual damages are more difficult to assess, the agreed amount is more likely to be enforced.[72] As two influential scholars have explained: "the greater the difficulty of estimating or proving damages, the more likely the stipulated damages will appear reasonable."[73]

Agreed damage clauses more commonly appear in contracts where the amount of actual damages may be difficult to calculate, particularly in situations where uncertain lost profits or intangible harm seems likely. For example, in construction contracts the consequences of delay can be hard to determine. Accordingly, these contracts frequently include a term fixing an amount of damages for each day, week, or month of delay in completing the project. The difficulty of proving lost profits due to a delay makes the agreed remedy more likely to be enforced than in situations where consequential damages may be easier to prove. The problem of determining the amount of actual damages is particularly acute in public works contracts where the injured governmental recipient of the breaching party's services is less likely to use the completed project to generate revenue.[74]

Provisions fixing an employee's damages in an employment contract due to wrongful discharge by the employer are more likely to be enforced, particularly where the harm to the employee amounts to more than his lost salary.[75] Wrongfully discharged employees suffer harm to their reputations or experience emotional distress, both of which are difficult to evaluate.[76] Likewise, an agreed remedy provision fixing the employer's recovery for an employee's early departure is more likely to be enforceable when the employee's unique abilities make the consequences of his or her absence difficult to discern.[77] The difficulty of determining the actual harm caused by an employee's breach of a covenant not to

---

[69] RESTATEMENT (SECOND) OF CONTRACTS § 356(1)(1981); U.C.C. § 2-718(1) (2012).

[70] Perfect Solutions, Inc. v. Jereod, Inc., 974 F. Supp. 77 (D. Mass. 1997).

[71] RESTATEMENT (SECOND) OF CONTRACTS § 356 cmt. b (1981). *E.g.*, Quaker Oats Co. v. Reilly, 274 A.D.2d 565 (N.Y. App. Div. 2000).

[72] RESTATEMENT (SECOND) OF CONTRACTS § 356 cmt. b (1981). *See, e.g, In re* Lappin Elec. Co., 245 B.R. 326, 329–31 (Bankr. E.D. Wis. 2000).

[73] Charles J. Goetz & Robert E. Scott, *Liquidated Damages, Penalties and the Just Compensation Principle: Some Notes on an Enforcement Model and a Theory of Efficient Breach*, 77 COLUM. L. REV. 554, 559 (1977).

[74] *See* City of Davenport v. Shewry Corp. 674 N.W.2d 79 (Iowa 2004); Priebe & Sons v. United States, 332 U.S. 407 (1947); Dave Gustafson & Co. v. State, 156 N.W.2d 185 (S.D. 1968).

[75] *E.g.*, Wassenaar v. Panos, 331 N.W.2d 357 (Wis. 1983).

[76] *See supra* § 12.04[D] Limit on Recovery for Emotional Distress.

[77] *E.g.*, Vanderbilt v. DiNardo, 974 F. Supp. 638 (M.D. Tenn. 1997) (college football coach); Cullman Broad. Co., Inc. v. Bosley, 373 So. 2d 830 (Ala. 1979) (radio announcer).

compete makes an agreed remedy provision particularly likely to be enforced.[78]

At the other end of the spectrum, agreed damage clauses rarely even appear in contracts for the sale of goods where substitute goods are readily available and damages based on the market value of the goods are usually readily ascertainable.[79] However, a term fixing the amount of a lost-volume seller's damages is more likely to be enforced where calculations of the seller's net revenue and reasonable overhead may otherwise be troublesome. Thus, a term permitting a lost-volume seller to retain the amount of the buyer's down payment is likely to be enforceable so long as the amount of the down payment is not disproportionate to the amount of any anticipated or actual lost profits.[80]

In contracts for the sale of goods, U.C.C. § 2-718(2) provides what is almost a statutory liquidated damages provision. It permits an aggrieved seller to retain a buyer's down payment in an amount up to 20% of the "total performance for which the buyer is obligated . . . or $500, whichever is smaller."[81]

For example, if Leslie gives Reprise Motors a $3,000 down payment on a car with a total price of $10,000 and then breaches, Reprise can keep only $500 of the $3,000 because 20% of the total price would have been $2,000, and $500 is less than $2,000.[82] If the total price had been only $1,000, and Leslie had made a $300 down payment, Reprise could retain only $200 (20% of the price) because 20% of the $1,000 price is less than the $500 maximum specified in § 2-718.[83]

A seller who can prove damages greater than the amount permitted to be retained under this provision is entitled to keep more.[84] If the price were $10,000 and Reprise Motors was able to demonstrate that its lost profit on the transaction would have been $2,700, it would be permitted to retain $2,700 of the $3,000 down payment, unfettered by the limits of the formula in U.C.C. § 2-718.[85]

Contracts for the sale of real estate also frequently provide for the seller's retention of a buyer's "earnest money deposit" (the term often used to describe a down payment) as liquidated damages. Here, it would seem that the relative ease of determining an injured seller's actual damages would make such a provision less likely to be enforced.[86] On the other hand, a seller who loses a sale may experience harms such as a continued obligation to pay real estate taxes or to maintain casualty and liability insurance on the premises, and other costs of maintenance

---

[78] *See, e.g.*, Raymundo v. Hammond Clinic Ass'n, 449 N.E. 2d 276, 384 (Ind. 1983); Gorman Publ. Co. v. Stillman, 516 F. Supp. 98, 108–09 (N.D. Ill. 1980).

[79] *See* H.J. McGrath Co. v. Wisner, 55 A.2d 793 (Md. Ct. App. 1947).

[80] *E.g.*, Rodriguez v. Learjet, Inc., 946 P.2d 1010 (Kan. Ct. App. 1997).

[81] U.C.C. § 2-718(2)(b) (2012).

[82] There is a standard joke told in the mathematics departments of the nation's universities that "there are three kinds of mathematicians: those who can count, and those who can't."

[83] U.C.C. § 2-718(2)(b) (2012).

[84] U.C.C. § 2-718(3)(a) (2012).

[85] *E.g.*, Neri v. Retail Marine Corp., 285 N.E.2d 311 (N.Y. 1972).

[86] *See supra* § 12.08[B] Contracts for the Sale of Goods — Breach by the Buyer.

and repair, as well as incidental expenses associated with finding another buyer.[87] Thus, courts have tended to enforce these provisions where the sum involved did not exceed 10% of the price.[88]

[3]   Reasonableness Compared to Anticipated or Actual Harm

The third prong of the test requires the amount of agreed damages to be reasonable compared to the anticipated or actual harm. If the specified amount is disproportionate to both, the clause will not be enforced.

The prevailing principle of this part of the test is that one size does not fit all. If the agreed amount is a fixed sum to be paid despite the potential for a wide degree of possible harm, it is easy for a court to conclude that the provision was intended as a penalty.[89] Where there was no rational basis for the agreed amount, based on the circumstances anticipated at the time the contract was formed, it is unenforceable.[90]

In the early British case of *Kemble v. Farren*,[91] the court refused to enforce a provision in an entertainer's employment contract that stipulated damages of £1,000 in the event of any breach. The sum was the same regardless of whether the breach was major or trivial. This made it clear to the court that the purpose of the fixed sum was to coerce performance rather than to compensate for losses caused by the entertainer's breach. Most important, the amount was the same whether the entertainer's breach occurred at the beginning of the term of his employment, when the harm to the theater owner might be grave, or near the end of the season, when it would be more negligible.[92]

Sometimes when faced with a "one size fits all" type of agreed remedy provision, courts construe the term narrowly and treat it as applying only in the case of a total breach.[93] In cases involving something short of total breach, this technique effectively sidesteps the issue of whether the provision is an unenforceable penalty. Likewise, even where the clause seems carefully tailored to the degree of breach, a court may sidestep the issue of its enforceability by interpreting the clause in a restrictive manner to have been intended to apply only to a narrow set of circumstances.

A notorious example of this occurred in *Massman Construction Co. v. City*

---

[87] 1 George E. Palmer, The Law of Restitution § 5.5 (1978).

[88] *See, e.g.*, Maxton Builders, Inc. v. LoGalbo, 502 N.E.2d 184 (N.Y. 1986); Vines v. Orchard Hills, Inc., 435 A.2d 1022 (Conn. 1980); Kelly v. Marx, 705 N.E.2d 1114 (Mass. 1999) (5% deposit as liquidated damages). *See generally* Arthur L. Corbin, *The Right of a Defaulting Vendee to the Restitution of Installments Paid*, 40 Yale L.J. 1013 (1931).

[89] *See* Energy Plus Consul., LLC v. Ill. Fuel Co., 371 F.3d 907, 909 (7th Cir. 2004); Wilt v. Waterfield, 273 S.W.2d 290 (Mo. 1954).

[90] *See* Kelly v. Marx, 705 N.E.2d 1114 (Mass. 1999).

[91] 130 Eng. Rep. 1234 (1829).

[92] 130 Eng. Rep at 1237. *See also* Britton v. Turner, 1834 N.H. LEXIS 48 (July 1834).

[93] *E.g.*, Hathaway v. Lynn, 43 N.W. 956 (Wis. 1889).

Council of Greenville,[94] where a contract for the construction of a bridge provided for liquidated damages of $250 per day for any delay. Construction was delayed, but completion of the connecting highway was delayed even longer, making the bridge unusable until long after its eventual completion. The court assumed that the agreed damages provision was not a penalty but treated it as dependent on the unarticulated assumption that the connecting highway would be finished before the scheduled opening of the bridge. Because this presupposed condition failed to occur, the agreed remedy provision was not enforced.[95]

The *Massman* decision also raises the question of the enforceability of liquidated damage provisions where no actual harm occurs, even though the clause may have been reasonable in light of the anticipated harm. The traditional answer has been that an agreed damages provision is enforceable if it is reasonable compared to the anticipated harm, even if the actual harm is greater or lesser than that predicted by the parties at the time the contract was made.[96]

The most difficult cases are those where the agreed amount is rationally premised on anticipated harm that simply does not occur. It has proven difficult for courts to ignore the 20/20 perspective that hindsight provides. In *Norwalk Door Closer Co. v. Eagle Lock & Screw Co.*,[97] the court acknowledged that it was not its role to use hindsight to evaluate the judgment of the parties at the time the contact was made, but still found it impossible to enforce a provision that it felt had a punitive effect because of the absence of any real harm.[98]

However, courts sometimes demonstrate flexibility in assessing whether the injured party has any suffered harm. For example, in *Wassenaar v. Panos*,[99] the court enforced an agreed damages clause in an action brought by an employee for wrongful discharge even though the employee was able to mitigate his harm by obtaining alternative employment. The court found that the employee had suffered harm because of differences beyond compensation relating to the opportunity for advancement and job security. These are situations where enforcement of an agreed remedy is particularly appropriate because of intangible harm that otherwise would be difficult to precisely calculate in monetary terms.

There will be times where the opposite situation is presented: the agreed amount is unreasonable compared to the anticipated harm but not disproportionate to the actual harm. Both the Restatement (Second) of Contracts[100] and U.C.C. § 2-718(1) provide for what courts have sometimes called a "second look" at the agreed remedy provision and permit enforcement if it is reasonable when compared to either the anticipated or the actual harm.[101] In *Equitable Lumber Corp. v. IPA*

---

[94] 147 F.2d 925 (5th Cir. 1945).

[95] *Id.* at 926. *See also* Lind Bldg. Corp. v. Pac. Bellevue Devs., 776 P.2d 977 (Wash. Ct. App. 1989).

[96] *E.g.*, Exar Corp. v. Nartron Corp., 89 F.3d 833 (6th Cir. 1996).

[97] 220 A.2d 263 (Conn. 1966).

[98] *Id.* at 268. *See also* Lind Bldg. Corp. v. Pac. Bellevue Devs., 776 P.2d 977 (Wash Ct. App. 1989).

[99] 331 N.W.2d 357 (Wis. 1983).

[100] RESTATEMENT (SECOND) OF CONTRACTS § 356(1) cmt. b (1981).

[101] U.C.C. § 2-718(1) (2012).

Land Development Corp.,[102] the court enforced the agreed remedy provision even though it was unreasonable in relation to the anticipated harm, because the agreed amount approximated the actual harm caused by the breach.[103]

Thus, some courts adhere to the traditional rule and evaluate agreed remedy provisions only in light of the anticipated harm, while others take a second look at the provision and permit enforcement if it is reasonable when compared to the actual harm. The cases seem about evenly split.[104] Still others refuse to enforce the provision, even though it seemed reasonable at the time of contract formation, if it is unreasonable when viewed in light of the actual harm.

Judicial skepticism of agreed remedy provisions has been tempered by academic support for them. There is considerable reason to believe that agreed remedy provisions encourage the formation of allocatively efficient agreements by providing an otherwise missing level of confidence that the transaction will be performed.[105] A seller who "puts his money where his mouth is," by making a commitment that he will pay if he is unable to perform, may well encourage a reluctant customer to become willing to deal with him precisely because of his willingness to put up a prize if he fails to perform. Such promises might encourage the formation of contracts with neophyte competitors who must offer such a bonus to gain a toehold share of the available market.[106]

Agreed remedy provisions may also serve to reduce prices by diminishing the risk to an aggrieved party of uncompensated intangible types of harm.[107] While these arguments have had a significant impact on academic scholarship regarding agreed remedy provisions, they have had little impact on the judges who are called upon to evaluate their enforceability.[108]

[C]   Alternative Performances and Bonuses[109]

Agreed remedy provisions are sometimes disguised as terms calling for alternative performances.[110] Where the recipient of the alternative performance was truly indifferent when the contract was made as to which alternative

---

[102] 344 N.E.2d 391 (N.Y. 1976).

[103] *Id.* at 395. *See* Ellen Peters, *Remedies for Breach of Contract Relating to the Sale of Goods Under the Uniform Commercial Code: A Roadmap for Article 2*, 73 YALE L.J. 199, 278 (1963).

[104] *See* Kelly v. Marx, 694 N.E.2d 869 (Mass. Ct. App. 1998)(appendix), *reversed*, 705 N.E.2d 1114 (Mass. 1999) (anticipated harm alone); Ann Morales Olazábal, *Formal and Operative Rules in Overliquidation Per Se Cases*, 41 AM. BUS. L.J. 503, 521–22 (2004).

[105] *See* Lake River Corp. v. Carborundum Co., 769 F.2d 1284 (7th Cir. 1985).

[106] *See* RICHARD A. POSNER, ECONOMIC ANALYSIS OF LAW 129 (6th ed. 2002).

[107] *See generally* Charles J. Goetz & Robert E. Scott, *Liquidated Damages, Penalties and the Just Compensation Principle: Some Notes on an Enforcement Model and a Theory of Efficient Breach*, 77 COLUM. L. REV. 554, 558–62 (1977); Phillip R. Kaplan, Note, *A Critique of the Penalty Limitation on Liquidated Damages*, 50 S. CAL. L. REV. 1055, 1057–58 (1977).

[108] *But see* Wasserman's, Inc. v. Twp. of Middletown, 645 A.2d 100 (N.J. 1994).

[109] Robert E. Scott & George G. Triantis, *Embedded Options and the Case Against Compensation in Contract Law*, 104 COLUM. L. REV. 1428 (2004).

[110] RESTATEMENT (SECOND) OF CONTRACTS § 356 cmt. c (1981).

performance would be forthcoming, the provision should be enforced without triggering analysis of it as a liquidated damages clause.[111] However, a provision intended to measure the value of the harm to the injured party in the event of nonperformance should be analyzed under the standards ordinarily used to evaluate liquidated damages clauses.

Alternatively, the parties might attempt to evade scrutiny by casting the contract in terms of a "bonus" for early completion rather than a "penalty" for delay.[112] Such provisions tend to escape scrutiny under the usual test for liquidated damages.[113] The difficulty of distinguishing between a true incentive for prompt early performance and a disguised penalty for delay, combined with the obvious commercial benefits of providing real incentives, argues strongly in favor of the general enforceability of agreed remedy provisions that were the result of arms-length bargaining between sophisticated parties.

[D]   Effect of Agreed Remedies on Specific Performance

It might be imagined that the inclusion of an enforceable agreed damages provision in a contract would make specific performance unavailable. The parties' agreement to a specific sum as a remedy for breach seems to acknowledge the adequacy of this sum as a remedy for breach. Nevertheless, most courts hold that the existence of an otherwise enforceable liquidated damages provision does not impair the availability of either specific performance or an injunction.[114] Parties who wish may expressly provide for the unavailability of equitable relief, and make payment of the agreed sum or performance of the duties otherwise specified in the contract alternative means of performing.[115]

[E]   Unconscionability of Liquidated Damages

Even where an agreed damages provision passes muster under these traditional tests, it is potentially vulnerable to attack if it is unconscionable. Unconscionability usually requires a showing that the term was unreasonably favorable to one party and was the product of an absence of reasonable choice by the other.[116] Thus, where an agreed damages provision would result in an apparent windfall to the injured party and there was unequal bargaining power when the contract was made, the fact that the clause was a reasonable estimate of the anticipated harm should not protect it from assault.

---

[111] *E.g.*, Carlyle Apts. Joint Venture v. AIG Life Ins. Co., 635 A.2d 366, 371 (Md. Ct. App. 1994).

[112] James P. George, *Rent Concessions and Illegal Contract Penalties in Texas*, 48 S. Tex. L. Rev. 645 (2007).

[113] *But see* Banta v. Stamford Motor Co., 92 A. 665, 667 (Conn. 1914).

[114] Restatement (Second) of Contracts § 361 (1981). *E.g.*, Bradley v. Health Coal., Inc., 687 So. 2d 329 (Fla. Dist. Ct. App. 1997).

[115] *See* Restatement (Second) of Contracts § 361 cmt. b (1981).

[116] *See generally supra* § 10.05 Unconscionability.

[F]   Agreements for Attorneys' Fees and Other Litigation Costs

Attorneys' fees and litigation costs are not generally recoverable as damages for breach of contract.[117] Despite this, the parties may make them recoverable by agreement.[118] An attempt to specify the amount recoverable as attorneys' fees will be subject to the same general test as any other provision fixing the amount of damages to determine if it is a penalty.[119]

[G]   Agreed Remedies in International Transactions

The United Nations Convention on the International Sale of Goods (CISG) does not address the enforceability of agreed remedy provisions, probably in recognition of differences in their treatment between common law legal systems, such as those existing in the United States and the United Kingdom, and those in civil law jurisdictions, such as those on the European continent. Under the civil law, penalty provisions are routinely enforced.

The UNIDROIT Principles of International Commercial Contracts (PICC)[120] seem to permit enforceability of an agreed remedy provision even if the nonbreaching party was not harmed, unless the amount is grossly excessive in light of the actual harm.[121] Likewise, Article 9.509 of the Principles of European Contract Law (PECL) specifies that "where the contract provides that a party who fails to perform is to pay a specified sum to the aggrieved party for such non-performance, the aggrieved party shall be awarded that sum irrespective of its actual loss."[122] This generous rule is buffered by language that permits the court to reduce the sum "to a reasonable amount where it is grossly excessive in relation to the loss resulting from the non-performance and the other circumstances."[123] Thus, both PICC and PECL take a retrospective approach to whether the agreed sum is "grossly excessive."

§ 14.04   ALTERNATIVE DISPUTE RESOLUTION[124]

Rather than agree to a specific remedy, the parties sometimes agree to a particular method for resolving their disputes, such as arbitration or mediation.

---

[117] Bernhard v. Farmers Ins. Exch., 915 P.2d 1285, 1297 (Colo. 1996).

[118] Oral Roberts Univ. v. Anderson, 11 F. Supp. 2d 1336, 1337 (N.D. Okla. 1997). *But see* Vermeer of S. Ohio, Inc. v. Argo Constr. Co., 760 N.E.2d 1 (Ohio Ct. App. 2001) (not enforceable where parties lacked equal bargaining power and similar levels of sophistication).

[119] *See* Equitable Lumber Corp. v. IPA Land Dev. Corp., 344 N.E.2d 391 (N.Y. 1976).

[120] *See* Joseph M. Perillo *UNIDROIT Principles of International Commercial Contracts: The Black Letter Text and a Review*, 63 Fordham L. Rev. 281 (1994).

[121] PICC Art. 7.4.13(1) (2004).

[122] PECL Art. 9.509(1) (2002).

[123] PECL Art. 9.509(2) (2002).

[124] Soia Mentschikoff, *Commercial Arbitration*, 61 Colum. L. Rev. 846, 848–54 (1961); Thomas J. Stipanowich, *Punitive Damages in Arbitration:* Garrity v. Lyle Stuart *Reconsidered*, 66 B.U.L. Rev. 953 (1986); W. Mark C. Weidemaier, *Arbitration and the Individuation Critique*, 49 Ariz. L. Rev. 69 (2007).

Binding arbitration has become a popular alternative to litigation, in part because it shifts some of the expense of initiating a dispute to the plaintiff.[125] Many agreements include a provision requiring the parties to submit any dispute that arises to a panel of arbitrators, whose decision, including any remedy they impose, will be binding. Arbitration provisions are typically enforceable, and despite initial judicial skepticism[126] and continuing challenges based on unconscionability,[127] courts now usually dismiss actions brought in violation of such a clause.[128]

Where one party attempts to impose an arbitration provision unilaterally on the other, as in the case of an employer requiring all disputes with employees to be submitted to binding arbitration, the provision may not be enforceable. A court may question whether the employee's silent acquiescence to this policy represented a real agreement to relinquish his or her right to press any claims against the employer in court.[129]

Arbitration clauses typically specify that the dispute will be resolved through an arbitration conducted according to the rules of the American Arbitration Association,[130] the American Arbitration Forum,[131] or pursuant to the Federal Arbitration Act.[132] Rules for arbitration typically provide for either a single arbitrator (usually in a smaller case) or a panel of three arbitrators, selected from a panel of experienced individuals willing to serve. The arbitrators are paid for their time, and the parties share the costs of the arbitration proceeding. Arbitration proceedings are similar to a trial in court except that the types of rulings that might dispose of the dispute prior to the conclusion of a complete trial are unavailable.[133] Arbitrators' decisions are subject to review in court but may be reversed only on extremely limited grounds, mostly involving misconduct by the arbitrators themselves.[134] Arbitration awards are enforced unless the arbitrators have exceeded the scope of

---

[125] Mark E. Budnitz, *Arbitration of Disputes Between Consumers and Financial Institutions: A Serious Threat to Consumer Protection*, 10 OHIO ST. J. DISP. RESOL. 267 (1995).

[126] Wilko v. Swan, 346 U.S. 427 (1953).

[127] Richard M. Alderman, *Pre-Dispute Mandatory Arbitration in Consumer Contracts: A Call for Reform*, 38 HOUS. L. REV. 1237 (2001); Charles L. Knapp, *Taking Contracts Private: The Quiet Revolution in Contract Law*, 71 FORDHAM L. REV. 761, 796 (2002); Stephan Landsman, *ADR and the Cost of Compulsion*, 57 STAN. L. REV. 1593, 1596 (2005).

[128] *See* Uniform Arbitration Act § 7, 7 U.L.A. 6 (2006). *See* Millennium Solutions, Inc. v. Davis, 603 N.W.2d 406 (Neb. 1999) (recognizing enforceability of arbitration agreements under the Uniform Arbitration Act, but refusing to enforce agreement entered into before effective date of legislation's adoption of the statute).

[129] *See, e.g,* Phillips v. CIGNA Invs., Inc., 27 F. Supp. 2d 345 (D. Conn. 1998). *But see* Morrison v. Circuit City Stores, Inc., 70 F. Supp. 2d 815 (S.D. Ohio 1999) (arbitration clause in employment contract signed by employee not unconscionable).

[130] http://www.adr.org (last viewed June 20, 2013).

[131] http://www.arbforum.com (last viewed June 20, 2013). The author has previously served as neutral arbitrator for the National Arbitration Forum.

[132] 9 U.S.C. §§ 1–14 (2006).

[133] Margaret Pedrick Sullivan, *The Scope of Modern Arbitral Awards*, 62 TUL. L. REV. 1113, 1125–31 (1988).

[134] *See* Federal Arbitration Act § 10, 9 U.S.C. § 10 (2006); Uniform Arbitration Act § 12 (2000).

their authority.[135] Arbitrators' decisions are only rarely accompanied by an explanation, so it is usually difficult to determine the basis for a panel's award.

Recently, arbitration clauses have been under attack as unconscionable. For example, in *Ingle v. Circuit City Stores, Inc.*,[136] the court found that an arbitration clause in an employment contract was unconscionable. The court used a "sliding scale" approach to substantive and procedural unconscionability, which the court explained "disregards the regularity of the procedural process of the contract formation, that creates the terms, in proportion to the greater harshness or unreasonableness of the substantive terms themselves."[137] Using this approach, "the more substantively oppressive the contract term, the less evidence of procedural unconscionability is required to come to the conclusion that the term is unenforceable, and vice versa."[138] The only procedural unconscionability was the superior bargaining power of Circuit City because of its role as employer and its use of the arbitration clause in its standard employment contract.

The court further concluded that several aspects of the arbitration clause were unreasonably one-sided. Several substantive terms of Circuit City's arbitration agreement were one-sided, including its coverage, its statute of limitations, its prohibition against class actions, its filing fee, the cost-splitting feature, the remedies available to the arbitrators, and the employer's one-sided power to modify or terminate it and choose litigation instead. While other courts have not been so critical of the same type of arbitration provision in employment contracts,[139] many courts are now willing to entertain challenges to arbitration clauses on grounds of unconscionability.[140]

---

[135] *See, e.g,* Garrity v. Lyle Stuart, Inc., 353 N.E.2d 793 (N.Y. 1976) (refusing to confirm an arbitration award of punitive damages assessed for breach of contract). *But see* Matter of Associated Gen'l Contractors, 335 N.E.2d 859 (N.Y. 1975) (refusing to question arbitrator's use of liquidated damages provision). *See generally* Stephen A. Hochman, *Judicial Review to Correct Arbitral Error — An Option to Consider*, 13 Ohio St. J. on Disp. Resol. 103 (1997); Thomas J. Stipanowich, *Rethinking American Arbitration*, 63 Ind. L.J. 425 (1988).

[136] 328 F.3d 1165 (9th Cir. 2003).

[137] *Id.* at 1171.

[138] *Id.*

[139] *E.g.*, Carter v. Countrywide Credit Indus., Inc., 362 F.3d 294 (5th Cir. 2004) (applying Texas law).

[140] *See* Steven J. Burton, *The New Judicial Hostility to Arbitration: Federal Preemption, Contract Unconscionability, and Agreements to Arbitrate*, 2006 J. Disp. Resol. 469; David Horton, *Federal Arbitration Act Preemption, Purposivism, and State Public Policy*, 101 Geo. L. J. 1217 (2013); Vonda Mallicoat Laughlin,, Annotation, *Claim of Unconscionability of Contract as Subject to Compulsory Arbitration Clause Contained in Contract*, 22 A.L.R.6th 49 (2007).

Chapter 15

EQUITABLE REMEDIES

§ 15.01 DEVELOPMENT OF EQUITABLE REMEDIES[1]

At early common law, money damages, was the only remedy available for breach of contract.[2] An award of damages is little more than a declaration that the plaintiff

---

[1] EDWARD YORIO, CONTRACT ENFORCEMENT: SPECIFIC PERFORMANCE AND INJUNCTIONS (1989); Melvin A. Eisenberg, *Actual and Virtual Specific Performance, the Theory of Efficient Breach, and the Indifference Principle in Contract Law*, 93 CAL. L. REV. 975 (2005); E. Allan Farnsworth, *Legal Remedies for Breach of Contract*, 70 COLUM. L. REV. 1145 (1970); Alan Schwartz, *The Case for Specific Performance*, 89 YALE L.J. 271 (1979); Peter Linzer, *On the Amorality of Contract Remedies — Efficiency, Equity, and the Second Restatement*, 81 COLUM. L. REV. 111, 114 (1981); Steven Shavell, *Specific Performance Versus Damages for Breach of Contract: An Economic Analysis*, 84 TEX. L. REV.

is entitled to recover money from the defendant. The judgment does not order the defendant to actually pay the money. Instead, it merely permits the plaintiff to begin to use a variety of other legal proceedings to seize the defendant's property and have it sold, to pay the amount of the judgment.[3] If the plaintiff wanted to force the defendant to perform his promise, the common law system provided no relief. Thus, if money was not a solution to the plaintiff's problem, the common law court system provided no recourse.[4]

When the normal legal rules are of little help, people look for alternatives.[5] When students are dissatisfied with a university's rules and procedures, they seek relief from the dean. In a similar manner, medieval plaintiffs, dissatisfied with the limitations of the rules and procedures of the common law court system sought recourse from the King or Queen. The monarch, like a modern dean, was usually far too busy with matters of state to become involved with minor disputes, especially those involving private parties. The job of finding solutions to these problems was delegated by the King or Queen to the Chancellor and his staff.[6]

In the course of dispensing justice, the Chancellor was free to resolve disputes in new and creative ways, bound only by the limits of his discretion. The Chancellor began issuing orders on the King's authority, compelling the King's subjects to perform contracts they had made. Alternatively, the Chancellor might restrain them from committing any breach. Thus, the alternative remedies of specific performance and injunctions, among others, became available from the Chancellor. And, unlike the "in rem" remedies available in the common law courts, the orders issued by the Chancellor operated "in personam," against the individual to whom the order was issued.[7]

As a result, a parallel court system developed. These equity courts were naturally reluctant to interfere with the work of the common law courts. Equity would not ordinarily intervene in disputes where a legal remedy already existed.[8] Thus, the rule developed that neither specific performance nor injunctive relief could be obtained if the normal legal remedy of money damages was adequate.[9] Where the remedy at law was adequate, the equity courts lacked jurisdiction over the dispute. Plaintiffs did not have a choice of remedies. Only if the normal remedy of money damages was inadequate would equity intervene.

---

831 (2006); Anthony Kronman, *Specific Performance*, 45 U. CHI. L. REV. 351 (1978).

[2] George T. Washington, *Damages in Contract at Common Law*, 47 L.Q. REV. 345 (1931).

[3] *See* JEFF FERRIELL & EDWARD J. JANGER, UNDERSTANDING BANKRUPTCY § 2.03 Judgments (3d ed. 2013).

[4] 1 DANIEL B. DOBBS, LAW OF REMEDIES § 2.1(1) (Practitioner's ed. 1993).

[5] Aside, *The Common Law Origins of the Infield Fly Rule*, 123 U. PENN. L. REV. 1474 (1975) (comparing baseball umpires' development of the infield fly rule as a result of the inadequacies of the official rules of baseball with the development of rules of equity due to the inadequacy of the common law).

[6] Historically, the Chancellor was a man. DANIEL B. DOBBS, LAW OF REMEDIES § 2.2 at 58 n.3 (2d ed. 1993). Apart from Mary (for a time), Elizabeth I, Victoria, and Elizabeth II, so was the monarch.

[7] *Id.* § 2.2.

[8] *See* A.W.B. SIMPSON, A HISTORY OF THE COMMON LAW OF CONTRACT 595–98 (1987 ed.).

[9] 1 W. HOLDSWORTH, HISTORY OF ENGLISH LAW 457 (7th Ed. 1956); EDWARD YORIO, CONTRACT ENFORCEMENT: SPECIFIC PERFORMANCE AND INJUNCTIONS 28 (1989).

The discretionary nature of the King's or Queen's justice led to other limits on the relief available in equity.[10] Like a thoughtful parent, the Chancellor was reluctant to issue an order that would be difficult to enforce. Accordingly, equity often refrained from exercising its jurisdiction if enforcement would be burdensome.[11] Likewise, the Chancellor was unwilling to provide assistance in situations where doing so would detract from the Chancellor's (or the King's or Queen's) moral credibility, such as where the plaintiff had engaged in some sort of improper conduct, where the contract was unfair, or where with the Chancellor's orders might be particularly burdensome.[12]

The distinction between law and equity was brought to the new world and found its way into the American Constitution. Article III of the United States Constitution extends the Judicial Power of the United States to "all cases in Law and Equity."[13] The Seventh Amendment ensures the right to a jury only "in suits at common law."[14]

The right to a jury trial was a key difference between actions at law and actions in equity. Unlike the common law courts where the jury determined the facts and the judge resolved questions of law, there were no juries in the courts of equity, where the Chancellor handled both jobs.[15]

Physical separation of the two court systems persisted well into the nineteenth century, when they were merged in both England and the United States.[16] Today, the separate judges, courts, and courthouses that at one time distinguished law and equity no longer exist. Instead, the same judges sit in both law and equity, commonly acting as both judge and chancellor in the same dispute.[17] Despite this merger, the availability of equitable remedies, such as specific performance and injunctions, still depends on the adequacy of the normal "legal" remedy of money damages.[18] Moreover, a judge's equitable discretion still depends on the moral and practical considerations developed by a long line of British Chancellors and American chancery judges.[19]

---

[10] Edward Yorio, *A Defense of Equitable Defenses*, 51 OHIO ST. L.J. 1201 (1990).

[11] EDWARD YORIO, CONTRACT ENFORCEMENT: SPECIFIC PERFORMANCE AND INJUNCTIONS 45–71 (1989).

[12] *See generally* Edward Yorio, *A Defense of Equitable Defenses*, 51 OHIO ST. L.J. 1201 (1990).

[13] U.S. Const., Art. III, § 2, cl. 1.

[14] U.S. Const., 7th Amend.

[15] EDWARD YORIO, CONTRACT ENFORCEMENT: SPECIFIC PERFORMANCE AND INJUNCTIONS 467 (1989).

[16] DANIEL B. DOBBS, LAW OF REMEDIES § 2.6(1) (1993). *See also* Charles Warren, *The Fusion of Law and Equity in United States Courts*, 6 N.C. L. REV. 283 (1928).

[17] Today, only four states maintain separate courts of law and equity. DOUGLAS LAYCOCK, MODERN AMERICAN REMEDIES, CASES AND MATERIALS 370 (3d ed. 2002).

[18] EDWARD YORIO, CONTRACT ENFORCEMENT: SPECIFIC PERFORMANCE AND INJUNCTIONS 30 (1989). *But see* Douglas Laycock, *The Death of the Irreparable Injury Rule*, 103 HARV. L. REV. 687 (1990).

[19] EDWARD YORIO, CONTRACT ENFORCEMENT: SPECIFIC PERFORMANCE AND INJUNCTIONS 101–126 (1989).

§ 15.02 TYPES OF EQUITABLE REMEDIES[20]

The two most common types of equitable remedies in contract cases are specific performance and injunctions. Other remedies such as subrogation, the imposition of an equitable lien, a constructive trust, or the appointment of a receiver to take control of a defendant's entire enterprise, are also available, but are used more rarely.[21]

[A]   Specific Performance

Specific performance compels a defendant to perform under the threat of imprisonment for contempt.[22] Unlike money damages, which substitute cash for performance, specific performance attempts to put the injured party in exactly the position it expected by forcing the defendant to perform.[23] In this respect, specific performance is a nearly perfect expectation remedy.

In many cases where the legal remedy is inadequate, practical enforcement of a decree of specific performance is easy. In a contract for the sale of real estate the defendant can easily be compelled to sign and deliver a deed. If the seller balks, the court can enter a decree transferring ownership of the property.[24] Specific performance of a promise to make a loan[25] or to convey chattels (goods) is similarly easy to enforce. The court can employ the offices of the sheriff to seize the defendant's property and deliver it to the plaintiff.[26] Although implementation of the remedy might be easier with some level of cooperation from the defendant, the court can easily take matters into its own hands and implement the desired result.

[B]   Injunctions

The early English Chancellors quickly realized that compelling performance of an obligation to render services was not so easy. This was because it was difficult for the court to discern whether the defendant had complied with the court's order to perform.[27]

Moreover, limitations on the court's jurisdiction that extended only to situations where the defendant's services were "unique" made evaluating the defendant's performance even more difficult. It is far more difficult to evaluate the

---

[20] E. Allan Farnsworth, *Legal Remedies for Breach of Contract*, 70 COLUM. L. REV. 1145, 1149–56 (1970); Anthony T. Kronman, *Specific Performance*, 45 U. CHI. L. REV. 351 (1978).

[21] Howard W. Brill, *Equity and the Restitutionary Remedies: Constructive Trust, Equitable Lien and Subrogation*, 1992 ARK. L. NOTES 1.

[22] *E.g.* Foster v. Gibbons, 33 P.3d 329 (Or. Ct. App. 2001). *See generally* 1 DANIEL B. DOBBS, LAW OF REMEDIES § 2.8 (Practitioner's ed. 1993).

[23] RESTATEMENT (SECOND) OF CONTRACTS § 357 cmt. a (1981).

[24] EDWARD YORIO, CONTRACT ENFORCEMENT: SPECIFIC PERFORMANCE AND INJUNCTIONS 57 (1989).

[25] *E.g.*, La Mirada Prods. Co., Inc. v. Wassall PLC, 823 F. Supp. 138 (S.D.N.Y. 1993).

[26] EDWARD YORIO, CONTRACT ENFORCEMENT: SPECIFIC PERFORMANCE AND INJUNCTIONS 101–26 (1989).

[27] *E.g.*, New Park Forest Assoc. II v. Rogers Enter., Inc., 552 N.E.2d 1215 (Ill. App. Ct.), *appeal denied*, 561 N.E.2d 694 (Ill. 1990).

performance of services that are unique[28] than to scrutinize those that are commonplace.[29] Accordingly, specific performance became unavailable in cases involving services and in other business relationships involving the need for continued cooperation between the parties or supervision by the court.[30]

In these situations the alternative equitable remedy of an injunction is sometimes used. Specific performance compels the defendant to perform. Injunctions encourage performance by restraining the defendant from conduct that is incompatible with full performance. For example, a cellist might not be compelled to play the cello at the plaintiff's theater, but she could be restrained from performing elsewhere.[31] Likewise, a professional football player might be enjoined from playing for a team in a rival league.[32] Though a court would probably find it difficult to determine whether the cellist was keeping beat with the rest of the orchestra, or whether a member of the team was trying to win, there would be no difficulty in discerning whether these defendants had gone to work for the plaintiff's competitors in violation of the court's injunction. Injunctions are therefore sometimes used to accomplish indirectly what cannot be achieved by specific performance.

Injunctions are also sometimes used to maintain the status quo while an action seeking specific performance is pending in court. Thus, the buyer of real estate might seek a short-term temporary restraining order or "TRO" and then a more durable "preliminary injunction," to prevent a seller from conveying land to a third party while the buyer's action to obtain specific performance is resolved.[33] Temporary restraining orders and preliminary injunctions are used for short-term relief to prevent the defendant from taking irreversible action in violation of a contract until a regular trial can be held.[34]

§ 15.03　ADEQUACY OF THE LEGAL REMEDY[35]

Equitable remedies are traditionally available only if the legal remedy of money damages is "inadequate."[36] Courts frequently describe this rule in terms of the

---

[28] *See* De Rivafinoli v. Corsetti, 4 Paige Ch. 274, 270 (N.Y. Ch. 1833).

[29] *See* N. Del. Indus. Dev. Corp. v. E.W. Bliss Co., 245 A.2d 431 (Del. Ch. 1968). *But see* Grayson-Robinson Stores, Inc. v. Iris Const. Corp., 168 N.E.2d 377 (N.Y. 1960) (confirming arbitrator's award of specific performance of a contract for landlord to construct a building for a tenant).

[30] *See generally* EDWARD YORIO, CONTRACT ENFORCEMENT: SPECIFIC PERFORMANCE AND INJUNCTIONS 58–61 (1989). *See also supra* § 12.08[D] Construction Contracts: Breach by the Builder — Cost of Performance or Difference in Value.

[31] Lumley v. Wagner, 42 Eng. Rep. 687 (1852); Duff v. Russell, 1891 N.Y. Misc. LEXIS 1888 (Mar. 9, 1891).

[32] Dallas Cowboys Football Club v. Harris, 348 S.W.2d 37 (Tex. Civ. App. 1961). *See* Am. Broad. Cos., Inc. v. Wolf, 420 N.E.2d 363 (N.Y. 1981) (sports commentator).

[33] *E.g.*, Walgreen Co. v. Sara Creek Property Co., 966 F.2d 273, 277 (7th Cir. 1992); *cf.* K.F.K. Corp. v. Am. Continental Homes, Inc. 335 N.E.2d 156 (Ill. App. Ct. 1975).

[34] *See* DANIEL B. DOBBS, LAW OF REMEDIES §§ 2.11, 12.8(1) (2d ed. 1993).

[35] *See* Anthony T. Kronman, *Specific Performance*, 45 U. CHI. L. REV. 351 (1978); Douglas Laycock, *The Death of the Irreparable Injury Rule*, 103 HARV. L. REV. 687 (1990); Thomas Ulen, *The Efficiency of Specific Performance: Toward a Unified Theory of Contract Remedies*, 83 MICH. L. REV. 341 (1984);

necessity for "irreparable injury" to the plaintiff, if equitable relief is not supplied.[37]

This jurisdictional limitation on the authority of a court of equity yields different results, depending on subject matter of the contract. Land, for example, is considered unique.[38] Because there is no substitute for a specific parcel of real estate, an award of money damages is not regarded as an adequate remedy for breach of a contract to sell land. Thus, specific performance became the customary remedy for breach of a contract involving real estate. Goods, on the other hand are only sometimes unique. Money can be used to purchase a ready substitute. As a result, specific performance is only rarely available as a remedy for breach of a contract for the sale of goods. As will be seen, different problems arise in connection with contracts for services.

The unique character of the subject matter of a contract makes money damages inadequate in two ways. First, the absence of a reasonable substitute makes it difficult to properly ascertain the market value of the land or goods involved. Without similar properties to use as the basis for a reasonable comparison, the market value cannot be determined. This presents a practical difficulty even today, in connection with some commercial real estate, and truly unique items of personal property. Even in connection with residential real estate, buyers frequently purchase a home because of its proximity to work, school, shopping, parks, transportation, and other facilities. A home in another location, even a few blocks away, might be entirely different. Second, in connection with unique property, there is a greater possibility that one of the parties will have personal aesthetic or sentimental interests for which there is no market value.[39] Features such as size, layout, interior traffic patterns, yard size, curb appeal, and "charm" play important roles in people's choice of where to live.

Even where the subject matter of the contract is not truly unique, market substitutes may not be readily available. The difficulty of obtaining a substitute can also make the legal remedy inadequate and thus justify an equitable remedy.[40]

Damages may also be difficult to calculate even where the land, goods, or services involved in the contract are not truly one of a kind, but where the harm caused by a breach is highly speculative. Thus, even where goods are not unique, specific performance or an injunction may be available to avoid the difficulty of proving speculative consequential damages.[41]

Edward Yorio, *In Defense of Money Damages for Breach of Contract*, 82 COLUM. L. REV. 1365 (1982); Alan Schwartz, *The Case for Specific Performance*, 89 YALE L.J. 271 (1979).

[36] RESTATEMENT (SECOND) OF CONTRACTS § 359 (1981); Doug Rendleman, *The Inadequate Remedy at Law Prerequisite for an Injunction*, 33 U. FLA. L. REV. 346 (1981).

[37] RESTATEMENT (SECOND) OF CONTRACTS § 359 (1981); Doug Rendleman, *The Inadequate Remedy at Law Prerequisite for an Injunction*, 33 U. FLA. L. REV. 346 (1981).

[38] RESTATEMENT (SECOND) OF CONTRACTS § 359 cmt. e (1981).

[39] RESTATEMENT (SECOND) OF CONTRACTS § 360 cmt. b (1981). *See, e.g.*, Cumbest v. Harris, 363 So. 2d 294 (Miss. 1978).

[40] *See* U.C.C. § 2-716 cmt. 2 (2012).

[41] *E.g.*, City Stores Co. v. Ammerman, 266 F. Supp. 766 (D.D.C. 1967), *aff'd*, 394 F.2d 950 (D.C. Cir. 1968); Oglebay Norton Co. v. Armco, Inc., 556 N.E.2d 515 (Ohio 1990).

These are not the only situations where the remedy at law is inadequate. Specific performance is also usually available in requirements and output contracts.[42] The difficulty of projecting the specific quantities likely to be required or produced in such contracts, and the difficulty of finding someone else willing to enter into a long-term exclusive dealing contract, makes them particularly good candidates for specific performance.[43] Similarly, the difficulty of calculating the extent of harm caused by breach of a covenant not to compete can make an injunction an attractive remedy.[44] The harm caused by the loss of the ability to control a corporation, following a breach of a contract to convey a block of shares, transcends the market value of the stock in ways that are hard to calculate, making these agreements also susceptible to specific enforcement.[45]

Any anticipated difficulty in actually enforcing an award of damages might also constitute grounds for equitable relief.[46] Thus, the defendant's financial insolvency might be enough to warrant an order of specific performance or an injunction.[47]

Despite the universal recital of the irreparable injury rule, some thoughtful scholars have questioned its vitality.[48] Their research suggests that decisions purporting to deny relief based on the adequacy of the legal remedy are really based on other grounds such as the harshness of granting the requested relief, the impracticality of judicial supervision, or other pragmatic concerns.[49] Based on economic principles of allocative efficiency, other scholars and a few courts[50] have argued in favor of expanding the availability of specific performance to cases where money damages might otherwise have been considered adequate.[51]

[A]　　　　Real Estate Contracts

In medieval England, land was critical and each parcel of real estate was considered unique.[52] Then, unlike today when tracts full of nearly identical homes abound, there was no adequate means of determining the market value of real

---

[42] *E.g.* Curtice Bros. Co. v. Catts, 66 A. 935 (N.J. Ch. 1907).

[43] *See* U.C.C. § 2-716 cmt. 2 (2012); Laclede Gas Co. v. Amoco Oil Co., 522 F.2d 33 (8th Cir. 1975); Tenn. Valley Auth. v. Mason Coal, Inc., 384 F. Supp. 1107 (E.D. Tenn. 1974).

[44] *See, e.g.*, Walgreen Co. v. Sara Creek Prop. Co., 966 F.2d 273, 277 (7th Cir. 1992); Fine Foods, Inc. v. Dahlin, 523 A.2d 1228 (Vt. 1986); Milton Handler & Daniel E. Lazaroff, *Restraint of Trade and the Restatement (Second) of Contracts*, 57 N.Y.U. L. REV. 669, 683–708 (1982).

[45] RESTATEMENT (SECOND) OF CONTRACTS § 360 cmt. b (1981).

[46] RESTATEMENT (SECOND) OF CONTRACTS § 360(c) (1981).

[47] *E.g.*, Miller v. LeSea Broad., Inc., 87 F.3d 224 (7th Cir. 1996); Estate of Brown, 289 A.2d 77 (Pa. 1972).

[48] Douglas Laycock, *The Death of the Irreparable Injury Rule*, 103 HARV. L. REV. 687 (1990).

[49] *Id.* at 692.

[50] Walgreen Co. v. Sara Creek Prop. Co., 966 F.2d 273 (7th Cir. 1992) (Posner, J.)

[51] Anthony T. Kronman, *Specific Performance*, 45 U. CHI. L. REV. 351 (1978); Thomas S. Ulen, *The Efficiency of Specific Performance: Toward a Unified Theory of Contract Remedies*, 83 MICH. L. REV. 341 (1984); Ian Macneil, *Efficient Breach of Contract: Circles in the Sky*, 68 VA. L. REV. 947 (1982); Peter Linzer, *On the Amorality of Contract Remedies — Efficiency, Equity, and the Second Restatement*, 81 COLUM. L. REV. 111 (1981); Alan Schwartz, *The Case for Specific Performance*, 89 YALE L.J. 271 (1979).

[52] E. Allan Farnsworth, *Legal Remedies for Breach of Contract*, 70 COLUM. L. REV. 1145, 1154 (1970).

estate. Furthermore, because the real value of land depended on its capacity to generate future income, establishing a precise "present value" was, and still is, highly conjectural. Land's value depended not only on both the weather and on the continued health of an available source of labor, but also at times on the risk of its seizure by an invading army.[53]

The rule was established early on, and persists today,[54] that the remedy at law of money damages is inadequate to compensate the buyer in a contract for the sale of land.[55] Accordingly, specific performance is nearly always available as a remedy for breach of a contract to transfer an interest in real estate.[56]

Where an aggrieved buyer enters into a contract to acquire the land for no purpose other than to resell it to someone else, it might appear that money damages would be adequate.[57] Even here however, most courts apply the rule that land is unique and that the remedy at law is inadequate,[58] though a few courts have ruled to the contrary.[59]

Interests in real estate take many forms. Specific performance is available regardless of the type of interest or the nature of the real estate involved. Thus, specific performance is available for a contract to purchase a nondescript condominium apartment[60] as well as for a lease of commercial real estate.[61]

When it is the buyer rather than the seller who is in breach, it might seem difficult to maintain the position that money damages are inadequate. In these cases the seller's expectation is almost always to receive money: payment of the price. For example, if a buyer reneges on his promise to pay $150,000 for land worth only $140,000, the seller would seem to be made whole if it receives the $10,000 difference plus whatever incidental damages may be incurred from having to place the land back on the market. Where there is a ready market of willing buyers for the land, courts have sometimes been reluctant to award specific performance to the seller.[62] Generally, however, courts award specific performance to the seller, compelling the buyer to take title and pay the entire price, instead of simply being liable for any difference in value between the contract price and the

---

[53] *See* Paradine v. Jane, 82 Eng. Rep. 897 (1647).

[54] *E.g.*, Sullivan v. Porter, 861 A.2d 625 (Me. 2004); Vigneaux v. Carriere, 845 A.2d 304 (R.I. 2004).

[55] *E.g.*, Gartrell v. Stafford, 11 N.W. 732 (Neb. 1882).

[56] RESTATEMENT (SECOND) OF CONTRACTS § 360 cmt. e (1981); Anthony Kronman, *Specific Performance*, 45 U. CHI. L. REV. 351 (1978).

[57] *E.g.*, Watkins v. Paul, 511 P.2d 781 (Idaho 1973). *Cf.* Miller v. LeSea Broad., Inc., 87 F.3d 224, 230 (7th Cir. 1996) (sale of television station for purpose of resale).

[58] Loveless v. Diehl, 364 S.W.2d 317 (Ark. 1962).

[59] Watkins v. Paul, 511 P.2d 781 (Idaho 1973); Meikle v. Watson, 69 P.3d 100 (Idaho 2003); Miller v. LeSea Broad., Inc., 87 F.3d 224 (7th Cir. 1996); Semelhago v. Paramadevan, 136 D.R.R.4th 1 (Canada 1996).

[60] Lindros v. Backus, 848 So. 2d 413 (Fla. Dist. Ct. App. 2003); Kalinowski v. An-Chi Yeh, 847 P.2d 673 (Haw. Ct. App. 1993).

[61] *E.g.*, City Stores Co. v. Ammerman, 266 F. Supp. 766 (D.D.C. 1967), *aff'd*, 394 F.2d 950 (D.C. Cir. 1968).

[62] *E.g.*, Suchan v. Rutherford, 410 P.2d 434 (Idaho 1966).

market value of the land.[63] Of course, in many cases, the buyer has backed out of the deal because it lacks the funds necessary to pay for the land, making specific performance highly impractical.

The seller's right to obtain specific performance was sometimes justified on the largely abandoned ground of "mutuality of remedy."[64] At one time the mutuality doctrine made specific performance unavailable to the plaintiff if it would not have been available to the defendant had the tables been turned.[65] It was thought that any effort to deny specific performance to sellers on grounds of the adequacy of their legal remedy would result in specific performance being made unavailable to buyers despite the unique nature of the property. The traditional requirement of mutuality of remedy, however, has now largely been abandoned,[66] even though outposts of the doctrine can still occasionally be found.[67] Expressions of the archaic doctrine now frequently support the seller's right to specific performance, on the theory that because it is available for a buyer, it should similarly be available to the seller.

Even though money is usually an adequate substitute for an aggrieved seller, finding a substitute qualified buyer for land is sometimes difficult.[68] Furthermore many landowners want to shed the burdens of taxes, insurance, maintenance, and potential liability associated with owning real estate, which are not inconsequential. Anyone who has ever been saddled with the continued ownership of an unwanted parcel of real estate will sympathize with an aggrieved seller's right to compel the buyer to take over the duties of ownership. Where a substitute buyer is readily available, most sellers will not seek specific performance. They will instead pursue the easier alternative of reselling the tract to an available buyer. Many courts still award specific performance to a seller, but only after insisting that the seller provide the court with information explaining the inadequacy of the damage remedy.[69]

---

[63] *E.g.*, Perroncello v. Donahue, 859 N.E.2d 827 (Mass. 2007); Humphries v. Ables, 789 N.E.2d 1025, 1034 (Ind. Ct. App. 2003).

[64] *See generally* John Norton Pomeroy, 5 Equity Jurisprudence §§ 2191–2194 (4th ed. 1919); Restatement (Second) of Contracts § 360 cmt. e (1981); Edward Yorio, Contract Enforcement, Specific Performance and Injunctions 281 (1989). "Mutuality of remedy" should not be confused with "mutuality of obligation." The former deals with whether the defendant could have obtained an equitable remedy against the plaintiff if the plaintiff were in breach. The latter deals with whether the defendant's promise is supported by consideration. *See supra* § 2.05[E][1] Illusory Promises.

[65] *See* J.B. Ames, *Mutuality in Specific Performances*, 3 Colum. L. Rev. 1 (1903).

[66] Restatement (Second) of Contracts § 363 cmt. c (1981). *E.g.*, Laclede Gas Co. v. Amoco Oil Co., 522 F.2d 33 (8th Cir. 1975) ("There is simply no requirement in the law that both parties be mutually entitled to the remedy of specific performance in order that one of them [may] be given that remedy"). *See* Arthur L. Corbin, 12 Corbin on Contracts §§ 1179–80 (Interim ed. 2002).

[67] Northcom, Ltd. v. James, 694 So. 2d 1329 (Ala. 1997).

[68] *See* Ludington v. LaFreniere, 704 A.2d 875 (Me. 1998) (evidence that the parcel would be difficult to resell).

[69] *E.g.*, Ludington v. LaFreniere, 704 A.2d 875 (Me. 1998).

[B]   Sales of Goods

Historically, a buyer of goods could obtain specific performance only if the goods were unique.[70] Thus, specific performance was available for breach of a contract for the purchase of a work of art[71] or a family heirloom,[72] but not for other items that are easily replaceable. Article 2 of the Uniform Commercial Code liberalizes the availability of specific performance beyond these circumstances, by also making it available in "other proper circumstances."[73]

Although the Code does not specify what other circumstances make specific performance appropriate, the Official Comments to § 2-716 indicate that "inability to cover" strongly suggests that equitable relief should be available.[74] Thus, even though the goods are not truly unique, if a substitute is nevertheless difficult to obtain because of "short supply and great demand," specific performance is warranted.[75]

This does not mean that a rise in the market price of the goods alone makes the legal remedy of money damages inadequate. If the goods are available, but at a significantly higher price, specific performance should be denied.[76] The money damage formulas of U.C.C. §§ 2-712 and 2-713, provide buyers with a sufficient remedy, so long as substitutes are available on the market.

The other proper circumstances specified by § 2-716 also encompass output and requirements contracts involving goods for which there is either a limited market or a particular source.[77] In the pre-U.C.C. case of *Curtice Brothers Co. v. Catts*,[78] the court awarded specific performance of a contract for the delivery of a farmer's entire crop of tomatoes to a local cannery where the goods, though hardly unique, could not be obtained in the open market "without serious interference with the economic arrangements of the [cannery]." In the U.C.C. decision in *Laclede Gas Co v. Amoco Oil Co.*,[79] specific performance of a long-term contract for a supply of propane gas was awarded, not because propane gas was difficult to find, but because of the buyer's inability to secure a similar long-term source of supply. Without specific performance the buyer would have faced the prospect of constantly fluctuating prices and the risk of limited supplies sometime in the uncertain future. An award of damages alone would have been based on uncertain future market values and left the buyer facing an unknown risk of consequential

---

[70] *See* Pusey v. Pusey, 23 Eng. Rep. 465 (1684).

[71] *See* RESTATEMENT (SECOND) OF CONTRACTS § 360 illus. 1 (1981).

[72] *In re* Marriage of Firestone, 511 N.E.2d 895 (Ill. App. Ct. 1987).

[73] U.C.C. § 2-716(1) (2012). *See* Harold Greenberg, *Specific Performance Under Section 2-716 of the Uniform Commercial Code: "A More Liberal Attitude" in the "Grand Style,"* 17 N. ENG. L. REV. 321 (1982).

[74] U.C.C. § 2-716 cmt. 2 (2012).

[75] *E.g.*, Sedmak v. Charlie's Chevrolet, Inc., 622 S.W.2d 694 (Mo. Ct. App. 1981).

[76] *See* Klein v. Pepsico, Inc., 845 F.2d 76 (4th Cir. 1988).

[77] U.C.C. § 2-716 cmt. 2 (2012).

[78] 66 A. 935 (N.J. Ch. Ct. 1907).

[79] 522 F.2d 33 (8th Cir. 1975).

loss due to the possibility of temporary shortages in the available supply over a long period of time.

Specific performance has also been granted where failure to obtain the goods from the seller would subject the buyer to financial hardship.[80] For example, in *Stephan's Machine & Tool, Inc. v. D & H Machinery Consultants, Inc.*,[81] the delay in finding a substitute would have disrupted the buyer's cash flow, causing it to default on its debts.   ·

Sellers are permitted to obtain specific performance — payment of the full contract price — in two situations. The first of these is where the buyer has accepted the goods.[82] If the buyer has taken the goods, and intends to keep them, there is no reason for the buyer to escape paying the price.

Second, if the buyer rejects the goods, the seller might still be entitled to recover the price if the goods have been destroyed,[83] or where for some other reason the goods cannot be resold.[84] Resale might be difficult or impossible where the goods were specially manufactured for the buyer and are therefore not suitable for resale to others. For example, in *Emanuel Law Outlines, Inc. v. Multi-State Legal Studies, Inc.*,[85] a publisher of bar exam review outlines was able to compel specific performance where the outlines had been prepared specifically for the buyer's bar review course and were not suitable for sale to others.[86]

Contracts for the international sale of goods are now nearly always governed by the United Nations Convention on the International Sale of Goods (CISG). Consistent with the practice in civil law jurisdictions on the European continent,[87] the CISG makes specific performance the normal remedy for breach of a contract for the sale of goods.[88] Thus, the buyer may require a breaching seller to deliver substitute goods[89] or to make any reasonable repair.[90] Likewise, the seller may require the buyer to take delivery of goods and pay for them.[91] Despite this, Article 28 restricts the availability of specific performance where it would be unavailable under the domestic law of the jurisdiction in which the court is

---

[80] *See* RESTATEMENT (SECOND) OF CONTRACTS § 360 illus. 9 (1981).

[81] 417 N.E.2d 579 (Ohio Ct. App. 1979).

[82] U.C.C. § 2-709(1)(a) (2012).

[83] *Id.*

[84] U.C.C. § 2-709(1)(b) (2012).

[85] 899 F. Supp. 1081 (S.D.N.Y. 1995).

[86] *See also* Alden Press, Inc. v. Block & Co., Inc., 527 N.E.2d 489 (Ill. App. Ct. 1988) (catalogs printed for delivery to buyer).

[87] John P. Dawson, *Specific Performance in France and Germany*, 57 MICH. L. REV. 495 (1959)

[88] CISG Art. 46(1) (1980). *See generally* John M. Catalano, Comment, *More Fiction Than Fact: The Perceived Differences in the Application of Specific Performance Under the United Nations Convention on Contracts for the International Sale of Goods*, 71 TUL. L. REV. 1807 (1997).

[89] CISG Art. 46(1) (1980).

[90] CISG Art. 46(3) (1980).

[91] CISG Art. 62 (1980).

located.[92] Thus, the CISG's more liberal policy toward specific performance is restricted by common law and U.C.C. rules that restrict its availability.

The CISG adds an additional procedural remedy, consistent with the civil law's "Nachfrist" or "additional time" rule that permits a buyer to "fix an additional period of time of reasonable length for performance by the seller of his obligations."[93] Once the buyer has formally extended the seller's time for performance, the buyer may not resort to other remedies — unless, of course, the seller gives notice that it will not perform during the extended time period.[94]

[C]   Services[95]

As with land and goods, equitable remedies are only available for breach of a contract for services if the remedy at law is inadequate. Services of many artists, athletes, and performers are unique — or at least sufficiently rare to make finding an adequate substitute difficult.[96] Services of most other laborers are not. If the services are not unique, money damages can almost always be used to obtain equivalent services from someone else. Because specific performance is generally unavailable when the legal remedy of money damages is adequate, equity will only intervene in the case of unique services for which no reasonable substitute was available, or where compensation is otherwise ill-suited to protect the plaintiff from harm.

[1]   Difficulty of Supervision

In contracts for services there is a dilemma not present in transactions involving land or goods. Ordering specific performance requires the court to supervise performance to determine whether the defendant is complying with the court's order. In cases involving services, this is difficult. Moreover, the more specialized the services are, the more difficult it is for the court to evaluate the quality of the work performed.

It would be relatively easy to supervise the work of a ditch digger. However, because of the wide availability of unskilled labor, the legal remedy of money damages is probably adequate for breach of a contract for these basic services. Supervising the performance of an opera star or a professional athlete, on the other hand, is far more difficult. Thus, where services are involved, specific performance is rarely available, even though the legal remedy of money damages may be inadequate.[97]

---

[92] CISG Art. 28 (1980).

[93] CISG Art. 47(1) (1980).

[94] CISG Art. 47(2) (1980).

[95] James T. Brennan, *Injunctions Against Professional Athletes' Breaching Their Contracts*, 34 BROOKLYN L. REV. 61 (1967).

[96] *See* James T. Brennan, *Injunction Against Professional Athletes Breaching Their Contracts*, 34 BROOKLYN L. REV. 61 (1967); Sharon F. Carton, *Damning with Fulsome Praise: Assessing the Uniqueness of an Artist or Performer as a Condition to Enjoin Performance of Personal Service Contracts in Entertainment Law*, 5 VILL. SPORTS & ENT. L.J. 197 (1998).

[97] London Bucket Co. v. Stewart, 237 S.W.2d 509 (Ky. Ct. App. 1951).

Apart from the problem of supervision, the Thirteenth Amendment to the United States Constitution, which prohibits "involuntary servitude," prevents specific performance of personal services contracts.[98] Even without this constitutional barrier, compelling a person to work for another offends our humanitarian sensibilities, even if it is not as despicable as the slavery or indentured servitude in our national history.[99] Thus, even where supervision does not seem unduly difficult, specific performance of a contract for services is always denied.[100]

[2] Injunction as an Alternative[101]

The unavailability of specific performance does not mean that the plaintiff must settle for money damages. Instead of granting specific performance, the court may issue an injunction preventing the defendant from engaging in conduct that is inconsistent with his or her duty to perform. A good example is supplied by the nineteenth-century dispute in *Lumley v. Wagner*.[102] The defendant was an opera star who signed an agreement to perform for three months for the plaintiff's opera company in a variety of specified roles. In addition to promising to appear at the plaintiff's theater, the defendant made an express promise not to use her talents in any other "theater, concert, or reunion," without the plaintiff's express consent. The court recognized that it could not force the defendant to perform, but it was willing to "specifically enforce" her promise not to perform at another theater for the duration of her agreement with the plaintiff.[103]

Later decisions recognized that an injunction was available even where there was no express negative covenant. In *Duff v. Russell*,[104] the defendant promised to perform seven shows a week at the plaintiff's theater. The practical difficulty of being in two places at the same time demonstrated that the defendant had made an implied covenant not to perform elsewhere for seven weeks, even though the contract was silent on the issue.

Where the services of artists, athletes, and other performers are involved,[105] the

---

[98] *See* Lea S. VanderVelde, *The Gendered Origins of the Lumley Doctrine: Binding Men's Consciences and Women's Fidelity*, 101 Yale L.J. 775, 794 (1992); Robert S. Stevens, *Involuntary Servitude by Injunction*, 6 Cornell L.Q. 235 (1921).

[99] *See* Am. Broad. Cos., Inc., v. Wolf, 420 N.E.2d 363, 366 (N.Y. 1981).

[100] N. Del. Indus. Dev. Corp. v. E.W. Bliss Co., 245 A.2d 431 (Del. Ch. 1968). *But see* Perez v. McGar, 630 S.W.2d (Tex. Ct. App. 1981) (ministerial act requiring delivery of copy of statement of facts by court reporter).

[101] Casey Duncan, Note, *Stealing Signs: Is Professional Baseball's United States-Japanese Player Contract Agreement Enough to Avoid Another "Baseball War"?*, 13 Minn. J. Global Trade 87, 103 (2003); Geoffrey Christopher Rapp, *Affirmative Injunctions in Athletic Employment Contracts: Rethinking the Place of the Lumley Rule in American Sports Law*, 16 Marq. Sports L. Rev. 261 (2006).

[102] 42 Eng. Rep. 687 (1852).

[103] *See* Lea S. VanderVelde, *The Gendered Origins of the Lumley Doctrine: Binding Men's Consciences and Women's Fidelity*, 101 Yale L.J. 775 (1991).

[104] 1891 N.Y. Misc. LEXIS 1888 (Mar. 9, 1891).

[105] Dallas Cowboys Football Club v. Harris, 348 S.W.2d 37 (Tex. App. 1961); Philadelphia Ball Club, Ltd. v. Lajoie, 51 A. 973 (Pa. 1902); Duff v. Russell, 1891 N.Y. Misc. LEXIS 1888 (Mar. 9, 1891).

question is not simply whether the performer's abilities are one of a kind, but whether a reasonably equivalent substitute is readily available. Early decisions, like *Philadelphia Ball Club, Ltd. v. Lajoie*,[106] which dealt with the economic struggle between owners and athletes in Major League Baseball, focused on the "unique and peculiar" character of several National League stars who threatened to jump to the new American League.[107]

More recent decisions focus not on whether the performer's skills are truly one of a kind, but on whether those of similar skill and ability are readily available.[108] In *Dallas Cowboys Football Club v. Harris*,[109] an injunction was granted based on testimony that the defendant's skills as a "defensive halfback," although "not unparalleled," were not readily available because other football players with skills similar to those of Harris were already playing for other teams.Thus, depending on the availability of a substitute, even a local performer may find himself or herself enjoined from working for a competing employer, unless performers with equivalent talents are available in the vicinity.[110]

It is not surprising that courts are reluctant to enjoin individuals from using their skills to earn a living.[111] Equitable relief in the form of an injunction is unavailable, even in the case of unique services, in the absence of an express or implied covenant by the employee not to provide his or her unique services to another. Express covenants of this type are frequently included in the contracts of professional athletes and other entertainers[112] as well as in endorsement contracts. Early decisions in contracts without express covenants refused to enjoin an employee from engaging in similar employment.[113] Even today, some courts are unwilling to use an injunction to indirectly compel performance that could not be specifically enforced.[114]

An injunction will also likely be available if the defendant has signed an enforceable covenant not to compete with the plaintiff. These agreements are generally enforceable when they are included in a contract for the sale of a business in order to protect the value of the goodwill sold to the buyer.[115] They are also enforceable in employment contracts to protect the employer's trade

---

[106] 51 A. 973 (Pa. 1902).

[107] C. Paul Rogers III, *Napoleon Lajoie, Breach of Contract and the Great Baseball War*, 55 S.M.U. L. REV. 325, 325 (2002).

[108] *E.g.*, Marchio v. Letterlough, 237 F. Supp.2d 580 (E.D. Pa. 2002).

[109] 348 S.W.2d 37 (Tex. App. 1961).

[110] *See* Pingley v. Brunson, 252 S.E.2d 560 (S.C. 1979) (relief denied where five other organists of comparable ability were available for hire in the area).

[111] *See* RESTATEMENT (SECOND) OF CONTRACTS § 367(2) (1981).

[112] *See, e.g.*, Am. Broad. Cos., Inc. v. Wolf, 420 N.E.2d 363 (N.Y. 1981).

[113] *See, e.g.*, Lumley v. Wagner, 42 Eng. Rep. 687 (Ch. 1852).

[114] Reier Broad. Co. v. Kramer, 72 P.3d 944 (Mont. 2003) (applying state statute preventing injunction "to prevent the breach of a contract the performance of which would not be specifically enforced").

[115] *E.g.*, Fine Foods, Inc. v. Dahlin, 523 A.2d 1228 (Vt. 1986).

secrets.[116]

However, they are enforceable only if they are limited in both duration and geographic scope to a range reasonably necessary to protect the goodwill or trade secrets of the plaintiff. The lost profits attributable to the breach of such a covenant are usually sufficiently speculative and uncertain that the remedy at law will be deemed inadequate, so that breach of the covenant will be enjoined.

[D]   Effect of Liquidated Damages[117]

It might seem as though the inclusion of an enforceable liquidated damages provision would impair the injured party's access to specific performance or an injunction.[118] However, these remedies remain available even though the contract contains a provision for liquidated damages,[119] unless the contract makes the liquidated damages provision the exclusive remedy.[120]

On the other hand, an aggrieved party is not usually able to obtain *both* specific performance and enforcement of a liquidated damages provision,[121] even though specific performance may not fully compensate the injured party for losses associated with any delay in receiving the other party's performance.

§ 15.04   BALANCING THE EQUITIES: PRACTICALITY AND FAIRNESS[122]

Equitable relief has always been regarded as discretionary;[123] it is not available as a matter of right, even where the legal remedy is inadequate.[124] In exercising their discretion, courts of equity have a strong tradition of considering the practical consequences and fairness of using specific performance or an injunction to compel performance.[125]

---

[116] *See generally* Hollingsworth Solderless Terminal Co. v. Turley, 622 F.2d 1324 (9th Cir. 1980).

[117] Ronen Avraham & Zhiyong Liu, *Incomplete Contracts with Asymmetric Information: Exclusive Versus Optional Remedies*, 8 Am. L. & Econ. Rev. 523 (2006).

[118] Fairway Devs., Inc. v. Marcum, 832 N.E.2d 581 (Ind. Ct. App. 2005).

[119] Restatement (Second) of Contracts § 361 (1981). *E.g.*, Bradley v. Health Coalition, Inc., 687 So.2d 329, 330, 332 (Fla. Dist. Ct. App. 1997).

[120] O'Shield v. Lakeside Bank, 781 N.E.2d 1114, 1121, (Ill. App. Ct. 2002).

[121] Perroncello v. Donahue, 859 N.E.2d 827 (Mass. 2007).

[122] J.B. Ames, *Mutuality in Specific Performance*, 3 Colum. L. Rev. 1 (1903); Arthur Leff, *Unconscionability and the Code — The Emperor's New Clause*, 115 U. Pa. L. Rev. 485, 530–33 (1967); Ralph A. Newman, *The Place and Function of Pure Equity in the Structure of Law*, 16 Hastings L.J. 401, 404–05 (1965); 1 J. Pomeroy, Equity Jurisprudence §§ 43–67 (5th ed. 1941); Emily L. Sherwin, *Law and Equity in Contract Enforcement*, 50 Md. L. Rev. 253, 285–87 (1991); Edward Yorio, *A Defense of Equitable Defenses*, 51 Ohio St. L.J. 1201 (1990).

[123] Edward Yorio, Contract Enforcement, Specific Performance and Injunctions 11–16 (1989).

[124] *E.g.*, Great Hill Fill & Gravel, Inc. v. Shapleigh, 692 A.2d 928, 930 (Me. 1997). *But see* Loveless v. Diehl, 364 S.W.2d 317 (Ark. 1962) (specific performance not available as of right, but nevertheless available "as *a matter of course*" for breach of a contract for the sale of real estate) (emphasis in original).

[125] Roger Young & Stephen Spitz, *SUEM — Spitz's Ultimate Equitable Maxim: In Equity, Good Guys Should Win and Bad Guys Should Lose*, 55 S.C. L. Rev. 175, 177 (2003) (listing maxims); Eugene

In exercising their discretion the English Chancellors took a practical approach, and American courts have followed their lead. Because they were dispensing the justice of the King or Queen, courts of equity were concerned with the fairness of the terms of the transaction involved in the request for relief.[126] Accordingly, the availability of equitable remedies frequently depended on the practicality and fairness of specific performance and injunctions.

These concerns have already been seen in the above discussion regarding the impracticability of attempting to supervise the performance of a personal services contract as well as with the potentially harsh effect of enjoining a person from making a living.[127] Equity's concern with practicality and fairness is expressed in a variety of other rules that limit the availability of equitable relief.

[A]   Mutuality of Remedy[128]

At one time, courts were unwilling to specifically enforce a contract against the defendant if specific performance would not have been available in favor of the defendant if it had been the plaintiff.[129] However, the "mutuality of remedy" doctrine has been almost completely rejected[130] and is now only rarely invoked.

A related rule, which retains its vitality, denies specific performance or an injunction in favor of a plaintiff whose own performance cannot be adequately assured.[131] For example, a court would be reluctant to grant specific performance of a contract for a credit sale of real estate, unless there were some adequate means of assuring payment by the buyer.[132] Also, in *Fitzpatrick v. Michael*,[133] the court denied specific performance of the defendant's promise to transfer her land, which had been given in exchange for the plaintiff's promise to provide her with what we would today refer to as "home health care" for the rest of her life, in part because the court could not ensure the plaintiff's continued performance of his part of the bargain.

[B]   Hardship

The availability of an equitable remedy may also depend on a comparison of the burdens compelled performance will impose on the defendant and the harm that will be suffered by the plaintiff if relief is denied.[134] Where the burden on the

---

Volokh, *Lost Maxims of Equity*, 52 J. LEGAL EDUC. 619, 619 (2002) (listing equally humorous maxims).

[126] *See* EDWARD YORIO, CONTRACT ENFORCEMENT, SPECIFIC PERFORMANCE AND INJUNCTIONS §§ 3.1–3.4 (1989).

[127] *See supra* § 15.03[C] Services.

[128] EDWARD YORIO, CONTRACT ENFORCEMENT: SPECIFIC PERFORMANCE AND INJUNCTIONS 127–42 (1989).

[129] *See* Northcom, Ltd. v. James, 694 So. 2d 1329, 1336 (Ala. 1997).

[130] *See* RESTATEMENT (SECOND) OF CONTRACTS § 363 cmt. c (1981).

[131] RESTATEMENT (SECOND) OF CONTRACTS § 363 (1981).

[132] RESTATEMENT (SECOND) OF CONTRACTS § 363 cmt. 2 illus. 1 (1981).

[133] 9 A.2d 639 (Md. 1939).

[134] RESTATEMENT (SECOND) OF CONTRACTS § 364(1)(b) (1981).

defendant is heavy, and the harm to the plaintiff relatively slight, relief may be denied.

Van Wagner Advertising Corp. v. S & M Enterprises,[135] provides a good example. A lessee of space on the side of a building in Manhattan sought specific performance to prevent a new owner from demolishing the building. The lessee used the space on the side of the building to display a billboard near the exit from a busy bridge coming into Manhattan, across the East River. Specific performance would have prevented a major metropolitan redevelopment project. The court concluded that the harm to the defendant resulting from compelling its performance of the lease contract would be disproportionate to the assistance provided to the plaintiff if specific performance were granted.[136]

However, in order to establish a defense based on hardship, the defendant must show that specific performance would create a hardship or injustice that is out of proportion to the relief sought. Showing that specific performance is merely inconvenient is not enough.[137]

Similarly, it has frequently been said that "equity abhors a forfeiture,"[138] and equitable relief has been denied where compelling performance would result in a forfeiture. Accordingly, specific performance is not available to compel performance of a liquidated damages provision that amounts to a penalty.[139]

[C]   Indefinite Terms[140]

Courts are similarly reluctant to order specific performance where the indefinite terms of the contract make it difficult to frame an appropriate order.[141] Thus, even though the terms are sufficiently definite to permit enforcement through an award of damages,[142] the court may refuse to order specific performance, if they are too indefinite for the court to determine whether its order has been followed.[143] If the court orders specific performance of a contract with imprecise terms, the defendant will find it necessary to engage in a guessing game about whether its performance complies with the court's order.

Some agreements will be sufficiently definite for the court to calculate an award

---

[135] 492 N.E.2d 756 (N.Y. 1986).

[136] *See also* Kilarjian v. Vastola, 877 A.2d 372 (N.J. Super. Ct. Ch. Div. 2004) (defendant suffered from physical infirmity). *But see* Minor v. Rush, 216 S.W.3d 210 (Mo. Ct. App. 2007) (financial hardship on defendants insufficient to preclude specific performance).

[137] Perel v. Brannan, 594 S.E.2d 899, 905 (Va. 2004) (specific performance of a restrictive covenant).

[138] Moran v. Holman, 501 P.2d 769 (Alaska 1972). *See also* E. Motor Inns, Inc. v. Ricci, 565 A.2d 1265 (R.I. 1989).

[139] Lewis v. Premium Inv. Corp., 568 S.E.2d 361 (S.C. 2002).

[140] Thomas G. Fischer, Annotation, *Specificity of Description of Premises as Affecting Enforceability of Contract to Convey Real Property — Modern Cases*, 73 A.L.R.4th 135 (1989).

[141] Restatement (Second) of Contracts § 362 (1981).

[142] Restatement (Second) of Contracts § 33(2) (1981). *See supra* § 4.11 Indefinite Terms and Agreements to Agree.

[143] Plantation Land Co. v. Bradshaw, 207 S.E.2d 49 (Ga. 1974) (description of real estate too indefinite for specific enforcement).

of money damages even if it is based on nothing more than the innocent party's reliance expenses, and yet still not sufficiently detailed for the court to compel performance. For example, in *Stanfield v. Fisher*,[144] a contract for the sale of "my farm," which purported to reserve the seller's title to the "small house and adjoining 10 acres," was too indefinite to permit specific performance but not too indefinite to permit an award of damages.[145]

[D]   Unfair Terms

Equitable relief may also be denied because of an unfair or otherwise disproportionate exchange in the transaction itself.[146] For example, the court denied specific performance of a contract for the sale of valuable mineral rights in *Wollums v. Horsley*, where the buyer took advantage of the seller's age, infirmity, and ignorance and made a contract to purchase the rights for far less than their value.[147] Decisions like *Wollums v. Horsley* denying specific performance because of a disparity in the values exchanged and an inequality of bargaining power provide a historical basis for more modern decisions that refuse to enforce a contract at all when it is unconscionable.[148]

[E]   Mistake

Specific performance or other equitable relief will also be denied where the contract was made pursuant to a mistake.[149] For example, in *Bailey v. Musumeci*,[150] the court denied specific performance to the seller where the buyer at an auction mistakenly bid on the wrong parcel of property, despite having exercised reasonable care in attempting to make sure he was bidding on the parcel he sought.

[F]   Unclean Hands

A plaintiff seeking equitable relief must approach the court with "clean hands."[151] Courts of equity are reluctant to advance the interests of a party who has engaged in inequitable, harsh, or unfair conduct in the creation or performance of the contract. This equitable clean-hands doctrine can be cited in a wide variety of circumstances, including those already mentioned, to deny specific performance to a plaintiff who has engaged in some sort of dishonest, overbearing, or otherwise

---

[144] 306 N.E.2d 187 (Ohio Ct. App. 1973).

[145] *But see* Kauka Farms, Inc. v. Scott, 352 S.E.2d 373 (Ga. 1987) (contract providing for reservation of a life estate in 20 acres immediately surrounding the seller's home could be specifically enforced).

[146] RESTATEMENT (SECOND) OF CONTRACTS § 364(1)(c) (1981).

[147] Wollums v. Horsley, 20 S.W.781 (Ky. 1892).

[148] *See* Campbell Soup Co. v. Wentz, 172 F.2d 80 (3d Cir. 1948). *See* Emily L. Sherwin, *Law and Equity in Contract Enforcement*, 50 MD. L. REV. 253, 285–87 (1991).

[149] RESTATEMENT (SECOND) OF CONTRACTS § 364(1)(a) (1981).

[150] 591 A.2d 1316 (N.H. 1991).

[151] *See generally* Zechariah Chafee Jr., *Coming into Equity with Clean Hands (Pts. 1 & 2)*, 47 MICH. L. REV. 877, 1065 (1949).

inequitable conduct. Plaintiffs who are guilty of misconduct are precluded from equitable relief. The early unconscionability cases were frequently based on this rationale.[152]

Courts thus deny equitable relief when "the requesting party has engaged in conduct 'savored with injustice touching the transaction.' "[153] A plaintiff seeking specific performance is held to a higher standard than one who will be satisfied with money damages. Courts sometimes express this rule by saying that "to receive equity [the plaintiff] must 'do equity' and must not come into court with 'unclean hands.' "[154]

For example, in *Village Medical Center, Ltd. v. Apolzon*,[155] the court denied specific performance to a seller who had conspired with the purchasers in the preparation of a "bogus" contract in an attempt to mislead a lien holder. And, in *Amoco Oil Co. v. Kraft*,[156] a lessee was prevented from asserting its fixed-price option to buy the property for only one-third of its value because the lessee had not only passed up the opportunity to exercise the option for 13 years, but had also knowingly permitted the property to be sold to a third party for three times the option price without exercising its right of first refusal.

[G]   Public Policy

The court might also deny equitable relief if enforcement of the contract is contrary to the public interest or otherwise in contravention of broad public policy.[157] Of course, if the contract is illegal, and would not be enforced by an award of damages, it is similarly unenforceable through an equitable remedy. But, some contracts are generally enforceable through an award of money damages, but may nevertheless not be specifically enforced.

An example of how the public interest might prevent a court from awarding specific performance is found in *Kakaes v. George Washington University*,[158] where the court refused to award a university professor "tenure by default" where doing so would have been contrary to the public interest against granting tenure to a person whom university officials considered unsuitable. In light of this interest, the court's award of damages, instead of directing the university to appoint the faculty member with tenure, was a suitable alternative.

In *Metropolitan Sports Facilities Commission v. Minnesota Twins Partnership*, the public interest cut in favor of equitable relief.[159] The Minnesota Twins and Major League Baseball were enjoined from taking any action that

---

[152] Campbell Soup Co. v. Wentz, 172 F.2d 80, 83–84 (3d Cir. 1948).

[153] Hawthorne's, Inc. v. Warrenton Realty, Inc., 606 N.E.2d 908, 912–13 (Mass. 1993).

[154] Boe v. Rose, 574 N.W.2d 834, 836 (N.D. 1998).

[155] 619 S.W.2d 188 (Tex. Ct. App. 1981).

[156] 280 N.W.2d 505 (Mich. Ct. App. 1979).

[157] RESTATEMENT (SECOND) OF CONTRACTS § 365 (1981).

[158] 790 A.2d 581 (D.C. Ct. App. 2002).

[159] Metropolitan Sports Facilities Commission v. Minnesota Twins Partnership, 638 N.W.2d 214 (Minn. Ct. App. 2002).

would have prevented the Twins from playing the 2002 major league baseball season at the Minneapolis Metrodome. In compelling performance, the court noted the parties' expectation that "the State, citizenry and fans would benefit substantially in [several] non-monetary ways" from the contract. And, in *United Water New Rochelle, Inc. v. City of New York*,[160] the court would not compel specific performance of a contract that would have resulted in an extended shutdown of a key source of water for municipalities with the right to draw water from the supply.

[H]   Performance Impracticable

Courts of equity are also mindful of the practical limitations on their authority. Thus, specific performance will not be awarded where performance is impossible, such as where the seller has already sold the land or goods involved in the dispute to a bona fide purchaser for value, and cannot recover it without the cooperation of that innocent party.[161]

Similarly, where complete performance has been rendered impossible due to an intervening event that destroyed a portion of the subject matter of the contract, the court may award specific performance but abate (reduce) the purchase price to the extent that the seller's insurance covers the loss.[162] Other courts, following the rule specified in the Uniform Vendor and Purchaser Act, simply excuse the parties from their obligations and permit them to renegotiate the contract under the circumstances as they exist after the casualty has occurred.[163]

§ 15.05   EQUITABLE REMEDIES IN INTERNATIONAL TRANSACTIONS[164]

Consistent with the practice in civil law jurisdictions on the European continent, the United Nations Convention on the International Sale of Goods makes specific performance the normal remedy for breach of a contract for the sale of goods.[165] Thus, the buyer may require a breaching seller to deliver substitute goods[166] or to make any reasonable repair.[167] Likewise, the seller may require the buyer to take

---

[160] 1999 N.Y. Misc. LEXIS 88 (Mar. 9, 1999).

[161] Grummel v. Hollenstein, 367 P.2d 960 (Ariz. 1962).

[162] Skelly Oil Co. v. Ashmore, 365 S.W.2d 582 (Mo. 1963).

[163] Unif. Vendor & Purchaser Risk Act § 1 (1941).

[164] Robert Bejesky, *The Evolution in and International Convergence of the Doctrine of Specific Performance in Three Types of States*, 13 IND. INT'L & COMP. L. REV. 353 (2003); Amy H. Kastely, *The Right to Require Performance in International Sales: Towards an International Interpretation of the Vienna Convention*, 63 WASH. L. REV. 607 (1988).

[165] CISG Art. 46(1) (1980). *See generally* John M. Catalano, Comment, *More Fiction Than Fact: The Perceived Differences in the Application of Specific Performance Under the United Nations Convention on Contracts for the International Sale of Goods*, 71 TUL. L. REV. 1807 (1997).

[166] CISG Art. 46(1) (1980).

[167] CISG Art. 46(3) (1980).

delivery of goods and pay for them.[168] As explained earlier, however, the CISG defers to the more limited availability of specific performance in the jurisdiction where the court is located.[169]

The UNIDROIT Principles of International Commercial Contracts take a similar approach and treat specific performance as a routinely available remedy.[170] Article 7.2.1 simply states that "where a party is obliged to pay money does not do so, the other party may require payment."[171] When the obligation is something other than the payment of money, Article 7.2.2 provides that the injured party may "require performance" unless performance is impossible, unreasonably burdensome, of a personal character, or where a substitute performance is reasonably available from another source.[172] As under the CISG, the court may order "repair, replacement, or other cure of defective performance."[173]

The Principles of European Contract Law contain similar provisions. Article 9.101 permits a creditor to "recover money which is due."[174] Specific performance of other obligations, including "remedying . . . a defective performance" is available subject to the same sort of exceptions specified in PICC.[175]

---

[168] CISG Art. 62 (1980).

[169] CISG Art. 28 (1980).

[170] *See* Joseph M. Perillo, *UNIDROIT Principles of International Commercial Contracts: The Black Letter Text and a Review*, 63 FORDHAM L. REV. 281, 304–06 (1994).

[171] PICC Art. 7.2.1 (2004).

[172] PICC Art. 7.2.2 (2004).

[173] PICC Art. 7.2.3 (2004).

[174] PECL Art. 9.101(1) (2002).

[175] PECL Art. 9.102 (2002).

Chapter 16

THIRD-PARTY BENEFICIARIES

§ 16.01   INTRODUCTION TO RIGHTS OF THIRD PARTIES[1]

[A]   Transactions Involving Third Parties

At first blush, it might seem that people who were not involved in the creation of a contract should not have any rights under it. The fundamental nature of a

---

[1] Arthur L. Corbin, *Contracts for the Benefit of Third Persons*, 27 YALE L.J. 1008 (1918); Melvin Aron Eisenerg, *Third-Party Beneficiaries*, 92 COLUM. L. REV. 1358 (1992); Peter Karsten, *The "Discovery" of Law by English and American Jurists of the Seventeenth, Eighteenth, and Nineteenth Centuries: Third*

contract results from the expression of mutual assent by parties to the terms of the same deal. Because a contract is a private undertaking, it would seem to follow that the legal relationship between the parties is personal to those directly involved in the transaction. If one of them fails to perform, it would not seem unusual to discover that the only person who had cause to complain about this was the other party to the agreement. While this is ordinarily true, there are several circumstances in which some third person, who was not originally involved in the contract, might have the right to enforce its terms.

Third parties can acquire rights under a contract in two ways. First, the original parties to the contract may agree that performance of the contract will benefit a third person. The third person is a "third party beneficiary" of the contract, and has the right to enforce it. Second, a new person might acquire rights, or even possibly duties, if one of the original parties transfers her rights or duties under the contract, to a new person. When this happens, the right to receive performance has been "assigned," or the duty to perform has been "delegated." Rules relating to "assignment of rights" or to "delegation of duties" must be consulted to determine the rights and obligations of the parties after the transfer. This chapter will consider the rights of third-party beneficiaries. The next chapter will examine the effect of assignments and delegations.[2]

[B]   Parties in a Third-Party Beneficiary Contract

In analyzing third-party beneficiary contracts, courts use a set of standard terms to refer to the parties. Consider the parties to a routine life insurance contract in which Ray purchases a policy from Perpetual Life Insurance Company, naming his wife Agnes as the beneficiary. Perpetual Life, the insurer, is the "promisor" because it has made the promise involved in the contract. Ray, whose life is insured, is the "promisee" — the person to whom Perpetual made its promise. Agnes, the person who will receive the benefits of the policy when Ray dies, is the third-party beneficiary. In analyzing any agreement involving a third-party beneficiary, one must identify the promisor, the promisee, and the third party whose rights to enforce the contract are in question.

[C]   Privity of Contract

The principal barrier to the establishment of the rights of third-party beneficiaries is the English common law principle of "privity of contract."[3] Privity of contract refers to the relationship between those who have entered into a binding legal agreement. The buyer and seller of a car are in privity of contract with one another. Members of the buyer's family, passengers, drivers of other cars on the same street as the buyer, and pedestrians walking across the street are not

---

Party Beneficiary Contracts as a Test Case, 9 LAW & HIST. REV. 327 (1991); Anthony J. Waters, *The Property in the Promise: A Study of the Third Party Beneficiary Rule,* 98 HARV. L. REV. 1109 (1985).

[2] *See infra* Ch. 17 Assignments and Delegations.

[3] Phalen v. United States Trust Co., 78 N.E. 943 (N.Y. 1906). *See* Arthur L. Corbin, *Contracts for the Benefit of Third Persons,* 27 YALE L. REV. 1008 (1918); Melvin A. Eisenberg, *Third Party Beneficiaries,* 92 COLUM. L. REV. 1358 (1992); Samuel Williston, *Contracts for the Benefit of a Third Person,* 15 HARV. L. REV. 767 (1902).

in contractual privity with the parties. Likewise, an employer and its employees are in privity of contract with one another, but the employee's family members are not. Nor are the employer's customers in privity with the employees. A builder and its customer are in privity of contract with one another, but the builder's subcontractors and suppliers are not in privity with the customer. The necessity of privity of contract between two individuals for an action based on contract to be brought had long been viewed as a fundamental tenet of the common law. The traditional rule was: "only a person who is a party to a contract can sue on it."[4]

Despite this long-standing rule, it is clear that there are many relationships between members of society that are derived from the formation of a contract even though the parties are not in strict contractual privity with one another. Life insurance contracts are a prime example. The main purpose for creating a life insurance contract is to establish the rights of a third person to the benefits of the policy upon the death of the insured. Construction performance bonds are another illustration. In these transactions, a bonding company makes a promise to a builder that if the builder does not complete one of its construction projects, the bonding firm will pay someone to finish it. Such "bonds" are a key method of protecting the owner of the project from the risk that the contractor will fail to complete the job, and be unable to pay any extra expenses of finishing the building. It is essential that such promises can be enforced by the owner of the project for whose benefit the promise was made.

In these, and other commonly recurring situations, it is not unusual for two parties to create a contract with the understanding that the agreement will operate for the benefit of some third person who is not directly involved in the creation of the contract. In the situation involving Sam's sale of his BMW to Barb for $20,000, Sam might want Barb to pay for the car by paying the $20,000 to Gail, to whom Sam owes a similar sum of money. While it might be possible to bring Gail into the negotiations over the deal for the car, it is much simpler if Sam and Barb can simply agree that Barb will fulfill her obligation to pay for the car by sending a check directly to Gail, together with a note indicating that she is receiving the payment in satisfaction of the debt Sam owes to her.

Alternatively, Sam might want Barb to send the $20,000 to his sister Claire, as a gift. While it probably would not be difficult to get Claire's assent to the overall transaction and make her a party to the contract, this seems like a silly waste of time. Unless the necessity of bringing Claire into the deal fulfills some important social or economic purpose, it is just as easy to let Sam and Barb set up this transaction on their own, with Barb's duty to pay running directly to Claire.

On the other hand, there are likely to be others who will be affected by a contract between Sam and Barb for the sale of his car for $20,000, even though

---

[4] Dunlop Pneumatic Tyre Co. v. Selfridge & Co., 1915 App. Cas. 847, 853 (H.L. 1915). For a full account of this history of the development of the law establishing the rights of third-party beneficiaries, see Vernon V. Palmer, The Paths to Privity: The History of Third Party Beneficiary Contracts at English Law (1992). *See also* Melvin Aron Eisenberg, *Third Party Beneficiaries*, 92 COLUM. L. REV. 1358 (1992); Gary L. Monserud, *Blending the Law of Sales with the Common Law of Third Party Beneficiaries*, 39 DUQ. L. REV. 111, 114–26 (2000); Anthony Jon Waters, *The Property in the Promise: A Study of the Third Party Beneficiary Rule*, 98 HARV. L. REV. 1109 (1985).

Sam and Barb might not have thought about the effect it will have on them. For example, Barb's friend Ed might be looking forward to getting a ride to work every day in Barb's BMW instead of having to walk or take the bus. And, the Mercedes-Benz dealership where Sam anticipates purchasing his new car seems likely to receive a benefit as a result of Sam's receipt of Barb's $20,000, which he plans to use as a down payment on his Benz. However, neither Ed nor the Mercedes-Benz dealership are able to sue either Sam or Barb if they breach their contract. Whatever benefit they may receive as a result of Sam and Barb's contract is purely incidental to Sam and Barb's purpose in making the deal. Neither of them intended the transaction to confer rights on Ed or the auto dealership.

In other circumstances, it may not be so clear whether a third party may enforce the contract. In the context of a sale of goods, the question of whether the end user of a product should have a claim against its manufacturer, *for breach of contract*, if the goods fail to live up to an express or implied warranty, even though the ultimate user purchased the goods from a retail outlet rather than directly from the manufacturer, is particularly controversial.[5] Likewise, in construction contracts, questions may arise over whether the owner of the contract may recover directly against a subcontractor due to the subcontractor's breach, even though the owner has made no direct deal with the subcontractor but instead has dealt directly only with the general contractor who engaged the subcontractor to perform part of the work. And, a subcontractor may seek to recover payment either directly from the owner or from an insurance company or bonding firm who provided the owner with a payment bond to ensure that payment was made to subcontractors and suppliers who contributed to the project. Further, there may be many members of the public who might seek to recover damages for a private utility's failure to provide promised services to the municipality, under the terms of a contract made between the utility and the city, for the benefit of local citizens.[6]

Privity of contract, therefore, is a shorthand way of saying that the plaintiff is not a party to the contract. A person not in privity cannot recover for breach of contract unless she establishes her rights as a third-party beneficiary.

§ 16.02   TYPES OF THIRD-PARTY BENEFICIARIES[7]

Exceptions to the general rule requiring the plaintiff to be in privity of contract with the promisor drew third parties into several traditional categories, based in

---

[5] *See supra* § 7.08[C][2] Vertical Privity; Harry M. Fletcher, *Enforcing Manufacturers' Warranties, "Pass Through" Warranties, and the Like: Can the Buyer Get a Refund?*, 50 Rutgers L. Rev. 397 (1998); Gary L. Monserud, *Blending the Law of Sales with the Common Law of Third Party Beneficiaries*, 39 Duq. L. Rev. 111 (2000).

[6] *See, e.g.*, Peter Breslauer, Note, *Finance Lease, Hell or High Water Clause, and Third Party Beneficiary Theory in Article 2A of the Uniform Commercial Code*, 77 Cornell L. Rev. 318 (1992); Kenneth J. Foster, Note, *Public Housing Tenants as Third-Party Beneficiaries: Considering Ayala v. Boston Housing Authority*, 27 New Eng. L. Rev. 85 (1992); Bernard E. Gegan, *Septembertide Revisited: The Third Party Beneficiary Caper*, 52 Syracuse L. Rev. 51 (2002) (publishing contract); Rachel Paras, Note, *Relief at the End of a Winding Road: Using the Third Party Beneficiary Rule and Alternative Avenues to Achieve Environmental Justice*, 77 St. John's L. Rev. 157 (2003).

[7] Melvin Aron Eisenerg, *Third-Party Beneficiaries*, 92 Colum. L. Rev. 1358 (1992); Harry G. Prince,

part on the characteristics of the parties in a few early cases. This classification scheme became crystalized in the first Restatement of Contracts, which divided third-party beneficiaries into three groups: (1) donee beneficiaries, (2) creditor beneficiaries, and (3) incidental beneficiaries.[8] The First Restatement permitted both donee beneficiaries and creditor beneficiaries to enforce contracts, but treated incidental beneficiaries under the traditional rule that denied recovery to a person who was not in privity with the promisor.[9] This classification system was never completely satisfactory, partially because of the difficulties in assigning beneficiaries to one of the three categories.

The Restatement (Second) of Contracts adopted a different test, based on determining whether the parties to the contract intended to confer benefits on the third party.[10] However, in implementing the new test, the Second Restatement reverts to an underlying analytical scheme quite similar to that used in the First Restatement but without the language of donee, creditor, and incidental beneficiaries. Furthermore, many modern courts persist in using the traditional labels.[11] Therefore, understanding the law of third-party beneficiaries still requires understanding the differences among these three categories, even though the Restatement has long since abandoned them.[12]

[A]　　Creditor Beneficiaries[13]

A creditor beneficiary is a third party who is a creditor of the promisee whose claim will be at least partially satisfied as a result of the promisor's performance. In entering into the third-party beneficiary contract the promisee seeks to ensure that one of its debts will be paid. Thus, the transaction is not intended to accomplish any kind of a gift.

The rights of creditor beneficiaries are frequently traced, at least in the United States, to *Lawrence v. Fox*,[14] which still serves as a useful illustration. Holly owed a debt to Lawrence. As a means of paying the debt, Holly lent $300 to Fox in return for Fox's promise to pay $300 to Lawrence. When Fox failed to pay,

---

Perfecting the Third Party Beneficiary Standing Rule Under Section 302 of the Restatement (Second) of Contracts, 25 B.C.L. Rev. 919 (1984); Orna S. Paglin, *Criteria for Recognition of Third Party Beneficiaries' Rights*, 24 New Eng. L. Rev. 63 (1989); David M. Summers, *Third Party Beneficiaries and the Restatement (Second) of Contracts*, 67 Cornell L. Rev. 880 (1982).

[8] Restatement of Contracts § 133 (1932).

[9] Gary L. Monserud, *Blending the Law of Sales with the Common Law of Third Party Beneficiaries*, 39 Duq. L. Rev. 111, 120–22 (2000).

[10] Restatement (Second) of Contracts § 302(1) (1981). *See* Hale v. Groce, 744 P.2d 1289 (Or. 1987).

[11] *See* Droplets, Inc. v. E*trade Fin. Corp., 939 F. Supp. 2d 336 (S.D.N.Y. 2013); CR-RSC Tower I, LLC v. RSC Tower I, LLC, 56 A.3d 170 (Md. 2012); Lovell Land, Inc. v. State Highway Admin., 969 A.2d 284 (Md. 2009);

[12] Melvin Aron Eisenberg, *Third Party Beneficiaries*, 92 Colum. L. Rev. 1358, 1381–84 (1992); Gary L. Monserud, *Blending the Law of Sales with the Common Law of Third Party Beneficiaries*, 39 Duq. L. Rev. 111, 122–26 (2000).

[13] M.H. Hoeflich & E. Perelmuter, *The Anatomy of a Leading Case*: Lawrence v. Fox *in the Courts, the Casebooks, and the Commentaries*, 21 U. Mich. J.L. Rev. 721 (1988); Anthony J. Waters, *The Property in the Promise: A Study of the Third Party Beneficiary Rule*, 98 Harv. L. Rev. 1109–23 (1985).

[14] 1859 N.Y. LEXIS 192 (Dec. 1859).

Lawrence sued Fox directly. Fox argued that Lawrence could not sue because there was no privity of contract between the two of them. In rejecting this defense the court said that "a promise made to one for the benefit of another, he for whose benefit it is made may bring an action for its breach."[15]

The court recognized that earlier decisions had seemed to limit the rights of a third party to situations where property had been transferred in trust for his or her benefit. Thus, if Holly had handed Fox the $300 and told him that he was to hold onto it for Lawrence's benefit, a trust would have been created. Lawrence, as the beneficiary *of the trust*, could have enforced his property rights in the fund. But a trust theory depended on the creation of an immediate property right in Lawrence's favor, and this had clearly not occurred on the facts of the case. The absence of a clear basis for establishing a trust left the court with no alternative, apart from denying relief to Lawrence altogether, to concluding that Lawrence was entitled to sue to enforce Fox's promise, even though the promise had been made to Holly. Although the court's analysis did not focus on Lawrence's status as a creditor of the promisee, the facts of the case lent themselves to the establishment of this distinction. After *Lawrence v. Fox*, third-party beneficiaries who were creditors of the promisee could sue to enforce a promise made for their benefit.

A good modern example of a third-party creditor beneficiary contract is found in the context of a credit life insurance policy. Credit life insurance policies are sometimes required by those who make loans to consumers, particularly when the amount of the borrower's down payment is small and there is a risk that the collateral provided for the loan will not be sufficient to fully satisfy the debt should the borrower die.

Suppose, for example, that Anita borrows a large sum of money from Richland Mortgage Company for the purchase of a home, but makes only a 5% down payment. As additional collateral, Richland might require Anita to obtain a life insurance policy, in the amount of the loan, naming Richland as the beneficiary. In consideration for Anita's payment of premiums, Perpetual Life Insurance Company issues the policy insuring Anita's life, but identifies Richland Mortgage as the "person" who will receive the policy's benefits. If upon Anita's death Perpetual Life refuses to pay, Richland Mortgage will be able to enforce Perpetual's promise. Just like Lawrence in *Lawrence v. Fox*, Richland is a creditor of the promisee, and the parties' intent in obtaining and paying for the policy was to satisfy Anita's debt to Richland Mortgage.

Another, more complicated example of a third-party creditor beneficiary contract occurs in construction settings.[16] Construction contracts sometimes permit the owner to withhold a specific portion of the price owed to the general contractor until the general contractor demonstrates that it has satisfied all of its obligations to subcontractors who worked on the project. The general contract might also require the owner to obtain a "payment bond" to make sure that money

---

[15] *Id.* at *11–*14.

[16] *See* Arthur L. Corbin, *Third Parties as Beneficiaries of Contractors' Surety Bonds*, 38 YALE L.J. 1 (1928).

is available to pay these subcontractors when the job is finished. The subcontractors are creditor beneficiaries of the payment bond, which is usually supplied by a commercial bonding firm. The payment bond ensures that funds are available for the payment of subcontractors if the owner becomes insolvent before paying them.[17]

Despite this practice, owners of a building under construction are not normally regarded as third-party beneficiaries of agreements between subcontractors or suppliers and the general contractor.[18] The owner's only recourse, if work is done badly, is against the general contractor with whom the owner has a contract.

Likewise, subcontractors and suppliers who have not been paid have no direct recourse against the owner, though they may be able to obtain a statutory mechanic's lien that is enforceable in an "in rem" action against the property itself.[19] Otherwise, subcontractors and suppliers[20] must obtain recovery, if at all, from the general contractor with whom they have a direct contractual relationship. If the general contractor has obtained a payment bond, many courts permit these suppliers of goods and services to recover from the surety, on the theory that the purpose of the bond was to ensure payment of these parties and thus insulate the owner from the risk that it would not receive payment from the contractor.[21] This is particularly true in connection with public contracts, where state and federal legislation usually requires a payment bond to be made payable in favor of workers, suppliers, and subcontractors.[22] However, in contracts involving private land, courts sometimes adhere to the traditional rule that the principal purpose of the bond is to protect the owner from mechanics liens. These decisions regard suppliers as mere incidental beneficiaries, without the right to enforce the bond.[23]

[B]   Donee Beneficiaries

At first, only creditors of the promisee had rights to enforce a contract as a third-party beneficiary. However, later decisions expanded this protection to those to whom the promisee intended to convey a gift. In *Seaver v. Ransom*,[24] a judge promised his dying wife that if she would execute her will as it had initially been prepared, he would pay $6,000 to his wife's favorite niece, who had inadvertently been excluded from the prepared will. The judge's promise was supported by the

---

[17] *See* W. Waterproofing Co. v. Springfield Hous. Auth., 669 F. Supp. 901 (C.D. Ill. 1987).

[18] *E.g.*, Pierce Assoc., Inc. v. Nemours Found., 865 F.2d 530 (3d Cir. 1988). *See* Melvin Aron Eisenberg, *Third Party Beneficiaries*, 92 Colum. L. Rev. 1358, 1402–05 (1992).

[19] *See* Melvin Aron Eisenberg, *Third Party Beneficiaries*, 92 Colum. L. Rev. 1358, 1396–1400 (1992).

[20] Suppliers who sell goods and other materials for incorporation into the project are frequently called "materialmen." *E.g.*, *Ex parte* Lawson, 6 So.3d 7 (Ala. 2008). *See also* C.T. Foster, Annotation, *Mechanic's Lien for Work on or Material for Separate Buildings of One Owner*, 15 A.L.R.3d 73 (1967).

[21] Daniel-Morris Co. v. Glens Falls Indem. Co., 126 N.E.2d 750 (N.Y. 1955). *See* Jean Fleming Powers, *Expanded Liability and the Intent Requirement in Third Party Beneficiary Contracts*, 1993 Utah L. Rev. 67.

[22] *E.g.*, Miller Act, 40 U.S.C. §§ 270a–270e (2006).

[23] Cretex Cos. v. Constr. Leaders, Inc., 342 N.W.2d 135 (Minn. 1984).

[24] 120 N.E. 639 (N.Y. 1918).

consideration of the wife's execution of the will as it had been initially drafted, even though it did not contain any bequest to the niece. The judge later passed away, without ever paying the $6,000 to his wife's niece, as he had promised. Although the niece was not a creditor of the judge's wife and could not have qualified as a "creditor beneficiary," the court ruled in her favor.

In *Seaver v. Ransom*, it was clear that unless the niece could enforce the dead judge's promise, no one would. The judge's wife, to whom the promise had been made, had already died. And, because the deceased judge was the executor of his wife's estate, it seemed highly unlikely that anyone else would take up the cause and sue to enforce the promise. The practical realities of this situation made a compelling case for enforcement of the judge's promise.

This feature of the case is in stark contrast to the situation in *Lawrence v. Fox*. There, Holly — the promisee — would have been able to recover from Fox for his failure to pay Lawrence. Holly was harmed by Fox's breach because without Fox's payment to Lawrence, Holly would have been vulnerable to an action to recover the debt he owed to Lawrence.[25]

Thus, a donee beneficiary is a third party to whom the promisee intended to convey a gift. As explained before, most life insurance policies purchased by parents and spouses to provide for the support of their surviving families are good examples of contracts made for the purpose of conferring a gift on the third-party beneficiary.[26] Unless donee beneficiaries have rights to enforce promises intended for their benefit, these types of life insurance policies could not be enforced at all. The only alternative would be to use the law of trusts as an awkward avenue for relief, and say that the promisor holds property in trust for the third-party beneficiary.[27]

In insurance contracts the person who owns and controls the policy — the owner of the policy — is frequently also the "insured." He is also the "promisee" for the purpose of third-party beneficiary analysis. The insurance company that issues the policy is the "insurer" and the "promisor." The person designated to receive the proceeds of the policy upon the death of the promisee is the "policy beneficiary" and is entitled to recover as an intended "third-party beneficiary" of the insurance contract. The beneficiary may not even be aware that the policy exists until the insured dies. Upon the death of the insured, the insurer has a duty to pay the face amount of the policy to the person named as the beneficiary.

Strict adherence to the rule of privity of contract would permit the insurer to escape paying the proceeds of the policy because the beneficiary could not properly seek to enforce a promise to which she was not a party. This would be absurd — and no one would buy life insurance. If the beneficiary of the policy could not sue, the only possible other plaintiff, the insured, would be dead. The insured's estate

---

[25] *See infra* § 16.05 Beneficiary's Rights Against the Promisee.

[26] RESTATEMENT (SECOND) OF CONTRACTS § 302 illus. 4 (1981). *E.g.*, Shea v. Jackson, 245 A.2d 120 (D.C. 1968).

[27] *E.g.*, Voelkel v. Tohulka, 141 N.E.2d 344 (Ind. 1957) (stating preference for third-party beneficiary theory in lieu of imposition of "constructive trust").

could sue, but the intended beneficiary of the policy might not be in line to receive the assets of the estate in probate.

No one would like this result. Widespread refusal to permit beneficiaries to enforce policies would remove any incentive for people to purchase these policies in the first place. The essential purpose of a life insurance policy is to provide for someone who is not a party to the policy agreement, but only after the death of the promisee. No sensible contract law system could tolerate blind adherence to formality under these circumstances, and it is not surprising that courts have long allowed beneficiaries of life insurance policies to sue for their enforcement following the insured's death.

As *Seaver v. Ransom* illustrates, the rule permitting donee beneficiaries to recover is not limited to situations involving life insurance. A donee beneficiary is someone to whom the promisee, by entering into the contract with the promisor, intends to confer a gift.[28] A modern example is a "gift certificate," purchased by one person and identifying someone else as the person who may redeem it. Another is the purchase of an item from an online store, with the store promising to deliver the item to someone else, frequently accompanied by a holiday or birthday "gift card."[29] Likewise, a divorcing couple's children are regarded as third-party donee beneficiaries of their parent's settlement agreement, if the agreement contains language providing for the children's support. This ensures the children's right of action to enforce the court's settlement decree.[30]

In cases involving done beneficiaries, it is sometimes difficult to see the consideration for the promise. However, on close examination of the transaction, the consideration is apparent. When Ray pays premiums to Perpetual Life Insurance Company in exchange for Perpetual's promise to pay $1 million to Ray's spouse, upon Ray's death, the premiums, made in exchange for Perpetual's promise, provide the necessary consideration. The fact that Ray's wife has paid nothing does not matter.[31] In *Seaver v. Ransom*, the consideration for the judge's promise was his wife's action in executing her will.

[C] Intended Beneficiaries[32]

As mentioned above, the Second Restatement of Contracts avoids referring to beneficiaries as either creditor or donee beneficiaries.[33] Instead, it refers to a third

---

[28] King v. Nat'l Indus., Inc., 512 F.2d 29, 33 (6th Cir. 1975) (applying Kentucky law); Martinez v. Socoma Cos., 521 P.2d 841, 845 (Cal. 1974) (applying the First Restatement).

[29] *See* RESTATEMENT (SECOND) OF CONTRACTS § 302 illus. 5 (1981). Use of the gift card shows that the store knew of the promisor's intent to benefit the third person as a donee.

[30] *E.g.*, Flanigan v. Munson, 818 A.2d 1275 (N.J. 2003); Hawkins v. Gilbo, 663 A.2d 9 (Me. 1995) (father's promise to spouse to pay child's college expenses).

[31] Tweeddale v. Tweeddale, 93 N.W. 440 (Wis. 1903).

[32] Ernest Jones, *Legal Protection of Third Party Beneficiaries: On Opening Courthouse Doors*, 46 U. CIN. L. REV. 313 (1977); Orna S. Paglin, *Criteria for the Recognition of Third Party Beneficiaries' Rights*, 24 NEW ENG. L. REV. 63 (1989); Jean F. Powers, *Expanded Liability and Intent Requirement in Third Party Beneficiary Contracts*, 1993 UTAH L. REV. 67; Harry G. Prince, *Perfecting the Third Party Beneficiary Standing Rule Under Section 302 of the Restatement (Second) of Contracts*, 25 B.C.L. REV.

person with the right to enforce the contract as an "intended beneficiary," regardless of whether he or she can be characterized as a creditor or donee.[34] It specifies that a third party has rights "if recognition of a right to performance in the beneficiary is appropriate to *effectuate the intention of the parties* and . . . the circumstances indicate that the promisee intends to give the beneficiary the benefit of the promised performance."[35]

This test avoids any concern with whether the promisee either held or manifested a true donative intent and replaces it with a rule that permits recovery if the promisee, for whatever motives, intended to confer rights on the third party.[36] Despite this, the Second Restatement still permits consideration of whether the promisee owed a duty to the third party, as part of the determination of whether the third party is permitted to enforce the contract.[37]

If the third party is not a creditor of the promisee, the Second Restatement encourages courts to examine all of the other circumstances to determine whether "the promisee" intended the third party to benefit from the contract.[38] Regardless of whether they have proclaimed adherence to the First Restatement's "creditor" and "donee" beneficiary categories, most courts have now adopted a standard based on the parties' intent to benefit the plaintiff.[39] Thus, the promisee's intent remains important, as it was in both *Lawrence v. Fox* and *Seaver v. Ransom.*

This revised approach might appear to be quite similar to the approach taken in the original Restatement, except for its terminology.[40] Under both classification schemes, a third party who is owed money can enforce a promise by the promisor, and a third party to whom the promisee intends to make a gift can do so as well. However, differences exist. First, it is now clear that the absence of a true donative intent is not critical to the establishment of third-party rights. Second, it is clear that intent to benefit the third party matters, though it is not entirely clear whether it is the intent of both parties or that of the promisee alone that controls. With respect to this second point, Restatement (Second) § 302(1)(b) clearly speaks in terms of the promisee's intent, but the preamble to § 302(1) refers to effectuating "the intent of the *parties*."[41]

---

919 (1984); Henry E. Smith, *The Language of Property: Form, Context, and Audience*, 55 STAN. L. REV. 1105 (2003).

[33] RESTATEMENT (SECOND) OF CONTRACTS, Introductory Note to Chapter 14 on Contract Beneficiaries (1981).

[34] RESTATEMENT (SECOND) OF CONTRACTS § 302 (1981).

[35] *Id.* (emphasis added).

[36] Melvin Aron Eisenberg, *Third Party Beneficiaries*, 92 COLUM. L. REV. 1358, 1383–85 (1992).

[37] RESTATEMENT (SECOND) OF CONTRACTS § 302(1)(a) (1981).

[38] RESTATEMENT (SECOND) OF CONTRACTS § 302(1)(b) (1981).

[39] *E.g.*, Scarpitti v. Weborg, 609 A.2d 147, 149 (Pa. 1992); Midwest Dredging Co. v. McAninch Corp. 424 N.W.2d 216, 224 (Iowa 1988). *See generally* Orna S. Paglin, *Criteria for the Recognition of Third Party Beneficiaries' Rights*, 24 NEW ENG. L. REV. 63 (1989).

[40] *See* Lovell Land, Inc. v. State Highway Admin., 969 A.2d 284, 297 (Md. 2009).

[41] RESTATEMENT (SECOND) OF CONTRACTS § 302(1) (1981) (emphasis supplied). *See* Melvin Aron Eisenberg, *Third Party Beneficiaries*, 92 COLUM. L. REV. 1358, 1382–84 (1992) (noting that the reasonable reliance test suggested by the comments to § 302 would effectively overrule many traditional third-party

Despite the Second Restatement's language, and the approach taken by most jurisdictions, some courts inquire into the intent of both parties to the contract. In *Grigerik v. Sharpe*,[42] the court specifically approved a jury instruction that required that "both the contracting parties intended the plaintiff to be a third party beneficiary of the contract." In doing so it emphasized that this was necessary to avoid any unfair surprise to the promisor. The court explained that "each party to a contract is entitled to know the scope of his or her obligations." The problem of protecting the promisor against unexpected liability might be better resolved through resort to the more conventional requirement, derived from *Hadley v. Baxendale*,[43] that the promisor must have reason to know of the promisee's intent that the third party will have the right to enforce the contract.[44]

Modern cases focusing on the parties' intent have expanded the scope of those who will enjoy third-party rights beyond those who fit neatly into the categories established by the First Restatement. However, as with contract law generally, the objectively manifested intent should govern, rather than some secret or otherwise undisclosed subjective intent.[45]

In many cases, where the performance promised by the promisor will be provided directly to the third-party beneficiary, the parties' intent will be easy to discern. This will cover all of the cases involving creditor beneficiaries and most of the cases involving donee beneficiaries where performance of the promise would require the promisor to transfer money or other property directly to the third party.

It is helpful to focus on the party who receives performance. For example, if Dave paints Myrna's house in exchange for Myrna's promise to pay Consumer Finance Co., to whom Dave's daughter, Carmen owes a debt, there might be a question about whether Consumer Finance Co. has the right to enforce Dave's contract against Myrna.[46] Carmen's creditor, Consumer Finance Company does not fit into the category of a creditor beneficiary because it is not one of Dave's creditors. Likewise, Dave's purpose in obtaining Myrna's promise to make payment to Carmen's creditors is primarily to confer a gift to Carmen, not to make a gift to Consumer Finance Company. Nevertheless, because Myrna's promised payment will run directly to Consumer Finanace Co, its status as an intended beneficiary is clear.[47]

Furthermore, where the terms of the contract specify the parties' intent to confer legal rights on a third party, their intent will be clear regardless of whether

---

beneficiary cases, including *Lawrence v. Fox* and *Seaver v. Ransom*); RESTATEMENT (SECOND) OF CONTRACTS § 302 cmt. d (1981).

[42] 721 A.2d 526 (Conn. 1998).

[43] 156 Eng. Rep. 145 (Ct. Exch. 1854). *See supra* § 12.04 Limits on Damages: Foreseeability.

[44] Kmart Corp. v. Balfour Beatty, Inc., 994 F. Supp. 634, 638 (D. V.I. 1998).

[45] *See generally* Jean Fleming Powers, *Expanded Liability and Intent Requirement in Third Party Beneficiary Contracts*, 1993 UTAH L. REV. 67.

[46] RESTATEMENT (SECOND) OF CONTRACTS § 302 illus. 6 (1981).

[47] *Id.*

performance of the contract runs directly to that person.[48] However, such express language will often be missing, and its absence should not reflect negatively on the parties' intent that the third party should have the right to enforce the contract.[49]

[D] Incidental Beneficiaries

Those who are not entitled to bring suit to enforce the contract are designated as "incidental" beneficiaries.[50] Incidental beneficiaries are not permitted to enforce a contract, despite the benefits they may receive from its performance, because they are not in privity with the contracting parties,[51] and because to impose this liability is beyond the parties' intent. Exposing the promisor to liability to strangers would expand his liability beyond anything he could have reasonably contemplated when the contract was made.

There are many cases where some third party might benefit from a contract, but where the parties neither manifested an intent to benefit the third party nor even considered the matter. A homeowner who hires a roofing contractor to repair the gutters on her home might realize that repairing her own gutters will prevent damage to her neighbor's foundation, but without additional information that shows that the homeowner had the work done with the purpose of protecting her neighbor's house, her neighbors are unlikely to have a cause of action if the roofer fails to properly complete the work.[52]

[E] Beneficiaries of Warranties for Goods[53]

Those who claim to be a third-party beneficiary of a contract for the sale of goods frequently do so in settings involving personal injury. In these situations, it is sometimes difficult to keep the plaintiff's contract claims, based on a breach of warranty, separate from claims based on negligence or strict product liability in tort. With respect to tort liability, at least, the privity barrier to relief has long since fallen.[54] In contract cases involving pure economic loss, this barrier remains

---

[48] *See In re* Estate of Cohen, 629 N.E.2d 1356, 1357 (N.Y. 1994) (contract explicitly conferred third-party beneficiary rights on "every [named] legatee"); Mowrer v. Poirier & McLane Corp., 114 A.2d 88 (Pa. 1955) (contract provided that purpose was to "protect" third party).

[49] *See* United States v. Huff, 165 F.2d 720 (5th Cir. 1948).

[50] RESTATEMENT (SECOND) OF CONTRACTS § 302 (1981).

[51] RESTATEMENT (SECOND) OF CONTRACTS § 315 (1981).

[52] RESTATEMENT (SECOND) OF CONTRACTS § 302 illus. 16 (1981).

[53] Alex Devience Jr., *The Developing Line Between Warranty and Tort Liability Under the Uniform Commercial Code: Does § 2-318 Make a Difference?*, 2 DEPAUL BUS. L.J. 295 (1990); David B. Gaebler, *Negligence, Economic Loss, and the U.C.C.*, 61 IND. L.J. 593 (1986); William K. Jones, *Products Defects Causing Commercial Loss: The Ascendancy of Contract over Tort*, 44 U. MIAMI L. REV. 731 (1990); Richard E. Speidel, *Warranty Theory, Economic Loss, and the Privity Requirement: Once More into the Void*, 67 B.U. L. REV. 9 (1987); William L. Stallworth, *An Analysis of Claims Instituted by Non-Privity Plaintiffs in Jurisdictions That Have Adopted Uniform Commercial Code Section 2-318 (Alternative A)*, 20 PEPP. L. REV. 1215 (1993); William L. Stallworth, *An Analysis of Warranty Claims Instituted by Non-Privity Plaintiffs in Jurisdictions That Have Adopted Uniform Commercial Code Section 2-318 (Alternatives B & C)*, 27 AKRON L. REV. 197 (1993).

[54] *See generally* William L. Prosser, *The Assault upon the Citadel: Strict Liability on the Consumer,*

in place to a much larger extent. However, the direct marketing efforts of manufacturers, whose advertising claims might form the basis for an express warranty, have sometimes led to the relaxation of the doctrine even where the loss is purely economic.[55]

In domestic contracts for the sale of goods, U.C.C. Article 2 supplies a complicated set of "uniform" alternatives that states might adopt and still claim to remain true to the code's principle of uniformity.[56] Article 2's rules address questions of "horizontal" privity, which deals with the right of those related to the buyer who might reasonably be expected to use, consume, or be affected by the product, such as a member of the buyer's family or a guest in his or her home, to recover from the seller.[57] They do not address the more difficult questions of "vertical" privity, which relates to the right of a buyer to recover from a remote defendant, other than his or her immediate seller, who is higher up in the chain of distribution of the goods, such as a distributor or manufacturer of the goods.[58]

The United Nations Convention for the International Sale of Goods (CISG), which applies to international commercial transactions involving the sale of goods, is silent about the rights of third parties.[59] Thus, the CISG takes no position on the right of downstream buyers and other third parties who suffer harm because of defective goods. Consistent with the CISG's exclusion of transactions involving consumers, it also excludes coverage of personal injury claims.[60] Article 4 provides that it only governs questions of formation of the contract and the rights and obligations of the immediate parties.[61] As a result, domestic law governing product liability still applies, perhaps including the rules in U.C.C. § 2-318 regarding privity.

In analyzing whether a third party may bring a claim against the seller, in a contract otherwise governed by the CISG, the principal inquiry would seem to be whether lack of contractual privity provides the seller with a defense. The seller's foreign location does not, standing alone, insulate the seller from a remote buyer's claim. If the seller is responsible to a remote party under domestic law, either because it has supplied an express product warranty, or because of its advertising about the qualities of the product, it would presumably be just as liable as a

---

69 Yale L.J. 1099, 1120 (1960); William L. Prosser, *The Fall of the Citadel (Strict Liability to the Consumer)*, 50 Minn. L. Rev. 791 (1966).

[55] *See, e.g.*, Randy Knitwear, Inc. v. Am. Cyanamid Co., 181 N.E.2d 399 (N.Y. 1962). *See generally* Richard Speidel, *Warranty Theory, Economic Loss, and the Privity Requirement: Once More into the Void*, 67 B.U.L. Rev. 9 (1987).

[56] U.C.C. § 2-318 (2012). *See supra* § 7.08[C] Absence of Privity.

[57] *See supra* § 7.08[C][1] Horizontal Privity.

[58] *See supra* § 7.08[C][2] Vertical Privity.

[59] Henry D. Gabriel, *The Inapplicability of the United Nations Convention on the International Sale of Goods as a Model for the Revision of Article Two of the Uniform Commercial Code*, 72 Tul. L. Rev. 1995 (1998). *See* Arthur Rosett, *Critical Reflections on the United Nations Convention on Contracts for the International Sale of Goods*, 45 Ohio St. L.J. 265, 293 (1984).

[60] CISG Art. 5 (1980).

[61] CISG Art. 4 (1980).

domestic seller who made the same claims.[62] Thus, the ability of a third party to pursue a claim would depend on domestic law.[63]

[F] Third-Party Beneficiaries in Specific Settings

The rights of third parties as intended beneficiaries are best understood in specific contractual settings. The most commonly recurring problems are those involving government contracts, construction deals, and contracts between professionals (such as lawyers), and their clients.

[1] Government Contracts[64]

Questions regarding a third party's rights are particularly difficult when a member of the public asserts the right to bring an action against someone who has contracted to supply goods or services to a governmental unit.[65] All such contracts are made to enhance the general public welfare, and it might be initially appealing to suggest that members of the public were intended to benefit from the contract and should be able to enforce it.

However, permitting individual citizens to bring an action against anyone who has a contract with a governmental agency would wreak havoc on these agencies, who would be unable to manage contracts with their suppliers on their own. Imagine the spectacle of a member of the general public bringing an action against a state employee (from the governor on down to the night janitor) for breach of his employment contract. On the other hand, where someone enters into a contract with the government to supply a direct benefit to members of the public, it is not so obvious that direct action by members of the public, who would have received those benefits if the contract had been performed, should not be allowed.

Judge Cardozo recognized the problem in *H.R. Moch Co. v. Rensselaer Water Co.*[66] There, the court denied recovery to the owner of a building that had been destroyed by fire due to the alleged failure of the water company to supply water to fire hydrants as it had promised the city. The court's reasoning was based in part on assumption that the water company was unlikely to have meant to expose itself to this type of potentially devastating liability.[67] Imposing liability on the

---

[62] Richard E. Speidel, *The Revision of UCC Article 2, Sales in Light of the United Nations Convention on Contracts for the International Sale of Goods*, 16 Nw. J. Int'l L. & Bus. 165 (1995).

[63] *See* Cedar Petrochemicals, Inc. v. Dongbu Hannong Chem. Co., 2007 U.S. Dist. LEXIS 51802 (S.D.N.Y. July 19, 2007).

[64] Robert S. Adelson, *Third Party Beneficiary and Implied Right of Action Analysis: The Fiction of One Governmental Intent*, 94 Yale L.J. 875 (1985); Melvin Aron Eisenberg, *Third Party Beneficiaries*, 92 Colum. L. Rev. 1358, 1406–1412 (1992).

[65] Gillian E. Metzger, *Privatization as Delegation*, 103 Colum. L. Rev. 1367 (2003); Nestor M. Davidson, *Relational Contracts in the Privatization of Social Welfare: The Case of Housing*, 24 Yale L. & Pol'y Rev. 263 (2006).

[66] 159 N.E. 896 (N.Y. 1928).

[67] *See also* Kornblut v. Chevron Oil Co., 62 A.D.2d 831 (N.Y. App. Div. 1978), *aff'd on opinion below*, 400 N.E.2d 368 (N.Y. 1979) (members of public were not intended beneficiaries of contract to provide auto repair service services to stranded motorists).

water company would have gone beyond its reasonable expectations, when it entered into the contract.[68]

Later cases have taken a similar approach.[69] In *Martinez v. Socoma Companies, Inc.*,[70] the court refused to permit residents of a blighted portion of Los Angeles to enforce a provision in an agreement between the defendant and the United States Department of Labor that required the defendant to hire "hard core unemployed residents" of the neighborhood. Similarly, in *Sussex Tool & Supply, Inc. v. Mainline Sewer & Water, Inc.*,[71] the plaintiff was not permitted to recover for damages it suffered as a result of a utility company's failure to maintain public access to the roads it had promised the city it would ensure during the completion of a construction project. There, the court explained that "the primary purpose of any public works contract is the benefit of the public [and that] [t]his characteristic has led courts and codifiers to fashion a more restrictive test to determine third-party rights in public contracts."

However, where the number of potential claimants is limited and the contract is sufficiently specific, liability has sometimes been imposed. *Koch v. Consolidated Edison Co.*[72] permitted the city itself to pursue a claim against a private electric utility for breach of its contract with the Power Authority of the State of New York to provide electric power to the city, where the contract specifically provided that its purpose was to "deliver power to . . . customers." But even this did not create a right of action in members of the public generally. And, in *Zigas v. Superior Court*,[73] the court permitted tenants in an apartment building, the construction of which had been financed with a federally insured mortgage, to enforce a provision in the mortgage documents that restricted the rent that the owner could charge. Here, the potential liability was confined, both in the extent of possible claimants and in the amount of potential liability, which the landlord could easily predict.

The Second Restatement takes the position that a person who contracts with a governmental agency to provide services to the public is not liable directly to a member of the public unless the contract expressly provides for this liability or unless the governmental agency is liable to individual citizens, and even then only if permitting "direct action" against the promisor is consistent with the policy of the law that authorized the governmental agency to enter into the contract.[74]

---

[68] *See also* Vaughan v. E. Edison Co., 719 N.E.2d 520 (Mass. Ct. App. 1999).

[69] *See also* Koenig v. City of S. Haven, 597 N.W.2d 99 (Mich. 1999) (no third-party beneficiary action for wrongful death due to failure of city to perform a "memorandum of understanding" with the Army Corps of Engineers to restrict the public from access to piers during dangerous inclement weather). *But see* Doyle v. South Pittsburgh Water Co., 199 A.2d 875 (Pa. 1964).

[70] 521 P.2d 841 (Cal. 1974).

[71] 605 N.W.2d 620 (Wis. Ct. App. 1999).

[72] 468 N.E.2d 1 (N.Y. 1984).

[73] 120 Cal. App. 3d 827 (1981).

[74] RESTATEMENT (SECOND) OF CONTRACTS § 313 (1981).

[2] Construction Contracts

Construction projects frequently involve a multiplicity of contracts which might create rights in third parties. For example, where Winkler Builders enters into a contract to build a house for Julie, it is highly likely that Winkler will enter into several subcontracts with a variety of service providers to perform various aspects of the overall construction project. If Ellen's Electric or Ron's Roofing fails to adequately perform their portion of the job, Julie may wish to bring a direct action against them to recover any damages she has suffered. Of course, most of the time, Julie will be able to recover from Winkler Builders for any defects caused by these subcontractors' defective goods or labor. However, if Winkler Builders is bankrupt, the issue becomes more critical.

The traditional rule requiring privity of contract usually applies to these situations, and prevents the owner from recovering from the general contractor's suppliers and subcontractors. The project owner's only recourse is against the general contractor it hired to complete the project. If defects in the building were caused by a subcontractor or a supplier, the owner must recover from the general contractor, with whom the owner has a direct contractual relationship. This leaves it to the general contractor to pursue recourse against its subcontractor, whose poor performance led to the problem.

This was the position taken recently in *Linden v. Cascade Stone Co., Inc.*[75] There, the homeowners brought both contract and tort claims against several subcontractors for water damage to their home that resulted from their defective performance. The plaintiff's tort action was dismissed under the "economic loss doctrine" that prevents plaintiffs from recovering in negligence in the absence of any personal injury or property damages.[76] The plaintiff's contract claims were also dismissed. The court explained that, because the subcontractor's performance would not discharge the general contractor's duty to the owner to deliver a completed building, the owner was not an intended beneficiary of the contract between the subcontractor and the general contractor. Despite this traditional rule, a few courts permit an owner to recover directly from a subcontractor for breach of contract.[77]

Another construction situation in which a similar issue is presented is where the owner serves as its own general contractor and enters into several prime contracts for various aspects of the work. For example, instead of hiring Winkler Builders to coordinate her home renovation project, Julie might decide to coordinate the project herself and hire Ron's Roofing, Lori's Lumber, Karl's Carpentry, Ellen's Electrical, and Mike's Masonry to provide the necessary materials and perform various parts of the work. Here, Julie is in direct contractual privity with each of these contractors and should have no trouble suing them for breach of their

---

[75] 699 N.W.2d 189 (Wis. 2005).

[76] Ralph C. Anzivino, *The Economic Loss Doctrine: Distinguishing Economic Loss from Non-Economic Loss*, 91 MARQ. L. REV. 1081 (2008).

[77] Keel v. Titan Constr. Corp., 639 P.2d 1228 (Okla. 1981); Syndoulos Lutheran Church v. A.R.C. Indus., 662 P.2d 109 (Alaska 1983); Jardel Ent., Inc. v. Triconsultants, Inc., 770 P.2d 1301 (Colo. Ct. App. 1988); Lin v. Gatehouse Constr. Co., 616 N.E.2d 519 (Ohio Ct. App. 1992).

contracts to perform separate parts of the job. Instead, in this type of case, the issue is whether one of the prime contractors can sue one of the others if defects in its performance create a problem for the first. These separate firms are not in direct contractual privity with one another. Their deals are with the owner, Julie.

Traditional rules of contractual privity prevent these contractors from recovering against one another.[78] However, as with owners' direct suits against subcontractors, some cases now permit separate prime contractors to recover from one other.[79] The likelihood that a direct action will be permitted is increased by language in the contract requiring each contractor to cooperate with the others.[80]

A similar issue arises in connection with the status of subcontractors and suppliers as third-party beneficiaries of the contract between the owner and the general contractor, if the general contractor fails to make payment for the goods and services they have provided in connection with the project. As with actions by the owner against these parties, most courts adhere to the traditional rule that subcontractors and material suppliers are not intended third-party beneficiaries. However, in these situations, state mechanics' lien statutes frequently provide the unpaid subcontractors and suppliers with a statutory lien against the real estate involved in the project. Their ability to obtain payment is usually protected by these liens, provided that they comply with whatever procedural steps they must take under the statutory lien law — usually filing notice of their liens in the real estate records of the county in which the land they have worked on is located.

As the court said in *Port Chester Electrical Construction Corp. v. Atlas:*

> It is old law that a third party may sue as a beneficiary on a contract made for his benefit. However, an intent to benefit the third party must be shown and, absent such intent, the third party is merely an incidental beneficiary with no right to enforce the particular contracts. . . . Generally it has been held that the ordinary construction contract, i.e., one which does not expressly state that the intention of the contracting parties is to benefit a third party — does not give third parties who contract with the promisee the right to enforce the latter's contract with another.[81]

And, as with other construction situations, some courts have defected from the traditional rule, and permitted subcontractors to bring direct actions against the owner.[82]

Suppliers and subcontractors might also have a direct right of action against a surety who has provided a payment bond to the general contractor. The ability of subcontractors, laborers, and suppliers to recover from the surety depends on the

---

[78] *E.g.*, J.F., Inc. v. S.M. Wilson & Co., 504 N.E.2d 1266, 1271 (Ill. App. Ct. 1987); Buchman Plumbing Co. v. Regents of Univ. of Minn., 215 N.W.2d 479, 484 (Minn. 1974).

[79] *See* Hanberry Corp. v. State Bldg. Comm'n, 390 So. 2d 277, 280 (Miss. 1980); Moore Constr. Co. v. Clarksville Dep't of Elec., 707 S.W.2d 1, 10–11 (Tenn. Ct. App. 1985).

[80] M.T. Reed Constr. Co. v. Va. Metal Prods. Corp., 213 F.2d 337, 338 (5th Cir. 1954).

[81] Port Chester Electrical Construction Corp. v. Atlas, 357 N.E.2d 983, 985–86 (N.Y. 1976).

[82] *E.g.*, Midwest Dredging Co. v. McAninch Corp., 424 N.W.2d 216, 226 (Iowa 1988).

language in the surety bond contract[83] and whether the owner obtained the bond solely to obtain protection against mechanics' liens, or to ensure that these third parties are paid. In government contracts in particular, these third parties are likely to have rights to enforce the contract, because state mechanics' lien laws do not apply to government contracts and thus the purpose of the bond must not have been to provide protection for such a lien. Thus, in *Western Waterproofing Co. v. Springfield Housing Authority*, in holding that subcontractors were third-party beneficiaries of a payment and performance bond contract that a surety supplied to the owner, the court said that the contract was made to provide a direct benefit — rather than an incidental benefit — to the subcontractor.[84]

[3]   Professional Services

Of particular interest to lawyers are cases that impose third-party beneficiary liability on lawyers and other professionals who fail to property perform contracts with their clients. One of the most famous illustrations is *Lucas v. Hamm*.[85] The intended beneficiaries of a will lost their rights under the will because it failed to comply with the rule against perpetuities. The court recognized third-party beneficiaries of those who would have inherited under the will, if it had been properly drafted.[86]

Further, in *Raritan River Steel Co. v. Cherry, Bekaert & Holland*,[87] accountants were held liable to a bankrupt company's creditors. The court ruled that the corporation intended its creditors to rely on the information supplied by the accounting firm and that the accounting firm shared this intent. Thus, the creditors were intended third-party beneficiaries of the agreement between the accounting firm and its client.

§ 16.03 DEFENSES AGAINST THIRD-PARTY BENEFICIARIES

Intended third-party beneficiaries have standing to recover damages they have suffered as a result of a breach of the contract, even though they are not in privity with the parties who created the contract. Giving third parties this right raises the

---

[83] *Supra* § 16.02[A] Creditor Beneficiaries.

[84] Western Waterproofing Co. v. Springfield Housing Authority, 669 F. Supp. 901 (C.D. Ill. 1987).

[85] 364 P.2d 685 (Cal. 1961). *Lucas v. Hamm* is also notable for its suggestion that the rule against perpetuities is so complex that an attorney's failure to prepare a will that avoids the adverse effects of the rule is not necessarily malpractice. "In view of the state of the law relating to perpetuities and restraints on alienation and the nature of the error, if any, assertively made by defendant in preparing the instrument, it would not be proper to hold that defendant failed to use such skill, prudence, and diligence as lawyers of ordinary skill and capacity commonly exercise." *Id.* at 690.

[86] *See also* Guy v. Liederbach, 459 A.2d 744 (Pa. 1983) (named legatees of a will treated as intended beneficiaries). *But see* Noble v. Bruce, 709 A.2d 1264 (Md. 1998) (estate beneficiaries could not maintain malpractice action against testator's attorney due to allegedly defective advice to testator concerning estate and inheritance tax consequences of estate plan).

[87] 339 S.E.2d 62 (N.C. Ct. App. 1986). *See* John W. Baby & John C. Ruhnka, *The Controversy over Third-Party Rights: Toward More Predictable Parameters of Auditor Liability*, 22 GA. L. REV. 149 (1987).

question whether the third party is vulnerable to defenses of the promisor or those of promisee. First, the promisor might assert a defense based on his or her contract with the promisee. Second, the promisor might wish to use a defense that the promisee has against the third party, typically a creditor beneficiary.

[A]   Defenses of the Promisor[88]

[1]   Breach by the Promisee

Normally, a promisor can assert against a third party any defenses that the promisor could assert against the promisee.[89] Suppose, for example, that Ray had entered into a life insurance contract with Perpetual Life, naming Agnes as the beneficiary. If Ray quit paying premiums before he died, there is little doubt that Perpetual — the promisor — can use this defense to avoid paying Agnes's claim. Payment of premiums is usually a condition to an insurer's obligation to fulfill the terms of the policy, and thus nonpayment excuses the insurer from its promise to pay.[90] Because the promisee would have no claim under the lapsed policy, the third party is in a similar position.

The same is true with respect to any defense the promisor might have based on the failure of any constructive condition of his or her duty to perform. Assume that Ready Roofers promises to install a new roof on Karen's house in exchange for Karen's payment of $5,000 to Franklin Bank, to whom Ready Roofers is indebted. If Ready Roofers materially breaches its contract to install Karen's roof, she can use this breach to avoid paying Franklin Bank. Her right to assert this defense against Franklin is the same as it would have been if Ready Roofers had tried to collect the $5,000 from her.[91]

Defects in the formation of the underlying contract are treated the same way.[92] If a promisor lacked capacity, or the promisee induced the promisor to enter into the contract through fraud, duress, undue influence, or other unconscionable conduct, the promisor can assert this defense against the third party. Its right to do so is not impaired because a third party is bringing the claim rather than the promisee.[93] Similarly, any available defense based on the statute of frauds, the absence of consideration, or the illegality of the contract, may be asserted against the third-party beneficiary.[94] And, the third-party beneficiary is equally likely to be bound by provisions in the contract requiring that any claim be brought in a particular forum or submitted to arbitration.[95]

---

[88] William H. Page, *The Power of the Contracting Parties to Alter a Contract for Rendering Performance to a Third Person*, 12 Wis. L. Rev. 141 (1937).

[89] Restatement (Second) of Contracts § 309 (1981).

[90] Restatement (Second) of Contracts § 309(2) (1981).

[91] *E.g.*, Rouse v. United States, 215 F.2d 872, 873 (D.C. Cir. 1954); Alexander H. Revell & Co. v. C.H. Morgan Grocery Co., 1919 Ill. App. LEXIS 268 (July 1919).

[92] Restatement (Second) of Contracts § 309(1) (1981).

[93] Rouse v. United States, 215 F.2d 872, 873 (D.C. Cir. 1954) (fraud).

[94] Restatement (Second) of Contracts § 309 cmt. a (1981).

[95] *E.g.*, Johnson v. Pa. Nat'l Ins. Cos., 594 A.2d 296 (Pa. 1991).

[2] Modifications and Vesting of Third-Party's Rights

A more difficult question is whether the promisor can raise a defense against a third-party beneficiary of the original contract based on a modification of the original contract. A classic example of the problem is supplied by *Copeland v. Beard*.[96] There, a landowner, whose property was subject to a mortgage debt, sold the property to a buyer, who "assumed" the mortgage. This means that the buyer promised the landowner (his seller), that he would pay the landowner's mortgage. This made the creditor who held the mortgage a third-party creditor beneficiary of the buyer's promise. Before the creditor learned of the transaction, the property was resold to a second buyer, who also assumed the debt. The creditor was also a third-party creditor beneficiary of the second buyer's promise. With the second commitment to repay the mortgage firmly in hand, the original landowner released the first buyer from his promise to pay the mortgage. Later, when the creditor sued the first buyer, the court was confronted with the question of whether the landowner's release of the first buyer from his promise to repay the mortgage was enforceable against the creditor. The court ruled that the creditor, who had neither relied upon the promise nor "accepted" it, was subject to the rescission of the contract between the initial parties, the landowner and the first buyer. The third-party beneficiary's rights had not "vested" and thus could be freely modified by the parties who made the third-party beneficiary contract – the original landowner and the first buyer.

Before a third-party beneficiary's rights have vested, the promisor and promisee are free to modify the terms of the contract and revise the third party's rights. And, as *Copeland v. Beard* illustrates, they are even free to rescind the contract and prevent the third party from asserting any rights to enforce the contract. However, after a third-party beneficiary's rights have vested, the original parties to the contract are prevented from altering the third party's rights without obtaining the third party's consent. Rules for determining when the third party's rights vest depend on the events that occur after the contract is made.[97]

Initially, third-party rights may not be altered if the terms of the original contract expressly prevent any discharge or variation of the promisor's duty without the third party's consent.[98] Thus, it is possible for the contract to prevent any deviation from its original terms, or to explicitly permit the promisor and promisee to change the terms of the beneficiary's rights, or perhaps to eliminate them entirely. Although life insurance contracts were at one time not thought to be susceptible to change, they now typically permit the insured to change the beneficiary, surrender it for cash, borrow against the policy, or assign it.[99]

Where the terms of the original agreement do not prevent the immediate parties from modifying their agreement, their power to do so ends when the third-party beneficiary:

---

[96] 115 So. 389 (Ala. 1928).

[97] *See generally* RESTATEMENT (SECOND) OF CONTRACTS § 311 (1981).

[98] RESTATEMENT (SECOND) OF CONTRACTS § 311(1) (1981).

[99] RESTATEMENT (SECOND) OF CONTRACTS § 311 cmt. c (1981).

- relies in some material way on the contract,

- expresses assent to the contract at one of the parties' request, or

- sues to enforce it.[100]

This is markedly different from the rule, articulated in the First Restatement, that the original parties could modify the ability of a creditor beneficiary to enforce a contract at any time before the creditor beneficiary had relied but could never modify the rights of a donee beneficiary, whose rights vested immediately upon the formation of the contract.[101] Some courts have fully embraced the Second Restatement's approach.[102] Other courts have been more resistant and have continued to adhere to the First Restatement's rule that a third-party donee beneficiary's rights vest immediately.[103]

A third-party beneficiary might easily take action in reliance on the contract. An obvious example would be where a creditor beneficiary entered into a novation with the promisee, releasing him from his original debt, in reliance on the promisor's commitment to satisfy the obligation. Suppose Barb promises to pay Sam's $20,000 debt to Claire as consideration for Sam's sale of his car to Barb. If Claire, upon learning of Barb's promise, releases Sam from his debt, Claire's reliance on Barb's promise prevents Sam and Barb from reducing the agreed price for the car.[104]

A third-party beneficiary's rights also vest when the third party "manifests assent to [the contract] at the request of the promisor or the promisee."[105] However, it is not clear what constitutes assent. The most difficult question is whether mere knowledge of the contract combined with a failure to object is sufficient. Some courts and commentators have said that it is not,[106] and have limited this aspect of the Restatement's rule to situations where the immediate parties to the contract have made a true offer to the third party to enter into an independent agreement with it to accept the benefits of the contract.[107]

Vesting via assent has proven to be a particular problem with respect to third-party beneficiaries who are minors or suffer from some other incapacity which makes them legally unable to give their consent. The normal rule that minors lack the capacity to give consent is based on a concern for their protection. Particularly

---

[100] RESTATEMENT (SECOND) OF CONTRACTS § 311(3) (1981). *E.g.* Olson v. Etheridge, 686 N.E.2d 563 (Ill. 1997). *See generally* Melvin Aron Eisenberg, *Third-Party Beneficiaries*, 92 COLUM. L. REV. 1358, 1414 (1992).

[101] RESTATEMENT OF CONTRACTS §§ 142–143 (1932). Despite the position of the First Restatement, this view about the vulnerability of creditor beneficiaries was not widely followed. *See* Melvin Aron Eisenberg, *Third-Party Beneficiaries*, 92 COLUM. L. REV. 1358, 1416–18 (1992).

[102] *E.g.*, Olson v. Etheridge, 686 N.E.2d 563 (Ill. 1997).

[103] *E.g.*, Biggins v. Shore, 565 A.2d 737 (Pa. 1989).

[104] RESTATEMENT (SECOND) OF CONTRACTS § 311 cmt. g (1981).

[105] RESTATEMENT (SECOND) OF CONTRACTS § 311(3) (1981). *E.g.* Copeland v. Beard, 115 So. 389 (Ala. 1928).

[106] Detroit Bank and Trust v. Chicago Flame Hardening Co., Inc., 541 F. Supp. 1278 (N.D. Ind. 1982); Melvin Aron Eisenberg, *Third-Party Beneficiaries*, 92 COLUM. L. REV. 1358, 1420–21 (1992).

[107] Melvin Aron Eisenberg, *Third-Party Beneficiaries*, 92 COLUM. L. REV. 1358, 1420–21 (1992).

in the case of donee beneficiaries, there would seem to be little reason to impose such a rule as a means of protecting minors from any adverse consequences of unwise decisions to accept the benefits of a gift. Some cases have therefore suggested that a minor's assent will be presumed.[108] However, if the circumstances surrounding the creation of the contract demonstrated that the immediate parties had preserved the right to alter the terms of the contract, this should be permitted.[109]

Not surprisingly, the parties are also prevented from modifying or rescinding their original agreement any time after the third party brings suit to enforce the contract.[110] Otherwise, the original parties could unfairly strip the beneficiary of his or her rights just as they were on the verge of being enforced.[111]

Once the third-party beneficiary's rights have vested, the original promisor and promisee cannot modify the agreement in a way that negatively impacts the third party without obtaining the third party's consent. In the insurance policy context, for example, once the beneficiary's rights have vested, the beneficiary could not be changed. Of course, if the insurance contract itself makes it clear that the promisee retains the right to change beneficiaries, then even after vesting, the promisee could make changes without getting the consent of the third party. As noted earlier, however, even after vesting the third party would still be subject to a defense that the policy had lapsed.

[B]   Defenses of the Promisee

The ability of the promisor to assert its own defenses that arise from the contract between the original parties is clear. The promisor's ability to assert defenses that are based on the promisee's relationship with the third-party beneficiary is another matter. This issue arises when the third party is a creditor beneficiary of the promisee, whose claim against the promisee is itself vulnerable to defenses based on the contract that gave rise to the beneficiary's claim against the promisee.

The problem is illustrated by *Rouse v. United States*,[112] which involved Rouse's assumption of a debt. The transaction started when a person named Winston issued a promissory note to Associated Contractors, who had installed a new furnace in Winston's home. Later, when Winston sold her house to Rouse, Rouse promised "to assume payment of $850 for [the] heating plant," thus agreeing to pay Winston's debt to Associated Contractors. After Rouse moved in, he discovered that Associated Contractors had done a poor job installing the furnace. Accordingly, he resisted paying the $850 debt he had assumed. If Winston had still lived in the house, there is no doubt that she would have been able to assert her

---

[108] RESTATEMENT (SECOND) OF CONTRACTS § 311 cmt. d (1981). *E.g.*, McDaniel Title Co. v. Lemons, 626 S.W.2d 686 (Mo. Ct. App. 1981).

[109] RESTATEMENT (SECOND) OF CONTRACTS § 311 cmt. d (1981).

[110] RESTATEMENT (SECOND) OF CONTRACTS § 311(3) (1981).

[111] *But see* Melvin Aron Eisenberg, *Third-Party Beneficiaries*, 92 COLUM. L. REV. 1358, 1418 (1992) (rejecting this view as unsupported by the case law and unsound).

[112] 215 F.2d 872, 873 (D.C. Cir. 1954).

defense either against Associated Contractors, who installed the furnace, or against the actual plaintiff in the case, the United States, who had acquired the contractor's rights.[113]

Whether Rouse was permitted to assert Winston's defense depended on the nature of Rouse's promise. Quoting Professor Corbin's treatise on contract law, the court said:

> if the promisor's agreement is to be interpreted as a promise to discharge whatever liability the promise is under, the promisor must certainly be allowed to show that the promisee was under no enforceable liability. . . . On the other hand, if the promise means that the promisor agrees to pay a sum of money to A, to whom the promisee says he is indebted, it is immaterial whether the promisee is actually indebted to that amount or at all.[114]

Because Rouse had promised to pay Associated Contractors $850 rather than the "debt owed by Winston," Rouse was not permitted to set up Winston's defense.

Thus, if Larry fraudulently induces Helen to agree to buy his house for $100,000 by lying about having taken steps to eradicate the termites that had infested the house, Helen will have a defense in any action brought by Larry to enforce their contract. If Helen lends $100,000 to Fred in exchange for Fred's promise to pay Larry the money she owes to him, Fred should be able to resist Larry's suit to enforce his promise to Helen. However, if Fred had promised, not to pay "Helen's debt" to Larry, but to pay $100,000 to Larry, without regard to any obligation that she might have owed, Fred will be unable to assert Helen's defense of fraud. The promisor's liability depends on the nature of the commitment it has made.

In situations involving a creditor beneficiary, passage of the statute of limitations on the third party's original claim against the promisee should not provide the promisor with a defense on its independent obligation, though this again should depend on the terms of the promisor's obligation. In *Spiklevitz v. Markmil Corp.*,[115] the court explained: "[w]here a person makes an agreement to pay off another's obligation, it creates a new and separate obligation; a right of action on this obligation accrues only from the date on which the new obligation becomes overdue." In effect, therefore, the new agreement by the promisor operates as a waiver of the portion of the period of limitation that has already run on the promisee's debt.

---

[113] The Federal Housing Administration (FHA) had guaranteed Winston's payment of the note. When payment was not made, Associated Contractors applied to the FHA to fulfill its guarantee. A surety, like the FHA in *Rouse v. United States*, upon payment of the guaranteed debt, obtains whatever rights the original creditor had against the obligor. This equitable right is known as a right of subrogation. The surety also enjoys a legal right of "reimbursement." *See* RESTATEMENT (THIRD) OF SURETYSHIP AND GUARANTY § 23 (1994).

[114] *Rouse*, 215 F.2d at 874.

[115] 357 N.W.2d 721, 723 (Mich. Ct. App. 1984).

§ 16.04   PROMISEE'S RIGHT TO ENFORCE THE CONTRACT

Because the parties to the original contract are the promisor and the promisee, it is not surprising that the promisee continues to have rights regardless of whatever claim of a third party might be successful.[116] However, the nature of the promisee's rights depends on the relationship between the promisee and the third party. If the promisee owes a debt to the third party, the promisor's failure to satisfy that debt will cause a direct harm to the promisee. An action by the promisee against the promisor, where the third party fails or refuses to proceed, will be permitted.

On the other hand, if a third party is a donee beneficiary, the promisee's damages will be limited. Still the promisee might be able to bring an action for specific performance,[117] or for restitution of any benefits the promisee has conferred on the promisor in exchange for his or her promise. Needless to say, the court will have to take steps to ensure that an overlapping action by the beneficiary does not result in double liability.[118]

§ 16.05   BENEFICIARY'S RIGHTS AGAINST THE PROMISEE

The right of the third-party beneficiary to recover from the promisee depends entirely on their relationship to one another and any contract or other obligation that may exist between them. Thus, if the third party is a donee beneficiary, it will not have a claim against the promisee on account of the promisor's failure to live up to the terms of its commitment.

However, if the third party is a creditor beneficiary, the creation of a duty on the part of the promisor to satisfy the promisee's debt does nothing in the absence of a novation to eliminate whatever obligation the promisee originally owed to the third party that gave rise to the promisor's agreement. Thus, in the facts of *Lawrence v. Fox*,[119] Lawrence would retain his right to recover from Holly to whom Fox made his promise. Whether Holly's satisfaction of Lawrence's original claim affects Fox's duties, depends, as it did in *Rouse v. United States*,[120] on the terms of Fox's commitment.[121]

---

[116] RESTATEMENT (SECOND) OF CONTRACTS § 305 (1981).

[117] RESTATEMENT (SECOND) OF CONTRACTS § 305 illus. 1, § 307 (1981). *E.g., In re* Marriage of Smith & Maescher, 21 Cal. App. 4th 100 (1993).

[118] RESTATEMENT (SECOND) OF CONTRACTS § 305 cmt. b (1981).

[119] 20 N.Y. 268 (1859).

[120] 215 F.2d 872, 873 (D.C. Cir. 1954).

[121] *See supra* § 16.03[B] Defenses of the Promisee.

§ 16.06   THIRD-PARTY BENEFICIARIES IN INTERNATIONAL TRANSACTIONS[122]

As explained above, the CISG is silent about the rights of third-party beneficiaries.[123] However, UNIDROIT's Principles of International Commercial Contracts address them directly. They recognize that "[t]he parties may confer . . . a right on a third party . . . by express or implied agreement."[124] Consistent with this rule, the beneficiary's rights are determined "by the agreement of the parties and are subject to any conditions or other limitations under the agreement."[125] Thus, the third-party beneficiary is subject to any defenses based on restrictions on the third party's rights that arise from the agreement itself. Further, the third party's rights are made explicitly subject to "all defences [sic] which the promisor could assert against the promisee."[126] But, the UNIDROIT Principles are silent about the ability of the promisor to assert defenses that might arise from the relationship between the promisee and the third party, such as where the promisee has some defense against a third-party creditor beneficiary based on the contract between the latter two parties. With respect to the vesting of third-party rights, the UNIDROIT Principles permit the parties to modify or revoke the third party's rights until the beneficiary has "accepted them or reasonably acted in reliance on them."[127] These rules are similar to those articulated in the Restatement (Second) of Contracts.

The Principles of European Contract Law (PECL) address these issues only to a limited extent. Article 6.110 permits a third party to "require performance of a contractual obligation when its right to do so has been expressly agreed upon between the promisor and the promisee, or when such agreement is to be inferred from the purpose of the contract or the circumstances of the case."[128] This, like the UNIDROIT Principles, seems to adopt the "intended beneficiary" approach found in the Restatement (Second) of Contracts.[129] The European contract principles do not speak directly to the promisor's right to assert defenses, but it would seem that the promisor would not lose rights that are derived from the contract itself, simply because a third party enjoys the rights to enforce the contract. More uncertain, as under UNIDROIT Principles, is the right of the promisor to assert the promisee's defenses.[130] PECL's rules on modification of a third party's rights are somewhat different from those in the UNIDROIT Principles. PECL Article 6.110(3) permits

---

[122] The question of whether treaties, which are a type of contract, should confer rights on third parties is discussed in Sital Kalantry, *The Intent-to-Benefit: Individually Enforceable Rights Under International Treaties*, 44 Stan. J. Int'l L. 63 (2008).

[123] *See supra* § 16.02[E] Beneficiaries of Warranties for Goods; Henry Mather, *Choice of Law for International Sales Issues Not Resolved by the CISG*, 20 J.L. & Com. 155, 159 (2001).

[124] PICC Art. 5.2.1(1) (2004).

[125] PICC Art. 5.2.1(2) (2004).

[126] PICC Art. 5.2.4 (2004).

[127] PICC Art. 5.2.5 (2004).

[128] PECL Art. 6.110(1) (2002).

[129] Restatement (Second) of Contracts § 302 (1981).

[130] *See supra* § 16.03[B] Defenses of the Promisee.

a promisee to "deprive the third party of the right to performance,"[131] but cuts this right to modify the third party's rights in any case where the third party has "received notice" that its rights are irrevocable,[132] or where either the promisor or the promisee "has received notice from the third party that [it] accepts the right."[133] PECL makes no mention of the effect of the third party's reliance on the contract.

---

[131] PECL Art. 6.110(3) (2002).

[132] PECL Art. 6.110(3)(a) (2002).

[133] PECL Art. 6.110(3)(b) (2002).

Chapter 17

ASSIGNMENTS AND DELEGATIONS

The right to receive performance under a contract can be transferred from one person to another, the same way as a property right.[1] Likewise, the duty to perform a contract can also be transferred to someone else, who assumes the responsibilities of original promisor. Through transfer or "assignment" of rights or "delegation" of duties, third parties can acquire either rights or duties created by the parties to the original contract.

Because of the common law doctrine of "privity of contract," adding parties presents conceptual problems that must be resolved. The privity doctrine prevented someone who was not a party to a contract from enforcing it.[2] The same reluctance to admit additional persons into a contract that once prevented third-party beneficiaries from asserting rights to enforce a contract, also affects the ability of parties to transfer their rights and duties to new people who were not involved in the original agreement.

The principal difference between the law of third-party beneficiaries and rules affecting assignments of rights and delegations of duties is the point in time when the third party was brought into the deal. In cases involving third-party beneficiary issues, the third party's rights are created at the same time the contract is formed.[3] In the case of assignments and delegations, the third party's rights are created after the contract is made. The ability to transfer contractual rights and duties raises a range of potential problems that did not exist when the privity doctrine was more important.

---

[1] If you have trouble thinking of the right to receive performance of a contract as a property right, consider your bank account. It's not really "your money" in the bank account. The money belongs to the bank, just like the money you borrowed from the bank belongs to you (well, maybe to your law school, by now). You have a contract with your bank. The terms of the contract require it to repay you, whenever you ask it to — "on demand." The contract a person has with her stockbroker works exactly the same way. The customer doesn't really own the stock in her "account." Instead, she owns what U.C.C. Article 9 refers to as a "security entitlement." Its parameters are defined by the stocks identified in the account and other details of the brokerage contract.

[2] *See* Lippy v. Soc'y Nat'l Bank, 651 N.E.2d 1364 (Ohio Ct. App. 1995) (privity of contract is the connection or relationship between two contracting parties that allows them to sue each other but prevents third parties from suing on the contract).

[3] Kester v. Kester, 108 S.W.3d 213, 226 (Mo. Ct. App. 2003).

§ 17.01   DISTINGUISHING ASSIGNMENTS AND DELEGATIONS[4]

The first problem in connection with assignments of rights and delegations of duties is distinguishing between the two. An "assignment" is the voluntary transfer of a party's right to receive a performance from another party to the contract.[5] When an assignment is made, the transferor's right to receive the performance is extinguished and is vested, instead, in the transferee.[6] The transferor is referred to as the "assignor;" the transferee is the "assignee."

A "delegation" occurs when one person transfers his contractual duty to someone else. The original obligor is the "delagor;" the new person, who has assumed the duty to perform the contract is the "delegee" or, the "delegate." In general, the delegation of a duty does not discharge the original obligor who entered into the contract.[7] Any particular transfer of some aspect of a contract may involve both an assignment of rights and a delegation of duties, merely an assignment of rights, or merely a delegation of duties.

[A]   Assignments of Rights

Generally, those who have acquired rights under an unperformed or "executory contract,"[8] are free to transfer them to someone else. In most cases, contractually acquired rights are fairly impersonal and ordinarily do not depend on the identity of the person who will *receive* the promised performance.

The transfer or "assignment" of a right is illustrated by the facts of a deal between Sam and Barb for the sale of Sam's car to Barb for $20,000. If Sam transfers his right to receive payment of the $20,000 from Barb, to his sister Carol, there has been an "assignment" of Sam's rights under the contract with Barb. After the assignment, Carol, rather than Sam, has the right to receive payment from Barb.[9] Consequently, Carol has the right to sue Barb if Barb fails to pay. Sam has no right to sue; as a result of the assignment, his rights are owned by Carol.

If, on the other hand, Barb transfers her right to receive the car from Sam, to Andrea, in exchange for $21,000, there has been an assignment of Barb's rights to Andrea. Once Barb assigns her rights Andrea owns the rights Barb once held to receive the car. If Sam fails to deliver it, it is Andrea who has the right to sue Sam due to his breach, not Barb.

In analyzing assignments, several sets of labels are used to refer to the parties.

---

[4] Arthur L. Corbin, *Assignment of Contract Rights*, 74 U. Pa. L Rev. 207 (1926); W.S. Holdsworth, *The History of the Treatment of Choses in Action by the Common Law*, 33 Harv. L. Rev. 997 (1920).

[5] Restatement (Second) of Contracts § 317 (1981). *See, e.g.*, Pub. Serv. Comm'n of Md., L.P., 825 A.2d 462, 469 (Md. 2003).

[6] Restatement (Second) of Contracts § 317(1) (1981).

[7] Restatement (Second) of Contracts § 318 (1981).

[8] An executory contract is one that has not yet been fully performed. *See supra* § 1.02[D] Executory Contracts.

[9] Restatement (Second) of Contracts § 317 illus. 1 (1981).

This terminology helps keep track of the parties' relationships to one another in connection with the assignment. Under one set of labels, the original contracting parties are known as the "obligor" and the "obligee." The obligee, the person who transfers the right to receive the obligor's performance, is also referred to as the "assignor." The person to whom those rights are transferred is the "assignee."

Using these labels in the transaction involving Sam's assignment of his right to receive the $20,000 price to Carol, Barb is the obligor; Sam, as the person to whom Barb originally owed the duty to pay the $20,000, is the obligee, and once he has made the assignment, is also referred to as the assignor; and Carol is the assignee.

These simple illustrations belie the complexity of modern commercial transactions involving assignments. A commonly recurring, but somewhat more complicated example, involves the relationship between commercial lenders and retailers who specialize in big-ticket consumer goods, particularly automobile dealers and their customers. When Sam buys a new Honda, he probably won't be able to pay cash for it, despite having recently received $20,000 from the sale of his old BMW. Instead, he is likely to have to borrow the balance of the purchase price of his new car and make monthly installment payments for several years. Or, he might purchase the car through an installment payment plan, promising to pay the seller, Suburban Motors, the $30,000 balance over a five-year period, with interest. Suburban Motors, not completely trustful that Sam will be able to make these payments, is likely to retain a "security interest" in the new Honda, giving Suburban the right to repossess the car and sell it to pay off the debt if Sam fails to make all of the agreed payments.[10]

However, Suburban Motors is a car dealership, and is not really in the business of lending money. As a result, it is ill-equipped to process Sam's monthly payments efficiently. Moreover, Suburban Motors probably has financial obligations of its own to meet and can't really afford to wait five years to receive full payment from Sam. It needs the money right away, so that it can pay its employees, pay the rent and utilities, and purchase additional cars from the manufacturer to sell to new customers. Consequently, Suburban is likely to want to "assign" its rights to receive payment from Sam to someone in a better position to handle this aspect of the transaction. Suburban, therefore, is likely to enter into an agreement with someone like the "Auto Finance Association" to take over the process of collecting Sam's monthly payments. In exchange for an immediate cash payment, possibly at some sort of discount below the face value of Sam's promise to pay $30,000, Suburban Motors will "assign" its bundle of rights against Sam to Auto Finance. Suburban Motors will go back to its usual business of selling cars, and Auto Finance will send notice to Sam that Suburban's rights under the contract he signed have been assigned to it.

After the assignment has been made, and notice has been supplied to Sam, Sam will make his regular monthly payments to Auto Finance. If Sam quits making payments, it will be Auto Finance who asserts the rights Suburban once held to repossess the car from Sam and to recover the balance due if the foreclosure sale

---

[10] Security interests are governed by Article 9 of the U.C.C. You will study them if you take a course in Secured Transactions or Commercial Law as a second- or third-year law student.

does not produce enough money to pay Sam's debt.

Here it should be noted that U.C.C. Article 9 applies to many assignments, particularly those like Sam's assignment to Carol of the right to receive $20,000 from Barb, and Suburban Motors' assignment to Auto Finance of its right to receive payment from Sam.[11] When the assignment is one governed by Article 9, a different set of labels is used to refer to the parties involved in the transaction.[12] In connection with the assignment of Suburban's right to collect Sam's installment payments to Auto Finance, Sam, who would be referred to as the "obligor" under the common law terminology, will be called an "account debtor."[13] If Sam has signed a promissory note, instead of a retail installment sales contract, he might also be referred to as the "maker" of the note.[14] Though it is highly counterintuitive in this limited context, Article 9 refers to Suburban Motors, the original obligee and assignor under the common law terminology, as the "debtor," even though Suburban Motors owes no debt.[15] Under Article 9 the "seller of accounts" or other similar payment obligations of this type is designated as a debtor, despite the fact that it owes no debt.[16] Auto Finance, the assignee, is referred to as a "secured party."[17] Although different labels are used by Article 9 to refer to the parties, the rules in Article 9 are the same as the common law rules governing assignments. Despite these more technical labels, in the traditional course in Contracts the traditional common law labels "assignor," "assignee," and "obligor" are usually used.

[B]   Delegations of Duties

A delegation of duties involves a transfer of a duty to render a performance of a contract to a third party.[18] The third party assumes the duty to perform. For example, if Winkler Builders enters into a contract to build a room addition on Julie's house, it might transfer ("delegate") the duty to Crash Construction Co. Crash will assume Winkler's obligation to build the addition at Julie's house. Crash's promise to Winkler probably also makes Julie a third-party beneficiary of Crash's promise. Thus, when duties are delegated, the obligee, to whom the delegated duty is originally owed, usually has the right to enforce the contract against the person who assumed the delegated duty, which, in this example, is Crash. As will be seen, because Julie's likelihood of receiving full performance may

---

[11] *See* U.C.C. § 9-109(a)(3) (2012).

[12] The common law terminology is likely to be used in your first-year Contracts course. However, if your Contracts professor also teaches Secured Transactions, he or she may use the Article 9 terminology. When you enroll in a course in Secured Transactions, which, of course, you should, the U.C.C. language will most likely be used. This guide is provided to assist you in anticipating the adjustment to the Code's technical language.

[13] U.C.C. § 9-102(a)(3) (2012).

[14] U.C.C. § 3-103(a)(5) (2012).

[15] U.C.C. § 9-102(a)(28)(B) (2012).

[16] If you take a course in Secured Transactions, where you will study Article 9 in earnest, you will see why this is true.

[17] U.C.C. § 9-102(a)(72)(D) (2012).

[18] *See* RESTATEMENT (SECOND) OF CONTRACTS § 318 (1981).

be impaired by the delegation, she may have the right to refuse to accept performance from Crash and to insist that Winkler do the job itself.

Rules about delegations of duties are more complicated than those dealing with assignments because people are more sensitive about who works for them than they are about who they work for or to whom they pay money. Julie may not care whether she writes a check to Winkler Construction or Builder's Finance Co., when the job on her house is finished, but she is likely to care about who is in her house every day, working on her room addition.

Julie may be anxious to learn that Winkler has transferred the duty to build her addition to Crash Construction. After all, Crash might have a reputation for shoddy work or may simply be unfamiliar to Julie, who chose Winkler because of recommendations from her friends and neighbors.

Where the extension of credit is involved, creditors are unlikely to appreciate depending on payment by someone whose credit score they have not checked. Sam probably won't care whether Barb or Andrea pays him the $20,000 in cash when he delivers the car, but if the example is changed so that payment at delivery is to be by personal check, then Sam may be more concerned about trusting Andrea, whom he may not even know, instead of Barb whom he knows and trusts. If payments are to be made over several months or years, Sam's concern will be more pronounced.

Like assignments of rights, the law governing delegations of duties has its own terminology. The person entitled to receive the performance that has been delegated is known as the "obligee." In the transaction involving a delegation to Crash Construction of Winkler's duty to build Julie's room addition, Julie is the obligee — the obligation is owed to her. Winkler is the original obligor and, as a result of the delegation, might also be referred to as the "delegator" of the transferred duty. Crash, to whom the duty has been delegated, is the "delegatee" or perhaps even more frequently, an "assignee," but this time of a duty. Use of this more general term however, requires care to ensure that it is understood that the assignment has resulted in a delegation of duties, not simply an assignment of rights.

[C] Assignment and Delegation Combined

Although an assignment of rights is different from a delegation of duties, the two might be combined in the same transaction, with the duty to provide a performance under a contract delegated to a person at the same time as an assignment of the rights to receive payment for the performance. When duties and rights are transferred together in this fashion, the entire contract has been assigned.

Consider Winkler Builders' delegation of its duty to install Julie's room to Crash Construction. Winkler might simply pay Crash for doing the job and retain the right to receive payment directly from Julie. However, it might make more sense for Winkler to assign the right to receive payment from Julie for the job together with the delegation of the duty to earn the right to Julie's payment by performing the duty to build the addition. This way, although Winkler will still have to worry about the quality of Crash's work, it can at least avoid liability to Crash if Julie fails to pay after the work is done.[19]

Assignments of rights are frequently combined with a delegation of the duties associated with those rights, such as when two businesses merge or when one company purchases another. The surviving firm normally agrees to satisfy the obligations of the company that is being purchased and also receives an assignment of the right to collect payment from past customers. For example, in *Macke Co. v. Pizza of Gaitherburg Inc.*,[20] a soft drink vendor, Virginia Coffee Service, Inc., was purchased by the Macke Co. The transfer resulted in a delegation of the Virginia Coffee shop's duty to deliver the soft drinks to the seller's customers and an assignment of the right to receive payment from the customers to the buyer, Macke Co.

Sally Beauty Co. v. Nexxus Products Co.,[21] involved a combined assignment and delegation as the result of Sally Beauty's purchase the stock of Best Barber & Beauty Supply Co. As part of the transaction, Sally Beauty received an assignment of all of Best's rights under a contract Best had with one its suppliers, Nexxus Products Co. Sally Beauty also assumed Best Barber's contractual duty to use its best efforts to distribute Nexxus's products.

Whether a particular assignment involves both a delegation of duties and an assignment of rights depends on an interpretation of the contract calling for the assignment. General language, calling for an assignment of "the contract" usually means that both rights and duties have been transferred.[22] In this regard, both the Second Restatement of Contracts and the U.C.C. provide that an assignment of "the contract" or of "all my rights under the contract" or an assignment in similar general terms should be regarded as both an assignment of rights and a delegation of assignor's duties.[23]

Of course, other language, or the accompanying circumstances may indicate a contrary intent.[24] However, in transactions like those in *Macke Co.* and *Sally Beauty Co.*, where the assignor is going out of business, the circumstances ordinarily lead to no other conclusion. Other circumstances might easily indicate that only an assignment of rights was involved. For example, where the assignment is made solely as a means of securing a loan, the assignment is construed as involving only the right to receive payment and not a delegation of the duty to perform the entire underlying contract. Thus, if Winkler Builders assigns its contract with Julie to the Beechwold Builder's Bank, as collateral for a loan used to buy the supplies and materials necessary to build Julie's addition, no one is

---

[19] This result, however, is not inevitable. Winkler and Crash might agree that if Julie doesn't pay, Winkler will make good on her obligation to pay for the work. This simply depends on how Crash and Winkler choose to handle the risk of nonpayment from Julie.

[20] 270 A.2d 645 (Md. Ct. App. 1970).

[21] 801 F.2d 1001 (7th Cir. 1986).

[22] *E.g.*, Rosenberg v. Son, Inc., 491 N.W.2d 71 (N.D. 1992).

[23] Compare U.C.C. § 2-210(3) (2012) *and* RESTATEMENT (SECOND) OF CONTRACTS § 328(1) (1981) (using nearly identical language).

[24] *Id.*

likely to think that Winkler delegated its duty to build the addition to the bank.[25] The bank has no experience in building room additions.

A further issue is whether the assignee's acceptance of a contract calling for the delegation of duties renders the assignee responsible as a third-party beneficiary of the contract providing for the assignment. While the general rule is that the delegate is liable, this rule is not universal.[26]

The parties can avoid any potential ambiguity about the issue with language that unequivocally assumes the obligation to perform the duties under the contract, or with language that expressly avoids such a commitment. Absent clear language to the contrary, the court should construe the language in the usual manner,[27] in light of the circumstances surrounding the transaction, any relevant usage of trade or course of dealing, and the economic realities of the transaction.[28]

§ 17.02   ASSIGNABILITY

Generally, contract rights are freely transferable.[29] However, there are a few exceptions to this general rule.[30] Public policy, unrelated to contract law, makes certain types of rights unassignable. Further, a contract right might not be assignable if its transfer would impair the likelihood of performance. In still other circumstances, the parties might enter into an agreement restricting the transferability of rights under the contract. This leads to questions about the enforceability of such a restriction.

[A]   Public Policy Restricting Assignment

An attempt to transfer some types of rights might conflict with countervailing public policies that serve purposes unrelated to contract law generally.[31] For example, the law imposes a general prohibition against assigning tort claims.[32] Permitting the assignability of personal injury claims has been thought to inappropriately encourage litigation.[33] However, some courts draw a distinction between assignments of a cause of action itself — which is nonassignable — and assignments of the proceeds from a personal injury claim — which is sometimes

---

[25] U.C.C. § 2-210(5) (2012); RESTATEMENT (SECOND) OF CONTRACTS § 328 cmt. b (1981).

[26] RESTATEMENT (SECOND) OF CONTRACTS § 328 cmt. c (1981).

[27] See supra § 6.02 Interpreting Express Terms.

[28] Chatham Pharm. v. Angier Chem., 196 N.E.2d 852 (Mass. 1964).

[29] E.g., Peterson v. Dist. of Columbia Lottery and Charitable Games Control Bd., 673 A.2d 664, 667 (D.C. 1996) (free assignability of right to receive lottery winnings).

[30] For example, when a lawyer retires from practice, she may sell her list of clients to her successor. The clients themselves, however, are not the property of the retiring lawyer. The clients remain free to choose a lawyer to represent them.

[31] RESTATEMENT (SECOND) OF CONTRACTS § 317(2) (1981). E.g., Managed Health Care Assoc., Inc. v. Kethan, 209 F.3d 923 (6th Cir. 2000).

[32] See Regie de l'assurance Auto. du Quebec v. Jensen, 399 N.W.2d 85 (Minn. 1987).

[33] E.g., Horton v. New S. Ins. Co., 468 S.E.2d 856 (N.C. Ct. App. 1996).

permitted.[34]

Likewise, most states prohibit the assignment of an employee's right to receive wages from his or her employer, usually creating an exception for court-ordered spousal or child support.[35] Other states draw a distinction between an assignment of wages already earned and those to be earned in the future, imposing the restriction only on future wages.[36]

Governmental entities are often reluctant to permit assignments of claims against them because they do not want to keep track of whom they owe a duty to pay. Consequently, governmental entities often prohibit assigning claims against them either by statute,[37] administrative regulation, or by specific provision in the agreement itself. Courts give effect to these restrictions more easily than when government is not involved, but as in cases involving nongovernmental reluctance to have to deal with assignees, invalidating the assignment as to the obligor (governmental entity) has no effect on the relationship between the assignor and the assignee.

[B] Assignment Resulting in Material Change in the Obligor's Duty[38]

The assignment of a right does not usually cause a material change in the risk of the obligor. This is particularly true of assignments of rights to receive payment. Thus, where Sam, after entering into an agreement to sell his car to Barb, assigns his right to receive Barb's payment, to Carol, it is unlikely that Barb will be harmed by the assignment. So long as Barb retains the right to receive delivery of the car before she makes payment, the risk to Barb remains unchanged.

In situations like this, where the assignment does not materially change the burden or risk on the obligor, nor affect the likelihood of the obligor's receipt of a return performance of the other party, the assignment is permitted.[39] Absent some reason to believe that Sam's assignment of his right to receive Barb's $20,000 to Carol will impair the likelihood of Barb receiving the car from Sam, there is no reason to prohibit the assignment. Even if Sam dislikes Carol, and is loath to pay her any money, the assignment does not materially affect his obligation in any way that the law will recognize.[40]

---

[34] *See* Charlotte-Mechlenburg Hosp. Auth. v. First of Ga. Ins. Co., 455 S.E.2d 655, 657 (N.C. 1995). *But see* Midtown Chiropractic v. Ill. Farmers Ins. Co., 847 N.E.2d 942 (Ind. 2006) (questioning the merits of this distinction).

[35] Restatement (Second) of Contracts, Introductory Note to Chapter 15 (1981). *E.g.*, Ohio Rev. Code § 1321.32 (2002).

[36] *E.g.*, *In re* Nance, 556 F.2d 602 (1st Cir. 1977) (commercial assignment of future and past wages owed to professional football player).

[37] *E.g.*, 31 U.S.C. § 203 (2000); 41 U.S.C. § 15 (2000).

[38] Larry A. DiMatteo, *Depersonalization of Personal Service Contracts: The Search for a Modern Approach to Assignability*, 27 Akron L. Rev. 407 (1994); Richard Epstein, *Why Restrain Alienation?*, 85 Colum. L. Rev. 970 (1985).

[39] Restatement (Second) of Contracts § 317(2)(a) (1981); U.C.C. § 2-210(2) (2012).

[40] *E.g.*, C.H. Little Co. v. Cadwell Transit Co., 163 N.W. 952 (Mich. 1917).

Likewise, the right to purchase goods or real estate is usually assignable.[41] Ordinarily the seller's obligation is not affected in any way by the identity of the person to whom title is to be delivered. Accordingly, Barb's right to receive title to Sam's car, in exchange for her payment of $20,000 cash, is freely assignable to Andrea. The same would be true if the contract were for the sale of real estate.[42] And, although an *offer* to enter into a contract is not generally regarded as assignable,[43] option contracts are widely regarded as freely assignable, at least in the absence of specific language making the option personal to the offeree.[44]

While delegations of duties might materially alter the risks involved in the transaction, simple assignments of rights, unaccompanied by a delegation of duties, rarely increase the obligor's risk.[45]

Nevertheless, in some situations it is easy to see how an assignment might affect the risk imposed on the obligor. Hazard and liability insurance policies are not generally assignable, for the obvious reason that the insurer's willingness to provide insurance at any price is likely to depend on the insurer's assessment of the likelihood the insured will engage in conduct that will give rise to a claim. Thus, a fire insurance policy on a home would not be assignable by the seller of the home to the new occupant, who, after all, may be an arsonist who has only recently been released from prison. Even in less obvious cases, however, the insured's rights under an insurance policy are generally regarded as not assignable.[46]

Requirements contracts are a particular problem in this regard, particularly where the assignee's requirements might be different from those of the assignor.[47] On the other hand, language in U.C.C. § 2-306(1), which prevents a buyer from demanding a quantity that is grossly disproportionate from any stated estimates or past quantities, would seem to protect the obligor from the risk that his or her obligations will materially change as a result of the assignment. Since adoption of the U.C.C., therefore, output and requirements contracts have come to be generally regarded as assignable.[48]

It may not always be obvious that an assignment is accompanied by a delegation of a duty. In the contract for the sale of Sam's car to Barb for $20,000, Barb's transfer of the contract to Andrea may involve a delegation to Andrea of the duty to pay for the car. If the terms of the contract required Sam to accept a personal

---

[41] RESTATEMENT (SECOND) OF CONTRACTS § 317 illus. 5 (1981) (assignment of buyer's right to purchase 250 tons of ice per week from seller).

[42] *E.g.*, Estate of Martinek, 488 N.E.2d 1332 (Ill. App. Ct. 1986).

[43] Cent. Bank & Trust Co. v. Kincaid, 617 S.W.2d 32 (Ky. 1981).

[44] *E.g.*, Black v. First Interstate Bank of Fort Dodge, Iowa, 439 N.W.2d 647 (Iowa 1989).

[45] RESTATEMENT (SECOND) OF CONTRACTS § 317 cmt. d (1981).

[46] Conrad Bros. v. John Deere Ins. Co., 640 N.W.2d 231, 236–37 (Iowa 2001).

[47] *See* Crane Ice Cream Co. v. Terminal Freezing & Heating Co., 128 A. 280 (Md. 1925) (ice cream manufacturer's rights to purchase its "requirements" of ice were not assignable to larger ice cream manufacturer who would reasonably be expected to require more ice than assignor had needed for its smaller operations).

[48] *See* U.C.C. § 2-210 cmt. 4 (2012) (suggesting that exclusive dealing contracts should be freely assignable in the absence of "material personal discretion").

check from Barb, delegating the duty to supply Sam with a check to Andrea may expose Sam to a bigger risk. On the other hand, if Barb will still be writing the check to Sam, with Andrea simply delivering Barb's check when Sam delivers the car, the additional risk to Sam is negligible. The general topic of the delegability of duties is discussed later in this chapter.[49]

[C]   Contractual Limitations on Assignments[50]

People usually prefer not to deal with strangers. As a result, they sometimes include a provision in their agreements prohibiting assignment. However, the law generally deplores efforts to restrain the free transferability of property. Thus, contractual prohibitions on the assignability of rights are construed narrowly. Unless the language explicitly prohibits the assignability of rights in addition to a delegation of duties, general language prohibiting assignment is construed to apply only to a delegation of duties and does not prevent the assignment of rights.[51]

Although the common law construes prohibitions on assignment narrowly, it does not make these restrictions unenforceable.[52] A contractual prohibition on assignment may help resolve doubt over whether an assignment will materially effect of the obligor's duties.[53] However, assignments of most payment rights are governed by U.C.C. Article 9[54] and U.C.C. § 9-406(d) makes agreements prohibiting assignments of Article 9 payment rights ineffective.[55] Contractual language prohibiting the assignment of an "account, chattel paper, [a] payment intangible, or [a] promissory note"[56] is unenforceable. This agreement is ineffective against the assignee; it also is ineffective against the assignor who cannot be sued for breach of the agreement not to assign his payment rights.[57] Accordingly, contractual prohibitions on the assignability of payment rights are enforceable only if the right to payment falls outside the broad scope of U.C.C. Article 9. Accordingly, if Julie's contract with Winkler Builders prevents Winkler from assigning his right to receive payment from Julie, the agreement is unenforceable in any respect. The same is true of nearly all other rights to receive payment for the sale of property or the performance of services.

Contractual restrictions on other types of rights, however, are enforceable. Thus, agreements preventing the right to receive other performances are

---

[49] *See infra* § 17.05 Limits on Delegating Duties.

[50] Arthur L. Corbin, *Assignment of Contract Rights*, 74 U. Pa. L Rev. 207 (1926); Grant Gilmore, *The Commercial Doctrine of Good Faith Purchase*, 63 Yale L.J. 1057 (1954); Edwin Goddard, *Non-Assignment Provisions in Land Contracts*, 31 Mich. L. Rev. 1 (1932); Grover C. Grismore, *Effect of a Restriction in Assignments in a Contract*, 31 Mich. L. Rev. 299 (1933); William S. Holdsworth, *The History of the Treatment of Choses in Action by the Common Law*, 33 Harv. L. Rev. 997 (1920).

[51] Restatement (Second) of Contracts § 322(1) (1981); U.C.C. § 2-210(4) (2012).

[52] Restatement (Second) of Contracts § 317(2)(c) (1981).

[53] Restatement (Second) of Contracts § 317 cmt. f (1981).

[54] U.C.C. § 9-109(a)(3) (2012).

[55] U.C.C. § 9-406(d) (2012).

[56] *Id.*

[57] U.C.C. § 9-406 cmt. 5 (2012).

enforceable. If Sam's contract with Barb, to sell his car to Barb for $20,000 prevents Barb from assigning the right to receive the car to anyone else, the restriction is enforceable. Barb, of course, can still enforce the contract with Sam, and then sell the car to whomever she likes. It is just her contract rights that cannot be assigned, not her title to the car once she owns it.

[D]   Partial Assignments

Partial assignments are problematic. They expose the obligor to the risk of a multiplicity of suits or claims based on the same contract, and thus increase his or her risk beyond what was contemplated by the original contract. For example, if Barb promises to pay $20,000 for Sam's BMW and then Sam assigns $10,000 of the amount due to Mike, $7,000 of the obligation to Nora, and $3,000 of the obligation to Ozzie, Barb has three creditors' claims to keep track of instead of the one she bargained for. As a result, at one time a partial assignment could be enforced only in equity.[58] The modern rule permits the assignment[59] but gives the obligor the right to insist that all assigned claims be brought together in the same action, or not at all. Thus, in the above example, Mike would not be able to sue Barb to recover the $10,000 assigned to him, without joining Nora and Ozzie in the action.[60]

[E]   Assignments in Sale of Goods Transactions

U.C.C. § 2-210 deals with assignments of rights and delegations of duties. With respect to assignments, it specifies that "unless otherwise agreed, all rights of either seller or buyer can be assigned, except where the assignment would materially change the duty of the other party, or increase materially the burden or risk on him or by his contract, or impair materially his chance of obtaining return performance."[61] This is consistent with the Second Restatement's approach.[62]

This language seems to make contractual agreements prohibiting assignment enforceable. However, § 2-210(b) is expressly subject to U.C.C § 9-406. Section 9-406 prohibits enforcement of agreements between an " 'account debtor' and an assignor."[63] This language, combined with the definition of "account debtor," applies to a broad range of rights to receive payment.[64] As the Official Comments to § 9-406(d) explain, it makes a contractual clause prohibiting assignment of an

---

[58] RESTATEMENT (SECOND) OF CONTRACTS § 326 cmt. b (1981).

[59] RESTATEMENT (SECOND) OF CONTRACTS § 326(1) (1981).

[60] RESTATEMENT (SECOND) OF CONTRACTS § 326 illus. 3 (1981). *See, e.g.*, Space Coast Credit Union v. Walt Disney World Co., 483 So.2d 35 (Fla. Dist. Ct. App. 1986).

[61] U.C.C. § 2-210(2) (2012).

[62] RESTATEMENT (SECOND) OF CONTRACTS § 317(2)(a) (1981). *See supra* § 17.02[B] Assignment Resulting in Material Change in the Obligor's Duty.

[63] U.C.C. § 9-406(d) (2012).

[64] *See* U.C.C. § 9-102(a)(3) (2012). Account debtor refers to a person obligated on "an account, chattel paper, or general intangible." The definitions of these terms cover a wide variety of payment obligations, other than the obligation to make payments on a promissory note, which is dealt with elsewhere in the code.

account "of no effect whatsoever."[65] However, restrictions on the transfer of other rights, such as the right to purchase the goods, are enforceable.

The United Nations Convention for the International Sale of Goods (CISG) does not address assignability of rights. Article 4 of the CISG limits its scope to "the formation of the contract of sale and the rights and obligations of the seller and the buyer arising from such a contract."[66] Thus, in resolving questions regarding assignability and the effectiveness of an assignment, reference must be made to the law that would otherwise be applied to either the transaction or to the assignment.[67]

§ 17.03   EFFECTIVENESS OF ASSIGNMENTS

Another set of issues regarding assignments deals with the steps necessary to make an assignment effective. As explained below, the issue is a particular problem in connection with gratuitous assignments — those made as a gift. Further, because assignments of most payment rights are governed by U.C.C. Article 9, its statute-of-frauds provision must be complied with, for assignments within its scope to be effective.

[A]   Effectiveness of Assignments Generally

Completing an effective assignment usually requires nothing more complex than an unequivocal manifestation of the obligee's intent to transfer the right involved to the assignee.[68] If Article 9 of the U.C.C. applies to the assignment, its formal requirements must be satisfied. These usually require the assignor to authenticate a writing or an electronic record that adequately describes the rights that are the subject of the transfer.[69] Depending on the form of the right transferred, the assignment may be accomplished through a transfer of possession of documents representing the transferred rights, as in the case of the assignment of a promissory note or tangible "chattel paper."[70]

Former U.C.C. § 1-206 prohibited the enforceability of any transfer of any type of personal property beyond the amount of $5,000, unless the transfer was memorialized in a writing signed by the party against whom enforcement was sought showing that the contract had been made and reasonably identifying the nature of the rights transferred.[71] Although this provision has been eliminated from the most recent revisions to U.C.C. Article 1, about one-third of the states have not yet adopted it. Further, some of the states that have adopted revised

---

[65] U.C.C. § 9-406 cmt. 5 (2012).

[66] CISG Art. 4 (1980).

[67] Henry Mather, *Choice of Law for International Sales Issues Not Resolved by the CISG*, 20 J.L. & Com. 155 (2001).

[68] Restatement (Second) of Contracts § 324 (1981).

[69] U.C.C. § 9-203(b)(3)(A) (2012). *See infra* § 17.03[C] Assignments of Rights to Payment Under U.C.C. Article 9.

[70] *See* U.C.C. § 9-102(a)(11) (2012).

[71] U.C.C. § 1-206 (2012) (eliminated from U.C.C. in 2001).

Article 1 have simply moved this statute-of-frauds provision elsewhere in their statutory scheme.

[1] Present Transfer of Future Rights

There is a distinction between an agreement promising to make a future assignment of existing rights, and a present transfer of those rights. A contract to make an assignment at some time in the future is not effective as a present assignment.[72] However, such a contract may be specifically enforceable in equity, subject to the normal requirement that the remedy at law is inadequate.[73] At the same time, a promise to make a future assignment is also different from a present transfer of future rights, which is effective as soon as the future rights come into existence.[74] Thus, the author of a bankruptcy law hornbook might enter into a contract promising that, should he be unable to repay a debt, he will transfer his right to receive royalties from sales of the book. This is a promise to make a future assignment. Alternatively, he might immediately transfer the right to receive future royalties from sales that have not yet been made. This is a present transfer of future rights.

[2] Authorized Agent Distinguished

A distinction also exists between an assignment and an agreement authorizing someone to act as an agent on the behalf of the obligee. For example, when a patient authorizes her insurance company to pay her doctor directly, there is no assignment.[75] The authorization simply establishes the right of insurance company to act on the patient's behalf. Like other agency relationships, it can be terminated at the will of the principal.

A check works the same way: it can be countermanded through a valid "stop payment" order from the bank's customer. A check is not an assignment of funds in the drawer's bank account. Thus, if Dan writes a check payable to Carmen, instructing Dan's bank to pay $300 to Carmen's order, the check is not an assignment of the money in Dan's bank account. Because there is no assignment, Carmen has no right against Dan's bank, if it refuses to pay the check.[76]

[B] Effectiveness of Gratuitous Assignments

[1] Gratuitous Assignments Described

Gratuitous assignments — those made as a gift — are particularly troublesome. An assignment is gratuitous if it is made without consideration and not given as security for or in satisfaction of a preexisting debt.[77] That is, it is gratuitous if it is

---

[72] RESTATEMENT (SECOND) OF CONTRACTS § 330(1) (1981).

[73] RESTATEMENT (SECOND) OF CONTRACTS § 330 cmt. c (1981).

[74] RESTATEMENT (SECOND) OF CONTRACTS § 330 cmt. d (1981).

[75] E.g., Kelly Health Care v. The Prudential Ins. Co. of Am., 309 S.E.2d 305 (Va. 1983).

[76] U.C.C. § 3-408 (2012).

[77] RESTATEMENT (SECOND) OF CONTRACTS § 332(5) (1981).

made as a gift. Assume, for example, that Sam sells his car to Barb in exchange for her promise to pay him $20,000 in 90 days, and assigns his right to the $20,000 to his sister Ellen, as a gift. This, of course, is an unusual transaction. Most assignments are not gratuitous. Consider the several types of assignments a business might make of its right to collect its accounts receivable from its customers. Rhonda's Roofing, a roofing contractor, might sell its right to receive payment from the customers it worked for in June to Commercial Finance Corp. in exchange for cash. Rhonda's Roofing needs the cash to meet its own obligations. The sale is supported by the consideration of Commercial Finance Corp.'s cash payment. If Rhonda's Roofing gives Commercial Finance Corp. a security interest in its accounts, as collateral for a line of credit promised to be made available to Rhonda's Roofing, the assignment as security is likewise given in exchange for Commercial Finance Corp.'s promise to make a loan. If, on the other hand, Rhonda's Roofing gives Commercial Finance Corp. a security interest in its accounts as security for a preexisting and previously unsecured debt owed to the finance company, there is no consideration for the assignment. However, because it was made as security for a preexisting debt, it is not a gift.[78] These assignments are governed by U.C.C. Article 9. As a result, their enforceability depends on whether the parties complied with Article 9.[79]

[2]   Revocability of Gratuitous Assignments

The problem with gratuitous assignments is that gifts are not complete until delivery. If Sam were to collect the $20,000 from Barb directly and then hand over the money to his sister Ellen, the gift would be complete at the time he delivered the cash to Ellen. However, a mere promise to give Ellen $20,000 is an unenforceable promise to make a gift.[80]

If Barb had signed a negotiable promissory note, representing her promise to pay the $20,000, Sam could indorse the note to Ellen and deliver it her. This would make Ellen a "holder" of the note[81] who is entitled to enforce it against Barb.[82] A gratuitous assignment like this can be accomplished via delivery of a writing, such as a negotiable promissory note, which is universally treated a symbol of the right to collect the $20,000 obligation.[83] Sometimes obligations are reduced to a particular written form — such as a promissory note — which is regarded as the exclusive symbol of the right involved. This makes physical delivery easy.

However, unless Barb's promise is represented by a similar type of writing, there is nothing tangible to deliver to Ellen to complete the assignment. A simple

---

[78] Restatement (Second) of Contracts § 332 cmt. h (1981). *See also* U.C.C. § 1-204(2) (2012) (formerly U.C.C. § 1-201(44)(b) (2012) ("value" given for transfer made "as security for or in total or partial satisfaction of a pre-existing debt").

[79] U.C.C. § 9-203(b) (2012). *See infra* § 17.03[C] Assignments of Rights to Payment Under U.C.C. Article 9.

[80] *See supra* § 2.04 Promises to Make a Gift.

[81] U.C.C. § 1-201(b)(21) (2012) (formerly U.C.C. § 1-201(20)).

[82] U.C.C. § 3-301 (2012).

[83] Restatement (Second) of Contracts § 332(1)(b) (1981).

written promise by Barb to pay the money, or a copy of the written contract between Sam and Barb for the sale of the car, is not the type of writing that symbolizes Barb's promise to pay in a way that would make delivery of the writing sufficient to complete the assignment. To qualify, it would have to be a negotiable promissory note, a check, or some other similar "reified" obligation that is recognized as transferrable by physical delivery of the piece of paper containing the obligation.[84] A simple contract for sale between Sam and Barb does not qualify.

If the obligation that is being assigned has not been "reified" in this manner, the assignment can be accomplished only through the delivery of a written assignment that is either signed or "sealed"[85] by the assignor.[86] If a gratuitous assignment is made through delivery of a signed writing making the assignment, the writing will have to be carefully drafted to make it clear that it manifests an intent to make a present transfer of the right involved and not simply a promise to make an assignment in the future.[87] A mere promise to make the assignment in the future is no more enforceable than any other promise to make a gift. Absent consideration, or some sort of foreseeable reasonable reliance on the promise, the promise to take future action is not enforceable. The language used must strip the assignor of ownership or control over the right assigned.[88] Thus, any "assignment" Sam signs must make it clear that he is relinquishing control over the obligation owed from Barb.

Notice to the obligor that it should make payment to the assignee will not normally be sufficient to make the assignment irrevocable. Such an order is no more effective to complete an assignment than a check, which is nothing more than a set of instructions to the drawer's bank, is effective to complete an assignment of funds held in the drawer's checking account.[89] Likewise, the language must go further than merely authorizing payment to the assignee.[90]

[C]   Assignments of Rights to Payment Under U.C.C. Article 9

Article 9 of the Uniform Commercial Code governs most assignments of rights to payment. Consequently, its rules are key to the enforceability of many assignments. Article 9's rules are not covered in detail in a standard first-year course in Contracts, but will surely be studied carefully in an upper-level course in Secured Transactions. Significantly, the Code's provisions on assignments are considered fair game by the drafters of the "Contracts" portion of the multi-state

---

[84] *See* Robert Charles Clark, *Abstract Rights versus Paper Rights Under Article 9 of the Uniform Commercial Code*, 84 YALE L.J. 445 (1975); James Steven Rogers, *Negotiability as a System of Title Recognition*, 48 OHIO ST. L.J. 197 (1987).

[85] *See supra* § 2.02[B] The Seal.

[86] RESTATEMENT (SECOND) OF CONTRACTS § 332(1)(a) (1981).

[87] RESTATEMENT (SECOND) OF CONTRACTS § 332 cmt. b (1981).

[88] *See* Lone Star Cement Corp. v. Swartwout, 93 F.2d 767 (4th Cir. 1938).

[89] U.C.C. § 3-408 (2012).

[90] *See* Kelly Health Care v. The Prudential Ins. Co. of Am., 309 S.E.2d 305 (Va. 1983).

bar exam.[91]

[1] Scope of Article 9 and Its Terminology

Most commercial assignments of rights to payment are governed by Article 9 of the Uniform Commercial Code. Article 9 applies regardless of whether the right to payment is in the form of an account,[92] a promissory note,[93] chattel paper,[94] or other intangible rights to payment.[95] Further, it applies regardless of whether the right to payment is transferred as collateral for a loan[96] or as an outright sale of the right to receive payment.[97] A few types of outright sales are explicitly excluded from Article 9.[98] Among these is an assignment of a right to payment under a contract to an assignee that is accompanied by a delegation of the duty to earn the right to payment by rendering the performance due under the contract.[99] Thus, if a painting contractor delegates a contract to another painter and transfers the right to receive payment for the work as part of the assignment of the entire contract, Article 9 does not apply. Article 9 does apply, however, to a wide range of transfers of various types of rights to payment, made as collateral for a loan, or as an outright transfer of ownership.

Many commercial assignments of rights to receive payment are made as collateral for a loan to the assignor. For example, Downtown Office Supply might borrow funds from State Bank and give the bank a "security interest" in all of its inventory and accounts receivable as collateral for the loan. If Downtown fails to repay the loan when it is due, State Bank will have the right to repossess the inventory[100] and the right to send notice to Downtown's customers to make any payments still owed to the store for items previously delivered directly to the bank.[101]

Under the common law, Downtown Office Supply would be referred to as the "assignor" of the accounts, and State Bank would be the "assignee." Article 9 uses somewhat different terms, referring to the assignor as the "debtor"[102] and the assignee as the "secured party."[103] The customer, an "obligor" in common law

---

[91] Despite this fact, many four- and five-credit first-year Contracts courses do not cover third-party beneficiaries or assignments at all, much less the particular provisions of Article 9 that govern them.

[92] U.C.C. § 9-102(a)(2) (2012).

[93] U.C.C. § 9-102(a)(65) (2012).

[94] U.C.C. § 9-102(a)(11) (2012).

[95] *See* U.C.C. § 9-102(a)(61), (42) (2012).

[96] U.C.C. § 9-109(a)(1) (2012).

[97] U.C.C. § 9-109(a)(3) (2012).

[98] U.C.C. § 9-109 cmt. 12 (2012).

[99] U.C.C. § 9-109(d)(6) (2012).

[100] U.C.C. § 9-609 (2012).

[101] U.C.C. § 9-607(a)(1) (2012).

[102] U.C.C. § 9-102(a)(28)(A) (2012).

[103] U.C.C. § 9-102(a)(72)(A) (2012).

terminology, is an "account debtor" under Article 9.[104] And, the underlying "account" or other right to payment that is the subject of the assignment is called "the collateral."[105]

Article 9 uses the same terminology when there is an outright sale of the debtor's accounts, even though no debt is owed. So, if Downtown Office Supply, rather than borrowing money from State Bank, instead simply sells its accounts receivable to Merchant's Finance Association in return for cash, with no obligation to make repayment,[106] Article 9 would still refer to the Downtown Office Supply as a "debtor."[107] Merchant's Finance, as the assignee or buyer of the accounts, would be termed a "secured party," even though there is no obligation of Downtown Office Supply to secure.[108] The customers who purchased items from Downtown Supply on credit and must eventually pay for the goods they purchased are "obligors" or, under Article 9, "account debtors."[109] And, even though the right to collect from them is not being used to secure repayment of any loan to Downtown Supply, it is still called "the collateral."[110] Thus, Article 9 uses the same terminology to refer to assignments of rights to receive payment regardless of whether the assignment was made to secure a loan or to transfer ownership of the underlying right to payment.

[2] Enforceability of Security Interests in Rights to Payment — "Attachment"

To be effective an assignment of a right to payment must "attach." Section 9-203(a) specifies that: "A security interest attaches to collateral when it becomes enforceable against the debtor with respect to the collateral, unless an agreement expressly postpones the time of attachment."[111] Article 9 imposes three requirements for an assignment of a right to payment to be enforceable against the assignor, called the "debtor": (1) value must be given, (2) the debtor must have rights in the collateral, and (3) usually, there must be an authenticated security agreement.[112]

The first requirement, that "value must have been given,"[113] is usually accomplished when the assignee (the "secured party") makes a loan to the debtor,

---

[104] U.C.C. § 9-102(a)(3) (2012).

[105] U.C.C. § 9-102(a)(12) (2012).

[106] In this situation, the finance company would have the right to collect the accounts directly from the office supply store's customers. U.C.C. § 9-605(a)(1) & cmt. 4 (2012).

[107] U.C.C. § 9-102(a)(28)(B) (2012) (" 'Debtor' means . . . a seller of accounts, chattel paper, payment intangibles, or promissory notes.").

[108] U.C.C. § 9-102(a)(72)(D) (2012) (" 'Secured party' means . . . a person to which accounts, chattel paper, payment intangibles, or promissory notes have been sold.").

[109] U.C.C. § 9-102(a)(3) (2012).

[110] U.C.C. § 9-102(a)(12)(B) (2012) ("accounts, chattel paper, payment intangibles and promissory notes that have been sold").

[111] U.C.C. § 9-203(a) (2012).

[112] U.C.C. § 9-203(b) (2012).

[113] U.C.C. § 9-203(b)(1) (2012).

or in a sale of the collateral, when the secured party pays for it.[114] The assignment of an account or other right to payment must comply with Article 9's statute of frauds. U.C.C. § 9-203 requires the assignor to "authenticate" a security agreement containing a description of the rights transferred.

The second requirement, that "the debtor has rights in the collateral,"[115] or has "the power to transfer rights in the collateral,"[116] is satisfied when the obligor ("account debtor") undertakes to make payment to the assignor ("debtor"). Thus, when a customer of our office supply store agrees to purchase 100 boxes of copy machine supplies, and promises to pay for them 30 days after they are delivered, the office supply store, as the debtor, "acquires rights" in the collateral.

The third requirement for attachment is a signed writing. The security interest does not attach and is not enforceable unless "the debtor has authenticated a security agreement that provides a description of the collateral."[117] This is usually accomplished with a signed written security agreement, describing the rights that are the subject matter of the assignment. By permitting an "authenticated" agreement, Article 9 permits this statute of frauds to be satisfied by electronic means.[118]

[3]　　Assignments of Future Rights

One of the most important features of Article 9 is that it permits assignments of future rights. Before Article 9, the law was highly resistant to the idea that a right to receive payment that had not yet been created could be assigned. Article 9 now expressly permits the assignment of "after-acquired collateral"[119] including rights of payment not yet earned.

This makes it possible for an obligeee, like Downtown Office Supply, to assign all of its accounts receivable, including those that will arise in the future. Each time Downtown Office Supply creates an account by entering into a new agreement to sell goods to a customer on credit, the assignee's security interest attaches to the new account. Such agreements are called "continuing" or "floating liens."[120] The assignee's or "secured party's" rights extend to any accounts or other payment rights described in the security agreement and acquired by the assignor by entering into agreements with customers in the future. Although the security interest does not "attach," and the assignment is not fully effective until the account is created, the extension of the security interest to such future rights avoids the necessity of entering into a new written security agreement each time a new account is created. Likewise, it permits the secured party to take steps to

---

[114] U.C.C. § 1-204 (2012) (formerly § 1-201(44)). Value includes "any consideration sufficient to support a simple contract." *Id.* Thus, a promise to make a loan or to pay for the accounts would also constitute value.

[115] U.C.C. § 9-203(b)(2) (2012).

[116] *Id.*

[117] U.C.C. § 9-203(b)(3) (2012).

[118] U.C.C. § 9-102(a)(7)(B) & cmt. 9(b) (2012).

[119] U.C.C. § 9-204(a) (2012).

[120] *See* U.C.C. § 9-204 cmt. 2 (2012).

protect its interest against the potentially competing claims of other secured parties who might obtain a subsequent assignment of the same accounts.

§ 17.04　ASSERTING DEFENSES AGAINST AN ASSIGNEE

Difficulties arise when the obligor asserts a defense to its obligation to pay. If Suburban Motors sells a defective Fleetstar automobile to Sam on credit, and then assigns the right to receive payment from Sam to Fleet Finance Company, Fleet Finance will probably send notice to Sam to make his regular monthly payments directly to it.[121] When Sam discovers that the car is defective, he will probably first try to have the car repaired. However, if the auto is truly a lemon and cannot be repaired, Sam will want to "revoke acceptance" and quit making payments for it.[122] If so, he will want to be able to assert this right against Fleet Finance, even though it had nothing to do with the sale or manufacture of the defective Fleetstar.

If the right to payment had not been assigned, it would have been clear that the Sam could assert his claim for breach of warranty as grounds for resisting payment to Suburban Motors.[123] His ability to avoid making payments to the finance company, in its role as assignee of the right to receive payment for the car, is less obvious. As will be seen, Sam's ability to resist payment depends on a variety of factors, including whether the transaction employed a negotiable promissory note, the language contained in the agreement, and whether Sam had purchased the car for his personal use or for his business. In some cases, it also might depend on the nature of his defense.

[A]　　　Transactional Defenses

The basic common law rule, codified in U.C.C. § 9-404, is that the assignee stands in the shoes of the assignor.[124] The assignee of a right to payment is "subject to all terms of the agreement between the account debtor [obligor] and assignor and any defense or claim in recoupment arising from the transaction that gave rise to the contract."[125] Accordingly, in the simple circumstances described above, Sam would be entitled to assert his defense against Fleet Finance, to whom his obligation to make payment had been assigned.

In a slightly different situation, an account debtor has a defense based on payment. Assume, for example, that Suburban Motors sold a different car to Moira, also on credit, and immediately sold the right to receive Moira's payments to Auto Finance Co. However, before Auto Finance had a chance to notify Moira of the assignment, she found a winning lottery ticket, cashed it in, and sent payment in full to Suburban Motors, who dishonestly cashed her check instead of advising

---

[121] U.C.C. § 9-607 permits a secured party in this situation to supply notice to the account debtor of the assignment and to direct it to make its payments directly to the secured party. U.C.C. § 9-607 (2012).

[122] *See supra* § 9.03[C] Revocation of Acceptance.

[123] *See* U.C.C. § 3-305 cmt. 3 (2012).

[124] RESTATEMENT (SECOND) OF CONTRACTS § 336(1). *See* Spanish Oaks, Inc. v. Hy-Vee, Inc., 655 N.W.2d 390, 403 (Neb. 2003); U.C.C. § 9-404 cmt. 2 (2012).

[125] U.C.C. § 9-404(a)(1) (2012) (formerly U.C.C. § 9-318(1)(a) (2000)).

her of the assignment to Auto Finance. Not surprisingly, Moira will be able to assert her defense of payment, or "discharge," against Auto Finance, when it sends her a statement demanding that she start making regular monthly payments on the assigned contract.[126] Moira has already fully performed her obligations, and Auto Finance will have to seek recovery from Suburban Motors, probably on a theory of conversion.

However, as an account debtor, Moira would not have been entitled to assert her defense of payment if she had received proper notice of the assignment from Auto Finance before sending her payment to Suburban Motors.[127] Article 9 applies to most such assignments. It specifies that the obligor cannot assert a defense of discharge with respect to payments made to the assignor after he or she has received an authenticated notification "that the amount due . . . has been assigned and that payment is to be made to the assignee."[128]

[B]   Defenses Based on Collateral Transactions

An account debtor might also want to assert defenses against an assignee, based on separate (collateral) transactions it had with the assignor. Assume for example that Lewis Landlord bought a new furnace for one of his rental units for $3,000 from City Heating & Cooling and signed an agreement promising to pay City Heating & Cooling in 60 days. City Heating & Cooling assigned the right to receive payment from Lewis to Merchant's Finance Co. Before Lewis's payment was due, City Heating & Cooling repaired an air-conditioning unit at one of Lewis Landlord's other apartment buildings, but did the job badly, resulting in the complete destruction of the air conditioner. When Merchant's Finance seeks to recover payment from Lewis for the price of the new furnace, Lewis will probably want to resist payment by asserting his rights against City Heating & Cooling for its botched job on the air conditioner.

Under U.C.C. § 9-404(a)(2), Lewis's ability to assert his claim based on the collateral (separate) transaction involving the air conditioner as a defense against Merchant's Finance Co.'s claim to recover payment for the furnace depends on whether Lewis's claim against City Heating & Cooling accrued before Lewis received notification of the assignment.[129] As a claim arising from a different transaction than the one involved in the assignment, Lewis's ability to assert his defense for the faulty work on the air conditioner is treated differently than defenses based on the transaction involving the purchase of the furnace.

The assignee's collection rights are subject to all of the obligor's claims and defenses that arose out of the transaction that was the subject of the assignment, other than discharge, regardless of whether or when the obligor received notice that the obligation was assigned.[130] The assignee takes free of the defense of

---

[126] U.C.C. § 9-406(a) (2012).

[127] RESTATEMENT (SECOND) OF CONTRACTS § 338 (1981).

[128] U.C.C. § 9-406(a) (2012).

[129] U.C.C. § 9-404(a)(2) (2012).

[130] U.C.C. § 9-404 cmt. 2 (2012).

discharge (usually through payment) if the payment and thus the discharge occurred before the obligor received notice of the assignment. And, the assignee takes free from claims based on collateral transactions — such as those arising from the faulty repair of the air conditioner — that did not accrue until after the obligor received notification of the assignment.[131]

[C]   Obligor's Freedom from Defenses

The obligor's ability to assert these defenses against an assignee is subject to several important exceptions. The first exception applies when the original agreement between the obligor and the assignor contains a so-called "waiver-of-defense" clause in which the obligor agrees not to assert any defense it might have against the assignor in an action to collect the amount otherwise due, brought by an assignee. The second exception is where the original obligation is in the form of a negotiable promissory note and the assignee has rights, under Article 3 of the U.C.C. as a holder in due course of the note. However, as explained below, these exceptions are subject to several important limitations.

[1]   Waiver-of-Defense Clauses

The obligor loses its ability to assert its defenses against an assignee if the obligor entered into "an enforceable agreement not to assert defenses or claims."[132] This type of "waiver-of-defense" clause would most likely be included in the terms of the original agreement between the obligor and the assignor. Assume, for example, that Computer Supply Co. sells new table computers to its customers, on credit. Its retail installment sales agreements contain language that permit Computer Supply to assign its right to receive payment for the computers to Merchant's Finance Co. The standardized agreement further provides that Computer Supply's customers waive their right to assert any claims or defenses they otherwise might have against Computer Supply because of a defect in items purchased by the customers, in a collection action brought by Merchant's Finance as Computer Supply's assignee.

This agreement not to assert defenses against an assignee is likely to enhance the willingness of the finance company to take the assignment. It will probably also increase the amount the finance company is willing to pay for the right to receive payment from the customer. If Merchant's Finance can successfully avoid the risk that Computer Supply's customers will be legally entitled to avoid payment for some reason, it will ultimately be able to collect more from Computer Supply's customers.

As a practical matter, if a customer agreed to pay $20,000 for 10 computers, it is unlikely that Merchant's Finance will agree to pay the full $20,000 face amount of the customer's account to Computer Supply. After all, the finance company wouldn't purchase any of the accounts unless it anticipated making a profit on the deal. In addition, Merchant's Finance will have to wait until the account is due to

---

[131] *Id.*

[132] U.C.C. § 9-404(a) (2012).

receive payment and must receive some compensation for the interest it could have earned during this delay on the amount it pays to the dealer. Furthermore, when Merchant's Finance buys the account, it takes on the "credit risk" that the customer will end up bankrupt and unable to pay the $20,000 when it falls due.[133] However, if the agreement between the Computer Supply and its customer includes an enforceable agreement not to assert any defenses the customer might have, the finance company will at least avoid the risk that Computer Supply is selling shoddy merchandise to its customers that will result in providing them with a defense to their obligation to pay for the goods.

Thus, Merchant's Finance might be willing to pay $19,500 to Computer Supply in exchange for the right to receive $20,000 from the customer 60 days after the computers are delivered. Computer Supply receives the $19,500 amount right away.[134] Without the waiver-of-defense clause, the finance company might be willing to pay only $19,000 for the right to collect the $20,000 due from the customer. The $500 difference that it pays with the waiver of defense clause in place permits Computer Supply to be more profitable, or may be passed on to its customers in the form of lower prices or better service to the dealer's customers, giving the dealer a competitive advantage in the marketplace.

However, these advantages are achieved only if the waiver-of-defense clause is enforceable. Waiver-of-defense clauses of this type are generally enforceable only if the assignee takes the assignment (1) for value, (2) in good faith, and (3) without notice of the customer's defense.[135] If the assignment was made as a gift, the assignee remains subject to the obligor's defenses to the same extent as if the waiver of defense clause had not been part of the original contract. Likewise, if the assignee had notice of the obligor's defense at the time the assignment was made, it remains subject to that defense notwithstanding the waiver of defense provision.

[2]   Holder-in-Due-Course Doctrine

The "holder-in-due-course" doctrine of U.C.C. Article 3 protects purchasers of negotiable promissory notes in much the same way as an enforceable waiver of defense clause protects assignees of other rights to payment. Under Article 3 a holder in due course takes a negotiable instrument free of all "personal" defenses such as breach of warranty, failure of consideration, and even most types of garden-variety fraud.[136] A "holder in due course" is a holder of a negotiable instrument, such as a promissory note, who takes the instrument (1) for value, (2) in good faith, and (3) without notice of any claim of ownership or defense to the

---

[133] In some transactions of this type, the assignor will agree to buy back any accounts that the assignee is unable to collect. Thus, the assignee sometimes has a right of recourse against the assignor. This right of recourse is useless when the assignor becomes bankrupt because it has developed a reputation for selling shoddy merchandise.

[134] The finance company in this situation is likely to insist on the right to screen each of the dealer's customers, to determine whether they are credit worthy, before becoming obligated to purchase the customer's account. In some situations, the finance company may have a representative on location at the dealer's store, to conduct this screening and decide whether to take an assignment of the account.

[135] U.C.C. § 9-403(b) (2012).

[136] U.C.C. § 3-305 (2012).

instrument.[137] Thus, if Computer Supply's customer, in the above example, signed a negotiable promissory note for the $20,000 purchase price of the computers, and Computer Supply indorsed it over to Merchant's Finance Co. for $19,500 cash, the finance company would most likely be a holder in due course of the customer's promissory note. Payment of the $19,500 would constitute full value.[138] As long as the finance company took the customer's promissory note in good faith and without notice that it was overdue or of any defense or claim to the instrument, it would qualify as a holder in due course and be invulnerable to most defenses that the customer might otherwise try to assert to resist payment of the note when it came due.

As with enforceable waiver-of-defense clauses, the holder-in-due-course doctrine facilitates the marketability of these types of obligations. A purchaser of such a note, who gives value, and is blissfully ignorant of any problems associated with the underlying obligation, earns the right to take free of defenses based on those problems. As a result, the customer will have to pay the full $20,000 amount of its promissory note to the finance company and bring whatever action it might have for breach of warranty against the computer dealer, if it is still in business.

[3] Preservation of Defenses

In transactions involving consumers, the ability of assignees of payment rights and holders in due course to take free of defenses has long been under attack. Two important rules prevent waiver of defense clauses and negotiable promissory notes from depriving consumer debtors of their defenses.

The first of these rules is the "close-connectedness doctrine." It is founded on the requirement that a holder in due course of a negotiable instrument acquire the instrument both in "good faith" and without "notice" of any defense of the obligor. If the assignee's business is too closely entangled with those of the assignor, the assignee is unable to assert that it was acting in good faith and without notice of the assignor's business practices that gave rise to the obligor's defenses.[139]

The second rule that preserves consumers' defenses against an assignee was promulgated by the United States Federal Trade Commission (FTC).[140] Sellers of goods and services are now required to include the following conspicuous language in any consumer credit contract:

---

[137] U.C.C. § 3-302(a) (2012). See WILLIAM H. LAWRENCE, UNDERSTANDING NEGOTIABLE INSTRUMENTS AND PAYMENT SYSTEMS § 6.01 (LexisNexis 2002).

[138] U.C.C. § 3-303(a)(1) (2012) ("An instrument is transferred for value if the instrument is transferred for a promise . . . to the extent the promise has been performed.").

[139] See, e.g., Commercial Credit Corp. v. Orange County Mach. Works, 214 P.2d 819, 821 (Cal. 1950); Calvert Credit Corp. v. Williams, 244 A.2d 494, 496 (D.C. 1968); Myron L. Erickson, Demise of Holder in Due Course, Waiver of Defense, and Interlocking Loan Lender Defenses in Consumer Transactions, 15 S. TEX. L.J. 236, 240–42 (1974).

[140] See generally Ford Motor Credit Co. v. Morgan, 536 N.E.2d 587 (Mass. 1989); William H. Lawrence & John H. Minan, The Effect of Abrogating the Holder-in-Due-Course Doctrine on the Commercialization of Innovative Consumer Products, 64 B.U. L. REV. 325 (1984).

NOTICE

ANY HOLDER OF THIS CONSUMER CREDIT CONTRACT IS SUB-
JECT TO ALL CLAIMS AND DEFENSES WHICH THE DEBTOR
COULD ASSERT AGAINST THE SELLER OF GOODS OR SER-
VICES OBTAINED PURSUANT HERETO OR WITH THE PRO-
CEEDS HEREOF. RECOVERY HEREUNDER BY THE DEBTOR
SHALL NOT EXCEED AMOUNTS PAID BY THE DEBTOR HERE-
UNDER.[141]

This language prevents assignees from asserting the rights of a holder in due
course and expressly negates the effect of any waiver-of-defense clause that the
assignor might attempt to insert in the consumer credit contracts it enters into with
its customers. Even more importantly, the required language may expose the
assignee to affirmative liability to the obligor for amounts the obligor has already
paid under the contract.

[4]   Defenses Based on Modifications

Once a contract has been assigned, there may be a question about whether
modifications entered into between the original parties, after the assignment, are
effective against the assignee without its consent. For example, if Industrial
Supply enters into a contract to sell goods to Franklin Manufacturing and then
assigns the right to receive payment from Franklin to Merchant's Finance Co., the
question is whether subsequent modifications between Industrial Supply and
Franklin are enforceable against the finance company.

The ability of the original parties to modify the contract is particularly
important where the underlying contract involves performance over a long period
of time, such as in a construction contract or a long-term requirements or output
contract for the sale of goods.[142] If the assignment is one within the scope of
U.C.C. Article 9, the answer is clear: "A modification of or substitution for an
assigned contract is effective against an assignee if the modification was made in
good faith."[143] The assignee's rights are simply changed in accordance with the
modification.

However, a modification is not enforceable if it was made after the assignor had
already earned right to payment by fully performing.[144] However, a good-faith
modification may be enforceable, even if the right to payment has been earned by
performance, if the account debtor had not yet been notified of the assignment
when the modification was made.[145]

Assume, for example, that a painting contractor, Fresh Finish, enters into a
contract with the Restful Night hotel chain to repaint all of the hotels in the chain
for a price of $5,000 for each of the 20 hotels in the chain, a total of $100,000. Before

---

[141] 16 C.F.R. § 433.2(a) (2014).

[142] *See* U.C.C. § 9-405 cmt. 2 (2012).

[143] U.C.C. § 9-405(a) (2012).

[144] U.C.C. § 9-405(b)(1) (2012).

[145] U.C.C. § 9-405(b)(2) (2012).

beginning work, Fresh Finish immediately assigns its right to receive payment from Restful Night to Union Finance Co., which pays Fresh Finish $95,000 cash for the assignment. After five hotels have been painted, Restful Night and Fresh Finish enter into a modification, reducing the price for the remaining 15 hotels to $4,800 each, in exchange for changes in the restrictions in the hours of the day the painting contractor can work. This good-faith modification is enforceable against the assignee. Any attempt to modify the amount to be paid for the first five hotels, for which the painter has already completed its work and earned the right to performance, however, is not enforceable against the finance company unless the hotel chain had not yet been notified of the assignment at the time the modification was entered into.

Even when the modification is effective against the assignee, it might be a breach of the contract between the assignor and the assignee. Thus, even though Restful Night will be able to satisfy its obligation by paying only Union Finance the sum of $97,000, Union Finance might be able to recover the additional $3,000 from Fresh Finish. Thus, the modification will still be effective, but the assignee will have a cause of action against the assignor for any damages it suffered as a result of the modification.[146]

§ 17.05   LIMITS ON DELEGATING DUTIES

Duties are generally delegable unless the delegation would conflict with public policy or would violate the terms of the original obligor's promise.[147] Contractual duties are frequently delegated to agents acting on behalf of the party to the contract, whether they are part of the original party's own organization, such as an employee, or part of another entity, as where a subcontractor performs part of a construction project undertaken by a general contractor. In most cases, the contract permits these delegations and even presumes that they will occur, at least so long as the original obligor retains a measure of control and supervision over the performance of the person who is actually performing the contract. In other situations, it makes little difference to the party who performs the duty, so long as the work complies with the requirements of the contract otherwise.

In other situations, performance is expected to be completed personally by the original parties to the contract. If the New York Yankees hire Alex Rodriguez to play baseball, the team is unlikely to be satisfied with anyone else to whom Rodriguez delegates his duty, regardless of how much confidence the team's star player has in his delegate's ability.

Accordingly, the law's restrictions on the assignability of contracts are more rigorous with respect to transfers of duties than they are with respect to assignments of rights. Although the rules are largely the same, the delegation of one party's duty is far more likely to have a material effect on the other party than an assignment of one party's rights to receive the other party's performance.

Assume, for example, that Sam agreed to accept payment for his BMW in the

---

[146] U.C.C. § 9-405(a) (2012).

[147] RESTATEMENT (SECOND) OF CONTRACTS § 318(1) (1981).

form of a personal check. If Barb assigns her entire contract for the BMW to Andrea, including the duty to pay for the car with a personal check, the risk to Sam that Andrea's check will bounce is materially different than his risk that Barb's check would have bounced. Sam may know Barb better than he knows Andrea. He may know them both well, but have more information about Barb's financial condition, her maturity, or her integrity than he has about Andrea. Thus, if Barb delegates her duty to pay for the car by check, in addition to assigning her rights to receive delivery of the car, Sam may be justified in being more reluctant in going through with his own end of the bargain with Andrea substituted for Barb.

If Sam goes through with the deal, despite the delegation of Barb's duties to Andrea, and Andrea's check is good, payment of the check will result in Sam receiving everything he was entitled to under his contract with Barb.[148] However, it would be unfair to Sam to force him to deliver the car to Andrea in exchange for her check and wait to see if the check clears. If Andrea's bank "dishonors" the check, Sam would have parted with the car without receiving payment. Sam could pursue a claim against Andrea to recover for the dishonored check, but once Andrea's check is dishonored, the likelihood that she will ever pay Sam the $20,000 is greatly reduced.

Sam could also pursue a claim against Barb, because Barb owed Sam a duty to pay $20,000 for the car, and that duty has not been discharged or released. Barb's assignment and delegation to Andrea is not a defense. The legal relation between Barb and Andrea is that of guarantor and obligor. As between the two of them, Andrea is primarily liable to Sam, and her failure to pay for the car causes Barb's obligation, as a guarantor of Andrea's promise, to mature when Andrea's check bounces. Accordingly, Sam may proceed against Barb to recover the $20,000.

A duty to pay a sum of money is normally fully delegable even though the person who will assume the duty is less reliable than the original obligor. The original obligor, after all, remains liable to perform the original contract.[149]

Because of these and other differences between assigning rights and delegating duties, the law is more likely to find that a duty cannot be delegated than it is to find that a right cannot be assigned. The duty may not be delegated if the obligee has a substantial interest in having the original obligor perform the promise or has a substantial interest in being in control of the performance of the promise.[150] Likewise, a provision in a contract restricting the obligor's ability to delegate its duties is considerably more likely to be enforceable than a mere restriction on the obligee's ability to assign its rights.

---

[148] RESTATEMENT (SECOND) OF CONTRACTS § 318 cmt. a & illus. 1–3 (1981).

[149] RESTATEMENT (SECOND) OF CONTRACTS § 318(3) (1981).

[150] RESTATEMENT (SECOND) OF CONTRACTS § 318(2) (1981).

[A]   Nondelegable Personal Duties[151]

"Personal" duties may not be delegated, without the consent of the obligee. These are "nondelegable" duties. Duties are personal if the obligee has a substantial interest in having the performance rendered by or under the control of a particular person.[152] Contracts involving personal services frequently anticipate that the skill, judgment, or discretion of a particular person will be involved in the performance of those services. Courts sometimes say that duties cannot be delegated if they involve the exercise of special knowledge, judgment, taste, skill, or ability.

Professional services in particular are not delegable.[153] An attending cardiac surgeon may not delegate his or her duty to perform open heart surgery to a new resident, unless the patient agrees. And, a lawyer may not delegate his or her duties to represent a client to another firm, regardless of the competence or ability of the other lawyer.[154] In many cases, however, the contract may expressly or impliedly authorize work to be performed by other lawyers in the same firm, as would ordinarily be done when a client engages a law firm to represent it in a business negotiation or a dispute over liability. Thus, personal duties are delegable if the contract permits, but this is nothing more than a matter of interpretation about the reasonable understanding of the client about how the representation will be handled. Likewise, artistic and athletic services will almost certainly involve an expectation that the obligor perform the services individually.[155]

Not every contract involving the rendition of services is nondelegable. As the court in *Taylor v. Palmer* aptly said:

> All painters do not paint portraits like Sir Joshua Reynolds, nor landscapes like Claude Lorraine, nor do all writers write dramas like Shakespeare or fiction like Dickens. Rare genius and extra-ordinary skill are not transferable, and contracts for their employment are therefore personal, and cannot be assigned. But rare genius and extraordinary skill are not indispensable to the workmanlike digging down of a sand hill or the filling up of a depression to a given level, or the construction of brick sewers with manholes and covers, and contracts for such work are not personal, and may be assigned.[156]

Thus, obligations, like the ditch digging in the streets of San Francisco involved in *Taylor v. Palmer*, which require mechanical skills or agreements to perform

---

[151] Larry A. DiMatteo, *Depersonalization of Personal Service Contracts: The Search for a Modern Approach to Assignability*, 27 Akron L. Rev. 407 (1994); Thomas H. Jackson, *Bankruptcy, Non-Bankruptcy Entitlements and the Creditors' Bargain*, 91 Yale L.J. 857, 896 (1992).

[152] Restatement (Second) of Contracts § 318(2) (1981); U.C.C. § 2-210(1) (2012).

[153] Deaton v. Lawson, 82 P. 879 (Wash. 1905).

[154] Fund of Funds, Ltd. v. Arthur Andersen & Co., 567 F.2d 225 (2d Cir. 1977); Johnston v. Baca, 85 P. 237 (N.M. 1906).

[155] *See generally* Rosetti v. City of New Britain, 303 A.2d 714 (Conn. 1972) (singling out artists, lawyers, doctors, and architects).

[156] Taylor v. Palmer, 1866 Cal. LEXIS 201, *11 (Oct. 1866).

ministerial acts that are readily susceptible to objective measurement, can be delegated.

In one widely reported case, the court held that the duty to supply a pizza shop with its requirements of carbonated beverages was readily delegable to one of the original parties' competitors, even though the pizza shop had dealt with the business to whom the duty had been delegated in the past and preferred not to do business with it.[157] Thus, where the delegation will not result in a substantial impairment of the rights of the other party to receive performance, it will be permitted.

In the context of modern business transactions, this rule may seriously impair the success of a corporate merger. Mergers and corporate acquisitions frequently involve the delegation of duties from one company, which will be eliminated in the merger, to the corporation that "survives" when the merger is complete. In *Sally Beauty Co. v. Nexxus Products Co.*,[158] the acquisition of one hair care product distributor by another was frustrated when the court held that the transaction would result in an impermissible delegation. Best Beauty & Barber Supply Co. was the exclusive distributor of products manufactured by Nexxus Products Co. When Best Beauty was acquired by a subsidiary of Nexxus's principal competitor, Alberto Culver, Nexxus balked and cancelled the exclusive distributorship agreement rather than have it performed by a company under the control of its principal business competitor. The court held that in this situation the merger substantially impaired Nexxus's right to receive its distributor's " 'best efforts' in promoting the sale of Nexxus products in" the geographic region involved in the contract.[159] Judge Posner laid out a vigorous dissent, questioning the propriety of summary judgment. He reasoned that the practical economic realities of the transaction might well lead to full performance of the duty and that the party to whom the contract had been delegated should have been given an opportunity to prove this to a jury.[160] His dissenting opinion is a good example of how principles of economic analysis are sometimes used to challenge existing contract doctrine.

[B] Delegation Creating Reasonable Grounds for Insecurity

In other situations, where one party has reasonable grounds for believing that the other party may be unable or unwilling to perform its contractual duties, the party who is uncertain about whether it will receive its return performance may make a demand for adequate assurances of future performance. If the necessary assurances are not provided, the aggrieved party is permitted to treat the other party's failure to supply assurance of future performance as a repudiation of its obligations under the contract.[161] The same approach can be used in connection with a delegation of a party's duties under a contract.[162] An assignment that

---

[157] Macke Co. v. Pizza of Gaithersburg, Inc., 270 A.2d 645 (Md. Ct. App. 1970).

[158] 801 F.2d 1001 (7th Cir. 1986).

[159] *Id.* at 1007.

[160] *Id.* at 1008.

[161] *See supra* § 9.06 Prospective Inability to Perform.

[162] U.C.C. § 2-210(6) (2012). The Uniform Computer Information Transactions Act (UCITA) takes

delegates performance creates reasonable grounds for insecurity and permits the other party to demand adequate assurance of future performance.

In a sale of Sam's BMW to Barb in which Barb delegates her rights and duties to Andrea, Barb's delegation may leave Sam uncertain about the prospect of receiving performance. This may be particularly true if the sale was to be on credit. Under this approach, Sam might treat Barb's delegation of her duties to Andrea as establishing reasonable grounds for insecurity under U.C.C. § 2-609. This would permit Sam to suspend his performance and demand adequate assurances of performance. If sufficient assurances are not provided, Sam may treat the contract as having been repudiated. Providing adequate assurances may require Andrea to prove her financial ability to pay for the car or to obtain a loan in the necessary amount from another source.

The facts of *Sally Beauty* raise another difficult question that might arise in the context of a corporate merger. Where the stock of a corporation is purchased by a new person, and management of the corporation comes under the control of new individuals, the result might be the same as it would have been had the assets of the corporation, including all of its contractual duties, been transferred to a new corporation. However, when the stock of one of the contracting parties is purchased, there is no real delegation of duties. The parties to the original contract remain intact, with the same corporate obligor performing the duties owed under the contract, even though the performance of those duties is being managed by a completely different set of individuals acting on behalf of the obligor.

Assume, for example, that GreenTree Landscape Inc. enters into a contract to design and install a new landscape design in Fred's backyard, and then the shares of GreenTree Landscape Inc. are purchased by a person known for his inability to make plants grow, who plans to take over the operation of the business. Fred may be legitimately concerned about the quality of goods and services he will receive from the business, under its new ownership. Here the question is whether the contract either expressly or impliedly required that the services be performed or supervised by the prior owners of GreenTree and, if not, whether the substitution of management gives Fred reasonable grounds for insecurity that may permit him to demand adequate assurances of performance of the contract.

[C]   Contractual Prohibition of Delegation

A contract not requiring the personal skill or judgment of the original obligor might nevertheless be rendered nondelegable by contractual language specifying that the duties under the contract may not be delegated.[163] Although restrictions on the assignment of contractual rights are viewed with skepticism, restraints on the delegability of duties are routinely upheld.[164] Some courts have taken a more liberal approach and have required that the other party act reasonably in deciding

---

the same approach. Carlyle C. Ring Jr., *Uniform Rules for Internet Information Transactions: An Overview of Proposed UCITA*, 38 Duq. L. Rev. 319, 356 (2000).

[163] Restatement (Second) of Contracts § 318(1) (1981).

[164] *E.g.*, First Fed. Sav. Bank v. Key Markets, Inc., 559 N.E.2d 600 (Ind. 1990) (shopping center lease).

whether to permit the delegation.[165] Broad language in a contract generally restricting its assignment will usually be construed narrowly in this regard, as a prohibition on delegation of the duty, not as a restriction on the assignability of rights.[166]

[D]   Delegations of Contracts for the Sale of Goods

U.C.C. Article 2 directly addresses delegations of duties arising from contracts for the sale of goods, within its scope. Section 2-210(1) generally permits a party to perform his or her duty "through a delegate." Consistent with the common law, there are exceptions when the agreement prohibits delegations or where "the other party has a substantial interest in having his original promisor perform or control the acts required by the contract."[167] As under the traditional common law rule, a simple delegation does not relieve the delegating party from its contractual duties.[168] This would require a novation, which can only be accomplished by the agreement of the other party to accept the delagee's *promise* as a substitute for the performance or the delegator. Moreover, the other party has the right to regard a delegation as "creating reasonable grounds for insecurity"[169] and may thus use the delegation to suspend performance and demand adequate assurances of performance under U.C.C. § 2-609.[170]

As with assignments, the CISG is silent about the delegability of contractual duties. Its scope is limited to questions regarding formation of the contract and the obligations of the original parties.[171] Thus, resolution of these issues depends on the local law that would otherwise apply to the delegation.[172]

§ 17.06   EFFECT OF DELEGATION

[A]   Third-Party Beneficiary Rights of the Obligee

A successful delegation of duties usually operates to create a third-party beneficiary contract for the benefit of the obligee.[173] Thus, absent circumstances that demonstrate otherwise, a delegation gives the obligee the right to recover against the delegate if the delegate fails to perform. The delegate's right to assert defenses that the original obligor might have had, as well as its right to assert its

---

[165] *E.g.*, Cheney v. Jemmett, 693 P.2d 1031 (Idaho 1984) (contract for installment purchase of real estate).

[166] RESTATEMENT OF CONTRACTS § 322(1) (1981); U.C.C. § 2-210(4) (2012).

[167] U.C.C. § 2-201(1) (2012).

[168] U.C.C. § 2-210(1) (2012).

[169] U.C.C. § 2-210(6) (2012).

[170] *See supra* § 9.06 Prospective Inability to Perform.

[171] CISG Art. 4 (1980).

[172] Henry Mather, *Choice of Law for International Sales Issues Not Resolved by the CISG*, 20 J.L. & COM. 155 (2001).

[173] RESTATEMENT (SECOND) OF CONTRACTS § 328(2) (1981).

own defenses, are governed by the normal rules associated with third-party beneficiary contracts.[174]

[B] No Release of the Original Obligor Absent Novation

It should be clear that the delegation of contractual duties to a delegate does not relieve the original obligor of its responsibilities under the contract.[175] As one court explained: "a simple assignment alone [is] insufficient to release [a party] from any further liability on [a] contract."[176] Thus, if the delegate fails to perform, the original obligor who made the delegation still owes a duty of performance to the obligee.

Thus, if, following Barb's delegation of her contractual duty to pay Sam $20,000 for the purchase of the car, Andrea fails to perform, Sam will still have a cause of action against Barb. The only way for Barb to escape liability in this situation is to establish that a "novation" has occurred. A novation means that a new or "substituted" contract has been made in which the liability of one person, in this case Barb, ceases in exchange for the substituted liability of another person, such as Andrea.[177] While novations certainly occur, they are found to exist only when it is clearly established that the obligor intended to substitute a new obligor for an old obligor. Why should Sam release Barb from liability just because Andrea appears at the door with her own personal check? Sam originally contracted with Barb, and she may be assumed to continue to expect that, in the final analysis, Barb will have to pay if Andrea does not.[178]

Establishing the existence of a novation requires a showing that the original contracting party, the obligee, expressly consented to the substitution. Very few implied novations will be encountered.

---

[174] *See infra* § 16.03 Defenses Against Third-Party Beneficiaries.

[175] RESTATEMENT (SECOND) OF CONTRACTS § 318(3) (1981). *See, e.g.*, Contemp. Mission, Inc. v. Famous Music Corp., 557 F.2d 918, 924 (2d Cir. 1977).

[176] Rosenberger v. Son, Inc., 491 N.W.2d 71, 74 (N.D. 1992).

[177] RESTATEMENT (SECOND) OF CONTRACTS § 280 (1981).

[178] Rosenberger v. Son, Inc. 491 N.W.2d 71, 75 (N.D. 1992).

TABLE OF CASES

[References are to pages.]

[References are to pages.]

[References are to pages.]

C

[References are to pages.]

[References are to pages.]

[References are to pages.]

[References are to pages.]

[References are to pages.]

[References are to pages.]

[References are to pages.]

N

[References are to pages.]

[References are to pages.]

[References are to pages.]

[References are to pages.]

[References are to pages.]

[References are to pages.]

[References are to pages.]

[References are to pages.]

TABLE OF STATUTES

[References are to page and note numbers.]

[References are to page and note numbers.]

[References are to page and note numbers.]

[References are to page and note numbers.]

[References are to page and note numbers.]

[References are to page and note numbers.]

[References are to page and note numbers.]

[References are to page and note numbers.]

[References are to page and note numbers.]

[References are to page and note numbers.]

[References are to page and note numbers.]

[References are to page and note numbers.]

[References are to page and note numbers.]

UNIFORM COMMERCIAL CODE (U.C.C.)—Cont.

UNIFORM COMMERCIAL CODE (U.C.C.)—Cont.

[References are to page and note numbers.]

[References are to page and note numbers.]

[References are to page and note numbers.]

INDEX

[References are to sections.]

[References are to sections.]

[References are to sections.]

[References are to sections.]

[References are to sections.]

[References are to sections.]

[References are to sections.]

[References are to sections.]

[References are to sections.]

[References are to sections.]

[References are to sections.]

[References are to sections.]

[References are to sections.]

[References are to sections.]

[References are to sections.]